The Routledge Companion to Business Ethics

The field of business ethics continues to expand intellectually and geographically. During the past five decades, scholars have developed and deepened their inquiries into the ethics of commercial and corporate conduct.

This *Companion* provides a novel overview of the discipline of business ethics, covering the major areas of the field as well as new and emerging topics. The eight thematic units range over an extraordinary set of subjects and include chapters on the history and pedagogy of business ethics, moral philosophy, the nature of business, responsibilities within the firm, economic institutions, the 2008 financial crisis, globalization, and business ethics in different regions of the world. Led by a well-respected editorial team, this unique volume gathers an international array of experts whose various critical approaches yield insights from areas such as public policy, economics, law, and history, in addition to business and philosophy.

With its fresh analyses, wide scope, and clarity of approach, this volume will be an essential addition to library collections in business, management, and applied ethics.

Eugene Heath is Professor of Philosophy at the State University of New York, New Paltz. He has published on eighteenth-century moral philosophers (Bernard Mandeville, Adam Ferguson, and Adam Smith) and on business ethics.

Byron Kaldis is Professor of Philosophy at the National Technical University of Athens, Greece. He works in the philosophy of science and the social sciences, political philosophy, ethics, and ontology.

Alexei Marcoux is Professor of Business Ethics and Society and Institute for Economic Inquiry Senior Scholar in Creighton University's Heider College of Business, Nebraska. His academic research focuses on the moral foundations of commercial transactions and methodological issues in business ethics.

Routledge Companions in Business, Management and Accounting

Routledge Companions in Business, Management and Accounting are prestige reference works providing an overview of a whole subject area or sub-discipline. These books survey the state of the discipline including emerging and cutting edge areas. Providing a comprehensive, up to date, definitive work of reference, Routledge Companions can be cited as an authoritative source on the subject.

A key aspect of these *Routledge Companions* is their international scope and relevance. Edited by an array of highly regarded scholars, these volumes also benefit from teams of contributors which reflect an international range of perspectives.

Individually, *Routledge Companions in Business, Management and Accounting* provide an impactful one-stop-shop resource for each theme covered. Collectively, they represent a comprehensive learning and research resource for researchers, postgraduate students and practitioners.

For a full list of titles in this series, please visit www.routledge.com/Routledge-Companions-in-Business-Management-and-Accounting/book-series/RCBMA.

Published titles in this series include:

THE ROUTLEDGE COMPANION TO TRUST
Edited by Rosalind Searle, Ann-Marie Nienaber and Sim Sitkin

THE ROUTLEDGE COMPANION TO TAX AVOIDANCE RESEARCH
Edited by Nigar Hashimzade and Yuliya Epifantseva

THE ROUTLEDGE COMPANION TO INTELLECTUAL CAPITAL
Edited by James Guthrie, John Dumay, Federica Ricceri and Christian Neilsen

THE ROUTLEDGE COMPANION TO BEHAVIOURAL ACCOUNTING RESEARCH
Edited by Theresa Libby and Linda Thorne

THE ROUTLEDGE COMPANION TO ACCOUNTING INFORMATION SYSTEMS
Edited by Martin Quinn and Erik Strauß

THE ROUTLEDGE COMPANION TO BUSINESS ETHICS
Edited by Eugene Heath, Byron Kaldis and Alexei Marcoux

The Routledge Companion to Business Ethics

*Edited by Eugene Heath, Byron Kaldis
and Alexei Marcoux*

LONDON AND NEW YORK

First published 2018
by Routledge
2 Park Square, Milton Park, Abingdon, Oxon OX14 4RN

and by Routledge
711 Third Avenue, New York, NY 10017

Routledge is an imprint of the Taylor & Francis Group, an informa business

© 2018 selection and editorial matter, Eugene Heath, Byron Kaldis and Alexei Marcoux; individual chapters, the contributors

The rights of Eugene Heath, Byron Kaldis and Alexei Marcoux to be identified as the authors of the editorial material, and of the authors for their individual chapters, has been asserted in accordance with sections 77 and 78 of the Copyright, Designs and Patents Act 1988.

All rights reserved. No part of this book may be reprinted or reproduced or utilised in any form or by any electronic, mechanical, or other means, now known or hereafter invented, including photocopying and recording, or in any information storage or retrieval system, without permission in writing from the publishers.

Trademark notice: Product or corporate names may be trademarks or registered trademarks, and are used only for identification and explanation without intent to infringe.

British Library Cataloguing-in-Publication Data
A catalogue record for this book is available from the British Library

Library of Congress Cataloging-in-Publication Data
Names: Heath, Eugene, editor. | Kaldis, Byron, editor. | Marcoux, Alexei M., editor.
Title: The Routledge companion to business ethics / edited by Eugene Heath, Byron Kaldis and Alexei Marcoux.
Description: 1 Edition. | New York : Routledge, 2018.
Identifiers: LCCN 2017038462| ISBN 9781138789562 | ISBN 9781315764818 (ebk)
Subjects: LCSH: Business ethics.
Classification: LCC HF5387 .R6767 2018 | DDC 174/.4—dc23
LC record available at https://lccn.loc.gov/2017038462

ISBN: 978-1-138-78956-2 (hbk)
ISBN: 978-1-315-76481-8 (ebk)

Typeset in Bembo
by Swales & Willis Ltd, Exeter, Devon, UK

Contents

List of figures   *xiii*
List of tables   *xiv*
List of contributors   *xv*
Acknowledgements   *xix*

    Introduction   1
    Eugene Heath, Byron Kaldis and Alexei Marcoux

PART I
The discipline of business ethics   5

1. The history of business ethics   7
   Bernard Mees

   The "idol of origins" 8
   Critics of capitalism 10
   Business ethics becomes a field of study 12

2. Theorists and philosophers on business ethics   23
   George Bragues

   Ancient and medieval suspicions of commerce 24
   The modern approval of business 27
   The late modern attack on business 31
   The philosophic epoch of business ethics 33

3. Theory and method in business ethics   38
   Nicholas Capaldi

   Hostility to business and business ethics 39
   The philosophical background 41
   The Enlightenment Project and contemporary ethics 44
   Exploration: the "new" normative methodology 46
   Two competing narratives of philosophical exploration 49
   An alternative method: explication 51

v

Contents

4 Teaching business ethics: current practice and future directions   60
   Darin Gates, Bradley R. Agle, and Richard N. Williams

   Business ethics: education vs. training 60
   The why, what, how, where, and when of business ethics education 62
   Strengthening a student's moral sense and commitment 67
   Moral blindness, self-deception, and unethical actions 70

PART II
Moral philosophy and business: foundational theories   77

5 Consequentialism and non-consequentialism   79
   Andrew Gustafson

   A brief overview of ethical theories 80
   Ethical theories of non-consequentialism and consequentialism 81
   Non-consequentialism and consequentialism in business ethics 85

6 Social contract theories   96
   Pedro Francés-Gómez

   A taxonomy of social contract approaches 96
   Justification of the social contract theory of business ethics 98
   How does it work? The elements of CBE 99
   Integrative Social Contracts Theory (ISCT) 103
   Application and criticism of Integrative Social Contracts Theory 105
   Other social contract theories in business ethics 106
   Concluding remarks: criticism and new directions 108

7 Can profit seekers be virtuous?   113
   Michael C. Munger and Daniel C. Russell

   Can profit seekers be virtuous? 114
   Profits in the entrepreneurial process 116
   Virtuously seeking profits 122
   Entrepreneurial virtue in commercial society vs. rent-seeking society 125

8 Feminist ethics and business ethics: redefining landscapes of learning   131
   Ming Lim

   Feminist ethics and the ethics of care 133
   Feminist ethics and business ethics 134
   Ethics of care: a way forward? 136
   Virtue, self, and other: implications for business ethics 137
   Etienne Wenger: learning a (virtue) ethics of relationship 140

9 Business ethics and religious belief   148
   Kenneth J. Barnes

   The Hebrew tradition 148
   The Christian traditions 151
   Islam 158
   Religions of Asia 159

PART III
Business ethics theories   **165**

10 Social responsibility   167
    Florian Wettstein

    Social responsibility defined 168
    Can corporations have moral responsibilities? Corporations as moral agents 169
    What are the social responsibilities of corporations? 171
    Making sense of CSR theory and practice 172
    New directions in CSR 176

11 Stakeholder thinking   184
    Kenneth E. Goodpaster

    Setting the stage 185
    Conscience: personal and institutional 187
    Is stakeholder thinking more an obstacle to than a proxy for
    *   corporate conscience? 188*
    From stakeholder to comprehensive moral thinking 194
    Implications for business education 197
    Appendix: the MBA Oath 203

12 Integrative Economic Ethics: concept and critique   204
    Alexander Lorch and Thomas Beschorner

    Integrative versus applied ethics 205
    Discourse, legitimization, and responsibility 207
    The micro level: the ethics of economic citizens 210
    The meso level: normative stakeholder management 211
    The macro level: republican liberalism and regulatory ethics 213

PART IV
Conceptual considerations   **221**

13 What is business?   223
    William Kline

    Business as an organization 224
    Business as an activity 228
    Stakeholder theory, participation rights, and fair decision procedures 232

Contents

14 The corporation: genesis, identity, agency ... 239
   Gordon G. Sollars

   Origins of the corporation 239
   Theories of the corporation 243
   Corporate moral agency 248

15 Alternative business organizations and
   social enterprise ... 257
   Dana Brakman Reiser

   The US experience described 258
   A critique of US specialized forms 263
   The European environment explored 265
   Evaluating European social enterprise forms 269

16 The ethics of entrepreneurship ... 275
   Christian Lautermann and Kim Oliver Tokarski

   Conceptions of entrepreneurship 276
   Expanded conceptions of entrepreneurship 277
   Core elements of entrepreneurship 279
   Ethical entrepreneurship: empirical considerations 280
   Ethical entrepreneurship: normative considerations 283

17 The contribution of economics to business ethics ... 290
   Joseph Heath

   Skepticism about business ethics 291
   The rational choice revolution 295
   The new modesty 300

PART V
Economic institutions: operations and effects ... 307

18 Property and business ... 309
   Bas van der Vossen

   Forms of ownership 309
   Two kinds of justification 311
   The conventionalist objection 317
   Intellectual property 318
   Concluding remarks: business and property 321

19 Creativity, innovation, and the production of wealth   326
    Knut Sogner

    Innovation and neoclassical economics 327
    The interactive approach to innovation 330
    Innovation institutionalized 333
    Living in an unsuccessful age? 337

20 Money and finance: ethical
    considerations   343
    Antonio Argandoña

    The legal and institutional framework 344
    The ethics of financial intermediaries 346
    The ethics of financial markets 351
    Alternative finance 353

21 Regulation, rent seeking, and business ethics   359
    Christel Koop and John Meadowcroft

    A typology of business ethics and regulation 361
    The business ethics of rent seeking 367
    Regulation, rent seeking, and institutional design 371

22 Business, nature, and environmental
    sustainability   376
    Joseph DesJardins

    Environmental goods as economic resources: where markets can work 377
    Environmental goods and intrinsic value: where markets won't work 378
    The ethics and environmentalism of sustainable development 381
    What sustainability is not 386

23 The economic crisis: causes and considerations   393
    Randall G. Holcombe

    Ethics and economics 394
    Public policy on mortgages and the 2008 crisis 395
    The role of the Fed in the crisis 398
    The financial industry bailout 399
    The auto industry bailout, and more 402
    The ethics of the policy response 403
    Housing policy and the political process 404
    Political capitalism 405

Contents

PART VI
Roles and responsibilities within the firm   **411**

24 Corporate governance   415
Ann K. Buchholtz

The primacy debate 416
Issues surrounding shareholders 418
Issues surrounding boards of directors 420
The nature and role of the CEO 422

25 Leadership and business ethics: are leaders wolves
for business ethics?   430
Valérie Petit and Sarah E. Saint-Michel

Theoretical foundations: desperately seeking ethics in leadership 431
The moral manager: navigating ethical leadership 433
The moral person: exploring the character of business leaders 437
Ethical leadership in the age of corporate social responsibility 438

26 Theoretical issues in management ethics   447
Joseph A. Petrick

Major management theories 447
Major ethics theories 450
Selected theoretical issues in management ethics 452

27 The ethics of managers and employees   459
Linda Klebe Treviño

Ethical awareness, judgment, motivation, and action 460
Managing ethical conduct through ethics and compliance programs 462
Ethical culture 463

28 Employee ethics and rights   474
Jeffrey Moriarty

Freedom of contract: Lochner's shadow 474
Starting and terminating the employment relationship 475
Compensation 478
The nature of work: meaningful work and workplace democracy 480
Privacy 482
Whistleblowing 484

29 Exploitation and labor   490
Benjamin Ferguson

How are laborers wronged? 491
What do firms owe their employees? 493
Who is responsible when workers are wronged? 501

30 Ethical issues in marketing, advertising, and sales 506
Minette Drumwright

Marketing, ethics, and marketing ethics 506
Criticisms of marketing 508
Conceptual and theoretical perspectives on marketing ethics 515

31 The accounting profession, the public interest, and human rights 523
Ken McPhail

Introducing accounting ethics 524
Introducing professions and the public interest 525
Expressions of the public interest 527
Accounting and human rights 529

PART VII
Multinational corporations and globalization 541

32 The globalization of business ethics 543
Kirk O. Hanson

Business ethics emerges in US business schools 544
A focus on business ethics emerges in US corporations 544
Interest in business ethics beyond the United States 545
Globalization becomes an economic reality 547
The growth of corporate global ethics programs 548
Defining a global ethic for business: challenges 550

33 Cross-cultural management ethics in multinational commerce 556
Terence Jackson

Foundations: Hofstede's cultural values approach in international
    management studies 556
Building on Hofstede's foundations 561
World Values Survey and modernization theory 563
Ethical judgments, algorithms, and codes of ethics 565

34 Corruption, bribery, and moral norms across
    national boundaries 573
Wesley Cragg

Bribery and gifts 575
Bribery: inherent characteristics 577
Bribery: a complex social, economic, and political reality 579
Addressing the paradox of bribery through legal reform 580
The pursuit of integrity in business and government: lessons
    and challenges 582
The character of corruption 585

Contents

PART VIII
Business ethics across the globe   591

35 Business ethics in China   593
    Yuqiao Xiang

    The new era in China and the rise of business ethics 593
    Theoretical trends in Chinese business ethics 598
    The future challenges of business ethics in China 602

36 Business ethics in South Asia: Gandhian trusteeship and its relevance
    for the twenty-first century   606
    S. Ramakrishna Velamuri

    Business ethics in South Asia: scholarship, teaching, and practice 608
    Gandhi's trusteeship framework 610
    Trusteeship: a critical appraisal 615
    Applicability of Gandhian trusteeship in the twenty-first century 617

37 Business ethics in Africa   624
    Minka Woermann

    Business ethics developments in Sub-Saharan Africa 625
    Business in Africa: contextual considerations and challenges 628
    Towards an African business ethics 634

38 Business ethics in Latin America   641
    Álvaro E. Pezoa

    Business ethics in Latin America: an approach to reality through the press 641
    Comparative data on public corruption 644
    Teaching and research 647
    *Corporate practices, Non-Governmental Organizations (NGOs)
        and government initiatives 648*
    Appendix: press citations 652

39 Business ethics in transition: communism to commerce in
    Central Europe and Russia   657
    Rodica Milena Zaharia

    Business ethics under communism 658
    Similarities among former communist countries 660
    Differences among former communist countries 664
    Business ethics and the EU 667

Index   674

Figures

3.1	The philosophical ordering of the universe and the priority of metaphysics	45
11.1	Google NGRAM of "stakeholder" in relation to "stockholder" and "shareholder"	184
11.2	A depiction of Gewirth's view of ethics	191
11.3	A depiction of stakeholder thinking along with shareholder thinking as part of the internal morality of the corporation	196
12.1	Two-level conception of corporate ethics	209
14.1	Owner shielding vs. entity shielding	248
26.1	Managerial competing values and integrity capacity framework	454

Tables

3.1	The competing narratives of Locke and Rousseau	52
4.1	Topical coverage in a selection of ethics textbooks	64
14.1	Types of theories (of the corporation)	243
21.1	Views of business ethics and regulation	365

Contributors

Bradley R. Agle, George W. Romney Endowed Professor, and Director of the Wheatley Institution Ethics Initiative, Brigham Young University, Provo, Utah, USA.

Antonio Argandoña, Emeritus Professor of Economics and Business Ethics, CaixaBank Chair of Corporate Social Responsibility, IESE Business School, University of Navarra, Barcelona, Spain.

Kenneth J. Barnes, Mockler-Phillips Professor of Workplace Theology and Business Ethics, Gordon-Conwell Theological Seminary, Boston, Massachusetts, USA.

Thomas Beschorner, Chair for Business Ethics and Director of the Institute for Business Ethics at the University of St. Gallen, Switzerland.

George Bragues, Assistant Vice-Provost and Program Head of Business, University of Guelph-Humber, Toronto, Canada.

Dana Brakman Reiser, Professor of Law, Brooklyn Law School, Brooklyn, New York, USA.

Ann K. Buchholtz (d. September 14, 2015) was Professor of Leadership and Ethics, and Research Director, Institute for Ethical Leadership, Rutgers University Business School, Newark, New Jersey, USA.

Nicholas Capaldi, Legendre-Soulé Distinguished Chair of Business Ethics, Loyola University, New Orleans, USA.

Wesley Cragg (d. August 26, 2017) was Senior Scholar, Professor Emeritus and Director, Canadian Business Ethics Research Network, Schulich School of Business and Department of Philosophy, York University, Toronto, Ontario, Canada.

Joseph DesJardins, Ralph Gross Chair in Business and the Liberal Arts, Professor of Philosophy, College of St. Benedict and St. John's University, Minnesota, USA.

Minette (Meme) Drumwright, Associate Professor, Stan Richards School of Advertising and Public Relations, University of Texas at Austin, Texas, USA.

Contributors

Benjamin Ferguson, Assistant Professor of Ethics, VU Amsterdam, the Netherlands.

Pedro Francés-Gómez, Professor of Moral and Political Philosophy, University of Granada, Spain.

Darin Gates, Visiting Fellow, The Wheatley Institution, Adjunct Professor of Philosophy and Computer Science, Brigham Young University, Provo, Utah, USA.

Kenneth E. Goodpaster, Professor Emeritus, Ethics and Business Law Department, Opus College of Business, University of St. Thomas, Minneapolis-St. Paul, Minnesota, USA.

Andrew Gustafson, Associate Professor of Business Ethics and Society, Heider College of Business, Creighton University, Omaha, Nebraska, USA.

Kirk O. Hanson, John Courtney Murray SJ University Professor of Social Ethics and Director, Markkula Center for Applied Ethics, Santa Clara University, California, USA.

Eugene Heath, Professor of Philosophy, State University of New York, New Paltz, USA.

Joseph Heath, Professor, Department of Philosophy and School of Public Policy and Governance, University of Toronto, Canada.

Randall G. Holcombe, DeVoe Moore Professor of Economics, Florida State University, Tallahassee, Florida, USA.

Terence Jackson, Professor of Cross Cultural Management, Middlesex University Business School, London, UK.

Byron Kaldis, Professor of Philosophy, Department of Humanities, Social Sciences and Law, The National Technical University of Athens, Greece, and Xiaoxiang Scholar, Moral Culture Research Center, Hunan Normal University, China.

William Kline, Associate Professor of Business Ethics, University of Illinois, Springfield, USA.

Christel Koop, Senior Lecturer in Political Economy, King's College London, UK.

Christian Lautermann, Research Associate, CENTOS—Oldenburg Center of Sustainability Economics and Management, Carl von Ossietzky University of Oldenburg, Germany.

Ming Lim, Associate Professor of Marketing and Management (Technology and Ethics), University of Liverpool Management School, UK.

Alexander Lorch, Scientific Director of the Kiel Center for Philosophy, Politics and Economics and Research Assistant at the Chair for Practical Philosophy, University of Kiel, Germany.

Alexei Marcoux, Professor of Business Ethics and Society, Institute for Economic Inquiry Senior Scholar, Heider College of Business, Creighton University, Omaha, Nebraska, USA.

Contributors

Ken McPhail, Associate Dean & Professor of Accounting, Alliance Manchester Business School, University of Manchester, UK, and Research Professor of Accounting, La Trobe University, Melbourne, Australia.

John Meadowcroft, Senior Lecturer in Public Policy, Department of Political Economy, King's College London, London, UK.

Bernard Mees, Associate Professor in Management, Tasmanian School of Business and Economics, University of Tasmania, Hobart, Australia.

Jeffrey Moriarty, Associate Professor and Chair, Department of Philosophy, Bentley University, Waltham, Massachusetts, USA.

Michael C. Munger, Director, Philosophy, Politics, and Economics Program, Duke University, Durham, North Carolina, USA.

Valérie Petit, Associate Professor of Leadership, Director of EDHEC Open Leadership Center, EDHEC Business School, Lille, France.

Joseph A. Petrick, Emeritus Professor of Management and Director of the Institute for Business Integrity, Wright State University, Dayton, Ohio, USA.

Álvaro E. Pezoa, Professor of Business Ethics and Corporate Responsibility and Director of the Center for Business Ethics, ESE Business School, Universidad de los Andes (Chile), and Research Fellow, W. Michael Hoffman Center for Business Ethics, Bentley University, Waltham, Massachusetts, USA.

Daniel C. Russell, Professor of Philosophy, Center for the Philosophy of Freedom, University of Arizona, Tucson, USA.

Sarah E. Saint-Michel, Associate Professor of Human Resource Management and Leadership, Université Paris I Panthéon-Sorbonne, Paris, France.

Knut Sogner, Professor of Economic History, Department of Law and Governance, BI Norwegian Business School, Oslo, Norway.

Gordon G. Sollars, Associate Professor of Management, Fairleigh Dickinson University, Teaneck, New Jersey, USA.

Kim Oliver Tokarski, Professor of Business Management and Entrepreneurship, Institute for Corporate Development, Bern University of Applied Sciences, Switzerland.

Linda Klebe Treviño, Distinguished Professor of Organizational Behavior and Ethics, Smeal College of Business, The Pennsylvania State University, University Park, Pennsylvania, USA.

S. Ramakrishna Velamuri, Professor of Entrepreneurship, China Europe International Business School (CEIBS), Shanghai, China.

Contributors

Bas van der Vossen, Associate Professor, Smith Institute of Political Economy and Philosophy, and Philosophy Department, Chapman University, Orange, California, USA.

Florian Wettstein, Chair and Professor of Business Ethics and Director, Institute for Business Ethics, University of St. Gallen, Switzerland.

Richard N. Williams, Professor of Psychology, and Director of the Wheatley Institution at Brigham Young University, Provo, Utah, USA.

Minka Woermann, Senior Lecturer, Department of Philosophy and Centre for Applied Ethics, Stellenbosch University, South Africa.

Yuqiao Xiang, Professor of the Research Institute of Ethics and Moral Culture, Hunan Normal University, Changsha, Hunan Province, China.

Rodica Milena Zaharia, Professor, Department of International Business and Economics, The Bucharest University of Economic Studies, and Executive Director of the Research Center in International Business and Economics (CCREI), Bucharest, Romania.

Acknowledgements

Eugene Heath and Alexei Marcoux wish to thank, respectively, Reva Wolf and Arianne Marcoux for their support and patience during the completion of this project; Byron Kaldis would like to thank little Chris Gabriel Kaldis for his understandable *im*patience and for providing a never-ending pleasurable distraction. For their collegial and helpful assistance, we also thank Natalie Tomlinson, our editor at Routledge, and her editorial assistants Isobel Fitzharris and Judith Lorton. For her cooperation in readying the chapters for publication, the editors thank Martha Teck, State University of New York at New Paltz, who not only found the time to assist but did so in a most efficient and agreeable way.

Introduction

Eugene Heath, Byron Kaldis and Alexei Marcoux

The discipline of business ethics continues to expand institutionally, geographically, and intellectually. During the past five decades, scholars in business ethics have developed and deepened their enquiries into the morals of commercial and corporate conduct. As markets have advanced globally, so have universities throughout the world sought to develop courses and research programs devoted to business ethics. As a result, scholars from Europe, Asia, Africa, and the Americas confer at international conferences, contribute to the same journals, and learn from one another. As commerce expands in both geographical reach and novelty, so do business norms come into tension with other social norms, raising fresh questions about the ethical contours of business practice.

There exists, therefore, a growing global audience for a single volume that examines the discipline as a whole, situates chief concerns within a larger economic and theoretical framework, and sets forth themes and concepts in a clear, engaging, balanced, and analytical fashion. This volume fulfills this aim. Its various chapters provide a lucid and comprehensive account of business ethics and place the relevant concepts, arguments, and themes within a larger context of economics, politics, and law. In so doing our authors provide fresh insights and analyses and do not shrink from exploring omissions and unsupported claims, or from suggesting new avenues of research. The volume offers, therefore, a frank assessment of the state of business ethics worldwide.

Such an assessment is, in fact, exactly what a reader should want and expect. After all, as a "companion" the volume should fulfill some of the features of any good companion, even of a friend. Aristotle suggested that friendship might exemplify pleasure, utility, or virtue, with the last manifesting true friendship. In a similar way, this volume should provide pleasures of discovery and enlightenment and promote the utility born of knowledge. Yet, in another extended sense, this volume offers a version of true companionship, at least for the reader who shares with the editors and contributors these aims: to discern what is good and right about exchange, production, and commerce; to learn about how and whether commercial societies may not only be productive but good; and to examine the state and character of business ethics across the globe.

Many of these subjects are, no doubt, contestable and worthy of a thoughtful and deliberate sifting. One of the editors' motivating concerns has been that too much of contemporary business ethics proceeds as if certain leading ideas and topics are mounted permanently at the center of the discipline—in no need of contestation, challenge, or reconsideration. Scholarly explorations simply cite some leading figure or figures and then proceed as if all were settled. Yet such assumptions have a way of discouraging robust inquiry and new perspectives; they lead to treading circular paths of affirmation and celebration, not to blazing new trails of thought and analysis. Certainly, the leading ideas of a discipline deserve a clear and fair hearing, but so do worthy challenges to these ideas. If business ethics is to continue forward, then its commitment should be less to leading figures of the discipline than to ideas, arguments, and analyses.

The *Companion* offers a broad and unmatched overview of the discipline of business ethics—what it *is* and what it may *become*. The authors, who hail from across the globe and from distinct generations, have been selected not only for their expertise but also because of their abilities to address business ethics in a balanced, fresh, and critical manner. In the almost forty chapters gathered in this volume our authors examine salient topics within or related to the discipline, note nascent themes, and provide a critical appreciation of significant ideas as well as an assessment of unexamined concepts, unexplored assumptions, or relevant subjects that have received insufficient attention from business ethics scholars. Notably, some chapters explore the larger context of economic institutions or the history of ideas as these relate to business ethics; others focus chiefly on law and ethics, or on practical aspects of business ethics, whether within the firm or across the globe; still others explore particular ethical issues arising in regions in which commercial engagements and business ethics are advancing. Each chapter offers a full bibliography, as well as a selection of "Essential readings"—works that provide the reader with a basis for further exploration of the topic at hand. In addition, each chapter also notes where in this volume the reader might turn if he or she wishes to find a related or complementary discussion.

The *Companion* consists of eight thematic units. The first includes chapters that introduce the discipline, recount its history, and take up central questions of pedagogy. The chapters in the second section address how ethical theories (e.g., deontological, consequentialist, as well as social contract, virtue, feminist theories, and religious perspectives) have been *applied* to the field of business; the third delves into normative theories specific to business (e.g., stakeholder theory, social responsibility, Integrative Economic Ethics). A fourth part explores essential conceptual considerations regarding business as an organization; the genesis, identity, and nature of the corporation; alternative conceptions of business organization; the varieties of ethical entrepreneurship; and the ways in which economic models may affect the arguments and conclusions of business ethicists. In the fifth division, the chapters focus on the institutions and operations of markets: property as the basis of exchange; money and finance; commercial and political decision-making and the role of regulation and rent seeking in competitive markets; business and the environment; innovation and productivity; and the nature of economic crises, using the financial collapse of 2008 as the focus. The sixth section takes up specific roles within business, with chapters focusing on management ethics (one chapter devoted to theoretical issues, and a second to practical questions), employee responsibilities and rights, the question of exploitation, the ethics of entrepreneurship, sales and advertising, accounting ethics, corporate governance, and leadership. The seventh section offers several chapters devoted to salient concerns of globalization: management across divergent cultures and outlooks; bribery and corruption across the globe; the role of multinational corporations and social responsibility in the global economy; and the globalization of business ethics. The eighth section offers chapters that describe the practice and scholarship of business ethics in countries and regions in transition.

What do the chapters of the *Companion* reveal? Most notably, the *Companion* exhibits the broad and interdisciplinary nature of business ethics and its relation to philosophy, management, economics, politics, law, and history. In a sense, of course, business ethicists already knew these facts about their discipline. However, the reminder is salutary and important:

The attentive business ethicist must cast an eye not only on some specific problem or issue but on how that problem or issue relates to underlying institutions, ethical and economic assumptions, as well as legal or cultural questions. These facts testify to the enduring importance of business ethics and the depth of its topics. The *Companion* reveals secondly how business ethics is not simply a North American phenomenon but also a European, South American, Asian, and African concern. Finally, the *Companion* reminds us that many seemingly settled topics of business ethics—including notions of corporate social responsibility, stakeholderism, even the very nature of business—remain avenues of exploration rather than alleys of assumptions. In this way, the *Companion* encourages a wide array of authors, a great variety of viewpoints, and a genuinely probing assessment of contentions too often regarded as incontestable. Through these effects the *Companion* aims to furnish what friends and companions provide: a steady and genuine resource from which to sift and to explore in an on-going attempt to realize goodness and to live rightly and well.

Part I
The discipline of business ethics

Focused on the ethics of commerce, business ethics (like other disciplines) has a history, theoretical tendencies, and preferred methods. The first two chapters in this section explore the history of business ethics and the way in which trade and commerce have featured in the thought of important philosophers. The next two chapters take up the current discipline of business ethics, both as a field of inquiry with particular theoretical assumptions and as field of pedagogy—business ethics in the classroom.

In the opening chapter, **The history of business ethics**, **Bernard Mees** delineates the broad history of business ethics, commencing from some of its oldest and most ancient sources and then considering elements of medieval thought. With the rise of industrialization there emerged both defenses and criticisms of business and the effects of commerce. Mees notes some of the signal works of the twentieth century that would lead ultimately to the institutionalization of business ethics in the universities and to the contemporary focus on issues of responsibility, leadership, and sustainability.

In Chapter 2, **Theorists and philosophers on business ethics**, **George Bragues** offers a complementary essay that focuses on the ideas and arguments of significant philosophers and thinkers. Bragues discerns a dual tendency emerging in the history of ideas, with the institutions and achievements of trade and business receiving both criticism and valorization. Aristotle viewed trade rather suspiciously, bequeathing to later thinkers, such as St Thomas Aquinas, a "circumscribed tolerance of business." However, early modern thinkers, such as Machiavelli and Mandeville, seek a reconsideration of whether virtue is a unique condition for prosperity, with later thinkers, including Locke, Hume, Kant, and Bentham, developing this reassessment further and offering a positive outlook on commerce. However, Rousseau and Marx offer a more critical perspective. Within the contemporary sphere, says Bragues, philosophers offer a "middle way" between the positive embrace of commerce and its rejection.

In the third chapter, **Theory and method in business ethics**, **Nicholas Capaldi** probes the discipline of business ethics, taking up both its genesis as a disciplinary field and its guiding assumptions. After noting the ambiguities of business ethics, as well as the general antipathy of intellectuals toward commerce, Capaldi situates contemporary business ethics within deeper tendencies of the modern philosophical outlook and delineates how business ethics has become an instance of the philosophical *exploration* of an underlying structure of conduct. After setting forth two opposing narratives of exploration, the Lockean and the Rousseauian, Capaldi suggests an alternative method of business ethics that rejects abstract applications of theory and seeks, instead, to *explicate* the implicit practices and norms of business.

Whether taught by philosophers or management scholars, business ethics is featured in most graduate business schools, as well as in many undergraduate curricula. In Chapter 4, **Teaching business ethics: current practice and future directions**, **Darin Gates, Bradley R. Agle, and Richard N. Williams** distinguish education from training and then canvas the purpose and content of business ethics education, noting its curricular location, academic levels, and methods. They offer counsel as to how education may reinforce a common-sense moral outlook and contribute to a greater awareness of moral blindness and self-deception.

Alexei Marcoux and Eugene Heath

1

The history of business ethics

Bernard Mees

In 1956 the first edition of Samuel Noah Kramer's bestselling *History Begins at Sumer: Thirty-nine Firsts in Recorded History* appeared, a good place if any to look for the origins of business ethics. The earliest written records acknowledged by historians come from the ruins of ancient Sumer, predating the earliest Chinese and European texts by many centuries. And the second-last of his historical firsts is, as Kramer labels it, the "The Pickaxe and the Plow: Labor's first victory." The passage, dating from the third millennium BC, takes a typical Sumerian form: that of a disputation. It begins with a pickaxe challenging a plow to see which implement is superior. The plow states that it is "the faithful farmer of mankind . . . the great nobles walk by my side, All the lands are full of admiration." The pickaxe, retorts in turn, that it is used in many more industries than the plow is, and furthermore:

> You, whose accomplishments are meager
>
> (but) whose ways are proud,
>
> My working time is twelve months,
>
> (But) the time you are present (for work) is four months,
>
> (While) the time you disappear is eight months,
>
> You are absent twice the time you are present.
>
> *(Kramer 1956: 345, trans. Kramer)*

The response of the plow (if any) is not recorded. The pickaxe won its case not just by arguing its broader utility, but particularly by pointing out that a pickaxe works much longer hours.

It is perhaps not customary to think of hours of work as particularly important in business ethics, but how many hours (and how hard) someone works has long been a key concern in commercial circles. One of the most widely accepted ethical judgements that prevails in the business world is that hard work is good and should be rewarded. Indeed a survey of American business ethics (Sutton et al. 1956), from the same year as Kramer's *History Begins at Sumer* first appeared, claimed that hard work was the only ethic broadly upheld in commercial life at the time. The valuing of hard work (as opposed to laziness) is one of the key moral issues still stressed in contemporary business, whether by Confucian cultural nationalists, Middle Eastern Islamic moralists or members of the boards of Western corporations. It reminds us that what constitutes ethical behavior in business can include both universal and ancient issues. At the same time, since what is judged morally good behavior in a business context is often contested and evolving, it may be given both a politically conservative and progressive assessment, as well as being a historically grounded, particular, and contested concern.

If business ethics is centrally concerned with "moral reasoning aimed at supporting managers' ethical obligations" (Green and Donovan 2010: 23), then issues such as work ethic remain central to its understanding. In fact, and as set forth in the first section of this chapter, discourses of business ethics are already evidenced at the dawn of recorded history and ancient philosophical traditions are widely referenced in contemporary business scholarship. In the subsequent section, we glimpse how similar discourses developed under the influence of industrialization; these became entwined with political philosophy as the number and size of organizations grew and increasing urbanization occurred. As characterized in the last section, a more focused tradition has arisen since the 1960s, and it has become a key concern of the business or management curriculum. These three periods of development are historically linked, with facets of present-day business ethics often having quite ancient intellectual histories.

The "idol of origins"

Rather than begin (with Kramer) at Sumer, historical surveys of business ethics tend to start with a reference to the Bible, the laws of the ancient Babylonian King Hammurabi, or to Aristotle, the fourth-century BC Greek author of the *Nicomachean Ethics* (e.g., De George 2006, but see also Abend 2013). But an older philosophical source would be Confucius (Kong Fuzi), the semi-legendary sixth-century BC author of the *Analects* (Confucius, trans. Lau 1979). The Confucian underpinnings of East Asian business ethics, however, have been contested by historians. Duty to the family (*xiao* or filial piety), for example, trumps any duty to uphold state law in traditional Confucian thinking: as Confucius comments in the tale of "Upright Gong" in the *Analects* (13.18) "fathers cover up for sons, and sons cover up for their fathers—'Uprightness' is to be found in that" (Rainey 2010: 25; Sarkissian 2010: 726). Indeed Confucius himself and his many followers (including later Confucian scholars such as Mencius) shared a disdain of merchants (Wang 2004). The notion of a Confucian business ethics often reflects a reconfiguration of the Confucian heritage by members of the Chinese diaspora (Dirlik 1995; Yao 2002; Makeham 2003; Wang 2004). How such understandings might apply in the People's Republic of China today remains something of a quandary when taken from a historical perspective (Sun 2005; Elstein and Tian 2017).

As the French medievalist Marc Bloch (1954: 24–35) explained, the "idol of origins" or the search for roots can often obscure historical understanding. But as Foucault (1972) observes, it is the continuity and discontinuity of discourses (such as ethics) that are a key focus in the history of ideas. From the Greek perspective, beginning a history of business ethics with Aristotle's assessment of commercial relationships in his *Politics* passes over the longstanding Greek traditions that date back to Homer. In the *Homeric Hymn to Hermes*, for example, the god most famous for his thievery states "I will take up whatever business is most profitable" (trans. Brown 1947: 72). In myth, Greek morality is typically daring, cunning, heroic and resourceful, but by the time of Aristotle's philosophical tracts it was logical, measured, considered and thoughtful. This distinction of *mythos* and *logos* (Fowler 2011) is characteristic of ancient Greek thought and is largely omitted from modern business-school accounts of Greek moral philosophy as if it were not a key tradition passed down from antiquity. But Hermes' Roman equivalent Mercury is usually thought to have been named for his association with *merx* or "merchandise"; hence *merchant* "a buyer of merchandise."

With the Greek and Chinese traditions, a third major influence on contemporary business ethics to have been passed down from ancient times is that of the Hebrew Torah and its associated texts. This religious collection from the last millennium BC was supplemented in the Christian tradition by four accounts of the life of Christ and a selection of other (mostly) first-century writings, but the Jewish and Christian scriptural traditions have long proved a treasure trove for moral teachings. From "A false balance is an abomination to the Lord but a just weight is his delight" (Proverbs 11:1) to "It is easier for a camel to pass through the eye of a needle, than for a rich man to enter into the kingdom of heaven" (Matthew 19:24), all manner of scriptural quotations, both parables and specific moral claims, have proved influential to understandings of Western business.

Perhaps most notably, however, from the perspective of historical continuity, is the work of the thirteenth-century philosopher St Thomas Aquinas. Aquinas sought to reconcile the ancient Greek tradition, particularly in the form bequeathed by Aristotle, with Christian Scripture. In doing so, he developed a theory of just price: "If someone would be greatly helped by something belonging to someone else, and the seller not similarly harmed by losing it, the seller must not sell for a higher price: because the usefulness that goes to the buyer comes not from the seller, but from the buyer's needy condition" (*Summa Theologica* ii-ii.77.1). Perhaps more importantly than advocating fairness in trading, however, Aquinas's *Summa Theologica* (ed. O'Sullivan 1952) was considered such a great work for generations to come that he rescued Aristotelian ethics for the Western world and encouraged the establishment of a continuous tradition of writing on business ethics.

Many of the world's non-Western ethical traditions can be seen to be preserved in a state more akin to ancient Greek *mythos* or the largely unstructured manner in which Biblical quotations have often been used by Christian preachers. The Islamic prohibition against the charging of interest (*riba*), for example, derives directly from the Qur'an (2:275) and more reflections on commercial ethics can be found in the Hadith (Sayings of the Prophet) such as "The seller and the buyer have the right to keep or return goods as long as they have not parted or till they part" (Al-Bukhari, trans. Khan 1997: iii, 293). Vedic concepts such as *karma* "action (cause and effect)" and *dharma* "(universal) law" are also important contributions to contemporary Indian understandings of business morality (Berger and Herstein 2014). Nonetheless, a developed tradition of business ethics comparable to the Thomist kind has not fully emerged in non-Western traditions—that is in the sense of major and in-depth studies of the *logos* of business practice. There are longstanding and distinctive discourses of received Confucian, Buddhist, Islamic, Taoist and Hindu ethics at the generic, personal or public levels, but these are not so clearly focused especially on commercial concerns. It is the continuity and focus brought to business ethics by Aquinas that makes him the founder of a considered continuous (or genealogical) tradition of writings on the morality of commercial dealings. The continuous nature of this tradition can be most obviously seen in the works of the late medieval business ethicist Johannes Nider (trans. Reeves 1966) who wrote an entire Thomist-inspired treatise, *On the Contracts of Merchants*, in the fifteenth century (Wren 2000), or John Locke's essay "Venditio" (1661), which still informs conceptions of public choice today (Guzmán and Munger 2014). But perhaps a more crucial contribution of Aquinas was reviving Aristotle's notion of *phronêsis* or "practical wisdom," a term translated by Aquinas into Latin as *prudentia* "prudence."

One of the most popular forms of early modern moral treatise was the instructional manual written for a territorial prince on how to be a good ruler, most famously Machiavelli's

The Prince (1523). These *Mirrors of the Kings* (*principium speculae*) and similar writings mostly date from the Middle Ages and the years leading up to the Enlightenment, and they customarily stress the importance of prudence, one of the four cardinal virtues of classical philosophy and Christianity. As Aquinas emphasized, judgments using reason for evil means or ends were considered to constitute cunning (*astutas*), not prudence (*Summa Theologica* ii–ii.55.3). Cunning (*mêtis*) was the key feature associated by the classical Greeks with Hermes, the god of merchants (Vergados 2012). But, like hard work, prudence has long come to have a traditional association with business ethics, particularly in the areas of accounting, finance and economics. The Thomist concept of prudence may have been narrowed when used in this way, but saving money for the future is still widely considered moral behavior (as opposed to recklessness); hence the "prudent man" rule so important to the development of English and American trust law (and to the law of fiduciaries generally), and the contemporary use of the term "prudential" to refer to a form of financial duty and regulation.

The traditional Western moral values of hard work, fairness and prudence (or thrift) have their equivalents in Chinese, Islamic and South Asian tradition, and are often thought of by sociologists today in terms of Max Weber's (1904/5) notion of a Protestant Work Ethic. Criticizing Weber, however, the British historian R.H. Tawney (1926) ascribed these values not to Protestantism (Weber relied on a lazy form of anti-Catholicism according to his critics; see Borutta 2013) but to changes in attitudes to the acquisition of wealth in early modern capitalism. More recent historians have traced out more fully how notions such as luxury were transformed from pejoratives (the medieval English meaning of *luxury* was "lechery, sinful self-indulgence") to something not only socially acceptable, but even desirable, indicating how transformative a rising focus on economic value was in early modern times (Berry 1994; Kovesi 2015). Similar influences on the development of moral understandings of the value of hard work, industry and thrift seem to recur in most societies. And while it may be difficult for a rich man to enter heaven, profit can still buy luxury, even if "all that glisters is not gold" as the medieval saying recorded by Shakespeare has it.

As in medieval morality plays, Shakespeare's works are often seen by historians as a key source for understanding early modern English morality. And one of the less appealing aspects of Shakespeare's *Merchant of Venice* is the ruse employed by the heroine Portia to make the Jewish money-lender Shylock give up his claim of a pound of flesh from the merchant Antonio. Portia's actions were judged moral to earlier audiences because of Shylock's profession and religion, reason enough to allow Portia to use such cunning against Shylock that he might beg once again "If you prick us, do we not bleed?" (Act III, scene I), but on the other hand for her to make the equally famous refrain "The quality of mercy is not strained" (Act IV, Scene I). The figure of Shylock, as the Jewish moneylender, represents one of the key European racial stereotypes that contributed to the twentieth-century picture of the Jew as being obsessed with money (Shapiro 1997; Reuveni 2010). Above all, the anti-Semitism of Shakespeare reminds us that business morals can change over time.

Critics of capitalism

The emergence of industrial capitalism in Europe in the late eighteenth and nineteenth centuries saw a new focus emerge in considerations of commercial ethics. Issues such as child labor and slavery were considered particularly concerning at the time, much as cigarette smoking, blood diamonds, arms trafficking and pornography remain morally charged issues in business today (cf. As-Saber and Cairns 2015). But much of the criticism of business practice since the emergence of industrial capitalism has derived from discourses that most strongly emerged during the rise of the nineteenth-century workers' movement, and of its supporters, particularly in the works of Karl Marx (1867). The key intellectual influence on the emergence of socialism, however, was the German philosopher G.W.F. Hegel.

Where much contemporary business ethics takes its cue from Immanuel Kant, it was his younger contemporary Hegel who had a greater influence on commercial concerns in the nineteenth century. The Western notion of progress dates back to the ancient period and writers such as St Augustine (Nisbet 1980), but Hegel's understanding that history was politically progressive, as well as economically and technologically advancing, particularly suited the emergence of a critique of business practice that focused on the lived experience of industrialization. Yet, as a transcendental idealist focused on the liberal self, Kant's understanding of the ethics of "good" and "right" has proved an impediment to the development of a wider, more socially grounded, understanding of business ethics. It was Hegel's absolute idealism that inspired more profoundly socialist thinkers such as Marx and hence was more influential in the nineteenth and early twentieth centuries. Kant's *Groundwork of the Metaphysic of Morals* (1785) was a seminal work in Western ethics, arguing that moral questions could be analyzed without recourse to God. "Left" Hegelians such as Marx went further, however, developing anti-religious explanations for ethical matters, decrying religion as an "opiate of the masses" that stopped his contemporaries from seeing that nineteenth-century industrialists had put all the "workers of the world" in "chains."

Where moral reformers such as the Welsh factory owner Robert Owen (Donnachie 2000) had seen the key problems of capitalism as being resolvable by supporting worker cooperatives, Marx (1867) saw the answer to the scourge of labor exploitation in the inevitable collapse of the capitalist system (apparently) presaged by the economic cycles of boom and bust that still typify the contemporary business world. Political economists such as Adam Smith (1776) and David Ricardo (1817) had acted as apologists for capitalism according to Marx, encouraging the "brutal" economic exploitation of factory-owning "parasites" in their endless pursuit of profit. Marx's critique (which held that factory managers were accomplices to "slavery") is not often viewed as part of the mainstream tradition of contemporary business ethics, but rather of political philosophy (Lippke 1995). His monumental work *Capital* (1867) is clearly labeled "A critique of political economy"—i.e., of the works of early economists—and is mainly a study in moral outrage. But in straying so far from the traditions of Aquinas, Kant and Hegel, it often seems a tradition that inhabits only the margins of business ethics discourse today.

Kant is the creator of a tradition of ethics that relies on reason rather than revelation (a common, albeit often unfair criticism of Aquinas). But Kant's influence on business ethics can be seen as negative rather than progressive. Most crucially, Kant (1785) argued that behaviors considered prudent by businessmen (e.g., "honesty is the best policy") could be considered unethical. Kant criticized traditional ethical thinking regarding how a "prudent merchant" behaved as confusing self-interest with principle and duty. Kant not only destroyed the tradition of civic philosophy represented in the genre of the *King's Mirror*, he was the main contributor to the "erosion of prudence" that undermined the Thomist tradition in the minds of many later philosophers (Pieper 1966; Hariman 2003). Kant gave philosophical ethics a new foundation on (ostensibly) rational grounds, but he robbed it of prudence and undermined the received Western philosophical understanding that matters of collective or civic virtue were often not be reducible to individual reason, agency and action.

Nonetheless, the emergence of the nineteenth-century worker movement did inspire action from religious leaders—the traditional gatekeepers of Western morality. Amidst a revival in Thomist thinking, in 1891 Pope Leo XIII issued the encyclical *De rerum novarum* or "On Capital and Labour" that sought to make the Catholic Church's position clear on key matters of political economy. In the neo-Thomist tradition, the Catholic Church is a public guarantor of moral behavior, and *De rerum novarum* forms the basis of Catholic social justice teaching, recognizing (among other matters) the role of trade unions in mitigating the worst effects of industrial capitalism. Reasserted and expanded upon by later works such as Pope St John Paul II's *Centesimus Annus* (1991), Catholic social justice teaching reflects a profound attempt to set out a form of business ethics in the tradition of Aquinas (Pontifical Council for Justice and Peace 2014).

Beginning on an ad hoc basis in the late nineteenth century, groups of Catholic employers' associations also came to be formed, which, by the 1950s, had begun to consolidate internationally (Gremillion 1961). Protestant organizations reacted similarly, realizing that a more considered articulation of Christian moral principles needed to emerge in order to influence contemporary business practice. By the early twentieth century, commercial scandals in the United States had encouraged the establishment of business ethics courses in places such as the Wharton School at the University of Pennsylvania, although these were largely soon forgotten (Abend 2014: 234–40). A former Protestant preacher, Edgar Heermance, produced the first attempt at a survey of American business ethics in 1926, in light of the mania for developing ethics codes that had swept the country in 1922–23 following a relaxation of American monopoly ("anti-trust") regulation that had encouraged the growth of trade associations. Several business ethics professors also produced similar studies (e.g., Taeusch 1931). But the early American business ethics movement seemed to be stillborn. When the William A. Vawter Foundation offered a prize in 1936 for the best business ethics study of the year, the entries proved so disappointing that the competition was never repeated (Abend 2013: 185–89). In his *Acquisitive Society* in 1921, Tawney had mocked the notion that business was a profession and hence could be subject to codes of conduct such as doctors and soldiers were. Most subsequent American commentary duly seemed to prove his point, works like Heermance's *Ethics of Business* (1926) quickly being forgotten.

Business ethics becomes a field of study

The key historical development in business ethics is its establishment as a field of study in university education. The breakthrough work that re-established business ethics as a continuous discourse in America dates to the postwar period and is widely held to have been a paper published by the Jesuit doctoral scholar Raymond Baumhart in the *Harvard Business Review* in 1961, which surveyed contemporary business moral values (McMahon 2002). Howard R. Bowen's *Social Responsibilities of the Businessman* (1953) had also proved an important work in establishing a new focus on the proper role of business in society. Bowen, an economist, had been asked to write the survey by a committee of the Federal Council of Churches and the book is rounded out with a response to Bowen's work by F. Ernest Johnson, a leading American religious studies educator of the day (Bowen 1953: 233–59; Limbert 1969; Acquier et al. 2011). The Federal Council of Churches was worried that the Protestant establishment was falling behind the Catholic Church in not providing more guidance on what upstanding Christian businessmen should consider ethical. Most of the discussion in the United States about business ethics in the 1950s and early 60s stressed the importance of religion as a key source of ethical guidance in business behavior (Clarke 1966; and cf. Carr 1968).

Over the course of the 1960s, however, two new pillars would be added to the anti-business canon developed by figures such as Marx. The environmental movement has a past that reaches back into the nineteenth century, but the appearance of marine biologist Rachel Carson's *Silent Spring* (1962) became a rallying point for a new generation of critics of business behavior. Focused especially on DDT and the harm that pesticides were doing to the natural environment, Carson's work remains a key contribution to the history of environmental activism (McGillivray 2004).

Carson neither founded the environmental movement, nor did she live to see her work become so iconic in early green circles. The emergence of the environmental movement, however, has been one of the most crucial developments in contemporary business ethics.

The other key critical work of the period was Ralph Nader's *Unsafe at Any Speed* (1965), a bestselling exposé of the contempt that American motor vehicle manufacturers had for public safety at the time. Far more than broader anti-corporate works such as J.K. Galbraith's *The Affluent Society* (1958), Nader's book seemed to galvanize the criticism of the American business community emerging on university campuses in the 1960s by a more questioning younger generation. Whereas books such as the American Management Association President Lawrence Appley's *Values in Management* (1968) seem almost bereft of any real understanding of commercial morality, Nader's book and the movement he inspired sparked a new era in business ethics.

Later expressions such as Dennis Gioia's (1992) account of his role in the 1970s Ford Pinto scandal built further on the tradition established by Nader. Nader's contribution, however, did not end with consumer protection. His *Taming the Giant Corporation* (penned in conjunction with Mark Green and Joel Seligman) popularized two new notions that had first been developed by business ethicists such as Richard Eells in the 1960s. The first and most pointed was Eells' notion of corporate governance (Eells 1960, 1962). With the popularization of the term by Nader and his followers, the expression was immediately taken up into business jargon by those seeking to find a way to prevent business collapses and the discrediting effect that journalistic exposés of scandals such as the Penn Central Transportation Company bankruptcy of 1970 inevitably generated (Sobel 1977). Nader also founded corporate activism groups such as Campaign GM that bought shares in listed corporations in order to try to influence the behavior of their boards (Schwartz 1971). Soon irate groups of stockholders had formed ethical and responsible investment bodies, and were calling on union-sponsored pension plans to use their stocks of "workers' capital" to civilize American business (Mees 2015). Begun as an ethical critique of US business, the corporate governance movement still has important ramifications for the moral understanding of what is now described in academic discussions as "financialization"—or "how an increasingly autonomous realm of global finance has altered the underlying logics of the industrial economy and the inner workings of democratic society" (van der Zwan 2014).

The other key contribution of Nader and his associates was his popularizing of the notion of the stakeholder. The basic notion that corporations had a range of broader constituencies than employees and owners had long been part of business discourse, and had been brought into particular focus by Eells in the early 1960s. But it was only in the light of Nader's activism that the idea of "stakeholder theory" began to appear in academic commentary, its first clear articulation even mentioning "Naderites" by name as one of the stakeholders of a corporation (Dill 1975). Given a more elaborate ethical basis by R. Edward Freeman in 1984, the stakeholder approach to business management is one of the key contributions of the new focus on business ethics that first achieved a wider public audience in the 1970s.

Ideas such as the social responsibility of business and the notion that businesses enjoyed a social contract with the communities they were situated in were further developed in the 1970s with the promotion of ideas such as Corporate Social Responsibility (Davis 1973; Carroll 1979) and Corporate Social Performance (Sethi 1975). On the other hand, a new focus on free markets, competition and the emergence of a literature of strategic management now threatened to take business ethics back to an earlier industrial age as a reformed version of nineteenth-century "classical" liberalism emerged. Many of the problems of capitalism experienced during the 1970s, especially those that became particularly prominent at the time of Western "stagflation" ("stagnant growth and high inflation"), encouraged new forms of business thinking as union influence, nationalization and public-sector involvement in key sectors of national economies were criticized and opposed. Many of the advocates of the new focus on entrepreneurialism, privatization and deregulation were demonized by their detractors as lacking a proper moral concern for the effects that industrial and economic liberalization had on the worst affected members of society. But the proposals for reform—of encouraging growth through heightened competition, increased labor-market flexibility and a particular focus on new business formation—were still seen as ethical by their promoters, whatever the claims of their critics.

The 1980s saw the full-fledged emergence of a renewal of capitalist thinking that was derided by its opponents as neoliberalism (Harvey 2005). The command economies of the old Soviet Block were castigated and attempts to develop more "mixed economies" (i.e., partly capitalist, party socialist) were blamed by figures such as Friedrich Hayek (1944, 1960) and Milton Friedman (1962) for holding Western countries back. For both Hayek and Friedman this was a moral as well as a political cause. In a television interview in 1979, Friedman explicitly argued that founding an economic system on greed did not seem to make much ethical sense, but no better economic system had since been developed. Where nineteenth-century advocates of utilitarianism such as John Stuart Mill (1863) saw their philosophical approach as supportive of socialism, precisely the reverse was argued by neoliberals. It was the utility of capitalism that made free markets and competition such a good and right thing for thinkers such as Friedman. Businessmen should act within the law and in line with the general expectations of the society they lived in, but, according to Friedman, socialism was wrong and advocates of Corporate Social Responsibility were enemies of success and growth (Friedman 1970).

In response, much ethical discourse has tended to become legalistic and contractual. Freeman's (1984) version of stakeholder theory explicitly references the theory of justice advocated by Rawls (1971), which is based in a long liberal ethical tradition of political philosophy that dates to early Enlightenment thinkers such as Thomas Hobbes (1651), John Locke (1690) and Jean-Jacques Rousseau (1762). A focus on human rights, particularly in terms of the United Nations' Universal Declaration of Human Rights of 1948, has buttressed the ethical and political response to the utilitarian form of economic neoliberalism that has held sway in much business thinking since the 1980s. Most business ethics textbooks published today duly take the traditions of utilitarianism, Kantian notions of universal rights and Rawls' theory of justice as their points of philosophical departure, as if this abstract tripartite approach reflects the lived reality of day-to-day business behavior, practice and morality.

Part of the reason for the emergence of this three-way normative demarcation in business ethics discourse is a reflection of the way in which the field was institutionalized in America in the 1980s. In response to the growing criticism of business associated with activists such as Nader, a renewed focus on business ethics appeared in the commercial curriculum. The great growth in business schools in the 1980s (with enrollments in business education quickly outstripping those of traditional liberal arts programs) also saw an opportunity emerge for philosophy graduates to move into a new form of academic career. The creation of hundreds of business ethics courses created a need for hundreds of business ethics scholars. This development inevitably led to the emergence of annual business ethics conferences and a range of specialist scholarly journals.

The first business ethics conference in the United States was held at the University of Kansas in 1976, the first annual conferences beginning in 1977 at Bentley College (now Bentley University) in Boston. The papers of the first conference proceedings (Hoffmann 1977; De George and Pichler 1978) show some confusion regarding what business ethics should comprise, with theologians, sociologists and even activists such as Nader appearing at the early meetings. But the influence of key contributors such as Norman Bowie (e.g., in Beauchamp and Bowie 1979) and Richard De George (De George 1982) would see a particular focus emerge on matters traditionally taught in philosophy courses such as Kantian, utilitarian and justice-based approaches to ethics. The canon of business ethics as it emerged from the early conferences, textbooks and academic outlets such as the *Journal of Business Ethics* (founded by Alex C. Michalos in 1982) remained philosophical and liberal (and not conservative or radical) in its approach. Rather than focus on social structures or the broader social science contributions to understanding the political economy, the main focus of business ethics would be idealistic and politically moderate (Lippke 1995).

It is clear from earlier attempts such as Wroe Alderson's (1964) assessment of the morality of marketing that the main focus of academic business ethics could have developed in other manners—the dominance of Kantian, utilitarian and Rawlsian approaches to business ethics is a relatively late development, part of a broader flowering of applied (philosophical) ethics since the 1970s. Yet one of the key problems with the normative American approach is also reflected in the emergence of psychological theories of ethics. Reflecting the dominance of consequentialist ethics (in the sense bemoaned by Elizabeth Anscombe in 1958), not only do textbook accounts of business ethics tend to neglect the longstanding Thomist tradition still embraced by many religiously influenced scholars, they also do not consider studies based on sociological evidence of how people actually behave.

There has been a recent focus on empirical studies in the leading academic journals—Heath (2008), for instance, calls for business ethics to be integrated with the findings of criminology. But much of the empirical literature remains psychologically based and tends to suffer from what critics have long dismissed as psychologism. Lawrence Kohlberg's (1976) model of stages of moral development, for example, essentially takes the developmental or stadial approach seen in Jean Piaget's (1923) theory of educational psychology and Abraham Maslow's (1943) hierarchy of needs, and applies it to morality. The notion of moral progress through a series of developmental stages assumes that people move from accepting contractual types of ethical understanding to a Kantian universalist form if they mature to the highest ethnocentrically Western stage.

Kohlberg's assumption that Kantian universalism represents a more advanced form of ethical reasoning than do utilitarian or contractual forms of moral understanding was one he could not support with experience or well-considered data. What studies there were of ethical reasoning in American society from his day suggest that most of his compatriots used religious, Kantian or justice-based forms of ethical reasoning, with no evidence that one form or the other could be shown to represent a more advanced type of ethical reasoning (Tipton 1982). Similar problems have affected more recent psychological approaches to business ethics with normative models of ethical reasoning increasingly being eschewed in empirical studies.

In response to the perceived failings of general frameworks of ethical reasoning, a more pragmatic approach to business ethics has developed alongside the philosophical and the psychological traditions. A renewed focus on codes of conduct emerged in the 1980s and 90s as the long-discredited notion of professionalizing business again acquired saliency. A focus also emerged on how to get business students to recognize ethical issues in the first place—to engage them further with ethical matters, to encourage them to form their own ethical voices. The widespread notion that the conduct of business was divorced from any ethical standards applicable in the general society (cf. the "separation thesis" of Freeman 1994) was reflected in expressions such as the 1980s adage that the description "business ethics" was an oxymoron (which first appeared in the *Wall Street Journal* in response to a survey of business ethics courses by Hoffmann; see Tannenbaum 1983). Notions such as "moral intensity" and studies of "ethical decision making" (Rest 1986; Jones 1991) found their way into the business ethics canon, adding more speculative function and scope to business ethics theorizing. Despite recourses to folksy notions such as "bad apples" and "bad barrels" (Treviño and Youngblood 1990), very little of this literature seemed to represent much of an advance in the academic project to elevate the moral standing of business practice.

It was, however, perhaps the notion of organizational culture that has had the most influence on such pragmatic approaches to the contemporary business ethics that have emerged under the influence of the business disciplines dominated by psychology. The notion that organizations have individual cultures was already present in the 1950s in the psychologically informed work of pioneers such as Elliot Jacques (1952). But it was the relaunching of the concept in the 1980s, especially by Edgar Schein (1985), that brought the notion of "ethical cultures" to the fore in business ethics discourse.

According to Schein's socializing model, executives who stress "values" and include them in recruitment specifications and codes of conduct will be able to influence the culture of an organization. The notion of organizational culture was much criticized in the 1990s, but still remains a key theme in the business ethics literature. Schein's model has been dismissed as stemming from a misunderstanding of Durkheimian sociology, as analytically wanting and as a product of the 1980s resurgent focus on issues such as how leaders can influence organizational behavior (Starkey 1998; Morrill 2008). Leadership theory in the 1980s went through a similar development as a new form of business literature emerged that was based on widely discredited notions such as "psychohistory" (i.e., the study of figures from the past in order to understand their psychological makeup); see, esp. Bass (1985). The new emphasis on leadership, however, saw the rebirth (and recasting) of the nineteenth-century notion of stewardship (Abend 2014: 332–347), or moral leadership as it had been described in the 1930s by Chester Barnard (Ciulla 2005).

Ethical leadership is an approach that seeks to bring the traditional notion of prudence back into the mainstream of moral discourse, but it does so in a very odd manner. In 1916, Henri Fayol had argued that prudence (*prévoyance*—the term is still used in French to refer to prudential matters) was a key feature of business administration. Mistranslated into English as "planning" (Fayol 1949), in the 1960s prudence was militarized (cf. Greek *strategia* "office of a general") and transformed into business strategy (Bracker 1980; Melé and Guillén Parra 2006). Where Machiavelli (Machiavelli, trans. Bondanella 2005: 82) had explained that prudence was principally concerned with the adjudication of risk ("Prudence consists in knowing how to recognize the nature of disadvantages, and how to chose the least sorry one as good"), the militarization of prudence as strategy occasioned the emergence of a key criticism of the strategic management literature. Stakeholder theory was initially articulated by figures such as Freeman (1984) in terms of business strategy, but what seemed increasingly lacking from business organizations was a recognition of personal responsibility among senior executives and their commitment to what Appleby had already described in the 1960s as "values."

The recent focus on ethical leadership has seen several strands of thinking emerge in what is often characterized as being one of the "positive" theories of leadership studies (Walumbwa and Wernsing 2013). In this discourse, leaders are encouraged to be ethical, model ethical behavior, set up and implement remuneration and promotion structures that reward accordance with ethical goals and otherwise encourage moral behavior—albeit in a manner akin to what sociologists call "social control." Kant's criticism of the prudent merchant as acting only instrumentally is lost in this new approach to ethical action as executives are encouraged to develop ideological and formal control systems in order to mandate particular ethical behaviors in the organizations they manage.

The continued concern with ethical behavior has generated a new vocabulary of corporate citizenship and corporate moral responsibility (French 1979; Banerjee 2007: 41–50). Prudence has also explicitly returned into business discourse under its Greek name of *phronêsis* (Cairns and Sliwa 2008). Yet the ethics of executive pay has not been influenced by such invocations in a noticeable way—it is only an interest in constraining excessive salaries among the trustees of pension funds that seems to have any prospect of bringing the explosion in executive remuneration that developed especially in the 1980s and 90s into any sense of perspective (Boatright

2010). International taxation arrangements that see multinational corporations shift profits to low taxing countries (transfer pricing) also seems more a matter of investment industry governance reform (particularly that championed by union-sponsored funds) than reflecting academic discourses of business morality.

The academic development of business ethics has also spawned considerable reflection on proper standards of behavior in business in non-Western traditions. In the 1980s, a revived form of Confucianism emerged in East Asia, a movement that has even seen a rehabilitation of Confucian tradition (officially demonized under Chairman Mao) in the People's Republic of China (Kang 2012). Where once most things Confucian were dismissed as holding China back, now a resurgence in historical consciousness has seen many East Asian scholars publish academic accounts of the influence of Confucian thought on Chinese, Korean and Japanese business practice. Abstract Confucian notions such as *li* "ritual, rules of propriety" have been brought into debates over non-Western business practice, enriching the particularist philosophical tradition at the expense of assumed universality. And issues such as bribery in cultures where gift-giving remains a traditional part of business life have also emerged as topics of particular interest in business ethics discourse, particularly in the context of China (Luo 2000; Elstein and Tian 2017).

Similar ideas and underpinnings have emerged since the 1990s in Islamic and South Asian academic discourse as ethical traditions of *mythos*, culture and text are brought to bear in new environments (e.g., Chakraborty 1997 and Hashim 2012). Approaches inspired by received non-Western ethical discourses remain a feature of the main business ethics journals. More research and thought, however, is still waiting to be applied to how Western discourses of business ethics might be accommodated with the moral traditions more broadly preserved in other cultures. The development of a properly diverse and international (rather than universalist and cosmopolitan) discourse of business ethics remains a challenge for the future.

Yet perhaps the most salient development in business ethics internationally since the 1980s is the notion of sustainability. Originally propounded by the Brundtland Commission (Brundtland 1987), the United Nations has adopted a three-pillar approach to sustainability—economic, social and environmental—which is emphasized by its Global Compact launched in 1999 by the UN's Ghanaian Secretary-General Kofi Annan. The global business ethics principles proposed by organizations such as the Caux Round Table have been brought together in a universalist manner under the Global Compact, which seeks to influence the behavior especially of multinational corporations. The UN's three pillars have been rebadged by accountants as "triple bottom line" reporting (Elkington 1997) and as matters of ESG (environmental, social and governance) risk in the investment industry (Waddell 2014). Other traditional concerns of business ethics, from working conditions to gender rights, have been increasingly brought under this much expanded discursive umbrella, as all manner of kinds of reputational, social and legal risk are construed as issues of business sustainability. The emergence of the discourse of sustainability has seen an important and emerging change occur in the way that business ethics is conceptualized as well as articulated presently.

According to the UN's Global Compact, sustainable business is environmentally, socially and economically responsible. Thus Corporate Social Responsibility, stakeholder theory and business prudence are all brought together in what is proposed to represent a unified framework. The ethical traditions of different countries and religions are left out of the UN framework in a cosmopolitan approach to business ethics that seems to assume that Kant was right and most other key writers on ethics were wrong. Nietzsche's warning that ethical reasoning is subject to a "genealogy of morals"—i.e., that a historically bound particularism better explains ethical understanding than Kantian universalism—is lost in any assumption that some sort of high tide has now been reached in the development of business ethics. More radical critics of sustainability such as Naomi Klein (2014) claim that the threat of climate change "changes everything"—that the discourse of sustainability simply reflects a business-as-usual approach that focuses only on the outliers—serial polluters and the most egregious violators of internationally accepted labor standards. The phenomena of greenwashing (Greer and Bruno 1996) and "ethical chic" (Hawthorne 2012) suggest that sustainability is not the answer to the longstanding moral concerns that recurrently emerge within and without business, a human activity that at its core has an essentially unethical feature—economic self-interest—that continually seems to need to be policed, interrogated and opposed.

Concluding remarks

The role of individual economic interest that is typically stressed in classical economics has rarely been seen as morally good. Yet some ancient discourses concerning business such as the value of hard work have remained longstanding ethical considerations in the commercial world. Other values and conceptualizations have undergone change over time, from the dismissal of "cunning" or the "erosion" of prudence, to the criticisms of industrial capitalism out of which both socialism and Catholic social justice teaching emerged. More recently, these issues have been revisited in the field of business ethics, a twentieth-century addition to the university curriculum that is often dominated by a form of applied philosophy that was not part of its original formulation. More focus on psychological understandings of ethics has also developed in light of the leading position that behavioral science has long had in management studies. But the most universal articulation of business ethics has come to be that which is associated with the United Nations and the environmental movement, with the discourse of sustainability representing the new cosmopolitan peak of the contemporary business ethics canon.

Essential readings

The history of business ethics has rarely been the subject of sustained inquiry. Morrell Heald (*The Social Responsibilities of Business*, 1970) and Gabriel Abend (*The Moral Background*, 2014) provide the only detailed histories of the business ethics of a period, both focusing on the USA. In "The History of Business Ethics," Richard De George (2006) sets forth a useful historical sketch of the development of the broader field, and Abend, in "The Origins of Business Ethics in American Universities, 1902–1936" (2013), offers a critique of the failing of many previous accounts. In his *The Catholic Movement of Employers and Managers* (1961), J.B. Gremillion presents one of the few historical surveys of the European (and Catholic) contribution of any substance. Christoph Luetge's *Handbook of the Philosophical Foundations of Business Ethics* (2013) provides the most detailed consideration of philosophical writings, but nothing similar is available yet from the behavioral perspective.

For further reading in this volume on the ideas and arguments of significant thinkers and philosophers on commercial ethics, see Chapter 2, Theorists and philosophers on business ethics. On the emergence of business ethics in the 1960s and 1970s, see Chapter 3, Theory and method in business ethics. For a critical assessment of the recent emergence of "sustainability" as a concept in business ethics, see Chapter 22, Business, nature, and environmental sustainability.

References

Abend, G. (2013). "The Origins of Business Ethics in American Universities, 1902–1936," *Business Ethics Quarterly* 23:2, 171–205.

Abend, G. (2014). *The Moral Background: An Inquiry into the History of Business Ethics*. Princeton, NJ: Princeton University Press.

Acquier, A., J. Gond and J. Pasquero (2011). "Rediscovering Howard R. Bowen's Legacy: The Unachieved Agenda and Continuing Relevance of Social Responsibilities of the Businessman," *Business & Society* 50, 607–46.
Al-Bukhari, M. (1997). *The Translation of the Meanings of Sahîh Al-Bukhâri: Arabic–English*, Muhammed Muhsin Kahn (trans.). Riyadh: Darussalam.
Alderson, W. (1964). "Ethics, Ideologies and Sanctions," *Report on the Committee on Ethical Standards and Professional Practices*, American Marketing Association, 1–20. Reprinted in R. Lavidge and R. Holloway (eds) (1969), *Marketing and Society: The Challenge*. Homewood, IL: Irwin, 74–85.
Anscombe, G.E.M. (1958). "Modern Moral Philosophy," *Philosophy* 33:124, 1–19.
Appley, L.A. (1968). *Values in Management*. New York, NY: American Management Association.
Aquinas, T. (1952). *The Summa Theologica*, Daniel J. O'Sullivan (ed.). Chicago, IL: Encyclopedia Britannica.
As-Saber, S. and G. Cairns (2015). "'Black International Business'—Critical Issues and Ethical Dilemmas," in Alison Pullen and Carl Rhodes (eds), *The Routledge Companion to Ethics, Politics and Organizations*. Abingdon: Routledge, 119–31.
Banerjee, S.B. (2007). *Corporate Social Responsibility: The Good, the Bad and the Ugly*. Cheltenham: Edward Elgar.
Barnard, C.I. (1934). *The Functions of the Executive*. Cambridge, MA: Harvard University Press.
Bass, B.M. (1985). *Leadership and Performance beyond Expectations*. New York, NY: Free Press.
Baumhart, R.C. (1961). "How Ethical are Businessmen?" *Harvard Business Review* 39:4, 6–19 and 156–76.
Beauchamp, T.L. and N. E. Bowie (eds) (1979). *Ethical Theory and Business*. Englewood Cliffs, NJ: Prentice Hall.
Berger, R. and R. Herstein (2014). "The Evolution of Business Ethics in India," *International Journal of Social Economics* 41:11, 1073–86.
Berry, C.J. (1994). *The Idea of Luxury: A Conceptual and Historical Investigation*. Cambridge: Cambridge University Press.
Bloch, M. (1954). *The Historian's Craft*, Peter Putnam (trans.). Manchester, UK: Manchester University Press.
Boatright, J.R. (2010). "Executive Compensation: Unjust or Just Right?" in George G. Brenkert and Thomas L. Beauchamp (eds), *The Oxford Handbook of Business Ethics*. Oxford: Oxford University Press, 161–201.
Borutta, M. (2013). "Settembrini's World: German and Italian Anti-Catholicism in the Age of the Culture Wars," *European Studies* 31, 43–67.
Bowen, H.T. (1953). *Social Responsibilities of the Businessman*. New York, NY: Harper & Bros.
Bracker, J. (1980). "The Historical Development of the Strategic Management Concept," *Academy of Management Review* 5, 219–22.
Brown, N.O. (1947). *Hermes the Thief: The Evolution of a Myth*. Madison, WI: University of Wisconsin Press.
Brundtland, G.H. (1987). *Our Common Future*. Oxford: Oxford University Press.
Cairns, G. and M. Sliwa (2008). "The Implications of Aristotle's *Phronêsis* for Organizational Inquiry," in D. Barry and H. Hansen (eds), *The Sage Handbook of New Approaches in Management and Organization*. Thousand Oaks, CA: Sage, 318–31.
Carr, A.Z. (1968). "Is Business Bluffing Ethical?" *Harvard Business Review* 46:1, 143–53.
Carroll, A.B. (1979). "A Three-dimensional Conceptual Model of Corporate Performance," *The Academy of Management Review* 4:4, 497–505.
Carson, R. (1962). *Silent Spring*. Boston, MA: Houghton Mifflin.
Chakraborty, S.K. (1997). "Business Ethics in India," *Journal of Business Ethics* 16:14, 1529–38.
Ciulla, J.B. (2005). "The State of Leadership Ethics and the Work That Lies Before Us," *Business Ethics: A European Review* 14:4, 323–335
Clarke, J.W. (1966). *Religion and the Moral Standards of American Businessmen*. Cincinnati, OH: Southwester.
Confucius (1979). *The Analects*, D.C. Lau (trans.). Harmondsworth, UK: Penguin.
Davis, K. (1973). "The Case For and Against Business Assumption of Social Responsibilities," *Academy of Management Journal* 16:2, 312–322.
De George, R.T. (1982). *Business Ethics*. New York, NY: Macmillan.
De George, R.T. (2006). "The History of Business Ethics," in Marc J. Epstein and Kirk O. Hanson (eds), *The Accountable Corporation*, 4 vols. Westport, CT: Praeger, Vol. II, 47–58.
De George, R.T. and J. A. Pichler (eds) (1978). *Ethics, Free Enterprise, and Public Policy: Original Essays on Moral Issues in Business*. New York, NY: Oxford University Press.
Dill, W.R. (1975). "Public Participation in Corporate Planning—Strategic Management in a Kibitzer's World," *Long Range Planning* 8, 57–63.

Dirlik, A. (1995). "Confucius in the Borderlands: Global Capitalism and the Reinvention of Confucianism," *Boundary 2*, 22:3, 229–73.

Donnachie, I.L. (2000). *Robert Owen: Owen of New Lanark and New Harmony*. East Linton, Scotland: Tuckwell.

Eells, R. (1960). *The Meaning of Modern Business: An Introduction to the Philosophy of Large Corporate Enterprise*. New York, NY: Columbia University Press.

Eells, R. (1962). *The Government of Corporations*. New York, NY: Free Press of Glencoe.

Elkington, J. (1997). *Cannibals with Forks: The Triple Bottom Line of 21st Century Business*. Oxford: Capstone.

Elstein, D. and Q. Tian (2017). "Confucian Business Ethics: Possibilities and Challenges," in E. Heath and B. Kaldis (eds), *Wealth, Commerce, and Philosophy: Foundational Thinkers and Business Ethics*. Chicago, IL: University of Chicago Press, 53–73.

Fayol, H. (1916). *Administration Industrielle et Générale: Prévoyance, Organisation, Commandement, Coordination, Controle*. Paris: Dunod & Pinat.

Fayol, H. (1949). *General and Industrial Management*, Constance Storrs (trans.). London: Pitman.

Foucault, M. (1972 [1969]). *The Archaeology of Knowledge*, A.M. Sheridan Smith (trans.). New York, NY: Harper & Row.

Fowler, R.L. (2011). "*Mythos* and *Logos*," *Journal of Hellenic Studies* 131, 45–66.

Freeman, R.E. (1984). *Strategic Management: A Stakeholder Approach*. Boston, MA: Pitman.

Freeman, R.E. (1994). "The Politics of Stakeholder Theory: Some Future Directions," *Business Ethics Quarterly* 4, 409–21.

French, P.A. (1979). "The Corporation as a Moral Person," *American Philosophical Quarterly* 16:3, 297–317.

Friedman, M. (1962). *Capitalism and Freedom*. Chicago, IL: University of Chicago Press.

Friedman, M. (1970). "The Social Responsibility of Business is to Increase its Profits," *The New York Times Magazine*, September 13, 32–33 and 122–124.

Galbraith, J.K. (1958). *The Affluent Society*. New York, NY: New American Library.

Gioia, D.A. (1992). "Pinto Fires and Personal Ethics: A Script Analysis of Missed Opportunities," *Journal of Business Ethics* 11:5–6, 379–89.

Green, R.M. and A. Donovan (2010). "The Methods of Business Ethics," in G.G. Brenkert and T.L. Beauchamp (eds), *The Oxford Handbook of Business Ethics*. Oxford: Oxford University Press, 21–45.

Greer, J. and K. Bruno (1996). *Greenwash: The Reality Behind Corporate Environmentalism*. New York, NY: Apex.

Gremillion, J.B. (1961). *The Catholic Movement of Employers and Managers*. Rome: Gregorian University Press.

Guzmán, R.A. and M.C. Munger (2014). "Euvoluntariness and Just Market Exchange: Moral Dilemmas from Locke's *Venditio*," *Public Choice* 158:1, 39–49.

Hariman, R. (2003). "Theory Without Modernity," in Robert Hariman (ed.), *Prudence: Classical Virtue, Postmodern Practice*. University Park, PA: Pennsylvania State University Press, 1–32.

Harvey, D. (2005). *A Brief History of Neoliberalism*. Oxford: Oxford University Press.

Hashim, M. (2012). "Islamic Perception of Business Ethics and the Impact of Secular Thoughts on Islamic Business Ethics," *International Journal of Academic Research in Business and Social Sciences* 2:3, 98–120.

Hawthorne, F. (2012). *Ethical Chic: The Inside Story of the Companies We Think We Love*. Boston, MA: Beacon.

Hayek, F.A. (1944). *The Road to Serfdom*. London: Routledge.

Hayek, F.A. (1960). *The Constitution of Liberty*. Chicago, IL: University of Chicago Press.

Heald, M. (1970). *The Social Responsibilities of Business: Company and Community, 1900–1960*. Cleveland, OH: Press of Case Western University.

Heath, J. (2008). "Business Ethics and Moral Motivation: a Criminological Perspective," *Journal of Business Ethics* 83:4, 595–614.

Heermance, E.L. (1926). *The Ethics of Business: A Survey of Current Standards*. New York, NY: Harper & Bros.

Hobbes, T. (1968 [1651]). *Leviathan*. Harmondsworth: Penguin.

Hoffmann, W.M. (ed.) (1977). *Business Values and Social Justice: Compatibility or Contradiction? Proceedings of the First National Conference on Business Ethics, March 11 and 12, 1977*. Waltham, MA: The Center for Business Ethics, Bentley College.

Hu, S. (2007). "Confucianism and Contemporary Chinese Politics," *Politics & Policy* 35:1, 136–153.

Jacques, E. (1952). *The Changing Culture of a Factory*. London: Tavistock.

John Paul II (1991). *Encyclical Letter Centesimus Annus of the Supreme Pontiff John Paul II: on the Hundredth Anniversary of Rerum Novarum*. Homebush, NSW: St. Paul Publications.

Jones, T.M. (1991). "Ethical Decision Making by Individuals in Organizations: An Issue-Contingent Model," *Academy of Management Review* 16, 366–95.
Kang, X.G. (2012). "A Study of the Renaissance of Traditional Confucian Culture in Contemporary China," in F. Yang and J. Tamney (eds), *Confucianism and Spiritual Traditions in Modern China and Beyond*. Leiden: Brill, 33–74.
Kant, I. (1964 [1785]). *Groundwork of the Metaphysic of Morals*, H.J. Paton (trans.). New York, NY: Harper & Row.
Klein, N. (2014). *This Changes Everything: Capitalism vs. the Climate*. New York, NY: Simon & Schuster.
Kohlberg, L. (1976). "Moral Stages and Moralization: the Cognitive-development Approach," in T. Lickona (ed.), *Moral Development and Behavior: Theory, Research and Social Issues*. New York, NY: Holt, Rinehart and Winston, 31–53.
Kovesi, C. (2015). "What is Luxury?: The Rebirth of a Concept in the Early Modern World," *Luxury: History, Culture, Consumption* 2:1, 25–40.
Kramer, S.N. (1956). *History Begins at Sumer: Thirty-nine Firsts in Recorded History*. New York, NY: Doubleday.
Leo XIII (1983 [1891]). *Rerum Novarum: Encyclical Letter of Pope Leo XIII on the Condition of the Working Classes*, Joseph Kirwan (trans.). London: Catholic Truth Society.
Limbert, P.M. (1969). "F. Ernest Johnson: Prophetic Interpreter of Christian Ethics (1885–1969)," *Religious Education* 64, 499–500.
Lippke, R.L. (1995). *Radical Business Ethics*. Lanham, MD: Rowman & Littlefield.
Locke, J. (1993 [1661]). "Venditio," in David Wooton (ed.), *Locke: Political Writings*, London: Penguin, 442–446.
Locke, J. (2003 [1690]). *Two Treatises of Government; and a Letter Concerning Toleration*. New Haven, CT: Yale University Press.
Luetge, C. (ed.) (2013). *Handbook of the Philosophical Foundations of Business Ethics*, 3 vols. Dordrecht: Springer.
Luo, Y.G. (2000). *Guanxi and Business*. Singapore: World Scientific.
MacGillivray, A. (2002). *Rachel Carson's Silent Spring*. Hauppauge, NY: Barron's.
Machiavelli, N. (2005 [1523]). *The Prince*, P. Bondanella (trans.). Oxford: Oxford University Press.
Makeham, J. (2003). "The Retrospective Creation of New Confucianism," in idem (ed.), *New Confucianism: A Critical Examination*. New York, NY: Palgrave Macmillan, 25–53.
Marx, K. (1867 [1992]). *Capital: A Critique of Political Economy*, B. Fowkes (trans.), 3 vols. London: Penguin.
Marx, K. and F. Engels (1888 [1848]). *Manifesto of the Communist Party*, S. Moore (trans.). London: Reeves.
Maslow, A.H. (1943). "A Theory of Human Motivation," *Psychological Review* 50, 370–396.
McMahon, T.F. (2002). "A Brief History of American Business Ethics," in Robert E. Frederick (ed.), *A Companion to Business Ethics*. Oxford: Blackwell, 342–52.
Mees, B. (2015). "Corporate Governance as a Reform Movement," *Journal of Management History* 21:2, 194–209.
Melé, D. and M. Guillén Parra (2006). "The Intellectual Evolution of Strategic Management and Its Relationship with Ethics and Social Responsibility," *Working Paper IESE* (D/658).
Mill, J.S. (1957 [1863]). *Utilitarianism*. Indianapolis, IN: Bobbs-Merrill.
Morrill, C. (2008). "Culture and Organization Theory," *Annals of the American Academy of Political and Social Science* 619, 15–40.
Nader, R. (1965). *Unsafe At Any Speed: The Designed-in Dangers of the American Automobile*. New York, NY: Grossmann.
Nader, R., M. J. Green and J. Seligman (1976). *Taming the Giant Corporation*. New York, NY: Norton.
Nietzsche, F. (1996 [1887]). *On the Genealogy of Morals: A Polemic*, D. Smith (trans.). Oxford: Oxford University Press.
Nisbet, R. (1980). *History of the Idea of Progress*. New York, NY: Basic Books.
Piaget, J. (1926 [1923]). *The Language and Thought of the Child*. London: Routledge & Kegan Paul.
Pieper, J. (1966). *The Four Cardinal Virtues*. Notre Dame, NJ: University of Notre Dame Press.
Pontifical Council for Justice and Peace (2014). *Vocation of the Business Leader: A Reflection*. Rome: Pontifical Council for Justice and Peace.
Rainey, L.D. (2010). *Confucius and Confucianism: The Essentials*. Oxford: Wiley-Blackwell.
Rawls, J. (1971). *A Theory of Justice*. Cambridge, MA: Belknap.
Reeves, C.H. (trans.). (1966). *Johannes Nider, On the Contracts of Merchants*. Norman, OH: University of Oklahoma Press.

Rest, J.R. (1986). *Moral Development: Advances in Research and Theory*. New York, NY: Praeger.
Reuveni, G. (2010). "Prolegomena to an "Economic Turn" in Jewish History," in G. Reuveni and S. Wobick-Segev (eds), *The Economy in Jewish History: New Perspectives on the Interrelationship Between Ethnicity and Economic Life*. New York, NY: Berghahn, 1–22.
Ricardo, D. (1951 [1817]). *On the Principles of Political Economy and Taxation*. Cambridge: Cambridge University Press.
Rousseau, J.-J. (1987 [1762]). *The Social Contract*, M. Cranston (trans.). Harmondsworth, UK: Penguin.
Sarkissian, H. (2010). "Recent Approaches to Confucian Filial Morality," *Philosophy Compass* 59, 725–34.
Schein, E.H. (1985). *Organizational Culture and Leadership*. San Francisco, CA: Jossey Bass.
Schwartz, D.E. (1971). "Proxy Power and Social Goals—How Campaign GM Succeeded," *St. John's Law Review* 45:4, 764–771.
Sethi, S.P. (1975). "Dimensions of Corporate Social Performance: An Analytic Framework," *California Management Review* 17, 58–64.
Shapiro, J. (1997). *Shakespeare and the Jews*. New York, NY: Columbia University Press.
Smith, A. (1904 [1776]). *An Inquiry into the Nature and Causes of the Wealth of Nations*. London: Methuen.
Sobel, R. (1977). *The Fallen Colossus: The Great Crash of the Penn Central*. New York, NY: Weybright & Talley.
Starkey, K. (1998). "The Limits of Corporate Culture: Whose Culture? Which Durkheim?" *Journal of Management Studies* 35:2, 125–36.
Sun, A.X.D. (2005). "The Fate of Confucianism as a Religion in Socialist China: Controversies and Paradoxes," in Fenggang Yang and Joseph B. Tamney (eds), *State, Market and Religions in Chinese Societies*. Leiden: Brill, 229–253.
Sutton, F.X. et al. (1956). *The American Business Creed*. Harvard, MA: Harvard University Press.
Taeusch, C.F. (1931). *Policy and Ethics in Business*. New York, NY: McGraw-Hill.
Tannenbaum, J.A. (1983). "Business Bulletin," *Wall Street Journal* May 5.
Tawney, R.H. (1921). *The Acquisitive Society*. London: Bell & Sons.
Tawney, R.H. (1926). *Religion and the Rise of Capitalism, a Historical Study*. London: Murray.
Tipton, S.M. (1982). *Getting Saved from the Sixties: Moral Meaning in Conversion and Cultural Change*. Berkeley, CA: University of California Press.
Treviño, L.K. and S.A. Youngblood (1990). "Bad Apples in Bad Barrels: A Causal Analysis of Ethical Decision-making Behavior," *Journal of Applied Psychology* 75, 378–385.
Vergados, A. (2012). "The *Homeric Hymn to Hermes*: Humour and Epiphany," in A. Falkner (ed.), *The Homeric Hymns: Interpretative Essays*. Oxford: Oxford University Press, 82–104.
Waddell, C.W. (2014). "Fulfilling Fiduciary Duties in an Imperfect World—Governance Recommendations from the Stanford Institutional Investor Forum," in J.P. Hawley, A.G.F. Hoepner, K.L. Johnson, J. Sandberg and E.J. Waitzer (eds), *Cambridge Handbook of Institutional Investment and Fiduciary Duty*. Cambridge: Cambridge University Press, 442–451.
Walumbwa, F.O. and T. Wernsing (2013). "From Transactional and Transformational to Authentic Leadership," in Michael G. Rumsey (ed.), *The Oxford Handbook of Leadership*. Oxford: Oxford University Press, 392–400.
Wang, G.W. (2004). "The Uses of Dynastic Ideology: Confucianism in Contemporary Business," in Frank-Jürgen Richter and Pamela C.M. Marr (eds), *Asia's New Crisis: Renewal Through Total Ethical Management*. Singapore: John Wiley and Sons, 51–62.
Weber, M. (1930 [1904/5]). *The Protestant Ethic and the Spirit of Capitalism*, Talcott Parsons (trans.). London: Unwin Hyman.
Wren, D.A. (2000). "Medieval or Modern? A Scholiast's View of Business Ethics, *circa* 1430," *Journal of Business Ethics* 28:2, 109–119.
Yao, S. (2002). *Confucian Capitalism: Discourse, Practice, and the Myth of Chinese Enterprise*. London: Routledge Curzon.
van der Zwan, N. (2014). "Making Sense of Financialization," *Socio-Economic Review* 12, 99–129.

2
Theorists and philosophers on business ethics

George Bragues

Ever since Socrates brought philosophy down from the heavens to deal with the human things, most of the thinkers who have made a name in that subject have reflected deeply on economic life and, particularly, on commerce. They sought to comprehend its origins and nature, its functions and consequences in the social order, along with its relation to the state. This is not to mention how the philosophers endeavored to gauge the proper role of commerce both in the larger community and in the lives of individuals. Even when they were not specifically addressing commerce, they were articulating ideas and theories applicable to it, mainly by providing enduring methods and principles of moral reasoning that help us grapple with situations neither known nor imagined by them. Consciously or not, these notions have been taken up in our time by business ethics, setting the terms of analysis and debate in the field. All the current discussion about corporate social responsibility, stakeholders, sustainability, shared value, living wages, and ethical consumption, draws upon the deposit of wisdom bequeathed to us by the great philosophers of the past. Much more could be mined, to be sure, but more than a few jewels from this deposit have managed to gain currency among business ethicists. Against that age-old stereotype of being an impractical and unworldly enterprise, against the conventional wisdom of our day that sees it as inextricably confined to its historical period, philosophy has much to say that is relevant (and even sympathetic) to our modern-day business civilization.

This should not be taken to mean that philosophy is necessarily at the ready to lend its support to commerce. Philosophy, after all, is the quest for knowledge about the most fundamental principles of reality. Its highest loyalty being to the cause of truth, it does not unhesitatingly render itself the servant of other forces that in any way threaten the fulfillment of its objective. This includes the currently prevailing mode of organizing our economic lives. Philosophy is not pre-programmed to offer counsel to those engaged in the production, buying, and selling of goods and services. Neither is that the case for those holding political offices charged with the task of overseeing commercial activity. It is not surprising, therefore, that the history of philosophy presents instances of friction with, indeed of outright rejection of, the occupations of business. In these, the very idea of business ethics is rendered tenuous, if not entirely ruled out of intellectual court. In the most extreme version of this mindset, business comes into view as so morally compromised that appending the word ethics to it is seen as a glaring contradiction of terms.

George Bragues

In this chapter I endeavor to tell the story of these dual tendencies in the history of philosophy, the one sympathetic and the other in tension with the project of business ethics. I also indicate some of the more notable ways in which these tendencies have been reflected and adopted by present-day business ethicists. This historical survey, along with the contemporary emanations of each phase, is divided into four chronologically ordered parts, each posing a distinct approach to commerce.

As such, the story of philosophy's relation to business turns out to be this: business begins under moral suspicion; it is then morally accepted and praised; from there, business is put beyond saving; it ends up being redeemable under specified conditions. Though the discipline continues to pull concepts from all of these stages, business ethics today is largely the offspring of this story's last chapter.

Ancient and medieval suspicions of commerce

It is tempting to attribute the stigma against business among the ancient philosophers to the fact that they lived in agrarian societies. Merchants were looked down upon in such societies as middlemen who merely moved around goods that others had produced. With land then being the principal asset, the necessity of defending and conquering it translated to a higher ranking of the martial virtues in the agrarian table of values. Even if amid the political turbulence of the time oligarchies and dictatorship would periodically displace the democracies of the ancient Greek city states, the latter type of regime exerted enough of an influence over people's minds to render suspicious any line of work that hindered an active participation in public affairs. Unlike the representative democracies of our day, the republics of the ancient world demanded a more politically engaged citizenry. This, in turn, required a degree of leisure that wealthy landowners could readily afford, but which merchants and artisans could not. Accordingly, the life devoted to matters of state, and all the virtues associated with that, was accorded higher esteem than the life devoted to money-making. The ancient philosophers, not being especially popular (as the fate of Socrates attests), did have to show respect for the moral code of the ruling elites (Melzer 2014). Even so, they did not put the virtue of courage on a pedestal and nor did they lend their unqualified support to the political life. To cite only the most prominent examples, Plato and Aristotle both concluded that the best life consisted in philosophizing. This suggests that when they questioned the morality of commercial pursuits, the ancients cannot properly be interpreted as giving theoretical voice to the prevailing *Weltanschauung*, or to the exigencies of the politico-economic order. They sought to give a verdict that anyone, regardless of time and place, could rationally accept.

This becomes clear once it is understood how the ancients framed their moral reflections under the lens of the *summum bonum*. Denoting the greatest good, that expression stands for whatever conduces to the utmost fulfillment of human beings given their nature and potentiality. Aristotle offers the paradigmatic account of this approach in his *Nicomachean Ethics*, where he maintains that figuring out what we ought to do is a matter of following the logic of our actions. Since everything we do is for the sake of something, and that in turn for something else, eventually as we progressively run through the purposes of our actions, we arrive at a goal that we pursue for its own sake—to wit, happiness. Ethics, then, is nothing else but the set of behavioural requisites for attaining a good life. Securing this entails that the appropriate mode of conduct become ingrained as a habit—that is, it must define a person's character. Aristotle, to be sure, was not the only one with a conception of what the good life meant. In the ancient philosophic scene, the Aristotelian view was chiefly opposed by the Epicureans and the Stoics. The Epicureans held that the *summum bonum* is to be found in pleasure, whereas the Stoics contended that it consists of virtue. Aristotle's compromise position—that happiness is essentially coterminous with virtue but also requires pleasure—proved the most influential in both the ancient and medieval traditions. Thus Cicero (1991 [44BC]), among Rome's most renowned statesman yet also its greatest philosopher, ended up adopting that middle stance in his moral teaching, most notably in his *De Officiis* (On the Duties). So, too, did St Thomas Aquinas (1920 [1265–1274]), whose voluminous writings grounded the thinking of the scholastics right through to the dawn of modernity in the seventeenth century.

By assigning pleasure a more auxiliary function as compared with virtue in the equation of human happiness, Aristotle passed on to his philosophic descendants a rather circumscribed tolerance of business. Were pleasure the highest good, then business would stand a better chance of gaining moral approval, inasmuch as the money to be earned furnishes the wherewithal to obtain all sorts of delights. But if virtue is the way to happiness, the place of money in a good life can only be to provide the material foundations of moral action. This is precisely where Aristotle ends up in his moral analysis of commerce. He proceeds there, first, by stressing the character of money as a mere means to other goods. "As for the life of the money-maker," Aristotle (1982) writes, "clearly the good sought is not wealth, for wealth is instrumental and is sought for the sake of something else" (1096a: 6–7). Not being an end in itself, money cannot constitute the *summum bonum*. The great danger, Aristotle warns, that the businessperson faces is that of succumbing to the temptation of seeking wealth as an end in itself, for then one is on a treadmill that no definite amount of accumulated riches can stop. "The cause of this disposition in men," Aristotle (1982 [fourth century BC]) says, "is that they are zealous for [mere] living but not for living well" (1257b41–1258a1). Aristotle recognizes that individuals do not pursue money only in order to live, but also with a view to buying pleasures and gaining honor, or what we nowadays refer to as status. Though happiness surely cannot be had without some measure of pleasure, we must choose between the different kinds of pleasure, which points to a good above pleasure. As for honor or status, which is the desire to be thought well of by our peers, that serves only to mentally enslave us to others. True fulfillment, Aristotle observes, must come from something more within our control, something like the satisfaction that comes from excelling in our actions, or realizing our highest possibilities as human beings. In other words, to live blissfully one must live virtuously.

What does this entail exactly? Aristotle's answer has already been signaled in noting his view that the *summum bonum* is to engage in philosophic reflection. This looks to have little to do with business until one recognizes the vision of human nature underlying it. Aristotle believes that the quality in which we human beings peculiarly excel is our rationality. It is what most distinguishes us from the animals; it is the source of the comparative advantage we have as a species (Aristotle 1982: 1097b22–1098a20). For Aristotle, therefore, virtue consists in nothing else than the exercise of reason in our actions.

There are two ways this can be done: by grasping the truth with our rational faculties, and by employing those faculties to regulate our desires and emotions. The first way comprises the intellectual virtues, whereas the second makes up the moral virtues. Even though Aristotle holds that the philosopher most fully realizes those qualities, this does not exclude people in other walks of life from exemplifying these traits, including businesspersons. Most applicable to these persons in Aristotle's catalog of the virtues would be prudence to make good decisions; self-control to regulate sensual impulses; courage to take reasonable risks; generosity to avoid an excessive attachment to money; sociability to be agreeable with colleagues and customers; and justice to transact fairly with others and give them what they deserve (Bragues 2006). Insofar as a virtue does not refer to a specific deed but rather to a habit, all of these traits come together to form an admirable character, someone for whom doing the right thing in light of the circumstances at hand comes as second nature. As a result, Aristotle's contribution to business ethics consists, not in providing a criterion to evaluate particular acts, but in putting the focus on the sorts of people we wish to see working in the economy.

Before this core idea made its way to us, however, it underwent significant modification. Cicero drew Aristotle's definition of happiness, as virtue accompanied by pleasure, into a life that encompasses what he called the honorable and the beneficial. In doing so, the Roman thinker brought a more lenient take on acquisitiveness, sanctioning the quest for riches so long as it does not jeopardize one's reputation or involve the perpetration of injustice. "Such expansion," he says, "of one's personal wealth as harms no one is not, of course, to be disparaged" (Cicero 1991 [44BC]: I.25). Cicero still found it demeaning for an individual to run a small business, but he thought leading an enterprise on a larger and more international scale to be respectable (I.151). In distinguishing between the honorable and the beneficial, Cicero also foreshadowed the tension that business ethicists nowadays are compelled to wrestle with between the moral and the profitable—the recurrent question of whether one can do well in business by doing good. To resolve that tension, Cicero examined a situation in which an exporter who has just arrived at Rhodes is faced with the question of whether to take advantage of the high price there for his corn or to disclose his knowledge that other merchants are on their way from Alexandria with similar produce (III, 50–53). Cicero explored a few other scenarios of this type, thus providing the first instance in Western philosophy in which attention is given to specific dilemmas in business ethics.

A more momentous development, no doubt, would come about with the subsequent emergence of Christianity in the Roman Empire. Initially, this represented a moral step back for business, inasmuch as the New Testament established the *summum bonum* in the next life, while memorably comparing the odds of a rich person getting into heaven as being worse than that of a camel going through the eye of a needle (Matthew 19:24). But once Aristotle's writings, which had mostly been lost, suddenly reappeared in the West during the 12th–13th centuries after having been preserved by Islamic scholars, the stage was set for an ascent in the moral status of business. To be sure, the integration of Aristotle into the Christian architectonic that was carried out by St Thomas Aquinas still conceived business as under a firm moral grip. Aside from reiterating Aristotle's condemnation of usury (i.e., lending on interest)—mainly on the argument that money cannot reproduce itself and that time is not something that can be bought or sold—Aquinas interpreted the latter's discussion of reciprocity in the exchange of goods as a theory of just price. According to this theory, it is not ethically licit for individuals and firms to charge whatever buyers are willing to pay, the right price being that which reflects the equality in value of the goods being exchanged (Aquinas 1920 [1265–1274]: II.II.77, A1). Qualifying this morally confining view, though, is the fact that Aquinas is notably less reluctant than Aristotle was in endorsing the admissibility of seeking profit in business, at least where that serves a virtuous purpose: "a man may intend the moderate gain which he seeks to acquire by trading for the upkeep of his household, or for the assistance of the needy: or again, a man may take to trade for some public advantage" (II.II.77, A4).

The Late Scholastic philosophers of the 14th–15th centuries—whose leading lights included Juan de Mariana, Luis de Molina and Francisco de Vitoria—would build on this more tolerant side of Aquinas. A notable example of this is how they construed the equality in exchange proviso of just price theory to mean the market price that buyers and sellers arrive at without coercion or fraud (Chafuen 2003: 82–92). In providing a robust ethical case against debasements of the currency, thus offering a sharp contrast to the technocratic approach surrounding monetary policy today, the Late Scholastics also defended the bedrock of a thriving commercial society, namely sound money (Oresme 1956 [1279]). Yet it must be admitted that in their rich and sympathetic analyses of commerce, unfortunately neglected for the most part in our day, the Late Scholastics did not go so far as to reverse the Aristotelian-Thomist stricture on usury. Still, they did chip away at it by glimpsing the pivotal point that a certain amount of money now is worth more than that same amount in the future (Chafuen 2003: 122–125). The complete repudiation in the Western philosophic corpus of the prohibition against the charging of interest had to await the 1787 publication of Jeremy Bentham's *Defense of Usury*.

Though representing the minority of business ethicists, significant contributions have been made to the discipline through the adaptation of ancient teachings. Overwhelmingly this has been sought by taking up Aristotle's emphasis on character, in what is typically called the virtue-ethics approach to business ethics. Certainly, a major figure in that movement has been Robert Solomon (1992), whose *Ethics and Excellence: Co-Operation and Integrity in Business* ignited a third way in business ethics between the reigning utilitarian and deontological methods. Edwin Hartman has followed in this third way with his *Virtues in Business: Conversations with Aristotle* (2013), while the list of scholarly articles with a virtue-ethics angle has continued to mushroom (Koehn 1995; Arjoon 2000; Moore 2005). Conspicuous by its absence in much of this literature, though, is Aristotle's conception of the good life as the cultivation of reason, or indeed any substitute for it. That has compounded the difficulty of settling upon the set of virtues that make up the character of the model businessperson. Amartya Sen (1999) and Martha Nussbaum (2011) have advanced the thesis that individuals should be afforded certain capabilities of obtaining happiness, which admittedly gets us closer to a list of the business virtues (Bertland 2009). Still, one cannot specify the means (capabilities) without first understanding the nature of the end (happiness).

With respect to the medieval thinkers, their impact on contemporary business ethics has been noticeably more limited than that of Aristotle. Partly this is owing to the pronounced secularism of the academy; and partly to the widespread belief that, just as the state ought to be separate from religion, so too must the company. What influence that Aquinas and the rest of the Scholastics have exercised has primarily reflected the applications to business of Alasdair MacIntyre's (1984) *After Virtue*, along with the body of accumulated politico-economic and moral reflections promulgated by the Catholic Church since 1891 known as Catholic Social Thought (Pontifical Council for Justice and Peace 2004).

The modern approval of business

Whether one understands it as the outcome of an evolution or as a sudden rupture with ancient and medieval thought, what cannot be doubted is that the corpus of modern philosophy presents us with a decidedly altered moral tone about business. Given the magnitude of the change, it is not surprising that it proved a tempestuous affair at the outset, with defenders of the old order decrying advocates of the new as radicals intent on overthrowing the cause of virtue. That was certainly the case with two crucial figures at the beginnings of modernity, Niccolò Machiavelli (1947 [1513]) and Bernard Mandeville (1924 [1732]). The first, the Italian Renaissance politician and writer famous for authoring *The Prince*, is not unknown to business ethicists, even if he is not generally regarded by them as any sort of appropriate moral guide. Interestingly enough, this assessment runs counter to the trend in the popular management literature, in which the handing down of Machiavellian lessons to business has become something of a cottage industry (Galie and Bopst 2006). Within the academic literature of business as a whole, Machiavelli's reputed advice is referred to most prominently in the field of organizational behavior, where individuals willing to adopt any unscrupulous means necessary to realize their particular ends is referred to as a Machiavellian personality. More quasi-scientifically, such people are known as

High-Mach types. These are identified through a variety of Likert scale personality assessments meant to single out individuals driven by a ruthless egotism (Gunnthorsdottir, McCabe and Smith 2002). With this measure, researchers can explore correlations between Machiavellianism and other personal characteristics as well as occupational status and job performance (Azia, May and Crotts 2002).

Only to the extent that Machiavelli is interpreted as arguing that politics is a separate realm from ethics with its own rules can it be said that the Florentine thinker has been taken up within business ethics. What comes to mind here is Albert Z. Carr's (1968) defense of bluffing, which features the analogous contention that business has its own rules distinct from those of private life. By contrast, that other controversial figure alongside Machiavelli at the ground floor of modernity, Bernard Mandeville, has been almost forgotten. With few exceptions, the eighteenth-century Dutch-Anglo philosopher figures nebulously at best in present-day business ethics as the one who first alluded to what Adam Smith would later call the invisible hand. Mandeville did so in the sub-title to his book *The Fable of the Bees*—which was *Private Vices, Publick Benefits*.

Their limited influence notwithstanding, Machiavelli and Mandeville both enable us to understand what really transpired intellectually to raise the moral standing of business. An important clue is given in the sub-title of Mandeville's book. It suggests that what had been called vice had to henceforth be seen as socially useful and that, by implication, what had been called virtue had to henceforth be seen as socially useless. By virtue here what Mandeville (1924 [1732]: 48–49) means is conduct in which a person subdues his or her selfish impulses, either to assist others or to obey the dictates of reason. Vice, on the other hand, is defined as conduct in which a person indulges selfishness. To Mandeville, what essentially distinguishes virtue from vice is the exercise of self-control. Though this dividing line might appear overstated and bordering upon the puritanical, he was right to pinpoint that morality had historically demanded an inner struggle against egoism. This was, to be sure, more pronounced in the medieval-Christian variant of that tradition, according to which the giving of self is the way to eternal bliss with God. Still, even among the ancient philosophers—who after all can be read as advocating a high-minded egoism by so closely tying virtue to personal fulfillment—individuals were called upon to resist the more common expressions of selfishness, whether in the seeking of pleasure, status, or wealth. What Mandeville (1924 [1732]: 35) perceived was that it is precisely these ordinary drives that conduce to economic prosperity, whereas self-denial ultimately leads to a deadly penury. Similarly in Machiavelli (1947 [1513]), who advised princes to respect private property and encourage commercial activity, we see the charge that the ancient medieval ideal is dangerously impractical: "he who studies what ought to be done rather than what is done will learn the way to his downfall" (44). By such criticisms, Machiavelli and Mandeville both hinted at the necessity of a transvaluation of values. Virtue had to cease being a means towards our natural flourishing as rational beings or our prospective communion with God. Instead, virtue had to become the instrument for worldly enjoyment and success. Selfishness, in all but its most nefarious forms, had to be made respectable.

The various systems of morality bequeathed to us by the modern philosophers are best seen as so many attempts to do just that. Three tasks were undertaken to this end. First, the ancient mission to define the *summum bonum* for human beings was abandoned, replaced by the view that no end exists to which all actions can be ordered to consummate our desires. Thomas Hobbes, the seventeenth-century British philosopher, set the tone: "For there is no such *Finis ultimus* (utmost ayme), nor *Summum bonum* (greatest good) as is spoken of in the Books of the old Morall Philosophers . . . Felicity is a continual progresse of the desire, from one object to another" (Hobbes 1985 [1651]: 160). Ends thus became relative and moral analysis turned its sights to where it largely remains today, including in business ethics—that is, with the question of how to regulate the means that individuals may choose towards their subjectively defined ends. Second, God had to be removed from the supporting structure of morality. Though some at the time expressed the atheist hope of accomplishing this through the complete secularization of society, the principal strategy that the modern philosophers adopted was toleration. To avoid social conflict over religious doctrine, the state was enjoined to be neutral and to respect the individual's right to privately practice his or her faith. The upshot was that moral arguments that impinged on public matters now had to be framed in terms that all persons, whatever their opinions on religion, could in principle accept. And third, some way had to be found to derive a set of moral obligations out of the confines of the self. With Hobbes, that which necessarily propels the self, to wit the desires that the self cannot help but endeavor to satisfy, became the source of a right to self-preservation. To more effectively satisfy this right, he argued, individuals give up the prerogative to promote their survival in any manner they deem fitting and agree to be bound by a social contract. For Hobbes, morality is identical to the terms of this contract. John Locke (1960 [1689]), the seventeenth-century British thinker often identified as America's philosophical inspiration, further developed this theory of the social contract, crucially modifying it by asserting a natural right to property.

Locke's defense of property rights is grounded on the claim that each of us owns one's self. Nobody is born to belong to another person. At the same time, however, Locke acknowledges that the earth and all its resources originally belonged to all human beings. So how does he go from ownership of the self to ownership of things? By mixing their labor with the world, Locke maintains that individuals acquire property rights to the bits of the world they work upon. Two conditions govern this process: the first is that no else already has established ownership over the resources appropriated; the second is that enough be left over for others to use. Not only does this second rule bar the monopolization of the earth, it prohibits the ownership of anything that would go to waste in one's possession. Implicit here is the claim that scarcity is a brute fact of the human condition. Describing the plight of being human, Locke speaks of "the penury of his condition" which in turn forces him "to subdue the earth" in order to live (Locke, 1960 [1689]: 332). Given these circumstances, to spoil something that is scarce is equivalent to taking something away from others that they could use. This spoilage proviso, Locke argues, was overcome with the introduction of money. Money does not spoil. Because of that, people are free to accumulate as much money as they want. And because those who pursue money harness the earth's materials to create a wealthier society, even those who lack property end up better off than they would be if no one were allowed to own things. Referring to pre-Columbian America, Locke observes: "a King of a large fruitful Territory there feeds, lodges, and is clad worse than a day Laborer in England" (Locke 1960 [1689]: 339). Thus, a natural right to property becomes a natural right to accumulate property without limit on the argument that its exercise in a monetary economy is consistent with the common good. No moral postulate has been more important historically than that of the right to property in providing an ethical sanction of business.

The exception to this, perhaps, is Adam Smith's invisible hand. Mandeville's adumbration of this has already been mentioned, but what Smith did was eliminate the paradox of maintaining that vicious acts produce social benefits. What Mandeville called vice, Smith (1981 [1776]: 540) referred to as, "the natural effort of every individual to better his own condition," an entirely commendable undertaking if pursued within the bounds of prudence and justice. Any individuals hoping to increase their fortunes through trade must do so by providing goods and services in exchange for which others are willing to pay. As this means an individual cannot prosper in the marketplace other than by attending to the wants of others, Smith holds that self-interest redounds to the public good even though no one consciously intends it. Indeed, Smith takes this claim further, insisting that the businessperson who does consciously intend the public good will likely fail to realize it. "I have never known much good done by those who affected to trade for the public good" (Smith 1981 [1776]: 456). Very few are the business ethicists that agree with this statement, defying as it does the precept of corporate social responsibility (or CSR) that normatively frames their discipline. Illustrating this is the critical stance that has overwhelmingly been taken against Milton Friedman's (1970) famous reprisal of Smith's argument in a *New York Times Magazine* essay entitled "The Social Responsibility of Business Is to Increase Its Profits." Thanks to the increasing recognition of corporate social responsibility in corporate law and among companies, the almost ritualistic practice has abated of highlighting Friedman's piece for attack as a prefatory to the study of business ethics. Of late, the more prevalent tack of addressing the challenge posed by Adam Smith has involved co-opting him by emphasizing the ethical dimension of his thought, manifest in *The Theory of Moral Sentiments* (Rothschild 2001). One way or another, business ethics has felt compelled to defuse the possibility of using Smith's authority to challenge the idea that managers ought to be socially conscious.

The modern philosophical movement subsequently produced two methods of analyzing moral dilemmas that have proven far more congenial to business ethicists. When first introduced, however, those were not put to the task of subordinating the quest for profit to the deliberate pursuit of social goals. Nowhere was this more evident than utilitarianism, a moral theory with roots as far back as the Epicureans of the ancient world and with its basic outlines having been suggested by the eighteenth-century Scottish philosophers, Frances Hutcheson (1738: 107–128) and David Hume (1957 [1751]: 40–58). But it was Jeremy Bentham who originally systematized utilitarianism in *An Introduction to the Principles of Morals and Legislation*. Starting from the premise that human beings live, "under the governance of two sovereign masters, *pain* and *pleasure*," Bentham infers that morality embraces those actions that, on balance, tend to bring about pleasure, whereas immorality embraces those actions that, on balance, tend to bring about pain (1948 [1789]: 1). Pleasures and pains are, in turn, subject to quantitative measurement by their intensity, duration, certainty, and proximity in time. Thus a given pleasure is greater to the extent that it is earlier, more intense, longer-lasting, and has a higher probability of occurring—and vice versa in the case of pain. Despite the hedonistic psychology, utilitarianism is not an egoistic ethic. While acknowledging that it is only our own pleasure and pain that we feel, Bentham maintained that individuals can feel the pleasure and pain of others as their own (1948 [1789]: 36 and 40). This affords Bentham the basis to pronounce that utility, defined as the quantity of pleasure, ought to be maximized among all persons comprising the group affected by an action, whether executed by an individual or an organization (1948 [1789]: 2–3). With the emergence of utilitarianism, therefore, the first seeds of doubt were planted against the modern philosophic effort to accept and harness selfishness for social purposes, even if Bentham and his early followers were all avid believers in Smith's invisible hand. Those seeds would sow demands for the substitution of more altruistic motives in economic life, demands that would subsequently become a core part of business ethics, as we shall see.

A more direct reproof of self-interest arose with Immanuel Kant. In this effort, the eighteenth-century German philosopher still kept to the modern philosophic strategy of looking to the self as the ground of morality; however, rather than honing in on the implications of our psychological propensities, Kant focused on our autonomy. Any ethic guided by our desires—whether for happiness, self-preservation, or pleasure—he categorized as heteronomous, that is, as a condition in which human beings are subject to a law outside themselves. If the self is to be autonomous, it has to follow a law it enacts for itself. This law must be universal, being meant for rational beings and to reflect the basic intuition that the rules of morality apply to everyone without exception. Kant's solution to this is the categorical imperative: "never act except in such a way that I can also will that my maxim should become a universal law" (Kant 1981 [1785]: 14). In thus envisioning what would happen if everyone else were allowed to perform a given act, Kant is not asking for an assessment of the consequences to all those that might be affected. Such a rule-utilitarianism is ruled out by Kant's aversion to a heteronomous ethics. What the universalization test is meant to check is whether any contradiction exists in generalizing the permissibility of an action. Suppose a man desperate for money obtains a loan while knowingly making a pledge of repayment that he will not keep. The moral turpitude of this conduct lies in this: if everyone could issue false promises, it would no longer make any sense to make promises as no one would accept them. Counterfeit promises, that is, cannot co-exist with the practice of issuing promises. Despite this and other illustrations, however, Kant left it notoriously unclear how a contradiction is supposed to be deciphered with the universalization formula.

Not surprisingly, then, another version of his categorical imperative has ended up gaining wider currency: "Act in such a way that you treat Humanity, whether in your own person or in the person of another, always at the same time as an end and never simply as a means" (Kant 1981 [1785]: 36). Kant was willing to tolerate self-interest in commerce, believing that it was part of a progressive historical process that would hopefully culminate in a world society characterized by a perpetual peace within which all persons are treated with dignity as ends in themselves (1983 [1795]: 37 and 124–125). Albeit less willing to tolerate self-interest than Kant, a good deal of business ethics today can be comprehended as an effort to realize an economy in which people are no longer solely used as means for the purposes of others.

The late modern attack on business

Before saying more about this Kantian legacy, as well as on some of the uses of utilitarianism made by business ethicists, it will be necessary to give a brief summary of the third philosophic chapter in the moral story of business. The importance of this phase is that it had to be overcome in order for business ethics to develop. For it is no coincidence that the subject did not originate until the 1960s and 1970s, precisely when the hold of Karl Marx on Western intellectuals began to fade. And, let there be no doubt, the nineteenth-century German philosopher and economist was the towering figure of the third chapter in our story. Yet he was not alone. Not to be forgotten is Jean-Jacques Rousseau, who launched the first all-out assault on modern philosophy's commendation of business, framing the moral vision and agenda that Marx later endeavored to systematize with the tools of classical economics. But if Marx had to be transcended, business ethics could, and indeed has, imbibed key elements of Rousseau's thought.

The eighteenth-century French philosopher's critique of modernity is most famously set forth in the *Discourse on the Origin and Foundations of Inequality*. He begins by adopting the same line of attack employed by other modern philosophers, taking his initial bearings from the self. He contends, though, that its true nature was distorted by previous thinkers: "All of them . . . speaking continually of need, avarice, oppression, desires, and pride, have carried over to the state of nature ideas they had acquired in society" (Rousseau 1964 [1754]: 102). With Hobbes and Locke among the presumed targets, Rousseau's charge is that philosophers did not go far enough in removing all the traits that human beings had absorbed through socialization and in stripping us down to what nature gave us. Once this is done, he maintains, human nature comes into view not as acquisitive and antagonistic, but as good and compassionate. Hence, the greed, vanity, and lust for power that pervades the human scene are due to the influence of society. Of all the social institutions that have shaped individuals throughout history, none has been more damaging, according to Rousseau, than private property: "What crimes, wars, murders, what miseries and horrors would the human race have been spared," he asks, if someone had stopped the first person from saying, "this is mine" (Rousseau 1964 [1754]: 141). This condemnation of private property as the source of human ills, beyond ending up as the fulcrum of Marxism, is tied to a suspicion of economic progress (not present in Marx) along with the nostalgia for a return to nature that has rightly been interpreted as the beginnings of environmentalism (LaFreniere 1990). Before Rousseau, one is hard pressed to find a philosopher who extolled nature in its uncultivated state to the extent that he did. Locke, for example, advocated the conquest of nature, observing that it, "furnished only the almost worthless Materials, as in themselves" (1960 [1689]: 340). By way of the environmentalist movement, Rousseau's spirit makes itself felt in business ethics today in the near-universal edict that corporations promote sustainability.

The main lineaments of Marx's theory are well known. So all that need be said here is that when private property was introduced, societies were divided into classes based on the ownership of the means of production. In capitalist societies, Marx claims, that class division is between those who own capital and those who do not; the first consist of the capitalists who earn profit and the second of the workers who, not having any other means of generating income, are forced to sell their labor to earn wages. Relying on Smith's and David Ricardo's labor theory of value, Marx held that the price any good commanded on the marketplace was due to the effort put into its production by workers. What this means is that the profit that the capitalist extracts out of that price is taken from the value created by the worker. In this way, capitalists exploit the working classes. Nothing can eliminate this injustice other than the overthrow of capitalism, for no matter how much it might be reformed, the oppression of labor is engrained into that system's drive for profit. However, because this regime is unsustainable, Marx held out the prospect that the forces of historical progress are inevitably leading to the end of capitalism, the elimination of private property, and the consequent realization of a classless society in which, "the free development of each is the condition for the free development of all" (1978 [1848]: 491).

Now, this being said, it is clear why business ethics had to await the fall of Marxist modes of thinking for it to develop as a discipline. On the Marxist view, after all, the task of the intellectual is to advance the revolution that history portends, whereas much of what transpires in business ethics is the giving of advice to capitalists—tantamount to consorting with the enemy. Moreover, ethical concepts are understood by Marx to be part of the cultural superstructure of society, a set of ideas whose function is merely to rationalize the underlying economic structure. That raises the question: why engage in moral analysis when the real action is taking place in the economic realm? Then, too, there is the fact that Marx paints a determinist picture of economic life whereby capitalists are trapped within a system in which they can do little else but take advantage of workers. Business ethics seeks to improve the conduct of firms as well as the individuals who work inside them. But there is little point in doing so if all the main players lack the freedom to mend their ways. No wonder that the recently published *Handbook of the Philosophical Foundations of Business Ethics* (Luetge 2013) contains only one article on Marxist business ethics.

It would be an exaggeration to say, however, that Marx has exercised no influence whatsoever on business ethics. His contention that employers have an inherent advantage over employees—inasmuch as the latter usually have fewer alternatives of contracting for work than the former do—is widely accepted by business ethicists. Witness their general opposition to the principle of employment-at-will and their support of measures, such as just-cause termination along with the right of workers to form unions and strike, which constrain the ability of employers to negotiate the hiring, pay and working conditions of their employees. In what he calls "radical business ethics," Richard L. Lippke (1995) appeals to the Marxian analysis of the capital-labor relationship to argue that advanced capitalist societies severely inhibit the realization of human autonomy. Not only does he allege that autonomy is hindered by the economic compulsion that the system exerts upon workers, Lippke also maintains that people's capacity to think for themselves is distorted by advertising and the concentration of ownership in media industries. While Lippke does not advocate the abolition of capitalism, he does stress the need for major structural changes, the institutionalization of worker participation in companies for example, which he thinks goes beyond what the general run of business ethicists are prepared to contemplate. Yet it would be a mistake to see only the influence of Marx at work here. Rousseau's shadow arguably protrudes even larger, for he is the one who introduced the ideal of autonomy into the Western intellectual aether. He, too, was the first to object that modern commercial societies undermine human autonomy—economically, by rendering everyone dependent on others through the division of labor; and psychologically, by inducing everyone to judge themselves based on what others think of them (Rousseau 1964 [1754]: 156).

The philosophic epoch of business ethics

Thus we arrive at the last epoch, during which business ethics has materialized into a burgeoning specialty. What is distinctive about the current era is that no philosopher, or even school of thought, can be identified whose ideas are predominantly etched into the contours of the field. No equivalent of an Aristotle, a Smith, or a Marx appears before us that directs, encapsulates, and lends substance to our epoch's moral approach to business. Instead what we have is a *zeitgeist* informed by various thinkers, an intellectual milieu conducing to a middle way between the modern praise of business and the late modern assailing of it. This middle way, an acceptance of business under substantial moral constraints enforced by regulations, not untypically features the appeal to earlier philosophic traditions to define those conditions—yet almost always a selective appeal.

A key turning point in this direction was John Stuart Mill. The nineteenth-century British philosopher and economist began his career firmly within the utilitarian camp founded by Jeremy Bentham that believed self-interest could be chiefly relied upon to promote the common good. But Mill (1994 [1871]: 324–357) ended his intellectual odyssey by arguing for the legitimacy of state intervention in those situations where individuals cannot be expected to understand their own interests correctly or be able to pursue them in voluntary concert with others. Indeed, he came to expect that the public would, over time, develop intellectually and morally to the point where businesses could all function successfully as worker-owned cooperatives (Mill 1994 [1871]: 147–156). With this, the adequacy of self-interest was undercut, but without the implication of a state-run socialism to supplant it. The operation of self-interest in business could be tutored and crafted into something more ethically elevated, without following the Marxist prescription.

Fortuitously enough, that prescription happened to lose credit around the time that John Rawls' *A Theory of Justice* was published in 1971. Prior to this, the influence of logical positivism among Anglo-American academics, with its contention that moral propositions can never be anything more than subjective beliefs, stifled the evolution of moral and political philosophy. Rawls single-handedly changed all that, not only reviving those subjects, but further pushing the gates that had been opened by the eclipse of Marx for the emergence of specialized fields of moral inquiry such as business ethics. One need only consider Rawls' teaching on justice—to wit, that inequalities in the distribution of resources are fair only if they work to the interests of less advantaged groups. This lent credence to the notion that business could find a licit place within a legitimate socio-economic system. Still, Rawls' philosophy—which comes closest in our time to playing the roles previously held by the works of Aristotle, Smith, and Marx—left the distinct impression that business is supposed to function in an environment in which self-interest and the pursuit of gain must bow down before the greater social imperative of treating everyone with equal concern and respect. In reaching his conclusions, Rawls combined utilitarianism, social contract theory, along with Kantian principles of human dignity. He argued that, of all the possible options, the allocation of goods that maximizes the welfare of the less advantaged is the one that persons would choose behind a veil of ignorance not knowing the social and natural assets that luck will assign them.

A similar attempt to marry time-tested philosophic theories is to be found in the central tenet of contemporary business ethics: the stakeholder theory of the firm. More popularly known under the banner of Corporate Social Responsibility (CSR), the stakeholder view aims to displace the shareholder theory of the firm that has long comprised the orthodoxy in economics and finance and which, until recently, was legally entrenched (*Dodge* v. *Ford* 1919). The shareholder theory envisions the firm as a nexus of individual contractors within which the highest duty of corporate managers is to the shareholders, the equity owners of the firm. By contrast, the stakeholder theory sees the firm as a legal privilege conditionally granted by the state, while asserting that corporate managers are ultimately obligated to conciliate the interests of multiple parties, namely all those affected by the firm's actions, the stakeholders. These include customers, employees, creditors, suppliers, governments, local communities, in addition to shareholders. In R. Edward Freeman's (2002) influential defense of the stakeholder theory, utilitarian arguments are employed to demonstrate that profit-maximizing for shareholders will not redound to the public interest owing to the presence of externalities and industry concentration. When there are externalities—which occur whenever the costs and benefits generated by an economic activity are felt by those not engaged in it—then the self-interest of companies will lead either to the underproduction of goods (when the benefits are externalized) or the overproduction of bads (when the costs are externalized), with pollution the standard instance of the latter. When industry concentration exists, whether in the form of oligopoly or monopoly, then self-interest will dictate that companies overcharge consumers for goods and produce less of them than is socially optimal. To overcome these dilemmas posed by externalities and industry concentration, stakeholder theory holds that firms must adopt a more socially conscious perspective in order to boost communal utility. Beyond this emendation of Bentham, the stakeholder theory also invokes Kant's maxim that everyone's ends be respected. It does so by raising all other agents affected by the firm to an equal status with the shareholders. When Freeman (2002: 414) objects against "the presumption in favor of financier rights," he insinuates that the traditional view lets shareholders use everyone else involved as mere means for their own purposes.

Bringing the idea of a social contract to bear as well, Freeman comes up with a corporate variation of the Rawlsian veil of ignorance. Individuals are conceived as being aware of the general facts of commercial life and the possibilities of market failures like externalities, but do not know what position vis-à-vis the firm they will end up occupying. Amongst the various alternative ways of organizing the firm, Freeman maintains that individuals, in order to hedge against the prospect of losing out by not becoming shareholders, would rationally opt for the stakeholder theory. The social contract tradition has also been summoned in business ethics by Thomas Donaldson and Thomas W. Dunfee (1994). Unlike Freeman, however, they envision two separate compacts, one macrosocial and the other microsocial, with the first providing the overarching norms for those that can be agreed to in the second. Another difference with Freeman is that what Donaldson and Dunfee call "integrative social contract theory" is put forward more as a technique for business ethicists to use as they deem theoretically fit, than it is to infer their own detailed set of ethical obligations for companies, even if they do make various suggestions that lean in the direction of corporate social responsibility.

Regrettably, in all this harnessing of time-tested ideas from the past, business ethicists show few signs of having gone beyond the level of general concepts. They have not yet come to grips with the complete scope of arguments that the philosophers marshalled to support their positions. Thus, for Hobbes and Locke, the obligatory force of the social contract, upon original consent to its terms, derives from the fact that it is generally in everyone's interests to continue to abide by it. This is why Locke (1960 [1689]: 460–470) argues that people reserve the prerogative to revolt if the state violates their rights, the preservation of the social contract no longer being in their interests; it is also why Hobbes (1985 [1651]: 199), though he denies a right of rebellion, nevertheless asserts that a person facing capital punishment has the right to evade the state's enforcement of that penalty, the social contract having been originally entered into to avoid death. Applying this reasoning to stakeholder theory, it is difficult to see why any rational shareholder would persist in agreeing, irrespective of whatever they initially signed up for under a veil of ignorance, to an arrangement in which management is not primarily obligated to them to maximize profits. As the last ones to be paid out of revenues, and therefore the bearers of the greatest risk among the firm's claimants, shareholders cannot ask for anything less than profit maximization if they hope to motivate corporate executives to generate a return on their investment. The solicitation of Kant by business ethicists is similarly remiss about his treatment of human dignity. It entirely neglects his insistence that treating people as ends-in-themselves entails that their property rights be respected almost absolutely, the chief limit being taxes to support the state and the poor. Such a conception of property rights is hard to square with the notion that shareholders ought to sacrifice profit for larger social goals (Kant 1991 [1797]: 136–137). Only with utilitarianism have business ethicists paid some heed to its original philosophic exponents. Even there, Mill's psychological assumption that individuals will become more socially minded as humanity progresses has been too uncritically accepted. Other thinkers sympathetic to utilitarianism, such as David Hume, had more modest expectations of human altruism but such views have received short shrift. These are just a few examples indicating that business ethicists have yet to thoroughly engage with the historical contributions to their field.

Concluding remarks

Despite not fully mining that legacy, business ethics shows all the marks of being influenced by the great philosophers. Veering from the celebration of commerce at one extreme to its condemnation at the other, and with qualified acceptance in between, what the philosophic tradition has to say about business ethics can be organized into four historical phases. In the first period, comprising the ancient and medieval thinkers, we see the initial clash between philosophy and business, albeit with this tension getting progressively eased as the Renaissance draws closer. This tension largely disappears in the second period encompassing the 17th to 18th centuries, during which early modern philosophers like John Locke, Adam Smith, Immanuel Kant, and Jeremy Bentham give moral sanction to commerce and establish the theoretical underpinnings for much of contemporary business ethics. Afterwards, we witness two distinct reactions to this philosophic alliance with commerce. Thus in the third period, beginning in the mid-eighteenth century with Jean-Jacques Rousseau and coming to fruition in the nineteenth century with Karl Marx, commerce is forcefully challenged. As for the fourth period, with its seeds sowed in the writings of the late John Stuart Mill in the nineteenth century and its latest manifestation in the figure of John Rawls, this tradition responds less radically to the consolidation of commercial societies. It does so by accepting the basic legitimacy of business, while simultaneously insisting upon the necessity of taming it with an array of political, economic, and moral checks. Business ethics belongs to this last phase, even if it looks to the first three for inspiration and guidance.

Essential readings

The essential works on the philosophic foundations and influences of business ethics include Aristotle's *Nicomachean Ethics* (1982), Adam Smith's *An Inquiry into the Nature and Causes of the Wealth of Nations* (1981 [1776]), Jeremy Bentham's *The Principles of Morals and Legislation* (1948 [1789]), Immanuel Kant's *Grounding for the Metaphysics of Morals* (1981 [1785]), Karl Marx and Friedrich Engels' *Manifesto of the Communist Party* (1978 [1848]), and John Rawls' *A Theory of Justice* (1971).

For further reading in this volume on the compatibility of virtue and profit-making business see Chapter 7, Can profit seekers be virtuous? On modern theories of ethics and their relation to business, see Chapter 5, Consequentialism and non-consequentialism. On Locke and Rousseau as offering competing visions of society see Chapter 3, Theory and method in business ethics.

References

Aquinas, T. (1920 [1265–1274]). *The Summa Theologica of St Thomas Aquinas*, Fathers of the English Dominican Province (trans.). Available at: www.newadvent.org/summa/.

Aristotle. (1982). "Nicomachean Ethics" in H.G. Apostle and L.P. Gerson (eds), *Aristotle Selected Works*. Iowa: The Peripatetic Press, 415–544.

Arjoon, S. (2000). "Virtue theory as a Dynamic Theory of Business," *Journal of Business Ethics* 28:2, 159–178.

Aziz, A., May, K. and Crotts, J.C. (2002). "Relations of Machiavellian Behavior with Sales Performance of Stock Brokers," *Psychological Reports* 90:2, 451–460.

Bentham, J. (1818 [1787]). *Defense of Usury*. London: Payne and Foss.

Bentham, J. (1948 [1789]). *The Principles of Morals and Legislation*. New York: Hafner Press.

Bertland, A. (2009). "Virtue Ethics in Business and the Capabilities Approach," *Journal of Business Ethics* 84:1, 25–32.

Bragues, G. (2006). "Seek the Good Life, Not Money: The Aristotelian Approach to Business Ethics," *Journal of Business Ethics* 67:4, 341–357.

Chafuen, A.A. (2003). *Faith and Liberty: The Economic Thought of the Late Scholastics*. Lanham, MD: Lexington Books.

Carr, A. (1968). "Is Business Bluffing Ethical?" *Harvard Business Review* 46, 143–153.

Cicero. (1991 [44BC]) in M.T. Griffin and E.M. Atkins (eds), *On Duties*. Cambridge: Cambridge University Press.

Dodge v. Ford Motor Co. (1919). 170 N.W. 668, 204 Michigan 459.

Donaldson, T. and Dunfee, T.W. (1994). "Toward a Unified Conception of Business Ethics: Integrative Social Contracts Theory," *Academy of Management Review* 19:2, 252–284.

Freeman, R.E. (2002). "A Stakeholder Theory of the Modern Corporation," in E. Heath (ed.), *Morality and the Market: Ethics and Virtue in the Conduct of Business*. New York, NY: McGraw Hill, 409–416.

Friedman, M. (1970). "The Social Responsibility of Business is to Increase Its Profits," *New York Times Magazine* 13, 32–33, 122–126.

Galie, P.J. and Bopst, C. (2006). "Machiavelli and Modern Business: Realist Thought in Contemporary Corporate Leadership Manuals," *Journal of Business Ethics* 65:3, 235–250.

Gunnthorsdottir, A., McCabe, K. and Smith, V. (2002). "Using the Machiavellianism Instrument to Predict Trustworthiness in a Bargaining Game," *Journal of Economic Psychology* 23:1, 49–66.

Hartman, E. (2013). *Virtues in Business: Conversations with Aristotle*. Cambridge: Cambridge University Press.

Hobbes, T. (1985 [1651]). *Leviathan*, C.B. Macpherson (ed.). New York, NY: Penguin.

Hume, D. (1957 [1751]). *An Inquiry Concerning the Principles of Morals*, C.W. Hendel (ed.). Indianapolis, IN: The Bobbs-Merrill Company, Inc.

Hutcheson, F. (1738). *An Inquiry into the Original of our Ideas of Beauty and Virtue*. Charlottesville, VA: Ibis Publishing.

Kant, I. (1981 [1785]). *Grounding for the Metaphysics of Morals*, J.W. Ellington (trans.). Indianapolis, IN: Hackett Publishing Company.

Kant, I. (1983 [1795]). *Perpetual Peace and Other Essays*, T. Humphrey (trans.). Indianapolis, IN: Hackett Publishing Company.

Kant, I. (1991 [1797]). *The Metaphysics of Morals*, M. Gregor (trans.). Cambridge: Cambridge University Press.

Koehn, D. (1995). "A Role for Virtue Ethics in the Analysis of Business Practice," *Business Ethics Quarterly* 5:3, 533–539.

LaFreniere, G.F. (1990). "Rousseau and the European Roots of Environmentalism," *Environmental History Review* 14:4, 41–72.

Lippke, R.L. (1995). *Radical Business Ethics*. Maryland, MA: Rowman & Littlefield.

Locke, J. (1960 [1689]). *Two Treatises of Civil Government*, P. Laslett (ed.). New York, NY: Cambridge University Press.

Luetge, C. (ed.) (2013). *Handbook of the Philosophical Foundations of Business Ethics*, 3 vols. Heidelberg: Springer.

Machiavelli, N. (1947 [1513]). *The Prince*, T.G. Bergin (ed.). Wheeling, IL: Harlan Davidson, Inc.

MacIntyre, A. (1984). *After Virtue*. Notre Dame: University of Notre Dame Press.

Mandeville, B. (1924 [1732]). *The Fable of the Bees*, F.B. Kaye (ed.). Oxford: Clarendon Press.

Marx, K. and Engels, F. (1978 [1848]). "Manifesto of the Communist Party" in R.C. Tucker (ed.) *The Marx–Engels Reader*. New York, NY: W.W. Norton & Company, 469–500.

Melzer, A. (2014). *Philosophy Between the Lines: The Lost History of Esoteric Writing*. Chicago, IL: University of Chicago Press.

Mill, J.S. (1994 [1871]). *Principles of Political Economy and Chapters on Socialism*. Oxford: Oxford University Press.

Moore, G. (2005). "Corporate Character: Modern Virtue Ethics and the Virtuous Corporation," *Business Ethics Quarterly* 15:4, 659–685.

Nussbaum, M. (2011). *Creating Capabilities: The Human Development Approach*. Cambridge, MA: Harvard University Press.

Oresme, N. (1956 [1279]). *The De Moneta of Nicholas Oresme and English Mint Documents*, C. Johnson (trans.). London: Thomas Nelson and Sons Ltd.

Pontifical Council for Justice and Peace (2004). *Compendium of the Social Doctrine of the Church*. Vatican City: Libreria Editrice Vaticana. Available at: www.vatican.va/roman_curia/pontifical_councils/justpeace/documents/rc_pc_justpeace_doc_20060526_compendio-dott-soc_en.html.

Rawls, J. (1971). *A Theory of Justice*. Cambridge, MA: Harvard University Press.

Rothschild, E. (2001). *Economic Sentiments: Adam Smith, Condorcet, and the Enlightenment*. Cambridge, MA: Harvard University Press.

Rousseau, J.J. (1964 [1754]). *The First and Second Discourses*, R.D. Masters (ed.). New York, NY: St Martin's Press.

Sen, A. (1999). *Commodities and Capabilities*. New York, NY: Oxford University Press.

Smith, A. (1981 [1776]) in R.H. Campbell and A.S. Skinner (eds), *An Inquiry into the Nature and Causes of the Wealth of Nations*, 2 vols. Indianapolis, IN: Liberty Fund.

Solomon, R. (1992). *Ethics and Excellence: Cooperation and Integrity in Business*. New York, NY: Oxford University Press.

3
Theory and method in business ethics

Nicholas Capaldi

What is the relationship between actual business practice and business ethics theorizing? How can or should business ethicists contribute to our understanding of business? These questions, which have been addressed insufficiently by business ethicists, manifest the aim of this chapter: to identify, clarify, and resolve some major tensions in what business ethicists do or think they are doing. The mainstream of business ethics, along with a smaller counterculture, reflects deeper disputes both within philosophy and about the nature of philosophy. It is essential to probe these disputes and to consider the intellectual frameworks that have guided much of contemporary business ethics.

There seems to be no universal agreement as to what business ethics *is* or on what business ethicists *should* do. This lack of agreement may reflect the fact that the field exhibits a fundamental ambiguity: Is business ethics descriptive or normative? Or is it some sort of combination (what I describe, below, as "exploration")? These questions yield still further clusters of queries.

1   Are scholars in business ethics trying to understand (descriptively) the norms inherent in extant business practice, or are they trying to judge (normatively) business practice from some external perspective, or are they focused on the practice of resolving ethical conflicts?
2   If they are engaged in describing the inherent norms of commerce, are they taking into account different historical and cultural contexts or do they have some abstract or generic version in mind? To what extent do business ethics scholars need to understand economics? Whose economics?
3   If business ethics scholars proceed along the normative route, are they identifying and critiquing those who fail to live up to standards (an internal critique) or are they challenging the inherent standards from some outside perspective (external critique)? Wouldn't this normative examination also presuppose some larger account of how commerce relates to other practices (Capaldi 2004)? Wouldn't a normative consideration have to privilege, at some point, either a particular practice or set of related practices (or the prioritization within practices), and wouldn't this raise the first and second issues—internal versus external critique—all over again at another level? Without the appeal to some privileged practices, one could not advance macro-level prescriptions as "business ethics."

4   Finally, if business ethicists are to be practitioners who advise or consult professionally to resolve ethical conflicts in business, they not only must address all three of the above issues, but also must have some understanding of what it means to be a practitioner (and in which specific dimensions of commerce). For example, a corporate business ethicist or consultant might be called upon (a) to identify and explain current extant norms, (b) to identify a conflict or potential conflict between the extant norm and some current form of commercial behavior, (c) to indicate why that norm does or does not apply to a particular case in hand, (d) to identify more than one applicable norm and how those norms might themselves be in conflict when applied to the case in hand, (e) to explain how similar cases in the past have been handled and the outcomes, and, of course, (f) to identify possible legal ramifications. Moreover, one would have to distinguish between a practitioner who approves of commerce as practiced and wants to make it work better (those who endow business ethics centers seem mostly to have this in mind) and someone who disapproves of commerce and thinks that the appropriate strategy is to goad students, workers, or professionals into some sort of reform (or rebellion), constructive or otherwise.

We shall approach these questions in the following ways. In the first section, we consider first the hostility to business that extends from intellectuals to business ethicists. The subsequent section takes up the philosophical background to this antipathy, canvassing the philosophical perspectives, from ancient to modern, that have framed this hostility. In so doing, we encounter something novel in the modern era: the appeal to expertise. In the third section, we examine the enlightened view of ethics and its tendency to both explain the world and to prioritize a view of ethics that demands the *exploration* of everyday conduct and practice. This idea of ethics has generated a new normative method in philosophy that includes applied fields such as business ethics. In the fourth section, we summarize how this normative method has yielded two broad narratives about society. However, as we point out in the last section, there is an alternative method that the business ethicist might employ and this we call *explication*.

Hostility to business and business ethics

With the opening questions in view, it is important to keep in mind that intellectuals maintain a long-standing opposition to commerce. This hostility extends from prominent members of the academy (see the discussions in Schumpeter 1975; de Jouvenel 1974; von Mises 2006; Nozick 1998) to scholars of business ethics. We cite as one example of this ingrained hostility a statement by George Brenkert, long-time editor of *Business Ethics Quarterly*, in an article on entrepreneurship:

> The argument for entrepreneurship and an entrepreneurial society is for a society in which some sub-set will provide leadership . . . the entrepreneurs will be the spark plugs, as it were, of this economy and society. Instead, then, of a Platonic society, which looked to its philosopher kings, our entrepreneurial society will look to its entrepreneur bosses.
> (Brenkert 2002: 17; see also McDonald 2017)

James Hoopes (2003) gives a broad but critical historical overview of the management literature of the twentieth century and documents the unwillingness of management gurus (e.g., Peter Drucker) to see profit as legitimate unless subordinated to another goal. Some anti-market advocates have wanted the US to be more like the European Union or Japan. Some other advocates maintain the corporation *should* be viewed as a social entity (Dodd 1932; Etzioni 1993; Clarkson 1995; Kuttner 1997). These advocates need not hold a specific ideology—or any ideology.

Some advocates of the stakeholder view of the firm may even operate under the assumption that they are *pro*-market (Donaldson and Preston 1995; Freeman and Phillips 2002). Yet these writers reject the notion that the chief object of business is to achieve a profitable product or service, and they insist that business, like other spheres of activity, must strive towards non-profit goals. In setting forth these assumptions they identify business ethics in terms of conflicts between profitability and other goals, demand that the problem be resolved through non-market structures (business should function less like business and more like political, religious or academic institutions), and then justify these appeals by drawing from disciplines other than economics.

Given this skepticism, if not outright hostility, to commerce, one might wonder why the field of business ethics exists at all? Despite a long history of ethical thought about commerce—even in business schools, as chronicled by Gabriel Abend (2013, 2014)—the idea of a self-conscious field of academic business ethics takes hold in the 1970s. (Biomedical ethics also emerges in this decade but its evolution reflects developments in medical technology, as set forth in Albert Jonsen 2003.) Prior to 1960, deliberation about ethical matters was left largely to centers of cultural authority operating independently of the academy: religion, the family, the professions, and other intermediate institutions. For many reasons, these traditional centers of authority became discredited. The intellectual movement of positivism along with the spectacular success of science and engineering contributed to their undermining. Even though positivism does not itself entail a specific account of morality, it does attenuate existing frameworks that do not measure up to the positivists' conception of what is rational (i.e., empirically verifiable). In addition, different religions offered different ethical responses. More to the point, starting in the 1960s every major religious denomination underwent its own internal revolt (e.g., Vatican II among Catholics). The overall direction of these revolts was towards liberalization and away from tradition, with regard to both theological and social issues.

Within universities there is historical opposition to including business education in the curriculum (Khurana 2007). Curiously, Alfred North Whitehead, who was a friend of Harvard Business School Dean Wallace Brett Donham, advocated the inclusion of a business faculty in the university in an address he gave in 1927 to the American Association of the Collegiate Schools of Business (Whitehead 1936). In 1936, Whitehead and Robert Maynard Hutchins debated this issue in the *Atlantic Monthly* (Whitehead 1936; Hutchins 1936). In opposition to Whitehead, Hutchins argued that the role of the university was to teach first principles, theory, and the unity of knowledge as opposed to facts and skills. Hutchins questioned whether business was even a profession, and he suggested that vocational practices should be taught on the job.

Business ethics[1] as a field within business schools originated in the 1960s at the University of California-Berkeley, where many in the "Business and Society" field were trained (see Epstein 1999 and Carroll 2008 on the importance of the 1960s). The early focus of business ethics centered on corporate social responsibility and social reform of the inequities of capitalism (Jones 1980). Members of Management departments initiated the Social Issues in Management division within the Academy of Management.

The financial scandals of the 1980s yielded a sudden demand for ethics training for business students. Philosophically trained business ethicists moved to tenured posts and even endowed chairs in business (Shaw 1996). As a consequence, the traditionally "hostile attitudes" of the university toward business (Shaw 1996: 490) were thus reinforced by the arrival of the philosophers. Business ethics was doubly conceived in sin, combining liberal Management scholarship with liberal Philosophy scholarship. Frequently, such scholarship employs a political model to "understand, assess, and perhaps modify the socioeconomic context . . . that frame[s] the moral choices that confront individuals" (Shaw 1996: 496), leading to critiques from a Marxist

(Lippke 1995) or from those who viewed the market as beset by immoral practices. Often the focus on corporate social responsibility is designed to affirm that firms should do more than maximize profits.

Currently, business ethics programs in American business schools reside mostly[2] in the Management discipline, with faculties drawn from two backgrounds: Philosophy and Management. The PhDs in Management reflect a social science methodology. This approach does not by itself reflect a normative management science—something that professionals could authoritatively teach business practitioners. In fact, the intellectual developments within philosophy have made the idea of normative management science tenable.

The philosophical background

Classical philosophy

The overriding perennial issue in normative philosophy is reconciling the individual with the community. The tendency among classical ethical views is to begin with an independently established ethical account and then measure actual practice against that ideal account: Plato alluded to the "Forms" and Aristotle claimed to have discovered a metaphysical teleological biology. The risk here is reducing philosophy to an ivory-tower exercise in ideology. However, classical philosophers could not locate commerce or trade within these external structures and so they had an inherent antipathy to the commercial practice of ancient times and would, I dare say, oppose it in its modern forms. Given his moral principles, it is not clear that Aristotle was justified in his antipathy (Miller 2017), and it may be the case that the outlooks of Plato and Aristotle, as typically understood, differed from the views of archaic writers, such as Homer and Hesiod (Peacock 2017).

Advocacy of an epistemological realism (truth as conformity of intellect to an external structure) leads to the classical and medieval conception that social structures should reflect external structure. This sort of realism tends, therefore, to prioritize the social over the individual. Societies come to be viewed as *enterprise* associations (Oakeshott 1975: Chapter 2, esp. 114–130), that is, as having a collective goal to which individuals must conform. The contrary belief that society is a *civil* association—eschewing a collective goal and existing to further the goals of its individual members—is a modern manifestation of the denial of epistemological realism and more consonant with the outlook that individual minds impose order on experience.

Medieval philosophy

Medieval Christendom sought to overcome classical philosophy's failure to achieve political harmony by invoking a theologically based natural law and by claiming that the Church was the institution for accessing it, thereby delegitimating the claims of the political realm to prioritization over the Church. This solution also failed—first, in the conflict generated between Church and state and, second, by succumbing to Church versus Church controversies.

For Christians, access to God's principles was a product of moral not just intellectual virtue. Moral virtue was achieved in a variety of ways including ascetic practice that emphasized self-sacrifice and self-denial partly as a way of achieving a form of disinterestedness. Those achieving this state were accorded recognition as spiritual mentors. Of course, there is a danger that asceticism becomes a form of pride. Nevertheless, the ascetic disposition remains a powerful stimulus to the ethical outlooks of members of religious communities: among contemporary clergy it leads to a critique of "consumerism," advertising, and profits, as well as advocacy of so-called stakeholderism (community) and public policies of redistribution (see, for example, Cavanaugh 2003; Pope Francis 2015).

In the later medieval period, "theology" meant rationalization of Christianity through the employment of classical Greek philosophy. To be a member of the intellectual elite, possessing intellectual virtue and moral virtue, meant that one was an "expert" of sorts, though the notion of ethical expertise would emerge more fully in the modern era. Recognition of the elite by the non-elite was facilitated by both the erudition and the ascetic lifestyle of those who claimed this status. The university developed in the late middle ages primarily to train clergy who thus constituted the ethical elite. The university thereby becomes the locus of ethical expertise. Modern universities claim this authority long after they have given up even the pretense of belief in the transcendent. To this day, faculty reflect a modern version of ascetic virtue in their widespread beliefs that universities are superior institutions because they are non-profits, that those who work for profit are morally or socially inferior, and that wealth is something to be shared or redistributed.

The danger of combining intellectual and moral virtue is the tendency for the former to subsume the latter. Morality becomes an intellectual exercise—the *application* of theory to practice or the reflective observance of rules or ideals. The emphasis is on having a correct and defensible theory rather than on how to act, a point explored notably by Michael Oakeshott (1991b). Ideals quickly turn into obsessions. Moral sensibility is inhibited or even eroded in favor of an elaborate casuistry. It is less important to behave well in a concrete manner than it is to chase an ideal or observe a rule.

Modern philosophy

The intellectual framework of the classical and medieval world not only proved inadequate in eliminating conflict on the practical level but was soon under attack on the theoretical level as well. Modern physics, as represented by René Descartes and Isaac Newton, denied the existence of final causes or a universal telos. In addition, the economy was being transformed from agriculture to industry and technology. Descartes himself urged mankind to make itself "the masters and possessors of nature" (*Discourse*, Part VI). In the fifth chapter of *Second Treatise of Government* (§40), John Locke pointed out how human labor created value. With the spread of enterprise in the seventeenth and eighteenth centuries, wealth and growth replaced poverty as the norm. Economics leaves the household, where it had been enclosed by classical thinkers, and becomes modern political economy as reflected in the title of Adam Smith's *Wealth of Nations* (1981[1776]).

The American Founders, especially James Madison, followed David Hume and Smith not only in prioritizing the individual, but in advocating that government be understood in economic terms rather than the economy being understood in political terms. A market economy works best when it exhibits competition; therefore, government ought to be understood as encompassing competing economic interests. Political institutions also require competition—states versus Federal government, divided branches of Federal government, a means of checks and balances. For the American Founders the role of government is to referee the conflict among economic interests (see Madison et al. 1987[1788], *Federalist Papers*, 10) not subordinate them to a non-existent collective good.

Within this intellectual and economic context, modern normative philosophy faced two theoretical problems: first, to account for the social, or at least inter-subjective, status of norms; and, second, to reconcile the individual good with the communal. (See Michael Oakeshott's synthesis of these two problems (1991c: 367–68), noting their origin in the work of Thomas Hobbes). With these two problems in mind, the following possibilities emerge.

First, one could always reassert the classical position, remaining both disdainful of and aloof from modern commerce. This is the position in mainline philosophy of Elizabeth Anscombe (1958) and Alasdair MacIntyre (1981). A somewhat simplified version of this position is the revival of Aristotelian virtue theory within business ethics. As illustrated in the work of Robert Solomon, it too ultimately prioritizes the community:

> The Aristotelian framework tells us that it is cooperation and not an isolated sense of individual self-worth that defines the most important virtues . . . in which the well-being of the community goes hand in hand with individual excellence . . . because of the social consciousness and public spirit of each and every individual.
>
> *(Solomon 2008: 75–76)*

As a second option, one could maintain the existence of a social and human teleology based upon theology yet divorced from any connection with physical nature (the position of the Catholic Church). This option is sometimes embraced by individuals ensconced in a non-profit institution in which they work unperturbed because of the beneficence of donors, all the while urging ascetic practice and the redistribution of resources.

Third, one could deny the existence of any *social* teleology but maintain a version of teleology within the individual. If so, ethics emerges as a form of contractual agreement (e.g., Hobbes maintains that personal survival is the all-encompassing end) among individuals who thereby claim negative rights (thus, limiting the state). Some scholars in philosophy and business ethics have pursued this version of neo-Aristotelian ethics, prioritizing the individual and applying this version of neo-Aristotelianism to business ethics (Machan 2007; Sternberg 2000; Miller 2017; 1995; Den Uyl and Rasmussen 2002), but much of their work has been marginalized perhaps because they do prioritize the individual.

As a fourth and last possibility, one can deny any form of teleology and claim that the social world is a construct of contracting individuals who claim negative rights but are willing on occasion to "adopt" a social perspective. The denial of teleology leads to a substitution of the notion of "moral philosophy" in place of "ethics," although subsequent linguistic usage is rarely this refined. Moral philosophy reasserts the fundamental social nature of morality and focuses on explaining how individuals can and may adopt the social perspective. For Smith and Hume it is through sympathy; for Immanuel Kant it is through transcendental reason.

For this last alternative, the remaining theoretical issue is whether the socially-constructed framework is substantive (as in Jean-Jacques Rousseau, the British idealists, or John Rawls) or procedural (Hume, Kant, J.S. Mill, Friedrich Nietzsche, F. A. Hayek, Oakeshott, James M. Buchanan). If one subscribes to the notion that the social order is substantive, then one is in position to argue for a framework in which positive rights (via the expanded power of the state) override all other claims. On the other hand, if one hews to the notion that the social order is procedural, then one can insist that negative rights are inherent within the individual and cannot be overridden (see, in particular, Buchanan 1975). Proceduralists prioritize the individual; substantivists prioritize the community or the alleged social compact. Proceduralists argue that substantivists indulge in either a covert teleology or a private political agenda. Substantivists argue that proceduralists are amoral or Darwinian in the pejorative non-teleological sense. Substantivists adopt the perspective of presumptive ethical experts; as such, they believe that there is both an overriding communal interest known to them and that, if necessary, the state should employ its monopoly on the legitimate use of force to foster and promote that interest. Proceduralists understand themselves to be advocates of interests, whether individual, group, or institutional, and beholden to voluntary and negotiated contracts.

For the proceduralist, the focus is business law, with ethics referenced to the evolving norms of an evolving marketplace. Should there be a conflict of ethics, there is no guarantee that it will be resolved, only managed.

The Enlightenment Project and contemporary ethics

Since the eighteenth century, the intellectual culture has been dominated by the belief in ethics experts and an authoritative and viable social technology. This belief, the Enlightenment Project (Becker 1962; MacIntyre 1981; Engelhardt 1986; Bloom 1987; Adorno and Horkheimer 1990; McCarthy 1998; Capaldi 1998), is the attempt to define, explain, and control the human predicament through scientific technology. It involves the intention to explain everything, without remainder, in scientific terms, to establish a social science to explain the social world, and to construct a social technology for the repair of and organization of the social world.

Since Descartes and Newton, among others, physical science has been successful in explaining, predicting, and controlling the physical universe. Presumably, there must be an analogous social science that will enable us to explain, predict, and control the human and social world, ultimately producing a social technology. This notion of Enlightenment with its companion science of society dominates the intellectual world, finds its locus in universities and research centers, and permeates all professions based on university education.

With regard to commerce, the Enlightenment Project promises to explain how there can be management science *and* how social scientists and philosophers can engage in normative theorizing and education. We can even, plausibly, educate students to do the "right thing." The authority claimed by philosophers was that they could see the large picture and, therefore, were uniquely positioned to determine policy for every institution—especially business—and resolve all apparent conflicts. Finally, the Enlightenment Project contains a bias in favor of government as occupying a principal perspective on society and thus capable of solving social problems and regulating the economy. For example, in addressing major ethical issues of modern commerce, the default position for many business ethicists is government regulation. Even if almost no one advocates central planning or government ownership, there is also scarcely any principled argument to limit government activity. Some defenders of stakeholder theory might challenge this conclusion (Freeman and Phillips 2002) but there is a difference between what a theorist might hold personally and the logic of the theory. If there is no limit as to who might be a stakeholder, then since the entire national or international economy can easily be construed as composed of stakeholders, the only institution that could resolve conflicts among stakeholders would be nation states or an international political authority. The most recent and celebrated book in economics, Thomas Piketty's *Capital* (2014) invokes the work of John Rawls (1971) to establish an argument eventuating in global economic regulation and significantly higher tax rates. The classic best statement about how government regulation is counterproductive, that of Cass Sunstein (1997), was written *not* to decry regulation but to improve it.

As in business ethics, the mainstream philosophical outlook also favors state activity, exemplified in John Rawls' later view, "Justice as Fairness: Political, not Metaphysical" (1985), receiving its full elaboration in *Political Liberalism* (1993) and *The Law of Peoples* (2001). For Rawls, it is possible to develop a political account of a democratic regime that will provide a kind of constitutional framework for dealing with disagreement about the most fundamental human problems. A similar approach is found in Richard Rorty's "The Priority of Democracy to Philosophy" (1991). We see this in business ethics in the works of Patricia

metaphysics
(identified with the philosophy of science) →
　　　　　epistemology →
　　　　　　　　　ethics →
　　　　　　　　　　　　political philosophy →
　　　　　　　　　　　　　　　　applied philosophy

Figure 3.1 The philosophical ordering of the universe and the priority of metaphysics.

Werhane (Werhane et al. 2003) in her opposition to employment at will. Employment at will permits employers to fire an employee without having to justify this to anyone; similarly, it also permits employees to quit or take a different job without having to justify this to anyone. To regulate employee hiring Werhane advocates an elaborate appeals process, one that will ultimately require regulation by the Department of Labor. One sometimes gets the impression that some business ethicists think part of the purpose of business ethics scholarship and teaching is advocating change in the law or the introduction of new laws—in short, a resort to government regulation.

Analytic philosophy is the current embodiment of the Enlightenment Project, with its ambition of universal explanation. For analytic philosophy, the correct philosophical ordering of the universe reveals the fundamental priority of metaphysics. Figure 3.1 reflects the priority of the ethical over the political but also the priority of the political over the economic, reinforcing again the notion that applied ethics will favor government regulation to make sure that economic practice conforms to larger social or political objectives.

Prior to 1970, many philosophers had either treated ethical issues as metaethical (the clarification of ethical discourse) or maintained that there was an alleged difference between facts and values. Both approaches seemingly precluded a normative science of ethics. All of that changed with the publication, in 1971, of Rawls' *A Theory of Justice*. Philosophers felt themselves newly empowered to engage in normative work. Medical ethics and business ethics became the major growth subfields in philosophy. Social scientists in general and management specialists in particular focused on methodological concerns and were quick to borrow from the discipline of philosophy the idea that they too could engage in normative work. One outcome is that almost everyone now teaching in American universities considers him or herself an ethics expert—and certainly so in relation to those working outside academe.

What accounted for this turn to normative philosophy and the temptation of expertise? Here, one must return to the Enlightenment Project. In physical science there are two major kinds of explanation: elimination and exploration. *Elimination* substitutes new ideas for older ones (e.g., the replacement of Ptolemy's geocentric view of the universe with Copernicus' heliocentric view or the replacement of everyday folk psychology with neuroscience). This is not useful in the social sciences because social theorists claim, initially, to be explaining our values not immediately replacing our values. *Exploration* begins with our ordinary understanding of how things work and then "explains" what is behind it, changing our ordinary understanding. The new understanding does not elaborate the old understanding, but replaces it by following the implications of some hypothetical model. The replacement "explanation" appeals to an underlying structure (e.g., the atomic theory explains chemical behavior and the behavior of gases). Exploratory explanations seek out the formal elements underlying the everyday world rather than accepting that the everyday world can constitute its own level of understanding. Everyday moral judgments are now viewed as epiphenomena, with the underlying sub-structure allegedly providing real scientific explanation.

Exploration had already been practiced in social science. By analogy with physical science, social scientists alleged that they were discovering the hidden sub-structure behind the everyday understanding of social activities. Now exploration arrives to philosophy, including applied philosophy.

Exploration: the "new" normative methodology

An important example of exploration is found in the work of Rawls. *A Theory of Justice* does not start with an explication of existing practice, but instead begins with an imaginary original position, an exploration of the hidden structure behind the epiphenomena of everyday moral judgments and intuitions ("reflective equilibrium"). Rawls' influence on business ethics can be seen prominently in the work of Thomas Donaldson, writing both alone (1982, 1989) and with Thomas Dunfee (Dunfee and Donaldson 1999). Without proceeding into the details of the Rawlsian account, I note that his ethical view is a restatement of the modern liberal worldview. Not to be outdone, Robert Nozick, Rawls' Harvard rival, offered *Anarchy, State, and Utopia* (1974), in which his (Lockean) hidden structure account is a restatement of the libertarian or classical liberal world view.

Suddenly, ethics was fun again. Philosophers with a more nuanced conception of the history of their discipline revisited the classics and reinterpreted them as if the canonical philosophers were offering theories as well. This was a new tour of the "grateful dead." Richard Hare (1981), and his student Derek Parfit (1986) "discovered" that metaethical views had (utilitarian) normative consequences. Some of Rawls' students (Thomas Nagel 1979; Onora O'Neill 1989; and Thomas Hill 1992) returned, or so they thought, to Kant. Elizabeth Anscombe had argued earlier (1958) that both the Kantian and utilitarian alternatives were guilty of errors that could be avoided by returning to Aristotle's account of virtue. Inspired by Anscombe were the neo-Aristotelian theories of Alasdair MacIntyre, in *After Virtue* (1981), followed by Martha Nussbaum (1986), Charles Taylor (1989), and Julia Annas (1993).

It is within this stream of thought that the curious notion of *applied philosophy* emerges, specifically in bioethics and in business ethics. An outgrowth of analytic philosophy, applied philosophy carries within its very name the idea that an independently arrived at and premeditated ethical theory will be "applied" to judging practice. However, this assumption distorts the historical resources of philosophy that might be of use. It takes the form of turning the ethical insights of important figures in the history of philosophy, such as Mill and Kant, into "theories" (utilitarianism, deontology, etc.), as if their insights were explorations and nothing more. This is a distortion because these ethical insights are rigidified into abstractions whose meaning becomes independent of the positions these philosophers actually espoused on public policy issues that are now discussed in business ethics. Mill, for example, had a great deal to say about such issues in his *Principles of Political Economy* (1848), the dominant textbook in economics and public policy in the last half of the nineteenth century. Instead of asking how Mill understood the application of philosophy to business ethics issues, "utilitarianism" has been turned into an independent exploratory theory. All too often business ethicists adopt models of utilitarianism or Kantianism that neither Mill nor Kant would recognize and which completely ignore what Mill and Kant (among others) have to say substantively about issues of business ethics. (For critical assessments of this practice, see the essays in Heath and Kaldis 2017.)

The obvious shortcoming of exploration (in social science or elsewhere) is that there is no way to confirm or disconfirm an exploration in the social world. We never reach a structural level that is observable or empirically verifiable. There are no formal criteria and no consensus we can appeal to in choosing among competing explorations. In fact, choosing among competing "higher" level explorations leads to an infinite regress. To an outsider it appears as if a hidden structure hypothesis is no more than a rationalization for a private agenda. Michel Foucault (1988) argued that the process is simply a power struggle. Bernard Williams complained (1985) that we are trying to wrench a moral consensus out of a divided culture. Both Anglo-American analytic philosophy and most versions of continental philosophy engage in the same type of thinking and make comparable errors.

We live in a morally pluralistic world. Not only is there no consensus nationally, or internationally, there may be no consensus account even within a particular moral agent. The belief that this is problematic or should be overcome by ethical theory is itself contestable. There does not appear to be a way of resolving this situation. Many if not most of these controversies reflect different foundational metaphysical commitments. As such, resolution is possible only by granting the initial premises and rules of evidence. Even if foundational metaphysical issues are not at stake, disagreements arise over different rankings of the good. Resolution does not appear feasible without begging the question, arguing in a circle, or engaging in infinite regress. We cannot appeal to consequences without knowing how to rank the impact of different approaches with regard to different moral interests (liberty, equality, prosperity, security, etc.), and we cannot appeal to preference satisfaction unless one already grants how one will correct preferences and compare rational versus impassioned preferences, as well as calculate the discount rate for preferences over time. Appeals to disinterested observers, hypothetical choosers, or hypothetical contractors will not avail. Truly disinterested decision makers will choose nothing. To choose in a particular way, the decision maker must be fitted out with a particular moral sense or at least a thin substantive account of the good. Intuitions are countered by contrary intuitions. Any particular balancing of claims can be opposed by a different approach to achieving a balance. Finally, in order to appeal for guidance from any account of moral rationality one must already have secured content for that moral rationality. The partisans of each position find themselves embedded within their own discourse so that they are unable to step outside of their own respective hermeneutic circles without embracing new and divergent premises and rules of inference. Many are convinced that they are committed to "reason" when what they are committed to is a particular set of premises and rules. Seeing only "flaws" in the positions of others who do not accept the same rules, they quite literally do not understand the alternative positions or even how there can be alternative positions.

Outside the academy, few take business ethics seriously, however much they may pay lip service to it. The evidence resides in casual conversations and humorous quips, though there is also evidence in print (Stark 1993; Badaracco and Webb 1995; Marino 2002; McDonald 2017). What concerns us here is why this dismissal of academic business ethics does not seem to bother academic business ethicists. Perhaps one reason that analytic exploratory business ethics does not aim to have an immediate and direct influence on business practice is that it aims to educate business students to hold an ideological position about business and to change business practice through the social and political transformation of society (see, for example, McDonald 2017; Khurana 2007). The ideology is an abstract principle or set of principles that has been independently premeditated. It provides without regard to the historical facts a specific political agenda, which also offers criteria for distinguishing the policies to be encouraged from those to be rejected. Social entrepreneurship is promoted as an alternative to, rather than an extension of, ordinary entrepreneurship. Rather than embracing liberal toleration, an ethical consumerism is advocated in the form of regular and ongoing boycotts on behalf of various social, political, environmental causes (Marcoux 2009). To be educated in such business ethics is to be taught how to articulate, defend, and implement the ideology. The ideology's content is drawn from a previous practice, the conversation of modern liberal and social democratic intellectuals.

For example, with regard to corporate governance, Christopher McMahon (1997) advocates co-determination, that is, "legally stipulating that boards of directors be composed in equal parts of representatives of employees and investors." Citing McMahon, Denise Rousseau and Andrea Rivero advance a political agenda to be superimposed on management: "democracy is the power of the people and is manifest in ways . . . that promote participation in and influence over the decisions affecting their everyday lives" (2003: 116). Further evidence of what could be called a "soft democratic socialism" of business ethics rests in the shareholder empowerment movement as designed to have the Securities and Exchange Commission impose further limitations on corporate directors (see Bainbridge 2012). Then there is the suggestion that executives have a fiduciary duty to the firm to limit their own compensation *prior* to accepting employment (Moriarty 2009).

Lest the charge of soft democratic socialism seem extravagant (but see Michael Freeden's account of the five themes embraced by socialists in Freeden 1998: 425–433), it is in many instances based upon the classical conception of philosophy and the notion of applied ethics exemplified in analytic philosophy. This can be seen in how the notion of distributive justice has been totally reconfigured. Aristotle understood distributive justice to mean the assigning of responsibilities and rewards to individuals based upon merit. In the contemporary world, however, the notion of merit has disappeared, replaced by adherence to environmental determinism. The contemporary version of distributive justice is the attempt to reconfigure society in such a way that all social goods are distributed on the basis of "fairness." There is no longer the notion of individuals with the power and responsibility to discipline or transform themselves or to achieve or acquire wealth through their own effort, planning, and self-control. Even the qualities of self-discipline, effort, and foresight are themselves taken as qualities whose original distribution appears as arbitrary. In this way, the free individual has been replaced by the "benevolent" welfare state. The most prominent advocate of this conception of distributive justice is Rawls. He has explicitly endorsed environmental determinism, famously claiming that the social world will always "affect the wants and preferences that persons come to have" (1999: 157). Moreover, "even the willingness to make an effort, to try, and to be deserving in the ordinary sense is . . . dependent on fortunate family and social circumstances." (Rawls 1971: 311–312). In most instances, distributivists remain vague about this doctrine. In so doing, they obscure the differences among various claims: (a) we are sometimes *influenced* by social circumstances (something no one would deny), (b) we are sometimes *determined* by social circumstances (controversial but not implausible), and (c) we are *always determined* by social circumstances. Given these alternatives, it would seem that (c) has to be held in order to justify consistently distributive justice.

With regard to economic growth, many business ethicists either deny or eschew the possibility of infinite growth. They maintain either that growth is finite, and therefore should be subject to government control and rationing on grounds of fairness, or that growth *should* be limited in order to achieve other, more worthy social objectives (Galbraith 1958; cf. Capaldi and Lloyd 2016, Chapter 11). According to anti-market advocates, the Environment (notice the capital "E") is a global ecological responsibility that cannot be adequately addressed by either markets or individual nation-states. The Environment requires that we conceive of the world as an enterprise association, necessitating either world government with global regulatory authority or a constrained view of civil society. Property rights may be overridden in the new globalization (see, for example, Werhane et al. 2010). The same argument for an implicit world government is used with regard to multinational corporations. Generally speaking, anti-market writers like to invoke the notion of universal human rights as embodied in the UN Universal Declaration of Human Rights, as in Pogge (2001).

Business ethicists of this stripe refer to themselves as liberals and claim to acknowledge the benefits of a market economy. What they seek is to regulate it through a democratically elected government. There are two reasons for this lack of frankness: an open acknowledgment of this soft socialism would immediately alienate the business world, and, second, there is no positive, consistent and coherent philosophical argument for this position. The literature is largely a negative and critical attack on the perceived weaknesses of a free market system. Thus, within business ethics the modern liberal or democratic socialist perspective dominates. This dominance helps to explain the prominence of Rawls as opposed to the relative neglect, among business ethicists, of the equally, if not more, gifted explorer, Nozick. There is some (classically liberal) opposition to this dominant view, though it is very much in the minority. More importantly, the left/right debate within business ethics *reflects* the fundamental modern historical debate originating between Locke and Rousseau and extending to the present.

Two competing narratives of philosophical exploration

The political economy of modernity is defined by the conflict between two competing narratives: the Lockean liberty narrative and the Rousseauian equality narrative (for an extended account of these, see Capaldi and Lloyd 2016).

The Lockean liberty narrative endorses:

(a) the **technological project** (the transformation of nature for human benefit);

> God, who has given the world to men in common, has also given them reason to make use of it to the best advantage of life, and convenience . . . it cannot be supposed He meant it should always remain common and uncultivated. He gave it to the use of the Industrious and Rational . . . not to the Fancy or Covetousness of the Quarrelsome and Contentious . . . for it is labor indeed that puts the difference of value on every thing . . . of the products of the earth useful to the life of man nine tenths are the effects of labor.
>
> *(Locke 1960[1690]: §26, 27, 34, and 40, respectively)*

(b) a **free-market economy** wherein property rights are fundamental. The right to private property is a democratic right based in effort rather than an aristocratic right based on the accident of inheritance. Private property is not theft, and a government dedicated to the preservation of property is not antidemocratic.

(c) a **limited government**. Liberty is the limitation of government power on behalf of individual liberty; in this context, recall Locke's endorsement of the right of revolution and his identification of the basic natural rights as life, liberty, and property.

(d) the **rule of law**. Government should have a representative structure in which the neutral rule of law replaces the biased rule of men. The rule of law is manifested not only in non-arbitrary, impartial, and universally applicable law but in the institutional arrangement of the separation of the branches of government and in the teaching of *self-imposed limits* on both the people and their chosen rulers as expressed in a doctrine of natural rights. In its Lockean formulation, these rights (e.g., life, liberty, property) are absolute, do not conflict, and are possessed only by individual human beings. Rights are morally absolute or fundamental because they are derived from human nature and God, and, as such, cannot be overridden; the role of these rights is to protect the human capacity to choose. Finally, such rights impose only duties of non-interference. The purpose of these rights is to limit

government; the responsibility of government is to refrain from violating your rights and stop others from violating your rights.
(e) **a culture of personal autonomy**. The dominant theme in Locke is that the best way of life is one in which the individual pursues happiness. He rejected the ancient view that one finds happiness by belonging or being with others.
(f) the identification of **a dysfunctional element** in human society (the "quarrelsome and contentious") and the attribution to that element of irresponsibility.

Whereas in Locke, all negotiation begins with the status quo, in Rousseau, that status quo's history is one of force and fraud, thereby tainting subsequent permutations of the economy. Whereas in Locke, once property rights are settled economic progress and growth for all commences, in Rousseau, the very nature of a market leads inevitably to economic inequality. Whereas Locke offers three pillars of liberty, Rousseau will offer three pillars of equality: political equality, economic equality, and cultural equality.

The Rousseauean equality narrative rejects:

(a) The **technological project**. In the *Discourse on the Sciences and Arts* (1750), Rousseau critiqued the technological project. Instead of satisfying genuine human needs, the arts and sciences express pride (promoting invidious self-comparison) and lead to luxury and the loss of human liberty. Within this development is the origin of inequality. This *First Discourse* emphasizes the huge costs to society—hypocrisy, moral pretense, and the loss of authenticity—in the development of the practical arts and sciences. The anti-technological attitude survives in the contemporary era as the environmental movement. Rather than a Lockean economy that allows for infinite growth wherein a rising tide raises all boats, we are offered a sustainable economy in which all are equal.
(b) A **free market economy**. Rousseau's *Discourse on the Origin of Inequality* (1754) carries his criticism of the liberty narrative one step further. He offers a hypothetical historical reconstruction in which the division of labor is blamed for economic inequality and private property is declared as a kind of theft. The inequality that first emerged as a result of the arts and sciences is now institutionalized as the product of a (Lockean) social contract by which the *few* rich bamboozle the *many*, who are poor, into an agreement that benefits only the wealthy. The liberty narrative in Rousseau's estimation is no more than a fraud.
(c) a **limited government**. Rousseau's own social contract is meant to displace this unhealthy hierarchy and inequality. Whether it is physical, material or intellectual inequality, Rousseau takes the presence of the inequality of condition as the point of departure in the "real" world of society. He questions whether the inequality can be justified, and answers that we cannot do so on the grounds provided by Locke.

Anticipating Rawls, Rousseau maintains that everyone should enter civil society not knowing what is in store for them ahead of time. The notion that certain privileged folks have constructed a false narrative in order to put one huge something over on the innocent and *victimized* many is central to the equality narrative. Effectively, this is the philosophical origin of victimization narratives. While Rawls uses the trappings of analytic philosophy and claims to be Kantian, he is restating Rousseau.

In his *Political Economy* (1755), Rousseau introduces the concept of the "general will." Central to the equality narrative, the general will shapes Rousseau's *Social Contract* (1762), becoming *the* standard by which all action is judged. Everyone gives up everything—especially private property—when leaving the state of nature to enter Rousseau's social contract. There is thus a conception of liberty in the Rousseau narrative but it is a "liberty *to*" participate in collective decision making. Lockean liberty, modern liberty in Constant's terms, is a "liberty *from*." The general will in the end embodies the ancient (and medieval) conception of a collective good, what Oakeshott describes (1975) as an enterprise association.

(d) the **rule of law**. But what are we to do if men, having been born free, are everywhere in chains? Can something be done to transform this condition? At the heart of both the *Political Economy* and the *Social Contract* is the claim that the so-called Lockean liberty narrative is actually a narrative of contractual slavery for the vast bulk of the population.

The only way to have a just society is for everyone upon entering civil society to give up everything and retain nothing. Thus, the Rousseau "correction" of Locke destroys the notion of unalienable rights because everyone alienates everything when leaving the state of nature. In their Rousseauean version, rights are not ends in themselves but a means to the achievement of ends. Merely prima facie, rights may be overridden and possessed by any entity, not just individual human beings. These rights become welfare rights, i.e., they may be such that others have a positive obligation to provide goods, benefits or means.

(e) **personal autonomy**. Right and wrong for Rousseau are no longer to be found in an individual choosing to dissent against the actions of a tyrannical prince or overbearing majority. Instead, right and wrong are decided by generalizing the wills of individuals as they become citizens of a collective project. Moreover, the general will never errs. It is for Rousseau the foundation for political economy. Market conditions do not dictate government policy; government policy dictates economic policy.

The individual is transformed into a willing citizen rather than into a Lockean calculating individual. The transformation is reinforced by quasi-religious festivals on behalf of the secular good. The general economic and political will is reinforced and uplifted by a civil religion that favors communal orthodoxy over individual dissent.

(f) **social dysfunction**. The origin of all social dysfunction is inequality, primarily economic and political inequality. Remove the inequality and the social dysfunction disappears.

The concepts of these two narratives, and some of their notable defenders, are summarized in Table 3.1.

An alternative method: explication

There is an alternative to philosophical exploration, namely the form of non-theoretical reflection championed by Hume (see Livingston 1985, 1998; and Capaldi 1992), the notion of spontaneous order articulated by Hayek (1973: 35–54), or the appeal to linguistic usage in Ludwig Wittgenstein's later philosophy (1953), among others. This form of reflection is "explication": the attempt to articulate the primordial practices existing prior to our theorizing about them. This mode of understanding social practices presupposes that all practices function with implicit norms: to explicate practice is to make explicit the implicit norms. (One analogue to explication is case law in Anglo-American jurisprudence.) In explication, we clarify what is routinely taken for granted in the hope of extracting from our previous practice a set of norms that can be used reflectively to guide future practice. Instead of changing our ordinary understanding, we come to know it in a new and better way. Explication is a kind of practical knowledge that takes human communal agency as primary, mediating practice from within practice itself. Unlike analytic philosophy, there is no theoretical account of the relation between theory and practice; practice is the pre-conceptual domain and there cannot be a conceptualization of the

Table 3.1 The competing narratives of Locke and Rousseau.

Issue	Locke/liberty	Rousseau/equality
Explanatory narrative	Explicate practice	Reform practice
Technology	Favor (Simon 1966)	Environmental concerns (Carson 1962; Gore 2006; Pope Francis 2015).
Markets	Favor (Hayek 2007[1944])	Market failure (Krugman 2009)
Politics	Libertarian	Communitarian (community as constitutive of the individual; collective good takes precedence over individual good)
Legislation	Equality of opportunity	Equality of result
Law	Rule of law incompatible with redistribution (Hayek 2007)	Distributive justice (fairness) (Rawls 1971, 2001; Dworkin 1986)
Role of government	Protect property rights	Protect third parties
Corporation	Nexus of contracting individuals (Coase 1937)	Social entity (Nader and Green 1976)
Purpose of corporation	Profitable product or service (Friedman 1970)	Common good (Drucker 1954)
Board of directors	Technical expertise to advise and consent (Bainbridge 2012)	Represent all stakeholders (Freeman and Phillips 2002)
Role of management	Primary fiduciary responsibility to shareholders (Friedman 1970)	Priority of distribution over production (Khurana 2007)
Relation of management to employees	Contractual autonomy, hierarchy (Coase 1937; Hoopes 2003)	Democratic participation (Rousseau and Rivero 2003).
Employees	Employment at will (Epstein 1984)	Collective bargaining (Werhane 2001)
Insider trading	Yes—enhances efficiency (Manne 1985)	No—incompatible with fairness (Werhane 1991)
Executive compensation	Supply and demand (Kay and Van Putten 2007)	Fairness (Piketty 2014)
Affirmative action/ diversity	If it improves productivity	Improve fairness (Boxill 2010)
Corporate Social Responsibility	If it contributes to bottom line	Serve common good
Entrepreneurship	Individual (Kirzner 1973; Phelps 2006)	Teams (Reich 1987)
Foreign outsourcing	Improves bottom line, workers, and local community (Maitland 2003)	"Sweatshops" (Arnold and Bowie 2003)

Source: Adapted from a table in Capaldi 2013.

pre-conceptual. Explication is itself a kind of practical knowledge that can be engaged in (successfully) only by those who have immersed themselves in the culture and have such practical know-how. This is Oakeshott's argument against rationalism (1991a), and a similar critique is to be found in Hayek (1973). To explicate is to begin with actual practices and with current law. For example, real-life firms strive to maximize profit and prioritize this over other corporate policies; real-life firms strive to comply with maximizing long-term shareholder value as

Theory and method in business ethics

stipulated in *Dodge* v. *Ford* (1919); real-life firms incorporated in Delaware follow Delaware law not some hypothetical legal universe.

The point of business ethics would then be to understand and explain commercial activity in the broadest possible sense, and, more particularly, to understand and explain the ethical norms that business people practice and to which they acquiesce. Business ethicists would thus discover business ethics in a manner analogous to the way a judge, through analysis of a line of previously decided cases, discovers the law. The analogy with the common law, noted only briefly here, is important; it resonates with the understanding of British thinkers such as Hume, who regarded experience as the funded knowledge of the past.

Explication is a philosophical activity to the extent that it seeks to reveal the role of business activity within the framework of our total experience. It is not a wholly theoretical endeavor. It involves knowledge of the tradition(s) of business behavior; comparative studies that get us to look more carefully at our traditions; and historical studies showing what people have said and thought, thus revealing a manner of thinking. The chief purpose of academic business ethics is less the solving of "moral problems" and the exposure of ethical error than it is the understanding of the inherent and evolving norms of commercial life.

As an explanatory activity, academic business ethics is not a practical enterprise, for we cannot automatically infer practical consequences from the understanding. To be a scholar of business ethics is not linked automatically to being a business ethics practitioner. Business ethics is immanent: it identifies the traditional norm(s) relevant to a particular situation or amends existing arrangements by further explication of the norms inherent in previous practice. Norms are not a permanent sub-structure; they can never be definitively explicated but are fertile sources of adaptation; they are an inheritance that does not entail its own future development.

Albert Carr's 1968 article, "Is Business Bluffing Ethical?" is an attempt at explication. Seeking to determine whether bluffing is ethical in business, Carr appeals to the actual practice of business people—both what they do and what they acquiesce in others doing. Carr *could* be understood as offering an actual-implied contract account of why bluffing is ethical, but in fact he is doing explication. It is not surprising that the reception of his approach in the exploration-dominated academic business ethics field has been almost uniformly negative. Like Milton Friedman's "The Social Responsibility of Business Is to Increase Its Profits," its pedagogical role is seen as offering an example of what-not-to-believe.

Explications are narratives that contain arguments within them, but the overall explication is not itself an argument. As with common law, one cannot refute an explication, but one can offer an alternative. An explication presupposes background agreement on what we are trying to achieve. Starting with a diagnosis of the problem at issue, it proposes a response: recommending this proposal by considering the consequences likely to follow from acting upon it and balancing these against those of at least one other proposal. Explication, therefore, is a problems-oriented approach. However, to teach business ethics in this way also presupposes that the instructor has presented a grand narrative of the role of commerce in the modern world and has identified the alternative philosophical approaches and explained why they are inadequate or reflect a wholly different agenda.

The most remarkable thing about explication is that it encourages us to retrieve the big picture as well as all of the crucial insights about modern market economies embedded in the works of great philosophers like Descartes, who went to the Netherlands, the most vibrant commercial center in Europe, to enjoy a greater liberty than available elsewhere, and whose technological project is discussed in the *Discourse on Method* (1931[1637]); like Locke, who reconceptualizes Christian labor as the technological project and recognizes the importance of private property; like Montesquieu, who relates market economies to law and politics; like Hume, who defends, in his seldom-read *Essays*, market societies against Rousseau's criticisms; like Adam Smith, who sets forth a sophisticated constructive critique of business people who fail to adhere to the norms of market practice and provides a wonderful and timeless critique of academics as unimaginative rent seekers; like Kant, who articulates the relationship among technology, markets, and international peace and their consistency with human freedom; like Hegel, who, influenced by Smith, articulates the importance both of the rule of law and individual autonomy; like J.S. Mill, who re-articulates the centrality of individual autonomy in *On Liberty* and offers a critique of socialism; as well as more recent philosophers like Hayek and Oakeshott.

Even if it is time to retrieve and extend the philosophical explication of business ethics, what happens if we find that there are incommensurable ethical communities? The answer is that you move to the political level, recognizing that once you are on the political-legal level all you will obtain is agreement on procedural norms that leave different ethical sub-communities or the members thereof to practice as they see fit within the larger procedural framework. Might there be specific communities in which there is serious conflict and confusion both about what is the right thing to do and about who are the mentors or whether the mentors could be misguided on a specific issue? The answer is yes. Depending upon how charitable one is, we can call these communities (a) dysfunctional, or (b) communities in crisis, or (c) disintegrating communities. This is a story for some other occasion.

Explicative methodology in business ethics aims to answer the following question: What are the norms inherent in current business practice? This does not preclude critique of such practices, but the critique of one practice would have to appeal to another practice, and in that special sense explication is an inherently conservative intellectual process. Such a method raises the following challenges.

1 Can the explication of business practice be carried out wholly from within the practice of business (which seems unlikely) or are we required to consider the larger cultural or social context within which business takes place?
2 In what sense is commerce itself a microcosm for understanding norms in general?
3 Are there not interesting and important differences across cultures that call for comparative analysis? There have been comparative studies in the business ethics literature and discussions of regional or national differences in business ethics norms in the various handbooks and guidebooks and companions (e.g., Robert Kolb's *The Sage Encyclopedia of Business Ethics and Society* (2008); or the series, published by Springer, on *Corporate Social Responsibility*: see, for example, Idowu et al. 2013).
4 In what sense is globalization influencing business practice?
5 Will there be consensus, convergence, or inevitably conflicting normative frameworks?

Concluding remarks

Given the inevitably partisan nature of exploration, some version of explication is the most fruitful method for business ethics research. Explication does not provide ready answers to our ethical problems but it does suggest a clear and non-partisan way of approaching complex issues. In this respect, it is worth keeping in mind that ethical issues are not the sort of thing about which one can have "expertise." There are spiritual and ethical mentors within a given community, all of whose members subscribe to a substantive view of what is right and what is wrong. To intellectualize those substantive views rarely provides genuine clarity or helpful guidance. Usually, the most valuable intellectual activity is a critique of previous attempts at over-intellectualization.

What positive philosophical meaning can be given to the practice of business ethics? A business ethicist can be either a scholar of business ethics or a business ethics practitioner. The scholar is not a practitioner but, in the broadest sense, an educator. The point of business education is to understand and explain market activity in the broadest sense. It is a philosophical activity that seeks to reveal the role of business activity on the map of our total experience. It is not a theoretical endeavor. It involves knowledge of our tradition of business practice. Comparative studies are valuable in getting us to look more carefully at our traditions. Historical studies show what people have said and thought, revealing a manner of thinking. The purpose of business education is less to expose errors than to understand assumptions and judgments. Business ethics education is an explanatory not a practical activity; we do not infer practical consequences from understanding or explanation.

Business ethics as a practice is immanent. That is, it either identifies the traditional norm(s) relevant to a particular situation or amends existing arrangements by explication of the norms inherent in practice. These norms cannot be accessed as a permanent sub-structure; they can never be definitively explicated. They are fertile sources of adaptation, for they are an inheritance that does not entail its own future development. An explication presupposes a general background agreement on what we are trying to achieve; it commences with a diagnosis of the problem at issue; it then proposes a response. It recommends this proposal by considering the consequences likely to follow from acting upon it; it balances these against those of at least one other proposal. You cannot refute an explication, but you can offer an alternative one.

Essential readings

One of the better anthologies on contemporary business ethics is that edited by George Brenkert and Tom Beauchamp, *Oxford Handbook of Business Ethics* (2010). Robert Kolb's *Encyclopedia of Business Ethics and Society* (2008, 2018) is great in scope and is a good place to start one's study of a subject. Although it is now out of print, the collection edited by Eugene Heath, *Morality and the Market: Ethics and Virtue in the Conduct of Business* (2002) gives special priority to readings from the history of Western thought that focus on the context, history, and operations of markets and business. In *Wealth, Commerce, and Philosophy: Foundational Thinkers and Business Ethics* (2017), Eugene Heath and Byron Kaldis enlist a rich collection of scholarly essays that reassess the contributions of significant thinkers to our understanding of the complex interplay of morals, markets, and commercial activity.

For further reading in this volume on the history of business ethics, see Chapter 1, The history of business ethics, and Chapter 32, The globalization of business ethics. For an account of major theorists on business ethics, see Chapter 2, Theorists and philosophers on business ethics. On the two dominant theories within business ethics, see Chapter 10, Social responsibility, and Chapter 11, Stakeholder thinking. For a theoretical perspective that prioritizes the idea of a neutral form of discourse in which the ethical determines the economic, see Chapter 12, Integrative Economic Ethics: concept and critique. A discussion of political versus economic decision making may be found in Chapter 21, Regulation, rent seeking, and business ethics. On some of the destructive consequences of twentieth-century politics, see Chapter 39, Business ethics in transition: communism to commerce in Central Europe and Russia. On the importance of lived practice and social learning, see Chapter 8, Feminist ethics and business ethics: redefining landscapes of learning.

Notes

1 I am indebted to Lori Verstegen Ryan (2006) for this history.
2 Less frequently, business ethics programs reside in marketing departments (e.g., Notre Dame University's Mendoza School of Business) or business law/legal studies departments (e.g., University of Pennsylvania's Wharton School, the Daniels School at the University of Denver). These departments have also, to an extent, shaped the field.

References

Abend, G. (2013). "The Origins of Business Ethics in American Universities, 1902–1936." *Business Ethics Quarterly* 23:2, 171–205.
Abend, G. (2014). *The Moral Background: An Inquiry into the History of Business Ethics*. Princeton, NJ: Princeton University.
Adorno, T.W. and M. Horkheimer (1990). *Dialectic of Enlightenment*, J. Cumming (trans.). New York: Continuum.
Annas, J. (1993). *The Morality of Happiness*. New York: Oxford University Press.
Anscombe, G.E.M. (1958). "Modern Moral Philosophy," *Journal of Philosophy* 33:124, 1–19.
Arnold D.G. and N.E. Bowie (2003). "Sweatshops and Respect for Persons," *Business Ethics Quarterly* 13:2 (April), 221–242.
Badaracco, J.L. and A.P. Webb (1995). "Business Ethics: A View from the Trenches," *California Management Review* 37:2 (Winter), 8–28.
Bainbridge, S. (2012). *Corporate Governance after the Financial Crisis*. New York: Oxford.
Becker, C. (1962). *The Heavenly City of the Eighteenth-Century Philosophers*. New Haven, CT: Yale University Press.
Bloom, A. (1987). *The Closing of the American Mind*. New York: Simon & Schuster.
Boxill, B. (2010). "Discrimination, Affirmative Action, and Diversity in Business," in G. Brenkert and T. Beauchamp (eds), *Oxford Handbook of Business Ethics*. Oxford: Oxford University Press, 535–562.
Brenkert, G. (2002). "Entrepreneurship, Ethics, and the Good Society," *The Ruffin Series of the Society for Business Ethics* 3, 5–43.
Brenkert, G. and T. Beauchamp (eds) (2010). *Oxford Handbook of Business Ethics*. Oxford: Oxford University Press.
Buchanan, J.M. (1975). *The Limits of Liberty: Between Anarchy and Leviathan*, in *The Collected Works of James M. Buchanan*, vol. 7 (1999). Indianapolis: Liberty Fund.
Business Round Table (1997). "Statement on Corporate Governance" (September) Washington, DC: The Business Roundtable of CEOs.
Capaldi, N. (1992). "The Dogmatic Slumber of Hume Scholarship," *Hume Studies* 18:2, 117–135.
Capaldi, N. (1998). *The Enlightenment Project in the Analytic Conversation*. Dordrecht: Kluwer Academic Publishers.
Capaldi, N. (2004). "The Ethical Foundations of Free Market Societies," *The Journal of Private Enterprise* 20:1 (Fall), 30–54.
Capaldi, N. (2013). "Pro-Market versus Anti-Market Approaches to Business Ethics," in C. Luetge (ed.), *Handbook of the Philosophical Foundations of Business Ethics*. Berlin: Springer, 1223–1238.
Capaldi, N. and G. Lloyd (2016). *Liberty and Equality in Political Economy: From Locke versus Rousseau to the Present*. Cheltenham: Edward Elgar.
Carr, A.Z. (1968). "Is Business Bluffing Ethical?" *Harvard Business Review* 46:1 (Jan–Feb), 143–153.
Carroll, A. (2008). "A History of Corporate Social Responsibility: Concepts and Practices," in *Oxford Handbook of Corporate Social Responsibility*, Crane, A. McWilliams, D. Matten, J. Moon, and D. Siegel (eds). Oxford: Oxford University Press, 19–46.
Carson. R. (1962). *Silent Spring*. New York: Houghton Mifflin.
Cavanaugh, W.T. (2003). "The Unfreedom of the Free Market," in D. Bandow and D. L. Schindler (eds), *Wealth, Poverty, and Human Destiny*. Wilmington, DE: ISI Books, 103–28.
Clarkson, M. (1995). "A Stakeholder Framework for Analyzing and Evaluating Corporate Social Performance," *Academy of Management Review* 20, 92–117.
Coase, R. (1937). "The Nature of the Firm," *Economica* 4:16, 386–405.
Den Uyl, D. and D. Rasmussen (2002). "Aristotelianism, Commerce, and the Liberal Order," in A. Tessitore (ed.), *Aristotle and Modern Politics*. South Bend, IN: University of Notre Dame Press, 278–304.
Descartes, R. (1931) [1637]. *Discourse on the Method of Conducting One's Reason Well and for Seeking the Truth in the Sciences*, in *The Philosophical Works of Descartes*, vol. 1, E.S. Haldane and G.R.T. Ross (trans.), 2 vols. Cambridge: Cambridge University Press.
Dodd, E.M. (1932). "For Whom are Corporate Managers Trustees?" *Harvard Law Review* 45:8, 1365–1372.
Donaldson, T. (1982). *Corporations and Morality*. Englewood Cliffs, NJ: Prentice-Hall.
Donaldson, T. (1989). *The Ethics of International Business*. New York: Oxford University Press.
Donaldson, T. and L.E. Preston (1995). "The Stakeholder Theory of the Corporation: Concepts, Evidence, and Implications," *The Academy of Management Review* 20:1 (January), 65–91.
Dunfee, T.W. and T. Donaldson (1999). *Ties that Bind: A Social Contracts Approach to Business Ethics*. Cambridge, MA: Harvard Business School Press.

Drucker, P. (1954). *The Practice of Management*. New York: Harper.
Dworkin, R. (1986). *Law's Empire*. Cambridge: Belknap Press.
Engelhardt, H.T. (1986). *Foundations of Bioethics*. New York: Oxford University Press.
Epstein, E.M. (1999). "The Continuing Quest for Accountable, Ethical, and Humane Corporate Capitalism," *Business & Society* 38, 253–267.
Epstein, R. (1984). "In Defense of the Contract at Will," *University of Chicago Law Review* 51:947.
Etzioni, A. (1993). *The Spirit of Community: Rights, Responsibilities, and the Communitarian Agenda*. New York: Crown Publishers.
Foucault, M. (1988). *Madness and Civilization: A History of Insanity in the Age of Reason*, Richard Howard (trans.). New York: Vintage Books.
Freeden, M. (1998). *Ideologies and Political Theory*. Oxford: Oxford University Press.
Freeman, R.E. and R. Phillips (2002). "Stakeholder Theory: A Libertarian Defense," *Business Ethics Quarterly* 12:3 (July), 331–349.
Friedman, M. (1970). "Social Responsibility of Business Is To Increase Its Profits," *New York Times* (Sept. 13, 1970).
Galbraith, J.K. (1958). *The Affluent Society*. New York, NY: Houghton, Mifflin Co.
Gore, A. (2006). *An Inconvenient Truth*. New York: Rodale.
Hare, R. (1981). *Moral Thinking*. Oxford: Oxford University Press.
Hayek, F.A. (1973). *Law, Legislation, and Liberty*, vol. 1, *Rules and Order*. Chicago, IL: University of Chicago Press.
Hayek, F.A. (2007) [1944]. *Road to Serfdom*. Chicago, IL: University of Chicago Press.
Heath, E. (2002). *Morality and the Market: Ethics and Virtue in the Conduct of Business*. New York: McGraw-Hill.
Heath, E. and B. Kaldis (eds) (2017). *Wealth, Commerce, and Philosophy: Foundational Thinkers and Business Ethics*. Chicago, IL: University of Chicago Press.
Hill, T.E. Jr. (1992). *Dignity and Practical Reason in Kant's Moral Theory*. Ithaca, NY: Cornell University Press.
Hoopes, J. (2003). *False Prophets: The Gurus who Created Modern Management and Why Their Ideas are Bad for Business Today*. New York: Basic Books.
Hutchins, R.M. (1936). Untitled Response to A.N. Whitehead, *Atlantic Monthly* (October), 582–588.
Idowu, S.O., N. Capaldi, L. Zu, A. Das Gupta (eds) (2013). *Encyclopedia of Corporate Social Responsibility*. Berlin: Springer.
Jennings, M. (2009). *Business: Its Legal, Ethical, and Global Environment*, 8th edition. Maon, OH: South-Western Cengage Learning.
Jones, T.M. (1980). "Corporate Social Responsibility Revisited, Redefined," *California Management Review* 22:3, 59–67.
Jonsen, A. (2003). *The Birth of Bioethics*. Oxford: Oxford University Press.
de Jouvenel, B. (1974). "The Treatment of Capitalism by Continental Intellectuals," in F.A. Hayek (ed.), *Capitalism and the Historians*. Chicago, IL: University of Chicago Press, 91–121.
Kay, I. and S. Van Putten (2007). *Myths and Realities of Executive Pay*. Cambridge: Cambridge University Press.
Khurana, R. (2007). *From Higher Aims to Hired Hands: The Social Transformation of American Business Schools and the Unfulfilled Promise of Management as a Profession*. Princeton, NJ: Princeton University Press.
Kirzner, I. (1973). *Competition and Entrepreneurship*. Chicago, IL: University of Chicago Press.
Kolb, R. (ed.) (2008). *The Sage Encyclopedia of Business Ethics and Society*, 1st edition (2nd edition 2018), 5 vols. Los Angeles, CA: Sage.
Krugman, P. (2009). *The Conscience of a Liberal*. New York: Norton.
Kuttner, R. (1997). *Everything for Sale: The Virtues and Limits of Markets*. Chicago, IL: University of Chicago Press.
Lippke, R.L. (1995). *Radical Business Ethics*. Lanham, MD: Rowman & Littlefield.
Livingston, D. (1985). *Hume's Philosophy of Common Life*. Chicago, IL: University of Chicago Press.
Livingston, D. (1998). *Philosophical Melancholy and Delirium: Hume's Pathology of Philosophy*. Chicago, IL: University of Chicago Press.
Locke, J. (1960) [1690]. *Second Treatise of Government*, Peter Laslett (ed.). Cambridge: Cambridge University Press.
Machan, T. (2007). *The Morality of Business*. New York: Springer.
MacIntyre, A. (1981). *After Virtue*. Notre Dame, IN: University of Notre Dame Press.
Madison, J., A. Hamilton and J. Jay (1987) [1788]. *The Federalist Papers*, I. Kramnick (ed.). London: Penguin.

Maitland, I. (2003). "The Great Non-Debate Over International Sweatshops," in W.H. Shaw (ed.), *Ethics at Work: Basic Readings in Business Ethics*, Oxford: Oxford University Press, 49–66.
Manne, H. (1985). "Insider Trading and Property Rights in New Information," *The Cato Journal* 4, 933–943.
Marcoux, A. (2009). "Is a Market for Values a Value in Markets?" *Reason Papers* 31 (Fall 2009): 97–107.
Marino, G. (2002). "The Latest Industry to Flounder: Ethics Incorporated," *The Wall Street Journal*, July 30.
McCarthy, J. (ed.) (1998). *Modern Enlightenment and the Rule of Reason*. Washington, DC: Catholic University of America Press.
McDonald, D. (2017). *The Golden Passport: Harvard Business School, the Limits of Capitalism, and the Moral Failure of the MBA Elite*. New York: HarperCollins.
McMahon, C. (1997). *Authority and Democracy: A General Theory of Government and Management*. Princeton, NJ: Princeton University Press.
Mill, J.S. (1848) [1965]. *Principles of Political Economy*, in *Collected Works*, Volumes II and III. Toronto: University of Toronto Press.
Miller, F.D. Jr. (1995). *Nature, Justice, and Rights in Aristotle's Politics*. Oxford: Oxford University Press.
Miller, F.D. Jr. (2017). "Aristotle and Business: Friend or Foe?" in, E. Heath and B. Kaldis (eds), *Wealth, Commerce, and Philosophy: Foundational Thinkers and Business Ethics*. Chicago, IL: University of Chicago Press, 31-52.
Moriarty, J. (2009). "How Much Compensation can CEOs Permissibly Accept?" *Business Ethics Quarterly* 19:2, 235–250.
Nader, R. and Green, M. (1976). *Taming the Corporate Giant*. New York: Norton.
Nagel, T. (1979). *Mortal Questions*. New York: Cambridge University Press.
Nozick, R. (1974). *Anarchy, State, and Utopia*. New York: Basic Books.
Nozick, R. (1998). "Why Do Intellectuals Oppose Capitalism?" *Cato Policy Report* 20:1 (Jan-Feb), 1, 9–11.
Nussbaum, M. (1986). *The Fragility of Goodness: Luck and Ethics in Greek Tragedy and Philosophy*. Cambridge: Cambridge University Press.
Oakeshott, M. (1975). *On Human Conduct*. Oxford: Oxford University Press.
Oakeshott, M. (1991a) [1947]. "Rationalism in Politics," in *Rationalism in Politics and Other Essays*, expanded edition. Indianapolis, IN: Liberty Fund, 5–42.
Oakeshott, M. (1991b) [1948]. "The Tower of Babel," in *Rationalism in Politics and Other Essays*, expanded edition. Indianapolis, IN: Liberty Fund, 465–487.
Oakeshott, M. (1991c) [1961]. "The Masses in Representative Democracy," in *Rationalism in Politics and Other Essays*, expanded edition. Indianapolis, IN: Liberty Fund, 363–383.
O'Neil, O. (1989). *Constructions of Reason: Exploring Kant's Practical Philosophy*. Oxford: Oxford University Press.
Parfit, D. (1986). *Reasons and Persons*. Oxford: Oxford University Press.
Peacock, M.S. (2017). "Wealth and Commerce in Archaic Greece: Homer and Hesiod," in E. Heath and B. Kaldis (eds), *Wealth, Commerce, and Philosophy: Foundational Thinkers and Business Ethics*, Chicago, IL: University of Chicago Press, 11–30.
Phelps, E.S. (2006). "Toward a Model of Innovation and Performance Along the Lines of Knight, Keynes, Hayek, and M. Polanyi," prepared for Conference on Entrepreneurship and Economic Growth, Max-Planck Institute and Kauffmann Foundation, Munich, May 8–9.
Piketty, T. (2014). *Capital*. Cambridge, MA: Harvard University Press.
Pogge, T. (2001). "Priorities of Global Justice," *Metaphilosophy* 32:1–2 (January), 6–24.
Pope Francis (2015). "Laudato si," w2.vatican.va/. . ./papa-francesco_20150524_enciclica-laudato-si.html.
Rawls, J. (1971). *Theory of Justice*. Cambridge, MA: Harvard University Press.
Rawls, J. (1985). "Justice as Fairness: Political not Metaphysical," *Philosophy and Public Affairs* 14:3, 223–251.
Rawls, J. (1993). *Political Liberalism*. New York: Columbia University Press.
Rawls, J. (1999). *Collected Papers*, S. Freeman (ed.). Cambridge, MA: Harvard University Press.
Rawls. J. (2001). *Justice as Fairness*. Cambridge, MA: Harvard University Press.
Reich, R. (1987). "Entrepreneurship Reconsidered: The Team as Hero," *Harvard Business Review* (May/June): 77–83.
Rorty, R. (1991). "The Priority of Democracy to Philosophy," in *Objectivism, Relativism, and Truth: Philosophical Papers*, vol. 1. Cambridge: Cambridge University Press, 175–196.
Rousseau, D.M. and A. Rivero (2003). "Democracy, a Way of Organising in a Knowledge Economy," *Journal of Management Inquiry* 12:2, 115–134.

Rousseau, J-J. (1750). *Discourse on the Sciences and Arts* in *The Discourses and Other Early Political Writings*, V. Gourevitch (ed. and trans.). Cambridge: Cambridge University Press.

Rousseau, J-J. (1754). *Discourse on the Origin and Foundations of Inequality Among Men* in *The Discourses and Other Early Political Writings*, V. Gourevitch (ed. and trans.). Cambridge: Cambridge University Press.

Rousseau, J-J. (1997) [1755]. *Discourse on Political Economy* in *The Social Contract and Other Related Political Writings*, V. Gourevitch (ed. and trans.). Cambridge: Cambridge University Press.

Rousseau, J-J. (1762). *The Social Contract* in *The Social Contract and Other Related Political Writings*, V. Gourevitch (ed. and trans.). Cambridge: Cambridge University Press.

Ryan, L.V. (2006). "Foundation and Form of the Field of Business Ethics," *Journal of Private Enterprise* 21:2, 34–49.

Schumpeter, J. (1975) [1942]. *Capitalism, Socialism, and Democracy*. New York: Harper Colophon.

Shaw, W.H. (1996). "Business Ethics Today: A Survey," *Journal of Business Ethics* 15:489–500.

Simon, J. (1996). "Can the Supply of Natural Resources be Infinite?" in *Ultimate Resource 2*. Princeton, NJ: Princeton University Press.

Smith, A. (1981) [1776] in R. H. Campbell, A.S. Skinner and W.B. Todd (eds), *An Inquiry into the Nature and Causes of the Wealth of Nations*, 2 vols. Indianapolis, IN: Liberty Fund.

Solomon, R.C. (2008). "Corporate Roles, Personal Virtues: An Aristotelian Approach to Business Ethics," in T. Donaldson, P. Werhane, and J. Van Zandt (eds), *Ethical Issues in Business: A Philosophical Approach*. Englewood Cliffs, NJ: Prentice-Hall, 66–77.

Stark, A. (1993). "What's the Matter with Business Ethics?" *Harvard Business Review* 71:3 (May-June), 38–40, 43–4, 46–8.

Sternberg, E. (2000). *Just Business: Business Ethics in Action*, 2nd edition. Oxford: Oxford University Press.

Sunstein, C.R. (1997). *Free Markets and Social Justice*. Oxford. Oxford University.

Taylor, C.M. (1989). *Sources of the Self: The Making of the Modern Identity*. Cambridge: Cambridge University Press.

von Mises, L. (2006) [1954]. *The Anti-Capitalist Mentality*. Indianapolis, IN: Liberty Fund, Inc.

Werhane, P.H. (1991). "The Indefensibility of Insider Trading," *Journal of Business Ethics* 10, 729–731.

Werhane, P. (2001). "Employer and Employee Rights in an Institutional Context" in T. Beauchamp and N. Bowie (eds), *Ethical Theory and Business*, Upper Saddle River, NJ: Prentice Hall, 366–375.

Werhane, P. (2005). "Intellectual Property Rights, Moral Imagination, and Access to Life-Enhancing Drugs," *Business Ethics Quarterly* 15:4.

Werhane, P., T.J. Radin and N. Bowie (2003). *Employment and Employee Rights*. New York. Wiley-Blackwell.

Werhane, P., S.P. Kelley, L.P. Hartman and D.J. Moberg (2010). *Alleviating Poverty Through Profitable Partnerships: Globalization, Markets and Economic Well-Being*. New York: Routledge.

Whitehead, A.N. (1936). "Harvard: The Future," *Atlantic Monthly* (September), 260–270.

Williams, B. (1985). *Ethics and the Limits of Philosophy*. Cambridge, MA: Harvard University Press.

Wittgenstein, L. (1953) in G.E.M. Anscombe and R. Rhees (eds), G.E.M. Anscombe (trans.). *Philosophical Investigations*, Oxford: Blackwell.

4
Teaching business ethics
Current practice and future directions

Darin Gates, Bradley R. Agle, and Richard N. Williams

Business ethics is a burgeoning field of study and practice with vibrant academic and practitioner communities. Due to a combination of pioneering leaders in business and academe, many resources are currently being expended to understand and manage ethics in business.[1] Unfortunately, however, we would argue that the actions of the unscrupulous in business have probably had a greater effect on the growth of the field than have its leaders. Every time there is a major scandal or controversy in business, or set of scandals or controversies (some of the "high" points include the mid 80s, early 90s, and the crisis of 2008), calls are made for reform, including further regulations (e.g., 1991 US Sentencing Guidelines, and Sarbanes-Oxley (2002)) and greater emphasis on ethics in companies and in business schools. Consequently, academic ethics organizations, and corporate ethics and compliance associations, are healthy and strong, allowing academic and business specialists to find conferences on the subject virtually every month of the year.

Included in the call for reform and greater resources is almost always a desire for greater education and training in business ethics. The American Association of Collegiate Schools of Business (AACSB) has responded with accreditation standards requiring that ethics be part of a business school's curriculum, and major businesses have responded by almost uniformly providing some level of ethics training. With this increase in resources has come a bevy of questions related to the what, why, where, when, and how of ethics education. In this chapter we will briefly discuss ethics training in organizations and then focus on how these questions are being addressed in the academic community, with much of the description drawing from experience within North America. In particular we will first address the history, current status, and future trends in business ethics education (including various aspects of behavioral ethics), and then delineate, in the subsequent section, an account of a business ethics pedagogy that should diminish the appeals to self-interest and to relativism, as well as alert students to the types of moral blindness and self-deception that often accompany unethical actions.

Business ethics: education vs. training

While discussions of trade, wealth, or the vocation of commerce have been around for millennia, the first attempt at formal, academic discussion of business ethics in the United States began with the introduction of business schools in the late 1800s and early 1900s (Khurana 2007). As Rakesh Khurana explains in his book *From Higher Aims to Hired Hands*, the original intent was to model these schools after professional medical and law schools, with a highly integrated professional code of ethics. However, such a vision never materialized, and business consequently evolved for decades without an explicit emphasis on ethics. The modern business ethics movement started primarily among philosophers in the 1970s and 1980s (for an alternative history see Abend 2014) and began to become much more common in business schools in the 1990s and 2000s. As the field has grown and attracted academics with varied backgrounds (e.g., law, psychology, marketing, business, sociology), a lively discussion has ensued regarding the purposes of and pedagogical approaches to the teaching of business ethics. In ensuing sections we will address the history, current status, and future directions of business ethics education (mainly in the US) through the lens of the major questions that tend to be asked about business ethics education, namely—why, what, how, where, and when.

As we discuss business ethics education, it is important to distinguish between education performed in an academic setting and ethics education (training) done within corporations. The number of organizational ethics training programs is on the rise: in 1986, the Center for Business Ethics found that only 44 percent of companies reviewed conducted training, whereas, most recently Weaver et al. (1999) found that 66–80 percent of firms offer such programs. However, very little work has been done to analyze the details or characteristics of these programs. The one outstanding attempt to investigate and assess details of ethics training was conducted by James Weber (2015). Weber examined employee ethics training programs among 70 US-based global organizations by asking members of the Ethics and Compliance Officer Association to describe various elements of their organizations' ethics training programs. We summarize selected results from Weber's (2015) research in the next three paragraphs of this section.

The adoption of employee ethics training has consistently increased and has now joined the ranks of organizational ethics policies as commonplace among large US business organizations. The ethics officers also report that their training seeks to empower employees to become more aware of ethical issues faced at work, to be better equipped with ethical decision-making skills, and thus better able to resolve ethical challenges faced at work. In conducting the training, a variety of approaches are used. By far the most common approach is using a computer-aided (online) training program. Engaging employees in a group setting to discuss general ethics topics or cases is also a common approach. Nearly half of the ethics training programs included lectures as the teaching approach.

Emphasizing group interaction is often an effective approach (as noted by other scholars, Elkjaer 2003; Morris and Wood 2011). However, the emergence of online or technology-enhanced training and the use of the lecture method without other, educationally proven, techniques is suspect. It is understandable that business organizations prefer web-related training approaches, since these can offer significant time and cost savings, but there is little evidence that such an approach is more or even as effective as face-to-face training in promoting ethics. Too often, businesses rely on short, infrequent, or at-orientation training sessions, which are also likely ineffective. One particularly troubling discovery is that only 30 percent of firms indicated that the impact or outcome of the ethics training programs is measured. When assessment is conducted at all, it generally relies on weak tools or metrics, rendering the effectiveness of such training questionable.

There also exists a strong consensus among ethics officers as to the challenges or obstacles faced in developing and offering an employee ethics training program. The most frequently mentioned obstacles were, in order: 1) finding the time to conduct the training, 2) acquiring sufficient resources (money), and 3) keeping the training program relevant and engaging for participants. Other ethics officers noted the challenge of administering their ethics training program given "multicultural diversity, variations of relevancy around the globe, and language differences." Finally, the challenge of "integrating the training into the work performed by the employees" and "coordinating ethics training with other training programs offered by the organization" were mentioned as well (Weber 2015: 34).

The why, what, how, where, and when of business ethics education

Why?

What are the purposes for teaching business ethics? Agle and Crossley (2011) provide a review of the objectives of ethics education. Their literature review finds 35 different objectives that have been set forth as the aims of a business ethics education. Their study suggests that the four most commonly mentioned objectives refer to 1) ethical decision-making skills (Warren 1995), 2) moral awareness (Sims and Felton 2006), 3) understanding of one's own values and principles (Hartman 2006), and 4) comprehending the place of business in society (LeClair et al. 1999). In addition to these four aims, other commonly noted objectives include the following: 1) the development of rhetorical skills in order to become effective advocates for ethical positions (Duska 2014), 2) the development of moral courage (Mason 2008), 3) advancing to moral leadership (Verschoor 2006), and 4) the attainment of moral character (Armstrong et al. 2003).

Many argue that greater moral awareness (e.g., Sims and Felton 2006), along with stronger cognitive abilities, both theoretical and practical, related to ethics (e.g., Heath et al. 2005; Berenbeim 2013), should be the objective of our ethics-education efforts. Such objectives are bolstered by empirical findings demonstrating that because of consumer capitalism, hyper-individualism, failures in education, and extreme moral relativism, young adults in America today are generally unable to identify and grapple effectively with moral issues (Smith 2011). Generally, the hope is that greater cognitive abilities will lead to more ethical behavior. While we continue to believe in this link, the empirical evidence of such a relationship has yet to be demonstrated. In fact, new research suggests that emotions and environment play a stronger role in ethical conduct than does cognition (Greene et al. 2001; Greene and Haidt 2002; Sonenshein 2007).

Moving into the future we believe that while a continuing emphasis will be placed on moral awareness and sound ethical decision-making, greater priority will be placed on understanding the drivers of unethical behavior and working to counter such behavior.[2] The two major trends moving us in this direction are behavioral ethics (e.g., De Cremer and Tenbrunsel 2012; Bazerman and Tenbrunsel 2011; Bandura 1999), and the positive reception that has followed a specific book, *Giving Voice to Values* (Gentile 2010). Behavioral ethics is the study of how individuals not only think but act when confronted with ethical issues. Arising primarily from the work of psychologists and economists, behavioral ethics accents phenomena such as ethical fading[3] (Bazerman and Tenbrunsel 2011), moral disengagement[4] (Bandura 1999), and neutralization techniques (Sykes and Matza 1957),[5] as well as behavioral tendencies such as cheating (Ariely 2012), pro-social behaviors (Grant and Gino 2010) and the effects of ego-depletion on such tendencies (Gino et al. 2011). Future educational efforts will provide greater emphasis on individuals understanding these behavioral tendencies in order to recognize and avoid them (Haidt 2014). We would argue, however, that as important as these insights are, behavioral ethics can never replace, but only supplement, normative business ethics (see Nagel 2013).

Authored by Mary Gentile, *Giving Voice to Values* is not just a book but a catalyst for a movement. A former ethics educator at the Harvard Business School, Gentile underwent a crisis of conscience while teaching ethics, wondering if her efforts were doing any good in making the business world a more ethical place. Her epiphany came years later while doing consulting work. She came to the realization that students needed a better understanding of how to *do* what is right (or, at least, to act in accordance with their values) under difficult circumstances. Her book, and subsequent teaching materials and cases, provide tools for helping students and businesspeople practice how they will "voice their values." Consequently, efforts are underway in academe and in business organizations to help individuals understand how to act in situations where demands made upon them are not in line with their values.

In order for ethics education to succeed in producing more ethical business people, it must be true that ethics can be taught. And yet, for many, the question of "Can ethics be taught?" seems to remain unanswered (Piper et al. 1993). Here, we need to distinguish between two questions, 1) can an ethics course teach someone to be ethical who has not already developed into a morally decent person? and 2) can such an ethics course teach a morally decent person to be more ethical? The former is highly dubious. The latter is almost certainly the case.

Numerous studies have concluded that there is a positive relationship between ethics courses and various aspects of ethical conduct. Weber (1990) was one of the first to review the business ethics education literature, concluding that, in general, such courses lead to some improvement in students' ethical awareness and moral reasoning. The positive impact of ethics teaching on ethical awareness and moral reasoning has been confirmed by several other studies (Rest 1986; Glenn 1992; Earley and Kelly 2004; Williams and Dewett 2005; Carroll 2005; Lau 2010). Ethics teaching has also been found to positively impact ethical sensitivity (Gautschi and Jones 1998) and an appreciation of the complexity of ethical issues (Carlson and Burke 1998). Other studies that suggest that ethics can successfully be taught include Langlois and Lapointe (2010), Mayhew and Murphy (2009), Wurthmann (2013), and May et al. (2014). However, despite the studies that suggest ethics can be taught, other research finds minimal to no effect from ethics instruction (Simha et al. 2012), including a meta-analysis of such studies performed by Waples et al. (2009).

The contradictory evidence does not necessarily imply that ethics *cannot* be taught, but rather that in such cases, ethics was *not taught effectively*. Analogously, just because some diet and exercise programs don't produce weight loss, one should not conclude that diet and exercise programs are not effective in helping with weight loss. So, the question is "How do we teach business ethics effectively?" In order to answer such a question, there is a pressing need for longitudinal research that explores the long-term effects of different pedagogical strategies and emphases on the multiple ethical outcomes of individuals (e.g., ethical awareness, sensitivity, decision-making, courage, leadership, etc.; see Agle et al. 2014).

What?

What is the content of business ethics education? Since current textbooks provide a perspective on what topics are currently being covered, we examined a sample of five leading ethics textbooks by authors with philosophy and management backgrounds. Table 4.1 provides a summary of the topical coverage of these textbooks.

Table 4.1 demonstrates that there is a continuing emphasis on ethical theory; real-world ethics cases; management issues involving human resources such as hiring, discrimination, employment rights, and occupational safety, and development of the corporate ethics infrastructure; marketing issues such as product safety, pricing, and advertising to vulnerable populations; corporate accountability and social responsibility; and specific topics such as whistleblowing, conflict of interest, privacy, and intellectual property rights. These topics tend to be the purview of the academic disciplines that have been most active in their examination of business ethics,

Table 4.1 Topical coverage in a selection of ethics textbooks.

	Boatright—Ethics and the Conduct of Business (7th edition).	Collins—Business Ethics: How to Design and Manage Ethical Organizations	Treviño and Nelson—Managing Business Ethics (5th edition).	Hartman and DesJardins—Business Ethics: Decision Making (3rd edition).	Donaldson, Werhane and Van Zandt—Ethical Issues in Business: a Philosophical Approach (8th edition).
Ethical theory	3	2	2	3	3
Specific ethics issues (1)	3	3	3	3	3
Marketing	3	2	2	3	2
Finance	3	1	1	2	1
Human resources (2)	3	3	3	3	3
CSR and stakeholder	2	2	3	3	2
Governance and accountability	3	1	3	3	2
International	2	2	1	1	2
Cases	2	3	3	3	3
Behavioral ethics	1	2	3	1	2
History	1	3	1	2	2
Corporate ethics management	3	3	3	3	3
Natural environment	1	3	1	3	3
Capitalism	1	2	1	1	2
Ethical culture	1	3	3	3	1
Ethical leadership (3)	1	3	3	1	1

Notes:

1—Indicates minimal topic coverage; 2—indicates moderate topic coverage; 3—indicates extensive topic coverage.

(1) Specific ethics issues—Whistle blowing, conflicts of interest, privacy, affirmative action, safety, intellectual property.

(2) Human resources—Hiring, discrimination, employment rights, occupational health.

(3) Ethical leadership—Specific attributes and qualities of ethical business leaders.

namely philosophy, management, marketing, and law. Other topics with less uniform coverage include ethical leadership; behavioral ethics; analysis of capitalism; corporate culture; issues related to the natural environment; international, religious, and cultural influences on business; history; and ethics in finance. Because of the explosion in research in behavioral ethics we expect the coverage of some of these topics to increase in coming years; however, barriers to this shift are evident. For example, given several books such as *All the Devils are Here* by Bethany McLean and Joe Nocera (2010) that suggest that a major cause of the financial crisis of 2008 was caused by unethical behavior in the finance industry, one would expect the emphasis on ethics in finance to have increased significantly after the most recent US recession and global financial market crisis. However, we are not aware of any important movement among finance professors to examine ethics. Other topics are more difficult to cover because the landscape is so large (e.g., cultural and religious influences as in VanBuren and Agle 1998; Weaver and Agle 2002; Culham 2013), or the pedagogical approaches for effectively teaching them are just now forming. For example, while complicated, the rise of behavioral ethics suggests that experiential learning will be a growing aspect of ethics education. Several examples of such efforts currently underway will be covered in our "how" section.

Where?

In recent years a lot of discussion has centered on the question of "where in the curriculum" should business ethics be handled. In general the debate has involved a question of stand-alone versus integration. While the idea of integration continues to be popular, and an idea we wholly endorse when combined with a stand-alone course, empirical research indicates that implementation continues to be problematic, particularly in areas such as accounting and finance (Rasche et al. 2013). In our experience, in order for integration to have a chance of succeeding, a school must have a contingent of ethics faculty, dedicated and trained, who can teach and assist their colleagues in integrating ethics material into their classes. However, if a pure integration model is attempted, and no required ethics classes exist, then it is also likely that the institution has no dedicated and trained ethics faculty members available. For this and other reasons, most commentators (e.g., Swanson and Fisher 2008) believe that a combination of stand-alone classes and integration is necessary to really meet the various objectives of business ethics education. In a very persuasive essay at the beginning of their edited volume on business ethics education, Diane Swanson and Dann Fisher argue that integration without stand-alone ethics courses will fail because of 1) the poor signal it provides to students (namely, that ethics isn't as important as other required topics), and 2) a lack of strong conceptual building blocks developed through extensive education by ethics educators.

In the context of this issue, Agle and Garff (2015) provide a much fuller discussion of how the various objectives of ethics can be met through the different elements of a student's academic experience. For example, students will likely a) learn ethical theory best through a stand-alone ethics course; but they will b) hone moral awareness through exposure to ethics in their various disciplinary classes (one's awareness is heightened when one is required to look for ethics in places where it is not advertised, as it is in an ethics course); they will then c) acquire corporate culture and grasp the moral infrastructure of organizational life through business school and university modeling (i.e., they see, experience, and are trained in the different elements of the university's code of ethics, learn about the role of the ethics ombudsman, see the ethics hotline, etc.).

Universities and business schools have the ability to demonstrate how to build a strong ethical culture, both formal and informal (Treviño and Nelson 2010). If students receive training in such things as academic plagiarism, appropriate and inappropriate sexual relations, appropriate and inappropriate interactions with faculty members, etc., they will have a much better understanding of how to provide and understand such training when they are in their subsequent business organizations. When taught the kinds of issues concerning students they might visit the university's ombudsman or call the ethics hotline (a professor has treated them unjustly or asked them to do something inappropriate, or they know that a fellow student is distributing a stolen exam, etc.), they will then be much better equipped to utilize those now common resources in organizations and to develop such resources as business leaders. The sharing of stories regarding university or college ethical dilemmas, failures, and successes, by administrators can also help to strengthen and illustrate such a culture (as developed further in Kiss and Euben 2010: 12).

When?

At what point in a student's academic experience is exposure to ethics education most effective? Although Agle and Garff (2015) provide a broad perspective on this question, coming down in favor of exposure throughout the academic experience, the question of the curricular location of the stand-alone ethics course remains an important one. In either undergraduate or graduate education, one can make the argument that the course should be placed toward the beginning of the curriculum as it provides fundamental principles that students should utilize throughout the rest of their coursework. Some might also argue that business ethics cannot really be taught effectively to students who don't yet understand business fundamentals. Thus, the appropriate approach is probably some hybrid of early exposure with more extensive coverage later in the curriculum.

How?

One could easily spend a lifetime reading the various books and articles on pedagogical approaches to ethics education. Such approaches include lecture (Burton et al. 1991); case studies (Falkenberg and Woiceshyn 2008); exposure to comic books (Gerde and Foster 2008), film (Hosmer and Steneck 1989; Gerde et al. 1996), and literature (Badaracco 2006); personal reflection and self-discovery (Calton et al. 2008); and service-learning (Vega 2007); etc. All of these approaches bring with them strengths as well as limitations. In our experience, we find that the most effective approach tends to be that which best utilizes an instructor's talents. However, "our experience" is not a particularly satisfying phrase. Thus, we argue again that such questions need to be answered through rigorous large-scale, multi-institutional, multi-instructor, longitudinal research. We renew our call for such efforts. Current efforts to help professors be more effective in their ethics teaching, with particular emphasis on the newer areas of behavioral ethics and Giving Voice to Values, include the following.

1 Business Roundtable Institute for Corporate Ethics in affiliation with the Darden School at the University of Virginia (www.corporate-ethics.org). The Darden School and the Business Roundtable Institute provide an extensive library of written and video materials regarding business ethics by many leaders in the field.
2 Ethics Unwrapped at University of Texas, Austin—this website (ethicsunwrapped.utexas.edu) provides a helpful set of videos explaining concepts in both behavioral ethics and Giving Voice to Values.
3 Giving Voice to Values—this website (www.babson.edu/Academics/teaching-research/gvv/Pages/home.aspx) provides a multi-faceted set of teaching materials related to the Giving Voice to Values curriculum, including cases, videos, readings, corporate examples, etc.

4   EthicalSystems.org. This collaboration of leading ethics scholars headquartered at the Stern School at NYU provides access to the latest research on organizational ethics.
5   Wheatley Institution Ethics Initiative at BYU (ethics.byu.edu). In concert with the Society for Business Ethics, the Wheatley Institution hosts a bi-annual conference on the teaching of business ethics. These conferences feature leading business ethics professors teaching a favorite business ethics class, providing a model for others to emulate. These exemplary classes are available on the website.

Strengthening a student's moral sense and commitment

We will now present a case for ways to improve the teaching of business ethics. In teaching such courses, we cannot simply assume that students will have a well-formed ethical sensibility, understanding, or commitment, and, even if they do, it is important to spend time strengthening a student's moral sense—that is, their sense of right and wrong.[6] If we fail to do so and move too quickly to the ethical dilemma stage involving complex cases, we can inadvertently create two undesirable results: 1) students may be led to conceive of business ethics in an exclusively cognitive manner, without a corresponding change in attitude or moral commitment; 2) students may end up thinking that being ethical in business is simply a type of game in which they learn to rationalize whatever they end up doing. This feeds into moral skepticism, moral relativism, and the view that ethical decision-making is merely an exercise in rhetorical skill. It's not that we must exclude the use of cases or ethical dilemmas at the start of such a course;[7] nor does it mean we should not provide students with the essential analytical skills necessary to guide them in dealing with such complex dilemmas. However, it does mean that we ought to present to students a sufficiently strong case that we all have a moral sense, a capacity to recognize certain principles of right and wrong. Furthermore, we need to teach in a way that encourages a stronger moral commitment. In the final section, we will discuss how focusing on moral blindness and self-deception can be one of the most effective ways to engage students.

The approach under consideration here would involve beginning a course by articulating some of the fundamental moral intuitions and principles found in almost all moral theories—for example, that all persons deserve *respect* and that there are minimal standards in terms of which we all expect others to treat *us* and which we in turn can be expected to treat others, and so on. The important thing is to articulate claims that most students should find fairly intuitive in order to strengthen their sense that there are universally valid moral principles The point is not that there are easy answers or absolute rules to determine every ethical decision, but rather to show students that there are moral principles that extend beyond individual preference, and across contexts, and can guide us in making such decisions. When we then turn to complex ethical dilemmas, students will more likely be able to navigate difficult decisions without recourse to ethical relativism and skepticism. It is important to present, at first, some of the fundamental insights from different moral teachings and principles in a fairly in-depth manner without simultaneously giving a too-detailed account of different moral systems. Students can easily become bewildered in a maze of moral theories if we go too fast into all the differences among them. However, a hasty overview of various moral theories (for example, simply spending a day covering a one-chapter overview of various moral theories) is also inadequate. We thus need to avoid presenting either a superficial sketch of moral theories—which leaves them with little more than a shallow understanding of ethics—or inundating them further into ethical theory than is needed in a business ethics course. Our argument is that giving students a good grounding in moral philosophy is essential, but that, before doing too much comparing and contrasting of all the different moral theories, it is crucial to find some way to help students come to appreciate that there is non-relativistic discernable status to principles of right and wrong.

Ethics and self-interest

As part of this approach, it is crucial to help students recognize both that 1) ethics is not *based on* self-interest, but also that 2) ethics is not necessarily contrary to self-interest. Establishing the first point is especially important in undercutting the move to *egoism* (or, more precisely, the move to adopting a position of *ethical egoism*), as well as the varieties of *relativism* that many students embrace. Business students can be especially attracted to ethical egoism since so much of business seems oriented toward self-interest. There are several ways to support the claim that our ethical systems and judgments are not essentially grounded in self-interest. One way is to point out that immoral or unethical actions are wrong regardless of how they may adversely harm the interests of those who engage in such actions. Take any serious ethical wrongdoing—murder, rape, fraud, and so on. When articulated in the right way, students can readily recognize that such actions are not wrong simply because these acts might harm *their own* interests in various ways (e.g., by leading to prison, etc.). They are wrong because of what such acts do to *others* who deserve the respect and regard called for in our fundamental duties not to harm others.

Another way to show that egoism is not the basis of moral action focuses on the implicit objectivity of moral judgments. Thomas Nagel provides an argument based on this approach. He points out that there is an "objective interest" we attribute to many of our needs and desires and that we are able to recognize an "objective element in the concern we feel for ourselves" (Nagel 1970: 83). Such objective interest shows up in the fact that when another person harms us, we not only dislike it, but we resent it (an argument first formulated by Adam Smith in 1759, see 1976: 79–83, 137). In other words, we think that "our plight [gives the other person] a reason" not to harm us. We can then recognize the importance of extending that "objective" status to the interests of others. This implies there are *reasons* to refrain from harming others (as well as reasons to help others) even when doing so has no apparent influence against or in favor of our own interests.

Here it is helpful (particularly in a business ethics course) to appeal to Adam Smith, who himself argues that ethical normativity cannot be based on self-interest. While it is true that, for Smith, the success of capitalism is based *largely* on self-interest, this success must come within certain limits on self-interest. In the *Wealth of Nations*, Smith states that "every man, as long as he does not violate the laws of justice, is left perfectly free to pursue his own interest in his own way, and to bring both his industry and capital into competition with those of any other man" (Smith 1981: 186).[8] In a passage from *The Theory of Moral Sentiments*, Smith writes: "one individual must never prefer himself so much even to any other individual, as to hurt or injure that other, in order to benefit himself, [even] though the benefit to the one [might] be much greater than the hurt or injury to the other" (1976: 138). Smith also refers to this sense of justice as "fair play" (1976: 83). Having a sense of fair play and the moral limits on self-interest are essential for Adam Smith and, arguably, to the success of capitalism.[9]

Here, it is helpful to make the case to students as to why capitalism cannot work effectively when based *merely* on self-interest without regard to the ethical limits on self-interest. How are moral limits essential to the success of capitalism? As many have argued, a business cannot truly succeed in the long-term without being ethical. As Robert Solomon puts it, "Though integrity does not guarantee success, there can be no success without it" (Solomon 1993: 174). Solomon adds: "This does not mean that virtue always prospers, but it does mean that the integrity of the corporation and the individual within the corporation is an essential ingredient in the overall viability and vitality of the business world" (21). Thus, while the ethical cannot be grounded simply in self-interest, it is nevertheless true that being ethical is almost always in one's real interest. As Norman Bowie argues, though conventional wisdom is that business should focus solely on the bottom line, if one does the right thing then profits are likely to result. While this is perhaps not the case in every instance, most often it seems to follow that those who are ethical are those who do very well (as evidenced in Bowie 1999: 23, 132–416). In any case, unethical practices will most likely lead to failure, and long-term success is not likely without an ethical commitment.[10]

Avoiding the slide to relativism

Establishing that ethics cannot simply be based on self-interest also helps indirectly to diminish support for normative ethical relativism; even so, it is important to address the issue with students, as well as in sessions devoted to training managers and executives. As Geert Demuijnk has recently argued, "the theoretical framework of cross-cultural management studies that has been the background of most of the teaching, executive training, consultancy" draws heavily on the work of Geert Hofstede and others who explicitly advocate a normative ethical relativism (2015: 824). However, as Demuijnk puts it: "The rejection of relativism and skepticism is a precondition for business ethics to get off the ground" (2015: 819). It is "only if people are convinced that not all ways of doing things are equivalent from a moral perspective [that] genuine discussions of business ethical issues will be taken seriously" (832). As Demuijnk also points out, the topic of ethical relativism is unfortunately neglected by many business ethics textbooks (819). He provides some striking examples to show the problems with ethical relativism (Demuijnk 2015: 828). For example, he shows that it would imply the permissibility of heinous practices that almost everyone would condemn, but also that even when such practices seem to be sanctioned by some culture, we can find those within such a culture who recognize the wrongness of such actions.[11]

Ethical relativists reject the claim that there are universally valid moral principles. However, as Louis Pojman shows, ethical relativism generates some absurd consequences (Pojman and Fieser 2012). Among other absurd results, if ethical relativism were true, we could not say that Gandhi (or any other moral exemplar) was any better than Hitler (or any other morally reprehensible person). Regarding ethical relativism, Joseph DesJardins (2014) articulates three confusions or "traps" that students can easily fall into. One of these "traps" involves "confusing respect, tolerance, and impartiality with relativism." As both DesJardins and Pojman point out, if ethical relativism were true, then condemnation of intolerance would simply be opinion and there could be no required *universal* norm of tolerance. As Pojman puts it, "From a relativistic point of view there is no more reason to be tolerant than intolerant, and neither stance is objectively morally better than the other" (Pojman and Fieser 2012: 21). Furthermore, since this very ideal of tolerance often motivates acceptance of ethical relativism, pointing out that universal tolerance does not logically follow from ethical relativism undercuts one major support for such a view.

The Golden Rule

Another way to strengthen a student's conviction that there are principles that everyone can accept is to focus on the Golden Rule, which can serve as a powerful tool to help students recognize the objective nature of those interests we share with others. In his essay, "Deception and

Withholding Information in Sales," Thomas Carson illustrates how pedagogically persuasive the Golden Rule can be in teaching business ethics. He argues that there are several prima facie duties in regard to selling products, each based on an appeal to the Golden Rule. For instance, to support the duty to warn customers regarding appropriate safety warnings and precautions for their products, he notes: "No one who values her own life and health can say that she does not object to others failing to warn her of the dangers of products they sell her" (Carson 2010: 171). Such examples present students with an intuitive way to recognize that there are indeed ethical principles relevant to business that they should accept.

It is essential, however, to formulate properly the Golden Rule since the simplest version is not without problems. As Harry Gensler and others have argued, application of the "literal" version ("do unto others as you would have them do unto you") can result in absurd consequences (Gensler 2011; Bruton 2004; Burton and Goldsby 2005). Gensler's revised version, which states, "Treat others as you would consent to be treated in the same situation" avoids most of the problems that the literal version can engender.

Even though it is an almost essential tool in helping students to see the universal nature of ethical principles, the Golden Rule is not the only moral principle we need, and it does have certain limitations. As Samuel V. Bruton notes, the problem with the Golden Rule is that it is based on preferences and wants. Thus, it would seem the Golden Rule would prohibit a business "from raising prices, even when their costs go up, on the grounds that customers would prefer that they not do so" (Bruton 2004: 183), or "prevent employers from firing unproductive employees who wish not to lose their job" (183) because clearly neither the employee nor the employer would want to be fired. It also faces difficulties when multiple stakeholders with different interests are involved. Such limitations in applying the Golden Rule can provide an effective transition to other basic ethical principles.[12]

One effective ethical principle to supplement the Golden Rule is Kant's Formula of Humanity as an End: we ought to treat humanity in oneself and in others always as an end, and never merely as a means. As Bruton argues, the imperative to treat the humanity of others as an "end" implies that respecting others' humanity is a "matter of adhering to standards that they could accept as rational beings." Conversely, to treat someone merely as a means is to treat that person in "accordance with rules or principles that the other could not reasonably accept" (Bruton 2004: 185). Thus, "Instead of focusing on preferences, the Formula of Humanity as an End relies on the notion of what people could or would accept. Though it is difficult to rigorously characterize "reasonableness," students should be able to grasp the intuitive difference between what is reasonable and what merely satisfies preference" (185).[13] To illustrate how the application of Kant's principle incorporates judgments that the Golden Rule cannot, Bruton returns to his previous example. He notes that because it would "be unreasonable even for employees not to accept the rule that says businesses may fire inadequate workers, one does not violate their humanity by doing so" (185). Introducing this Kantian principle in this way helps students see the connection between the Golden Rule and other fundamental ethical principles. Even with its limitations, the Golden Rule principle provides one of the best ways to help students appreciate the significantly objective status of ethics.[14]

Moral blindness, self-deception, and unethical actions

A good business ethics course will not only strengthen students' recognition that there are principles they should accept as right; it will also educate them on the common forms of self-deception and moral blindness that we tend to engage in when we go against what we know is right. In relation to the 2007 Duke University business school cheating scandal, Terry Price argues:

> In ethics, the general requirements—the *what* of morality—are often quite straightforward. Indeed we would be hard pressed to find anyone in our society, let alone a university-level student, who was unaware of the general prohibition on cheating. However, the application of these requirements to individuals—the *whom* of morality—can be significantly murkier. I dare say that it would not be difficult at all to find students who genuinely believe that their circumstances justify them in violating the prohibition on cheating.
>
> *(Price 2007)*

Moral blindness and self-deception often occur as the individual shifts from a reflection on right and wrong in general to a consideration of right or wrong *for me* in some particular situation. Thus, it is crucial to alert students to the types of rationalizations and justifications that often prevent us from *seeing* and *acting* on what is right in particular situations. Such moral blindness has been an important emphasis in recent years for those doing behavioral business ethics (see De Cremer and Tenbrunsel 2012). In the book *Blind Spots*, for example, Max Bazerman and Ann Tenbrunsel effectively point out some of the ways we are often influenced by psychological patterns that contribute to unintentional wrongdoing. They refer to such limitations as "bounded ethicality." As they explain, "most instances of corruption, and unethical behavior in general, are unintentional, a product of bounded ethicality and the fading of the ethical dimension of the problem" (Bazerman and Tenbrunsel 2011: 19). Such bounded ethicality refers to the "cognitive limitations that can make us unaware of the moral implications of our decisions" (30). Articulating these cognitive limitations that generate moral blindness is crucial in the context of business ethics courses and training programs.

As examples of such "bounded ethicality," Bazerman and Tenbrunsel point to cognitive biases that make us think we are more ethical than we really are (37): overly discounting the future (56), recollection biases (72), as well as the everyday egocentrism that leads us "to make self-serving judgments regarding allocations of credit and blame" (50). Closely related to this phenomenon is the notion of "ethical fading," which occurs when the *ethics* of a situation fade, and we interpret the situation under another description—such as a business, or legal decision. According to Bazerman and Tenbrunsel, ethical fading is usually caused by external forces like those that contributed to the Ford Pinto case, in which intense competition led Ford managers to overlook the ethical nature of a decision to prioritize the costs of recalling and replacing fuel tanks over the costs to those who might be harmed by malfunction (36). Another example would be the time pressures surrounding the decisions that led to the Space Shuttle O-Ring disaster (14). But such ethical fading is also influenced by compliance systems (113), rewards systems, one-dimensional goals (107), and pressures from the informal culture of a business (117). Bazerman and Tenbrunsel recommend various strategies to help prevent ethical fading and the effects of bounded ethicality (104–117; 160–163).

Such moral blindness is often due to *self-deception*. Tenbrunsel and Messick claim that "self-deception is at the core of ethical fading" (2004: 233). Such self-deception either "eliminate[s] negative ethical characterizations or distort[s] them into positive ones" (232). This allows us to disguise "the moral implications of a decision" and thus "behave in a self-interested manner and still hold the conviction that [we] are ethical persons" (225).

One contemporary philosopher, C. Terry Warner, gives a particularly compelling account of how self-deception and moral blindness occur. His account of self-deception and self-betrayal (the foundation for work done by the Arbinger Institute—see Arbinger 2015) argues that self-deception involves distortions for which we are responsible. His emphasis is less on the type of external pressures and psychological patterns that we find in *Blind Spots*, and more on how some forms of moral blindness are our own creations rather than inevitable consequences of the circumstances. His account provides students with a way to understand both that they are moral *agents* and that their own actions profoundly influence their moral perception of the world.

A good business ethics course should do what it can to alert students to the types of self-deception and moral blindness to which we are all susceptible. In our experience, such a focus is one of the best ways to truly engage students and help them internalize the ethical.

Concluding remarks

We began this chapter with a brief overview of the current trends in business ethics education and then presented a case for a pedagogy that strengthens a student's understanding that ethics is neither based on self-interest nor simply relative to individuals or cultures. Finally, we showed the importance of recognizing common forms of moral blindness and self-deception. This approach responds to the new emphasis being placed on behavioral ethics.

However, there remain issues that need to be considered concerning teaching business ethics. First, since business is increasingly international, an emphasis on international understanding will need to increase. While some have done some very helpful work on international business ethics, there is still more to be accomplished. Clearly, as we have argued in this chapter, there are universal principles that should apply internationally. Nevertheless, there are still many questions to be answered concerning how to apply basic moral principles in cultures that differ from our own. What, for example, does *respect* require of us in the face of different traditions?

Second, the field needs to do a much better job of assessing the effectiveness of ethics teaching. While there are many short-term studies, there is a dearth of longitudinal studies looking at various groups, and different types of educational interventions (type of curricula, type of educational institutions, etc.). These studies are badly needed, yet are expensive in terms of both time and money, and require significant commitment on the part of researchers.

Essential works

Essential works on business ethics education include Thomas R. Piper, Mary C. Gentile and Sharon D. Parks, *Can Ethics Be Taught?* (1993), Ronald R. Sims, *Teaching Business Ethics for Effective Learning* (2002), and Mary C. Gentile, *Giving Voice to Values* (2010). For newer collected works on the subject, see Diane Swanson and Dann Fisher (eds), *Advancing Business Ethics Education* (2008), Charles Wankel and Agata Stachowicz-Stanusch (eds), *Management Education for Integrity* (2011), and Diane Swanson and Dann Fisher (eds), *Got Ethics? Toward Assessing Business Ethics Education* (2011). Broader works that deal with moral education in business schools and universities include Rakesh Khurana, *From Higher Aims to Hired Hands* (2007), Elizabeth Kiss and J. Peter Euben (eds), *Debating Moral Education* (2010), and Derek Bok, *Our Underachieving Colleges* (2006).

For further reading in this volume on the aims and objectives of business ethics education, see Chapter 3, Theory and method in business ethics. On education and moral blindness in management, see Chapter 27, The ethics of managers and employees. For a discussion of moral myopia in marketing, see Chapter 30, Ethical issues in marketing, advertising, and sales. On theoretical perspectives in ethics see the selection of chapters in Part II: Moral philosophy and business: foundational theories. Further discussion of business ethics and education (and the idea of business as a profession) may be found in Chapter 11, Stakeholder thinking. On Geert Hofstede, cross-cultural management, and relativism, see Chapter 32, The globalization of business ethics.

Notes

1 Weber (2015) found that 70 out of 71 large US-based global corporations contacted had ethics training programs in place. Seventy percent of top business schools have an ethics requirement, and 57 percent require at least one stand-alone ethics course (Litzky and MacLean 2011).
2 As Kiss and Euben point out, "A more complex understanding of moral development has led to a tendency to replace a singular emphasis on moral reasoning with models of moral education that combine cognitive, affective, volitional, and behavioral capacities." See Kiss, E. and Euben, J. (eds) (2010: 11).
3 We will return to a discussion of ethical fading in a later section of this chapter.
4 "Moral disengagement" includes distorting consequences, euphemistic language, and advantageous comparison.
5 "Neutralization techniques" refers to the way one justifies wrongdoing through a denial of the victim, denial of injury, along with an appeal to higher loyalties, etc.
6 When we use the term "moral sense," we are not endorsing any particular meta-ethical position (e.g., any particular position on a "moral sense," as did some philosophers of the eighteenth century—Francis Hutcheson is the chief example). We intend a broad use of the term that could apply to most moral theories ranging from that of Aristotle, with his notion of practical reason, to that of Kant, with his concept of moral reason.
7 For a good discussion of using the case method, see Goodpaster 2002.
8 See also Smith 1981[1776], pp. 82–3. It is worth noting that Smith's notion of self-interest is not necessarily a narrow one, but would likely include one's small circle of family and friends.
9 For excellent sources on Adam Smith on self-interest and business, see Heath (2013), Bragues (2010), and Solomon (1993).
10 Joseph DesJardins points to the Malden Mills case as evidence that being ethical does not *always* lead to success (DesJardins 2014).
11 One example Demuijnk gives is that of an Amazon tribe (the Suruwaha) that buries children alive if they have some physical defect (because they think they have no souls). He points to a report in which a family went to great lengths to avoid complying with an order to kill their child as evidence that people *within* that culture recognized the wrongness of such actions.
12 It is possible that Gensler's formulation of the Golden Rule can address such concerns. However, this is a debate for another time.
13 Of course, some moral philosophers (for example, David Hume or Thomas Hobbes) accept only an instrumental conception of reason. On such views, this point would be more difficult to make. Kant, among many other moral philosophers, does not accept such an instrumental notion of reason.
14 There are many other ways one might strengthen a student's recognition that there are common moral principles. Another approach might focus on W.D. Ross's account of prima facie duties. Robert Audi (2009) illustrates the effectiveness of this approach.

Bibliography

Abend, G. (2014). *The Moral Background: An Inquiry into the History of Business Ethics*. Princeton: Princeton University Press.
Agle, B.R. and T. Crossley (2011). "Business Ethics Education, Why Bother? Objectives, Pedagogies, and a Call to Action," *Proceedings of the Conference on Leveraging Change—The New Pillars of Accounting Education*, Toronto.
Agle, B.R. and P. Garff (2015). "Matching Business Ethics Education Objectives and Pedagogy: Utilizing the Entire University Experience in Creating Stronger Moral Agents," Working Paper.
Agle, B.R., D.W. Hart, J.A. Thompson, and H. Hendricks (eds) (2014). *Research Companion to Ethical Behavior in Organizations: Constructs and Measures*. Northampton: Edward Elgar Publishing.
Arbinger (2015). *Leadership and Self-Deception*, 2nd edition. San Francisco, CA: Berrett-Koehler Publishers.
Ariely, D. (2012). *The Honest Truth about Dishonesty*. New York, NY: Harper-Collins.
Armstrong, M.B., J.E. Ketz, and D. Owsen (2003). "Ethics Education in Accounting: Moving Toward Ethical Motivation and Ethical Behavior," *Journal of Accounting Education* 21:1, 1–16.
Audi, R. (2009). *Business Ethics and Ethical Business*. Oxford: Oxford University Press.
Badaracco, J. (2006). *Questions of Character*. Cambridge, MA: Harvard Business School Press.
Bandura, A. (1999). "Moral Disengagement in the Perpetration of Inhumanities," *Personality and Social Psychology Review* 3:3, 193–209.

Bazerman, M.H. and A.E. Tenbrunsel (2011). *Blind Spots: Why We Fail To Do What's Right and What To Do About It*. Princeton, NJ: Princeton University Press.
Berenbeim, R. (2013). "Ethics Classes Don't Need to Make Students More Ethical To Be Worthwhile." Available at: www.ethicalsystems.org/content/ethics-classes-don't-need-make-students-more-ethical-be-worthwhile.
Boatright, J. (2012). *Ethics and the Conduct of Business*, 7th edition New York: Pearson.
Bok, D. (2006). *Our Underachieving Colleges*. Princeton, NJ: Princeton University Press.
Bowie, N. (1999). *Business Ethics: A Kantian Perspective*. Oxford: Blackwell Publishers.
Bragues, G. (2010). "Adam Smith's Vision of the Ethical Manager," *Journal of Business Ethics* 90, 447–460.
Burton, B.K. and M. Goldsby (2005). "The Golden Rule and Business Ethics: An Examination," *Journal of Business Ethics* 56:371–383.
Burton, S., M.W. Johnston and E.J. Wilson (1991). "An Experimental Assessment of Alternative Teaching Approaches for Introducing Business Ethics to Undergraduate Business Students," *Journal of Business Ethics* 10:7, 507–517.
Bruton, S. (2004). "Teaching the Golden Rule," *Journal of Business Ethics* 49:2, 179–187.
Calton, J., S. Payne and S. Waddock (2008). "Learning to Teach Ethics from the Heart," in Swanson, D. and Fisher, D., *Advancing Business Ethics Education*. Charlotte, NC: Information Age Publishing.
Carlson, P.J. and F. Burke (1998). "Lessons Learned From Ethics in the Classroom: Exploring Student Growth in Flexibility, Complexity and Comprehension," *Journal of Business Ethics* 17, 1179–1187.
Carroll, A. (2005). "An Ethical Education," *BizEd* 4:2, 36–40.
Carson, T. (2010). *Lying and Deception*. Oxford: Oxford University Press.
Ciulla, J.B. (2011). "Is Business Ethics Getting Better? A Historical Perspective," *Business Ethics Quarterly* 21:2, 335–343.
Collins, D. (2012). *Business Ethics: How to Design and Manage Ethical Organizations*. Somerset, NJ: John Wiley and Sons.
Culham, T. (2013). *Ethics Education of Business Leaders*. Charlotte, NC: Information Age Publishing.
De Cremer, D. and A. Tenbrunsel (2012). *Behavioral Business Ethics: Shaping an Emerging Field*. New York: Routledge.
Demuijnk, G. (2015). "Universal Values and Virtues in Management Verses Cross-Cultural Relativism: An Educational Strategy to Clear the Ground for Business Ethics," *Journal of Business Ethics* 128, 817–835.
DesJardins, J. (2014). *An Introduction to Business Ethics*. New York: McGraw Hill.
Donaldson, T., P. Werhane and J. Van Zandt (2007). *Ethical Issues in Business: A Philosophical Approach*, 8th edition New York: Pearson.
Duska, R. (1991). "What's the Point of a Business Ethics Course?" *Business Ethics Quarterly* 1:4, 335–354.
Duska, R. (2014). "Why Business Ethics Needs Rhetoric: An Aristotelian Perspective," *Business Ethics Quarterly* 24:1, 119–134.
Earley, C.E. and P.T. Kelly (2004). "A Note on Ethics Educational Interventions in an Undergraduate Auditing Course: Is There an 'Enron Effect'?" *Issues in Accounting Education* 19:1, 53–71.
Elkjaer, B. (2003). "Social Learning Theory: Learning as Participation in Social Processes," in Mark Easterby-Smith and Marjorie Lyles (eds), *The Blackwell Handbook of Organizational Learning and Knowledge Management*. Malden, MA and Oxford, UK: Blackwell Publishers, 38–53.
Falkenberg, L. and J. Woiceshyn (2008). "Enhancing Business Ethics: Using Cases to Teach Moral Reasoning," *Journal of Business Ethics* 79:3, 213–217.
Garrod, A. (ed.). (1993). *Approaches to Moral Development: New Research and Emerging Themes*. New York: Teachers College Press.
Gautschi, F.H. and T.M. Jones (1998). "Enhancing the Ability of Business Students to Recognize Ethical Issues: An Empirical Assessment of the Effectiveness of a Course in Business Ethics," *Journal of Business Ethics* 17:2, 205–216.
Gensler, H. (2011). *Ethics: A Contemporary Introduction*. New York: Routledge.
Gentile, M. (2010). *Giving Voice to Values*. New Haven, CT: Yale University Press.
Gerde, V.W. and R.S. Foster (2008). "X-men Ethics: Using Comic Books To Teach Business Ethics," *Journal of Business Ethics* 77:3, 245–258.
Gerde, V.W., J.M. Shepard, and M.G. Goldsby (1996). "Using Film to Examine the Place of Ethics in Business," *Journal of Legal Studies* 14:2, 199–214.
Gino, F., M.E. Schweitzer, N.L. Mead and D. Ariely (2011). "Unable To Resist Temptation: How Self-control Depletion Promotes Unethical Behavior," *Organizational Behavior and Human Decision Processes* 115:2, 191–203.

Glenn, J. (1992). "Can a Business and Society Course Affect the Ethical Judgment of Future Managers?" *Journal of Business Ethics* 11:3 (March), 217–223.
Goodpaster, K.E. (2002). "Teaching and Learning Ethics by the Case Method," in N. Bowie (ed.), *The Blackwell Companion to Business Ethics*. Oxford: Blackwell Publishers, 117–141.
Grant, A.M. and F. Gino (2010). "A Little Thanks Goes a Long Way: Explaining Why Gratitude Expressions Motivate Prosocial Behavior," *Journal of Personality and Social Psychology* 98:6, 946.
Greene, J.D., R.B. Sommerville, L.E. Nystrom, J.M. Darley and J.D. Cohen (2001). "An fMRI Investigation of Emotional Engagement in Moral Judgment," *Science* 293:5537, 2105–2108.
Greene, J. and J. Haidt (2002). "How (and Where) Does Moral Judgment Work?" *Trends in Cognitive Sciences* 6:12, 517–523.
Haidt, J. (2014). "Can You Teach Businessmen to be Ethical?" Available at: www.washingtonpost.com/blogs/on-leadership/wp/2014/01/13/can-you-teach-businessmen-to-be-ethical/.
Hartman, E. (2006). "Can We Teach Character? An Aristotelian Answer," *Academy of Management Learning and Education*, 5:1, 68–81.
Hartman, E. (2013). *Virtue in Business: Conversations with Aristotle*. Cambridge: Cambridge University Press.
Hartman, L and J. DesJardins (2011). *Business Ethics: Decision Making for Personal Integrity and Social Responsibility*, 2nd edition. New York: McGraw Hill.
Hasnas, J. (2013). "Teaching Business Ethics: The Principles Approach," *Journal of Business Ethics Education* 10, 275–304.
Heath, E., B. Hutton, D. McAlister, J. Petrick and S. True (2005). "Panel: Philosophies of Ethics Education in Business Schools," *Journal of Business Ethics Education* 2:1:13–20.
Heath, E. (2013). "Adam Smith and Self-Interest," in C.J. Berry, M.P. Paganelli and C. Smith (eds), *The Oxford Handbook of Adam Smith*. Oxford: Oxford University Press, 241–264.
Hosmer, L.T. and N.H. Steneck (1989). "Teaching Business Ethics: The Use of Films and Videotape," *Journal of Business Ethics* 8:12, 929–936.
Kant, I. (1994). *Ethical Philosophy*, J.W. Ellington (trans.). Indianapolis, IN: Hackett.
Khurana, R. (2007). *From Higher Aims to Hired Hands*. Princeton, NJ: Princeton University Press.
Kiss, E. and J. Euben (eds) (2010). *Debating Moral Education*. Durham, NC: Duke University Press.
Langlois, L. and C. Lapointe (2010). "Can Ethics be Learned? Results From a Three-Year Action-Research Project," *Journal of Educational Administration* 48:2, 147–163.
Lau, C.L. (2010). "A Step Forward: Ethics Education Matters!" *Journal of Business Ethics* 92:4, 565–584.
LeClair, D.T., L. Ferrell, L. Montuori and C. Willems (1999). "The Use of Behavioral Simulation to Teach Business Ethics," *Teaching Business Ethics* 3, 283–296.
Litzky, B.E. and T.L. MacLean (2011). "Assessing Business Ethics Coverage at Top U.S. Business Schools," in D.L. Swanson and D.G. Fisher (eds), *Toward Assessing Business Ethics*. Charlotte, NC: Information Age Publishing, 133–142.
Mason, R.G. (2008). "Considering the Emotional Side of Business Ethics," in D.L. Swanson and D.G. Fisher (eds), *Advancing Business Ethics Education*. Charlotte, NC: Information Age Publishing.
May, D.R., M.T. Luth and C.E. Schwoerer (2014). "The Influence of Business Ethics Education on Moral Efficacy, Moral Meaningfulness, and Moral Courage: A Quasi-Experimental Study," *Journal of Business Ethics* 124:1, 67–80.
Mayhew, B.W. and P.R. Murphy (2009). "The Impact of Ethics Education on Reporting Behavior," *Journal of Business Ethics* 86:3, 397–416.
McLean, B. and J. Nocera (2010). *All the Devils are Here*. New York: Portfolio/Penguin.
Morris, L. and G. Wood (2011). "A Model of Organizational Ethics Education," *European Business Review* 23:3, 274–286.
Nagel, T. (1970). *The Possibility of Altruism*. Princeton, NJ: Princeton University Press.
Nagel, T. (2013). "You Can't Learn About Morality from Brain Scans: The Problem with Moral Psychology," *The New Republic*, Nov 1.
Piper, T.R., M.C. Gentile and S.D. Parks (1993). *Can Ethics Be Taught?* Boston, MA: Harvard Business School.
Pojman, L. and J. Fieser (2012). *Ethics: Discovering Right and Wrong*. Boston, MA: Cengage Learning.
Price, T. (2007). "How to Teach Business Ethics," *Inside Higher Education*, June 4.
Rasche, A., D.U. Gilbert and I. Schedel (2013). "Cross-Disciplinary Ethics Education in MBA Programs: Rhetoric or Reality," *Academy of Management Learning and Education* 12:1, 71–85.
Rest, J.R. (1986). *Moral Development: Advances in Research and Theory*. Toronto: Praeger Publishers.
Sarbanes-Oxley Act (2002). PL 107-204, United States Statutes 116 Stat 745.

Shaw, W. and V. Barry (2013). *Moral Issues in Business*. Boston, MA: Cengage Learning.
Simha, A., J.P. Armstrong and J.F. Albert (2012). "Attitudes and Behaviors of Academic Dishonesty and Cheating—Do Ethics Education and Ethics Training Affect Either Attitudes or Behaviors?" *Journal of Business Ethics Education* 9, 129–144.
Sims, R.R. (2002). *Teaching Business Ethics for Effective Learning*. Westport, CT: Quorum Books.
Sims, R.R. and E.L. Felton, Jr. (2006). "Designing and Delivering Business Ethics Teaching and Learning," *Journal of Business Ethics* 63, 197–312.
Smith, A. (1976 [1759]) in D.D. Raphael and A.L. Macfie (eds), *The Theory of Moral Sentiments*. Indianapolis, IN: Liberty Fund.
Smith, A. (1981 [1776]) in R.H, Campball, A.S. Skinner and W.B. Todd (eds), *An Inquiry into the Nature and Causes of the Wealth of Nations*, 2 vols. Indianapolis, IN: Liberty Fund.
Smith, C. (2011). *Lost in Translation*. Oxford: Oxford University Press.
Solberg, J., K.C. Strong, and C. McGuire, Jr. (1995). "Living (Not Learning) Ethics," *Journal of Business Ethics* 14, 71–81.
Solomon, R. (1993). *Ethics and Excellence: Cooperation and Integrity in Business*. Oxford: Oxford University Press.
Sonenshein, S. (2007). "The Role of Construction, Intuition, and Justification in Responding To Ethical Issues at Work: The Sensemaking-Intuition Model," *Academy of Management Review* 32:4, 1022–1040.
Stanwick, P. and S.D. Stanwick (2013). *Understanding Business Ethics*. New York: Prentice Hall.
Swanson, D. and D. Fisher (eds) (2008). *Advancing Business Ethics Education*. Charlotte, NC: Information Age Publishing.
Swanson, D. and D. Fisher (2011). *Got Ethics? Toward Assessing Business Ethics Education*. Charlotte, Information Age Publishing.
Sykes, G.M. and D. Matza (1957). "Techniques of Neutralization: A Theory of Delinquency," *American Sociological Review* 22, 664–670.
Tenbrunsel, A. and D.M. Messick (2004). "Ethical Fading: The Role of Self-Deception in Unethical Behavior," *Social Justice Research* 17:2, 223–236.
Treviño, L. and K. Nelson (2010). *Managing Business Ethics: Straight Talk about How to Do It Right*, 5th edition. Somerset, NJ: John Wiley and Sons.
Van Buren, H. and B. Agle (1998). "Measuring Christian Beliefs that Affect Managerial Decision-making: A Beginning," *International Journal of Values Based Management* 11:2, 159–177.
Vega, G. (2007). "Teaching Business Ethics Through Service Learning Metaprojects," *Journal of Management Education* 31:5, 647–678.
Verschoor, C. (2006). "IFAC Committee Proposes Guidance for Achieving Ethical Behavior," *Strategic Finance* 88:6, 19.
Wankel, C. and A. Stachowicz-Stanusch (2011). *Management Education for Integrity*. Bingley, UK: Emerald Publishing.
Waples, E.P., A.L. Antes, S.T. Murphy, S. Connelly, and M.D. Mumford (2009). "A Meta-Analytic Investigation of Business Ethics Instruction," *Journal of Business Ethics* 87:1, 133–151.
Warner, C.T. (2013). *Oxford Papers*. Farmington, UT: The Arbinger Institute.
Warren, R.C. (1995). "Practical Reason in Practice: Reflections on a Business Ethics Course," *Education and Training* 37:6, 14–22.
Weaver, G.R. and B.R. Agle (2002). "Religiosity as an Influence on Ethical Behavior in Organizations: A Theoretical Model and Research Agenda," *Academy of Management Review* 27:1, 77–97.
Weaver, G.R. and L.K. Treviño (1999). "Attitudinal and Behavioral Outcomes of Corporate Ethics Programs: an Empirical Study of the Impact of Compliance and Values-Oriented Approaches," *Business Ethics Quarterly* 9:2, 315–335.
Weber, J. (1990). "Measuring the Impact of Teaching Ethics to Future Managers: A Review, Assessment, and Recommendations," *Journal of Business Ethics* 9:3, 183–190.
Weber, J. (2015). "Investigating and Assessing the Quality of Employee Ethics Training Programs Among US-Based Global Organizations," *Journal of Business Ethics* 129:1, 27–42.
Williams, S.C. and T. Dewett (2005). "Yes, You Can Teach Business Ethics: A Review and Research Agenda," *Journal of Leadership and Organizational Studies* 12, 109–120.
Wurthmann, K. (2013). "A Social Cognitive Perspective on the Relationships Between Ethics Education, Moral Attentiveness, and PRESOR," *Journal of Business Ethics* 114:1, 131–153.

Part II
Moral philosophy and business
Foundational theories

Introduction

One of the main branches of philosophical enquiry, moral philosophy studies ethical conduct from both a theoretical and applied perspective. Since business ethics is a prominent area of applied moral philosophy, it is imperative to understand the theoretical background behind an ethics of business. The chapters in Part II present and examine the foundational theories that historically comprise the subject area of moral philosophy. The distinct kinds of moral theorizing, or schools of ethics, include consequentialism, non-consequentialism, contractarianism, virtue theory, and, most recently, feminism. The discussions in this Part reveal how business ethics has drawn upon the first principles and basic theses of these theories. In addition, and because much ethical conduct bears the influence of a religious background, this section includes a chapter on the role of religion in shaping business ethics.

In the first chapter, **Consequentialism and non-consequentialism**, **Andrew Gustafson** presents the viewpoints of two competing visions as to what makes an action, trait, or policy right or wrong—the consequentialist and its opposite, the non-consequentialist. Both schools of morals have a principal and developed version, utilitarianism and deontology, respectively. The chapter starts with an overview of ethical theories focusing on their history, kinds, and ramifications, and proceeds to present and critically discuss both consequentialism and non-consequentialism, tracing the main theoretical varieties of each. Gustafson points out that in business ethics the prevailing view seems to be in favor of a non-consequentialist rather than a consequentialist perspective. He proceeds to analyze extensively and in detail how the two opposing moral standpoints are employed in business ethics.

In Chapter 6, **Social contract theories**, **Pedro Francés-Gómez** examines the contribution of social contract theory to contemporary debates in business ethics. After distinguishing between classical and contemporary versions of the political and moral theory that grounds contractarian thought, he explains how contractarianism has been applied to business ethics in general and how this application is justified by its proponents. Francés proceeds to discuss in detail the constitutive elements of any contractarian approach, as well as a variety of particular contractarian theories of business ethics. The most prominent of these is the so-called "integrative social contracts theory" (ISCT). Francés outlines its proposed applications as well as the criticisms voiced against it, even from those within the contractarian camp. The chapter closes with a picture of some alternative paths of current contractarian theory.

Michael C. Munger and **Daniel C. Russell** open Chapter 7, **Can profit seekers be virtuous?**, by arguing that under appropriate conditions profit seeking in business can be compatible with being a virtuous person. They argue for this thesis by examining profit, the character of businesspersons, and the place of virtue within a competitive market (with a focus on virtuous *intent* in entrepreneurship). If profit seeking is no vice, then is there such a thing as entrepreneurial virtue? The authors answer this question positively (but critically) by drawing a distinction between a commercial versus a rent-seeking society. They delineate the place of entrepreneurial virtue in commercial society and describe how the rent-seeking society proves corrosive to virtue.

In Chapter 8, **Feminist ethics and business ethics: redefining landscapes of learning**, **Ming Lim** considers how feminism can shed light on business ethics by illuminating neglected features of human conduct in commercial, and, more generally, in economic activities. She points out the concrete contributions—philosophical and empirical—that feminist theory has made to business ethics, in particular, a reorientation towards a fuller appreciation of the moral experiences of women. She examines, on the one hand, feminist ethics and its relationship to the ethics of care, and, on the other, the complex, critical, and ambivalent relationship between feminist ethics and business ethics. To accomplish a reorientation of business ethics, she draws from a theory of social or situated learning within "communities of practice" in which a person's social identity is constantly re-fashioned through a dynamic process of exchange that can be facilitated within organizations or commercial enterprises.

In Chapter 9, **Business ethics and religious belief**, **Kenneth J. Barnes** observes that, some obvious differences apart, there are crucial similarities among the global religions regarding their stances vis à vis commercial conduct. The chapter starts by examining the Jewish tradition and moves on to Christianity and Islam before closing with an examination of Asian religious traditions, namely Hinduism, Buddhism, Taoism and Confucianism. The author provides a detailed discussion of an extensive material, both scriptural and practical, taken from each religious tradition and its moral assessment of economic life in general, including, where relevant, any specific perspectives on activities of business or trade.

Byron Kaldis

5

Consequentialism and non-consequentialism

Andrew Gustafson

Business persons tend to focus on results, or consequences, so business practice is naturally consequence-driven. To engage in commerce is to act with a vision of an end to be achieved—for example, to create valuable goods and services, to make a profit, or to attain the firm's goals for the quarter. In the academic field of business ethics, few would claim to be consequentialists, and, in fact, most find consequentialism in tension with ethics not a source of it, in part because consequentialism is often associated with a focus on either happiness or utility—oftentimes economic—rather than ethical values. Given the perceived association between consequentialism and economic utility, as well as the apparent links between business and specific results, many come to the view that business practice itself is often inherently in tension with ethics.

Traditionally, the consequentialist asserts that the rightness or wrongness of an action, rule, or policy is entirely dependent upon its consequences, or results. Truth telling is right, a consequentialist might say, because lying ultimately leads to bad results. Utilitarianism is a standard consequentialist ethic, holding that actions are right if they have the greatest probability of bringing about the greatest happiness for the greatest number. The non-consequentialist, in contrast, is one who thinks that the rightness or wrongness of an action (rule, policy) is not determined by its consequences but by some feature inherent to the action itself. Telling the truth is good in itself, not merely because it brings good results (although that may be an added benefit). We do not determine morality by an action's benefit to us or others; its rightness or wrongness is found in something other than consequences. Typically, duty-based, law-based, or rights-based theories are considered non-consequentialist.

We can find elements of consequentialist and non-consequentialist thinking in business itself. Of course business is about results, and in many cases one is praised for good results and chastised for bad ones—one's good intentions are not so important, particularly if one has poor results. On the other hand, it is not uncommon to hear business people say that they chose such and such an action that cut into profits "because it was simply the right thing to do."

It will be useful to explain more clearly consequentialist and non-consequentialist theories of ethics, and then highlight some of the key examples of how they have been applied in the field of business ethics. To that end, the first section below furnishes a brief overview. Section two provides explanations of both consequentialist and non-consequentialist ethical theories. In the third section each of these types of theories are applied to business ethics. The concluding remarks raise some questions about non-consequentialism, as well as some contemporary developments in business ethics theory.

A brief overview of ethical theories

In terms of the history of modern ethical theory, one could say that consequentialism has been the preeminent approach, starting from Jeremy Bentham's theory of utility and that of J.S. Mill, to Henry Sidgwick's utilitarianism in the 1800s and up until 1971 with John Rawls' critique of utilitarianism in *A Theory of Justice*. Since Rawls' work, much of English-speaking ethical theory has been a reaction to consequentialism; in fact, non-consequentialist Kantian ethics have been revived after Rawls (Wood 2007). Some might place the revival of non-consequentialist virtue theory at the feet of Elizabeth Anscombe who launched a critique of modern ethical theory in "Modern Moral Philosophy" (1958), but others might point to Alisdair MacIntyre's *After Virtue* (1981). Regardless of how one construes that history of theory, there is no doubt that non-consequentialist theories have quite certainly dominated academic business ethics literature since the 1970s. Consequentialism is rarely used as a basis of business ethics, and this is perhaps because business decision-making "without ethics" is typically construed as a utilitarian calculus with an aim of wealth maximization for the firm.

There are many possible varieties of consequentialism. We may disagree about *which* ends should be achieved or expected or *whose* consequences should be considered, but typically the two key consequentialist ethics are utilitarianism and egoism. Traditionally, utilitarianism considers the probability of benefit to all people, but egoism considers only the individual. In addition, there are variations that suggest that the universe of concern might be one's firm. Bentham, Mill or Sidgwick are classic utilitarians: the best thing to do is whatever brings about the greatest happiness for the many. Ayn Rand was an egoist who argued that each person ought to do whatever is in his or her own *rational* interest. The main difference then, between utilitarianism and egoism concerns whose happiness is the basis of moral intention: that of the agent alone or that of the larger society? The egoist is concerned only with the consequences to himself, not others, while the utilitarian is concerned with the consequences to the many (either as a whole, or as a sum total of the individuals).

A further distinction to be made between different types of consequentialism turns on a distinction between an action and a rule (governing actions). Are we to judge each individual act by the measure of how it contributes toward the greatest happiness principle? Or should we use the greatest happiness principle to determine general rules that are then to be applied to determine our actions? Such rules, by the way, would be empirically derived from looking at consequences of types of acts as they have occurred throughout history and over the long-term, such as "don't lie" or "don't steal." The first type is act-consequentialism, and the second is rule-consequentialism (the rules being empirically derived from what typically happens when, for example, one lies).

Non-consequentialist theories of ethics find the basis of ethics in some sort of rules not based on consequences. The basis of the rules may be some intrinsic Good (Plato 1974 [fourth century BCE]) or some fundamental rights (Rawls 1971); or these rules may be entailed by the commands of reason (Immanuel Kant 2012 [1785]), or derived from natural law (Thomas Aquinas 2000 [thirteenth century CE]), self-evident intuitions (W.D. Ross 1965) or the emergent results of universal sentiments (Francis Hutcheson 2003 [1728]); for others, such rules may be the commands of God (Duns Scotus 1986 [thirteenth century CE]).

The intuitive appeal of non-consequentialism is that happy consequences and ethical behavior do not, in fact, seem to be necessarily connected. Doing the right thing often is difficult, and one pays a price for genuinely ethical conduct. There are principles or behaviors that appear to be valued in themselves, not because of any resultant outcomes. For example, we may think it right to keep promises even when it will cost us; we demand fair and costly trials for criminals even when it seems obvious they are guilty; and we seek to preserve the rights of individuals or minorities when it will cost the majority a great deal. Situations such as these illustrate the non-consequentialist intuition that consequences are not a good guide to determine the ethical course of action.

On the other hand, the intuitive appeal of consequentialism is that we do typically think that the results count: we provide rights to minorities because such rights make for a happier society overall; we keep promises because lying usually ends up with trouble. Look what happens to the boy who cries wolf too many times when there is no wolf: when the wolf actually shows up and he cries "wolf!" then no one believes him. In discussions about public policies, social values, right ways of living, and correct actions we constantly support our viewpoint by turning to the consequences as reasons: "ethical business is good (i.e., profitable) business!"; "honesty is the best policy." When faced with a difficult decision we often judge what to do based on what will cause the least harm, or the most happiness—this is how we conduct ourselves with others and reason ethically on a regular basis.

Ethical theories of non-consequentialism and consequentialism

Non-consequentialism

As mentioned above, there are many types of non-consequentialism. Some are oriented around rules, others around rights. Deontologists believe there are certain principles or rules that must be obeyed. The deontologist believes he can give reasons to justify the rule, and provide a means to discover the rules as well, by reason in most cases (Kant 2012), although at times other empirical or intuitive means enable us to discover the basic principles that must be followed. Some think these principles are inviolable, while others such as W.D. Ross (1965) think rules can be overridden at times by other rules.

Kantian non-consequentialism

Kant, and contemporary Kantian ethicists such as Christine Korsgaard (1996) or Allen Wood (2007), see the duty to follow rules as fundamental to one's ethics. For Immanuel Kant, the only intrinsically good thing (good in itself) is a good will. Good intentions are not only more important than consequences, it is the intention that carries moral significance. We praise the one who tries to do good, often even if the person does not achieve it; yet someone who attempts to harm but accidentally produces a good result receives no praise (perhaps even condemnation). Kant's categorical imperative states that at all times, in every case, one has an ethical obligation as a reasonable being to act only in accord with principles that are universalizable: One is rationally obligated not to do what one could not wish everyone to do, and to do that which one can rationally expect everyone to do without contradiction.

His second formulation, which he believes follows from the first, is that we should treat persons only as ends, not merely as means to our own ends—people must be treated with dignity and respect as individuals. In Kant's ethics we find a deep concern for the individual and her freedom and sociality. This latter notion of sociality is quite important, for Kant also argues that we should see each other as a member of a kingdom of ends, and when I act I should think not merely of myself, but of every person I meet as an end in himself, and all others should conceive of everyone else the same way.

There are criticisms of Kant's ethics—that it is too rigid, that rules can conflict, that emotions are neglected, and even that it slips into consequentialism. But the beauty of Kant's theory is that it seems to capture the importance of the dignity of the individual person while also seeing us all as responsible for one another in society. And it attempts to do this purely on the basis of rationality, not empirical consequences. Insofar as we judge people on their intentions more than we do on what they accomplish, Kant has captured a very important aspect of morality.

Contractarian non-consequentialism

Social contract theorists are also typically considered non-consequentialists. They typically believe that moral principles or rules are achieved by agreement or consensus, and that rationality compels us to make these agreements and stick to them. In other words, reason directs us to those rules that are ultimately in the self-interest of each person in the covenant. Thomas Hobbes was a classic contractarian, while Rawls (1971) and David Gauthier (1986) are more contemporary. One can think of social contract theory in this way: an egoist is concerned primarily about himself—he believes that the right way to act is to act in the way that generates the most good for himself alone; however, the problem he faces in getting all that he wants is, quite simply, you, me, and all other people. Due to the presence of others, he is forced to negotiate and get the best that he can—by negotiating he arrives at a social contract that ensures rights for all social actors participating. Each person gives up some potential power in order to receive some guaranteed rights in society. These rights provide moral norms regarding how we should treat one another.

Although there are criticisms of social contract theory—for example, its starting point assumes a fictional hypothetical situation with a decision-maker who is sexless, raceless, and essentially disembodied of personal attributes—but it does provide a framework for thinking about the shared foundations of ethical obligations.

Virtue ethics non-consequentialism

Virtue theorists, it is often said, are outside of the consequentialism/non-consequentialism discussion because they are concerned with the development of ethical character, or the development of personal virtues, not acts per se. Consequentialists and non-consequentialists, in contrast, are portrayed as focused on acts. However, since virtue ethics is teleological, implying thereby an end or a goal to be pursued, some have categorized it as consequentialistic. For Aristotle, happiness is the end in itself: it is not pursued for some other end, but it is achieved when humans fulfill their proper function, which is to be rational (and so free) beings. We pursue rationality and virtue because it will ultimately bring us happiness. But there are also reasons to see virtue ethics as fundamentally non-consequentialist. After all, the virtuous person should possess certain dispositions and character traits; he is not required to achieve a particular state of affairs. So a courageous individual who does a heroic act may face the bad consequence of death even as the person manifests the virtue of courage. For traditional virtue ethicists the world is constructed in a certain fashion, with rules of nature not unlike the "laws" of physics or biology that provide a blueprint of correct or excellent behavior. Nature's determination makes particular actions or ways of being in the world right or proper, and others wrong or improper—in other words, unnatural, unhealthy, or inappropriate to the one doing those actions. Dishonesty is wrong not merely because of the consequences of lying, but because it goes against the created order of nature and the world as it was intended (by nature in Aristotle's case, or by God in Aquinas' case).

Criticisms of virtue ethics are various. Some contend that virtues are culturally-relative, others that virtues do not provide clear rules or guides to action, and others suggest that the appeal to personal excellence is ultimately self-centered. Nonetheless, virtue ethics has enjoyed a powerful revival in the last few decades.

Consequentialism

Consequentialist approaches to ethics judge the right or good by the consequences. There are at least two key initial concerns: what is the consequence desired? and for whom? Or, put another way, what is the value theory we have (is it happiness, pleasure, preference satisfaction, profit, or efficiency?), and who is within the universe of concern for which we are deciding (myself, my family, the firm, the club, society at large?).

Egoism

The egoist claims that the individual is the locus of concern. There are three types of egoism to distinguish: psychological egoism, rational egoism, and ethical egoism. Psychological egoism is not a normative (ethical) theory, but a descriptive claim that all people are motivated only by their perceived self interest. Although Hobbes is often considered a social contract theorist, at root he was a psychological egoist: "No man giveth but with intention of good to himself; because gift is voluntary; and of all voluntary acts the object to every man is his own pleasure" (Hobbes 1994 [1651]: Ch. 15, par. 16). Ethical egoism is the view that we *ought* to act on our own self interest. Ayn Rand set forth a version of ethical egoism that emphasized an individual's rational long-term self-interest. In the title of one of her books (*The Virtue of Selfishness: A New Concept of Egoism* 1964), Rand sought to indicate her own brand of egoism, according to which the individual should "exist for his own sake, neither sacrificing himself to others nor sacrificing others to himself" (Rand 1964: 3). Although Rand and ethical egoism is often caricatured as something brutish, scholars such as Douglas Rasmussen and Douglas Den Uyl, as well as Tara Smith, have provided more careful analyses of her thought (Rasmussen and Uyl 1987; Smith 2006).

Utilitarianism: Jeremy Bentham

When defining utilitarianism, it is useful to consider Jeremy Bentham and John Stuart Mill. Mill's definition of utilitarianism is quite clear:

> The creed which accepts as the foundation of morals, Utility, or the Greatest Happiness Principle, holds that actions are right in proportion as they tend to promote happiness, wrong as they tend to produce the reverse of happiness. By happiness is intended pleasure, and the absence of pain; by unhappiness, pain, and the privation of pleasure.
> *(Mill 1998 [1861]: Utilitarianism, Ch. 2)*

Bentham puts no restrictions on what should or shouldn't bring pleasure; since it is purely subjective what one may find pleasurable, one man may like to write poetry, another to bet on horses. Bentham developed a utilitarian calculus, a numerical tool to calculate the pleasures and pains of particular acts. His goal was to quantify pleasure cumulatively: we calculate the relative pleasure and pain of all people involved to determine which action or policy would most likely yield the most happiness, and then we legislate accordingly, always keeping the greater happiness of the majority in mind.[1] In some cases a particular choice may cause more pain to me than to others (for example, the government destroys my house in order to build a highway), but we realize that, given the great pleasure others will receive, it is the right thing to do, despite my personal loss.

Given Bentham's approach, critics say that utilitarianism undermines justice, runs roughshod over the minority, and ignores individual rights, treating individuals as a means to the greater happiness rather than ends in themselves. Some have urged that the doctrine is too demanding, because in most cases in which one enjoys some idle hour or amusement, one could be bringing about more pleasure for the many. Moreover, the *motivation* to act in utilitarian fashion remains a problem: why would I sacrifice my own pleasure in order to bring pleasure to the many? Finally, critics point to the great difficulty utilitarians face in providing an adequate means of determining how to do the utilitarian calculus.

Utilitarianism: John Stuart Mill

Knowing these criticisms of Bentham's utilitarianism helps us understand how John Stuart Mill's utilitarianism differs from that of his predecessor. Mill contended that some types of happiness are qualitatively superior to others, and some capacities for happiness are more important to preserve than others. Higher pleasures include those of the intellect and imagination, as well as noble feelings and benevolent sentiments. When asked how to determine which are higher and which lower, Mill says we must ask those who are experienced with both types. Mill suggests Epicurus (d. 270 BC) as a model hedonist, since Epicurus saw friendship, fidelity, and generosity, for example, as essential to a truly happy life.

Mill sees impartiality (more recently referred to as "agent neutrality") as essential if one is to be capable of sacrificing what one loves most for a higher good. In this vein, Mill regards Jesus Christ as an exemplar of such selflessness. Ethical action (as well as rules and principles) arise from what brings about the best interests of humanity:

> Not only does all strengthening of social ties, and all healthy growth of society, give to each individual a stronger personal interest in practically consulting the welfare of others; it also leads him to identify his feelings more and more with their good, or at least with an even greater degree of practical consideration for it. He comes, as though instinctively, to be conscious of himself as a being who of course pays regard to others. The good of others becomes to him a thing naturally and necessarily to be attended to, like any of the physical conditions of our existence.
>
> *(Mill 1998 [1651]: 3.10.32)*

Some critics tend to portray all utilitarians as act-utilitarians—as though each action is uniquely calculated—but many utilitarians claim that we must establish rules, based on the greater happiness principle. Both Mill and Bentham were in favor of creating legislative rules based on human experience of what actions tend to bring about happiness (or less unhappiness) for the many. Mill's distinction between higher and lower pleasures, in conjunction with what many scholars view as his implicit version of rule-utilitarianism, suggests a better way to respond to typical criticisms (Miller 2011). Mill believes justice is valuable to society, and a society committed to preserve justice and various classic individual rights (including those of property, assembly, and religious freedom, among others) will encourage the capacity to aspire and attain the higher forms of happiness. In addition, we glean from experience and from history that lying generally is not the right policy, so we should avoid it, as a rule.

With regard to motivation, Mill's answer—like that of Aristotle, Plato, and ethicists throughout history—is that we must work hard to train the young and instill in them social concern and values, all for the sake of the greater happiness of society. There is no doubt that doing any utilitarian calculation, at least with any precision, is difficult; however, the allusion to mathematical precision may be misleading and unnecessary. As Aristotle says, "We must not expect more precision than the subject-matter admits" (*Nichomachean Ethics* I. 3).

So utilitarianism is not without difficulties, but also not without defenders. It can provide rules for action based upon a goal of achieving the greatest happiness for the many. Those rules may include supporting individual rights, justice, truth-telling, kindness, respect, and many other types of behavior that throughout history have helped to establish greater happiness for the many.

Non-consequentialism and consequentialism in business ethics

Business tends in its activity and goals to be focused on results—and while these results can include the interest or satisfaction we find in our business activities, a basic consequence typically sought is profit. In this sense then, business has a consequential value as its goal. For many academic business ethicists, this is a utilitarianism of business values—a myopic concern with profit, at the expense of human concern for others. So consequentialism is often seen as a nonstarter for business ethics theories, for it will either be egoistic, and concerned only with self, or it will be utilitarian and so only concerned with profit. But this is an unfair portrayal of utilitarian ethics, and a myopic misleading view of consequentialist ethics.

In the business ethics literature there is surprisingly little literature written from a consequentialist perspective, although there is a great deal of literature that criticizes it. Non-consequential theories such as Kantian deontological theory, contractarianism, and virtue theory dominate the scholarly considerations of business ethics. The reasons for this have much to do with a general rejection of any sort of consequentialism. Although business may be conceived as a collective egoism whose collectivity is demarcated by the boundaries of the firm, egoism is typically associated with selfishness and greed—in other words, egoism is typically seen to be anti-ethical—exactly what ethics is trying to resist. The utilitarian concern with happiness is often considered to be at base hedonistic—or merely concerned with self-indulgent pleasure—and thus in conflict with ethics. Even though John Stuart Mill's utilitarianism focuses on a rich and diverse conception of the greater happiness of the many, for many in business (and for some scholars in business ethics), utilitarianism is often associated with a narrow economic utilitarianism that is reduced, by many critics, to a mere concern for profit maximization complemented with an ethical indifference to others.

Non-consequentialism in business ethics

Non-consequentialism is clearly the predominant ethical outlook in academic business ethics, at least since the 1970s when the field first emerged, right after the so-called "normative turn" that followed Rawls' critique of utilitarianism. Norman Bowie developed a Kantian approach to business ethics (Bowie 1999), and his influence continues through his students (Arnold and Harris 2012). Thomas Donaldson and Thomas Dunfee (1999) developed the contractarian approach, rooted in Hobbes, Jean-Jacques Rousseau and Rawls, and more recently scholars such as Nien-hê Hsieh (2004) have developed a Rawlsian approach. Robert Solomon (1993), Edwin Hartman (2015) and many others have developed virtue ethics approaches to business ethics.

Andrew Gustafson

The Kantian approach in business ethics

Norm Bowie is clearly the pioneer in this field, and his students have gone on to help establish Kantian business ethics as the predominant approach among many business ethicists. Bowie claims that a Kantian practicing businessman should adhere to promises and contracts, refrain from deceit or fraud, and conduct himself in a way that he could will to be standard practice. In addition, when it comes to the treatment of others, Bowie says a Kantian approach will give great autonomy to employees, and great respect to customers and suppliers, in line with treating all people as an end, not merely as a means (in this case, a means to profit). One should pay fair wages, pay bills briskly, give respectful and timely customer service, and do all of this for the sake of duty, not merely for repeat business or reputation. Furthermore, Bowie applies Kant's notion of a kingdom of ends to the corporation: "Because an organization is a community of persons, whatever else an organization is, it should be a moral community" (Bowie 1999: 89). This has significant implications for how a business should be run. As he says, "A Kantian would morally object to a hierarchical structure that requires those lower down to carry out the orders of those above, more or less without question" (Bowie 1999: 12). Additionally, Bowie suggests that all companies use open-book management, where the employees all have access to all accounting documents of the company (Bowie 1999: 54).

Bowie provides a list of characteristics of a company run with a Kantian approach:

1. The business firm should consider the interests of all the affected stakeholders in any decision it makes.
2. The firm should have those affected by the firm's rules and policies participate in the determination of those rules and policies before they are implemented.
3. It should not be the case that, for all decisions, the interests of one stakeholder automatically take priority.
4. When a situation arises where it appears that the interest of one set of stakeholders must be subordinated to the interests of another set of stakeholders, that decision should not be made solely on the grounds that there is a greater number of stakeholders in one group than in another.
5. No business rule or practice can be adopted which is inconsistent with the first two formulations of the categorical imperative.
6. Every profit-making firm has a limited, but genuine, duty of beneficence.
7. Every business firm must establish procedures designed to ensure that relations among stakeholders are governed by rules of justice.

(Bowie 1999: 90)

But there are criticisms to be raised with Bowie's approach. The difficulty with considering the interest of all affected stakeholders (1) is that it seems to be a nearly impossible responsibility to have to consider the ways one's decision affects even the most remote stakeholders every time one makes a business decision. And the more stakeholders one considers, the more difficult the decision would be—buying from one supplier may adversely affect the supplier's competitors, all of whom employ human beings who are indirect stakeholders in this purchasing decision (Langtry 1994). The difficulty of having all affected by the firm's rules participate in their determination is that this would make corporate governance extremely time consuming and inefficient. A problem with claim (6) is that Bowie slips from talking about all individuals as parts of a kingdom of ends to making the company, which is itself a kingdom of ends, into an agent in the kingdom of ends. Sometimes he talks about corporations having "a duty of beneficence to society in return" (Bowie 2008: 11). On other occasions he describes the firm as a kingdom of ends (Bowie 1999: 87). Perhaps the company has limited duties, rights, and is a person as a legal fiction. But surely Bowie does not think a corporation as an entity possesses the *same sort* of dignity or responsibility as a human—we would not mourn the death of company as we would a human.

Bowie himself thinks the greatest challenge to a Kantian approach is that it is too demanding, particularly when it comes to purity of motive, but a more practical concern is simply how to take account of or judge someone else's intentions (Bowie 2017). For Kant, we judge one's behavior to be ethical not on the basis of achieving some goal, but on the basis of what one was intending. A good intention or good will is the only purely good thing for Kant. But this is not particularly congruent with business. Business behavior is generally judged from an external perspective—John will get a raise if he meets his sales goals, not if he had purity of heart in desiring to meet those goals. Part of the reason businesses judge based on performance, not purity of intention, is that they have no means to access the inner workings of one's heart. They can, however, see what the results are. If one uses external behaviors for judging performance, then this is a fundamental problem for Kantianism in general, and Bowie's Kantian business ethics in particular. And it is quite difficult to see how one could do anything to judge others for merit or demerit apart from simply taking their word on what their intentions were in a given case. In this sense, Bowie and Kantian ethics seem to have a subjectivity problem—only the subject acting can possibly know what his intentions are, and so only he will be able to determine if his actions are morally praiseworthy or blameworthy.

Bowie illustrates his Kantian non-consequentialism with some examples from commerce (Bowie 1999). However, these seem to rely on consequentialist arguments. In the first of three examples, Bowie describes how he observed bad checks posted on a wall at a restaurant; that restaurant, he points out, no longer accepts *any* checks. In another example, drawn from Poland, he relates how he learned of a bank failure caused by many people taking out loans and not paying them back. Finally, he reports the testimony of economists who claim that Hong Kong will not remain a central worldwide hub of finance unless China supports Hong Kong's long-standing tradition of strictly upholding the laws. From these examples, Bowie argues, "If a maxim for an action when universalized is self-defeating, then the contemplated action is not ethical. That is Kant's conceptual point. And when enough people behave immorally in that sense, certain business practices like the use of checks or credit become impossible" (Bowie 1999: 20). However, each of these examples seems to point out a conditional consequent that we want (to write checks, receive loans, conduct business in Hong Kong), and then argues in reverse that if we seek to maintain these desirable goods, then we shouldn't engage in certain actions (writing bad checks, reneging on loans, or disregarding the tradition of law in Hong Kong). This exemplifies consequentialist reasoning: we shouldn't write bad checks because we enjoy the option of writing checks, and so on. Bowie, like Kant, wants the ethical principles to be based in reason, and kept formal, but his illustrative argument seems to slip into the reality of the empirical and to employ tacitly a consequentialist mode of reasoning. (For a defense of Kant against consequentialist readings, see Kirstein 2005: 139–55, as well as the discussion in Timmermann 2007: 161–3 and 2014).

A social contract approach to business ethics

Donaldson and Dunfee's *Ties that Bind* (1999) is the classic contractarian approach to business ethics. Donaldson and Dunfee hold that while ethical attitudes and cultural expectations may develop and change over time, there are transcultural concepts that do not. For example, what is considered to be irresponsible polluting may shift or adjust according to the culture, but certain macro-concepts, such as the dignity of all persons, remain constant and serve, thereby, as stable boundaries (or "hypernorms") for the micro-concepts of a culture (Donaldson and Dunfee 1999). Because societies do have these macro-concepts or hypernorms, contractualism then attempts to acknowledge the importance of shifting values and expectations, while not slipping into mere cultural relativism. The hypernorms for society (and thus business) can be "discerned" according to Donaldson and Dunfee, by observing whether particular characteristics feature in some norm. Such features might include widespread consensus, support by industry, NGOs, government groups, consistency with the laws of many countries, and so forth (Donaldson 1999).

Non-contractarians generally find a few things problematic about social contract theory. First, it is doubly hypothetical—a hypothetical conclusion of a hypothetical meeting of all involved. All involved did not get together, and no decision was actually made, but through thoughtful reason (if not conjecture) the parties come up with binding rules for morality. One is reminded of Ronald Dworkin's famous objection to social contract theory that a doubly hypothetical agreement cannot bind any actual person (Dworkin 1975: 18). Feminists like Alison Jaggar claim that the hyper-idealization of the hypothetical actors in the hypothetical agreement discounts the concrete differences among people, and particularly ignores those special concerns of the disenfranchised (Jaggar 1989: 91). Amartya Sen has argued that social contract theory spends far too much time imagining what an ideal world should look like, and has very little concrete advice to alleviate the social ills of the actual world (Sen 2009: 53).

But these criticisms are in some ways misplaced. For one thing there is a concern for the disenfranchised in the work of Rawls, and especially in the work of Nien-hê Hsieh (2004), among others. And Donaldson has done careful work trying to show that universal trans-cultural values might be distinguished from mere cultural ones—and his distinction between conflicts of development and conflicts of tradition is helpful (Donaldson 1996). More often than not the arguments rest on some suggested basic principles, rooted in supposedly shared intuitions about how we want the world to be, or what seems right to us.

Certainly the social contract approach has done a great deal to help businesses consider the notion of social responsibility. Although that notion remains popular, there are many who find it to be a category mistake: companies, these critics say, are not the sorts of beings that can have "social responsibility"—only people can have social responsibilities (see, for example, Friedman 1970). In addition, utilitarians will see in social contract arguments appeals to outcomes that seem thoroughly concerned with the greater happiness of the many—in other words, social contract arguments can be seen as a species of utilitarianism that takes individual rights as basic to the happiness-producing capacity of a society in general.

The virtue approach in business ethics

Robert Solomon (1993) and many others have worked to develop this approach, which has generally followed the more general revival of virtue theory in philosophy. Solomon's book *Ethics and Excellence* (1993), as well as his more popular *A Better Way to Think About Business* (1999), were landmark books for virtue ethics business ethicists. Virtue ethicists such as Solomon usually rely on the Greek philosopher Aristotle. In short, their view is that business, as a part of our social lives, is about more than money—one must think of one's practices in business as an essential part of living the good life. A flourishing or excellent life will bring fulfillment and deep satisfaction. But an excellent life is not simply making the most money possible, and in business we must remember this as well, according to the virtue ethicists. As Solomon puts it, "Business is about integrity as well as profits, and the profits mean little if their cost sacrifices integrity . . . Business serves people and not the other way around, and it is value and virtue that make business life rewarding and meaningful" (Solomon 1999: xiii).

Virtue ethics is a powerful theory of personal moral development. It does not allow us to bifurcate our personal and business values, but regards virtuous business practices as an essential aspect of a flourishing life. Recent work applying virtue ethics to business include the historical and broadly interdisciplinary account of Deirdre McCloskey (2006), as well as Alejo José Sison's *Happiness and Virtue Ethics in Business: The Ultimate Value Proposition* (2014), in which he suggests ways for businesses to cultivate the virtues of their employees, and argues that pursuing virtue will bring about the greatest business value. A typical criticism of virtue ethics is that it is difficult to see how to apply it practically in the business world but Edwin Hartman's *Virtue in Business: Conversations with Aristotle* (2015) does an admirable job of applying virtue ethics to business practice in concrete ways. Both Sison and Hartman's works also interact with the field of moral psychology, which is essential.

Consequentialism in business ethics (utilitarianism)

Academically, utilitarianism is the leading consequentialist ethical theory, yet in the business ethics literature utilitarianism almost always plays the role of foil—the appropriate object of criticism and response.[2] There are few contemporary business ethicists who show any interest in supporting a utilitarian business ethics.[3] This is perhaps because there are indeed so many economists who promote what is often called a utilitarian calculus by which business should make choices according to what will bring about the greatest social utility, as determined in purely economic terms. This economic utilitarianism is often cast by stakeholder business ethicists in an unfavorable light in relationship to business ethics: market utilitarianism is seen to be in favor of "policies that deregulate private industry, protect property rights, allow for free exchanges, and encourage competition" and on this economic utilitarian view "Efficiency is simply another word for maximizing happiness" (DesJardin 2013: 35).

Clearly at a popular level "utilitarian" has come to mean something like "concerned not with aesthetic or other such values, but with least-expensive effectiveness" as in "we chose our car based on utilitarian reasons—it's no Lexus, but it was inexpensive and it gets us from point A to point B." However, there is much more to utilitarianism than efficiency, or, even more crudely, financial efficiency, although some of the criticisms of utilitarianism in the business ethics literature fail to see this.

But how does utilitarianism apply to business? What kind of ethical direction can a mandate to seek pleasure and avoid pain provide to business practice? We know that a fundamental principle of Mill's utilitarianism is that we contribute to the greater happiness and to sustaining a happiness-producing society. We should do this impartially, not giving special concern to ourselves, but considering all with equal weight when making a judgment. Even our discussions of justice and what rights one should be granted are based on concerns for utility, or the greater happiness—which is why Mill wrote the classic work *On Liberty*, arguing that a society that protects individual liberty against the tyranny of the masses will actually provide the greatest possibility of happiness

We see this already in our laws. We take drivers' licenses away from people who get too many speeding tickets, because their speeding is considered a danger to society. We take away people's freedom and put them in jail when they commit crimes that pose a great threat to society. We give people citizenship in our country when they demonstrate some concern and respect for others in the country, and some willingness to contribute to the general happiness of society by paying taxes, being good citizens, etc. We grant people freedom to vote, own land, have guns, trade stocks, run companies, and all sorts of freedoms so long as they do not use these freedoms against the greater happiness of society. In the United States, the Sarbanes-Oxley legislation (2002) specifically provides for the possibility that the Securities and Exchange Commission (SEC) can bar unfit executives and limit pay, among other legal provisos. The fundamental argument for this power to take away freedom is that the greater happiness of society is being protected. Other acts of legislation, across a variety of nations, are undertaken with an appeal to the public welfare or the greater happiness.

If one wants to develop a utilitarian business ethics approach, it seems that the best candidate would be a rule-utilitarianism that acknowledges qualitative distinctions of pleasure and upholds principles of justice, fairness, and liberty. Such an approach can not only bring about an environment more capable of enabling happiness (than a market or society that does not uphold justice, fairness and liberty), and it has the advantages of helping determine the right rules of conduct and of providing reasons that are broadly compelling to our basic desire for good overall outcomes.

With respect to business practices, the utilitarian approach can be adopted at three different levels: a) the individual level, guiding personal business practices towards others; b) the corporate level, giving direction to company policies that affect the greater happiness of those inside the company; and c) the macro level, considering the effect of the company on the greater happiness of society. A utilitarianism properly understood could be quite adept at providing ethical support and guidance for many aspects of business practices at the individual, corporate, and macro levels. Adopting the utilitarian approach at each of these levels, one can then grasp how utilitarianism might provide a basis by which to address the following questions or concerns.

1. For the business firm, which rules or virtues provide a plausible path to greater happiness? A company run on Mill's utilitarian ethics will be managed by principles of justice, fairness, honesty, and integrity, and together these principles should provide more happiness to stakeholders as well as to their communities. Employees are treated fairly, stockholders are not swindled by dishonest executives, and suppliers and customers are able to trust the company to provide a good product or service at a fair price.
2. What are my personal obligations to others? Business practice conducted according to established rules made on the basis of a concern for the greater happiness provides the conditions for thoughtfully considering personal obligations to others, to duties, and to any specific rights that we should respect.
3. Within the firm, are there reasons to offer particular recognition to specific groups or to encourage diversity? A utilitarian-run business may find a basis to support the concerns of minority viewpoints and liberties, and to prohibit discrimination insofar as Mill's utilitarianism sees diversity and support of individual liberty to be the basis of a happier community. (Mill, of course, is more concerned with diversity of opinion and lifestyle and political voice in society, not race or gender diversity in firms).
4. How can a business value dignity? A company run for the sake of the greater happiness will consider the relative contribution to the firm of its employees (necessary for determining promotions and salary increases) and provide a basis for valuing and encouraging the dignity of individuals (on the importance of dignity to Mill's utilitarianism, see Capaldi 2017). Because of this, utilitarianism provides an ethic for workplace management that makes sense in decision making.
5. What sort of culture should a company cultivate? Because utilitarianism embraces a cohesive social community as the basis of all decision making, it emphasizes the importance of corporate vision and corporate culture as the foundation of ethical behavior in the workplace.

6   What are our corporate social responsibilities? It seems natural for a company that is run with a concern for the greatest happiness to be concerned about its social responsibility, but, given various and sometimes ill-defined appeals to CSR, a utilitarian would want to see clear social benefit, not mere window dressing, nor would a utilitarian suffer pressures to submit to an ideology that didn't actually provide social benefit.

7   What are the effects of our actions, corporate or individual, on the natural environment? A utilitarian concern for the greatest happiness helps establish a broader conception of the effects of our actions that may even include those who in the future will face the environmental effects of our behaviors today.

Concluding remarks

We have examined the typical consequentialist and non-consequentialist ethical theories, addressed some criticisms and responses, and considered the ways that consequentialism and non-consequentialism, typically construed, have been utilized in business ethics. In his great work, *On Liberty* John Stuart Mill wrote that it is essential to constantly be challenged with atypical positions because, if that new stance is right, then one has a chance to exchange error for truth; if the atypical view is wrong, there will be a "clearer perception and livelier impression of truth, produced by its collision with error" (Mill 2002: 75). With this in mind, I have two concluding comments. I suggest, first, that many if not all views of non-consequentialism can be ultimately reduced to consequentialism. We can call this viewpoint reductive consequentialism. Second, I highlight some recent work of the market failures approach of Joseph Heath as a type of consequentialism that I believe to be crypto-utilitarian as well.

Recently Philip Pettit has argued for "the inescapability of consequentialism" (Pettit 2012); he is not the only one to think that most ethical theories in the end depend on consequentialism (Sosa 1993; Portmore 2009; Dreier 2011). Consequentialists actually have a long history of regarding non-consequentialism as not possible, or, perhaps more positively, of thinking that even though non-consequentialists *believe* they are not consequentialists, they in fact are. (Of course this is not accepted by most Kantians, see, for example, Timmerman 2014.) Mill actually claimed Kant was a consequentialist who didn't realize it, because ultimately in Mill's eyes, "All he [Kant] shows is that the consequences of their universal adoption would be such as no one would choose to incur." (Mill 1998: 1.4.32). On Mill's reading, Kant turns out to be a rule-utilitarian, because universalizing "bad" maxims, more often than not, results in consequences we would not desire, not consequences that are, in some sense, contradictory or impossible.

Although contractarians like Rawls reject aspects of utilitarianism, ultimately they are concerned about consequences. Hobbes argues for the Leviathan due to its efficacy. And contractarians from Rawls to Scanlon (1998) have since argued for or against various political structures or rules based on what the consequences of those structures or rules would be. If it is true that contractualism is a form of forced-negotiation egoism, by which one must compromise and try to get the best deal possible through a social contract, then contractualism certainly seems to be a consequentialist ethic.

Virtue ethics can be conceived as a consequentialist ethic, insofar as it is teleological. In Aristotle we find little concern for society except insofar as it is important for me to fulfill my own potential as a social being. Self-sacrifice is not promoted, except insofar as it will gain one honor in a noble death. Quite clearly virtue ethics for Aristotle has a consequence or aim—happiness—in the broad sense of that word. Aristotle's deep understanding of the relation between behavior and habit influenced Mill, and it is no surprise that the author who cited Christian and Stoic authors, as well as Epicurus (1998: 2.4. 1–20), had read the works of Aristotle long before he read the works of Bentham. Mill's utilitarianism brought a broader and deeper conception of social happiness into the utilitarian calculus, thanks, in no small part, to Aristotle.

Second, an interesting recent example of a consequentialist approach to business ethics is Joseph Heath's market failures approach (Heath 2013, 2014). He attempts to derive ethical rules or limits for business practice from the pursuit of a healthy market efficiency itself, rather than to impose it from everyday morality, which may not always usefully apply to business. Market efficiency and the avoidance of market failures are fundamental: to profit from market failures is "morally objectionable, not because it violates some duty of loyalty to the customer (as stakeholder theory would have it), but because it undermines the social benefits that justify the profit orientation in first place" (Heath 2014: 88–89). The market-failures approach urges businesspersons to maintain a healthy market, not to exploit or corrupt it. Specifically, in addition to obeying laws enacted to protect the general good of society, individuals and companies need to follow ethical imperatives such as these: to minimize negative externalities; to reduce information asymmetries; and, among other imperatives, to refrain from opposing appropriate regulation aimed at correcting market imperfections, and to shun the imposition of protectionist measures or the establishment of barriers to market competition. In short, Heath says, "If all companies fully internalized all costs, and charged consumers the full price that the production of their goods imposed upon society, I believe it would be impossible to make the case for any further 'social responsibility' with respect to the environment" (Heath 2014: 90).

Heath obviously has a consequence in mind that guides his theory of business practice, namely, Pareto-optimal markets. It is hard to pin down what the underlying justification is for the market-failures approach other than that it will lead to Pareto-optimal markets in theory, which would provide more balanced outcomes for everyone—specifically, a state of affairs in which resources are allocated in such a way that it is impossible to make any one better off without making another worse off. It appears that the market failure approach is crypto-utilitarian, if the reason for pursuit of Pareto-optimality is that it is in the end best for the overall market (the many).

Non-consequentialists are convinced that there must be transcendent truths such as rules, principles or rights that can be established and maintained without reference to consequences. Consequentialists believe that such rules, principles and rights can be grounded only on the basis of consequences. It is a wonderful world we live in where we find so many different approaches trying to discover the excellent, good and right ways to practice business. For some, responsibility, duty, and reason are the basis of business ethics. For others rights, justice, and social responsibility are the essentials. The virtue ethicists believe excellence, virtue, and flourishing provide the best tools for thinking about business. And the utilitarians believe the pursuit of the greatest happiness for the many is the most cogent and best means to conceive of ethical business. Although there are clearly distinctions between these varieties, they all have in common a pursuit of ethical business practices.

Essential readings

The essential readings in consequentialism and non-consequentialism include the classic texts of John Stuart Mill, *Utilitarianism* (1998 [1861]), and Immanuel Kant (2012 [1785]), *Groundwork of the Metaphysics of Morals*. For contemporary discussion, see J.J.C. Smart and Bernard Williams, *Utilitarianism: For and Against* (1973); Samuel Scheffler, *Consequentialism and Its Critics* (1988); and Julia Driver, *Consequentialism* (2012). For applications to business ethics, one may consult Jeffery

Smith (ed.) *Normative Theory and Business Ethics* (2008); Dennis Arnold and Jarred Harris (eds) *Kantian Business Ethics* (2012); and Andrew Gustafson, "In Defense of a Utilitarian Business Ethic" (2013).

For further reading in this volume on utilitarian thinkers and their conceptions of business, see Chapter 2, Theorists and philosophers on business ethics. On common sense moral intuitions, moral awareness, and moral blindness, see Chapter 4, Teaching business ethics. On the relation of moral theories and management theories, see Chapter 26, Theoretical issues in management ethics. On economic analysis and its implications for corporate conduct (including the "market failures" approach to business ethics), see Chapter 17, The contribution of economics to business ethics.

Notes

1 Bentham's earliest writings emphasize this majoritarian element. In his essay of 1774, "A Comment on the Commentaries and A Fragment on Government," he defines utilitarianism as a "fundamental axiom, it is the greatest happiness of the greatest number that is the measure of right and wrong" (Bentham 1977 [1774]: 393). For more on the importance of happiness for the greatest number in Bentham see J.H. Burns 2005.
2 In the recent book *Normative Theory and Business Ethics* (Smith 2008) utilitarianism did not even merit an essay, although it was criticized in many of the papers included.
3 Exceptions would be Thomas Jones and Will Felps (2013), William Shaw (1999), the current author (2013), and other "stealth utilitarians" who at times advocate utilitarianism (see Boatright 2006).

References

Anscombe, E. (1958). "Modern Moral Philosophy," *Philosophy* 33:124, 1–16.
Aquinas, St. T. (2000) [thirteenth century CE]. *Treatise on Law*, Richard Regan (trans.), Indianapolis, IN: Hackett Publishing.
Aristotle (2014) [fifth century BCE]. *Nicomachean Ethics*, Roger Crisp (ed. and trans.). Cambridge: Cambridge University Press.
Arnold, D. and J. Harris (eds) (2012). *Kantian Business Ethics: Critical Perspectives*. Northampton, MA: Edward Elgar Press.
Bentham, J. (1977) [1774]. "A Comment on the Commentaries and A Fragment on Government," in J.H. Burns and H.L.A. Hart (eds), *The Collected Works of Jeremy Bentham*. Oxford: Oxford University Press, 3–351.
Boatright, J. (2006). "What's Wrong—and What's Right—with Stakeholder Management," *Journal of Private Enterprise* 22.2, 106–130.
Bowie, N. (1999). *Business Ethics: A Kantian Perspective*. New York: Riley-Blackwell.
Bowie, N. (1991). "Challenging the Egoistic Paradigm," *Business Ethics Quarterly* 1:1, 1–21.
Bowie, N. (2017). "Why Kant's Insistence on Purity of the Will Does Not Preclude an Application of Kant's Ethics to For-Profit Businesses," in E. Heath and B. Kaldis (eds), *Wealth, Commerce, and Philosophy: Foundational Thinkers and Business Ethics*. Chicago, IL: University of Chicago Press, 263–281.
Burns, J.H. (2005). "Happiness and Utility: Jeremy Bentham's Equation," *Utilitas* 17:1 46-61.
Capaldi, N. (2017). "J.S. Mill and Business Ethics," in E. Heath and B. Kaldis (eds), *Wealth, Commerce, and Philosophy: Foundational Thinkers on Business Ethics*. Chicago, IL: University of Chicago Press, 301–320.
Cummiskey, D. (1996). *Kantian Consequentialism*. New York: Oxford University Press.
Desjardins, J. (2013). *An Introduction to Business Ethics*. New York: McGraw-Hill.
Donaldson, T. (1996). "Values in Tension: Ethics Away from Home," *Harvard Business Review* Sept/Oct, 48–62.
Donaldson, T. and T. Dunfee (1999). *Ties that Bind: A Social Contract Approach to Business Ethics*. Boston, MA: Harvard Business Press.
Dreier, J. (2011). "In Defense of Consequentializing," in M. Timmons (ed.), *Oxford Studies in Normative Ethics*. Oxford: Oxford University Press, 97–11.
Driver, J. (2012). *Consequentialism*. New York: Routledge.

Duska, R. (2009). "Revisiting the Egoism Question in Business," in Dennis Arnold and Jarred Harris (eds), *Kantian Business Ethics*. Northampton, MA: Edward Elgar, 18–34.

Dworkin, R. (1975). "The Original Position" in N. Daniels (ed.), *Reading Rawls*. Oxford: Basil Blackwell, 16–52.

Friedman, M. (1970). "The Social Responsibility of Business Is to Increase Its Profits," *New York Times Magazine* (September 13).

Gauthier, D. (1986). *Morals by Agreement*. Oxford: Oxford University Press.

Gustafson, A. (2013). "In Defense of a Utilitarian Business Ethic," *Business and Society Review* 118:3, 325–360.

Hartman, E. (2015). *Virtue in Business: Conversations with Aristotle*. Cambridge: Cambridge University Press.

Heath, J. (2013). "Market Failure or Government Failure? A Response to Jaworski," in *Business Ethics Journal Review* 1:8, 50–56.

Heath, J. (2014). *Morality, Competition, and the Firm: The Market Failures Approach to Business Ethics*. Oxford: Oxford University Press.

Hobbes, T. (1994) [1651]. *Leviathan*. Indiana, IN: Hackett.

Hsieh, N. (2004). "The Obligations of Transnational Corporations: Rawlsian Justice and the Duty of Assistance," *Business Ethics Quarterly* 14:4, 643–661.

Hutcheson, F. (2003) [1728]. *An Essay On the Nature and Conduct of the Passions and Affections: With Illustrations On the Moral Sense*, Knud Haakonssen (ed.). Indianapolis: Liberty Fund.

Jaggar, A. (1999). "Feminist Ethics: Some Issues for the Nineties," *Journal of Social Philosophy* 20:1–2, 91–107.

Jones, T. and W. Felps (2013). "Stakeholder Happiness Enhancement: A Neo-Utilitarian Objective for the Modern Corporation," *Business Ethics Quarterly* 23:3 349–379.

Kant, I. (2012) [1785]. *Groundwork of the Metaphysics of Morals*, Mary Gregor and Jens Timmermann (trans.). Cambridge: Cambridge University Press.

Kirstein, S.J. (2005). *Kant's Search for the Supreme Principle of Morality*. Cambridge: Cambridge University Press.

Korsgaard, C. (1996). *Sources of Normativity*. Cambridge: Cambridge University Press.

Langtry, B. (1994). "Stakeholders and the Moral Responsibilities of Business," *Business Ethics Quarterly* 4:4, 431–443.

MacIntyre, A. (1981). *After Virtue: A Study in Moral Theory*. Notre Dame: University of Notre Dame Press.

McCloskey, D. (2006). *The Bourgeois Virtues: Ethics for an Age of Commerce*. Chicago, IL: University of Chicago Press.

Mill, J.S. (1998) [1861]. *Utilitarianism*, R. Crisp (ed.). New York: Oxford University Press.

Mill, J.S. (2002) [1859]. *On Liberty*. New York: Dover.

Miller, D. (2011). "Mill, Rule Utilitarianism, and the Incoherence Objection," in B. Eggleston, D. Miller and D. Weinstein. (eds), *John Stuart Mill and the Art of Life*. New York: Oxford University Press, 94–118.

Pettit, P. (2012). "The Inescapability of Consequentialism," in U. Huer and G. Lang (eds), *Luck, Value, and Commitment: Themes from the Ethics of Bernard Williams*. New York: Oxford University Press, 41–70.

Plato (1974) [fourth century BCE]. *The Republic*, G.M.A. Grube (trans.). Indianapolis, IN: Hackett Publishing.

Portmore, D.W. (2009). "Consequentializing," *Philosophy Compass* 4:2, 329–47.

Rand, A. (1964). *The Virtue of Selfishness*. New York: Signet.

Rand, A. (1989). *The Voice of Reason: Essays in Objectivist Thought*, L. Peikoff (ed.). New York: New American Library.

Rasmussen, D. and D. Den Uyl (1987). *The Philosophic Thought of Ayn Rand*. Champaign, IL: University of Illinois Press.

Rawls, J. (1971). *A Theory of Justice*. Boston, MA: Belknap Press.

Ross, W.D. (1965). *The Right and the Good*. Oxford: Clarendon Press.

Scanlon, T.M. (1998). *What We Owe to Each Other*. Cambridge, MA: Belknap Press of Harvard University Press.

Scheffler, S. (1982). *The Rejection of Consequentialism*. Oxford: Clarendon Press.

Scheffler, S. (1988). *Consequentialism and Its Critics*. New York: Oxford University Press.

Scotus, D. (1986) [thirteenth century BCE]. *On the Will and Morality*, Allan B. Wolte (trans.). Washington, DC: Catholic University of America Press.

Sen, A. (2009). *The Idea of Justice*. Boston, MA: Belknap Press of Harvard University.

Shaw, W. (1999). *Contemporary Ethics: Taking Account of Utilitarianism*. Malden, MA: Blackwell.
Sison, A.J. (2014). *Happiness and Virtue Ethics in Business: The Ultimate Value Proposition*. Cambridge: Cambridge University Press.
Smart, J.J.C. and B. Williams (1973). *Utilitarianism: For and Against*. New York: Cambridge University Press.
Smith, J. (ed.) (2008). *Normative Theory and Business Ethics*. Lanham, MD: Rowman and Littlefield Press.
Smith, T. (2006). *Ayn Rand's Normative Ethics: The Virtuous Egoist*. New York: Cambridge University Press.
Solomon, R. (1993). *Excellence and Ethics: Cooperation and Integrity in Business*. New York: Oxford University Press.
Solomon, R. (1999). *A Better Way to Think About Ethics: How Personal Integrity Leads to Corporate Success*. New York: Oxford University Press.
Sosa, D. (1993). "Consequences of Consequentialism," *Mind* 102:405, 101–22.
Timmermann, J. (2007). *Kant's Groundwork of the Metaphysics of Morals: A Commentary*. Cambridge: Cambridge University Press.
Timmermann, J. (2014). "Kantian Ethics and Utilitarianism," in B. Eggleston and D. E. Miller (eds), *The Cambridge Companion to Utilitarianism*. Cambridge: Cambridge University Press.
Wood, A. (2007). *Kantian Ethics*. New York: Cambridge University Press.

6
Social contract theories

*Pedro Francés-Gómez**

Originating in the works of political philosophers such as Thomas Hobbes, John Locke and Jean-Jacques Rousseau, the modern social contract tradition received renewed attention in the twentieth century in the works of James Buchanan (1975), John Rawls (1971) and David Gauthier (1986). The underlying idea is that practical authority must ultimately be derived from individual consent. Contractarian business ethics (henceforth, CBE) takes classical and contemporary theories of social contract as models for normative business ethics theory. This chapter covers the tradition of contractarian business ethics from the appearance of Thomas Donaldson's *Corporations and Morality* (1982) to current debates.

Before delving into this "tradition" of business ethics, a brief taxonomy of social contract theories and their employments in business ethics is presented. After this initial roadmap of the territory, the chapter turns to the justifications of the social contract in business ethics. The third section sets forth the major elements common to CBE theories. The subsequent section focuses on the influential theory of Thomas Donaldson and Thomas Dunfee, the Integrative Social Contracts Theory, followed by section five that is devoted to developments and criticisms of this theory. A sixth section summarizes other approaches to CBE. A concluding section summarizes significant critical stances towards CBE and indicates new directions of inquiry within the tradition.

A taxonomy of social contract approaches

The general idea of the social contract in ethics is that a certain prescription is morally obligatory for the agent if it derives from an agreement to which the agent herself can rationally consent. The first distinction is between actual and hypothetical contracts. Within actual contracts, consent may be explicit (as when an employee signs a code of ethical conduct as part of her contract with a company) or implicit. If implicit, the will of the consenting party must be inferred from her conduct: for example, acquiescence to company (or market customary) attitudes and behavior, willing participation in certain benefits, and so on. Hypothetical consent refers to the agreement that the agent would have found rational to accept in an imaginary *ex ante* situation. The so-called "original position" is often imagined as an earlier time when relevant conventional norms did not exist, and knowledge about individual real circumstances was null or limited.

Most social contract theories in political and moral philosophy are of the hypothetical variety (Kersting 1994). In this way, the social contract works like a mental experiment that helps us to understand the demands of practical reason in relation to a certain normative question: what are the limits of state authority? What is a just society? In business ethics the normative questions may be, for example: What is the ethical basis of economic activity in general? What are the moral rules for international commerce? How should a corporation be governed?

Both actual and hypothetical social contract theories assume that normative authority derives from the consent of individuals. One crucial difference is that actual consent can be revoked or reversed as a matter of fact, while hypothetical consent, as an attempt to capture the demands of reason, is thought to represent unchangeable principles.

Based on the work of Harvard philosopher Thomas Scanlon (1998), social contract theories have come to be described as "contract*ual*" or "contract*arian*" (Ashford and Mulgan 2012). The contractarian version of the social contract, which assumes that individual rationality equates to self-interest, tries to derive morality out of an agreement among self-interested agents (Gauthier 1986). On the other hand, the contractual version, drawing upon Kant's account of the social contract, assumes that moral agreement is based on mutual recognition as rational autonomous agents sharing basic moral capacities.

Within the territory of business ethics, the social contract typically adopts at least three forms that differ according to who are the parties to the agreement and what the object of agreement is about:

1 the agreement among all citizens by which the basic institutions of society are created or authorized;
2 the agreement between the corporate world as a whole and the civil society as to the rights and duties of the corporation and the society;
3 the agreement among prospective constituents of a business firm to create that particular organization and its basic governance principles.

According to version 1, a social contract may include businesses and markets as basic social or legal institutions; this contract would specify the normative framework for these institutions, including the ethical framework. Businesses and their market activities are in this case the *object* of agreement. In version 2, there is a reciprocal relationship between civil society and businesses: civil society gives businesses legitimacy and—through the legal system—protection of private property; in turn, businesses deliver goods and services, jobs, and public revenue through taxes. However, in version 3 the general framework of free market and capitalism is taken for granted. In this context, the question is whether and under which conditions individual agents would agree to create hierarchical organizations for economic purposes. The idea is that business firms, and in particular large corporations, are the product of an original contract among all the parties involved, that is, all stakeholders.

The social contract in business—in any of these versions—has been used to lend support to normative stakeholder theory (Mansell 2013). However, there is no logical connection between the social contract argument and the stakeholder approach to management (Boatright 2000). Contractarian business ethics may be supportive of any approach to management, or it may be neutral. In fact, social-contract scholars *tend* to support stakeholder theory, and Edward Freeman has employed Rawlsian notions of contract to defend his view about the corporation (Freeman 1994; Freeman and Evan 1990).

Finally, Gjalt De Graaf (2006) introduced a distinction between *constitutive* and *heuristic* uses of the social contract. The constitutive use assumes that moral obligations are established by the social contract. This would be obvious in actual social contracts, and less so in hypothetical versions. The heuristic use takes the social contract as an epistemic tool: it helps us to discover or clarify our obligations, but it does not purport to explain or justify their origin.

These distinctions are often blurred. It would be impossible to find one theory that can be squarely classified in one side of each of the several taxonomies. However, these distinctions may be useful in describing the approaches below.

Justification of the social contract theory of business ethics

The first question about the application of the social contract to business ethics is: Why is this philosophical foundation to be preferred to other moral theories? Scholars in the field usually refer to four types of reasons.

1. The poor results obtained by other moral theories when applied to business ethics.
2. The strong analogy between large corporations and the modern state (itself the primary object of the social contract arguments).
3. The potential of the social contract theory as the normative core of stakeholder theory.
4. The fact that the method and premises of the social contract argument draw upon familiar economic concepts.

Theme 1 is mentioned by Dunfee and Donaldson (1995). The difficulties the (non-contractarian) approaches encounter in the field of business ethics are due to the "artifactual" and plural nature of modern corporations. Ethical theories were developed to deal with "natural" ways of life. This is why an attempt to apply broad ethical theories to "hard-core business problems, such as nepotism, bribery in Third World cultures, drug-testing, or insider trading, usually reach vague, unsatisfying conclusions" (Dunfee and Donaldson 1995, 173; see also Freeman 1994, 415).

Theme 2 focuses on the size and power of large corporations, their potential impact on the lives of millions, their bureaucratic nature and hierarchical structure. The exercise of power in the corporate context is analogous to the political exercise of power—in fact, according to the defenders of a "political" view of business ethics, corporate power is just one form of political power (Heath et al. 2010). This power is exercised over subjects that may not share a single view of the good life; in fact, they may not share the same culture, language, religion, etc. However, they are supposed to accept the legitimacy of their superiors' commands and behave cooperatively in order to produce a certain collective result. The need for justification of the power exercised by and within these organizations is thought to be analogous to the need of justification of the political power of the modern state. The social contract is the model of justification of the modern state, therefore it suggests itself as a model for the justification of the power of large corporations.

Surely smaller companies are not analogous to modern states in the same way. However, the analogy is frequently extended, stressing that medium-sized enterprises are the daily arena of truly "political" struggles around issues like gender discrimination, cultural diversity accommodation, distribution of cooperatively-generated wealth, respect of labor and other individual rights, etc.

Along with analogies, there exist differences. Above all, the state is the supreme social institution. Remove the state and you get an anarchic "state of nature." Therefore, the state must establish its own sovereignty. Firms, on the contrary, operate in a (more or less stable and legitimate) legal environment. You may very well remove one or all firms, and no anarchy ensues. The social-contract theorists generally argue that the analogies are sufficient to warrant the importation of the method from political philosophy. Taking as the main object of business ethics the large publicly owned corporation operating at a global level serves to reinforce the analogy (and the argument). Therefore, CBE is often presented as a philosophical argument for (or against) the legitimacy of large corporations.

Theme 3 has been emphasized by Freeman (1994) but also by others (Donaldson and Dunfee 1999; Sacconi 2011a; Phillips 2003). Of the three branches of stakeholder theory—instrumental, descriptive and normative (Donaldson and Preston 1995)—it is the normative that concerns us here: stakeholders of the firm are entitled to a fiduciary relationship with the management analogous to the relationship that legally exists between shareholders and management. This claim runs counter to the formal definition of firms in most legal systems, and its usage gives rise to serious debate (Marcoux 2003; Mansell 2013). Defenders of stakeholder theory, therefore, would need a re-definition of the firm (Post et al. 2002). At this point, a heuristic use of the social contract might help to check whether a group of independent and rational agents would or would not consent to the sort of legal and economic system that gives shareholders the prerogatives they actually enjoy. Of course, it may be entirely possible that rational agents would *reject* stakeholding and choose exactly the economic system we now have, corporate law included. But the stakeholder theorist trusts that rational agreement would not legitimize the *status quo*.

Finally, reasons included in theme 4 have been put forward by contractarian scholars such as Lütge (2005, 2012b). Lütge stresses the fact that contractarianism requires weaker premises than any other philosophical foundation of business ethics, and those premises are common to the economic theory of rationality. His sort of contractarianism takes individual self-interest as the only normative premise. Lütge concurs with Heugens et al. (2006) that a contract approach is the natural one in the realm of business, where "contractual obligation" is a well-understood notion. Additionally, some of the work in CBE is done by using the tools of economics—game theory in particular (Binmore 1999).

A further related reason is that CBE is liable to some form of empirical validation (Dunfee and Donaldson 1995; Heugens et al. 2006). Empirical tests of normative theories may not be obvious, but a well-defined social contract theory must make some empirical assumptions about how individuals would behave in certain circumstances. Empirical discoveries can potentially support or falsify the theory or some of its premises (Faillo et al. 2015; Francés-Gómez et al. 2015).

How does it work? The elements of CBE

CBE comes in a variety of forms. It is worth having a statement of the standard way to understand the idea of a social contract of business. This section deals first with the CBE as a general method for business ethics, and then explains the key contractarian elements: the idea of a state of nature, or original position; individual rationality and rational agreement by unanimous consent; the content of agreement; the basic normative content of CBE theories; and the issue of compliance.

The social contract as a method of business ethics

The social contract can be seen as a method of ethics (Donaldson 1982: 39), a way to justify ethical norms. Dunfee and Donaldson (1995: 178) dubbed it a "critical theoretical tool."

As a method, it has its rules. Ben Wempe (2005) argues that it has been used with little discipline and rigor in our field—although recent work by Lorenzo Sacconi (2011a, 2011b), Christoph Lütge (2015), as well as John Bishop (2008), represent an effort to discipline CBE. According to Wempe's analysis, the argument should describe with precision,

1   the level of justification: rational or moral, universal or local;
2   the object of justification: a certain business conduct, rules of corporate governance, the governance scheme of a particular organization, corporations in general, and so forth;
3   the addressees of justification: all affected by the norm or institution, the public in general, the members of a certain organization, members of a certain community, and so forth.

Once these questions are clear, the social contract argument should be loyal to its internal logic, as defined by the premises and logical steps we describe below. In this logic, the key element is consent: "Consent is the justificatory linchpin of any social contract method, whether the contract proposed is hypothetical or real" (Dunfee and Donaldson 1995: 179).

The state of nature

Common to any description of the state of nature is the idea that the *status quo* represents a sub-optimal state. In Paretian terms, no person in the state of nature has anything to lose by shifting to a "social state." If any individual would be made worse off by such a shift, then that would make unanimity, the only possible decision rule for an *original* contract, impossible. After all, if the original state were *Pareto-optimal*, there would exist no reason to abandon it, even if that state were unfair for a majority.

In CBE the "state of nature" was defined by Donaldson (1982) as a state of "individual production" inferior to a state in which all agree to allow the existence of firms provided that they respect employees' and consumer's rights. Agents in the state of individual production see themselves primarily as *potential* employees and consumers. Donaldson's characterization of the state of individual production sets the standard for Rawlsian theories in business. Other common ways of imagining what the business state of nature looks like is to think of it as a state in which market failures prevail (Lütge 2015; Child and Marcoux 1999) or as one beset with transaction costs (Sacconi 2000). Freeman (1994) models his theory of "Fair Contracts" after Rawls', and seems to accept Donaldson's view of the state of nature as one with no or little value creation through business organizations. These accounts describe a real or fictional situation in which business transactions are less than efficient, so that all involved would benefit from agreeing to adopt new norms or institutions.

Individual rationality and agreement

The state of nature invites the construction of a cooperative scheme. By definition, in the hypothetical state of nature the social norms we seek to justify are absent; only individual will and individual rationality, operating through mutual consent, can be used as the cement of new societal schemes. An agreement among equals is the only way out. The same idea works in actual social contracts, with the exception that social rules may exist. Sometimes they make possible the new normative structure created by the contract.

According to the logic of the social contract, the parties in the original position engage in a process—it may be bargaining or deliberation—in order to agree on a cooperative scheme. The rules of this negotiation vary according to distinct versions, but it is common to assume that individual rationality implies some form of self-interest. Even in the contractual, as opposed to the contractarian, tradition, the parties are assumed to be defending their interests, and assuming that others do the same. The agreement must be, therefore, *mutually advantageous*.

Some thinkers use game theory to describe negotiation and its outcome. Sacconi (2011b) uses Nash bargaining theory as a proxy for rational bargaining. Lütge (2005, 2012a, 2012b) adheres to James Buchanan's version of a rational constitutional contract, based on microeconomic analysis (Buchanan 1975). Others offer an argumentative defense of what they believe rational people would agree to in the "corporate state of nature." Paul Neiman (2013) provides an effective illustration of this, with a theatrical representation of the hypothetical negotiation between a corporate shark and a community activist.

Regarding the parties to the agreement, forms 2 and 3 of CBE leave ambiguous the identities of the contracting parties (Bishop 2008: 196). Donaldson (1982) provides an extreme example of such vagueness. At the beginning of the chapter when he introduces the social contract in business, he refers to an agreement between "business" and "society," both taken as general abstract entities; however, in his illustration of such an agreement he refers to a tacit agreement between a single company (GM) and the whole of society. Moreover, as the chapter progresses, he introduces the "state of individual production," populated by "rational people" who, the reader learns, are the ones drafting the contract. On the other hand, some scholars (Sacconi 2011a; Phillips 2003) are clear that their theories are *about* the firm, so that the contracting parties are those directly involved or affected: the stakeholders. Yet, even in these cases, the exact extension of these contracting parties is not easy. This can be considered an unavoidable characteristic of types 2 and 3 of CBE. After all, the standard social contract is applied to the state, and political communities are, once constituted, very precise about who is a citizen and who is not; so the standard argument can be reconstructed as an agreement among all the citizens, as exemplified only in form 1 of CBE. When the object of justification is *not* the political community, this precision is impossible. The very nature of business makes it an open activity. Even the business corporation, formally defined by its charter and nexus of legal contracts, is a fluid notion compared with the state.

The content of the contract

Social contract theories diverge about the content of the contract. Small differences in the characterization of the original position and the rationality of the contracting parties result in remarkable differences in the substance of any agreement. The content of the contract depends crucially on the *aim* of the theory (Wempe 2005). The aim determines how the premises are conceived and how the decision procedure is envisioned. But, in the case of CBE, there is no unanimity about theoretical aims. Wempe (2005: 128) proposes three questions that, due to their similarity with the questions addressed by the hypothetical social contract in political philosophy, could be chosen as the theoretical aim of hypothetical CBE: 1) the accommodation of mutually exclusive claims posed by different stakeholders (wages vs. dividends, and the like); 2) the weighing of incommensurable values when making business and economic choices (workplace safety vs. profit; environmental sustainability vs. economic growth); 3) the resolution of which background institutions will make cooperative behavior in business possible. (These three theoretical aims refer to no specific business norm or even a specific commercial institution; rather, these are general procedures for fair adjudication or fair dealing. For a more substantive content of the social contract, actual contracts would be required.)

A common way to express the general aim of the social contract is to talk of a distributive agreement. For example, in Rawls' *Theory of Justice*, the aim of the original contract is to set up a mutually beneficial cooperative scheme, so the parties must agree about how to distribute all the benefits derived from cooperation. The object of the agreement is therefore a distributive principle. Once agreement is reached around this principle, the parties can design the cooperative scheme and the individual rights and responsibilities it involves in order to carry out that distribution in an efficient manner. In this way, the agreement can be seen, *ex post*, as instituting the moral rules of the group—the minimum morality implied by rights and duties—while the purpose of the contract, *ex ante*, remains, at least in the abstract, that of selecting a fair distributive procedure.

Compliance

The fourth key element in CBE is compliance. It is one thing to accept the contractarian or contractual argument as a rational method of discovery or construction of the ethical norms that structure common life, but another to suppose that such argument can *motivate* ordinary agents to behave morally. This concern points to a challenge for the social contract method, especially its contractarian version which assumes a consent motivated only by rational self-interest: Since it may be rational to make a contract and then, at a later time, rational to break it, is there any way in which *a priori* consent can generate a moral motivation to comply with the agreed contract? Or must the contractarian, to insure compliance, argue for some independent source of moral motivation?

Some business ethicists seem to think that this concern is about a more general question—whether or not to accept or reject *any* moral constraints. Dunfee, for example, characterizes the problem thus: "A related, but distinctly different issue is whether individuals would in fact comply with the social contract. This is the standard "why should I be ethical?" question raised in the context of social contract theory. Assumptions that managers are often egoistic make this question particularly pertinent in business ethics" (Dunfee 1991: 29). Dunfee implies that, once we have a sound theory that justifies the obligations derived from the contract, then the only worry is that agents may reject their justified obligations due to their egoism. However, this sort of worry would seem to hold for *any* ethical theory; it is not particular to the social contract argument.

The specific worry about the social contract argument, especially its contractarian form, is that it rests the basis of obligation on individual rationality. This very rationality may preclude compliance! To put it simply: the source of the authority of ethical norms is the agent's rational consent; consent is rational if the ethical norms secure mutual benefits; mutual benefit implies improvement over—at least, not degeneration of—the *status quo* for everyone. However, if the conditional of mutual benefit does not hold, then compliance with a contracted ethical obligation could be directly harmful for the agent (in the long run and all things considered) and, thus, the rationally self-interested agent may claim not to be obliged.

The social contract argument is not complete until this challenge is conveniently met. Sacconi (2011b) is the philosopher that most conscientiously completes his CBE proposal by meeting this challenge. His analysis starts with the assumption that economically rational individuals may deviate whenever there are incentives to do so in the *ex-post* situation. Deviation must be expected even if we assume that the agreement is fair, because a fair agreement may leave many *ex post* decisions open to the parties, in order to attain efficiency. Yet allowing such decisions would make the social contract unstable, since self-interested agents may use the leeway they have to improve their lot by exploiting others (recall that the contractarian argument assumes non-moral agents as the parties to the contract). Knowing of this eventuality at the moment of original contract, rational contractors may bring the issue of stability to *ex ante* negotiation. In so doing, they would focus on self-enforcing agreements, namely, those, and only those, that rational contractors know would elicit general compliance under normal circumstances and are therefore feasible *ex post*. Sacconi shows that stability, and therefore willing compliance, can be expected only around basically egalitarian solutions, where asymmetries of power are minimized.

Despite Sacconi's efforts, the most common way to address the issue of compliance with the social contract is to defer its solution to implementation policy at the level of real social contracts.

Integrative Social Contracts Theory (ISCT)

The result of the joint work of Thomas Donaldson (1982, 1989, 1994), who pioneered the adaptation of Rawls' argument to business ethics, and Thomas Dunfee (1991), who had proposed that extant—that is, actual—social contracts are the source of business ethics norms, Integrative Social Contracts Theory (ISCT) purports to be a comprehensive theory of business ethics, covering foundational issues and applications, including norm identification and an algorithm for ethical decision. Additionally, the authors claim that the theory would justify stakeholder approaches (1999, Chapter 9), as do other scholars (Van Buren III 2001; Agle et al. 2008). The expression "integrative" suggests the nature of the theory: it is based on the idea of a "hypothetical social contract whose terms allow for the generation of binding ethical obligations through the recognition of actual norms created in real social and economic communities" (Dunfee 2006: 304). Extant social contracts are called "micro-social contracts." The hypothetical social contract that lends legitimacy to these is labeled "macro-social contract."

Their view is that rational contractors would accept the validity of community-based norms as long as they meet some conditions. The macro-social contract establishes the conditions under which micro-contracts can be taken as legitimate sources of ethical business norms.

Dunfee (1991) emphasized that business communities are ethical communities. Formal contracts and legal provisions are not the only source of mutual normative expectations common to commerce. Dunfee introduced the term "extant social contracts" to refer to the implicit agreements through which participants in economic practices tacitly accept common norms. These norms establish prima-facie duties for the members of the community. But the world economy requires some universal moral standards: minimum common rules that establish a framework for a global market. This minimum morality may challenge the legitimacy of some community-based norms. Although their account draws explicitly upon Michael Walzer's (1994) idea of "thick" and "thin" moralities, Donaldson and Dunfee reject the charge of relativism as leveled against Walzer's approach. Despite the community-based origin of actual ethical norms, they offer a validity criterion—the macro-contract—that purports to be universal and rational.

Why did they choose a *hypothetical* social contract to establish the universal minimum morality of business (the macro-social contract)? Donaldson and Dunfee argue that global business is pursued in a context of plural values. Therefore, the normative theory that supports or condemns extant social contracts must be valid for agents with different world-views and convictions. A social contract, by focusing only on the economic rationality of agents and on their mutual recognition as potential partners in business, may claim general acceptance.

The key concepts of the theory derive from its strategy of applying the hypothetical social contract to the justification/criticism of business practices. The parties to the hypothetical contract are economic rational agents seeking to establish the ethical basis for "today's business world" (Donaldson and Dunfee 1999: 26). Unlike Rawls, the parties may know who they are, and what political, religious or philosophical options they embrace; the only veiled knowledge concerns the economic community to which they belong.

The agreement will be guided by the parties' awareness that economic activity requires some ethical framework, and their knowledge that people possess *bounded moral rationality*: agents cannot typically pursue long arguments or complex calculations before every decision. Many times, they will have only partial knowledge of the facts before deciding. In these circumstances, usually the right thing to do is to comply with the relevant extant social contract—the normative view of the community to which one belongs. This is desirable for an additional reason: *ceteris paribus*, economic activity should be aligned with the cultural, religious or philosophical attitudes of the agents involved.

This overarching macro contract would have four clauses: 1) Economic communities possess a *moral free space*. Within this space they can establish their ethical norms through one or several *micro-social contracts*. 2) The creation of norms at this micro level must be based on *consent*, and buttressed by a universal right to *voice* and *exit*. 3) Norms belonging to micro-contracts are legitimate—and therefore obligatory for the participants in the relevant community—if they are compatible with "hypernorms." 4) In case of conflict between legitimate norms, priority must be established according to the spirit of the macro-social contract.

Except for the third clause, these contentions express procedural standards by which economic communities consent to substantive norms. These standards assume the value of individual autonomy by granting rights of voice and exit. Of course, it may appear that respect for individual autonomy reveals a substantial—as opposed to merely procedural—value. But it is possible to see voice and exit rights as a corollary of the notion of consent itself, so they would not essentially change the procedural content of clause 2.

However, clause 3, setting forth the notion of "hypernorms" remains the most controversial element in the theory, as the authors have readily admitted (see Dunfee 2006; Agle et al. 2008). These norms seem to introduce a genuinely substantive limit—one *not* based on agreement—on the content of the micro-social contracts. To be fair, not all hypernorms would be substantive in this sense. There are three types of hypernorms: structural, procedural and substantive. Structural hypernorms have to do with background political and social institutions (property law, for example). Procedural hypernorms refer to the conditions that make micro-contracting possible. The rights of voice and exit are examples of these. Substantive hypernorms, however, include fundamental concepts of the right and the good such as promise-keeping, truth-telling, and respect for human dignity. This type of hypernorm poses a problem for the hypothetical social contract argument, as generally understood in moral and political philosophy. These norms do not immediately follow from the hypothetical contract as described in the theory (Wempe 2005). In fact, Donaldson and Dunfee do not suggest that substantive hypernorms are instituted by agreement. The authors offer a guide as to how to recognize them; but their authority is independent of consent.

Substantive hypernorms are presented by Donaldson and Dunfee as "convergent" principles that the macro contractors would *recognize* as belonging to a minimum universal morality. So it seems that a minimum universal morality is simply assumed, as if emerging from a "global" extant social contract. But if this is so, a doubt arises about the necessity of the hypothetical social-contract argument. Why couldn't these "convergent principles" be used as the only legitimacy check for community-based norms? What does the hypothetical contract *add* to the minimum universal morality on which all economic agents converge anyway? These questions elicit many of the critical responses to ISCT.

No other notion is as controversial as hypernorms. The notion of moral free space perhaps requires some clarification: it refers to a) the collective freedom to establish ethical norms by consent, and to b) the individual freedom to join economic communities. Moral free space understood as a) amounts, according to Boatright (2000), to a communitarian view of business ethics. Understood as b), it is the opposite, since it implies the liberal view that individuals choose to belong to a certain community (professional, corporate, industry, national). This choice should not be mistaken for a piecemeal acceptance or rejection of each and every norm supported by the community; rather, any such choice would be all-encompassing. Based on this encompassing will, the individual can be held accountable for her individual failures to comply with tacitly accepted standards. In sum, the notion of moral free space purports to explain why business ethics norms can legitimately vary, but also why free individuals are actually bound by ethical norms imposing constraints on their actions.

Application and criticism of Integrative Social Contracts Theory

Donaldson and Dunfee's ISCT offers a theoretical foundation of business ethics and a relatively clear guide for managerial decision in a wide range of functional areas and cultural contexts. Their ISCT has been applied to the following issues and problems: gender discrimination (Mayer and Cava 1995); differences in moral reasoning and ethical standards across cultures (Bucar et al. 2003; McCarthy and Puffer 2008; Spicer et al. 2004), including bribery (Dunfee et al. 1999: 14–32); distribution of life-saving pharmaceuticals in developing countries (Danis and Sepinwall 2002); downsizing (Van Buren III 2001); and deviant behavior in organizations (Warren 2003).

The impact of the theory is better measured, however, by the number and range of criticisms it has received. The core of the theory was published in 1994, so even the book *Ties that Bind* (1999) dealt with some early criticism: in explaining substantive hypernorms, Donaldson and Dunfee (1999, Chapter 3) mention—and try to respond to—several critical comments, among them Mayer (1994), Nelson (1996), Rynning (1996) and Taka (1996). An excellent summary of critical reactions to *Ties that Bind* is Dunfee (2006). Again, most criticism concerns hypernorms.

The *method* of ISCT has been much scrutinized (Conry 1995; Marens 2007; Velasquez 2000; Frederick 2000). Most critics point in one way or other to what Wempe (2005) defines as "discipline" in the use of the argument. The normative force of the argument of the social contract rests on how normative conclusions are plausibly derived from empirical assumptions about the parties, combined with the collective objective served by the agreement. Critics observe little precision in the definition of the individuals entering the contract or in the passage from their common aim to the conclusion about the content of the contract. Contemporary social contract theories devote great attention to the definition of the original position—it must be realistic despite being completely fictional—because the acceptability of the normative consequences of the theory crucially depends on the acceptability of the premises. However, Donaldson and Dunfee describe the original position in just a couple of passages in a twenty-two page chapter (1999, Chapter 2). Part of the vagueness is due to the use of the two concepts of contract (actual and hypothetical) in one single theory (Velasquez 2000; Boatright 2000). Wempe (2005) concludes that the structure of the original position as defined by Donaldson and Dunfee does not entail their conclusion.

The ISCT is challenged also by scholars defending a "political" approach to business ethics drawing upon Jürgen Habermas' discourse ethics. Contractarian business ethics is expected to be a "political" theory of business ethics, in part due to the political origin of the social contract argument. However, ISCT remains—the objection goes—too removed from the political dimension of business. In practice, it focuses on managerial decision making; in theory, it is very abstract and speculative, granting no place to actual political struggles within corporations or among corporations and other social institutions. Andreas Scherer and Guido Palazzo (2007) argue that Donaldson and Dunfee design a "mono-logical" theory of fair economic behavior, a theory whose method is no different from the armchair philosophy of the seventeenth century. They propose instead a dialogical approach that would be true to the fact that corporations often include opposing, sometimes conflicting, interests, so that seldom can they be equated with "communities" where consensual norms simply emerge. Gilbert and Behnam (2009) offer a revision of ISCT according to a Habermasian view of ethics and fairness. Note that, in ISCT, micro-norms are supposed to have spontaneously evolved as local practices, while macro-principles are rationally discoverable. Neither is given a deliberative origin. This is in contrast with standard stakeholder theory, which emphasizes the role of stakeholder dialogue. Overlooking the role of deliberation is thus seen both as a theoretical mistake and a practical problem for the theory.

As noted above, the nature and function of hypernorms is probably the most contested issue in the theory. These norms are theoretically questionable from different points of view. The contractarian objects that they introduce substantive values not directly derived from agreement (Van Oosterhout et al. 2006; Marens 2007); the communitarian, that they introduce universal values over and above local ones (Douglas 2000; Husted 1999). The realist may complain about the indefinite and weak philosophical foundation of these norms (Conry 1995; Boatright 2000; Soule et al. 2009). The relativist may deny their universal character (Douglas 2000). From a deliberative perspective, such norms set aside any universal insights that might be gained from normative discourse (Scherer 2015).

Beyond theoretical worries, they are questionable in practice. Some scholars complain that the proposal for their identification does not yield clear-cut results; for example, Dunfee (2006: 305–308) shows how the problem of identification has plagued attempts to apply hypernorms as management guides in many fields. In fact, some authors sympathetic to the general aim of ISCT have proposed re-defining the theory without hypernorms (Husted 1999; Soule et al. 2009).

These references are not meant to be exhaustive or representative of all the criticism towards ISCT. They intend to show that ISCT sets the stage for a deep discussion about CBE as a method for business ethics. Even if the project of integrating actual and hypothetical contracts remains highly problematic, Donaldson and Dunfee's work is an ineludible reference for any social contract approach to business and corporate ethics.

Other social contract theories in business ethics

In this section a brief characterization of other relevant CBE theories will be offered. De Graaf's distinction (2006) between heuristic and constitutive social contract will be used to group these theories. To appreciate the differences, it is essential to focus on the theoretical aims of each.

Heuristic CBE

For heuristic CBE, the language of the social contract simply helps to make sense of a complex normative reality in a way that fits our common notions of mutuality, reciprocity, and fairness. But this usage implies no commitment to particular views about the ultimate source of value.

For example, Freeman's allusion to the social contract is explicitly framed in a pragmatist approach to value (Freeman and Evan 1990). His declared objective is to overcome the separation thesis—the idea that a business decision can be fully justified from an economic point of view while being unethical (and vice-versa). This objective requires re-describing the corporation in terms that avoid distinguishing between an economic and an ethical component of decisions. Portraying the corporation as the result of a social contract conveys the idea that the network of stakeholders constitutes a moral community, rather than a bunch of economic agents interacting for profit. The rhetoric of the social contract facilitates understanding the value-creation activity of corporations as part of an acceptable way of life, while relinquishing the possibility of "finding some moral bedrock" for business, "for there are no foundations for either business or ethics" (Freeman 1994: 418).

Not far from this pragmatist view, Lütge's defense of "order ethics" can be cited as another form of a purely heuristic use of (some elements of) the social contract. The aim here is to define "corporate responsibility" as a branch of the larger set of rules that secure social order. Lütge's theory claims to be contractarian in the sense that it adopts the view of society as a cooperative venture for mutual benefit, and shares the analysis of social dilemmas based on games and individual self-interested behavior. Lütge adopts Bruce Ackerman's (1980) version of the original contract as an agreement to help design a framework of rules that transforms Prisoner's Dilemma-like situations into co-ordination games where individual self-interest is aligned with social benefit. Order ethics is guided by the question of how to increase mutual benefit in the long run. The best solution from a contractarian point of view is for corporations to commit themselves to public policies and rules carefully designed to include incentives (punishment and reward) that make compliance the rational move for each participant, therefore securing stability and predictability (Lütge 2012a).

Cited by Donaldson and Dunfee as one of the forerunners of CBE, Michael C. Keeley (1988) seeks to provide a theory of organizations that is more empirically grounded than rival approaches that utilize organic or mechanistic models. Keeley advances a view of organizations as a series of contracts among people. These empirical contracts are often formal and explicit, but the implicit variety also exists. To view organizations as social contracts, Keeley suggests, offers a better metaphor and a better tool to deal with normative questions than rival accounts. Even if his theory points to empirical contracts as sources of mutual obligations, the device of the hypothetical contract is used heuristically to explain the network of individual rights that define an organization's structure and legitimize individual claims. As Keeley states, "the key theoretical question here is: What concrete rights would self-interested participants agree to support *if* they were in a position to freely negotiate a set of rules for mutual benefit?" (Keeley 1988: 19).

Constitutive CBE

The work of Robert Phillips represents an application of the contract argument to more concrete questions. In seeking to provide an ethical foundation for stakeholder management (and one that avoids Freeman's pragmatism), Phillips combines tacit consent with Rawls's principle of fairness (Phillips 2003: 86). Yet, *contra* Rawls, he applies this notion not to the basic structure of society but to other social institutions such as business firms. Phillips contends that if one is engaged in a cooperative scheme and accepts its benefits, then one thereby consents to the obligations that the scheme may impose. The functioning of tacit consent as obligation-generating device is parallel to Donaldson and Dunfee's view of micro-social contracts (Phillips 2003: 100–106).

Arguably the most sophisticated attempt to bring the formal argument of the social contract to bear on corporate responsibilities, the work of Lorenzo Sacconi (2000, 2011a, 2011b) delineates a detailed contractarian explanation of the responsibilities of corporations based on a hypothetical contract. If we imagine an original contract among all constituents of a firm, then that agreement would specify how the firm should be governed and who is to profit from the firm's operation. In particular, the constitutional contract of the firm would specify the status, scope, and requirements of formal "Corporate Social Responsibility (CSR)" policies. As explained above, Sacconi's theory aims also at explaining compliant behavior.

In his 2011 version, Sacconi's argument adopts an explicit Rawlsian form. The *status quo* is represented by production *without* firms (via a nexus of one-to-one contracts); such a state is inefficient due to transactions costs. The device of the hypothetical contract behind a veil of ignorance is then applied to this *status quo*. What governance structure would be chosen by *all* constituents of the firm, if they had to agree on a "constitution" for the firm, without knowledge of their position in the resulting governance structure? The veil of ignorance obscures which party will end up having some pre-contractual asset (capital, knowledge, education, ability, etc.) to be invested.

Sacconi treats this problem as a bargaining game. If the players of this game are rational, then a solution can be found. The bargaining game was defined by Nash as the problem of finding a distribution of utility that maximizes the product of utilities of the bargaining parties, subject to the restriction that no party gets a utility lower than the *status quo* (Nash 1950). The original position guarantees impartiality because each bargainer must adopt the position of anyone (since by stipulation she can end up being anyone), therefore the bargaining solution would be fair.

Fairness is not only the result of an impartial original position but a rational requirement to secure compliance in the *ex post* situation. A basically egalitarian solution to the bargaining problem faced by the original contractors will elicit a rational preference for compliance by facilitating a reciprocal expectation of compliance that can activate, in turn, the pro-social attitudes of economic agents.

Concluding remarks: criticism and new directions

Contractarian business ethics is in part made up by the dialogue among its proponents. Donaldson's first theoretical foray in 1982 was criticized as inconsequential and incomplete; Keeley's social contract theory of organizations has been accused of smuggling a theory of rights (Wempe 2005). Dunfee thought Donaldson's Rawlsian approach too removed from the real workings of business ethics. And their joint publications immediately encountered suspicion and questions.

Virtually all contractarian theories of business ethics have been challenged by proponents of alternative CBE theories. The following two samples illustrate this. George W. Watson et al. (1999) took up one of the themes Donaldson and Dunfee proposed for future research: the empirical validation of the theoretical assumptions of ISCT. Watson et al. conducted a survey to check the perceived fairness in several downsizing scenarios. Their conclusion is that any perception of fairness is influenced more heavily by the predominant individualistic or communitarian ideology of the subjects than by any other variable. This result can be interpreted as questioning the social consensus at the micro level that the theory of extant social contracts seems to assume. Individual factors influence moral judgment more than social identities.

De Graaf (2006) sets forth a representative philosophical criticism. Drawing upon Wempe's (2005) complaint that CBE had not been "domain-specific" enough, De Graaf contends that CBE has simply used some concepts developed in the social contract tradition without any adaptation to the domain of business ethics and without any serious discussion of their meta-ethical or anthropological assumptions. This causes conceptual weakness in CBE. De Graaf points out, for example, that the concept of autonomy used in all-encompassing social contract theories is not even required for a social contract explanation of business norms; a clear idea of individual responsibility would be enough.

Apart from this internal dialogue, CBE has received a constant downpour of criticism from opponents to the contract hypothesis and the stakeholder view of the corporation. In his robust criticisms of the stakeholder perspective, Samuel Mansell (2013) argues for a shareholder view of corporations. He dismisses as unnecessary the elaboration of hypothetical mental experiments about the firm and contends that a genuine moral basis for the market is at odds with the assumptions of social contract theory.

More recently, Abraham Singer (2015) challenges the Rawlsian brand of CBE (Bishop 2008; Neiman 2013, for example). Rawls maintained that the corporation was a private association and not a part of the basic structure. Corporations would be subject to the principles of justice as these are applied via constitutional or legal provisions; however, there is no basis in Rawls' theory for asserting that either the form of corporate governance, or the very ends of the corporation, can be chosen by its members with no further limits. Since so many theories of CBE assume a Rawlsian framework, it must be clarified to what extent that framework is compatible with the ethics of the firm or corporation.

Apart from these types of criticisms, one may well consider whether the original theories of CBE have provided new avenues of exploration. After all, Donaldson and Dunfee suggested that contractarian theories would engender "promising research directions for CBE" (1994: 178). Although it is not clear that these hopes have been fulfilled, it would still be pertinent to explore, for example, the nature of consent in business ethics, our understanding of the empirical foundations of ethical behavior in organizations, and the link between contractarian thought and stakeholder management.

Two issues that are receiving fresh attention are "contractarian assumptions and moral psychology," and "managerial utility and contractarian business ethics." These topics both raise questions as to how the norms derived from the social contract are (or are *not*) compatible with moral psychology. These questions have received further impetus from advances in behavioral business ethics and new experimental methods in ethics. Some connections between an *ex ante* agreement and actual *ex post* behavior can be tested in the laboratory, as Marco Faillo et al. (2015) show. The experimental program in CBE is one of the most promising and distinctive contributions in the field (for an overview, see Francés-Gómez et al. 2015).

Recommended reading

Thomas Donaldson and Thomas Dunfee's *Ties that Bind. A Social Contracts Approach to Business Ethics* (1999) is required reading. The *Précis* that the authors wrote also comes in handy: "Précis for: *Ties that Bind*" (2000). In his essay, "In Defense of a Self-disciplined, Domain-specific Social Contract Theory of Business Ethics," (2005), Ben Wempe offers a nice tool to navigate the tradition and provides a useful comparison with classic theories. A critical, philosophically informed, and aptly illustrative study is Samuel Mansell's *Capitalism, Corporations and the Social Contract* (2013). For a recent critical exploration of the possible uses and interpretations of the social contract model in business see Nien-hê Hsieh, "The Social Contract Model of Corporate Purpose and Responsibility" (2015).

For further reading in this volume on modern theories of ethics, including Hobbes' social contract, see Chapter 2 Theorists and philosophers on business ethics. On contractualism as a species of non-consequentialism, see Chapter 5 Consequentialism and non-consequentialism. On the use of social contract theories in cross-cultural contexts, see Chapter 32 The globalization of business ethics.

Note

* This work was made possible thanks to funding from the Spanish Ministry of Economy (DGICYT) through the research project BENEB FFI2011-29005 and BENEB2 FFI2014-56391-P. I am grateful to César González Cantón for references about ISCT; and to Eugene Heath and Alexei Marcoux for their help and suggestions.

References

Ackerman, B. (1980). *Social Justice in the Liberal State*. New Haven, CT, Yale University Press.
Agle, B.R., T. Donaldson, R.E. Freeman, M.C. Jensen, R.K. Mitchell and D.J. Wood (2008). "Dialogue: Toward Superior Stakeholder Theory," *Business Ethics Quarterly* 18:2, 153–190.
Ashford, E. and T. Mulgan (2012). "Contractualism," in Edward N. Zalta (ed.), *The Stanford Encyclopedia of Philosophy* (Fall 2012 edition). Available at: http://plato.stanford.edu/archives/fall2012/entries/contractualism/.
Binmore, K. (1999). "Game Theory and Business Ethics," *Business Ethics Quarterly* 9:1, 31–35.
Bishop, J.D. (2008). "For-profit Corporations in a Just Society: A Social Contract Argument Concerning the Rights and Responsibilities of Corporations," *Business Ethics Quarterly* 18:2, 191–212.
Boatright, J. (2000). "Contract Theory and Business Ethics: A Review of *Ties that Bind*," *Business and Society Review* 105:4, 452–466.
Bucar, B., M. Glas and R.D. Hisrich (2003). "Ethics and Entrepreneurs. An International Comparative Study," *Journal of Business Venturing* 18, 261–281.
Buchanan, J. (1975). *The Limits of Liberty: Between Anarchy and Leviathan*. Chicago, IL: The University of Chicago Press.
Child, J.W. and A.M. Marcoux (1999). "Freeman and Evan: Stakeholder Theory in the Original Position," *Business Ethics Quarterly* 9:2, 207–223.
Conry, E.J. (1995). "A Critique of Social Contracts for Business," *Business Ethics Quarterly* 5:2, 187–212.
Danis, M. and A. Sepinwall (2002). "Regulation of the Global Marketplace for the Sake of Health," *Journal of Law, Medicine & Ethics* 30:3, 1–10.
De Graaf, G. (2006). "The Autonomy of the Contracting Partners: An Argument for Heuristic Contractarian Business Ethics," *Journal of Business Ethics* 68:3, 347–361. Available at: http://doi.org/10.1007/s10551-006-9018-4.
Donaldson, T. (1982). *Corporations and Morality*. Englewood Cliffs, NJ: Prentice Hall.
Donaldson, T. (1989). *The Ethics of International Business*. Oxford: Oxford University Press.
Donaldson, T. (1994). "When Integration Fails: the Logic of Prescription and Description in Business Ethics," *Business Ethics Quarterly* 4:2, 157–169. Available at: http://doi.org/10.2307/3857487.
Donaldson, T. and T. Dunfee (1994). "Toward a Unified Conception of Business Ethics: Integrative Social Contracts Theory," *Academy of Management Review* 19:2, 252–284. Available at: http://doi.org/10.5465/AMR.1994.9410210749.
Donaldson, T. and T. Dunfee. (1999). *Ties that Bind. A Social Contracts Approach to Business Ethics*. Boston, MA: Harvard Business School Press.
Donaldson, T. and T. Dunfee (2000). "Précis for: *Ties that Bind*," *Business and Society Review* 105:4, 436–443.
Donaldson, T. and L.E. Preston (1995). "The Stakeholder Theory of the Corporation: Concepts, Evidence and Implications," *Academy of Management Review* 20:1, 65–91.
Douglas, M. (2000). "Integrative Social Contracts Theory: Hype Over Hypernorms," *Journal of Business Ethics* 26:2, 101–110.
Dunfee, T.W. (1991). "Business Ethics and Extant Social Contracts," *Business Ethics Quarterly* 1, 23–51.
Dunfee, T.W. (2006). "A Critical Perspective of Integrative Social Contracts Theory: Recurring Criticisms and Next Generation Research Topics," *Journal of Business Ethics* 68:3, 303–328.
Dunfee, T.W. and T. Donaldson (1995). "Contractarian Business Ethics: Current Status and Next Steps," *Business Ethics Quarterly* 5:2, 173. Available at: http://doi.org/10.2307/3857352.
Dunfee, T.W., N.C. Smith, and W.T.J. Ross (1999). "Social Contracts and Marketing Ethics," *Journal of Marketing* 63, 14–32.
Evan, W. and E. Freeman (1993). "A Stakeholder Theory of the Modern Corporation: A Kantian Analysis," in T.L. Beauchamp and N.E. Bowie (eds), *Ethical Theory and Business* 4th edition. Englewood Cliffs, NJ: Prentice Hall, 75–84.
Faillo, M., S. Ottone and L. Sacconi (2015). "The Social Contract in the Laboratory: An Experimental Analysis of Self-enforcing Impartial Agreements," *Public Choice* 163:3–4, 225–246.
Francés-Gómez, P., L. Sacconi and M. Faillo (2015). "Experimental Economics as a Method for Normative Business Ethics," *Business Ethics: A European Review* 24, 41–53. Available at: http://doi.org/10.1111/beer.12096.
Frederick, W.C. (2000). "Pragmatism, Nature and Norms," *Business and Society Review* 105:4, 467–479.
Freeman. E. (1994). "The Politics of Stakeholder Theory: Some Future Directions," *Business Ethics Quarterly* 4:4, 409–421.

Freeman, R.E. and W.M. Evan (1990). "Corporate Governance: A Stakeholder Interpretation," *Journal of Behavioral Economics* 19:4, 337–359.
Gauthier, D. (1986). *Morals by Agreement*. Oxford: Clarendon.
Gilbert, D.U. and M. Behnam (2009). "Advancing Integrative Social Contracts Theory: A Habermasian Perspective," *Journal of Business Ethics* 89:2, 215–234.
Heath, J., J. Moriarty, and W. Norman (2010). "Business Ethics and (or as) Political Philosophy," *Journal of Business Ethics* 3, 427–452.
Heugens, P.P.M.A.R., J. Van Oosterhout, and M. Kaptein (2006). "Foundations and Applications for Contractualist Business Ethics," *Journal of Business Ethics* 68:3, 211–228.
Hsieh, N. (2015). "The Social Contract Model of Corporate Purpose and Responsibility," *Business Ethics Quarterly* 25:4, 433–460.
Husted, B.W. (1999). "A Critique of the Empirical Methods of Integrative Social Contracts Theory," *Journal of Business Ethics* 20:3, 227–235.
Keeley, M. (1988). *A Social-Contract Theory of Organizations*. Notre Dame, IN: University of Notre Dame Press.
Kersting, W. (1994). *Die politische Philosophie des Gesellschaftsvertrags*. WBG, Darmstadt (Spanish translation: *Filosofía política del contractualismo moderno*, México, Plaza y Valdés, 2001).
Lütge, C. (2005). "Economic Ethics, Business Ethics and the Idea of Mutual Advantages," *Business Ethics: A European Review* 14:2, 108–118.
Lütge, C. (2012). "The Idea of a Contractarian Business Ethics," in C. Lütge (ed.), *Handbook of the Philosophical Foundations of Business Ethics*, 3 vols Dordrecht: Springer, vol. 2, 647–658.
Lütge, C. (2012b). *Wirtschaftsethik ohne Illusionen : ordnungstheoretische Reflexionen*. Tübingen: Mohr Siebeck.
Lütge, C. (2015). *Order Ethics of Moral Surplus. What Holds a Society Together?* Lanham, MD: Lexington Books.
Mansell, S.F. (2013). *Capitalism, Corporations and the Social Contract. A Critique of Stakeholder Theory*. Cambridge: Cambridge University Press.
Marcoux, A. (2003). "A Fiduciary Argument Against Stakeholder Theory," *Business Ethics Quarterly* 13, 1–24.
Marens, R. (2007). "Returning to Rawls: Social Contracting, Social Justice, and Transcending the Limitations of Locke," *Journal of Business Ethics* 75:1, 63–76.
Mayer, D. (1994). "Hyper-norms and Integrative Social Contracts Theory," *Proceedings: International Association for Business and Society*, annual conference, Hilton Head, SC.
Mayer, D. and A. Cava (1995). "Social Contract Theory and Gender Discrimination: Some Reflections on the Donaldson/Dunfee Model," *Business Ethics Quarterly* 5:2, 257–270.
McCarthy, D.J. and S.M. Puffer (2008). "Interpreting the Ethicality of Corporate Governance Decisions in Russia: Utilizing Integrative Social Contracts Theory to Evaluate the Relevance of Agency Theory Norms," *Academy of Management Review* 33:1, 11–31.
Nash, J. (1950). "The Bargaining Problem," *Econometrica* 18:2, 155–162.
Neiman, P. (2013). "A Social Contract for International Business Ethics," *Journal of Business Ethics* 114:1, 75–90.
Nelson, J. (1996). "A Communitarian Contract for Business: Conditions Necessary and Sufficient," paper presented at Society for the Advancement of Socio-Economics Meeting, HEC School of Management, Jouy-en-Josas, France.
Phillips, R. (2003). *Stakeholder Theory and Organizational Ethics*. San Francisco, CA: Berrett-Koehler Publishers.
Post, J.E., L.E. Preston and S. Sachs (2002). *Redefining the Corporation. Stakeholder Management and Organizational Wealth*. Stanford: Stanford University Press.
Rawls, J. (1971). *A Theory of Justice*. Cambridge, MA: Harvard University Press.
Rawls, J. (1999). *The Law of Peoples*. Cambridge, MA: Harvard University Press.
Rynning, H. (1996). "Political Liberalism and Integrative Social Contracts Theory," in J. Lodgson and K. Rehbein (eds), *Proceedings of the Seventh Annual Meeting of the International Association for Business and Society*. Santa Fe, NM, 113–118.
Sacconi, L. (2000). *The Social Contract of the Firm*. Berlin: Springer.
Sacconi, L. (2011a). "A Rawlsian View of CSR and the Game Theory of its Implementation (Part I): The Multi-Stakeholder Model of Corporate Governance" in L. Sacconi, M. Blair, R. E. Freeman and A. Vercelli (eds), *Corporate Social Responsibility and Corporate Governance. The Contribution of Economic Theory and Related Disciplines*. New York: Palgrave Macmillan, 157–193.
Sacconi, L. (2011b). "A Rawlsian View of CSR and the Game Theory of its Implementation (Part II): Fairness and Equilibrium," in L. Sacconi, M. Blair, R. E. Freeman and A. Vercelli (eds), *Corporate*

Social Responsibility and Corporate Governance. The Contribution of Economic Theory and Related Disciplines. New York: Palgrave Macmillan, 194–252.

Scanlon, T. (1998). *What We Owe to Each Other.* Cambridge, MA: Harvard University Press.

Scherer, A.G. (2015). "Can Hypernorms Be Justified? Insights from a Discourse–Ethical Perspective," *Business Ethics Quarterly* 25:4, 489–516.

Scherer, A.G. and G. Palazzo (2007). "Toward a Political Conception of Corporate Responsibility: Business and Society Seen From a Habermasian Perspective," *Academy of Management Review* 32:4, 1096–1120.

Singer, A. (2015). "There Is No Rawlsian Theory of Corporate Governance," *Business Ethics Quarterly* 25:1, 65–92.

Soule, E., M. Hedahl and J. Dienhart (2009). "Principles of Managerial Moral Responsibility," *Business Ethics Quarterly* 19:4, 529–552.

Spicer, A., T.W. Dunfee and W.J. Bailey (2004). "Does National Context Matter in Ethical Decision Making? An Empirical Test of Integrative Social Contracts Theory," *Academy of Management Journal* 47:4, 610–620.

Taka, I. (1996). "A New Direction of Integrative Social Contracts Theory," *Journal of Japan Society for Business Ethics* 3, 3–15 (in Japanese).

Van Buren III, H.J. (2001). "If Fairness Is the Problem, Is Consent the Solution? Integrating ISCT and Stakeholder Theory," *Business Ethics Quarterly* 11:3, 481-499.

Van Oosterhout, J.H., P.P.M.A.R. Heugens and M. Kaptein (2006). "The Internal Morality of Contracting: Advancing the Contractualist Endeavor in Business Ethics," *Academy of Management Review* 31:3, 521–539.

Velasquez, M. (2000). "Globalization and the Failure of Ethics," *Business Ethics Quarterly* 10:1, 343–352.

Walzer, M. (1994). *Thick and Thin: Moral Arguments at Home and Abroad.* Notre Dame, IN: Notre Dame University Press.

Warren, D.E. (2003). "Constructive and Destructive Deviance in Organizations," *Academy of Management Review* 28:4, 622–632.

Watson, G.W., J.M. Shepard, and C.U. Stephens (1999). "Fairness and Ideology: An Empirical Test of Social Contracts Theory," *Business & Society* 38:1, 83–108.

Wempe, B. (2005). "In Defense of a Self-disciplined, Domain-Specific Social Contract Theory of Business Ethics," *Business Ethics Quarterly* 15:1, 113–135.

7

Can profit seekers be virtuous?

Michael C. Munger and Daniel C. Russell[1]

Cicero, in *On Duties* III.15, tells of a man who asked the price of an estate he was trying to buy. When the seller named the price, the buyer replied that the price was too low and insisted on paying more. "There is no one," Cicero writes, "who would deny that this was the act of a good man, but people do deny that it was the act of a wise man, just as if he had sold for less than he could have. This, then, is that mischievous doctrine: they consider some people to be good, and other people to be wise," that is, worldly-wise: shrewd, sharp, and calculating.[2] Is that mischievous doctrine correct, or can profit seekers be virtuous people as well as clever people?

In popular thinking, the answer is that they can't. People see profit seekers as *wise* for their effectiveness but non-profits as *good* for their noble intentions (Aaker et al. 2010), and profitable firms are seen as creating little value for the rest of society, sometimes for no other reason than that those firms are profitable (Bhattacharjee et al. unpublished). So, in popular thinking, profit seekers cannot be virtuous because *what they do is bad*: taking from society by whatever amount they profit. But even if profit seekers made positive contributions to society, many would still say they couldn't be virtuous, because *what they intend isn't good*—they intend only to make profits. At best profit seeking is no virtue. At worst, it is a vice. Or so says the mischievous doctrine.

We believe the mischievous doctrine is false. Profit seekers *can* also be virtuous people, if three conditions are all met:

1 the exchanges are truly voluntary, or "euvoluntary," in a sense we shall explain;
2 the profits are "real" profits, earned through a competitive market process, and not "rent seeking" profits, obtained through a privilege-based political process; and
3 the intent of the profit seeker is virtuous.

When the first two conditions are met, profits arise from creating value for others, unlike rent seeking that extracts value from others.[3] Under these conditions, what profit seekers do is not bad—on the contrary, it is beneficial. More than that, profit seekers act with virtuous intent when they intend to earn real profits by participating in a competitive process that creates real value rather than by seeking rents. Also, while there is never a guarantee that profit seekers will be virtuous persons, market forces that limit profit opportunities to real profits are far more favorable to good character than political forces that reward rent seeking (Arnold 1987).

113

Virtue, in the sense we intend it, is founded in character. For our purposes, then, the most useful definition of virtue is that provided by Miguel Alzola:

> Roughly, a virtue is a deep-seated trait of character that provides (normative) reasons for action together with appropriate motivations for choosing, feeling, desiring, and reacting well across a range of situations. The traits of character traditionally postulated as virtues have at least two fundamental features. First, they have a tendency to influence conduct. The virtues characteristically yield appropriate behavior. If someone is, say, honest, we assume that he has a character of a certain sort that makes us expect that he habitually behaves honestly (when he acts in character) over time. Second, character traits are global in the sense that someone who possesses the trait of, say, benevolence is inclined to behave in a benevolent manner across a broad range of circumstances.
>
> *(Alzola 2012: 380)*

The question posed by Cicero is, in effect, whether the virtuous character can seek profit, so we turn now to an example of profit seeking.

Can profit seekers be virtuous?

Profiting as taking: the mancgere

Sharon Turner's *History of the Anglo-Saxons* preserves an eleventh-century account of the retail merchant, or "mancgere," which is simultaneously a defense and an indictment of his trade:

> "I say that I am useful to the king, and to ealdormen, and to the rich, and to all people. I ascend my ship with my merchandise, and sail over the sea-like places, and sell my things, and buy dear things which are not produced in this land, and I bring them to you here with great danger over the sea; and sometimes I suffer shipwreck, with the loss of all my things, scarcely escaping myself."
>
> "What things do you bring to us?"
>
> "Skins, silks, costly gems, and gold; various garments, pigment, wine, oil, ivory, and orichalcus [brass], copper, and tin, silver, glass, and suchlike."
>
> "Will you sell your things here as you brought them here?"
>
> "I will not, because what would my labour benefit me? I will sell them dearer here than I bought them there, that I may get some profit, to feed me, my wife, and children."
>
> *(Turner 1836: 115–16)*

It's all there: risk, greed, profit. The mancgere of 1050AD is the epitome of the middleman in any age, buying cheap and selling dear without improving the product. Admittedly, his customers may concede that he deserves something for packaging and transporting goods, but he doesn't only charge for transportation; he charges the highest price he can. Isn't the mancgere preying on other people, adding no real value?

Aristotle said that in a fair trade the things traded must be of equal worth (1934/1999, *Nicomachean Ethics* V.5), which naturally raises the concern that in commercial trade the only way to make a profit is to sell a thing for more than it is worth:

[Acquisition] has two forms: one that concerns commercial trade, and another that concerns household management. The latter is necessary and well regarded, whereas the former mode of exchange is rightly objected to, since it is not natural but operates at the expense of others.

(Aristotle 1995, Politics I.10, 1258a38-b2)

The age-old complaint is not that middlemen *trade* but that they trade *for profit*. Profits are made "at the expense of others" and so profit seeking is a vice. And yet the mancgere objects that he is no parasite—in fact, he insists he is "useful." But though the mancgere may be wise, could he also be good?

Sharpening the question

Unlike other approaches to "business ethics," a virtue-based approach calls attention to what business does to the character of businesspeople, and the assessments range from pessimistic to optimistic.[4] The pessimistic answer is that while businesspeople need virtues, unfortunately virtue is exogenous to business—at best business won't improve one's character, and at worst it may corrupt it. Alasdair MacIntyre (1981: Chapter 14) argued that virtues are excellences of doing well at things that are worth doing for their own sake and are shared within a community and a tradition. But business is something people do for the sake of other things, like profits, and because those other things aren't shareable business doesn't unite people but separates them into winners and losers. Virtue therefore doesn't grow within business, but at best must *infiltrate* business from the outside.

Not all pessimists are *that* pessimistic, though. Geoff Moore (2002) observes that besides obligatory profit seekers, businesses also house people who love the very practice of law (say), or fishing, or other crafts with shareable rewards and a heritage of their own. But while this view makes room for virtue *within* a business, there still seems to be no such thing as virtue that *belongs* to business: on the *business* side of a business, virtue is still exogenous. So the pessimistic answer is that some are wise, others are good, and the difference is profit seeking.

By contrast, optimists think that virtue is endogenous to business. Edwin Hartman (2015: Chapter 5) argues that although business goes on for the sake of other goods—"to get some profit," in the mancgere's unvarnished words—that doesn't have to keep businesspeople from also treating the very work *of business* as a craft. On the contrary, even crafts like law and fishing are worth doing for their own sake only because they also serve some further purpose. Why should managing or accounting be any different? If anything, businesspeople may be especially prone to getting wrapped up in their work, because, as Deirdre McCloskey (2006: 461, 469) puts it, "the bourgeoisie thinks of work as a calling," a calling with an ancient and noble heritage (see also Solomon 1992: Chapter 13; Swanton 2016).

What's more, despite the "dog-eat-dog" cartoon of business life, the life-blood of everyday business is not so much competition as cooperation, both within and between firms.[5] Getting work done requires cooperative relationships, but not every contingency that might destroy those relationships can be written into contracts ahead of time. One of the most valuable business assets is therefore "social capital"—being known to be reasonable, honest, and trustworthy. Most business relationships extend over long periods, requiring that both parties expect to benefit from the relationship. This means that those who make and sell products must develop and exhibit the virtues we associate with social capital (Storr 2009). Those who do not will lose customers and suffer a decline in the value of their reputations and brand names.

Not only does virtue support business. Business also supports virtue, as one must work with different people, come to reasonable agreements, resolve and avoid disputes, put long-term gains ahead of short-term temptations, and constantly try to discover what other people want and how to bring it to them at a low cost.[6] And even though profit per se may not be the direct object of for-profit work, profit can be ennobling, evidence of the virtuous intent to do something so valuable that others will find it worth paying for (Brennan 2012; McCloskey 2006: 476).

But what about the mancgere? There is nothing to stop him from treating his business as a craft, but that wasn't the complaint; there is nothing to stop the mancgere from being honest in his dealings, or from doing valuable work, but that wasn't the complaint either. The complaint was about the very intent of seeking profit—*that* intent is at best no virtue and at worst a vice.[7] So far, optimists have been somewhat quieter on this question, and that's surprising considering how deep and enduring the suspicion of profit has been in human history. Worse, it risks giving pessimism the last word: virtue requires virtuous intent, but what profit seekers intend is at best nothing good and at worst something bad.

Our aim is to extend the optimistic answer even to this further and tougher question: not whether there is just any respect in which a profit seeker can also be virtuous, but whether one can be virtuous *in respect of seeking profits*. For that reason, we focus on entrepreneurship, which is actually *defined* in terms of profit seeking. Entrepreneurial profit is not merely profit in the accounting sense of revenue in excess of costs; rather, it is profit in excess of the next-best profit-making opportunity. In other words, by definition entrepreneurs seek *extraordinary* profits, as opposed to ordinary profits available from ordinary opportunities. Can the intent to realize entrepreneurial profits be a virtuous intent?

The best work on virtue and profit is informed by the economics of profit seeking, and assesses profit seeking in comparison with alternative intents. We hope to continue in that spirit, by arguing that the key to seeing the potential virtue in the intent to seek profits is to appreciate the difference between seeking real profits versus seeking artificially created rents. And the first step is to understand what real profits are and why they get created in the first place.

Profits in the entrepreneurial process

Euvoluntary exchange: the prison camp

Imagine people making direct exchanges (as in Aristotle's "household management") that we can all agree are fair. Would the entrance of a middleman who exchanges for profit inject unfairness where there was none before? A British economist, Richard Radford (1945), described a natural experiment of just that sort, in a POW camp during World War II. Every month, prisoners received identical Red Cross packets with milk, beef, cigarettes, and other goods. Everybody in the camp therefore had the same endowments, but preferences differed, making mutually beneficial trades possible. Suppose Allan prefers beef to milk, and Barry has beef but prefers milk. There is increased value—to both men—in correcting the mistake in allocation that would result from Barry eating beef when he could have had milk, or from Allan drinking milk when he could have had beef.

Such a trade is fair because it is truly voluntary: no one is stealing, defrauding, or threatening, and neither is so desperate to trade that he is "coerced by circumstances." This notion of *euvoluntary* exchange accommodates the moral suspicion that trade is not *truly* (*eu-*) voluntary when there are profound asymmetries in bargaining power. Guzman and Munger (2014) argue that exchange is euvoluntary if, but only if, all the following conditions are met:

1 conventional ownership of items, services, or currency by both parties;
2 conventional capacity to transfer and assign this ownership to the other party;
3 both parties receive value at least as great as they anticipated when they agreed to exchange;
4 no large-scale or dangerous uncompensated costs imposed on third parties (negative externalities);
5 no one is forced to exchange by threat ("If you don't trade I'll shoot!"); and
6 no one will be harmed by failing to exchange ("If I don't trade I'll starve!").

Categories (1)–(4) are standard requirements in the common law of contracts, and categories (5) and (6) could be summarized as the common-law requirement of "no duress."

Because each party to a euvoluntary exchange is truly free to walk away from it, the exchange will take place only if *each party* will be better off for it. In fact, Radford made a striking observation about exactly that:

> Very soon after capture people realized that it was both undesirable and unnecessary, in view of the limited size and the equality of supplies, to give away or to accept gifts of cigarettes or food. 'Goodwill' developed into trading as a more equitable means of maximising individual satisfaction.
>
> *(1945: 191)*

The prisoners discovered that exchange was *more equitable* than relying on gifts or charity. They were right, because *truly* voluntary exchanges clearly make *both* parties better off.

Enter the entrepreneur: the itinerant padre

But what if neither party is aware of the potential trade opportunity? Radford (1945: 191) explains that the prisoners faced exactly this problem shortly after their capture—and an unlikely entrepreneur discovered a profit opportunity:

> We reached a transit camp in Italy about a fortnight after capture and received ¼ of a Red Cross food parcel each a week later. At once exchanges, already established, multiplied in volume. Starting with simple direct barter, such as a non-smoker giving a smoker friend his cigarette issue in exchange for a chocolate ration, more complex exchanges soon became an accepted custom. Stories circulated of a padre who started off round the camp with a tin of cheese and five cigarettes and returned to his bed with a complete parcel in addition to his original cheese and cigarettes; the market was not yet perfect.

With the "itinerant padre," a middleman enters the picture. The padre is an *arbitrageur*, "discovering sellers and buyers of something for which the latter will pay more than the former demand" and keeping the difference as profit (Kirzner 1973: 39). If anything looks like profiting "at the expense of others," arbitrage does: the product is not improved, just resold at a higher price. It certainly looked that way to the other prisoners: "Taken as a whole," Radford (1945: 199) says, "opinion was hostile to the middleman."

That hostility is paradoxical. On the one hand, the itinerant padre didn't steal from people's bundles; he didn't force anyone to give him what he wanted; he didn't misrepresent any of the goods he was trading; there was no disparity in bargaining power. Since each exchange the padre made was euvoluntary, his trading partners must have been better off. But, on the other hand, no new rations entered the camp, so how could the padre return with an extra Red Cross parcel—his profits—*except* at the expense of others?

That latter perspective is incorrect, though. Yes, middlemen buy cheap and sell dear, without improving the product, so they appear to profit without creating value. But that appearance is misleading. Suppose Allan was willing to *pay six cigarettes* for a tin of beef, and Barry would *accept three cigarettes* for his tin of beef. The padre, by searching across trade opportunities, found he could sell beef to Allan for five cigarettes after buying it from Barry for four. Allan and Barry were better off by one cigarette each and the padre "profited" one cigarette by finding the euvoluntary exchange opportunity to correct the misallocation.

But wouldn't Allan and Barry have been *even better* off without the middleman, exchanging with each other directly? The problem is that the exchange between Allan and Barry cannot be taken for granted, because finding those opportunities was costly and uncertain—in other words, transactions costs were high. They "traded" via the padre because each valued relief from trouble (where will I find the trade?) and risk (is there a trade to be found?) more than the profits they paid to the padre. Put into perspective, the individuals who traded benefited enormously from the padre's activities, and the padre earned his profits by specializing in the valuable but underappreciated service of arbitrage, lowering transactions costs for others.

But then why was opinion "hostile to the middleman"? Frédéric Bastiat (1850/2011) argued that such problems are generic, because people focus on what is easy to see and ignore what is hard to see. In the camp, the profits were visible and concentrated: an extra parcel in the hands of the padre. By contrast, the benefit to consumers was invisible and scattered: greater satisfaction with each parcel, for dozens of people across the camp. The story of the itinerant padre illustrates that we cannot understand the gains on one side of a euvoluntary exchange in isolation from the gains on the other side. Unfortunately, that is exactly how people tend to see them: gain implies offsetting loss, rather than mutual benefit.

Profit seeking as service-provision: the verger

But even if entrepreneurs deserve profits, do they really deserve *extraordinary* profits? Entrepreneurs seek opportunities no one else has noticed—which means they capture extraordinary profits while competitors scramble to catch up. Wouldn't consumers be better off if entrepreneurs could earn profits but not extraordinary profits?

That reasoning confuses cause and effect, because it takes extraordinary profits for entrepreneurs to try to discover new ways of creating value in the first place. Somerset Maugham (1952) illustrated this aspect of entrepreneurship in his short story, "The Verger." In the story, Mr Foreman has worked well as a verger at St Peter's Church for more than 30 years. A new vicar is assigned to St Peter's, and is shocked to learn that the verger cannot read or write. Foreman is sacked, and wanders, dejected. He looks to buy a cigarette, but notices there are no tobacco shops anywhere on the busy street. Risking his meager savings, Mr Foreman opens a shop, and makes considerable profits. Before long, he opens another, and then several more, amassing a small fortune. His bank manager urges him to invest the money, but Foreman demurs, saying he can't manage other investments since he cannot read. The banker, amazed, wonders what Foreman might have done if he had been literate. "'I can tell you that sir,' said Mr Foreman, a little smile on his still aristocratic features. 'I'd be verger of St Peter's.'"

Mr Foreman's strategy was simple: find a busy street with no tobacconist, and open a shop there. He invented nothing, and brought no new products into the country. What he really sold was convenience, not tobacco. No one else had noticed the misallocation of commercial space.

"Correcting misallocations" is really shorthand for the multiplicity of services that are easy for consumers to overlook but costly—and risky—for entrepreneurs to provide. Israel Kirzner (1973) observed that entrepreneurship is the exercise of alertness to new possibilities waiting "around the corner" that would create value for others if they were noticed and realized. Entrepreneurs like Mr Foreman exercise alertness to new ways of bringing people things they want. Entrepreneurs also exercise alertness through innovation, imagining new things that people might want. Innovation corrects misallocations by discovering new uses or combinations of available resources to satisfy demand that has so far gone unnoticed. In both of these ways, entrepreneurs specialize in the unusual service of imagining an alternative future on behalf of others. But until someone earns profits for correcting a misallocation, it's not clear that there *is* a misallocation to correct. This has to be discovered, and profits are motivation for and signal of such a discovery. The discovery process is therefore ultimately driven by consumers, not entrepreneurs, because an entrepreneur who thinks he has discovered something consumers want, but then loses money, was wrong.

Israel Kirzner (1973: 32) described entrepreneurs as trying to discover what people will find worth paying for, even when those people don't know what that will be. But anyone who invests resources in guessing the future risks losing that investment, in addition to the lost opportunity to invest in safer alternatives. So entrepreneurs don't just exercise alertness and make new discoveries on behalf of consumers. They do so *while also* relieving consumers of the *risks* of alertness and discovery.

This fact about entrepreneurial profits is important to understand but easy to overlook. A world where we could enjoy new products and services *without also* paying entrepreneurs extraordinary rates of profit doesn't, and couldn't, exist. The prospect of ordinary profit could never motivate someone to take entrepreneurial risks, because ordinary profit just is what's available from lower-risk investments. A world without entrepreneurial *profits* is a world without entrepreneurs.

Profit, incentive, and desert

But just how "extraordinary" do entrepreneurial profits need to be? Even if profit spurs entrepreneurs to create value, do they really need the hope of the enormous profits they sometimes earn? Did the verger need to amass *so great* a reward for bringing new shops to the neighborhood (and *tobacco* shops at that)? Did the padre need *nothing less* than an extra Red Cross parcel to induce him to trade? Did Bill Gates need *that much* money to create Microsoft?

This is to ask what the *price* of entrepreneurial services should be. As tempting as it is, though, it is a mistake to guess in advance of euvoluntary exchange what "the price" of anything should be. In fact, another service that entrepreneurs provide is to *discover prices*. When transactions costs in the camp are high, milk will sell at different prices in different places. Price disparities create arbitrage opportunities by signaling misallocations. But as the padre bought and sold milk, "the price" of milk was discovered, because it leveled out across the camp. And, of course, another price discovered through entrepreneurial activity is the price of *entrepreneurial services themselves*— a price that fell to zero once prisoners began trading via bulletin board instead.

But aren't entrepreneurial profits often out of all proportion to the merits of entrepreneurs? Absolutely; Mr Foreman was mostly lucky, and even clever entrepreneurs may be only marginally cleverer than others who didn't see the opportunity (von Mises 1952: 120–1). Isn't there something wrong with disproportionate profits for entrepreneurs who do so little to merit them?

There would be, *if* profits had to be justified by personal merit. In reality, the justification for entrepreneurial profits is the benefits entrepreneurs create for consumers: the greater the misallocation corrected, the greater the profit (Arnold 1987: 398). Put another way, the question is not whether the success of any particular entrepreneurial success carries moral weight. The question is whether the *institution* of entrepreneurship carries moral weight. Individual entrepreneurs would then be deserving if their profits were acquired within an institution that carries weight.[8] And that institution *does* carry weight, because profits taken by entrepreneurs are a tiny fraction of the benefits entrepreneurship creates.

Private and public middlemen

Within a process of profit and loss, entrepreneurs are not net takers but net creators of value. But wouldn't consumers be even better off with a different process altogether? Wouldn't consumers pay lower prices, uninflated by entrepreneurial profits, if products and services were more under the direction of public functionaries seeking the public good, and less under the control of private entrepreneurs competing for their private good?

Frédéric Bastiat asked exactly this question, focusing on perhaps the worst entrepreneur imaginable: one who profits from importing food during famine.

> "What can be the use," they say, "of leaving to the merchants the care of importing food from the United States and the Crimea? Why do not the State, the departments, and the towns, organize a service for provisions and a magazine for stores? They would sell at a just price, and the people, poor things, would be exempted from the tribute which they pay to free, that is, to egotistical, individual, and anarchical commerce."
>
> *(1850/2011: 19)*

There is a misallocation of resources—hungry people in one place, grain grown by farmers in hopes of selling to hungry people in another place—so there is a valuable service to be provided in correcting that misallocation. Bastiat's question is how to provide it:

> When the hungry stomach is at Paris, and corn which can satisfy it is at Odessa, the suffering cannot cease till the corn is brought into contact with the stomach. There are three means by which this contact may be effected. First, the famished men may go themselves and fetch the corn. Second, they may leave this task to those to whose trade it belongs. Third, they may club together, and give the office in charge to public functionaries.
>
> *(1850/2011: 20)*

The first option is no option at all, so the question is whether to hire private entrepreneurs or public functionaries. Since entrepreneurs will take profits above cost, surely public functionaries should provide the service at cost, passing the savings on to hungry Parisians?

The problem, though, is that the cost of delivering grain to Paris is determined by the incentives and information the method of delivery creates. The profit and loss process creates information and incentives to be cheap and fast. Because competition constantly drives prices down, profit seeking forces entrepreneurs to keep finding new ways to reduce costs and transport grain as cheaply and quickly as possible. By contrast, public functionaries have no such incentive to reduce costs; their "price" will always be their "cost," because the process outlaws profits. Within the political process, the main incentive is to avoid expensive efforts to improve quality, expedite delivery, or reduce prices. Worse, for political reasons the non-price costs to consumers—queuing, favoritism, discrimination—may even go up.

When comparing the services of private and public functionaries, it's important not just to focus on the costs that are seen but to look for the savings that are not seen. Profits are a cost we can see, but that cost is less, often much less, than the costs of forgone innovations we never see.

Putting competition in its place

But even if the process of entrepreneurial competition is better at providing some services, isn't *unrestricted* competition wasteful? Shouldn't governments subsidize the most promising entrepreneurial ventures—wouldn't that bring consumers the benefits of entrepreneurship without the wasteful proliferation of entrepreneurial startups, most of which will fail anyway?

It *would* make sense to eliminate waste owing to entrepreneurial experimentation and failure *if* there were a less costly way of discovering which ventures would make the best use of the resources invested in them. The problem is that no such way could exist, because the only way that entrepreneurs ever manage to see around corners is within the entrepreneurial *process* of trial and error, profit and loss.

The political process works by inhibiting or even preventing competition, which of necessity turns away innovation. In the 1950s, Japan's Ministry of International Trade and Industry decided to "rationalize" Japan's automobile industry by limiting it to just two manufacturers. This "streamlining" left no room for an entrepreneur named Soichiro, who was allowed to make other sorts of machines but forbidden to make cars. Nonetheless, in 1959 he produced his first car, and he eventually made enough profits that he was allowed to open a car company too, but only after overcoming terrible obstacles from a government that had decided it didn't need this new company called Honda. The reason the company exists today is that Soichiro Honda created value. How do we know? Because he earned profits, creating cars that cost him less to make than people were willing to pay for them.

But what about ideas that are so obviously good that there's no need for an entrepreneurial discovery process? The problem is that ideas are "obviously" good only in hindsight. One of the earliest personal computers—designed and built in a garage—was a metal box that attached by a wire to a television screen. It had no fixed memory and only 16 kilobytes of RAM, but its designers Steve Wozniak and Steve Jobs put it on sale in 1976 for $666 (about $3,000 today). By all appearances they had no chance of success, and if they had asked the government whether they should go ahead the government would have said no, because voters didn't know they wanted that metal box.

Political decision-making works at the median: any new possibility must always wait until the median politician and the median voter are convinced it's a good idea. If personal computing had been put to the vote in 1985, more than 90 percent of American households would have voted no, and it wasn't until 2003 that a majority of American households had personal computers (File 2013). Entrepreneurial decision-making works at the margin: new possibilities spring to life as soon as there are just enough people who value them more than it costs to provide them.

But what about the failed entrepreneurial ventures that competition inevitably creates—aren't those failures wasteful? Actually, those failures are very valuable, because they provide information as to which discoveries do, *and which do not*, produce value. In hindsight, an invention like the smartphone has obvious value, but there would have been no smartphone in the absence of discoveries made possible by both the successes and failures—such as the short-lived Apple "Newton"—of different approaches to the mobile technology market. Make no mistake: state provision really does reduce the waste of failed entrepreneurial ventures. But that "waste" is the price of discovery. Restricting competition chokes off discovery and locks in existing misallocations of resources, which are even more wasteful. The difference between entrepreneurship and politics is not the presence or absence of "waste," but the availability or unavailability of information that signals which allocations of resources bring more satisfaction to consumers.

Virtuously seeking profits

It is no vice for entrepreneurs to seek profits, but is there such a thing as entrepreneurial *virtue*? Thomas Aquinas was pessimistic:

> Business, taken by itself, has a certain sordidness about it because, due to its purpose, it doesn't entail any respectable or necessary goal. Nevertheless, even if profit, which is the goal of business, doesn't entail anything respectable or necessary due to its purpose, it doesn't entail anything vicious or opposed to virtue due to its purpose, either.
>
> *(2012,* Summa Theologiae *II–II.77.4)*

Entrepreneurs may create benefits for others, and someone who was an entrepreneur could even act virtuously—but not *because* he was an entrepreneur. Virtuous action requires not just doing good but also the intent to do good for its own sake (Aristotle 1934/1999, *NE* II.4), so that the act is done for the right reason (II.6). Virtuous acts require virtuous intent. True—but what exactly is virtuous intent?

Virtuous intent: the "what" and the "how"

Giving to help the needy is an act with virtuous intent; giving as a pretense of concern for the needy is not. The difference is *what one intends to do*: to help in the one case and to show off in the other. But besides what one intends to do, there is also the question of *how one intends to do it*. Suppose the money donated to help the needy had already been promised to another in repayment of a debt. Being "generous" by giving away someone else's money is unjust, so virtuous intent involves not only what one intends to do but also how one intends to do it.

What's more, it is possible to act with virtuous intent, even when what one intends to do is nothing special. Someone who walks for exercise does something that is neither virtuous nor vicious on its face, but how he intends to do it will *make* it one or the other. Does he intend to go for a walk even though it means breaking a promise to take his kids to a ballgame? Does he intend to walk for exercise even though his regimen calls for lifting weights? Does he intend to walk briskly no matter how many people he bowls over? Here, how someone intends to do something makes the *entire* difference as to whether his intent is virtuous or not.

Nor is how-one-intends-to-do-it any less important than what-one-intends-to-do—on the contrary, virtue makes its greatest impact on our lives in how we do everyday things. To restrict virtuous intent to the what-one-intends-to-do variety is to think of virtuous actions as rare cases involving special goals, islands in an ocean of character-neutral behavior. But in the circumstances of real life, character is in everything we do, like how one does one's job: honestly, fairly, diligently, even if, like most jobs, it doesn't involve any specifically virtuous goal. Of course, there are some actions that we cannot do in a virtuous way at all (Aristotle 1934/1999, *NE* II.6, 1107a8-27); there is no virtuous way of stealing or defrauding. These are the islands where what-we-intend-to-do really does make all the difference, when it is vicious on its face. But, for the most part, life happens on the ocean of actions that are neither virtuous nor vicious on their face, but only *become* virtuous or vicious depending on how we go about them.

The Stoic philosophers of ancient Greece and Rome thought of virtuous intent in exactly this way—in fact, walking with virtuous intent was one of their favorite examples:

> Right actions are things like these: being prudent, being temperate, fair dealing, being joyful, doing good, being in good spirits, walking prudently, and anything that is done with correct reasoning.
>
> (Arius Didymus 2002, Summary of Stoic Ethics *11e*)

The Stoics liked examples like "walking prudently" precisely because of their humdrum nature. The Roman statesman and Stoic philosopher Seneca was especially fond of reminding people that virtue inheres in everyday acts, because virtue and vice lie in all the choices we make as we go through our day.

> When I choose the sort of clothes it's appropriate to choose, when I walk as I should, when I dine as I ought, it's not the dinner or the walk or the clothes that are good, but my intention in these acts, insofar as they observe on each occasion a manner suitable to right reason. Indeed, mankind is naturally a neat, tasteful animal, and so while neat clothes are not good in their own right, the selection of neat clothes is, because goodness is not in a thing, but in a certain sort of selection.
>
> (Seneca 1989, Letters *92.11–12*)

There is nothing virtuous or vicious in eating dinner, getting dressed, or going for a walk. But it is always a matter of character *how we choose to do* each of these things, in what Seneca called the "selection" of them. Here, how-we-intend-to-do-it is what makes it virtuous or vicious.

Entrepreneurial intent: seeking real profits

Aquinas was right to say that there is neither virtue nor vice in what profit seekers do. But to say no more than that would be to ignore—as pessimists about business virtue do ignore—the ways in which profit seekers can be virtuous in *how* they intend to seek their profits (see also Swanton 2016). First of all, entrepreneurs can be virtuous in seeking profits when they intend to earn those profits *within a process that ties profits to value created for consumers.*

An ancient parable depicts vicious people seated around a table spread with food, but because their spoons are as long as the people are tall, they starve in front of this magnificent feast because they can't get their spoons back to their mouths. Strikingly, virtuous people sit before an identical feast with identical spoons, but they all eat sumptuously because each uses his spoon to feed the person across from him.

There is a difference in virtue between the people around these two tables, but the difference is not in what they intend to do. The difference is in how they intend to do it. At both tables, each person sits down *to eat*; the virtuous diners are not virtuous for sitting down to a dinner they only intend someone *else* to eat. What makes the virtuous diners virtuous is their intent to feed themselves *by participating in a positive-sum process*, a process of giving and receiving. Their intent is virtuous, not because of what they intend to do but because of how they intend to do it.

Adam Smith perceived a similar intent in everyday buying and selling:

> It is not from the benevolence of the butcher, the brewer, or the baker, that we expect our dinner, but from their regard to their own interest. We address ourselves, not to their humanity but to their self-love, and never talk to them of our own necessities but of their advantages.
>
> (1776/1904, Wealth of Nations: *I.2.2*)

If we look at the selling side of exchange in isolation, we'll focus on what the butcher, brewer, and baker intend to do—"that I may get some profit"—and that makes it hard to see what could be virtuous about being a butcher, brewer, or baker. But Smith offered a subtler perspective, putting both sides of exchange into clearer view: "Whoever offers to another a bargain of any kind, proposes to do this: Give me that which I want, and you shall have this which you want, is the meaning of every such offer." Both parties intend to seek their own advantages, but Smith focused on how each of them intends to do so, sitting down to eat by offering to feed the person across the table. What makes Smith's insight great is his perception of the *reciprocity* embedded in truly voluntary exchange within a competitive process of profit and loss, where people persuade others to meet their needs by first offering to meet theirs.

Entrepreneurial intent: forbearance from rent seeking

The flip-side of the intent to seek real profits is a second variety of virtuous entrepreneurial intent: the *intent to forbear from rent seeking*.[9] What is a "rent," and what is "rent seeking"?

Earlier we distinguished between accounting profits, which are simply revenues above cost, and economic or entrepreneurial profits, which are in excess of the next-best profit opportunity. But a second and perhaps more important difference is that accounting profits include revenues from *all* sources, even those that result from restraint of trade, government subsidies, or higher prices due to trade protection, regulation, or price controls. An economist would deny that these are real profits, because instead they are "rents." Rents are excess of revenues over cost that the firm is not entitled to receive, save by virtue of its effectiveness in political lobbying. Rents are a transfer from taxpayers to firms, in the form of either direct subsidies or artificially high prices.

Wherever the political process replaces the entrepreneurial process, it also eliminates entrepreneurial profits. But that doesn't mean that profit seeking is thereby banished. Instead, participants focus on *rent seeking*, as accounting "profits" now come from obtaining favors from bureaucrats instead of creating value for consumers. The political process doesn't eliminate profit seeking; it just turns it into rent seeking.

The political process doesn't eliminate competition either, but makes it more wasteful. Tollison (1982) defined rent seeking as competition for artificial prizes created by public functionaries, rather than competition that creates value for consumers. For example, in many American states it is illegal to braid hair commercially without a license, and licensure often requires 1,000 hours or more of training in hair-braiding (Bayham 2005). Occupational licenses of this sort make it difficult and costly for new competitors to enter the market, and as a result consumers pay higher prices and established businesses make greater profits—not real profits, but rent seeking profits that create no value. On the contrary, rent seeking destroys value for consumers by misallocating resources, like the time and talents spent obtaining a braider's license, or lobbying the legislature to make unlicensed braiding illegal.

To ask whether it can be virtuous to seek profits within the entrepreneurial process is really to ask, "Compared to what alternative process?" (as posed by Arnold 1990). The difference between the entrepreneurial process and the political process is not profit seeking, or competition, but the shapes that profit seeking and competition take within these processes. In both processes, profit seekers try to avoid competition, reduce risk ("sometimes I suffer shipwreck"), and acquire capital. One way to avoid competition is to correct misallocations that no competitor has noticed yet; but another is to create misallocations by lobbying for laws that erect barriers to entry. One can reduce risk by exercising prudence; but the assurance of a taxpayer-funded bailout can make it prudent to take even more risks. One way to acquire capital is by selling stock to people betting with their own money; but another is to obtain subsidies from politicians who bet with taxpayers' money.

When exchanges are euvoluntary, and free of artificial constraints—subsidies, barriers to entry, restrictions on who can produce, etc.—entrepreneurs can earn real profits only by creating value for consumers who are free to turn down the exchange unless they think it will make them better off. It is not real profits but rents that really do come "at the expense of others." So it is not profit seeking but rent seeking that cannot be virtuous, because rent seeking cannot create value.

By contrast, it takes virtue to earn real profits when this means forgoing the opportunity to seek rents. Of course, virtue requires more than a resolve not to do wrong, but then, forgoing rent seeking is more than merely "not doing wrong." Rents do still count as accounting profits, so the pressure to seek rents can be enormous, whether that pressure comes from shareholders dissatisfied with managers who forgo more profitable rent seeking opportunities, or from public functionaries looking to sell favorable policies or extort bribes. Faced with such pressures, entrepreneurial virtue requires a particular strength of personal character, a fiercely independent desire to forgo rent seeking opportunities. Profit seeking in its pure form is virtuous; rent seeking in most of its forms is vicious, and the character of the virtuous entrepreneur naturally and habitually seeks out profits arising from creating value while eschewing accounting profits accruing to rents. The way this distinction cashes out in the real world may be murky, but the analytic distinction as a tendency of *character* is clear.

Entrepreneurial virtue in commercial society vs. rent-seeking society

Of course, nothing we have said guarantees that entrepreneurs will be virtuous. Actually, the absence of such guarantees is precisely our point: the entrepreneurial process offers no guarantee of entrepreneurial virtue, but neither does the political process. So the remaining question is, which of these two non-ideal processes is less detrimental to the character of entrepreneurs?

Commercial society

It is a paradox of entrepreneurship that those who seek profits as a proximate goal are less successful, and actually make smaller profits, than those who are committed to creating value. Profits are a byproduct of a focus on creating value, because successful sellers need healthy, successful customers. In this way, commercial society regularly selects for entrepreneurs whose main assets are character and a reputation for probity.

The first venture capitalist with that job title was Georges Doriot, who co-founded the American Research and Development Corporation in 1946. The company's objective was to connect people sitting on piles of cash accumulated during World War II with servicemen returning with lots of energy and big ideas. The transactions costs were high—investors didn't know which ideas were likely to be profitable, and the new entrepreneurs had few contacts with investors—so Doriot and ARDC undertook to rate investment opportunities and target those with the greatest chances of success. Doriot's own description of his strategy is striking: the correct estimates count character more than the quality of the idea itself.

> "Always remember that someone, somewhere, is making a product that will make your product obsolete," was typical Doriot advice.... "Doriot taught me the commitment and sense of responsibility needed to succeed in business," said American Express Chairman James Robinson III. Former Ford chairman, Philip Caldwell, said, "I can still hear him saying, in his French-accented voice, 'Gentlemen, if you want to be a success in business, *you must love your product*.'"
>
> *(Fisher 2007: 147, emphasis added)*

Doriot's view of venture capital emphasized the importance of caring about the idea itself, and emphasized character as if it were an asset in its own right. The reason for his emphasis was simple: he doubted his ability, and anybody else's, to predict consumers' reaction to an idea, particularly one that was genuinely new. "A grade-A man with a grade-B idea is better than a grade-B man with a grade-A idea. . . . When someone comes in with an idea that's never been tried, the only way you can judge is by the kind of man you're dealing with" (Fisher 2007: 147).

This insight has far-reaching implications for other transactions as well. The problem of enforcing agreements in an uncertain business environment elevates character and reputation to the status of an asset, one that might even be listed on a balance sheet as brand name or "good will" (for further discussion, see Maitland 1997: 21–25). When financier J.P. Morgan was asked before Congress in 1912 whether loans were "based primarily upon money or property," he replied, "No, sir, the first thing is character. . . . Because a man I do not trust could not get money from me on all the bonds in Christendom" (US House of Representatives 1912).

Again, none of this is to say that most managers or CEOs of corporate enterprises cultivate these character traits. Commercial society offers no guarantee that only virtue will be rewarded with commercial success. In fact, a system of impersonal relations, with separation of ownership and control and contracts that focus on short-run gains measured by changes in stock price, may have the effect of winnowing out the entrepreneurial virtues in favor of much less attractive character traits. But the question is, how favorable is the process of profit and loss to the good character of entrepreneurs, compared with the alternative bureaucratic process?

Rent-seeking society

While nothing guarantees virtue, rent seeking society is actively corrosive to virtue, because one can "profit," or even just survive, only at the expense of others. Perhaps the most striking illustration of rent seeking society is found in the remarkably candid statements by Dwayne O. Andreas, CEO of farm and chemical giant Archer-Daniels-Midland Corporation. Mr Andreas saw courting politicians as an important part of his job (Weiner 1996), and ADM's political importance as a sign of his success: "How is the government going to run without people like us? We make 35 percent of the bread in this country, and that much of the margarine, and cooking oil, and all the other things" (Carney 1995). James Bovard put it this way: "ADM's political strategy has long been based on the ideas that politicians should control prices and markets, and that ADM and Andreas should control politicians" (Weiner 1996).

To his credit, Mr Andreas made no effort to justify his rent seeking by saying "everyone does it." In fact, no one "did it" as much, or as successfully, as ADM. His reasoning was that the political environment, and especially the food industry where ADM had positioned itself as "the supermarket to the world," was not really a market system at all:

> There isn't one grain of anything in the world that is sold in a free market. Not one! The only place you see a free market is in the speeches of politicians. People who are not in the Midwest do not understand that this is a socialist country.
>
> *(Carney 1995)*

If entrepreneurs can be virtuous within a process governed by profit and loss, the question is, could virtuous entrepreneurs survive within political processes that are governed by rent seeking? In a modern setting, where there are very few limits on the scope and magnitude of subsidies, bailouts, and regulatory assistance in creating barriers to competition, it may be impossible to avoid acting as both an economic *and* a political entrepreneur. In that environment, one profit-making opportunity is to serve consumers within the entrepreneurial process, but another is to seek rents within the political process. If a virtuous entrepreneur forgoes rents that shareholders perceive as accounting profits, the firm's stock price will be reduced, at least compared with ADM-style management, leaving that firm susceptible to hostile takeovers by firms less hesitant to seek those rents. Rent seeking society thereby *selects against* entrepreneurial virtue, so even if it is possible to be a virtuous entrepreneur, in that environment there is a real question as to whether virtuous entrepreneurship is sustainable.

The key, then, is to ensure that government does not encourage such adverse selection by offering rents to the highest bidder. But this requires virtue on behalf of government officials, and it is a virtue we should not expect to observe: offering rents to producers in exchange for quasi-legal payments, campaign contributions, and other forms of political support captures enormous competitive advantages for incumbent politicians (Buchanan 2003). Thus, while entrepreneurial virtue is possible, it may not be sustainable (even with the best will in the world) in publicly traded firms within an expansive regulatory environment that rewards rent seeking.

So, the mischievous doctrine is false: profit seeking can be virtuous as well as clever. The really difficult question is, can *politicians* be virtuous? Will the political system say *no* when rent-seekers come asking for (say) an occupational licensing requirement that has no basis in merit but serves only to restrict competition, raising prices and harming consumers? What would help entrepreneurs be virtuous is for politicians to be virtuous enough to take politics out of the economic process and leave entrepreneurs no option but to earn profits by creating something that other people want to buy. The crucial question about *entrepreneurial virtue*, therefore, is whether there is any hope of *political virtue*, since it is in everyday political vice that the worst dilemmas of character originate for entrepreneurs.

Concluding remarks

So far, most work on virtue and for-profit business—pessimistic and optimistic alike—has been done in the shadow of MacIntyre's approach. But we hope to have shown that there is no benefit in defining virtue and business in such a way that never the twain could meet; we would prefer to conclude, with Alzola, that in for-profit business, "Virtue is possible" (see Alzola 2012: 396).

Putting that behind us, for all that we have said here several questions still await exploration, in multiple disciplines:

- Can profit seeking be virtuous when exchange is *not* euvoluntary—when there are serious disparities in bargaining power?
- Can it be virtuous not just to make a profit but to try to *maximize* the profit one collects from consumers?
- Does behavioral evidence bolster or undermine the idea that commercial exchange supports virtue?
- Do for-profit ventures make for better or worse neighbors, say, in the wake of a natural disaster?
- Is profit an effective motivator within various types of organizations?
- To what extent is profit the primary motive of people in business?

Essential readings

Essential works on the values of virtue and character in entrepreneurship include Cicero, *On Duties*, Book III; Burton Folsom, *The Myth of the Robber Barons* (2010); Edwin Hartman, *Virtue in Business* (2015); Deirdre McCloskey, *The Bourgeois Virtues* (2006); and Gordon Tullock, *Rent seeking* (1993). For a comprehensive review of many of the best arguments against our position, see Allen E. Buchanan, *Ethics, Efficiency, and the Market* (1985), Chapters 2 and 3.

For further reading in this volume on Aristotle's conception of virtue, see Chapter 2, Theorists and philosophers on business ethics. On virtue as a kind of non-consequentialism, see Chapter 5, Consequentialism and non-consequentialism. For a discussion of virtue in business leadership, see Chapter 25, Leadership and business ethics. On conceptions of entrepreneurship, see Chapter 16, The ethics of entrepreneurship. On political decision-making and rent seeking, see Chapter 21, Regulation, rent seeking, and business ethics. On political decision making and the economic crisis, see Chapter 23, The economic crisis: causes and considerations.

Notes

1 For their constructive comments on earlier drafts, we thank Julia Annas, Jonathan Anomaly, Peter Boettke, Geoffrey Brennan, Ed Friedman, Jerry Gaus, Brian Kogelmann, Mark LeBar, Tristan Rogers, Dave Schmidtz, Danny Shahar, John Thrasher, Mario Villarreal-Diaz, Lawrence White, and the editors of this volume.
2 All translations are original, except Bastiat (1850/2011). The translated versions given in the bibliography are for the use of the reader.
3 "Rent seeking" is variously defined; for background see Krueger (1974), Tollison (1982), and Tullock (1967, 1993). For our purposes, the definition of rent seeking is "the pursuit of artificially high accounting profits obtained through special privileges or protection from competition awarded through political action by state actors." A classic example is the special combination of subsidy and protected monopoly position awarded to Edward Collins to deliver US mail by steamship in the nineteenth century, as described in Folsom (2010, Chapter 1).
4 Maitland (1997). For general overview of virtue in business, see Audi (2012); Hartman (2013), (2015); Kline (1998); Solomon (1992).
5 Brennan (2016); Choi and Storr (2016); Hartman (2015), Chapters 3, 5; Klein (2003); Rose (2016); Solomon (1992), Chapter 6.
6 Brennan (2016); Choi and Storr (2016); Koehn (2005); McCloskey (2006, 1–53, 507–8); Maitland (1997); Smiles (1859, Chapter 8); Solomon (1992, Chapters 19–22).
7 For example, although Solomon is generally an optimist, he agrees with Aristotle that profit seeking is "parasitic," especially when one doesn't "make" anything (1992, 13–16, 101–3).
8 See Nozick (1974, 151–2); Schmidtz (2008, 198–9); see also Marx (1875/1970, Part I, §§1, 3).
9 Cf. Hartman (2013, 259–60); Heath (2013, 119–20). See also Heath (2014, 71).

References

Aaker, J., K.D. Vohs and C. Mogilner (2010). "Nonprofits are Seen as Warm and For-Profits as Competent," *Journal of Consumer Research* 37:2, 224–37.
Alzola, M. (2012). "The Possibility of Virtue," *Business Ethics Quarterly* 22:2, 377–404.
Aquinas (2012). *Summa Theologiae*. Latin-English edition, translated and published by The Aquinas Institute, Rochester, NY.
Aristotle (1995). *Politics*, E. Barker, rev. by R.F. Stalley (trans.). Oxford: Oxford University Press.
Aristotle (1934/1999). *Nicomachean Ethics* 2nd edition, H. Rackham (trans.). Loeb Classics, Cambridge, MA: Harvard University Press.
Arius Didymus (2002). *On Stoic and Peripatetic Ethics: The Work of Arius Didymus*, W.W. Fortenbaugh (trans. and ed.). New Brunswick, NJ: Rutgers University Studies in Classical Humanities.
Arnold, N.S. (1987). "Why Profits are Deserved," *Ethics* 97:2, 387–402.
Arnold, N.S. (1990). "Economists and Philosophers as Critics of the Free Enterprise System," *The Monist* 73:4, 621–41.
Audi, R. (2012). "Virtue Ethics as a Resource in Business," *Business Ethics Quarterly* 22:2, 273–91.
Bastiat, F. (1850/2011). "What is Seen and What is Not Seen," in *The Bastiat Collection*, 2nd edition, 1–48. Auburn, AL: Ludwig von Mises Institute.

Bayham, V. (2005). "A Dream Deferred: Legal Barriers to African Hairbraiding Nationwide." Institute for Justice. Available at: http://ij.org/report/a-dream-deferred/.
Bhattacharjee, A., J. Dana and J. Baron (unpublished). "Is Profit Evil? Associations of Profit with Social Harm." Available at: www.sas.upenn.edu/~danajd/antiprofit.pdf.
Brennan, J. (2012). "For-Profit Business as Civic Virtue," *Journal of Business Ethics* 106:3, 313–24.
Brennan, J. (2016). "Do Markets Corrupt?" in J. Baker and M. White (eds), *Economics and the Virtues*. Oxford: Oxford University Press, 236–55.
Buchanan, A. (1985). *Ethics, Efficiency, and the Market*. Totowa, NJ: Rowman and Littlefield.
Buchanan, J. (2003). "Politics without Romance," *Policy* 19:3, 13–18.
Carney, D. (1995). "Dwayne's World," *Mother Jones* July/August issue.
Choi, S. and V.H. Storr (2016). "Can Trust, Reciprocity, and Friendships Survive Contact with the Market?" in J. Baker and M. White (eds), *Economics and the Virtues*. Oxford: Oxford University Press, 217–35.
Cicero (Marcus Tullius) (1991). *On Duties*, E.M. Atkins (trans.). New York, NY: Cambridge University Press.
File, T. (2013). "Computer and Internet Use in the United States," US Census Bureau. Available at: www.census.gov/prod/2013pubs/p20-569.pdf.
Fisher, K.L. (2007). *100 Minds that Made the Market*. Woodside, CA: Business Classics.
Folsom, B. (2010). *The Myth of the Robber Barons*. Herndon, VA: Young America's Foundation.
Guzman, R.A. and M.C. Munger (2014). "Euvoluntariness and Just Market Exchange: Moral Dilemmas from Locke's *Venditio*," *Public Choice* 158:1, 39–49.
Hartman, E. (2013). "The Virtue Approach to Business Ethics," in D. Russell (ed.), *The Cambridge Companion to Virtue Ethics*. Cambridge: Cambridge University Press, 240–64.
Hartman, E. (2015). *Virtue in Business*. Cambridge: Cambridge University Press.
Heath, E. (2013). "Virtue as a Model of Business Ethics," in Christoph Lütge (ed.), *Handbook of the Philosophical Foundations of Business Ethics*. Berlin: Springer, 109–29.
Heath, E. (2014). "The Qualities of Virtue and its Rivals," in N. Karlson, M. Norek, and K. Wennberg (eds), *Virtues in Entrepreneurship*. Stockholm: Ratio, 58–80.
Kirzner, I. (1973). *Competition and Entrepreneurship*. Chicago, IL: University of Chicago Press.
Klein, S. (1998). "Emotions and Practical Reasoning: Implications for Business Ethics," *Business & Professional Ethics Journal* 17:3–29.
Klein, S. (2003). "The Natural Roots of Capitalism and its Virtues and Values," *Journal of Business Ethics* 45:4, 387–401.
Koehn, D. (2005). "Integrity as a Business Asset," *Journal of Business Ethics* 58:1, 125–36.
Krueger, A. (1974). "The Political Economy of the Rent seeking Society," *American Economic Review* 64:291–303.
MacIntyre, A. (1981). *After Virtue*. Notre Dame, NJ: University of Notre Dame.
Maitland, I. (1997). "Virtuous Markets: The Market as School of the Virtues," *Business Ethics Quarterly* 7:1, 17–31.
Marx, K. (1875/1970). "Critique of the Gotha Programme," in *Karl Marx and Frederick Engels: Selected Works*, vol. 3. Moscow: Progress Publishers.
Maugham, S. (1952). "The Verger," in *Complete Short Stories of Somerset Maugham*. New York: Doubleday.
McCloskey, D. (2006). *The Bourgeois Virtues*. Chicago, IL: University of Chicago Press.
Moore, G. (2002). "On the Implications of the Practice-Institution Distinction," *Business Ethics Quarterly* 12:1, 19–32.
Nozick, R. (1974). *Anarchy, State, and Utopia*. New York, NY: Basic Books.
Radford, R.A. (1945). "The Economic Organisation of a P.O.W. Camp," *Economica* (new series) 12:48, 189–201.
Rose, D. (2016). "Virtues as Social Capital," in J. Baker and M. White (eds), *Economics and the Virtues*. Oxford: Oxford University Press, 202–16.
Schmidtz, D. (2008). "The Institution of Property," in *Person, Polis, Planet: Essays in Applied Philosophy*. New York, NY: Oxford University Press, 193–210.
Seneca (Lucius Annaeus) (1989). "Letters," *Epistulae Morales*, R. M. Gummere (trans.). Loeb Classics. Cambridge, MA: Harvard University Press.
Smiles, S. (1859). *Self-Help*. Boston, MA: Ticknor and Fields.
Smith, A. (1776/1904). *An Inquiry into the Nature and Causes of the Wealth of Nations*, E. Cannan (ed.). London: Methuen & Co.

Solomon, R. (1992). *Ethics and Excellence*. New York, NY: Oxford University Press.
Storr, V. (2009). "Why the Market? Markets as Social and Moral Spaces," *Journal of Markets & Morality* 12:2, 277–296
Swanton, C. (2016). "Virtues of Productivity versus Technicist Rationality," in J. Baker and M. White (eds), *Economics and the Virtues*. Oxford: Oxford University Press, 185–201.
Tollison, R. (1982). "Rent Seeking: A Survey," *Kyklos* 35:4, 575–602.
Tullock, G. (1967). "The Welfare Costs of Tariffs, Monopolies and Theft," *Western Economic Journal* 5:224–232.
Tullock, G. (1993). *Rent Seeking*. Brookfield, VT: Edward Elgar.
Turner, S. (1836). *History of the Anglo-Saxons*, 6th edition. London: Longman, Rees, Orme, Brown, and Green.
US House of Representatives (1912). "Testimony of J.P. Morgan Before the Bank and Currency Committee of the House of Representatives, at Washington, DC; Appointed for the Purpose of Investigating an Alleged Money Trust in 'Wall Street.'" Cross-Examined by Samuel Untermyer, Attorney for the Committee. December 18 and 19, 1912. Washington, DC: United States Government Printing Office.
von Mises, L. (1952). *Planning for Freedom*. South Holland, IL: Libertarian Press.
Weiner, T. (1996). "Dwayne's World: Influence of Archer-Daniels is Wide as Well as Deep," *The New York Times* 16 January.

8
Feminist ethics and business ethics
Redefining landscapes of learning

Ming Lim

As we approach the second decade of the twenty-first century, the field of business ethics continues to gain momentum in business practice, university curricula, and in governmental and nongovernmental organizations worldwide (Holland and Albrecht 2013). Nearly every Fortune 500 company has established corporate social responsibility commitments and mission statements (EABIS 2012) and the impacts of global financial and environmental crises, business misconduct, gender discrimination, pay inequality, whistle-blowing and corruption continue to be named by the next generation of business executives and leaders as some of the most troubling ethical issues of our time (Crane and Matten 2004). The theoretical, philosophical, pedagogical and cultural impetus for a fresh understanding of business ethics is, arguably, coming from developments in a number of sub-disciplines and intellectual streams. One of the most prominent of these developments is feminist ethics.

Feminist theories of ethics encompass a fairly wide range of concepts. Among these are: relationality, responsibility, care and the experience of diverse others, including those in positions of power and privilege. What makes feminist ethics *feminist*, however, is its reorientation of traditional ethics towards a more balanced or fuller appreciation of the moral experiences of women. While business ethics is about the application of ethical principles to problems and dilemmas in business, feminist theories of ethics emphasize the dangers of addressing or approaching these problems from traditional, unexamined ontological and epistemological assumptions about male/female differences that perpetuate women's oppression and marginalization. As a corollary, feminist ethics of business facilitates fresh thinking on how businesses can disrupt, rather than simply perpetuate, strict oppositional boundaries between "male" and "female" approaches and perspectives to business issues. Feminist ethics is especially critical of sex-based gender roles that naturalize the assignation of traditional female roles to women because women are somehow associated with "feminine" traits such as sensitivity, gentleness, passivity, or domesticity. One consequence of this kind of stereotypical thinking is that women do not receive the kind of public respect and recognition—material, professional and positional—accorded to men.

In other words, the underlying problem with traditional ethics—and the assignation of social and economic roles based on 'male' and 'female' traits—is that it is almost always based on essentialist notions of the female subject (Card 1991: 5). Traditional notions of female identity and what constitutes "ethical" choices for women are heavily inscribed in social and cultural discourses and practices bound to sexual (rather than gendered) difference. According to Rosalyn Diprose (1994), arguments from sexual difference tend to mask and perpetuate the subordination of women and the value of their experiences; indeed, saying that a woman is "different" from a man can imply that she is less productive and her contributions less significant than those of a man. Rethinking the female subject thus presents business ethics with new conceptual and empirical challenges. The key purpose of this chapter is to chart a course through some of the current debates around the issue of how business ethics is shaped, and potentially transformed, by feminist ethics.

In recent years, feminist theories of ethics have enlarged the scope of business ethics both philosophically and empirically. Philosophically, feminist ethics continues to expand our notions of "good business": the broadening of stakeholder theories of business owes much to recent work by feminist researchers on the need to consider the many "others" that business affects, including persons and groups beyond shareholders, investors, and executives (Carroll 2004). Empirically, feminist ethics has reshaped the agenda of business ethics by highlighting issues of pay inequality, diversity, and sexism. The battle for gender equality in the workplace, for example, has gained prominence within employment laws and statutes in the European Union, due in no small part to the increasing awareness of women's challenges in professional domains that have very little, if anything, to do with sex but everything to do with socially and discursively constructed notions of gendered behavior, capabilities, and abilities.

Feminist scholarship is also generating greater awareness of how businesses treat, nurture, and represent the voices and concerns of diverse segments of society, including minority groups, women and so on (on women and work, see Hakim 2004; Goldin 2014). The contributions of Alison Jaggar (1992) to the articulation of women's experiences as equally worthy of moral consideration as those of men can hardly be improved upon in this respect. Jaggar (1992) notes that traditional ethics have all too often focused on, and thus privileged, men's moral issues, values, and judgements to the detriment and neglect of women's. Therefore, feminist ethicists must address the imbalance while not making the mistake of overrating either men's *or* women's morality. Feminist ethics seeks to rethink and reimagine the epistemological and ontological assumptions of traditional ethics, including the limitations of privileging rules, laws, and regulations to the neglect of partial, emotional, and complex moral issues. Failure to rethink traditional ethics, in other words, impoverishes everyone, not just women.

From this vantage point, traditional notions of "business ethics" also need to change. Empirically, however, much remains to be explored with regards to how feminist ethics contributes to the moral grounding of business, and, thus and thereby, to a practice-based ethics founded upon virtue, responsibility, and relationship.

The first section of the chapter focuses on key debates in feminist ethics, specifically a feminist ethics versus an ethics of care. In the second section we set forth several ways in which feminist ethics has intersected with business ethics, including both positive and negative assessments of capitalism and the market economy. A third section returns to the topic of an ethics of care—as developed in the work of Carol Gilligan (1982)—and notes how such an ethic is part of a relational turn that some have used as a model for the business firm. That relations between and among others may prove crucial to a feminist business ethics is then approached in the final two sections. Section four takes up the views of Alasdair MacIntyre whose account of virtue is compatible with a feminist ethics that focuses on relations and strikes a balance between a moral universalism and an ethical particularism. The final section brings together the chapter's themes of feminist ethics, business ethics, and the ways in which we practice our ethical commitments in negotiation with others by drawing upon the ethical frameworks proposed by social philosopher and business theorist Etienne Wenger. A mutually constitutive, reflexive, relationship of individuals to their communities and social systems presents a promising research opportunity for advancing "landscapes of practice," as Wenger puts it (Wenger-Trayner et al. 2015: 13), that incorporate a feminist ethics of commercial conduct that is not reducible to an ethics of care.

Feminist ethics and the ethics of care

Feminist theories of ethics may be characterized, broadly speaking, as attempts to overturn, disrupt, and critique traditional theories of ethics that marginalize or exclude women's experiences. The distinction between sex and gender is, again, salient to the discussion because behaviors or traits deemed "feminine" or "masculine" are neither necessary nor essential correlates of females or males, respectively (for an opposed view, see Goldberg 1993; see also Hakim 2007). To the extent that women, for one reason or another, have had to display certain traits such as self-sacrifice, care, or the nurturance of others' interests above their own (and to a much greater degree than men), then so have women been gendered as being *naturally* caring, nurturing and so on. Feminist ethics disputes the essentialist and naturalizing tendency to attribute caring traits exclusively—or primarily—to women and not to men. This gendering of traits perpetuates stereotypes of women as the "caring sex" while ignoring a far more fundamental issue of "*who* cares for *whom*" (Tong 1996: 72, my italics).

Carol Gilligan's groundbreaking, if controversial, work (1982) makes an important contribution to the question of whether, and how, women might respond differently from men in situations calling for moral decision-making. She found that there were different "voices" that emerge in ethical deliberations, one of which was a voice of "care," distinct from one based on abstract, universal rules. It is important to note that Gilligan refrained from identifying this "voice" as uniquely feminine, although she has been misread as saying exactly that. She merely noted that there was evidence that an ethics of care was more evident in "women's voices" (1982: 2).

Over a decade after her 1982 book, Gilligan (2011) made a distinction between a feminine ethic and a feminist ethic. A feminine ethic derives from a fundamentally asymmetrical relationship between the person who cares and those she cares for. To "care," in this context, entails (among other features) the sacrifice of one's interests and even one's well-being for the sake of others, as well as the subordination of one's self-development to that of the other. Relationships built upon this definition of care are unequal because the one who is presumed to carry feminine traits is defined by an ethical *lack*, a lack of agency insofar as the one who cares for the other feels incapable of making the choice *not* to put the other's interest(s) above her own. Furthermore, an ethics of care assumes separation between selves: the self that cares and the self that receives care.

By contrast, feminist ethics is not defined by the kind of asymmetrical ethical relations that underpin an ethics of care (Borgerson 2007; Sherwin 1996). Indeed, "conflating feminist ethics with care ethics has resulted in misapprehension, theoretical misunderstanding, and, most importantly, missed opportunities to benefit from feminist ethics' extensive and flexible assets," Janet L. Borgerson argues (2007: 477). What exactly are the "assets" feminist ethics offers that an ethics of care does not?

According to Rosemarie Tong (1993), the answer lies in an ontology and epistemology founded upon the idea of relationship rather than hierarchical difference. The hierarchy in a relationship founded on the care-giver and the cared for, for example, is masked because the caring relationship is structured as ethically benign. Yet, as Tong (1993) cautions, *all* of us are intersubjectively related; from an ethical perspective, therefore, hierarchical relations should be interrogated. To the extent that women have been subordinated and oppressed by systems and structures controlled by men, this insight is even more urgent than it might otherwise be.

Women need to be liberated from the ontology implied by the "ethics of care," in other words. In this sense, therefore, feminist ethics can provide a much-needed, alternative ontology to that of the ethics of care.

Feminist ethicists argue that women's experiences should not be essentialized as different (i.e., less important, less valid, less reasonable, etc.) from those of men. Traditional epistemologies of sexual difference leave oppositions based on gender intact, but feminist ethics places "gender differences" under sharp scrutiny, questioning the epistemological grounds for gender-based arguments that purport to encourage "ethical sensitivity" towards women's issues (see Collins 2000). Even more crucially, feminist ethics transcends, according to Borgerson, the gap between business ethicists' concerns with lived experiences of ethical dilemmas, on the one hand, and traditional ethical principles of universality and abstract reason.

Feminist ethics and business ethics

Feminist ethics today has come a long way from the historical concerns of feminism, namely, those focused on women's rights, female empowerment, and the deconstruction of masculinist discourses of power, privilege, influence, and rights (Dobson and White 1995; Wicks et al. 1994; Gilligan 1982). Moreover, in the case of business ethics more particularly, feminist ethics is discussed by a number of scholars as a powerful lens with which to re-examine business practice and governance (Machold et al. 2008; Liedtka 1999; Dobson and White 1995). Both feminists as well as non-feminists have weighed in on the vexed question as to how feminist theory shapes (or can be integrated) into business ethics. A few broad lines of argument can, however, be discerned.

One line of discussion focuses on whether or how feminist ethics might contribute to business ethics. For example, some scholars are skeptical about the utility of including feminist agendas in business ethics research. Chimezei Osigweh and Loren Falkenberg (1995), for example, contend that feminist ethics entrenches gender dichotomies and thus fails to recognize the shifting balance of power towards the rights of minorities. In their view, business ethics transcends gender dichotomies and acknowledges minority rights.

By contrast, a number of leading feminist ethicists emphasize that feminist ethical theory and business ethics can, and should be, deeply integrated because the two domains share common conceptual and empirical concerns related to care for others and to the representation of minority voices. Thus, these scholars have argued that feminist theory can play a pivotal role in enriching business ethics (Burton and Dunn 1996; Borgerson 2007) precisely because feminist concerns for neglected or minority or marginalized "others" broadens the scope of traditional business ethics. Still others have called for business ethics to "integrate" into feminist ethics (Rabouin 1997: 247).

Another strand of argument focuses on whether feminism and capitalism can be friends. From a broad perspective informed by economics and history, some feminists have hailed commerce as an agent for ethical (not merely material) progress. The seminal work of Deirdre McCloskey (2006) positions the rise of capitalism as an engine for ethical advancement: capitalism, in other words, "improves our ethics" (2006: 22). McCloskey exhorts us to remember that "(c)apitalists ended slavery and emancipated women and founded universities and rebuilt churches, none of these for material profit and none by damaging the rest of the world" (2006: 32).

Of course, feminism has an historical connection with movements on the anti-capitalist left (for example, Ehrenreich 1976). Critics of a market-based view, such as that adumbrated by McCloskey, maintain that a class-based system like capitalism will always tend to subordinate women's interests to those of men; the only way for women to be as powerful as men is to replace capitalism with socialism, by which is meant challenging patriarchy and inequality inherent in capitalism with the recognition that all work undertaken by all classes of women—especially domestic and/or emotional labor—is valuable and should be free from exploitation and the threat of violence (Ehrenreich 1976; Hochschild 1989). Implicit in the critiques of capitalism by socialist/Marxist feminists is that men and women are paid unequally for their work and that such inequalities can be ameliorated only by expanding the role of public or state control.

Both past and recent research shows, however, that the lowest-paid categories of work in contemporary societies are those associated with informal services such as care-giving, occupational categories that are represented disproportionately by women (ILO Report 2015, 2016). In its 2016 report, the ILO found that:

> Gender stereotypes of women and expectations by society that they will shoulder larger care responsibilities, lack of role models, a work culture that expects long working hours, the undervaluation of traditionally "feminine" skills and inadequate work–family measures limit the possibilities for women to overcome segregation and participate on an equal footing in political, social and economic life and decision-making and reach top-level positions.
>
> *(ILO Report 2016: 10)*

The ethical foundation for this phenomenon, from a feminist viewpoint, lies in how epistemological categories of "male" versus "female" value continue to be perpetuated in the world of work. In other words, the precepts of traditional ethics—which (over)rate social and cultural constructions of masculinity (autonomy, will, intellect, war, domination) above traits deemed to be feminine (caring, sharing, emotion, peace, the body)—continue to hold sway over much of the developed and developing world. In traditional ethics itself "male" ways of moral reasoning that emphasize norms, rules, universality, and impartiality are privileged over "female" ways of moral reasoning that focus on relationships, responsibilities, particularity, and partiality (Jaggar 1992, 1991).

A third strand of discussion focuses on practical questions related to women in the workplace. In capitalist and post-capitalist societies, feminist ethics treads a thin line between two competing imperatives: moral respect for diverse workforces, for minority rights, for women's rights and so on, on the one hand; and the constant pressure to satisfy shareholder, regulatory and profitability demands, on the other. In a point of difference with feminist ethics, business ethics is, ultimately, focused on business, albeit business conducted in as virtuous and socially responsible a manner as possible. Interestingly enough—and perhaps as a response to the "business" in business ethics—feminist scholars have begun to tackle the practical requirements of business, addressing issues such as autonomy, power, personal identity and corporate social responsibility in tandem with issues related to an ethics of care (e.g., Grosser 2016; Banerjee 2010). Thus, contemporary arguments put forward by feminists take in a much wider scope of concern than "women's issues" or feminine qualities.

In keeping with this broad social agenda, feminist ethics strives for nothing less than a fundamental questioning of a community's taken-for-granted moral assumptions and norms (Card 1999). What underpins the feminist ethical project and its application to commerce is not merely the desire to challenge male bias in the moral treatment of issues usually relegated to that sphere of experience called "women's issues" but a determination to examine and critique the ontology and epistemology of ethics altogether, giving weight and value to women's experiences in terms of sexuality, reproductive rights, work and employment, taking note, especially, of the multiple ways in which women experience oppression by virtue of class, race, sex as well as gender. In other words, it is "essential that feminist ethics should address certain hitherto neglected issues or areas of life" (Card 1999: 85) as experienced by women.

In summary, feminist ethics is inclusive of women's perspectives, reasoning and lived experiences (Derry 2002). Women's voices as well as political and socio-economic dimensions of justice and equality (including care ethics) are inextricably part of the fabric of a feminist ethic that differs in fundamental respects from a masculinist perspective (Noddings 1994; Tronto 1999, 1993; Held 1993). The question of a distinctively "woman's voice" in ethics, however, raises other issues pertaining to the "self," and "identity," and how these are articulated and expressed in professional as well as domestic settings.

Ethics of care: a way forward?

Carol Gilligan's book, *In a Different Voice* (1982, 1990), set off new debates among feminist ethicists. She found that boys and girls responded differently to morality-related questions, that many women feared "a morality of rights and non-interference" that appeared to justify "indifference and unconcern" whereas, "from a male perspective, a morality of responsibility appears inconclusive and diffuse" (Gilligan 1990: 22). Women, Gilligan argues, face particular problems in distinguishing between "the created or socially constructed feminine voice" and "a voice they hear as their own" (1990: xvii), although women *do*, she stresses, hear the difference.

Elucidating the point about male–female differences further, Gilligan presents a division based on two selves. For women, the self is relational while, for men, the self is set apart from others—all moral action follows from this division (Gilligan 1982, 1990). The autonomous self is defined against others; the aim is to play a game of defined rules in accordance with abstract principles of what is acceptable and unacceptable. Gilligan's empirical research found, in this context, that men were twice as likely as women to be willing to engage in actions regarded as unethical, to be more competitive in business decision-making and to regard such decision-making as more of a game than an issue of relationships between people. Set against this tendency of men is the feminine self, or "voice," consciously joined to others—not hierarchically—but in a web of interrelationships that govern women's ethical choices much more, it appears, than they do men's. The ethical orientation for this feminine voice is conceptualized in terms of care; the masculine orientation is conceptualized as ethics of rights or justice.

Many questions have been raised about the nature of this difference identified by Gilligan (1982): in what does it consist and does it apply to other settings? For Mary Swigonski and Salome Raheim (2011: 15), care ethics is deeply contextual:

> Care-focused . . . decision making embodies attention to the environment and focuses on the unique and particular features of a situation. Moral decisions are made on the basis of these features. Care grounded in contextual decision making begins from the standpoint of the concrete other and views every individual as unique with a concrete history, identity, and affective constitution. Feelings, along with rationality, become morally central. Care emphasizes maintaining relationships and takes the concerns of others as a basis for action, starting from the standpoint of the ones who need care or attention. Within relationships, care is manifest as both attitude and action, both disposition and practice.

For John Dobson and Judith White, care ethics is part of a relationship-based value system that makes what they call the "*feminine* firm" morally desirable. It is the value system that is found in "feminine firms" (1995: 463).

For many feminists, the ethic of care, although attractive as a concept, is problematic because it makes universalizing claims about "woman" as category and about women's experiences (Friedman and Bolte 2007). An even more devastating critique comes from Robin Derry (1996) who suggests that "the notion of a 'Feminist Firm'" may be more productive (1996: 101) than that of the "feminine firm" proposed by Dobson and White (1995). In essence, Derry argues that conceptualizing behavioral traits as "feminine" or "masculine" is not in fact helpful for business ethics. What is needed is to note how such terms can be used to justify unethical ways of behaving within business organizations. Although men and women do approach business problems and realities differently, business ethicists can, with the help of feminist theory, help move the needle towards greater ethical transparency by enabling women to assert their voices instead of continuing to see women as part of a game still "controlled by men" (Derry 1996: 102).

Feminist ethics, therefore, is not exclusively—or even primarily—focused on women in a caring role. Yet, the ethic of care is still a prolific and persistent branch of feminist theory that spans many disciplines. Marilyn Friedman and Angela Bolte (2007) argue that care survives its critics because an ethic of care: a) focuses on aspects of humanity historically ignored by dominant discourses written by men largely uninvolved in care practices (e.g., childrearing); b) goes beyond critiquing masculinist values and provides a substantive ethic; c) is distinct from the three existing dominant paradigms of morality (utilitarian, Kantian, and virtue theories); and d) brings close personal interrelations to focus in philosophies of ethics, decentering humanist values of objectivity and universality. In these ways, the ethic of care aligns with management functions as characterized in relationship management theory (e.g., Ledingham 2003) or in dialogic theory of communication (e.g., Kent and Taylor 2002). The notion of care has even emerged (in name and theory) in public relations literature: for example, Timothy Coombs and Sherry Holladay have recently argued that "The ethic of care's focus on interdependence, mutuality, and reciprocity mirrors our perspective on public relations" (2013: 40). In addition, care is situated and local, aligning it also with goals for culturally immersed and sensitive research, as well as an orientation to social change (Robinson 2011). These authors have situated care as a socially embedded construct but leave unexplored the question of how it can be effectively challenged unexplored.

As already noted, some scholars remain less convinced by this account of the ethic of care than Dobson and White. Derry (1996), for instance, takes umbrage at what she sees as their simplistic binarification of women as good and men as hopelessly flawed. Somewhat sarcastically, she paraphrases Dobson and White's argument as one in which

> Women can save us from the error of our ways. A concern for relationships, nurturing communities, care, and trust, could redeem our competitiveness, material greed, consumption obsession, and distrust. Dobson and White argue that a feminine approach would improve the economic and moral standing of the firm. Among the potential improvements would be greater cooperation, collaboration, mutual support and trust, all leading to a decrease in costs associated with theft, absenteeism, poor morale, and excessive competitiveness.
>
> *(Derry 1996: 105)*

Virtue, self, and other: implications for business ethics

Following on the distinction between feminist ethics and an ethic of care, it is essential to probe a little deeper the question of how the self is positioned vis-a vis the "other" in society and the implications of such theorizing for an understanding of virtue. In so doing, we can gain a better sense of how a feminist ethic may draw from an ethics of virtue, which itself places emphasis on relations with others. How does the self balance a sense of morality with personal interest? How, in other words, do we balance our private wants and needs with social obligations to behave in a predictable but acceptable way?

The virtue theory of Alasdair MacIntyre combines an account of the importance of recognizing the universal validity of morality with a canny awareness of the contextual, often unpredictable nature of human behavior. The enlightenment notion of "some shared impersonal standard in virtue" (MacIntyre [1981] 2007: ix) refers to a context that can be said to no longer exist in a meaningful way. Instead, MacIntyre calls for an understanding of the "situatedness of all enquiry" (MacIntyre [1981] 2007: xii) and the varying standards of truth and the justifications put forward for those truths by those who claim moral or managerial authority. Historical understanding and awareness is required to challenge managerial claims of expertise that rely for their legitimacy and power on unjustified (and outdated) generalizations of a law-like nature (MacIntyre 1985: 206, 210).

For MacIntyre, the cultivation of "internal" goods can, and should, harmonize and be integrated with, the pursuit of "external" goods. Indeed, both kinds of activities are mutually reinforcing of each other. Internal goods (such as love, practices of self-cultivation, and so on) require some level of participation in the acquisition and consumption of external goods (such as money and prestige). However, external goods should not dominate one's life pursuit to the detriment or neglect of internal goods. Both are "goods" and both are genuinely good, depending on the uses to which they are put. As MacIntyre contends:

> It would be a large misconception to suppose that allegiance to goods of the one kind necessarily excluded allegiance to goods of the other . . . Thus the goods of excellence cannot be systematically cultivated unless at least some of the goods of effectiveness are also pursued. On the other hand it is difficult in most social contexts to pursue the goods of effectiveness without cultivating at least to some degree the goods of excellence.
>
> *(MacIntyre 1988: 35)*

MacIntyre's argument can be extended usefully to business practice and to feminist ethics. To the extent that one's desire is to seek the betterment of society and community through the conduct of one's business, commerce can be a vehicle for expressing the virtues associated with the desire for internal goods as well a means for acquiring external goods (Arrow 1975).

Scholars have noticed the trend—in business-ethics theory—from a normative, rule-based approach to rationality towards a virtue-ethics approach (e.g., Klein 1989; Murphy et al. 2007). Deirdre McCloskey (2006), for instance, proposes that the capitalist system itself produces virtue in a way that other market systems do not, and, indeed, produces specific virtues that enable the larger good of society—virtues like prudence, temperance, justice, courage, love and faith. Thus, capitalism encourages the expression of virtue. At the same time agents do not act in a vacuum. They are always acting within specific contexts or connections. This is why the concept of "virtue-ethics" in contexts as deeply embedded within society as business and politics requires further redefinition, in my view. It is not enough, epistemologically or practically, to theorize virtue as a desire to act according only to internalized motivation. A virtue-based organization is thus at the same time, situationally dynamic; such an organization inspires and nurtures the individual's motivation to cultivate and to exercise excellence of character and virtuous qualities.

The notion of virtuous agency requires, therefore, additional probing. How is the agent positioned in relation to the society? How can ethics be consistently practiced when conditions in commerce and politics can be volatile and unpredictable and where the temptation to do what seems most expedient and self-serving lurks in every corner? A feminist theory of ethics, by emphasizing inherent intersubjective relationships and responsibility, encourages the conditions that also facilitate greater interpersonal awareness of ethical conduct between ourselves and others. Greater interpersonal awareness can be profoundly helpful in anchoring right commercial conduct. This orientation towards intersubjectivity seems to lead us up the right path: a lived understanding of experiential relational responsibility towards others is perfectly in keeping with a feminist theory of business ethics that emphasizes the universal value of moral action. Intersubjectivity is not limited to the expression and exercise of virtue between individual agents, however; it also implies a standard that is universally valid and desirable. In the words of the political philosopher Seyla Benhabib, a feminist ethics is a finely-poised balance between "moral universalism (and) ethical particularism" (2004: 16).

But we can go further still. How can businesses operationalize a caring feminist ethics of business? In a time of global challenges, when concepts and limits of tolerance are being stretched like never before by ecological crises, mass migration, terrorism, and citizenship claims and rights across a spectrum of differences, the role of business in balancing ethical dilemmas has become ever more acute. Andrew Wicks' diagnosis of the issue can hardly be disagreed with and is worth quoting at some length:

> Firms of today are struggling to create and manage a diverse workforce, foster teamwork and cooperation, create trust and empowerment, and share power and accountability (i.e., decentralization). All of these efforts require training and modeling of the sort which caring requires (indeed, many of them are forms or extensions of caring), yet each resists the creation of universal decision rules to get at the heart of the matter.
>
> *(1994: 529)*

Wicks is correct, in my view, in emphasizing, effectively, the importance of organizational learning to enable virtuous conduct within firms. He is also right to caution against taking an overly prescriptive, mechanistic approach to such efforts. That is to say, a sense of sociality and connectedness founded upon a feminist ethic, has to be balanced with systems to ensure fidelity and compliance with ethical conduct.

While forms of belongingness can, and should be, embedded in firms and communities, broad consensus (impartially laid down, enforced and communicated) must still operate in a fair, transparent and sustainable fashion. Business ethics, in other words, must be businesslike. This requirement notwithstanding, however, we can still work towards instantiating caring systems and community-led programs that facilitate and produce (largely) benevolent, compassionate and humane business practices and environments, supported by policies that are not only (or overwhelmingly) dominated by utilitarian or instrumental ends.

The enactment(s) of virtuous business conduct takes place through processes of engagement and negotiation. Although debates and negotiations about the meanings of "good," "just," and "fair" may often be tacit rather than explicit in business practice, notions of what constitutes ethical conduct in business often emerge as a result of dialogue and mutual engagement. Furthermore, these subtle negotiations of the "best way" or "the best outcome possible" between individuals and groups in the context of practice take place both internally and externally. Internally, communities configure and reconfigure norms of conduct; externally, they position and reposition themselves within broader networks of influence (Wenger 1998). When these processes of configuration are somehow aligned in a common purpose, business practices of all kinds work smoothly without each person having to share, or even consent to, the same values or beliefs. Consensual systems and rules exist as a social lubricant to ease our professional relations with each other.

Nonetheless, there is more to understand about how independent subjects form ethical relationships with others in social life. How are the relationship(s) between employers, managers and customers structured, for instance? Do these structures reflect gender roles or gender biases? How do colleagues at work arrive at a consensus about how they interact to achieve good outcomes in a range of professional areas? What ethical rules, if any, help support the smooth, harmonious and virtuous functioning of these relationships? And how do we *learn* these rules of participation?

Etienne Wenger: learning a (virtue) ethics of relationship

One of the most workable, and inspiring, illustrations of such a system of learning is that developed by the Swiss educationist and social theorist Etienne Wenger. Wenger (1998) has developed a constellation of concepts based on "situated cognition," "communities of practice" and "regimes of competence" that have illuminated the processes by which individuals and groups view, negotiate with, and work with others in organizations.

Wenger's concept of "communities of practice," especially, has had a strong and enduring impact upon how businesses can nurture innovation as well as an ethics of respect based upon mutual sharing and learning. "Communities of practice," according to Wenger are "groups of people who share a concern, a set of problems, or a passion about a topic, and who deepen their knowledge and expertise in this area by interacting on an ongoing basis" (Wenger et al. 2002: 4). Continual engagement with others around a common professional purpose (or social mission) is the foundation of communities of practice. But the theory of these communities goes much further than this: it explains how actors can, as a result of group interactions, *learn* to allow their social identities to be changed and, on that basis, change their social world. This interaction between "self" and "world" is ethical in a profound sense because it involves questions of what is good for the organization, what is most innovative, most harmonious, and so on. But this interaction may also serve as the basis for rethinking the traditional workplace and for making it a place in which women and men will succeed.

Thus, an ethics of learning is inextricably bound up with social identity. Social identity, as Wenger conceives the concept, is both a *process* and an *outcome* of all kinds of negotiations (some harmonious, some not) between oneself and others (Wenger 1998). This process of negotiation takes place in diverse settings and comes to the fore explicitly in professional situations, e.g., contract negotiations, political diplomacy, work teams and so on. Wenger's theory of social identity is, first and foremost, premised upon an ethical relation between "self" and "other" that is finely balanced between autonomy of the individual self and responsibility for others. Wenger proposes that individuals and societies can negotiate (jointly) for a certain kind of social ethics that emerges out of the respectful learning of the other's differences—gender differences as well as differences in the perception, resolution and communication of ethical issues and dilemmas. When individuals are empowered to learn from, and through, these differences as part of a trajectory of meaning-making conversations, activities, tools and other means of engagement, a more robust organization is the result (Wenger and Snyder 2000). Everyone is a worker and everyone is a manager—the conventional hierarchies can loosen and even dissolve (Wenger and Snyder 2000).

It is important to remind ourselves that Wenger describes this negotiated identity-formation as a *learned* activity. As a result of this learning, I negotiate my identities with others, allowing them to change my understanding of them and their understanding of me. In this way, a certain phenomenology of self is fused with a pragmatic, situated, yet deeply caring, practical ethics of business. From a feminist perspective, Wenger's theory of learned identity and meaning-making adds a rich perspective to—extends the boundaries of—notions of relationship and interconnectedness, all of which inhere in notions of virtue discussed so far.

For Wenger, simply engaging with the social world, with community, with work and so on—including, but certainly not limited to, businesses and schools—changes one's social identity (Wenger 1998). This change in my social identity is both a cause and a consequence of the way I relate to others. In this way, Wenger argues, my *ethical* relation to the world changes in a dynamic process of exchange with others. I am obliged to reflect upon how I do right by others and how I do good (or otherwise) for and to others. My relations of participation with others become reified, acceptable and, thus and thereby, virtuous (Wenger 1998). Wenger, however, does not intend "communities of practice" to be normatively interpreted as "good" or "bad": his framework helps businesses see, instead, how they might be failing or succeeding in engaging with their members to the extent that networks of interests are either functioning well or less well in meeting organizational objectives (see Probst and Borzillo 2008). By definition, communities of practice are *epistemologically* non-hierarchical although they are likely, of course, to be organizationally and functionally structured in layers or hierarchies.

Intra-organizational networks, however, are only part of the story for Wenger. True communities of practice are forged out of individuals' willingness to adjust or modify their professional identities, which is particularly fruitful in the context of business and industry. Further, others' identities are also changed as a result of their interactions with oneself. For Wenger, *community* is what emerges out of this mutually reciprocal process of identity-making. In other words, community is the all-important concept that allows human individuals to develop virtuous social identities. These identities become legitimized and endure through repertoires of practice using shared resources (objects, purposes, aspirations, places, texts, and so on). Through these repertoires and practices, one learns what matters and why it matters. This learned practice forms part of a history of memories. In other words, learning is not an abstract set of rules and theories; to enter the discursive, symbolic and emotional life of any community, that community must encourage participation and relationship among others with a common interest in achieving a set of goals.

Learning is thus the accumulation of facts, activities, and tools by an agent in a world made up of certain systems and structures; it is the *mutually constitutive relationship* between agents (their activities, concerns and interests) and the world (Lave and Wenger 1991). In this relation of participation, the social and the individual constitute each other. This mutual constitution of subject and object is enabled by a certain reification (in the form of common or collective rules, memories and artifacts). When the rules of a community combine naturally and easily with their reification (or participatory enactments), a "regime of competence" results. This, then, is how learning takes place and takes root in a community, business, workplace or group. For Wenger, this relationship forms the ethical horizon of how we conduct ourselves in every professional setting.

Ethics, therefore, is a set of evolving, dynamic, continually changing, *learned* relationships. And "relationship" is most productive as a concept when it is anchored to learning as a reflexively participatory practice that can be consciously invoked to solve business problems and to reflect upon ethical issues within organizations, especially, and not in spite of, the random and messy conditions under which businesses operate. What makes the process *ethical*—and not merely about encouraging desirable attributes or modes of behavior such as honesty or punctuality or productivity—is its reflexivity: relationships, according to Wenger, enable us to reflect upon our contributions and behaviors within organizations and, thus, to trigger a process of peaceful, collectively beneficial change. Even more than that, our relationships become a way of holding up a mirror to the organizations in which we work. They allow others around us to understand the organization better, to see it through our eyes, so to speak.

Because of the nature of communities "in" practice, therefore, Wenger's concepts can enrich a feminist ethics of business. Business ethics, as a field, has conceived of organizations in a somewhat static fashion, as groups or collectives of actors who work (or aim to work) towards "sustainability" or "corporate social responsibility" or similar goals. Yet, as Wenger explains, ethical corporate behavior must take into account the ways in which different actors, male and female, negotiate a common set of meanings and purposes and, by doing so, change their organizational practices for (long-lasting) good. Individuals, groups and the wider organization and societies in which they operate can be reconceived as *intersubjectively constitutive*, in other words. With this ontology of understanding, Wenger's framework offers an alternative to hierarchical thinking and disempowering binary distinctions consisting of unequal power relations. By explaining how organizational actors can be reflexively engaged in their organizations, Wenger and his collaborators have mapped out a viable way to allow ethics to be part of organizational learning practice, and thus and thereby, for such learning to evolve as the individuals and groups in organizations engage in new identity-making projects and practices.

Wenger's framework of ethics also makes several powerful contributions to feminist ethics. First, it enables *mutuality* and *reciprocity* between the personal self and her or his professional identity. Communities of practice, in effect, can soothe the constant feminist anxieties that circulate around doing what women need and want to do and what women feel obliged to do as a "social being in a social world," to borrow one of Wenger's phrases. As Gilligan (1982) discovered in her research, women often feel unable to manage the tensions between the private and the public or professional personae they adopt. Women's ready-made or spontaneous communities of interest can be conceived of as professional communities of practice, as, indeed, millions of women have found out. Wenger's theory allows us to see that both men's as well as women's networks in business can be mutually constitutive within, and beyond, the organization. Practical activities of mutual engagement based on this understanding can loosen unhelpful hierarchies and provide common metrics of valuation, reward, and recognition across gender boundaries.

Second, communities of practice add a dimension of *dynamicity* to feminist concerns. As women's repertoires of communicative competence develop within organizations, they form new networks, associations, and alliances that co-evolve with those of men. Relations of professional caring can grow as a result of shared learning, especially if these are institutionalized and given professional recognition. Wenger's theory of social identity and the ethics of practical community mean that women can find new freedom as leaders, ambassadors, and champions of an organizational ethics based on social cognition rather than socially-constructed roles of power and privilege. Interestingly, it has been argued that the very process by which individuals enact masculinities and femininities emerges out of participation in legitimate communities of practice (Paechter 2003). The "learning of particular forms of masculinity and femininity" has implications for our bodily and professional identity (Paechter 2003: 69).

Wenger notes, however, that the process of learning a shared ethics of practice is far from assured. It is often fraught with risks and dysfunction of all kinds. But it is inherently productive because it keeps the "improvisational logic" of shared competence alive. Shared competence refers to the domain of common interests or expertise that individuals use to interact with each other for the purpose of achieving a set of goals or objectives. Further, competence goes beyond the assemblage or specified portfolios of competencies that enable organizations to achieve their goals. Rather, competence is tied to issues of power and to how communities hold individuals accountable. Wenger emphasizes further that definitions of "competence" and "accountability" are inextricably linked to questions of power (Wenger 2012). As he says,

The definition of the regime of accountability and of who gets to qualify as competent are questions of power. Every learning move is a claim to competence, which may or may not function — i.e., be considered legitimate by the community or change the criteria for competence that the community has developed. From this perspective, a community of practice can be viewed as an unstable equilibrium among a set of experiences, each with a more or less effective claim to the competence that defines the community. Learning and power imply each other.

(Wenger 2012: 8)

For the individual, the learning process has meaning and value because it reflects her or his personal engagement with the situation at hand. For the group, long-held or taken-for-granted behaviors can be disrupted and, therefore, changed, by individuals' insights or experiences (Lave and Wenger 1991). The process of situated learning is, therefore, potentially transformative for all concerned.

Just as feminist ethics challenges ontologies of dualism (self versus others, individual agency versus community will), so does Wenger's epistemology offer an innovative approach to feminist business ethics that offers an account of how communities of practice can create and reify virtuous conduct. The potential for gender issues to be abrasive or inflammatory becomes softened when people understand that ethical problems are resolved through learned engagement rather than through fixed categories of understanding: "feminine," "masculine," "male," "female," and so on. The worlds of business, education, commerce and industry can benefit enormously from the notion that ethics is about sharing competencies rather than solving problems, even those rooted in gender inequality or asymmetrical relations between individuals (as is often theorized under an "ethics of care"). Wenger offers new possibilities for a feminist ethics that is practical, reflexive, participatory, and self-enhancing. Too often, individuals experience the world of work as constraining and artificial. Learning to negotiate between the spaces of social morality and workplace participation might be one of the best ways to magnify the concepts of caring, responsibility, relationship and trust discussed in this chapter.

Concluding remarks

The productive tensions and overlaps between feminist ethics, a feminine ethic of care and business ethics carry profound implications for commercial practice. By reviewing some of the key debates in these fields, we can position feminist ethics in a way that fully exploits its potential for enabling meaningful ethical progress in commercial settings and workplaces of all kinds. Many scholars (e.g., Lentricchia 1989; McCloskey 2006) provide compelling evidence that capitalism is rarely as it is caricatured by its critics. As MacIntyre has argued, virtue is grown and encouraged not by rigidly adhering to law-like rules (although these have a role to play in modern life) but by a horizon of history and context. Universal rules need to be situated within varying standards of truth that acknowledge the unpredictability of human nature.

The pursuit of internal goods, as MacIntyre argues, is compatible with the consumption of external goods: even virtue requires a certain level of social comfort. In our time—and in a similarly insightful manner—moral economists such as McCloskey have demonstrated how capitalism can enable moral flourishing. Capitalism lends itself to a certain enabling mechanism for the cultivation of internal virtue (Solomon 1992; McCloskey 2010). Feminist ethics, by insisting upon the inclusion of the concerns and interests of non-state actors (minorities, working mothers, care givers, the disabled and other marginalized groups) within mainstream systems of production and consumption, adds new depth and nuance to the consideration of virtue in social life. If it is harder for some groups to access material (external) goods than others, how do we re-theorize "business ethics" from the perspective of women and marginalized others? How can we ensure that capitalism allows the moral flourishing of all, recognizing the experiences of women as well as men? These are questions to be explored and researched further. In the meantime, a process of collective learning can take place to provide additional insight for social change. Wenger's work is fruitfully considered from this perspective.

From his perspective, a feminist theory of care, although valuable because it makes a commitment to social change, still leaves intact a moral hierarchy. By arguing for common interests based on negotiated, learned social identities, Wenger's framework loosens the bonds of hierarchy. Social learning within caring communities becomes a productive and useful means for embedding social change in commerce. Collaboration and teamwork in business environments may well be strengthened if systems of learning that nurture virtues such as love, justice and compassion are actively encouraged rather than sidelined or ignored altogether (Wenger and Snyder 2000). Wenger's theory of social identity, learning, and the ethics of community practice has provided a means by which we can re-imagine the ethics of commercial conduct. A social theory of identity aligns well with current work in feminist ethics that emphasizes contextual appreciation of the desirability of cultural and political sensitivity towards others, including, but not limited to, those who are socially, historically and economically marginalized or disempowered (Warin and Gannerud 2014; Borgerson 2007; Bacchi and Beasley 2005).

New areas of exploration would include an even bolder vision of feminist firms now and in the future. These would be led, organized, and managed by both men and women who have diverse learning styles and goals. Some of the most pressing—and enduring—inequalities suffered by women in the workplace, for example, may be addressed if we recognize that the sources of the problems lie not merely in the glacial rate of institutional, legal and political change but in our collective failure to implement systems of learning and norms of moral identity that support progressive, non-sexist forms of corporate behavior. When such gaps are recognized and addressed, businesses and workplaces will make further progress in gender equality and ethical performance. A productive, flourishing, empirically grounded feminist ethics of business, in other words, must combine care, collaboration, teamwork and a system of social learning in order to be capable of thriving both in, and through, individuals in a business setting.

Essential readings

For a lucid account of the functions and moral basis for feminist ethics, see Alison Jaggar's chapter on "Feminist Ethics" in Lawrence Becker and Charlotte Becker (eds), *Encyclopedia of Ethics* (1992). Rosemarie Tong's *Feminine and Feminist Ethics* (1993) provides a clear exposition of the epistemological overlaps as well as differences in the feminine versus feminist conceptions of ethics. The cross-fertilization of arguments between feminist ethics and business ethics is covered by Robin Derry in her chapter on "Feminist Theory and Business Ethics" in *The Encyclopedia of Business Ethics* (2002) edited by Robert Frederick. For the latest work on how feminist ethics informs business and corporate governance, see Subhabrata Bobby Banerjee's "Governing the Global Corporation: A Critical Perspective," (2010) and Kate Grosser's "Corporate Social Responsibility and Multi-Stakeholder Governance: Pluralism, Feminist Perspectives and Women's NGOs" (2016).

For further reading in this volume on the relation of virtue and business, see Chapter 7, Can profit seekers be virtuous? On moral awareness, see Chapters 4, Teaching business ethics and 27, The ethics of managers and employees. For a discussion of exploitation in the labor market, see Chapter 29, Exploitation and labor. For a view of business ethics that prioritizes lived practice rather than the application of theories, see Chapter 3, Theory and method in business ethics.

References

Arrow, K. (1975). "Gifts and Exchanges," in E.S. Phelps (ed.), *Altruism, Morality, and Economic Theory*. New York, NY: Russell Sage Foundation, 13–28.

Bacchi, C. and C. Beasley (2005). "Biotechnology and the Political Limits of 'Care,'" in Margrit Shildrick and Roxanne Mykitiuk (eds), *Rethinking Feminist Bioethics: The Challenge of the Postmodern*. New York, NY: MIT Press, 49–64.

Banerjee, S.B. (2010). "Governing the Global Corporation: A Critical Perspective," *Business Ethics Quarterly* 20, 265–274.

Beadle, R. and G. Moore (2006). "MacIntyre on Virtue and Organization," *Organization Studies* 27:3, 323–340.

Benhabib, S. (2004). *The Rights of Others*. Cambridge: Cambridge University Press.

Borgerson, J. (2007). "On the Harmony of Feminist Ethics and Business Ethics," *Business and Society Review* 112:4, 477–509.

Burton, B.K. and C.P. Dunn (1996). "Feminist Ethics as Moral Grounding for Stakeholder Theory," *Business Ethics Quarterly* 6:2, 133–147.

Card, C. (ed.) (1991). *Feminist Ethics*. Lawrence, KS: University Press of Kansas.

Card, C. (1999). *On Feminist Ethics and Politics*. Lawrence, KS: University Press of Kansas.

Carroll, A.B. (2004). "Managing Ethically with Global Stakeholders: A Present and Future Challenge," *Academy of Management Executive* 18, 114–120.

Collins, D. (2000). "The Quest to Improve the Human Condition: the First 1500 Articles Published in Journal of Business Ethics," *Journal of Business Ethics* 26, 1–73.

Coombs, W.T. and S.J. Holladay (2013). *It's Not Just PR: Public Relations in Society*. New York, NY: John Wiley and Sons.

Crane, A. and D. Matten (2004). *Business Ethics: A European Perspective*. Oxford: Oxford University Press.

Derry, R. (1996). "Toward a Feminist Firm: Comments on John Dobson and Judith White," *Business Ethics Quarterly* 6:1, 101–9.

Derry, R. (1997). "Feminism: How Does it Play in the Corporate Theatre?" In A.L. Larson and R.E. Freeman (eds), *Women's Studies and Business Ethics Towards a New Conversation*. New York, NY: Oxford University Press, 11–29.

Derry. R. (2002). "Feminist Theory and Business Ethics," in R. Fredrick (ed.), *A Companion to Business Ethics*. Oxford: Blackwell Press, 81–87.

Diprose, R. (1994). *The Bodies of Women: Ethics, Embodiment and Sexual Difference*. New York, NY: Routledge.

Dobson, J. and J. White (1995). "Toward the Feminine Firm: an Extension to Thomas White," *Business Ethics Quarterly* 5:3, 463–78.

EABIS (2012). "Leaders' Forum: Sustainability: Brand, Reputation and Customer Perceptions," *The European Business Network for Corporate Social Responsibility*. Available at: www.csreurope.org/eabis-2012-leaders%E2%80%99-forum-sustainability-brand-reputation-and-customer-perceptions#.WPykII-cFdg [accessed 08 April 2017].

Ehrenreich, B. (1976). "What is Socialist Feminism?" Working Papers on *Socialism and Feminism*. Available at: www.marxists.org/subject/women/authors/ehrenreich-barbara/socialist-feminism.htm [accessed 20 April 2017].

Friedman, M. and A. Bolte (2007). "Ethics and Feminism," in L. Alcoff and E.F. Kittay (eds), *The Blackwell Guide to Feminist Philosophy*. Oxford: Blackwell Press, 81–101.

Gilligan, C. (1982, 1990). *In A Different Voice: Psychological Theory and Women's Development*. Cambridge, MA: Harvard University Press.

Gilligan, C. (2011). *Joining the Resistance*. Cambridge: Polity Press.

Goldberg, S. (1993). *Why Men Rule: A Theory of Male Dominance*. Chicago, IL: Open Court.

Goldin, C. (2014). "A Grand Gender Convergence: Its Last Chapter," *American Economic Review* 104:4, 1091–1119.

Grosser, K. (2016). "Corporate Social Responsibility and Multi-Stakeholder Governance: Pluralism, Feminist Perspectives and Women's NGOs," *Journal of Business Ethics* 137:1, 65–81.

Hakim, C. (2004). *Key Issues in Women's Work: Female Heterogeneity and the Polarisation of Women's Employment*. London: Glasshouse Press, Routledge Cavendish.

Hakim, C. (2007). "Dancing with the Devil: Essentialism and other Feminist Heresies," *British Journal of Sociology* 58:1, 123–132.

Held, V. (ed.) (1993). *Justice and Care: Essential Readings in Feminist Ethics*. Boulder, CO: Westview Press.

Hochschild, A.R. (with A. Machung) (1989). *The Second Shift: Working Families and the Revolution at Home*. London: Penguin Viking Books.

Holland, D. and C. Albrecht (2013). "The Worldwide Academic Field of Business Ethics: Scholars' Perceptions of the Most Important Issues," *Journal of Business Ethics* 117:4, 777–788.

ILO Report (2015). "Women and the Future of Work: Women +20 and Beyond." Available at: www.ilo.org/wcmsp5/groups/public/---dgreports/---dcomm/documents/briefingnote/wcms_348087.pdf [accessed 10 May 2017].

ILO Report (2016). "Women at Work: Summary of Trends." Available at: www.ilo.org/wcmsp5/groups/public/---dgreports/---dcomm/---publ/documents/publication/wcms_457086.pdf [accessed 11 May 2017].

Jaggar, A. (1991). "Feminist Ethics: Projects, Problems, Prospects," in C. Card (ed.), *Feminist Ethics*. Lawrence, KS: University Press of Kansas, 78–106.

Jaggar, A. (1992). "Feminist Ethics," In L. Becker and C. Becker (eds), *Encyclopedia of Ethics*. New York, NY: Garland Press, 363–364.

Kent, M.L. and M. Taylor (2002). "Toward a Dialogic Theory of Public Relations," *Public Relations Review* 28:1, 21–37.

Klein, S. (1989). "Platonic Business Theory and Virtue Ethics," *Business & Professional Ethics Journal* 8:4, 59–82.

Lave, J. and E. Wenger (1991). *Situated Learning: Legitimate Peripheral Participation*. Cambridge: Cambridge University Press.

Ledingham, J.A. (2003). "Explicating Relationship Management as a General Theory of Public Relations," *Journal of Public Relations Research* 15:2, 181–198.

Lentricchia, F. (1989). "Lyric in the Culture of Capitalism," *American Literary History* 1:1, 63–88.

Liedtka, J.M. (1999). "Feminist Morality and Competitive Reality: A Role for an Ethics of Care?" *Business Ethics Quarterly* 6:2, 179–200.

Machold, S., P.K. Ahmed and S.S. Farquhar (2008). "Corporate Governance and Ethics: A Feminist Perspective," *Journal of Business Ethics* 81:3, 665–678.

MacIntyre, A. (1985). *After Virtue*, 2nd edition. London: Duckworth.

MacIntyre, A. (1988). *Whose Justice? Which Rationality?* London: Duckworth.

MacIntyre, A. (1990). *Three Rival Versions of Moral Enquiry*. London: Duckworth.

MacIntyre, A. (2007) [1981]. *After Virtue*, 3rd edition. Notre Dame, IN: University of Notre Dame.

McCloskey, D.N. (2006). *The Bourgeois Virtues: Ethics for an Age of Commerce*. Chicago, IL: University of Chicago Press.

McCloskey, D.N. (2010). *Bourgeois Dignity: Why Economics Can't Explain the Modern World*. Chicago, IL: University of Chicago Press.

Murphy, P.E., G.R. Laczniak and G. Wood (2007). "An Ethical Basis for Relationship Marketing: A Virtue Ethics Approach," *European Journal of Marketing* 41:1–2, 37–57.

Noddings, N. (1984). *Caring: A Feminine Approach to Ethics and Moral Education*. Berkeley, CA: University of California Press.

Osigweh, C.A.B. and L. Falkenberg (1995). "Does Feminism Belong in Business Ethics?" *Employees, Responsibilities and Rights Journal* 8:2, 97–110.

Paechter, C. (2003). "Masculinities and Femininities as Communities of Practice," *Women's Studies International Forum* 26:1, 69–77.

Probst, G. and S. Borzillo (2008). "Why Communities of Practice Succeed and Why They Fail," *European Management Journal* 26:5, 335–347.

Rabouin, M. (1997). "Lyin' T(★)gers, And 'Cares' Oh My: The Case for Feminist Integration of Business Ethics," *Journal of Business Ethics* 16:3, 247–261.

Robinson, F. (2011). "Discourse Ethics and Feminist Care Ethics in International Political Theory," *Millennium: Journal of International Studies*, 39:3, 845–860.

Sherwin, S. (1996). "Feminism and Bioethics," in S.M. Wolf (ed.), *Feminism and Bioethics: Beyond Reproduction*. Oxford: Oxford University Press, 47–66.

Solomon, R.C. (1992). "Corporate Roles, Personal Virtues: An Aristotelian Approach to Business Ethics," *Business Ethics Quarterly* 2, 317–339.
Swigonski, M.E. and S. Raheim (2011). "Feminist Contributions to Understanding Women's Lives and the Social Environment," *Women and Social Work* 26:1, 10–21.
Tong, R. (1993). *Feminine and Feminist Ethics*. Belmont, CA: Wadsworth.
Tong, R. (1996). *Feminist Approaches to Bio-ethics: Theoretical Reflections and Practical Applications*. Boulder, CO: Westview.
Tronto, J. (1993). *Moral Boundaries: A Political Argument for an Ethic of Care*. New York, NY: Routledge.
Tronto, J.C. (1999). "Care Ethics: Moving Forward," *Hypatia* 14:1, 112–119.
Warin, J. and E. Gannerud (2014). "Teaching and Care: A Comparative Global Conversation," *Gender and Education* 26:3, 193–199.
Wenger, E. (1998). *Communities of Practice: Learning, Meaning, and Identity*. Cambridge: Cambridge University Press.
Wenger, E. (2012). "Communities of Practice and Social Learning Systems: The Career of a Concept." Available at: http://wenger-trayner.com/wp-content/uploads/2012/01/09-10-27-CoPs-and-systems-v2.01.pdf [accessed 20 April 2017].
Wenger, E. and W. Snyder (2000). "Communities of Practice: the Organizational Frontier," *Harvard Business Review* (January–February), 139–145.
Wenger, E., R. McDermott and W. Snyder (2002). *Cultivating Communities of Practice: A Guide to Managing Knowledge*. Boston: Harvard Business School Press.
Wenger-Trayner, E., M. Fenton-O'Creevy, S. Hutchinson, C. Kubiak and B. Wenger-Trayner (eds) (2015). *Learning in Landscapes of Practice: Boundaries, Identity and Knowledgeability in Practice-based Learning*. Abingdon, Oxford: Routledge.
Wicks, A.C., D.R. Gilbert and R.E. Freeman (1994). "A Feminist Reinterpretation of the Stakeholder Concept," *Business Ethics Quarterly* 4:4, 475–97.

9
Business ethics and religious belief

Kenneth J. Barnes

A consideration of business ethics from the perspective of historic religions is fraught with difficulties, not least because business as we understand it today bears little resemblance to the economic activity of ancient times. Similarly, the ethical frameworks inherent in religious systems are often amalgamations of various influences ranging from parochial traditions and interpretations of religious texts to the influence of culture, scientific discovery and philosophical inquiry. In this manner, religion incorporates both doctrinal texts as well as elements of practice. Additionally, religious ethics may be informed by voices outside religious communities themselves, such as the influence of Neo-Platonism and Aristotelian virtue ethics on Christianity, as just one example among many.

Despite these difficulties, it is possible to discern a range of similarities among the so-called global religions,[1] as well as certain particularities, relating to the ethics of economic activity and commerce. It is no easy task to harmonize the philosophical and theological underpinnings of each system's approach to the needs or concerns of contemporary business ethics. At best, we will offer summary perspectives on some of the global religions, emphasizing textual sources primarily. In so doing we shall note the believed relations between deity and humanity, how the economic activities of production and trade are conceived, and some of the moral boundaries that circumscribe one's relations to self and others. The chapter focuses first on the Jewish tradition, moving subsequently to a consideration of early Christianity (Jesus, Paul) and then examining later developments including the thought of Aquinas, the Protestant Reformers (Luther and Calvin), as well as more recent Catholic social teaching. A third section focuses on Islamic belief and business ethics, and the final section takes up religious traditions of Asia (Hinduism, Buddhism, Taoism, and the Confucian tradition). The chapter concludes with a brief consideration of the relevance and impact of religion and spirituality within the contexts of two over-riding socio-economic phenomena: globalization and secularism.

The Hebrew tradition

Judaism's theology as it relates to economic activity begins with the creation narratives of the *Torah* (i.e., the biblical "Pentateuch") and are directly related to the nature of God as one who created all things by an act of will (Gen. 1:1) and humanity which was in turn created by God in

God's image, in order to have dominion over and cultivate the earth. In this construct, which is itself realized through a series of divinely sanctioned covenants, God is the suzerain-creator of the universe and humankind (Gen. 1:26–31/2:5). This notion is demonstrated in the Sabbath principle of Genesis 2:2, whereby the last day of the week is consecrated, i.e., made "holy" in deference to God's example. Humankind is expected to imitate the practices of the Creator in the ordering and rhythm of economic life.

The writer of the Book of Ecclesiastes poses the following rhetorical question:

> What does the worker gain from his toil? I have seen the burden God has laid on men. He has made everything beautiful in its time. He has also set eternity in the hearts of men; yet they cannot fathom what God has done from the beginning to end. I know that there is nothing better for men than to be happy and do good while they live. That everyone may eat and drink and find satisfaction in all his toil—this is the gift of God.
>
> *(Eccl. 3:9–13)*

In this verse, the writer clearly notes the intrinsic value of work, in spite of its "burdensome" nature. As a "gift of God" work generates goodness both through its creative merit and its utility (in order to "eat and drink"). The writer sees in economic activity the participation of humankind in the creation fiat, begun by God "from the beginning" and made "beautiful in its time." These images provide a very powerful metaphor for economic activity as procreative, in the sense that it is a continuation of the Lord's work, whether its specific purpose is practical or aesthetic.

It remains true, of course, that work (however blessed) is not equivalent to economic activity or trade more generally. Yet work, as understood by the writer of Ecclesiastes, is productive; it is not merely pointless toil. In this sense of productivity, work is an essential element of economic activity, even necessary to trade, and such activity is fundamental to what it means to be created in the image of God. In this sense, it could be argued, work, while corrupted by sin (see Genesis 3), helps to establish and to maintain a *dignity* consistent with humankind's unique position within the creation order and has value beyond mere subsistence. Hence, from the earliest writings, individuals are identified not only by their names but often by their occupations as well. Abel, for instance, is described as a shepherd, Cain a farmer, Noah a vintner, Oholiab an engraver, Malkijah a goldsmith, Bezalel a builder, and so on.

Although work is seen as intrinsic to one's "being"—Isaiah even envisions economic activity in paradise (Is. 2:4/65:21)—there is an undoubted utility to work, and by inference to trade and wealth creation, in so far as these have an essential connection to work. In the first instances of creation, we see the necessity of human activity in the fulfillment of the creation fiat:

> Now no shrub had yet appeared on the earth and no plant had yet sprung up . . . for there was no one to work the ground.
>
> *(Gen. 2:5)*

The impression given above is that the very purpose of vegetation was both the nourishment of humankind and humankind's procreative, economic activity; however, the latter was corrupted by the Fall of Man and what was originally intended as a purely productive endeavor is now beset by the curse of divine sanction:

> Cursed is the ground because of you; through painful toil you will eat food from it all the days of your life. It will produce thorns and thistles for you, and you will eat the plants of the field. By the sweat of your brow you will eat your food until you return to the ground.
>
> *(Gen. 3:17–19)*

A full consideration of this account would require a full description of the status quo prior to and after the Fall. But at a minimum there are several implications to this event, the first being the disruption of the divine order. Now there is enmity between creatures where harmony was the original intention; where plenty was originally envisioned, now there is scarcity and "painful toil." In Judaic thinking, these two factors are fundamental to understanding both the necessity of economic activity itself and the need for the ethical regulation of that activity (to be explored below).

However, the reality of both scarcity and harsh economic conditions did not exclude the development of commerce or the creation of wealth. In fact, the latter is envisioned in the creation narrative (Gen. 2:13) where reference is made to the existence of gold, pearls and onyx whose only purposes are as decorative adornments or as currency. From the earliest narratives of the *Torah* one sees the combination of human migration (often in search of basic necessities) and the interaction of various peoples (groups) resulting in the creation of markets and the exchange of goods, sometimes resulting in the creation of great wealth (Gen. 13:2, for example).

The tension between wealth and scarcity, however, is not without its ethical implications in the Hebrew tradition, as evidenced by the example of Joseph (son of the Hebrew patriarch Jacob/Israel) who, while in the service of Pharaoh, exercised the virtues of both thrift and stewardship:

> During the seven years of abundance the land produced plentifully. Joseph collected all the food produced in those seven years of abundance in Egypt and stored it in the cities. In each city he put the food grown in the fields surrounding it. Joseph stored up huge quantities of grain . . . The seven years of abundance in Egypt came to an end, and the seven years of famine began, just as Joseph had said. There was famine in all the other lands, but in the whole land of Egypt there was food.
>
> *(Gen. 41:47–54)*

The example of Joseph would set the tone for later developments in the regulation of economic life among the Hebrew people, including the institution of the Jubilee (Lev. 25:1–54) and the tithe (Lev. 27:30), but the great portion of Judaism's teaching regarding ethical business conduct revolves around one's moral duties, which brings us to the roles of Hebrew law and custom in grounding and constraining economic activity.

There are many facets to the dutiful exercise of one's economic responsibilities in Hebrew literature. Foremost among them is a prohibition against the inhumane exploitation of workers, rooted in the slavery experience of Jews prior to the Exodus. The conditions of the Hebrew people are explained in considerable detail from their physical "affliction" under their Egyptian "taskmasters" (Ex. 1:11–12) to the systematic slaughter of their newborn sons (Ex. 1:22); however their lamentations toward God do not go unnoticed (Ex. 2:23–25) and it is under the tutelage of their deliverer Moses[2] that they receive the commandments under which they are to conduct every aspect of their lives, including economic activity.

Space here does not permit an exhaustive review of all 613 "commandments" traditionally ascribed to the *Torah* or even those that specifically relate to economic activity, but a cursory review of the most salient prohibitions (so-called "negative commandments") and obligations (so-called "positive commandments") is helpful in understanding both the parochial and the broader influence of those provisions on our current understanding of business ethics today.

Firstly, it is important to understand that the ethical requirements found in Scripture do not take place in a theological vacuum; they relate instead to the previously discussed constructs of covenant between God and humankind and contain all of the customary "blessings" (for obedience) and "curses" (for disobedience) one would expect to find therein. And so, the prohibitions against thievery, dishonesty and covetousness for instance, found in the Decalogue (Ex. 20:15–17), are closely aligned to one's other communal responsibilities and devotion to God. Similarly, those who obey the ethical precepts established in the Law are expected to reap benefits from their obedience while those who break them may expect the wrath of God to befall them.

Throughout the Scriptures one sees a constant tension between the rights of individuals to benefit from their economic activities, and their broader obligations to seek the good of others, especially those who are less fortunate, both within the community and outside of it. So, while a person has the right to own property, that individual is also required to treat those under his care with dignity and respect (Ex. 21–22). Private gain is not to be at the expense of others nor is it to be the result of dishonest behavior (Ex. 23:1–10/Prov. 11:1); and the long-term benefits to individuals, communities and even nature itself are to be placed above the short-term benefits of any given person; hence there are prohibitions against the unfair treatment of strangers, widows and orphans (Ex. 22:21–24); restrictions on usury (Ex. 22:25–27); as well as the establishment of the "sabbatical year" (Ex. 23:10–12) and the aforementioned Jubilee (Lev. 25:1–54).

While the rights of the poor and the oppressed are upheld, there are stern warnings against behavior that could lead to self-destruction, such as slothfulness (Prov. 19:15/20:13/24:30–34), drunkenness (Prov. 23:21); hubris (Is. 13:11) and avarice (Prov. 1:8–18).

In short, the teachings of Judaism bear significant similarities to some features in the virtue ethics of Aristotle, in that the Hebrew people are expected to conduct themselves in all things, including in their business dealings, with prudence (Prov. 8:12–19), justice (Prov. 8:15–21), courage (Neh. 13:15–22) and temperance (Prov. 23:1–35). These ethical recommendations would be codified in the thirteenth century by St Thomas Aquinas, whose teachings have greatly influenced the Christian understanding of business ethics as we shall now explore.

The Christian traditions

Our biographical knowledge of Jesus is limited to the Gospel accounts, but these were concerned more with the mission, ministry, and teachings of Jesus than with details of his personal life. Jesus does appear to have had a working knowledge of the economic realities of his day. He often used work-related settings in his parables, such as the parable of the laborers (Matt. 20:1–16) and the parable of the talents (Matt. 25:14–30), and demonstrated an understanding of the "practicalities" of economic activity, even as they related to such things as paying one's taxes (Matt. 17:24–27/Matt. 22:15–22). Additionally, while equally comfortable in the company of both the rich and the poor, the powerful and the downtrodden, Jesus had a very difficult relationship with the religious establishment of his day, especially the Sadducees, whose management of the Temple he clearly objected to (John 2:13–22) and the Pharisees whose excessive burden on the poor he flatly rebuked (Matt. 15:1–9).

In short, Jesus' teachings on the ethics of economic activity were those of a prophet determined to root out injustice wherever he found it, to warn those who had acquired wealth through unrighteous means, to encourage those with wealth to use it wisely and in the service of God and neighbor, to assure the victims of a corrupted religious, political and economic system, and lastly to encourage his followers to keep economic activity in eschatological perspective.

When Jesus famously turned over the tables of the "money-changers" and drove out those conducting business (specifically "selling doves") in the Temple courts (Matt. 21:12/Mark 11:15/John 2:15), he was making a specific statement against injustice and those who would take advantage of poor pilgrims whose currencies were no doubt exchanged at a cost and who had no choice but to purchase a dove for their birth-offering, quoting the Old Testament prophets, Isaiah and Jeremiah, in the process. When he implored a rich young man to "sell [his] possessions and give to the poor," and the man refused, he lamented that "it is easier for a camel to go through the eye of needle than for someone who is rich to enter the kingdom of God" (Matt. 19:21–23, NIV). When he commended the tax-collector Zaccheus for "giving half of [his] possessions to the poor" and promising that "if [he] has cheated anybody out of anything [he] will pay back four times as much" (Luke 19:8–9), Jesus was warning against the dangers inherent in both the accumulation and the mismanagement of wealth.

It is in the Sermon on the Mount (Matt. 5:1–6:27), however, where one sees the clearest expression of Jesus' ethical principles. First, in the so-called Beatitudes (Matt. 5:3–12), Jesus specifically addressed the poor, the downtrodden, the meek, the disadvantaged and the lowly faithful and promised them that a reward awaits those who have faith, persevere and seek after righteousness.

However, it is Jesus' ethic of wealth that is most striking. While he did not condemn the accumulation of wealth per se, he gave a strong warning against the dangers of pursuing wealth at the expense of pursuing righteousness:

> Do not store up for yourselves treasures on earth, where moths and vermin destroy, and where thieves break in and steal. But store up for yourselves treasures in heaven . . . For where your treasure is, there your heart will be . . . No one can serve two masters. Either you will hate the one and love the other, or you will be devoted to the one and despise the other. You cannot serve both God and money . . . Therefore I tell you, do not worry about your life, what you will eat or drink; or about your body, what you will wear . . . For the pagans run after all these things, and your heavenly Father knows that you need them. But seek first his kingdom and his righteousness, and all these things will be given to you as well.
> (Matt. 6:19–33)

This "other-worldly" emphasis is typical of Jesus' entire life and ministry. He even states to Pontius Pilate, at the trial that would ultimately lead to his execution, "my kingdom is not of this world" (John 18:36). Yet his ethical teaching is still applicable to business and other forms of economic activity, in that he consistently spoke to motives of the heart: justice, selflessness, fairness, obedience to the moral law, and to the futility of pursuing wealth as an end unto itself. These are themes that would be built upon by his followers, both the Apostles and later adherents to the faith.

The teachings of the Apostle Paul

While he may have been the self-proclaimed "Apostle to the Gentiles," prior to his conversion to Christianity, Saul of Tarsus (the Apostle Paul) was vehemently opposed to the sect he believed to be an apostate cult within Judaism. A Roman citizen and a Jew by birth, he was a student of the Pharisaic scholar Gamaliel, charged by the Temple authorities to root out and condemn followers of Jesus of Nazareth. Once converted, however, he used his intimate knowledge of *Torah* and his command of the Greek language to spread the Gospel across Asia Minor, Southern Europe and eventually the center of the Empire—Rome itself. It may be argued that, were it not for Paul, Christianity would have remained a small Jewish sect and not become the global religion it is today.

Paul's ministry across cultures required a slightly different approach from the methods employed by the Jerusalem church. Paul's message implored Christians to embrace a holistic version of Christianity that would sanctify every aspect of life, including economic activity. Writing to the church at Colossae he stated:

> Since, then, you have been raised with Christ, set your hearts on things above ... there is no Gentile or Jew, circumcised or uncircumcised, barbarian, Scythian, slave or free, but Christ is all, and is in all ... And whatever you do, whether in word or deed, do it all in the name of the Lord Jesus ... work at it with all your heart, as working for the Lord.
>
> *(Col. 3:1–23)*

Elsewhere Paul prided himself on the fact that throughout his ministry he remained involved in economic activity and trade (Acts 18:1–4, 1 Thes. 2:9–12). He regularly shared the Gospel in the public square, including the "marketplace" (Acts 17:16–34) and, like Jesus, sometimes used work analogies to make a theological point (1 Cor. 3:6–14). Paul also recognized the importance of people using their individual gifts and callings to serve the common good (1 Cor. 12:4–31) and saw "honest work" as part of Christian discipleship. While he did not condemn wealth, he made a stern warning against greed, which he defined as a form of idolatry (Eph. 4:17–28/2 Thes. 3:6–13) and cautioned his readers that "love of money is the root of all kinds of evil" (2 Tim. 6:10). As we will explore below, leaders of the sixteenth century Reformation would later emphasize Paul's more positive view of economic activity; however it was the more sceptical view of economic activity, advanced largely by Christian monastic communities, that dominated ethical thinking for centuries.

Thomas Aquinas and the influence of virtue ethics

St Thomas Aquinas is generally considered the greatest theologian of his day and, along with St Anselm of Canterbury, one of the "fathers" of Christian scholasticism. He wrote specifically about economic activity on several occasions, addressing for instance the question of whether those in religious orders should engage in "secular" business activities:

> We must conclude therefore that it is unlawful for either monks or clerics to carry on secular business from motives of avarice; but from motives of charity, and with their superior's permission, they may occupy themselves with due moderation in the administration and direction of secular business.
>
> *(Summa Theologica: 2–2.187.2)*

While this was a relatively positive view of business, he generally viewed economic activity as a mere utility:

> Manual labor is directed to four things. First and principally to obtain food ... Secondly, it is directed to the removal of idleness whence arise many evils ... Thirdly, it is directed to the curbing of concupiscence, inasmuch as it is a means of afflicting the body ... Fourthly, it is directed to almsgiving.
>
> *(Summa: 2–2.187.3)*

However, it is within the context of Aquinas' teachings on virtue (and specifically "justice") that he speaks most directly to issues of wealth and commerce:

> in distributive justice something is given to a private individual, in so far as what belongs to the whole is due to the part, and in a quantity that is proportionate to the importance of the position of that part in respect of the whole. Consequently in distributive justice a person receives all the more of the common goods, according as he holds a more

> prominent position in the community. This prominence in an aristocratic community is gauged according to virtue, in an oligarchy according to wealth, in a democracy according to liberty, and in various ways according to various forms of community. Hence in distributive justice the mean is observed, not according to equality between thing and thing, but according to proportion between things and persons: in such a way that even as one person surpasses another, so that which is given to one person surpasses that which is allotted to another.
>
> (Summa: 2–2.61.2)

In this passage Aquinas justifies inequality between persons as long as the proportion of that inequality is consistent with communal norms (a widely held belief in medieval times). However, he also addresses the relationship between buyers and sellers, lenders and debtors:

> A voluntary transfer belongs to justice in so far as it includes the notion of debt, and this may occur in many ways. First when one man simply transfers his thing to another in exchange for another thing, as happens in selling and buying. Secondly when a man transfers his thing to another, that the latter may have the use of it with the obligation of returning it to its owner. If he grant the use of a thing gratuitously, it is called usufruct in things that bear fruit; and simply borrowing on loan in things that bear no fruit, such as money, pottery, etc.
>
> (Summa 2–2.61.3)

Here Aquinas sees no sin in the exchange of goods (i.e., between buyer and seller) but supports the traditional view against usury, as money (in this view) is considered economically neutral/barren/arid (i.e., not inherently "fruit-bearing").

Some later generations have reverted to the entire codex of Aquinas' writings on the so-called "cardinal virtues" (prudence, justice, courage and temperance) to suggest an ethical framework applicable to modern economic activity. However, beyond recognizing certain themes consistent in Aquinas' work (some of which shall be noted below), it would be an exercise in eisegesis to read too much into Aquinas' teachings on business ethics, beyond those instances where he, himself, makes specific references.

While scholastic teaching on work, trade, usury, and commerce would stand relatively unchallenged for centuries, as with every other aspect of Christian theology, the Reformation of the sixteenth century changed the ethical landscape considerably and irreversibly as we explore below.

The influence of Martin Luther

When Martin Luther challenged the authority of the Roman See over the issue of indulgences, he inadvertently started a process of intellectual inquiry and theological heterodoxy that would become known as the Reformation. No longer content with accepting the doctrines of previous generations, reformers employed the newly established ideas of humanism to discern what the Scriptures had to say about every imaginable aspect of life, including economic activity.

In Luther's case, he was particularly concerned about the evolution of a sacred/secular divide that he saw as both perpetuating a corrupt class of clerical elites and the artificial compartmentalization of the Christian life. Citing the writings of the Apostle Paul (Col. 3) as well as the first epistle of St Peter (1 Pet. 2–3), he stated in a treatise known as *The Babylonian Captivity of the Church* that,

> the works of monks and priests, however holy and arduous they may be, do not differ one whit in the sight of God from the works of the rustic laborer in the field or the woman going about her household tasks . . . all works are measured before God by faith alone.
>
> *(Luther 1520: 3.42)*

He believed strongly that every aspect of economic activity if performed in accordance with one's Christian beliefs and in an attitude of thankfulness toward God, was no less than an act of worship. In a letter to an old friend and barber in Wittenberg, named Peter Beskendorf, Luther assured his friend that:

> the believer when he is working fears and honors God and remembers God's commandments so that he does not deal unjustly with his neighbor, steal from him, take advantage of him, or misappropriate what belongs to him. Such thoughts undoubtedly make his work prayer and praise as well.
>
> *(Luther 1535 [1960]: 125)*

However, despite his high view of work, Luther, like all those who preceded him, opposed usury and was deeply concerned about the just and righteous conduct of business people. In a pamphlet published in 1524, Luther reminded his followers that:

> It should not be: I will sell my wares as dear as I can or please, but thus: I will sell my wares as dear as I should, or as is right and proper. For thy selling should not be a work that is within thy power and thy will, without all law and limit, as though thou wert a god bounden to no one; but because thy selling is a work that thou performest to thy neighbor it should be restrained within such law and conscience that thou mayest practise it without harm or injury to thy neighbor, but heed rather that thou do him no injury which is thy gain.
>
> *(Luther 1524: 19)*

Here Luther appealed directly to their sense of "prudence" (defined by Aquinas as "knowing what to want and what not to want"), their sense of "justice," their sense of "temperance" and their sense of "courage" (which Aquinas regarded as anything "at enmity with virtue itself").

Luther also appealed in this pamphlet to "conscience," which he equated to the influence of Law in the regulation of human conduct. Conscience is an important ethical principle in that it presumes all people, regardless of religious beliefs, are capable of making moral decisions, a view supported by the sixteenth-century Swiss Reformer, John Calvin, who wrote:

> The end of the natural law, therefore, is to render man inexcusable, and may be not improperly defined—the judgment of conscience distinguishing sufficiently between just and unjust, and by convicting men on their own testimony depriving them of all pretext for ignorance.
>
> *(1983, Inst. II.2.xxii)*

As we shall explore below, Calvin's teaching would leave an indelible imprint on the nature of economic activity in the English-speaking world and on the nature of capitalism in particular.

Kenneth J. Barnes

The influence of John Calvin and reformed thinking

The French-born theologian and pastor who served in Geneva, Switzerland, from 1536 to 1564, Calvin was perhaps most famous for his masterful work of systematic theology known as *The Institutes of the Christian Religion* (*c.*1559). In this exhaustive tome Calvin covers every aspect of the Christian life, including such things as the relationship between God and humanity, the nature and function of the church, the duties and responsibilities of government and the rights and responsibilities of all people, both those within the community of faith and those outside of that community.

In reading the *Institutes* along with Calvin's many commentaries on the Bible, one recognizes a theology that is both supportive of previous generations' views and one that challenges those views as they relate to ethics and economic activity. For instance, Calvin had this to say about work:

> (God) does not disparage man's labor or his effort and planning. For any virtue of ours is worthy of praise if we employ it in our zeal for fulfilment of duty . . . Adam was put into the garden to cultivate it . . . God approves . . . the labor men undertake . . . and offer to him as an acceptable sacrifice.
>
> *(2005 [1557]:* Commentary, Ps. 127*)*

Here Calvin offers an affirmation of Luther's view, even as he held a more expansive or liberal view regarding personal property and the accumulation of wealth, stating:

> This commandment, therefore, we shall duly obey, if, contented with our own lot, we study to acquire nothing but honest and lawful gain; if we long not to grow rich by in-justice, nor to plunder our neighbour of his goods, that our own may thereby be increased . . . but let us contribute to the relief of those whom we see under the pressure of difficulties, assisting their want out of our abundance. Lastly, let each of us consider how far he is bound in duty to others, and in good faith pay what we owe.
>
> *(1983,* Inst. *3.8.46)*

In this passage Calvin left open the possibility of virtuous people acquiring great wealth, provided that wealth was not at the expense of others or the result of impure motives. He also stakes out the principle notion that those who do possess great wealth bear the burden of responsible stewardship, or, as Jesus himself said: "to whom much is given, much is expected" (Luke 12:48).

When it came to the issue of usury however, Calvin made the greatest departure from his predecessors. For Calvin, an outright ban on usury was inconsistent with Biblical teaching in that there were some instances where the Jewish people were permitted to charge interest (Deut. 23:20). Consequently, Calvin believed that the charging of interest was permissible as long as the lender adhered to the following constraints: not to charge interest on loans to the poor or the needy; and to meet the obligation to assist the welfare of others, and otherwise ensure that a loan was consistent with the law of charity, as well as "natural justice" (i.e., "golden rule"). In addition, Calvin believed that a borrower's net gain should ultimately meet or exceed the lender's net gain; the interest rate should not be determined simply by the world's (i.e., "the markets") standards, but by "God's standards" (charity being the first consideration); and that the lender always consider the impact of any loan on the community as well as on the individual borrower, operating always within the civil law. While restrictive by today's standards, Calvin's view of usury was significantly more liberal than the prevailing view of the church up to that point.

As Max Weber rightly observed in *The Protestant Ethic and the Spirit of Capitalism* (2011 [*c.*1904]), the potent combination of Luther's view of "calling," Calvin's liberal views on usury, the "this-worldly asceticism" of various Protestant sects, the advancement of technological innovation, and the settlement of territories rich in natural resources, produced a pool of highly motivated, highly skilled workers. When combined with well-financed entrepreneurs, orderly societies, and an economic system built on "thrift," "stewardship," honesty, and "fair dealing," the overall outcome was unparalleled economic development and unprecedented wealth creation.

Sadly the ethical foundations of that system soon eroded and the result was an economic engine that could be as exploitative and capricious as any system that preceded it. It was in this context that Catholic social teaching emerged in the late nineteenth and early twentieth centuries.

Contemporary Catholic social teaching and the "Encyclicals"

Papal encyclicals have existed since the earliest days of the church. Several relatively recent ones deal specifically with the ethics of economic activity. The first one to consider is entitled *Rerum Novarum* (1891) issued by His Holiness Pope Leo XIII on the condition of the working classes, noting that after the end of the medieval period and the demise of the trade guilds, and in light of the decline of religious teaching on ethics, workers were "handed over . . . to the inhumanity of employers," the result of which was the concentration of economic power in the hands of the few, who have "laid a yoke almost of slavery on the unnumbered masses of non-owning workers." The condition, however, was not seen as hopeless, and although he harshly condemned the misguided attempts of "socialists" to impose on society an "unnatural" economic hegemony via excessive state intervention, he suggested a combination of both legal remedies (including the notion of a "living wage") and an appeal to "wholesome morality . . . justice . . . [and the] equitable distribution of public burdens" (i.e., taxes), as well as the progressive development of industry and trade.

A later encyclical by Pope Paul VI entitled *Populorum Progressio* (1967) would build on Pope Leo's previous encyclical but with a more prophetic tone. In this encyclical the rich nations were called to task over a variety of evils, from colonialism to environmental abuse and an appeal was made for the institutions of international cooperation to place economic justice at the top of their agendas. Similarly, Pope John Paul II wrote two interesting and influential encyclicals entitled *Laborem Exercens* (1981) and *Centesimus Annus* (1991). The former addressed issues relating to the intrinsic dignity of work, while the latter celebrated the 100th anniversary of the aforementioned work of Leo XIII, and set forth a stronger endorsement of a market economy than previous encyclicals. A later encyclical of Pope Benedict XVI entitled *Caritas in Veritate* (2009) addressed problems inherent in the global financial system. The most recent encyclical, however, Pope Francis' *Laudato si'*, offers a stinging criticism of developed nations, a critical assessment of the environmental impact of industrialization, and an appeal to the wealthy nations to assist poorer countries who suffer disproportionately from environmental degradation.

The fundamental principle underlying these encyclicals is a concept known as "subsidiarity," whereby responsibility for the remedy of social ills should always begin with the most local and least complex organization. In the case of *Rerum Novaum* that would have primarily meant individuals and families, companies and their employers, voluntary societies, as well as local and national governments.

During the past few decades some have urged that the Church devote itself to liberation, including liberation from markets (Gutiérrez 1973), but others have responded with strong defenses of a market economy (Booth 2007; Sirico 2012). Nonetheless, what is common among all Judeo-Christian teaching as it relates to economic activity, work, wealth and what we would call "business ethics" today, is the notion that economic activity is part of God's divine plan; that it is indelibly linked to both the *imago dei* and the *missio dei*. It is also acknowledged that economic activity has, with the rest of creation, been corrupted by sin (i.e., the existence of evil and the selfish motives of people). The effects of such corruption, such as "envy," "malice," "avarice," "selfishness," and "exploitation", must be guarded against through both moral teaching and the rule of law. Despite this corruption however, human beings are still endowed with the ability to make moral decisions, whether through the exercise of right reason or the benefit of religious instruction. Consequently, business ethics must be based upon a combination of universally held beliefs concerning "right and wrong," "mutuality and reciprocity," "prudence," "justice," "courage," "temperance," and "love of neighbor" and those beliefs need to be embodied in both law and custom.

Islam

While recent history has highlighted the many differences between Islam and the other Abrahamic faiths, when it comes to the question of ethics, and business ethics in particular, the similarities are striking.

Born out of the political, religious and tribal complexities of the Arabian peninsula in the late sixth and early seventh century, Islam was founded upon the *Quran* (which Muslims believe to be the last revelation of God) and the *Sunnah*, containing the "*hadiths*" (i.e., teachings) of the Prophet. From these sources come the basic tenets of the faith (sometimes referred to as the "five pillars"), including an unequivocal monotheism (*shahada*), a commitment to regular prayer (*salat*), a commitment to charitable giving (*zakat*), a requirement to fast (*sawm*), and a call to pilgrimage (*hajj*). However, they also contain other doctrines similar in nature to the Judeo-Christian principles mentioned above. Among them is the *ontological* nature of ethics, rooted in the belief that humanity is a race of "viceregents" ("*khilafa*"'—Quran 2:30) to the creator (*Allah*), who are charged with the imitation of the Prophet, described as the "excellent model" ("*ouswatoun hasana*"—Quran 33:21) of "wisdom" ("*hikmah*"—Quran 2:151), sent to "perfect moral character" (as noted in the collected sayings, *hadith*, of Muhammad, #45).

Rafik I. Beekun describes the Prophet's character traits as being consistent with Aristotelian virtues and identifies them as "trustfulness and integrity" including a command to avoid hypocrisy as well as outright lying; "trustworthiness," including the exercise of good stewardship of natural resources as well as wealth; "justice," or the recognition of one's "rights"; "benevolence," in keeping with every person's "human dignity"; "humility"; "kindness," and "patience," including endurance during times of hardship (Beekun 2012: 1012).

Perhaps the most significant similarity, however, between Islam and the other Abrahamic faiths (especially Judaism) is the importance of "law" in the ethical regulation of human affairs. Like *Torah* in the Hebrew tradition, *Sharia* is a legal code derived from Islam's holy texts. Similarly, just as Talmudic scholars have interpreted the tenets of *Torah* for the purposes of providing guidance to Jewish believers on the application of the law, so too do Islamic scholars regularly interpret *Sharia* via a methodology known as *Usul Al-fiqh*.

Among the most important precepts of *Sharia* is the principle responsibility of Muslims to "prevent harm" (*daf' al-darar*), not only to an individual but to another's property as well. It specifically prohibits retaliatory actions (i.e., "two wrongs don't make a right") and elevates the public good over an individual's personal benefit.

While the application of *Sharia* law is often associated with specific proscriptions, Muatasim Ismaeel and Katherine Blaim suggest that there is actually a degree of "flexibility and adaptability" inherent in Islamic ethics and base their thesis on the tri-level nature of religious obedience (*deen*), specifically that which is obligatory (*islam*), that which is complementary (*iman*) and that which is an embellishment (*ishan*). According to Ismaeel and Blaim:

> Islamic ethics consist of some clear rules on rights and wrongs (deontology, obligation, Islam level), general guidelines that help Muslims decide what is right and wrong by themselves (consequentialism, values, iman level) and motivation and inspiration of Muslims toward moral living based on spiritual experience (virtue theory, virtue component, ishan level).
>
> *(Ismaeel and Blaim 2010: 1093)*

The three levels of ethics mirror the emphases in Judeo-Christian ethics, but there are, of course, significant differences between the Islamic approach to ethics and that of Judaism and Christianity. For instance, in Islam there is no concept of "holiness" as an emulation of the Deity. While this is fundamental to Judeo-Christian thinking, to Muslims "holiness" is a trait unique to Allah and the best humanity can do is submit to the will and precepts of the Deity. Lastly, more in keeping with Jewish tradition but in sharp contrast to Protestant thinking, the charging of interest (*riba*) is strictly prohibited. However, "*riba*" is not just prohibited in financial transactions such as loans (*riba al-qarud*), it is also prohibited in other areas of economic activity such as trade (*riba al-buyu*) and constitutes a general prohibition against any form of exploitative gain. It would seem clear, however, that the Islamic tradition has in general looked favorably on commerce (Quddus and Rashid 2017: 124).

In fact, the ethical principles of Islam applicable to business are very similar to those of the other Abrahamic faiths and are rooted in the nature of the Deity, the nature of humanity and humanity's obligations to both itself and the Deity as well as a strong eschatological belief in the temporal nature of human existence and an impending day of divine eternal judgment. Some but not all, of these elements are also to be found in the religions of the East.

Religions of Asia

Hinduism and business ethics

Hinduism is the world's third largest religion with approximately one billion adherents and is perhaps the world's oldest as well, with origins dating back to the Vedic religions of the second millennium BCE. As with Buddhism (which in many ways is derived from Hinduism), it is an extremely complex web of ancient traditions, philosophies, theologies and customs that over the centuries have evolved into a codex of beliefs more than a unified belief-system per se. There isn't a single Deity, nor is there a founder or prominent prophet. There isn't a single set of moral precepts or rituals. There are, however, four basic elements of belief, known as the *puruṣārtha* (i.e., life's primary objectives), that are generally shared among Hindus of various persuasions, and they include: *dharma* (which includes the pursuit of virtue and morality); *artha* (which incorporates economic activity as something both fundamental and worthwhile); *kama* (which roughly translated means the enjoyment of life); and *moksha* (which results in self-realization and liberation from life's burdens). While *moksha* is one's ultimate goal, unlike in Buddhism where there is a sense of gradual attainment, in Hinduism there is more of a creative tension between the ascetics of *moksha* and the aesthetics of *dharma, artha*, and *kama*.

As this tension relates to ethics and business ethics in particular, there is a very high view of work and of wealth creation, not simply because their pursuit is itself desirable, but because they stave off the effects of vice (and therefore promote virtue) and help people and societies enjoy life. Provided work is itself virtuous (i.e., not injurious to others) and provided it is conducted morally, the symbiosis between the four elements of *puruṣārtha* should, in theory, produce a virtuous and harmonious economic environment, in a way not unlike the teachings of the Tao (see below).

Buddhism and business ethics

Developed over centuries across the Indian sub-continent, China and Southeast Asia, Buddhism[3] is a complex constellation of religious beliefs and traditions based upon the fifth-century BCE life and teachings of Siddhartha Gautama, a.k.a. the Buddha. The primary goal of Buddhism is to assist its adherents in their pursuit of *nirvana* (or, in the case of Mayhayana Buddhism, "Buddhahood"), which may be described as a state of being free from the insatiability of human desire, known as *dukkha*. By following the "Noble Eightfold Path" (or the "Bodhisattva Path") Buddhists seek to attain a mental and spiritual purity that is free of all desire, encumbrance and external conditioning.

Unlike the monotheistic religions, Buddhism has no concept of a God of creation, nor does it recognize sin as such, and there is no eschatological understanding of time. Unlike the Abrahamic faiths, ethics are not rooted in a desire to please or obey a Deity, but instead are seen as part of a process designed to bring enlightenment. Buddhism, however, does profess a kind of universal law called *dharma* that, while difficult to translate precisely, may be seen as a kind of revelation that leads one along a virtuous path. Similarly, in order to disrupt the endless cycle of death and rebirth, Buddhists seek to attain merit through the cultivation of good thoughts and actions known as *karma*.

These beliefs have resulted in very strong ethical precepts, many of which are specifically applicable to business and economic activity in general. They include notions of "right speech, right action and right livelihood" (Harvey 2000: 3), as well as specific prohibitions against stealing, lying and causing harm (either to one's self, others or the environment). Work (even "toil") is seen as having merit, with service to others being a particularly high calling. There are also expectations that those who seek enlightenment and an eventual state of "non-self" would seek to be generous in nature and exercise reciprocity and fairness in all things. However, what is most striking about the Buddhist approach to ethics is the emphasis not merely on actions but on one's thoughts and motivations. Consequently, greed, envy, malice, selfishness, anger, etc. are as prohibited as the actions they may produce. These principles are also evident in Hinduism (see above).

Taoism and business ethics

Taoism (Daoism) is an ancient Chinese religion based largely upon the writings of Laozi entitled *Tao Te Ching* (c. fifth century BCE), which roughly translated means "book of the virtuous way." It is a relatively short document divided into two sections: *Tao Ching* (i.e., "book of the way") and *Te Ching* (i.e., "book of virtue"). Together they propose a road to harmony between competing forces in the universe (sometimes alluded to as *yin yang*). While there is no God (in the theistic sense) in Taoism, there is a very strong ontological understanding of the universe as expressed in the following quotation from the *Tao Te Ching*:

> There was something formless and perfect before the universe was born. It is serene. Empty. Solitary. Unchanging. Infinite. Eternally present. It is the mother of the universe. For lack of a better name, I call it the Tao. It flows through all things, inside and outside, and returns

to the origin of all things. The Tao is great. The universe is great. Earth is great. Man is great. These are the four great powers. Man follows the earth. Earth follows the universe. The universe follows the Tao. The Tao follows only itself.

(Laozi 1988: Ch. 25)

The goal of the follower therefore is not to emulate the Tao as one would emulate a God or a prophet, but to "cultivate" the Tao within in order to perfect one's virtue:

Cultivate Virtue in your own person, and it becomes a genuine part of you. Cultivate it in the family and it will abide. Cultivate it in the community and it will live and grow. Cultivate it in the state, and it will flourish abundantly. Cultivate it in the world and it will become universal.

(Laozi 1961: Ch. 54)

Virtue in the Taoist tradition involves a kind of detachment from the world and particularly from the desire for what one might call "success" in the West. Instead, followers are encouraged to seek a path of serenity and moderation in all things, including the pursuit of wealth. Followers are encouraged (although not commanded) to be gentle and kind; efficient in business; avoid great wealth; avoid covetousness; embrace the simple; be humble; avoid all extremes, excesses and extravagances; be frugal; be faithful; and perhaps most of all, be merciful.

There is little emphasis on either proscriptions or commands but there is great emphasis on personal development and character and how the cultivation of that character will benefit each individual. There is very little ritual in Taoism and much less emphasis on the ethical responsibility of communities. It is largely in these two areas that Taoism differs significantly from the other great Chinese belief-system, Confucianism.

Confucianism and business ethics

Confucianism is the term used to describe the followers of the ancient Chinese scholar K'ung Ch'iu (Kongzi) or Confucius (c. fifth century BCE), who was himself a devotee of Zhougong, patriarch of the Zhou Dynasty (c. eleventh century BCE). Confucius did not see himself as a religious leader or a moral philosopher, but as a guardian of ancient Chinese wisdom, tradition and ritual (2003, *Analects* 7.1). During his lifetime he travelled extensively, sometimes in the service of the state but mostly as an exile, and was purported to have encountered Laozi (the founder of Taoism) whose teachings he found impractical. Instead of the passive, individualistic approach of Laozi, Confucius sought and ultimately developed a world-view that saw human potential as unlimited and human virtue as the ultimate expression of the divine (*Tian*). Most importantly, however, Confucius saw culture as both the repository and the perpetuator of that world-view and, unlike Laozi, sought to actively influence culture (including the institutions of government and economic activity) through a combination of education and ritual.

Confucius is credited with writing several major works, including the so-called "Five Classics" (*Book of Changes, Book of Poetry, Book of History, Book of Rites* and *Spring and Autumn Annals*), but it is from *The Analects* (*Lunyu*) that we receive most of his teaching on ethics. Confucian ethics include such concepts as altruism (*ren*), justice (*yi*), filial piety (*xiao*), righteousness (*yi*) and honesty (*xin*). Although he had little to say specifically about business (other than that it is to be "honored"—Confucius 2003, *Analects* 1.5), the general principles of Confucianism are applicable to all aspects of life, including economic activity. For Confucius, however, the cultivation of virtue must always happen within the context of relationships (*guanxi*). However, the application of Confucian principles to business is not obvious (see Elstein and Tian 2017), even though many scholars think otherwise (Chan 2008).

Concluding remarks

It is obvious from the material above that both significant differences and striking similarities exist between the global religions as they pertain to the sources, purpose, authority, nature and application of ethical principles. For the monotheistic religions, there is a much greater emphasis on the tension between the "holiness" of the Deity and humankind's need for ethical constraint. In the Eastern religions there is a greater emphasis on human potential and the ability to cultivate virtue and create virtuous cultures, including, one would assume, virtuous business cultures. In the monotheistic religions there is a greater emphasis on "law" and the need to establish specific codes of conduct, while in the Eastern religions there is a greater emphasis on character and one's innate ability to act ethically. As divergent as these emphases may seem however, it is important to note that they are not strict dichotomies, and elements akin to Eastern religions are present in the monotheistic religions and vice versa.

What are even more significant however are the similarities that exist across all religious traditions. All of the aforementioned religions have an *ontological* element to their beliefs as they all profess, in one way or another, a connection to what Professor Paul Tillich referred to as "the ground of being" (Tillich 1952); a connection that sees in economic activity and in its associated ethics something that is fundamental to what it means to be human. There is also a *teleological* element to their beliefs surrounding work, worth and wealth as being necessary to human purpose and fundamental to human flourishing. Lastly, there is a broad but nearly universal *deontology*, rooted in each religion's moral code, dedicated to the quest for "goodness" in all its forms and applicable to every sphere of life. The global religions constitute the scriptural, historic, ritualistic and cultural soil from which all ethics, including business ethics spring. The challenge today, however, is how against a backdrop of secularization and globalization may these ancient voices still be heard?

It is clear that one phenomenon above all others is challenging the ethical landscape of business today—globalization. The ability (and it would seem necessity) of individuals, companies, and nations to conduct business across national and cultural boundaries is happening on an unprecedented scale. The question that often arises is: how may cultural differences be overcome without causing religious or political conflict? One popular suggestion is to jettison all vestiges of religion in favor of a totally secular approach. However, there are problems associated with that strategy. In the first place, secularism is itself a worldview and while it seems a simple solution to a difficult problem, it flies in the face of the fact that religious observance, while declining in the West, is actually growing worldwide and, as we have seen above, religion and culture are indelibly linked. Secularism is also based upon the notion that globalization and religious belief are somehow incompatible, which is more an *a priori* assumption than an established fact.

Globalization refers to the vast and complex constellation of powerful and influential businesses, capital, governments, organizations and institutions, but it is also a vast network of individual people, with minds and wills and consciences. It is ultimately the morality of the decisions those individual people make, and the virtuousness of the cultures they form, that will determine what kind of global business environment we create. As the traditional guardians of virtue, ethics and morality, religious faiths are uniquely placed to influence the future of the global economy, not merely because faith communities have political strength in numbers, but because their traditional values still have currency in the marketplace of ideas.

Essential readings

For general introductions to religion and business ethics see Scott B. Rae and Kenman L. Wong, *Beyond Integrity, a Judeo-Christian Approach to Business Ethics* (1996) and T. O'Brian and S. Paeth, *Religious Perspectives on Business Ethics: an Anthology* (2007). For perspectives on Judaism, see Aaron Levine and Moses L. Pava (editors), *Jewish Business Ethics: The Firm and Its Stakeholders* (1999). Christian views may be found in the following works: Scott Rae and Kenman Wong, *Business for the Common Good, a Christian Vision for the Marketplace* (2011); Philippe de Woot, *Spirituality and Business, a Christian Viewpoint* (2013); and Theodore Roosevelt Malloch, *Spiritual Enterprise: Doing Virtuous Business* (2008). For an insightful (and, for some, prophetic) critique of modern economic systems from a religious perspective, one should read Donald Hay, *Economics Today: a Christian Critique* (2004). For a textbook on economics from a Christian perspective, see Shawn Ritenour's *Foundations of Economics: A Christian View* (2010). On Islam, see Gillian Rice, "Islamic Ethics and the Implications for Business" (1999). On Asian religion, see Rajeev Dehejia and Vivek Dehejia, "Religion and Economic Activity in India: an Historical Perspective" (1993), and James Autry and Stephen Mitchell, *Real Power: Business Lessons from the Tao Te Ching* (1998). In Eugene Heath and Byron Kaldis's recent collection, *Wealth, Commerce, and Philosophy* (2017), one finds chapters devoted to exploring the thought of Confucius, Augustine, Ibn Khaldun, and Aquinas in relation to business ethics, trade, and wealth.

For further reading in this volume on the business ethics in the history of thought, see Chapter 1, The history of business ethics. On medieval and scholastic views of markets and trade, see Chapter 2, Theorists and philosophers on business ethics. On the role of religious societies and business ethics in Latin America, see Chapter 38, Business ethics in Latin America. On Gandhi's use of Hindu ideas in his views on markets, see Chapter 36, Business ethics in South Asia. For a brief discussion of Islamic finance, see Chapter 20, Money and finance: ethical considerations. On the erosion of civil society and religious belief in the former Soviet republics, see Chapter 39, Business ethics in transition: communism to commerce in Central Europe and Russia. On cross cultural management, see Chapter 33, Cross-cultural management ethics in multinational commerce.

Notes

1 For the purposes of this chapter, the term "global religions" shall refer to the Abrahamic traditions (Judaism, Christianity and Islam), Buddhism, Hinduism, Taoism and Confucianism.
2 Although Mosaic authorship of the *Torah* is disputed by many contemporary scholars, Moses is traditionally associated with the transmission of the Law to the Hebrew people.
3 Space does not allow for even a cursory explanation of the many variations in the beliefs and practices of Buddhists, Hindis, etc. The brief outlines provided are extremely basic and designed chiefly for comparative purposes vis-à-vis Abrahamic monotheism.

References

Aquinas, T. (1989). *Summa Theologiae: A Concise Translation*, T. McDermott (ed.). Notre Dame, IN: Ave Maria Press.
Autry, J. and S. Mitchell (1998). *Real Power: Business Lessons from the Tao Te Ching*. New York, NY: Riverhead Books.
Beekun, R.I. (2012). "Character Centered Leadership: Muhammad (p) as an Ethical Role Model for CEOs," in *Journal of Management Development* 31:10, 1003–1020.
Bible, New International Version (NIV). Colorado Springs, CO: International Bible Society.
Booth, P. (ed.) (2007). *Catholic Social Teaching and the Market Economy*. London: Institute of Economic Affairs.

Breyfogle, T.S. (2017). "The Earthly City and the Ethics of Exchange: Spiritual, Social, and Material Economy in Augustine's Theological Anthropology," in E. Heath and B. Kaldis (eds), *Wealth, Commerce, and Philosophy: Foundational Thinkers and Business Ethics*. Chicago, IL: University of Chicago Press, 75–94.

Calvin, J. (1983). *Institutes of the Christian Religion*, H. Beveridge (trans.). Grand Rapids, MI: Wm. B. Eerdmans.

Calvin, J. (2005) [1557]. *Commentary on the Book of Psalms*, 5 vols., J. Anderson (ed.), Vol. 5. Grand Rapids, MI: Christian Classics Ethereal Library.

Chan, G.K.Y. (2008). "The Relevance and Value of Confucianism in Contemporary Business Ethics." *Journal of Business Ethics* 77:3, 347–60.

Confucius (2003). *Analects*, E. Slingerland (trans.). Indianapolis, IN: Hackett.

Dehejia, R. and V. Dehejia (1993). "Religion and Economic Activity in India: an Historical Perspective," *American Journal of Economics and Sociology* 52:2, 145–153.

De Woot, P. (2013). *Spirituality and Business, a Christian Viewpoint*. Leeds: GSE Research Ltd.

Dillenberger, J. (1962). *Martin Luther, Selections from His Writings*. New York, NY: Anchor.

Elstein, D. and Q. Tian (2017). "Confucian Business Ethics: Possibilities and Challenges," in E. Heath and B. Kaldis (eds), *Wealth, Commerce, and Philosophy: Foundational Thinkers and Business Ethics*. Chicago, IL: University of Chicago Press, 53–73.

Encyclicals of the Church. Papal Documents. Available at: www.vatican.va/offices/papal_docs_list.html.

Freemantle, A. (1963). *Papal Encyclicals in Their Historical Context*. New York, NY: Mentor-Omega.

Gutiérrez, G. (1973). *A Theology of Liberation*. Maryknoll, NY: Orbis.

Hadith Silsilat Al-Ahadeeth Al-Saheehah [Collected Sayings of Muhammad] (1985). Complied M.N. Al-Albani, J. Badawi (trans.). Beirut: Al-Maktab Al-Islaami.

Harvey, P. (2000). *Introduction to Buddhist Ethics*. Cambridge. Cambridge University Press.

Hay, D. (2004). *Economics Today: a Christian Critique*. Vancouver: Regent.

Heath, E. and B. Kaldis (eds) (2017). *Wealth, Commerce, and Philosophy: Foundational Thinkers and Business Ethics*. Chicago, IL: University of Chicago Press.

Ismaeel, M. and K. Blaim (2012). "Toward Applied Islamic Business Ethics: Responsible Halal Business," in *Journal of Management Development*, 31:10, 1090–1100.

Kardong, T. (1996). *Benedict's Rule and Commentary*. Collegeville, PA: Liturgical Press.

Laozi (1961). *Tao Te Ching*, J. Wu (trans.). Available at: http://terebess.hu/english/tao/_index.html.

Laozi (1988). *Tao Te Ching*, S. Mitchell (trans.). Available at: http://terebess.hu/english/tao/_index.html.

Levine, A. and M. Pava (1999). *Jewish Business Ethics: The Firm and Its Stakeholders*. Lanham, MD: Jason Aronson, Inc.

Luther, M. (1535 [1960]). *Letters of Spiritual Counsel*, T.G. Tappert (ed.). Philadelphia, PA: Westminster.

Luther, M. (1520). *The Babylonian Captivity of the Church*. Available at: www.lutherdansk.dk/Web-babylonian%20Captivitate/Martin%20Luther.htm.

Luther, M. (1524) [1897]. "On Trade and Usury," W.H. Carruth (trans.), in P. Carus (ed.,), *The Open Court Magazine* 11:1 (January), 16–34.

Malloch, T. (2008). *Spiritual Enterprise: Doing Virtuous Business*. New York, NY: Encounter.

O'Brian, T. and S. Paeth (2007). *Religious Perspectives in Business Ethics: an Anthology*. Lanham, MD: Rowman and Littlefield.

Quddus, M. and S. Rashid (2017). "The Ethics of Commerce in Islam: Ibn Khaldun's *Muqaddimah* Revisited," in E. Heath and B. Kaldis (eds), *Wealth, Commerce, and Philosophy: Foundational Thinkers and Business Ethics*. Chicago, IL: University of Chicago Press, 115–134.

Rae, S. and K. Wong (1996). *Beyond Integrity, A Judeo-Christian Approach to Business Ethics*. Grand Rapids, MI: Zondervan.

Rae, S. and K. Wong (2011). *Business for the Common Good, a Christian Vision for the Marketplace*. Downers Grove, IL: Intervarsity Press.

Rice, G. (1999). "Islamic Ethics and the Implications for Business," *Journal of Business Ethics* 18:4, 345–358.

Ritenour, S. (2010). *Foundations of Economics: A Christian View*. Eugene, OR: Wipf and Stock.

Schlag, M. (2017). "Thomas Aquinas: The Economy at the Service of Justice and the Common Good," in E. Heath and B. Kaldis, (eds), *Wealth, Commerce, and Philosophy: Foundational Thinkers and Business Ethics*. Chicago, IL: University of Chicago Press, 95–114.

Sirico, Rev. R. (2012). *Defending the Free Market: The Moral Case for a Free Economy*. Washington, DC: Regnery.

Tillich, P. (1952). *The Courage to Be*. New Haven, CT: Yale University Press.

Weber, M. (2011). *The Protestant Ethic and the Spirit of Capitalism*, S. Kalberg (ed.). Oxford: Oxford University Press.

Part III
Business ethics theories

Introduction

In its history as a self-conscious academic discipline, business ethics has proceeded through different theoretical phases. Its initial phase saw business ethicists engaged straightforwardly in applied ethics, offering arguments for or against business practices or institutions by applying some version of Kantian, utilitarian, contractarian, or virtue-ethics-informed arguments. Although this approach remains vital in business ethics, it was supplanted as a main activity for academic business ethicists by a shift toward "bespoke" theory making: business ethicists began developing business-ethics-specific theories tailored to the peculiar venues and practices of commerce. Examples of these include shareholder theory, stakeholder theory, and what Thomas Donaldson and Thomas Dunfee dubbed "integrative social contracts theory." Although the development of these theoretical constructs is not wholly devoid of inspiration from mainstream ethical theory (see, e.g., the treatment of integrative social contracts theory in Chapter 6, Social contract theory), neither may they rightly be said to be mere applications of it. Whether more recent theoretical developments in business ethics continue the bespoke phase or constitute a new direction in business ethics theory remains to be seen.

At a higher level of abstraction, an important and unresolved question is the conceptual relationship between business ethics and corporate social responsibility (CSR). Are they two different names for the same thing? Does one circumscribe the other and, if so, which circumscribes which? These questions take on added importance with the emergence of sustainability as yet another banner under which ethical concern is expressed.

In this section's opening chapter, **Social responsibility**, **Florian Wettstein** lays out the widely varying terrain of CSR, undertaking the difficult task of defining social responsibility as well as connecting the concept of CSR to foundational questions surrounding whether corporate entities may be regarded properly as moral agents. He explores subsequently the content of CSR (what *are* the social responsibilities of corporations?) and examines the relationship between what CSR scholars pursue *academically* and what business firms pursue *practically* under the heading of CSR. Wettstein closes with a consideration of emergent trends in CSR.

In the next chapter, **Stakeholder thinking**, **Kenneth E. Goodpaster** explores both the promise and the limits of stakeholder thinking as a moral paradigm in business ethics. This he does through the intriguing lens of *conscience*. If failures of business ethics are failures of conscience, the question arises as to whether stakeholderism is a conscience-supporting or a conscience-impeding model of business decision making. Goodpaster considers the relationship between stakeholderism and comprehensive moral thinking and concludes with a consideration of the implications of stakeholder thinking for business education.

If the emergence of stakeholder theory marked a turn toward venue- or practice-specific theory in business ethics, perhaps the subject of Chapter 12, **Integrative Economic Ethics: concept and critique**, by **Alexander Lorch and Thomas Beschorner**, reconnects business ethics to larger questions of ethics and political philosophy. Delineating Integrative Economic Ethics' attempt to link fine-grained questions of business ethics to basic questions of just political and economic institutions, Lorch and Beschorner take their reader through multiple levels of social and ethical analysis to discover the strengths and weaknesses of a perspective that seeks to embed the principles of markets into the larger considerations illuminated by discourse ethics.

Alexei Marcoux

10
Social responsibility

Florian Wettstein

In 1972, Dow Votaw, a pioneer in corporate social responsibility research, lamented the increasingly inflationary use of the term "Corporate Social Responsibility" (CSR). However, despite (or perhaps precisely because of) the term being referred to in excess there seemed little clarity about its meaning:

> The term is a brilliant one; it means something, but not always the same thing, to everybody. To some it conveys the idea of legal responsibility or liability; to others, it means socially responsible behavior in an ethical sense; to still others, the meaning transmitted is that of "responsible for," in a causal mode; many simply equate it with a charitable contribution; some take it to mean socially conscious; many of those who embrace it most fervently see it as a mere synonym for "legitimacy," in the context of "belonging" or being proper or valid; a few see it as a sort of fiduciary duty imposing higher standards of behavior on businessmen than on citizens at large.
>
> *(Votaw 1972: 25)*

Despite dating back more than 40 years, Votaw's assessment seems as accurate today as it was then. Even more has been written on CSR in the meantime, even more companies have signed up to the idea, even more approaches and interpretations are being offered in the now vast literature on the concept. Some of these conceptualizations overlap or complement each other, but, overall, there seems as little convergence among different approaches to CSR today as then.

Navigating and making sense of this heterogeneous field is no trivial task. Considering the breadth and depth of the discussion, it is hardly realistic for this chapter to aim at providing a complete overview of, or even a comprehensive introduction to, CSR. Any such overview or introduction must discriminate by necessity in order to remain manageable; it has to select carefully what to address and what not to address, what ideas and approaches to include or not to include, what arguments to emphasize and which to marginalize. As a consequence, this chapter aims to provide a systematic starting point for readers so that they can make sense of the CSR discussion and grasp core issues and problems connected to it. Even if it is not possible, in a short chapter such as this, to offer a full understanding of the CSR debate, the selected contents are, in my view, essential to a deeper understanding of that discussion and thus provide entry points for readers who seek a more thorough engagement.

The chapter will, first, attempt to provide a formal (rather than substantive) definition of the term "social responsibility." In the second section, the chapter will address the most basic prerequisite for corporations to be able to have social responsibilities in the first place. That is, it will tackle the question of whether or not corporations are moral agents. The third section will look at the definitional issue from a more substantive angle. What are the social responsibilities of companies? This will be followed by a broad overview of existing approaches and theories of CSR. Thus, section four will provide two basic taxonomies—one classifying CSR theory and one CSR practice. The fifth section will engage with new directions in CSR research. More specifically, it will explore three new and increasingly influential approaches in the broader discussion on corporate responsibility: Creating shared value, political CSR, and business and human rights.

Social responsibility defined

"Social responsibility" is an inherently fuzzy concept. Even on its own, the term "responsibility" is notoriously ambiguous and multi-dimensional. Generally, we can distinguish four common uses of the term. First, in referring to a responsible person, we commonly mean reliable, good, virtuous or reasonable. That is, we refer to the morally favorable traits of someone's character (Frankena 1973: 71). Second, a person can be responsible for a specific past action or incidence, meaning that the person can be blamed for causing it. Third, when referring to a person having a responsibility to engage in certain types of activities or to bring about specific consequences in the future we use the term synonymously with obligation. Finally, in a very basic sense, a responsible person is a person who is capable of being ascribed responsibility. Responsibility, in this basic sense, means having a basic capacity to reason.

Responsibility in a moral sense is closely associated with ascribing praise or blame. That is, praise or blame are our typical (even natural) responses to someone having caused, with his or her actions, a negative (blameworthy) or positive (praiseworthy) outcome. In other words, we tend to view someone as morally responsible (in the second backward-looking sense above) if it is appropriate to either praise or blame that person for a certain action or outcome. Thus, moral responsibility in this sense is akin to blameworthiness or praiseworthiness (Eshleman 2014).

Now, to what does *social* responsibility refer? Similar to the meaning of "responsibility," the meaning of "social" is multi-faceted and contested as well. Without dwelling too much on content, we can access the term from two basic directions. First, "social" in connection with the term "responsibility" can refer to the *foundation* or *source* of that particular responsibility; and, second, it can refer to its *addressee* and thus to the basic nature or quality of the activities required of an agent to meet the responsibility.

Turning first to the question of foundations, Richard DeGeorge distinguishes between three sources that give rise to three different kinds of (corporate) responsibility: moral, social, and legal (DeGeorge 2010: 198–204). DeGeorge argues that they often overlap, but should not be confused conceptually. *Moral responsibility*, according to DeGeorge (2010: 198–99), arises from ethical grounds. It is independent from what the law says and what is socially mandated. A company that dumps toxic waste into a river inevitably causes harm and thus violates its moral responsibilities irrespective of whether or not this practice is prohibited by law or socially accepted by the people and communities whose river is being polluted. *Social responsibility*, on the other hand, derives from social demands and expectations. It is what society explicitly or implicitly expects of businesses. Finally, and perhaps most straightforward, *legal responsibility* derives from what is mandated by law.

This distinction particularly between social and moral responsibility as outlined by DeGeorge, while conceptually useful, seems problematic from a normative point of view. At any given time, social demands (that is, what society expects of businesses) overlap considerably with moral requirements (that is, what businesses ought to do based on ethical considerations), but may not coincide fully. Social demands may exceed moral requirements or vice versa. For example, people might be too optimistic about what a company can reasonably achieve in regard to supply chain responsibility in the short term and thus set the bar too high for businesses. On the other hand, we may find certain tax avoidance strategies as acceptable simply because they are common practice. However, this does not mean that such strategies are also morally legitimate. So, how ought businesses to deal with situations in which social demands run counter to basic moral requirements? What if social demands are unjust, discriminatory, or offensive? Does it still make sense in such cases to claim that companies have an actual *responsibility* to meet such socially harmful demands and expectations? It seems that to turn social demands into actual social *responsibilities* for business, they ought to be justifiable also from a moral point of view; at the very least, I would argue that they cannot run counter to some of the most fundamental moral principles without losing their normative status as actual responsibilities. Hence, while it makes sense to distinguish between social and moral demands and expectations, it may be problematic to do so also in regard to social and moral responsibilities.

Concordantly, I would argue that the term "social" in social responsibility does not refer to the foundation of the responsibility, but rather to the quality of the required action or the nature of its expected impact. Social responsibility in this second sense is a responsibility for *social action*, that is, for action that expresses concern for and has a positive impact on society (DeGeorge 2010: 200). More specifically, the responsibility to engage in a socially beneficial (or non-harmful) activity should possess its own moral justification (or demonstrated moral compatibility) that does not rest solely on the appeal to the purported social benefit.

If, as we have argued, social responsibility ought to be grounded or at least justified morally, the question arises whether or not companies can, in fact, be ascribed moral or social responsibilities. This question is synonymous with the question of whether or not corporations are moral agents, since only moral agents are capable of having and discharging social or moral responsibility. This fundamental prerequisite of the corporate social responsibility discussion will be addressed in the next section.

Can corporations have moral responsibilities? Corporations as moral agents

Morally grounded responsibility can be ascribed only to moral actors, that is, to actors capable of acting intentionally. Thus, while corporate legal responsibility merely presupposes that corporations are recognized as legal persons in law, social or moral responsibility requires more than that: it requires that companies can be viewed not merely as legal, but as moral persons or, alternatively, as moral agents. Therefore, the question that precedes all other questions about the form and content of corporate social responsibility is to what extent the characteristics of moral agents apply also to collective actors such as companies and other organizations.

On one end of the spectrum are those who hold that corporations are merely aggregates of individuals (see Werhane 2015: 13). Accordingly, they argue that only individuals can be bearers of moral responsibility but not corporations as entities (see, e.g., Velasquez 1983; Friedman 1962, 1970). On this view, it would be conceptually wrong to assign moral responsibility to a corporation because all corporate acts are, in fact, the acts of individuals within the company. The same goes for corporate intentions, which, as they argue, are always the shared intentions of individuals. Manuel Velasquez (1983) also sees practical danger in such a position: seeing corporations as moral agents who can be blamed and held morally responsible creates a corporate veil that shields individuals within the company from being held responsible for their wrongdoings.

A slightly different argument is advanced in the "structural restraint view" (see Donaldson 1982: 24). This account of the corporation is based on a similar position about the moral agency, or lack thereof, of companies. As opposed to Velasquez's view, which claims that morality in organizations is always reducible to individual intentions of its members, the structural restraint view holds that the way companies are set up prevents them from utilizing moral considerations in their decision-making. According to this account, corporations are built to maximize the achievement of a given set of goals at the expense of all other moral considerations (Donaldson 1982: 25). Such a view has recently been espoused, for example, by Joel Bakan (2004), who portrays corporations as psychopaths that are programmed for the sole pursuit of profits and power.

On the other end of the spectrum are those who argue that corporations are to be viewed as "full-fledged moral persons" with equal standing and the same privileges, rights and duties as human beings (see, e.g., French 1979).[1] Peter French argued that corporations can be held morally responsible based on their corporate intentionality, which he perceived as distinct from the intentionality of any one of its members. Internal decision-making structures, according to French (1979: 212), *incorporate* the acts of its individual members and are thus the basis of corporate intentionality. Having such internal decision-making structures, corporations are capable of acting based on corporate reasons, which are irreducible to the reasons of its individual members. Therefore, corporate decisions are morally relevant in the sense that corporations can be ascribed moral responsibility that is equally irreducible to the responsibility of its individual members.

A middle ground between these two extreme views would be to attribute moral agency to corporations but not full-fledged moral personhood akin to human beings (Donaldson 1982). Such a position seems sensible. Moral persons are ends in themselves. Based on this, it would seem cynical to claim moral personhood for corporations (DeGeorge 2010: 112). Donaldson (1982) argued that in order to qualify as a moral agent, a company needs to embody a process of moral decision making, which is characterized by two elements: first, the capacity to use moral reasons in decision-making, and, second, the capacity to control (within the decision-making process) not only the actual activities and behavior of the company but also the structure and policies that guide such behavior. This second condition corrects a practical danger inherent to the structural restraint view. As Donaldson puts it:

> A corporation which, despite having the requisite amount of control, failed to correct faulty procedures in its product safety division and procrastinated until a consumer was injured ought not be let off the moral hook by disclaiming moral agency. Only if the decision-making process of a corporation were thoroughly mechanistic and fit perfectly the Structural Restraint model, or if the corporation were thoroughly fragmented and lacked any significant decision-making mechanisms, would the corporation be analogous to the sick or insane person who could not tell right from wrong.
>
> *(Donaldson 1982: 31)*

Based on this account, Donaldson proposes that companies should be required to meet these conditions for moral agency, in order to qualify as corporations. That is, they ought to meet the conditions for moral agency in order to become incorporated.

In summary, while there has been an ongoing discussion on corporate moral agency since at least the 1970s, there is a broad consensus today both among scholars as well as in the broader public that we can hold corporations morally responsible for what they do. While this view may more often be informed by intuition, rather than by a well-grounded philosophical account of moral agency, it does find broad support also in the scholarly discussion on the issue.

What are the social responsibilities of corporations?

After clarifying that corporations, as moral agents, can have moral and social responsibilities, it is now time to look into what CSR entails.

Historically, the discussion on corporate social responsibility dates back to the 1950s. More specifically, Howard R. Bowen's 1953 book on *The Social Responsibilities of the Businessman* is commonly regarded as the first text to address the topic in depth. For Bowen, social responsibility "refers to the obligations of businessmen to pursue those policies, to make those decisions, or to follow those lines of action which are desirable in terms of the objectives and values of our society." Since Bowen, countless alternative definitions have been proposed. Generally, early approaches to CSR tended to have a rather philanthropic outlook (Carroll 1999). Business was seen to have a responsibility not only to abide by the law but to benefit society by donating a part of their profits to social causes. In more recent times, such charitable approaches to CSR have been criticized as inadequate or at least insufficient (see, e.g., Ulrich 2008: 402–404).

Thus, more recent approaches have rightly pointed out that CSR is less about charity than the way a corporation conducts its core business. As such, it concerns and affects everything from recruiting employees, to goal-setting processes, the design of incentive and reward systems, to product development and distribution, and so on (see, e.g., Waddock and Rasche 2012). Thus, rather than being supplemental to a company's business activities, CSR ought to be integrated at the very core of them (see, e.g., Grayson and Hodges 2004). This is not to say that a well-designed philanthropic program cannot be a part of a holistic CSR strategy (see, e.g., Carroll 1998), but it hardly is the core or even the essence of it.

Opinions vary considerably regarding the content and focus of CSR. It is safe to say that the specific social responsibilities of companies are dependent on context and situation. Prominently, the European Commission (2011) recently put forth a broad definition of CSR as "the responsibility of enterprises for their impacts on society." The idea of "impacts" is defined both in negative and positive terms: corporations ought to avoid adverse consequences for both society and the environment and to strive to increase their positive effects on others. Generally, as Andreas Scherer and Guido Palazzo (2007: 1096) have pointed out, CSR serves as something like an "umbrella term" for all those debates that deal with the "responsibilities of business and its role in society." Similarly, Jan Jonker (2005) refers to CSR as a "sensitising concept," that is, "a term that draws attention to a complex range of issues and elements that are all related to the position and function of the business enterprise in contemporary society. As such, this umbrella term helps to identify and address what needs to be debated" (Jonker 2005: 20).

Under this CSR umbrella countless standards and initiatives have formulated a wide range of norms, principles, and issues that corporations ought to respect and consider when conducting their business. It makes sense to look at such standards to get an idea about what specific responsibilities CSR may entail and what issues it may address. Most of such standards entail provisions regarding the proper treatment of workers and employees, prohibiting exploitative and unsafe working conditions as well as the use of sweatshops and child labor. Many subsume environmental responsibilities as a part of CSR, encouraging businesses to reduce their environmental footprint and work toward climate neutrality. Some standards are specifically geared toward stakeholder relations and the company's impact on the communities in which it operates. Human rights impacts of companies have become a core concern of many CSR standards, such as the UN Global Compact, the Organisation for Economic Cooperation and Development (OECD) Guidelines for Multinational Companies and, most recently, the UN Guiding Principles on Business and Human Rights. There is a tendency for such standards to become more expansive over time, that is, to cast the net of potential corporate responsibility ever wider. For example, while the UN Global Compact initially comprised of only nine broad principles, it has later added a tenth principle addressing anti-corruption efforts by businesses. In a similar manner, tax avoidance has been addressed more frequently under the CSR umbrella as well in recent times (see, e.g., Preuss 2010). Another trend is the formulation of industry-specific standards to address issues and problems particular to certain industries: for example, freedom of expression for the information and communication technology sector; access to essential drugs for pharmaceutical companies; or free, prior and informed consent of local communities to mining projects; or the use of force by private and public security contractors.

Making sense of CSR theory and practice

There are countless approaches and theories of CSR in the vast literature on the topic. This section attempts to make conceptual sense and provide an overview of the CSR landscape by, first, developing a basic taxonomy that helps classifying CSR theories and, second, introducing two conceptual models that have done the same in regard to CSR practice.

CSR theories

There are many ways one could order and classify CSR theories. For example, Elisabet Garriga and Domènec Melé (2004; see also Melé 2008) distinguish between instrumental, political, integrative and ethical theories of CSR. The four categories roughly resemble four different perspectives from which to theorize CSR: economic, political, social and ethical. Duane Windsor (2006) starts from a similar vantage point, but distinguishes between only three basic categories of theories: ethical responsibility theory, economic responsibility theory, and corporate citizenship (in essence, a political responsibility theory). Peter Ulrich (2008) advances a normative taxonomy that proceeds from functional, instrumental, charitable and corrective approaches to integrative approaches. Ulrich's categorization does not classify existing theories along certain conceptual traits, but assesses the normative merit of different approaches to CSR. The more holistically an approach challenges the dominant shareholder-value-maximization doctrine of the corporation, the higher its normative status.

The following overview of CSR theories draws, in varying degrees, on these previous attempts, rearranging their insights and adding new thought to them. It groups theories along two dimensions: the *foundations* on which they are built and their basic *aims*. Accordingly, within both dimensions, a number of sub-categories are distinguished.

Foundation

The CSR theories can be distinguished based on the foundation from which they derive corporate responsibilities. Three different foundations, which provide three different (moral) justifications for CSR, can be distinguished in this regard (see also Hsieh and Wettstein 2014).

Purpose-based accounts derive the responsibilities of companies from the distinct purpose or function that companies are assigned in society. Narrow accounts interpret corporate purpose exclusively in economic terms, e.g., as the creation of wealth for society or, more narrowly, as the creation of value only for its owners. Accordingly, such accounts tend to define the respective corporate responsibilities in equally narrow terms. Milton Friedman's (1970) view that "there is one and only one social responsibility of business—to use its resources and engage in activities designed to increase its profits so long as it stays within the rules of the game, which is to say, engages in open and free competition without deception or fraud" can be viewed as representative of such interpretations. On the other hand, more expansive accounts tend to stress the social, rather than merely the economic, role and purpose of corporations. Accordingly, they tend to frame also the social responsibilities of companies in broader terms. Ulrich (2008: 410) argues that the purpose of business enterprises is more than merely providing goods for payment. Rather, as he argues, business activity must be guided by "a vision of real-life practical values which ought to be created, be it on the level of fulfilling fundamental human needs or on the level of enlarging the abundance of human life." Thus, underlying business activity is an "idea of value creation which aims to make a genuine contribution to the quality of life in society" (Ulrich 2008: 410–11).

Power- or influence-based accounts portray companies as increasingly powerful actors in economic, social and even political terms and argue that such power must be accompanied by shouldering more (public) responsibility within and for society (Kobrin 2009: 350). At minimum, such accounts argue for the responsible and legitimate use of corporate power (Davis 1960). However, such approaches often embrace accounts of corporate responsibility that reach decisively beyond "do no harm" provisions for business (see, e.g., Wettstein 2012; Wood 2012). Especially where state institutions are weak or entirely absent, such accounts tend to argue that corporations ought to step in to fill, at least in part, the social and political void.

Relational accounts derive corporate responsibility not from purpose or power but from the kind of relations between corporations and their social environment. Contractual accounts argue that corporate responsibilities derive from a broad social contract between society and business. The most prominent theory in this category is Donaldson and Dunfee's (1999) Integrated Social Contracts Theory (ISCT), which applies social contract thinking to the international context and thus provides a frame to derive the social responsibilities specifically of multinational companies. Theories that emphasize the fiduciary duty of managers to shareholders can also be framed in contractual terms. Directly opposed to theories stressing shareholder primacy is the broad field of stakeholder theories (Freeman 1984; Donaldson and Preston 1995; Phillips 2011). Stakeholder approaches perceive shareholders as only one among many groups to which companies have morally significant relations. Accordingly, such groups too may have legitimate stakes or claims in the company alongside, or in some cases prior to, shareholders. The main challenges of stakeholder theories are connected to the identification and prioritization of stakeholder groups (see Phillips 2003) as well as to the balancing of the respective stakeholder responsibilities. However, stakeholder approaches grapple with certain limitations and thus have been faced with fundamental challenges and criticisms (Norman 2013, 2004; Marcoux 2003). For example, it has been argued that they do not provide much insight into the role of business in finding solutions for large-scale societal problems (Walsh 2005). Goodpaster (2009) has framed this as the lack of what he calls "comprehensive moral thinking," that is, as a lack of reflection about the larger social implications of corporate decision making and the influence of business behavior on the system as a whole. This apparent gap in stakeholder thinking may be addressed more convincingly by purpose-based and influenced-based outlooks as outlined above.

Aim and outlook

An alternative way to group CSR theories is based on their basic aim and outlook. Four different approaches can be distinguished: normative, instrumental, managerial, and institutional. While the first two aim at providing a justification for CSR (one ethical, the other economic), the third and fourth are concerned more with its operationalization and implementation (one from a managerial, the other from an institutional perspective).

Normative approaches to CSR emphasize the intrinsic importance of corporate responsibility by appeal to moral principles, ideals and values, rather than instrumental utility (for example, to advance corporate profits). Advocates for these accounts argue for corporate responsibility not because it makes economic sense but because they see a moral obligation for companies to conduct their business in a responsible manner—irrespective of the financial costs or benefits this may imply. For example, stakeholder theories have been framed both in normative and strategic terms. Although Freeman's (1984) original account had a strategic outlook, others (Donaldson and Preston 1995) have reformulated stakeholder thinking toward a normative perspective. Stakeholder interests, from a normative point of view, ought to be taken seriously for their own sake and based on their legitimacy, but, from a strategic perspective, the adequate consideration of stakeholder demands and interests is seen to be instrumental to the maximization of profits.

Strategic or instrumental approaches stress the so-called business case for CSR, that is, they highlight the economic or financial value of CSR for companies. According to this view, corporations should not primarily adopt CSR because it is the "right thing to do," but because it is good for business. Accordingly, instrumental approaches argue that social responsibilities ought to be taken into consideration by companies only if they are consistent with the profit maximization aim (Garriga and Melé 2004). There is a long list of studies that have tried to prove a causal link between CSR and increasing financial returns, but evidence has been mixed (see, e.g., Orlitzky et al. 2003; Rost and Ehrmann 2015) and the methodology and general conceptual soundness of such correlations has frequently been questioned (see, e.g., Vogel 2005). Generally, a business case for CSR can be framed in two basic ways (see Paine 2000). The positive argument stresses the potential of CSR to increase profits, for example, by emphasizing reputational gains or increased productivity of employees. The negative argument, on the other hand, perceives CSR more as a tool to mitigate risk and associated costs that may arise from litigation, reputational damage, customer boycotts or generally from naming and shaming by civil society organizations.

Managerial approaches to CSR are less concerned with normative or instrumental justifications or the philosophical foundations of CSR than with its application and operationalization within the organization (see, e.g., Waddock and Rasche 2012; Paine 1994). Such approaches have been put forth first of all by strategy or general management scholars, rather than by business ethicists or philosophers.

Institutional approaches form perhaps the most recent group of CSR theories and have gained considerable influence in the field in recent years (e.g., Brammer et al. 2012). Such approaches seek neither to justify CSR nor to probe its managerial implications. Rather, they analyze the conditions under which CSR can be institutionalized in organizations, industries, and markets; explain how organizations strive for and achieve legitimacy; and explore how different institutional settings can either foster or hinder the effective diffusion of CSR practices throughout society. Institutional approaches have attracted scholars in organizational behavior and sociology to the field of CSR.

CSR practice

What is the actual practice of CSR? Although it is difficult to gather direct data on the extent to which corporations integrate CSR in their operations there is some evidence. Along with earlier studies (Williams and Aguilera 2008; Visser 2008), one of the better and more recent gauges is the 2014 report on new business models for the twenty-first century developed by the highly acclaimed Economist Intelligence Unit (EIU). The EIU surveyed 285 senior executives from corporations across the globe (with 27 percent headquartered Western Europe, 24 percent in the US, 20 percent Asia-Pacific, 12 percent Latin America, 11 percent Middle East and Africa, and 6 percent in Eastern Europe), on their approaches, achievements, and future plans in regard to corporate *sustainability*. However, in this survey "sustainability" is defined as a company's commitment to environmental, social, and governance (ESG) goals. Thus, depending on how broadly we define the scope of CSR, the survey suggests a significant overlap with CSR goals. (Most of the prevailing CSR standards such as the UN Global Compact or the OECD Guidelines for Multinational Enterprises specify norms in all three ESG domains.) The EIU reports that overall commitment to sustainability principles remains high even as more and more companies face increasing obstacles to embedding them in their business. As a result, 52 percent of surveyed companies now say that "immediate financial goals are currently more urgent." Somewhat surprisingly, perhaps, the EIU observes that the expansion of sustainability practices in the past two years has come predominantly from developing economies. Twenty percent of the firms surveyed publish their sustainability goals and performance at least once a year. However, a third of them doubt that their sustainability strategies will stand the test of time. The report states that almost two thirds of the firms are reviewing new strategies and business models to ensure long-term sustainability, but only a very small number have actually followed up and revised their overall strategies accordingly.

If we turn from actual practice to a theoretical taxonomy of CSR practice, then we find a number of contributions that analyze how, as a matter of practice, companies evolve and progress as responsible organizations. Such studies set forth taxonomies to classify companies according to their position on a corporate responsibility spectrum.

In a widely cited paper, Simon Zadek (2004) showed that companies evolve on a "path to corporate responsibility" along five consecutive stages from "defensive" to "compliant," "managerial," "strategic," and finally to the highest stage—"civil." At the *defensive stage*, as Zadek points out, companies are often caught off-guard by criticism about their social or environmental conduct and, as a consequence, react with denial and rejection of such criticism. At the *compliance stage*, corporations start to realize that denial may not make the criticism disappear. So they switch to what we could call a strategy of appeasement. However, their response is often rather superficial and focused merely on the protection of the firm's reputation. At the *managerial stage*, companies develop a deeper understanding of the problem. They begin to understand that real solutions will not transpire from communications or legal departments, but from the managers of the core business. For example, it is unlikely that adopting a standard on responsible sourcing will lead to a profound transformation of such practices without adjusting incentive structures and goal-setting accordingly. At the *strategic stage*, companies start to realign their core business strategies in order to address responsible business practices. Finally, at the *civil stage*, corporations promote collective action, that is collaboration within and across industries, in order to lift their whole industry or even the marketplace as such to a higher level of responsibility; they may even see a role for business to contribute together with other institutions to solving broader societal problems.

Similar to Zadek's typology, Mirvis and Googins (2006) distinguish five stages of corporate citizenship. At the *elementary stage*, citizenship activity within a corporation is episodic and responsibility programs are not well developed. There is little awareness regarding citizenship issues and companies merely aim at complying with the law. At the *engaged stage* of citizenship, companies become aware and start to engage with corporate responsibility, although in a largely reactive manner. At the *innovative stage* companies start to broaden their citizenship agenda and deepen their involvement, displaying high levels of innovation and moral learning. However, there remains little integration of citizenship programs with the core business strategies, corporate culture, and management systems of the company. At the *integrated stage* "companies take serious steps to drive citizenship into their lines of business. In operational terms, this involves setting targets, establishing key performance indicators, and monitoring performance through balanced scorecards" (Mirvis and Googins 2006: 115). Furthermore, at this stage corporate efforts are driven increasingly by values rather than by a business case. Finally, at the *transformative stage*, corporations display bigger aspirations to change the way business is done by fusing their citizenship and business agendas. Similar to Zadek's typology, Mirvis and Googins point out that at this final stage, corporations partner and collaborate extensively with other institutions to drive a common responsibility agenda.

New directions in CSR

After classifying and outlining some of the major approaches and theories of CSR in the previous section, let us now take a closer look at three recent developments in the CSR discussion, each of which has the potential to provide novel insights that might push the debate into new directions.

Creating shared value

In a 2006 essay in *Harvard Business Review*, with a follow-up contribution to the same journal in 2011, Michael Porter and Mark Kramer (2006, 2011) introduced the "Creating Shared Value" (CSV) approach. Particularly in their 2011 contribution, the authors intend nothing less than to redefine business and to reinvent capitalism itself, in order to regain trust for what they perceive as a system (and its players) under siege. In essence, CSV is built on the proposition that companies should create "economic value in a way that also creates value for society by addressing its needs and challenges" (Porter and Kramer 2011: 64). Business ought to address social challenges and concerns from a value perspective, rather than to treat them as peripheral matters (66). Or, more bluntly stated, it should turn social problems into business opportunities (Crane et al. 2014: 130). Porter and Kramer subsequently propose three ways in which companies can create shared value: first, by reconceiving products and markets, second, by redefining productivity in the value chain, and, third, by building supportive industry clusters at the company's locations.

To be sure, CSV is not actually meant to be a CSR approach. On the contrary, it is to be understood as a more or less direct critique of CSR. The authors perceive CSR to be peripheral to business and largely ineffective, so they propose CSV as a way to move *beyond* CSR—by shifting social issues and challenges to the very center of the business equation. "Shared value" as the authors assert, "is not social responsibility . . . but a new way to achieve economic success" (Porter and Kramer 2011: 64).

Taken at face value, this seems a reasonable suggestion; and perhaps Porter and Kramer are correct in claiming that "most companies remain stuck in a "social responsibility" mind-set in which societal issues are at the periphery, not the core" (2011: 64). From that perspective, CSV may indeed reduce the level of hesitation among companies to address social issues proactively and through their core business processes. However, it is at least questionable whether doing away with the idea of responsibility altogether in favor of the similarly fuzzy idea of "shared value" ultimately is the right response to this diagnosis.

Against this background, it is not surprising that CSV has been criticized harshly by a number of scholars, especially in the business ethics field. For example, Crane et al. (2014: 133) acknowledge that the CSV concept has succeeded in drawing more attention to the social dimension of doing business, thereby elevating this dimension to a strategic level. Nevertheless, they see it as a "reactionary" rather than transformational approach to solve what Porter and Kramer (2011: 64) perceive as a current trust and legitimacy crisis of business. More specifically, as they contend, the approach is, first, unoriginal and based on a caricature of CSR that emphasizes only its philanthropic dimension but ignores its connection to the core business of a company. Second, the win–win orientation of the approach ignores potential trade-offs between economic and social value-creation, which might ultimately "drive corporations to invest more in easy problems and decoupled communication strategies than in solving broader societal problems" (Crane et al. 2014: 137). Third, they lament the naiveté of the approach in taking business compliance with laws and social norms simply as a given, when, in fact, this remains an unresolved challenge. Finally, the authors criticize CSV for being based on a shallow conception of the corporation's role in society, because it does not challenge the traditional competitive logic of doing business in a fundamental manner but rather affirms and bolsters it. After all, social problems, according to CSV, are relevant to companies only if they can be transformed into win–win opportunities. Thus, as they argue, CSV "wants to rethink the purpose of the corporation without questioning the sanctity of corporate self-interest" (Crane et al. 2014: 140).

Political CSR

It is perhaps not a coincidence that the above-cited critique of CSV and especially its alleged reaffirmation of a narrow economic role of the corporation has been voiced by a group of scholars, some of whom have been involved decisively in shaping a new research stream that has been labeled "political CSR." Political CSR challenges a narrow economic interpretation of the role and purpose of companies. Instead, it is based on the observation that companies are increasingly involved in activities and tasks that are public in nature and formerly thought to be reserved for governments to discharge (see, e.g., Matten and Crane 2005; Scherer and Palazzo 2007). In short, corporations are turning into political actors, involved particularly in the governance of those spaces that increasingly elude governmental reach and control in what is often referred to as a "post-Westphalian" order:

> political CSR suggests an extended model of governance with business firms contributing to global regulation and providing public goods. It goes beyond the instrumental view of politics in order to develop a new understanding of global politics where private actors such as corporations and civil society organizations play an active role in the democratic regulation and control of market transactions. These insights may enrich the theory of the firm with a more balanced view on political and economic responsibilities in a globalized world.
> *(Scherer and Palazzo 2011: 901)*

Traditional notions of CSR, which build on the presumption of strong and reliable state institutions as well as a shared value basis, increasingly fail to deal adequately with the distinct challenges of this "post-national constellation" (Scherer and Palazzo 2011: 905). As a consequence, this constellation, as the authors suggest, has profound implications also for the theorization of CSR.

This being said, the thought that corporations are politically relevant actors with political responsibilities is nothing new per se. Peter Drucker outlined the political nature of the company in 1946. In the "Concept of the Corporation" he denotes the business corporation as an institution,

> [. . .] which sets the standard for the way of life and the mode of living of our citizens; which leads, molds and directs; which determines our perspective on our own society; around which crystallize our social problems and to which we look for their solutions.
>
> *(Drucker 1993: 6)*

Similarly, in the 1960s, Dow Votaw (1961) urged that we understand the corporation as a political institution:

> Only if we have a thorough familiarity with the corporation as a political institution, as well as an economic and social one, can we hope even to recognize the effects that it has had and will have on the rest of society.
>
> *(Votaw 1961: 106)*

Political CSR generates for CSR theory a change in perspective that could be conceptualized along three lines: first, political CSR widens the *scope* of corporate responsibility. That is, relative to traditional conceptions of CSR, it includes a broader set of issues and problems within a company's sphere of responsibility. Among the issues and problems that traditional notions of CSR tend to exclude are those connected to the provision of public goods and services. In contrast, for example, the perspective of political CSR encourages pharmaceutical companies to do more than merely provide effective drugs at a reasonable price or to donate essential drugs to low-income countries; rather, companies are encouraged to participate in broad coalitions—both public and private—whose aims encompass a holistic improvement of local health systems including access to medicine in the Global South. Such issues have traditionally been perceived as the exclusive domain of governments. Second, political CSR increases the *extent* of corporate responsibility. Corporations do not merely bear responsibility for problems they have directly caused, but increasingly also for issues to which they are merely connected. This enlarges the extent of responsibility, for example, along a company's value chain. Thus, corporations are increasingly seen as having a responsibility not only in regard to the working conditions in their own subsidiaries but also in the factories of their suppliers, their contractors and sub-contractors. Third, political CSR advocates for a change in the *nature* of corporate responsibility. More specifically, it moves from a focus "merely" on the social responsibilities of business to a perspective of political responsibility, which is typically framed as a communicative and inherently collaborative kind of responsibility, expressed particularly through the involvement of companies in governance tasks (see Scherer and Palazzo 2007).

Business and human rights

Human rights are one of those domains previously thought to be of concern only to governments. However, since the mid-1990s there has been an increasingly influential debate on business responsibilities for human rights. This debate emerges in the 1990s and for reasons similar to those motivating the advocates of political CSR: "The root cause of the business and human rights predicament today," as former UN Special Representative on Business and Human Rights (SRSG) John Ruggie (2008: 3) puts it, "lies in the governance gaps created by globalization—between the scope and impact of economic forces and actors, and the capacity of societies to manage their adverse consequences." And he goes on: "These governance gaps provide the permissive environment for wrongful acts by companies of all kinds without adequate sanctioning or reparation" (Ruggie 2008: 3; see also Fasterling and Demuijnck 2013: 800; Ramasastry 2015: 243; Simons and Macklin 2014: 9–16). Despite this resemblance to political CSR arguments, the business and human rights debate has been largely driven by legal perspectives rather than by CSR scholars (Wettstein 2012). Only recently has the debate caught on in other fields such as business ethics, CSR, and international relations, especially since the publication of the "Protect, Respect and Remedy Framework" (Ruggie 2008) and its operationalization via the "UN Guiding Principles on Business and Human Rights" (Ruggie 2011).

Two decades later this debate has turned into one of the most dynamic and perhaps most interdisciplinary discussions in the broader realm of corporate responsibility. While its focus is narrower than that of CSR more generally, it has some important lessons in store for conventional CSR conceptions (Wettstein 2016). First, its more narrow concern, particularly with human rights responsibility, helps focus the debate as well as the tools and instruments that emerge from it. Second, governments have been involved much more directly in agenda-setting processes for this debate than is the case for CSR. This is partly due to governments still being perceived as the primary bearer of human rights responsibility. Thus, the very definition and conceptualization of corporate human rights responsibility must necessarily address the role of governments. As a consequence, governments have a direct stake in the discussion and thus are more involved in driving it forward. Third, "business and human rights" has brought the law back into the corporate responsibility equation. While for CSR the law can be viewed as a frame or a background condition, exploring the active and productive use of the law for encouraging and enforcing human rights responsibility of companies has been at the very center of the agenda in business and human rights from the start.

Currently, the debate offers different avenues for research for scholars concerned with corporate responsibility. First, there has been an ongoing discussion both on the foundations (moral, political, legal) of attributing human rights responsibility to corporations (see, e.g., Muchlinski 2001; Wettstein 2009; Hsieh 2015) as well as on the scope and nature of corporate human rights responsibilities (see, e.g., Santoro 2009; Bilchitz 2010; Wettstein 2012). Second, there is a more specific debate, both critical and affirmative, on the UN Guiding Principles and their implementation as well as their interpretation in different industries and contexts. Third, there is a debate particularly on legal questions connected to business and human rights. Most prominent among them are questions on the extraterritorial application of domestic law for the protection of human rights abroad and issues and challenges connected to the emerging practice of foreign direct liability cases. In such cases corporate headquarters are sued in their home states for alleged human rights violations committed by their foreign subsidiaries abroad. Furthermore, there has been an ongoing debate on whether or not a legally binding international treaty on business and human rights will be necessary to close the governance gaps effectively. While the SRSG has been skeptical about the merit of such attempts, others have argued that a treaty would address the governance gaps more adequately than a voluntary initiative such as the Guiding Principles.

Concluding remarks

Theorizing corporate social responsibility is an ongoing project. The concept evolves as society evolves and it will therefore never be finished. Today, as we are in the midst of profound global transformations, the implications for how we perceive the purpose and the responsibilities of corporations may be equally profound. Some of the newer directions in corporate responsibility as outlined above have, to various degrees, started to integrate these transformations into their theorizing of the role of corporations in society. Generally, the evolution and growth of the debate on corporate social responsibility, from its beginnings in the 1950s to its current state, has been not only impressive but telling. The way we perceive and theorize the role and responsibilities of corporations says a lot about the state and outlook of our society in general. This alone indicates the inherently social (not merely economic) roots and implications of business.

It was not the aim of this contribution to steer the debate in new directions, but to take stock of what has been done so far. As the global integration of societies continues at rapid speed and the internet and communication technology revolutionizes the ways we live and interact, the views on the corporation will evolve further and nurture new ideas and approaches to CSR. Thus, despite, or perhaps because of, the sometimes criticized "fuzziness" of the concept, research on CSR—conceptual, empirical, and normative—will remain highly relevant for years to come, not only for the sake of understanding corporations better, but for getting a better grasp of society in general.

Essential readings

There is a vast and diverse body of literature on CSR. Andrew Crane et al. *The Oxford Handbook of Corporate Social Responsibility* (2008) provides an excellent introduction to and overview of the field. *Corporate Responsibility: The American Experience*, by Archie B. Carroll et al. (2012), is essential for everyone with an interest in the history of CSR. While the book focuses on the US context, many of its insights are of general relevance. As a contrast, Andrew Crane and Dirk Matten, in *Business Ethics: A European Perspective* (2004) provide a European perspective on CSR, although from a more general business ethics perspective. In *The Market for Virtue* David Vogel (2005) shifts the perspective from the company to the market environment and assesses how market forces can facilitate or hinder responsible business practices and CSR. John M. Kline, in *Ethics for International Business* (2010), deals with the particular challenges of CSR in a global context. The discussion on political CSR connects in very direct ways to Kline's international account. Andreas G. Scherer and Guido Palazzo's essay, "Toward a Political Conception of Corporate Responsibility" (2007) outlines the rationale and basic outlook of this new research stream. For those concerned with questions of implementation and "how it is done" on the ground, consult Sandra Waddock and Andreas Rasche's *Building the Responsible Enterprise* (2012) for helpful insight in how to build the responsible enterprise.

For further reading in this volume on the nature of a corporation, see Chapter 14, The corporation: genesis, identity, agency, and on the nature of business more generally, Chapter 13, What is business? On economic theories of the firm and the goals or aims of the corporation, see Chapter 17, The contribution of economics to business ethics. On the corporation as a locus of the social contract or as existing in contractual relation with society, see Chapter 6, Social contract theories. On human rights in the international context, see Chapter 31, The accounting profession, the public interest, and human rights. On socially responsible investment vehicles, see Chapter 20, Money and finance: ethical considerations. For some considerations on the idea of responsibility and leadership, see Chapter 25, Leadership and business ethics. For a brief discussion as to how the subject of business ethics is regarded as distinct from that of corporate social responsibility, see Chapter 38, Business ethics in Latin America.

Note

1 Note that Peter French eventually distanced himself from the claim that corporations are moral persons analogous to human beings and embraced a weaker account of corporations as moral agents (Arnold 2006: 280).

References

Arnold, D. (2006). "Corporate Moral Agency," *Midwest Studies in Philosophy* 30:1, 279–291.
Bakan, J. (2004). *The Corporation: The Pathological Pursuit of Profit and Power*. New York, NY: Free Press.
Bilchitz, D. (2010). "Corporations Have Positive Fundamental Rights Obligations?" *Theoria* 57:125, 1–35.
Brammer, S., G. Jackson and D. Matten (2012). "Corporate Social Responsibility and Institutional Theory: New Perspectives on Private Governance," *Socio-Economic Review* 10/1:3–28.
Bowen, H.R. (1953). *The Social Responsibilities of the Businessman*. New York, NY: Harper and Row.
Carroll, A.B. (1998). "The Four Faces of Corporate Citizenship," *Business and Society Review* 100/101:1–7.
Carroll, A.B. (1999). "Corporate Social Responsibility: Evolution of a Definitional Construct," *Business and Society* 38:3, 268–295.
Carroll, A.B., K.J. Lipartito, J.E. Post, P.H. Werhane and K.E. Goodpaster (2012). *Corporate Responsibility: The American Experience*. Cambridge: Cambridge University Press.
Crane, A. and D. Matten (2004). *Business Ethics: A European Perspective*. Oxford: Oxford University Press.
Crane, A. et al. (2010). *The Oxford Handbook of Corporate Social Responsibility*. Oxford: Oxford University Press.
Crane, A., G. Palazzo, L.J. Spence, and D. Matten (2014). "Contesting the Value of 'Creating Shared Value,'" *California Management Review* 56:2, 130–149.
Davis, K. (1960). "Can Business Afford to Ignore Corporate Social Responsibilities?" *California Management Review* 2, 70–76.
DeGeorge, R.T. (2010). *Business Ethics*, 7th edition. Upper Saddle River, NJ: Prentice Hall.
Donaldson, T. (1982). *Corporations and Morality*. Upper Saddle River, NJ: Prentice Hall.
Donaldson, T. and L.E. Preston (1995). "The Stakeholder Theory of the Corporation: Concepts, Evidence, and Implications," *The Academy of Management Review* 20:1, 65–91.
Donaldson, T. and T.W. Dunfee (1999). *Ties that Bind: A Social Contracts Approach to Business Ethics*. Cambridge, MA: Harvard Business School Press.
Drucker, P.F. (1993). *Concept of the Corporation*. New Brunswick, NJ; London: Transaction Publishers.
Eshleman, A. (2014). "Moral Responsibility," in Edward N. Zalta (ed.), *The Stanford Encyclopedia of Philosophy* (summer 2014 edition). Available at: http://plato.stanford.edu/archives/sum2014/entries/moral-responsibility/.
European Commission (2011). "A Renewed EU Strategy 2011–14 for Corporate Social Responsibility." Available at: http://eur-lex.europa.eu/LexUriServ/LexUriServ.do?uri=COM:2011:0681:FIN:EN:PDF.
Fasterling, B. and G. Demuijnck (2013). "Human Rights in the Void? Due Diligence in the UN Guiding Principles on Business and Human Rights," *Journal of Business Ethics* 116:799–814.
Frankena, W.K. (1973). *Ethics*, 2nd edition. Englewood Cliffs, NJ: Prentice-Hall.
Freeman, E. (1984). *Strategic Management: A Stakeholder Approach*. Boston, MA: Harper Collins.
French, P.A. (1979). "The Corporation as a Moral Person," *American Philosophical Quarterly* 16:3, 207–215.
Friedman, M. (1962). *Capitalism and Freedom*. Chicago, IL: University of Chicago Press.
Friedman, M. (1970). "The Social Responsibility of Business Is To Increase Its Profits," *The New York Times Magazine* (13 September), 32–33, 122–126.
Garriga, E. and D. Melé (2004). "Corporate Social Responsibility Theories: Mapping the Territory," *Journal of Business Ethics* 53, 51–71.
Goodpaster, K.E. (1991). "Business Ethics and Stakeholder Analysis," *Business Ethics Quarterly* 1:1, 52–71.
Goodpaster, K. (2009). "Corporate Responsibility and its Constituents," in G. Brenkert and T.L. Beauchamp (eds), *The Oxford Handbook of Business Ethics*, Oxford: Oxford University Press, 126–157.
Grayson, D. and A. Hodges (2004). *Corporate Social Opportunity! 7 Steps to Make Corporate Social Responsibility Work for your Business*. Sheffield: Greenleaf Publishing.
Hsieh, N. and F. Wettstein (2014). "Corporate Social Responsibility and Multi-national Corporations," in D. Moellendorf and H. Widdows (eds), *The Routledge Handbook of Global Ethics*, New York, NY: Routledge, 251–266.
Hsieh, N. (2015). "Should Business Have Human Rights Obligations?" *Journal of Human Rights* 14:2, 218–236.
Jonker, J. (2005). "CSR Wonderland. Navigating between Movement, Community, and Organization," *Journal of Corporate Citizenship* 20, 19–22.
Kline, J.M. (2010). *Ethics for International Business. Decision Making in a Global Political Economy*. New York, NY and London: Routledge.

Kobrin, S.J. (2009). "Private Political Authority and Public Responsibility: Transnational Politics, Transnational Firms and Human Rights," *Business Ethics Quarterly* 19:3, 349–374.

Marcoux, A. (2003). "A Fiduciary Argument against Stakeholder Theory," *Business Ethics Quarterly* 13:1, 1–24.

Matten, D. and A. Crane (2005). "Corporate Citizenship: Toward an Extended Theoretical Conceptualization," *Academy of Management Review* 30:1, 166–79.

Melé, D. (2008). "Corporate Social Responsibility Theories," in A. Crane, D. Matten, A. McWilliams, J. Moon, and D. S. Siegel (eds), *The Oxford Handbook of Corporate Social Responsibility*, Oxford: Oxford University Press, 47–82.

Mirvis, P. and B. Googins (2006). "Stages of Corporate Citizenship," *California Management Review* 48:2, 104–126.

Muchlinski, P. (2001). "Human Rights and Multinationals: Is There a Problem?" *International Affairs* 77:1, 31–47.

Norman, W. (2004). "What Can the Stakeholder Theory Learn from Enron?" *Éthique et économique/Ethics and Economics* 2:2, 1–14.

Norman, W. (2013). "Stakeholder Theory," in H. LaFollette (ed.), *The International Encyclopedia of Ethics*, Chichester: Wiley-Blackwell, 5002–5011.

Orlitzky, M., F.L. Schmidt, and S.L. Rynes (2003). "Corporate Social and Financial Performance: A Meta-analysis," *Organization Studies* 24:3, 403–441.

Paine, L.S. (1994). "Managing for Organizational Integrity," *Harvard Business Review* 72:2, 106–117.

Paine, L.S. (2000). "Does Ethics Pay?" *Business Ethics Quarterly* 10:1, 319–330.

Phillips, R.A. (2003). *Stakeholder Theory and Organizational Ethics*. San Francisco, CA: Berrett-Koehler.

Phillips, R.A. (ed.). (2011). *Stakeholder Theory: Impact and Prospects*. Cheltenham UK, Cambridge, MA: Edward Elgar.

Porter, M.E. and M.E. Kramer (2006). "The Link Between Competitive Advantage and Corporate Social Responsibility," *Harvard Business Review* (December), 78–92.

Porter, M.E. and M.R. Kramer (2011). "Creating Shared Value. How to Reinvent Capitalism—and Unleash a Wave of Innovation and Growth," *Harvard Business Review* (January–February), 62–77.

Preuss, L. (2010). "Tax Avoidance and Corporate Social Responsibility: You Can't Do Both, or Can You?" *Corporate Governance: The International Journal of Business in Society* 10:4, 365–374.

Ramasastry, A. (2015). "Corporate Social Responsibility Versus Business and Human Rights: Bridging the Gap Between Responsibility and Accountability," *Journal of Human Rights* 14:2, 237–259.

Rost, K. and T. Ehrmann (2015). "Reporting Biases in Empirical Management Research: The Example of Win-Win Corporate Social Responsibility," *Business & Society* 56:6, 840–888.

Ruggie, J.G. (2008). "Protect Respect and Remedy. A Framework for Business and Human Rights," A/HRC/8/5. Available at: www.reports-and-materials.org/sites/default/files/reports-and-materials/Ruggie-report-7-Apr-2008.pdf.

Ruggie, J.G. (2011). "Guiding Principles on Business and Human Rights. Implementing the United Nations 'Protect, Respect and Remedy' Framework." Available at: www.businesshumanrights.org/media/documents/ruggie/ruggie-guiding-principles-21-mar-2011.pdf.

Salazar, J. and B.W. Husted (2008). "Principals and Agents: Further Thoughts on the Friedmanite Critique of Corporate Social Responsibility," in A. Crane, D. Matten, A. McWilliams, J. Moon, and D. S. Siegel (eds), *The Oxford Handbook of Corporate Social Responsibility*, Oxford: Oxford University Press, 137–155.

Santoro, M.A. (2009). *China 2020: How Western Business Can—and Should—Influence Social and Political Change in the Coming Decade*. Ithaca, NY: Cornell University Press.

Scherer, A.G. and G. Palazzo (2007). "Toward a Political Conception of Corporate Responsibility: Business and Society Seen from a Habermasian Perspective," *Academy of Management Review* 32:4, 1096–1120.

Scherer, A.G. and G. Palazzo (2011). "A New Political Role of Business in a Globalized World: A Review and Research Agenda," *Journal of Management Studies* 48:4, 899–931.

Simons, P. and Macklin, A. (2014). *The Governance Gap: Extractive Industries, Human Rights, and the Home State Advantage*. London; New York, NY: Routledge.

The Economist (2005). "Profit and the Public Good." Available at: www.economist.com/node/3555259.

The Economist Intelligence Unit (2014). "New Business Models: Shared Value in the 21st Century." Available at: www.economistinsights.com/sites/default/files/EIU%20-%20ENEL-New%20business%20models%20for%20the%2021st%20century%20WEB_0.pdf.

Ulrich, P. (2008). *Integrative Economic Ethics. Foundations of a Civilized Market Economy*. Cambridge: Cambridge University Press.

Velasquez, M. (1983). "Why Corporations Are Not Morally Responsible for Anything They Do," *Business & Professional Ethics Journal* 2:3, 1–18.

Visser, W. (2008). "Corporate Social Responsibility in Developing Countries," in A. Crane, A. McWilliams, D. Matten, J. Moon, D.S. Siegel (eds), *The Oxford Handbook on Corporate Social Responsibility*. Oxford: Oxford University Press, 473–499.

Vogel, D. (2005). *The Market for Virtue. The Potential and Limits of Corporate Social Responsibility*. Washington, DC: Brookings Institution Press.

Votaw, D. (1961). "The Politics of a Changing Corporate Society," *California Management Review* 3:3, 105–118

Votaw, D. (1972). "Genius Becomes Rare: A Comment on the Doctrine of Social Responsibility Pt. I," *California Management Review* 15:2, 25–31.

Waddock, S. and A. Rasche, A. (2012). *Building the Responsible Enterprise: Where Vision and Values Add Value*. Stanford, CA: Stanford University Press.

Walsh, J.P. (2005). "Book Review Essay: Taking Stock of Stakeholder Management," *Academy of Management Review* 30:2, 426–438.

Werhane, P. (2015). "Corporate Moral Agency and the Responsibility to Respect Human Rights in the UN Guiding Principles: Do Corporations Have Moral Rights?" *Business and Human Rights Journal* 1:1, 5–20.

Wettstein, F. (2009). *Multinational Corporations and Global Justice: Human Rights Obligations of a Quasi-Governmental Institution*. Stanford, CA: Stanford University Press.

Wettstein, F. (2012). "CSR and the Debate on Business and Human Rights: Bridging the Great Divide," *Business Ethics Quarterly* 22:4, 739–770.

Wettstein, F. (2016). "From Side Show to Main Act: Can Business and Human Rights Save Corporate Responsibility?" in D. Baumann-Pauly and J. Nolan (eds), *Business and Human Rights—From Principles to Practice*, 78–87. London: Routledge.

Wettstein, F. and K.E. Goodpaster (2009). "Freedom and Autonomy in the 21st Century: What Role for Corporations?" in *Markus Breuer, Philippe Mastronardi and Bernhard Waxenberger (eds), Markt, Mensch und Freiheit. Wirtschaftsethik in der Auseinandersetzung*. Berrn: Haupt, 117–134.

Williams, C.A. and R.V. Aguilera (2008). "Corporate Social Responsibility in a Comparative Perspective," in A. Crane, A. McWilliams, D. Matten, J. Moon and D.S. Siegel (eds), *The Oxford Handbook on Corporate Social Responsibility*. Oxford: Oxford University Press, 452–472.

Windsor, D. (2006). "Corporate Social Responsibility: Three Key Approaches," *Journal of Management Studies*, 43:1, 93–114.

Wood, S. (2012). "The Case for Leverage-Based Corporate Human Rights Responsibility," *Business Ethics Quarterly* 22:1, 63–98.

Zadek, S. (2004). "The Path to Corporate Responsibility," *Harvard Business Review* (December), 125–132.

11
Stakeholder thinking

Kenneth E. Goodpaster

In this chapter I examine a broad set of approaches to organizational decision making that I will refer to as "stakeholder thinking." Stakeholder thinking is a normative ethical approach to decision making that emphasizes corporate responsibilities to individuals, groups, and institutions including, when applicable, fiduciary obligations owed to investors and shareholders. I favor the phrase "stakeholder thinking" over "stakeholder theory" because it is more generic.[1] Understood in this way, stakeholder thinking is frequently offered as a proxy for what some would call the "conscience" of the corporation.[2]

One way to get an historical perspective on stakeholder thinking is to view a Google NGRAM of the frequency of the use of the word "stakeholder" in relation to "stockholder" and "shareholder" since 1850. It seems clear from Figure 11.1 below, that the 1970s saw the genesis of the *language* of stakeholder thinking and it has grown dramatically since then. In the post-WWII period, the language of "shareholders" has gradually displaced the language of "stockholders." Stakeholder thinking emerged during this period by contrasting itself with *fiduciary* shareholder thinking as a view about corporate *governance*. Eventually, however, it emerged as a view about how managers should make decisions.

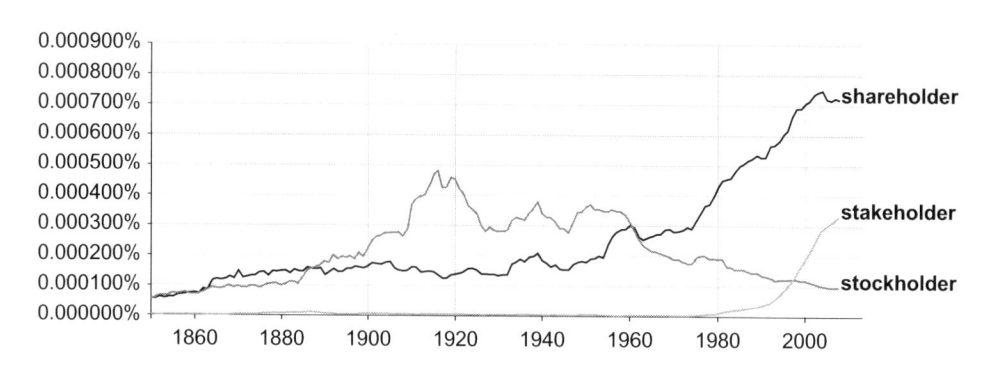

Figure 11.1 Google NGRAM of "stakeholder" in relation to "stockholder" and "shareholder."

Throughout this chapter I will affirm the distinctiveness of fiduciary obligations, while suggesting that the nature of business obligations that go "beyond" them need not and should not be expressed as impartial fiduciary duties to stakeholder groups. Furthermore, I will argue that stakeholder thinking, often celebrated as a *successor* to the shareholder paradigm, is itself in need of a successor along with the shareholder paradigm. This successor—which is, in fact, the very framework that underlies these paradigms—I will call *comprehensive* moral thinking. A recent illustration of this mindset can be found in the reflective practice of John Mackey, CEO of Whole Foods (Mackey and Sisodia 2013).

The first section of the chapter sets the stage historically and conceptually regarding stakeholder thinking. In the next section I clarify the idea of conscience, suggesting that its essence lies in what Josiah Royce, at the end of the nineteenth century, called "the moral insight." We are then in a position to offer a concise account of *corporate* conscience. In the third section I point out how stakeholder thinking is more of an *obstacle* to corporate conscience than a *proxy* for it. This discussion also reveals several criteria that an adequate account of corporate conscience must satisfy: a) moral substance/depth; b) specification of both the domain and the range (agents and recipients) of non-fiduciary duties, and c) a more robust and practical view (than markets and laws afford) of the "goods and services" for which a business economy exists. In the fourth section I offer suggestions about a comprehensive approach to corporate conscience based on two principles, human dignity and the common good. In the last section I draw out some implications for business education.

Setting the stage

> Twenty years ago, [I held] that corporate powers were powers in trust for shareholders while Professor Dodd argued that these powers were held in trust for the entire community. The argument has been settled (at least for the time being) squarely in favor of Professor Dodd's contention.
>
> *(Adolf Berle 1954: 169)*

The quotation above from Adolf Berle indicates that the debate between Berle (at Columbia) and E. Merrick Dodd (at Harvard Law School)—a foreshadowing of what today is called the shareholder–stakeholder debate—dates back at least to the 1930s.[3]

The term "stakeholder" seems to have originated in a 1963 internal memorandum at the Stanford Research Institute (SRI). It defined stakeholders as "those groups without whose support the organization would cease to exist" (Freeman and Reed 1983: 89). Professor R. Edward Freeman, in his book *Strategic Management: A Stakeholder Approach*, expanding on the SRI characterization, defined the term this way: "A stakeholder in an organization is (by definition) any group or individual who can affect or is affected by the achievement of the organization's objectives" (Freeman 1984: 46). Examples of stakeholder groups (beyond stockholders) are employees, suppliers, customers, creditors, competitors, governments, and communities. It is useful to note that these two definitions of "stakeholder" are not the same, and that one of the characteristics of "stakeholder thinking" from its inception has been disagreement over the *breadth* of its primary idea. Indeed some have argued that the stakeholder concept can easily extend to "the whole of the human race" (Langtry 1994: 432). Such a broad view would provide a recipe for decisional paralysis. On the other hand, a narrower interpretation can reduce ethics to clashes of competing interest groups (Heath 2006).

In addition to the unresolved questions of narrowness or breadth in defining "stakeholder," there are questions about applying stakeholder thinking to corporate *governance* in contrast to applying it to corporate *management*. This distinction is clarified by John Boatright this way:

> Stakeholder management goes wrong by (1) failing to appreciate the extent to which the prevailing system of corporate governance, marked by shareholder primacy, serves the interests of all stakeholders, and (2) assuming that all stakeholder interests are best served by making this the task of management rather than using other means.
>
> *(Boatright 2006: 107)*

The suggestion here is that the economic and legal structure of the modern corporation, its *governance* structure, is and should be distinct from the principles by which the *management* of the corporation operates, its *decision-making* norms (Stone 1991).

Despite these tensions about meaning, many would argue that the most significant normative generalization in post-WWII business ethics is represented by the phonemic shift from *stock*holder to *stake*holder. Corporate responsibility was often defined by business practitioners as primarily the *fiduciary* responsibility of managers to stockholders. *Stakeholder* thinking seems to insist that decision makers widen their perspectives to include other affected parties. Indeed, today, it is common to claim that the *essence* of business ethics lies in extending *stock*holder concern to *stake*holders generally. With this extension in mind, there exists a wide literature on the meaning and implications of the shift from stockholder to stakeholder thinking. The literature addresses questions such as the following:

> Is stakeholder thinking a *descriptive/empirical* perspective on decision making? Or is it *normative*?
> *(Donaldson and Preston 1995)*

> And if normative, is it moral or non-moral?
> *(Donaldson and Preston 1995)*

> Is any theory of stakeholding truly a *theory* in any meaningful sense of that term?
> *(Norman 2013)*

> How should we *identify* (and perhaps even *rank order*) the principal stakeholders in a business context?
> *(Freeman 1984, 2014; Langtry 1994)*

> How should we *weigh* potentially conflicting stakeholder interests?
> *(Heath 2006; Freeman et al. 2007)*

> Does stakeholder thinking *generalize* beyond business corporations to other organizational forms (unions, government or public sector entities, NGOs)?
> *(Hasnas 2013)*

> What does stakeholder thinking imply (if anything) for corporate *governance*, e.g., for representation on corporate boards?
> *(Stone 1991; Boatright 2006; Agle et al. 2008)*

> What are the implications of stakeholder thinking for the traditional *fiduciary* obligations of management and the board?
> *(Goodpaster 1991, 2007a, 2010; Marcoux 2003; Paine 2003)*

> Should stakeholder thinking influence the business school *curriculum*?
> *(Smith and Rönnegard 2014)*

These and other questions indicate the conceptual variety and range of the stakeholder literature (Hasnas 2013).

Conscience: personal and institutional

> In the society of organizations, each of the new institutions is concerned only with its own purpose and mission. It does not claim power over anything else. But it also does not assume responsibility for anything else. Who, then, is concerned with the common good?
> *(Peter Drucker "The Age of Social Transformation,"*
> The Atlantic Monthly, November 1994: 7)

Webster's Unabridged Dictionary defines "conscience" as "the inner sense of what is right or wrong in one's conduct or motives, impelling one toward right action: *to follow the dictates of conscience.*"

I believe that at the core of conscience lies a pair of complementary tensions that needs to be managed—a tension on the personal level between self-love and love of others and on the public corporation level between shareholders and non-shareholding stakeholders (see Goodpaster 2007a: Chaps 3, 4; Goodpaster 2007b). At the personal level, "self-love" should not be confused with mere self-interest or selfish desires, just as "love of others" should not be confused with merely satisfying the desires of others. Love is about looking after the *good*, not simply the desires, of the loved one. In this respect, both self-love and love of others are normative concepts. This clarification should help us at the *institutional* level when we contrast fiduciary obligations to stockholders with obligations to stakeholders. The contrast is *not* between corporate selfishness and corporate altruism. Instead, it is a *moral* distinction between an institution's fiduciary duties to its providers of capital and its duties to other stakeholder groups that are morally grounded in different ways.

Nineteenth-century Harvard philosopher Josiah Royce believed that all of ethics was grounded in what he called the *moral insight* (a precursor to what philosophers in the twentieth century called the "moral point of view"). Royce described the moral insight this way:

> The moral insight is *the realization of one's neighbor*, in the full sense of the word *realization*; the resolution to treat him unselfishly. But this resolution expresses and belongs to the moment of insight. Passion may cloud the insight after no very long time. It is as impossible for us to avoid the illusion of selfishness in our daily lives, as to escape seeing through the illusion at the moment of insight. We see the reality of our neighbor, that is, we determine to treat him as we do ourselves. But then we go back to daily action, and we feel the heat of hereditary passions, and *we straightway forget what we have seen*. Our neighbor becomes *obscured*. He is once more a *foreign power*. He is *unreal*. We are again deluded and selfish. This conflict goes on and will go on as long as we live after the manner of men. Moments of insight, with their accompanying resolutions; long stretches of delusion and selfishness: That is our life.
> *(Royce 1865: 155–6, emphasis added)*

Royce's idea of the moral insight lies at the foundation of the "Golden Rule," the oldest and most widely shared ethical precept known to us. His language in the above passage is significant, and it will be relevant in the remaining parts of this chapter and as we consider, in the next section, some shortcomings of stakeholder thinking.

Over the past two centuries Western society has become what Peter Drucker referred to as a "society of organizations" (1978: 12). Personal or individual actors on the public stage have been joined (if not replaced) by institutional or organizational actors. If we join the idea of a "society of organizations" with the fact that, by 1868, corporations were firmly established under American law as "legal persons," it is not surprising to find that corporations are today expected to behave with *consciences* analogous to individual persons (Goodpaster and Matthews 1982).

The "legal personhood" of the corporation is not the same as moral personhood. Moral personhood requires that the corporation have a degree of discretion or freedom under the law and in practice, so that the ideas of responsibility and conscience can make sense. Without such discretion, corporate leaders might be constrained to make decisions solely on the basis of non-moral economic considerations. Only an organization that is relatively free can be asked to be *responsible*; an organization that is merely an arm of the state can only be compliant. As corporate law scholar Lyman Johnson has pointed out:

> It is . . . the very discretion afforded by law that makes discussions of corporate responsibility possible and meaningful. Without such discretion—as, for example, if managers really were legally required to maximize profits—advocacy of socially responsible behavior would truly be academic because managers would be prohibited from engaging in such conduct.
>
> *(Johnson 2011: 17–18)*

Organizations are in some ways macro-versions (projections) of ourselves as individuals—human beings writ large. We can sometimes see more clearly in organizations certain features that we want to understand better in ourselves, but often the reverse is true. Managers and leaders can often benefit from what we understand about ourselves as individuals. I have referred to this analogical approach in the past as the "moral projection" principle. Formally, it can be stated as follows:

> *Moral Projection Principle*. It is appropriate not only to describe organizations and their characteristics by analogy with individuals, it is also appropriate normatively to look for and to foster moral attributes in organizations by analogy with those we look for and foster in individuals.
>
> *(Goodpaster 2005: 363–364)*

Corporate responsibility is the projection of moral responsibility in its ordinary (individual) sense onto a corporate agent. Corporate conscience can evolve from purely self-referential status (e.g., public relations) through the status of an environmental constraint (e.g., legal or regulatory requirements) to being an authentic, independent management concern. Such an evolution represents a maturation process analogous to the development of conscience in individuals (Piaget 1932). Sociologist Philip Selznick articulated this idea six decades ago (1957) when he wrote about "character formation" as an important area of exploration for those who would understand the decision making of organizations. Leadership, according to Selznick, was about institutionalizing values. We are now in a position to look more critically at the suggestion that stakeholder thinking should be adopted as a proxy for managerial decision making and corporate conscience.

Is stakeholder thinking more an *obstacle to* than *a proxy for* corporate conscience ?

> So we must think through what management should be accountable for; and how and through whom its accountability can be discharged. The stockholders' interest, both short- and long-term, is one of the areas, to be sure. But it is only one.
>
> *(Peter Drucker,* Harvard Business Review, *September 1988: 73)*

Given the context of stakeholder thinking and the idea of corporate conscience limned above, one might think that the former is a solid candidate for operationalizing the latter. But all is not sweetness and light when it comes to overlaying stakeholder thinking onto corporate conscience. Indeed, some have argued that the two are not only incongruent, but that stakeholder thinking is actually an obstacle to responsible (conscientious) corporate decision making. And there are a number of other concerns about the adequacy of stakeholder thinking in its conventional formulations that may give us pause.

A fiduciary argument against stakeholder thinking

There is a paradox in stakeholder theory:

> It seems *essential*, yet in some ways *illegitimate*, to orient corporate decisions by ethical values that go beyond fiduciary shareholder obligations to a concern for stakeholders generally.
> *(Goodpaster 1991: 63)*

The paradox arises because there is an ethical problem whichever way management chooses to go. The mindset behind the paradox is conflicted by a concern that the "impartiality" of *stakeholder* thinking simply cuts management loose from certain well-defined bonds of "partial" (fiduciary) *shareholder* accountability (Goodpaster 2007a: Chap. 4). My suggested way out of the paradox was to distinguish between two different kinds of ethical obligations—fiduciary and non-fiduciary—and to argue that management's fiduciary obligations to shareholders were *different in kind* from management's obligations to non-shareholding stakeholders (Goodpaster 1991: 67).

This line of argument stands out as a significant challenge to a commonly held version of stakeholder thinking, namely, the view that the fiduciary relationship between management and shareholders is not distinctive, and that the conscience of the corporation should instead be guided by a "multi-fiduciary" view. A multi-fiduciary view (for example, Evan and Freeman 1988: 103–4) holds that management has fiduciary duties to investors, yes, but also to other stakeholders like employees, customers, suppliers, local communities, and perhaps even the natural environment. Alexei Marcoux (2003), among others (Hasnas 1998; Heath 2006), has argued that such a view of stakeholder thinking is either incoherent or morally inadequate.

Marcoux's critique of the multi-fiduciary stakeholder view is based on his analysis of the nature of fiduciary duties. He argues that the attribution of fiduciary duties to physicians, lawyers, and others (including managers and boards of directors) calls for partiality toward their beneficiaries—and that this is incompatible with concurrent fiduciary duties to multiple third parties (impartiality) (Marcoux 2003: 19). Marcoux points out that "[t]o act as a fiduciary means to place the interests of the beneficiary ahead of one's own interests and, obviously, those of third parties, with respect to the administration of some asset(s) or project(s)," adding that:

> The multi-fiduciary stakeholder theory, rather than extending the fiduciary duties of managers to non-shareholding stakeholders (because it is conceptually and practically impossible), *eliminates* fiduciary duty altogether in favor of a consequentialist-like weighing and balancing of admittedly competing stakeholder interests.
> *(Marcoux 2003: 3; 5, original emphasis)*

Marcoux's argument does more than shed light on the special character of the fiduciary relationship. In the course of marshaling his argument against multi-fiduciary stakeholder theory, he makes a number of observations that relate to Royce's moral insight—the working of conscience, both personal and institutional. Three of these observations deserve special emphasis:

Vulnerability, moral substance and depth;

Contractual incompleteness; and

Non-fiduciary obligations.

Throughout his discussion of the moral warrant for fiduciary duties, Marcoux emphasizes the vulnerability of the beneficiaries of those duties: "Vulnerability consists . . . in deficits of control and information that arise from the relationship, even in the absence of physical, mental, or financial weakness" (Marcoux 2003: 10). Taking advantage of a patient, a client or an investor by subordinating their interests either to the interests of the fiduciary (self-dealing) or to a quasi-utilitarian impartial calculation is emphatically morally wrong (Marcoux 2003: 11). One interpretation of this wrongness is that denying protection to the vulnerable does not respect their *reality*. Perhaps another way to make this point would be to say that fiduciary duties relate to beneficiaries *directly*, not *indirectly* through an impersonal calculus.

This is reminiscent of Royce's account of the moral insight. My beneficiaries are not illusory or "unreal" as would be the case if I responded to their vulnerability using impersonal public policy reasoning. Marcoux insists that fiduciary duties are *morally substantial* (and elsewhere, *morally deep*) because they apply quite independently of "what benefits society in general" (Marcoux 2003: 12, 19). Royce tells us that we "see the reality of our neighbor . . . we determine to treat him as we do ourselves." But often "we straightway forget what we have seen. Our neighbor becomes obscured" (Royce 1865: 155–6). For Royce, as for Marcoux, the substance or depth of our moral perception is direct, unmediated, and action-guiding.

In a similar spirit, Marcoux argues that "shareholders are the object of the fiduciary duties of managers because their contracts with the firm are fundamentally incomplete," meaning that foreseeing and enumerating the ways in which the shareholders can be taken advantage of is virtually impossible (by comparison with other stakeholder groups such as suppliers, employees, and customers) (Marcoux 2003: 13, 18). The fiduciary duties of doctors to patients, lawyers to clients, and managers to shareholders cannot be reduced to contractual obligations—the vulnerabilities of the beneficiaries are more indefinable. This seems to be why we refer to fiduciary relationships as the basis for fiduciary duties—and why Marcoux describes them as morally substantial and morally deep.

Finally, Marcoux acknowledges that managers may have extensive *non-fiduciary* obligations to stakeholders, but he insists that "the relationship of non-shareholding stakeholders to the firm is of a morally different kind" (Marcoux 2003: 16, emphasis added). The nature of non-fiduciary obligations to non-shareholding stakeholders may well be extensive—and the relative "weights" of those obligations are not easily determined without significant contextual information. Indeed, such obligations might be as morally substantial (or morally deep) as fiduciary obligations, even if they are different in kind. As we shall see, this last point helps us to articulate "comprehensive moral thinking" adumbrated in the next section.

In summary, Marcoux's fiduciary argument against conventional stakeholder thinking appears to be rooted in a fundamental respect for those who are vulnerable, such as patients in relation to doctors, clients in relation to lawyers, and investors in relation to managers. The "partiality" of the fiduciary relationship is not, of course, unconditional. This is what allows us to explore non-fiduciary relationships "of a morally different kind." It remains to be seen a) whether these relationships with other stakeholders are "impartial" or simply "different," and b) how best to "weigh" fiduciary duties in relation to non-fiduciary duties.

Let us now turn to a second cautionary critique of stakeholder thinking as a proxy for corporate conscience, its under-specification regarding both the parties responsible and the parties to whom the responsibility is owed.

The domain and the range of moral transactions

More than thirty-five years ago, University of Chicago philosopher Alan Gewirth insightfully conceptualized the field of ethics as having to do with transactions between *agents* and *recipients*: "where what is affected is the recipient's freedom and well-being, and hence his capacity for action" (Gewirth 1978: 129). Applying Gewirth's perspective to a discussion of corporate conscience, as in Figure 11.2 below, means that we need to attend to both *agents* (e.g., corporations and business leaders) and *recipients* (e.g., customers, employees, suppliers, etc.) as we scrutinize stakeholder thinking. An adequate stakeholder view needs to identify both those whose responsibility is to *do* stakeholder thinking (moral agents or actors)—and the relevant stakeholder groupings themselves (moral recipients).

Occasionally stakeholder thinkers will insist that business organizations cannot (and so should not) see themselves as responsible for achieving objectives that are beyond their spans of control (Nagel 1986; Goodpaster 2010). A long-defended maxim in moral philosophy is that "ought" implies "can."

Environmental protection, public health, minimization of poverty, a culture of respect for life and liberty—these are aspirations for which no institution in any single sector (economic, political, civic) can be asked to take full responsibility. Realizing these aspirations would require the collaboration of institutions across sectors—which means that individual institutions have partial but not complete responsibility for the result. Business is responsible *to* the common good but not completely *for* it (for a similar distinction, see Donaldson and Walsh 2015: 198).

Stakeholder thinking can overlook business responsibilities for collaborative action—largely because it is framed in terms of what a corporation should do in relation to its own stakeholders.

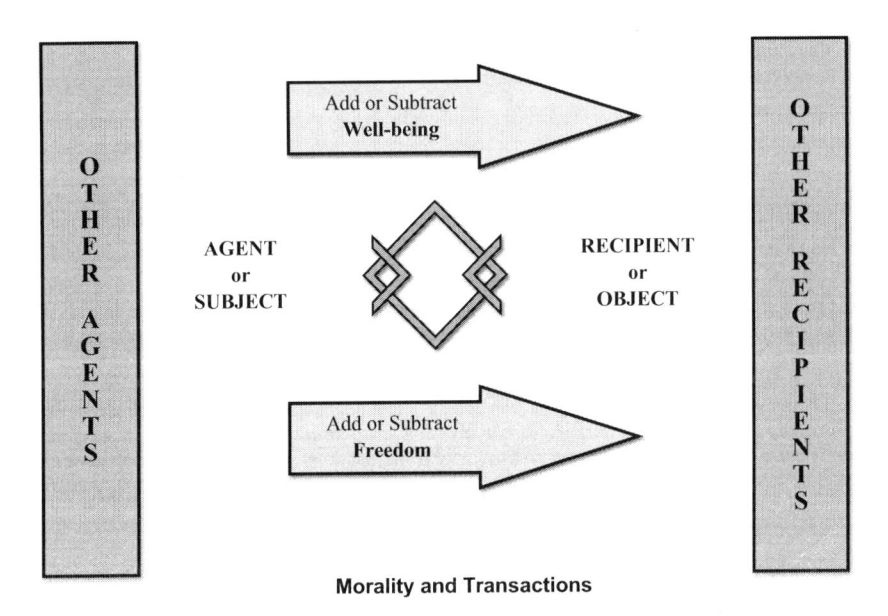

Figure 11.2 A depiction of Gewirth's view of ethics.

Source: As adapted from Goodpaster 1985a: 166.

This is not simply a matter of how broadly or tightly the corporation understands *its own* stakeholders. Indeed, the notion of the community as a stakeholder of any corporation would seem to open the gates to a very broad interpretation of "affected parties." The point in this context is not about the breadth of a given business's set of stakeholders, but about a given business's *co*-responsibility with other institutions for freedom and wellbeing in the human community (Goodpaster 2010, 2016). Businesses must do their part in support of the human community, even if that "part" takes them beyond their responsibilities to their typical stakeholding groups. If the problems facing humankind are problems that call for multi-sector cooperation, then responsible institutions need to develop new collaborative skills. They must develop a kind of "peripheral moral vision" and a willingness to work with other institutions to achieve what can only be accomplished *together*.

In summary, the grammar of stakeholders can be liberating, but it can also *blind* companies by shaping their ethical awareness in advance and thereby inhibiting moral imagination—an imagination that can see more deeply the relationships among social sectors (agency) and between companies and their stakeholders (fiduciary obligations and non-fiduciary obligations). Stakeholder thinking tends to "standardize" the relationships between businesses and their stakeholders using a consequentialist formula ("affect or affected by") to identify moral relevance. But moral relevance may well take other, more *qualitative*, forms, e.g., attention to the vulnerable, keeping a promise, commitment to human dignity and the common good (Goodpaster 2010, 2016).

On the *recipient* side of moral transactions, the usual stakeholders whose freedom or well-being are under scrutiny include individuals, organized groups (e.g., labor unions) and, occasionally, whole societies (e.g., the water supply of a nation or the global climate). Recipients are those whose freedom or well-being deserve *consideration*. Two principal contexts in which stakeholder thinking often reveals a too-narrow ethical awareness of recipients are: consideration for non-human beings, and consideration for institutions or corporations themselves (Goodpaster 2007a: Chap. 1).

I use the phrase "moral consideration" (or the phrase "moral considerability") deliberately to signal a level of moral awareness and concern that may or may not rise to the level of attributing moral *rights* to the recipient in question (Goodpaster 1978). Debates about animal rights, for example, can be spirited, but we need *not* take a position in those debates in order to accord to non-human living creatures some level of moral consideration. It seems clear to most of us on reflection that animals are part of the ecosystem that we inhabit and that we have certain stewardship responsibilities toward them. Stakeholder thinking as it is conventionally deployed, especially in business ethics, often excludes animals as a category deserving consideration alongside employees, consumers, suppliers, and shareholders. Also, while it is frequently true that considerations about ecological awareness can enter into stakeholder thinking as concern for future generations, it does not go without saying or argument that *all* of our stewardship responsibilities can be translated in this way.

Another context in which moral considerability can be overlooked by stakeholder thinking relates to our conduct toward corporations themselves. Much of business ethics, appropriately, attends to the responsibilities of corporations toward those parties affected by corporate decision making. But corporations themselves are often affected parties (stakeholders, moral recipients), for example in legal and judicial contexts as well as contexts like boycotts or labor strikes involving public displays of disapproval. Indeed, corporate competitors can come under moral scrutiny both as agents and recipients in the marketplace—even when the value of their competitiveness itself is affirmed.

The point to be made here in connection with moral recipients is *not* that corporations are identical in all respects with human beings as bearers of rights. There is much room for debate over the moral "personhood" of organizations. What is plausible, however, is that stakeholder thinking needs to accord moral consideration to organizations, just as it needs to accord moral consideration to non-human living creatures.

As we saw above, Royce's moral insight (the "realization of one's neighbor") implies that conscience does not discriminate in its answer to the question "Who is my neighbor?" It is inclusive rather than marginalizing. Let us now turn to a third cautionary critique of stakeholder thinking: its lack of a normative account of value.

Stakeholder interests and the open question argument

The significance for stakeholder thinking of an underlying view of goodness (benefits and costs) often goes unnoticed, or at least unspoken. Views about goodness may be sidestepped in favor of a morally neutral appeal to something like "stakeholder choices, wants, desires, preferences, or satisfactions." Perhaps such appeals escape notice because in an economic context, market reasoning and legality tend to dominate, and market reasoning and legality are quite at home with neutrality about what is good. Something has market value, it is often said, "if people are willing to exchange money for it." Something is legal if the laws, as interpreted by the courts, say it is legal. To illustrate, let us take three principal stakeholder categories: customers, employees, and shareholders.

If "market value and legality" prevail in the provision of "goods and services" for customers or consumers then the quality of those goods and services in relation to fulfilled human lives is set aside or replaced by the current desires of customers.[4] It is clear that markets and the law can and have underwritten the "goods" of pornography and cocaine, and the "services" of prostitution and drug-dealing. But these do not serve human freedom or well-being. An alternative? Companies seek to provide goods that are truly good and services that truly serve (Goodpaster 2011). But this calls for *normative* stakeholder thinking to develop an account of true goodness and true service.

If "market value and legality" prevail in the provision and design of employment, then the quality of that employment in relation to fulfilled human lives may be set aside or replaced by labor market imperatives driven more by efficiency than by humanity. An alternative? Companies appreciate the dignity of work and principles like subsidiarity (Pontifical Council 2012, §80 and Naughton et al. 2015). But this calls for normative stakeholder thinking about the freedom and well-being of employees' lives that is deeper and more substantial than market value and legality.

If "market value and legality" prevail as metrics of fiduciary obligations to shareholders, then enhancing stock price and avoiding derivative lawsuits (legal actions brought by shareholders on behalf of a corporation against some or all of the officers of the corporation typically for offenses such as fraud or some form of fiduciary failure) become tests of corporate responsibility. Executive stock options may benefit from this pursuit, but it is not clear whether the vulnerability of shareholders is being exploited. The alternative? Providing care and loyalty to shareholders, bearing in mind both their responsibilities and their rights and—if I am a financial advisor—not assuming that wealth maximization *alone* serves the true interests of my beneficiaries. But again, this calls for normative stakeholder thinking about fiduciary *and* non-fiduciary obligations to investors.

Normativity about goods and services

Business decision makers need to understand that their normative views about goods, services, the dignity of work, and environmental responsibility are essential, and, whether they realize it or not, executives make assumptions constantly about what counts as "the good" for human beings (and how human goods are to be prioritized). Stakeholder thinking, as a systematic norm for business ethics, needs to offer a thoughtful account of the moral ground of business—what "good" business is supposed to do for people—be they customers, employees, or shareholders. It does not go without saying that simply satisfying stakeholder preferences is morally acceptable (Goodpaster 2010). In his encyclical, addressed to "all persons of good will," Pope John Paul II put the matter this way: "Of itself, an economic system does not possess criteria for correctly distinguishing new and higher forms of satisfying human needs from artificial new needs which hinder the formation of a mature personality" (*Centesimus Annus* 1991, §36).

Stakeholder thinking as a proxy for corporate conscience cannot give *carte blanche* to serving the desires and demands of customers, employees, investors, or other stakeholder groups (even if the desires and demands of these groups were homogeneous, which they seldom are). It is clear that some "goods and services"—however much there might be a *market* for them—do not add value to the lives of such stakeholders, and stakeholder thinking that ignores the value-added issue is problematic. To be sure, there is room in this context for divergent views about "true goods and services." The point is not to defend a dogmatic paternalism about human goods but to emphasize the importance of what Marcoux calls moral depth or substance in the stakeholder as much as in the shareholder realm.

Philosophically, this critique of stakeholder thinking is reminiscent of the "Open Question Argument" used over a century ago by G.E. Moore in his classic treatise *Principia Ethica* (1903). Moore could say regarding "goods" and "services" today: "Yes, these products and services or these corporate policies are supported by the market, but are they good?" Or "Yes, this corporate behavior is permitted by the law, but is it right?"

The third critique of stakeholder thinking as a proxy for corporate conscience, therefore, is that it must, but frequently does not, help decision makers to discern "true goods" for customers, dignified work for employees, and reasonable returns for shareholders.[5] To do this, it seems clear, the advocate of stakeholder thinking in business must offer a *normative* account of human persons and their well-being.

Returning again to Royce's moral insight (the "realization of one's neighbor"), we can see that corporate conscience—by not fleeing from normativity—maintains or renews its awareness and avoids forgetting or obscuring the human (and non-human) reality of agents and recipients in the business system.

From stakeholder to comprehensive moral thinking

> The development of peoples depends, above all, on a recognition that the human race is a single family working together in true communion, not simply a group of subjects who happen to live side by side.
>
> *(Pope Benedict XVI,* Caritas in Veritate, *§53)*

We have seen how stakeholder thinking might limit ethical awareness and inhibit moral imagination; we have also noted a tendency in stakeholder thinking to *avoid* normativity in relation to the content of stakeholder "interests, wants, and desires." These criticisms are not trivial. But a more positive view of stakeholder thinking is that it provides us with a platform for a "transition" to a larger vision.

In 2008 Thomas Donaldson wrote of a "Normative Revolution" in our understanding of the business economy:

> [M]anagers must ascribe some *intrinsic* worth to stakeholders. That is to say, a stakeholder, such as an employee, must be granted intrinsic worth that is not derivative from the worth they create for others. Human beings have value in themselves. Their rights stand on their own. These rights themselves are morally and logically prior to the way in which respecting their rights may generate more productivity for others or the corporation.
>
> *(Donaldson 2008: 175–76, original emphasis)*

In some ways, with his use of the phrase "intrinsic worth," Donaldson is extending Marcoux's observation about the moral depth of the fiduciary relationship to shareholders, by applying it to stakeholders whose relationship to the corporation is non-fiduciary. This is a non-fiduciary version of Royce's "realization of one's neighbor." Now we can clarify how "comprehensive moral thinking" extends management's perspective, this time with special attention to the relationships among stakeholders in a wider human community.

Stakeholder thinking, without negating fiduciary thinking, expands the horizons of corporate responsibility: goods and harms for multiple parties. It emphasizes that many have "stakes" in corporate decision making, both fiduciary (in the case of shareholders) and non-fiduciary (in the case of employees, customers, suppliers, etc.). This is perhaps the most salutary contribution of stakeholder thinking to business and organizational ethics (Hasnas 2013).

Because of this expanded decision-making horizon, stakeholder thinking prepares us for a more holistic approach to corporate conscience, offering a stepping stone to enrichment on both the agent side of Gewirth's moral transactions and on the recipient side. This more holistic approach is what I will call *comprehensive moral thinking*.

Hugh Heclo (2008) offers an interpretation of institutions and institutional thinking that helps to clarify comprehensive moral thinking. Heclo points out that institutions by their nature have a normative dimension:

> by virtue of participating in an institutional form of life, there are more and less appropriate ways of doing things. These obligations are a kind of *internal morality* that flows from the purposive point of the institution itself.
>
> *(Heclo 2008: 85, emphasis added)*

The "internal morality" of institutions is best understood using what W.D. Ross called prima facie obligations in relation to our participation in other institutions, e.g., the norms of family, work, and community (Ross 1988 [1930]). Also, in addition to the requirements of the "internal morality" of institutions in relation to one another, there is a deeper morality to which *all* institutions must be subject. To quote Heclo again:

> Since institutions exist for people, they are to be judged along a moral continuum of good and bad according to what is needed for human beings to flourish as human beings. In order to deserve the designation of good, institutions ought to be doing what is good for us as human beings.
>
> *(Heclo 2008: 153)*

Figure 11.3, on the following page, depicts stakeholder and shareholder thinking as part of the internal morality of the corporation—and *comprehensive* moral thinking as an external check on "what is needed for human beings to flourish as human beings."

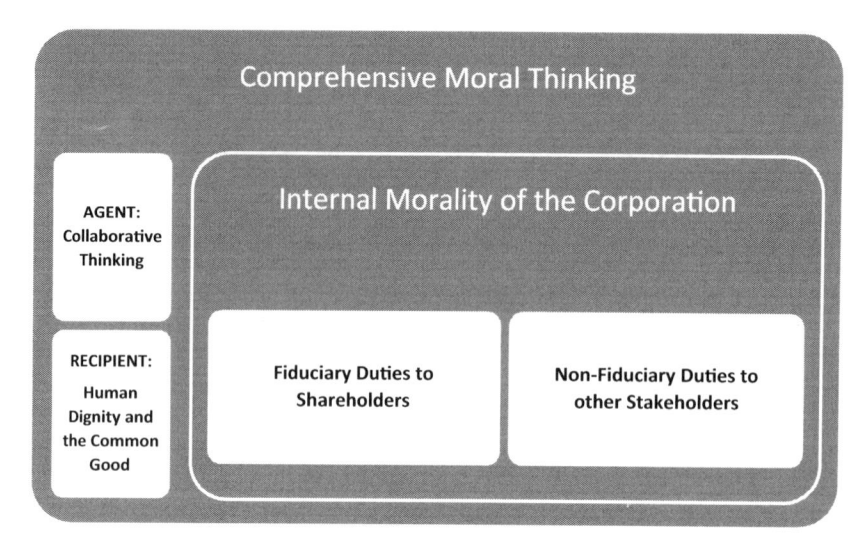

Figure 11.3 A depiction of stakeholder thinking along with shareholder thinking as part of the internal morality of the corporation.

If we were to diagram the proposition, "Corporations are responsible to their stakeholders," then comprehensive moral thinking would be depicted as shifting both the subject *and* the object of corporate responsibility. The shifting of the *subject* calls for attempts at collaboration with other responsible institutions. This often means sharing responsibility between private and public sectors. It can also mean engaging moral-cultural institutions (family, school, media, church), since usually no one of these sectors or institutions can achieve the common good alone. Comprehensive moral thinking means looking at society and its problems through a first-person-plural lens: "*We* need to address this issue." Instead of thinking solely from within their institutional boundaries (according to their internal morality), corporate leaders (and, *mutatis mutandis*, political leaders and NGO leaders) who think collaboratively must migrate toward a more embracing perspective. To be persuasive, of course, this idea must be thoroughly vetted to avoid abuses of collaboration. The anti-trust regulatory framework in the US exists to preserve competition and to prevent collaboration *against* the common good.

The shifting of the *object* of corporate responsibility calls for more than the satisfaction of multiple stakeholders.[6] It calls for seeing shareholders and other stakeholders as parts of a global community of interdependent participants each of whom deserves to be treated with dignity—the principal implication of Royce's moral insight, "realizing one's neighbor."

The essence of the common good lies in the social nature of human beings, in our willingness to collaborate and also in our willingness to sacrifice when maximization strategies prove to be dysfunctional. On this point, philosopher Richard Norman once suggested that the sacrificing of one's interests to something like a shared common good need not be thought of as a sacrifice to something *external*:

> Commitments to our friends or our children, or to causes in which we believe, may be a part of our deepest being, so that the experience of devoting ourselves to them is less like *sacrifice* and more like *fulfilment*.
>
> *(Norman 1983: 249, emphasis added)*

Norman implies that the "deepest being" in each of us reaches for the same moral insight—and ultimately the same basis for conscience.

An example of comprehensive moral thinking

During 1983 and 1984, Velsicol Chemical Corporation, a Chicago-based producer of agricultural chemicals, proposed a "One World Communication System" for pesticide labeling. The idea was to create an industry-wide system of pictograms for agricultural workers in developing countries who were often illiterate or could not understand the precautionary information on conventional labels.

From the point of view of Velsicol's stakeholders—customers, farm employees, local communities, and shareholders—the company's labeling innovation was a success. But it was expensive, and a more comprehensive view seemed to call for more. Industry practices were not uniform and there were many hidden casualties in developing countries. A solution to this problem would require collaboration between industry (private sector) and government (US and host country public sectors). In the eyes of Velsicol, each had partial responsibility for solving the problem.

Unfortunately, enthusiasm for Velsicol's pictogram initiative was not sufficient to move the idea forward, either at the National Agricultural Chemical Association (NACA) or at the US Environmental Protection Agency. The result was that Velsicol's CEO was forced on economic grounds to discontinue the project (Goodpaster 1985). The company's comprehensive moral thinking could have led to fewer lives lost to the misuse of these hazardous chemicals—a reflection of concern for human dignity and the global common good. The problem was not solved because coordination of corporate (and government) efforts was not achieved. Several executives at Velsicol, disheartened at this outcome, left the company.

The Velsicol case, of course, is an example of a company's *lack of success* in influencing its industry association and its government. It also illustrates the distinction between a company's *categorical* responsibility and its *qualified* (or *conditional*) responsibility for seeking comprehensive solutions. The very nature of comprehensive moral thinking—thinking outside what Heclo calls the internal morality of an institution—calls for collaborative efforts on the part of responsible institutions in several sectors. When efforts at collaboration are unsuccessful, then perhaps no further responsibility remains: "Ought categorically" implies "can"—but "ought conditionally" simply implies "must try."

Implications for business education

> Why were we so reluctant to try the lower path, the ambiguous trail? Perhaps because we did not have a leader who could reveal the greater purpose of the trip to us. For each of us the sadhu lives. What is the nature of our responsibility if we consider ourselves to be ethical persons? Perhaps it is to change the values of the group so that it can, with all its resources, take the other road.
>
> *(Bowen McCoy, "The Parable of the Sadhu,"*
> Harvard Business Review, *1983: 108)*

Bowen McCoy suggests that one of the key roles of leadership lies in revealing the greater purpose of the trip and reminding the group of that greater purpose. Leadership is cultivated, in part, through education. So, in this concluding part, I offer thoughts as to how the discussions set forth in the previous sections might be employed to influence business education, and so ultimately the formation of future business leaders. There are at least three ways in which comprehensive moral thinking might influence business ethics pedagogy.

Challenging market logic and legal compliance

Business school faculty have an opportunity to go beyond "information transfer" and to challenge both "market value" and "legal requirement" as surrogates for corporate conscience. They can press students to search for criteria that go deeper. In so doing, students and faculty must take some risks as they come to terms with their often-unexpressed views about human well-being. Classroom debates can be encouraged about the sufficiency of both market incentives and compliance with legislation (such as, within the United States, *Sarbanes–Oxley* and *Dodd–Frank*) for preventing irresponsible business conduct in the realms of corporate governance and consumer financial protection. Faculty can use readings and case studies that encourage self-discovery for students, inviting them to go beyond market and legal measures of goodness, whether for customers, employees, shareholders (see, for example, the *McGraw-Hill Create* online database). Writing assignments can be given that call for an answer to the question: "What are the norms, beyond market effectiveness and legal compliance that I, as a future business leader, would be prepared to defend or reject for my company?"

For those who are apprehensive about encouraging students to "get normative" regarding economic and legal frameworks, it is useful to remember that when normative ethical judgments (about products and services, the dignity of work, the common good) are *not* addressed or defended with thoughtful reasons, they do not disappear. Rather, they "go underground" and become *unexamined* moral assumptions. We owe it to our students to assist them in their own leadership formation. Business leaders inevitably make moral judgments, but they need to be grounded in a solid understanding of the human person.[7]

Challenging the sufficiency of fiduciary and stakeholder thinking

The business ethics student should take seriously the imperatives of fiduciary shareholder *and* non-fiduciary stakeholder obligations while thinking more broadly about the societal contributions of economic, political, and civic institutions.

Students can be asked whether the Moorean question "This corporate decision most satisfies our shareholders and our other stakeholders, but is it right?" is an *open* question.

> Analyzing business decisions solely in terms of their likely impact on specific categories of affected parties ("interest groups") *can miss morally relevant information*. Much as the "Stockholder Proviso" warned us about reducing ethical decisions to fiduciary duties, the "Stakeholder Proviso" warns of another kind of reduction and invites more *comprehensive* moral thinking.
>
> (Goodpaster 2010: 741, original emphasis)

As we noted previously, the word "comprehensive" signifies two things in this context: acknowledging the value of private sector collaboration with other societal institutions, and appreciating human dignity and the common good as overarching normative ideals that may exceed the reach of stakeholder satisfaction.

The bold idea of management as a profession

The third implication for business education may be the most straightforward and the most radical: challenging students to "reimagine" their careers in the vocabulary of professions, callings, even vocations.[8] The best scholarly work on this topic was published in 2007 by Harvard Business School professor, Rakesh Khurana (see Khurana 2007). More recently, Khurana and Nitin Nohria have advocated eloquently for the professionalization of management (Khurana and Nohria 2008). Craig Smith and David Rönnegard comment:

> Khurana and Nohria advocate making management a true profession, which would include the teaching of a formal body of knowledge and a commitment to a code of conduct. The latter, a "Hippocratic Oath for managers," has inspired an MBA Oath movement, to which over 300 institutions have committed as of 2013. Khurana and Nohria (and the authors of the MBA Oath) are careful to frame their code such that it . . . emphasizes that corporate purpose has much to do with value creation. They write: "By turning managers into agents of society's interest in thriving economic enterprises, we get out of the bind of viewing them as agents of one narrowly defined master (shareholders) or many masters (stakeholders)."
>
> *(Smith and Rönnegard 2014: 23)*

A careful reading of the MBA Oath, included as an Appendix to this chapter, reveals a vision that respects not only fiduciary thinking and stakeholder thinking, but comprehensive moral thinking, e.g., "I will protect the human rights and dignity of all people affected by my enterprise" and "I will remain accountable to my peers and to society for my actions and for upholding these standards."[9]

But a caveat may be in order on this topic. As attractive as the idea of "management as a profession" may be, some would challenge it on the grounds that first, many skilled practitioners of management have no formal education in a technical body of knowledge, and, second, the idea of business managers enforcing something like the MBA Oath through a gatekeeping body may not comport well with our convictions about the importance of entrepreneurship. This being said, we should remember that the argument for the *fiduciary* relationship between managers and shareholders draws on an analogy between management and *professions* like law and medicine.

Concluding remarks

Nobel Laureate poet T.S. Eliot, in "Choruses from the Rock" (1934), observed that humankind is forever "dreaming of systems so perfect that no one will need to be good." The power of this poetic phrase can be appreciated in the present context as we ask corporate leaders to think more comprehensively: to see that stakeholder and shareholder frameworks are ultimately meant to *serve*, not to *supplant*, the pursuit of human dignity and the common good. These frameworks reveal the need for a broader perspective from which the inevitable pushes and pulls of prima facie obligations can be negotiated. This perspective looks carefully at business as an *institution*—at the horizon of moral considerability and at society's need for institutional collaboration. This perspective *remembers why* we create the systems (economic, political, and cultural) that we do, lest in Royce's words, we "obscure the reality of our neighbor."

Kenneth E. Goodpaster

Essential readings

The richness of the literature on the theme of stakeholder thinking (and its strengths and weaknesses) makes identifying "essential" readings difficult. However, taking into account the categories of *shareholder thinking, stakeholder thinking*, and *comprehensive moral thinking*, the following works prove, respectively, most essential. Alexei Marcoux's article "A Fiduciary Argument against Stakeholder Theory," (2003) offers a deeper level of understanding of the obligations of management to shareholders than most articles or books on the subject. And Goodpaster's essay, "Business Ethics and Stakeholder Analysis" (1991), provides useful background to the subject of fiduciary duties. R. Edward Freeman's *Strategic Management: A Stakeholder Approach* (1984) is the source of a large literature in defense of stakeholder thinking (as well as a dissenting literature). And Joseph Heath's article "Business Ethics Without Stakeholders" (2006) explains a plausible *substitute* for stakeholder thinking that deserves serious consideration. On the subject of comprehensive thinking, Hugh Heclo's *On Thinking Institutionally* (2008) is indispensable. Finally, on the educational importance of comprehensive moral thinking and management as a profession, Rakesh Khurana's book *From Higher Aims to Hired Hands* (2007) merits close attention.

For further reading in this volume on the legal personhood of corporations, see Chapter 14, The corporation: genesis, identity, agency. On the predominance of stakeholder theory in sub-Saharan Africa, see Chapter 37, Business ethics in Africa. For critical consideration of the compatibility of managerial responsibilities with duties to stakeholders, see Chapter 13, What is business? On the need for managers to have ethical awareness, see Chapter 27, The ethics of managers and employees. On the subject of business ethics education and on challenges to moral awareness, see Chapter 4, Teaching business ethics: current practice and future directions. On moral myopia and advertising, see Chapter 30, Ethical issues in marketing, advertising, and sales.

Notes

1 The reference to *fiduciary* duties to shareholders applies, of course, only to organizations that *have* shareholders. For other organizational forms, the definition of stakeholder thinking can be adjusted simply to "those who can affect or be affected by an organization's decision making."
2 Another measure of the significance and ubiquity of stakeholder thinking is that, as of August 2016, Google Scholar lists 629,000 books and articles since 1980 when searched under "stakeholder."
3 It was also implicit in the work of (among other contemporary writers) Chester Barnard, *The Functions of the Executive* (1938).
4 This distinction appears in the literature in different ways. *Interests* may be taken as normative in relation to *preferences*. Alternatively, the *truly valuable* goods and services may be taken as normative in relation to goods and services that have *market value*.
5 "Reasonable" in relation to shareholder returns is here meant to signal the need for normative judgment about dividends or stock appreciation strategies that take seriously the health and resiliency of the corporation as a whole—in contrast to short-sighted "maximizing" behavior that could end up undermining the corporation. The 2015 scandal surrounding Volkswagen's automobile emissions would be a case in point.
6 In the words of Benedict XVI in the encyclical *Caritas in Veritate* (2009) "In an increasingly globalized society, the common good and the effort to obtain it cannot fail to assume the dimensions of the whole human family, that is to say, the community of peoples and nations, in such a way as to shape the earthly city in unity and peace ..." (§7).
7 Oxford philosopher Mary Midgley explains the vital productive role of moral judgment: "The power of moral judgement is, in fact ... *a necessity*. When we judge something to be bad or good, better or worse than something else, we are taking it as an example to aim at or avoid. Without opinions of this sort, we would have no framework of comparison for our own policy, no chance of profiting by other people's insights or mistakes. In this vacuum, we could form no judgments on *our own* actions" (Midgley 1981: 72,

emphasis added). As one of the editors of this volume observed: "The choice isn't between doing philosophy and not doing philosophy. It's between doing philosophy badly and haphazardly to one's detriment and doing it well and carefully to one's good."

8 Pope Francis, in his speech to the Joint Session of the US Congress, 24 September 2015, said: "Business is a noble vocation, directed to producing wealth and improving the world ... especially if it sees the creation of jobs as an essential part of its service to the common good."

9 Worth mentioning in this connection are the *United Nations Principles for Responsible Management Education* (*UNPRME*). These principles, like the *MBA Oath*, reflect a comprehensive moral framework, and represent a "quasi-oath" not for *individuals* but for educational *institutions*.

References

Agle, B.R., T. Donaldson, R.E. Freeman, M.C. Jensen, R.K. Mitchell, and D.J. Wood (2008). "Dialogue: Toward Superior Stakeholder Theory," *Business Ethics Quarterly* 18:2 (April), 153–190.

Barnard, C. (1938). *The Functions of the Executive*. Boston, MA: Harvard University Press.

Berle, A. (1954). *The 20th Century Capitalist Revolution*. New York, NY: Harcourt, Brace, and World.

Boatright, J.R. (2006). "What's Wrong—and What's Right—with Stakeholder Management?" *Journal of Private Enterprise* 22:2 (Spring), 106–130.

Dodd, E.M. (1932). "For Whom are Corporate Managers Trustees?" *Harvard Law Review* 45:7, 1145–1163.

Donaldson, T. (2008). "Two Stories," Part IV of "Dialogue: Toward Superior Stakeholder Theory," (with B. R. Agle, T. Donaldson, R. E. Freeman, M. C. Jensen, R. K. Mitchell and D. J. Wood), *Business Ethics Quarterly* 18:2 (April), 153–190.

Donaldson, T. and L.E. Preston (1995). "The Stakeholder Theory of the Corporation: Concepts, Evidence, and Implications," *The Academy of Management Review* 20:1 (January), 65–91.

Donaldson, T. and J.P. Walsh. (2015). "Toward a Theory of Business," *Research in Organizational Behavior* 29:35, 181–207.

Drucker, P.F. (1978). "We Have Become a Society of Organizations," *Wall Street Journal*, January 9 (Eastern edition).

Drucker, P.F. (1988). "Management and the World's Work," *Harvard Business Review* 66 (September), 65–76.

Drucker, P.F. (1994). "The Age of Social Transformation," *The Atlantic Monthly* 274:5 (November 1994), 53–80.

Eliot, T.S. (1934). "Choruses from the Rock," *The Complete Poems and Plays 1909–1950*. Orlando, FL: Harcourt Brace & Company.

Evan, W. and R.E. Freeman (1988). "A Stakeholder Theory of the Modern Corporation: Kantian Capitalism," in Tom L. Beauchamp and Norman Bowie (eds), *Ethical Theory and Business*, 3rd edition. Englewood Cliffs, NJ: Prentice Hall, 75–93.

Freeman, R.E. (1984). *Strategic Management: A Stakeholder Approach*. New York, NY: HarperCollins.

Freeman, R.E. (2014). "Stakeholder Theory," in the *Encyclopedia of Management*, 3rd edition. Vol. 2. Hoboken, NJ: John Wiley and Sons, 1–6.

Freeman, R.E. and D.L. Reed (1983). "Stockholders and Stakeholders: A New Perspective on Corporate Governance," *California Management Review* 25:3, 88–106.

Freeman, R.E., J. Harrison, A. Wicks (2007). *Managing for Stakeholders: Survival, Reputation, and Success*. New Haven: Yale University Press.

Gewirth, A. (1978). *Reason and Morality*. Chicago, IL: University of Chicago Press.

Goodpaster, K. (1978). "On Being Morally Considerable," *Journal of Philosophy* 75 (June), 308–25.

Goodpaster, K. (1985a). "Toward an Integrated Approach to Business Ethics," *Thought* 60:237 (June), 161–180.

Goodpaster, K. (1985b). "Velsicol Chemical Corporation (A)," *HBS Case Services*, 9-385-021.

Goodpaster, K. (1991). "Business Ethics and Stakeholder Analysis," *Business Ethics Quarterly* 1:1 (January), 53–73.

Goodpaster, K. (2005). "Moral Projection, Principle of," in C. Argyris, W. Starbuck and C.L. Cooper (eds), *The Blackwell Encyclopedia of Management*, 2nd edition. Vol. 2. Malden, MA: Blackwell Publishing, 363–64.

Goodpaster, K. (2007a). *Conscience and Corporate Culture*. New York, NY: Wiley-Blackwell.

Goodpaster, K. (2007b). "Conscience," in Robert W. Kolb (ed.), *The Encyclopedia of Business Ethics and Society*, Vol. 1. Thousand Oaks, CA: Sage, 407–410.

Goodpaster, K. (2010). "Two Moral Provisos" *Business Ethics Quarterly* 20:4 (October), 741–42.

Goodpaster, K. (2011). "Goods That Are Truly Good and Services That Truly Serve: Reflections on Caritas in Veritate," *Journal of Business Ethics* 100:1, 9–16.

Goodpaster, K. (2016). "Human Dignity and the Common Good: The Institutional Insight," presented at the 40th Anniversary Conference for the Center for Business Ethics at Bentley University, July 24–26.

Goodpaster, K. and J. Matthews (1982). "Can a Corporation Have a Conscience?" *Harvard Business Review* 60:1 (May–June), 132–141.

Hasnas, J. (1998). "The Normative Theories of Business Ethics: A Guide for the Perplexed," *Business Ethics Quarterly* 8:1 (January), 19–42.

Hasnas, J. (2013). "Whither Stakeholder Theory? A Guide for the Perplexed Revisited, *Journal of Business Ethics* 112, 47–57.

Heath, J. (2006). "Business Ethics Without Stakeholders," *Business Ethics Quarterly* 16:4 (October), 533–557.

Heclo, H. (2008). *On Thinking Institutionally*. Boulder, CO: Paradigm Publishers.

Johnson, L. (2011). "Law and the History of Corporate Responsibility," Minneapolis, MN: CEBC History of Corporate Responsibility Project Working Paper No. #6.

Khurana, R. (2007). *From Higher Aims to Hired Hands: The Social Transformation of American Business Schools and the Unfulfilled Promise of Management as a Profession*. Princeton, NJ: Princeton University Press.

Khurana, R. and N. Nohria (2008). "It's Time to Make Management a True Profession," *Harvard Business Review* 86 (October), 70–77.

Langtry, B. (1994). "Stakeholders and the Moral Responsibilities of Business," *Business Ethics Quarterly* 4:4 (October), 431–443.

Mackey, J. and R. Sisodia (2013). *Conscious Capitalism: Liberating the Heroic Spirit of Business*. Boston, MA: Harvard Business School Press.

Marcoux, A.M. (2003). "A Fiduciary Argument against Stakeholder Theory," *Business Ethics Quarterly* 13:1 (January), 1–24.

McCoy, B. (1983). "The Parable of the Sadhu," *Harvard Business Review* 75:3, 103–08.

Midgley, M. (1981). "On Trying Out One's New Sword," in *Heart and Mind: The Varieties of Moral Experience*. New York, NY: St Martin's Press, 69–75.

Moore, G.E. (1903). *Principia Ethica*. Cambridge: Cambridge University Press.

Nagel, T. (1986). *The View from Nowhere*. New York, NY: Oxford University Press.

Naughton, M., J. Buckeye, K. Goodpaster and D. Maines (2015). *Respect in Action: Applying Subsidiarity in Business*. St. Paul, MN: UNIAPAC and University of St. Thomas. Available at: www.stthomas.edu/cathstudies/cst/research/publications/subsidiarity/.

Norman, R. (1983). *The Moral Philosophers*. Oxford: Oxford University Press.

Norman, W. (2013). "Stakeholder Theory," in Hugh LaFollette (ed.), *International Encyclopedia of Ethics*. London: Blackwell, 5002–5011.

Paine, L.S. (2003). *Value Shift*. New York, NY: McGraw-Hill Publishing Company.

Piaget, J. (1932). *The Moral Judgment of the Child*. London: Routledge and Kegan Paul.

Pope Benedict XVI (2009). *Charity in Truth: Caritas in Veritate, Encyclical Letter*. San Francisco, CA: Ignatius Press, §53.

Pope Francis (2015). "Speech to a Joint Session of the US Congress, 24 September," *Libreria Editrice Vaticana*.

Pope John Paul II (1991). *Centesimus Annus: Encyclical Letter Addressed by the Supreme Pontiff John Paul II to His Venerable Brothers in the Episcopate, the Priests and Deacons, Families of Men and Women Religious, All the Christian Faithful and to All Men and Women of Good Will on the Hundredth Anniversary of Rerum Novarum*. Sherbrooke, Quebec: Éditions Paulines, §36.

Pontifical Council for Justice and Peace (2012). *Vocation of the Business Leader: A Reflection*, 3rd edition St. Paul, MN: John A. Ryan Institute for Catholic Social Thought.

Ross, W.D. (1988) [1930]. *The Right and the Good*. Indianapolis, IN: Hackett Publishing.

Royce, J. (1865). *The Religious Aspect of Philosophy*, reprinted 1965. Gloucester, MA: Peter Smith.

Selznick, P. (1957). *Leadership in Administration*. New York, NY: Harper & Row.

Smith, N.C. and D. Rönnegard (2014). "Shareholder Primacy, Corporate Social Responsibility, and the Role of Business Schools," *Journal of Business Ethics* 16 (November), 1–42.

Stone, C.D. (1991). *Where the Law Ends: The Social Control of Corporate Behavior*. Long Grove, IL: Waveland Press.

Appendix: the MBA Oath

As a business leader I recognize my role in society.

- My purpose is to lead people and manage resources to create value that no single individual can create alone.
- My decisions affect the well-being of individuals inside and outside my enterprise, today and tomorrow.

Therefore, I promise that:

- I will manage my enterprise with loyalty and care, and will not advance my personal interests at the expense of my enterprise or society.
- I will understand and uphold, in letter and spirit, the laws and contracts governing my conduct and that of my enterprise.
- I will refrain from corruption, unfair competition, or business practices harmful to society.
- I will protect the human rights and dignity of all people affected by my enterprise, and I will oppose discrimination and exploitation.
- I will protect the right of future generations to advance their standard of living and enjoy a healthy planet.
- I will report the performance and risks of my enterprise accurately and honestly.
- I will invest in developing myself and others, helping the management profession continue to advance and create sustainable and inclusive prosperity.

In exercising my professional duties according to these principles, I recognize that my behavior must set an example of integrity, eliciting trust and esteem from those I serve. I will remain accountable to my peers and to society for my actions and for upholding these standards.

This oath I make freely, and upon my honor.

12
Integrative Economic Ethics
Concept and critique

Alexander Lorch and Thomas Beschorner

Initially developed by Jürgen Habermas[1] and Karl-Otto Apel[2], discourse ethics remains one of the most influential critical theories of the twentieth century. Habermas' book *The Theory of Communicative Action* (1981) and his later *Remarks on Discourse Ethics* (1991/1992, 1993)[3] describe how his ethical theory *does not* instruct people "upon *what* they decide but *how* they come to these decisions" (our emphasis, Baert 2001: 85) in fair conditions of discourse. This differentiation between "what" and "how" points to two important streams in normative ethics: material ethics on the one hand and formal or process-oriented ethics on the other hand. Material ethics tells us what to do, one example of which is the Ten Commandments of Christian ethics. These commandments set forth ethical *norms*: "Thou shalt not kill" or "Thou shalt not steal." Process-oriented approaches in ethics, such as discourse ethics, do not focus primarily on concrete moral norms, but on the procedures that yield normative principles. Kantian ethics offer a good example: employ the categorical imperative in order to consider which acts are one's genuine moral duties.

The same is true for discourse ethics. Here, moral norms are approached by first invoking the moral principle of *open debate among equal citizens* in which *fair processes of deliberation* take place in a *power-free realm*. In opposition to both Christian and Kantian ethics, discourse ethicists reclaim a modernized approach to ethics. It is not a "God given" moral law within us that we should follow, but a moral principle emergent from within the interaction of concrete citizens. In other words, Habermas and others ask: How can we organize a society that enables open discourse and open criticism as the precondition for just practices (moral norms)? With respect to deliberations and open discourses, another key component of Habermas comes into play: "communicative actions," as opposed to strategic actions. Strategic actions are characterized by power-relations and a process of negotiation and exchange between two or more parties (as we know from economics), but "ideal communication communities" base their interaction on a fair and power-free discourse. Actors do not negotiate, they deliberate.

This general philosophical background has relevance to business ethics. Several authors have made use of discourse ethics while applying it to the economic context and to businesses. These examples include Darryl Reed (1999a, 1999b) with respect to normative stakeholder theories; Thomas Beschorner (2006) with respect to organizational issues; Dirk Ulrich Gilbert and Andreas Rasche (2007) on the question of social standards; John Mingers and Geoff Walsham

(2010) on ethical information systems; Gilbert and Michael Behnam (2009) with a perspective on "advancing integrative social contracts theory"; and, most prominently in the international debate, Andreas Georg Scherer and Guido Palazzo (2007), on a "political conception of corporate responsibility . . . from a Habermasian perspective."

In this chapter we will outline another discourse ethical approach in business ethics, *Integrative Economic Ethics* (Ulrich 2008a, 1997). Developed by Peter Ulrich, a philosopher and professor emeritus at the University of St Gallen (Switzerland), Integrative Economic Ethics is currently less present in the international debate than the parallel contributions mentioned above. However, although Ulrich's ideas might have attracted little international attention in the English-speaking world, his work is extraordinarily influential within the business ethics communities of German-speaking countries. The deep theoretical grounding of Ulrich's perspective warrants a closer examination. First, Integrative Economic Ethics is not only an application of discourse ethics to the business world, but an attempt to challenge economic rationality on the basis of communicative action. Second, the "transformation" of an instrumental (calculative) rationality into a communicative rationality allows Ulrich to develop a moral point of view that allows him to criticize mainstream economic theory. Third, Ulrich's theory is not merely a (narrow) view of business ethics but it includes multiple levels of economic and ethical analyses: a micro level of individual ethics, a meso level of the corporation, and a macro level of political regulations.

In five sections we discuss salient elements of Integrative Economic Ethics. We will first discuss Ulrich's term "integrative" and his understanding of integrative ethics in opposition to "applied ethics." Based on Ulrich's understanding of business ethics as a mode of "economic enlightenment" we will then sketch, in section two, the different "loci" of responsibility (micro, meso, and macro) in the concept of Integrative Economic Ethics. We will then further illustrate Ulrich's approach by employing these three loci. In the third section we discuss the micro level (the individual's rights and responsibilities), then turning, in the next section, to the meso level of businesses, noting in particular Ulrich's perspectives on stakeholder management. In a fifth section we provide an account of the macro level of political regulation at which Ulrich urges a form of republican liberalism that connects to ideas of a social market economy, as developed after World War II by German "ordoliberals." The concluding remarks outline some strengths and weaknesses of Integrative Economics Ethics and sketch possible further research perspectives.

Integrative versus applied ethics

Over the past 25 years Peter Ulrich has developed an impressive oeuvre that constitutes a general theory of business ethics based on discourse ethical ideas. In his earliest book, *The Firm as Quasi-Public Institution* (1977), Ulrich takes a critical stand on methodological ideas in management sciences. A stronger orientation toward ideas of discourse ethics later enabled him to work out a fruitful conception of business ethics (Ulrich 1993, 1997, 2000; Ulrich and Breuer 2004) that he called *Integrative Economic Ethics*.[4] With its systematic and comprehensive philosophical foundation it serves as an all-encompassing guide to philosophical considerations regarding the nature of a just economy, as well as offering assessments of contestable claims of mainstream economic theory, including the premise of economic rationality. In sum, Ulrich offers a holistic approach to discussing questions of business and ethics.

Integrative Economic Ethics is a rather unconventional appellation, so it is important to understand what is expressed by both terms, "integrative" and "economic ethics." The theory is called "economic ethics" to convey the fact that it discusses economic actors (i.e., business firms or individual managers) in terms of conventional categories of business ethics (e.g., legitimacy, responsibility, permissibility, and so on), even as it situates the discussion in a broader, holistic, approach to ethics and economic thought. Ulrich's main statement, laid out in his two major works (Ulrich 1993, 2008a) and countless papers, is that the underlying logic of the market and the way we think about economic policy and business decisions are all imbued with normative claims. It is therefore not sufficient to talk about ethical actions or decisions in a business setting if we do not also critically discuss the larger normative context in which these decisions are embedded. *Integrative* Economic Ethics therefore discusses first and foremost the underlying normative assumptions of economics, such as "good" market practices, efficiency and the rationality of markets (including, for example, the imperatives of market growth, profit maximization, the necessity of competition, and so on). The chief task of ethics in this context is to "enlighten" and critically reflect on the normative foundations of the inherent logic of the market as a foundation for economic ethics.

Ulrich's terminology draws upon an established category utilized in German-speaking debates on economic ethics: "*Wirtschaftsethik*" is a general term that encompasses all questions related to economic ethics. Questions of economic ethics are then discussed in various sub-fields, labeled institutional or regulatory ethics ("*Ordnungsethik*"—i.e., questions of economic policy and regulations), business ethics ("*Unternehmensethik*"—questions of business conduct, corporate social responsibility, corporate citizenship, etc.), and individual ethics ("*Individualethik*"—questions of consumer ethics, leadership ethics, virtues, etc.). These categories are important for understanding Ulrich's aim: to establish a universal moral point of view that gives a unified perspective for all questions that touch upon economic settings or arrangements, thereby providing an "ethically rational *orientation* in politico-economic thinking without abandoning reflection in the face of the implicit normativity of 'given' economic conditions." (Ulrich 2008a: 3–4, emphasis added)

The point of departure for Ulrich is the specific moral point of view laid out in Kantian ethics; this perspective is to be used in all economic considerations. The headline of the introduction to Peter Ulrich's book *Integrative Economic Ethics* (2008a) offers to give "orientation in economic-ethical thinking." This caption, which alludes to Immanuel Kant's famous essay, "What Does it Mean to Orient Oneself in Thinking?" (Kant 1786), implies that the first intent and general direction of Integrative Economic Ethics is to discuss ethical questions of business and society in a foundational philosophical manner that will, thereby, offer an ethical orientation, a perspective that prioritizes critical moral reasoning shorn of interests and partialities.

Ulrich spends a considerable effort to lay down a thorough clarification of the moral point of view,[5] set within a Kantian understanding of rational autonomy. He states that a moral point of view can be grounded only within the self-critical reason of man. Ulrich thus adopts the Kantian perspective as "a moral point of view that all people can recognize as valid and binding because it is rationally well founded" (Ulrich 2008a: 37). This moral point of view is then further developed, in discourse ethics, from an *individual* moral point of view (Kant) to an *interpersonal* and formal process of reasoning according to which questions of legitimacy are to be resolved in ideal communication communities (cf. Habermas 1981), as characterized briefly in the opening paragraphs of this chapter.

Once established, this moral point of view is used in two major ways. It is used, first, to illuminate and critically discuss the normative assumptions of economic theory and practice, offering thereby an alternative view on the benefits and drawbacks of the logic of markets, competitiveness, and other axioms of economics. In this way, the moral point of view orients our economic and ethical reasoning. Such orientation not only suggests *how* to act in a given setting but it also provides legitimacy: According to discourse ethical assumptions, legitimacy stems from deliberation and consensus, not from the adherence to an axiom of economic theory or principle of conduct. Thus, Ulrich's Integrative Economics Ethics offers, along with his critique of economic reason, a critical discussion of utilitarian ethics as the foundation for economic theory (both in micro- and macroeconomics), at least as it is reflected in appeals to the "greatest happiness of the greatest number," or to corollary claims concerning the maximization of wealth, profits, or need fulfillment. In this way, Integrative Economic Ethics can be comprehended, in part, as an exercise in "economic enlightenment" attained through discussion and critique of these and other moral or economic assumptions.

Second, following his critique of economic theory, Ulrich's moral point of view is used to establish a different, and more appropriate, foundation for an ethically sound economy. Ulrich contends that the moral point of view, as he understands it, should legitimate an understanding of a liberal-republican polity based on Kantian republicanism and the discursive lifeworld ('*Lebenswelt*'). Such an approach partakes from both Habermas's thought and Rawls' (1999) conception of political liberalism and his theory of justice (see below). Amongst other things, this approach has led to a republican understanding of businesses as citizens, a perspective that has sparked intense debates of corporate citizenship in German business ethics.

The term "integrative" is meant to differentiate this approach further from traditional methods of applied ethics. Integrative Economic Ethics is not meant as an addition or supplement to economic rationality, nor is it set forth as but an alternative perspective to common business decisions (as if it were just another department next to accounting or marketing). For Ulrich, ethics is *integrative*, present in every single human action and thought, hence also in every economic action and economic thought. For Ulrich, serious (business) ethics can thus be established only by an unconditional critical (self-) reflection of normative economic assumptions. It is henceforth "not enough simply to 'apply' ethics to the sphere of economic activity as the alternative to or corrective for economic rationality" (Ulrich 2008a: 3). Integrative Economic Ethics must rather be an integral part of all economic thinking, business actions, and policymaking.

Discourse, legitimization, and responsibility

As we have seen above, Peter Ulrich aims to develop a moral point of view that provides the basis and justification for concrete actions in businesses. Following Habermas, Ulrich's main idea is to prioritize the idea of *fair and power-free discourses*. As a consequence, he criticizes an unscrutinized dominance of market economies in modern societies. Such societies are based on two crucial pillars: property rights and the free exchange of properties. Nonetheless, Ulrich does not regard property rights, per se, as problematic; they become problematic only if private economic actions lead to negative (intended or unintended) consequences or side effects. Consequently, Ulrich characterizes firms as quasi-public institutions (Ulrich 1977). Whether listed as corporations or small family businesses, firms are privately owned, but their business activities (can) result in negative external effects for the whole society as many past and recent business scandals have shown. In other words, due to negative external effects (social or ecological), not to mention limitations of the classical nation state to regulate these effects on a constitutional level, businesses increasingly need to legitimate their economic activities. It is important to note here that Ulrich is trying to make a case for ethics (and not for business success). He is not interested in the practical question of how businesses can gain or regain legitimacy merely in order to increase their reputation (the "business case") but in a practical question of conduct: What is the right thing to do?

On a theoretical level, Ulrich regards the main problems of modern economics as its underlying orientation toward a calculative or utilitarian ethics. In contrast, Ulrich suggests, economics should be grounded on *communicative ethics*; it needs to be transformed from an economic into a *socioeconomic rationality*: "Any action or institution is rational in a socioeconomic sense *if free and responsible citizens could have consensually justified it as a legitimate way of creating value in a rational process of deliberation*" (Ulrich 2002: 19, emphasis added). This explication of the moral point of view indicates that individual interests should not be followed if there is no *general* agreement on them in a given discourse community—that is, if they are not legitimate. Rational moral discourse (the legitimacy of actions) precedes any rational decision in an economic sense (utility or profit maximization) (Ulrich 1997: 13, 2000).

This normative component is not taken into account in economics since economic rationality is "purely" based on the normative logic of the exchange of benefits. In contrast, Ulrich stresses, as does Habermas, categorical orientations toward normative principles: One should act on a principle because the principle is understood to be *right*. In other words, Ulrich attempts to work out "regulative ideas" of businesses as (corporate) citizens rather than regarding them simply as "pure" economic actors within an economic system. He especially emphasizes "normative logics of human interaction" that are "justice-based" rather than power-based, and that are grounded on "intersubjective obligations" rather than maximizing private interests (Ulrich 2002: 21).

With regard to a first concrete "application" of the concept of integrative business ethics, Ulrich distinguishes different loci of socioeconomic responsibility: On the constitutional (macro) level, he follows the social market system adumbrated by the school of ordoliberalism and he embraces, as well, the so-called concept of *Vitalpolitik* ("policies aimed at 'vital' prerequisites for a good life"). With a parenthetical reference to Wilhelm Röpke, one of the major architects of postwar "ordoliberalism," Ulrich proposes the (re-)embeddedness of the market economy "into a higher overall order, which cannot be based on supply and demand, free prices and competition" (Ulrich 2002: 29). In addition and complementary to a political-economic framework, Ulrich develops a corporate ethics, with at least two important elements: at the first level a demand for corporate social responsibility (or, as Ulrich puts it, "business integrity"); at the second level, a call to the "political co-responsibility" of firms. Figure 12.1, on the next page, reproduces both elements.

Business integrity includes the search for legitimate value creation, so this pursuit is, in this sense, a legitimate practice to find business opportunities: "Thus, a possible *synthesis between ethics and economics* ("the business case") is not criticized per se but it is rather seen as valuable for the firm *and* society" (Ulrich 1994: 93–94, 1996). However, Ulrich makes it clear that business practices must be grounded in *deontological values* that subject business strategies to the light of moral principles. In other words, individuals and firms should be bound, by moral necessity, to certain "good" business principles.

This idea can be illustrated with a simple example: Let us assume corruption and bribery are seen as immoral practices of businesses, and let us also assume, further, that company X shares this understanding and has included a non-corruption policy in its statement of corporate values. In the hypothetical scenario in which bribery of a public official appears as an option, the corporation could determine what to do by adopting a strict business case perspective and undertaking a cost-benefit calculation (e.g., how big is the contract, what is the likelihood that the bribery will be discovered?) to determine what to do. But such a perspective (and such a calculation) might direct the firm towards morally questionable acts. However, from Ulrich's perspective, the company could under no circumstances make such a deal; no matter how big this business is

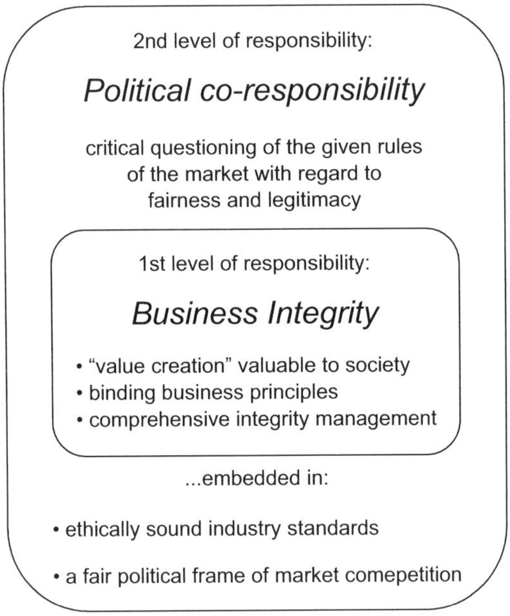

> **2nd level of responsibility:**
>
> *Political co-responsibility*
>
> critical questioning of the given rules of the market with regard to fairness and legitimacy
>
> > **1st level of responsibility:**
> >
> > *Business Integrity*
> >
> > - "value creation" valuable to society
> > - binding business principles
> > - comprehensive integrity management
>
> ...embedded in:
>
> - ethically sound industry standards
> - a fair political frame of market comepetition

Figure 12.1 Two-level conception of corporate ethics.

Source: Ulrich 2002:31.

or how unlikely it is to be caught. Business integrity demands a broader perspective, including a categorical adherence to deontological values.

The level of *political co-responsibility* of firms in Ulrich's concept of corporate ethics is linked with the above-mentioned idea of embeddedness and corporate citizenship. For Ulrich, the social responsibility of businesses is related to their contributions to just institutions on a political level. Businesses should not merely act according to the rules of the game but ought to be "game changers" through active political participation as corporate citizens (for more details see below). The commitment and engagement of companies to develop ethically sound standards within their industries or their participation in multi-stakeholder initiatives are important examples of the political co-responsibility of firms. Such co-responsibility should involve the search for legitimate collective solutions and an approach to business ethics that is not limited to the "internal" CSR performance of a company.

Neither the constitutional level nor one of the two levels in Ulrich's corporate ethics are, however, the main loci of fairness. Suitable political arrangements and corporate ethics assist in the realization of justice in modern societies, but they do not have an independent moral status—they do not function, so to speak, as "moral judges." After all, the crucial element in Peter Ulrich's republican business ethics is the *critical public*. Ulrich does not build his ethical approach on a set of material norms, by which we are to render judgments, but on a formal principle of discussion and deliberation. Habermas' "ideal speech situation" is the yardstick to measure the circumstances of "real communication." It represents an ideal type of open debate for all and without any constraints (Baert 2001: 88).

To grasp more fully how Ulrich's ethics might be "applied" to the three levels of responsibility, we turn first to the micro level of the individual. As noted above, and as we see below, Integrative Economic Ethics is less a technique to be *applied* than a normative orientation.

The micro level: the ethics of economic citizens

Integrative Economic Ethics imbues the question of a political order with the specific perspectives of citizens and their civic virtues. Ulrich conceives of society as (striving for) a free and democratic political order based on liberal principles. In accordance with the Kantian moral point of view,

> interpersonal obligations can be founded only on the observation of the same inviolable freedom of all men in the sense of their right to pursue the 'possibility of human existence' to the full. This is in accordance with the autonomous personal commitment of every moral subject to the conditions of the general freedom of all men.
>
> (Ulrich 2008a: 14)

This general freedom of all men then necessarily leads to a liberal political framework that Ulrich calls *Republican Liberalism*, linking it to the political liberalism proposed by Rawls (1999) but drawing upon fruitful discussions between liberalism and communitarianism (see, for example, Honneth 1993; Forst 2002), while also adding important elements of republicanism (Pettit 1997). For Ulrich, individual freedom is understood chiefly as positive freedom (cf. Berlin 2002), but he adds to this liberal paradigm an emphasis on social communities (communitarianism) and a prioritization of civic virtues and the responsibilities of *citoyens* (republicanism). Both aspects are fundamentally necessary for an appropriate liberal conception. Contrary to traditional liberal thought and in line with discourse ethics, Ulrich does not accept the reduction of the individual to some "atomistic" existence that is just "set" in society or whose freedom is "endangered" by the state or by others. According to Ulrich, being a member of both a pluralistic society and the political arena are essential for every individual.

With that said, Ulrich also deploys these same republican and liberal elements against the tendencies of communitarianism to exaggerate community—individual citizen rights (including rights against the state) are still paramount and it remains everyone's *individual* responsibility as citizens to participate in a shared *res publica* (Ulrich 2008a: 274ff.). The free and democratic society thus depends on the civic sense and political participation of its citizens: "Republican freedom is conceived as the politically constituted greatest possible equal freedom of all citizens. It includes, and is indeed a precondition for, their entitlement to active participation as citizens of the state (*citoyens*) in the democratic self-determination of a well-ordered life with others in a free society" (282). Thus, elements of all three lines of thought (liberalism, communitarianism, and republicanism) coalesce into a version of republican liberalism that upholds a conception of positive freedom (participatory self-determination of legitimate ends) that is in turn dependent on a sense of civic virtues (279).

While Ulrich's reference to a formal (rational) ethics "leaves the settlement of all material questions to the public use of reason (Kant, Rawls) by mature and responsible citizens of the *res publica*" (Ulrich 2008a: 283), individuals must adhere to a *minima moralia* in order to uphold the regulative idea of a reasoning public. In short, citizens need to be willing 1) to reflect on their preferences and attitudes and be willing 2) to reach an agreement on impartial, fair principles and procedural rules in a deliberative process. Furthermore, they need the inclination 3) to compromise in areas of dissent and 4) to accept the need for the legitimation of their acts, practices, and institutions (299).

One final point is extremely important. For Ulrich, civic virtues are not only necessary conditions for dealing with political matters in the public sphere but within the economy too.

Since in discourse ethics the deliberative process is what gives legitimacy to any action, civic virtues are also *economic citizen virtues* insofar as business activities always have public relevance for Ulrich:

> [T]he idea of a neat and tidy separation between the political citizen (as homo politicus) and the economic citizen (as homo oeconomicus) turns out to be the symptomatic expression of a privatistically reduced self-understanding of the bourgeois who has lost his awareness of the priority and indivisibility of his status as a citoyen. The core of a republican economic ethics consists precisely in reflecting on the indispensable republican civic ethos in the self-understanding of the economic agents and putting it into practice. From this point of view, all economic agents essentially share a responsibility that cannot be delegated. Their shared responsibility refers to the quality of societal processes of deliberation, particularly in regard to debates concerned with the general economic, social and political conditions for the legitimate pursuit of private economic interests.
>
> *(Ulrich 2008a: 300)*

It is this *integrity* of the individual that is the regulative idea of the individual dimension of Ulrich's economic ethical approach. All citizens need to adhere to the principles of the deliberative process in all areas of their life, including the economic, whether as employees, managers, or consumers.

The meso level: normative stakeholder management

In the debate on business ethics it is now widely accepted that businesses face legitimate claims by actors other than shareholders. This paradigmatic change incorporates a shift from a shareholder value approach to a stakeholder one (Freeman 1984; Freeman and McVea 2001; Freeman 2004). The business of business is not merely business (see the opposite position by Friedman 1970). It is, rather, to strike a balance (itself not well-defined) between different claims of various stakeholder groups. But why should firms take stakeholder interests into account?

In management theory, a *strategic* response is dominant. On this strategic view, a firm should attend to (or respect) the interests of stakeholders because doing so tends to have a bottom line pay-off. Within the last two decades, a corporation is better off, even with its increased power,[6] if it responds to the correlative and increased interest of "critical" components of society. For example, one might conceive of nongovernmental organizations (NGOs) as the professionalized voices of some members of civil society. One of the NGOs' main goals is the mobilization of the public (and consumers) to put pressure on (multinational) corporations in order to launch concrete business practices for greater social justice. A telling example of mobilization of consumer power through NGOs is the Brent Spar case of Royal Dutch Shell in 1995 (for details see the case studies of Paine 1999a, 1999b; and Beschorner 2005). Of course, from a strategic point of view, increasing societal pressure in favor of just business practices may entail economic costs for firms, with relatively higher costs imposed on smaller firms. Nonetheless, it is economically smart from the business perspective to deal with these societal demands and to incorporate relevant organizational measures within the firm. Consequently, elements of risk management to avoid "negative attention" by stakeholder groups have been integrated in traditional management systems. In this sense, the social responsibility of firms is a certain type of "smart management" to prevent harming the corporate image and to improve the firm's reputation. In this way, the social responsibility of firms is related to the power and spheres of influence of certain stakeholders. Businesses take ethical issues into account if—and only if—they "pay."

If we turn from the strategic to the normative consideration of stakeholders, then it could be argued that the negative external effects of business practices—social as well as ecological (world) problems—need to be ameliorated, if not solved. In instances of incomplete law or regulation, Ulrich argues that firms have the moral obligation to avoid negative external effects resulting from their practices. The author criticizes the strategic stakeholder approach due to its orientation on the stakeholders' bargaining power. Basing stakeholder dialogues on power (the more powerful a stakeholder is, the more (s)he has to say) obviously leads to moral conundrums: Why should some stakeholders have a louder voice then others? Or, even, why should some stakeholders be excluded from a discourse while others are allowed to articulate their demands? Obviously, these are not legitimate practices from a discourse ethical point of view. One argument must count as one argument. In contrast to the power-based arguments in traditional strategic management Ulrich suggests a critical approach, as a form of *regulative idea*, that verifies "who *ought* to assert entitled stakes to the business (thus not merely: who *can* assert the stakes due to his or her power)" (our translation, Ulrich 1997: 443).

As we have stated above—regarding Habermas' ideas—a discourse does not take into consideration *all* interests of *all* participants. Thus, a discourse is more than a mere dialogue in which (some) parties are engaged in a conversation; rather, it is an ideal dialogue in which normative criteria define the circumstances for a moral conversation. It is important to note that, in discourse, certain stakes or interests have the status of "candidates" who will then be justified according to the question whether or not it supports a greater good (beyond the mere self-interests of the participants). More precisely, Habermas and Ulrich suggest a twofold test of the specific stakes within discourses: first, the normative propositions that emerge must be deemed *responsible* in the sense that they are consensually justified as legitimate in a rational process of (power free) deliberation. All participants "re-spond" (dialogical) to the question of whether or not the norm can be seen as satisfied for *all* affected. Second, the renunciation of one's own interests must be *reasonable* (Ulrich 2000: 13). It would be unreasonable if the norm would lead to the negligence of some actors or their interests. After all, the economic interests of a firm are not per se unreasonable. In fact, these interests are quite reasonable if the existence of the firm is at stake. Nonetheless, in a discourse ethical perspective, the firm's interest must also always be regarded with respect to the first criteria, taking into account whether the interest is merely selfish (e.g., in favor of just one stakeholder, the shareholders) or whether it reflects a more general interest.

For discourse ethicists, two aspects are important here: First, the ideal dialogue does not lead to an absence of specific interests of the participants, but it makes these interests visible (Habermas 1993: 57–58). Second, as the term "candidates" signalizes, Habermas' and Ulrich's variant of discourse ethics is not absolutistic in the sense that one specific moral standard has to be applied. In fact, every normative proposal—even those that might seem absurd, such as more child labor or excluding males or females from a board of directors—can be discussed. Every proposition has the status of a candidate—a candidate for concrete moral practices. However, whether or not the proposition is legitimate depends on whether it is responsible and reasonable (as just noted). The dialogic perspective indicates, for example, that profit seeking is not per se an illegitimate practice, since the existence of firms depends on a certain margin of profit. Profit seeking might also be seen by the discourse participants as satisfactory to all those affected. However, it could be assumed, though without any certainty, that participants in a discourse (including workers for example) might not agree upon an idea of profit maximization if this entailed the exclusion of any consideration of the interests of stakeholders other than shareholders.

To conclude, first, Ulrich emphasizes in contrast to the strategic perspective the relevance of communicative action (deliberation versus bargaining). The German term for deliberation, "argumentative *Verständigung*," includes both understanding and consensus. Second, Ulrich underlines the non-identity between real and ideal communication communities, between the "Is" and the "Ought" (Ulrich 1997: 80–82 and 448, 1999: 84) which allows him, third, to characterize the moral point of view as a "regulative idea" that aims at bridging practices of the real world with the normative orientations of the ideal. It is in this sense that Ulrich's approach, as noted previously, is not a technique that is *applied* in certain situations but a more holistic orientation by which individuals may sift, consider, and legitimate the practices that engage and underlie their lives and societies.

The strengths of Ulrich's strict ethical perspective can be seen as a more general critique that takes into account the *ends* of business activities as well as the *means* of business practices. Such a critique is relevant from a theoretical as well as practical point of view. From a theoretical perspective, Ulrich conceptualizes the embeddedness of firms in a broader societal context (and not merely within the economic system) and honors contributions of businesses toward a "good society." Ulrich develops his idea from a pure "moral point of view" without accepting somewhat empirical circumstances that might prevent concrete moral practices. It is important for him to rethink what business ethics should be, and this leads to a diminished focus on practical solutions. Ulrich regards this "full play" of ethics as the specific strength of Integrative Economic Ethics. Others, however, regard the neglect of "real communication communities" as a particular weakness of Ulrich's concept.

From a rather practical point of view, Peter Ulrich's normative position questions *core aspects of business practices*. These practices include the ethical quality of products and services, the production processes (including workplace issues) and the sales process. In a practical sense, these normative claims may point to an *ontological basis for corporate values* as a fundamental aspect of business activities. Such corporate values may, for example, result in an explicitly formulated corporate philosophy and other institutional arrangements for just business practices. In sum, and in his own words, Peter Ulrich stands for a "critical stakeholder approach which emphasizes the difference to strategic management orientations and undertakes fundamental reflections for management sciences while it avoids categorical confusions and shortcomings" (our translation, Ulrich 1997: 448).

The macro level: republican liberalism and regulatory ethics

Any form of market economy needs some sort of justified political and social framework. The aim of Integrative Economic Ethics is to embed or situate the market within an overall ethical and political conception, legitimated by the moral point of view:

> The justification of a certain order of the market economy consists in embedding the market in an overall conception, taking into account both the market and the non-market elements of well-coordinated socio-economic interactions in a society. The determination of such a conception, and in particular of the precise role which can be ascribed to the market as a partial coordination mechanism within it, is the task of institutional politics. The problem is obviously of a normative kind: as with every legitimate form of politics, regulatory politics must be oriented on justified normative principles. The clarification of the corresponding orientational problems is the task of regulatory ethics.
>
> *(Ulrich 2008a: 315)*

Due to its strong social and political impetus and its discourse ethical foundation, Integrative Economic Ethics lays out a substantial critique of classic economic paradigms and discusses the problems of a neoliberal market order at great length (Ulrich 2008a, Chapter 8). Given the inherent political limits of liberal economics (with its presumption against political control over market processes) and taking into account the substantial empirical shortcomings of communism and socialist economies, Ulrich turns to concepts of a political order that are less dogmatic and more open to interpretation.

One such alternative approach is the paradigm of a "social market economy." This economic order, which has accompanied German political thought for the past sixty years, strives to resolve the challenge of constituting and moderating a just market economy. The social market economy, as articulated by the ordoliberal school of economic thought (Lorch 2014), can be considered to be one of the more successful approaches of a "third way" (Giddens 1998) operating between the binary opposition of "capitalism vs. communism." Ordoliberalism and its fruitful elaboration of a social market economy is thus the point of departure for an application of Integrative Economic Ethics to questions of market regulation. To understand this fit, a short introduction of ordoliberalism is necessary.

During and after World War II the "ordoliberals," attempted to revitalize economic thinking in Germany (Röpke 1966; Rüstow 1950; Müller-Armack 1946). These thinkers laid the theoretical foundation for the unique economic success story of the post-war German economy—the "*Wirtschaftswunder*" (or the "economic wonder" see Sally 1996; Ptak 2004). (The major ordoliberal thinkers were also members of the renowned Mont Pelerin Society that reinvented and broadcast liberal political and economic thought—their efforts are today commonly known as neoliberalism (Plickert 2008; Mirowski and Plehwe 2009)). With their focus on a "third way" between laissez-faire capitalism and socialist planning, the ordoliberals considered how seemingly economic decisions—about government policies, business practices, and the ends of business—were, in fact, deeply related to the general order of society. With the German society and economy devastated after World War II, the ordoliberals realized that the government had to think about how to rebuild not only its economy but society as a whole. They consequently discussed and debated both historical ideal types of society and economy—the liberal unbound market economy as well as the planned socialist economy. With their analysis of the two historical forms they came to the conclusion that both ideologies contributed to the social crises of their time. Nonetheless, the "third way" of the ordoliberals remains closely related to traditional liberal thought. Setting off from the idea of individual freedom, the ordoliberals set out to "reinvent liberalism from the ground up" (our translation, Miksch 1949: 163).

The ordoliberal version of the social market economy became a framework for the post-war German economic and social order. Essential to this ideal was an awareness of the interconnectedness of the economy with all other spheres of society (i.e., politics, law, culture, etc.). The economy is not disconnected from society (as it was considered to be in laissez-faire liberalism) but an integral part of society, dependent on social and political forces it cannot (re-)produce on its own. For the social market economy, the terms "social" and "market economy" are not in a hierarchical order but are equals:

> Even though the opinion has been voiced in Germany that all that is needed in order to resolve social problems is the fulfillment of economic principles, one should see clearer today that this instrumental view cannot live up to the task at hand. We are not only talking about shaping an economical order, rather we need to incorporate it into a holistic societal design.
>
> *(our translation, Müller-Armack 1952: 462)*

Developing a theory of the social market economy as a socially "embedded economy," the ordoliberals incorporated strong normative statements about how society in general was supposed to be structured in order to be able to embed a productive and competitive market order (see, for example, one of the few English publications by the ordoliberal thinkers, that of Müller-Armack 1978). Ordoliberals thus discussed different kinds of social norms, values, and individual virtues necessary for a competitive market order to be beneficial for all.

The ordoliberal line of thought turns out to be a natural fit to the political and social imperatives of Integrative Economic Ethics, with its emphasis on a republican order of equally free citizens and the moral significance of the interconnectedness of the economy with all other fields of society, not to mention the discursive perspective on social norms and values as a necessary underlying foundation of the social market economy. The ordoliberal perspective, in other words, matches Ulrich's critiques of mainstream economics and of laissez-faire capitalism, and it expresses his search for an embedded market order.

In an attempt to modernize and refresh the thoughts of ordoliberals with regards to a social market economy, Integrative Economic Ethics therefore discusses ways to connect this more historical approach to society and economy and enriches it with its own idea of republican liberalism. Although the *general impetus* of the social market economy, to connect economic thought with ethical considerations of society and morals in general, remains useful, the *normative foundations* and the *specific solutions* discussed by ordoliberals may seem outdated and not helpful by today's philosophical, social, and political standards. Specific ordoliberal normative thoughts (e.g., that the political order be imbued with values of Christian religion, of chivalry, and of rural life) may seem peculiar by today's more pluralistic standards (see Lorch 2014 for a critical discussion of the normative assumptions of ordoliberalism). Yet Ulrich's approach transcends the historical attempt of the ordoliberal school by adding a republican liberalism as the philosophical and normative foundation for a modern social market economy. In Ulrich's version the processes of deliberation, not material norms, take priority: the values of the political order cannot be determined before any of these processes have taken place.

Concluding remarks

Following Ulrich's critical discussion of ordoliberal thought and his attempt to strengthen the social and political aspects of economic policy, there are various recent attempts to discuss this important line of ordoliberal economic thought and integrate it into the larger body of ideas that is Integrative Economic Ethics (Thielemann 2010; Lorch 2014). More generally, the approach of Integrative Economics Ethics has had a tremendous and lasting impact on German debates of economic and business ethics. However, Ulrich's approach has received little international attention. This is a shame, considering its unique and important contributions to a holistic philosophical approach to business ethics.

One reason for the lack of visibility and exposure of Integrative Economic Ethics arises from issues of translatability. Ulrich's theory is firmly set in German philosophical debates situated within a tradition that is typically indebted to either Kant or critical theorists (chiefly Habermas). It is difficult not only to explain adequately what "economic ethics" really is, but also to translate the extensively used German terms such as *Lebenswelt* that do not have a direct equivalent in the English language.

Ulrich's approach has, on the other hand, influenced important international scholars of business ethics such as Florian Wettstein (2009), a former student of Ulrich, working on questions of business and human rights, as well as Scherer and Palazzo (2007), most prominently working on concepts of political CSR. In a sense, the notion of political CSR is well established in Integrative Economic Ethics and can be directly traced to the thorough political-philosophical works of Ulrich.

Nonetheless, Integrative Economic Ethics has also received its fair share of criticisms due to its firm and resolute philosophical interpretation of discourse ethics as the basic condition for legitimate action and its insistent critique of economic rationality. Ulrich demands, à la Kant, a very self-conscious, autonomous economic actor, yet he gives little advice on how to deal with the inevitable conflicts between ethics and economic rationality, leaving many readers unsatisfied with the practical implications of his approach. As true of discourse ethics, the condition of ideal communication communities has been accused of overburdening the individual, resulting in endless "practical discourses" that leave the individual economic actor incapable of acting (e.g., Nutzinger 1994; Nutzinger 1996; Osterloh 1996; König 1999). This line of criticism, however, has to be regarded with some ambivalence: on the one hand, we agree with Ulrich on the importance of stressing the moral point of view as a regulative idea since making any compromises, such as confusing the moral point of view with empirical facts, "given" conditions, and so on, would indeed lead to a halt in ethical reflection and thus to "ethical suicide" (Kersting 1993). On the other hand, we agree with Ulrich's critics that he is not assertive enough in dealing with actual cases and practices. Ulrich's theory thus needs to respond more fully to the criticism that it might be somewhat out of touch with everyday business situations. For practitioners, it can be unclear how the theoretically appealing idea of ideal speech situations of discourse ethics can be translated to specific business situations or conflicts. Ulrich's approach may sound entirely reasonable, a model for what everyone wants, at least in theory, yet it does not entail any direct consequences for business practices.

In two lesser-known articles, Peter Ulrich (2004a, 2004b) proposes what he calls "grass root reflections," which attempts to connect the concept of the ideal communication community with concrete moral orientations of "flesh and blood" agents. Actions, Ulrich states, are de facto always grounded on the moral orientations of the actors. This idea, and the possible extension of Integrative Economic Ethics toward a normative theory of practices, has recently sparked new discussions (Beschorner et al. 2015). But, considering the breadth and depth of Integrative Economic Ethics, there still appears to be lots of room for further advancements, discussions, and applications of this important approach to business ethics.

Essential readings

The essential theoretical foundation of Integrative Economic Ethics can be found in Peter Ulrich: *Integrative Economic Ethics: Foundations of a Civilized Market Economy* (2008a), also available in German (Ulrich 2008b) and Spanish (Ulrich 2008c). For a thorough review of Ulrich's theory see Jeffery Smith's book review of the same (2013). The philosophical basis of Integrative Economic Ethics is found in Jürgen Habermas, *Theory of Communicative Action* (1981, 2 vols). We also recommend Habermas' (short) book *Justification and Application: Remarks on Discourse Ethics* (1993) for an introduction to discourse ethics. For a brief introduction to the general idea of a social market economy, we recommend Alfred Müller-Armack's article, "The Social Market Economy as an Economic and Social Order" from 1978. Wilhelm Röpke's book *A Humane Economy: The Social Framework of the Free Market* (1960) is a great introduction to ordoliberal thought.

For further reading in this volume on motivation and rationality and their roles in economic theory, see Chapter 17, The contribution of economics to business ethics. On the idea that firms and agents are embedded in social relations, see Chapter 8, Feminist ethics and business ethics: redefining landscapes of learning through practice. On the very idea of enlightenment and disinterested rationality, see Chapter 3, Theory and method in business ethics. For an account of business as embedded within the culture of central European nations both before and after communism, see Chapter 39, Business ethics in transition: communism to commerce in Central Europe and Russia. For a discussion of how entrepreneurship is a moral notion, see Chapter 16, The ethics of entrepreneurship. For a discussion of how stakeholder thinking may prove an obstacle to a comprehensive ethical perspective, see Chapter 11, Stakeholder thinking. On a political interpretation of social responsibility, see Chapter 10, Social responsibility.

Notes

1 For a very helpful introduction to the work and life of Jürgen Habermas see Baert (2001).
2 We do not discuss Apel's position here. In contrast to Habermas, Apel suggests developing a universal moral point of view based on cultural invariances (cf. Apel 1980). This research strategy tends to lead to fundamentalism and seems—at least for business ethics issues—not adequate. Habermas' approach is in this sense more moderate since, as we will see, he attempts to reconstruct his version of Discourse Ethics in relation to lifeworlds (in plural!). See Scherer (2005).
3 We refer to the German original first published in 1991. Quotes and specific Habermasian terms are taken from the English translation by Ciaran Cronin, published in 1993 by MIT Press.
4 There are unfortunately very few publications by Ulrich in English; see for example Ulrich 1998; 2002; 2008a; 2009.
5 The concept of a moral point of view that is understood in a rational ethical sense can be found in Baier (1958).
6 In the 1980s the number of transnational corporations has tripled from 10,000 to 30,000 (Arrighi 1999). In 2001, the United Nations Conference on Trade and Development (UNCTAD) in its World Development Report counted 62,000 transnational corporations and 820,000 foreign affiliates. Merger and acquisition activities of businesses and increasing profits have also led to an increasing (financial) power of firms. For example, the revenue of Exxon Mobil in 2002 (205 billion dollars), the world's largest corporation, is higher than the GDP of countries such as Denmark (172), Indonesia (173), Turkey (184), or Saudi Arabia (188) in the same year (numbers by IMF).

References

Apel, K.-O. (1980). *Towards a Transformation of Philosophy*. London: Routledge & Kegan Paul.
Arrighi, G. (1999). "Globalization and Historical Macrosociology," in J.L. Abu-Lughod (ed.), *Sociology for the Twenty-first Century, Continuities and Cutting Edges*. Chicago, IL: University of Chicago Press, 117–133.
Baert, P. (2001). "Jürgen Habermas," in A. Elliott and B.S. Turner (eds), *Profiles in Contemporary Social Theory*. London; Thousand Oaks, CA; New Delhi: Sage, 84–93.
Baier, K. (1958). *The Moral Point of View: A Rational Basis of Ethics*. Ithaca, NY: Cornell University Press.
Berlin, I. (2002). *Liberty: Incorporating Four Essays on Liberty*. Oxford: Oxford University Press.
Beschorner, T. (2005). "Social Responsibility of Firms," in J. Beckert and M. Zafirovski, (eds), *International Encyclopedia of Economic Sociology*. London: Routledge, 618–622.
Beschorner, T. (2006). "Ethical Theory and Business Practices: The Case of Discourse Ethics," *Journal of Business Ethics* 66:1, 127–139.
Beschorner, T., P. Ulrich, and F. Wettstein (eds) (2015). *St. Galler Wirtschaftsethik. Programmatik, Positionen, Perspektiven*. Marburg: Metropolis.
Enquête-Kommission Globalisierung der Weltwirtschaft (2002). "Schlussbericht. Globalisierung der Weltwirtschaft—Herausforderungen und Antworten." Berlin: Deutscher Bundestag.
Forst, R. (2002). *Contexts of Justice: Political Philosophy Beyond Liberalism and Communitarianism*. Berkeley and Los Angeles, CA: University of California Press.
Freeman, R.E. (1984). *Strategic Management: A Stakeholder Approach*. Marshfield, MO: Pitman.
Freeman, R.E. (2004). "The Stakeholder Approach Revisited," *Zeitschrift für Wirtschafts- und Unternehmensethik* 5:3, 228–241.
Freeman, R.E. and J. McVea (2001). "A Stakeholder Approach to Strategic Management," in M.A. Hitt, R. E. Freeman and J.S. Harrison (eds), *The Blackwell Handbook of Strategic Management*. Oxford: Blackwell Business, 189–207.

Friedman, M. (1970). "The Social Responsibility of Business Is to Increase its Profits," *The New York Times Magazine*, September 13, 32–33, 122–126.

Giddens, A. (1998). *The Third Way: The Renewal of Social Democracy*. Cambridge: Polity.

Gilbert, D.U. and M. Behnam (2009). "Advancing Integrative Social Contracts Theory: A Habermasian Perspective," *Journal Of Business Ethics* 89:2, 215–234.

Gilbert, D.U. and A. Rasche (2007). "Discourse Ethics and Social Accountability: The Ethics of SA 8000," *Business Ethics Quarterly* 17:2, 187–216.

Habermas, J. (1981). *Theory of Communicative Action*, Vol. 1: *Reason and the Rationalization of Society*, T A. McCarthy (trans.). Boston, MA: Beacon Press.

Habermas, J. (1981). *Theory of Communicative Action* Vol. 2: *Lifeworld and System: A Critique of Functionalist Reason*, T. A. McCarthy (trans.). Boston: Beacon Press.

Habermas, J. (1991/1992). *Erläuterungen zur Diskursethik*. Frankfurt a.M.: Suhrkamp.

Habermas, J. (1993). *Justification and Application: Remarks on Discourse Ethics*. C. P. Cronin (trans.). Cambridge, MA: MIT Press.

Honneth, A. (ed.) (1993). *Kommunitarismus: eine Debatte über die moralischen Grundlagen moderner Gesellschaften*. Frankfurt a.M.: Campus.

Kant, I. (1786). "What Does it Mean to Orient Oneself in Thinking?" in A. Wood and G. di Giovanni (eds), *Religion and Rational Theology, The Cambridge Edition of the Works of Immanuel Kant*. Cambridge: Cambridge University Press, 1–18.

Kersting, W. (1993). "Moralphilosophie, angewandte Ethik und Ökonomismus," *Zeitschrift für Politik* 43:2, 183–194.

König, M. (1999). "Ebenen der Unternehmensethik," in H.G. Nutzinger, Hans and Berliner Forum zur Wirtschafts- und Unternehmensethik (eds), *Wirtschafts- und Unternehmensethik: Kritik einer neuen Generation. Zwischen Grundlagenreflexion und ökonomischer Indienstnahme*. München: Hampp, 55–73.

Lorch, A. (2014). *Freiheit für alle. Grundlagen einer neuen Sozialen Marktwirtschaft*. Frankfurt/ New York, NY: Campus.

Miksch, L. (1949 [2008]). "Versuch eines liberalen Programms," in N. Goldschmidt and M. Wohlgemuth (eds), *Grundtexte zur Freiburger Tradition der Ordnungsökonomik*. Tübingen: Mohr Siebeck, 163–170.

Mingers, J. and G. Walsham (2010). "Toward Ethical Information Systems: The Contribution of Discourse Ethics," *MIS Quarterly* 34:4, 833–854.

Mirowski, P. and D. Plehwe (eds) (2009). *The Road from Mont Pèlerin: The Making of the Neoliberal Thought Collective*. Cambridge, MA: Harvard University Press.

Müller-Armack, A. (1946). *Wirtschaftslenkung und Marktwirtschaft*. Hamburg: Kastell.

Müller-Armack, A. (1952 [2008]). "Stil und Ordnung der Sozialen Marktwirtschaft," in N. Goldschmidt and M. Wohlgemuth (eds), *Grundtexte zur Freiburger Tradition der Ordnungsökonomik*. Tübingen: Mohr Siebeck, 457–466.

Müller-Armack, A. (1978). "The Social Market Economy as an Economic and Social Order," *Review of Social Economy* 36:3, 325–331.

Nutzinger, H.G. (1994). "Unternehmensethik zwischen ökonomischem Imperialismus und diskursiver Überforderung," in Forum für Philosophie (ed.), *Markt und Moral. Die Diskussion um die Unternehmensethik*. Bern, Stuttgart, Wien: Haupt, 181–214.

Nutzinger, H.G. (1996). "Zum Verhältnis von Ökonomie und Ethik. Versuch einer vorläufigen Klärung," in H.G. Nutzinger (ed.), *Naturschutz—Ethik—Ökonomie*. Marburg: Metropolis, 171–196.

Osterloh, M. (1996). "Vom Nirwana-Ansatz zum überlappenden Konsens. Konzepte der Unternehmensethik im Vergleich," in H.G. Nutzinger (ed.), *Wirtschaftsethische Perspektiven III. Unternehmensethik, Verteilungsprobleme, methodische Ansätze*. Berlin: Duncker & Humblot, 203–229.

Paine, L.S. (1999a). "Royal Dutch/Shell in Transition (A)," *Harvard Business Online*, Case 300–039.

Paine, L.S. (1999b). "Royal Dutch/Shell in Transition (B)," *Harvard Business Online*, Case 300–040.

Pettit, P. (1997). *Republicanism: A Theory of Freedom and Government*. Oxford: Oxford University Press.

Plickert, P. (2008). *Wandlungen des Neoliberalismus. Eine Studie zu Entwicklung und Ausstrahlung der "Mont Pèlerin Society."* Stuttgart: Lucius & Lucius.

Ptak, R. (2004). *Vom Ordoliberalismus zur Sozialen Marktwirtschaft. Stationen des Neoliberalismus in Deutschland*. Opladen: Leske + Budrich.

Rawls, J. (1999 [1971]). *A Theory of Justice*, revised edition. Cambridge, MA: Harvard University Press.

Reed, D. (1999a). "Stakeholder Management Theory: A Critical Theory Perspective," *Business Ethics Quarterly* 9:3, 453–483.

Reed, D. (1999b): "Three Realms of Corporate Responsibility: Distinguishing Legitimacy, Morality and Ethics," *Journal of Business Ethics* 21, 23–35.

Röpke, W. (1960). *A Humane Economy: The Social Framework of the Free Market*. Chicago, IL: H. Regnery Co.

Röpke, W. (1966). *Jenseits von Angebot und Nachfrage*, 4th edition. Erlenbach-Zürich: Rentsch.

Rüstow, A. (1950). *Das Versagen des Wirtschaftsliberalismus*, 3., rev. edition F.P. und G. Maier-Rigaud (trans. and eds) (2001). Marburg: Metropolis.

Sally, R. (1996). "Ordoliberalism and the Social Market: Classical Political Economy from Germany," *New Political Economy* 1:2, 1–18.

Scherer, A.G. (2005). "Neuere Entwicklungen der Diskursethik und deren Beitrag zur Lösung des philosophischen Grundlagenstreits zwischen Universalismus und Relativismus in der interkulturellen Ethik," in: T. Beschorner, B. Hollstein, M. König, M.-Y. Lee-Peukerand, O. Schumann (eds), *Wirtschafts- und Unternehmensethik. Rückblick—Ausblick—Perspektiven*. München: Hampp, 213–231.

Scherer, A. and Palazzo, G. (2007). "Towards a Political Conception of Corporate Responsibility: Business and Society Seen from a Habermasian Perspective," *Academy of Management Review* 32:4, 1096–1120.

Smith, J. (2013). "Book Review: Integrative Economic Ethics: Foundations of a Civilized Market Economy by Peter Ulrich," *Business Ethics Quarterly* 23:1, 151–154.

Thielemann, U. (2010). *Wettbewerb als Gerechtigkeitskonzept: Kritik des Neoliberalismus*. Marburg: Metropolis.

Ulrich, P. (1977). *Die Grossunternehmung als quasi-öffentliche Institution: eine politische Theorie der Unternehmung*. Stuttgart: Schäffer-Poeschel.

Ulrich, P. (1993). *Transformation der ökonomischen Vernunft: Fortschrittsperspektiven der modernen Industriegesellschaft*, 3rd revised edition. Bern: Haupt.

Ulrich, P. (1994). "Integrative Wirtschafts- und Unternehmensethik - ein Rahmenkonzept," in Forum für Philosophie (ed.), *Markt und Moral. Die Diskussion um die Unternehmensethik*. Bern: Haupt, 75–107.

Ulrich, P. (1996). "Unternehmensethik und 'Gewinnprinzip,'" in H.G. Nutzinger (ed.), *Wirtschaftsethische Perspektiven III—Unternehmensethik, Verteilungsprobleme, methodische Ansätze*. Berlin: Duncker & Humblot, 137–171.

Ulrich, P. (1997). *Integrative Wirtschaftsethik. Grundlagen einer lebensdienlichen Ökonomie*. Bern: Haupt.

Ulrich, P. (1998). "Integrative Economic Ethics—Toward a Conception of Socio-Economic Rationality," Working paper of the Institut für Wirtschaftsethik, University of St Gallen, No. 82, St Gallen.

Ulrich, P. (1999). "Zum Praxisbezug der Unternehmensethik," in G.R. Wagner (ed.), *Unternehmensführung, Ethik und Umwelt*. Wiesbaden: Gabler, 74–94.

Ulrich, P. (2000). "Integrative Wirtschaftsethik: Grundlagenreflexion der ökonomischen Vernunft," *Ethik und Sozialwissenschaft* 11:4, 555–566.

Ulrich, P. (2002). "Ethics and Economics," in L. Zsolnai (ed.), *Ethics in the Economy. Handbook of Business Ethics*. Bern, Switzerland: Peter Lang, 9–37.

Ulrich, P. (2004a). "Prinzipienkaskaden oder Graswurzelreflexion?—Zum Praxisbezug der Integrativen Wirtschaftsethik," in P. Ulrich, P. and M. Breuer (eds), *Wirtschaftsethik im philosophischen Diskurs. Begründung und 'Anwendung' praktischen Orientierungswissens*. Würzburg: Königshausen und Neumann, 127–142.

Ulrich, P. (2004b). "Wirtschaftsethische Graswurzelreflexion statt angewandte Diskursethik: Persönliche Sicht einiger Differenzen zwischen St. Galler und Berliner Position," in T. Bausch (eds), *Wirtschaft und Ethik: Strategien contra Moral?* Münster: LIT-Verlag, 21–41.

Ulrich, P. (2008a). *Integrative Economic Ethics: Foundations of a Civilized Market Economy*, James Fearns (trans.). New York, NY: Cambridge University Press.

Ulrich, P. (2008b). *Integrative Wirtschaftsethik: Grundlagen einer lebensdienlichen Ökonomie*. Bern: Haupt.

Ulrich, P. (2008c). *Ética Económica Integrativa: Fundamentos de una economía al servicio de la vida*. L. A. Panchi Vasco (trans.). Quito, Ecuador: Ediciones Abya-Yala.

Ulrich, P. (2009). *Civilizing the Market Economy: The Approach of Integrative Economic Ethics to Sustainable Development*. Discussion Papers of the Institute for Business Ethics/Berichte des Instituts für Wirtschaftsethik, Nr. 114. St Gallen.

Ulrich, P. and Breuer, M. (eds) (2004). *Wirtschaftsethik im philosophischen Diskurs—Begründung und "Anwendung" praktischen Orientierungswissens*. Würzburg: Königshausen + Neumann.

Wettstein, F. (2009). *Multinational Corporations and Global Justice: Human Rights Obligations of a Quasi-Governmental Institution*. Stanford, CA: Stanford University Press.

Part IV
Conceptual considerations

Introduction

In retrospect, it is interesting to consider what the founders of the self-conscious academic business ethics discipline took to be the cornerstones of their field's subject matter. An outgrowth of the business-and-society literature and the corporate social responsibility (CSR) movement, the emergent business ethics focused almost exclusively on for-profit corporations whose shares are traded on public exchanges. This focus had a variety of consequences for what were taken to be central topics of business ethics. From the *for-profit* emphasis comes much ethical analysis of the profit motive and whether its effects are pro- or anti-social. From the *corporate* emphasis comes an identification of the economy with the activities of firms on the S&P 500—and an ethical analysis of business that is often indistinguishable from an ethical analysis of bigness. From the *publicly-traded* emphasis comes an extended consideration of whether shareholders, who can readily dispose of their shares on public stock exchanges, merit being the objects of corporate directors' and officers' fiduciary duties. From *all* of these together come a sense that the academic discipline of economics is hostile ground on which to find business ethics insight. But what happens to business ethics when different aspects of the for-profit, publicly-traded-corporation focus are relaxed and no longer serve as anchor points for business ethics analysis? What happens when habitual antipathy is jettisoned and business ethicists look at economics with fresh eyes? The chapters in this section may be read as invitations to explore these questions.

This section opens with Chapter 13, **What is business?** In this chapter, **William Kline** considers the different senses in which we use the word "business" and how focusing on the idea of business as either organization or activity may shift the ground under our understanding of the subject matter of business ethics. He delineates the conditions for engaging in business and offers a critique of stakeholderism for its failure to appreciate the very activity of doing business. In addressing the nature of business, Kline not only changes the questions we ask but the answers we're inclined to give to the questions we already ask.

In Chapter 14, **The corporation: genesis, identity, agency**, Gordon G. Sollars connects business ethics to theories of the corporation with a careful survey of the corporation's historical antecedents and emergence. He addresses longstanding disagreements about whether the corporate identity is better understood as an entity or as an aggregation of persons, and traces the implications of these alternatives for understanding different normative schemes of corporate governance. Sollars also retraces an important debate over whether the corporation, as distinct from the persons who compose it, may be the locus of moral agency.

In Chapter 15, **Alternative business organizations and social enterprise**, **Dana Brakman Reiser** takes the discussion outside the investor-owned, for-profit firm by considering the varieties of alternative business organizations and social enterprises. Although social enterprises are not wholly unconcerned with profits, each by some device mitigates organizational focus on financial returns in pursuit of some other social or environmental objective. Concomitant with the emergence of social enterprise has been the design and promotion of alternative business organization governance models designed to support bifurcated aims of social enterprises. Contrasting and critiquing both American and European forms, Brakman Reiser provides a historical treatment of the emergence of these alternative business organizations for social enterprise and identifies the peculiar legal implications of each for organizational governance.

In Chapter 16, **The ethics of entrepreneurship**, **Christian Lautermann and Kim Oliver Tokarski** counter the narrowly big-corporate tendencies of business ethics by exploring entrepreneurship. Unpacking the term from its French and German roots as a form of "undertaking," they find entrepreneurship pregnant with normative significance: *what* should be undertaken, and to what *end*? Offering an overview of both classic and contemporary conceptions of entrepreneurship, Lautermann and Tokarski identify both narrowly economic and broadly social-cultural conceptions of entrepreneurship. They suggest that an understanding of entrepreneurship as a broadly social endeavor allows an escape from the tendency to view social entrepreneurship as *a priori* altruistic and ethical but ordinary for-profit entrepreneurship as selfish and unethical. Lautermann and Tokarski close by considering both the ethical implications of empirical work on entrepreneurial decision making and the way entrepreneurship appears through the lenses of normatively pragmatic, virtue-ethical, and value-pluralist perspectives.

In the last chapter of this section, **The contribution of economics to business ethics**, **Joseph Heath** discusses the ways in which the discipline of economics relates to business ethics. Locating the source of business ethicists' distrust of economics in economists' skepticism about the need for or efficacy of business ethics (in the first instance by way of Adam Smith's invisible hand), he identifies less and more radical versions of this skepticism and the different theoretical paradigms of economics that generate them. However, of these theoretical paradigms, the one most important to driving some of the common concerns of business ethicists and economists is, according to Heath, rational choice theory. An outgrowth of the twentieth-century development of decision and game theory, rational choice theory (and related developments like experimental economics) effectively forced economics and economists to "get normative" and to see the significance of norms at work in market relations. They also provided the tools so useful for work in political philosophy and in business ethics. Heath closes with a consideration of the sources of a new modesty in the economists' assessment of the role of ethics in business.

Alexei Marcoux

13
What is business?

William Kline

In business ethics the concept of "business" is just as important as "ethics" in determining what businesses ought to do. What business *is* constrains what it can do. If "ought" implies "can," then the answer to "What is business?" sets the parameters for what business ought to do. Our problem is that much like "ethics," there are different theories about, and meanings of, "business."

In the early seventeenth century, in his *Novum Organum* (1620), Francis Bacon warned against judgment biases arising from the natural looseness of words. Words mean different things to different people, and this leads to personally biased conclusions as well as fruitless debates as people using the same word are actually talking or writing about distinct things—the proverbial apples and oranges. Bacon aptly names these judgment biases, "Idols of the Market." Such biases are idols of the market because they arise out of ambiguities in communication and, apparently, Bacon thought nothing symbolizes this better than the hurley-burley exchanges and negotiations of a seventeenth-century market. Bacon's warning has relevance to the understanding of business. In order to avoid confusion, business ethicists must choose, articulate, and argue for a theory of business just as they do with ethics. Given the richness of the term and actual practice of business, this is no easy task.

The *Oxford English Dictionary* lists at least twenty-two entries for "business," thereby reaffirming Bacon's apt nomenclature. Nonetheless, this list of entries is finite, so the meaning of "business" has boundaries: not everything is business. Clarifying what constitutes these boundaries will help us to better identify what should and should not count as business, and why.

To organize the discussion, I will use the observation of Al Gini and Alexei Marcoux (2012) that "business" can refer to both organizations and activities. Accordingly, this chapter will first examine two prominent views of business as an organization: business may be identified with corporations or it may be understood in terms of a theory, the transaction costs theories of the firm. I will argue that both are deficient conceptions of business. Consideration will then be given to business as an activity. I will argue that rules define the scope of business activities. Activities that violate these rules are not merely unethical, they are not business at all. I then explore how these rules provide the bases for what business is: attempting to profit by producing a good or service for trade. The final section of this chapter will examine the implications of stakeholder theory for our very understanding of business as an activity.

William Kline

Business as an organization

Business as the corporation

In the business ethics literature, and in popular critiques, the organizational structure overwhelmingly identified as business is the large publicly traded corporation. Robert Solomon captures the essence of this focus: "the consequences of the activities of a giant corporation are always so pervasive and powerful that, unlike similar actions by a smaller company, virtually everything it does becomes an ethical issue" (1997: 50–51, see also Solomon 1999; Hasnas 2013). Archie B. Carroll (1999) points to the same fixation on the corporation in his account of how the concept of "social responsibility" in *business* ethics evolved, from the 1950s to the end of the 1990s, into the idea of *corporate* social responsibility. As to why this change occurs he notes only that, "In the early writings on CSR, it was referred to more often as social responsibility (SR) than as CSR. Perhaps this was because the age of the modern corporation's prominence and dominance in the business sector had not yet occurred or been noted" (1999: 269). According to Zhenzhong Ma, from 2002 to 2006 the most influential papers published in business ethics shifted their focus to corporate social responsibility and corporate performance (2009: 258). The framing of this issue as one of *corporate* social responsibility combined with the publication and citation of influential articles on corporate social responsibility mutually reinforce each other. The end result is that the business ethics literature tends to focus on the large publicly traded corporation. As Richard DeGeorge (2015) has put it, "business ethics sought to provide an explicit ethical framework within which to evaluate business, and especially corporate activities."

Two major background arguments serve as the foundation underlying the focus on the corporation. The first argument involves the proposition that we no longer live in Adam Smith's world of small shopkeepers (Solomon 1997: 304). The second involves the supposed observation that large corporations have far greater effects on people's lives than single small proprietorships. We shall examine each of these arguments in turn and find them both wanting.

The claim that we are no longer a nation of small shopkeepers does not stand up to careful scrutiny. According to business census data there are close to as many jobs provided by firms hiring 500 and fewer employees as there are persons employed by firms larger than 500 (Caruso 2015). In the United States approximately 56.1 million people earn their living in firms of less than 500 employees. To assert that we now have corporations larger than Adam Smith ever conceived also overlooks that we have far more small businesses than he had ever known possible. Assuming away the real statistical distribution of extant business organizations is not a justification for disproportionately focusing on large publicly traded corporations.

This leaves us with the claim about relative impacts. There is truth to the claim that scholarly focus on large publicly traded corporations is justified due to their potential influence relative to that of a small firm. The actions or policies of one very large firm will have greater ramifications than those of one very small firm. If the local steel mill or coal mine closes, the local town is in for a great deal of misery, but not so if the local hardware store closes. When Union Carbide makes a mistake with chemicals, as it did in Bhopal, India 1984, thousands are hurt or killed. This scale of impact does not occur with local "mom and pop" shops, or so the argument goes.

The argument about influence or impact overlooks how business ethics should consider not just the corporate firm but the actions of individuals and small businesses, as well as the effects of collective action, especially those resulting from laws and government policies. Millions of people are employed and pay taxes due to mid- and small-size firms. Moreover, licensing, taxing, zoning, minimum wage, and other policy decisions have a broad impact on small businesses, an influence that is left largely unnoticed due to the focus on large corporations.

For example, in 2007, almost a million Mattel toys were recalled due to the presence of lead (Story 2007). This incident served as the justification for Congress to pass the Consumer Product Safety Improvement Act (CPSIA), which purportedly imposed stricter testing standards for toys. However, with the focus on large corporations it has been largely overlooked how, with the imposition of stricter testing standards, many smaller toy companies, that never had these problems, went out of business due to the high costs of compliance (Wayne 2009). Comparing a single large firm to a single small company, for purposes of measuring "impact," is a mistake. Laws, regulations, and ethical judgements usually do not apply only to a single firm whether large or small. In consequentialist reasoning, it is essential to take into account the totality of effects that may occur, an entirely contingent and empirical matter that depends upon a host of factors that go beyond the single data point concerning the size of a single company. Although the standard reasons for examining corporations may be important, they are poor reasons for ignoring the other half of the economy.

Business is more than large publicly traded corporations. Business includes firms of many sizes and legal forms. So any account of *business* should identify all of these firms as a type of organization, a *business* organization that is structurally or functionally different from other organizations that are not seen as a business. Transaction cost theory, while often eschewed by ethicists, holds the promise of identifying certain economic elements that distinguish an organization as a business regardless of size. Given its stature and prevalence, this theory cannot be ignored in the quest to examine what business as an organization is. The next section explores this theory on its own terms; although there is much to learn from it, such a theory of the firm is not, in fact, a theory of business.

The theory of the firm—and business

A transaction cost theory of the firm explains the existence of "firms" in terms of how expensive it is to conduct all transactions within the open market. According to Ronald Coase, it is the existence of such transaction costs that explain the existence of firms (1937a). Broadly understood, transaction costs are the costs of coordinating individuals to complete a task in the market; these include, but are not limited to, the price of locating people, negotiating individual contracts, and the costs of ensuring compliance with those contracts.

To overcome these costs firms make contracts with employees to place them under the authority of managers who then may, within the limits set by the contract, order the employee to perform various tasks. This is why, for Coase, "The essence of the contract is that it should only state the limits to the power of the entrepreneur" (1937a: 391). Once the contract allows for discretionary authority—authority to allocate resources not based on prices but on the judgment of the entrepreneur or manager—the transaction is no longer within the market. By this reasoning even two people can constitute a firm if the contract allows for discretionary authority.

There is a problem, though, if the presence of discretionary authority, the "supersession of the price mechanism," (1937a: 389) is the hallmark of the firm. In fact, a focus on discretionary authority actually blurs the line between market transactions and transactions within the firm, since *every* contract between buyer and seller (not just employer and employee) embodies some form of discretionary authority. To see this let us consider two simple examples. In the first example you hire someone to clean your house. You stipulate each task, research the price for each task, sum these discrete prices, and offer a specific total price for someone to do those exact tasks; you then find a person who will do those tasks for that price. Allowing for the fact that those willing to do the work may try to negotiate, this example captures many of the costs Coase associates with market transactions and is a feasible example of what he considers a market transaction. Consider a second example. In this case you advertise for a cleaner, stipulating that only house cleaning is involved and perhaps other limitations to what you can ask of the potential employee. You go into the market and advertise, negotiate, and find someone who will do all those tasks allowed within the scope of the contract. Although the act of hiring the person is conducted according to the price mechanism, all future interactions involve you telling the cleaner what to do, thereby substituting your authority for price allocation. This latter example exhibits the nature of the firm, albeit in the limiting case of two individuals.

The problem these examples generate is that the nature of a task and of a price is not a given natural fact. With regards to the first example, it is doubtful that any task can be so completely described as not to require some direction outside of contractual stipulations. Contracts are always incomplete. Furthermore, it would seem that a contract would stipulate, in the case of ambiguity, whose judgment must be consulted. There are issues the contracting agent is free to decide on his own, and there are others that will require the decision of the principal. Take the cleaning example again: the meaning of the term "clean"—its operational implications—is subject to the judgment of both the principal and agent. Some areas may be so important for the principal that both principal *and* agent carefully inspect the agent's work to make sure the principal's standard is met. Such scrutiny, though, is not possible for the entire area being cleaned and in those areas it is the judgment of the cleaner that, effectively, prevails. Both principal and agent exercise discretionary authority over resource allocation. Even for market contracts, as represented by Coase, discretionary authority is present and hence there is supersession of the price system. Therefore, if discretionary authority is present in any contract, then by this account any contract constitutes a firm; however, if this is the case, then the presence of discretionary authority within contracts does not distinguish the firm from the market.

Coase posits discretionary authority as the defining element that removes contracts from the market and places them within the firm. However, as we have just seen, this does not provide a clear distinction between the firm and the market. Another possibility for distinguishing the firm from the market arises from the fact that all contracts are incomplete. Since all contracts are incomplete, principals must monitor performance to ensure contracts are executed in a manner that satisfies the principal's interests. Such monitoring, which itself is a transaction cost, is minimized (or reduced) if it is done within a firm. Therefore, it is argued, the firm exists precisely because it is the organizational means of ensuring contractual compliance. To focus on the subset of transaction costs related to ensuring contractual compliance is to work within the ambit of *agency* theory. If transaction costs are what separate the firm from the market, then it may be that agency theory's focus on the costs of compliance provides the defining feature(s) of the firm.

Oliver Williamson argues, like Coase, that transaction costs are the reason firms exist. Unlike Coase, though, Williamson argues that it is because of monitoring and enforcement costs that firms take transactions out of the market and place them within the firm (1975, 1985). The need to monitor and enforce contracts thus becomes the distinguishing feature of the firm. However, as we have seen with the example of the cleaner, the need for monitoring does not end at making contracts that supposedly take transactions out of the market. Agency theory steps in to argue that monitoring is necessary within the firm as well because agents still face opportunities to advance their own interests at the expense of the principal. Jensen and Meckling argue that "positive monitoring . . . costs will result in the manager of a corporation possessing control over some resources which he can allocate (within certain constraints) to satisfy his own preferences" (1976: 309). This is apparently why Joseph Heath calls business a "criminogenic" environment (2008, 2009): opportunities for cheating, theft, and self-dealing supposedly abound within the firm. On a slightly less criminal note, Armen Alchian and Harold Demsetz contend that it is the problem of shirking in teams that necessitates monitoring and the organization of the firm (1972: 782). Differences in interests between principles and agents give rise to the necessity of spending resources on performance monitoring and contract enforcement even within the firm. These "agency problems" are a particularly important subset of the transaction costs used to explain the nature of the firm.

Some business ethicists counter that agency theory, with its focus on contract monitoring and compliance, is a morally deficient conception of the firm. Critics argue that the agency problems postulated by agency theory arise out of the unwarranted assumption that agents are egoistic utility maximizers. "Agency theorists act as if all people are psychological egoists. They assume that agents will act on their own behalf rather than on behalf of their principals for whom they are agents" (Bowie 2013: 32, see also Ghoshal and Moran 1996: 17). According to Ian Maitland et al., "Williamson's market strikingly resembles Hobbes's state of nature" (1985: 61). Apparently, it is this incorrect model of human behavior that then leads to an incorrect, unethical, understanding of the firm.

Critics are correct that a utility maximization model of human nature is present within the agency theory literature. (For example see Jensen and Meckling 1976: 308). In fact, the assumption goes back much farther. In the business literature, Adolf Berle and Gardiner Means (1933) are often credited with the original observation of the divergence in interests between principals and agents because of the profit motive, i.e., self-interest. In philosophy the argument that everyone would cheat dates back as far as Plato's dialogue *Republic* with its tale of the Ring of Gyges. One of the interlocutors, Glaucon, tells the story of a Lydian Shepherd, the agent, who discovers a ring of invisibility he uses to satisfy his own preferences by assassinating the king, the principal, and taking over the kingdom. While Glaucon argues that nobody would do any differently than act like the Lydian Shepherd, we need not make the assumption of universal egoism for agency problems to be real. The ring is not imaginary, it is metaphorical. Master keys, computer knowledge, promotions to the executive ranks, and business trips all bring with them reduced monitoring and associated risks.

While there is a rich history of assuming agents are psychological egoists, the business ethics critique falls short of the mark and is not the real reason we should reject agency theory (or transaction costs) as the defining theory of the firm. The need for monitoring does not rest on everyone being a cheat. Human nature could be mostly "good" but it only takes a certain percentage of "bad apples" to hurt or ruin a business. Ghoshal and Moran, reach the same conclusion: Transaction costs theory "does not require that all individuals are so inclined, but only that some, sometimes, are" (1996: 19). Joseph Heath argues similarly that rationality does not require egoism, even if "agency theorists often do make unflattering empirical assumptions about individual preferences" (2009: 500). Egoism, Heath argues, is not the problem. Two altruists with different opinions of what constitutes the good would still face an agency problem. "[W]hat creates the need for incentives in principal–agent relations, strictly speaking, is not the fact that the principal and the agent have egoistic preferences, but merely the fact that they have *different* preferences (2009: 500, original emphasis). The conclusion that firms must monitor and enforce contracts requires only a reasonable assessment of interest divergence and a sufficient estimated risk of harm such a divergence can cause, not the universal assumption that human nature is necessarily cutthroat. Contract monitoring and enforcement are essential within the firm even without the morally dubious assumption of utility maximization. The real reason for rejecting agency theory (and thus the transaction costs view) as a defining notion of the firm lies elsewhere.

The tendency of some transaction costs theorists to focus on agency problems conveys the impression that preventing self-dealing is *the core* problem that defines business. The firm exists to monitor and enforce the performance of contracts. Even critics of these theories, like Heath, seem to subscribe to the notion that self-dealing is somehow a more urgent problem in business than in other walks of life. What philosophy shows us, though, is that this problem is not unique to business. Governments, nonprofits, and almost any human interaction present opportunities for acting on divergent interests. There is no empirical evidence to show that business organizations are any more "criminogenic" than any other organization. Business organizations may need to monitor agents, but for the same reasons so do non-business organizations. The monitoring of contracts neither distinguishes the firm from the market nor distinguishes business from other hierarchical non-business firms. Transaction costs as captured in agency theory do not provide the distinguishing characteristic(s) of business as opposed to other types of organizations and therefore should be rejected as providing an account of what a business organization is. The economic theory of the firm, therefore, is not a theory of business.

What makes an organization "business" is not a function of size, legal form, the presence of discretionary authority to allocate resources outside the price system, or the need to monitor contractual performance. In order to tell if an organization is a business organization we need to look more at the activities of the organization and what people do in these organizations. As Alexei Marcoux states: "Business firms differ from other kinds of organizations not principally in their organizational features, but in what they are organized to do—business" (2006: 57). We need to examine business as an activity.

Business as an activity

Rules and activities

Business exists because certain normative rules classify the actions that define the practice of business. For example, Joseph Heath argues that the principal–agent relationship is not simply an empirical matter, but must be defined in terms of who ought to be served and who ought to serve. "It is not clear . . . [that] the 'principal–agent' relationship can ever be normatively neutral" (2009: 505). Once the rule is set the proper action of who serves whom is defined. Legal theorist H.L.A. Hart makes the same point with respect to signing contracts: Rules concerning what constitutes a proper signature tell people how to write their name such that it constitutes the signing of a contract and not merely scribbling (1961: 28). Douglass North argues that institutions set "the rules of the game in society" (1990: 3) and thereby set the context of exchange and contract.

> A hierarchy of rules—constitutional, statute law, common law . . . —together will define the formal structure of rights in a specific exchange. Moreover, a contract will be written with enforcement characteristics of exchange in mind. Because of the costliness of measurement, most contracts will be incomplete; hence informal constraints will play a major roles (sic) in the actual agreement. These will include reputation, broadly accepted standards of conduct . . . and conventions that emerge from repetitive interaction.
>
> *(North 1990: 61)*

Rules, both formal and informal, determine what activities count as business, hence an examination of what activities constitute business is, in part, an examination of these rules. These rules do not exhaust the concept of business, but any examination of the nature of business activity is certainly incomplete without their examination.

Business exists within the market, and even if it may be regulated by a state it is not an institution *of* the state.[1] Business is an institution of the market. A market is not a place, it is a normative stipulation of the rules of a certain type of engagement.

> The market is where people go to buy, sell, truck, and barter. In short, the market is the realm of voluntary exchange. As such, coercion—the use or threat to use physical force to attain one's ends—is *definitionally* outside the bounds of market activity.
>
> *(Hasnas 2013: 286, italics mine)*

Markets exist because of a host of rules but two central rules for business are those concerning voluntary trade and property rights.

For an exchange to count as a business exchange it must be voluntary. We should not pretend there is an easy solution to the question of what counts as voluntary and what counts as coercive. Our purpose here is not to define the line between coercion and free choice. Rather, it is to identify that the existence of business depends on normative judgements, e.g., is the trading voluntary? Looking to law and to common language supports the claim that rules of voluntary trading are central in our discussions of what counts as business activities. For example, children are legally excluded from certain economic activities precisely because, prior to the age of reason, children may not be fully capable of giving voluntary consent. Similar concerns may apply to some adults. The condition of a person's mental state or that individual's external circumstances can affect the voluntary nature of trade. An undeveloped capacity to reason, emotional or psychological duress, or radically insufficient knowledge—for example, a situation in which one's options are severely limited—may reduce the sense in which one may exercise a genuinely voluntary choice.

The other central rule, or set of rules, defining the context of a business exchange is property rights. Trading in the market is not simply trading possession of a good or service, it is also trading a set of rights to the good or service in question. Sometimes rights are completely transferred such that the recipient may do whatever she wants with the purchase. Other times the transfer of rights is not complete leaving the seller some rights (e.g., leases), or reserving those rights to a third party (e.g., homeowners' associations). Either way, for a property right to be exchanged it must be legitimately possessed in the first place. No claim is made here about what the set of property rights must be, their origins, their philosophical justification, or whether they must be "absolute." The distinction we make here follows that of the philosopher David Hume: that there are property rights is essential for the stability necessary for markets, what those specific property rights are is another question (1998 [1751]: Appendix. 3.10). Property rights make clear who has legitimate claim to various goods and services and this sets the stage for who is permitted to trade such goods and services.

One serious challenge to property rules concerns unpleasant or harmful effects on third parties, "negative externalities." Pollution provides a classic instance of these externalities. However, purported secondary effects like crime, and even cultural shifts, can be the subject of discussion and debate on externalities and whether a specific trade, or the regime of trading, is entirely voluntary. Karl Marx and Friedrich Engels (1848) rue the effects of trading itself on society in general. In a different vein, Ronald Coase (1937b) discusses the problem of negative externalities and who should pay for them. While some negative externalities may be addressed through payments and clarification of property rights, it is not entirely clear that every effect of trade can be made voluntary. On the same note, it is not always the case that property rights can be clearly defined via philosophy or even determined by some empirical or historical facts of the matter—and yet a decision will still need to be made.

With both voluntary trades and property, the institutions of civil society will need to make decisions where facts and theories are incomplete. In business dealings, property rights will need to be settled, and exchanges will need to be judged voluntary or not. This is another problem for ethicists: these decisions will, in some instances, be difficult, even messy and, in other cases, seemingly morally arbitrary. As David Hume notes, when an appeal to public utility provides no clear answer to problems of property or trade,

> positive laws are often framed to supply its place, and direct the procedure of all courts of judicature. Where these too fail, as often happens, precedents are called for; and a former decision, though given itself without any sufficient reason, justly becomes a sufficient reason for a new decision. If direct laws and precedents be wanting, imperfect and indirect ones are brought in aid; and the controverted case is ranged under them by analogical reasonings and comparisons, and similitudes, and correspondencies, which are often more fanciful than real . . . and the preference given by the judge is often founded more on taste and imagination than on any solid argument.
> *(1998 [1751]: Appendix 3.10)*

The rules of property rights and what constitutes a voluntary trade will therefore consist of a host of historically contingent factors. Such a conventional account of business faces at least two problems. First, the rules of the market have fuzzy boundaries and will not always yield a definite conclusion as to whether a certain activity is actually business or not. Second, this account relies on real-world, historically bound, processes and decisions that at least prima facie may appear morally arbitrary. Those who argue that determinations of rights and value distributions must be ethical "the whole way down" will not be satisfied with this account as it currently stands. To the extent that this warrants further argument and discovery we agree, but abandoning these rules entirely would also entail fundamentally changing the practice and concept of business.

Producing a good or service for trade

Within the rules of the market, attempting to profit by producing a good or service for trade is business.[2] To execute an exchange the goods or services to be traded must be produced by each party to the transaction. How they go about producing and trading X is literally their business. A farmer who grows food just for herself is not trading and is not in business. If she gives away the food she is engaging in charity and if she is violating the rights of others in the process she is engaging in criminal activity. If she grows the food and then trades it with the intent to profit she is engaging in business.

Production of a good or service for trade is motivated by the desire to profit. The most basic formulation of this motivation is that each party to a trade expects to be better off as a result of the exchange. This point is captured by the historian Fernand Braudel:

> the merchant's problem remained the same: at the end of the day, the goods travelling towards him . . . had to fetch a price which would not only cover incidental expenses, purchasing price and transport costs, but also the profit the merchant hoped to obtain from the whole operation. If not, what was the point of risking one's money and peace of mind?
> *(Braudel 1982: 169)*

Luca Pacioli refined and advocated double-entry bookkeeping in Renaissance Europe because "the goal of every businessman who intends to be successful, is to make a lawful and reasonable profit" (1494: 4).[3] Given the universal adoption of double-entry bookkeeping, Pacioli seems justified in his claim.

Business activity seeks profit. However, intent without action is empty. It is not the intent itself, but the activities required by this intent, that define business. First, making a profit requires *doing* something. Profit, and loss, are not activities of business. They are the outcomes of doing business: producing a good or service for trade (Kline 2006, 2009). Second, the intentional pursuit of profit requires keeping track of inputs, outputs, and to whom they are owed—the practice of accounting.

Accounting is not a separate activity that is superimposed upon the activity of producing a good or service for trade. Accounting is constitutive of business, consisting of both tracking resources and recording who possesses the rights necessary for production and trade. These two aspects of accounting are what accounting historian Richard Mattessich (1989) identifies as the duality of accounting.

Tracking resources, the first part of the duality of accounting, is assessing how one's resources are depleted through costs and augmented through revenues. Whatever specific actions businesses choose, these actions need to be measured as to the impact they have on either costs or revenues. The tracking of resources

> expresses the one-to-one correspondence between an empirical event (such as a sale and purchase, or the transfer of goods and services from one department or process to another), on one side, and some representational scheme—be it a token accounting system of ancient Mesopotamia or a computerized matrix accounting system in the twentieth century—on the other side.
>
> *(Mattessich 1989: 78)*

As Richard Mattessich reminds us, we should not conflate "accounting" with modern double-entry bookkeeping. Merchants were keeping track of accounts using "single-entry" methods well before double-entry was developed. Accounting even predates writing. Through extensive archeological analysis Denise Schmandt-Besserat (1996) argues that prehistoric humans were keeping track of accounts using three-dimensional objects, such as tiny square blocks and cones placed in containers, to record what we now call credits and debits. Even double-entry accounting has its origins in earlier Arabic and Hindu business practices of which Luca Pacioli himself was aware (Gleeson-White 2012). Accounting is constitutive of business across both times and cultures.

Resources are always limited and the business person needs to know how to allocate them. With the first part of the duality, tracking resources, accounting collects and reflects diffuse information in a form that is at the heart of making business decisions. Without this information there is simply no way to know whether business activity is generating a profit or a loss. Tracking revenues and costs is epistemically constitutive of doing business, but it is only half of what accounting does. Accounting also keeps track of who owns what and this is the second part of the duality of accounting.

"The second kind of duality seems not so much to arise out of a physical transfer, but of the fact that every asset belongs to somebody" (Mattessich 1989: 78). Rules of the market require respecting the rights of others e.g., property rights and contractual obligations. "[I]t was the need to keep a record of goods sold on credit . . . which inspired the first account books" (Braudel 1982: 572). Business activity requires not only knowing the relation between revenues and costs but knowing the relationships between buyers and sellers, thus respecting property rights by recording who is owed what. Creditors and debtors must be accounted for. Contractual obligations must be paid. It is in the settling of accounts that property rights are ultimately transferred which then makes possible the further voluntary trading of goods and services. Knowing who owns what is not an ancillary activity of business, it is central to producing a good or service for trade.

Trading is a constitutive activity of business but trading is not the equivalent of business. To trade, potential trading partners must be sufficiently incentivized to produce and engage in voluntary trade. This expectation of gain requires knowledge of the costs of the good or service produced and how it relates to the expected gains from trade. One cannot record a gain, or a loss, if one does not know the initial baseline for judgment. If there is something called "business" that is distinct from "trading" one key difference is in tracking resources and their ownership i.e., accounting. Accounting as a constitutive activity of business is born out of the desire to gain, or at the very least not lose, from trade.

The intent to profit, and the distribution of profit, are contentious issues in business ethics, especially for stakeholder theorists. Based on the rules of property rights and voluntary trade, attempting to profit by producing a good or service for trade allows for the existence of a multitude of business organizations and practices. Such variation would include the possibility that in business organizations managers will have sole authority to determine resource allocation. It also includes the possibility that managers will have a fiduciary responsibility to maximize profits for the owners of the business.[4] However, stakeholder theorists argue that these are morally impermissible ways to conduct, and organize, business. The next section will argue that stakeholder *arguments* actually go one step deeper. To be consistent with their own arguments, stakeholder theorists should conclude that any theory permitting fiduciary obligations solely between owners and managers, and the managerial authority to execute those duties, are in fact not theories of business at all. It would follow, then, that stakeholder arguments that reject fiduciary theories of business would also imply that the historical development of formal and informal institutions has allowed an aberration to occur in the form of firms that uphold fiduciary obligations. In both theory and practice stakeholder theory seeks to redefine the scope of what we identify as business organizations and activities. Stakeholder theory is thus not merely an argument that some business activities are currently unethical, it is ultimately an attempt to redefine *the meaning* of "business."

Stakeholder theory, participation rights, and fair decision procedures

Stakeholder theory can be legitimately viewed and employed from multiple perspectives (Heath and Norman 2004). We cannot hope to address them all. Rather, the strategy here is to identify some elements of stakeholder theory that have a direct impact on the question, "What is business?" Since we have already identified the importance of rules and norms in defining business, a natural starting place is with normative stakeholder theory. Normative stakeholder theory has ontological as well as ethical implications for business activity.

One ontological implication follows from the denial of what has come to be called the "separation thesis." The "separation thesis" is "the view that matters of economic value are somehow distinct from ethical values" (Harris and Freeman 2008: 541; see also Freeman et al. 2010). Freeman argues "The whole point of the stakeholder approach is to deny the Separation Thesis" (1994: 412). On the stakeholder view, neither the concept nor the activities of business are morally neutral. Ethics is a constitutive part of what business is. Arguing against the separation thesis also comports with the argument of this paper: The rules that define the activity of business are not ethically neutral. Ethics is part of what business is. "Business" is not a morally neutral term. Normative stakeholder theory, in conjunction with the rejection of the separation thesis, is not just a theory about what business should do, it is an argument of what "business" is, or at least, should be.

Normative stakeholder theory is a story about the nature of business and value creation, but there is not just one such "stakeholder story." Rather stakeholder theory can employ different moral theories—normative cores—to adjudicate among the interests of different stakeholders (Freeman 1994: 413; 1997; Freeman et al. 2010: 213). Thus, stakeholder stories about business and value creation change depending on the normative core utilized. Stakeholder theory, though, is not neutral with regard to potential normative cores. The rules governing property rights and voluntary trade would be rejected as a normative core of stakeholder theory. After all, this normative core would yield the definition of business activity as producing a good or service for trade with the intent to profit. However, stakeholder theorists typically oppose this conception of business. There are at least two reasons why and both have implications for what constitutes business: profit distribution and managerial authority.

John Hasnas identifies two substantive normative implications of stakeholder theory.

> Managers of an organization do not have an exclusive fiduciary duty to any one stakeholder group, but rather, are obligated to ensure that the value created by the organization is distributed among all normative stakeholders and that all normative stakeholders have input into the managerial decisions that determine how the organization attempts to create value.
>
> *(2013: 52)*

Jeffrey Moriarty (2012) likewise identifies both a general distributive and a separate, but connected, procedural element in stakeholder theory. These elements cut across normative stakeholder theories regardless of the specific normative core. They also function as constraints on what can be in the normative core and thus as constraints on what stories count as business. We shall examine each in turn.

Procedure and stakeholder voice[5]

Stakeholder theory argues it is morally unacceptable for managers to make unilateral decisions that affect others in an enterprise that depends upon joint cooperation (Gould 2002: 13). The right of exit is morally insufficient. Stakeholders must have a substantive voice in business activities that affect them. In stakeholder theory voluntary contracts cannot be the "last word" in defining managerial authority. Some set of basic rights must carry over into the activities of business and delineate which voluntary agreements count as business and which do not. John Rawls identifies a generally accepted list of these basic rights in *A Theory of Justice* (1971).

According to Rawls, the first basic right is that "each person is to have an equal right to the most extensive basic liberty compatible with a similar liberty for others" (1971: 60). While this includes a right to private property, it also includes rights like voting and free speech. And while Rawls (1993) rejects the application of his theory to business, Moriarty (2005) counters that for purposes of justice the difference between business and the state is one of degree not kind, so that these basic liberties are applicable within business. Additionally, while some theorists directly refer to Rawls to make this same point, others do not. For example, Carol Gould argues that there is a "prima facie requirement of democratic participation" in business (2002: 13). Bruce Barry (2007) argues that free speech should be protected within a business, even when that speech is critical of the very same business enterprise. Stakeholders deserve a voice in business decisions because of this background of participatory rights. In stakeholder theory, political decision making is constitutive of business. The normative rules of the polity at large, not just the market, define what constitutes business activity. Business becomes a political arena where doing business *is* doing politics.

William Kline

Fair distribution versus negotiation

Concomitantly with participation rights in stakeholder theory comes the idea that a distribution of the value business creates must be "fair." Freeman and Evan (1990) and Freeman (1994; 1997) use a Rawlsian "veil of ignorance" argument to establish what would constitute a fair contract. Child and Marcoux (1999) argue that Freeman, and Freeman and Evan, fail to appropriately construct a relevant "veil of ignorance" argument for business and that their arguments fail internally. But if veil of ignorance arguments can still be generally applied to business, then specific arguments against Freeman and Evan leave the door open for other possible formulations and this is exactly what we see in the literature (Cohen 2010; Evans and Evans 2014).

Veil of ignorance arguments are a direct replacement, if not condemnation, of the very real practice of negotiation. Negotiation is a multivariable problem involving the preferences of both agents, knowledge about competing agents, information about relevant supply and demand, substitution possibilities, and a host of persuasive skills. The information, resources, and skills brought to the negotiating table will be asymmetrical and conducted under incomplete information. Central to a veil-of-ignorance strategy is removing all such specific knowledge of the decision maker's position in the world, leaving just a basic knowledge of social science and the basic goods of human life (Evans and Evans 2014; Freeman 1994; Rawls 1971). Since all specific knowledge is removed from the bargainers, they also have the same preference orderings. A multiple party bargaining situation is reduced to a single ideal agent parametrically deciding which rules secure those outcomes consonant with a purportedly rational preference ordering and a stipulated level of risk aversion. All human communication is removed from the process which is, in fact, no longer a bargaining problem.

The art of negotiating lays bare the communicative and interactive nature of actual business transactions. Bargaining requires the use of strategic rationality (Elster 1985), whereby agents realize how their own actions affect the actions of others. In bargaining situations, outcomes are determined by the joint action of all parties. In these situations agents must learn the rules of the game, the various possible outcomes, their own valuation of these outcomes, and the most likely preferences of the other bargainer in relation to these outcomes. In this process communication between contracting parties has a real effect.[6] Decision making behind the veil wipes this all away. Interestingly enough, standard game theory representations do so as well since they assume that both parties value the objective possible outcomes equally and that communication does not matter; this however is just an assumption akin to assuming that the firm's cost of discovering the market price is zero. However, in actual negotiations, getting the best deal means discovering the minimum my interlocutor will accept. This will depend on factors such as how wealthy or poor the person is, her related alternative options, and how well she negotiates. Information asymmetries are unavoidable since agents only have limited and dispersed knowledge regarding any economic problem they face (Hayek 1945). It is precisely the importance of these information and preference asymmetries in negotiations that unsettle many ethicists, and it is thus the fundamental nature of forming voluntary agreements that stakeholder theory and the doctrine of fair contracts attempts to replace. Choosing from behind a veil of ignorance is not, therefore, business activity.

Stakeholder theory correctly identifies that what business is and does is not ethically neutral. Furthermore, stakeholder theory argues against traditional managerial authority and an exclusive fiduciary duty of management to maximize profits for owners. Attempting to profit by producing a good or service for trade allows for, but does not dictate, such an organizational structure. Stakeholder theory, then, is in opposition to the definition of business advanced in this chapter. Furthermore, to the extent that rational and fair distribution of profits is advocated, stakeholder theory pits itself against the practice of business as it has historically developed. What remains is not so much a theory of business as a transformation of business into a form of ideal political theory. Freeman is correct to state that the current organization and practice of business is not meant to survive the implementation of normative stakeholder theory (Freeman 1994: 415, 418.). In fact, it is not clear that "business" is meant to survive at all.

Concluding remarks

Business ethics is about both business and ethics. Just as there are disagreements about what ethics is and requires, so too is there disagreement about what business is and requires. Focusing solely on the corporation is too narrow. Alternatively, transaction cost theories of the firm are too broad in scope, explaining why organizations exist but not telling us what business is. It is the activities of organizations and individuals that really define what business is. What counts as business activity, though, is at least in part defined by two institutional rules of the market: property rights and voluntary trade. Within this institutional framework, attempting to profit by producing a good or service for trade answers the question "What is business?" Business is the activity of attempting to profitably solve problems. Within the proper institutional framework, the activities of production, voluntary trade, accounting, and negotiation are constitutive elements of the attempt to make a profit from these solutions (be they in the form of a good or a service). The activity of seeking profitable solutions through trade will give rise to a multitude of business organizations including, but not limited to, those where residual earnings go to the owners and managers have a fiduciary obligation to maximize profits.

R. Edward Freeman claims that we need to (re)conceptualize this "value-creation" process (1994). In fact, the phrase "value-creation" is part of this reconceptualization of "business." While stakeholder theory continues to use the word "business" it is difficult to see how those versions that argue for democratic decision making and "rational" profit distribution resemble what has historically evolved as business. Instead, these versions of stakeholder theory posit a rationalist ideal conception of "value creation" to replace the historical and conventional practice of business as it has developed in the world.

Many would herald such a change based on a belief that a liberal institutional framework and the activities it permits are morally deficient. We should not forget, though, that rules concerning property rights and voluntary trade have evolved over the centuries in part to mediate ethical disputes. Furthermore, the activities of business require the exercise of a host of virtues we have not been able to examine here. Assuredly there are ethical critiques of the current institutional framework of business and not every business action is virtuous. Just because something has evolved the way it has does not absolve it from ethical examination and refinement. Still, arguing for a reconceptualization of business implies that we truly understand what business is in the first place. Given the complexity of law, history, and the massive diversity of actual business activities, claims to such a complete understanding should be regarded skeptically. On-going scholarship and research suggests our understanding of business is far from complete. Rather than reconceptualizing business, we would do better to deepen our understanding of what it is in the first place.

Essential readings

Essential works on transaction cost theory include Ronald Coase, "The Nature of the Firm" (1937a), Oliver Williamson, *Markets and Hierarchies: A Study in the Economics of Internal Organization* (1975), and Michael Jensen and William Meckling, "Theory of the Firm: Managerial Behavior, Agency Costs and Ownership Structure" (1976). Essential works on business as an activity include William Kline "Business Ethics from the Internal Point of View" (2006), and Alexei Marcoux "The Concept of Business in Business Ethics" (2006). Essential works on stakeholder theory include R. Edward Freeman et al. *Stakeholder Theory: The State of the Art* (2010), and John Hasnas, "Whither Stakeholder Theory? A Guide for the Perplexed Revisited" (2013).

For further reading in this volume on the firm as a set of contracts, see Chapter 6, Social contract theories. On agency theory and the firm, see Chapter 17, The contribution of economics to business. On motivation in business, see Chapter 21, Regulation, rent seeking, and business ethics. For a discussion of exchange and profit, see Chapter 7, Can profit seekers be virtuous? On the status and justifications of property rights, see Chapter 18, Property and business. For an account of accounting as a profession, see Chapter 31, The accounting profession, the public interest, and human rights.

Notes

1 The counter argument would be that under a system of state-owned enterprises, e.g., socialism, business would be an institution of the state. This counterpoint hinges on the extent to which business can exist without markets. The historic argument on this point is the economic calculation debate (Lavoie 1985). What we see today, though, is many state-owned enterprises firmly operating within larger markets. These state enterprises may be hybrids of some sort, if you will, but still subject to the observation at the beginning of this section: Any examination of even state-owned "business" is incomplete without understanding the rules of the market. It makes no difference to the argument at hand whether or not states create markets. Understanding business still requires understanding that market institutions set the parameters of what is defined as business activity.
2 "Produce" here is meant quite broadly as in "producing a witness." For our purposes, it is *not* a synonym for manufacturing.
3 Luca Pacioli (144–1517) was a Venetian mathematician who wrote *Particularis De Computis Et Scripturis* (1494), which both refined and advocated double-entry bookkeeping. It is because of Pacioli's work that double-entry bookkeeping was adopted across Western Europe, replacing earlier forms of single-entry bookkeeping.
4 Friedman (1970) is perhaps the most famous argument in favor of management's fiduciary obligation to owners.
5 A.O. Hirschman defines "voice" quite broadly as "any attempt at all to change, rather than to escape from, an objectionable state of affairs" (1970: 30). This chapter explores a subset of voice options dealing with direct stakeholder participation in managerial decisions.
6 As an example of how important communicating is to negotiation, and the very real impact it can have, see Babcock and Laschever (2007).

References

Alchian, A. and H. Demsetz (1972). "Production, Information Costs, and Economic Organization," *The American Economic Review* 62:05, 777–795.
Babcock, L. and S. Laschever (2007). *Women Don't Ask: Negotiation and the Gender Divide*. Princeton, NJ: Princeton University Press.
Bacon, F. (1620) [1902]. *Novum Organum*. New York, NY: P.F. Collier.
Barry, B. (2007). "The Cringing and The Craven," *Business Ethics Quarterly* 17:2, 263–96.
Berle, A. and G. Means (1933). *The Modern Corporation and Private Property*. New York, NY: Macmillan.
Bowie, N. (2013). *Business Ethics in the 21st Century*. New York, NY: Springer.
Braudel, F. (1982). *The Wheels of Commerce*, Vol. 2: *Civilization and Capitalism, 15th–18th Century*. New York, NY: Harper & Row.
Carroll, A.B. (1999). "Corporate Social Responsibility: Evolution of a Definitional Construct," *Business & Society* 38:3, 268–95.
Caruso, A. (2015). "Statistics of U.S. Businesses Employment and Payroll Summary: 2012," *Economy-Wide Statistics Briefs*. United States Census Bureau. Available at: www.census.gov/content/dam/Census/library/publications/2015/econ/g12-susb.pdf [accessed 08 December 2015].

Child, J. and A. Marcoux (1999). "Freeman and Evan: Stakeholder Theory in the Original Position," *Business Ethics Quarterly* 9:2, 207–23.
Coase, R. (1937a). "The Nature of the Firm," in R. Coase (ed.), *The Firm, the Market, and the Law*. Chicago, IL: The University of Chicago Press, 33–55.
Coase, R. (1937b). "The Problem of Social Cost," in R. Coase (ed.), *The Firm, the Market, and the Law*. Chicago, IL: The University of Chicago Press, 95–156.
Cohen, M.A. (2010). "The Narrow Application of Rawls in Business Ethics: A Political Conception of Both Stakeholder Theory and the Morality of Markets," *Journal of Business Ethics* 97:4, 563–579.
De George, R.T. (2015). "A History of Business Ethics," Santa Clara University, Markkula Center for Applied Ethics. Available at: www.scu.edu/ethics/focus-areas/business-ethics/resources/a-history-of-business-ethics/ [accessed 21 October 2016].
Elster, J. (1985). *Ulysses and the Sirens: Studies in Rationality and Irrationality*, revised edition. Cambridge: Cambridge University Press.
Evans, D. and G. Evans (2014). "Stakeholder Interests from Behind the Veil: A Rawlsian Approach to Ethical Corporate Governance," *Management and Organizational Studies* 1:2, 148–154.
Freeman, R. (1994). "The Politics of Stakeholder Theory: Some Future Directions," *Business Ethics Quarterly* 4:4 (October), 409–421.
Freeman, R. (1997). "A Stakeholder Theory of the Modern Corporation" in T. Beauchamp and N. Bowie (eds), *Ethical Theory and Business*, 5th edition. Upper Saddle River, NJ: Prentice Hall, 66–76.
Freeman, R. and W. Evan (1990). "Corporate Governance: a Stakeholder Interpretation," *Journal of Behavioral Economics* 19:4, 337–59.
Freeman, R., J. Harrison, A. Wicks, B. Parmar and S. De Colle (2010). *Stakeholder Theory: The State of the Art*. Cambridge: Cambridge University Press.
Friedman, M. (1970). "The Social Responsibility of Business is to Increase Its Profits," *New York Times Magazine*, September 13.
Ghoshal, S. and P. Moran (1996). "Bad For Practice: A Critique Of The Transaction Cost Theory," *Academy of Management Review* 21:1, 13–47.
Gini, A. and A. Marcoux (2012). *The Ethics of Business: A Concise Introduction*. Lanham, MD: Rowman & Littlefield.
Gleeson-White, J. (2012). *Double Entry: How the Merchants of Venice Created Modern Finance*. New York, NY: W.W. Norton.
Gould, C.C. (2002). "Does Stakeholder Theory Require Democratic Management?" *Business and Professional Ethics Journal* 21:1, 3–20.
Hart, H.L.A. (1961). *The Concept of Law*. Oxford: Clarendon Press.
Harris, J. and R. Freeman (2008). "The Impossibility of the Separation Thesis," *Business Ethics Quarterly* 18:4, 541–48.
Hasnas, J. (2013). "Whither Stakeholder Theory? A Guide for the Perplexed Revisited," *Journal of Business Ethics* 112:1, 47–57.
Hayek, F. (1945). "The Use of Knowledge in Society," *American Economic Review* 35:4, 519–30.
Heath, J. (2008). "Business Ethics and Moral Motivation: A Criminological Perspective," *Journal of Business Ethics* 83:4, 595–614.
Heath, J. (2009). "The Uses and Abuses of Agency Theory," *Business Ethics Quarterly* 19:4, 497–528.
Heath, J. and Norman, W. (2004). "Stakeholder Theory, Corporate Governance and Public Management: What Can the History of State-Run Enterprises Teach Us in the Post-Enron Era?" *Journal of Business Ethics* 53:3, 247–65.
Hirschman, A. (1970). *Exit, Voice, and Loyalty: Responses to Decline in Firms, Organizations, and States*. Cambridge, MA: Harvard University Press.
Hume D. (1998) [1751]. *An Enquiry concerning the Principles of Morals*, T. Beauchamp (ed.). Oxford: Oxford University Press.
Jensen, M. and W. Meckling (1976). "Theory of the Firm: Managerial Behavior, Agency Costs and Ownership Structure," *Journal of Financial Economics* 3:4, 305–360.
Kline, W. (2006). "Business Ethics from the Internal Point of View," *Journal of Business Ethics* 64:1, 57–67.
Kline, W. (2009). "Business as an Ethical Standard," *Journal of Private Enterprise* 24:2, 35–48.
Lavoie, D. (1985). *Rivalry and Central Planning: The Socialist Calculation Debate Reconsidered*. Cambridge: Cambridge University Press.
Ma, Z. (2009). "The Status of Contemporary Business Ethics Research: Present and Future," *Journal of Business Ethics* 90: Sup. 3, 255–65.

Maitland, I., J. Bryson, and A. Van De Ven (1985). "Sociologists, Economists, and Opportunism," *The Academy of Management Review* 10:1, 59–65.
Marcoux, A. (2006). "The Concept of Business in Business Ethics," *Journal of Private Enterprise* 21:2, 50–67.
Marx, K. and F. Engels (1848) [2002]. *The Communist Manifesto*. London: Penguin Classics.
Mattessich, R. (1989). "Accounting and the Input-Output Principle in the Prehistoric and Ancient World," *Abacus* 25:2, 74–84.
Mill, J.S. (1869) [1991]. "On Liberty," in J. Gray (ed.), *John Stuart Mill On Liberty and Other Essays*. Oxford: Oxford University Press, 5–130.
Moriarty, J. (2005). "On the Relevance of Political Philosophy to Business Ethics," *Business Ethics Quarterly* 15:3, 455–73.
Moriarty, J. (2014). "The Connection Between Stakeholder Theory and Stakeholder Democracy: An Excavation and Defense," *Business & Society* 53:6, 820–52.
North, D. (1990). *Institutions, Institutional Change, and Economic Performance*. Cambridge: Cambridge University Press.
Oxford English Dictionary. Available at: www.oed.com/ [accessed 29 November 2016].
Pacioli, L. (1494) [1994]. *Particularis De Computis Et Scripturis*, G. A. Jeremy (trans.) Cripps. Seattle, WA: Pacioli Society.
Rawls, J. (1971). *A Theory of Justice*. Cambridge, MA: Harvard University Press.
Rawls, J. (1993). *Political Liberalism*. New York, NY: Columbia University Press.
Schmandt-Besserat, D. (1996). *How Writing Came About*. Austin, TX: University of Texas Press.
Solomon, R. (1997). *It's Good Business: Ethics and Free Enterprise for the New Millennium*. Boston, MA: Rowman & Littlefield.
Solomon, R. (1999). *A Better Way to Think about Business: How Personal Integrity Leads to Corporate Success*. New York, NY: Oxford University Press.
Story, L. (2007). "Lead Paint Prompts Mattel to Recall 967,000 Toys." Nytimes.com. The *New York Times*, 2 August. Available at: www.nytimes.com/2007/08/02/business/02toy.html [accessed 21 October 2016].
Wayne, L. (2009). "Burden of Safety Law Imperils Small Toymakers," *New York Times*, October 31, p. B1.
Williamson, O. (1975). *Markets and Hierarchies: A Study in the Economics of Internal Organization*. New York, NY: The Free Press.
Williamson, O. (1985). *The Economic Institutions of Capitalism*. New York, NY: The Free Press.

14

The corporation

Genesis, identity, agency

Gordon G. Sollars

The term "corporation" has been used to designate any group of persons united for some purpose. Within the business ethics literature the term is sometimes used synonymously with the terms "company" or "firm" simply to denote an organization with a business purpose, with some authors explicitly highlighting ethical issues of such organizations without regard to their legal form (Hartman 1996). The modern business corporation[1], however, is a legally recognized organization with a class of investors (shareholders) who typically elect a committee (board of directors) that provides the highest level of management oversight for the activities related to the corporation. Investors' shares may be publically bought and sold, or "closely held" by members of the corporation (Klein et al. 2006). The corporation has become the dominant form of business organization (Hansmann 1996).

These features of the corporation make salient questions of identity and agency. Ethical issues concerning responsibility arise from the difference between collective and individual action. Is the corporation best thought of as a sort of single entity or as some aggregate of persons? If an entity, is the corporation a moral agent somehow separate from the persons who act on its behalf? To what degree may shareholders be held liable for actions presumed to be taken either by the corporation or by its directors or employees? This chapter will briefly outline the historical antecedents of the modern business corporation, analyze its identity as understood by current theories, and explore the sense in which a corporation engages in moral action.

Origins of the corporation

Historically, the general description of the corporation is that of an association of persons, treated in some legal respects as a single person. Members of a corporation were individuals united for some common purpose, be it religious, governmental, or commercial. This section begins with the early origins of the corporation as a device to deal with the interaction between a common purpose and property law, and continues through the addition to the corporation of the modern features of joint-stock ownership, shareholder limited liability, and general incorporation, each feature to be defined below.

Arguably, the need for something like the corporation arose from the first combining of associations with property ownership (Seymour 1903). Property held in common by an aggregate of individuals would, over time, tend to pass to heirs who might not hold the aims or purposes that motivated those in the original aggregate. Ultimately, ownership of the property by any individuals still sharing the original purpose would be lost. This concern was addressed by the understanding that it was the association itself, in some sense, that owned the property, rather than individual members of the association having common ownership.

The need for this understanding arises from the rules specific to common property, in both Roman civil and English common law, according to which each owner has an undivided inheritable interest in the common property. Another form of property, joint property or "property by the entireties," would have addressed the problem of dispersed ownership across persons without a shared purpose, but at the expense of creating a different problem. With joint property, an owner's property interest at death is absorbed into that of the remaining owners, so that a group of owners would retain control as members died. However, the rules for joint property traditionally required that all the owners take title at the same time; the attempt to include new persons as property owners would thereby transform the ownership from joint to common. Other forms of property besides common and joint are, of course, imaginable. Within the existing property framework of both Roman and English law, however, treating an association as an entity capable of property ownership in its own right was apparently less of a conceptual obstacle than the development of an additional form of property.

The English law borrowed heavily from Roman law with regard to the corporation (Seymour 1903). In Roman law, the idea of the corporation as an association of persons with a continuing existence not identical to its current members was applied in a wide variety of contexts: municipalities, religious societies, and groups of artisans. This same wide application was repeated centuries later in England (Seymour 1903; Williston 1888a).

Within England, the concept of the corporation was first applied to religious organizations (Seymour 1903). By the reign of King Henry IV (1399–1413), the idea was applied to municipal associations, perhaps driven by the governance requirements stemming from the increasing populations of cities and towns (Seymour 1903). In addition to owning property, corporations could make ordinances or by-laws (Anonymous 1702; Williston 1888a). By 1466 the corporate concept was being applied to trade guilds (Seymour 1903).

The continuing application of the same term to cover a variety of kinds of associations suggests that the distinction between "business" and "political" associations was not sharp. One of the first treatises on the corporation stated that the "general intent and end of all civil incorporations is for better government; either general or special." By "special government," the author referred to the "managers of particular things" such as trade guilds (Anonymous 1702). The label of "government" was appropriate because, e.g., guilds had the power to regulate the conduct not only of members but also of any person engaged in the trade in question. As corporations for commerce began being formed, they were created by a charter from the king or by Parliament that typically granted a monopoly over trade in a geographic area (Williston 1888a).

An alternative to the corporation was the common law partnership. The need for a charter from the king or Parliament made forming a corporation time-consuming and expensive; the partnership was formed by contract. The easy availability of the partnership form, however, was counterbalanced by other factors brought into focus because the partnership was not viewed as an entity but an aggregate of persons linked by contract. A partnership was dissolvable by any one of the partners, or by a partner's death, and each partner's actions bound the partnership as a whole. The issues raised by these factors were manageable when partnerships were small, but as commerce expanded, especially with regard to foreign trade, the need for capital grew beyond what a small number of persons could provide.

These new requirements for capital were met by the issue of "joint stock"[2] that could be purchased by investors, thereby combining the capital from potentially a large number of persons. Initially, the issue, or "subscription," of joint stock was for the life of a single project, with a pro rata division of profits at the end. The Royal African Company, trading by around 1660, hired its ships for each voyage, and was an instance of this initial practice. Later, the joint stock was subscribed for a term of years, as with the Russian Company, which owned ships used over several voyages, with old stock being sold to new buyers at the end of the term (Walker 1931; Williston 1888a). The use of joint stock was a method of financing not tied to the corporate legal form of organization, but also available to partnerships (Walker 1931).

One such joint-stock company, the South Sea Company, was a corporation chartered by Parliament in 1711, and it combined a trading monopoly over South America with a debt-for-equity swap of short-term government debt for shares of the company (Dale 2004). The value of the company's shares first rose spectacularly and then fell disastrously in 1720, which led to the appellation "bubble" being applied, first to the event and then to joint stock companies more generally ("bubble companies"). With the so-called "Bubble Act" of 1720, Parliament prohibited the use of joint stock by unincorporated companies[3] and adopted a policy of limiting access to incorporation (Harris 1994). As a result, few corporations were chartered during the eighteenth century, except for the building of canals (Handlin and Handlin 1945).

The policy appears to have had more effect than the legal prohibition. Although the Bubble Act specified harsh penalties for violations, there is a record of only one criminal prosecution under the Act during the eighteenth century (Harris 1994). With corporate status difficult to obtain, unincorporated companies raised the needed amounts of capital by issuing stock. Indeed, the term "joint-stock company" typically referred to an unincorporated company (Shannon 1954). These companies, strictly speaking illegal, were nevertheless applying to Parliament for the right to sue and be sued in the name of a company officer before the Bubble Act was repealed in 1825 (Shannon 1954), suggesting that these companies were widely tolerated due to their economic advantages. By 1825, when the Bubble Act was repealed, the total investment in unincorporated joint-stock companies has been estimated at between "£160 million and £200 million" (Shannon 1954).

Because partnership law was applied to the unincorporated joint-stock company, the substantial investment in these companies presents something of a challenge to the idea that limited liability is essential for obtaining investment by large numbers of persons who will have no active participation. By 1808 at least one company had 8,000 shareholders, and by mid-century there were about 1,000 joint-stock companies. On the other hand, the legal exposure of shareholders may have had little practical consequence given the procedural difficulties in bringing suit against large partnerships present in English law at that time, as each partner had to be named explicitly (Blumberg 1986).

Limited liability and general incorporation

Under limited liability a shareholder's financial liability for debts of the corporation is capped at the value of the shareholder's investment; assessments against the corporation can reach only those assets in the corporate name, not others held by the shareholder. The most common alternative, unlimited liability, applies to partnerships, in which debts of the partnership may fall on a partner individually and without limitation to the amount of his investment in the partnership. The availability of limited liability for members for debts of the corporation was not uniform. The English legal authorities Edward Coke and William Blackstone did not mention limited liability as a necessary element of the corporation (Blumberg 1986), nor is it listed as such by early treatises (Anonymous 1702; Kyd 1793) on the corporation. Some corporate charters expressly stated that their members were liable, while other charters expressly stated that members were not (Blumberg 1986). Authorities differ over what default rule for member liability applied. H.A. Shannon (1954), as noted previously, holds that the default was limited liability; Samuel Williston (1888b) argues that members of a company could be held liable for debts of a corporation, at least in courts of equity, if not courts of law. Interestingly, shareholders of railway companies, as a category, were granted limited liability from the beginning of the industry, perhaps because of the relatively large amounts of capital required, but also because of the recognized "public usefulness" of the railroads (Shannon 1954).

Attitudes began to change quickly, however, in the middle of the nineteenth century, perhaps because of the growing number of small capitalists. Between 1855 and 1857, Parliament passed the first legislation that allowed for general incorporation by simply registering a "memorandum of association" that stated the purpose of the corporation and whether liability was to be limited. Almost at once, incorporation with the certainty of limited liability was made easy to obtain (Shannon 1954).

Incorporation and limited liability in the United States

Incorporation was much more common in the US than in England. In the 20 years after the Revolutionary War, some 350 companies were incorporated in various states. Prior to 1809, corporate charters were routinely granted to companies involved in building canals, turnpikes, toll-bridges, and water supplies, as well as in banking and insurance, activities that required relatively large aggregations of capital, unlike manufacturing which at that time did not (Blumberg 1986; Dodd 1948). Some charters explicitly mentioned limited liability, but others were silent on the point. The default rule remains unclear, although there is evidence that shareholder liability for corporate debts depended on whether the charter granted the corporation the power to make assessments for additional capital against the members (Dodd 1948; Handlin and Handlin 1945).

A detailed understanding of the development of the corporation in the US during the nineteenth century is made difficult by several factors. First, incorporation was a matter of state law, and the various legislatures made changes to their laws of incorporation at different times (Dodd 1948). Second, at that time, shareholders did not initially pay the entire par value for their shares, instead being assessed for the remaining amounts over time; however, assessments could also be made by the corporation for amounts in excess of the par value (Blumberg 1986). Third, in addition to the two extremes of liability, limited and unlimited liability, there were regimes of double, triple, and proportional liability (Blumberg 1986; Dodd 1948).

The existence of proportional liability, by which a shareholder is liable only for that percentage of shares held in relation to the total shares outstanding, is particularly notable given later theoretical interest in this regime (Hansmann and Kraakman 1991; Sollars 2001). Proportional liability occurred in various state and business contexts during the nineteenth century, and was the law for all companies chartered or doing business in California until the early 1930s. The early enforcement procedure of shareholder liability allowed any creditor to sue any shareholder for the full claim, which encouraged the targeting of the wealthiest shareholders and proved unworkable. Over time, however, courts of equity developed the "creditors' bill" procedure, invoked on behalf of all of a corporation's creditors, where proportional liability was applied (Blumberg 1986).

The difference in timing among the states in the movement from unlimited, multiple, or proportional towards limited liability potentially constitute a "natural experiment" regarding the effect of limited liability. Although there are no detailed statistical studies for the 19th century directly on this point, general comparisons suggest that a state's economic activity was not strongly affected by the liability regime selected (Blumberg 1986). Both E. Merrick Dodd (1948) and Phillip Blumberg (1986) suggest, however, that the lack of effect was a product of the overall lower levels of investment in the nineteenth century relative to the twentieth.

Some states had some kind of general incorporation laws rather than the requirement for special charters as early as 1800 (Handlin and Handlin 1945). A majority of the states did not have general incorporation, however, until after the Civil War, and some industries such as railroads were not included. By 1875, however, almost no state required special charters (Hamill 1999). Incorporation came to be viewed throughout the US as merely legal formality rather than a constituting event. The availability of general incorporation has, especially in the latter decades of the twentieth century, promoted the idea that the function of corporate law is to simply acknowledge the identity of a voluntary association, rather than to bring into existence by special legislative action an entity existing only at the pleasure of the state. The nature of corporate identity is considered next.

Theories of the corporation

Theories of the corporation begin with a question of the nature of corporate identity: is the corporation an entity distinct in some sense from its components, or is the corporation an aggregate resolvable without residue into those components. As indicated in Table 14.1, below, entity theories may be further divided into those that view the corporation as an "artificial person," or those that take the corporation to be a "natural" or "real" entity of some kind. Aggregate theory looks through the corporation to its shareholders or, in the modern version, to all those individuals or groups that conduct transactions with the corporation.

As noted in the previous section, the artificial person theory appears in the earliest writings on the corporation. Edward Coke refers to the corporation as existing "only in intendment and consideration of the law" (Williston 1888a), and older treatises state that the corporation is "framed by a policy or fiction of law" (Anonymous 1702, capitalization updated), or is "vested, by a policy of the law, with the capacity of acting, in several respects, as an individual" (Kyd 1793, spelling updated). As such, a corporation can be given the legal right to own property in the same manner as a natural person. In addition to retaining control of property, the artificial person can sue or be sued using a single name, rather than the names of all the members, as would be required with a partnership. During the period that the Bubble Act was legally in force (1720–1825), joint-stock companies could not be incorporated, and such companies often asked Parliament for the right to sue and be sued in the name of a single company officer. Furthermore, the life of the artificial person can be made indefinite in length, and thus independent of the lives of any of the members, allowing for greater continuity than the partnership.

Table 14.1 Types of theories (of the corporation).

Types of theories		
Entity		Aggregate (includes "nexus-of-contracts" theory)
Artificial person (includes "concession" theory)	Real entity (includes corporation as "moral person")	

In the US, Chief Justice Marshall advanced the artificial person theory with his classic statement that, "A corporation is an artificial being ... existing only in contemplation of law," which has "only those properties which the charter of its creation confers upon it, either expressly, or as incidental to its very existence."[4] As noted previously, until the 1850s, in both the US and England, legal incorporation required in most situations a case-by-case action by the state. Further, incorporation up until about that time often included some grant of legal monopoly, and, before general incorporation statutes became the norm, corporate charters might list specific privileges and restrictions. Putative actions of a corporation that were inconsistent with the charter were deemed *ultra vires*[5] ("beyond the powers") and thus not legally actions of the corporation.

Against this background, within the artificial-person conception the term "concession theory" is often used to highlight that special privileges not available by contract are being granted by the state. The concession variant of the artificial-person theory explains how an association can be imbued with properties that partnerships, formed by contract, do not have. For example, while partners face unlimited liability for the debts of a partnership, the state may concede limited liability to corporate shareholders. The question of whether limited liability could be available by contract is considered below.

At the same time, Marshall's legal opinion may be read as giving support to a theory of the corporation as an aggregate rather than an entity. Marshall describes the corporate charter of Dartmouth College as "plainly a contract" among the parties, one specifying how property is to be used.[6] As general incorporation statutes widely displaced specific legislative acts of chartering during the nineteenth century, the artificial person theory, especially in its concession form, lost relevance. Thus, in 1882 Justice Field stated, "Private corporations are, it is true, artificial persons, but ... the courts will always look beyond the name of the artificial being to the individuals whom it represents."[7] The aggregate theory limited the power of the state to regulate a corporation, since such regulation fell upon the property rights of the contracting parties. Further, as incorporation became more available and charters less specific, the idea of the charter as a contract made possible a closer analogy between the corporation and the partnership, which had always been viewed as an aggregate of individuals.

Although the aggregate theory would return to have a vigorous life in the later decades of the twentieth century, the nineteenth-century version was supplanted by the entity theory. Morton J. Horwitz (1992) argues that, for various legal and economic factors, the analogy made by the aggregate theory between the corporation and the partnership began to break down in the late 19th and early twentieth centuries. In particular, Horwitz stresses the difference in liability between the partnership and the corporation after the middle of the nineteenth century, pointing to Chief Justice Taney's concern, expressed as early as 1839, over the (lack of) analogy. Limited liability seemed to some as logically connected to the idea of the corporation as an entity (Horwitz 1992). If general incorporation—the formation of a corporation without an explicit act of a legislature—made the concession theory implausible, perhaps the corporation was a real entity.

The idea of corporation as a real entity was the dominant conception in France and Germany in the nineteenth century, and was brought to the attention of theorists in England and the United States by Frederick Maitland's translation of a portion of a multivolume German text (Gierke 1913), which included an influential introduction by Maitland. The real-entity theory views the corporation not as a creation of the law, but rather as having an existence that may be recognized by law. The basis for the existence varies with the details of the particular theory. Arthur Machen (1911) argues that the corporation must have a separate existence from its components in order to explain its continuity over time. Harold Laski (1916) simply argues that "we are compelled" to treat the corporation as an entity, as reflected in language and legal decisions. In Otto von Gierke's view the corporation is a "living organism" (Gierke 1913: xxvi). Of particular interest in the context of agency discussed below are real-entity theories grounded in the possibility that the corporation is a moral person (French 1979; Maitland 1905; Phillips 1992).

Real-entity theory grew in influence during the first several decades of the twentieth century. John Dewey (1926) began an attack on the real-entity theory, however, arguing that the law need be concerned only with the consequences of attaching various aspects of personhood to the corporation, rather than with the logical implications stemming from the "nature" of an entity. This focus on consequences rather than on the articulation of a theory of corporate personality proved highly influential, undercutting most theorizing over corporate identity until the 1980s (Bratton 1989; Phillips 1994),[8] when interest in the aggregate theory returned through the influence of economics on the law (Coase 1960; Posner 1973).

Building upon the insights of Ronald Coase (1937), Armen Alchian and Harold Demsetz (1972) constructed a "team production" theory of the firm. In team production, inputs to the production process by team members create a joint product that is not easily separable into the contribution of each. Because individual contribution is hard to measure, each team member has an incentive to shirk, leaving the work to the others. This difficulty can be overcome if there is a party to monitor the production, and that monitor has the proper incentive if it can claim the residual amount of the joint product after all other input costs are paid. Because the monitor is the "one party who is common to all the contracts of the joint inputs," the firm is a "contractual organization of inputs" (Alchian and Demsetz 1972).

Michael Jensen and William Meckling (1976) endorsed Alchian and Demsetz's focus on contractual relationships, famously referring to the firm as a "nexus of a set of contracting relationships." Jensen and Meckling highlight the "agency costs" introduced when Alchian and Demsetz's unitary "monitor" is replaced by shareholders (with the residual claim) and a manager acting on their behalf. Jensen and Meckling argued that the problem of containing agency costs, present in all of the firm's contractual relations, not simply those involving team production, better explained the role of the firm.

Jensen and Meckling stated that they viewed organizations such as the corporation as "legal fictions," whereby the law considered an organization to be an individual, suggesting the artificial person theory. At the same time, however, they undercut the idea of the firm as an "entity" by claiming that trying to distinguish what was "inside" versus "outside" a contractual nexus did not make sense. In any event, legal scholars identify the "nexus-of-contracts" idea with the aggregate theory (Bainbridge 1997; Bratton 1989; Millon 1990). What is important is the content of the contractual relations among the parties, not the fictional nexus.

Margaret Blair and Lynn Stout (1999) present a team-production theory of the corporation, adding the idea of firm-specific investments to Alchian and Demsetz's earlier work. Firm-specific investments are costly commitments to develop assets, including human assets, for a particular use, such that their value would be greatly reduced in any alternative use. Team members will make these investments up-front only if they have some assurance that they will receive corresponding benefits from the greater production value the investments make possible, and not have their efforts exploited after the fact.

Blair and Stout argue that their approach is consistent with contract theory, but stress the problems that team members would face in trying to account for all aspects of their interactions by means of explicit contracts. Contracts that provide, *ex ante*, a fixed allocation of the joint production to each member will encourage shirking; contracts that provide for *ex post* allocation are subject to rent seeking, as each team member tries to get a larger share of the produced value. Seeing these difficulties, team members can give up control of the assets and production to a third party, e.g., a corporation's board of directors, who will allocate the corporation's residual value among the members. Given that the corporation holds the residual, their theory might be thought of as a kind of "weak-form" entity theory, rather than as a contract theory.

Corporate governance

Theories of corporate identity pay a role in issues related to corporate governance. The nexus-of-contracts theory is widely understood to support a shareholder-centric view for the corporation's directors. The contract theory identifies corporate law as private law, intended only to set the ground rules for the contracting parties, rather than public law, which could impose outside constraints, not simply on the corporation's conduct but on its internal goals and organization. A sole fiduciary duty of directors to shareholders is not essential to the contract theory, however, as it views such duties as "corporate assets" that can be "bargained for and auctioned off" to others (Macey 2014). The entity view can be used to support the idea of broader duties by the directors. If corporate law is public law, then the corporate entity can be structured to mandate a stakeholder-centric view (Freeman 1984).[9]

Theoretical fitness

The accuracy of contract view as a descriptive theory of law has been strongly questioned. A major issue is the status of mandatory rules in corporation law. State incorporation laws allow for great flexibility in choosing the initial content of the articles of incorporation. However, there are some default rules that cannot be altered, such as quorum requirements for voting by directors or shareholders, or that share votes cannot be sold apart from the sale of the underlying shares (Easterbrook and Fischel 1991). Since the parties to a contract may set its terms without being subject to third-party interference by the state, the presence of mandatory rules in state incorporation laws has led to arguments that the contract theory does not fit the facts (Bratton 1989; Brudney 1985; Eisenberg 1999; Gordon 1989). Defenders have argued that the mandatory rules are unimportant or should be made optional (Bainbridge 1997; Butler and Ribstein 1990; Romano 1989).

Limited liability for shareholders of the corporation presents another issue of fit, one with more direct normative implications. Although state law provides limited liability to shareholders, the advocates of contract theory maintain that limited liability could be achieved purely by contract. Thus, these contract advocates [contractarians] do not view limited liability as a concession granted to a corporate entity by the state, but rather see the body of corporate law as a "standard form contract" (Easterbrook and Fischel 1991) in which limited liability is one term. Having a "standard form" provided by law is simply a convenience that could be replaced by having corporate officers insert limited liability clauses into every contract with the corporation's creditors. Critics of contract theories, however, have argued that limited liability is the mark of an entity not an aggregate (Horwitz 1992).[10] With the partnership, the paradigm of an aggregate association, partners had unlimited liability for the debts of the partnership.

For voluntary creditors, the contract advocates can point to both theory and historical practice. The voluntary creditor has the opportunity to assess the financial status of a would-be debtor company, to adjust the terms of credit accordingly, and to decide whether to enter a contract or not (Posner 1976). Historically, since the Bubble Act prevented joint-stock companies in England from incorporating, such companies were subject to the law of partnerships. These companies began to routinely insert clauses in their contracts with creditors limiting the liability of the members to the amount already invested in the company, and such clauses were upheld (Blumberg 1986).

Not all creditors are voluntary, however. The tort victim makes no choice to interact with the company (corporation or partnership), and has a claim against it, not for the payment of debt, but for damages. Tort claims are satisfied from the assets of the company, but, if the total claim exceeds the company assets, partners are liable to pay the difference from their other assets, while shareholders have no liability.

Contract advocates try to account for this difference in the treatment of involuntary creditors in various ways. Some (Hessen 1979; Pilon 1979) attempt to dissolve the problem by arguing that tort liability should fall only on those who actively "control" a business, regardless of whether it is a corporation or a partnership. Frank Easterbrook and Daniel Fischel (1991) argue that limited liability is economically efficient, at least for corporations with publicly traded shares; their implicit premise is that rules that, on balance, enhance welfare should be adopted. Larry Ribstein (1991) presents versions of both of these arguments.

These claims are contested even by some who are broadly accepting of the nexus-of-contracts view of the corporation. Thus, Henry Hansmann and Reinier Kraakman (1991) argue that a rule of limited liability is not economically efficient for either the close or publically-traded corporation as compared with a rule of proportional liability. Most analyses of the merits of limited versus unlimited liability assume "joint and several" liability, where each shareholder is liable for the entire claim. Under proportional liability, although liability is not capped, shareholders are liable only for the proportion of the claim represented by their proportion of the total shares.

Vicarious liability may also be based upon the receiving of benefits as well as control. Pilon (1979) tries to undercut this argument by claiming that the corporation's benefit, its profit, is used to pay others ("creditors, customers, taxpayers") as well as shareholders, and so would not confer vicarious liability uniquely upon shareholders. This argument, however, misunderstands the economic concept of profit: profit is what remains after all other contractual or legal claims are paid. As the residual claimants, only shareholders have the possibility of unbounded gains. For this reason, Sollars (2001) argues that shareholders should have proportional liability for tort claims in excess of a corporation's assets.

Whatever the relative merits of these arguments regarding limited liability, there is a more serious challenge to the idea that the corporation can be, or, failing that, should be viewed strictly as a composition of contracts. This comes from a different aspect of asset protection than limited liability, one that, although present through history, has only been analyzed relatively recently. Figure 14.1 presents the situation using the terminology of "owner shielding" and "entity shielding" (Hansmann and Kraakman 2000; Hansmann, Kraakman, and Squire 2006). When the role of the firm is played by a corporation, the firm's creditors are unable to reach the personal assets of the shareholders; access is cut off by owner shielding. When the role of the firm is played by a partnership, the owners' non-firm assets can be reached. Limited liability is the paradigm case of owner shielding.

There is, however, a different kind of asset shielding, one that is directed not at the creditors of the firm, but at the personal creditors of the firm's owners. This is illustrated in Figure 14.1 by the term "entity shielding." With entity shielding, the owner's personal creditors are unable to reach the assets of the firm. Hansmann et al. (2006) argue that entity shielding is crucial to a firm being able to obtain credit. Without entity shielding, firm creditors face the risk that a creditor of any of the owners could disrupt the firm by pressing a claim that an owner might only be able to satisfy by means of liquidating her ownership interest. The corporation provides entity shielding to its shareholders since personal creditors of the shareholders are unable to reach the corporation's assets.[11]

Although owner shielding or limited liability is available to the corporation with regard to voluntary creditors, at least in principle, by means of contract, Hansmann et al. (2006) argue

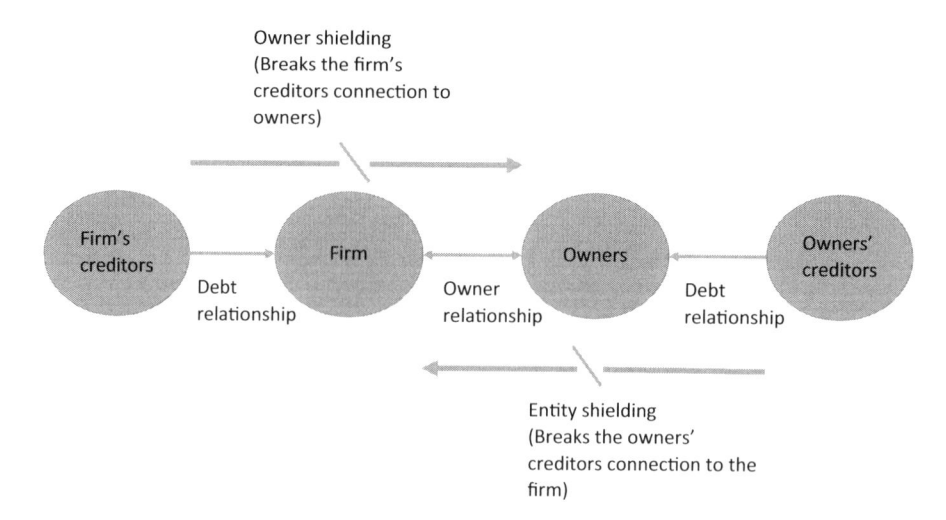

Figure 14.1 Owner shielding vs. entity shielding.

that it is not possible to obtain entity shielding by contract. The reason is not simply because the transactions cost of inserting limiting terms in all of the contracts that potentially millions of owners have with each of their creditors is exponentially greater than the cost of putting analogous terms in every contract between one firm and its creditors. More importantly, each owner has a temptation to free-ride by omitting the limiting term from his personal credit contracts. While the firm's cost of credit will be reduced if all owners ensure that the limitation term is in each contract with their personal creditors, each owner will individually obtain better credit from personal creditors by leaving out the term. This problem of collective action undercuts a potential firm creditor's belief that an entity-shielding term has been included in every contract the firm's owners have with their creditors. Hansmann et al. (2006) conclude that entity shielding must be viewed as a rule of property law, not available by contract.

Although this argument shows the inability of contract law to serve in principle as the sole foundation for corporate identity, it does not necessarily provide an argument for the real-entity theory. The corporation might still simply be an artificial person constructed by law. Arguments for the real-entity theory may be found, however, in discussions of corporate agency.

Corporate moral agency

Can a corporation be a moral agent? In particular, is a corporation morally responsible, or, at least, liable for "its" actions? Is it proper to blame or praise a corporation for its actions? The theories of corporate identity discussed above play a role in answering these questions. With the aggregate theory, actions that might be ascribed to a corporation can be ascribed instead without loss of meaning to various natural persons who make up the aggregate that is the corporation in question.[12] Any so-called corporate actions could be reduced without remainder to the actions of those persons. With the entity theory, a corporation itself acts, even if the actions of various persons are a necessary condition for that act. If the corporation itself acts, then it is at least logically possible that it can act morally (or immorally).

The possibility that the corporation is a moral agent seems to argue against the aggregate theory, and the artificial person (or concession) theory as well (Phillips 1992). Under the aggregate theory, corporate actions may be re-described as the actions of corporate directors, employees, or shareholders taken as permitted under the agreements or contracts that construct the corporation. Under the artificial person view, courts and legislatures may ascribe agency to various parties connected to the corporation with or without using a consistent moral underpinning. If a corporation is a real entity, however, then it is possible that it might take actions with moral import, which, whatever the law might say, cannot in fact be re-described as the actions of others.

Peter French (1979)[13] embraces a strong form of the entity theory with the argument that a corporation is actually a moral person. He argues that a corporation is a moral person if it has intentions that cannot be properly attributed to the biological persons who compose it. A corporation has an internal decision (CID) structure, combining policy and decision-making, so that "[w]hen operative and properly activated . . . accomplishes a subordination and synthesis of the intentions and acts of various biological persons into a corporate decision" (French 1979). Further, French contends that "the melding of disparate interests and purposes gives rise to a corporate long range point of view." Thus, a corporation may have its own intentions, and so be a moral person.[14]

Patricia Werhane (1985) endorses a weaker form, denying that intentionality is a sufficient condition for moral personhood, but accepting that a corporation is an entity that can nevertheless have moral responsibility.[15] For Werhane, the corporation performs secondary actions that result from the primary actions of moral persons, but these secondary actions are not simply reducible to the primary ones. Corporate actions are not the sum of individual actions because "of the anonymity of the individual actions, the ways in which each is changed through the actions of others . . . and the ways in which goals are interpreted at each stage of activity" (1985). Thus, a corporation could take a (secondary) action that is immoral, even though it results from a "series of blameless primary actions" (1985).

Manuel Velasquez (2003) rejects the claim that a corporation is a moral person, taking issue, for example, with the idea that a corporation is a "real individual entity," and with the claim that corporations manifest intentionality. Velasquez claims that arguments for real-entity status for corporations rely upon this premise: "(P1) If X has properties that cannot be attributed to its individual members, then X is a real entity distinct from its members" (2003).

This premise is false, he argues, because collections of objects X routinely have properties that do not hold for the members of X, yet we do not think that all such collections are entities. Even the property of a continuing identity over time is not enough for the corporation to be a real entity. Velasquez uses the example of a pile of sand replica of the "Great Pyramid of Cheops" that has some grains of sand carefully replaced so that its shape is retained. He states that, "clearly, the pile of sand is not an individual entity but merely an aggregate of entities" (2003).

The entity advocate might argue that Velasquez's "clearly" simply reveals a competing intuition. Such an advocate might reply that "clearly" the pile of sand *in the shape* of the Great Pyramid is an individual entity. After all, Velasquez seems to refer to the Great Pyramid itself as an entity, yet it might be described as "merely" a pile of blocks. The advocate is concerned not with *any* property of X, but with those properties that provide some structure to X, for example, French's CID, which are claimed to provide intentionality.

Regarding intentionality, Velasquez grants that intentions are attributed to groups, even in situations where the same intention cannot properly be attributed to members of the group. He dismisses this as metaphorical or "as if" intentionality. Thus, we may say that a car is "trying" to start or that a toy robot that continues to move its legs when stopped by an object "thinks" there is nothing blocking its path; but these are analogies, not a claim that the objects have "intentions and beliefs in any literal sense" (2003). The "intentionality" of corporate CID structures is no more literal than that of the car or robot.

William G. Weaver (1998) replies by taking the (metaphorical) bull by the horns, adopting a functionalist perspective. Relying on Daniel Dennett's (1987) idea of the "intentional stance," Weaver argues that corporations are complex enough systems to warrant ascriptions of the same sort of intention that we ascribe to arguably more complex human beings.

Velasquez claims to explain the attributions of intention to corporations without recourse to "ghostly group agents," "group minds," or "group intentionality" (2003). In his view, the burden is upon real entity theorists to prove his explanation incorrect. Velasquez claims that those arguing for corporate moral agency do so mostly through examples in which they argue individuals are blameless, yet something wrong has been done. When seen "with the eyes of an individualist," however, these same examples reveal individuals morally responsible for the wrong (2003).

Entity advocates need not, however, argue from the existence of "ghost agents" or "group minds." Nor are they committed to any premise like Velasquez's P1. The motivation behind their examples is the concern that a wrong may occur that is not properly attributable to any of the individuals who make up a corporation, yet the corporation is in some way "attached" to the wrong. Thus, Philip Pettit worries that failure to hold a corporation responsible may leave a "deficit in the accounting books" (2007) of responsibility. If the corporation is a moral agent, then responsibility for the residual wrongdoing that remains after all individual responsibility has been properly allocated may be assigned to the corporation. Moreover, the possibility would exist that, by holding a corporate moral agent accountable for such wrongs, their occurrence could be minimized.

When no individual moral responsibility may properly be assigned, Velasquez's (2003) response is that such incidents are simply cases of accidents, and the effects of treating them otherwise will be pernicious. Velasquez's own example is that of National Semiconductor, which the Department of Defense claimed had falsified records to cover up inadequate semiconductor chip-testing procedures. The company agreed to pay a fine, but not to identify any individuals involved. The CEO claimed that the responsibility rested with the company as a whole, although there was evidence that pointed to at least some specific persons. The acceptance of corporate responsibility thwarted the possibility of banning certain culpable individuals from working on such projects in the future.

The potentially bad effects of a theory are not, however, an argument against its being true. Entity advocates can agree that individuals may be morally responsible in such situations, and perhaps some individuals should have been held accountable as well as National Semiconductor. Furthermore, advocates can at least point to the possibility that if corporate moral agency is ignored, there is a "perverse incentive" to mask or attenuate individual responsibility in the way that the internal relationships of a corporation are structured (Pettit 2007).

Entity advocate M.J. Phillips (1995) reworks French's (1984) example of the Air New Zealand Mount Erebus crash. Phillips grants that in French's account there is actually no left-over corporate responsibility for the crash; in Phillips' re-imagining, each of several persons with some responsibility for informing the captain of Flight 901 of the changed conditions reasonably thinks that one of the others will do so. Apparently, then, the crash could have resulted from the interactions of various persons in the corporation, but no individual was responsible. Phillips notes, however, that such a situation of individuals with overlapping responsibilities is the result of the organization's design, which, in turn, is attributable to some individuals. These individuals could suffer from the same kinds of excusing factors, e.g., "group think" and "risky-shift" (Phillips 1995) in the design activities that absolve the operations personnel from individual responsibility. If justifiable ignorance by persons responsible for an organization's design may be excused from responsibility, why would it not excuse the corporation as well?

Phillips's answer is that, if the corporation is an entity, then, given its network structure and information processing power, it can and should be held to a higher standard than individuals (1995). The problem with this claim is that the very cases Phillips wants to point to are those in which the corporation failed to foresee the consequences. Why is this evidence of corporate responsibility rather than evidence that, even with the "superhuman intelligence" (1995) of a corporation, the event was not foreseeable? Why should human beings, with their limited intelligence, believe that they can set the parameters of foreseeability for a super intelligence?[16] In hindsight, of course, even ordinary human intelligence might see that a design change in the organization would have prevented some wrong. That the needed change was missing, however, is some evidence that the corporate "superintelligence," as it was in fact structured, was not sufficient to foresee the problem. Perhaps corporations are entities with superintelligence, but our own limited intelligence leaves us without a way to determine a foreseeability criterion for their responsibility.

After his own detailed recounting of this decades-long debate, John Hasnas (2012) attempts to cut through the metaphysical knot of corporate moral responsibility by asking the pragmatic question of what purpose is served by attributing moral responsibility to a corporation. Hasnas argues that the reason must be in order to justify some kind of punishment. In punishing a corporation, however, we engage in collective punishment. As the prosecution of Arthur Anderson makes clear, the vast majority of the accounting firm's employees suffered for an incident over which they had only the most tenuous connection. Hasnas sees corporate punishment, whether imposed to enhance corporate self-regulation or to denounce wrongdoing as violating the liberal Kantian principle that individuals may not be used merely as a means (2012).

Hasnas' attempt to refocus the debate using the firm anchor of a shared Kantian insight might flounder, however, for Pettit (2007) seems quite willing to contemplate the propriety of collective punishment.[17] Pettit distinguishes between making a proper ascription of moral responsibility to a person and punishing the person; his primary concern is with the degree of responsibility that is appropriate to attribute to a corporation rather than how it would be best punished. Thus, he holds that, retributivism is a "backward looking" doctrine "that bears primarily on when someone is fit to be held responsible in criminal law," while consequentialism is a "forward-looking" doctrine of "how someone who is fit to be held responsible should be sanctioned" (2007). Arguably, then, despite Hasnas' claim that the purpose of acknowledging corporate moral responsibility is to justify corporate punishment, Pettit might be seen as trying to properly account for the existence of a moral responsibility that is not exhausted by individual responsibility.

Pettit seems at places, however, to ignore his own distinction. He argues that even when there is no "deficit" in the total responsibility account to be filled by a corporate entity, there is reason to hold corporations responsible because of the "perverse incentive" mentioned above. However, such a concern is forward looking, undercutting a claim that his argument is only to establish the proper ascription of moral responsibility. Furthermore, Pettit stresses the importance of a forward looking "developmental rationale" (2007) that would prompt individuals to form a group in order that corporate responsibility could be properly applied.

Some other recent attempts to establish corporate moral responsibility include a "political" theory (Dubbink and Smith 2010) and a "non-agency" theory (Dempsey 2013). Wim Dubbink and Jeffery Smith (2010) argue for what they call a political account of corporate moral responsibility, based upon the need to maintain social coordination in a global business context where governmental regulation is ineffective. They view corporations as "administers of duty" that are capable of voluntarily incorporating moral principles into their decision making. Dubbink and Smith call their argument pragmatic, claiming to sidestep the contentious issue of whether a corporation can meet the requirements typically taken as necessary for individual moral responsibility.

At key points in their argument, however, they rely upon the idea that a CID—a corporation's internal decision structure—provides the corporation with the ability to act on reasons, to act voluntarily, and to exercise a (limited) form of self-governance. The problem with these claims is that an opponent of corporate moral responsibility, such as Velasquez, would deny that the CID provides such capabilities to an entity, but rather is a description of rules governing individual interactions. Without facing a direct argument for the existence of a corporate entity, the opponent can deny any "deficit" in moral responsibility that requires corporate moral responsibility.

James A. Dempsey (2013) denies that the corporation is an intentional agent, but holds nevertheless that moral responsibility may properly be ascribed to it. He argues that "non-agential moral responsibility" may be ascribed to a corporation when it is sufficiently complex to generate a "remainder" responsibility over and above any individual responsibility. As noted above, however, remainder responsibility may be countered by the claim that a wrong was simply accidental, or that we lack the intelligence needed to specify a criterion of foreseeability for a corporation.

Dempsey claims that for some specific corporate rule it could be "impossible to determine . . . how given individuals should be held responsible for its existence and operation" (2013: 342). Unfortunately, the relation intended between "impossible" and "should" seems unclear. On the one hand, a given individual "should" be held responsible by actually holding him responsible; this cannot be impossible generally. On the other hand, the epistemic impossibility in some cases of determining which individuals had the responsibility does not imply that those unknown individuals do not bear all of the responsibility without remainder.

Concluding remarks

The initial concept of the corporation was a solution to the problem of how to retain property for some purposeful use over time. Recent scholarship has refined this idea by introducing the concepts of owner shielding, whereby a shareholder's personal assets are protected from claims by corporate creditors, and entity shielding, whereby the corporation's assets are protected from claims by a shareholder's creditors. Analysis of the origins of the modern corporation suggest that the owner shielding provided by limited liability may not be a necessary feature of the corporation, but debate continues (Grundfest 1992; Hansmann and Kraakman 1992). Additional research concerning proportional liability might be helpful; this author is aware of only one historical analysis of the California situation (Weinstein 2005).

Regarding the debate between aggregate and real entity theories, although the aggregate theory, through the nexus-of-contracts concept, has arguably become the dominant view, the need for entity shielding has highlighted a crucial aspect of the corporation that is not contractual in nature. As for the matter of corporate governance, the team production theory of the corporation presents an exciting possibility for reconciling the shareholder-centric view of the corporation with the idea of increased discretion for board directors that is often associated with the stakeholder view. If director discretion increases the total value of a corporation by enticing more firm-specific investment, shareholders might prefer, somewhat paradoxically, that directors not have a shareholder-centric view.

No similar breakthrough seems near regarding the debate over corporate moral responsibility. Questions concerning the conditions for determining moral agency implicate basic philosophical disagreements over the nature of entities and actions that research in business ethics alone seems unlikely to settle.

Suggested readings

There is no single work that presents a history of the corporation from its genesis in ancient times to the present; the interested reader must focus on specific periods or topics. Standard references that treat aspects of the early corporation are E.B. Seymour, "The Historical Development of the Common-Law Conception of a Corporation" (1903), and Samuel Williston, "History of the Law of Business Corporations before 1800" (1888a). The English Bubble Act is analyzed in a paper by Ron Harris "The Bubble Act: Its Passage and Its Effects on Business Organization" (1994), and a book-length discussion is given by Richard Dale, *The First Crash* (2004). Phillip Blumberg, "Limited Liability and Corporate Groups" (1986), provides a comprehensive introduction to the history of limited liability in both England and the United States.

Readers interested in theories of corporate identity can begin with M.J. Phillips, "Corporate Moral Personhood and Three Conceptions of the Corporation" (1992). This essay combines ethical and legal perspectives in contrasting the artificial entity (or concession), real entity, and aggregate theories, while making clear Phillips' preference for the real entity theory. The most influential statement of the real entity theory is given by Peter A. French, "The Corporation as a Moral Person" (1979). The starting point for the contemporary aggregate theory is the seminal "nexus-of-contracts" article by Michael Jensen and William Meckling, "Theory of the Firm: Managerial Behavior, Agency Costs and Ownership Structure" (1976). Their treatment is difficult for the non-economist, but more accessible discussions of the aggregate theory are given by Roger Pilon, "Corporations and Rights: On Treating Corporate People Justly" (1979), and William W. Bratton, "The 'Nexus of Contracts' Corporation" (1989).

Reading in corporate moral agency should begin with Peter A. French, *Collective and Corporate Responsibility* (1984) or "The Corporation as a Moral Person" (1979), which present the corporation as a fully-fledged moral agent, consistent with his view of the corporation as an entity with intentions. In *Persons, Rights, and Corporations* (1985), Patricia Werhane argues that the corporation is an entity with moral responsibility. Manuel Velasquez, in "Debunking Corporate Moral Responsibility" (2003), challenges the claim that corporations are entities with intentions. For aggregate theories that resolve ascriptions of corporate responsibility into those of natural persons, see Robert Hessen, *In Defense of the Corporation* (1979), and Roger Pilon "Corporations and Rights" (1979).

For further reading in this volume on philosophical justifications of property, see Chapter 18, Property and business. On the legal structures of non-profit corporations and corporations with a social mission, see Chapter 15, Alternative business organizations and social enterprise. On divergent views of the corporation and its relations to social responsibility, see Chapter 10, Social responsibility. On the nature of business, see Chapter 13, What is business?

Notes

1 Space allows for only a description of the business corporation as it developed in England and the US.
2 Walker (1931) suggests that the term stems from the practice of requiring guild members, beginning shortly after the Norman Conquest, to share purchases of goods with each other, paying out a common or joint fund.
3 This prohibition may seem unusual, given that the South Sea Company was itself incorporated. What has come to be called the "Bubble Act," however, was passed by Parliament shortly before the crash, apparently largely through the lobbying efforts of the directors of the South Sea Company, who were concerned that the proliferation of unincorporated joint-stock companies would adversely affect the company's ability to raise additional capital (Harris 1994).
4 *The Trustees of Dartmouth College* v. *Woodward*, 17 US.518, 636 (1819).

5 Under the *ultra vires* doctrine a corporation could not take actions outside the scope of its charter. See, for example, Horwitz (1992).
6 *The Trustees of Dartmouth College*, 17 US at 643.
7 The Railroad Tax Cases: *County of San Mateo v. Southern Pacific R. Co.*, 13 F. 722, 743–44 (1882).
8 Bratton (1989) holds that until late in the twentieth century the accepted doctrine used either the entity or aggregate theories depending on the "facts of the situation," which is consistent with Dewey's (1926) analysis.
9 Note, however, that Freeman (1984) argues that this viewpoint should be adopted voluntarily by corporate management.
10 Some contract advocates (Hessen 1979; Ribstein 1991) argue specifically against the concession theory. Even if limited liability is available by contract, however, some other version of the entity theory could be correct.
11 A shareholder's creditor might be able to obtain the owner's shares, but reaching corporate assets would require obtaining at least a majority of the shares.
12 One potential complication is that the identity of the persons who took the action(s) described as a "corporate act" could be unknown, either initially or after considerable investigation. Such a situation might legitimize talk of blaming a corporation (Pfeiffer 1995). A through-going proponent of an aggregate theory, however, could simply refer to "persons unknown who are members of the corporation."
13 Partially in response to the criticisms that follow, French (1995) has modified his theory, and in later work refers to corporations as moral actors or agents rather than persons.
14 Ladd (1970) had previously argued that corporations could form intentions, but denied that their structure allowed them to form moral intentions.
15 Donaldson (1982) takes a similar position.
16 Hayek calls the idea that all the relevant facts could be known to one mind the "synoptic delusion" (Hayek 1973, 14–15).
17 Pettit (2007) states that "ascribing group responsibility will be all the more powerful, of course, if the ascription of guilt is attended by a penal sanction of some kind."

References

Alchian, A.A. and H. Demsetz (1972). "Production, Information Costs and Economic Organization," *The American Economic Review* 62:5, 777–95.

Anonymous (1702). *The Law of Corporations: Containing the Laws and Customs of all the Corporations and Inferior Courts of Record in England*. London: The assigns of Richard and Edward Atkins.

Bainbridge, S.M. (1997). "Community and Statism: A Conservative Contractarian Critique of Progressive Corporate Law Scholarship," *Cornell Law Review* 82, 856–904.

Blair, M.M. and L.A. Stout (1999). "A Team Production Theory of Corporate Law," *Virginia Law Review* 85, 247–328.

Blumberg, P.I. (1986). "Limited Liability and Corporate Groups," *The Journal of Corporation Law* 11 (Summer), 573–631.

Bratton, W.W. (1989). "The 'Nexus of Contracts' Corporation: A Critical Appraisal," *Cornell Law Review* 74, 407–465.

Brudney, V. (1985). "Corporate Governance, Agency Costs, and the Rhetoric of Contract," *Columbia Law Review* 85, 1403–1444.

Butler, H.N. and L.E. Ribstein (1990). "Opting Out of Fiduciary Duties: A Response to the Anti-Contractarians," *Washington Law Review* 65, 1–72.

Coase, R. (1937). "The Nature of the Firm," *Economica* 4, 386–405.

Coase, R. (1960). "The Problem of Social Cost," *Journal of Law and Economics* 3, 1–44.

Dale, R. (2004). *The First Crash: Lessons from the South Sea Bubble*. Princeton, NJ: Princeton University Press.

Dempsey, J. (2013). "Corporations and Non-Agential Moral Responsibility," *Journal of Applied Philosophy* 30:4, 334–350.

Dennett, D.C. (1987). *The Intentional Stance*. Cambridge, MA: MIT Press.

Dewey, J. (1926). "The Historic Background of Corporate Legal Personality," *The Yale Law Journal* 35:6, 655–73.

Dodd, E.M. (1948). "The Evolution of Limited Liability in American Industry: Massachusetts," *Harvard Law Review* 61, 1351–1379.

Donaldson, T. (1982). *Corporations and Morality*. Englewood Cliffs, NJ: Prentice-Hall.
Dubbink, W. and Smith, J. (2010). "A Political Account of Corporate Responsibility," *Ethical Theory and Moral Practice* 14, 223–246.
Easterbrook, F.H. and D.R. Fischel (1991). *The Economic Structure of Corporate Law*. Cambridge, MA: Harvard University Press.
Eisenberg, M.A. (1999). "The Conception that the Corporation is a Nexus of Contracts," *Iowa Journal of Corporation Law* 24, 819–36.
Freeman, R.E. (1984). *Strategic Management: A Stakeholder Approach*, E.M. Epstein (ed.), Pitman Series in Business and Public Policy. Boston, MA: Pitman Publishing Inc.
French, P.A. (1979). "The Corporation as a Moral Person," *American Philosophical Quarterly* 16:3, 207–15.
French, P.A. (1984). *Collective and Corporate Responsibility*. New York, NY: Columbia University Press.
French, P.A. (1995). *Corporate Ethics*. Fort Worth, TX: Harcourt Brace College Publishers.
Gierke, O. (1913). *Political Theories of the Middle Age*, Frederick W. Maitland (trans.). London: Cambridge University Press. Original edition 1900, reprint 1913.
Gordon, J.N. (1989). "The Mandatory Structure of Corporate Law," *Columbia Law Review* 89, 1549–99.
Grundfest, J.A. (1992). "The Limited Future of Unlimited Liability: A Capital Markets Perspective," *Yale Law Journal* 102, 387–425.
Hamill, S.P. (1999). "From Special Privilege to General Utility: A Continuation of Willard Hurst's Study of Corporations," *American University Law Reivew* 49, 81–180.
Handlin, O. and M.F. Handlin (1945). "Origins of the American Business Corporation," *Journal of Economic History* 5:1, 1–23.
Hansmann, H. (1996). *The Ownership of Enterprise*. Cambridge, MA: Belknap Press.
Hansmann, H. and R. Kraakman (1991). "Toward Unlimited Shareholder Liability for Corporate Torts," *Yale Law Journal* 100, 1879–1934.
Hansmann, H. and R. Kraakman (1992). "Do the Capital Markets Compel Limited Liability? A Response to Professor Grundfest," *Yale Law Journal on Regulation* 102, 427–436.
Hansmann, H. and R. Kraakman (2000). "The Essential Role of Organizational Law," *Yale Law Journal* 110, 387–440.
Hansmann, H., R. Kraakman, and R. Squire (2006). "Law and the Rise of the Firm," *Harvard Law Review* 119, 1333–1403.
Harris, R. (1994). "The Bubble Act: Its Passage and Its Effects on Business Organization," *The Journal of Economic History* 54:3, 610–627.
Hartman, E.M. (1996). *Organizational Ethics and the Good Life*, R. Edward Freeman (ed.), The Ruffin Series in Business Ethics. New York, NY: Oxford University Press.
Hasnas, J. (2012). "Reflections on Corporate Moral Responsibility and the Problem Solving Technique of Alexander the Great," *Journal of Business Ethics* 107, 183–195.
Hayek, F.A. (1973). *Law, Legislation and Liberty*, Vol. 1, *Rules and Order*. Chicago, IL: The University of Chicago Press.
Hessen, R. (1979). *In Defense of the Corporation*. Stanford, CA: Hoover Institution Press.
Horwitz, M.J. (1992). *The Transformation of American Law, 1870–1960: The Crisis of Legal Orthodoxy*. New York, NY: Oxford University Press.
Jensen, M. and W. Meckling (1976). "Theory of the Firm: Managerial Behavior, Agency Costs and Ownership Structure," *The Journal of Financial Economics* 3, 305–60.
Klein, W.A., J.M. Ramseyer, and S.M. Bainbridge (2006). *Business Associations*. New York, NY: Foundation Press.
Kyd, S. (1793). *A Treatise on the Law of Corporations*, 2 vols, Vol. 1. London: Printed for J. Butterworth.
Ladd, J. (1970). "Morality and the Ideal of Rationality in Formal Organizations," *The Monist* 54:4, 488–516.
Laski, H.J. (1916). "The Personality of Associations," *Harvard Law Review* 29:4, 404–26.
Macey, J.R. (2014). "Corporate Social Responsibility: A Law & Economics Perspective," *Chapman Law Review* 17, 331–353.
Machen, A.W. (1911). "Corporate Personality," *Harvard Law Review* 24:4, 253–67.
Maitland, F.W. (1905). "Moral Personality and Legal Personality," *Journal of the Society of Comparative Legislation* 6:2, 192–200.
Millon, D. (1990). "Theories of the Corporation," *Duke Law Journal* 39:2, 210–262.
Pettit, P. (2007). "Responsibility Incorporated," *Ethics* 117 (January), 171–201.
Pfeiffer, R.S. (1995). *Why Blame the Organization?: A Pragmatic Analysis of Collective Moral Responsibility*. Lanham, MD: Littlefield Adams Books.

Phillips, M.J. (1992). "Corporate Moral Personhood and Three Conceptions of the Corporation," *Business Ethics Quarterly* 2:4, 435–459.

Phillips, M.J. (1994). "Reappraising the Real Entity Theory of the Corporation," *Florida State University Law Review* 21, 1061–1123.

Phillips, M.J. (1995). "Corporate Moral Responsibility: When It Might Matter," *Business Ethics Quarterly* 5:3, 555–576.

Pilon, R. (1979). "Corporations and Rights: On Treating Corporate People Justly," *Georgia Law Review* 13 (Summer), 1245–1370.

Posner, R. (1973). *Economic Analysis of Law*, 1st edition. Boston, MA: Little Brown.

Posner, R.A. (1976). "The Rights of Creditors of Affiliated Corporations," *University of Chicago Law Review* 43 (Spring), 499–526.

Ribstein, L.E. (1991). "Limited Liability and Theories of the Corporation," *Maryland Law Review* 50, 80–130.

Romano, R. (1989). "Answering the Wrong Question: the Tenuous Case for Mandatory Corporate Laws," *Columbia Law Review* 89, 1599–1618.

Seymour, E.B. (1903). "The Historical Development of the Common-Law Conception of a Corporation," *The American Law Register* 51:9, 529–51.

Shannon, H.A. (1954). "The Coming of General Limited Liability," in E.M. Carus-Wilson (ed.) *Essays in Economic History*. London: Edward Arnold, 358–379.

Sollars, G.G. (2001). "An Appraisal of Shareholder Proportional Liability," *Journal of Business Ethics* 32, 329–345.

The Trustees of Dartmouth College v. Woodward (1819). United States Supreme Court, 17 US.518, 636.

Velasquez, M. (2003). "Debunking Corporate Moral Responsibility," *Business Ethics Quarterly* 13:4, 531–562.

Walker, C.E. (1931). "The History of the Joint Stock Company," *The Accounting Review* 6:2, 97–105.

Weaver, W.G. (1998). "Corporations as Intentional Systems," *Journal of Business Ethics* 17, 87–97.

Weinstein, M.I. (2005). " Limited Liability in California 1928–1931: It's the Lawyers," *American Law and Economics Review* 7, 439–83.

Werhane, P.H. (1985). *Persons, Rights, and Corporations*. Englewood Cliffs, NJ: Prentice-Hall.

Williston, S. (1888a). "History of the Law of Business Corporations before 1800 (Part 1)," *Harvard Law Review* 2:3, 105–124.

Williston, S. (1888b). "History of the Law of Business Corporations before 1800 (Part 2)," *Harvard Law Review* 2:4, 149–166.

15
Alternative business organizations and social enterprise

Dana Brakman Reiser*

Despite Milton Friedman's famous quip that "the social responsibility of business is to increase its profits" (Friedman 1970), many businesses seek to improve society, help the less fortunate, and be responsible corporate citizens (CECP 2014; Brakman Reiser 2009). These efforts have a long history; the earliest corporations were chartered with social or community-oriented goals at their center (Rana 2013). Some foundations created with wealth generated by large companies have become household names, like the Ford, Rockefeller and Gates Foundations. But corporate charitable activity is not limited to these legendary scions.

Businesses pursue social and environmental goals in different ways, depending on their size, orientation and public exposure. Philanthropy is often an important part of these efforts (Brakman Reiser 2009). Cash and in-kind donations to local, national and international charities from 272 companies surveyed, including 62 of the top 100 companies in the Fortune 500, totaled over $24 billion in 2015 (CECP, *Giving in Numbers* 2016). Some rely on separately-incorporated nonprofit foundations, which have their own boards of directors and can make grants out of income on their endowment on an extended time horizon. Many, including even very small businesses, simply contribute funds or in-kind donations to charities directly.

Depending on a company's goals for its philanthropic activity, it may focus on local charities or ones that complement its business model in some way. Employee-matching programs and cause-related marketing campaigns even endeavor to align a company's philanthropy with the charitable interests of its employees or customers, respectively. In whatever way a business structures its philanthropy, these efforts are generally tax-favored and offer additional public relations and marketing benefits.

In addition to philanthropy, many large and especially multinational companies devote significant resources to corporate social responsibility (CSR). Corporate social responsibility is a company's efforts to integrate social and environmental concerns into its business operations (Schwab 2008). Corporate social responsibility programs may spur innovation within a company to make it a more positive force in society. These programs have initiated changes in companies' supply chains, manufacturing processes, employee relations and a variety of other activities (Brakman Reiser 2009). Although sometimes expensive, these efforts can provide both short-term public relations value and long-term savings for the companies that undertake them.

Philanthropic contributions and corporate social responsibility efforts are sufficient to meet the desires of many businesses to pursue social or environmental goals along with their profit objectives. A growing number of entrepreneurs, business managers, and investors, however, want to create businesses with even greater social and environmental commitments (Brakman Reiser and Dean 2017). Many names are used to describe these businesses, including "for-benefit companies," "blended enterprises," and "mission-driven businesses." This chapter refers to these firms as "social enterprises," defined here as businesses that integrate profit-making goals and a social mission in a single for-profit entity.

An entire chapter could have been devoted to exploring the term "social mission" or indeed the word "social" itself. Some would argue all businesses have a social mission, as they produce goods and services that benefit society, provide opportunities for gainful employment and contribute to the tax base. Other views of what is social and what is a truly social mission will be far narrower, focused on each person's conception of the good—which conceptions can conflict with each other. Rather than wade too deeply into this philosophical quandary, this chapter takes its definition of "social mission" as serving interests and constituencies beyond those of investors in the enterprise.[1] Such groups include, but are not limited to, employees, customers, a local community, the environment, and society at large. Social enterprise, thus defined, has grown substantially across the globe in recent years (Defourny and Nyssens 2010; Kerlin 2006). Early on, this growth was fueled by the success of microfinance, pioneered by Grameen Bank and others in Asia and Latin America (Defourny and Nyssens 2010). Today, entrepreneurs spanning many continents and myriad industries helm businesses that include a social mission as a key component of their business models.

This chapter is devoted to a particular development that has accompanied this growth of social enterprise in the United States and Europe: the creation of alternative organizational forms intended to be more hospitable to their dual aims than traditional for-profit or nonprofit ones. It begins by situating these efforts in the legal context of US and European law. With this background in place, the chapter will describe, compare and contrast several quite different new organizational forms launched in a variety of jurisdictions. Finally, it will assess how much support forms like these can provide to social enterprises and offer suggestions for reform.

The US experience described

Nonprofits

In the United States, organizations pursuing a social mission are frequently established as nonprofits. For US nonprofits of any substantial size, the most common legal form is the nonprofit corporation, though nonprofits can and do form as charitable trusts and many small and new nonprofits are unincorporated nonprofit associations (Fremont-Smith 2004). Nonprofit corporations share many features of their for-profit counterparts, and are governed by a board of directors subject to a charter and bylaws.

Despite these similarities, however, and even though social goals are part of what impels founders to create social enterprises, nonprofit forms will be unsuitable for these for-profit businesses. Perhaps most importantly, nonprofit organizations may not distribute their net earnings to those who control them (RMNCA 1987; I.R.C. § 501(c)(3)). This limitation has been styled the "nondistribution constraint" (Hansmann 1996). The nondistribution constraint prohibits equity share issuance; thus, nonprofit corporations must be financed through donations, earned revenue, and borrowing. This check on capital formation is a serious drawback to organizing a social enterprise as a nonprofit.

Alternative business organizations and social enterprise

Of course, there are potential benefits of nonprofit forms. In particular, US nonprofits can qualify to receive substantial tax benefits, such as federal income, estate and gift tax exemptions, state property tax exemption, and the ability to receive tax-deductible contributions from individuals and entities. In exchange for these benefits, however, comes a significant regulatory burden.

To be eligible for these tax benefits, a nonprofit must pursue charitable purposes. Permissible charitable purposes vary somewhat by jurisdiction, but most are similar to the federal tax system's requirement of a "religious, charitable, scientific, testing for public safety, literary, or educational purposes, or to foster national or international amateur sports competition ... or for the prevention of cruelty to animals" (IRC § 501(c)(3)). Again, depending on the relevant tax benefit regime, pursuing non-charitable purposes is prohibited, limited, or otherwise triggers a loss of tax benefits. Entities found to be overly commercial may be ineligible for tax exemption, and even if entity-level exemption is maintained, income from unrelated business activities is taxed at regular rates (IRC § 511). Similarly, property owned by a nonprofit must be used for charitable purposes to be exempt from state property taxation (Brody 2002). In addition, federal and state tax benefits are accompanied by public reporting obligations and limitations on commercial and political activity (IRC § 501(c)(3); Fremont-Smith 2004). Unless a social enterprise will be financed largely through tax-deductible donations and will engage in few activities that stray beyond tax regulators' notions of charity, nonprofit forms will be more hindrance than help.

For those developing social enterprises, defined again as businesses that integrate profit-making goals and a social mission in a single entity, for-profit choices in the US have until recently been limited to corporations, various kinds of partnerships, and limited liability companies. In the past several years, however, a number of new legal forms have been developed intended to house these social enterprises. These forms are in their infancy, and contain many features that will need improvement if they are to serve the needs of social enterprises better than existing ones.

Specialized forms for social enterprise

The first specialized form for social enterprise developed in the United States was the low-profit limited liability company, or L3C (Brakman Reiser 2010; Murray and Hwang 2011; Tyler et al. 2015). This form is a twist on the limited liability company (LLC), a for-profit form available across the US that offers adopters both limited personal liability and pass-through tax treatment (Tyler et al. 2015). Mandatory rules for LLCs' governance are few, and adopting entities use an operating agreement to set ownership terms by contract (Tyler et al. 2015).

Legislation adopting the L3C form sits atop existing LLC legislation, but adds four special components. In the words of the first L3C statute, adopted in Vermont in 2008, an adopting entity "significantly further[s] the accomplishment of one or more charitable or educational purposes," and "would not have been formed but for the company's relationship to the accomplishment of charitable or educational purposes" (11 VSA § 3001 (27)(A)). In addition,

> [n]o significant purpose of the company is the production of income or the appreciation of property; provided, however, that the fact that a person produces significant income or capital appreciation shall not, in the absence of other factors, be conclusive evidence of a significant purpose involving the production of income or the appreciation of property.
>
> *(11 VSA § 3001 (27)(B))*

Finally, political and legislative purposes are barred (11 VSA § 3001 (27)(C)). If an existing L3C stops complying with the additional L3C components, however, it simply transforms into an ordinary LLC (11 VSA § 3001 (27)(D)). Moreover, L3Cs must self-monitor and enforce these mandates; no compliance regime is included in L3C legislation.[2]

The components of L3C statutes in large part derive from another regime, US tax law's regulation of "program-related investments (PRIs)." Program-related investments are a special category of expenditures available to private foundations, a subcategory of tax-exempt nonprofit organizations subject to a range of special rules (Internal Revenue Code (IRC) § 509). Principal among these is the requirement that private foundations make "qualifying distributions" equal to five percent of the fair market value of their net assets each year (IRC § 4942). Most qualifying distributions are grants to nonprofit, tax-exempt public charities. In contrast, PRIs may be loans, purchases of equity or other types of investments and may be made to for-profit entities, but also count toward the five percent floor (Brewer et al. 2014; Tyler 2010).

Of course, not just any investment in a for-profit is a PRI—only an investment meeting requirements almost precisely aligned with the four components of L3C law (US Treas. Reg. §53.4944-3)—and investing foundations are required to exercise additional oversight on such investments. In addition to counting toward the annual spending requirement private foundations must meet, PRIs are exempt from possible treatment as "jeopardy investments," risky investments of the foundation's assets that can lead to penalty excise taxes (IRC § 4944(c)). Incorrect PRI classification by a private foundation, however, runs the risk of very serious penalties. Thus, many private foundations have been hesitant to employ them (Murray and Hwang 2011), and some advisors caution doing so without obtaining a private letter ruling through lengthy and expensive Internal Revenue Service process (Bishop 2010).

The overlap of the L3C statute's core components and the requirements for PRI treatment is deliberate. The creators of the L3C concept intended it to be an organizational form ready-made to receive PRIs. They hoped the IRS would bless investments in L3Cs as PRIs per se and thereby encourage the expansion of their use by foundations (Brewer et al. 2014; Lang 2014). Perhaps unsurprisingly, given the absence of any enforcement apparatus to ensure L3Cs comply with the PRI requirements, the IRS has not provided a blanket ruling or other assurance that investments in L3Cs will meet the PRI standards.

Although the IRS has not blessed the L3C as a PRI vehicle, the form enjoyed some success with state legislatures. Between 2008 and 2011 nine states adopted L3C legislation, following a pattern very similar to the initial Vermont statute (Americans for Community Development 2012). Since 2011, however, no new adoptions have appeared and North Carolina repealed its L3C statute (Brewer et al. 2014; Tyler et al. 2015).

This waning of the L3C's popularity coincided with the arrival of another specialized form of legislation on the scene: the benefit corporation (Brakman Reiser 2013; Brakman Reiser 2011a). The benefit corporation, as its name suggests, is an incorporated legal form. While incorporated entities are also taxable as a matter of default under US law, they can qualify for pass-through treatment under Subchapter S (Eustice and Kuntz 2015). Many social enterprises, the lion's share of which are small and have few owners, will have no difficulty doing so. Corporate shareholders enjoy limited liability, and corporate statutes set a few important mandatory rules and a somewhat sticky default framework for matters of governance. The benefit corporation statutes follow these patterns, but vary certain aspects of standard for-profit corporate law to suit the needs of social enterprises.[3]

Firstly, benefit corporation statutes require adopting entities to pursue a "general public benefit" in addition to their profit-making purposes (Model Benefit Corporation Legislation (MBCL); § 201(a)). General public benefit is defined as "[a] material positive impact on society and the environment, taken as a whole, assessed against a third-party standard, from the business and operations of a benefit corporation." Benefit corporations may elect to identify a specific public benefit, such as protecting the environment or supporting the arts, that they plan to pursue, but need not do so (MBCL § 201(b)).

Secondly, benefit corporation statutes impose different obligations on fiduciaries. They instruct directors that they

> shall consider the effects of any action or inaction upon (i) the shareholders of the benefit corporation, (ii) the employees and work force of the benefit corporation, its subsidiaries, and its suppliers, (iii) the interests of customers as beneficiaries of the general public benefit or specific public benefit purposes of the benefit corporation, (iv) community and societal factors, including those of each community in which offices or facilities of the benefit corporation, its subsidiaries, or its suppliers are located, (v) the local and global environment, (vi) the short-term and long-term interests of the benefit corporation, including benefits that may accrue to the benefit corporation from its long-term plans and the possibility that these interests may be best served by the continued independence of the benefit corporation; and (vii) the ability of the benefit corporation to accomplish its general public benefit purpose and any specific benefit purpose.
>
> *(MBCL § 301(a)(1))*

Importantly, benefit corporation statutes do not instruct directors to prioritize any of these considerations over others. The legislation guarantees benefit corporation directors significant discretion to pursue the social mission of their enterprises if they so choose, but do not require them to do so. So long as directors consider the needs of employees, the community, etc., they may then decide to act instead to maximize shareholder value. Consideration, not action, is the mandate. Further, directors are not personally liable for a benefit corporation's failure "to pursue or create general public benefit or specific public benefit" (MBCL § 301(c)).

These social purpose and fiduciary duty requirements expressly reject the shareholder value maximization paradigm many identify with US for-profit corporations. Yet, it is worth noting that ordinary for-profit corporate statutes do not explicitly limit the objectives of adopting entities to maximizing shareholder value, and do not instruct fiduciaries to pursue this shareholder wealth maximization exclusively or otherwise. Indeed, many corporate scholars argue for-profits need not single-mindedly pursue shareholder value maximization, pointing to the breadth of fiduciaries' discretion (Elhauge 2005) and the unique facts involved in the few cases where courts have rebuked them for failing to do so (Stout 2012). Still, the trope of shareholder value maximization runs strongly through for-profit law and lore (Brakman Reiser 2013; Strine 2012). Further, the values of the marketplace undergird it, as for-profit corporate fiduciaries who fail to maximize shareholder value may watch share prices fall and find their companies subject to a takeover motivated by extracting greater value. For all of these reasons, social enterprise founders worry the force of shareholder value maximization will push them to abandon their social goals (Page and Katz 2010). By their foundational purpose and fiduciary duty requirements, benefit corporation statutes attempt to cast off this burden.

Some benefit corporation statutes also add new content to standard for-profit law to address enforcement. They often, but not always, include a new right of action: the benefit enforcement proceeding (MBCL § 305).[4] When such a provision exists, benefit enforcement proceedings are the exclusive means by which directors may be challenged for their failures to pursue general or specific public benefits (MBCL § 305(a)), though personal liability remains unavailable. The benefit corporation itself, directors, shareholders and others designated in the benefit corporation's charter or bylaws may bring an action making such a challenge, but are limited to obtaining injunctive relief (MBCL § 305)(b), (c)).

Although this limited additional right of action is often included in benefit corporation statutes, their primary model for enforcement is disclosure (Brakman Reiser 2011a). Benefit corporations are required to issue annual benefit reports to shareholders, and to post these reports on any organizational website (MBCL §§ 401, 402). The report must describe the benefit corporation's efforts to pursue general public benefit, along with the extent of its success in doing so. Although this assessment is made by the benefit corporation itself, it must be made with reference to a "third-party standard": "[a] recognized standard for defining, reporting, and assessing corporate social and environmental performance" (MBCL § 102). Under the Model Act, this standard must be created by an entity independent of the benefit corporation that uses it (i.e., not a controlled subsidiary or, say, a company run by the CEO's sister), and must be made transparent to the public (MBCL § 102).[5]

Information-forcing is also the hallmark of an important precursor of the benefit corporation idea—the similarly-named "B Corp" (Brakman Reiser 2013). In fact, a B Corp is not a legal form at all, but a trademarked name available to businesses with a social mission through a certification and licensing process run by B Lab. B Lab is a nonprofit organization dedicated to "us[ing] the power of business to solve social and environmental problems" (B Corp website 2017). The certification process requires at least two steps. Aspiring B corporations must revise their articles of incorporation to require directors to consider a range of impacts and constituencies when acting in their fiduciary roles (B Corp website 2017). Applicants must also complete a B Assessment and achieve a score of 80 out of a possible 200 points. This detailed survey asks questions ranging from recycling policies to employment conditions to governance, and varies depending on an applicant's size and industry (B Corp website 2017). Applicants who make the required changes and score highly enough on the B Assessment may license the B Corp mark for a sliding-scale fee based on annual sales, promote themselves as B Corps, and access a number of benefits available to the B Corp community (B Corp website 2017). Successful applicants may keep the certification for two years, and 10 percent of entities are subject to a random audit by B Lab. (B Corp website 2017).

The similarity between the names "benefit corporation," a state legal form, and "B Corp," a private trademark available for use as a certification, has led to much confusion. The overlapping names and some of their overlapping content, however, is easily explained. B Lab has been heavily involved with developing and promoting the benefit corporation form (B Corp website 2017). Further, the B Assessment is one tool benefit corporations formed under state law can use as the third-party standard against which they must assess themselves. Importantly, though, none of these state forms require B Lab to certify an entity in order for it to qualify as a benefit corporation (Brakman Reiser 2013). Benefit corporations must only use a third-party standard to assess themselves. At the time of this writing, over 2,100 B corporations exist around the world (B Corp website 2017).

Benefit corporation statutes have been widely adopted since Maryland's first-in-the-nation legislation was enacted in 2010. In the US, entity formation laws are enacted at the state rather than the federal level, so state legislatures are the site of the action. At the time of writing, 31 states have benefit corporation legislation on the books and more are considering adopting a statute (Benefit Corp Information Center 2015). In 2013 a key development in the march through US state legislatures occurred when Delaware adopted legislation enabling the "public benefit corporation" (Plerhoples 2014). This variation on the benefit corporation form is important because Delaware is the state of incorporation of choice for major and publicly-traded US corporations (Delaware Department of State 2015). When Delaware joined this party, it was viewed by some as powerful evidence of the importance and legitimacy of specialized forms for social enterprise (Murray 2014; Plerhoples 2014).

Like L3Cs and benefit corporations, the Delaware public benefit corporation is a state legal form of organization that permits an adopting entity to have a dual purpose. A Delaware public benefit corporation pursues profits, but also identifies a "public benefit" to pursue in its corporate charter (8 Delaware Code § 362). The statute also gives a tripartite instruction to public benefit corporation directors. As they manage their corporations, they must "balance" the financial interests of shareholders, the interests of other stakeholders impacted by the firm's conduct, and the public benefit the firm identifies in its charter (8 Delaware Code § 365). Delaware's new form does not include any special enforcement proceedings, but does require shareholders to be sent a report on the company's public benefit progress every two years (8 Delaware Code § 366).

It remains to be seen how popular the public benefit corporation will become in Delaware or elsewhere. (In the US, entities can form under any state's law, so a social enterprise in Utah that finds the Delaware public benefit form attractive can form under it from afar.) Indeed, despite the popularity of the various specialized legal forms among state legislatures, the adoption of these forms by actual social enterprises has been slow (Brakman Reiser and Dean 2017). The most recent figures available show that at most only about 4,500 organizations have adopted any of these specialized forms since the inception of the first one in 2008 (Murray 2016). These low figures could be explained as the very gradual uptake of a new and untested legal concept, and time will tell. An alternative explanation, however, suggests that while these forms are an attractive legislative product, they do not sufficiently resolve the concerns social entrepreneurs have identified with using standard for-profit forms to house social enterprise. Primary among these are corporate objectives and capital access.

A critique of US specialized forms

The "two masters" problem

One of the main arguments for the development of specialized forms has been the need to permit fiduciaries to pursue a dual mission, both profit and social purpose. With a purely nonprofit or for-profit enterprise, the argument goes, purity of mission is also necessary. Of course, this view is somewhat overstated. Nonprofits certainly may earn profits; in fact, fully 50 percent of the income of US public charities in 2012 came from earned revenues from tuition payments, ticket sales, patient revenue, etc. (McKeever and Pettijohn 2014). For-profits may make charitable contributions, engage in corporate responsibility and, as discussed earlier, are not legally bound to a strict requirement to maximize profits for shareholders. Yet, there are legal and practical limits that a social enterprise pursuing dual missions of profit and social purpose might encounter. Nonprofits cannot have shareholders or distribute the profits they earn to members or others in control. Also, ultimately, for-profits who dismiss the profit concerns of their investors do so at their peril. The market will punish such actions, even if the law is unlikely to do so.

The US hybrid forms thus explicitly permit the expression of these dual objectives and fiduciaries' pursuit of them in an attempt to develop an organizational form more suited to social enterprise. Solving this one problem, however, has generated another. Having two goals, especially goals that will often conflict, complicates the role of managers and the discipline of fiduciaries. When faced with a decision, like where to locate production facilities for the growing product of a promising social enterprise, should managers choose more expensive local production to generate jobs for their community? Or, should they opt for production offshore that would increase profits and generate a complex mix of benefits and problems in the off-shore location? Depending on the production process employed, this choice may also have environmental implications.

Managers, even those managers who are directors or officers with a legal obligation as fiduciaries, typically have great discretion in such operational decisions (Elhauge 2005). But, in an environment with a primarily profit-making objective, this single bottom line can focus the mind and improve decision-making confidence. For nonprofit fiduciaries, the single bottom line of serving organizational mission plays a similar function, but is significantly more difficult to identify and evaluate. They must determine their mission, a contested process to which multiple constituencies have appropriate contributions to make, and then measure their progress toward it, a daunting task (Brakman Reiser 2011b).

For a dual purpose social enterprise, combining the goals of profit and purpose complicates fiduciaries' jobs even further. This challenge of the "two masters" problem has been recognized at least since biblical times.[6] But US hybrid forms do nothing to mitigate it. The L3C statutes say nothing explicit regarding fiduciary duties (11 VSA § 3001 (27)); benefit and public benefit corporation statutes instruct fiduciaries to "consider" or "balance" these concerns, with no guide star or prioritization to set the course (MBCL § 301(a); 8 Del. Code § 365). Moreover, these forms offer little or nothing in the way of remedies, relying heavily on self-directed and non-monitored reporting to shareholders and (sometimes) the public, and locating any ability to challenge fiduciaries' management of the enterprise solely in shareholder suits for non-monetary relief (Brakman Reiser 2013). This discretion may be sufficient to placate fiduciaries' concerns about a lack of guidance, as it essentially removes any concern that failures to pursue profit or purpose will be subject to legal remediation. In fact, this even greater freedom of decision may make these forms particularly attractive to managers seeking to further reduce the already quite limited exposure they face for accountability for poor decision-making. The almost complete lack of accountability, however, should trouble another important constituency—investors.

The capital access problem

Another major motivation behind the development of social enterprises in general and the specialized legal forms that house them in particular, is capital formation. The essential argument here is that nonprofits, due to their reliance on donations, debt and surpluses from earned revenue, are insufficiently capitalized to respond effectively to the serious problems facing society—from education, to climate change, to the many consequences of the ever-widening gaps in wealth and income. For-profit entities keen to marry profit for investors with social value suggest that we might harness vast pools of investment capital to address these vital societal issues. This promise will be realized only, however, if investors controlling this capital are also persuaded that social enterprises can effectively produce both profit and social value—and are willing to bet their money on it (Tyler et al. 2015).

Assuming dual purpose investors, often called "impact investors," exist in large numbers, they face great uncertainty when considering a specific investment. They are asked to hand over their money (perhaps for a rate of return lower than that pure for-profits would offer) to an entrepreneur set on pursuing both profit to share with them and also a social purpose—an aim difficult to achieve and perhaps even harder to evaluate. To do so, significant trust is required (Brakman Reiser and Dean 2017). Indeed, there are questions of trust on both sides, as entrepreneurs dedicated to dual mission may find the thought of investment, and particularly equity investment, bittersweet. The addition of new investors carries its own risks. They may fail to share in, or even abandon, the entrepreneur's commitment to mission if it begins to cut too much into profits, thereby pushing the entrepreneur away from the social goals she holds dear (Brakman Reiser and Dean 2017).

Both entrepreneur and investor need trust and assurances, but these needs are not addressed by the current American forms of social enterprise. Because there is no prioritization of social good required at the entity or fiduciary level and precious little enforcement in any event (Brakman Reiser 2013, Brakman Reiser and Dean 2017), investors must find some other route to assure themselves they can trust managers. Moreover, either managers (in the L3C) or investors (in benefit and public benefit corporations) can remove the mission component from the entity unilaterally (Brakman Reiser 2013; Brakman Reiser and Dean 2017). While these forms were developed with the aim of aiding capital formation, they do little to solve the trust problems that inhibit the key actors in the capitalization process (Brakman Reiser and Dean 2017).

Unless specialized forms prove effective at resolving the two-masters problem and providing assurances needed for capital formation, they will also have a difficult time fulfilling the final desire behind these forms: branding (Brakman Reiser 2013, Brakman Reiser & Dean 2017). With every business seeking to paint itself as "one of the good guys," the marketplace of self-proclaimed social enterprises could become quite crowded with poseurs. Certainly one goal of these forms is to serve as a signal for consumers, investors, employees and others to identify trustworthy dual-purpose enterprises. Such a brand, if effective, would be extremely valuable for all involved. But, without prioritization and enforcement, it is hard to imagine any of these specialized organizational forms serving as an effective brand.

Indeed, a single brand may be a mirage. These various constituencies are often looking for different kinds of information, and the appropriate standards may vary not only on the dimensions addressed here but also further by industry or geography. Ironically, for this branding purpose, private certification may be a superior solution, bringing us back to the world of B Lab and the B Corp certification, as well as some of the many other entities seeking to measure, mark and brand social enterprises.

The European environment explored

European nations each have an extensive list and a long tradition of standard nonprofit and for-profit legal forms. Nonprofit forms include all manner of associations and foundations, as well as companies limited by guarantee and various others (Hopt and von Hippel 2010). Each of these forms, however, comes with the familiar and problematic limitation for social entrepreneurs that profits may not be distributed to owners (Defourny and Nyssens 2013). In addition, some European countries limit commercial or "trading" activities by nonprofit entities (Framjee 2009; Coates and Van Opstal 2009; Kerlin 2006; Hopt and von Hippel 2010). For-profit forms are myriad too. Although European Union (EU) company forms have been slow to launch (Kirshner 2010; Bratton et al. 2009),[7] each member state offers its own version of a private and public company and various types of partnerships (Bratton et al. 2009). Despite this plethora of legal options available to house social enterprises, European nations experienced pressure similar to that in the US to develop specialized forms. Nearly all of the forms that have emerged, however, are meaningfully distinct from those seen Stateside.[8]

Cooperatives

The effort to develop specialized forms to house social enterprises has earlier roots on the Continent than possibly anywhere else, especially in Italy. Social enterprise organizations began taking on the cooperative form there as early as the 1970s and 1980s, due to its inherently attractive combination of the ability to engage in commercial activity and pursue community aims, while offering owners limited liability and a role in governance (Borzaga and Santuari 2001).

This activity culminated, however, in the passing of landmark 1991 legislation recognizing the "social cooperative" as a new and distinct Italian legal form (Law 8 November 1991, No. 381).

Social cooperatives under this law were required to operate "for the general benefit of the community and for the social integration of citizens" (Borzaga and Santuari 2001). This law also breaks down the class of social cooperatives into two types. Type A social cooperatives deliver social services, typically healthcare or education, and may take on outside, non-member, investors. Type B social cooperatives engage in "work integration," providing training and work opportunities for individuals, at least thirty percent of whom must be disadvantaged (Borzaga and Santuari 2001; Cafaggi and Iamiceli 2008).

Social cooperatives formed under the 1991 law may make distributions of profits to owners, albeit limited ones.

> [T]he Act states that the amount of profits to be divided must not exceed 80 percent of the total; that the rate of profits for each share cannot be higher than 2 percent of the rate applicable to the bonds issued by the Italian Post Service; and that no assets can be distributed should the co-op be wound up.
>
> *(Borzaga and Santuari 2001: 171)*

Cooperatives are also required to disclose information regarding their activities to members and to report financial information to the Enterprises' Register Office (Cafaggi and Iamiceli 2008). As of 2008, there were 13,938 active social cooperatives in Italy (Carini et al. 2012).

Decision-making power in social cooperatives is decentralized. Originally, all cooperatives were required to conform to a so-called "tripartite" system of administration and control, which contemplated three governing bodies: the member assembly, the board of directors and the board of supervisors (Fici 2006). This multistakeholder approach represents the interests of different classes of stakeholders, though the power of cooperative members predominates. Cooperative members must make up at least a majority of the board, whereas the roles played by financing members and voluntary working members are specifically limited. Since a 2003 reform, social cooperatives may choose among three different governance models in which members have differing degrees of authority to monitor directors and enforce compliance. In addition to the original tripartite model, dualistic and monistic models are available, but external auditing is required for cooperatives adopting the new models (Cafaggi and Iamiceli 2008).

The 1991 Italian social cooperative law was highly influential across Europe (Defourny and Nyssens 2013). Forms like France's "collective interest cooperative society," Greece's "social cooperative with limited liability," and Poland's "social cooperative" share with the Italian law the commitments to mission primacy, limitations on distributions, and a multistakeholder approach to governance (Defourny and Nyssens 2013; Kerlin 2006). In these countries and others, social entrepreneurs are using social cooperatives to deliver on dual goals of social good and profit.[9]

Despite the influence its 1991 social cooperatives law commanded across Europe, in 2006 Italy enacted a new piece of social enterprise legislation to pursue quite different purposes. This law enacts a nationwide definition of "social enterprise," which is not dependent upon the form taken by a particular entity. Instead, the new social enterprise definition includes

> any kind of private organisation (e.g., associations, foundations, co-operatives, non-co-operative companies) which permanently and principally operates an economic activity aimed at the production and distribution of social benefit goods and services while pursuing general interest goals.
>
> *(Cafaggi and Iamiceli 2008: 24)*[10]

For economic activity to be the enterprise's principal operation, this activity must generate 70 percent of the organization's revenues (Cafaggi and Iamiceli 2008). Importantly here, although social cooperatives that qualify may still make limited distributions, the social enterprise category is otherwise asset-locked. Profits and surplus must be used to benefit mission, not distributed to owners (Cafaggi and Iamiceli 2008). This sets the Italian national definition of social enterprise somewhat at odds with its use by many American commentators, and with the definition in this chapter. The Italian social enterprise legislation also has only limited requirements related to stakeholders and governance (Cafaggi and Iamiceli 2008).

Company forms

Belgium and the United Kingdom have diverged from the cooperative path and instead utilized a company model. Belgium's social purpose company (Société à Finalité Sociale ("SFS")) designation was enacted in 1995 (Doeringer 2010; Defourny and Nyssens 2013). Adopting the SFS designation allows socially-minded organizations including nonprofits to engage in unlimited commercial activity (Coates and Van Opstal 2009); such activities by non-SFS Belgian nonprofits are legally restricted (Doeringer 2010).

As a designation only, when a company registers as an SFS, it does not change its underlying legal form. Instead, it simply accepts limits on its ability to distribute profits and additional reporting requirements. An SFS-designated entity must state in its articles that its members seek limited or no profit, and that any profit distributions will not exceed an annual return of six percent on an investor's principal (Doeringer 2010). In addition, upon dissolution, residual assets must be transferred to a company or charity that furthers the SFS's social purpose (Doeringer 2010). Disclosure requirements mandate production of an annual report indicating how the SFS furthered its social goals. Yet the report is not required to contain any specific content and no regulator polices such reports or whether an organization's activities align with its social purposes more generally (Coates and Van Opstal 2009). By the mid-2000s, only about 400 SFS registrations had been filed with the Belgian government (Defourny and Nyssens 2008).

The UK's Community Interest Company (CIC), in contrast, is a specialized legal form subject to oversight by a dedicated regulator. The CIC was established by amendments to UK company law adopted in 2004 (Companies Act 2004) and, to date, over 15,000 CICs have been created (CIC Regulator 2014/2015). The CIC form relies on company law as its basic framework, adding requirements that the adopting entity pursue a "community benefit," observe an asset lock on some of its capital and caps dividends, as well as mandated stakeholder involvement. The CIC status does not confer any tax benefits on companies that adopt it, whether formed as companies limited by shares or limited by guarantee, and they are subject to entity-level tax (UK CIC Regulator Guidance 2016: Ch. 2; Companies Act 2004 § 36).[11]

In 2014, however, the UK did begin to provide tax benefits to investors in CICs, among other types of social ventures, through a new scheme of tax relief for social investments (Finance Act 2014, Schedule 11, ¶257J). Thereby, eligible investors are permitted to deduct thirty percent of the cost of their investment in a CIC or other eligible entity (HMRC Guidance 2015). In addition, investors may defer paying tax on capital gains on such investments or even avoid paying capital gains tax on the investment entirely (HMRC Guidance 2015).

The CICs, like other UK companies, are governed by a board of directors and all directors are fiduciaries. Like other company directors, CIC directors must exercise their management and supervisory duties with "reasonable care, skill and diligence," and avoid conflicts of interest or other situations of potential disloyalty (Companies Act 2006). The role of CIC directors is unique, however, because they are also responsible for preserving the CIC's ability to meet the community interest test (UK CIC Regulator Guidance 2016: Ch. 9). This test, necessary to form as a CIC, requires that "a reasonable person might consider that its activities (or proposed activities) are being carried on for the benefit of the community" (UK CIC Regulator Guidance 2016: Ch. 4). The CICs must report on their community interest achievements to the Regulator annually (UK CIC Regulator Guidance 2016: Ch. 8).

The CIC Regulator directs adopting entities to include stakeholders in its governance (UK CIC Regulator Guidance 2013: Ch. 9). The specific form of stakeholder involvement is not mandated, with the idea that CICs of various types and sizes will flourish using diverse techniques to involve stakeholders in governance. Yet, the CIC Regulator has offered suggestions on how stakeholder governance roles might be articulated. Its Guidance suggests that adequate information may be provided:

> by simple methods such as circulating news letters and holding stakeholder meetings or more sophisticated methods such as setting up a web site with dialogue facilities or issuing formal consultation documents before taking a major policy decision. Alternatively, stakeholder groups can be given official standing under a company's constitution (for example, by requiring that they are consulted before the directors or members make certain types of decisions).
>
> Other stakeholders could be included with the members in the circulation of the company annual report and accounts and invited to attend an open forum linked to the company's annual general meeting.
>
> In many organisations the setting up of user and advisory groups or a club committee separate from the board of directors can be an effective way of bringing stakeholders into the running of the organisation.
>
> A wide view should be taken of who may be affected by your activities and should include not only those who currently benefit but also potential beneficiaries. You should also consider those indirectly affected such as the other residents of the area of your operations.
>
> *(UK CIC Regulator Guidance 2016: Ch. 9)*

Information on a CIC's efforts to include stakeholders in governance must be provided in its annual community interest report to the Regulator for review (UK CIC Regulator Guidance 2016: Ch. 8).

Perhaps the most potent components of the CIC structure relate to financing. The CICs' assets are subject to an "asset lock," prohibiting a CIC from disposing of assets for less than fair market value consideration, except in pursuit of the community benefits the CIC is designed to pursue or in a transfer to a charity or another CIC (UK CIC Regulator Guidance 2016: Ch. 6). This "fundamental" feature means that even beyond dissolution, a CIC's assets are perpetually devoted to community benefit (UK CIC Regulator Guidance 2016: Ch. 6).

In addition, dividends paid to members of a CIC limited by shares are permissible only to the extent the Regulator so authorizes (Companies Act 2004 § 30). The Regulator has issued a number of regulations limiting dividends, most recently in October 2014. Although the Regulator initially applied per-share dividend caps, and then increased these caps after consultation in 2010, the most recent changes removed the per-share dividend cap entirely. Now, the only cap on dividends mandates the total dividend declared for all shares must not exceed thirty-five percent of distributable profits in any given year (UK CIC Regulator Guidance 2016: Ch. 6). A cap on performance-related debt payments was also increased (UK CIC Regulator Guidance 2016: Ch. 6). The various caps and changes to them represent the Regulator's attempt to balance the competing desires to incentivize investments in CICs and to maintain their focus on producing benefits for the community.

Evaluating European social enterprise forms

The European experience with social enterprise is diverse, with a range of cooperative forms, company forms, and designations that layer over legal forms taken by individual entities. Many of these forms emphasize a multistakeholder approach to governance not found in American forms and all place restraints on profit distribution, while US forms do not. These differences also affect the type of work European social enterprises perform, the capital they can raise, and the branding they are able to offer.

European social cooperatives tend to be focused on traditional charitable work rather than innovating new business ideas (Esposito 2013; Defouny and Nyssens 2013; Defourny and Nyssens 2008). Of course, the mission primacy embedded in these forms makes some business activities unrealistic. However, the founding statutes also often encourage the view that social cooperatives are essentially charitable in nature, such as in Italy's direction to social cooperatives to engage in social service or work integration activities or the even more extreme Portuguese social solidarity cooperative's prohibition on all distributions (Cafaggi and Iamiceli 2008). Additionally, the strong norm of multistakeholder governance in European social cooperatives may be perceived as an obstacle to effective operation of a business.

The European experience also showcases the tension between maintaining a social purpose and raising capital. The UK CIC Regulator's decade-long struggle to identify dividend limitations for CICs that will focus adopting entities on pursuing community benefit without turning off investors is, perhaps, the most dramatic example. The financial limitations on CICs mean they offer investors something quite different from ordinary equity. Investors can buy these shares and participate in profits, but only to the extent of capped dividends—not the full amount of a CIC's profits its directors might choose to distribute; and share ownership entitles investors to no residual claim. CICs' inclusion in the new social investment tax regime suggests that even with increased dividend caps, stimulating investment in these social enterprises remains difficult. Some authors likewise attribute the lack of uptake of Belgian SFS designations to the challenges these organizations will face in raising capital (Esposito 2013; Doeringer 2010).[12]

Finally, with so much diversity of form and meanings, it is difficult to imagine social enterprise branding emerging at the European level. Instead, branding effects, if any, will need to occur country by country. It will be interesting, in this regard, to track the development of the new Italian social enterprise designation. Its attempt to bring under one umbrella the many forms being taken by organizations using economic activity to pursue social good is unique. Italy has long been at the vanguard of European legal innovation for social enterprises, so the space is well worth watching.

Concluding remarks

Businesses have long deployed corporate philanthropy to pursue social goals along with their profit-making objectives, and in recent decades many have adopted corporate social responsibility programs to include social and environmental considerations as part of their business decision-making. Businesses, entrepreneurs, and investors who seek to more fully integrate these dual goals, or prioritize social missions, are now forming social enterprises.

States throughout the US and countries across Europe have responded with a range of dual purpose entity forms. Social cooperatives common across Europe can be used in this vein, but until these break free from their traditionally-limited social service and work-integration emphases, business entrepreneurs will make little use of them. The UK's community interest company was developed precisely for this purpose, and has seen significant adoption on the ground. It is still, however, much more commonly used by companies limited by guarantee, and the effort to attract capital to CICs limited by shares remains a work in progress.[13]

Hybrid forms have been a great legislative success story in the United States, with at least some form being adopted by over half the states in less than a decade. However, the acceptance by entrepreneurs has not been nearly as fulsome or fast. Unless the legislation enabling these forms is revised to require prioritization of social good and to provide a reliable enforcement mechanism, these forms will continue to have little to offer social enterprise founders and investors. More targeted reforms, like financing arrangements that reassure entrepreneurs and investors of their mutual commitments, show greater promise (Brakman Reiser and Dean 2017). Likewise, in the absence of an enforcement regime that establishes government forms of social entrepreneurship as a reliable sorting mechanism, private certification systems will likely grow to brand social enterprises for a range of audiences.

Essential works

The essential works on US social enterprise law include Dana Brakman Reiser and Steven Dean, *Social Enterprise Law: Trust, Public Benefit, and Capital Markets* (2017), Cass Brewer, Elizabeth Minnigh, and Robert Wexler, *Social Enterprise by Nonprofits and Hybrid Organizations* (2014), and materials found on the websites of B Lab and the Benefit Corporation Information Center. For comprehensive comparative analysis of social enterprise in the US and Europe, see Jacques Defourny and Marthe Nyssens, "Conceptions of Social Enterprise and Social Entrepreneurship in Europe and the United States: Convergences and Divergences" (2010), Janelle A. Kerlin, "Social Enterprise in the United States and Europe: Understanding and Learning from the Differences" (2006), and Carlo Borzaga and Jacques Defourny. *The Emergence of Social Enterprise* (2001). Extensive guidance on the UK community interest company form is provided at the CIC Regulator website.

For further reading in this volume on the legal frameworks of corporations, see Chapter 14, The corporation: genesis, identity, agency. On the idea of the "social" and "social responsibility" see Chapter 10, Social responsibility. On the responsibilities of fiduciaries, see Chapter 24, Corporate governance. On the question of the nature of business, especially in relation to the "two masters" problem, see Chapter 13, What is business?

Notes

* I am grateful for the support of the Brooklyn Law School Dean's Summer Research Program and for the dedicated research assistance of Susan Miller.

1 For a more thorough investigation of the social mission concept and its relationship to ethical questions, consult Chell et al. (2014), Fayolle and Matlay (2010), Praszkier and Nowak (2012), and Spence (2014).
2 The Illinois L3C regime is an interesting outlier. It deems L3C fiduciaries "trustees" required to register and report under its Charitable Trust Act and subject to enforcement by the state attorney general (Ill. Comp. Stat. 180/1-26(d); Lane 2011; Tyler 2010).
3 Benefit corporation statutes currently exist in over half the states, and vary somewhat in their particulars. To describe the basic features of these statutes, references to the Model Benefit Corporation Legislation will suffice. When adoptions by particular states are relevant, those state statutes will be referenced.
4 Some states, like Maryland, do not include enforcement proceedings (Maryland Code 2013).
5 The Model Act also requires the standard to comprehensively address the various considerations directors must consider in their decision-making and to be developed by an entity with appropriate

expertise and which uses a "multistakeholder approach" (MBCL § 102). A number of state benefit corporation statutes, especially those earlier adopted in time, do not contain these additional requirements (Colorado Revised Statutes § 7-101-501; Maryland Code, Corporations and Associations, § 5-6C-01 et seq.; McKinney's New York Business Corporation Law § 1701 et seq.).

6 "No one can serve two masters. Either you will hate the one and love the other, or you will be devoted to the one and despise the other. You cannot serve both God and money" (Luke 16:13).
7 The European Union has not created any EU-wide social enterprise forms or designations (Esposito 2013), as it has done for public limited liability companies and standard cooperatives (Fici 2013). The EU has left the development of specialized forms to member countries and has instead offered support for the emerging social enterprise trend in Europe by funding research (Defouny and Nyssens 2013) and supporting activities such as the construction of databases and formation of expert panels (European Commission Website 2015).
8 One recent exception is Italy, which enacted a provision allowing for a new corporate form closely aligned with a benefit corporation or social purpose corporation model in late 2015, see Law 28 December 2015 (Stability Law), n. 208, article 1, par. 376–384. According to the legislation, it aim[s] to promote the establishment and encourage the spread of companies, hereinafter referred to as "Società Benefit," which, by performing an economic activity, pursue one or more objectives of common benefit besides sharing profits, and which operate in a responsible, sustainable and transparent manner toward people, communities, territories and the environment, cultural heritage and social activities, entities and associations and other stakeholders.
9 In 2012, France had 190 organizations registered as collective interest cooperative societies and Greece had 113 limited liability social cooperatives (European Commission Report 2012).
10 As of 2011, 769 organizations were registered as "social enterprise" in Italy (Borzaga and Galera 2012).
11 Notably, even if formed as a company limited by guarantee, a CIC is expressly prohibited from being deemed a charity under UK tax law (Companies Act 2004 § 26(3)(a)).
12 Of course, other factors also may be at work in the lack of adoption of the SFS designation (Coates and Van Opstal 2009; Defourny and Nyssens 2008).
13 As of 2016, 9,987 CICs still on the public register were companies limited by guarantee; only 3,068 were companies limited by shares (CIC Regulator 2016/2017).

References

Americans for Community Development, *Laws*. Available at: www.americansforcommunitydevelopment.org/legislation.html.
B Corp website. Available at: www.bcorporation.net.
B Corporation "Today Marks a Tipping Point in the Evolution of Capitalism," *B Lab Blog*. Available at: www.bcorporation.net/blog/today-marks-a-tipping-point-in-the-evolution-of-capitalism [accessed 17 July 2013].
B Lab. (2015). *The Nonprofit Behind B Corps*. Available at: www.bcorporation.net/what-are-b-corps/the-non-profit-behind-b-corps.
Bainbridge, S. (May 5, 2012). "The Shareholder Wealth Maximization Norm," *Professorbainbridge.com Blog*. Available at: www.professorbainbridge.com/professorbainbridgecom/2012/05/the-shareholder-wealth-maximization-norm.html.
Benefit Corp Information Center (2015). *State By State Legislative Status*. Available at: www.benefitcorp.net/state-by-state-legislative-status.
Bishop, C. (2010). "The Low-Profit LLC (L3C): Program Related Investment By Proxy Or Perversion?" *Arkansas Law Review* 63, 243–67.
Borzaga, C. and G. Galera (2012). "The Concept and Practice of Social Enterprise. Lessons from the Italian Experience," *International Review of Social Research* 2:2, 85–102.
Borzaga, C. and J. Defourny (eds) (2001). *The Emergence of Social Enterprise*. London and New York: Routledge.
Borzaga, C. and A. Santuari (2001). "Italy: From Traditional Co-operatives to Innovative Social Enterprises," in C. Borzaga and C. Defourny (eds), *The Emergence of Social Enterprise*. London & New York: Routledge, 166–181.
Brakman Reiser, D. (2009). "For-Profit Philanthropy," *Fordham Law Review* 77:5, 2437–73.
Brakman Reiser, D. (2010). "Governing and Financing Blended Enterprise," *Chicago-Kent Law Review* 85:2, 619–55.
Brakman Reiser, D. (2011a). "Benefit Corporations—A Sustainable Form of Organization?" *Wake Forest Law Review* 46:3, 591–625.

Brakman Reiser, D. (2011b). "Charity Law's Essentials," *Notre Dame Law Review* 86:1, 1–64.
Brakman Reiser, D. (2013). "Theorizing Forms for Social Enterprises," *Emory Law Journal* 62:4, 681–39.
Brakman Reiser, D. and S. Dean (2017). *Social Enterprise Law: Trust, Public Benefit, and Capital Markets*. New York, NY: Oxford University Press.
Bratton, W., J. McCahery and E. Vermeulen (2009). "How Does Corporate Mobility Affect Lawmaking? A Comparative Analysis," *American Journal of Comparative Law* 57, 347–85.
Brewer, C., E. Minnigh and R. Wexler (2014). *Social Enterprise by Nonprofits and Hybrid Organizations*. Arlington, VA: Tax Management Inc., a division of The Bureau of National Affairs, Inc.
Brody, E. (ed.) (2002). *Property-Tax Exemption for Charities*. Washington, DC: The Urban Institute Press.
Cafaggi, F. and P. Iamiceli (2008). "New Frontiers in the Legal Structure and Legislation of Social Enterprises in Europe: A Comparative Analysis," *European University Institute Working Papers* 2008/16.
Carini, C., E. Costa, M. Carpita and M. Andreaus (2012). "Italian Social Cooperatives in 2008: A Portrait Using Descriptive and Principal Component Analysis," Eurcise, Working Paper No. 035 (2012).
CECP, in association with The Conference Board (2014). *Giving in Numbers: 2016 Edition*. Available at: http://cecp.co/wp-content/uploads/2016/11/GIN2016_Finalweb-1.pdf?redirect=no.
Chell, E., L. Spence, F. Perrini and J. Harris (2014). "Social Entrepreneurship and Business Ethics: Does Social Equal Ethical?" *Journal of Business Ethics* 133:4, 1–7.
Coates, A. and W. van Opstal (2009). "The Joys and Burdens of Multiple Legal Frameworks for Social Entrepreneurship. Lessons from the Belgian Case," EMES Conferences Selected Papers Series, ECSP-T09-01. Colorado Revised Statutes § 7-101-501.
Companies (Audit, Investigations, and Community Enterprises) Act 2004. United Kingdom.
Companies Act 2006. United Kingdom.
Defourny, J. and M. Nyssens (2008). "Social Enterprise in Europe: Recent Trends and Developments," *Social Enterprise Journal* 4:3, 202–28.
Defourny, J. and M. Nyssens (2010). "Conceptions of Social Enterprise and Social Entrepreneurship in Europe and the United States: Convergences and Divergences," *Journal of Social Entrepreneurship* 1:1, 32–53.
Defourny, J. and M. Nyssens (2013). "Social Co-operatives: When Social Enterprises Meet the Co-operative Tradition," *Journal of Entrepreneurial and Organizational Diversity* 2:2, 11–33.Delaware Code Annotated, Title 8, §§ 361–68.
Delaware Department of State (2015). Division of Corporations, About Agency, available at: https://corp.delaware.gov/aboutagency.shtml.
Doeringer, M. (2010). "Fostering Social Enterprise: A Historical and International Analysis," *Duke Journal of Comparative & International Law* 20, 291–329.
Elhauge, E. (2005). "Sacrificing Corporate Profits in the Public Interest," *New York University Law Review* 80:3, 733–869.
Esposito, R. (2013). "The Social Enterprise Revolution in Corporate Law: A Primer on Emerging Corporate Entities in Europe and the United States and the Case for the Benefit Corporation," *William & Mary Business Law Review* 4, 639–714.
European Commission (2007). *Study On Practices And Policies In The Social Enterprise Sector In Europe*. Vienna.
European Commission. (2012). *Social Economy—Laying the Groundwork for Innovative Solutions to Today's Challenges*. Paris.
European Commission website (2015). *Social Entrepreneurship*. Available at: http://ec.europa.eu/internal_market/social_business/index_en.htm#maincontentSec3.
Eustice, J. and J. Kuntz (2015). *Federal Income Taxation of S Corporations*. London: Thomson Reuters.
Fayolle, A. and H. Matlay (2010). *Handbook of Research on Social Entrepreneurship*. Cheltenham, UK and Northampton, MA: Edward Elgar.
Fici, A. (2006). "The New Italian Law on Social Enterprise," Innovative Social Enterprise Development Network Working Paper 3.
Fici, A. (2013). "Italy," in Cracogna, D., Fici, A. and Henry, H. (eds), *International Handbook on Cooperative Law*. Berlin: Springer.
Finance Act 2014. United Kingdom.
Framjee, P. (2009). "Trading—A Survivor's Guide: Guidance Notes on Charity Trading in the U.K.," *International Journal of Not-for-Profit Law* 11:3. Available at: www.icnl.org/research/journal/vol11iss3/special_3.htm.
Fremont-Smith, M. (2004). *Governing Nonprofit Organizations*. Cambridge and London: Belknap.

Friedman, M. (1970). "The Social Responsibility of Business is to Increase its Profits," *New York Times Magazine* (September 13).

Hansmann, H. (1996). *The Ownership of Enterprise*. Cambridge, MA: Harvard University Press.

HM Revenue & Customs (HMRC) and HM Treasury, *Guidance: Social Investment Tax Relief*, (Updated 27 March 2015). Available at: www.gov.uk/government/publications/social-investment-tax-relief-factsheet/social-investment-tax-relief.

Hopt, K. and T. von Hippel (eds) (2010). *Comparative Corporate Governance of Nonprofit Organizations*. New York, NY: Cambridge University Press.

Illinois Comprehensive Statutes 180/1-26(d).

Internal Revenue Code (IRC) §§ 501(c)(3), 509, 511, 4942, 4944. United States.

Kerlin, J. (2006). "Social Enterprise in the United States and Europe: Understanding and Learning from the Differences," *Voluntas* 17, 247–263.

Kirshner, J. (2010). "'An Ever Closer Union' In Corporate Identity?: A Transatlantic Perspective on Regional Dynamics and the Societas Europaea," *St. John's Law Review* 84, 1273–1345.

Lane, M. (2011). *Social Enterprise: Empowering Mission-Driven Entrepreneurs*. Chicago, IL: American Bar Association Publishing.

Lang, R. (2014). *An Explanation of the L3C*. Available at: www.americansforcommunitydevelopment.org/downloads/Explanation%20of%20the%20L3C%20(021714-2).pdf.

Law 8 November 1991, No. 381. Italy.

Law 28 December 2015 (Stability Law), n. 208, article 1, par. 376–384. Italy.

Maryland Code, Corporations and Associations, § 5-6C-01 et seq.

McKeever, B. and Pettijohn, S. (2014). *The Nonprofit Sector in Brief*. Urban Institute. Available at: www.urban.org/sites/default/files/alfresco/publication-pdfs/413277-The-Nonprofit-Sector-in-Brief—.PDF.

McKinney's N.Y. Business Corporation Law § 1701 et seq. Model Benefit Corporation Law (MBCL). Available at: www.benefitcorp.net/attorneys/model-legislation.

Murray, J.H. (2014). "Social Enterprise Innovation: Delaware's Public Benefit Corporation Law," *Harvard Business Law Review* 4, 345–69.

Murray, J.H. (2016). "The Social Enterprise Market," *Maryland Law Review* 75:2, 541–589.

Murray, J.H. and E.I. Hwang (2011). "Purpose With Profit: Governance, Enforcement, Capital-Raising And Capital-Locking In Low-Profit Limited Liability Companies," *University of Miami Law Review* 66, 1–52.

Page, A. and R. Katz (2010). "Freezing Out Ben & Jerry: Corporate Law and the Sale of A Social Enterprise Icon," *Vermont Law Review* 35:1, 211–50.

Plerhoples, A. (2014). "Delaware Public Benefit Corporations 90 Days Out: Who's Opting In?" *U.C. Davis Business Law Journal* 14, 247–77.

Praskier, R. and A. Nowak (2012). *Social Entrepreneurship: Theory and Practice*. New York, NY: Cambridge University Press.

Rana, S. (2013). "Philanthropic Innovation And Creative Capitalism: A Historical And Comparative Perspective On Social Entrepreneurship And Corporate Social Responsibility," *Alabama Law Review* 64, 1121–74.

Regulator of Community Interest Companies (UK), *Annual Report 2016/2017*. Available at: www.gov.uk/government/uploads/system/uploads/attachment_data/file/630211/cic-17-2community-interest-companies-annual-report-2016-2017.pdf (referenced as CIC Regulator 2016/2017).

Revised Model Nonprofit Corporation Act (RMNCA) (1987).

Roe, M. (2001). "The Shareholder Wealth Maximization Norm and Industrial Organization," *University of Pennsylvania Law Review* 149, 2063–81.

Schwab, K. (2008). "Global Corporate Citizenship: Working with Governments and Civil Society," *Foreign Affairs* 87:1, 107–18.

Spence, L. (2014). "Business Ethics and Social Responsibility in Small Firms," in E. Chell and M. Karataş-Özkan (eds), *Handbook of Research on Small Business and Entrepreneurship*. Cheltenham, UK and Northampton, MA: Edward Elgar.

State of Delaware, Department of State. *Division of Corporations: About Agency*. Available at: http://corp.delaware.gov/aboutagency.shtml.

Stout, L. (2012). *The Shareholder Value Myth*. San Francisco, CA: Berrett-Koehler Publishers, Inc.

Strine, Jr., L. (2012). "Our Continuing Struggle with the Idea That For-Profit Corporations Seek Profit," *Wake Forest Law Review* 47, 135–72.

Tyler, J. (2010). "Negating the Legal Problem of Having 'Two Masters': A Framework for L3C Fiduciary Duties and Accountability," *Vermont Law Review* 35:1, 117–61.

Tyler, J., E. Absher, K. Garman and A. Luppino (2015). "Producing Better Mileage: Advancing The Design And Usefulness Of Hybrid Vehicles For Social Business Ventures," *Quinnipiac Law Review* 33, 235–337.

UK Office of the Regulator of Community Interest Companies (2016). *Information and Guidance Notes, Chapter 2: Preliminary Considerations*. Available at: www.gov.uk/government/uploads/system/uploads/attachment_data/file/605412/12-1334-community-interest-companies-chapter-2-preliminary-considerations.pdf (referenced as CIC Regulator Guidance 2016: Ch. 2).

UK Office of the Regulator of Community Interest Companies (2016). *Information and Guidance Notes, Chapter 4: Creating a Community Interest Company (CIC)*. Available at: www.gov.uk/government/uploads/system/uploads/attachment_data/file/605414/13-781-community-interest-companies-chapter-4-creating-a-cic.pdf (referenced as CIC Regulator Guidance 2016: Ch. 4).

UK Office of the Regulator of Community Interest Companies (2016). *Information and Guidance Notes, Chapter 6: The Asset Lock*. Available at: www.gov.uk/government/uploads/system/uploads/attachment_data/file/605418/14-1089-community-interest-companies-chapter-6-the-asset-lock.pdf (referenced as CIC Regulator Guidance 2016: Ch. 6).

UK Office of the Regulator of Community Interest Companies (2016). *Information and Guidance Notes, Chapter 8: Statutory Obligations*. Available at: www.gov.uk/government/uploads/system/uploads/attachment_data/file/605420/13-711-community-interest-companies-guidance-chapters-8-statutory-obligationstions.pdf (referenced as CIC Regulator Guidance 2016: Ch. 8).

UK Office of the Regulator of Community Interest Companies (2016). *Information and Guidance Notes, Chapter 9: Corporate Governance*. Available at: www.gov.uk/government/uploads/system/uploads/attachment_data/file/211749/13-712-community-interest-companies-guidance-chapter-9-corporate-governance.pdf (referenced as CIC Regulator Guidance 2016: Ch. 9).

United States Treasury Regulation § 53.4944-3.

Vermont Statutes Annotated (VSA) § 3001(27).

Vogel, D. (2005). *The Market for Virtue*. Washington, DC: The Brookings Institution Press.

Young, D. (2009). "Alternative Perspectives on Social Enterprise," in J. Cordes and E. Steuerle (eds), *Nonprofits and Business*. Washington, DC: The Urban Institute Press.

16
The ethics of entrepreneurship

Christian Lautermann and Kim Oliver Tokarski*

The central quality of entrepreneurship derives from the literal meaning of the word—*entreprendre* in French, *unternehmen* in German—which simply means to undertake or to get things done. So, if entrepreneurship is about getting things done, then immediately two major questions result: 1) "What things?" and 2) "What for?" It is obvious that these two questions have ethical or normative implications, so there is good reason to consider the ethics of entrepreneurship. Oddly enough, however, entrepreneurial ethics has been a generally neglected topic within business ethics and entrepreneurship research. Yet it has begun to emerge more recently. Empirical research and conceptual theorizing about the ethical issues of entrepreneurship have been presented in a body of literature emergent from the early 1990s (Dees and Starr 1992).

The literature is wide in scope and of variable quality, but it suggests that the ethics of entrepreneurship is a genuine field of inquiry within the family of critical social sciences and ethics, not just a subfield of business ethics. In this sense, entrepreneurship is not a mere economic phenomenon but also a social one. Since the path-breaking work of economic thinkers such as Joseph A. Schumpeter (1934), Ludwig von Mises (1949), Israel Kirzner (1973) and Peter F. Drucker (1985), who regarded the entrepreneur in terms of economic function, there has arisen a growing discussion of the entrepreneur both as economic and social agent. Within this literature one encounters empirical considerations of the decision-making processes of entrepreneurs, as well as moral perspectives on the implications of the two questions posed above.

This chapter will consider these topics, beginning in the first section with an overview of the classic conceptions of entrepreneurship as well as more recent ones found in business and management literature. In the second section we portray some of the ways in which the conception of entrepreneurship has been extended or broadened to include activities that may not appear economic. The third section offers a synoptic account of four core elements in any kind of entrepreneurial activity. In the fourth section we take up some of the recent empirical literature on the ethics of entrepreneurial decision-making. The last section sets forth some normative perspectives for assessing the things that entrepreneurs might pursue and for what ends.

Christian Lautermann and Kim Oliver Tokarski

Conceptions of entrepreneurship

The classic conception of the entrepreneur is found in the work of economists. Perhaps the first to introduce the notion was Richard Cantillon (1755) who conceptualized the entrepreneur as an economic risk-bearer. Some fifty years later Jean-Baptiste Say (1803) explored the notion of the entrepreneur in terms of coordinating resources for productive profit-making (see the study by Bert Hoselitz (1960) for a consideration of early instances of entrepreneurship, as well as the work of Robert Hébert and Albert Link (1988)). Schumpeter develops the notion in terms of creativity and innovation: the entrepreneur carries out innovations that interrupt the equilibrium of a functioning market. Von Mises draws a distinction between simply managing resources efficiently and being attuned or alert to a divergence or discrepancy between the sum of the factors of production and the prices that the good might receive in the market (von Mises 1949: 289–294). The insights of von Mises have been developed more fully in Kirzner's notion of entrepreneurial alertness (1973): the entrepreneur is alert to profit-making opportunities and in acting on these he moves the market closer to equilibrium. Drawing from Say's account and, like von Mises, pointing to the power of consumer decision-making, Peter Drucker contends (1985) that the entrepreneur, whether an individual or an organization, shifts resources to their most profitable uses. Along with Frank Knight's distinction between uncertainty and risk, not to mention his emphasis on entrepreneurial judgment (1921, 1942), there is the more recent study by William J. Baumol (1990) on conditions for entrepreneurship (and see also Foss and Klein 2012). All of these works are essential for anyone who wishes to comprehend the theoretical and historical contours of the idea of entrepreneurship. Much subsequent scholarship that deals with the characteristic traits or typical behavior of entrepreneurs is, in a real sense, derivative of the classic works of economists.

As we shift from economic theory to the emerging literature on entrepreneurial ethics we find that discussions of the entrepreneur become more loosely related to any theoretical function or specific role. In the management and business literature the notions of entrepreneurship range from the narrow (entrepreneurs as self-employed business people) to the wide-ranging (entrepreneurship as a universal and creative activity). Since the late 1980s empirically oriented contributions to entrepreneurship have assumed an individualistic approach that focuses on business entrepreneurs as those "who described themselves as self-employed" (Longenecker et al. 1988: 66). The classic economic conception did not regard the entrepreneur simply as "self-employed" even though such a description, which reflects the entrepreneur's abandonment of the steady paycheck for the uncertainties of enterprise, may draw nonetheless from Knight's distinction between risk and uncertainty (Knight 1921).[1] More generally, entrepreneurship has been characterized, often vaguely, as "the embodiment of individualism in the realm of economic activity" (Velamuri 2002: 125). An individualistic and economic understanding, which drew its force from the classic economists, proved dominant until recently: "Entrepreneurs . . . carry out economic tasks that increase employment, create new organizations, uncover new production processes and perform other business activities which improve material well-being" (Hannafey 2003: 101). From this general perspective, it is often inferred that entrepreneurship has its "home" in the economic sphere and should not be "extended inappropriately to other spheres" (Brenkert 2002: 24).

Alongside the economic conception is the prominent image of the entrepreneur as individual "hero." The idea of entrepreneurs as extraordinary performers is common not only in public perception, but also in ethics-related research: "entrepreneurs [are understood] as mavericks who resist conformity to bureaucratic structures and rules" (Longenecker et al. 1988: 65). This picture, of course, must draw from descriptions of the great early theoreticians of entrepreneurship, especially Schumpeter with his "plus ultra" innovator who seeks to create his own realm (Schumpeter 1997 [1911]: 137), or Kirzner's resource mobilizer who becomes aware of changed patterns of resource availability and economic possibilities (Kirzner 1974). In fact, the entrepreneur as creative agent is an important element in some of the ethical questions regarding entrepreneurship. For example, the notion of the entrepreneur as a discrete type of agent helps to distinguish him from the capitalist (cf. Gasparski 2010: 25–27 with reference to von Mises1949) or the small business manager (Carland et al. 1984). These distinctions are helpful to a consideration of morally relevant internal psychological states, including intuitive awareness, ambition, and desire for control, as well as external factors such as accountability or reputation (Steinbauer et al. 2014).

These economic considerations of entrepreneurship would seem to incorporate tacit ethical concerns and assumptions that, effectively, respond to the two questions posed at the beginning of this chapter. However, any such response carries implications that proceed beyond a seemingly narrow economic function and to broader conceptions of entrepreneurship. Therefore, to grasp the full range of ethical issues regarding entrepreneurship, it may be necessary "to shift the focus away from 'entrepreneurs' and onto the much broader phenomenon of entrepreneurial action or 'entrepreneuring' in its societal and institutional contexts" (Watson 2013: 16).

Expanded conceptions of entrepreneurship

The economic perspective focuses, typically though not necessarily, on functions and outcomes, especially of individual endeavor. However, Marta Calás et al. (2009: 553) raise a question that points to a broader conception: "What would happen, theoretically and analytically, if the focus . . . were reframed from entrepreneurship as an economic activity with possible social change outcomes to entrepreneurship as a social change activity with a variety of possible outcomes?" Given the emergence of entrepreneurial ventures that are community-based or cooperative, the scope of entrepreneurship may be extended beyond "entrepreneurship as [only] creative market action" (Dunham 2007: 15) or as reliant "on functionalist and positivist assumptions that define entrepreneurship as an economic activity" (Goss et al. 2011: 212). The theoretical move from individualism to an entrepreneurship that is social, cultural, and historical (Clarke and Holt 2010: 317–318) allows us to discern entrepreneurship in a broader light. From this perspective, entrepreneurship discloses a shared "new world" (Spinosa et al. 1997) and offers "a new or reconfigured set of practices that many or most people then come to 'take for granted'" (Solomon 1999: 174).

Within this extended conception, the organizing processes of change and transformation prove broader than what was assumed when entrepreneurship was relegated to business (Goss et al. 2011: 212). For this reason, one may add to the classic notions of innovation and value creation, the notion of entrepreneurship as *emancipation* from the status quo (Rindova et al. 2009). Of course, as Richard Swedberg points out, even the young Schumpeter had stressed that "in other areas of society than the economy" there are "dynamic" people undertaking new things (Swedberg 2006: 33). Advancing this idea, Michela Betta et al. have proposed "that any innovative practices that lead to personal development and growth should be understood as a form of entrepreneurship" (2010: 234). This view ranges over various social phenomena and might include practices such as establishing a new lifestyle after a personal crisis or systematic efforts to achieve new career goals. But such an expansive view is contestable in that it may include too much. For instance, George Brenkert remarks that entrepreneurship should not be expanded too far: "I don't think that we should allow the term to apply to everyone . . . Consequently, accounts such as von Mises's and Kirzner's, which identify entrepreneurship with an ability characteristic of human action, should be rejected" (Brenkert 2002: 9). Whether or not this is a correct reading of von Mises or Kirzner—each of whom notes an entrepreneurial element in all human action without extending entrepreneurship to any or all *activities*—the statement does mark an opposing side of the debate.

Although various authors have defended a broader notion of entrepreneurship, some of their statements do prove vague, as when entrepreneurship is characterized as, "the capacity to be 'active and get things done,' thus acting as an entrepreneur . . . belongs to every man and woman" (Johansson 2009: 1209), or when it is characterized in terms of "a more humanistic conception of not just people in business but all economic agency . . . [so] that to an extent we are all entrepreneurs, only some of us become professional at the task" (Machan 1999: 600). Another scholar (Velamuri 2002: 128) opines that "entrepreneurship, in its most generic form, takes place in all areas of activity and inquiry. . . . Any creative act, in its essence, is an entrepreneurial act" referring thereby to Peter Drucker, who anticipates how "[i]nnovation and entrepreneurship are . . . needed in society as much as in the economy, in public-service institutions as much as in businesses" (1985: 254).

It is one thing to expand the notion of entrepreneurship, but does such expansion entail *no* distinction between social and commercial entrepreneurship? Social entrepreneurship is commonly described as pursuing a social mission, creating social value, or tackling social problems in an innovative fashion or an entrepreneurial way. However, there is disagreement on the definition and the uniqueness of social entrepreneurship as a theoretical concept: except for the attribute "social" the conceptual differences among established fields of entrepreneurship (economic, social, institutional) remain unclear; empirically most of the examples in one field could be treated as ventures in other fields (Dacin et al. 2010). Some have conceptualized social entrepreneurship and business entrepreneurship in terms of altruistic motivation: entrepreneurship becomes "social" because of its altruistic direction compared with the business version (Tan et al. 2005), but this interpretation assumes that economic entrepreneurship is *not* altruistic in the first place (Velamuri 2002). Other attempts to distinguish the two do not get beyond the already cited motivation, or organizational structure (profit vs. nonprofit), or the reiteration of sector (business vs. social) (cf. Lautermann 2013). Yet other scholars have suggested that a distinction could be forged in terms of value *creation*, as in social entrepreneurship, as opposed to value *capture*, in commercial entrepreneurship (Santos 2012; Agafonow 2014). Still others have proposed that any division of entrepreneurship is "artificial," for "social entrepreneurship and business entrepreneurship in the private arena are not necessarily dichotomous but rather a continuum" (Surie and Ashley 2008: 238). However, this last suggestion is unpersuasive at least as long as one regards the social and the economic as distinct and opposed realms.

Nonetheless, and contrary to an attempt to distinguish one form of entrepreneurship from another, if the notion is treated as a broad social activity from the outset, then one may proceed to an ethics of entrepreneurship that overcomes the tendency to separate theoretically the poles of social/altruistic/ethical from those of economic/selfish/unethical. It is that very tendency, by the way, which is often expressed in an idealized moral portrayal of social entrepreneurs as "a priori ethical," thereby blessed with the moral potential to solve social problems or meet social needs (Dey and Steyaert 2016; Bacq et al. 2016).

However, if one starts, as we suggest, from the assumption that entrepreneurship is a social activity, then all that remains to do is to consider, reflect on, or assess the qualities of different forms of entrepreneurship in terms of their "social" merits, benefits, or values—all part of an ethics of entrepreneurship.

Core elements of entrepreneurship

The two questions that entrepreneurship raises, noted at the commencement of this chapter, arise from the idea of an *undertaking*, or getting things done: What things are undertaken, and to what purposes are they pursued? To revisit these questions allows us to set forth four features of any notion of entrepreneurship.

1   The first feature follows from the first question: As a form of social action, entrepreneurship is fundamentally about the *creation* of goods or values. The things created through entrepreneurship may be valued good or bad, better or worse, a point developed by Baumol (1990); at the same time other things of value or worth, or things of little value may be destroyed. It is therefore a basic ethical question of entrepreneurship: "What values are being created (or destroyed) through entrepreneurship? and for whom?" Since other forms of social action can be regarded as value creating (e.g., politics, arts, science), we need to explore further features in order to grasp the *entrepreneurial* way of value creation.

2   One could assume that any instance of entrepreneurship is but an instrumental activity designed to bring to fruition some good or value. But there is a larger or deeper concern about the creative activity of entrepreneurship: the activity itself has some inherent value. The purpose of entrepreneurship is not merely an instrumental one of bringing about some product: after all, in many instances of entrepreneurship the good that results is not known prior to the activity but emerges in the course of the activity. The inherent value of creative activity rests in its very exercise: freedom. In this sense, entrepreneurship is a matter of "breaking free from authority and breaking up perceived constraints . . . of an intellectual, psychological, economic, social, institutional, or cultural nature" (Rindova et al. 2009: 479). Entrepreneurship is not only about "dealing with resistance or opposition" (Brenkert 2002: 11) or about a challenge to "prevailing beliefs and values, disrupting the status quo" (Dunham 2007: 22) but is *emancipatory*. In this way, emancipation emerges "as a defining principle of entrepreneuring" (Goss et al. 2011: 213). The effects of the emancipatory practice may allow for the independence or sovereignty of a much larger group than the entrepreneurs themselves. Of course, the overcoming of constraints may introduce new constraints, but the emerging constraints are (typically) not intended or even anticipated but a side-effect of the entrepreneurial activity.

The first two core features of entrepreneurship are therefore 1) *creativity/change* and 2) *emancipation/liberation*. The latter has only recently become an *explicitly* conceptualized quality of entrepreneurship. Leaving a permanent job and going into business for oneself emancipates one from a subordinate position in a management structure. Schumpeter too mentions the entrepreneur's "dream and will to found a private realm" which can be (among others) an expression of "freedom" (Schumpeter 1997 [1911]: 138, authors' translation). The notion of creativity has a long history, most prominently in terms of the Schumpeterian emphasis on innovation. The same is true for the two further features of entrepreneurship that emerge once one answers a corollary query, "*How* are things getting done?" This question indicates the third and fourth features.

3   Things are accomplished by *taking a risk*. As a core feature of entrepreneurship, risk has probably the longest history, as the first documented usage of the word "entrepreneur" is attributed to the Irish-French economist Cantillon (1755; and see Tarascio 1985). More important for our current treatment of entrepreneurial risk is the theory of uncertainty developed by Knight one and a half centuries later. Several ethical questions arise including

the appropriate relation between risk and reward, as in the case of entrepreneurial profit (Arnold 1987). Other related and basic ethical questions that follow on risk and uncertainty concern the evaluation of any threats or potential harms that may arise from the entrepreneurial process and who is affected by them. Such questions also lead to examination, empirically, of the living conditions and the quality of life of both *self-employed* entrepreneurs who voluntarily abandon the safety of their regular paycheck and bear the uncertainties of their own enterprise, as well as *precarious* entrepreneurs who are forced to make themselves dependent on creditors or procurers in order to survive. An important focus of analysis in this respect is how personal risks are conditioned or structured by power relations and institutions which, in turn, can be the object of entrepreneural efforts (institutional entrepreneurship).

4   By *seizing an opportunity*. Mainly due to the oeuvre of Israel Kirzner, the discovery, creation and exploitation of opportunities are recognized as some of the most common features of entrepreneurship and as well-established concepts in entrepreneurship studies (Foss and Klein 2012: Ch. 3; cf. Shane 2005). The utilization of one's perception and alertness have been successfully applied to the other (non-economic) fields of social, sustainable, and institutional entrepreneurship and play a central role in the literature on the ethics of entrepreneurship. In as much as mobilizing and exploiting resources is the common way to seize opportunities entrepreneurially, the most obvious ethical issue related to this is not only what is *noticed* but the *means* and *consequences* of the accompanying utilizations and exploitations: Under what circumstances is the use of informational advantage justified? What role do differences or deficits in market regulation play in the legitimacy of opportunity exploitation? May one use government powers to enact a regulation that would thwart competition or gain a competitive advantage? Under what conditions may personal connections be used to create opportunities that others do not have access to? Can the assumed benefits of exploiting an opportunity justify jeopardizing or compromising others' wellbeing?

In sum, entrepreneurship can be understood as a creative and emancipatory undertaking promoted by taking risks and seizing opportunities. These four features provide thematic cornerstones for a consideration of the ethics of entrepreneurship and they guide recent efforts "to reframe entrepreneurship theory into a more critical and reflexive mode" (Goss et al. 2011: 212). The very features of entrepreneurship indicate a critical and reflexive approach that must take into account that creation may be accompanied by destruction, emancipation may lead to new domination, risk may generate courage or recklessness, and that the seizing of opportunity may sometimes be mere opportunism but sometimes much more. To appreciate ambiguities and contradictions need not detract from the overall orientation of an approach to entrepreneurship guided by the hope of a desirable future: "the task of entrepreneurship is to move us from the world we have to live in to the world we want to live in" (Sarasvathy 2002: 96).

Ethical entrepreneurship: empirical considerations

Having discussed the general scope and core elements of entrepreneurship, and before we broach some normative ethical perspectives, we pause with a summation of empirical research on entrepreneurial ethics, focusing chiefly on the ethical decision-making attitudes and strategies of entrepreneurs. Many of these studies focus on the narrower practice of business entrepreneurship, but their conclusions offer significant and interesting considerations on the empirical context of decision making. In this context, it is important to note that entrepreneurs often do not face issues arising from the separation of ownership and control; many entrepreneurs own the majority stake in their companies. Because of this link between entrepreneurship and ownership, it is often thought that the actions of an entrepreneur may provide a more direct image of his or her own ethical perspectives than the activity of a person situated within a large organization or publically held company (Bucar and Hisrich 2001).

One research stream in entrepreneurship studies analyzes the traits of entrepreneurs. Entrepreneurs are often characterized by positive traits, such as self-confidence and a high need for achievement: these individuals are action oriented and make decisions on their own, without consultation with others. Even if entrepreneurs have many values in common with other actors in business, like managers, entrepreneurs may be more independent and even egoistic when the decision has clear financial relevance (Ayios et al. 2014). They also tend to rationalize behavioral traits—egoism, selfishness, domination, or opportunism—that others view more critically (Longenecker et al. 1988). In many instances these attributes are regarded by the entrepreneurial agents as the very traits that enable creativity and innovation in the face of challenge and doubt.

Psychological and social factors

As noted earlier in the chapter, entrepreneurs are often stereotyped in heroic terms or as persons who possess traits such as low aversion to high risk. This often leads to the (implicit) assumption that an entrepreneur must be a rule-breaker if he or she wants to be innovative and successful in the entrepreneurial process (Zhang and Arvey 2009). It is also often assumed that entrepreneurs rely more on their individual opinions and values than do managers, especially those in large organizations (Bucar et al. 2003: 8). Nonetheless, there seems to be no (globally) clear picture regarding whether there is a difference between the ethical attitudes and behaviors of entrepreneurs versus managers, either in small businesses or large companies, especially when studies analyze these dimensions cross-culturally.

For example, some cross-cultural studies, such as that of Robert Hisrich and Mikhail Gratchev (2001), show that US and Russian entrepreneurs differ in terms of their attitudes and their adherence to ethical codes. However, when Branko Bucar et al. (2003) analyzed the differences of ethical attitudes between entrepreneurs and managers across the United States, Russia, and Slovenia, it turned out that entrepreneurs and managers differed significantly in only a few cases. This might seem surprising given that one may assume that entrepreneurs and managers encounter distinct situations. Yet several studies indicate that only minor differences exist between actors in small rather than large businesses (Longenecker et al. 1989; Bucar et al. 2003; Longenecker et al. 2006), especially when the small firm represents the entrepreneur and the large stands for the manager (e.g., Bucar and Hisrich 2001; Crane 2009). However, in Bucar and Hisrich's study (2001), entrepreneurs and managers differed only slightly regarding their ethical perceptions and judgment (as noted in previous findings of Hisrich and Gratchev 2001).

Nonetheless, there are some significant differences. Entrepreneurs seem to be more likely to maintain their ethical attitudes than are managers. Managers tend to sacrifice their personal values in favor of those of the company more than entrepreneurs do (Bucar and Hisrich 2001). Similar findings in studying Canadian entrepreneurs and managers have been presented (Crane 2009). Canadian entrepreneurs and managers differed only slightly in terms of ethical attitudes, yet to a greater degree than managers the entrepreneurs did perceive some specific practices as unethical, such as exaggerating the performance of a company's product (or service) or criticizing unfairly a competitor's products.

Ethical decision-making

The concepts and processes of ethical decision-making and ethical judgment have long been studied in different disciplines (e.g., business, medicine). In the case of entrepreneurs, faced with the risk of business failure, they are often confronted with ethical dilemmas distinct from those encountered by managers. If so, then one might expect different modes of decision-making in distinct contexts. For example, entrepreneurs often rely on personal judgments of right and wrong, rather than organizational codes (Robinson et al. 2007).

Groundbreaking research on the development of models to explain the ethical decision-making process, commonly of individuals (in organizations), has been done by O.C. Ferrell and L.G. Gresham (1985). Within the context of moral development there have been numerous additional studies (Rest 1986; Treviño 1986: Hunt and Vitell 1986; Bommer et al. 1987; Dubinsky and Loken 1989; Jones 1991; Hunt and Vitell 2006). Most of the research has been done in the context of marketing ethics, though Linda Trevino's general model (1986) is an exception. James Rest (1986) established a four-component model, which comprises recognizing moral issues, making moral judgments, establishing moral intent, and implementing moral actions. Thomas Jones (1991) developed an issue-contingent model of ethical decision making in organizations that includes variables of individual moral intensity, recognition, judgment, and intent, as well as organizational factors.

During the past three decades, scholars have analyzed the areas of ethical decisions made by entrepreneurs during the start-up and growth phase. Dinah Payne and Brenda Joyner (2006) suggest that ethical (and social) responsibility enters into decision-making along four distinct categories related either to the individual, the organization, the product (service), or stakeholders more generally. The results of Payne and Joyner's study also show that the ethics (or values) acknowledged (explicitly or tacitly) by entrepreneurs are similar to those of society in general. A confirming study revealed that between small business owners and their customers there was a high degree of similarity in ethical judgments (Humphreys et al. 1993). Other studies of ethical decision making include Kuratko and Goldsby (2004) and Robinson et al. (2007).

Despite these various studies, ethical decision making in entrepreneurship is not well understood. Due to the uncertain context in which the entrepreneur acts and enterprises operate, entrepreneurs are disposed to adopt distinctive/diverse cognitive approaches to decision making (McVea 2009). For many entrepreneurs working within a new or small organization (without structures, processes, or routines) and lacking established ties with stakeholders, there is no well-established organizational culture (see, for example, Henderson 1999; Brush et al. 2001; Gruber 2003). Therefore, the entrepreneur cannot rely upon organizational culture in making ethical choices. Furthermore, there are no established company ethical codes to rely on when making ethical decisions (Buchholz and Rosenthal 2005).

Among the ethical difficulties that entrepreneurs encounter is that they must build a reputation and demonstrate legitimacy if they are to acquire resources and build up trust (Rutherford et al. 2009). Reputation serves as an economic resource, a means of social recognition, a mechanism of control, and as a means of status amongst other owner-managers. An entrepreneur must overcome any liabilities and gain legitimacy with investors and stakeholders. However, sometimes the means for doing so may include questionable ethical conduct—telling lies or misrepresenting facts to present the company in a better and more appealing way (Rutherford et al. 2009).

If the entrepreneur must have a vision of some sort, then so must he or she have a story to tell about it. In fact, it is often assumed that entrepreneurs should be good storytellers to acquire funds and backing to engage in a venture. Empirical findings show that a good story helps entrepreneurs in acquiring funds for initiating and sustaining the entrepreneurial process.

Thus, storytelling is an important instrument through which entrepreneurs can acquire additional resources. Nevertheless, the stories told by entrepreneurs do not seem always to be true. A major theme in ethical decision making is the intentional misrepresentation of reality—lying. Of course, lying is distinct from exaggeration or the expression of an overly optimistic attitude about the future. Moreover, the commitment to realize one's vision is distinct from both lying and exaggeration. The chief concern, as some have noted, is that an entrepreneur will lie to a (potential) investor to get the needed resources (Martens et al. 2007; Lounsbury and Glynn 2001; Pollack and Bosse 2014). Entrepreneurs do, in fact, face a dilemma: Should they lie to acquire the needed resources? Or should they be honest to potential investors and face a risk that these investors will not provide funds for the company? With respect to questions such as these, it is necessary to examine, if only summarily, some of the perspectives from which to evaluate the ethics of entrepreneurship.

Ethical entrepreneurship: normative considerations

Moving from empirical research to the ethical theorizing of entrepreneurship, we should recall the central implication of the four features of entrepreneurship. Entrepreneurial creativity raises the question of the values created, entrepreneurial emancipation expresses the desirable purpose of exercising and gaining freedom, entrepreneurial risk affects the well-being of entrepreneurs and their stakeholders, and entrepreneurial opportunities may be seized in various ways. Consequently, entrepreneurship is an inherently normative, value-laden, and thus ethical concept.

How might one consider the ethics of entrepreneurship? We suggest considering three theoretical approaches to the ethics of entrepreneurship: pragmatism, virtue ethics, and value pluralism. These approaches may be characterized independently of one another even as they may be able to be fused in a more sophisticated theory.

Pragmatism

Entrepreneurial creation occurs within economic and social contexts, takes place over time, and involves improvisation and experimentation. These factors have inclined some to adopt a pragmatist approach to entrepreneurial action that focuses on experimentation, experience, contingency, and habits (Buchholz and Rosenthal 2005: 314). The pragmatist approach suggests that entrepreneurial valuations and judgments are continually tested and altered through a practical process of experimentation: "ethics is something which is done by social entrepreneurs on a day-to-day basis rather than possessed once and for all" (Dey and Steyaert 2016: 628). Moreover, the role of contingency appears in a different light and obtains an unexpected ethical significance. Contingency—understood as "possibility without necessity"—leaves the entrepreneurial agent a certain flexibility between the extremes of autonomy and adaptation (Harmeling 2011: 296); in this sense, contingency itself becomes a resource that can help create new values (Harmeling et al. 2009). In this view the agent's values and preferences are not fixed (as in traditional economic notions) but discovered and formed in the process of entrepreneurship. Therefore, Buchholz and Rosenthal (2005) call their pragmatist union of entrepreneurship and moral decision-making a "process approach to ethics." If we apply the experimental experience-based approach of pragmatism to ethical questions regarding entrepreneurial action, eventually one is pushed to assess relevant elements of experience, including "the primacy of habit and repetition in shaping behavior, including habits of thinking" (Surie and Ashley 2008: 239).

Virtue ethics

Habituation, says Aristotle, is essential to the cultivation of virtues and character. In the Aristotelian tradition (which has been adopted in some of the recent organizational and business ethics literature) virtues are considered exemplary human qualities that are developed and exercised, as Aristotle counseled, via habituation within a good community. Although virtue ethics as a theory has a richer intellectual heritage than pragmatism, within the entrepreneurship literature the discussion is often limited to a listing of virtues compared with certain entrepreneurial traits (e.g., Hicks 2009: 53; Crockett and Anderson 2004: 12; see also Karlson et al. 2015). Such practical moral capabilities or virtues—both during and after their full development—become effective for the entrepreneur's actions, character, and life. At a general level of the ethical assessment of entrepreneurship, basic moral capabilities such as "moral sensitivity" and "moral imagination" have been suggested (Buchholz and Rosenthal 2005: 311–312); perhaps the most comprehensive capacity is that of phronesis, i.e., practical wisdom or prudence (cf. Dunham 2010; Dunham et al. 2008).

Practical wisdom (or prudence) is often presented as a kind of entrepreneurial super-virtue as it constitutes "a skill for discernment required of every entrepreneur: the exercise of judgment in particular cases" (Crockett and Anderson 2004: 12). Practical wisdom integrates both ethical and pragmatic qualities of the agent in context. Thus, it "can be defined as the capacity to understand and act upon what is both *good and feasible for oneself and others* in particular situations" (Dunham 2010: 523, emphasis in original). In this respect wise or prudent entrepreneurship entails the pursuit of opportunities in order to achieve a greater good. Some link practical wisdom to entrepreneurial judgment (Machan 1999: 604), though others have noted only that practical wisdom (or prudence) and entrepreneurial discernment share a commonality: each requires the agent to observe a complicated context of particulars and to see beyond the limits of self (Heath 2015: 74). The general contention remains: to understand the entrepreneur as acting and creating within particular conditions is to grasp that ethics is not external to entrepreneurship but inherent in the theory.

Value pluralism

The ethics of entrepreneurship has to deal with the potentiality and the changeability of both good and bad as possible directions of any entrepreneurial process. The very fact of emancipation may entail new values or a new *competing* value. Another normative perspective on entrepreneurship, and one that may complement the pragmatic and even some virtue ethics approaches—such as Alasdair MacIntyre's account (1985: 187) of historically grounded social practices—is that which embraces the idea of value pluralism. One of the most notable of value pluralists was Isaiah Berlin (1969) but his focus was on political liberalism. However, the notion that there may be plural and incommensurable values may be applied to individual and social choice more generally: "Only with a pluralism of values is it possible to view conflicts of values as an area of tension able to serve as a source for new values" (Wempe 2005: 216). Laura Dunham (2007: 15–16) explains concisely the relevance of this argument to our subject: "[E]ntrepreneurship is fundamentally involved with a confrontation between prevailing beliefs and values. As that confrontation ultimately results in the shaping of new values and beliefs across the broader society ... the role of ethics ... inspire[s] creativity, experimentation and imagination." Although this sort of claim may prove too grand, if not too dramatic, it arises as part of the suggestion that the very "process" of entrepreneurship "entails an exploration of the multiplicity of incommensurable values ..." (Dunham 2010: 525).

To get a sense of the applicability of value pluralism to entrepreneurial activity, one should consider some of the challenges that new creations pose. Neither the high-tech startup introducing a green technology to fight climate change or the community enterprise offering a new social service to citizens can ever be sure whether the innovation will be accepted as beneficial or disliked as reprehensible—even though the entrepreneurs had the best intentions and a promising vision. Green technologies might come into conflict with other social values, even ecological ones: for example, wind power vs. nature conservation. Any well-meant social service that appeared undoubtedly decent at the time can turn out to be considered inappropriate due to unpredicted cultural changes: for example, consider a home economics school for women that will be evaluated differently from the perspective of a feminist as opposed to that of a non-feminist. Instead of juxtaposing the ethical to the unethical, the value pluralist suggests that the plurality (and even ambivalence) of valuation should be taken into ethical consideration. Entrepreneurship (as a creative emancipatory practice) is a particularly good case for illustration.

Concluding remarks

Entrepreneurship was once considered a province of the economic, but as an activity it is not singularly economic or commercial. In fact, it rests on various social conditions and assumptions and appears in various guises. But in every instance it manifests a response to the questions: What things are being done? And for what purpose? These questions help to illuminate ethical concerns and these may be enriched by insights from pragmatism, virtue ethics, and pluralism. In this way, it becomes possible to take into consideration as integral features of entrepreneurship the normative value issues regarding the good life. The ethics of entrepreneurship is an integrative and critical reflection on multiple values and the good life. This chapter has sought to outline the ethics *of* entrepreneurship as the consideration of the empirical conditions and the valuational issues relevant to entrepreneurship theory. In this respect, the future task of the proposed ethics of entrepreneurship will be a systematic critical reflection of the conditions, manners, types, and effects of entrepreneurship with regard to the good (or the better) action, the good person, community, society, and world: in short, the good life.

Essential readings

The classic discussion of the entrepreneur is found in Joseph Schumpeter's *The Theory of Economic Development* (1911). On the entrepreneur as alert to opportunity, see Israel M. Kirzner, *Competition and Entrepreneurship* (1973). For an economic account of entrepreneurship that takes into consideration the contributions of both Kirnzer and Frank Knight, see the book by Nicolai J. Foss and Peter G. Klein, *Organizing Entrepreneurial Judgment* (2012). The pioneering contribution to the emerging field of ethics and entrepreneurship is probably the essay of J.G. Dees and J.A. Starr, "Entrepreneurship through an Ethical Lens: Dilemmas and Issues for Research and Practice" (1992). The most recent overview of the field is that of Jared Harris, Harry Sapienza, and Norman Bowie, "Ethics and Entrepreneurship" (2009). For an overview on the ethical decision-making of entrepreneurs, see Robert Steinbauer, Nicholas Rhew, Eric Kinnamon, and Francis Fabian, "The Conflicting Drivers of Entrepreneurial Ethics" (2014). On ethical entrepreneurship from a pragmatist perspective, see Rogene A. Buchholz and Sandra B. Rosenthal, "The Spirit of Entrepreneurship and the Qualities of Moral Decision Making" (2005) and Susan S. Harmeling, Saras Sarasvathy and R. Edward Freeman, "Related Debates in Ethics and Entrepreneurship: Values, Opportunities, and Contingency" (2009). From a virtue ethics approach see Laura C. Dunham, "From Rational to Wise Action" (2010) and George Brenkert, "Innovation, Rule Breaking and the Ethics of Entrepreneurship" (2009).

For further reading in this volume on entrepreneurship, virtue and profit, see Chapter 7, Can profit seekers be virtuous? On the significance of Joseph Schumpeter to entrepreneurship and innovation more generally, see Chapter 19, Creativity, innovation, and the production of wealth. Those interested in the entrepreneur as a leader should consult Chapter 25, Leadership and business ethics: are leaders wolves for business ethics? Considerations of moral entrepreneurship may be found in Chapter 8, Feminist ethics and business ethics: redefining landscapes of learning.

Notes

* The authors thank the editors of this volume for their patience and assistance in bringing this chapter to completion.

1 We owe this insight to Alexei Marcoux.

References

Agafonow, A. (2014). "Toward A Positive Theory of Social Entrepreneurship: On Maximizing Versus Satisficing Value Capture," *Journal of Business Ethics* 125:4, 709–713.
Anderson, A.R. and R. Smith (2007). "The Moral Space in Entrepreneurship: an Exploration of Ethical Imperatives and the Moral Legitimacy of Being Enterprising," *Entrepreneurship and Regional Development* 19:6, 479–497.
Arjoon, S. (2000). "Virtue Theory as a Dynamic Theory of Business," *Journal of Business Ethics* 28:2, 159–178.
Arnold, N.S. (1987). "Why Profits are Deserved," *Ethics* 97:2, 387–402.
Ayios, A., R. Jeurissen, P. Manning and L.J. Spence (2014). "Social Capital: A Review from an Ethics Perspective," *Business Ethics: A European Review* 23:1, 108–124.
Bacq, S., C. Hartog and B. Hoogendoorn (2016). "Beyond the Moral Portrayal of Social Entrepreneurs: An Empirical Approach to Who They Are and What Drives Them," *Journal of Business Ethics* 133:4, 703–718.
Baumol, W.J. (1990). "Entrepreneurship: Productive, Unproductive, Destructive," *Journal of Political Economy* 98:5, 893–921.
Berlin, I. (1969). "Two Concepts of Liberty," *Four Essays on Liberty*. London: Oxford University Press [new edition 2002].
Betta, M., R. Jones and J. Latham (2010). "Entrepreneurship and the Innovative Self: a Schumpeterian Reflection," *International Journal of Entrepreneurial Behaviour and Research* 16:3, 229–244.
Bommer, M., C. Gratto, J. Gravander and M. Tuttle (1987). "A Behavioral Model of Ethical and Unethical Decision Making," *Journal of Business Ethics* 6:4, 265–280.
Brenkert, G.G. (2002). "Entrepreneurship, Ethics, and the Good Society," *The Ruffin Series of the Society for Business Ethics* 3, 5–43.
Brenkert, G.G. (2009). "Innovation, Rule Breaking and the Ethics of Entrepreneurship: Special Issue Ethics and Entrepreneurship," *Journal of Business Venturing* 24:5, 448–464.
Brush, C.G., P.G. Greene and M.M. Hart (2001). "From Initial Idea to Unique Advantage: The Entrepreneurial Challenge of Constructing a Resource Base," *Academy of Management Executive* 15:1, 64–78.
Bucar, B. and R.D. Hisrich (2001). "Ethics of Business Managers vs. Entrepreneurs," *Journal of Developmental Entrepreneurship* 6:1, 59–82.
Bucar, B., M. Glas and R.D. Hisrich (2003). "Ethics and Entrepreneurs: An International Comparative Study," *Journal of Business Venturing* 18:2, 261–281.
Buchholz, R.A. and S.B. Rosenthal (2005). "The Spirit of Entrepreneurship and the Qualities of Moral Decision Making: Toward A Unifying Framework," *Journal of Business Ethics* 60:3, 307–315.
Calás, M.B., L. Smircich and K.A. Bourne (2009). "Extending the Boundaries: Reframing 'Entrepreneurship as Social Change' through Feminist Perspectives," *Academy of Management Review* 34:3, 552–569.

Cameron, K.S., J.E. Dutton, and R.E. Quinn (eds) (2003). *Positive Organizational Scholarship: Foundations of a New Discipline*. San Francisco, CA: Berrett-Koehler.

Cantillon, R. (2015) [1755]. *Essay on the Nature of Trade in General*, Antoin Murphy (trans. and ed.). Indianapolis, IN: Liberty Fund.

Carland, J.W., F. Hoy, W.R. Boulton and J.A.C. Carland (1984). "Differentiating Entrepreneurs from Small Business Owners: A Conceptualization," *Academy of Management Review* 9:2, 354–359.

Carr, P. (2003). "Revisiting the Protestant Ethic and the Spirit of Capitalism: Understanding the Relationship between Ethics and Enterprise," *Journal of Business Ethics* 47:1, 7–16.

Clarke, J. and R. Holt (2010). "Reflective Judgement: Understanding Entrepreneurship as Ethical Practice," *Journal of Business Ethics* 94:3, 317–331.

Crane, F.G. (2009). "Ethics, Entrepreneurs and Corporate Managers: A Canadian Study," *Journal of Small Business and Entrepreneurship* 22:3, 267–274.

Crockett, C. and A.R. Anderson (2004). "The Added Value of Virtue," *Journal of Research in Marketing and Entrepreneurship* 6:1, 5–17.

Dacin, P.A., M.T. Dacin and M. Matear (2010). "Social Entrepreneurship: Why We Don't Need a New Theory and How We Move Forward From Here," *Academy of Management Perspectives* 24:3, 37–57.

Dees, J.G. and J.A. Starr (1992). "Entrepreneurship Through an Ethical Lens: Dilemmas and Issues for Research and Practice," in D.L. Sexton and J.D. Kasarda (eds), *The State of the Art of Entrepreneurship*. Boston, MA: PWS-Kent, 89–116.

Dey, P. and C. Steyaert (2016). "Rethinking the Space of Ethics in Social Entrepreneurship: Power, Subjectivity, and Practices of Freedom," *Journal of Business Ethics* 133:4, 627–641.

Drucker, P.F. (1985). *Innovation and Entrepreneurship: Practice and Principles*. New York, NY: Harper & Row.

Dubinsky, A.J. and B. Loken (1989). "Analyzing Ethical Decision Making in Marketing," *Journal of Business Research* 19:2, 83–107.

Dunham, L. (2007). "The Ethical Dimensions of Creative Market Action: A Framework for Identifying Issues and Implications of Entrepreneurial Ethics," *Business and Professional Ethics Journal*, 26:1–4, 3–39.

Dunham, L. (2010). "From Rational to Wise Action: Recasting Our Theories of Entrepreneurship," *Journal of Business Ethics* 92:4, 513–530.

Dunham, L., J. McVea and R.E. Freeman (2008). "Entrepreneurial Wisdom: Incorporating the Ethical and Strategic Dimensions of Entrepreneurial Decision-making," *International Journal of Entrepreneurship and Small Business* 6:1, 8–19.

Ferrell, O.C. and L.G. Gresham (1985). "A Contingency Framework for Understanding Ethical Decision Making in Marketing," *Journal of Marketing* 49:3, 87–96.

Foss, N. and P. Klein (2012). *Organizing Entrepreneurial Judgment: A New Approach to the Firm*. Cambridge: Cambridge University Press.

Gasparski, W.W. (2010). "Entrepreneurship from a Praxiology Point of View," in W.W. Gasparski, S. Kwiatkowski, and L.V. Ryan (eds), *Entrepreneurship. Values and Responsibility* New Brunswick, NJ: Transaction Publishers, 23–36.

Goss, D., R. Jones, M. Betta and J. Latham (2011). "Power as Practice: A Micro-sociological Analysis of the Dynamics of Emancipatory Entrepreneurship," *Organization Studies*, 32:2, 211–229.

Gruber, M. (2003). "Research on Marketing in Emerging Firms: Key Issues and Open Questions," *International Journal of Technology Management* 26:5/6, 600–620.

Hannafey, F.T. (2003). "Entrepreneurship and Ethics: A Literature Review," *Journal of Business Ethics* 46:2, 99–110.

Harmeling, S. (2011). "Contingency as an Entrepreneurial Resource: How Private Obsession Fulfills Public Need," *Journal of Business Venturing* 26:3, 293–305.

Harmeling, S., S. Sarasvathy and R.E. Freeman (2009). "Related Debates in Ethics and Entrepreneurship: Values, Opportunities, and Contingency," *Journal of Business Ethics* 84:3, 341–365.

Harris, J.D., H.J. Sapienza and N.E. Bowie (2009). "Ethics and Entrepreneurship," *Journal of Business Venturing* 24:5, 407–418.

Heath, E. (2015). "The Qualities of Virtue and its Rivals: Business, Entrepreneurship, and Business Ethics," in N. Karlson, M. Norek, and K. Wennberg (eds), *Virtues in Entrepreneurship*, 58–80. Stockholm: Ratio.

Hébert, R.F. and A.N. Link (1988). *The Entrepreneur: Mainstream Views and Radical Critiques*. New York, NY: Praeger.

Henderson, A.D. (1999). "Firm Strategy and Age Dependence A Contingent View of the Liabilities of Newness, Adolescence, and Obsolescence," *Administrative Science Quarterly* 44:2, 281–314.

Hicks, S. (2009). "What Business Ethics Can Learn from Entrepreneurship," *The Journal of Private Enterprise* 24:2, 49–57.

Hisrich, R.D. and M.V. Gratchev (2001). "Ethical Dimension of Russian and American Entrepreneurs," *Journal of Small Business and Enterprise Development* 8:1, 5–18.

Hoselitz, B.F. (1960). "The Early History of Entrepreneurial Theory," in Joseph J. Spengler and William R. Allen (eds), *Essays in Economic Thought: Aristotle to Marshall*. Chicago, IL: Rand McNally & Company, 234–257.

Humphreys, N., D.P. Robin, R.E. Reidenbach and D.L. Moak (1993). "The Ethical Decision Making Process of Small Business Owner/Managers and their Customers," *Journal of Small Business Management* 31:3, 9–22.

Hunt, S.D. and S. Vitell (1986). "A General Theory of Marketing Ethics," *Journal of Macromarketing* 6:1, 5–16.

Hunt, S.D. and S.J. Vitell (2006). "The General Theory of Marketing Ethics. A Revision and Three Questions," *Journal of Macromarketing* 26:2, 143–153.

Johansson, A.W. (2009). "Regional Development by Means of Broadened Entrepreneurship," *European Planning Studies* 17:8, 1205–1222.

Jones, T.M. (1991). "Ethical Decision Making by Individuals in Organizations: an Issue-contingent Model," *Academy of Management Review* 16:2, 366–395.

Karlson, N., M. Norek and K. Wennberg (eds) (2015). *Virtues in Entrepreneurship*. Stockholm: Ratio.

Kirzner, I. (1973). *Competition and Entrepreneurship*. Chicago, IL: University of Chicago Press.

Kirzner, I. (1974). "Producer, Entrepreneur, and the Right to Property," *Reason Papers* 1:1, 1–17.

Knight, F. (1921). *Risk, Uncertainty, and Profit*. Boston, MA: Hart, Schaffner and Marx.

Knight, F. (1942) "Profit and Entrepreneurial Functions," *Journal of Economic History* 2: Supplement, 126–132.

Kuratko, D.P. and M.C. Goldsby (2004). "Corporate Entrepreneurs or Rogue Middle Managers? A Framework for Ethical Corporate Entrepreneurship," *Journal of Business Ethics* 55:1, 13–30.

Lautermann, C. (2013). "The Ambiguities of (Social) Value Creation: Towards an Extended Understanding of Entrepreneurial Value Creation for Society," *Social Enterprise Journal* 9:2, 184–202.

Lehnert, K., Y. Park and N. Singh (2015). "Research Note and Review of the Empirical Ethical Decision-Making Literature. Boundary Conditions and Extensions," *Journal of Business Ethics* 129:1, 195–219.

Longenecker, J.G., J.A. McKinney, and C.W. Moore (1988). "Egoism and Independence: Entrepreneurial Ethics," *Organizational Dynamics* 16:3, 64–72.

Longenecker, J.G., J.A. McKinney, and C.W. Moore (1989). "Ethics In Small Business," *Journal of Small Business Management* 27:1, 27–31.

Longenecker, J.G., C.W. Moore, J.W. Petty, L.E. Palich and J.A. McKinney (2006). "Ethical Attitudes in Small Businesses and Large Corporations: Theory and Empirical Findings from a Tracking Study Spanning Three Decades," *Journal of Small Business Management* 44:2, 167–183.

Lounsbury, M. and M.A. Glynn (2001). "Cultural Entrepreneurship Stories, Legitimacy, and the Acquisition of Resources," *Strategic Management Journal* 22:6/7, 545–564.

Machan, T.R. (1999). "Entrepreneurship and Ethics," *International Journal of Social Economics* 26:5/6, 596–609.

MacIntyre, A. (1985). *After Virtue: A Study in Moral Theory* 2nd edition. London: Duckworth.

Martens, M.L., J.E. Jennings and P.D. Jennings (2007). "Do the Stories They Tell Get Them the Money They Need? The Role of Entrepreneurial Narratives in Resource Acquisition," *Academy of Management Journal* 50:5, 1107–1132.

McVea, J.F. (2009). "A Field Study of Entrepreneurial Decision-Making and Moral Imagination," *Journal of Business Venturing* 24:5, 491–504.

Morris, M.H., M. Schindehutte, J. Walton and J. Allen (2002). "The Ethical Context of Entrepreneurship: Proposing and Testing a Developmental Framework," *Journal of Business Ethics* 40:4, 331–361.

Payne, D. and B.E. Joyner (2006). "Successful US Entrepreneurs: Identifying Ethical Decision-making and Social Responsibility Behaviors," *Journal of Business Ethics* 65:3, 203–217.

Pollack, J.M. and D.A. Bosse (2014). "When Do Investors Forgive Entrepreneurs for Lying?" *Journal of Business Venturing* 29:6, 741–754.

Rest, J.R. (1986). *Moral Development: Advances in Research and Theory*. New York, NY: Praeger.

Rindova, V., D. Barry and D.J. Ketchen, Jr. (2009). "Entrepreneuring as Emancipation," *Academy of Management Review* 34:3, 477–491.

Robinson, D.A., P. Davidsson, H. van der Mescht and P. Court (2007). "How Entrepreneurs Deal with Ethical Challenges—An Application of the Business Ethics Synergy Star Technique," *Journal of Business Ethics* 71:4, 411–423.

Rutherford, M.W., P.F. Buller, and J.M. Stebbins (2009). "Ethical Considerations of the Legitimacy Lie," *Entrepreneurship: Theory & Practice* 33:4, 949–964.

Santos, F.M. (2012). "A Positive Theory of Social Entrepreneurship," *Journal of Business Ethics* 111:3, 335–351.

Sarasvathy, S.D. (2002). "Entrepreneurship as Economics with Imagination," *The Ruffin Series of the Society for Business Ethics* 3, 95–112.

Sarasvathy, S.D. (2004). "Making It Happen: Beyond Theories of the Firm to Theories of Firm Design," *Entrepreneurship: Theory and Practice* 28:6, 519–531.

Say, J.-B. (1850) [1803]. *A Treatise on Political Economy; or the Production, Distribution, or Consumption of Wealth*, C.R. Prinsep (trans.) (from 4th French edition). Philadelphia, PA: Lipincott, Grambo & Co.

Schumpeter, J.A. (1997) [1st edition 1911]. *Theorie der Wirtschaftlichen Entwicklung: Eine Untersuchung über Unternehmergewinn, Kapital, Kredit Zins und den Konjunkturzyklus*. Berlin: Duncker und Humblot. [English edition: *The Theory of Economic Development* (1936), Redvers Opie (trans.). Cambridge, MA: Harvard University Press.]

Shane, S.A. (2005). *A General Theory of Entrepreneurship: The Individual-Opportunity Nexus*. Cheltenham: Edward Elgar.

Solomon, R.C. (1999). "And Now for Something Completely Different: From Heidegger to Entrepreneurship," *Business Ethics Quarterly* 9:1, 169–177.

Spinosa, C., F. Flores and H.L. Dreyfus (1997). *Disclosing New Worlds: Entrepreneurship, Democratic Action, and the Cultivation of Solidarity*. Cambridge, MA: MIT Press.

Steinbauer, R., N.D. Rhew, E. Kinnamon and F. Fabian (2014). "The Conflicting Drivers of Entrepreneurial Ethics," *Journal of Ethics and Entrepreneurship* 4:1, 57–72.

Surie, G. and A. Ashley (2008). "Integrating Pragmatism and Ethics in Entrepreneurial Leadership for Sustainable Value Creation," *Journal of Business Ethics* 81:1, 235–246.

Swedberg, R. (2006). "Social Entrepreneurship: the View of the Young Schumpeter," in C. Steyaert and D. Hjorth (eds), *Entrepreneurship as Social Change. A Third Movements in Entrepreneurship Book*. Cheltenham: Edward Elgar, 21–34.

Tan, W.L., J. Williams and T.-M. Tan (2005). "Defining the 'Social' in 'Social Entrepreneurship': Altruism and Entrepreneurship," *International Entrepreneurship and Management Journal* 1:3, 353–365.

Tarascio, V.J. (1985). "Cantillon's Essai: A Current Perspective," *Journal of Libertarian Studies* 7:2, 249–257.

Treviño, L.K. (1986). "Ethical Decision Making in Organizations: A Person-Situation Interactionist Model," *Academy of Management Review* 11:3, 601–617.

Velamuri, S.R. (2002). "Entrepreneurship, Altruism and the Good Society," *The Ruffin Series of the Society for Business Ethics* 3, 125–143.

Verduyn, K. (2015). "Entrepreneuring and Process: A Lefebvrian Perspective," *International Small Business Journal* 33:6, 638–648.

von Mises, L. (1949). *Human Action*. New Haven, CT: Yale University Press.

Watson, T.J. (2013). "Entrepreneurial Action and the Euro-American Social Science Tradition: Pragmatism, Realism and Looking Beyond 'the Entrepreneur,'" *Entrepreneurship and Regional Development*, 25:1–2, 16–33.

Welsch, H.P. (2010). "The Twelve Tribes of Entrepreneurship," in W.W. Gasparski, S. Kwiatkowski and L. V. Ryan (eds), *Entrepreneurship: Values and Responsibility*. New Brunswick, NJ: Transaction Publishers, 37–61.

Wempe, J. (2005). "Ethical Entrepreneurship and Fair Trade," *Journal of Business Ethics* 60:3, 211–220.

Zhang, Z. and R.D. Arvey (2009). "Rule Breaking in Adolescence and Entrepreneurial Status: An Empirical Investigation," *Journal of Business Venturing* 24:5, 436–447.

17
The contribution of economics to business ethics

Joseph Heath

To say that the relationship between economics and business ethics has been antagonistic would be to risk enormous understatement. Perhaps the low point was reached in 1978, the year the Ford Motor Company lost the first of two important "Pinto" lawsuits, after having failed to issue a product recall to fix a known problem with the fuel tank in their vehicles that made them likely to explode in the event of a rear-end collision. During the trial it was discovered that the company had decided against a recall, based on the calculation that the cost of effecting the repairs was greater than the value of the anticipated loss of life (Birsch and Fielder 1994). Public outrage reached such a fever pitch that the State of Indiana decided to press criminal charges against Ford—a legal novelty at the time. To this day, the "Ford Pinto case" remains a staple of the business ethics curriculum, a seemingly uncontroversial example of a corporation putting the search for profit ahead of basic human decency. And yet that same year, Milton Friedman, recent recipient of the Nobel prize in economics, gave a public lecture in which he offered a spirited defense of Ford (Friedman 1978). He lamented the public fixation on the fact that it would have cost only $11 per vehicle to fix the fault. What if it had cost $1000? or $10,000 or $1,000,000? Should Ford have gone ahead and fixed it at any price? Obviously there is some point at which the repair would be too expensive—consumers would rather drive the unsafe vehicle than pay to have it modified. So the question is not really one of principle, Friedman argued, everyone agrees that there is some point at which doing the repair is not cost-effective. The only question was whether the number chosen by Ford is one that actually matched consumer preference.

To this day, many business ethicists regard this response as being "beyond the pale." It is, in any case, illustrative of the antagonistic relationship that prevailed, for a long time, between economists and business ethicists. And yet, to say that the relationship was antagonistic is not to say that it was unfruitful. Indeed, one of the reasons that Friedman's argument antagonized so many people is the fact that, while morally counterintuitive, it is very far from being incoherent. Furthermore, Friedman was doing more than just pointing to a supposed incompatibility between the pious homilies of ethicists and the harsh realities of the marketplace. He was using a recognizably "economic" style of reasoning—treating "safety" as just another commodity that consumers are only willing to pay so much for—to attack the claims made by ethicists, suggesting that they were offering little more than a knee-jerk reaction to the case, without having thought through the implications of their view. In this respect his argument echoed Friedrich Hayek's (1986) suggestion that "moral" evaluation of market relations was essentially atavistic, a throwback to a more primitive assessment of social relations, based on a failure to adjust to the changed conditions of a modern complex economy. Thus economists have done much more than just offer a counterpoint to the perspective of business ethicists, they have in many cases advanced a significant challenge to the entire enterprise.

My objective, in the first section of this chapter, will be to outline the major points on which economists have challenged business ethicists. I will, of course, be speaking rather loosely about the two groups, since there have always been economists who are quite sympathetic to business ethics (e.g., Arrow 1973; Baumol and Blackman 1991; Sen 1993), while within the field of business ethics there is a surprisingly strong libertarian tradition of theorists who are quite happy to endorse positions of the sort espoused by Friedman and Hayek (e.g., Hasnas 2009). Nevertheless, what I would like to show is that the mainstream economic perspective, at around the time that Friedman offered his defense of the Ford Motor Company, was one that offered at least three significant challenges to any sort of naive application of standard philosophical ethical theories in the context of marketplace interactions. Indeed, in these early debates, economists played much the same role that skeptics have played throughout the history of philosophy—a role that is, I will suggest, ultimately salutary, insofar as it prevents anyone from resting content with merely conventional or dogmatic convictions. Furthermore, while philosophers have usually been forced to posit a hypothetical skeptic with whom to engage, business ethicists often enjoyed the advantage of being able to find a real live one working just down the hall.

However, as I will show in the second section, part of the force of this "economic" critique of business ethics was, in fact, a reflection of the limitations of economic science as it was practiced at the time. Much of it was due to the fact that economists were wedded to a deeply unrealistic model of rational action, which led them to deny that certain types of moral considerations could motivate human conduct. Part of it was also due to the fact that they were operating, in effect, without any coherent "theory of the firm," and so had little understanding of the challenges that managers actually face running corporations (which is to say, trying to get large groups of people to act cooperatively). Subsequent advances in economic science, ranging from the rise of behavioral economics to the development of agency theory, have changed all of this, and laid the groundwork for a much more positive, collaborative relationship between economists and business ethicists. Thus, in the final section, I will trace out the most important changes, then show some of the ways in which these newer, more sophisticated economic ideas have enriched the discussion about corporate social responsibility, regulation and compliance, and managerial authority.

Skepticism about business ethics

The most obvious challenge to business ethics arises from Adam Smith's "invisible hand," argument, which suggests that individuals, in seeking to advance their own interests in the context of a well-structured market economy, generally promote the public interest, and so there is no need for any of the special constraints or obligations imposed by morality. Ethics has no place in business, it is claimed, not because there is anything wrong with ethics, but simply because there is no need for it in a market economy. (Markets are, as the philosopher David Gauthier put it, "moral-free zones" (1982).) Business ethics, from this perspective, is otiose. This suggestion was made somewhat before Smith by Bernard Mandeville, who in his *Fable of the Bees* (1728) suggested that the economy transforms private vices into public virtues. Mandeville, however, despite having coined a catchy phrase, did not have a very good argument in support of his position. Smith, by contrast, had not only a catchy phrase but also a powerful argument. In *The Wealth of Nations* he suggested that when individuals pursue their self-interest, in the context of a market economy, they are led as though "by an invisible hand" to promote the common good, even though this is "no part" of their intention ([1776] 1843: 194). Because of this, Smith suggested, people should be left free to engage in economic transactions on whatever terms they like.

This is the claim. But what is the argument? What is this extraordinary trick through which the invisible hand of the market spins straw into gold, or, more prosaically, reconciles egoism and altruism? The key to understanding it, Smith observed, is to examine the impact that self-interested behavior has on the *prices* at which goods and services trade. Consider, for instance, how the system of free contracting ensures that scarce resources are put to their best use. Suppose that, in a predominantly agricultural economy, a limited amount of fertilizer suddenly becomes available. Who should get it? The obvious answer is that it should be put to use wherever it will do the most good, which is to say, wherever it will produce the greatest increase in agricultural output. One way of figuring this out is to conduct an in-depth study in order to assess the potential productivity gains on each individual farm. Another way is simply to sell the fertilizer to the highest bidder. In doing so, one is essentially forcing each individual farmer to do an assessment of the potential productivity gains on his own farm, because in order to know how much to bid, each farmer has to know how much of an increase in output he can expect. It is the potential increase in output, and hence of revenue, that creates the budget for purchasing fertilizer. There is, of course, an enormous amount of "noise" that can interfere with the smooth operation of the price mechanism—as there is with any other social institution. For example, the farmers may be wrong in their estimates (although, in general, they will probably produce better estimates than anyone else could). Nevertheless, the *general tendency* in a market economy will be for resources to flow, not to the richest, or to the biggest, or to the most powerful, but to the person who is able to get the most out of them when it comes to increasing production and providing goods that other people want to buy. Thus the self-interest of the farmers is not just compatible with, but actually tends toward the promotion of, the general good.

The Smith argument was generalized, most influentially, by Hayek, who drew a distinction between "spontaneous" and "made" orders (1973). The most important aspect of the distinction, in his view, was that spontaneous orders rely only upon a basic set of ground rules, but that, once these are established, all further action within the system can be driven by the incentives that individuals face. "Made" orders, by contrast, are governed by rules that specify, in detail, what individuals are obliged to do at each point of decision. A great deal of confusion arises, Hayek claims, when people try to apply moral rules that are appropriate in the context of made orders to actions undertaken within spontaneous orders. He argues that the concept of "social justice," as applied to the distribution of income, arises from a category error of precisely this sort. The market economy is a spontaneous order that rests upon a system of property rights and contract law. Once those ground rules are specified, there is simply no further question that can arise about whether the outcomes that result are "right" or "wrong," "just" or "unjust." It follows from this analysis that, to the extent that it attempts to engage in moral analysis of the outcome of free contracting, or goes beyond an insistence upon the sanctity of property and contract, "business ethics" is based upon a category error.

The second major challenge to business ethics arising from an "economic" perspective is closely related to the "invisible hand" argument, although not quite the same. It stems from the observation that markets are competitively organized domains of interaction. Indeed, the economic analysis of the deleterious effects of monopoly demonstrates the importance of preserving this competitive dimension. Suppose, for instance, that instead of competing against one another for the fertilizer two farmers decide to be nice and to share it, dividing it equally among themselves. Rather than submitting rival bids, they submit a joint bid, one that will (naturally) reflect the average increase in production that the two of them expect from their shares. From the point of view of everyday morality, this may seem like the right thing to do, but from a societal perspective it is actually quite counterproductive. First, it means that agricultural production will not be maximized—since half of the fertilizer will be going to the less productive farmer, who is not able to get as much use out of it. Second, by failing to bid the price up, the farmers send the wrong signal to fertilizer producers, suggesting that the social value of fertilizer is much less than it actually is. The consequence will be an underproduction of fertilizer and a further misallocation of productive resources. This suggests that, if one understands morality in simplistic terms, such as an injunction to "do unto others as you would have them do unto you," then morality is not only unnecessary in a market economy, it is positively harmful. Behaving in a narrowly self-interested way (e.g., bidding aggressively against other producers and consumers) is not just permissible in a market economy, it is actually required, in order to maintain the competitive dynamic that allows the price system to function.

More generally, the fact that one is engaged in a competition seems to provide at least partial exemption from many of the moral norms that structure everyday social interaction. A market economy, from this perspective, can be compared with a sporting competition, or a game in which participants adopt an *adversarial* orientation. Frank Knight made this observation in an influential article on "The Ethics of Competition." ("Some of the criticisms brought against existing society amount to condemning a foot-race as unfair because someone has come out ahead" (1935: 605).) Albert Carr put the point even more provocatively in a 1968 *Harvard Business Review* article, in order to consider whether "business bluffing" was ethical. He drew the analogy to a poker game where participants have a similarly adversarial orientation: "No one expects poker to be played on the ethical principles preached in churches. In poker it is right and proper to bluff a friend out of the rewards of being dealt a good hand. A player feels no more than a slight twinge of sympathy . . . It was up to the other fellow to protect himself" (1968: 145). Similarly, many have argued that deception in advertising, or strategic misrepresentation in negotiations, are morally acceptable elements of business practice, simply because the institutional context of business is one that relieves individuals of many everyday-moral obligations (Gini and Marcoux 2012: 79–81). Thus, in order to make the case for business ethics, one must show that the moral judgments one is making are not merely the naive projection of commonsense virtues or the "ethical principle taught in churches" to marketplace interactions.

Last but not least, economists have cast doubt upon the enterprise of business ethics by endorsing, as a methodological precept, a model of rational action that classifies as irrational a very large range of moral concerns. The conception of practical rationality as expected utility-maximization (or the so-called *homo economicus* model of action) claims that the value of an action is entirely a function of its probable consequences, but that the action itself can have no intrinsic value. While this does not rule out the possibility of altruistic preferences, it does imply that the phenomenon of commitment, as well as genuine rule-following, is either illusory or irrational (Sen 1977; Heath 2009: 46–48, 2015: 270). This implies, in turn, that any form of deontological morality (i.e., one that conceives of morality as a set of rules or constraints on the pursuit of self-interest) is *eo ipso* irrational.

This critique, it should be noted, is far more radical than either of the two discussed above. The invisible hand argument and the poker analogy may have convinced many economists that there was no place for moral concerns in assessing behavior in the market, but this provides no reason to doubt that morality is important in other domains, such as family life or democratic politics. The utility-maximization model, however, suggests that deontological morality is something of a ruse, or an elaborate self-deception. At the limit, this analysis pushes in the direction of the sort of pro-capitalist Nietzscheanism that one can find in the work of Ayn Rand, where any constraint on selfishness is portrayed as the consequence of a plot perpetrated by the weak against the strong (1964). More commonly, however, it created an atmosphere in the economics profession that encouraged "debunking" analyses of moral constraints—so that whenever economists encountered an instance of putative moral action, they would search for some underlying "self-interested" motive that was taken to provide the real explanation for the phenomenon (e.g., Becker 1973).

Now of course one might wonder how much mischief this sort of methodological commitment could really produce. After all, economics aspires to be a positive science. Overestimation of the importance of extrinsic incentives in motivating the conduct of others is a common cognitive bias (Heath 1999), and while it is somewhat perverse for economists to want to elevate it to the level of a methodological imperative, one might think that the worst that could result is simply the production of a great deal of bad social science. And yet the consequences extended much further, because the methodological postulate in question is embedded in a *normative* theory of rationality. The classification of moral constraints as irrational therefore generated a tendency among economists to think that "moral" preoccupations are only for the tender-minded and sentimental, those who are incapable of the more disciplined style of thinking exemplified by economic analysis. This generated a certain *déformation professionel* among economists, the effects of which can be seen to this day. Steven Levitt, for instance, in *Freakonomics*, suggested that morality "represents the way that people would like the world to work, whereas economics represents how it actually does work" (Levitt and Dubner 2005: 11). Notice the implication— that morality is not something that is actually *in* the world; it is an illusion that economics teaches us to overcome by focusing on the self-interested motives that actually drive individual behavior (for discussion, see Heath 2009: 47).

Finally, it should be noted that not all economists have been committed, over the years, to doing purely "positive" research. In particular, work done within the tradition of "welfare economics" has an obvious normative dimension. Thus one might wonder why there was not more disagreement within the profession over the tendency to denigrate morality. The answer lies in the important status of the "Pareto efficiency" principle in normative analysis, and the assumption, once widespread amongst economists, that it could be introduced as a merely technical postulate, or else that it could be derived from the instrumental conception of rationality. This led many economists to believe, incorrectly, that they had succeeded in emancipating themselves from any and all specifically moral theories. Throughout the nineteenth century, economics had been classified as one of the "moral sciences," a description that seemed particularly apt given the close connection between economics as it was practiced and philosophical utilitarianism. However, a series of conceptual revolutions in the late twentieth and early twentieth centuries allowed economists to free themselves from many of the more controversial aspects of utilitarianism (Blaug 1985: 299–303). First of all, the "marginalist revolution" provided the foundations for the modern concept of utility, which breaks, once and for all, with the Benthamite commitment to hedonism. The Pareto principle ("if a transformation of the social state makes at least one person better off, and does not make anyone worse off, then it is to be preferred") also allowed economists to drop the commitment to aggregationism that is central to classical utilitarianism. Not only did this enable them to avoid committing themselves to controversial utilitarian claims about how to handle transformations in which some are made better off while others are made worse off, it also provided a normative principle that could be applied without requiring interpersonal comparisons of utility. Since the latter appears to require some form of value theory, the shift to Paretianism freed economists from the need to pronounce on the question so memorably posed by John Stuart Mill, of whether "it is better to be Socrates dissatisfied than a fool satisfied" (1863: 14).

The Pareto efficiency principle could fairly be described as an extremely *minimalist* normative principle. Many economists, however, took the fact that it avoids *controversial* value judgements to suggest that it avoids *all* value judgments, and is therefore somehow "scientific" or "objective" (As my undergraduate economics textbook stated approvingly, back in the 1980s, "Because it is possible to talk about efficient and inefficient allocations, but not about better or worse distributions of income without introducing normative considerations, much of economics concerns efficiency and neglects effects on the distribution of income" (Lipsey et al. 1988: 478).) This type of error was aided and abetted by the unfortunate tendency to confuse "efficiency" in the engineering sense, which is a purely instrumental criterion, with "efficiency" in the social, or Pareto sense, which most evidently is not. Thus many economists became convinced that welfare economics was exempt from the general rule that all normative analysis was value-laden, and hence non-rational, "subjective," or "biased" (Blaug 1985: 591).

Furthermore, once economists persuaded themselves that they could help themselves to the Pareto principle, many felt that this allowed them to ignore all other moral concerns by essentially subsuming them under the Pareto principle, treating them as just "preferences" that needed to be satisfied. For instance, instead of treating equality as a normative principle coeval with the efficiency principle, it was instead treated as a type of efficiency concern, by supposing that certain people in society have a "taste for equality," which has some claim to satisfaction just like any other preference (Kaplow and Shavell 2002: 21). Of course, no one ever tried to pursue this analysis very far, which is not surprising since the preference interdependencies being introduced would have created insuperable difficulties. It was mainly used as a way of dismissing all other normative concerns, and thus maintaining a sort of "efficiency monism." This ruled out any serious consideration of questions of distributive justice, but it also had the effect of ruling out business ethics, to the extent that the latter introduced concerns that went beyond Pareto efficiency.

All of these trends led to the widespread perception, among economists, that they had no reason to concern themselves with moral questions. This was true even among those who were doing explicitly normative work. Furthermore, because this was tied to the emergence of modern utility theory and the emancipation of economics from its association with utilitarianism, there was a tendency among economists to think of business ethicists as simply people who did not understand modern economics very well. And in fairness it should be acknowledged that there has never been any shortage of business ethicists who fit the description. Nevertheless, the dismissal proved to be unsustainable, and over time even mainstream economists became dissatisfied with it.

The rational choice revolution

If one had to point to a single factor that was the most important in transforming the relationship between economics and business ethics, the most obvious candidate would be the development and diffusion of "rational choice" theory in the 1980s and 90s. Just to be clear on terminology: the term "decision theory" refers to the model of rational action based on an axiomatic representation of the instrumental conception of practical rationality (which is to say, the view that conceives of practical rationality as calculation of the best means to the attainment of pregiven ends). Game theory is the term used to refer to the extension of the decision-theoretic model to solve social interaction problems (or to solve "strategic" rather than "parametric" choice problems). Both conceive of rational action as expected utility-maximization, in the modern sense of the term "utility," which defines it in terms of a subjective preference ordering. Thus decision and game theory represent the most abstract articulation of the basic model of rational action underlying microeconomic analysis (and from which many basic microeconomic results can be derived.) "Rational choice theory" is a somewhat more vague term, often used to refer to the application of this model of action outside of the economist's traditional domain of analysis (e.g., to voting, crime, marriage, etc.).

The development of decision and game theory in the twentieth century had wide-ranging implications. For economists, it provided a unifying framework that allowed them to express a wide range of results in a more parsimonious fashion. For instance, the analysis of the "prisoner's dilemma" game made it possible to see that Paul Samuelson's (1954) theory of public goods, Mancur Olson's (1965) analysis of the logic of collective action, and Garrett Hardin's (1968) tragedy of the commons, were all just special instances of a more general class of interactions, viz. ones in which individual utility-maximization does not produce outcomes that are Pareto efficient. And while this was a profound insight, it also tended to undermine some of the confidence that many economists had traditionally held about the robustness of "spontaneous orders" (Cowen and Crampton 2002). During the 1930s, the sociologist Talcott Parsons had posed the question, whether Adam Smith's "propensity to truck and barter" or Thomas Hobbes' proclivity for "force and fraud" was the more fundamental human tendency (1949: 90–94). If it were the latter, then the only truly spontaneous order would be the Hobbesian state of nature, in which life was "solitary, poor, nasty, brutish and short." The analysis of the prisoner's dilemma led to a dramatic resurgence of interest in Hobbes, and a tendency to think that a spontaneous *order* is almost a contradiction in terms. Left to their own devices, people produce only disorder or anomie. To the extent that markets are orderly, it is because they are carefully regulated institutions.

All of the attention paid to the prisoner's dilemma was also important in driving home the point that the Pareto principle is irreducibly normative, not merely technical, and that it cannot be derived from the instrumental conception of rationality. Indeed, what theorists found so fascinating about the prisoner's dilemma is the fact that a group of agents, acting rationally according to the instrumental conception, could wind up with an outcome that is worse for all of them (i.e., Pareto inefficient), even when this was perfectly foreseeable. Early on, the tendency to conflate rationality and Pareto efficiency was sufficiently strong that many theorists described the prisoner's dilemma as a "paradox" (e.g., Campbell and Sowden 1985). And yet, over time, they began to realize that there was nothing paradoxical about it. As Thomas Schelling put it, "Things don't work out optimally for a simple reason: there is no reason why they should." Even if everyone acts rationally, "there is no mechanism that attunes individual response to some collective accomplishment" (1978: 32). Thus the prisoner's dilemma went from being considered a paradox to something more like a metaphor for the human condition. At the same time, it showed that the concerns that had traditionally motivated welfare economists were essentially moral, and thus of the same order as those that animated business ethicists. This meant that, if it was legitimate to talk about efficiency, then it was equally legitimate to talk about distributive justice, or individual rights, or any other sort of normative principle (a point that was articulated, quite influentially, by John Rawls in *A Theory of Justice* (1971)).

The second major consequence of rational choice theory stemmed from the fact that it allowed theorists to model small-scale interactions, rather than looking at markets in the aggregate or the entire economy (as the older "general equilibrium" models in economics had done). This in turn gave rise to the discipline of "experimental economics," which involved putting test subjects in interactions that had the structure of an abstract game model, then seeing whether their actions corresponded at all to the predictions of theory. At this point the vague complaints that many people had about the economic model of rational action being "unrealistic" could be given much more precise expression (Rabin 1998). Of course, the action-theoretic model is normative, and so the mere fact that experimental subjects do not act perfectly rationally does not invalidate it. Nevertheless, there are many experimental techniques that offer indirect confirmation or disconfirmation. For instance, if subjects are given more time to reflect, or repeat opportunities to play the game, or aids to help them calculate outcomes, then their actions should more closely approximate "normative" play. Yet what emerged from this research program were a set of highly persistent "anomalies," or deviations from instrumental rationality, many of which confirmed the complaints that critics of the economic model had long been advancing (Dawes and Thaler 1988; Kahneman 2011).

The most important consequence of this, with respect to business ethics, is that the economic "debunking" of morality was itself debunked. Moral norms, in other words, were shown to have an important and measurable impact on people's actions (Sally 1995). "Public goods" games showed that people have a strong (but not universal) propensity to act cooperatively, even in one-shot games, with strangers whom they have never met and will never meet again. Every attempt to explain away this result by suggesting an indirect concern for consequences was painstakingly tested and ruled out (Bowles and Gintis 2013: 22–23). (For example, the possibility of repeated interaction was shown to have an impact on choice, but one that was independent of the basic cooperative disposition.) Second, the "ultimatum" (and later "dictator") game showed that experimental subjects exhibit a concern for fairness in their choices, which may trump their tendency to pursue their pecuniary interests. And again, experimental work showed that these results were real, robust, and easily replicated (Henrich et al. 2004).

What was striking about these two experimental games is that the type of behavior elicited was "moral" in the deontological sense. In other words, it was not only pro-social, but it entered into practical deliberation through a norm that prescribed particular actions, independent of their consequences. In other words, it matched the description of morality as a "principled constraint on the pursuit of self-interest" (Gauthier 1986). Furthermore, it was shown to have not just a measurable but a significant effect on individual choice in interactions that had an obvious "economic" dimension. This constituted tangible proof that morality is not just wishful thinking, but that it is part of the world, and, indeed, that in order to understand human social interaction it is necessary to have a model of action that has some way of representing moral concerns.

To illustrate the difference this acknowledgment makes, consider the longstanding debate over "efficiency wages"—the fact that paying slightly above-market wages can have a positive impact on productivity, and therefore result in net savings to the firm (Akerlof and Yellen 1986). In 1982 George Akerlof suggested a simple explanation for the phenomenon, which appealed to informal norms of reciprocity. He argued that labor contracts were a type of "partial gift exchange," in which the employer offered wages and the worker in return gave "an honest day's work." By taking the initiative in raising wages, the employer could, in turn, provoke greater work effort (or reduce shirking) by making workers feel as though they owed something to the firm (based on the principle that "one good turn deserves another"). While intuitively quite plausible, this explanation was for a long time resisted by economists. Many preferred to observe that, by raising wages, the firm also created an economic rent associated with the employment position (Shapiro and Stiglitz 1984). This generates greater aversion to being fired among employees, who know that they would be unlikely to secure another job at the same wage rate elsewhere. This should, in turn, intensify work effort.

Now if one compares these two explanations, both have an element of plausibility to them, and of course they are not exclusive. And yet the second was strongly favored over the first by economists (e.g., Milgrom and Roberts 1992: 250–253; Fisher and Waschik 2002: 291), largely because it avoided any reference to "norms" and to moral incentives, appealing only to the self-interest of workers. In other words, it was preferred not on empirical but rather on *a priori* grounds, because it was felt to be scientifically more respectable (or more parsimonious). All of this was based, however, on the mistaken idea that moral norms cannot influence behavior, but that there is always a motive of self-interest at work underlying any apparently moral action. It is this idea that experimental game theory was able to debunk, once and for all.

Another major consequence of the development of game theory was the ability it provided to develop a rigorous analysis of the internal structure of the firm, which had previously been a "black box" in economic analysis. Again, taking my undergraduate economics textbook as a guide to where mainstream economic thinking was in the 1980s, one can see how weak—and in many ways, positively misleading—economic thinking about the firm used to be. The discussion starts out with an analysis of individuals, claiming that both consumers and producers want to maximize utility. At some point, however, consumers simply get grouped together into households, who are given a *joint* utility function, and said to want to maximize consumption (Lipsey et al. 1988: 46). In the same way, producers are grouped together into firms, given a joint utility function, and said to want to maximize profits. This move obviously papered over a rather important issue, which is how one moves from a set of individual utility functions to a joint utility function. More perniciously, it encouraged the tendency to conflate the profit orientation of firms with the self-interest of individuals, making it seem, for instance, as though a modern professionally managed corporation is motivated by "greed," in the same way as Smith's butcher or baker. This is obviously not so, since the "separation of ownership and control" in the typical large firm ensures that operational decisions are made by managers, while the profits go to shareholders. This gives rise to a number of complex incentive alignment problems, but it also undermines any simplistic (or naively moralizing) understanding of corporate motives. This point was made by Adolf Berle and Gardiner Means in 1932, but did not receive much uptake in the economic literature until many decades later.

Similarly, Ronald Coase had laid out the basic structure of the modern theory of the firm in 1937. His view was, in turn, updated by Oliver Williamson in the 1970s, becoming the "transaction cost" theory (Williamson 1973, 1985). There was, however, rather limited uptake of this work among economists at the time, due to the fact that the theory lacked microfoundations. The suggestion that the boundary of the firm will adjust in order to minimize aggregate transaction costs can easily be made to sound either naively functionalist or panglossian. Agency theory changed all this by offering a formal representation of the organizational hierarchy that exists within the firm (as a set of iterated "principal–agent" relations). This offered a clear representation of the circumstances and mechanism through which the firm could serve as a transaction cost-minimizing organizational form, while at the same time providing a framework that could account for the well-known exceptions to the transaction-cost-minimization rule, such as money-losing mergers and acquisitions that seem to be motivated by an empire-building impulse among managers (Eisenhardt 1989). The latter could be characterized in terms of "agency problems," which is to say, situations in which the incentives provided by the organization fail to create an appropriate alignment of objectives between principals (in this case, shareholders) and agents (managers).

Of course, no sooner had the "black box" of the firm been opened than economists began to find social structures that appeared to defy economic modeling, even with the advanced tools of modern game theory. Armen Alchian and Harold Demsetz (1972) were quick to announce, optimistically, that there was nothing interesting to be found inside the box—they described firms as no more than "privately owned markets," and declared the suggestion that they harbor any sort of distinctive authority relations to be an illusion. But this turned out to be just another case of methodologically induced blindness (Singer 2015). The firm is full of "anomalies," which agency theory has struggled mightily to explain. Being an application of the rational choice model, the principal–agent framework focuses exclusively on extrinsic incentives, while ignoring (i.e., failing to model) the effect of such deontic motivations as loyalty, conceptions of fairness, "work ethic," professionalism, or obedience to authority. As a result, it was not long before a series of limitative results began to appear, showing that it was impossible to create a hierarchical organization using extrinsic incentives alone, but that some sort of "intrinsic" motive was in every case necessary (Holmström 1982; Gibbons 1998).

The more realistic understanding of the firm that emerged from these studies created an obvious point of *rapprochement* with business ethics. One of the most important trends in management theory (and education) in the last two decades of the twentieth century had been an emphatic rejection of Taylorism, and a shift toward more participatory and team-focused management techniques. Much of this began with the popularization, in the late 80s, of Japanese management practices, which informed such approaches as "Total Quality Management." Talk of corporate "values" and "mission" became commonplace—a trend that of course engaged the work of business ethicists, who had spent a great deal of time trying to articulate notions of corporate "integrity," "social responsibility," "citizenship," etc. Traditional rational choice theory, however, dismissed all of this as "cheap talk" (i.e., non payoff-relevant communication), which could have no influence on individual action. With the tools of modern experimental economics, however, it was easy to demonstrate the falsity of these claims (Sally 2005). For instance, in "public goods" games, many of the incentive structures recommended by orthodox game theory as a way of enhancing cooperation—such as iteration of the game—actually turned out to undermine it. Meanwhile, simple verbal interventions, such as allowing the players to talk to one another, or even having a person come into the room and order the participants to cooperate, were shown to greatly enhance cooperation (Sally 1995). "Cheap talk," it turns out, can actually be quite valuable (Bowles and Gintis 2013: 30). This suggested, in turn, that business ethicists and management theorists may have been on to something, in suggesting that the "values" promoted within an organization could have an impact on employee performance and behavior.

Finally, it is important to note the very significant changes that occurred among economists over the course of the twentieth century in the understanding of Smith's "invisible hand." It is important to recognize that the claims Smith made about the reconciliation of private self-interest and the public good were essentially a conjecture. Although he provided some supporting rationale, his arguments fell far short of proving that the reconciliation was possible in all cases, or on the scale of an entire economy. Indeed, the question remained outstanding until the 1950s, when Kenneth Arrow and Gerard Debreu developed their mathematical proof of what is known, informally, as the "invisible hand theorem" (Blaug 1985: 594) but more formally as the "first fundamental theory of welfare economics" (Arrow and Debreu 1954). They were able to show that individual utility-maximizing action, in the context of a competitive market economy, would produce an outcome that is Pareto-optimal.

This theorem was an enormous achievement (not least because they were able to prove that markets generate Pareto-optimality and not just utilitarian "greatest happiness"). It is a well-known feature of the theorem, however, that it was proven with the aid of a truly formidable set of idealizing assumptions. As a result, the interpretation of the theorem tended to go in different directions. Some took it as a straightforward vindication of Smith's claims, and hence as an argument against government "intervention" in the market, as well as license to treat commercial exchange as a "moral-free zone." Others, however, read it in exactly the opposite direction—as proof that real-world markets will never be perfectly efficient and so there will always be room for improvement through non-market means. Consider just one example: in order to avoid dealing with the question of transportation costs, Arrow and Debreu decided to treat commodities at different spatial locations, and at different times, as different commodities. And yet the model also assumes a sufficiently large number of producers of each commodity that no one can expect to influence the price through her supply decisions (and an equally large number of buyers). The requirement, however, that there be a very large number of suppliers and buyers, ready to contract over any good at *every* distinct point in space and time, is very difficult even to visualize. While it simplifies the mathematics, it also shows that the model is not just a slight idealization of the real world, but that it in fact bears little resemblance, and quite possibly violates the laws of physics. Thus an obvious way of reading the result is to take it as a demonstration of the practical impossibility of a perfectly efficienct market.

Finally, Richard Lipsey and Kelvin Lancaster's proof of the "general theory of second-best" (1956) showed that if one of the optimality conditions required for the first fundamental theorem was not satisfied, then there should no presumption that satisfying the others would produce an outcome that was more efficient than that which could be achieved by violating them. Put more colloquially, they showed that if a perfectly competitive market could not be achieved, then creating a market that was as close as possible to perfectly competitive offered no assurances that the outcome would be as close as possible to perfectly efficient. This result did a great deal to dampen down sweeping and bombastic appeals to the "invisible hand," by showing that, in general, the case for free markets must be made on a piecemeal basis in an empirical fashion. This had a significant impact on debates over regulation by suggesting that, in cases of market imperfection, interventions that, in a sense, made the market even more imperfect, could actually improve efficiency. It had important implications for business ethics as well, for essentially the same reason.

The new modesty

If one were to describe the net effect of all of these developments in the science of economics, perhaps the most important consequence would be that it encouraged much greater modesty among economists. Indeed, the late 70s, when Milton Friedman made his remarks about the Ford Pinto, may well be looked back upon as the apogee of economic immodesty. Events as well conspired to push economists in the direction of greater modesty—from the stagflation of the 1970s, the near-complete failure to offer useful advice to communist states seeking to make the transition to capitalism, the ongoing frustration of efforts to promote development in Africa, and of course the financial crisis of 2008. As a result, there is now much greater opportunity for fruitful collaboration between economists and business ethicists, and many ways in which economic theory can inform the reflections of ethicists. While much of this work remains in its infancy, in this final section I would like to describe some of the more promising avenues of research—areas in which economic theory has made, and continues to make, a constructive contribution to moral reflection.

A good starting point would be the more nuanced understanding of the "invisible hand" that results from the proof of the first fundamental theorem. The implications for business ethics are fairly straightforward, and were pointed out early on by Kenneth Arrow himself. In his article, "Social Responsibility and Economic Efficiency" (1973), Arrow observed that the set of conditions that must be satisfied in order for the result to obtain describe both the scope *and the limits* of the invisible hand. In cases where the conditions are not satisfied, he wrote, "the classical efficiency arguments for profit maximization do not apply... and it is wrong to obfuscate the issue by invoking them" (1973: 308). He focused in particular on two types of situation in which the simple rule of maximizing profits is socially inefficient: the case in which costs are not paid for, as in pollution, and the case in which the seller has considerably more knowledge about his product than the buyer, particularly with regard to safety. In these situations it is clearly desirable to have some idea of social responsibility, that is, to experience an obligation, whether ethical, moral, or legal.

(1973: 309)

In this article Arrow lays out in admirably straightforward terms the rudiments of what I have described elsewhere as the "market failures" approach to business ethics (Heath 2015). The idea, simply put, is that when the invisible hand is working properly, then there is no need for firms to deviate from the goal of profit-maximization, but when market conditions are such that the pursuit of profit is not compatible with the "general good," then firms are under a moral obligation to exercise some constraint in the range of profit-seeking strategies that they employ, restricting themselves to ones that would be available if the market were not so impaired. There is, of course, also an argument to be made for regulation in such cases, except that the law is a rather blunt and cumbersome instrument (Norman 2011). Thus business ethics, at least with regard to market transactions, takes an essentially interstitial form, proscribing conduct that would be ruled out either by an ideal market or by an ideal regulatory regime, but which for practical reasons happens not to be ruled out by real-world markets or real-world regulations.

This approach conceives of ethics as essentially a "governance mechanism" that complements the legal structure of the market. As Steen Thomsen puts it, there is a degree of substitutability between "alternative kinds of ethical codes as well as between ethical codes and other institutional arrangements. The implication is that there will be a rationale for ethical codes when alternative governance mechanisms (pure markets, hierarchies, government, the prevailing social ethic) fail to achieve a social optimum" (2001: 156). This analysis applies to market transactions, but can also be generalized to corporate governance. Indeed, Thomsen joins others, such as Allen Buchanan (1996), in thinking that principal–agent theory provides a powerful heuristic for understanding the role that ethics plays within organizations. In effect, the limitative results of agency theory show that without some kind of principled constraint on the pursuit of self-interest, firms could not function. Ethics, in this respect, serves as the "glue" that keeps large organizations together, allowing them to operate cohesively. Thus Buchanan writes that "the most important and distinctive ethical principles that are applicable to bureaucratic organizations express *commitments* on the part of persons working in bureaucracies that function to *reduce the risks* that the behavior of bureaucrats, understood as agents, imposes upon the principals whose agents they are. . ." (1996: 422).

These are all examples of views that take their inspiration directly from modern economic theory. But there have also been many indirect effects. In particular, the development of the economic theory of the firm has had an enormous impact on corporate law over the past three decades. While the "law and economics" movement brought some discredit upon itself by overextending the analysis into domains that were a poor fit (such as the criminal law), in the area of corporate law it has done an enormous amount to enrich our understanding. Frank Easterbrook and Daniel Fischel's influential work, *The Economic Structure of Corporate Law* (1991), while not uncontroversial, changed the terms of the debate over the legal structure of the firm in fundamental ways. One of the more facile ways of dismissing business ethics was to suggest that managers had no choice but to act unethically since they were legally obliged to maximize profits for shareholders (Hinkley 2002; Bakan 2004). This was often bolstered through reference to the Michigan Supreme Court decision *Dodge* v. *Ford*. This had always been somewhat dubious (the mere fact that *Dodge* v. *Ford* is a Michigan court decision, not Delaware, should have been grounds for suspicion (Stout 2008)), but Easterbrook and Fischel provided what can only be described as a decisive refutation of the idea that corporate law imposes a profit-maximization mandate upon managers. The goal of the firm, in their view, is whatever the parties involved have contracted to do. As they put it, somewhat pithily

> An approach that emphasizes the contractual nature of a corporation removes from the field of interesting questions one that has plagued many writers: what is the goal of the corporation? Is it profit, and for whom? Social welfare more broadly defined? Is there anything wrong with corporate charity? Should corporations try to maximize profit over the long run or the short run? Our response to such questions is: who cares?
>
> *(1991: 35–36)*

Again, what is important is not whether the view is uncontroversial, but that it changes the terms of the debate in a provocative way, and creates an opening for a more interesting dialogue with views that have been championed by business ethicists, such as multifiduciary stakeholder theory (Freeman 1998).

This entire current of thinking in corporate law has, in fact, dramatically shifted the way that scholars think about the profit orientation of firms. Michael Jensen (2000) argued that the importance of profit needs to be understood, not in terms of the property rights of shareholders, but by the need to provide an "objective function" to guide managerial decision-making. He went on to elaborate the implications of this analysis for debates in business ethics, developing a spirited attack on stakeholder theory (2002). In a similar vein, although with a less confrontational tone, John Boatright has articulated what he refers to as the "public policy" argument for shareholder primacy (2002). What is striking about the argument is that, like the stakeholder theorists, he starts out with a general concern for social welfare. The position that he winds up taking, regarding the "social responsibilities" of management, therefore stems from differences in his economic analysis of the structure of the firm, and not from any fundamental differences in moral outlook.

These are just two examples of the more sophisticated arguments that have emerged in recent years in defense of the traditional norm of shareholder primacy. Critics of this doctrine, however, have not been resting either. While "stakeholder theory," in its early formulations, was a purely normative approach to business ethics, more sophisticated advocates have, in recent years, suggested that it may also offer a more compelling reconstructive account of the structure of the firm. Advocates of "team production theory," most influentially Margaret Blair and Lynn Stout (1999), have argued that the central function of the firm is to serve as a repository of asset-specific investments on the part of *all* patron groups, not just investors. They develop this analysis as part of an *economic* theory of the firm—just one that weights the evidence differently from the more orthodox version, put forward by theorists like Easterbrook and Fischel. A doctrine such as this provides far more sophisticated conceptual underpinnings for a multifiduciary stakeholder theory, by suggesting that the latter is not merely an ethical theory, but one that also articulates the underlying normative principles of corporate law.

Concluding remarks

The examples provided in the previous section in no way constitute a survey of the field. They are intended merely to show how modern economic theory has informed contemporary thinking in business ethics, in ways that move beyond the purely antagonist relations that prevailed for a long time. Of course, it may remain true that the majority of economists and business ethicists want nothing to do with one another. As Max Planck observed, "science advances one funeral at a time." Nevertheless, one can see that the research frontier has moved decisively in the direction of increased collaboration between the two disciplines. This is as it should be. After all, Smith's greatest lesson was to have shown that the operations of the market are not transparent, and certainly not visible to the casual observer. Part of the joy of studying economics lies in the discovery that actions have complicated, unexpected, and sometimes perverse consequences. At its best, economics is the science dedicated to tracing these consequences, pushing the analysis beyond where common sense and naive intuition alone can take us. To the extent that business ethicists are interested in the consequences of our actions, then they obviously cannot afford to ignore the teachings of economists. The only way to engage in moral assessment of actions is to understand them in their context, and, in the case of market behavior, it is economics that provides our understanding of this context.

Essential readings

The most trenchant and clear presentation of the tension between economic reasoning and business ethics can be found in David Gauthier, "No Need for Morality: The Case of the Competitive Market" (1982). In order to move beyond this antagonism, the most interesting contributions are generally those written by economists addressing issues in business ethics, such as Kenneth Arrow, "Social Responsibility and Economic Efficiency" (1973), Amartya Sen, "Does Business Ethics Make Economic Sense?" (1993) and Michael Jensen, "Value Maximization, Stakeholder Theory, and the Corporate Objective Function" (2002). Discussions in corporate law provoked by modern theories of the firm, such as Frank Easterbrook and Daniel Fischel, *The Economic Structure of Corporate Law* (1991), or Margaret Blair and Lynn Stout, "A Team Production Theory of Corporate Law" (1999), are also essential.

For further reading in this volume on a view of business ethics that situates economics within normative thought, see Chapter 12, Integrative Economic Ethics: concept and critique. For a discussion of the ways in which evolutionary economics contributes to a theory of innovation, see Chapter 19, Creativity, innovation, and the production of wealth. For further reading on the idea of a commercial versus a rent-seeking society, see Chapter 7, Can profit seekers be virtuous? On economic analysis and regulation, see Chapter 21, Regulation, rent seeking, and business ethics. On practical rationality, economic motivation, and the theory of the firm, see Chapter 13, What is business? On the contribution of economic analysis to an understanding of the financial crisis of 2008, see Chapter 23, The economic crisis: causes and considerations.

References

Akerlof, G. (1982). "Labor Contracts as Partial Gift Exchange," *Quarterly Journal of Economics* 97, 543–569.
Akerlof, G. and J. Yellen (eds) (1986). *Efficiency Wage Models of the Labor Market*. Cambridge: Cambridge University Press.
Alchian, A.A. and H. Demsetz (1972). "Production, Information Costs, and Economic Organization," *American Economic Review* 62, 777–795.
Arrow, K.J. (1973). "Social Responsibility and Economic Efficiency," *Public Policy* 21, 303–318.
Arrow, K.J. and G. Debreu (1954). "Existence of an Equilibrium for a Competitive Economy," *Econometrica* 22, 265–290.
Bakan, J. (2004). *The Corporation*. New York, NY: Free Press.
Baumol, W.J. and S.A.B. Blackman (1991). *Perfect Markets and Easy Virtue*. Cambridge, MA: Blackwell.
Becker, G. (1973). "A Theory of Marriage," *Journal of Political Economy* 81, 813–846.
Berle, A. and G. Means (1932). *The Modern Corporation and Private Property*. New York, NY: Transaction.
Birsch, D. and J.H. Fielder (eds) (1994). *The Ford Pinto Case*. Albany, NY: SUNY Press.

Blair, M.M. and L.A. Stout (1999). "A Team Production Theory of Corporate Law," *Virginia Law Review* 85, 248–328.
Blaug, M. (1985). *Economic Theory in Retrospect*, 4th edition. Cambridge: Cambridge University Press.
Boatright, J. (2002). "Ethics and Corporate Governance: Justifying the Role of the Shareholder," in N.E. Bowie (ed.), *The Blackwell Guide to Business Ethics*. London: Blackwell, 38–60.
Bowles, S. and H. Gintis (2013). *A Cooperative Species*. Princeton, NJ: Princeton University Press.
Buchanan, A. (1996). "Toward a Theory of the Ethics of Bureaucratic Organizations," *Business Ethics Quarterly* 6, 419–440.
Campbell, R. and L. Sowden (eds) (1985). *Paradoxes of Rationality and Cooperation*. Vancouver: UBC Press.
Carr, A.Z. (1968). "Is Business Bluffing Ethical?" *Harvard Business Review*, January–February, 143–53.
Coase, R. (1937). "The Nature of the Firm," *Economica*, New Series 4:16, 386–405.
Cowen, T. and E. Crampton, (eds) (2002). *Market Failure or Success*. Cheltenham: Edward Elgar.
Dawes, R.M. and R.H. Thaler (1988). "Anomalies: Cooperation," *Journal of Economic Perspectives* 2, 187–197.
Easterbrook, F. and D. Fischel (1991). *The Economic Structure of Corporate Law*. Cambridge, MA: Harvard University Press.
Eisenhardt, K.H. (1989). "Agency Theory: An Assessment and Review," *Academy of Management Review* 14, 51–74.
Fisher, T.C.G. and R.G. Waschik (2002). *Managerial Economics*. London: Routledge.
Freeman, R.E. (1998). "A Stakeholder Theory of the Modern Corporation," in M. Clarkson (ed.), *The Corporation and its Stakeholders*. Toronto: University of Toronto Press.
Friedman, M. (1978). *Free to Choose, Lecture 3*, "Is Capitalism Humane?" Available at: www.freetochoose.tv/program.php?id=mfs_3&series=mfs.
Gauthier, D. (1982). "No Need for Morality: The Case of the Competitive Market," *Philosophic Exchange* 3:3, 41–54.
Gauthier, D. (1986). *Morals by Agreement*. Oxford: Oxford University Press.
Gibbons, R. (1998). "Incentives in Organizations," *Journal of Economic Perspectives* 12, 115–132.
Gini, A. and A. Marcoux (2012). *The Ethics of Business: A Concise Introduction*. Plymouth: Rowman and Littlefield.
Hardin, G. (1968). "The Tragedy of the Commons," *Science* 162, 1243–1248.
Hasnas, J. (2009). "The Mirage of Product Safety," in G. Brenkert and T. Beauchamp (eds), *The Oxford Handbook of Business Ethics*. Oxford: Oxford University Press, 677–697.
Hayek, F. (1973). *Law, Legislation and Liberty*, Vol. 1, *Rules and Order*. Chicago, IL: University of Chicago Press.
Hayek, F.A. (1986). "The Moral Imperative of the Market," in M.J. Anderson (ed.), *The Unfinished Agenda: Essays on the Political Economy of Government Policy in Honour of Arthur Seldon*. London: Institute of Economic Affairs, 56–89.
Heath, C. (1999). "On the Social Psychology of Agency Relationships: Lay Theories of Motivation Overemphasize Extrinsic Incentives," *Organizational Behavior and Human Decision Processes* 78, 25–62.
Heath, J. (2009). *Economics Without Illusions*. New York, NY: Random House.
Heath, J. (2015). *Morality, Competition, and the Firm*. New York, NY: Oxford University Press.
Henrich, J., R. Boyd, S. Bowles, C.F. Camerer, E. Fehr and H. Gintis, (eds) (2004). *Foundations of Human Sociality*. Oxford: Oxford University Press.
Hinkley, R. (2002). "How Corporate Law Inhibits Ethics," *Business Ethics* 16:1, 4–5.
Holmström, B. (1982). "Moral Hazard in Teams," *Bell Journal of Economics* 13, 324–340.
Jensen, M.C. (2000). *A Theory of the Firm*. Cambridge, MA: Harvard University Press.
Jensen, M.C. (2002). "Value Maximization, Stakeholder Theory, and the Corporate Objective Function," *Business Ethics Quarterly* 12, 235–256.
Kahneman, D. (2011). *Thinking Fast and Slow*. New York, NY: Farrar, Straus and Giroux.
Kaplow, L. and S. Shavell (2002). *Fairness Versus Welfare*. Cambridge, MA: Harvard University Press.
Knight, F. (1923). "The Ethics of Competition," *The Quarterly Journal of Economics* 37, 579–624.
Levitt, S.D. and S.J. Dubner (2005). *Freakonomics*. New York, NY: William Morrow.
Lipsey, R.G. and K. Lancaster (1956). "The General Theory of Second Best," *Review of Economic Studies* 24, 11–32.
Lipsey, R.G., D.D. Purvis and P.O. Steiner (1988). *Economics*, 6th edition. New York, NY: Harper & Row.
Mandeville, B. (1728). *The Fable of the Bees, or, Private Vices, Publick Benefits*. London: J. Tonson.

Milgrom, P. and J. Roberts (1992). *Economics, Organization and Management.* Upper Saddle River, NJ: Prentice Hall.
Mill, J.S. (1863). *Utilitarianism.* London: Parker, Son and Bourn.
Norman, W. (2011). "Business Ethics as Self-Regulation: Why Principles that Ground Regulations Should Be Used to Ground Beyond-Compliance Norms as Well," *Journal of Business Ethics* 102, 43–57.
Olson, M. (1965). *The Logic of Collective Action.* Cambridge, MA: Harvard University Press.
Parsons, T. (1949). *The Structure of Social Action,* Vol. 1. New York, NY: Free Press.
Rabin, M. (1998). "Psychology and Economics," *Journal of Economic Literature* 36, 11–46.
Rand, A. (1964). *The Virtue of Selfishness.* New York, NY: Signet.
Rawls, J. (1971). *A Theory of Justice.* Cambridge, MA: Belknap.
Reilly, B.J. and M.J. Kyj (1990). "Economics and Ethics," *Journal of Business Ethics* 9, 691–698.
Sally, D. (1995). "Conversation and Cooperation in Social Dilemmas: A Metaanalysis of Experiments from 1952 to 1992," *Rationality and Society* 7, 58–92.
Sally, D. (2005). "Can I Say 'Bobobo' and Mean 'There's No Such Thing as Cheap Talk?" *Journal of Economic Behavior and Organization* 57, 245–266.
Samuelson, P.A. (1954). "The Pure Theory of Public Expenditure," *Review of Economics and Statistics* 36, 387–389.
Schelling, T. (1978). *Micromotives and Macrobehavior.* New York, NY: W.W. Norton.
Sen, A. (1977). "Rational Fools," *Philosophy and Public Affairs* 6, 317–344.
Sen, A. (1993). "Does Business Ethics Make Economic Sense?" *Business Ethics Quarterly* 3, 45–54.
Shapiro, C. and J.E. Stiglitz (1984). "Equilibrium Unemployment as a Worker Discipline Device," *The American Economic Review* 74:3, 433–444.
Singer, A. (2015). "The Form of the Firm." Toronto, unpublished dissertation.
Smith, A. (1843) [1776]. *An Inquiry into the Nature and Causes of the Wealth of Nations.* Edinburgh: Thomas Nelson.
Stout, L.A. (2008). "Why We Should Stop Teaching Dodge v. Ford," *Virginia Law and Business Review* 3, 164–176.
Thomsen, S. (2001). "Business Ethics as Corporate Governance," *European Journal of Law and Economics* 11, 153–64.
Williamson, O.E. (1973). "Markets and Hierarchies: Some Elementary Considerations," *American Economic Review* 63, 316–325.
Williamson, O.E. (1985). *The Economic Institutions of Capitalism.* New York, NY: The Free Press.

Part V

Economic institutions

Operations and effects

Introduction

Business takes place not in abstraction, but within the context of a number of institutions. It also takes place within what we might think of as the ultimate context: the natural environment. What should business ethicists *say*, if anything, about the background institutions within which business is done? What should business ethicists *know* about those institutional backdrops, regardless of whether these institutions will be the subject of business ethics analysis and argument? What does the natural environment *mean* for business ethics? The chapters in this section turn the analytical spotlight onto the contexts shaping business practice.

The section opens with Chapter 18, **Property and business**. **Bas van der Vossen** explores the institution without which trade, and therefore commerce, would be impossible—property. He considers the various forms of property ownership and the two basic kinds of justification that are offered for property ownership, as well as some recurrent objections. As Van der Vossen elucidates, intellectual property presents peculiar conceptual and justificatory challenges that the business ethicist must take into account.

In Chapter 19, **Creativity, innovation, and the production of wealth**, **Knut Sogner** turns the focus to innovation and the institutional infrastructure that promotes or frustrates it. He considers how innovation is treated within neoclassical economics and how this may obscure (but also shed light on) what innovation is and how it emerges. Sogner also takes up research on the topic of interaction and its role in promoting innovation. Among the dreams of both *dirigiste* planners and corporate strategists is the institutionalization of the processes of innovation—to build and operate what is effectively a constant-output innovation machine. Sogner addresses the question of whether innovation is the sort of thing that can be institutionalized.

Money is not just a medium of exchange. Its form and the institutional rules surrounding it do much to shape the business landscape and, at the margin, what can function as a business model. In Chapter 20, **Money and finance: ethical considerations**, **Antonio Argandoña** describes the institutional framework of finance and identifies ethical issues arising from financial intermediation and within financial markets. He considers also the emergence of alternative finance and its implications.

Economic institutions

In the following Chapter (21), **Regulation, rent seeking, and business ethics**, **Christel Koop and John Meadowcroft** counter the often naïve view of business–government relations that informs much of business ethics analysis and argument. Beginning with a typology of business ethics views about regulation, the authors then consider the ethics of seeking and resisting regulatory initiatives. They close by considering the implications of decades of research into rent-seeking behavior for institutional design.

How should we value the natural environment? What are the implications for business practice? In Chapter 22, **Business, nature, and environmental sustainability**, **Joseph DesJardins** seeks to expose both the power and the limits of markets as vehicles for the valuation of environmental goods. He also undertakes the important work of identifying the strengths of sustainability as a framework for understanding environmental responsibilities, as well as its profound failings as an all-purpose framework within which to subsume what are historically understood to be questions of business ethics or corporate social responsibility.

The most significant economic event of the early twenty-first century is the financial crisis of 2008. In Chapter 23, **The economic crisis: causes and considerations**, **Randall G. Holcombe** disaggregates the roles of the various private and public actors whose actions or policies either contributed to or exacerbated the most significant economic decline of recent memory. Not content to delve only into the causes, he considers also how attempts to ameliorate the crisis were fraught with ethical significance. He closes by identifying the implications of an emergent *political* capitalism—a politico-economic system in which capitalist business models built on securing political favors are the rule rather than the exception.

Alexei Marcoux

18
Property and business

Bas van der Vossen

Property rights define the economy. Economic exchange lies at the core of commercial activity. We trade real property and we exchange manufactured objects, services, intellectual goods, and other things. These forms of exchange are organized around, and made possible by, the parties' property rights. These rights specify our prior holdings, the forms of exchange into which we can enter, and they protect what we might get out of the exchange. They define and protect the consumer's purchase, the producer's income, and the exchange itself. And a settled system of property determines when economic activity creates problematic externalities, what might be the appropriate scope of regulation, what are the limits of acceptable tax policy, and so on.

Any theory of business ethics must, therefore, contend with the idea of property. If business itself is organized around property, a theory of how business ought to be done will presuppose a certain view of property rights. While all such theories (must) accept that a system of private property exists, not all will agree on the moral qualities of that system. Whereas some shareholder theorists have suggested, famously, that businesses ought to maximize their profits in accordance to what their private possessions allow, stakeholder theorists have challenged this view by pointing out that the moral demands on businesses go beyond what a private property economy allows. The viability of these and other theories of business ethics will depend in part on their fit with the best theories of property.

This chapter gives an overview of the main foundational theories of property. As I will show, there are two major *families* of justification for property (with each family, of course, having many different members). After laying out those two families and their potential problems, I will consider some of the issues that reside in intellectual property, turning subsequently to explore one way in which a theory of business ethics may either be in tension or fit with such a justification of property. In particular, I will look at the tensions that stakeholder theory, on at least one version of that theory, might create.

Forms of ownership

Before we turn to the justifications of property, however, we should begin to reflect on what property is. What's the nature of property, and private property in particular?

Property rights are complex. Even a relatively simple form of ownership such as the possession of a car can be violated or negated in a variety of ways. Your car can be stolen or damaged, you can be prevented from using it, you can be prohibited from selling it or giving it away, your car can be wrongfully expropriated by the government, and so on. Each of these violates or negates your property rights. But they affect your ownership in very different ways.

We can put this in more technical terms using the Hohfeldian analysis of rights (Hohfeld 1919).[1] When someone steals or damages your car, they thereby deny your *claim-right* to exclude them from your possessions. When you are wrongfully prevented from using your car, this denies your *liberty* to use what you own. When the law prohibits a sale, it thereby denies your *power* to transfer your rightful possessions to others. And when the government wrongfully expropriates you, it thereby violates your *immunity* against having your rights unilaterally altered or extinguished.

Systems of private property standardly afford owners all these elements of ownership. However, this analysis masks a still greater complexity. Property rights confer different kinds of liberties, claims, powers, and immunities on owners. We can have rights to possess, use, or manage our property, rights to the income we can garner using it, rights to the capital that the property represents, and so on (Honore 1961). These rights will involve several kinds of Hohfeldian incidents. The right to possess, for example, will typically involve both the claim-right to exclude and the immunity against expropriation. A right to the income one can make using property will typically involve the power to (temporarily) transfer the property to others, or the right to use the property, in exchange for payment, as well as other rights protecting this power (such as, again, the claim-right to exclude and the immunity against having these rights annulled).

There is great variation among different legal regimes in how rights to property are organized. The law can recognize, alter, or abridge various claim-rights, liberties, powers, and immunities with respect to different parts and aspects of ownership. One might thus have the liberty to grow crops on one's land, but lack the liberty to build a structure without a permit. An owner may have a claim that others not trespass on his property, but also be subject to an easement that gives others the liberty to walk across the property in designated places. One may have the power to transfer, but not be immune from, government expropriation through eminent domain. One can be a partial or shared owner, as a shareholder in a firm. One can be a conditional owner, as the holder of a mortgage-backed security. The list goes on.

Some philosophers have concluded from this complexity that there is no "core" to property rights. Instead, it is said, property rights are like a bundle of sticks, with each stick representing one of these many possible incidents. But the bundle can be put together in many different ways, and none of the sticks is really essential. As long as the bundle is recognizable as a property right, any one incident (or stick) may be present or absent (Grey 1980).

Others have challenged this thought. Some say that, while no particular incident is essential, at least the presence of certain incidents requires the presence of others (Attas 2006). Others maintain a stronger view and say that some incidents really are the "core" of property. Perhaps, for example, the right to exclude is practically unavoidable if property rights are to function as they should (Schmidtz 2011). As John Locke famously writes in section 138 of *The Second Treatise*: "I have truly no *Property* in that, which another can by right take from me, when he pleases, against my consent" (Locke 1988 [1698]).

This dispute (regarding the bundle versus core theories) matters for the broader moral relevance of property rights, including for theories of business ethics. To the extent that property lacks a common core, it will be more difficult to argue that a policy, legal regime, or moral theory is in conflict with it. After all, as long as the theory does not altogether negate rights of possession, there will be some form of property with which it is consistent. And one form is as good as any. On the other hand, if Locke is right that property rights must empower owners to exclude others, such objections can have real force.

It is important here to distinguish between two questions. One question is whether the presence of any particular incident is necessary for any given *right* to qualify as a property right. Another, and quite independent, question is whether the presence of any particular incident is necessary for a *system* to qualify as a system of property rights.

With respect to the first question, it may well be plausible that no particular incident is necessary for a given right to qualify as a property right. Rights of ownership may be composed and decomposed in myriad ways. One reason for a specific configuration of a property right is government regulation. Private ownership of nature preserves, for example, is typically heavily curtailed to prevent forms of use, exploitation, and change of the land. Another reason is private contract. Suppose you take out a mortgage with a bank to buy a house. The bank can transform the mortgage loan into collateralized debt obligations, making a number of entities the shared owner of your house in the event of your nonpayment. All of these effectively unpack what was once a thick bundle of incidents into several separate sticks.

Answering this first question in the negative, however, does not mean we must answer the second in the negative as well. For it is possible that any recognizable property *system* must have certain general or recurrent features, even if the rights within that system need not all share those features.

As we will see below, it is very plausible that for a system of property to be acceptable or justified, it will have to contain a number of regularly occurring features. But even at the conceptual level, it is true that any recognizable system of property will have certain regularly occurring features. The rights with which we began are good initial candidates. A society that generally abolishes or even heavily curtails people's rights to exclude others, to use their possessions, and their powers to enter into economic exchange, has not just changed one form of property into another. It will have effectively abolished it altogether. And, by extension, a theory of business ethics that seriously undercuts the ability of owners to exclusively hold and determine the use of their possessions will be in clear tension with private property as well. In this sense, the features of use, exclusion, and exchange form the "core" of property.

Two kinds of justification

This point about the rights to use, exclude, and transfer is conceptual in nature. It claims only that an economic system recognizable as a system of property will generally contain these rights. It leaves open, of course, whether or not there should be such a system. This latter question is one of justification.

Roughly speaking, justifications of property rights can be grouped into two kinds. The first offers a justification that moves from persons to property, so to speak. Here we begin by identifying something of moral importance about owners or their connection to the particular thing that is owned, and we end up with a view about why their property rights should be respected. The second kind moves in the opposite direction. Here, the justification begins with something of importance about rights of ownership and tries to deduce the morally important status of individuals as owners from this.

From person to property

Arguments that adopt the first approach attempt to ground rights of ownership in some morally important fact or feature about the owner. On this view, a justified system of property consists of rights that ought to be respected because they directly represent morally relevant facts about owners.

No doubt this is highly abstract. Consider, then, the most famous version of this argument. In Chapter V of *The Second Treatise*, Locke argues that property rights come about as the result of people working on things that were previously unowned (Locke 1988 [1698]). Suppose there is a piece of land that no one has appropriated yet, and you clear it, till it, and plant some crops. The result, Locke argued, is that you not only own the crops you produce, but the land as well. By laboring, you appropriate.

There is considerable controversy about precisely why Locke thought that laboring constitutes appropriation. Most commentators focus heavily on section 27, where Locke writes that laboring involves the "mixing" of something one already owns (one's labor) with something unowned (the land), thereby pulling the unowned into the sphere of what is owned. This is probably the most straightforward version of the from-person-to-property approach. It sees appropriation as quite literally the extension of the (already owned) self into the (previously unowned) external world.

On this reading, the Lockean view is that we ought to respect property because it represents previously performed labor. If you steal a car you are taking someone's work without consent. If you prevent them from using their car, you are denying them the ability to enjoy what they worked for. If you block exchange you prohibit free and equal persons from disposing of their labor as they please. In each case, to violate a property right means violating (the extension of) a person's rights over her person.

Other arguments for property take a similar form. Compare G.W.F. Hegel's view that the ultimate foundation of property lies not in the respect for mixed labor, but the recognition of others' free wills (Hegel 1967 [1821]). Hegel saw property rights as protecting the physical imprint an autonomous will makes on the external world—the objective manifestation of subjects. When we plan, say, to cultivate some land, carrying out that plan requires changes to the world. Property rights, on this Hegelian view, protect the physical manifestation of our wills in the external world. As such, they make our freely chosen plans practically possible.

On Hegel's view, to violate someone's property rights, then, is to interfere with their autonomous plans, and thus their ability to live freely by their own will. Contrary to Locke, who saw property as the extension of our physical selves, Hegel sees property as the extension of our mental selves. Instead of connecting property with labor, he connects it with our will or autonomy.

Both Locke and Hegel adopt a person-to-property approach in that they see the moral significance of property rights as directly based in some morally significant fact about individual owners. The justification of property rights, in other words, derives from normatively significant features of the persons who do or can possess them. For Locke, property rights protect our labor from being taken away by others. For Hegel, property rights protect our will from being interfered with by others.

Theories that take this approach have many attractions. One advantage is that they promise a very solid foundation for property rights. The rights over our bodies, labor, and the exercise of our autonomy or free will are all widely accepted. Given the controversial nature of disputes that invoke property rights—such as disputes over taxation, economic regulation, or the moral limits of for-profit enterprise—such a solid grounding is more than welcome.

Another advantage is that these views offer a clear mechanism for distinguishing legitimate from illegitimate forms of property. Suppose person P holds object O and we wish to know if P is justified in claiming O as his property. All we need to do is find out whether P mixed his labor or will with O, or whether O was legitimately transferred to P by someone else who had a rightful claim to O. If the answer is yes, then P has a right to O. If not, then P's claim to O is void.[2]

Unfortunately, the person-to-property approach also suffers from some well-known and recurring problems. For one, views of this kind seem poorly suited to justifying anything close to what we would intuitively recognize as at least potentially legitimate holdings. That is, the theory will fail to recognize as legitimate numerous cases in which there really does seem to be a genuine property right. And it may identify cases as involving genuine property rights where there really seem to be none. Put more precisely, the kinds of property-grounding facts or features on which this approach relies seem to be neither necessary nor sufficient for genuine property rights.

Consider these in turn. First, there are numerous examples where real property rights seem to exist, yet there is no direct connection to the owner's labor, will, or what have you. One example is the filing of a patent by a pharmaceutical corporation that has created a certain chemical compound. These bring about a property right, but it seems quite beside the point to say that this represents the corporation's mixing its labor with or extending its free will into the external world. After all, the point of the patent is to protect the idea or invention more than some particular physical object.[3]

Of course the friend of the person-to-property approach might insist here that patents ought to be abolished anyway. But many other standard cases of ownership suffer from the same problems. Imagine, for instance, a system of acquisition by which people become owners by submitting a deed application to a local registry. Or consider something like a finders-keepers rule according to which those who happen upon an object or resource become the owner, such as through "telepossession," the appropriation of sunken treasure through the use of remote video cameras.[4] There seems to be no meaningful way in which these cases involve the mixing of labor or the extending of a free will.[5]

Second, just as the person-to-property connection is not necessary for genuine property rights to exist, it is also not sufficient. Consider again Locke's suggestion of labor-mixing. As Robert Nozick (generally a follower of Locke) has famously pointed out, it cannot be true that mixing what one owns with what is unowned leads to the unowned becoming owned. Nozick's example involves pouring a can of tomato juice into the ocean. Even if I own the tomato juice, and even though the ocean belongs to nobody, I lose the tomato juice—I do not gain the ocean. Examples like this abound. You might spill some paint on a rock, you might dump waste in a forest, you might go for a hike and leave your backpack on a log. In such cases (good or bad), we seem to introduce things that are owned into things that are unowned. Yet, contrary to what Locke's labor mixing-argument would seem to imply, the result is not the extension of ownership but its loss.

The problem these cases pose for person-to-property approaches is that they seem incapable of offering a *principled* distinction between instances of appropriation and instances of waste, abandonment, or loss. As far as labor-mixing (or Hegelian will-extending) is concerned, appropriation, spillage, and abandonment all look the same. But this simply is not a plausible conclusion.

The point that these problems raise is a general one. Property rights can exist in the presence or absence of morally significant facts about owners. And people can possess these significant facts with or without enjoying property rights. The person-to-property approach thus fails to line up correctly its justifying account with the actual property rights that need justification.

The stories I have recounted here are, of course, vast simplifications of the actual arguments offered by Locke and Hegel. And other versions of these stories can be told too. Some of these will no doubt be more plausible than the ones I have just told. A Hegelian might say, for instance, that since the exercise of our autonomy or free will requires interaction with the physical and social world, the point of property is to enable or guarantee to us that ability. A Lockean might point out that property rights matter not just because of particular laboring acts, but because they protect and encourage the kind of productive activity that labor represents.

Such variations certainly fit the spirit of these arguments, and I agree they are more plausible. There may even be grounds for interpreting Hegel's and Locke's own views along these lines. But note that these stories involve a crucial *reversal* of the direction of justification. For these reconstructions no longer attempt to show that all justified property rights directly represent a connection with the owner. Instead, they aim to show that a system of property in general does something that is morally important. The rights of individual owners are morally significant because the system as a whole has morally significant features. This is the second approach to justifying property.

From property to person

Arguments that adopt this second approach typically take as their starting point the function or purpose fulfilled by a system of property rights. The conclusions they derive about the moral standing of individual property holders are defended as best fitting this function. On this more systemic view, then, property rights are primarily seen as things that are meant to solve a problem. The moral significance of property rights follows from the ways in which they solve those problems. As such, this approach reasons from ideas about the system of property as such to the rights of individuals.

We can illustrate this second approach by drawing an analogy, perhaps more familiar to students of business ethics, from the law and economics literature. One standard defense of shareholders' property rights in corporations argues that a number of potential problems that can plague firms are best (or most efficiently) solved by creating a relation of fiduciary care to shareholders (Hansmann 1996). Here, too, the justification of ownership is supposed to follow from an argument about the social desirability of its function.[6]

This approach traces back to at least David Hume. For Hume, the system of property overcomes two important problems. First, we naturally find ourselves in a condition of "moderate scarcity." That is, while there is (or can be) enough for all of us to survive and even live prosperously, there is not enough for all of us to just get whatever we want. Second, when dealing with this scarcity, we do not care for other people quite as much as we care for ourselves. Our capacity for altruism is limited.

In a world without property rights, these two problems are very severe indeed. When the world's resources are available in common, one person's gain necessarily means another person's loss. When I take a bushel of wheat from the commons, what is available to you has decreased. And if the commons do not produce enough for all of us to be satisfied, and we all look out for ourselves first, we are facing a toxic situation. Every person's attempts at providing for his or her own needs threatens the like ability of others.

This kind of zero-sum world is something we have reason to avoid. Commonly held resources tend to suffer from collective action problems, sometimes called the "tragedy of the commons" (Hardin 1968). The tragedy is that, while each person has reason to keep the commonly held resource intact, each has an incentive to overuse the resource. Our combined actions thus predictably lead to the destruction of the resource. The logic of the problem is similar to that of a prisoners' dilemma (only worse because of the increased number of players). Because no individual has the ability to exclude others from the resource, no individual has control over how the resource is used overall. The resulting uncertainty about the total use of the resource creates incentives for each individual to maximize his use of the resource, thereby leading, predictably, to the destruction of that resource.

Let's make this concrete. Think about your options as someone who shares access to the resource. One option is to restrict your use to a level that would help preserve the resource for later. Of course this means forgoing some benefit now, but that may be worth it since preserving things can offer a lot of benefits later. But this is very dangerous. For others may not similarly restrict their use, leading to the resource being depleted anyway. And that would be a terrible outcome as you lose both the future benefits and the benefits you are thinking of forgoing.

So here is your other option. You can avoid this terrible outcome by maximizing your own use of the resource. Probably this will not matter much anyway. If others end up restricting their use, your overuse will likely not destroy the resource. And if others do not restrict their use, at least you got yours. It seems, then, that your choice is pretty clear—whatever the others might do, you should use as much of the resource as possible.

The tragedy of the commons is that everyone is in this position. Everyone is incentivized to overuse a commonly held resource. As a result, commonly held resources—and the livelihood they might represent for users—tend to be depleted, mismanaged, or otherwise destroyed. The situation is such that if each does what is good for him or her, the outcome will be bad for everyone. Individually rational behavior leads to collectively irrational outcomes.

Frequently, environmental problems are a result of tragedies of the commons. David Schmidtz (1994) discusses a case involving the unregulated fishing of coral reefs in the Philippine and Tongan Islands. Because each fisherman has an incentive to overfish, and cannot reduce their own fishing with the assurance that others will do the same, they all end up overfishing. The result is the destruction of the reef and the fishermen's livelihood it represents. The same dynamic contributes to other problems, such as the cutting down of rainforests, or humanity's inability to reduce carbon emissions. (For discussion of these problems and the role property can play in solving them, see Schmidtz and Willott 2008).

The key function of property rights (and, for Hume, justice more generally) is to avoid this kind of world of rival and zero-sum interactions and to create a world where our interactions are mutually beneficial or positive-sum in nature. Systems of property avoid the zero-sum world, and therefore the tragedy of the commons, because they allow individuals to use and exclude others from their possessions. Since each person has the right to use only his or her discrete part of the world, one person's rightful use no longer reduces what is available to others.

Suppose, then, that the resource in question is a forest whose trees are used for lumber. If the forest is commonly owned, individual users have reason to cut down so many trees as to destroy the forest. But if they split up the forest into discrete parcels, each owner can control how many trees are cut down on his or her lot. Consequently, it makes sense for them to cut down only so many trees as are renewable over time.

Second, property rights foster mutually beneficial interactions. Since we need people's permission to use what is theirs, they will typically allow such use only if they think it in their interest. If you want some of my lumber, I might ask for some of your wheat in return. As a result, your use of my land no longer diminishes but enhances my ability to provide for my needs. Property systems thus encourage positive-sum or mutually beneficial interactions.

Of course, property rights need not be unique in this sense. Other solutions to tragedies of the commons can be imagined, and some have actually worked in practice too. Because fish that travel great distances cannot be confined within an owner's lot, it is hard to see how assigning property rights over the oceans, say, might help to avoid overfishing. And sometimes it can make sense for communities to want to manage certain resources together.

That being said, cases in which these alternative solutions succeed are more exception than rule. Successful collective resource management is rare and fragile (Ostrom 1990). And most resources do not swim away like fish. What is more, even if they do, property systems can

315

develop sophisticated responses.[7] There is no sense in claiming that property is the only solution humanity might invent to the tragedy of the commons. But there is little more sense in denying that it is by far the most effective response that has proven to be useful in a widespread way.

From the point of view of a moral justification for property, the following two points matter most. First, systems of private property contain far greater economic promise than their rivals. They promise, that is, to do more than just maintain the stock of resources. Because owners know that they may be able to reap the full benefits of their holdings, ownership incentivizes them to invest time and money and increase the resource's total productivity, for example by removing the underbrush, fighting common diseases, protecting one's lot against potential poachers who might cut trees at unsustainable rates, and so on.

The first argument for private property, then, is that it avoids a world in which all or most of our resources are subject to tragedies of the commons, and replaces it with one in which exclusionary rights lead to productive benefits. Life under an economic system characterized by property thus promises standards of living that are vastly superior to life under non-propertied systems.

Second, a much less commonly recognized justification offered by these arguments is more theoretical in nature. When people's livelihoods depend on what they can extract from commonly held resources, the achievement of their goals, ambitions, even their very survival come to be in conflict. To use again the example above, because person A's cutting down of trees to sell for lumber means there is less for B to cut down, A's livelihood necessarily comes at the expense of B's, and vice versa.

When social relations are zero-sum in this way, conflict looms. The threat of conflict is not simply an immediate hazard of physical confrontation (although, at the limit, fighting does loom) but a more philosophical sense of conflict—including fundamental disagreements over values, aims, and desires—that threatens the very possibility of justice. Though not much of a defender of property, John Rawls famously emphasized that a just society is a cooperative venture for mutual advantage (Rawls 1999 [1971]: Ch. 2, sec. 14), a place in which our ends become mutually reinforcing rather than rival. Leaving resources in common possession pushes us in quite the opposite direction.[8]

Property rights thus help create the conditions of justice by dividing the social world into discrete parcels. As a result, A's use of the resources available to A does not reduce the resources available to B. Stronger still, since if A wants to use B's resources, A will need to secure B's permission, such use will require terms that B considers in his interest to accept. The effect is that A's interaction with B will be to their mutual advantage.

Here, then, we find the second version of the property-to-persons argument. Individual owners can rightfully insist on their property rights because these rights are essential components of a harmonious and just social order. Because owners are authorized to make decisions about their several possessions, property rights express the moral demand that people must enter into such mutually acceptable relations.

This second property-to-person argument, then, adds something crucial to the first. The justification of property lies not only in the avoidance of tragedies of the commons, but in *how* property systems avoid them.

Note, finally, that while these arguments cannot conceive of property as an *extension* of the person, they can capture at least part of the intuition that ownership is a deeply personal affair. For our holdings represent personal projects, sacrifices, and decisions. We put time, effort, and ideas in our work, all of which is represented by the money we make. The numbers on our 401(k) slip may look like mere numbers, but they represent past sacrifices and future plans or goals. Whenever property rights are infringed, whether it be by other people or the government, we are directly affected in intimate and personal ways. In this sense, then, there is an immediate connection between respecting people, their work, and their choices, and respecting their possessions.

The conventionalist objection

Both the person-to-property and the property-to-person approaches aim to show that property rights are among our basic moral rights. On either view, property rights pose genuine moral demands similar to other important moral rights, such as rights over our bodies, our rights to freedom of action, belief, and speech.[9]

The very idea that property rights are fully fledged moral rights has been subjected to several critiques. Some of these, such as Marxist critiques, seek to reject property altogether, or even object to the very idea that people might possess rights (Marx 1978 [1844]). The worry behind these arguments is that rights in general, and property in particular, put people in antagonistic relations to one another, relations that are inimical to our living together in justice and harmony.

Less radical critiques accept that property might play an important role in society, but reject their moral foundations. According to these arguments, property rights are not among our basic moral rights, but mere conventions or legal creations, and, as such, are more malleable. They can be altered, interpreted, determined, taken away, reallocated, and strongly curtailed by the law without moral problem. Because this challenge sees property rights as mere conventions or legal creations, I label it the conventionalism-charge. (See, e.g., Murphy and Nagel 2004; Donaldson and Preston 1995.)

The upshot of the conventionalist objection is best understood in terms of a point about the order of justification. Suppose we ask what justice requires for the distribution of material goods in society. A number of things will go into answering that question. For instance, one might want the distribution to be consistent with everyone having good opportunities in life, with everyone having enough to avoid living in desperate circumstances, with some kind of equality obtaining, and with people being free to choose their occupations.

Let us call these the "inputs" of distributive justice, the basic ingredients that go into bringing together a full view of what justice might demand. The two approaches to justifying property discussed above see people's property rights as figuring among these inputs. That is, if achieving a just distribution is a question of people's opportunities, living standards, or equality, it is also a question of respecting people's property. Property, we might say, is among the premises in a longer argument about distributive justice.

The conventionalist objection seeks to reverse this order. It sees property rights as mere legal or conventional allocations, the justice of which depends on how they conform to the (different) inputs of justice. Those inputs express the demands of justice—they are the premises in the argument—and property is what we end up with once those principles are correctly applied—it is what rolls out of such an argument. However, the objection goes, because property rights function as the conclusion of a logically prior (and independent) argument about distributive justice, they themselves cannot be invoked to protest against policies of taxation, redistribution, and the like. To do so would be to make a simple mistake.

The conventionalist objection is more often asserted than defended. But its intuitive appeal is not hard to see. Any introduction to property law shows just how complicated and sophisticated the legal rules of property can—and need to—get. And this sophistication is hard to imagine without an equally complicated, sophisticated, and detailed legal system or state. Thus, the charge goes, property is something created by the law, not something pre-existing that it must protect and enforce.

This objection can be made more precise in slightly different ways. The lesson against person-to-property arguments, for example, is said to be that these justifications are radically incomplete. There is simply no way, it seems, in which we can derive such complicated and detailed views about property from arguments about individuals mixing their labor, extending their free wills, and so on. As a result, these arguments cannot support actual property rights. (See, e.g., Fried 2004; Railton 1985.)

Similarly, and contrary to property-to-person arguments, the charge holds that the benefits of property are really the result of a well-functioning state. Without a state, we lack the detailed solutions and enforcement needed to avoid tragedies of the commons, resolve conflicts, and promote productivity. But if the state is itself central to property rights fulfilling their function in the first place, then those rights cannot be coherently claimed against that legal system. Property, again, is a mere convention (Murphy and Nagel 2004).

Despite its initial appeal, the conventionalism charge is deeply problematic. While it is plausible that the philosophical arguments above are insufficient by themselves to settle all potential property disputes, this does not defeat them as justifications for property rights. These are philosophical theories and were never intended to resolve all practical problems with which the law deals. Asking them to do so would surely be asking too much of philosophical theories. Instead, their point is to identify moral boundaries within which a just legal system can specify, interpret, and settle our property rights. These theories aim to identify a scheme of justification within which a legal system can appeal to concrete facts to make particular judgments and evolve legal principles implementing the general scheme of justification.[10]

This feature is not unique to property. Consider other standard liberal rights, such as our rights to free movement, free speech, privacy, and more. The precise contours of these rights, too, are not derivable from their philosophical justifications. Different legal systems can protect, say, the right to free speech in different ways without injustice. This version of the conventionalism charge thus seems to prove too much. It threatens not only property rights, but liberal rights in general. (As such, it is closer to the more radical and less plausible Marxist objections.)

The upshot is that the conventionalism charge can simply be conceded as harmless, if not irrelevant. The (obvious) fact that property rights need specification does not threaten their status as important moral rights. It is one thing to say that a legal system backed up by a state is necessary to specify property rights with the kind of detail that we need in practice. It is quite another to say that property rights are entirely a creation of the law or state. Even if the former claim is true—and it is an empirical matter whether it is true—the latter is not.

Intellectual property

The discussion above has focused largely on ownership in tangible objects, such as land, resources, companies, and the like. However, ownership of non-tangible things is becoming increasingly important. Some of the largest and most valuable parts of the economy are organized around the existence and enforcement of patents and copyrights. Pharmaceutical companies, the entertainment industry, and technological firms all heavily rely on the enforcement of these rights.

The basic problem such forms of intellectual property are supposed to solve is not hard to see. Most economically valuable ideas and applications are not easy to find. In order to develop, say, a new kind of medication, large amounts of time, energy, and resources need to be invested. However, once developed, the recipe and application of this new medication are easily copied by others.

This creates a double-edged sword. On the one hand, since the marginal cost of applying and reapplying the idea behind the medication is virtually zero, it can be very cheap to produce it in large quantities. In this sense, the low cost of copying ideas is a boon, for it makes new medication potentially available to lots of people at a very low price.

On the other hand, this also creates a problem of free-riding. If the marginal cost of producing the medicine is very low, the price of the medication in a competitive market will be very low as well. And this may make it impossible to recoup the (often significant) investment in researching and developing the idea. As a result, companies will rationally avoid investing in the research and development of new medication. Better to wait for others to come up with innovations, and then copy them at low cost. Since all companies are in this position, few new kinds of medication will be developed.

Intellectual property rights, on their most popular defense, can strike an appropriate balance between these two effects. By awarding owners a temporary right to preclude others from freely copying and using the idea, they achieve two things. First, they end the collective action problem by creating an artificial monopoly for their creators. As monopolists, the holders of intellectual property are in a position to demand higher prices in the market. Higher prices enable them to recoup their investment and incentivizes the necessary research, development, and creative activity. Second, when the intellectual property expires, the idea becomes publicly available for commercial exploitation, thus enabling the availability of these goods at very low prices under competitive conditions. The combination of these virtues will lead, so this defense goes, to more and more ideas becoming freely available over time.

This argument is both similar to and subtly different from the argument that property rights serve to avoid the tragedy of the commons. The argument is subtly different because those previous arguments concerned the potential overuse of already existing resources. Property rights are defended to overcome the scarcity of these resources. By contrast, the present argument concerns the creation of new resources. Here scarcity is artificially created by protecting the ideas from being copied.

Nevertheless, the motivation behind the two arguments is similar. Property in ideas, just as property in tangible objects, aims at preventing the socially destructive use of valuable resources, and increasing the stock of useful goods available to mankind. Whereas in the former case, the problem concerns the overuse of already existing goods, in the latter case the problem concerns a kind of overuse that makes the creation of the resource less likely.

Intellectual property rights are highly controversial (as evidenced in a recent collection of essays, Mossoff 2013). One controversy concerns the practical use of these rights and, in particular, their duration. When the Copyright Act was first enacted in the United States, the duration of copyright was fourteen years. Now, in some cases, copyright protection can last over a century. The reasons behind these extensions are often said to be less about the recouping of investments and more about companies' lobbying Congress to keep in place their most profitable copyrights.

Other concerns about intellectual property rights focus on particular kinds of ideas. Consider new kinds of medication that could, if made cheaply, save millions of people's lives. Is there not something perverse about large pharmaceutical companies charging high prices for these products when the marginal cost of production is very low? Perhaps, then, we should exclude things like life-saving medicine from the scope of patents.[11]

On its face, however, the proposal to allow patents for all but the most important ideas is potentially disastrous. If the free-riding problem is real, and the free availability of ideas discourages the investment of resources into their development, then this proposal will lead to the production of all but the most important things. And this, of course, is precisely the opposite of what we want. Even if there is something distasteful about artificially inflating the price of this kind of medication—as there surely is—the alternative is far worse (compare Rosenberg 2004).

It is worth noting here that this line of reasoning has far-ranging implications for how we think about property rights. For the concern that there is something bad about excluding people from potentially life-saving resources is not unique to the case of patents. In fact, it is a perfectly general feature of systems of property. All such systems, we saw, allow people to exclude others from the things they possess, and at times the burdens for non-owners of being excluded can be great.

It is important to avoid posing a false dilemma here. We are not faced with a choice of absolute rights to exclude non-owners from our property come what may, or the abolition of the system of property altogether. It is possible, for instance, to support a system of property while admitting that there can be circumstances in which those rights may be justifiably infringed. Consider an example. Suppose that your life is in danger, and you are in immediate need of medical attention. And suppose that the only way you can make it to the hospital is to walk across my land. Even though you may not be able to ask me for permission—indeed, even if I were to explicitly tell you no—it is clearly permissible for you to cross my land.

But if my property rights cannot in general stand in the way of your survival, then the case for patents to life-saving ideas would seem to be similarly imperiled. After all, if we can infringe property rights in one case to save a life, why not also in the other? We live—tragically—in a world in which there are quite literally always people whose lives could be saved if only the requisite resources were available. So why not exempt life-saving medication from the patent system?

This challenge raises a question about the proper place and scope of exceptions. On the one hand, it seems true that the very benefits that justify property rights in the first place require a rule of exclusion. On the other hand, there do seem to be cases where exigent circumstances can justify exceptions to this rule. How far can those exceptions reach before they overthrow the rule and, with it, the entire practice?

The first step towards a solution is to realize that if the practice as a whole is to survive, we cannot violate the rule for every possible exception. We can, and should, recognize exceptions when important things like people's lives are at stake, but only if such recognition is consistent with upholding the more general rule of respect for property that makes saving lives possible in the first place. This means that we cannot simply generalize the truth that property can give way to emergencies into the falsehood that property rights cannot apply to potentially life-saving goods.

Note, moreover, that nothing in this argument precludes companies or philanthropists using their property rights in order to help people—or even it being morally desirable or required that they use their property in such ways. Just as I can—and, if I reasonably can, then I should—agree to let you cross my land to get to the hospital, so too wealthy parties can—and, if they reasonably can, should—make patent-protected medication cheaply available. And indeed, there are examples where companies do just this. Since 1987, Merck & Co Inc. has produced and distributed over 2 billion treatments of the river blindness drug Mectizan around the world without charge.

A third and final challenge to intellectual property rights also focuses on potentially life-saving medication, but focuses on a different problem. This objection, offered by Thomas Pogge (2002: Ch. 9), holds that the patent system does not encourage the right kind of innovations. Since patents encourage the production of medication because of the artificially high prices these will command, the system incentivizes the production of medication for which the most purchasing power exists. The system will thus likely be very good at producing, say, new kinds of skin cream that helps rich Westerners avoid wrinkles, but bad at manufacturing the kinds of medicine that would cure diseases that affect only the poorest. That is, while the patent system may well lead to a greater total stock of goods, it may also fail to bring about the right kinds of goods.

Pogge has proposed an alternative regime for producing life-saving medicine, what he calls a Health Impact Fund. The idea is to create a central fund out of which large awards could be paid to companies that have a measurable impact on public health. Such a regime, Pogge argues, would better encourage the production of medicine aimed at helping the poor. Indeed, because companies get paid not just for inventing new kinds of medication, but for the impact these have on public health, the Fund might improve the delivery of medication too.

One problem with Pogge's proposal, Nobel-laureate Angus Deaton (2015: Ch. 7) points out, is that it is very difficult to disentangle what precisely caused improvements in public health. When improvements occur, they are usually the result of the interaction of many different factors, making it hard to know which caused what. This is doubly true in very poor countries where statistical measuring techniques are poor as well. As a result, a Health Impact Fund might not be very good at matching its awards with products that genuinely improve public health.

Another problem is analogous to the problems with patents identified by Pogge. While patents incentivize companies to serve people in proportion to their aggregate purchasing power, a Health Impact Fund would encourage companies to be seen or measured to have an impact. But to be seen to have an effect is not the same as actually having a real impact. So where the patent system might incentivize the development of luxury products, the Health Impact Fund creates a different problem. It incentivizes companies to introduce their products in places where health improvements are already imminent for other reasons, to manipulate statistics and other measuring tools, and other ways of capturing the prize.

Concluding remarks: business and property

Property rights are central to questions about business ethics. They constrain how we can ethically run our own businesses, as well as treat the businesses of others. We must make sure not to defraud, deceive, pollute, steal, or damage the possessions of others. And within those limits, we must leave others free to run their businesses as they choose. The laws and regulations for which businesses can ethically lobby must be consistent with property rights and their justification.

There are differences in the degree to which theories of business ethics fit this idea of property. At its most extreme, one might hold in the tradition of E. Merrick Dodd (1932) that control of a corporation, say, ought not to lie with the shareholders but with society at large. On such a view, corporations are closer to public institutions that ought to be subject to standards of providing common benefits than private possessions that owners can use for their own gain. If, at the other extreme, we follow Milton Friedman's famous thought that the terms of business ethics are largely set by the terms of private property, we might indeed say that "there is one and only one social responsibility of business—to . . . increase its profits so long as it stays within the rules of the game" (Friedman 2002: 133).

On other views, the relation will be more complicated. Consider the following version of stakeholder theory, which aims "to broaden management's vision of its roles and responsibilities to include interests and claims of non-stockholding groups" (Mitchell et al. 1997: 855). On this view, companies morally ought to take into consideration the interests of all the "groups and individuals who benefit from or are harmed by, and whose rights are violated or respected by, corporate actions" (Freeman 1998: 129).

The suggestion, here, is that managers have moral obligations to take into account the interests of a variety of groups that surround the firm. But consider the incentives that this creates. These will include:

a. an incentive to be *among* those who have a stake in how the firm acts;
b. an incentive to *maximize* the extent of one's stake;
c. an incentive to *prevent others* from having or developing a stake in how the firm acts; and
d. an incentive to *minimize* the extent of the stakes of others.

The rationale behind these incentives is the same throughout. The extent to which one stands to gain from the way businesses operate depends on the size of one's proportional stake. One gains more, that is, the larger the numerator and the smaller the denominator of one's share of the total stake in the business's operations. At the limit, the point at which one's interests are served *best*, the proportional size of one's stake will be 1.

The incentives above mirror the different ways one can move in this direction. One can increase the numerator by, first, making sure one is counted among the stakeholders. Once you are counted, the business in question will have to serve your interests. Second, one can increase this by maximizing the interests one has in how the business operates. The larger your stake, the more you stand to gain from the business decisions. One can decrease the denominator in two analogous ways. First, one can limit the ability of others to become among the stakeholders. Fewer stakeholders means fewer claimants to the business pie. And second, one can work to make others' stakes as small as possible. With others receiving smaller slices, more of the pie is left for one to gain.

A theory of business ethics that creates these incentives need not explicitly *deny* that individuals are the owners of private, and thus exclusive, property. It can grant this while claiming, for instance, that the owners of said property ought to use stakeholder theory as their guide for action. Nevertheless, there is an undeniable tension between the two ideas. For the dynamic created by stakeholder theory precisely reproduces the tragedy-of-the-commons situation discussed above. And this tragedy was the very reason for defending property rights on the property-to-person approach.

Stakeholder theory thus threatens to undo the very solution property rights was supposed to provide. It encourages behavior that renders our ends zero-sum or rival once again. Your gain comes at my expense, and my gain means you must lose. It follows that the more a firm's decisions become a matter of weighing the interests of various stakeholders, the more those holders' stakes come to stand in conflict. This is to make everybody's business everybody's business. And when everybody's business is everybody's business, tragedies of the commons arise.[12]

None of this is to say, of course, that it is wrong for businesses to take the interests of stakeholders into account. As said above, part of the point of property is to empower owners to decide how they want to use their possessions, and they can—and sometimes should—exercise their rights for the benefit of others. There is a place in our lives for rights and duties, and there is a place for virtue and plain old decency. But we must not lose sight of the place of these demands. The ethics of business cannot override or undercut the central motivation of the kind of property rights on which companies, exchange, and productivity are based in the first place.

Essential readings

The most important treatment of property rights remains Chapter V of John Locke's *Second Treatise of Government* (1988 [1698]). A great overview and critical discussion of arguments in favor of private property rights remains Jeremy Waldron, *The Right to Private Property* (1988). The locus classicus for the "tragedy of the commons" is Garrett Hardin's essay, "The Tragedy of the Commons" (1968). For discussion on the person-to-property and the property-to-person types of justification, see my discussion in "What Counts as Original Appropriation?" (2009).

For a key modern discussion that takes the property-to-person approach, see David Schmidtz, "The Institution of Property" (1994).

For further reading in this volume on whether stakeholder theory is compatible with business ownership, see Chapter 13, What is business? For a consideration of the moral scope of stakeholder thinking, see Chapter 11, Stakeholder thinking. On property and its relation to the forms of the corporation, see Chapter 14, The corporation: genesis, identity, agency and Chapter 15, Alternative business organizations and social enterprise. For a discussion of market and non-market responses to environmental problems, see Chapter 22, Business, nature, and environmental sustainability. On freedom of contract in employment relations, see Chapter 28, Employee ethics and rights. On Mahatma Gandhi's conception of property, see Chapter 36, Business ethics in South Asia: Gandhian trusteeship and its relevance for the twenty-first century. On the social and moral effects of collectivization, including the idea of a "property deficit," see Chapter 39, Business ethics in transition: communism to commerce in Central Europe and Russia. On the relevance of property to the development of business in Africa, see Chapter 37, Business ethics in Africa.

Notes

1 Hohfeld proposed an analytical understanding of rights as relations between parties. On this analysis, one party's liberty-right (sometimes called a privilege) to something entails the absence of a claim-right in another to the same thing. A claim-right to something, further, entails a duty for another party to that thing. (Consequently, a party's liberty-right to do something entails that the same party does not have a duty not to do it.) Third, a power-right denotes a party's ability to change a juridical or moral relation in some party. When one party has a power, this entails a liability for some party (a liability to have their juridical or moral position changed by the power-holder). Finally, an immunity-right protects one against the use of a power. When one has an immunity, some party has a disability (i.e., the absence of a power to change the immunity-holder's juridical or moral relation).

2 Alexei Marcoux has suggested to me that early stakeholder-theoretic criticisms of equity owners' claims to management's fiduciary care might be interpreted as person-to-property arguments in negative form. That is, they deny that shareholders in a corporation possess the morally relevant features that would justify a property right in the firm being managed in their interests because (for example) they lack a morally substantial relationship to the success of the firm.

3 This sets aside even more vexing questions about whether corporations can possess the kind of morally significant free will that gives this argument its punch.

4 See *Columbus-American Discovery Group Inc. v. Atlantic Mutual Ins. Co.*, 1992 (974, F. 2d 450–4th Cie 1992).

5 Perhaps a hard-nosed friend of the person-to-property approach might insist that these kinds of ownership, too, should be abolished. But this just seems silly. If we are going to accept a robust system of property rights at all, there is little point in restricting it to only those for which there is a direct connection with labor, the will, or what have you.

6 Thanks to Alexei Marcoux for pointing this out to me.

7 Compare the way the common law treats questions about who owns a wild animal killed in a hunt: the person who pursues the animal by giving chase or the person who killed and carried it away when it happened by him? The classic case here is *Pierson v. Post* (3 Cai. R. 175, 2 Am. Dec. 264; N.Y. 1805), decided on appeal in favor of Pierson, the person who killed the fox pursued by Post. Or consider the related question about who owns gas that is extracted from a field spanning multiple people's properties. Here, the party who captures the gas is considered the owner. In both cases, the justification that's offered for the rule takes a clear property-to-person form, namely the socially beneficial use of natural resources. For related discussion see Rose (1996).

8 Thus Hume emphasized that even though property rights mean that I cannot just take what I want or need, "it will be for my interest to leave another in the possession of his goods, provided he will act in the same manner with regard to me" (Hume (1978 [1739]), book III, part II, sec. II).

9 Hume, of course, thought that there was an important difference between rights over our persons and rights over our possessions. The latter were "conventional" in the sense that they come into existence

only after a certain man-made practice is in place, the former "natural" in that they require no such thing. This distinction is often confused for the view that our property rights are somehow less secure than our other rights. Nothing of the kind follows from Hume's argument (see Hume (1978 [1739]), book III).

10 Thanks to Alexei Marcoux for helpfully putting the point this way.
11 While he did not put his point in terms of the patent system, the idea here is analogous to a famous argument by Peter Singer. In his discussion of the moral significance of famines around the world, Singer argued that if we can save a person's life without giving up something of moral significance, then we ought to do it. This means that relatively rich people (people like you and me, that is) ought to give away what we own up to the point that saving another life no longer justifies the sacrifice we are about to make. At the limit, this might endanger property rights as well. As Singer put it: "the prevention of the starvation of millions of people outside our society must be considered at least as pressing as the upholding of property norms within our society" (Singer 1972: 237).
12 Sometimes stakeholder theorists argue that the demands on business are limited because the business cannot be required to trade them off against each other (Freeman 2009: 66). But this does not remove the problem, as we face a kind of arms race to get one's stake as large as possible as quickly as possible. The result is the same: wastefully maximized demands, dependencies, and zero-sum interaction.

References

Attas, D. (2006). "Fragmenting Property," *Law and Philosophy* 25, 119–49.
Deaton, A. (2015). *The Great Escape*. Princeton, NJ: Princeton University Press.
Dodd, E.M. Jr (1932). "For Whom are Corporate Managers Trustees?" *Harvard Law Review* 45, 1145–1163.
Donaldson, T. and L.E. Preston (1995). "The Stakeholder Theory of the Corporation: Concepts, Evidence, and Implications," *Academy of Management Review* 20, 65–91.
Freeman, R.E. (1998). "A Stakeholder Theory of the Modern Corporation," in M.B.E. Clarkson (ed.), *The Corporation and its Stakeholders*. Toronto: University of Toronto Press, 125–138.
Freeman, R.E. (2009). "Managing for Stakeholders," in T.L. Beauchamp, N.E. Bowie, and D.G. Arnold (eds), *Ethical Theory and Business* (8th edition). New Jersey: Pearson, 56–68.
Fried, B. (2004). "Left-Libertarianism: A Review Essay," *Philosophy & Public Affairs* 32:66–92.
Friedman, M. (2002). *Capitalism and Freedom*. Chicago, IL: University of Chicago Press. 40th anniversary edition.
Grey, T.C. (1980). "The Disintegration of Property," in J.R. Pennock and J.W. Chapman (eds), Nomos XXII: *Property*. New York, NY: New York University Press, 69–85.
Hansmann, H. (1996). *The Ownership of Enterprise*. Cambridge, MA: Belknap Press.
Hardin, G. (1968). "The Tragedy of the Commons," *Science* 162, 1243–8.
Hegel, G.W. F. (1967 [1821]). *The Philosophy of Right*, T.M. Knox (trans.). Cambridge: Cambridge University Press.
Hohfeld, W.N. (1919). *Fundamental Legal Conceptions*, W. Cook (ed.). New Haven, CT: Yale University Press.
Honore, A.M. (1961). "Ownership," in A.G. Guest (ed.), *Oxford Essays in Jurisprudence*. Oxford: Oxford University Press, 107–47.
Hume, D. (1978 [1739]). *A Treatise of Human Nature*, L.A. Selby-Bigge and P. H. Nidditch (eds). Oxford: Clarendon Press.
Locke, J. (1988 [1698]). *Two Treatises of Government*, Peter Laslett (ed.). Cambridge: Cambridge University Press.
Marx, K. (1978 [1843]). "On the Jewish Question," in R. Tucker (ed.), *The Marx-Engels Reader*. New York, NY: Norton & Company, 26–46.
Mitchell, R.K., B.R. Agle, and D.J. Wood (1997). "Toward a Theory of Stakeholder Identification and Salience: Defining the Principle of Who and What Really Counts," *The Academy of Management Review* 22:4, 853–886.
Mossoff, A. (ed.) (2013). *Intellectual Property and Property Rights*. Northampton, MA: Edward Elgar.
Murphy, L. and T. Nagel (2004). *The Myth of Ownership: Taxes and Justice*. Oxford: Oxford University Press.

Ostrom, E. (1990). *Governing the Commons: The Evolution of Institutions for Collective Action*. Cambridge: Cambridge University Press.

Pogge, T. (2002). *World Poverty and Human Rights*. Polity Press.

Railton, P. (1985). "Locke, Stock and Peril: Natural Property Rights, Pollution and Risk," in M. Gibson (ed.), *To Breathe Freely*. Tolowa, NJ: Rowman & Littlefield.

Rawls, J. (1999 [1971]). *A Theory of Justice*. Cambridge, MA: Harvard University Press.

Rose, C. (1996). *Property and Persuasion: Essays On The History, Theory, And Rhetoric Of Ownership*. Boulder, CO: Westview Press.

Rosenberg, A. (2004). "On the Priority of Intellectual Property Rights, Especially in Biotechnology," *Politics, Philosophy and Economics* 3, 77–95.

Schmidtz, D. (1994). "The Institution of Property," *Social Philosophy and Policy* 11:2, 42–62.

Schmidtz, D. (2011). "Property," in G. Klosko (ed.), *The Oxford Handbook of the History of Political Philosophy*. Oxford: Oxford University Press, 599–610.

Schmidtz, D. and E. Willott (2008). "Reinventing the Commons: An African Case Study," in D. Schmidtz, *Person, Polis, Planet: Essays in Applied Philosophy*. Oxford: Oxford University Press, 211–227.

Singer, P. (1972) "Famine, Affluence, and Morality," *Philosophy & Public Affairs* 1:3, 229–243.

van der Vossen, B. (2009). "What Counts as Original Appropriation?" *Politics, Philosophy and Economics* 8, 355–373.

Waldron, J. (1988). *The Right to Private Property*. Oxford: Clarendon Press.

19
Creativity, innovation, and the production of wealth

*Knut Sogner**

"Adam Smith did not see the Industrial Revolution coming"—so said my undergraduate teacher in economic history in 1985. In his seminal book *The Wealth of Nations* (1776), Smith lays some of the crucial groundwork for the modern science of economics, but he does not systematically address innovation. Yet parallel to his writing this treatise, the British production system began to usher forth profound changes in the organization of production and in the goods produced. While Smith discussed efficiency, the Industrial Revolution involved innovative change that radically shifted what was achievable in terms of the production of wealth.

During the latter half of the eighteenth century the Industrial Revolution was in embryonic form, so it is understandable that Smith might not have discerned the potential of his very own conception, the natural system of liberty. Yet he did write profoundly about the possibilities of economic change (in particular specialization and how specialization might lead to innovation) and growth. Compared with many modern economists his is a broad and historical approach. Yet economics—with its account of the mechanisms that create balance between what is produced and what is consumed (or, more correctly, between supply and demand)—is hardly able to grasp the many and messy undertakings that alter the supply system, that part of the economy that creates and produces the goods and services under the demand of consumers.

Creativity and innovation help to increase productivity, thereby changing the way in which people earn their livelihoods as well as the goods and services they enjoy. To understand creativity and innovation one must move beyond standard models employed by economists. One must consider, for example, the transformative possibilities engendered by science as well as the ways in which politics and law function to allow, encourage, or incentivize creative acts and beneficial interactions (Fagerberg et al. 2005).

Over the last quarter century new fields of research have emerged that seek to understand positive change in the economy (Fagerberg et al. 2012). The common agenda is to find out how and why innovation, in the broadest sense, happens. The scholars who pursue this agenda range from those interested in corporate success to those who want to understand why nations and societies grow rich. This is, therefore, a vast and heterogenous arena, but this chapter will concentrate on what may be termed *Schumpeterian* innovation, after the Austrian-American economist Joseph Schumpeter. The chapter will, therefore, focus on processes of creativity and entrepreneurship that have, either through intended purpose or as actual result, effected real changes in the production of goods and services—innovation. These sorts of innovations may arrive in a cluster, accumulating during a discrete slice of time, and lead to such radical changes of the economy that we may speak of an "industrial revolution."

Schumpeter contributed at least three concepts that guide much research on innovation: the "entrepreneur" as agent of innovation (Schumpeter 1934, but see Hébert and Link 2009 for predecessors); a distinction between adaptive and creative economic behavior (Schumpeter 1947); and the idea that innovations be institutionalized within large corporations (Schumpeter 1943/1976). Schumpeter places these concepts in larger economic landscapes, revealing thereby how processes of creativity and change prove relevant to the whole society. A very important distinction in Schumpeter's definition of innovation is that invention and innovation are not the same. A new chemical entity, a new way to produce energy, or a novel food recipe, are inventions until the required processes of commercialization turn them into innovations. Indeed, the definition of an innovation is the introduction of something new in the economy (even if the new entity is but a novel reconfiguration of old entities).

While Schumpeter was active in the first part of the twentieth century, his rise to the center stage of a scholarly enterprise devoted to the study of innovation and change is a consequence of the shift from post-war growth to crises and volatility that occurred from the 1970s onwards (Van der Wee 1986). Innovation has been seen as more than a necessary tool to solve issues of economic stagnation or to redo old economic structures that contribute to climate change and pollution. In fact, innovation may be regarded as a new tool to achieve economic equality. While revolution and redistribution were leftist political goals for centuries, innovation is a new tool to change the society for the better (Phelps 2013; Mazzucato 2014).

This chapter offers an historic introduction to the broad field of innovation studies with an eye towards ethical matters. Four fundamental issues are highlighted. In the first section, I delineate how the concept of innovation has little place within the framework of standard economic models, yet innovation is crucial to the total economy. In the second section, I take up some theoretical approaches, emerging in the 1980s, that construe the phenomena of innovation as occurring within specific circumstances. This is the "interactive" approach. In the subsequent section, I focus on how innovation has been seen, by some, to be institutionalized within the large corporation or, in other cases, within clusters of small companies or even the nation state, noting as well how some scholars have argued for cultural or ethical frameworks as catalysts of innovation. In the final section, I canvas some of the debate as to whether or why innovation has failed to return economic growth to the wealthy nations.

Innovation and neoclassical economics

Whether the global economy is assessed over time or over geographical space, creative change is both apparent and, for the most, welcomed. Over the last two centuries the global economy has grown, and large populations, though not in all regions, increasingly have become accustomed to a comfortable life. But, as Schumpeter argued, economics as a science provides little entrance to the idea of economic or productive creativity. Striving to be an exact and encompassing science, economics has been long concerned with static efficiency, namely how best to use available resources to produce some given product (Baumol 2002). The standard model in contemporary economics requires that companies take prices as given and behave in the most efficient way. To this end, the standard models require economic agents, whether individuals or firms, to *adapt* to a given set of production goals in the most efficient manner.

Much—but certainly not all—of how economists see the world goes back to Adam Smith (Smith 1776/1981; Roncaglia 2001). The wealth of nations, Adam Smith claimed, was measured against the background of a country's population (per capita), and was the result of division of labor and specialization. By dividing work processes into several different tasks and having the workers specialize in specific operations, productivity (production measured against effort) would rise. This, of course, entailed a kind of innovation. Smith was concerned, in particular, about labor productivity, i.e., the amount of labor going into the production of a unit of something. Efficiency was the goal. The wealth of nations was not, consequently, dependent on balance of foreign trade or on amassing trade surpluses, two contentions defended by Smith's mercantilist predecessors. Foreign trade is only a part of what goes on in an economy, but Smith set out to cover the whole picture.

Smith's approach shifts the balance of economic thinking on growth and wealth from focusing on the guidance of the state or the directives of a ruler (not to mention the accrual of gold via exports) to a framework that emphasizes law, competition, and the improvement of individual lives. The processes of corporate expansion and growth that led to a division of labor is part of what is referred to by Smith's famous appeal to the "invisible hand": An economy characterized by acts of self-interest and the pursuit of profit leads actors and companies, via the mechanisms of the market economy, to put their efforts into activities that best serve society. The potential problem of a society where every actor seeks profit maximization is countered by competition within the rule of law that prohibits fraud and coercion. Competition among companies to supply a certain product increases supply and thereby lowers prices. The involved companies then adjust the supply accordingly. These mechanisms work throughout the economy and, in the end, profits for the sale of all products reach the same natural level. Economic actors constantly adjust their behavior according to the natural profit rate. The totality of adjustments of sellers and buyers reaches, thereby, a level of balance, in technical terms, an "equilibrium."

Smith argued against state-led economies and for the benefits of the free market. In a free market economy, each agent may employ his or her own local or situational knowledge in the pursuit of self-interest (broadly understood). The cumulative result is a powerful dynamic force for creating wealth; in the long run, a centrally directed economy is unable to duplicate or match this result. The only real direct role for the state is to thwart collusion and provide crucial public goods. Smith—who readily acknowledged the presence of self-interest as a potential problem—was under no illusion that companies would not try to avoid competition. For Smith the counteractive mechanism of competition is the key that justifies the self-interest promoted by a free market economy.

In a market economy, the balance achieved between supply and demand, and the underlying mechanisms described by Smith, gives an approximation of where economics has developed up until the present. The understanding of the economy as a system that balances supply and demand in a sort of a circular flow proceeds from Smith's earlier analyses, even as current economics is much more detailed and technical, and capable of taking into account aspects not addressed by Smith. The current model of perfect competition makes assumptions that Smith did not employ: No firm is large enough to dominate price setting; each has the same information, the same cost structure and produces equivalent goods and services, all performed in conditions with freedom of entry and exit. These mechanisms lead to situations where every company would experience prices as given. Companies are *adaptive*, but they are certainly not *innovative*.

It is against this model that Joseph Schumpeter's idea of "creative response" acquires its force: "And whenever the economy or an industry or some firms in an industry do something else, something that is outside the range of existing practice, we may speak of *creative response*" (Schumpeter 1947: 150, italics original). Creative responses are actions that forge new paths, for example, moving from horse-drawn wagons to steam trains or to the internal combustion engine in automobiles. A creative response is, in fact, an act of *entrepreneurship*, a term that Schumpeter uses in a wider and more profound sense than simply as a new venture creation. Schumpeter views creativity and innovation as tightly interwoven. Creativity—entrepreneurship—drives innovation.

In his path-breaking book *The Theory of Economic Development* (1934), Schumpeter treats the entrepreneur as having a dual role. The entrepreneur is a flesh and blood human being who takes risks and acts in an intentional and creative way. However, the entrepreneur's action fulfills a function that could almost be termed a systemic and integral part of Schumpeter's approach to macroeconomics. Indeed, group entrepreneurial actions, motivated by economic circumstance, prove powerful enough to be the drivers of economic cycles. Crises create opportunities, and the entrepreneurs take them. Joseph Schumpeter also coined a phrase, "creative destruction," to emphasize, thereby, the need for an economy to renew itself (Schumpeter 1943/1976: 83). Economic crises may "rinse" the economy of old methods and products and usher forth novel approaches and goods, aided throughout by entrepreneurial activity.

Schumpeter's creative response is also applicable to the role of the business firm. The business firm may in principle perform exactly the same entrepreneurial role as the individual entrepreneur, and with their extra clout their impact is often greater. There is, of course, a literature about business innovation—innovation *within* the firm—and how companies may organize themselves better through the use of the resources they possess and the capabilities they contain (Penrose1959/1995; Lazonick 2005; Barney and Clark 2007; Teece 2009). But there exists no easy recipe for how to facilitate growth-creating business innovation *throughout* society. (For the purpose of this chapter, the business firm is included in the discussion alongside individual entrepreneurs.)

Schumpeter offers a break with the neoclassical model. Creative behavior, he maintains, is about individual acts and novel practices; these new acts and activities rely, in part, on differences in belief (including information, hunches, and knowledge). Yet individual innovations cannot be foreseen or anticipated, only explained after the event itself. For these reasons, innovation is difficult to include in models of the economy, whether a part or a whole. In this sense, neoclassical economics assumes that all producers simply produce the same goods and do so in an efficient way. Yet for the entrepreneur products are not the same and it may be worthwhile for the creative person to consider how or whether new techniques or products might prove viable. The entrepreneur faces uncertainty, not risk, a distinction characterized aptly by Frank Knight:

> The essential point for profit theory is that insofar as it is possible to insure by any method against risk, the cost of carrying it is converted into a constant element of expense, and it ceases to be a cause of profits and loss. The uncertainties which persist as causes of profit are those which are uninsurable because there is no objective measure of the probability of gain or loss.
>
> *(Knight 1951/2013: 116)*

It remains true that Schumpeter's entrepreneurs may create what in certain instances (temporal or geographical) amount to monopolies. The aim of monopoly profit is one of the main attractions of innovation. Those who come first on the market with a brilliant new product may reap enormous profits because of the lack of competition. Not simply self-interest but greed is not unknown in the entrepreneurial world. If one places uncertainty of outcome at center stage, then a pursuit of profit, including a putatively monopoly profit, suggests that processes of innovation may come fraught with difficult and morally ambiguous challenges.

Entrepreneurial people may not necessarily be nice. The fulfilment of novel projects and processes may require a firm and steady hand; in fact, the sort of "creative destruction" described by Schumpeter may also lead to the neglect of ethical sensitivity. It may turn out that self-interest is not fully constrained by competition. In such cases, there is an argument that the sort of rule breaking that may take place may be ethically defensible because it can create new paths of actions, both morally and economically (Brenkert 2009). But being close to strong-minded entrepreneurs can expose employees, collaborators and relatives to ruthless or cold obsession. These dimensions are not much included in the histories and handbooks of entrepreneurship (Casson et al. 2006; Hébert and Link 2009; Landstrøm and Lohrke 2010), though some of the American "robber barons," active during the turn of the twentieth century, were entrepreneurs. If there is this "dark side" to entrepreneurship, then it might be approached through the consideration of these questions:

> For example, when does persistence become rigidity that stifles the building and sustaining of nurturing relationships? When does entrepreneurial passion turn into a dysfunctional obsession? . . . Finally, when does the entrepreneur's need for dominance and achievement lead to engaging in fraud and corruption that undermines the well-being of the community and society?
>
> *(Wright and Zahra 2011: 4)*

Even taking the above into account, the creative entrepreneur by and large remains a heroic figure because of his—and increasingly her—role as promoter of change in the economy. Fulfilling an entrepreneurial role has been increasingly valued in society, even if there is a "dark side."

The importance of entrepreneurial innovation has re-emerged since the decade of the 1970s. During the immediate postwar era, the economies of the Western nations were characterized, for almost two decades, by solid economic growth led, in part, by governments' fine-tuning their budgets, as well as corporate willingness to play along with government objectives. However, from the late 1960s, growth became more difficult, and ever since the steep rise of oil prices in 1973 many of the rich countries have struggled with unemployment and stagnation. The economic crisis of the 1970s changed many people's (not necessarily economists') perception of the value of economics as a predictive and useful science in a national planning sense. Economists such as Ludwig von Mises (1949), F.A. Hayek (1960) and Milton Friedman (1962), who for a long time had criticized postwar Western economics for being too dominated by the state and for ignoring the role of decentralized decision-making for allocating resources, came to prominence (Van der Wee 1986). Schumpeter and his ideas were mere shadows in the background, however, in the turn to market-based solutions and deregulation of the late 1970s and early 1980s (Frieden 2006). This was an era of highly visible political reformers such as Ronald Reagan and Margaret Thatcher, and most Western countries tried their hand at withdrawing the state from taking direct action in the economy. By and large, this was a political and economic undertaking to promote international competitiveness and entrepreneurship: trim the public sector and thereby increase the room for private entrepreneurship. Even so, in most countries economic growth remained lower than in previous decades. There was no new industrial revolution in the form of solid and transformational economic growth. There was a need for new thinking about how innovation and creativity could promote economic growth.

The interactive approach to innovation

Individuals such as Bill Gates, Steve Jobs and others are often seen as "game-changers" in the economy, creative agents emblematic of the innovative entrepreneur. However, the academic understanding of innovation has moved beyond the heroic individual to develop a more contextual approach to understanding innovation and entrepreneurship. This sort of approach focuses on circumstance and how situational opportunity provides conditions for innovation. Often called the "interactive approach," because of how situational opportunity presents connections and relations among individuals, companies, and circumstances, this perspective also focuses on how the people involved in these creative processes are generally normal wage-earning employees who are, so to speak, "just doing their jobs."

Such an approach gained prominence in the early 1980s with the evolutionary account of innovation offered by two economists, Richard R. Nelson and Sidney G. Winter. In *An Evolutionary Theory of Economic Change* (1982), they built on earlier work by Armen Alchian (1950), who had argued that the economy should be construed as an evolving system with analogues to biological evolution: selection mechanisms for actions from units or organisations (companies) that have established routines and are searching for new and better ways to do business.

Although influenced by Alchian, and by Schumpeter as well, Nelson and Winter also acknowledged their debt to two other economists, whose work exemplified the Austrian School of economic thought rather than the neoclassical. These were Israel Kirzner and F.A. Hayek. Kirzner has long recognized the signal importance of entrepreneurship to the economy. It is, he argued, through the actions of entrepreneurs that opportunities are recognized and acted on. Kirzner criticizes Schumpeter's approach to entrepreneurship as not sufficiently attentive to the dynamic of the market economy and to the crucial role of entrepreneurial alertness: "Instead of identifying the profits captured ex post by the entrepreneur, we must focus attention on the profit possibilities which serve to attract the entrepreneur" (Kirzner 1971: 208; see also Kirzner 1973). Kirzner shares with his forerunner Hayek a micro understanding of the economy's core processes. Hayek characterizes the economy not as one coherent whole, oriented to a specific end, but as several smaller "economies" connected by the price mechanism. Price changes are bits of information that lead to changes in the actions of individuals, organizations, and firms. The actual market order is not a world of perfect information. Competition is not, therefore, a static state but a process for discovering facts in the form of what is desirable and achievable, and how (Hayek 1945, 1978). Together Kirzner and Hayek portray the economy as a constantly changing entity in which entrepreneurship is an important way of achieving change.

For Nelson and Winter, innovation is a result of corporations striving to improve their profits through new products. The economic actors are profit seekers, as in mainstream economics. But they are acting in a world of bounded rationality—a world without full information—in which striving for innovations creates differences among companies. Learning from interacting with the environment is important. Companies develop unique knowledge that creates differences among firms and among their products; such differences, mutations in the biological jargon, are either selected or discarded in the market based on their specific characteristics. This is a model of an evolving and changing economy, with companies that act differently from each other, within an economy operating with "selection mechanisms" in addition to price.

During the 1980s, Nelson and Winter's approach was developed in close communication with Chris Freeman and Nathan Rosenberg, scholars who, among others, were influenced by Schumpeter. A British economist, Chris Freeman, perceived that Schumpeter's cycles of creative destruction were parts of long waves resting on shifts in technological foundations (Freeman and Soete 1997; Freeman and Louçã 2001). Fundamental kinds of technology were introduced into the economy as innovations altering long-term growth patterns. Freeman identified several such historical waves, two of which merit notice. The second great wave of innovation, taking place from the 1840s to the 1890s, rests on the industrial revolution with its resultant growth in the numbers of professional engineers, institutes of technology, as well as in the steady rise of mass primary education and the emergence of railways, telegraph, and the use of steam power, coal and iron. In the 1990s, according to Freeman, a fifth long wave came forth based on global research and development networks, lifetime education and training, information highways, digital networks, microelectronics, and gas and oil. The technical and institutional context provided by Freeman and associates could be combined with the evolutionary approach of Nelson and Winter.

For several decades Freeman has developed and maintained a global center for innovation studies, namely the Science Policy Research Unit (SPRU) at University of Sussex in Brighton, UK. Together, Freeman and the SPRU blended Schumpeter and science and technology studies (STS), as originally influenced by Thomas Kuhn's book, *The Structure of Scientific Revolutions* (1962). Kuhn demonstrated that science was not developing only according to its own internal logic, but through the formation of paradigmatic regimes involving subjective beliefs that were not necessarily rooted in unquestionable scientific facts. Freeman's long waves could be seen as "techno-economic paradigms" (Freeman 1989), an expression that for a time was much employed in the field.

During the 1980s several independent academic developments came to support the approach of Nelson and Winter, and Freeman too. A common theoretical position was to place particular emphasis on different types of contextual features: locality, nation-state, communication networks, or institutional settings. Innovation was seen as a result of interactive processes of various kinds in which "learning" is the key, often via a feedback mechanism, through personal communication, or from a particular situation, be it geographical, national, legal, or cultural. Market-signals, technological knowledge, access to skills, initial markets, illustrate the advantages that firms and individuals could gain from positive interactions within such situations.

The appeal to situation or context provided, in effect, a critique of another view propagated first by Vannevar Bush in 1945: that the root cause of technological and economic progress was science ("Science as the Endless Frontier"), and that a nation would advance so long as science progressed. But in fact many students of science and technology rejected Bush's theory. The influential historian of technology Thomas P. Hughes wrote a book about the electrification of Western society called *Networks of Power* (Hughes 1983; see also Hughes 1986) in which he emphasized not the advance of science itself but the complex web of actors and processes of technology and their responses to different circumstances.

Possibly the seminal contribution to the interactive approach is one that takes into account both economics and business—that of Stephen J. Kline and Nathan Rosenberg. In their essay, "An Overview of Innovation" (Kline and Rosenberg 1986), they summarize recent work on economics and technology (to which Rosenberg in particular had contributed significant elements, even influencing Nelson and Winter, as in Rosenberg 1976, 1982). Kline and Rosenberg point out that a central assumption of much science policy has been the belief that science and technology developed in tandem: as suggested by Vannevar Bush, science provided a basic input that laid the groundwork for technology and development, and from that would follow production and marketing. However, according to Kline and Rosenberg, this assumption of linearity was not correct. As they contend,

> An improved model of innovation indicates not one, but rather five major pathways that are all important in innovation processes. These paths include not only the central-chain-of-innovation [research-development-production and marketing], but also the following:
>
> > numerous feedbacks that link and coordinate R&D with production and marketing;
> >
> > side-links to research all along the central-chain-of-innovation;

long-range generic research for backup of innovations;

potentiation of wholly new devices or processes from research; and much essential support of science itself from the products of innovative activities, i.e., through the tools and instruments made available by technology.

(Kline and Rosenberg 1986: 303)

From the perspective of a company, Kline and Rosenberg proposed a more complex process of interaction than the traditional view that gave a special role to science. Innovations coming out of companies were not necessarily an application of a scientific insight, but of longer and more complex processes that involved very different departments and included both internal and external relations. The department of marketing, for example, could be the initial mover of something that would lead to a number of further responses and developments over time. In the end, marketing could influence the direction of science. An illustrative example of how the interactive approach turns traditional presuppositions on their head might be glimpsed in the simple fact that the science of thermodynamics developed because of the existence of the steam engine, not the other way round as the conventional view had assumed (Nelson 1993: 7).

Out of the interactive approach grew the recognition of the economic relevance of feedback mechanisms, intentional communication, even unintended and positive spillovers from activities, also called externalities—whatever one called the relations between companies, their networks, customers, and their wider surroundings, be they other companies, universities, suppliers, or individuals. Yet this sort of approach to innovation did not point only to seemingly opaque or difficult-to-understand micro processes but to larger patterns as well. In this sense, the interactive approach also could be seen as indicative of larger patterns of economic developments: The interactive approach was coupled with institutional analyses; in this way, national, regional or local environment became relevant to innovation studies. This contextual emphasis led, in the late 1980s, to the concept of a "system of innovation."

Innovation institutionalized

The rise of institutionally focused innovation studies changed the field. Schumpeter had identified the elusive entrepreneur, but the institutional approach made it possible to look for complex business and social arrangements; suddenly, law, regulations and public policy mattered. There was a clear shift from the uneasy search for the creativeness of the individual to the attempt to identify what kind of stable arrangements held the key to institutionalize positive processes of innovation.

In fact, Schumpeter did influence the turn to institutionalization. Although his last important book, *Capitalism, Socialism and Democracy* (1943/1976) did not focus on innovation, Schumpeter predicted there that innovation would be increasingly institutionalized in the research and development function of large corporations. He did not mince words:

The perfectly bureaucratized giant industrial unit not only ousts the small or medium-sized firm and "expropriates" its owners, but in the end it also ousts the entrepreneur and expropriates the bourgeoisie as a class which in the process stands to lose not only its income but also what is infinitely more important, its function. The true pacemakers of socialism were not the intellectuals or agitators who preached it but the Vanderbilts, Carnegies and Rockefellers.

(Schumpeter 1943/1976: 134)

If innovation could be institutionalized in large corporations, then in Schumpeter's estimate there was no need for independent entrepreneurship. While Schumpeter's earlier book introducing the entrepreneur was written as a young man early in the twentieth century, *Capitalism, Socialism and Democracy* came more than thirty years later, after he was established as a professor at Harvard. The rise of American big business had influenced Schumpeter to such a degree that he made quite a turnaround. And Schumpeter, the macro analyst, did indeed, unlike most of his pupils, name some of the "robber barons" among the important entrepreneurs of the past. Entrepreneurship (also) called for forceful people.

Innovation and the corporation

One of the most powerful arguments for the innovative might of the large corporation came from the Harvard Business School historian, Alfred Chandler. Through several articles and three important books, with the telling titles *Strategy and Structure* (1962), *The Visible Hand* (1977), and *Scale and Scope* (1990), Chandler argued that the rise of the large vertically integrated corporation in the USA created economic advantages that explained why the United States became the richest economy in the world. Combining large marketing operations, strong research and development, and an elaborate and meritocratic management structure, the large corporation was able to reach a level of efficiency no other corporate system could. Large American corporations had lowered unit costs so much that they offered cheaper and often better products than would a competitive market constituted by smaller companies. This outcome ran counter to the standard economics argument that such a situation—oligopolistic competition—would in itself lead to higher prices. Chandler acknowledged that (large) firms would benefit from smaller transaction costs than otherwise obtainable through market transactions. However, his main argument was that big businesses not only appropriated the innovative work of smaller corporations but also created functions and capabilities that were not available in the market—hence the title *The Visible Hand* (Chandler 1977).

In 1977 when *The Visible Hand* was published, the belief in the superiority of the large corporation was beginning to crumble. By 1990, when Chandler published *Scale and Scope*, the vertically integrated large-scaled American corporation was hardly a model any more. It was associated with the Keynesian economic policy of the postwar period whose fine-tuning of the economy had catered to stable political and economic conditions for large corporations. Already in the 1980s an important critique had claimed that the success of Chandler's big companies was as much a result of ideology and fashion as real economic forces (Piore and Sabel 1984). Through flexible specialization, it was argued, communities of companies located within easy distance of each other could utilize scale and scope advantages while also providing a flexibility that proved to be a comparative advantage to the big business corporation in the face of unexpected and changing market conditions.

The rise of the huge information technology (IT) sector in Silicon Valley was based on such a flexible specialization concept. Companies were smaller, people moved between companies, universities provided knowledge, and vertical specialization replaced vertical integration as some companies provided components for many other companies. Of course, no one would call Silicon Valley an example of flexible specialization any more. Apple, Intel, Cisco, Google, to name a few, have become giants that outwardly resemble Chandler's big businesses (although they are very different from the traditional large corporation in that the firms of Silicon Valley are financially orientated, vertically specialized and innovate in part through the acquisition of firms).

Within mainstream economics, Chandler's positive view of large corporations has hardly been taken seriously. One important exception is the influential economist William J. Baumol, who writes about corporations, and in particular those of a certain size (see *The Free-Market Innovation Machine* 2002). Chandler's younger colleague at Harvard Business School, Clayton Christensen, has argued that large and established corporations are inherently vulnerable (Christensen 1997/2006). He cites examples of larger and successful corporations with leading technology that, in the longer run, fall victim to disruptive innovation. Smaller less established companies that get a foothold in the market with cheaper and less advanced products in the same segment may build their positions gradually and in the end assume a dominant position. The new firms have a different customer base and have a different product strategy and lower costs. The old firms might be aggressive, change-oriented and resourceful, but may fall into the trap of listening too intently to (part of) their customer base (a "squeaky wheel bias," see Heath 2006), leading them on what in the longer run is an unproductive path.

Systems and clusters of innovation

One of the pivots to institutionalism emerged with a focus on complex aggregations of firms, particularly those called "systems of innovation" or "clusters." Explanations of these systems or clusters combine an interactive approach with the institutional-political approach exemplified by "flexible specialization" noted above: Communities or networks of companies are understood within political and institutional contexts. The system of innovation approach, applied by several authors coming from the SPRU-based network (see above, p. 332), and utilized in Harvard-based Michael Porter's cluster theory, emerged in tandem in the late 1980s and early 1990s (Dosi et al. 1988; Lundvall 1992; Nelson 1993; Porter 1990). By and large, the two approaches are similar in that each emphasizes interactions between companies and their environments—including other companies and organizations, as well as the legal and regulatory context. In early formulations each approach had a clear footing in national (and regional) institutions. For example, factor conditions (education levels, infrastructure), the initial market, relevant business surroundings, and patterns of governance and labor relations reflected national laws and historical traditions. Many countries, in the latter part of the twentieth century, also enacted industrial policies whose assumptions and constraints reflected national priorities.

Although there are great similarities between Porter and the SPRU-based network, there remain significant differences. For Michael Porter a cluster represented local aggregations of companies in the same sector. A combination of intentional collaboration and unintentional knowledge flows from the local activity of people changing jobs, interacting with subcontractors (who in turn cater to more than one customer), and communicating with the community. Schools, universities and a specialized infrastructure would give the companies in these clusters additional advantages compared with companies without such fruitful surroundings. For Porter competition among companies within the cluster was also important. Porter's approach was reminiscent of the famous and influential English economist Alfred Marshall's concept of industrial districts, back when the British industrial company—located in particular areas, characterized by vertical and horizontal specialization, as well as a competitive climate—represented the state of the art in global production systems. In the British industrial districts, Marshall said, "mysteries of the trade become no mysteries; but are as it were in the air" (Marshall 1961: 271, quoted from Lazonick 2005: 35).

However, the theories of the SPRU scholars emphasized a national-systems-of-innovation approach that was much more loose-knit and flexible than Porter's clusters. It is fair to claim that Porter's approach represented a more neoclassically inclined approach in which competition was included, while the SPRU approaches were more or less influenced by evolutionary economics. In the evolutionary perspective, developments would prove more random than in a tightly knit Porter-cluster, but the broader national institutional setting would be a strong constraining factor. Two of the pioneers in this national approach, Bengt-Åke Lundvall and Charles Edquist, provided an interpretation of Danish innovative developments:

> The process of technical change in Denmark is organized neither by big firms nor by the state. It is quite self-organized. The only reasonably strong coordinating block in the economy has been the export-oriented, and cooperatively organized, agroindustrial sector.
> *(Edquist and Lundvall 1993: 281–2)*

As noted previously, much work has been done to develop the perspective of innovation as local, regional or sectoral systems (Asheim and Gertler 2005; Malerba 2005). To render the interactive perspective relevant to local, regional or sectoral requires examining smaller entities with numerous interactions. Such an approach may be employed in a different research environment, such as the examination of long-term innovation processes in the state of Minnesota, as detailed by Andrew Van de Ven and colleagues in *The Innovation Journey* (1999).

Open innovation and aggregations

Another and related approach that has gathered a lot of interest outside of academia is Henry Chesbrough's "Open innovation": if companies open up their processes of innovation and bring others in, they can share the burden and stimulate each other (Chesbrough 2003). To invite others in may serve as a tool with which a common solution, brought forward by several partners, stands a better chance to succeed as a viable product or a process. Open innovation is also a way of sharing or spreading risks: putting one's economic eggs in more than one basket through establishing external relations. The ideas behind open innovation are very similar to the innovation/cluster-approach, and reflect as well the older notion of flexible specialization. Clearly, much of what has been written and thought about innovation over the last thirty years plus is inspired by the remarkable rise of the IT businesses of Silicon Valley in California.

Aggregations are good at a particular type of innovation—small and gradual improvements that spread among companies, where no single company or innovation is of particular importance. Such piecemeal and accumulated improvements are found in the progressive development, over the twentieth century, of cars and airplanes, goods typically manufactured by international businesses whose breakthroughs (some more important than others) exemplify gradual or incremental development (Nelson 1993). Positive changes are often the result of everyday work by normal employees, not the outcomes of risk-taking entrepreneurs obsessed by some particular idea. The other type of innovation is the radical sort—a new drug, or a remarkable new innovation that changes the rules of the game in a specific sector. For either kind of development, piecemeal or revolutionary, the chances of success are greater if the firm is located within the right region and nation for that kind of activity. The support of the surrounding factors, firms, and people are important for the whole process from breakthrough through product development and marketing.

Law, culture, and ethics

Constructing aggregations may seem like a good idea to promote economic development. However, the examples of the successful institutionalization of innovation in these clusters and systems come from Western countries. This fact points to a larger institutional framework distinct from locality and the interactive support therein. Without a well-functioning legal system (the rule of law), entrepreneurial activities and processes of innovation are hardly possible. Many countries have the right legal frameworks, at least in script, but poor countries often lack the means—including the actual political willingness—to enforce effectively the property rights and contract law essential for economic experimentation, development, and innovation (Cooter 2005). Without these basic protections of one's efforts and of potential rewards, why should anyone undertake to develop new ideas or experiment with new techniques of production? After all, as Schumpeter reminds us, innovation challenges the status quo and defies those whose power rests on the preservation of the status quo.

Framing innovation as nationally facilitated and constrained leads to the grand synthetic grasps of, for example, David S. Landes' *The Wealth and Poverty of Nations: Why Some Are So Rich and Some Are So Poor* (1998), or Daron Acemoglu and James A. Robinson's *Why Nations Fail: The Origin of Power, Prosperity and Poverty* (2012). Approaches such as these introduce into the discussion different cultural habits and institutional settings among the nations and regions and treat these as relevant to innovation and the realization of economic growth. Landes' book in particular has been controversial because he explains that the West is richer than the rest through the early adoption of a capitalist culture with a technological aptitude. Acemoglu and Robinson argue, on the other hand, for an institutional explanation, dividing countries between those that have inclusive and those that have extractive economic and political institutions. The latter countries, which are also poorer, function for the benefit of an elite rather than for industrious people.

In a recent three-volume account of the great economic growth experience of the last 200 years, Deirdre McCloskey has argued that shifts in ethical values explain how ingenuity through individual effort has been unleashed. The rise of individual liberty through new political constitutions (as in France, and the United States, Norway, among other nations) and the ensuing development of ideas, gave rise to what McCloskey calls "the double ideas of liberty and dignity" (2016: xxxiii). Dignity incorporates both a pride and a moral fulfillment in one's work and effort, especially of the commercial sort. The rise of the new, proud, and commerce-oriented individual emerged most fully in the eighteenth and nineteenth centuries but these ideas found their earliest roots in England and the Netherlands. The changing ideas about the moral value of commerce as a human activity (*from* being disreputable and unproductive activity *to* a worthy and creative pursuit reflective of the Judeo-Christian idea that human beings are made in God's image) would inspire waves of innovation that account for the wealth of the West today. McCloskey's twin appeals to specific political institutions and ethical ideas serves to directly refute Landes' long-term cultural approach. Her argument against Acemoglu and Robinson's institutional explanation suggests, similarly, that it omits the constitutive role of ethics in guiding and justifying the everyday activities of individuals. For McCloskey, differences in productive capacity rests in very significant part on whether political institutions allow the freedom to produce and exchange and whether the majority of the people believe in and work for the principles that such institutions express (McCloskey 2006, 2010 and 2016, and see especially her "Exordium," in the book of 2016).

Living in an unsuccessful age?

So mankind, especially in the Western nations, has grown richer. But what is happening in the world today? Do communities of companies—a system, cluster, or ecosystem—belonging to a kind of geographical entity create more economic growth than the companies not situated within such contexts? It is fair to say that they do, at least in most circumstances. To a great degree, these institutionalized arrangements have grown up through long term and complex processes. They have stood the test of time and the test of competition. But are they reflective more of successful and particular historical processes than of examples that may be, so to speak, exported as solutions for less successful localities, regions, or companies? One cautionary note is that economic growth in the Western world has not been impressive over the last couple of decades.

In a recent book the American economist Robert J. Gordon argues that the American economy since about 1970 has not produced the same economic growth as in previous decades (Gordon 2016). The innovations of the last four to five decades are simply not up to the standard of the innovations of the special century following the American Civil War. This is not an entirely new argument, as Tyler Cowen has argued a similar conclusion (Cowen 2011), but Gordon supports his argument with massive empirical work. As Gordon summarizes,

> Our central thesis is that some inventions are more important than others, and that the revolutionary century after the Civil War [for example, the introduction of electricity into daily life] was made possible by a unique clustering, in the nineteenth century, of what we will call the "Great Inventions". This leads directly to the second big idea: that economic growth since 1970 has been simultaneously dazzling and disappointing. This paradox is resolved when we recognize that advances since 1970 have tended to be channeled into a narrow sphere of human activity having to do with entertainment, communications, and the collection and processing of information. For the rest of what humans care about—food, clothing, shelter, transportation, health, and working conditions both inside and outside the home—progress slowed down after 1970, both qualitatively and quantitatively.
>
> *(Gordon 2016: 2)*

Gordon finds that the contributors to growth have changed over time. For example, inventions (which, in the terminology of this article are innovations, i.e., they are taken into use in the economy) and technical change have contributed less since 1970 than in the period before. He draws this conclusion by comparing what is called "total factor productivity"—the contribution of everything that is not labor, and capital, often understood to be improvements in techniques, methods, knowledge and such.

Gordon believes the potential for continued improvements has decreased because so many fundamental advances (for example, safe drinking water, improvements in transportation) can happen only once. He paints a grim picture of our current age, and points to the growing social divide in the USA. He suggests that a *second* industrial revolution, starting at the end of the nineteenth century and extending into the twentieth, should be recognized as particularly important compared with what went on before and what came after.

Whether the American economy (or that of other nations) will explode again with productive creativity will have to resolve itself. Gordon does not really explain why such a special century emerged or why he is pessimistic about the future possibility of presently unknown and important innovations. His book details the improvements that contributed to the special century, but there is not one clear lesson to be taken from his account, a point iterated by a fellow economist (Margo 2016).

What is particularly noteworthy from the perspective of this chapter is the overlap in time frame of the perspectives of Gordon and Alfred Chandler. Gordon's special century matches Chandler's claim that the rise and innovative efficiency of big business was an important growth factor for United States. Does Chandler's rise of big business help explain Gordon's special century? And, consequently, when the fortunes of big business waned during the troubled times of the 1970s, never really to come back in favor, does that explain the lack of rise in productivity?

There is no easy answer to those questions, but there is another theme that Gordon and Chandler share about development in the USA and the Western world since the 1970s: The rise of inequality. For Gordon this is manifest in the per capita living standards. For Chandler, the power shift from a meritocratic leadership group to shareholders was a negative move undermining the grasp and innovative strength of big business (Chandler 1990). Shareholder value, as a concept, has become isolated as singularly important but in previous periods it was part of a larger concern—the creation of corporate value, comprising shareholders, managers, and other employees working together as a whole. Efficiency seems to be prioritized in shareholder capitalism, possibly to the detriment of innovation.

Gordon is right in emphasizing future unpredictability. The essence of innovation is unpredictability. The reason "the unforeseen innovations" are not already here is because of our inability to imagine them. That is the core of what innovation is. But it is food for thought that our preoccupation with innovation comes at a historical time when, seemingly, not enough innovation is delivered to keep the economy growing as fast as we became accustomed to up until the 1970s.

Concluding remarks

Innovation and creativity are at the same time alluring and frightening. On the one hand, innovative goods and processes, and the aspirations to realize these, suggest progress; they renew hope and offer something to strive for or to anticipate. On the other hand, they also suggest the crumbling of known entities, with its concomitant uncertainty, anxiety, and apprehension. Whether such processes and novel events pose more difficult psychological if not ethical challenges than more stable economic situations is difficult to say.

It is a well-known fact that change may be challenging. It is worth remembering that the mighty movement forward for long-term economic growth, the Industrial Revolution of the late eighteenth century, was shaped by an earlier period known as the Enlightenment (Mokyr 2009). For all the harsh conditions and tragic individual outcomes of the long ascent of the industrial economy, the development of the economy was shaped by attitudes and ideas of how better societies could be created. These aspirations played a role in making industrial society sustainable, and such positive caution should be applicable to our own future. Maybe Robert Gordon's "slow growth" conclusion should be seen as proof of the failure of the economic policies created in the 1970s for increased competition. In particular, an attempt to capture ways that innovation may be institutionalized can appear as futile in light of that slow growth. Perhaps even the attempt to realize clusters, systems of innovation, even specific benefits from the free market may remain difficult to realize. No wonder some innovation scholars are crying for more action from the state (Mazzucato 2014; Schot and Steinmueller 2016). Yet, in a genuinely liberal economy there will always be a need for Schumpeter's entrepreneurial action and for creative responses, at least if the economy is to continue to grow.

Essential readings

Innovation studies begin (and may even end) with Joseph Schumpeter's *The Theory of Economic Development: An Inquiry into Profits, Capital, Credit, Interest, and the Business Cycle* (1934). There Schumpeter outlines the essence of entrepreneurship and economic innovation. Richard Nelson and Sidney Winter's *An Evolutionary Theory of Economic Change* (1982) is a landmark in the establishment of the field of innovation studies. In "Exploring the Emerging Knowledge Base of 'the Knowledge Society,'" *Research Policy* (2012), Jan Fagerberg, Hans Landstrøm and

Ben R. Martin provide an excellent overview of entrepreneurship and innovation studies. There also exists a number of insightful handbooks and histories, two of which merit attention: Jan Fagerberg, David C. Mowery and Richard R. Nelson (eds), *The Oxford Handbook of Innovation* (2005) and Robert F. Hébert and Albert N. Link, *A History of Entrepreneurship* (2009).

For further reading in this volume on the nature, ethics, and conditions of innovative entrepreneurship, see Chapter 16, The ethics of entrepreneurship. On the role of the entrepreneur in society, see Chapter 7, Can profit seekers be virtuous? On the ways in which current economics has influenced our understanding of business ethics, see Chapter 17, The contribution of economics to business ethics. For a discussion of economic motivation and obstacles to economic progress, see Chapter 21, Regulation, rent seeking, and business ethics. For an account of recent innovations in the organizational forms of corporations, see Chapter 15, Alternative business organizations and social enterprise. On intellectual property rights, see Chapter 18, Property and business.

Note

* I thank Bjørn T. Asheim and Beniamino Callegari for comments on my first draft.

References

Acemoglu, D. and J.A. Robinson (2012). *Why Nations Fail: The Origins of Power, Prosperity and Poverty*. London: Profile Books.
Alchian, A. (1950). "Uncertainty, Evolution, and Economic Theory," *Journal of Political Economy* 58:3, 211–221.
Asheim, B.T. and M.S. Gertler (2005). "The Geography of Innovation: Regional Innovation Systems," in J. Fagerberg, D.C. Mowery and R.R. Nelson, (eds), *The Oxford Handbook of Innovation*. Oxford: Oxford University Press, 291–317.
Barney, J.B. and D.N. Clark (2007). *Resource-Based Theory: Creating and Sustaining Competitive Advantage*. Oxford: Oxford University Press.
Baumol, W.J. (2002). *The Free-Market Innovation Machine: Analyzing the Growth Miracle of Capitalism*. Princeton, NJ: Princeton University Press.
Brenkert, G.G. (2009). "Innovation, Rule Breaking and the Ethics of Entrepreneurship," *Journal of Business Venturing* 24, 448–464.
Carlsson, B. (ed.) (1995). *Technological Systems and Economic Performance: The Case of Factory Automation*. Dordrecht: Kluwer Academic Publishers.
Casson, M., B. Yeung, A. Basu and N. Wadeson (eds) (2006). *The Oxford Handbook of Entrepreneurship*. Oxford: Oxford University Press.
Chandler, A.D. Jr. (1962). *Strategy and Structure: Chapters in the History of the American Enterprise*. Cambridge, MA: The MIT Press.
Chandler, A.D. Jr. (1977). *The Visible Hand: The Managerial Revolution in American Business*. Cambridge, MA: Belknap Press.
Chandler, A.D. Jr. (1990). *Scale and Scope: The Dynamics of Industrial Capitalism*. Cambridge, MA: Belknap Press.
Chesbrough, H. (2003). *Open Innovation. The New Imperative for Creating and Profiting from Technology*. Boston, MA: Harvard Business School Press.
Christensen, C.M. (1997/2006). *The Innovator's Dilemma*. New York, NY: HarperCollins.
Cooter, R.D. (2005). "Innovation, Information and the Poverty of Nations," *Florida State University Law Review* 33, 373–393.
Cowen, T. (2011). *The Great Stagnation: How America Ate All the Low-Hanging Fruit of Modern History, Got Sick, and Will (Eventually) Feel Better*. New York, NY: Penguin Publishing Group.
Dosi, G., C. Freemann, R. Nelson, G. Silverberg and L. Soete (1988). *Technical Change and Economic Theory*. London: Pinter Publishers.
Edquist, C. and B. Lundvall (1993). "Comparing the Danish and Swedish Systems of Innovation," in Richard R. Nelson (ed.), *National Innovation Systems: A Comparative Analysis*. Oxford: Oxford University Press, 265–298.

Fagerberg, J., D.C. Mowery and R.R. Nelson (eds) (2005). *The Oxford Handbook of Innovation*. Oxford: Oxford University Press.

Fagerberg, J., H. Landström and B.R. Martin (2012). "Exploring the Emerging Knowledge Base of 'the Knowledge Society,'" *Research Policy* 41, 1121–1131.

Freeman, C. (1989). *Technology Policy and Economic Performance: Lessons From Japan*. London and New York, NY: Pinter Publishers.

Freeman, C. and F. Louçã (2001). *As Time Goes By: From the Industrial Revolutions to the Information Age*. Oxford: Oxford University Press.

Freeman, C. and L. Soete (1997). *The Economics of Industrial Innovation*, 3rd edition. Cambridge, MA: The MIT Press.

Frieden, J.A. (2006). *Global Capitalism: Its Fall and Rise in the Twentieth Century*. New York, NY: W.W. Norton & Co.

Friedman, M. (1962). *Capitalism and Freedom*. Chicago, IL: University of Chicago Press.

Gordon, R.J. (2016). *The Rise and Fall of American Growth. The US Standard of Living Since the Civil War*. Princeton, NJ: Princeton University Press.

Hayek, F.A. (1945). "The Use of Knowledge in Society," *The American Economic Review* 35:4 (September), 519–530.

Hayek, F.A. (1960). *The Constitution of Liberty*. Chicago, IL: University of Chicago Press.

Hayek, F.A. (1978). "Competition as a Discovery Procedure," in *New Studies in Philosophy, Politics, Economics and the History of Ideas*. Chicago, IL: University of Chicago, 179–190.

Heath, J. (2006). "Business Ethics Without Stakeholders," *Business Ethics Quarterly* 16:3, 533–557.

Hébert, R.F. (2011). "Review of Hans Landström and Franz Lohrke," in *Historical Foundations of Entrepreneurship Research*. Cheltenham, UK: Edward Elgar, EH.NET (http://eh.net/).

Hébert, R.F. and A.N. Link (2009). *A History of Entrepreneurship*. London: Routledge.

Hughes, T.P. (1983). *Networks of Power: Electrification in Western Society*. Baltimore, MD: Johns Hopkins University Press.

Hughes, T.P. (1986). "The Seamless Web: Technology, Science, Etcetera, Etcetera," *Social Studies of Science* 16:2 (May), 281–292.

Jones, G. and R.D. Wadhwani (2008). "Entrepreneurship," in G. Jones and J. Zeitlin (eds), *The Oxford Handbook of Business History*. Oxford: Oxford University Press, 501–528.

Kirzner, I.M. (1971). "Entrepreneurship and the Market Approach to Development," in F.A. Hayek, Henry Hazlitt, Leonard R. Read, G. Velasco and F.A. Harper (eds), *Toward Liberty: Essays in Honor of Ludwig von Mises on the Occasion of his 90th Birthday*, Vol. 2. Menlo Park, CA: Institute for Humane Studies, 194–208.

Kirzner, I.M. (1973). *Competition and Entrepreneurship*. Chicago, IL: University of Chicago Press.

Kline, S.J. and N. Rosenberg (1986). "An Overview of Innovation," in Ralph Landau and Nathan Rosenberg (eds), *The Positive Sum Strategy. Harnessing Technology for Economic Growth*. Washington, DC: National Academy Press, 275–306.

Knight, F.H. (2013 [1951]). *The Economic Organization*. New Brunswick and London: Transaction Publishers, (original edition, New York, NY: Augustus M. Kelley).

Kuhn, T.S. (1962). *The Structure of Scientific Revolutions*. Chicago, IL: The University of Chicago Press.

Landes, D.S. (1988). *The Wealth and Poverty of Nations: Why Some Are So Rich and Some Are So Poor*. New York, NY, and London: W.W. Norton & Co.

Landström, H. and F. Lohrke (2010). *Historical Foundations of Entrepreneurship Research*. Cheltenham, UK: Edward Elgar.

Landström, H. and M. Benner (2010). "Entrepreneurship Research: a History of Scholarly Migration," in H. Landström and F. Lohrke (eds), *Historical Foundations of Entrepreneurship Research*. Cheltenham, UK: Edward Elgar, 15–45.

Lazonick, W. (2005). "The Innovative Firm," in J. Fagerberg, D.C. Mowery and R.R. Nelson (eds), *The Oxford Handbook of Innovation*. Oxford: Oxford University Press, 29–55.

Lundvall, B. (ed.) (1992). *National Innovation Systems: Towards A Theory of Innovation and Interactive Learning*. London: Pinter Publishers.

Malerba, F. (2005). "Sectoral Systems: How and Why Innovation Differs Across Sectors," in J. Fagerberg, D.C. Mowery and R.R. Nelson (eds), *The Oxford Handbook of Innovation*. Oxford: Oxford University Press, 380–406.

Margo, R.A. (2016). "Review of Robert J. Gordon," *The Rise and Fall of American Growth: The US Standard of Living since the Civil War*. Princeton, NJ: Princeton University Press, EH.Net (http://eh.net/).

Marshall, A. (1961). *Principles of Economics*, 9th (variorum) edition. London: Macmillan.
Mazzucato, M. (2014). *The Entrepreneurial State: Debunking Public vs. Private Sector Myths*. London: Anthem Press.
McCloskey, D.N. (2006). *The Bourgeois Virtues: Ethics for an Age of Commerce*. Chicago, IL: University of Chicago Press.
McCloskey, D.N. (2010). *Bourgeois Dignity: Why Economics Can't Explain the Modern World*. Chicago, IL: University of Chicago Press.
McCloskey, D.N. (2016). *Bourgeois Equality: How Ideas, Not Capital or Institutions, Enriched the World*. Chicago, IL: University of Chicago Press.
Mokyr, J. (2009). *The Enlightened Economy: An Economic History of Britain, 1700–1850*. New Haven, CT: Yale University Press.
Moore, J.F. (1996). *The Death of Competition: Leadership & Strategy in the Age of Business Ecosystems*. New York, NY: HarperBusiness.
Nelson, R.R. and S.G. Winter (1982). *An Evolutionary Theory of Economic Change*. Cambridge, MA: The Belknap Press of Harvard University.
Nelson, R.R. (1993). *National Innovation Systems: A Comparative Analysis*. Oxford: Oxford University Press.
Penrose, E. (1959/1995). *The Theory of the Growth of the Firm*. Oxford: Oxford University Press.
Phelps, E.S. (2013). *Mass Flourishing: How Grassroots Innovation Created Jobs, Challenge, and Change*. Princeton, NJ: Princeton University Press.
Piore, M.J. and C.F. Sabel (1984). *The Second Industrial Divide: Possibilities for Prosperity*. New York, NJ: Basic Books.
Porter, M.E. (1990). *The Competitive Advantage of Nations*. London: Macmillan.
Rogers, E.M. (2003). *Diffusion of Innovations*, 5th edition. New York, NY: Free Press.
Roncaglia, A. (2001). *The Wealth of Ideas: A History of Economic Thought*. Cambridge: Cambridge University Press.
Rosenberg, N. (1976). *Perspectives on Technology*. Cambridge: Cambridge University Press.
Rosenberg, N. (1982). *Inside the Black Box: Technology and Economics*. Cambridge: Cambridge University Press.
Schot, J. and E. Steinmueller (2016). "Designing Innovation Policy for Transformative Change," briefing note. Available at: www.sussex.ac.uk/webteam/gateway/file.php?name=3640-spru-briefing-note-web.pdf&site=25.
Schumpeter, J.A. (1934) [1911]. *The Theory of Economic Development. An Inquiry into Profits, Capital, Credit, Interest, and the Business Cycle*. Cambridge, MA: Cambridge University Press (originally published in German).
Schumpeter, J.A. (1943/1976). *Capitalism, Socialism and Democracy*. London: George Allen & Unwin.
Schumpeter, J.A. (1947). "The Creative Response in Economic History," *The Journal of Economic History* Vol. 7, No. 2, 149–159.
Smith, A. (1981) [original 1776]. *An Inquiry into the Nature and Causes of The Wealth of Nations*, R.H. Campbell, A.S. Skinner and W.B. Todd (eds), 2 Vols. Indianapolis, IN: Liberty Fund.
Teece, D.J. (2009). *Dynamic Capabilities & Strategic Management. Organizing for Innovation and Growth*. Oxford: Oxford University Press.
Van de Ven, A.H., D.E. Polley, R. Garud and S. Venkataraman (1999). *The Innovation Journey*. New York, NY: Oxford University Press.
Van de Wee, H. (1986). *Prosperity and Upheaval: The World Economy, 1945–1980*. Harmondsworth, UK: Viking.
von Mises, L. (1996) [1949]. *Human Action: A Treatise on Economics*, ed. Bettina Bien Greaves. Indianapolis, IN: Liberty Fund.
Wright, M. and S. Zahra (2011). "The Other Side of Paradise: Examining the Dark Side of Entrepreneurship," *Entrepreneurship Research Journal* 1:3, 1–5.

20
Money and finance
Ethical considerations

Antonio Argandoña

Financial institutions and markets render vital services to the economy: they provide funds for consumption and investment, they facilitate access to payment systems, offer custom-designed risk-return combinations for asset management, and manifest an outstanding capacity for innovation in products and services, among many other virtues. Finance is concerned with money, credit, assets, debt, risk, banks, investment, and a variety of investment funds, but it goes further than that: "financing an activity really is creating the architecture for reaching our goals, and providing stewardship afterwards to protect and conserve the achievement of that goal" (Shiller 2012: 6). So finance has a social and moral significance. But it also has its dark side: it is often accused of being cold and even heartless, its managers sometimes prove willing to shade the truth and take whatever advantage lies open to them, and the apparent concentration of power in major financial institutions may work to the detriment of those without enough power or wealth.

But this is nothing new. Since ancient times people have criticized usury (charging abusive interest on loans), worried about the power of owners of capital, and fretted over the ways in which money and wealth elicit greed and profligacy (on medieval usury, see Munro 2003). Finance creates opportunities for huge profits, sometimes at the expense of other people, or undertakes excessive risks whose unraveling can ruin families and companies. In recent years, the criticisms have become stronger, particularly after the financial crisis of 2008,[1] not to mention the manipulation of Libor and exchange rates, bankers' collusion in money laundering and tax evasion operations, or the supposed capture of legislators and regulators by the bankers' lobby. So there are many reasons to undertake an ethical reflection on finance.

Financial ethics is the body of principles, norms and virtues that guide the behavior of financial agents and organizations towards goals that are not only efficient and profitable, but also good, fair or proper. From the economic viewpoint, people make financial decisions based primarily on their preferences and a set of constraints (resources, relative prices and costs, regulations). Ethics is not one restriction imposed from outside, but an essential component of profitable and responsible decisions. Ethical principles (honesty, integrity, justice, truthfulness, prudence, responsibility, stewardship, accountability and many others) are common to all decisions, and they are not different from those of general ethics, but their content and application must take into account the specific circumstances of each case (Argandoña 1995b). For example, fairness is required of a judge, not to mention a sports referee, as well as an account manager with a fiduciary duty towards his client or a broker who sells a standard bond to an unknown customer. In each of these instances, fairness is required but the contents of that virtue will be different in each type of case (see Heath 2010 on fairness in finance).

The ethical analysis of financial decisions arises from the theories and principles of philosophical or religious ethics, but these decisions cannot be analyzed in isolation from some exogenous variables. One of these is the set of ideas and values shared in the community that influences people's attitudes: many shortcomings of financial institutions and markets reflect the social environment. For example, if citizens show an individualistic and selfish character, those working in finance will show similar moral biases.

Another relevant variable when judging financial ethics is the set of theories that provide a rationale for financial practices (Mackenzie 2008). These theories share with economics the goal of efficiency, along with some basic assumptions, such as a narrow conception of rationality, the identification of good with the maximization of wealth, an instrumentalist interpretation of science and an alleged ethical neutrality (Ryan et al. 2010). Financial models are considered ethically neutral, but the assumptions underlying them imply conceptions of the person and society, their motivations and behaviors, and these have ethical implications. The criticisms that some theories have received during the recent crisis were due not only to technical faults, but to the alleged promotion of immoral behavior from within the models (Dembinski 2009).

In this chapter we outline the ethical issues raised by modern finance. In the first section we delineate the legal and institutional framework of the system. In a longer second section we consider the roles of financial intermediaries, such as banks and investment vehicles, noting in addition particular questions that arise with specific financial instruments (such as derivatives), along with issues related to risk. A third section broaches two practices of financial markets, speculation and high-frequency trading. In the fourth section we introduce, briefly, some alternative models of finance.

The legal and institutional framework

Financial markets and intermediaries operate within a legal and institutional framework that determines how costs, benefits, and risks are shared among the parties. This framework includes external institutions such as the rule of law, property, contract legislation, and a national currency established by a central bank. Along with supervisory institutions, regulations, and crisis management procedures internal to each bank, this framework both undergirds and creates ethical obligations.

Although legality does not mean morality, for law and ethics pursue different goals, there is nonetheless a relationship between ethics and regulation (Davies 2001; Kane 2014). In some instances, high ethical standards may make some regulations redundant: ethics substitute for regulation. However, it is more common for them to be complementary: ethics goes beyond the law and addresses problems that the law must not be concerned with, because they involve people's conscience (including inner attitudes or values) or their personal discretion. However, in other cases, ethics may demand more than the law either because there are circumstances that the law cannot consider or because there exist supererogatory duties that the law should not command. Finally, there are many examples of situations in which a regulation (or a change in regulation) would not only affect risks and returns but promote, even unintentionally, immoral behavior (Koehn 2010).

Regulations may create ethical obligations for those who are bound by them: if they are not unnecessary, arbitrary or unfair, regulations and laws must be obeyed, even if they are imperfect or impose unreasonable costs on agents. But regulations may also create perverse incentives or moral hazards (for example, when one bank takes more risk because the taxpayers, not the shareholders, will bear the burden of rescue in case of a crisis), or opportunities for rent seeking (the grant of legal advantages to some entities at the expense of others or of all citizens, as summarized in Tollison 2012).

There are also ethical duties regarding the basic framework of finance, including a general duty to maintain the proper legal and regulatory framework suitable for a free and decent society. More specific obligations might include drawing up a standard concerning banks' equity or creating a deposit insurance institution; such endeavors have ethical content in so far as they bear important consequences for citizens' welfare and condition their behavior.

Money is an important component of the economic system's legal and institutional framework. The word "money" has several different meanings: it may refer to a means of payment, or to income, wealth, or power, or it may suggest a cause of happiness, among other meanings. Given these senses, money may serve either as a means or an end. In a narrow sense, it refers to *currency*, the means used to make payments and to facilitate exchange. In this sense money serves a social function: it is liquidity, universal purchasing power, a means for achieving disparate ends; as such, money is also a creator of opportunities, allowing people to exercise individual freedom and collaborate impersonally in other people's projects.

As a means of exchange, it is better to have more money than less. However, money is more than a tool: it represents wealth, power, prestige, and security. Money is a motivator for many actions, at least in the sense that it represents the power to acquire things or attain a status. And in some instances, not necessarily the best, the desire for money may constitute the end itself.

As a means of payment and a store of value money plays a key role in the lives of people, so the ethical principles of ownership should be applied to it. Moreover, money is based on trust: we accept coins, notes and deposits as money because other people also accept them. Trust in money is built on three pillars, one institutional and legal, one based on trust in banks, and another that relies on the stability of its purchasing power.

The legal framework of money includes legislation on currency counterfeiting, public guarantees on deposits, mechanisms for preventing bank crises and other policies and structures. Trust in banks is necessary because they play a prominent role in the money creation process.[2] But confidence in banks is subject to limitations: they only keep a very small part of their deposits in a liquid form (fractional reserve banking),[3] which sometimes makes them unable to reimburse those deposits, and they also keep only a small part of their assets as shareholders' equity, which may raise a risk of insolvency. This may cause losses to depositors, blockages in the payment system and paralysis of financing mechanisms in the economy, destroying trust.

Finally, the use of money as a means of exchange is based on the expectation that its purchasing power will be stable, that is, the inflation rate will be low. Inflation causes many economic and ethical harms: it leads to unfair income and wealth distribution, it is a non-democratic and unfair tax on currency, and it generates inefficiencies that may lead to a deterioration of citizens' standard of living. There has been a general agreement among economists that, in the medium and long term, inflation is caused by excessive growth of the quantity of money; controlling this process is the job of monetary policy, which is implemented by the central bank.

Originally, money is a spontaneous non-state creation, as explained by Hayek (1976) and others (Lietaer and Lunne 2013). This spontaneity is seen in many developments that have taken place in recent decades. Here we will mention only three: e-money, private and social currencies, and virtual monies.

E-monies (*PayPal, Apple Pay, Google Wallet* and many others) are means of payment of limited acceptance, bereft of any legal backing, and a form of mobile money. Various types of social, community or cooperative currencies have been developed by retail associations or local governments in several countries, often with a social purpose, such as providing credit to local companies, fostering proximity of trade and consumption or encouraging fair trade (for example, the Swiss *Wir* that has been operating since the 1930s, the *Wörgl* in Austria, or the *Bristol Pound* in Great Britain). Digital currencies have also flourished; the best known is the *Bitcoin*, a virtual international currency exchanged by digital means and not backed by any government but by a person-to-person network of users.

The questions that ethics raises about these currencies are similar to those it asks about traditional currencies: What is their social function (their contribution to the life and the economy of citizens)? Do they create excessive or poorly understood risks that prove difficult to hedge against (counterfeiting, inflation or depreciation)? Are they used for permissible or ethical ends (as opposed to fraudulent or illicit purposes)? And what is the basis of the trust that underlies their use? It is not enough that a currency fulfills a social function to be accepted as ethically correct (see Angel and McCabe 2014).

The ethics of financial intermediaries

The financial system is the set of markets and institutions that make up financial activities. Its social function is to efficiently satisfy the needs of the suppliers and demanders of funds, namely to allocate savings in profitable controlled-risk investments; to finance consumption, production or investment projects; to provide means of payment for the economy, and to manage and control risk. The fulfilment of these tasks gives legitimacy to the system and translates into ethical responsibilities for all the agents.

There are many varieties of financial institutions, but all have some common characteristics: they all operate within a network of institutions and markets and each receives funds from clients (creditors) and lends them to other clients (debtors), thereby incurring risk but also the potential for profit. This simple explanation allows us to identify three areas of ethical responsibilities common to all institutions: duties to their customers, duties to other actors, and internal duties of governance (management and control).

The main principle in the relationships of banks with their customers is that the interest of the latter must take precedence over the interest of the first. Their professional relationships are based on contracts that should be governed by principles of justice or fairness, which entails that both parties must comply with the terms of the contract (see Koehn 1994). In finance those contracts have usually non-explicit terms, such as shared interests (both parties expect to gain from the relationship), mutual respect and impartiality (equitable treatment of different customers) and reciprocity (the relationship may be repeated in the future, as discussed in Johnson 2015).

Financial institutions have more complete information about their products (and their risks) than do their clients and may use this asymmetric information for their own benefit at the expense of the clients' interests. This entails the obligation of providing the customers with the full, fair, accurate, complete, objective, relevant, timely and understandable information they need to make rational decisions,[4] as well as negative obligations such as avoiding misrepresentation, confusion or concealment of important information, fraud, manipulation, price-rigging, insider trading,[5] conflicts of interest and other practices. Another moral duty refers to the appropriate use of sensitive (and confidential) information about the customer.

Financial intermediaries often have greater power than their clients and can abuse that power, not respecting the other party's freedom to choose, contract, undertake and exchange. Abuse of power may take place when drafting the contract but also in performing it: for example, the right to monitor the borrower to ensure the return of credit does not entitle the bank to interfere unduly in the debtor's business, and the emergence of difficulties in paying back the loan does not allow undue harshness against a defaulting client. Procedural justice demands equitable, but not necessarily equal, treatment of its various customers.

Some financial institutions have special duties to specific clients. For example, commercial banks must safeguard and diligently manage their deposit holders' funds and provide services of liquidity management. Banks' obligations related to their lending activities include the honest examination of applications, prudent decision-making in granting loans (fairness in setting interest rates, charges, installments, guarantees, collateral, etc.), monitoring the borrower and fair treatment in the event of default.

In a highly interconnected world, the actions of a financial institution can have negative impacts on many others—or, with a positive language, they should cooperate for the common good of the industry; for example, poor management of liquidity or solvency in one bank can cause a general panic that endangers others. Problems may occur if all banks adopt the same models of analysis that meet rational criteria when applied to one institution, but whose application may generate a uniform but unmerited risk in other banks, i.e., a systemic risk. Other forms of harm occur when a bank seeks a special regulatory treatment that may be unfair to competitors and may allow the exploitation of clients; or practices regulatory arbitrage (taking advantage of locations where regulations are more lax) compromising the system's stability; or obstructs the orderly functioning of the markets impairing their social role as devices for the dissemination of information and the discovering of opportunities for all (Kleinau 2014).

These responsibilities towards other actors are important even when each institution is unable to understand all the consequences of its decisions on others; these responsibilities fall primarily on the supervisors, but this does not preclude holding the institution itself ethically responsible, especially when it is "too-big-to" or "too-connected-to" fail. Nevertheless, even if stability is a public good, it is not the only one; there are others, such as growth and innovation. A culture that fosters stability above all else may not be the best.

The ethical duties of banks to their customers and other entities turn ultimately into internal obligations for boards and managers. In general, financial crises draw justifiable attention to external shocks, but such crises also raise questions about failures in the management of incentives (conflicts of interest, remuneration schemes, agency problems), problems of information and control (transparency, risk management and supervision), and lapses in accounting (tampering with financial statements), among others. These problems point also to an information asymmetry between the bank's shareholders and its managers, when the latter may obtain a short-term personal gain at the cost of long-term risks or losses for the organization.

The solution to these problems requires, at the organizational level, the establishment of good practices to avoid opportunism and conflicts of interest, and also a culture of high ethical standards. If agents have acquired solid virtues it will be easier for them to identify emerging ethical problems, assess their consequences, look for alternatives and take the best decision, and also develop the will to effectively implement it. Prudence or practical wisdom is probably "the banker's characteristic virtue" (Termes 1995: 130); the second is justice or fairness, and it is accompanied by honesty, integrity, good faith, truthfulness, diligence or professionalism and accountability, among others. These virtues manifest themselves in everyday conduct and they reflect, more generally, a society in which there is trust. As a public good produced and enjoyed by all, trust depends also on institutional factors, including the rule of law, a fair judicial system, and a dependable framework of financial regulation.

Commercial banks, shadow banks, investment banks

Commercial banks are the financial intermediaries par excellence, so it is not surprising that there are important discussions of bank ethics in the literature (Cowton 2002; Green 1989; Koslowski 1995, 2011). Traditionally banks were financed by deposits, granted medium and long-term credit to households and companies, maintained close relationships with their customers and were integrated into their local communities. However, this model has undergone significant mutations in recent decades, due to innovations in products and processes, technological change (that, for example, expanded customers' opportunities, encouraged greater appetite for risk, short-term outlook and less loyalty to banks), new means of payment (which might render obsolete one of the banks' main functions) and deregulation (which opens up new opportunities for the other intermediaries and increases competition).

The reaction of many commercial banks to these changes has been to adapt their business models to those of their non-bank competitors, and this has also changed their principles and behavior. For example, securitization provided opportunities for obtaining finance by routes other than deposits and changed the banking model from "originate-to-hold" (*hold* the credit on its balance sheet until its due date) to "originate-to-distribute" (*convert* the credit into collateral for a security, sell it and take the risk off the balance sheet); the use of automated procedures for granting loans has weakened personal relationships, replacing, thereby, an ethos of service with a sales-driven culture.

As a result of these changes, the culture of many commercial banks has changed: they are financed impersonally in wholesale markets and lend impersonally through securities, use sophisticated risk models, pursue purely short-term financial targets and stop working with their local communities.

The term "shadow banking" does not imply any negative legal or moral judgment. It is used to designate those organizations (investment banks, brokerage houses, finance companies, structured investment vehicles and many others) that provide banking services to specific clients but neither receive deposits nor handle payment systems, which puts them outside of the official backstop system (the central bank as source of liquidity, along with deposit guarantee programs). They operate in a less regulated environment than commercial banks, though often are owned and managed by them, and have lower costs, substantial competitive advantages and opportunities for big profits (Poszar et al. 2013).

The ethical problems affecting shadow banking are similar to those of commercial banks, although more acute, because its business model is more aggressive, the risk level higher, the leverage greater, and the equity levels lower. Shadow banks are highly connected with other institutions, which may create systemic risk, and they may also be prone to problems related to opacity, herd behavior or conflict of interests.

Investment banks undertake a broad range of operations with other financial intermediaries and private customers: they help private companies obtain financing by means of public share offers; they trade with institutional investors on the secondary markets; they act as market makers, adding depth and liquidity to the market; they trade in derivatives; they facilitate transactions on the repo markets and provide clearing services to other financial institutions, and they also carry out operations on their own behalf. They are usually large organizations, with a considerable resource-generating capacity and a powerful influence on the economy.

Investment banks have often been criticized due to the risks they take and transmit to the rest of the system, the complexity of their products, the opacity of their operations and their interconnection with many markets and institutions, which leads to negative knock-on effects (Painter 2010; Reynolds and Newell 2011).

Investment funds, mutual funds, exchange-traded funds, hedge funds

Investment funds are collective investment institutions that hold portfolios containing only financial or real-estate assets; investors buy shares in these funds, thereby becoming co-owners of that portfolio.[6] Mutual funds target modest investors who cannot manage their wealth personally and offer them diversified portfolios with yields that are higher than could be obtained on their own. Pension funds receive employees' savings to provide them income when they retire. In exchange-traded funds investors buy and sell the fund's shares on the stock market; their assets consist of participations in indexes; they are diversified products, easy to operate and with low costs.

The ethical problems that usually arise with respect to these funds include putting managers' interests before that of clients' (for example, a manager strategically executes his own trade prior to the request of a client), generating unnecessary trades (churning) to collect more commissions, or dealing unfairly with an investor. Excessive risk-taking is not frequent due to the strictness of regulations.[7]

Hedge funds have undergone rapid growth in recent years. They are usually large, have a small number of high net worth clients and impose strict terms on them, in particular for the withdrawal of funds. They operate under lax regulations, they are heavily leveraged, their strategies are opaque and they offer high yields with high risk. They charge high commissions and their managers also have other incentives tied to the fund's performance.

Hedge funds came under strong criticism in the recent financial crisis for their size and power, aggressive strategies, high potential profits (and losses) and the risks they take or transfer to other participants. They were also criticized for the lack of transparency of their operations, although this is not relevant for the market's efficiency when such information concerns the fund's internal strategy and is accepted by its participants. Possible agency problems (putting the interests of the managers ahead of those of the customers) and conflicts of interest (for example, when managers carry out proprietary trading that can cause lower profits for clients) may also arise (see Donaldson 2010 on the ethical problems of hedge funds).

Financial derivatives and securitization

Derivatives are financial instruments in which an asset's value depends on or is derived from the value of another underlying asset, index, or interest rate. There are many types of financial derivatives; the best known are forward contracts (buying or selling at a price fixed beforehand, with delivery at a specified time in the future), futures (the same operation with standardized products in organized markets), options (the right, but not the obligation, to buy or sell something at a given time in the future at a specified price) and swaps (two parties agree to swap financial instruments at a given time in the future at a specified price: for example, a contract at a fixed interest rate for another contract at a variable rate). Derivatives have been used for centuries to hedge risks: for example, farmers sell their harvest beforehand in the futures market at a fixed price to protect themselves against an eventual drop in prices.

Derivatives are morally legitimate products which, like many others, can be used inappropriately, becoming "toxic assets."[8] Sometimes they are viewed with mistrust, perhaps because their operation is not properly understood: for example, a future is a zero-sum contract, what one party wins the other party loses, but it enables the risk to be borne by the party who is best able to do so, with a compensation. Another reason for criticism is their speculative use and the potentially high risk: for example, when an option is financed with debt, the gain can be very high, but the loss, if it happens, could be also very high.

Securitization consists of pooling credits that form part of a financial institution's assets (mortgages, auto loans or credit card-linked debt, for example), taking them out of its balance sheet and transferring them to a "special purpose vehicle" (SPV) to act as collateral for derivatives sold to investors. Securitization is a good technical and ethical practice, which allows financial institutions to transfer the risk to other investors, reduce their equity requirements and obtain liquidity to fund new operations. However, this practice can also be used in an imprudent way: for example, in the years of strong real-estate growth in the US, driven by low interest rates and policies promoting the extension of family homeownership, subprime loan originators, who were paid by the quantity and amount of loans granted, regardless of risk of default thereof, had an incentive to conceal the potential borrowers' true risk, and even to encourage them to make misleading statements. Mortgage lenders were not diligent in controlling those risks because, via securitization, mortgages and risk would disappear from their balance sheet.

During placement of the collateralized debt obligations (CDOs) and other derivatives in the years before the financial crisis of 2008, basic rules of prudent investment were also disregarded, such as ascertaining the nature and scope of the risk. The rating agencies, which played a central role in the design and valuation of derivatives, committed big mistakes: the sophisticated criteria used were not appropriate, and conflicts of interest arose because the agency had to assess the products submitted to it by the same banks that had to pay their fees. The derivative portfolios' risk was hedged by credit default swaps (CDSs), in which the issuer undertook to compensate the investor if the asset on which the contract was based lost value or defaulted, in exchange for a premium. Not only were they complex; the CDSs created the illusion that the hedged assets were secure, increasing their imprudent use.

Risk management

All financial transactions involve expectations about the future and therefore carry a risk. This risk may be understood both as hazard and opportunity: sometimes, it is worth accepting risk to get a higher return; other times, it is best to protect oneself from it, pass it on to someone else or, simply, avoid it. The goal of risk management is to prevent the losses that may occur in the future because of the risk and to ensure that the occurrence of critical events does not endanger the organization's survival (see Boatright 2012 and Young 2010).

Risk is not just a technical issue but also an ethical one, because of its consequences on the agent's welfare and on others, and it may even endanger the functioning of the financial system as a whole (systemic risk). A bank's portfolio risk, for example, is borne not only by its shareholders but also by its creditors and even by other agents who act as counterparties in its operations, but decisions on these risks are frequently taken by the bank managers without considering the interests of other stakeholders.

The nature and level of risk must be known, identified, and evaluated in order to decide the best strategy: accept it (if, for example, the institution has enough capital buffer to cover the possible losses), or protect oneself against it (balancing the assets and liabilities, or monitoring borrowers, as the banks do, or passing on the risk through securitization, hedging with derivatives or taking out insurance). There are also immoral forms of risk transfer, by deceit, abuse of power, product opacity or creating moral hazard.

Prudence is the main virtue of the risk manager: excessive risk-taking may be an imprudent action, even if it does not lead immediately to losses. Currently, most regulators delegate an important part of risk control to the financial institution; this reduces the costs for the bank but does not lessen its responsibility, and may increase costs for others, including the taxpayers.

Sound risk management (both technically and ethically) and the exercise of accountability contribute positively to the creation of trust.

Using complex mathematical models has made risk management easier, but it has also created new problems. Sometimes it has been forgotten that the results of these models are dependent on their underlying assumptions and on the information used to calibrate them. Decisions have been left to experts who do not always have the appropriate experience. Reliable models may create the illusion of safety and lead to excessive risk-taking; moreover, each manager sees only the part of the problem that affects him, so that the protection of his institution may be compatible with the creation of greater systemic risks. Finally, the widespread use of similar models based on the same assumptions may create situations of herd behavior, leading to excessive optimism during booms and panic during crashes.

The ethics of financial markets

Financial markets put buyers and sellers in contact with each other, either directly or through intermediaries (brokers, dealers, market makers). The main contribution of these markets to the welfare of society is setting prices and providing information to the market participants and to the society.

Sometimes it is argued that markets are unethical, due to the suspicion that the people who operate in them are moved by greed. But one should not confuse a legitimate personal interest with greed. Moreover, markets are only a means to achieve buyers' and sellers' goals; the morality of transactions depends on the goals of the agents and on the means used; if the parties operate in suitable conditions of freedom and access to information, both gain from the exchange and they contribute to efficient resource allocation.

The markets' proper operation depends on a suitable legal and institutional framework that guarantees fair treatment and avoids manipulative, fraudulent, or misleading conduct. Fairness in financial markets is defined by a set of freedoms and rights: freedom from coercion, misrepresentation, and non-rational impulses, as well as rights to (roughly) equal information, intellectual processing power, bargaining power, as well as efficient prices (Shefrin and Statman 1993). The weight of these responsibilities falls upon regulators, but the participants' duties cannot be ignored: for example, they must not commit fraud or deceit, or abuse a dominant position due to asymmetric information; they should not engage in opportunistic behavior when they can breach a contract with impunity; and they should take into account possible externalities that transfer to a third party the costs generated by the decision maker. Here we will discuss two typical problems of financial markets: Speculation and high frequency trading.

Speculation

Speculation is a routine practice on the financial markets.[9] Strictly speaking, it is the purchase (or sale) of an asset without performing a simultaneous hedging operation, with the hope that its price will be higher (or lower) in the near future, while at the same time running the risk that the expectation may not be fulfilled. But often people call speculation, improperly, any operation involving buying low and selling high.

A grocery store does this, but its profit is often justified by the service rendered by providing consumers with the products they want. The moral justification of speculation is based on the exercise of free initiative: whatever their motivation, each party expects to win on the exchange, and the other party makes it possible. Obviously, if a person buys cheap because he expects its price increase and this occurs, he will gain in the operation, and the seller will relatively lose, but this does not mean that the buyer has behaved unfairly, unless he has engaged in immoral practices such as price rigging, hoarding or spreading false news to cause shortages: the morality of the operation will depend, above all, on having observed the rules of justice in exchange. Thus, speculation contributes to the social function of the market: it provides liquidity (it facilitates the parties to buy or sell whenever they want without excessive cost) and information to the market, and this improves efficiency.

Speculation is sometimes criticized by the sheer amount of profit that the speculator may earn, quickly and effortlessly (but with risk), but a moral assessment of these actions is not determined simply by the amount of profits, so long as they have been obtained by fair means (on the morals of profits see the divergent views of Arnold 1987 and Brown 1992). Another aspect is risk: speculators take on a risk, but this is not necessarily immoral, as we said before; the fact that some speculators are ruined has more to do with their misjudgment of the circumstances than with the market's morality.

Electronic and high frequency trading

New information technologies expand and accelerate the possibilities of analysis, decision-making and communication; consequently, finance is becoming more interconnected, faster and more complex—and less human. This may be an advantage in terms of the addition of speed, memory, or power coupled with the subtraction of emotion, distraction, and error. But this does not lessen the moral responsibility of the people who use these technologies.

In the recent decades the growth of electronic trading has provided easy access to the markets without the intervention of intermediaries; this increased competition and developed continuous, integrated and more efficient markets. Afterwards, supercomputers were introduced that operate at superspeed using complex algorithmic programs, and it is here that new moral problems arise.[10]

A particularly significant form of the use of this technology is high frequency trading (sometimes referred to as "HFT"). These are sophisticated programs that carry out operations in a fraction of second and do it thousands of times a day by holding numerous positions open for very short periods of time. By locating the intermediaries' computers very close to the markets' computers, they receive orders a few milliseconds before slow traders; if, for example, a buying order arrives, they can place another order before the selling order arrives from a slower trader, obtaining a minimal profit per unit but multiplied by a very large number of operations. In addition, they anticipate market movements, placing many orders that forestall the actions of slow traders, running ahead of them to get a profit.

High frequency trading is a rent-capturing procedure at the expense of slower traders, and its social benefits are extremely debatable (Angel and McCabe 2013; Cooper et al. 2016; Liu 2014; and Madonna 2013). They provide arbitrage opportunities, identifying small price differences, but the millisecond lead does not provide any significant benefit in liquidity terms; neither does the reduction in transaction costs, due to the narrower spread between bids and ask prices. Furthermore, stuffing the market with fictitious orders can be a type of deception: for example, a trader can launch a large number of fictitious purchase orders to create the false impression that he is trying to make that purchase and cause sales orders from other traders, although the released orders will be canceled immediately. And these practices heighten operations' endogeneity, giving markets a life of their own, disconnected from the agents' financial needs,[11] and may have destabilizing effects, triggering a chain reaction processed by computers, without human intervention—but with human responsibility—in response to an erratic market movement.

Computers and networks perform vital functions in financial markets: they provide access to more and faster information, they reduce costs and give empowerment to customers. But they can also have negative effects: speed may accentuate volatility, increase risk, hamper some agents' free access to the market and unfairly discriminate among operators. The technical advantages of computers are undeniable but, from the ethical viewpoint, it is the person's agency, initiative and freedom that may be at stake, because it is the person who designs the programs and endorses its use who is ultimately responsible for the decisions made by computers.

Alternative finance

Ethical banking, ethical funds, socially responsible investment, crowdfunding, microfinance

Over the course of history, many investors have felt responsible for the use of their money and did not wish to become collaborators with or accomplices to possible immoral dealings of the companies they financed; or, taking a positive approach, they wished their wealth to be used in economically and socially beneficial activities. From the other side of the market, the investors' demands have been mirrored with the provision of ethically and socially responsible investment products and in the actions of organizations that try to manage themselves in accordance with ethical standards.

Investors with these concerns often see the financial world as something complex and opaque, in which questionable ethical practices abound. To correct this, new models of financial institutions and products have emerged, such as ethical or sustainable banking, ethical funds, socially responsible investment, impact investing and many others. Their goal is to direct resources towards broader goals than profit, offering savers the possibility of cooperating for the good of the activities they invest in, without sacrificing financial return. The adjectives *ethical, sustainable*, or *responsible* differentiate these institutions, but this does not mean that other organizations are not ethical, sustainable or responsible, or that the organizations that do have these adjectives live up to them in everything they do.[12]

Initially, attention was focused on negative investment criteria, excluding business involved in the production of weapons, tobacco, or pornography, or industries that pollute. Later on, positive criteria were added, so that investment would be made preferentially in socially desirable activities, such as community development, fair trade or renewable energies. And, more recently, shareholder activism was included to get companies to apply environmental, social and governance (ESG) criteria in their actions.

There have been many highly varied innovations in the field of alternative finance. For example, crowdfunding, person-to-person lending and social lending consist of raising funds in a flexible way through the social media, often by means of a large number of small contributions, in order to finance economic, social or hybrid projects. Their ethical appeal arises from their possible social goals and the involvement of communities interested in the project, although they are sometimes criticized for the high interest rates charged to borrowers, uncertainty on guarantees, lack of transparency about the projects and ex-post accountability, and the possible use for illicit activities (as in instances of crowd-funding: Hossain and Oparaocha 2017).

Originally, microcredit consisted of granting small loans to entrepreneurs with the collective guarantee or social control of a group of small entrepreneurs; the commitment to return the funds provided was taken very seriously, and the interest rate was usually high, as justified by the operation's risk and the interest charged by alternative sources. Microfinance includes microcredits and other instruments (savings, payment systems, insurance) to which their recipients do not have access for geographical reasons or lack of income or collateral. The ultimate goal of microfinance was to combat poverty and foster development by financing sustainable micro-enterprises.

Microfinance has been highly praised (Grameen Bank, one of the pioneer institutions, and its founder, Muhammad Yunus, were awarded the Nobel Peace Prize in 1976) but it also received criticism, not so much for its goals as for its procedures and results (Argandoña 2010; Schmidt 2012). As a tool for development, it was expected that microfinance institutions were able to cover their costs and make a profit that would attract new investors, ensuring their economic sustainability. But the expectation of a profit and the pressure of investors changed the nature of the lending operations from the creation of microenterprises to more general consumer credit, in competition with commercial banks; interest rates increased and pressures to repay the debt became more aggressive. Behind those developments were changes in the ownership of the institutions, which often ceased to be social enterprises, foundations, or NGOs in order to become for-profit banks.

The expected social results of microcredit have not always been achieved, perhaps because expectations were too high, or because a region's development depends on more than the existence of small projects targeting a local market that can end up becoming saturated. Microcredit can be used to stabilize a middle class of small entrepreneurs and create jobs, but the debt burden on the poorest limits their ability to eliminate poverty. The future of microfinance is yet to be determined, but now we know more about its possibilities and limitations.[13]

Islamic finance

Islamic finance is a radical alternative to Western finance, based on the principles of *Sharia* or Islamic law. It is not intended as a mere correction of the capitalist model as it is based on religious principles: *Sharia* seeks to develop a way of life, a collective morality and a spirituality. Any human activity, including economic operations, must seek human good and apply principles of justice, equality, harmony and moderation to achieve balance between material and spiritual needs. Islamic finance includes both moral principles and legal regulations that are applied to any activity and, in particular, to the financial institutions created and managed in accordance with *Sharia* (on the ethical implications of Islamic finance, see Hassan and Kayed 2009; Rice 1999; and Wilson 1997).

Sharia prohibits any financial activity related to the production of or trade in non-permitted goods, such as pigs, alcohol and gambling. Money does not beget money; consequently, it is forbidden to charge interest (*riba*) on a loan. Costs, profits, and risks must be shared between the parties to the contract: the concept of justice does not refer only to the procedure but also to the results and, above all, it must create value for society. Islamic banks do not just lend money to their customers; they also establish close relationships with them, including a partnership in the business, dispensing advice and providing supervision. Financial institutions are at the service of the community and not only of individuals, and responsible finance includes controlling the behavior of lenders and borrowers, avoiding, for example, over-indebtedness.

Concluding remarks

In the preceding pages we have explained the nature of several ethical issues arising in finance. Such issues are not morally different from other human decisions, because there are no autonomous moral principles for different activities. Nonetheless, each financial asset or endeavor has its own character, whether because of the nature of the transaction, the product itself, the sponsoring institutions, or the circumstances of the overall market. And through it all reside human relationships.

Good financial professionals act for the benefit of their clients. In so doing, these professionals must ask themselves questions such as these: Is it wise for a householder without a regular job to commit a significant portion of his income on a mortgage to buy a home? Do investors have any specific responsibility for the activities of the company in which they place their money? Does the expectation of a great profit justify highly leveraged option trades? Is it lawful to sell a complex financial asset to a client without financial education or experience? The answers to these queries have an economic dimension in terms of variables such as income and expenses, yields and risks, solvency and liquidity. But they also have a moral dimension—the fair, the prudent, and the responsible—which looks toward the flourishing of individuals and the common good of society. This ethical dimension has become more complex in recent decades but it cannot be compromised for some economic variable or reduced to some technical decision of risk and return.

Finance needs ethics not just to soothe investors' consciences but to improve the industry's practices, to develop solid legal and regulatory (not to mention theoretical) frameworks, to sustain appropriate institutional and cultural foundations, and to create the atmosphere of trust without which finance cannot succeed. Good ethics is good finance: not necessarily because it contributes to greater returns, but, above all, because it is a condition for the good management of financial institutions and for the full life of all individuals.

Essential readings

Financial ethics is a very broad field. The reader can find excellent analysis of the most relevant issues in John R. Boatright, *Ethics in Finance* (2014) and John Hendry, *Ethics in Finance: An Introduction* (2013). Several edited collections offer incisive accounts and analyses, including A. Argandoña (ed.), *The Ethical Dimension of Financial Institutions and Markets* (1995a), Boatright (ed.), *Financial Ethics: Critical Issues in Theory and Practice* (2010) and Andreas R. Prindl and Bimal Prodhan (eds), *Ethical Conflicts in Finance* (1994), among others. With a focus on financial intermediaries, see Christopher J. Cowton and Paul Thompson, *Ethical Banking: Progress and Prospects* (1999) and Peter Koslowski, *The Ethics of Banking: Conclusions from the Financial Crisis* (2011).

For further reading in this volume on the institutions that frame the financial system, see Chapter 18, Property and business and Chapter 21, Regulation, rent seeking, and business ethics. On the causes of the 2008 financial crisis, see Chapter 23, The economic crisis: causes and considerations. On the relation of religious belief (including Islam) to money lending and markets, see Chapter 9, Business ethics and religious belief. On issues related to risk and accountability, see Chapter 31, The accounting profession, the public interest, and human rights.

Notes

1 There are many studies of the ethical side of the recent crisis: for example, Argandoña (2016), Donaldson (2012), Graafland and van de Ven (2011), Kolb (2010), Nielsen (2010). See also Chapter 23 in this volume.
2 On the history, status, and function of money, see Guido Hülsmann (2008).
3 Divergent perspectives on fractional reserve banking may be found in Murray N. Rothbard (2008) and Lawrence White (1989).
4 In each case, what this information will be depends on factors such as the customer's ability to understand the transaction and its potential outcomes.
5 On the ethical problems of insider trading, cf. Engelen and van Liedekerke (2010), McGee (2008).
6 Bonvin and Dembinski (2002) and Dembinski et al. (2003) discuss the ethical responsibilities of investors.
7 On the ethics of funds, cf. Hess (2010), Johnsen (2010). Particular ethical issues are discussed by Almeder and Snoeyenbos (1987) on churning; Boatright (1999), Carson (1994) and Palazzo and Rethel (2008) on conflicts of interest.
8 Overdahl (2010) and Raines and Leathers (1994) deal with the ethical issues of derivatives; Cvjetanovic (2014) and Murdock (2013) address specific derivatives in the recent crisis. On the ethical aspects of securitization, cf. Buchanan (2015), Nielsen (2010) and Schwarcz (2009). The ethical failures of rating agencies in the valuation of derivatives are explained in Scalet and Kelly (2012) and Strier (2008).

9 Angel and McCabe (2010) and Koslowski (1995) discuss the ethics of speculation. A particular case is that of short selling (selling securities or other financial instruments that are not currently owned, and subsequently repurchasing them) (Angel and McCabe 2009). This practice adds another ethical issue: the possibility that the short sale will trigger an overreaction in the market, accentuating the fall of the price of the security.
10 Hurlburt et al. (2009), Kraemer et al. (2010) and West (2014) analyze the ethical issues arising from the use of new information and communication technologies in the financial markets.
11 Dark pools are electronic trading networks that facilitate anonymous trading, hiding it from the market to prevent their strategy from becoming known; they are, somehow, defense mechanisms against high frequency operators (Koehn and Koehn 2014).
12 The ethics of socially responsible investing is treated, among others, by Louche and Lydenberg (2010), Mackenzie and Lewis (1999), Sandbu (2012), Sparkes (2002) and Vandekerchkove et al. (2011). For critical perspectives on this form of investing, see Entine (2005).
13 Microfinance is related to bankarization and financial inclusion, which seeks to enable all citizens to access a variety of financial products as a means to overcome significant obstacles to their opportunities, security and participation.

References

Almeder, R.F. and M. Snoeyenbos (1987). "Churning: Ethical and Legal Issues," *Business & Professional Ethics Journal* 6:1, 22–31.
Angel, J.J. and D. McCabe (2009). "The Business Ethics of Short Selling and Naked Short Selling," *Journal of Business Ethics* 85:1, 239–249.
Angel, J.J. and D. McCabe (2010). "The Ethics of Speculation," *Journal of Business Ethics* 90:3, 277–286.
Angel, J.J. and D. McCabe (2013). "Fairness in Financial Markets: The Case of High Frequency Trading," *Journal of Business Ethics* 112:4, 585–595.
Angel, J.J. and D. McCabe (2014). "The Ethics of Payments: Paper, Plastic, or Bitcoin," *Journal of Business Ethics* 132:3, 603–611.
Argandoña, A. (ed.) (1995a). *The Ethical Dimension of Financial Institutions and Markets*. Berlin: Springer.
Argandoña, A. (1995b). "The Treatment of Ethical Problems in Financial Institutions and Markets," in A. Argandoña (ed.), *The Ethical Dimension of Financial Institutions and Markets*. Berlin: Springer, 1–26.
Argandoña, A. (2010). "Microfinance," in J.R. Boatright (ed.), *Financial Ethics: Critical Issues in Theory and Practice*. Hoboken, NJ: John Wiley and Sons, 419–434.
Argandoña, A. (2016). "Three Ethical Dimensions of the Financial Crisis," in A.G. Malliaris, L. Shaw and H. Shefrin (eds), *The Global Financial Crisis: Neglected Ideas from Economics, Psychology, and Values*. New York, NY: Oxford University Press, 2016 413-428.
Arnold, N.S. (1987). "Why Profits Are Deserved," *Ethics* 97:2, 387–402.
Boatright, J.R. (1999). "Financial Services," in M. Davis and A. Stark (eds), *Conflict of Interest in the Professions*. New York, NY: Oxford University Press.
Boatright, J.R. (ed.) (2010). *Financial Ethics: Critical Issues in Theory and Practice*. Hoboken, NJ: John Wiley and Sons.
Boatright, J.R. (2012). "The Ethics of Risk Management: A Post-Crisis Perspective," in BBVA Foundation, *Values and Ethics for the 21st Century*. Madrid: BBVA Foundation, 473–496.
Boatright, J.R. (2014). *Ethics in Finance*. Oxford: Wiley Blackwell.
Bonvin, J-M. and P.H. Dembinski (2002). "Ethical Issues in Financial Activities," *Journal of Business Ethics* 37:3, 187–192.
Brown, G.A. (1992). "Are Profits Deserved?" *Journal of Business Ethics* 11:2, 105–114.
Buchanan, B.G. (2015). "Securitization: A Financing Vehicle for All Seasons?" *Journal of Business Ethics* DOI 10.1007/s10551-015-2636-y.
Carson, T.L. (1994). "Conflicts of Interest," *Journal of Business Ethics* 13:5, 387–404.
Cooper, R., M. Davis and B. Van Vliet (2016). "The mysterious ethics of high-frequency trading," *Business Ethics Quarterly* 26:1, 1–22.
Cowton, C.J. (2002). "Integrity, Responsibility and Affinity: Three Aspects of Ethics in Banking," *Business Ethics: A European Review* 11:4, 393–400.
Cowton, C.J. and P. Thompson (1999). *Ethical Banking: Progress and Prospects*. London: Financial Times Business.

Cvjetanovic, M. (2014). "Collateralised Debt Obligations (CDOs): An Update," *Moral Cents*, Seven Pillars Institute, 3:1, 29–52.
Davies, H. (2001). "Ethics in Regulation," *Business Ethics: A European Review* 10:4, 280–287.
Dembinski, P.H. (2009). *Finance: Servant or Deceiver? Financialization at the Crossroads*. London: Palgrave Macmillan.
Dembinski, P.H., J.-M. Bonvin, E. Dommen and F.-M. Monnet (2003). "The Ethical Foundations of Responsible Investment," *Journal of Business Ethics* 48:2, 203–213.
Donaldson, T. (2010). "Hedge Funds," in J.R. Boatright (ed.), *Financial Ethics: Critical Issues in Theory and Practice*. Hoboken, NJ: John Wiley and Sons, 239–252.
Donaldson, T. (2012). "Three Ethical Roots of the Economic Crisis," *Journal of Business Ethics* 106:1, 5–8.
Engelen, P-J. and L. van Liedekerke (2010). "Insider Trading," in J.R. Boatright (ed.), *Financial Ethics: Critical Issues in Theory and Practice*. Hoboken, NJ: John Wiley and Sons, 199–221.
Entine, J. (ed.) (2005). *Pension Fund Politics: The Dangers of Socially Responsible Investing*. Washington, DC: AEI Press.
Graafland, J.J. and B.W. Van de Ven (2011). "The Credit Crisis and the Moral Responsibility of Professionals in Finance," *Journal of Business Ethics* 103:4, 605–619.
Green, C.F. (1989). "Business Ethics in Banking," *Journal of Business Ethics* 8:8, 631–634.
Hassan, M.K. and R.N. Kayed (2009). "The Global Financial Crisis, Risk Management and Social Justice in Islamic Finance," *ISRA International Journal of Islamic Finance* 1:1, 33–58.
Hayek, F.A. (1976). *The Denationalisation of Money*. London: Institute for Economic Affairs.
Heath, E. (2010). "Fairness in Financial Markets," in J.R. Boatright (ed.) *Financial Ethics: Critical Issues in Theory and Practice*. Hoboken, NJ: John Wiley and Sons, 163–178.
Hendry, J. (2013). *Ethics in Finance. An Introduction*. Cambridge: Cambridge University Press.
Hess, D. (2010). "Pension Funds," in J.R. Boatright (ed.), *Financial Ethics: Critical Issues in Theory and Practice*. Hoboken, NJ: John Wiley and Sons, 359–372.
Hossain, M. and G. Oparaocha (2017). "Crowdfunding: Motives, Definitions, Typology and Ethical Challenges." *Entrepreneurship Research Journal* 7:2. Available at: https://doi.org/10.1515/erj-2015-0045.
Hülsmann, J.G. (2008). *The Ethics of Money Production*. Auburn, AL: Ludwig von Mises Institute.
Hurlburt, G.F., K.W. Miller and J.M. Voas (2009). "An Ethical Analysis of Automation, Risk, and the Financial Crises of 2008," *IEEE IT Professional* 11, 14–19.
Johnsen, D.B. (2010). "Mutual Funds," in J.R. Boatright (ed.), *Financial Ethics: Critical Issues in Theory and Practice*. Hoboken, NJ: John Wiley and Sons, 339–358.
Johnson, T.C. (2015). "Reciprocity as a Foundation of Financial Economics," *Journal of Business Ethics* 131:1, 43–67.
Kane, E.J. (2014). "Regulation and Supervision: An Ethical Perspective," in A.N. Berger, P. Molyneux and J.O.S. Wilson (eds), *Oxford Handbook of Banking*. New York, NY: Oxford University Press, 2nd edition, 505–526.
Kleinau, C. (2014). "Ethics in Finance: Applying Ethical Theory to Guide Decisions and Analysis in Finance." Available at: http://ssrn.com/abstract=2512668.
Koehn, D. (1994). *The Ground of Professional Ethics*. London: Routledge.
Koehn, D. (2010). *Living with the Dragon: Thinking and Acting Ethically in a World of Unintended Consequences*. New York, NY: Routledge.
Koehn, J.L. and D. Koehn (2014). "Ethical Issues with Dark Liquidity and the Ethics of Possible Remedies," *Moral Cents*, Seven Pillars Institute 3:2, 3–29.
Kolb, R.W. (ed.) (2010). *Lessons from the Financial Crisis: Causes, Consequences, and Our Economic Future*. Hoboken, NJ: John Wiley and Sons.
Koslowski, P. (1995). "The Ethics of Banking. On the Ethical Economy of the Credit and Capital Market, of Speculation and Insider Trading in the German Experience," in A. Argandoña (ed.), *The Ethical Dimension of Financial Institutions and Markets*. Berlin: Springer, 180–232.
Koslowski, P. (2011). *The Ethics of Banking: Conclusions from the Financial Crisis*. New York, NY: Springer.
Kraemer, F., K. van Overveld and M. Peterson (2010). "Is There an Ethics of Algorithms?" *Ethics and Information Technology* 13:3, 251–260.
Lietaer, B. and J. Lunne (2013). *Rethinking Money: New Currencies Turn Scarcity into Prosperity*. San Francisco, CA: Berrett-Koehler.
Liu, T.C.W. (2014). "The New Financial Industry," *Alabama Law Review* 65:3, 567–623.
Louche, C. and S. Lydenberg (2010). "Responsible Investing," in J.R. Boatright (ed.), *Financial Ethics: Critical Issues in Theory and Practice*. Hoboken, NJ: John Wiley and Sons, 393–417.

Mackenzie, C. and A. Lewis (1999). "Morals and Markets: The Case for Ethical Investing," *Business Ethics Quarterly* 9:3, 439–452.
Mackenzie, D. (2008). *An Engine, Not a Camera. How Financial Models Shape Markets.* Cambridge, MA: MIT Press.
Madonna, L. (2013). "The Ethics of High Frequency Trading," *Moral Cents*, Seven Pillars Institute, 2:1, 17–25.
McGee, R.W. (2008). "Applying Ethics to Insider Trading," *Journal of Business Ethics* 77:2, 205–217.
Munro, J.H. (2003). "The Medieval Origins of the Financial Revolution: Usury, Rentes, and Negotiability," *The International History Review* 25:3, 505–562.
Murdock, C.W. (2013). "Credit Default Swaps: Dubious Instruments." *Harvard Business Law Review Online*, 133–141. Available at: http://lawecommons.luc.edu/cgi/viewcontent.cgi?article=1460&context=facpubs.
Nielsen, R.P. (2010). "High-Leverage Finance Capitalism, the Economic Crisis, Structurally Related Ethics Issues, and Potential Reforms," *Business Ethics Quarterly* 20:2, 299–330.
Overdahl, J.A. (2010). "Derivative Contracts," in J.R. Boatright (ed.), *Financial Ethics: Critical Issues in Theory and Practice.* Hoboken, NJ: John Wiley and Sons, 223–238.
Painter, R. (2010). "The Moral Responsibilities of Investment Bankers," *University of St. Thomas Law Journal* 8:1, 5–28.
Palazzo, G. and L. Rethel (2008). "Conflicts of Interest in Financial Intermediation," *Journal of Business Ethics* 81:1, 193–207.
Poszar, A., T. Adrian, A. Ashcraft and H. Boesky (2013). "Shadow Banking," *Federal Reserve Bank of New York Policy Review Staff Report No. 458.*
Prindl, A.R. and B. Prodhan (eds) (1994). *Ethical Conflicts in Finance.* Oxford: Blackwell.
Raines, J.P. and C.G. Leathers (1994). "Financial Derivative Instruments and Social Ethics," *Journal of Business Ethics* 13:3, 197–204.
Reynolds, J.N. and E. Newell (2011). *The Ethics of Investment Banking.* Houndmills, UK: Palgrave Macmillan.
Rice, G. (1999). "Islamic Ethics and the Implication for Business," *Journal of Business Ethics* 18:4, 345–358.
Rothbard, M.N. (2008). *The Mystery of Banking.* Auburn, AL: Ludwig von Mises Institute, 2nd edition.
Ryan, L.V., A.K. Buchholtz and R.W. Kolb (2010). "New Directions in Corporate Governance and Finance: Implications for Business Ethics Research," *Business Ethics Quarterly* 20:4, 673–694.
Sandbu, M. (2012). "Stakeholder Duties: On the Moral Responsibility of Corporate Investors," *Journal of Business Ethics* 109:1, 97–107.
Scalet, S. and T.F. Kelly (2012). "The Ethics of Credit Rating Agencies: What Happened and the Way Forward," *Journal of Business Ethics* 111:4, 477–490.
Schmidt, R.H. (2012). "Ethics in Microfinance," in BBVA Foundation, *Values and Ethics for the 21st Century.* Madrid: BBVA Foundation, 523–558.
Schwarcz, S. (2009). "The Future of Securitization," in R.W. Kolb (ed.), *Lessons from the Financial Crisis: Causes, Consequences, and Our Economic Future.* Hoboken, NJ: John Wiley and Sons, 595–600.
Shefrin, H. and M. Statman (1993). "Ethics, Fairness and Efficiency in Financial Markets," *Financial Analysts Journal* 49:6, 21–29.
Shiller, R.J. (2012). *Finance and the Good Society.* Princeton, NJ: Princeton University Press.
Sparkes, R. (2002). *Socially Responsible Investment. A Global Revolution.* Chichester, UK: John Wiley and Sons.
Strier, F. (2008). "Rating and the Raters: Conflict of Interest in the Credit Rating Firms," *Business and Society Review* 113:4, 533–553.
Termes, R. (1995). "Ethics in Financial Institutions," in A. Argandoña (ed.), *The Ethical Dimension of Financial Institutions and Markets.* Berlin: Springer, 118–135.
Tollison, R. (2012). "The Economic Theory of Rent Seeking," *Public Choice* 152:1, 73–82.
Vandekerchkove, W., J. Leys, K. Alm, B. Sholtens, S. Signori and H. Schäfer (eds) (2011). *Responsible Investment in Times of Turmoil.* New York, NY: Springer.
West, J. (2014). "Quantitative Method in Finance: From Detachment to Ethical Management," *Journal of Business Ethics* 129:3, 599–611.
White L.H. (1989). *Competition and Currency: Essays on Free Banking and Money.* New York, NY: New York University.
Wilson, R. (1997). "Islamic Finance and Ethical Investment," *International Journal of Social Economics* 24:11, 1325–1342.
Young, P.C. (2010). "Risk Management," in J.R. Boatright (ed.), *Financial Ethics: Critical Issues in Theory and Practice.* Hoboken, NJ: John Wiley and Sons, 495–508.

21
Regulation, rent seeking, and business ethics

Christel Koop and John Meadowcroft

In the autumn of 1979, US car maker Ford was struggling to compete with cheaper imports from Japan and was considering asking the US government for protection from this unwelcome foreign competition. Ford's chief economist at the time, William A. Niskanen, wrote a memo to the company's executives arguing that Ford should maintain its historic commitment to free trade. He stated that if Ford should lobby the government, it should be for the removal of existing tariffs on steel, engines and other components that the company presently imported (Simison 1980). Niskanen warned that the government did not give away special favours for free, so any protection the company secured would come with conditions attached that Ford would eventually regret. Moreover, he argued that for the business to seek special privileges from government would be morally wrong. He wrote: "A common commitment to refrain from seeking special favors serves the same economic function as a common commitment to refrain from stealing" (Simison 1980: 18).

Niskanen's analysis suggests that business ethics—broadly defined as the "reflection on the ethical dimension of business exchanges and institutions" (Brenkert and Beauchamp 2010: 3)[1]—has an important place in the relationship between firms and governments. While, in the short term, a business or sector might benefit from protection from government, Niskanen argued that, in the long run, such special privileges would prove more costly than the steps required to make a business genuinely competitive. Moreover, he believed that businesses had a moral responsibility not to lobby government for special privileges and hence such behavior, while legal, was nevertheless unethical.

Niskanen's account of ethical business practice would seem to contrast with Milton Friedman's (1970) famous dictum that "the social responsibility of business is to increase its profits." In an article that would introduce the shareholder theory in business ethics, Friedman argued that a business cannot have social responsibilities because only individuals have responsibilities. Questions about the social responsibility of businesses in fact amount to questions about the social responsibility of particular individuals. Corporate executives employed by firms are responsible to the shareholders of those corporations and those shareholders wish to see a return on their investment. To pursue other ends, Friedman argued, would be to put the agent's interests over those of the principal and this would be morally wrong—business employees are employed to pursue their employer's interests.

Friedman's analysis would seem to condone businesses lobbying government in pursuit of special privileges. As long as such lobbying was done within the law and the award of special privileges increased the returns of shareholders then Friedman's account of the appropriate role of business would seem to offer no basis to object. The executives at Ford appeared to have agreed with Friedman's analysis, as they decided to ignore Niskanen's advice and also decided that his services were no longer required.

Niskanen's experience at Ford and Friedman's injunction that "the social responsibility of business is to increase its profits" raise critical questions of business ethics in the relationship between firms and government, particularly given the size and scope of contemporary governments and their willingness to intervene in the economy. Governments in capitalist economies have the power to regulate business conduct in a number of ways.[2] They may impose taxes on businesses, they may grant businesses subsidies, and they may introduce rules that prescribe certain types of business conduct, whether aimed at the production process or the products themselves. All of these regulatory tools can dramatically increase or decrease the costs of production, lead to the closure of or birth of whole industries, and significantly affect a country's international competitiveness. Moreover, by using the regulatory tools at their disposal, governments may grant some businesses or sectors special privileges and protections—what are often termed "rents"—that may greatly influence the profitability of the firms so privileged vis-à-vis their competitors and affect the operation of the economy as a whole. In sum, governments can have a profound impact on business, and, consequently, on the fates of individual men and women. As George Stigler starkly put it:

> The state—the machinery and power of the state—is a potential resource or threat to every industry in the society. With its power to prohibit or compel, to take or to give money, the state can and does selectively hurt or help a vast number of industries.
>
> *(1971: 3)*

As intervention in the economy can take different forms, governments must decide how they are to deal with businesses, and businesses must decide how they are to deal with government. Much may depend on how governments understand businesses: as enterprises that involve the pursuit of private gain irrespective of the social consequences, thus requiring external intervention to ensure its activities are consistent with the public interest, or as enterprises that—wittingly or unwittingly—produce socially beneficial outcomes without the need for much external direction and control. How businesses approach their dealings with government may similarly depend upon how they understand the appropriate role of government and whether they believe lobbying government for particular regulatory regimes or special privileges—in other words, rent seeking—is morally right or wrong.

In this chapter we look at different ways of understanding the role of business in a modern economy, and the implications this has for business ethics, the appropriate scope and nature of government regulation, and the business ethics of rent seeking. We develop a two-by-two typology of views of regulation and business ethics based on 1) different perspectives on the motivation of firms, and 2) different perspectives on the type of obstacle—market or government failure—that is considered more detrimental to the economy. We link these perspectives to different (positive and normative) views of business ethics and government regulation. In the second section, we link the questions of business ethics and regulation to rent seeking—a prominent but controversial form of business engagement with the regulatory process. The scope and form of rent seeking may be contingent on economic calculations, but the decision on whether or not to engage in it will also depend on the motivation of a firm and its willingness to be involved in what some consider "inappropriate practices." We conclude the chapter by reflecting on the policy implications of our analysis. Government regulation is nowadays ubiquitous. To the extent that businesses shape regulation with a view to their own special interests, the regulatory process can introduce new inefficiencies. We argue that institutional structures—governmental and corporate ones—may mitigate these problems, but are themselves highly sensitive, thus necessitating caution.

A typology of business ethics and regulation

Views of the role of business ethics in the economy—positive and normative—vary considerably from one part of the social science literature to another. Similarly, and partially following from these views, positions on the potential and desirability of government regulation vary. We argue that this variation can be attributed largely to differences in 1) perspectives on the motivation of firms, and 2) perspectives on the sort of obstacle that is most detrimental to the economy—market or government failure. In this section, we develop a two-dimensional heuristic typology linking perspectives on business motivation and economic obstacles to positions on the role of business ethics and government regulation. Our typology seeks to capture the most important variation in these positions and to clarify the sources of the variation.

The perspectives we distinguish are ideal-typical and many observers hold views that lie somewhere between the extremes. For instance, in their seminal work on *Responsive Regulation* (1992), Ian Ayres and John Braithwaite theorize the conditions under which different perspectives on the motivation of firms can be taken (see also Parker 2013). Nonetheless, as analytical constructs, the ideal types can help us identify the sources of views on regulation and business ethics as well as the position of these views in the broader debate on the topic.

Let us now turn to the typology itself. First of all, two ideal-typical perspectives on what actually drives business can be distinguished in the literature: 1) firms are amoral entities motivated by the maximization of purely economic goals, and 2) firms are moral entities driven by conceptions of appropriateness and legitimacy (cf. Ayres and Braithwaite 1992: 19; DeGeorge 2010: Ch. 1; Kagan and Scholz 1980). Underlying these perspectives are different logics of action: the "logic of consequences" and the "logic of appropriateness" (e.g., March and Olson 2008). Following the logic of consequences, action is driven by rational choice, cost-benefit analysis and utility maximization. As Thomas Risse puts it, "[t]his is the realm of instrumental rationality whereby the goal of action is to maximize or optimize one's own interests and preferences" (2000: 3). The logic of appropriateness, by contrast, emphasizes the institutionalized environment in which action takes place. Action is motivated by the social norms and rules that apply to the situation; by "internalized prescriptions of what is socially defined as normal, true, right, or good, without, or in spite of calculations of consequences and expected utility" (March and Olson 2008: 689). In other words, actors seek "to do the right thing"—or to be ethical—rather than to maximize utility. The norms and rules do not only directly affect behavior, but they also constitute the identity and preferences of actors (Risse 2000: 4–5).

The logic of consequences is linked to a view of firms as utility maximizers; a view that is dominant in economics. Utility typically takes a very specific form; namely, the form of (expected) profit. This is most explicit in the assumption of profit maximization in the neoclassical theory of the firm. It is argued that firms seek to maximize profit since they crucially depend on it; otherwise, they risk going bankrupt or being subject to hostile take overs. Moreover, in modern corporations, with their separation of ownership and control, managers seek to maximize profit because it is this form of utility that the owners—with whom they have a fiduciary relationship—are interested in.

The assumption of profit maximization has not been without criticism. According to managerial theories of the firm, which focus on the role of managers, firms pursue other objectives than (just) profit maximization. Under conditions of organizational complexity, uncertainty and separation of ownership and control, managers may maximize their own personal utility rather than the firm's profit (e.g., their salary, prestige, perks, or security) (e.g., Baumol 1962; Williamson 1963; cf. Jensen and Meckling 1976).[3] The type of objective will also depend on organizational form, with considerable differences between for-profit and not-for-profit organizations and state-owned companies.

What most managerial modifications have in common with standard neoclassical models is the assumption of utility maximization. Though utility does not need to mean profit, it tends to be defined in purely economic terms. Indeed, action is assumed to follow a consequential logic. The models also all portray firms as amoral entities. Business conduct is driven by economic considerations; not by considerations of what is the right or ethical thing to do. This does not mean that firms are immoral: they may act morally, but only if it is, one way or another, economically beneficial. For instance, if companies can benefit from changes to the production process that lead to less pollution, or from introducing a strategy of corporate social responsibility, they are expected to choose these options. However, if companies can reduce their costs or increase their output by exploiting externalities in the form of pollution or exploitation of workers, they are expected to do so (see, e.g., Jensen 2002: 239). Even compliance with the law may be a function of economic calculation, with the law being disobeyed "when the gain derived from the crime exceeds the potential pain of being caught and punished" (Kagan and Scholz 1980: 356).

The economic conception of the firm as amoral entity—a conception that leaves little room for ethical reflection in business—is shared by some branches of the applied ethics literature and by many practitioners. First of all, it is shared by postmodern scholars who take an ethically nihilistic perspective on business, "contending that most of free enterprise is governed by executives and managers who only care about profits and their own well-being and think of ethical issues in business as either externalities or as irrelevant altogether" (Werhane 2012: 48–49). Second, it is represented in the shareholder theory of business ethics (e.g., Friedman 1970). As we set out below, this theory not only conceives of the firm as an amoral entity, but it also considers the limited scope of ethical reflection in business desirable. Finally, the conception is dominant in business itself, particularly in the Western world. For many observers, so Richard DeGeorge points out, "[corporations] are not unethical or immoral; rather, they are *amoral* insofar as they feel that ethical considerations are inappropriate in business" (2010: 3; italics original).

A different perspective on business motivation is presented by scholars who assume that rules of appropriate behavior play an important role in the economy. Sociological institutionalism, for instance, emphasizes that companies are deeply affected by the institutionalized environment in which they operate and that is governed by shared conceptions of what is normal and right (e.g., Meyer and Rowan 1977; DiMaggio and Powell 1983). This implies that ethics play an important role in business. This is echoed in what DeGeorge calls "the myth of amoral business" (2010: Ch. 1). The conception of the firm as amoral entity may prevail, but it is, according to DeGeorge, heavily flawed. Not only do scandals such as the Enron one suggest that we, as members of society, believe ethics should play a role in business, but the responses of businesses to ethical pressure by, for instance, environmental and consumer organizations, demonstrate that ethics do matter (2010: 4–5).

Much of the business ethics literature—and, as we set out later, particularly the stakeholder theory—regards firms as moral entities that base their choices on their (conscious or unconscious) assessment of what is appropriate for them to do in a specific situation rather than on cost-benefit analysis. In this context, firms are sometimes portrayed as seeking to act like "good citizens." Though conceiving firms as citizens is not unproblematic—particularly in the case of multinational corporations—Pierre-Yves Néron and Wayne Norman find it useful as it captures the fact that "corporations are real members *of some kind* of our communities, with the power to contribute to or to diminish the common good, and the right to influence political and legal processes" (2008: 16; italics original). As such, the conception is relevant for empirical and normative analyses of firm behavior.

The concept of organizational legitimacy is also central in the "appropriateness perspective." As John Meyer and Brian Rowan explain, companies are driven to incorporate—either ceremonially or substantially—practices and procedures that are associated with prevailing rationalized and institutionalized concepts of organizational work, even when conformity to institutionalized rules conflicts with efficiency criteria (1977: 340). Conforming to the rules, so Mark Suchman points out, can lead companies to be regarded as "natural and meaningful" and can "increase their legitimacy and long-term survival prospects, independent of the immediate efficacy of the acquired practices and procedures" (1995: 576). Crucially, the practices are introduced for reasons of appropriateness rather than for instrumental reasons, even though they can enhance firms' survival (cf. Bowie 1999: 120–121).

The question of what sort of behavior we should expect is somewhat open if we take the second perspective. Firms would do what is considered to be "right" in a given situation, but conceptions of what is right may vary over time and across countries and sectors. That is, firms are generally expected to incorporate "good practices" such as ensuring health and safety at work, protecting consumers and the environment, and committing themselves to some of corporate social responsibility, but there will be context-specific variation. Also, firms are, in general, law-abiding, particularly if the law reflects socially shared conceptions of what is normal and right. Yet, if laws are considered to be inappropriate—for instance, because they are regarded as arbitrary or unreasonable—companies may "rebel" (cf. Kagan and Scholz 1980: 360).

The distinction between the two perspectives of business motivation is, so we argue, crucial to but not sufficient for a good understanding of the variation in views of business ethics and regulation. A second analytical distinction is needed; one that follows from the question of whether market or government failure is the more important obstacle to a well-functioning economy. Market failure refers to situations where resources are not allocated in the most efficient way; in other words, where market activity leads to outcomes that could still be improved upon from a societal perspective (see Bator 1958). Examples include monopoly power, negative externalities, predatory pricing and other forms of anti-competitive behavior, and information inadequacies. Government failure, by contrast, is about situations in which government intervention in the economy creates allocative inefficiencies. Capture by industry is the best-known source, but failure may also result from excessive bureaucracy, information asymmetry between regulators and regulatees, coordination problems, and policies that enhance anti-competitive behavior, moral hazard, overcapitalization, and crowding out (e.g., Majone 1994: 79).

The first ideal-typical perspective emphasizes market failure as the crucial obstacle. We find this perspective in a rather pure form in public interest-based approaches to policy-making, where (regulatory) policies are considered to be introduced for reasons of public interest, including the creation of markets and the correction of market failure (see Baldwin et al. 2012: 41–42). The perspective also prevails in the business ethics literature, which focuses much more on market failure than on government failure (cf. Jaworski 2013). Market failure is, in these literatures, seen as a major problem for the economy, while government failure is largely assumed away. Policy makers are regarded as capable and willing to act in the public interest, as well as trustworthy and disinterested. They may act in the public interest for reasons of appropriateness, but their "responsiveness" may also be a consequence of institutionalized mechanisms such as elections. Moreover, the attitudes may be public sector-specific, as argued in studies on public sector motivation (e.g., Perry and Wise 1990). All in all, as Robert Baldwin and his colleagues put it:

> It is a vision that implies a highly benevolent view of political processes. It assumes some form of objective knowledge that can establish the presence of 'market failure' and that can respond with the appropriate instruments. The 'public interest' world is a world in which bureaucracies do not protect or expand their turf, in which politicians do not seek to enhance their electoral or other career prospects, in which decision-making rules do not determine decisions, and . . . in which business and other interest groups do not seek special exemptions or privileges.
>
> *(2012: 41)*

The alternative holds that government failure is the key problem: markets may not always be perfect, but government intervention leads to worse outcomes. Explanations of government failure focus on the role of (private) interests or on the role of policymakers' (lack of) knowledge. Public choice (or private interest) approaches criticize the assumption of disinterested policy makers, arguing instead that the latter—like everyone else—seek to pursue their own interests rather than some sort of public interest. While politicians seek to maximize re-election chances, bureaucrats aim to maximize their budget, turf or autonomy.

This perspective has been most famously advanced in the so-called "economic theory of regulation," which centers on regulatory capture as failure. The theory was introduced by Chicago school economist George Stigler (1971), and further developed by authors such as Sam Peltzman (1976). Stigler's core and still prominent argument is that "as a rule, regulation is acquired by the industry and is designed and operated primarily for its benefit" (1971: 3). The author explains that both industry and other interest coalitions put effort into averting unfavorable policy outcomes, but industry is more successful in shaping policy because it is more concentrated, more resourceful, and more vigorous in exercising pressure for it has more to lose (cf. Olson 1965). Policy makers, on the other hand, will give in to industry demands because they are either indifferent or electoral beneficiaries.

Concerns about government failure may also be knowledge-based. Even if policy makers wish to pursue the public interest, they may not be able to do so because of insufficient information or an insufficient capacity to process the information. At a general level, the argument is that allocative efficiency is hard to identify and achieve; for instance, because there are multiple and clashing conceptions of the public interest (Baldwin et al. 2012: 42). A more specific mechanism behind government failure is presented by F.A. Hayek (1945). Hayek argues that information about economic needs and preferences is incomplete and dispersed among many people, which is why it is impossible for government to design a system that is capable of collecting and analyzing all pieces of information, and responding quickly to changes. The market, on the other hand, can coordinate economic activity by means of its price system, "a kind of machinery for registering change, or a system of telecommunications which enables individual producers to watch merely the movement of a few pointers . . . in order to adjust their activities to changes of which they may never know more than is reflected in the price movement" (1945: 527). Hence, markets can achieve much higher levels of allocative efficiency than governments can.

Combining the different perspectives, we can come to four different positions on the role of business ethics and regulation. These positions incorporate positive as well as normative elements, and are summarized in Table 21.1.

Table 21.1 Views of business ethics and regulation.

		Most important obstacle	
		Market failure	Government failure
Motivation of firms	To maximise utility (profit)	A. • Minimal or no role for business ethics. • High levels of regulation are needed, with an enforcement strategy of tough sanctions.	B. • Minimal or no role for business ethics. • Shareholder theory. • Government should (largely) stay away from regulation.
	To "do the right thing"	C. • Business ethics play, and should play, a role. • Stakeholder theory. • Some regulation is needed, with an enforcement strategy of co-operation and suasion.	D. • Business ethics play a role and should be fully relied upon. • Government should rely on self-regulation and business ethics and play, at most, a guiding role.

The upper left-hand cell (Type A) brings together a view of firms as utility maximizers with a view of market failure as the key obstacle to the functioning of economies. This combination of perspectives is prominent in those parts of the economics literature that focus on market failure and regulation—that is, parts that do not assume perfect markets. The view of firms as economic utility maximizers does not leave much room for ethical considerations—business ethics are not (or hardly) considered to play a role. Yet, letting firms operate in the way they naturally tend to operate leads to suboptimal economic outcomes as market failures will be exploited. Therefore, high levels of government regulation are needed to avoid market failure. Self-regulation by industry, on the other hand, cannot be relied upon as it will be used in the interest of the industry; for instance, to protect the industry from competition by making it harder for new entrants to enter the market. Government failure is not or hardly taken into consideration. Moreover, as firms are seen as driven by cost-benefit analyses that are also used to determine whether or not to comply with the law, an enforcement strategy that focuses on hard sanctions is needed. That is, only by making sure that compliance pays off can government regulation be successful; any other strategy will be exploited (see Kagan and Scholz 1980: 354).

A rather different view of business ethics and regulation can be found in the upper right-hand cell (Type B). Observers here are associated with the same conception of firms as utility maximizers, but government failure is considered to be the key problem. The economy, according to this view, works most efficiently if we let firms maximize their economic utility. Ethics do not play a role in business, and this is how it should be as ethical considerations may move firms away from utility maximization and may, thus, lead to suboptimal outcomes. Such a view is traditionally associated with Adam Smith's *Wealth of Nations*:

> As every individual . . . endeavours as much as he can both to employ his capital in the support of domestic industry, and so to direct that industry that its produce may be of the greatest value; every individual necessarily labours to render the annual revenue of the society as great as he can. He generally, indeed, neither intends to promote the public interest, nor knows how much he is promoting it. By preferring the support of domestic to that of foreign industry, he intends only his own security; and by directing that industry in such a

manner as its produce may be of the greatest value, he intends only his own gain, and he is in this, as in many other cases, led by an invisible hand to promote an end which was no part of his intention. Nor is it always the worse for society that it was not part of it. By pursuing his own interest, he frequently promotes that of the society more effectually than when he really intends to promote it.

(1981 [1776]: IV.ii.9)

Smith puts emphasis on the positive externalities of utility maximization by economic actors. Government, on the other hand, should be minimal and should largely stay away from the regulation of business. Regulation would make things worse as it moves the focus of business away from competition and towards co-operation to extract favors from government, for which the consumer pays the price.

In a similar vein, Friedman (1970) advises not to move away from the maximization of utility and, in particular, the maximization of profit. He argues that corporate executives are responsible for conducting business in accordance with the preferences of their principals—the owners—who typically have an interest in profit maximization. Friedman's argument does not end here, though: firms' pursuance of other interests than those of the owners may reduce economic efficiency. That is, promoting "desirable social ends" is a form of taxing and spending; yet, corporate executives have neither the authority nor the expertise to engage in such activities. Thus, serving broader interests may lead to worse outcomes than serving the interests of the owners. Following from this, the shareholder theory in business ethics states that it is the responsibility of corporate managers to act according to the preferences of the shareholders, and thus to maximize profit.[4]

The next cell (Type C)—at the lower left-hand side—captures conceptions of firms as moral entities combined with concerns about the detrimental effect of market failure. Even though firms seek to be "good citizens," market failure—which is more of an unintended consequence here—is a crucial problem. Following these views, some government regulation is needed, but self-regulation can also be relied on, with business ethics playing, and having to play, an important role (cf. Norman 2011). Moreover, if government regulation can take forms that enhance ethical reflection and "good behavior" by firms, such forms should be preferred for they are more effective and efficient (Ayres and Braithwaite 1992: Ch. 2). Equally, the preferred enforcement strategy is one based on co-operation and persuasion, including reminders of what "good citizenship" looks like. Such a strategy will be more successful than a strategy of deterrence (as advocated under Type A) as the latter undermines companies' good will and sense of responsibility.

This position characterizes many approaches to business ethics, and the stakeholder theory in particular. Developed in various forms by authors such as Edward Freeman (1984), Archie Carroll (1989) and Norman Bowie (1999), the theory emphasizes firms' responsibility towards a broad range of stakeholders, not just shareholders. These include at least employees, customers, suppliers, and the local community, and sometimes also the media, government, special interest groups, and competitors (e.g., Freeman 1984: 25). The theory has a normative, instrumental and descriptive dimension (Donaldson and Preston 1995). The normative argument is that firms—and managers in particular—have moral obligations towards different categories of stakeholders. The key moral dilemmas in business are, consequently, about reconciling obligations in cases where stakeholders have conflicting interests (Heath 2014: 68). The normative foundations are somewhat diverse, with authors having relied on, for instance, Kantian and Rawlsian ethics (e.g., Bowie 1999; Evan and Freeman 1988; Phillips 1997). The theory also has an instrumental dimension, with authors linking, though not always demonstrating, the stakeholder focus to organizational success and survival (e.g., Freeman 1984; Bowie 1999: 120–121; cf. Jensen 2002).

In other words, taking ethics into consideration can lead to better outcomes for the firm. Finally, in descriptive terms, the theory seeks to explore stakeholder relations, holding that firms do, indeed, act upon their obligations towards various stakeholders. In other words, firms are moral entities that are not (solely) driven by economic utility maximization.

Even more directly representative of Type C is Joseph Heath's (2014) market-failures approach to business ethics. Heath not only argues that firms are moral entities, but also focuses attention on the detrimental effect of market failure. He points out that the purpose of the market is to promote Pareto efficiency, and such efficiency can be seen as a virtue because of its win-win characteristic (2014: 3). Indeed, we value the profit orientation of firms because it contributes to competition in the market and, thus, to Pareto efficient outcomes. Yet, only in some circumstances does the market produce efficient outcomes by means of an "invisible hand"; most areas of economic activity suffer from market failure. Therefore, government regulation is introduced. But regulation cannot deal with all imperfections: regulatory policies are characterized by imperfect contracting, while high levels of regulatory enforcement are too costly (2014: 16). This is where moral obligation enters: insofar as regulation leaves open the possibility of exploiting market failure, firms have the ethical responsibility to refrain from such behavior and to comply beyond the law.

Finally, the lower right-hand cell (Type D) combines an emphasis on government failure with a view of business firms as "rule-followers." This position is not prominent in the literature, but is fully compatible with the view that ethics can and should play a crucial role in the economy. Firms are not only considered to have most knowledge of their own market, but they are also seen as moral entities seeking to do the right thing. This puts firms in a perfect position to contribute to "moral markets" (cf. Zak 2008). Government intervention in the economy should be limited as such intervention is likely to enhance rather than correct distortions of the price signal.[5] Such government failure is not so much the result of policy makers pursuing their own self-interest, but rather a consequence of knowledge problems and unintended consequences of intervention. Policy makers may seek to pursue the public interest, but are prevented from doing so because of, for instance, a lack of knowledge of the sector. Only light forms of regulation that are voluntary in nature may find support here as these may serve as a reminder of what ethical behavior in business is. For instance, governments may want to introduce voluntary environmental standards or promote strategies of corporate social responsibility.

The business ethics of rent seeking

Government regulation incentivizes firms to engage with governments (and regulatory agencies) to try to influence the regulatory process, including by means of individual or collective lobbying. Business engagement with the regulatory process—whether initiated for economic or ethical reasons—may help ensure that regulation efficiently and effectively targets market failure. Businesses may provide sector-specific information about how the market works and what the implications of different types of interventions may be, and this may reduce the likelihood of government failure. Yet, business involvement in the regulatory process may also lead to the promotion of special interests, and this may shift regulation away from what is most beneficial for society. Such attempts to frame regulations in a way that is beneficial for individual businesses are usually described as an example of rent seeking: "non-voting, non-criminal activities that individuals or firms engage in with the purpose of either changing the laws or regulations, or how the laws and regulations are administered, for the purpose of securing a benefit" (Brennan 2016: E3).

Rent seeking constitutes one of the most prominent and controversial forms of business engagement in politics and policy-making. In economic theory (as opposed to everyday language), a rent describes a payment made to the owner of a resource over and above what that resource could command in an alternative usage. Rents may be found in commercial settings: for instance, the sole baker in a remote village sets the price for bread to maximise profits and, in the short term, may be able to reap exceptional returns if there is no convenient alternative source of bread; but, in the long term, the existence of exceptional profits should motivate other producers to establish competing bakeries or inspire consumers to source alternative supplies of bread or substitute products. In this way, over time, market competition should eliminate economic rents. In the marketplace, rent seeking is said to have socially beneficial consequences because it acts as a spur to entrepreneurial activity that dissipates rents. The overall outcome of this process is increased efficiency as resources move to more productive uses as signalled by the utility-maximizing activities of producers and consumers.

In the political realm, however, rent seeking is generally understood to be more pernicious. Political rents do not exist "naturally," but are deliberately created by government, usually via the allocation of a monopoly right or special privilege to a particular individual, group or firm. For example, a car manufacturer may try to persuade the government to ban foreign imports; or milk producers may lobby for government subsidies to protect their profits. In contrast to economic rents, once a monopoly right or special privilege has been granted, it may be exploited repeatedly, with little prospect of erosion or dissipation. As political rent seeking is institutionalized, it does not trigger the same competitive processes as economic rent seeking. Rather, the removal of political rents will require political action, but as vested interests are created in the process of rent seeking, such change may be hard to achieve.

Until very recently there was almost no discussion of the ethics of corporate rent seeking in the business ethics and corporate social responsibility literature. This led John Boatright to conclude that "[e]ither there is nothing morally wrong with rent seeking, or the moral wrong in rent seeking has escaped attention" (2009: 541). A notable exception to the neglect of rent seeking in discussion of business ethics has been Heath's (2014) market-failures approach to business ethics. As described above, according to this approach businesses should refrain from engaging in activities that create market failures. Rent seeking—for example, seeking a monopoly privilege from government—is said to create a market failure because it introduces inefficiencies into the marketplace and for this reason business managers should eschew such behavior.

Peter Jaworski (2013) has objected that Heath incorrectly classifies rent seeking as a market failure when it should properly be understood as a government failure:

> Tariffs and protectionist measures, and, we might say, the successful extraction of rents in general when they contribute to socially inefficient outcomes, cannot be described as a *market* failure. Instead, these are properly described as instances of *government* failure . . . the choice to grant these special favours to certain firms is controlled not by market, but by government actors and institutions.
>
> *(2013: 4; italics original)*

Nevertheless, Heath and Jaworski are in agreement that rent seeking constitutes unethical behavior. Jaworski's intention is to highlight the essential role of government in the process of rent seeking. For Jaworski, the "primary wrong" in rent seeking is the actions of "public agents [who] violate their duties to be good stewards or effective custodians of tax dollars" by distributing rents (2014: 475). But he also argues that rent seekers themselves should bear some of the responsibility for the social costs imposed by rent seeking:

Just as it would be wrong for me to try to pressure my doctor to write me a prescription for painkillers, so it would be wrong for businesses to try to pressure public actors to create or distribute rents that generate social waste, or promote market inefficiencies.

(2014: 475)

It is surely legitimate and even desirable for businesses to be involved in the process via which government regulates their sector of the economy, but the ethical question raised by Jaworski concerns how businesses should balance their own interests and the interests of others (e.g., competitors, consumers) in their interactions with government. If businesses have specialist knowledge that regulators (or their political principals) do not possess, should they exploit the information asymmetry to frame regulation in their interests in ways that would constitute rent seeking?

To answer this question, it is necessary to identify the moral wrong(s) that have led scholars to judge rent seeking to be unethical. Rent seeking is usually considered unethical for two principal reasons: 1) it is economically wasteful; and 2) it involves the exploitation of those who must pay for the rents obtained.

Rent seeking is considered economically wasteful because resources devoted to it could have been put to an alternative use and, as such, rent seeking imposes opportunity costs that may hold an economy within its production possibility frontier—in other words, make society poorer than it would be otherwise. Indeed, it has been argued that a definitional characteristic of rent seeking is that it is inherently wasteful. Nobel laureate James Buchanan, for example, stated that, "[t]he term *rent seeking* is designed to describe behavior in institutional settings where individual efforts to maximize value generate social waste rather than social surplus" (1980: 4; italics original).

The assimilation of rent seeking and waste originates in the first conceptualisation of rent seeking in response to Arnold Harberger's (1954, 1959) analysis of the social cost of monopoly. Prior to Harberger's work economists assumed that the welfare losses resulting from monopolies were relatively large, but Harberger's formal and empirical analysis suggested that previous research had significantly over-estimated these costs. According to Harberger, the "additional" income derived by monopolists from the higher prices consumers paid compared to a genuinely competitive market was a zero-sum transfer from consumers to producers that did not impose a cost on society as a whole. The social cost of monopoly, therefore, was simply the opportunity cost of the trades that were foregone because consumers expended resources paying inflated monopoly prices.

Gordon Tullock's (1967) ground-breaking article first applied (what has become known as) the concept of rent seeking to challenge Harberger's calculation of the social cost of monopoly. Tullock argued that it was a mistake to regard transfers as zero-sum without any accompanying social cost. While one can formally show, as Harberger did, that transfers simply move resources from one individual to another with no apparent net loss to society, Tullock argued that such an approach failed to take into account the fact that the availability of transfers led people to invest resources in seeking transfers or attempting to prevent transfers.

Tullock (1967, 1971) used the analogous case of theft to illustrate the error of Harberger's approach. In economic terms, theft is a transfer that "produces no welfare triangle at all, and hence would show a zero social cost if measured by the Harberger method" (1967: 228). But it does not follow that theft is costless to society because individuals expend resources in the activity of theft and in protecting themselves against theft. Such expenditure imposes opportunity costs on society—that money could have been spent on alternative uses. The expenditure of resources in the pursuit of transfers, and in resisting transfers away, has become known as

"Tullock Costs," in recognition of Tullock's role in establishing the scholarly literature in which these costs are identified and analysed. Tullock Costs are the costs of rent seeking, separate and above the costs of monopoly identified by Harberger.

It is argued that the presence of Tullock Costs means that rent seeking is always negative-sum because resources are spent in the pursuit of rents and in attempts to avoid rent extraction. The costs of rent seeking include the resources expended by successful *and unsuccessful* rent seekers, as well as resources spent resisting the rent seeking of others (Krueger 1974; Tollison 1982; Fang 2002). It would then appear to be simply axiomatic that resources spent on rent seeking constitute a loss to society. In the words of William Mitchell: "It is readily apparent that whenever a more valued employment is possible, something is being 'wasted'" (1990: 95). Rent seeking, then, is considered unethical because it is essentially unproductive from society's point of view; it is simply the expenditure of effort in the attempt to capture a share of already existing resources.

Rent seeking is also claimed to be unethical because the already existing resources that rent-seekers attempt to capture have been produced by others, so that if rent seeking is successful then those producers will have worked to produce a benefit that others will consume. Hence, rent seeking is said to involve the routine exploitation of large sections of the population by organized interest groups who harness the power of the state to extract benefits funded by others (e.g., Buchanan 1996; Clark and Lee 2006). According to Buchanan, when "[a] coalition of special interests, each with concentrated benefits, can succeed in majoritarian settings in imposing generalized costs on all members of the polity," this constitutes "the exploitation of the many by the few" (1996: 71; see also Brennan and Buchanan 1980; Buchanan and Congleton 1998).

Normative weight may be added to this claim by the fact that rent extraction tends to be either horizontal, involving transfers from one non-poor group to another, or regressive in that the poor will pay a higher proportion of their income in rents than the non-poor. Higher food prices as a result of subsidies to farmers, for example, will have a greater impact proportionately on the incomes and living standards of the poor than the non-poor because the former spend a greater proportion of their income on essentials like food (e.g., DeBow 1992: 11–12; Rodríguez 2004).

Rent seeking is therefore deemed morally wrong because it involves the imposition of costs on others to produce the benefit consumed by the recipient of the rent. It is for this reason that Niskanen in his advice to Ford discussed at the outset of this chapter, and in accordance with the views of many other economists and political scientists, argued that businesses should refrain from rent seeking, even if such actions were not illegal and would be in the financial interests of the firm. It may also be significant that Milton Friedman (1962, Chapter IV) argued against government protections and special privileges for business in the form of monopolies, tariffs and subsidies. This suggests that even on Friedman's own terms the social responsibility of business is not as clear-cut as his famous article would suggest; it would seem to follow from Friedman's opposition to the government allocation of protections and special privileges that business managers and shareholders do have a moral responsibility not to engage in rent seeking, even if such behavior is perfectly legal.

Setting out the moral wrong usually identified in rent seeking does not end the ethical analysis, however. Separating rent seeking from contributing to the regulatory process, for example, may be difficult. Safety regulations, for example, may genuinely help to protect consumers from hazardous products, but may also create costs of market entry that shield incumbent firms from market competition. If a firm participates in the regulatory process that creates regulations that have both public and private benefits, should it be considered a public-spirited contributor to regulation or an immoral seeker of special privileges? As it stands, there has been very little theoretical or empirical engagement with such nuances concerning the appropriate relationship between government and business in contemporary economies.

Regulation, rent seeking, and institutional design

In a context in which regulation is at least partially embraced by government, businesses have to decide how they are to deal with the regulatory process. On the one hand, we have observed that the presence of regulation triggers engagement aimed at avoiding or shaping the rules; on the other hand, business engagement may itself lead to new or expanded regulation that, at least partially, serves the industry that lobbied for it. Rent seeking may be the most contentious and prominent form of industry-serving government intervention. However, there is widespread agreement in the economic literature that rent seeking is wasteful and involves the exploitation of those who fund the rents created. From an ethical perspective, it is also hard to justify rent seeking. Yet, once we accept that ethics matter—that is, once we accept that firms are (also) moral entities—the scope of rent seeking may not be as large as the economic argument suggests. That is, we should expect there to be a category of firms that care about ethical behavior and largely refrain from rent seeking for these reasons, even if they could conceivably benefit from it economically.

Nonetheless, empirical analysis suggests that rent seeking takes place on a large scale. This raises the question of whether and how government can deal with it. One answer is that there should be no more regulatory intervention—or no more intervention targeting specific groups in society. As it depends on the existence of regulation, rent seeking may indeed disappear. However, if we accept that market failure is a problem, and that regulation has the potential to reduce such failure, we may lose something important in the process. Another answer, therefore, is that we should focus on institutional design—both in a formal and an informal sense.

First, the regulatory process itself may be formally regulated so as to avoid rent seeking. That is, to the extent that policymakers are interested in escaping rent seeking, they may introduce structures that institutionalize their commitment to stay away from rents. This may take broadly two forms. On the one hand, business engagement in the regulatory process can be reduced by getting rid of lobbying, revolving doors and other mechanisms that can facilitate rents. Yet, besides the fact that this is difficult if not impossible to implement, it will also reduce the sector-specific expertise that business engagement contributes to regulatory policies. On the other hand, business engagement can be balanced by actively broadening the range of interests that are involved in the regulatory process. This may, for instance, take the form of requirements in terms of diversity of the background of the members of executive, supervisory or advisory boards, or the form of the (financial or other) support for consumer organisations. It may also take the form of transparency requirements, which make it more challenging for businesses to convince policy makers to grant them favours. Yet, the second strategy is not easy: getting the balance right is notably difficult and incumbent business interests may still be de facto dominant.

Second, governments may seek to strengthen informal institutions—including norms—that make rent seeking less attractive. If rent seeking can be challenged on ethical grounds, norms of appropriate business behavior may be emphasized in the regulatory process and, based on the literature on suasion, firms may be regularly reminded what constitutes "good citizenship." Yet again, this is not straightforward. As the literature on "responsive regulation" suggests, a strategy of suasion may work for some companies, but could be exploited by other companies that prioritise profit-making (e.g., Ayres and Braithwaite 1992).

Clearly, designing institutions to avoid rent seeking is a major challenge, and we may never fully solve the problem. An important note of optimism may be injected if we consider that the literature on rent seeking was developed during the second half of the twentieth century when the scope and size of the state was expanding throughout the Western democracies. The economists and political scientists who first studied rent seeking saw it as an important driver of that state expansion; that is, demands for more state intervention, protections and privileges were judged to be leading to bigger and bigger government. The trajectories of contemporary democracies towards ever-bigger government were thought by some scholars to even threaten economic and political freedom (Hayek 1944; Olson 1982). But, in fact, from the standpoint of the present, it can be seen that many states have shrunk since the 1970s and 1980s; the empirical evidence seems to show that when rents reach a certain level then counter-veiling pressures will emerge that can lead to a process of rent destruction. Rent seeking, then, may rise and fall in a cyclical manner (Alves and Meadowcroft 2014; Murphy et al. 1993).

Concluding remarks

The relationship between government and business is an essential feature of the modern economy. Government regulation of the economy may have the potential to solve market failures, but it also has the potential to introduce new pathologies—what are known as government failures. It is important, then, to judge the *relative* merits of intervention and non-intervention; the potential costs of market failure and government failure.

The temptation to seek rents, like the temptation to steal, will likely always be present. Moral injunctions against rent seeking, like moral injunctions against theft, may be effective to deter some people from rent seeking, but institutional design that takes seriously the problem of government failure, as well as the problem of market failure, will surely also be necessary.

Essential readings

In their book, *Responsive Regulation*, Ian Ayres and John Braithwaite (1992) build on the differences in motivations of firms to develop their influential theory on responsive regulation. Robert Baldwin, Martin Cave and Martin Lodge cover the full scope of the positive study of regulation in *Understanding Regulation* (2012). In *Morality, Competition, and the Firm* (2014), Joseph Heath takes market failure as the guiding principle for regulation as well as for business ethics and engages with the idea of rent seeking. The classic articles on the theory and practice of rent seeking are those by Anne O. Krueger, "The Political Economy of the Rent-Seeking Society," (1974) and Gordon Tullock, "Welfare Costs of Tariffs, Monopolies and Theft" (1967).

For further reading in this volume on the ethics of rent seeking, see Chapter 7, Can profit seekers be virtuous? On the nature of the business firm and the motivation of business agents, see Chapter 13, What is business? For a discussion of economics and market failures, see Chapter 17, The contribution of economics to business ethics. On the contribution of US government policy toward the economic crisis of 2008, see Chapter 23, The economic crisis: causes and considerations. For discussions of recent instances of the intersection of politics and markets, see Chapter 35, Business ethics in China; Chapter 37, Business ethics in Africa; Chapter 38, Business ethics in Latin America; and Chapter 39, Business ethics in transition: communism to commerce in Central Europe and Russia.

Notes

1 Such reflection may be done by business actors themselves (the focus of Niskanen's argument), but it is also what the scholarly literature on business ethics does. Green and Donovan (2010: 22) explain that this literature not only seeks to understand the ethics of business actors and organisations, but also aims to improve "the quality of business managers' ethical thinking and performance."

2 Broadly speaking, the term "regulation" refers to one actor's intervention in, or steering of, the activities of another actor. Such interventions may be based on rules (e.g., product standards) or take the form of incentives (e.g., environmental taxes); they may be carried out by governments or by private-sector actors; and they may be directed at activities in the private or the public sector. Yet, looking at the actual usage of the concept in the social sciences, scholars tend to refer to something more specific: regulation is primarily used to refer to forms of intervention that are carried out by government agencies over economic activities—in short, government regulation of business (Koop and Lodge 2017). It is also this meaning that we have in mind here. Business regulation, in this chapter, may be rule-based or incentive-based. When it comes to the term "businesses," we primarily think of privately owned for-profit firms.

3 Not all economists working with the profit maximization assumption believe that it provides an accurate description of firms' behavior; some solely believe that it is appropriate to use the assumption for the reason that, in the long run, only profit-making firms survive (e.g., Alchian 1950). This is also reflected in Friedman's *as if* logic (1953: pt. 1): Firms may not actively seek to maximize profit, but as those firms that survive are the ones that attained the highest profits, we can model firms as if they aim at profit maximization. Interestingly, Kaneda and Matsui (2003) find that firms with profit maximization objectives are not the ones whose realized profits are largest. The authors conclude that the *as if* logic and the managerial theory are, in fact, compatible.

4 As set out in the introduction, Friedman adds that such profit maximization should conform to the "basic rules of society" (1970: 33). Such conformity does not go far beyond compliance with the law, even though deception is rejected, even if legal. A different conclusion on deception is drawn by authors such as Albert Carr (1968). For Carr, bluffing and other legal forms of deception are part of the business game. As in a poker game, bluffing does not reflect on the personal morality of the bluffer.

5 Peter Jaworski (2013) points to the importance of taking government failure into consideration in the business ethics literature. Though not a representative of the position described here, Jaworski argues that analysing government failure "will help us to turn our critical gaze on government actors and the role they play in generating socially non-optimal outcomes" (2013: 5).

References

Alchian, A.A. (1950). "Uncertainty, Evolution, and Economic Theory," *Journal of Political Economy* 58:3, 211–221.

Alves, A.A. and J. Meadowcroft (2014). "Hayek's Slippery Slope, the Stability of the Mixed Economy and the Dynamics of Rent-Seeking," *Political Studies* 62:4, 843–861.

Ayres, I. and J. Braithwaite (1992). *Responsive Regulation: Transcending the Deregulation Debate*. New York, NY, and Oxford: Oxford University Press.

Baldwin, R., M. Cave and M. Lodge (2012). *Understanding Regulation: Theory, Strategy, and Practice*, 2nd edition. Oxford: Oxford University Press.

Bator, F.M. (1958). "The Anatomy of Market Failure," *Quarterly Journal of Economics* 72:3, 351–379.

Baumol, W.J. (1962). "On the Theory of Expansion of the Firm," *American Economic Review* 52:5, 1078–1087.

Boatright, J.R. (2009). "Rent Seeking in a Market with Morality: Solving a Puzzle about Corporate Social Responsibility," *Journal of Business Ethics* 88:S4, 541–552.

Bowie, N.E. (1999). *Business Ethics: A Kantian Perspective*. Malden, MA: Blackwell.

Brenkert, G.G. and T.L. Beauchamp (2010). "Introduction," in Brenkert and Beauchamp (eds), *The Oxford Handbook of Business Ethics*. New York, NY: Oxford University Press, 3–18.

Brennan, G. and J.M. Buchanan (1980). *The Power to Tax: Analytical Foundations of a Fiscal Constitution*. Cambridge: Cambridge University Press.

Brennan, J. (2016). "Morality, Competition, and the Firm: The Market Failures Approach to Business Ethics by Joseph Heath (review)," *Kennedy Institute of Ethics Journal* 26:1, E1–E4.

Buchanan, J.M. (1980). "Rent Seeking and Profit Seeking," in James M. Buchanan, Robert D. Tollison and Gordon Tullock (eds), *Toward a Theory of the Rent-Seeking Society*. College Station, TX: Texas A&M University Press, 3–15.

Buchanan, J.M. (1996). "Distributional Politics and Constitutional Design," in Vitantonio Muscatelli (ed.), *Economic and Political Institutions in Economic Policy*. Manchester, UK: Manchester University Press, 70–78.

Buchanan, J.M. and R.D. Congleton (1998). *Politics by Principle, Not Interest: Towards Nondiscriminatory Democracy*. Cambridge: Cambridge University Press.

Carr, A.Z. (1968). "Is Business Bluffing Ethical?" *Harvard Business Review* 46:1, 143–153.
Carroll, A.B. (1989). *Business and Society: Ethics and Stakeholder Management*. Cincinnati, OH: South-Western.
Clark J.R. and D.R. Lee (2006). "Expressive Voting: How Special Interests Enlist their Victims as Political Allies," in G. Eusepi and A. Hamlin (eds), *Beyond Conventional Economics: The Limits of Rational Behaviour in Political Decision Making*. Cheltenham, UK: Edward Elgar, 17–32.
DeBow, M.E. (1992). "The Ethics of Rent Seeking? A New Perspective on Corporate Social Responsibility," *Journal of Law and Commerce* 12:1, 1–21.
DeGeorge, R.T. (2010). *Business Ethics*, 7th edition. Prentice Hall, NJ: Pearson.
DiMaggio, P.J. and W.W. Powell (1983). "The Iron Cage Revisited: Institutional Isomorphism and Collective Rationality in Organizational Fields," *American Sociological Review* 48:2, 147–160.
Donaldson, T. and L.E. Preston (1995). "The Stakeholder Theory of the Corporation: Concepts, Evidence, and Implications," *Academy of Management Review* 20:1, 65–91.
Evan, W.M. and R.E. Freeman (1988). "A Stakeholder Theory of the Modern Corporation: Kantian Capitalism," in T. Beauchamp and N. Bowie (eds), *Ethical Theory and Business*, 2nd edition. Englewood Cliffs, NJ: Prentice Hall, 75–93.
Fang, H. (2002). "Lottery versus All-Pay Auction Models of Lobbying," *Public Choice* 112:3–4, 351–371.
Freeman, R.E. (1984). *Strategic Management: A Stakeholder Approach*. Boston, MA: Pitman.
Friedman, M. (1953). *Essays in Positive Economics*. Chicago, IL: Chicago University Press.
Friedman, M. (1962). *Capitalism and Freedom*. Chicago, IL: University of Chicago Press.
Friedman, M. (1970). "The Social Responsibility of Business Is To Increase Its Profits," *The New York Times Magazine*, September 13.
Green, R.M. and A. Donovan (2010). "The Methods of Business Ethics," In G.G. Brenkert and T.L. Beauchamp (eds), *The Oxford Handbook of Business Ethics*. New York, NY: Oxford University Press, 21–45.
Harberger, A.C. (1954). "Monopoly and Resource Allocation," *American Economic Review*, 44:2, 77–87.
Harberger, A.C. (1959). "Using the Resources at Hand More Effectively," *American Economic Review* 49:2, 134–146.
Hayek, F.A. (1944). *The Road to Serfdom*. London: Routledge.
Hayek, F.A. (1945). "The Use of Knowledge in Society," *American Economic Review* 35:4, 519–530.
Heath, J. (2014). *Morality, Competition, and the Firm: The Market Failures Approach to Business Ethics*. Oxford: Oxford University Press.
Jaworski, P.M. (2013). "Moving Beyond Market Failure: When the Failure is Government's," *Business Ethics Journal Review* 1:1, 1–6.
Jaworski, P.M. (2014). "An Absurd Tax on our Fellow Citizens: The Ethics of Rent Seeking in the Market Failures (or Self-Regulation Approach)," *Journal of Business Ethics* 121:3, 467–476.
Jensen, M.C. (2002). "Value Maximization, Stakeholder Theory, and the Corporate Objective Function," *Business Ethics Quarterly* 12:2, 235–256.
Jensen, M.C. and W.H. Meckling (1976). "Theory of the Firm: Managerial Behavior, Agency Costs and Ownership Structure," *Journal of Financial Economics* 3:4, 305–360.
Jones, T.M. (1995). "Instrumental Stakeholder Theory: A Synthesis of Ethics and Economics," *Academy of Management Review* 20:2, 404–437.
Kagan, R.A. and J.T. Scholz (1980). "The 'Criminology of the Corporation' and Regulatory Enforcement Strategies," in E. Blankenburg and K. Lenk (eds), *Organisation und Recht: Organisatorische Bedingungen des Gesetzesvollzugs*. Jahrbuch für Rechtssoziologie und Rechtstheorie VII. Opladen, Germany: Westdeutscher Verlag, 352–377.
Kaneda, M. and A. Matsui (2003). "Do Profit Maximizers Maximize Profit? Divergence of Objective and Result in Oligopoly." Available at: http://www.amatsui.e.u-tokyo.ac.jp/profit50.pdf.
Koop, C. and M. Lodge (2017). "What is Regulation? An Interdisciplinary Concept Analysis," *Regulation & Governance* 11:1, 95–108.
Krueger, A.O. (1974). "The Political Economy of the Rent-Seeking Society," *American Economic Review* 64:3, 291–303.
Majone, G. (1994). "The Rise of the Regulatory State in Europe," *West European Politics* 17:3, 77–101.
March, J.G. and J.P. Olsen (2008). "The Logic of Appropriateness," in R.E. Goodin, M. Moran and M. Rein (eds), *The Oxford Handbook of Public Policy*. Oxford: Oxford University Press, 698–708.
Meyer, J.W. and B. Rowan (1977). "Institutionalized Organizations: Formal Structure as Myth and Ceremony," *American Journal of Sociology* 83:2, 340–363.

Mitchell, W.C. (1990). "Interest Groups: Economic Perspectives and Contributions," *Journal of Theoretical Politics* 2:1, 85–108.

Murphy, K.M., A. Shleifer and R.W. Vishny (1993). "Why Is Rent-Seeking So Costly to Growth?" *American Economic Review* 83:2, 409–414.

Néron, P. and W. Norman (2008). "Citizenship, Inc.: Do We Really Want Businesses to Be Good Corporate Citizens?" *Business Ethics Quarterly* 18:1, 1–26.

Norman, W. (2011). "Business Ethics as Self-Regulation: Why Principles That Ground Regulations Should Be Used to Ground Beyond-Compliance Norms as Well," *Journal of Business Ethics* 102:S1, 43–57.

Olson, M. (1965). *The Logic of Collective Action: Public Goods and the Theory of Groups*. Cambridge, MA: Harvard University Press.

Olson, M. (1982). *The Rise and Decline of Nations: Economic Growth, Stagflation and Social Rigidities*. New Haven CT: Yale University Press.

Parker, C. (2013). "Twenty Years of Responsive Regulation: An Appreciation and Appraisal," *Regulation & Governance* 7:1, 2–13.

Peltzman, S. (1976). "Towards a More General Theory of Regulation," *Journal of Law and Economics* 19:2, 211–240.

Perry, J.L. and L.R. Wise (1990). "The Motivational Bases of Public Service," *Public Administration Review* 50:3, 367–373.

Phillips, R.A. (1997). "Stakeholder Theory and a Principle of Fairness," *Business Ethics Quarterly* 7:1, 51–66.

Risse, T. (2000). "'Let's Argue!' Communicative Action in World Politics," *International Organization* 54:1, 1–39.

Rodríguez, F. (2004). "Inequality, Redistribution and Rent-Seeking," *Economics and Politics* 16:3, 287–320.

Simison, R.L. (1980). "Ford Fires an Economist," *Wall Street Journal*, July 30, p. 18.

Smith, A. (1981) [1776]. *An Inquiry into the Nature and Causes of the Wealth of Nations*, R.H. Campbell, A.S. Skinner, and W. B. Todd (eds), 2 vols. Indianapolis, IN: Liberty Fund.

Stigler, G.J. (1971). "The Theory of Economic Regulation," *Bell Journal of Economics and Management Science* 2:1, 3–21.

Suchman, M.C. (1995). "Managing Legitimacy: Strategic and Institutional Approaches," *Academy of Management Review* 20:3, 571–610.

Tollison, R.D. (1982). "Rent Seeking: A Survey," *Kyklos* 35:4, 575–602.

Tullock, G. (1967). "Welfare Costs of Tariffs, Monopolies and Theft," *Western Economic Journal* 5:3, 224–232.

Tullock, G. (1971). "The Cost of Transfers," *Kyklos* 24:4, 629–643.

Werhane, P.H. (2012). "Norman Bowie's Kingdom of Worldly Satisficers," In D.G. Arnold and J.D. Harris (eds), *Kantian Business Ethics: Critical Perspectives*. Cheltenham, UK: Edward Elgar, 48–57.

Williamson, O.E. (1963). "Managerial Discretion and Business Behavior," *American Economic Review* 53:5, 1032–1057.

Zak, P.J. (ed.) (2008). *Moral Markets: The Critical Role of Values in the Economy*. Princeton, NJ: Princeton University Press.

22
Business, nature, and environmental sustainability

Joseph DesJardins

The relation between business and the natural environment mirrors that of the wider society. It is not surprising, therefore, that this relation has changed dramatically since the early twentieth century. At one time, the environment was understood simply as a collection of natural resources to be used in production, with a value established by market forces. Today, spurred on by the global movement towards sustainable development and a broader ethical approach to the natural world, many businesses have taken on environmental responsibilities as part of their strategic mission and the environment itself as an essential stakeholder. Indeed, in many business contexts, sustainable development, and its cognate, environmental sustainability, is thought to provide a comprehensive account of the social and environmental responsibilities of business.

This evolution in thinking about business's environmental responsibilities accompanied significant transformations in the ways public policy, corporate social responsibility, the role of business in society, and environmental ethics have been understood. The story of business, ethics, and the natural world thus involves an account of a broader social evolution as well.

This chapter suggests that the diversity of environmental values and topics is too broad to be accurately captured by a single framework of *sustainability*. Instead, I offer a more pragmatic approach, suggesting that business's responsibilities regarding environmental issues are best explained and addressed by a range of differing philosophical, environmental, and policy strategies. As a consequence, I suggest that both business and environmentalists ought to approach the movement towards sustainability with caution.

The first section of this chapter explores the role of economic markets in achieving environmental goals. What functioned for much of the twentieth century as the dominant model of business's social responsibilities holds that economic markets, at least well-ordered markets, provide the most effective strategies for achieving social goals. This first section examines the ethical foundations for this market-based approach to environmental responsibilities and examines a range of ethical and environmental issues that challenge the adequacy of even well-regulated markets. The following section examines some environmental goods that are considered so valuable that they ought to be exempted from the usual trade-offs that occur in the market. This section describes various regulatory schemes that have been employed to achieve the goal of protecting certain environmental goods. The third section introduces the framework of sustainable development and the ethical and environmental values that underlie this movement.

Subsections examine a range of business responsibilities that are thought to follow from the ethical and environmental commitments of sustainable development. Of course, the framework of sustainability has become ubiquitous in contemporary business settings, yet it is easily misapplied and misunderstood. The next section considers how the concept of sustainability has been so misused that it asks both too little and too much of business. A final section offers some concluding reflections on the present and future state of business's environmental responsibilities.

Environmental goods as economic resources: where markets can work

Through the middle of the twentieth century, the prevailing economic and policy understanding in most of the industrialized world was that the chief value of the natural environment was to provide resources for human use. This widespread understanding denied that environmental goods had any inherent value; they were valued only instrumentally for their utility in serving human ends. Natural objects were natural resources, understood as economic commodities that, like other commodities, could be used and exchanged to further human welfare.

In this context, ethical and policy prescriptions generally followed the familiar model of market utilitarianism. As with all other resources, economic markets were thought to offer the best means for allocating natural resources among competing uses, especially in situations where their availability was limited by conditions of scarcity or production costs. Efficient markets would guarantee that resources would be allocated to uses that produced optimal satisfaction, or maximal utility. From this it followed that the responsibility of business regarding the natural environment mirrored business's social responsibility more generally. Business had no direct social responsibility regarding the natural world other than to obey the law and fulfil its function in the market economy. By pursuing profits within the law, business would help achieve the market's goal of an optimal allocation of environmental costs and benefits.

Consider, for example, deciding which land use would produce the greatest social benefit. Should a particular wooded area be preserved as woodland, harvested for timber, cleared for agricultural use, or cleared for housing or commercial development? Advocates for a market solution would argue that the land ought to go to those willing to pay most for it (O'Toole 1988). Willingness to pay indicates the degree of value that society places on a resource, and by allocating resources to those who most value it, markets ensure an optimal utilitarian outcome. Resources get used in ways that produce maximum overall satisfaction. The preservationist answer amounts to a waste of resources that could otherwise serve human interests. So, if commercial developers are willing and able to pay most for some land it is because society, working through the social preferences expressed in the market, values the commercial development over any alternatives.

Or consider how market mechanisms would work against the depletion of resources. As the supply of a natural resource dwindles, the price would increase. Increasing price creates incentives to find a lower-cost alternative. Defenders of market mechanisms argue that human ingenuity, an indefinitely renewable resource if anything is, will find substitutes before any natural resource is fully exhausted (see Simon 1998; Shahar 2012; Schmidtz 2012a).

Of course, a range of conditions must be met in order to ensure that markets will, in fact, attain this utilitarian end. Markets must be open, competitive and free. Participants must be informed and exchanges must be free from fraud and deception. Property rights must be appropriately assigned and protected. Negative externalities must be internalized, but, if they are not, then the victims of these externalities should receive compensation. It is fair to characterize much of environmental regulation throughout the twentieth century as aiming to ensure competitive and efficient markets and to prevent such market failures.

Some of the earliest US environmental regulations, developed in the first decade of the twentieth century, reflected this approach to business and the natural world. Gifford Pinchot, appointed by President Theodore Roosevelt as the first head of the US Forest Service, advanced a conservationist environmental policy that was explicitly utilitarian and designed to address market failures. The two biggest failures in the eyes of Roosevelt's progressive polices were a lack of competitive markets in situations where natural resources were controlled by a few monopolistic companies, and the exploitation of resources associated with the problem of the commons. Pinchot promoted environmental regulation as "a planned and orderly scheme for national efficiency, based on the elimination of waste, and directed toward . . . the greatest good of the greatest number for the longest time" (Pinchot 1914: 25). The policies that followed held that natural resources ought to be managed for the common good, not for the benefit of the few, and ought to be managed to long-term benefits, rather than exploited for short-term profit.

This utilitarian approach to economic and environmental regulation spread beyond the forestry and timber industry to other natural-resource-intense industries, including mining, oil and gas, wildlife and fisheries management, and water use. It remains a plausible public policy and business strategy for situations in which parties compete for resource usage and in which the natural objects involved are valued only for their instrumental use (Ostrom 1990).

It can be helpful to think in terms of means and ends to understand the ethical foundations of this market-based approach. The ends of both business and environmental policy are determined by the preferences of individual human beings. Some people desire to use land for a housing development, some desire a public park, and some prefer commercial development. On this model, business decisions and public policy should be arranged to produce the greatest satisfaction of those preferences as possible. Efficiently functioning markets are considered to be the best means to achieve those ends, but regulations may be required to prevent a variety of market failures and to ensure that markets do, in fact, function efficiently. The ethical foundations for this approach were decidedly utilitarian. The value of natural objects stems only from the happiness derived from the uses to which humans can put them, and policy ought to be set in ways that achieve the optimal use of those resources.

Environmental goods and intrinsic value: where markets won't work

At first glance, a similar ethical approach underlies a wave of US environmental regulations that arose in the middle of the twentieth century, including such landmark laws as the Clean Water Act and Clean Air Act. As public goods, both air and water were subject to market failures associated with the problem of the commons. Well-regulated markets would provide an optimal allocation of clean air and water. Thus, environmental regulation aimed at controlling air and water pollution could be understood as addressing common market failures. But, unlike such environmental goods as timber, land, wildlife, and fisheries, a strong case can also be made that clean air and water are not mere commodities to be allocated according to market demand, but are central human goods that ought to be protected as human rights. Breathable air and drinkable water are not mere personal preferences that are fungible and whose value is determined by willingness to pay. They are important human needs.

This suggests a different ethical foundation for environmental values and for the environmental responsibilities of business. If some environmental goods are the objects of human rights and are not merely fungible commodities, then markets alone will offer them an inadequate protection. The ethical implication is that some environmental goods, and clean air and water are examples, have an intrinsic rather than merely an instrumental value. As such, they should function as side-constraints on how business and markets operate, limiting what goods can be subjected to market exchanges. From this perspective, business's pursuit of profit should be constrained not only by legal responsibilities, but also by responsibilities established by rights to clean air and water. Like obedience to the law, respect for rights is part of the background conditions required for conducting business.

This alternative philosophical framework entails a very different approach to business and public policy (Arnold and Bustos 2005). The utilitarian and market approach takes all ends as equally deserving, and seeks an optimal overall satisfaction of those ends as the ethically responsible approach. But an approach that takes some environmental goods as the objects of human rights would thus seek to protect those goods from the utilitarian trade-offs that occur within the market. Under a utilitarian philosophy, regulations function to correct market failures and help make markets more efficient. A second philosophy of governmental regulation, what is often referred to as a *standards enforcement* approach, mandates that all business activity must meet certain minimal standards. These standards become part of the rules under which business and markets operate and cannot be subjected to market trade-offs. In addition to these environmental regulations, governmental regulations regarding consumer product safety, food and drug safety, workplace safety, and the minimum wage are other examples of this standards enforcement approach.

These philosophical issues are manifested in legal and public policy debates concerning government regulation and business's environmental responsibilities. In particular, these disputes lie at the heart of debates over the role of cost benefit analysis in setting government regulatory standards. Starting with the Reagan administration in the 1980s, US regulatory standards have required the use of cost benefit analysis to determine appropriate environmental standards. Those sympathetic to the utilitarian and market approach argue that regulatory standards ought to be set only at the point at which the benefits outweigh the regulatory costs. Opponents argue that the goods protected by some environmental regulations, and health and safety are obvious examples, are not commodities to be priced in the market. Environmental standards ought to be set on the qualitative ethical grounds of health and safety, not the quantitative grounds of costs and benefits (see Sagoff 2008; Kelman 1981; and Schmidtz 2012a).

Consider, for example, setting allowable lead levels in water or arsenic levels in air. If clean water and air are treated as mere resources or commodities, then the utility that they provide is reasonably traded off against other benefits that might be lost in the pursuit of clean water and air. Cost benefit analysis would measure the benefits of various levels of water or air contamination, measure the costs of each level, and then set regulatory standards so as to optimize net overall benefits.

Critics who hold that healthy and safe air and water are rights and not commodities to be subjected to financial trade-offs contend that the standards ought to be set on such grounds as the levels of contamination at which health impairment occurs (Sagoff 2004). Once those safe levels are established, then it is reasonable to rely on a cost-effectiveness strategy to determine the most efficient means of achieving those ends. Cost effective analysis takes the ends as given and seeks the most efficient means to attain those ends. It differs from cost benefits analysis, which subjects the ends themselves to a financial calculation. This alternative would argue that market and economic considerations come in to play after the ends of policy have been determined, but they ought not be used to determine the ends themselves (Kelman 1981).

Cap and trade policies for controlling water and air pollution, including greenhouse gas emissions, are perhaps the best known examples of such cost-effective strategies. On this approach, overall levels of allowable pollution are established on scientific grounds. This is the overall "cap" on allowable air pollution. Business and industries are then granted permits to emit such contaminants at a level at which overall emissions meet the cap. But, a market for these permits is established that allows more efficient businesses to sell, or "trade," their unused permitted pollution to those firms that are unable to meet their own permitted levels. Cap and trade therefore creates a financial incentive for businesses to become more environmentally efficient while still meeting overall pollution targets.

A number of considerations support the latter approach over the market-based utilitarian and cost benefit approach. First, protecting such environmental goods as clean water and air and exempting them from market trade-offs recognizes the central value that health and safety play in every human life. Second, this provides at least an important first step in guaranteeing equal access to these central goods, rather than allocating them according to ability to pay. This protects citizens least able to pay from being placed in the potentially coercive position of having to trade-off health and safety for wages or other financial goods. Third, it avoids the mistake of assuming that all human values can be measured and quantified in economic terms and the immense practical difficulties that face any attempt to calculate the costs of such things as global warming, air pollution, or groundwater and aquifer contamination. Fourth, it allows a means for preventing harms from occurring in the first place, rather than relying on market failures to provide information about harms after the fact, often too late to reverse what could have been avoidable harms (Kaswan 2011).

Along with the Clean Air Act and the Clean Water Act, the 1970s also witnessed the creation of another far-reaching environmental law, the Endangered Species Act of 1973. At first glance, the Endangered Species Act might also appear to be a response to market failures. Many species, fisheries most dramatically, suffered from the problem of the commons (Ostrom 1990). Overfishing and exploitation by commercial fishing pushed numerous species to the brink of extinction and regulation was needed to avoid this market failure. But the Endangered Species Act was much broader than a resource conservation action similar to Pinchot's management of forests. It offered protection of *all* endangered species, whether they were commercially harvested or not. Like the Clean Air and Clean Water acts, this regulation created a principled limitation on markets and business activity, establishing side constraints on business by exempting some goods from economic trade-offs. In this case, living species were the goods recognized as non-fungible, and having an inherent value.

Philosophically, there are two ethical foundations for offering an in-principle protection for species. First, one could argue that some species have a moral standing that deserves to be protected by moral rights and that, as a result, these species ought to be treated as ends in themselves. This would represent a revolutionary change from the old model in which natural objects were valued merely as means to human ends. This approach would hold that businesses have a direct ethical responsibility not to violate rights, be they human or animal. Similar to human rights, animal rights create a range of strict ethical duties on business.

This approach is perhaps best seen in cases involving the ethical treatment of animals in the food industry and in consumer products and pharmaceutical research. A plausible case has been made that business has a strong ethical duty not to inflict undue pain and suffering on animals, even in those cases that would prove to be more efficient and profitable (Singer 1975). While disputes continue, both consumer demand and political consensus seems to have moved business away from the worst abuses of factory farming of animals and the use of animals in research.

A second approach to protecting animals would avoid debates about animal rights and remain anthropocentric in its environmental values. This approach would argue that the ethical status of animals derives not from their standing as moral beings, but from other intrinsic values that humans attribute to them. Thus one might argue that all living beings have an inherent value established by religious, spiritual, aesthetic, or symbolic considerations and that this value overrides their value as a commodity (Sagoff 2008).

The challenges to the approach that attributes rights to species is that in its most plausible version only some species, those with certain minimal cognitive capacities or those with developed central nervous systems are the most commonly defended examples, would qualify as rights-holders (Regan 2004). A rights-based approach to environmental regulation faces more significant challenges when the environmental goods being protected are not individual animals but aggregates like species, or ecological wholes such as wetlands, wilderness areas, forests, or watersheds. Attributing rights to all species or to these natural objects probably stretches the concept of ethical rights beyond recognition. It is more reasonable to defend such natural goods on other, non-moral, value grounds. However, attributing non-moral religious, spiritual, aesthetic or symbolic values to natural objects risks making that judgment appear to be subjective and relativistic. If environmental values are subjective, then it would seem to follow that they are personal preferences that do not deserve special status when competing against other subjective consumer preferences. This conclusion would suggest that leaving such policies to the workings of the market would remain a favored policy prescription.

In practice, this controversy seems to have been resolved in the political sphere, at least for a number of widely-held preservationist environmental values. There is a broad consensus that many distinctive natural areas deserve protection against the normal trade-offs that occur in economic markets. They are valued as ends in themselves, not as mere instruments for overall social utility. In the United States, for example, one can think of national parks such as Yosemite, Yellowstone, the Grand Canyon, or wilderness areas such as the Everglades (Florida) or Boundary Waters (Minnesota) as examples of natural environmental goods that society has a duty to protect, even if no cost benefit analysis can establish that benefits outweigh the costs. Such goods are preserved for their beauty, for what they symbolize, for their historical significance, for the inspiration that they create rather than for their usefulness or for the income they can generate.

As the discussion so far suggests, by the late twentieth century a wide range of environmental values were making a claim on both regulatory law and on the social responsibility of business. Conservationist values, similar to those advocated by Gifford Pinchot at the turn of the last century, hold business responsible for the long-term, efficient, non-exploitive and non-wasteful use of natural resources. Values such as equality, equal opportunity in the pursuit of happiness, and stewardship underlie much of this approach. Human rights to such goods as a livable environment and clean water and air offer a different ethical foundation for other environmental responsibilities. The ethical status of animals can create other responsibilities, especially in the area of agriculture and consumer products. Preservationist environmental values, in which some natural objects should be preserved from commercialization, add yet other responsibilities to business.

To some, this wide range of environmental responsibilities, and the values that underlie them, might appear as little more than an ad hoc inventory of demands being placed on business (Hoffman 2005). In recent decades, therefore, the idea of environmental sustainability has been promoted as offering a more comprehensive and coherent theory of business's environmental responsibility (Hawken 1993).

The ethics and environmentalism of sustainable development

Current interest in sustainability can be traced to "Our Common Future," the 1987 report of the United Nations World Commission on Environment and Development (the "Brundtland Report"). Brundtland defined sustainable development as that which "meets the needs of the present without compromising the ability of future generations to meet their own needs" (World Commission on Environment and Development 1987).

The Brundtland Report was based on two critical observations about the dominant model of economic development, a model that interprets development merely in terms of aggregate economic, or GDP, growth. First, the Brundtland Commission argued that an economic model that equated development with undifferentiated economic growth was, in fact, failing to meet the real needs of hundreds of millions of people in the developing world. Second, the Commission cited growing evidence that by disregarding the capacity of the natural environment to produce resources and absorb wastes, the prevailing model of economic development was jeopardizing future generations' abilities to meet their own needs. The alternative is an economic model that gives priority to human needs while respecting the biophysical limits of the earth's biosphere and conserving natural resources for long-term sustainable use.

The Brundtland Report offered recommendations for macroeconomic policy at the global level, but it was intended also to have implications for every level of analysis, from individual decisions to organizational behavior as well as to global economic policy. That goal has more than been fulfilled. Today, we can regularly find the adjective "sustainable" used to modify every business division, including management, marketing, accounting, operations, and strategy. One management textbook cites over 500 different activities modified by the word "sustainable" (Young and Dhanda 2012: 2). Sustainability reporting among large firms is commonplace, supplementing if not replacing the traditional annual report. For example, one Ernst & Young report claims that 95 percent of the 250 largest global corporations issue annual sustainability reports (Ernst & Young 2013). New business segments have been created in sustainability consulting, ranking, investing, and measurement. *Forbes* magazine publishes an annual ranking of the top 100 sustainable firms, the "Global100." The Global Reporting Initiative (GRI) has created a sustainability measurement and assessment tool that is widely used by business and non-governmental organizations (NGOs) throughout the world. The "triple bottom line" (TBL), another well-known benchmarking framework, is also widely used by business and in sustainability consulting.

The Brundtland Commission defended its recommendations by appeal to values with deep roots in traditional economic thinking. In terms that echoed Gifford Pinchot, the Brundtland diagnosis was that too much economic activity treats the natural environment as if its productive capacity were practically infinite. Mounting evidence suggests that we have been spending down our environmental capital at such a rate that much of it may soon be incapable of continuing to generate the resources required to meet human needs. The natural environment provides materials and services that are essential for economic activity, and a rational economic policy should avoid expending those resources at rates faster than which they can be replenished or than which substitutes can be found. Sustainable development is a strategy aimed at creating an economic system that can meet needs without so disrupting and exploiting natural ecosystems that they are no longer sufficiently productive.

Thus, a portion of the Brundtland report can be understood as an extension of early twentieth century conservationist environmentalism and can therefore be seen as an extension of economic and environmental models previously described. Where conservationists such as Pinchot focused on forestry and other specific natural resources, the Brundtland Report broadened the concern to such factors as cropland fertility, aquifer reserves, ocean fisheries, as well as the capacity of the atmosphere and oceans to absorb pollutions and wastes such as carbon dioxide.

All economic activity exists within, and depends upon, the earth's biosphere. The guiding principle is that resources cannot be used, nor wastes created, at rates exceeding the biosphere's capacity to replace resources or absorb wastes (Daly and Farfley 2010). As a result, a prudent business should operate in ways that do not threaten the capacity of the natural environment to produce resources, or absorb wastes, at rates sufficient to sustain human well-being. This insight provides a foundation for making a business case for adopting the sustainable development agenda. On a time horizon broader than that found in quarterly earnings reports, a prudent business ought to take steps to operate in an environmentally responsible manner.

But long-term self-interest is not the only value that underlies the Brundtland report. The Brundtland vision of sustainable development was also advocated as a matter of economic justice. Unlike the utilitarian account of justice implicit in the model of economic development aiming for aggregate GDP growth, Brundtland's model of economic development advocates a needs-based version of inter-generational justice. According to this perspective, society has an ethical responsibility not simply to grow the economy, but to prioritize meeting human needs in economic activity. This needs-based approach to economic justice, with roots in Plato, the Christian gospels, and Karl Marx, rejects economic growth as an ethically sufficient measure of economic development. Meeting human needs takes priority over meeting those expressed preferences found in market demand and, according to Brundtland, the needs of future humans have an ethical status equal to the needs of present generations.

Embedded in the Brundtland Report was a "carrot and stick" approach to business. On the one hand, Brundtland provided a vision of the future that innovative and entrepreneurial business could use to create a long-term business strategy. Brundtland was effectively providing business with a roadmap for long-term sustainable success. On the other hand, Brundtland also called on global policy makers, ranging from institutions such as the United Nations, World Bank and International Monetary Fund to national governments, to use their legal, policy, and regulatory resources to change the model of global economic development from one focused on GDP growth to one focused on meeting human needs. Implicit in this call was the threat of greater regulation and adverse public policy aimed at industries and companies that were unable, or unwilling, to transform themselves into environmentally sustainable companies.

Business responsibilities within sustainable development

A significant environmental agenda for business is encouraged by the Brundtland model and a number of business strategies have been developed to describe the many possibilities open for businesses within a sustainable economy (Hawken 1999; McDonough 1998). Some of these strategies involve familiar conservationist and efficiency goals, but others involve innovative and entrepreneurial approaches.

The fundamental tenet of sustainable development is that the economy exists as a subsystem of the biosphere and, as a result, there are biophysical factors governing the rates at which resources can be provided to the economy and wastes can be absorbed back into the biosphere. In general terms, the conservationist foundation of sustainability creates direct duties regarding resource use and responsibilities for wastes and by-products created. Within the sustainability model, the responsibilities of business can be framed in these terms.

The normative principle for sustainable resource use is to reduce the amount of resources used and wastes produced. As a general rule of thumb, reducing resource use and waste creation and becoming more efficient in both materials and energy use will lead to reduced costs for business. To the degree that markets are forced to internalize environmental externalities and capture the true costs of energy and resources, a strong business and financial case can be made for the sustainable development agenda. As environmental resources become more scarce their costs should rise, making a reduction in resource use economically, as well as environmentally, more efficient.

To the degree that sustainable resource use is efficient and a business case can be made for adopting sustainable practices, market mechanisms and economic incentives discussed previously can be an effective public policy tool for moving towards a sustainable future. For example, government regulation aimed at internalizing environmental externalities or eliminating subsidies are obvious steps. Thus, a carbon tax that internalizes the externalities associated with carbon emissions might be one strategy that business might anticipate. Eliminating subsidies that support the fossil fuel or nuclear power industry, or providing comparable incentives or subsidies for alternative energy sources, would be other regulatory strategies using market incentives to achieve more efficient energy use. Other appropriate regulatory steps might include establishing standards to prevent harms and to thwart free riders or implementing cap and trade policies that use market forces to help achieve pollution reduction targets. Requiring licenses to use or harvest resources is another policy means for maintaining a sustainable supply of resources at prices that mirror the market.

In general terms, under the sustainable development model three principles are commonly referenced as appropriate guides to business practice (Hawken 1999; McDonough 1998). Resource productivity, or what is sometimes called eco-efficiency, is the principle that business should seek to produce goods and services with ever more efficient uses of environmental resources. If energy is the primary natural resource used by every business, then a sustainable energy policy is the area in which business is likely to reap the most benefits from eco-efficient practices.

Biomimicry is a second principle that should guide sustainable business practice. Biomimicry holds that the life-cycle of economic goods should mimic the biological life-cycle of natural objects, a cycle that is a closed system of production from natural objects and full re-absorption back into the biosphere for continued safe and productive use. Ecological systems are sustainable when they remain in equilibrium by fully recycling and reabsorbing the products of biological processes. In the words of sustainable business advocate and designer Bill McDonough, "waste equals food" (McDonough 1998: 88). Just as natural systems fully recycle such natural elements as carbon, nitrogen, and water through the biological processes of plant growth, decay, and photosynthesis, economic systems must also fully reincorporate the products back into the productive systems. At present, the climate parameters necessary for stable economic development, especially in the crucial areas of food and water production, are threatened by the increasing discharge of carbon dioxide into the atmosphere. Thus, in the most obvious case, reducing and eliminating the production of carbon dioxide and other greenhouse gases should be a primary obligation for sustainable business.

A related area of responsibility under the biomimicry principle concerns life-cycle responsibility for all products. Under the sustainable development agenda, a strong case could be made that business should be liable for any harm caused to the productive capacity of the biosphere by anything that they first brought into the commercial stream. The ideal is to design products that can be reused and fully recycled back into the production process once their economic lives end. In cases where this is not possible, products ought to be designed in ways that what remains after their productive life can be fully and quickly absorbed back into the biosphere.

Finally, a principle of dematerialization directs businesses to reduce their use of physical resources. Dematerialization re-conceptualizes consumer demand as a demand for services rather than material goods, and an entrepreneurial business model shifts towards a service model. Thus, for example, rather than selling cars, air conditioners, or cell phones, a sustainable business leases cars, cooling and telecommunication services. The products themselves remain as capital owned by the business rather than being sent out into the commercial stream never to be considered again. This creates an incentive to create longer-lasting products that can be reconditioned and reused, rather than products with built-in obsolescence.

Business responsibilities within sustainable development: meeting needs

A more problematic aspect of the Brundtland model of sustainable development is the needs-based account of economic justice. At first glance it is unclear that business should be seen as having responsibilities in this regard. Consumer preferences rather than human needs are what get expressed in the market place and a business that ignores consumer demand to pursue human needs risks its own financial demise. Expecting business to have a responsibility to meet needs creates a dilemma. On one hand, if needs do not get expressed by individuals in the market, then a business seeking to meet needs would face the real possibility of financial ruin by producing goods and services that people do not want. On the other hand, if we trust individuals to be the best judges of their own needs, then business will serve needs by fulfilling its role by meeting consumer demand.

But framing the situation in this way is too simplistic. Incorporating a wide range of human needs into an account of business's social responsibility may well ask too much of business, at least within a political and economic system that values individual liberty. Yet, a plausible and defensible distinction can be made between needs and mere consumer preferences. Whether one relies on a thin theory of primary goods as defended by John Rawls, or a thicker theory as found in a capabilities approach defended by Martha Nussbaum and Amartya Sen, a case can be made that human dignity and well-being requires certain basic goods (Rawls 1971; Nussbaum 2000; Sen 1995). Indeed, any but the most radical *laissez faire* theories of economic justice will make an ethical distinction between market preferences and human goods. In the present case, the sustainable development model might provide guidance for a limited account of human needs, an account that would provide ethical directions for business's environmental responsibilities.

I suggest that the human needs most threatened by environmental disruption, and therefore the human needs most reasonably incorporated into business's responsibilities under the sustainable development agenda, are the human needs for adequate and healthy food, water, air, and energy. Accordingly, we have reason to think that businesses operating in these areas have particular responsibilities under the model of sustainable development.

Let us reflect on human needs and consumer demand in the food industry as an example. Starting in Book II of Plato's *Republic*, philosophers have recognized that adequate food is a paradigmatic example of a basic human need. An economic or political system failing to provide adequate food would be, by any measure, a failed economic or political system. Of course, this need for food gets expressed by an extensive range of marketplace preferences, some less healthy than others. What responsibilities does a business have for creating, selling, and marketing food?

Consider that a wide variety of artificial food colorings, artificial sweeteners, food additives, and artificial preservatives have been linked to human health problems. Food with high fat, high salt, and high sugar content are also linked to health problems. Yet, there is a market demand for all such foods. We can make a plausible prima facie case that a responsibility to meet human needs would preclude creating, selling, and marketing products linked to health problems, even if a market for unhealthy food exists. For example, in 2015 General Mills announced that it would be phasing out the use of synthetic artificial dyes and flavors in its breakfast cereals and replacing them with natural colors and flavors (Hamblin 2015). Assuming a market demand for colorful cereal exists, General Mills still had the discretion to choose to meet that demand in a way that met needs by reducing health risks posed by artificial colors and flavors.

Under the sustainable development model, business can be said to have responsibilities not only to conserve natural resources and reduce wastes, but also to fashion products that help people meet their needs, or, at a minimum, do not thwart meeting needs. Arguing that business simply passively responds to the consumer demands expressed in the market adopts too narrow an understanding of the realities of business management. Such a view underestimates the fluidity and diversity of consumer demand, the range of discretion that business has in meeting that demand, and under-estimates the influence that business has in shaping, if not creating, consumer demand.

Before moving on, we should recognize that there can be situations that involve tensions among the sustainable development goals themselves. In some cases serving the goal of meeting human needs operates in tension with conserving environmental productivity. Issues ranging from industrial food production to the use of coal and other fossil fuels for energy production seem to serve the goal of meeting human needs while undermining the earth's productive capacity. I suggest that these might be understood as transitional technologies. In an ethically and environmentally best case, humans would abandon such environmentally disruptive practices in favor of more environmentally benign techniques for meeting human needs. Organic farming, localized community agriculture, and solar power would be part of a long-term sustainable future. But shifting to these models too quickly, especially in the face of increasing global population, would threaten real harm to the needs of hundreds of millions of people. As the global economy transitions to a more sustainable future, responsible businesses should, and entrepreneurial businesses will, begin the transition to that future. In the meantime, a case can be made for continuing the less than optimal practice.

What sustainability is not

While sustainable development as envisioned by the Brundtland Commission entails a wide range of environmental responsibilities, it does not cover every environmental value that might create responsibilities for business. Unfortunately, the rush towards sustainability as a comprehensive environmental business philosophy often confuses this fact by attempting to incorporate every conceivable environmental good under the guise of sustainability. It will be helpful to clarify some of the confusion regarding the environmental implications of the concept of sustainability.

First, significant misunderstanding occurs whenever the modifier "sustainable" is divorced from the noun "development," and gets turned into a generic goal of "sustainability" (Barkemeyer 2014; DesJardins 2016). As a stand-alone concept, the word "sustainable" lacks any normative meaning. To be sustainable simply means having the capacity to endure, and whether this is a good thing or not depends wholly on what it is that endures. It would be an ethically good thing if the effort to eradicate childhood cancer is sustained; it would be an ethically bad thing if a terrorist organization is sustainable.

As a result, we should be alert to the possibility that the imperative for business to become "sustainable" might be little more than a call for business to continue doing what it is doing and to manage risks to profits posed by environmental factors. This error is commonly found when businesses themselves speak of sustainability, especially when speaking to their shareholders in annual reports. It is also especially popular among consulting groups who offer sustainability consulting and advisory services.

But risk management is not equivalent to sustainable development in the normative and environmental sense promoted by Brundtland. Sustainable development requires significant change in the *status quo* by establishing positive environmental responsibilities for business. Risk management simply advises business to mitigate the risks posed by environmental considerations. However, a business can manage risks in many ways, including the risks posed by operating in a more environmentally responsible manner. Given that even an environmentally dirty business can be sustainable if operating within a broadly sustainable economy, one risk-management strategy would be to become a free rider in an otherwise environmentally clean system. Another strategy is to engage the political system to counter the requirements of sustainable development.

Risk management assumes the survival of a business as a given and seeks strategies for minimizing the risks posed by environmental degradation to that survival. In contrast, the business case for sustainable development accepts the environmental ends that were outlined by Brundtland, and seeks to make a financial case to strive for that end. But the survival of any particular business or industry should not be a given under the sustainable development agenda.

A second misused notion of "sustainability" occurs when a much more extensive range of social and environmental responsibilities than was imagined by Brundtland is subsumed under the concept of sustainable business. For example, the United Nations promotes sustainability as a broad call for "social development," which includes an extensive range of human, labor, social, and cultural rights. The Global Reporting Initiative (GRI), which works with the United Nations and many business organizations to create sustainability benchmarks, offers another example of how far the concept of sustainability has grown. The GRI describes its work as helping "businesses, governments and other organizations understand and communicate the impact of business on critical sustainability issues such as climate change, human rights, corruption and many others" (Global Reporting 2016). In addition to the UN's list of human and other rights, GRI advises business that sustainable business practices include responsibilities to local community engagement, labor rights, initiatives to counter corruption and anti-competitive behavior, and commitments to product safety, ethical marketing, and ethical sourcing (Global Reporting Index G4 2015).

In these and many other cases, sustainability has come to be used as a synonym for the much broader notion of corporate social responsibility. But the ethical foundation of sustainable development is very different from the ethics that underlies judgments of human rights, corruption, labor rights, cultural rights, community engagement, ethical marketing, and so on. Good ethical reasons can be given for respecting human rights, engaging in the local community, avoiding corruption, etc., but they are distinctively different from the reasons for pursuing a policy of environmental conservation. At a minimum, intellectual consistency requires that we distinguish the ethical case for sustainable development from the ethical case for a much wider claim for human, labor, and cultural rights.

More importantly for present purposes, significant confusions arise whenever the original concept of *sustainable development* gets replaced with the problematic concept of *environmental sustainability*. This is problematic because it transforms the narrow conservationist ethics of sustainable development into a wide agenda that includes every imaginable environmental cause. Examining what, exactly, is to be sustained by "environmental sustainability" demonstrates how overextended this concept is. What would it mean to sustain "the environment"? The earth and its natural environment itself will exist, will be "sustainable," regardless of anything human beings might do. As long as there is a planet Earth, there will be a natural environment that will be sustained, although it might not be an environment conducive to human flourishing. The general concept of environmental sustainability is ethically vacuous unless and until the aspects of that environment that are to be sustained are specified.

Brundtland's sustainable development agenda, of course, has an obvious answer to this. Environmental sustainability for Brundtland refers to sustaining the productive (and absorptive) capacity of nature so that the earth's environment can sustain human life. Sustaining human life is the entire point of the conservationist approach to environmentalism. Environmental objectives beyond this conservationist and anthropocentric goal would fall outside the ethical approach found in Brundtland and, therefore, like the broader ethical and cultural goals described previously, stand in need of an alternative ethical defense. Calling on business to take responsibility for such issues as preservation of wilderness and other natural objects, the ethical treatment of animals, protecting endangered species, and preserving biodiversity are beyond what is required by the sustainable development model. This fact is more than a mere academic distinction because, in practice, it can lead to different and even competing prescriptions for socially responsible businesses.

The tension between the conservationist goals of sustainable development and broader preservationist goals of some environmentalists can appear most dramatically in the area of food and agriculture. The "green revolution" of the late twentieth century was largely responsible for producing sufficient food resources to meet the needs of an exploding global population. This was a technology-driven revolution that relied on the heavy use of pesticides, fertilizers, fossil fuels, and genetics. By any measure, these food technologies were successful in meeting the human need for food in both the short- and long-term. But many people object to these technologies on environmental and ethical grounds, citing human health risks, the potential for abuse from powerful agribusiness corporations, and environmental preservation.

If technologies involved in synthetic pesticide use or genetically modified crops cause harm to human health then they would be incompatible with the conservationist ethics of sustainable development. Business has a duty to avoid causing harms to human health under any ethical framework, including the sustainable development agenda. Similarly, to the degree that large agribusinesses abuse their market power, the ethical foundation embedded in sustainable development would provide sufficient grounds for regulation.

But business responsibilities are less clear in cases where those technologies that do help food production threaten harms only to other environmental values. These debates play out in a number of areas, including GMO foods, the loss of local biodiversity caused by economic and development, and the conversion of natural areas to agriculture. Does business have a responsibility to forego activities that serve the sustainable development agenda if the means involved impose costs on certain aspects of the natural environment?

A well-known example concerns the case of genetically modified "golden rice." In 2009 the World Health Organization (WHO) estimated that as 190 million children were affected by vitamin A deficiency (VAD), a condition that can lead to blindness and death (WHO 2009). Golden rice is genetically modified in a way that synthesizes beta-carotene, making it a significant source of vitamin A. Because rice is an inexpensive, readily available, and familiar food in many of the regions where VAD is prevalent, golden rice would seem an ideal solution to meet the needs of some of the world's poorest and malnourished people. Yet because it is a GMO food, opposition among many environmentalists has essentially put an end to golden rice production in many of the world's poorest regions. Greenpeace, for example, called golden rice "environmentally irresponsible" (Greenpeace 2013). What responsibilities would a company like Syngenta, one of the developers of golden rice, have regarding this genetically modified food source?

In cases such as these it is unclear what a socially and environmentally responsible business ought to do. The point is that arguments must be made and decisions must be defended. Little is gained, and clarity at least is lost, by appeals to a generic concept of sustainability or environmentalism. If only for the sake of intellectual and ethical integrity, we should be clear to distinguish the goals and values embedded in the sustainable development movement from those of a wider environmentalism.

As in other cases, this analysis must be done on a case-by-case basis, with the ultimate resolution depending on the facts of each case. Again, if the values underlying environmental objections to such technologies as golden rice or synthetic pesticides rests with potential harms to humans or abuse of market power by business, then the conflict with sustainable development is only apparent rather than real. But if the harm is to non-human nature and the environmental values with preserving nature for its own sake, then real conflicts are possible.

In these situations I would argue that a strong prima facie case can be made that the needs of actual human beings trump other environmental values that rest on claims regarding the interests of nonhuman life or the intrinsic value of nature itself. The actual harms done to humans caused by malnutrition and vitamin A deficiency should have a moral priority over harms that would be caused by the potential loss of native rice species. I would suggest that even within the Brundtland paradigm, the needs of actual people override the needs of future people, especially if the equal opportunity of those future people to satisfy their own needs is protected.

But many other environmental issues are simply independent of that agenda. For example, some cases involving the preservation of biodiversity and natural areas lie outside the responsibilities that follow from a commitment to sustainable development. In simple if somewhat stark terms, one can easily imagine an economically and environmentally sustainable society with fewer plant and animal species and fewer hectares of preserved wild areas. This is not to say that there are no good reasons to preserve biodiversity and natural areas. The question is whether the reasons for preserving biodiversity or a particular natural area rise to the level that they create an ethical responsibility for business. There is, of course, an avenue open for those who wish to protect and preserve biodiversity and undeveloped natural areas. As was the case with the Clean Air, Clean Water, and Endangered Species Acts, legal avenues provide one option to exempt environmental goods from economic trade-offs.

Consider the case of a purported business responsibility to preserve a rainforest or an endangered species. It would be difficult to imagine making an in-principle case that in all circumstances businesses have a positive duty to preserve natural areas, or even a negative duty to refrain from any action that disrupts a rainforest or that threatens the survival of a species. In the case of a rainforest, surely the answer in such a case would depend on various factors—the harms caused by the disruption, the size of the area disrupted, the amount of forest left undisturbed, the uses to which the land will be put, the type of business enterprise causing the disruption, and the connection that the business has to the activities disrupting the forest. In the case of species preservation, the case would depend on which species (the white rhinoceros or the tuberculosis bacteria?), the role it plays in the wider ecosystem (honey bees are different from starlings), and the actions causing the threat (overuse of lawn pesticides or damming a river to provide water for agriculture?) and whether the business is engaged in any activities that are responsible for the species loss.

The challenge, of course, is to determine if there is any decision procedure or methodology for analyzing and resolving future debates between the conservationist program of sustainable development and other preservationist environmental objectives. How and when does a business determine its environmental responsibilities in cases of opposing environmental values? It is not clear that the sustainable development paradigm provides a single method or framework for determining the full range of business responsibility toward the natural environment.

Concluding remarks

There is a tendency, in ethics as in so many other areas of thought, to seek clarity in the form of a single unified theory or framework (Stone 1987; Light and Katz 1996). We are inclined to think that there should be *a* correct theory of ethics, of CSR, of environmentalism. This chapter suggests that there are a variety of ethical approaches, each bringing important insights and values, which are relevant to the question of businesses' environmental responsibilities. Perhaps the story of the development of US environmental policy accurately reflects an underlying philosophical story but it seems more likely that the perspective incorporates more voices than some would have us believe.

Competitive economic markets can be a powerful and efficient tool for some public policy decisions. All things being equal, markets can provide very effective and equitable means for allocating resources among competing demands. But, of course, all things are not always equal. Some values—certainly human rights, aesthetic, symbolic, spiritual, cultural values, perhaps some animal rights—are not simply "competing demands" clamoring for satisfaction. Rightfully, such goods deserve special exemption from the calculating trade-offs that markets can so efficiently accomplish. The challenge, both politically and philosophically, lies in making a persuasive case for such exemptions. Perhaps the story reveals that the best we can hope for comes from the practical wisdom that emerges from ethical individuals, well-regulated markets, sound public policy, a well-functioning democracy, and humane organizations.

The movement towards sustainable development offers some hope for a future form of business that is, at least, environmentally benign if not strong. Sustainable development acknowledges the need for a robust economic system to keep pace with the needs of a growing human population. It contains reasonable environmental and social justice constraints on economic development. It has gained significant, although far from universal, traction among both the business and environmental communities. Work done under the banner of sustainable development has already provided many models for innovative and entrepreneurial business. Properly focused, the sustainable development framework can offer an ethically, environmentally, and economically substantive vision of the future.

Essential readings

As environmental policy and regulation developed in the 1970s and 1980s, a corresponding scholarly literature established the ethical framework for debates concerning businesses' environmental responsibilities. Important texts from these years established the essential parameters for the ethical and policy debates that persist to this day and provide cogent analyses well worth continued study. Contributions to the defense of the free market approach against the regulatory approach include Richard Stroup and John Baden, *Natural Resources: Bureaucratic Myths and Environmental Management* (1983), William Baxter, *People, Penguins, and Plastic Trees* (1974), and Randal O'Toole, *Reforming the Forest Service* (1988), as well as Julian Simon's later work, *The Ultimate Resource* (1998). Mark Sagoff's *Economy of the Earth* (2008, originally published 1988) remains, in my opinion, the single best philosophical critique of the market-based approach to environmental issues. Sagoff's more recent work, *Price, Principle and the Environment* (2004), expands and updates some of the arguments referenced in this chapter. Philosophically thoughtful and rigorous treatments of the non-economic value of the natural environment include Holmes Rolston's *Conserving Natural Value* (1994); Roderick Nash, *The Rights of Nature* (1989), and Eugene Hargrove, *Foundations of Environmental Ethics* (1989). Herman Daly's *Beyond Growth: The Economics of Sustainable Development* (1996) provides a readable introduction to ecological economics, the economic model that underlies sustainable development. David Schmidtz and Elizabeth Willott's *Environmental Ethics: What Really Matters, What Really Works* (2012) provides a comprehensive collection of classic and contemporary essays on environmental ethics and policy.

For further reading in this volume on sustainability as an emerging topic of current business ethics, see Chapter 1, The history of business ethics. On the underlying assumptions that animate debates on the role and value of markets and of regulation, see Chapter 21, Regulation, rent seeking, and business ethics. On the relation of economic theory to the moral assumptions of business ethics, see Chapter 17, The contribution of economics to business ethics. For a consideration of recent work of Chinese scholars on our relations to the environment, see Chapter 35, Business ethics in China.

References

Arnold, D. and K. Bustos (2005). "Business Ethics and Global Climate Change," *Business and Professional Ethics Journal* 24:1&2, 103–130.
Barkemeyer, R.H. (2014). "What Happened to the 'Development' in Sustainable Development? Business Guidelines Two Decades After Brundtland," *Sustainable Development* 22, 15–32.
Baxter, W. (1974). *People, Penguins, and Plastic Trees*. New York, NY: Columbia University Press.
Daly, H. (1996). *Beyond Growth: The Economics of Sustainable Development*. Boston, MA: Beacon Press.
Daly, H. and J. Farfley (2010). *Ecological Economics* 2nd edition. Washington, DC: Island Press.
DesJardins, J.R. (2016). "Is it Time to Jump off the Sustainability Bandwagon?" *Business Ethics Quarterly* 26:1, 117–135.
Ernst & Young (2013). *Sustainabilty Reporting: The Time is Now*. New York, NY: Ernst & Young.
Global Reporting (2016). "About GRI." Available at: www.globalreporting.org/information/about-gri/Pages/default.aspx [accessed 02 February 2016].
Global Reporting Index G4 (2015). Global Reporting Index G4: *Sustainability Reporting Guidelines 2015*. Available at: www.globalreporting.org/resourcelibrary/GRIG4-Part1-Reporting-Principles-and-Standard-Disclosures.pdf, p. 3. [Accessed 19 January 2016].
Greenpeace (2013). *Golden Illusion: The Broken Promise of "Golden" Rice*. Amsterdam: Greenpeace International.
Hamblin, J. (2015). "If Our Bodies Could Talk," *The Atlantic* (Digital), June 23. Available at: www.theatlantic.com/health/archive/2015/06/general-mills-to-phase-out-artificial-cereal-dyes/396536/.
Hargrove, E. (1989). *Foundations of Environmental Ethics*. New York, NY: Prentice Hall.
Hawken, P. A. (1993). *Ecology of Commerce: A Declaration of Sustainability*. New York, NY: Harper Collins.
Hawken, P.A. (1999). *Natural Capitalism*. Boston, MA: Little Brown.
Hoffman, A. (2005). "Business Decisions and the Environment: Significance, Challenges, and Momentum of an Emerging Research Field," in G. Brewer and P. Stern (eds), *Decision Making for the Environment*. Washington, DC: National Academies Press, 200–229.
Kaswan, A. (2011). "Reconciling Justice and Efficiency: Integrating Environmental Justice into Domestic Cap and Trade Programs," in D. Arnold (ed.), *The Ethics of Global Climate Change*. New York, NY: Cambridge University Press, 232–254.
Kelman, S. (1981). "Cost Benefit Analysis: An Ethical Critique," *Regulation: American Enterprise Institue Journal on Government and Society* (January/February), 33–40.
Light, A. and E. Katz (1996). *Environmental Pragmatism*. New York, NY: Routledge.
McDonough, W.M. (1998). "The Next Industrial Revolution," *The Atlantic* (October), 82–92.
Nash, R. (1989). *The Rights of Nature*. Madison, WI: University of Wisconsin Press.
Nussbaum, M. (2000). *Women and Human Development: The Capabilities Approach*. Cambridge: Cambridge University Press.
Ostrom, E. (1990). *Governing the Commons: The Evolution of Institutions for Collective Action*. Cambridge: Cambridge University Press.
O'Toole, R. (1988). *Reforming the Forest Service*. Washington, DC: Island Press.
Pinchot, G. (1914). *Training of a Forester*. Philadelphia, PA: Lippincott.
Rawls, J. (1971). *A Theory of Justice*. Cambridge, MA: Harvard University Press.
Regan, T. (2004). *The Case for Animal Rights* 2nd edition. Oakland, CA: University of California Press.
Rolston, H. (1994). *Conserving Natural Value*. New York, NY: Columbia University Press.
Sagoff, M. (2004). *Price, Principle and the Environment*. Cambridge: Cambridge University Press.
Sagoff, M. (2008). *The Economy of the Earth* 2nd edition. New York, NY: Cambridge University Press.
Schmidtz, D. (2012a). "A Place for Cost-Benefit Analysis," in D. Schmidtz (ed.), *Environmental Ethics: What Really Matters, What Really Works*. New York, NY: Oxford University Press, 387–400.
Schmidtz, D. (2012b). "The Institution of Property," in D. Schmidtz and E. Willott (eds), *Environmental Ethics: What Really Matters, What Really Works*. New York, NY: Oxford University Press, 406–419.

Schmidtz, D. and E. Willott (eds) (2012). *Environmental Ethics: What Really Matters, What Really Works.* New York, NY: Oxford University Press.

Sen, A. (1995). *Inequality Reexamined.* Oxford: Oxford University Press.

Shahar, D. (2012). "Free Market Environmentalism pace Environmentalism," in D. Schmidtz and E. Willott (eds), *Environmental Ethics: What Really Matters, What Really Works.* New York, NY: Oxford University Press, 438–445.

Simon, J. (1998). *The Ultimate Resource* 2nd edition. Princeton, NJ: Princeton University Press.

Singer, P. (1975). *Animal Liberation.* New York, NY: Harper Collins.

Stone, C. (1987). *Earth and Other Ethics: The Case for Moral Pluralism.* New York, NY: Harper and Row.

Stroup, R. and J. Baden (1983). *Natural Resources: Bureaucratic Myths and Environmental Management.* San Francisco, CA: Pacific Insitute for Public Policy Research.

World Commission on Environment and Development (1987). *Our Common Future.* Oxford: Oxford University Press.

World Health Organization (WHO) (2009). "Global Prevalence of Vitamin A Deficiency in Populations At Risk 1995–2005," *WHO Global Database on Vitamin A Deficiency.* Geneva, World Health Organization.

Young, S. and K. Dhanda (2012). *Sustainability: Essentials for Business.* Thousand Oaks, CA: Sage.

# 23

The economic crisis
Causes and considerations

Randall G. Holcombe

The economic downturn that began in 2008 had its origins in the housing market. A substantial run-up in housing prices early in the 2000s followed by a collapse in housing prices as the economy slid into a recession led to defaults on mortgages, which in turn led to a collapse in the value of mortgage-backed securities that put many financial institutions, and perhaps the financial system more generally, in peril. Factors that led to problems in the housing market can be traced back decades, to many government policies that affected how financial institutions qualified buyers for mortgages and how the market for mortgages operated. The crisis was global in scope, but began with the housing market in the United States, and at least some of the international problems arose because foreign investors were holding US mortgage-backed securities. The causes of the economic crisis that will be discussed in this chapter focus on US housing policies, even while recognizing the international scope of the crisis.

The factors that led to the crisis will be discussed within an ethical context. Doing so requires, first, a link that connects ethics with economic policy. Perhaps the most common link in the popular media has been to focus on the greed of those in the financial industry who made mortgage loans to unqualified buyers when the lenders knew, or should have known, the borrowers could not afford them, and on the investment banks that packaged these mortgages into securities that, as the crisis unfolded, were labeled as toxic. Making an ethical judgment on the behavior of those in the financial industry is not as clear-cut as it might first appear, as Boudewijn De Bruin (2015) notes, partly because those in the industry surely did not foresee the ultimate consequences of their activities due to the uncertainties that always underlie economic decisions. Another major factor is that the government's public policy decisions pushed mortgage lenders to make the very types of loans and to create the mortgage-backed securities that precipitated the financial collapse. Not only that, policymakers often praised the issuing of those mortgages that later proved to be toxic as a desirable policy outcome.

This chapter focuses heavily on the ethics of the government policies that led up to the financial crisis, rather than the ethics of those in the financial industry. John A. Allison (2013), who was the CEO of a major financial institution at the time the crisis hit, offers substantial criticism of those in his industry, but also finds fault with government policies that led those in the industry to make decisions that critics, in hindsight, viewed as ethically questionable.

Without passing judgment on those in the industry, this chapter looks at the ethical foundations of decades of housing policies that provided the incentives for those in the industry to engage in those activities that led up to the crisis.

Ethics and economics

The making of ethical judgments about economic policies requires some ethical criteria, and, broadly speaking, two types of criteria have been applied to judge economic activities. One type is procedural, judging economic activity and economic outcomes to be ethical if the process that produced the outcomes is ethical. The second applies some criteria to judge economic outcomes as either ethical or not. One type passes an ethical judgment on the procedure, the other an ethical judgment on the outcome. Consider some ways in which economic outcomes are judged as ethical. For one example, one might look at a Gini coefficient, which is a measure of income inequality, or the share of income going to the top 10 percent or the top 1 percent, to decide whether the distribution of income is fair. An excellent example is Thomas Piketty (2014) who looks at the distribution of income and wealth generated by a capitalist economy and judges it to be unfairly skewed to benefit those at the top. As a result, he calls for very progressive income and wealth taxes to rectify the inequity. Another example is Amartya Sen's (1985) capabilities approach to evaluate economic welfare. According to this approach, people should have sufficient resources to allow them to be full participants in a society, and Sen calls for income redistribution to produce this outcome. Yet another example is William J. Baumol (1986), who judges the fairness of economic outcomes based on whether some envy the economic situations of others. All these approaches illustrate how an ethical judgment may be rendered by invoking a standard or set of criteria by which to assess some outcome as ethical or not.

An alternative approach is to pass judgment on whether the procedure by which the outcome is generated is ethical. Fair outcomes are the result of fair procedures, taking this approach. John Rawls (1971) and James Buchanan (1975) both take a procedural approach to economic outcomes, arguing that if people agree to the procedure that produces the outcome then the outcome is fair.[1] This procedural approach to ethics goes back at least to John Locke (1690), whose ideas lay the foundation for Murray N. Rothbard's (1982) judgment that the only way people may ethically interact with one another is through voluntary agreement. Based on Rothbard's idea, market transactions are ethical because everyone who participates in them can, by that fact, be said to agree to the transactions, but government interference with markets is not, because government action is based on coercion. What constitutes a fair procedure is a separate issue, and the brief discussion in this paragraph shows that different scholars have different ideas. The key point is that a procedural approach to ethics concludes that an outcome is ethical if the procedure that produces it is ethical.[2]

Is a procedure determined to be ethical (or not) based on the outcome it produces, or is the outcome judged to be ethical (or not) based on the procedure that generates the outcome? Sometimes the ethical criteria behind a judgment are unclear. Joseph E. Stiglitz (2012), for example, is obviously disturbed by the outcome of inequality, as his title, *The Price of Inequality*, shows, but his analysis also points at government policies that favor the 1 percent over the 99 percent as the cause. He objects to the procedure, but it also appears that he would object to the outcome regardless of the procedure that generated it. While it is common to judge outcomes as unfair or unethical without analyzing the procedures that produced the outcomes, a number of writers who discuss the aftermath of the financial crisis clearly do point to unethical procedures, including David A. Stockman (2013) and John A. Allison (2013) on the political right, and Jacob S. Hacker and Paul Pierson (2010) and Martin Gilens (2012) on the political left. This chapter will consider these two broad ways of making ethical judgments in an analysis of the factors that led up to the 2008 crisis.

Public policy on mortgages and the 2008 crisis

Stan J. Liebowitz (2009) provides a very comprehensive analysis of the government policies that set the stage for problems in the mortgage market that led to the economic crisis. Essentially what happened is that, over a period of decades, underwriting standards for mortgages were increasingly weakened so that people who would not have qualified for mortgages previously were able to qualify and buy homes. This weakening of underwriting standards was the result of a series of policy decisions dating back to the 1930s, but which had increasingly greater impacts leading up to the meltdown in the housing market.

During the Great Depression the housing construction industry suffered a serious decline, partly because banks were reluctant to offer mortgages to people who, in poor economic conditions, might not be able to continue making their mortgage payments. In 1934 the federal government created the Federal Housing Administration (FHA) to guarantee mortgages against default. Banks could then make FHA mortgage loans without having to be concerned about the possibility of default. The FHA mortgages tended to be available for lower-income home buyers, and for less expensive homes, because the program had limitations on borrowers' incomes and the size of mortgages that it would insure.

In 1938 the federal government created the Federal National Mortgage Association, known as Fannie Mae, to buy FHA mortgages. Fannie Mae was converted into a privately-held corporation in 1968. In 1970 the federal government authorized Fannie Mae to purchase private mortgages in addition to FHA mortgages, and also established the Federal Home Loan Mortgage Corporation, known as Freddie Mac, with the same capabilities as Fannie Mae, to create a more competitive market. The federal government became increasingly involved in efforts to facilitate people's buying their own homes.

Fannie Mae created the first mortgage-backed security in 1981, which allowed investors to buy an investment whose income was generated by a large number of loans in the security. The idea was to spread the risk of default. While any one mortgage might default, leaving its holder without the income from the mortgage, in the aggregate few mortgages would default, so by holding a security backed by a large number of mortgages the risk of default was minimized. And, by lowering the risk of default, financial institutions would be more willing to hold mortgages in the form of mortgage-backed securities, further encouraging the issuance of mortgages.

The ethical motivation for the FHA, Fannie Mae, and Freddie Mac, was outcome-based. They would allow more people to become homeowners, and boost the residential construction industry. There was no thought that the former procedure for purchasing residential housing was unfair or unethical, nor was there any idea that the process under these new organizations would be fairer or more ethical. These policies fall closely in line with Sen's (1985) capabilities approach to ethics: more people would have the capability to participate in home ownership, which has often been associated with "the American dream." To the degree that these programs placed taxpayer dollars at risk, one might raise ethical questions on procedural grounds. Why should taxpayers be put in the position of assuming any risk of default so that individuals could become homeowners?

The next major development was the Community Reinvestment Act (CRA) that was passed in 1977. The CRA prohibited "red lining," the exclusion of certain areas within a bank's market region from its mortgage business. When the CRA was passed, it appeared that many banks were unwilling to offer mortgages to home buyers in certain areas; primarily low-income areas and areas with a sizeable minority population. After the passage of the CRA, banks began receiving a score measuring their CRA compliance, providing banks with an incentive to make sure their mortgage business did not give the impression of discrimination. Lending patterns might give the impression of discrimination if few loans were granted in areas with large minority populations, for example, even if those areas also had more low-income and poorly-qualified borrowers. The reporting requirements were expanded in 1991 so that banks' mortgage rejection rates by race were readily available, and, using this data, news organizations began reporting that mortgage rejections were higher for minorities than for whites.

Data on race-based mortgage rejection rates does not take into account that, for various historical reasons, minority homebuyers may be less credit-worthy than whites, but the Federal Reserve Bank of Boston published data in 1991 indicating that even after taking other factors into account, rejection rates were still higher for minority buyers.[3] While subsequent analysis of this study concluded that it might exaggerate the degree of discrimination, some economists, such as Munnell et al. (1996) found some evidence of race-based discrimination, while others, such as Day and Liebowitz (1998) concluded that after taking account of all of the characteristics of borrowers, lenders did not discriminate. Regardless, one result was that banks lowered their lending standards to enable more minority borrowing, by lowering downpayment requirements and relaxing standards used to measure creditworthiness.

Looking at the potential for discrimination from an ethical standpoint, one can see that the motivation has a procedural element, in that discrimination implies that the process is biased. However, in the Federal Reserve Bank of Boston data and follow-up studies, the way this bias was measured was to look at the outcome to see if minority borrowers appeared to suffer worse outcomes than others. The study did not identify any flaws in the procedures that banks used to qualify mortgage loans, but rather concluded that the procedure must be flawed because of the outcome it generated. Thus, the policy implication was that the procedure should be changed to produce the outcome that policy makers demonstrated that they wanted. After all, with banks being scored on their record of minority lending, banks would not want to give the appearance of discrimination. From an ethical standpoint the focus was on the outcome, not on the procedure. If the outcome appears biased, then the procedure must be changed to eliminate the biased outcome.

Shortly after the initial data came out, the Federal Reserve Bank of Boston (1992) issued a brochure, "Closing the Gap: A Guide to Equal Opportunity Lending," in which it notes,

> Failure to comply with the Equal Credit Opportunity Act or Regulation B can subject financial institutions to civil liability for actual and punitive damages in individual or class actions. Liability for punitive damages can be as much as $10,000 in individual actions and the lesser of $500,000 or 1 percent of the creditor's net worth in class actions.

There were clear incentives for banks to expand their lending to less credit-worthy customers, and that same brochure provided a substantial amount of advice on how to do so. The brochure says, "Special care should be taken to ensure that standards are appropriate to the economic culture of urban, lower-income, and nontraditional consumers." Clearly, the idea here is to modify procedures to effect a desired outcome.

Lenders have an obvious incentive to make loans only to borrowers who will be able to pay them back. This is one reason that, prior to the 1990s, it was almost mandatory that mortgage borrowers put 20 percent down on the purchase of a house. In the event of a foreclosure, this provided a cushion so that the bank could sell the house and recover its investment. Further, as long as housing prices are rising, the lender is increasingly safer in the mortgage, partly because in the event of a foreclosure the house will be worth more, but mostly because rather than default on the mortgage, the owner can sell the property at a profit to pay off the mortgage. The reader knows how this turned out. The collapse in housing prices in 2008 eliminated that cushion and created the "toxic" mortgage-backed securities that contributed so substantially to the financial crisis.

There is more to this story, however. As banks were increasingly encouraged to lower their lending standards for mortgages, Fannie Mae and Freddie Mac were increasingly entering the secondary market and buying mortgages. Thus, banks could sell their mortgages to Fannie or Freddie and did not have to be as careful to make sure home buyers could continue to repay their mortgages. If a bank had to hold its mortgages to maturity, it would want to be confident that the borrower would be able to continue to pay on the mortgage for decades into the future, but when banks had the opportunity to sell their mortgages within a few months after they were issued, the risk to the banks of making mortgages that might eventually go bad was much less.

Fannie and Freddie bundled the mortgages they purchased to create mortgage-backed securities. The idea was that with a large number of mortgages backing the security, while some would fail it would be a small number, so the payback on the securities would be more certain and entail less risk than for any individual mortgage. As long as housing prices kept rising, the risk on those securities was minimal. Selling those securities on the market enabled Fannie and Freddie raise money, and to issue more mortgages.

The rating agencies rated those securities as very safe based on their recent histories during a time when housing prices were rising. In hindsight it became apparent that the safety of those securities was overrated, and their values plummeted as the housing market collapsed and foreclosures piled up. With the market rapidly deteriorating in 2008, the mortgage-backed securities became difficult to value, to the point where few buyers were willing to buy them even as many sellers wanted to sell. As the market for them disappeared, they were labeled toxic assets and were the target of the Troubled Asset Relief Program (TARP) that was hastily approved by Congress in October 2008.

As we have underlined so far, public policy in the mortgage market was designed to produce the outcome of increasing home ownership by making mortgages more accessible, especially for minorities and low-income borrowers. The focus was on the outcome rather than the process. Theodore Day and Stan J. Liebowitz (1998) commented, a decade before the major crisis,

> After the warm fuzzy glow of 'flexible underwriting standards' has worn off, we may discover that they are nothing more than standards that led to bad loans. . . . It will be ironic and unfortunate if minority applicants wind up paying a very heavy price for a misguided policy based on badly mangled data.

Their premonition proved to be accurate as lending policy led many people to take on mortgages that ultimately they were unable to pay off.

Another irony in these events is that after the mortgage market meltdown, banks were accused of predatory lending—trying to entice homebuyers into taking on mortgages that the banks knew the borrowers would have trouble repaying. And banks may have actually been doing this, because that is what federal mortgage policy was pushing them to do. In order to get an outcome that policymakers viewed as more equitable, they were pushing lenders to engage in procedures that critics later labeled as unethical: "predatory lending."[4]

Was there some ethical problem with the process by which mortgages were being approved prior to the 1990s? There is no good evidence that any specific policies were discriminatory; the evidence critics cited was in the outcome—that low-income and minority applicants were rejected at higher rates than whites. Thus, flexible underwriting standards were introduced to make the mortgage market more accommodating to those groups, not because there was any evidence that the process was treating them unfairly but because there was evidence that they did not have outcomes comparable with white borrowers.

The role of the Fed in the crisis

The Federal Reserve Bank (Fed) played a big role in the housing bubble through its interest rate policies throughout the first decade of the 2000s. Interest rates tend to move together, and the rate the Fed targets directly is the federal funds rate, which is the rate banks charge to lend reserves to each other. During the 1990s the rate was generally around 5 percent, and in response to the economic downturn in the early 2000s the Fed lowered this rate to 1.75 percent in 2002, and eventually to 1 percent in 2004. The rate went up to about 5 percent in 2006–07, but when the economic crisis hit in 2008 the rate plunged to near zero, where the Fed has held it through 2016.

Housing markets appeared to be one bright spot during the recession that began in 2001, and the bubble in housing prices during the 2000s was largely a product of the low interest rates the Fed maintained. Housing prices more than doubled from 2000 to 2007 before the collapse in the housing market.[5] The interest rate on a 30-year fixed-rate mortgage fell from an average of more than 8 percent in 2000 to 5.8 percent in 2004, and to below 4 percent in 2013.[6] For potential home buyers whose cost of ownership includes a monthly mortgage payment, the decline in the mortgage rate substantially lowers the monthly payment, which increases the demand for housing and therefore the price of housing. The lower mortgage rates meant that the interest cost of buying a home was lower, but the lower interest cost was offset, and often more than offset, by an increased sales price.

Rising prices for real estate encouraged speculators into the market who would buy houses to flip them—sell them again shortly after they were purchased—at a profit. This would work as long as housing prices kept rising, and one factor that kept them rising was the speculative demand. Looking at past prices, potential buyers, including but not limited to speculators, believed they should buy now to get in before prices went up even more. When the bubble burst, speculators found themselves with mortgages they could not pay off by re-selling their houses, leading them to default. In addition, the bubble caused many people to buy more expensive homes than they could comfortably afford, feeling that housing was a good investment in a rising market, as Emmons et al. (2011) note. The housing collapse brought with it the severe recession in 2008, and the downturn put many people in a position where they could not afford to continue paying their mortgages. Had housing prices not collapsed, they could have sold their homes, paid off their mortgages, and made some profit, but with the housing downturn many people owed more on their mortgages than their homes were worth, so they defaulted on their mortgages and their homes went into foreclosure.

Had the Fed not maintained its low interest rate policy, mortgage rates would not have declined and so housing prices would not have risen, or, at least, would not have risen as much as they did. Indeed, there is a strong argument that all of the increase in housing prices was due to the Fed's low interest rate policy. Individuals correctly view the cost to them of buying a house with a mortgage as the monthly payment, so if the interest component of the monthly payment goes down, the same house will still cost the same to the borrower if the purchase price rises to offset the lower interest rate. This policy prompted the initial increase in housing prices, which then led to a speculative bubble that kept housing prices rising further.

The Fed's low interest rate policy was driven by its desire to prevent the economy from sliding into a more serious recession, which, ironically, was exactly what happened as a result of their policy. The prolonged low interest rates in the early 2000s may have kept the recession that began in 2001 from being more severe, but it set into motion economic events that led to the very severe downturn in 2008. The lower interest rates early in the decade were the catalyst for the unsustainable rise in housing prices and the bursting bubble.

John B. Taylor (2014) argues that the Fed's policy was entirely motivated by an attempt to create a favorable outcome, and procedural issues were not a consideration. The initial lowering of interest rates in the early 2000s was an attempt to keep the 2001 recession from becoming more severe, and to promote a stronger recovery after the recession bottomed out. Rising housing prices during the decade were, in general, viewed as a sign of a healthy recovery, despite a concern that housing was becoming increasingly unaffordable for many Americans. Indeed, while Fed policy was the driving force making housing increasingly unaffordable, Congress, along with Fannie and Freddie, was working to develop policies that would allow more people to buy that unaffordable housing. The collapse came when that housing did actually prove to be unaffordable. Two policy goals were in conflict with each other. The policy goal of supporting a weak economy by keeping interest rates low, which also supported housing prices and was viewed as a desirable outcome, was in conflict with the goal of providing affordable housing for lower-income Americans and non-traditional borrowers.

The Fed's policy of maintaining an economic recovery and producing economic growth with low interest rates, which would stimulate business activity, was aiming at this outcome, without any reference to ethical issues associated with the process. The Fed's low interest rate policy did have distributional consequences (and still has them, as of this writing) as a result of their procedures. Lower interest rates are designed to help businesses and borrowers in general, but they lower the incomes of lenders and, especially, people who live on income from fixed income assets, such as retirees. People with savings accounts, or retirees who receive income from interest payments on bonds, are made worse off by a policy that holds down interest rates. So, from an ethical standpoint, one would want to judge how the interests of retirees and low-income individuals, who are the groups that rely most heavily on the return from fixed interest investments, are weighed against the interests of business people and those who rely on the overall health of the economy. The evidence shows that Fed policy was aimed at benefiting borrowers at the expense of lenders.

Of course most people have a direct interest in the overall health of the economy, so, on that basis, a utilitarian calculation of the Fed's goals might rate them approvingly. However, if one weighs the interests of stockholders, who, as Piketty (2014) argues, tend to be upper-income individuals, against bondholders and others who save with fixed interest assets, often lower-income individuals, the utilitarian calculus may not come out so much in favor of the Fed. Its policies have clearly favored upper-income interests over lower-income interests since the beginning of the twenty-first century. The irony is that its policies that had the intention of supporting the overall economy for the good of everyone laid the foundation for the 2008 collapse that was detrimental to everyone, but that nevertheless favored the rich over the poor.

The financial industry bailout

As the economy entered into a steep decline in 2008, the federal government, in concert with the Fed, engaged in a series of bailouts to keep firms from failing. Most of the bailout support went to the financial industry, but the bailouts of General Motors and Chrysler were high profile events, and the stimulus package approved by Congress in 2009 supported many other firms through government spending rather than explicit bailouts. The bailouts started in March 2008 when the Treasury negotiated a deal for J. P. Morgan to purchase the failing Bear Stearns by guaranteeing a floor under the possible losses that could be incurred by J. P. Morgan. Bear Stearns would have been forced into bankruptcy without the bailout (Allison 2013: Ch. 15).

The Bear Stearns deal was minor compared with the American International Group (AIG) bailout. On September 16, 2008, the Federal Reserve Bank of New York agreed to lend AIG $85 billion in exchange for a nearly 80 percent ownership of AIG. American International Group was a major insurer of mortgage-backed securities owned by financial institutions, and when the housing market meltdown caused the value of those securities to plummet, AIG found itself with liabilities well in excess of its assets. The $85 billion loan kept AIG from bankruptcy, and officials in the Treasury Department and Fed argued that the loan was necessary to prevent a financial collapse that could lead to another Great Depression.

The Fed's bailout of AIG was unprecedented in several respects. First, the Fed was designed to be a lender of last resort to commercial banks that were members of the Federal Reserve System, and AIG was neither a bank nor a member of the system. Second, the Fed had never taken an equity interest in any company. Its role had always been as a regulator, a bank for member banks, and, more recently (since the nation went off the gold standard), the regulator of the quantity of money in the money supply. With the AIG bailout, the Fed had vastly overstepped the boundaries within which its actions had always taken place. Why did the Fed do this? Another possibility was to have the Treasury finance the bailout, but the Fed is nominally independent and can act on its own whereas the Treasury is a department of the US government. Appropriations for a Treasury bailout would have had to have been approved by Congress, and the thought was that it would have taken too long. So, the Fed acted, setting aside its long-standing procedures because it wanted to produce a particular outcome.

In November of 2008 the Treasury committed $40 billion of its own to the AIG bailout, and the Fed agreed to purchase more than $50 billion in mortgage-backed securities. The Fed's purchase of mortgage-backed securities was another unprecedented action. The Fed had always limited its purchases to securities issued by the federal government. It had long used purchases and sales of government securities as a primary tool for regulating the quantity of money in the economy, partly because of the relative safety of government securities as investments and partly to make its actions neutral with regard to private businesses in the economy. If the Fed had purchased corporate bonds, for example, it would have differentially benefited the corporations whose bonds it bought. But, by purchasing mortgage-backed securities, the Fed departed from its position of neutrality explicitly for the purpose of aiding those who held the securities.

One of the most underappreciated major changes that occurred during the meltdown was the unprecedented increase in the scope of actions undertaken by the Fed as it set aside long-standing procedures because it wanted to produce a specific outcome. It was no longer the neutral lender of last resort in the banking system, and regulator of banks and the money supply. It was actively engaged in economic planning, keeping some firms afloat, like AIG, supporting some businesses over others, like the holders of mortgage-backed securities, but at the same time judging that other firms, like Lehman Brothers, did not merit that same level of support. Lehman Brothers declared bankruptcy on September 15, 2008, because it was unable to refinance loans it needed to remain solvent. Using contemporary terminology, the Fed judged that AIG was "too big to fail"; Lehman Brothers was not. The focus was on the outcome, setting aside well-established procedures.

Another major bailout program was the federal government's Troubled Asset Relief Program (TARP) that was rammed through Congress on October 3, 2008. A sense of panic set in after the Lehman Brothers bankruptcy, and it took just a little over two weeks for Congress to pass TARP. The TARP program, engineered by the Bush administration, authorized up to $700 billion to purchase mortgage-backed securities for the purpose of bailing out financial institutions that held them. With the decline in the value of mortgage-backed securities after the housing market meltdown, financial institutions that held them were in danger of becoming insolvent. Banks are required by the Fed to use "mark to market" accounting principles to value their assets, which means that assets are valued according to the market's current price for them, rather than what the bank paid or what the bank expected to earn on them over their lifetimes. With the housing market collapse, banks holding mortgage-backed securities saw the market value of those securities fall, and as a result, banks risked having the value of their assets fall below the value of their liabilities, which would have led to their being closed down by the Federal Deposit Insurance Corporation. However, without the "mark to market" regulation, banks could have valued the securities they held based on the dividends they expected to receive over the life of the security plus the eventual payoff when the security matured, but with "mark to market," the decline in the market value of those securities meant that they had to be valued based on the going market price. Purchase of those "toxic" securities would help to recapitalize the banks.

The Treasury ran into difficulties in trying to determine how to value the securities and how they might be purchased, so the program was modified and the Treasury purchased equity positions in nine large banks. Not all of those banks wanted to give equity interest to the Treasury, but the judgment was that if some banks were able to choose not to participate, that would send a signal that the participating banks were in weaker financial condition, so the banks were "persuaded" to participate. Ultimately, hundreds of banks received TARP funds, even though they may not have wanted to participate in the program. Allison (2013: 170–171) describes how vaguely-worded mandates caused banks to fear regulatory problems if they did not take TARP funds. Allison, who was chairman of BB&T bank at the time, says,

> we were contacted by our regulators. . . . The essence of the message was that although BB&T had substantially more capital than it needed under long-established regulatory standards . . . the regulators were going to create a new set of capital standards. They did not know what those standards would be. . . . They had a regulatory team in place to reexamine our capital position immediately unless we took TARP funding. The threat was very clear.

Banks were intimidated into participating in TARP whether or not they wanted to.

The motivation behind the bailout of the financial market was purely outcome-based. The perception was that the economy was in danger of slipping into a depression, so extraordinary measures were called for to try to contain the damage that was being felt in the financial sector, and to keep it from spreading, as much as possible, to the rest of the economy. There was the perception that there were procedural problems that led up to the financial crisis, and the biggest procedural reaction was the passage of the Dodd-Frank Act in July 2010, which strengthened regulations in the financial industry. As Allison notes (2013: 193), one big issue Dodd-Frank does not address is the problem of "too big to fail" organizations, so this particular regulatory act overlooks one of the major problems behind the 2008 financial crisis.

The ethical aspects of the financial bailout received significant attention, producing the Occupy Wall Street movement that began in 2011 as a protest against the government policies that bailed out the 1 percent, as the movement's language put it, at the expense of the 99 percent. The Wall Street fat cats had their firms bailed out, they kept their jobs and their substantial salaries; meanwhile, individuals who could not pay their mortgages during the economic downturn were foreclosed and thrown out of their homes. If homeowners cannot pay their mortgages, is the ethical thing to do to foreclose on them, but have the federal government bail out the people who invested in those mortgages?

The auto industry bailout, and more

Perhaps more visible than the financial industry bailouts were the bailouts of General Motors (GM) and Chrysler. Those bailouts began in December 2008 when the Bush administration committed $13 billion in TARP money to bail out GM. The bailouts continued under the Obama administration in 2009, with more than $50 billion committed to GM. Ultimately, GM declared bankruptcy in June of 2009 and the US government took a 61 percent equity interest in the reorganized company. By 2014 the government had sold all of its interest in the company, tallying a loss of $10.3 billion in the process (Beech 2014). The government also lost more than $12 billion bailing out Chrysler, which it ultimately gave to Fiat in exchange for intellectual property and Fiat's $4.4 billion payment to the United Auto Workers (UAW) (Bertau 2014).

One irregularity in the GM bankruptcy was that the UAW received about $10 billion in GM stock after the bankruptcy, whereas bondholders prior to the bankruptcy received nothing.[7] Normally, in bankruptcy proceedings, the claims of bondholders would have to be satisfied before the claims of workers or their unions, but that did not happen in this case because the bankruptcy terms were dictated by the administration rather than in bankruptcy court. Needless to say, many bondholders were outraged by this.

James Sherk and Todd Zywicki (2012) explain that bankruptcy law requires that creditors' claims retain the same order in bankruptcy as outside bankruptcy, which is known as "absolute priority rule." Secured creditors are given priority over unsecured creditors, and Chrysler's bonds were secured, which meant that the bondholders should have been paid in full before any payments went to the UAW, which was an unsecured creditor. While GM's bonds were unsecured, bankruptcy law also treats similarly-situated creditors similarly, but the UAW received a much more generous settlement than GM's bondholders. These irregularities were the result of the bankruptcy being administered as a part of the TARP program rather than going through a bankruptcy court as would normally be the case.

Again, policies were dictated by the outcomes policymakers wanted to see rather than based on any issues that policymakers had with the procedures that led up to the outcomes. General Motors and Chrysler were deemed too big to fail, while many smaller firms were failing as the recession deepened. Despite long-standing legal procedures governing bankruptcy, in these cases the desires of the administration for a particular outcome—in this case, one that placed the claims of the UAW ahead of bondholders—determined the policy. Bankruptcy laws have not been changed as a result of the GM bailout. Bondholders still have a legal claim ahead of workers and their unions in bankruptcy proceedings. It was just in this case that an exception was made, because policymakers preferred an outcome different from the one that would have occurred had the normal rules of bankruptcy been followed.

The bailouts in the financial and auto industries were the most visible rescue programs during the recession, but many others were thrown a lifeline through stimulus program spending. Shortly after his election, President Obama pushed the American Recovery and Reinvestment Act of 2009 that provided $831 billion in stimulus spending to help ease the economy through the recession. The money was aimed at a variety of areas, including education, health care, energy, and infrastructure. The stimulus program was aimed at producing an outcome rather than altering a procedure. People received stimulus money not because they were treated unfairly by the market process, or because they did something to deserve it, but rather because, during the recession, the thought was that the stimulus spending would result in a more desirable outcome—a shallower recession. Nobody was suggesting that policies were implemented because there were any issues with the process, except that the process did not produce an outcome desired by policymakers.

The ethics of the policy response

The chapter noted at the outset that ethical judgments can be made regarding outcomes or procedures. Looking at the decades-old policy measures leading up to the recession, it is apparent that economic policy focuses heavily on the outcome, and attempts to design a procedure less to ensure that the procedure itself is ethical than to produce the outcome policymakers prefer. Sometimes the outcome policymakers prefer is driven by a view toward fairness, especially toward those at the bottom of the income distribution. Certainly, the government's housing policies stretching back decades can be viewed this way, and appear consistent with outcomes that might emerge from Rawls' (1971) views on justice—an idea that will be taken up in the next section. But there is no indication that policymakers judged procedures in the housing market to be unjust or unethical, beyond their observing that the outcomes produced by those procedures were not to their liking.

Consider the housing policies that led up to the housing market boom and subsequent collapse. The creation of Fannie Mae and Freddie Mac, the Community Reinvestment Act, the judgment that lending discrimination is based on the share of minority loans rather than the procedure for making those loans, the reduction in downpayment requirements—all of these policies were aimed at generating outcomes policymakers deemed desirable, rather than rectifying procedures they deemed to be undesirable. The procedures were judged by the outcomes they produced.

Why did the housing market exhibit the bubble in the early 2000s, leading up to the collapse in the second half of the decade? Strong arguments can be made that faulty procedures led up to the bursting of the housing market bubble and the resulting financial crisis. Policies were implemented for decades that facilitated people obtaining home mortgages that they were ill-equipped to handle, yet the policy response did not give these procedures much scrutiny, and essentially left them in place.

Some people blamed financial institutions for pushing people into mortgages they could not afford, but people apply for mortgages from banks rather than the other way around. And if, once those people applied, they did get mortgages they could not afford, one can see that the policies pushing both parties in that direction had been building for decades. Is it ethical to design procedures that lead people into mortgages they are unable to handle? Policies that did so were the result of policymakers judging the procedures in the mortgage industry by the results they produced. One can debate whether there is an ethical justification for the results policymakers were trying to produce, but it is apparent when looking at the history of government policies toward home ownership that the ends justified the means.

Taking into account the policy responses to the economic downturn that began in 2008, it is apparent that the concern was always the outcome, not the procedure. The concern of policymakers was to try to cushion the economy from falling more deeply into the recession. They wanted a particular outcome, and policies were designed to produce that outcome, not to address the procedural issues that led to the problems to begin with. While the financial regulation in Dodd-Frank did address procedures, it did not address the major procedural problems that led up to the financial crisis. The focus was on the outcome, and procedures were designed solely with the intent of producing the outcome policymakers desired. The ends would justify the means.

Randall G. Holcombe

Housing policy and the political process

The preceding analysis places a good deal of the blame for the economic crisis on housing policies that were developed decades earlier—some as early as the 1930s. This analysis is not unique in this regard, and many economists have pointed toward issues in the home mortgage market as major causes. Some observers have blamed the mortgage lenders for extending mortgages to unqualified buyers, and while it is easy to see that this happened, it is also easy to see that decades of government policies nudged them in that direction. The motivation was to allow more Americans to be able to own their own homes. How much blame should fall on government policy and how much should fall on the mortgage lenders who responded to that policy could be debated, but up until the collapse of the housing market politicians were touting increasing home ownership as a desirable outcome.

One perspective on the goal of increasing home ownership, especially for those who might have trouble qualifying for a mortgage under traditional standards, is that such policies would be supported under a Rawlsian (1971) veil of ignorance. If we step behind a veil of ignorance to design housing policies, and behind that veil we know nothing about our own personal characteristics, we might favor policies that give lower-income individuals a greater opportunity for home ownership. Behind a veil of ignorance, people know nothing about their own personal characteristics. They might be rich or poor, intelligent or stupid, tall or short, physically gifted or disabled. They do not know their race or gender, or anything of their individual characteristics. Behind the veil, it is easy to imagine people deciding that they would like to make it as easy as possible for those at the bottom end of the income and wealth scales to become homeowners.

This veil of ignorance exercise would suggest that the nation's housing policies were designed to further the interests of those at the bottom end of the income distribution, but the poor have relatively little political clout, and public policy tends to respond to interest groups who have the power to deliver votes and campaign contributions to those who make the policies. The policies that create more homeowners do not only benefit the homeowners themselves. They also benefit real estate agents, who have substantial lobbying power, the construction industry, and the banking and financial industry that profits from the financing of the homes. In fact, public policy is not made from behind a veil of ignorance, but is the result of bargaining among parties who all know their own interests. Stiglitz (2012) and Stockman (2013) both analyze the economic crisis and place blame on government policies that favor the elite at the expense of the masses. Stiglitz, writing from the political left, uses the language of Occupy Wall Street to describe policies that favor the 1 percent over the 99 percent, while Stockman makes similar observations and calls the system "crony capitalism."

Following Gary S. Becker (1983), the legislature might be viewed as a marketplace where different political interests reveal their demands for public policy outcomes. Politicians weigh the political support they gain or lose among various interest groups and pass policies that maximize their political support. In contrast with the veil of ignorance approach to public policy, the actual political decision-making process favors politically powerful interests. One can imagine government as an omniscient benevolent despot that produces public policies that are in the public interest, but in fact public policies are produced through a political process in which the interests of various groups are weighed by politicians who have their own interests (including, but not limited to, a desire to be reelected).

This line of reasoning suggests that the political forces behind the housing policies that led to the economic crisis were those who had economic power: the bankers, the builders, the real estate professionals. They were able to use their economic power to influence the political process to produce public policies favorable to themselves, as Holcombe (2015) explains.

Those with limited economic power, who faced difficulties in buying and financing their own homes, also have limited political power, and are unlikely to play a big role in steering public policy. Public policy is made by balancing the political interests of various groups, and the weight they represent in the balance depends on the political benefits they can bring to policy-makers. The interests of those who can deliver votes and campaign contributions weigh more heavily than those who cannot.

Political capitalism

This idea that public policy is oriented toward supporting the economic elite is not new. In an interesting analysis of the Progressive era, spanning roughly from the end of the nineteenth century up to World War I, Gabriel Kolko (1963) takes issue with the conventional wisdom on Progressivism, which argues that government was regulating the economically powerful to curb their might for the benefit of those who had less power. Kolko argues that Progressive era regulation was designed to stabilize the status quo, so that the economic elite would be protected from competition and able to retain their positions at the top of the economic hierarchy. Kolko called the resulting economic arrangements "political capitalism," which is a system under which the economic and political elite work together to protect each other's interests. Kolko (1965) argues that the regulation of the railroads, which began at the end of the nineteenth century, was undertaken for the benefit of the railroads, a view that is echoed by Richard White (2011). So, the idea that economic policy is designed for the benefit of the economic elite applies to policies that far-predate the 2008 financial crisis.

This idea was popularized in the Occupy Wall Street movement that began in 2011. In the language of the Occupy movement, public policy was designed to benefit the 1 percent at the expense of the 99 percent. Looking at the policy response to the economic crisis, the claim has some support. After the housing market bubble burst, the economy went into a recession and unemployment rose. People who lost their jobs were unable to make their mortgage payments, and, with housing prices down, many of them found themselves underwater and could not sell their houses to repay their lenders. They defaulted on their mortgages and were foreclosed. Meanwhile, in contrast to the 99 percent (to use the Occupy language), the financial institutions holding those mortgages were bailed out. It is easy to perceive that the economic elite—those rich fat-cat Wall Street bankers—were on the receiving end of government bailouts to cover their losses, while ordinary Americans lost their homes and were offered no helping hand from the federal government.

Two books published after the economic collapse offer an interesting commentary because they come from opposite ends of the political spectrum, yet offer very similar ideas on the causes of the nation's economic and political problems and on the effects. Stiglitz (2012), writing from the perspective of the political left, is obviously concerned about economic inequality, and places much of the blame for inequality on the policies of the federal government. Stockman (2013), writing from the political right, offers a very similar analysis. Both cite the same government policies that favor insiders and the economic and political elite over the general public, and both conclude that those policies are undermining the nation's market economy and threatening its democratic government. Considering their very different political views, their similarities on the causes and consequences of the nation's economic and political challenges are striking, as Holcombe (2014) notes.

Stiglitz and Stockman analyze the policies leading up to the economic crisis in some detail, and both are critical of the cronyism that generates policies that favor the elites over the masses. While they do not use the term, both are describing what Kolko called political capitalism: an economic and political system that works for the advantage of the economic and political elite. Ralph Nader (2014) refers to this political capitalism as the "corporate state," and notes that those speaking out against it span the left–right political spectrum. Nader argues that this left–right political coalition will be unstoppable, leading to the dismantling of the corporate state. It is interesting to see how much common ground across the political spectrum there is in pointing the finger toward government policy as the primary cause of the economic crisis.

In discussing ethical issues related to the crisis the distinction was made between ethical criteria that judged the procedures versus those that judged outcomes. It should be apparent that the parties determining public policy in political capitalism are focused on outcomes, but not outcomes based on any ethical criteria. Rather, they are judging how the outcomes of public policy will directly affect them. Political capitalism promotes policies that favor the economic and political elite, by increasing their wealth and by stabilizing their position at the top of the hierarchy. This is consistent with the events that saw the bailout and subsequent resurgence of too-big-to-fail firms, while foreclosing on homeowners who fell behind on their mortgage payments during the downturn.

Public policies are produced through a political process in which policymakers weigh the interests of voters, of lobbyists, and include their own interests to decide what policies to enact. The process is driven by interests, rather than by ethical considerations. When one evaluates how the actual political process works, rather than engaging in wishful thinking about how it might ideally work, it should not be surprising that the process focuses on outcomes more than procedures, that procedures are designed to produce particular outcomes rather than have an ethical foundation, and that even the outcomes policymakers try to engineer are not based on ethical considerations, but rather look at the interests of their supporters and themselves.

Concluding remarks

The economic crisis began in the housing industry, with a bubble in housing prices in the early 2000s and a collapse of the housing market in 2008. A look at the history of federal government housing policies shows a series of policies dating back to the 1930s that were designed to facilitate the purchase of single family homes. Those policies accelerated with the Community Redevelopment Act passed in 1977, followed by the more active role played by Fannie Mae and Freddie Mac in the home mortgage market. There was increasing Congressional pressure on mortgage lenders to extend mortgages to buyers who were more and more marginal, partly justified by some perception of discrimination in the mortgage market and partly driven by a public policy that viewed home ownership as the American dream and wanted more Americans to realize that dream. As long as home prices kept rising negative fallout from these policies was minimal, because people who found themselves in a position of being unable to meet their mortgage payments could sell their homes, pay off the remaining mortgage balance and leave the transaction with a profit. After the housing bubble burst, many financially-strapped homeowners, often suffering other economic problems due to the recession, found themselves under water on their mortgages, owing more than the value of their houses. They defaulted on their mortgages and were foreclosed, but the holders of the mortgages found themselves owning houses whose values were less than the mortgages.

The housing policies the federal government implemented were driven by a desire to achieve certain outcomes. From an ethical standpoint, policymakers looked at racial differences in homeownership rates and viewed them as a sign of discrimination, but, more broadly, viewed extending home ownership to more people as a desirable goal. Why was this goal desirable? Because there was political support for it, not only from those who could buy homes, but from the real estate industry, from bankers, from the construction industry, and other influential political groups. The focus was on producing politically popular outcomes, not on any problems with the procedures that led to those outcomes. Procedures were changed as a result, but, again, not because of any issues with the procedures themselves but because they did not lead to the outcomes policymakers wanted.

The mortgages were often bundled into mortgage-backed securities that were owned by banks and other financial institutions, and when the market value of those securities fell many of those financial institutions were on the brink of insolvency. This led to unprecedented bailouts, and the role of the Federal Reserve Bank is especially noteworthy because of its extension from a regulator and lender of last resort to an organization that targeted some for help while ignoring others, essentially picking winners and losers rather than acting as a neutral regulator and monetary authority. Again, the justification was outcome-based. Some firms were viewed as too big to fail and got the federal lifelines, while many others went under during the economic crisis. The motivation was not that in some way the procedures that had led up to the crisis were unethical or unfair, but rather that the outcome was undesirable so action needed to be taken.

The policy response of the federal government faced substantial criticism from throughout the political spectrum because of the perception that those policies were targeted to benefit the economic and political elite at the expense of the masses. The policies were indeed based on trying to achieve a certain outcome, but it should come as no surprise that the political process tends to favor those who have political power and political connections. This cronyism, perhaps better called political capitalism, is an outcome-based system, but it is not based on judgments of what would be an ethical outcome, but rather on what best benefits the cronies.

Essential readings

An excellent discussion of policies that led to the economic crisis is found in Stan J. Liebowitz, "Anatomy of a Train Wreck: Causes of the Mortgage Meltdown" (2008). John A. Allison, *The Financial Crisis and the Free Market Cure* (2013), gives the perspective of a large-bank CEO on the policies leading up to the crisis and the government's response. David A. Stockman, *The Great Deformation: The Corruption of Capitalism in America* (2013) offers an especially critical assessment of those policies, calling them crony capitalism. Boudewijn de Bruin, *Ethics and the Global Financial Crisis: Why Incompetence Is Worse than Greed* (2015), evaluates the ethics of those in the financial industry, offering a conclusion that is expressed in his subtitle.

For further reading in this volume on the institutions and laws governing money and finance, see Chapter 20, Money and finance: ethical considerations. On competing narratives (Locke vs. Rousseau) concerning the role of the state in the economy, see Chapter 3, Theory and method in business ethics. On political decision-making, see Chapter 7, Can profit seekers be virtuous? On ways of conceptualizing of government regulation, as well as issues of market failure and government failure, see Chapter 21, Regulation, rent seeking, and business ethics.

Notes

1 Rawls (1971) goes beyond his procedure to give specific outcomes he believes would result from that procedure, but he is criticized by James Buchanan (1975), who says one cannot know what will emerge from this hypothetical procedure. Considering this topic further would be an unnecessary digression. The point is that Rawls' agreement from behind a veil of ignorance, and Buchanan's renegotiation from anarchy, describe procedures that produce fair outcomes, and the fairness of the outcome is a result of the fairness of the procedure.

2 In distinguishing between historical versus patterned theories of justice, Robert Nozick (1974) offers a parallel distinction.
3 Congress passed the Home Mortgage Disclosure Act (HMDA) in 1990, and the Federal Reserve Bank of Boston's HMDA data appeared to show discrimination against minorities. See Day and Liebowitz (1998) for a discussion.
4 See Emmons et al. (2011) for an analysis that finds households more at fault for overreaching than lenders for predatory lending.
5 The S&P/Case-Shiller Home Price Index, 2000=100, rose to more than 200 in its 20-city composite, and more than 225 in its 10-city composite, by 2007 before the collapse in prices. The index can be found at us.spindices.com/index-family/real-estate/sp-case-shiller.
6 Mortgage rate data from www.freddiemac.com/pmms/pmms30.htm, accessed June 20, 2014.
7 Patrice Hill, "GM's Union Recovering After Stock Sale," *Washington Times*, November 25, 2010. The article reports that one-third of the stock the UAW received was sold for $3.4 billion in the week before the article was published, which would value the entire amount of stock they received at greater than $10 billion.

References

Allison, J.A. (2013). *The Financial Crisis and the Free Market Cure*. New York, NY: McGraw-Hill.
Baumol, W.J. (1986). *Superfairness*. Cambridge, MA: MIT Press.
Becker, G.S. (1983). "A Theory of Competition Among Pressure Groups for Political Influence," *Quarterly Journal of Economics* 98:3, 371–400.
Beech, E. (2014). "U.S. Government Says It Lost $11.2 Billion on GM Bailout," *Reuters*, April 30.
Bertau, J. (2014). "Auto Bailout Gives Away Chrysler," *Newsmax*, January 13.
Buchanan, J.M. (1975). *The Limits of Liberty: Between Anarchy and Leviathan*. Chicago, IL: University of Chicago Press.
Day, T. and S.J. Liebowitz. (1998). "Mortgage Lending to Minorities: Where's the Bias?" *Economic Inquiry* 36:1, 1–27.
De Bruin, B. (2015). *Ethics and the Global Financial Crisis: Why Incompetence Is Worse than Greed*. Cambridge: Cambridge University Press.
Emmons, W.R., K. Fogel, W.Y. Lee, L. Ma, D. Rorie and T.J. Yeager (2011). "The Foreclosure Crisis in 2008: Predatory Lending or Household Overreaching?" *The Regional Economist*, July, Federal Reserve Bank of St. Louis, 12–16.
Federal Reserve Bank of Boston (1992). *Closing the Gap: A Guide to Equal Opportunity Lending*. Boston, MA: Federal Reserve Bank of Boston.
Gilens, M. (2012). *Affluence and Influence: Economic Inequality and Political Power in America*. New York, NY: Russell Sage Foundation and Princeton University Press.
Hacker, J.S. and P. Pierson (2010). *Winner-Take-All Politics: How Washington Made the Rich Richer—and Turned Its Back on the Middle Class*. New York, NY: Simon & Schuster.
Holcombe, R.G. (2014). "What Stiglitz and Stockman Have in Common." *Cato Journal* 34:3, 569–579.
Holcombe, R.G. (2015). "Political Capitalism," *Cato Journal* 35:1, 41–66.
Kolko, G. (1963). *The Triumph of Conservatism: A Reinterpretation of American History, 1900–1916*. New York, NY: The Free Press.
Kolko, G. (1965). *Railroads and Regulation: 1877–1916*. Princeton, NJ: Princeton University Press.
Liebowitz, S.J. (2009). "Anatomy of a Train Wreck: Causes of the Mortgage Meltdown," in Randall G. Holcombe and Benjamin Powell (eds), *Housing America: Building Out of a Crisis*. New Brunswick, NJ: Transaction Publishers, 287–321.
Locke, J. (1960 [1690]). *Two Treatises of Government*. Cambridge: Cambridge University Press.
Munnell, A.H., G.M.B. Tootell, L.E. Browne and J. McEneaney (1996). "Mortgage Lending in Boston: Interpreting HMDA Data," *American Economic Review* 86:1, 25–53.
Nader, R. (2014). *Unstoppable: The Emerging Left-Right Coalition to Dismantle the Corporate State*. New York, NY: Nation Books.
Nozick, R. (1974). *Anarchy, State, and Utopia*. New York, NY: Basic Books.
Piketty, T. (2014). *Capital in the Twenty-First Century*. Cambridge, MA: Harvard University Press.
Rawls, J. (1971). *A Theory of Justice*. Cambridge, MA: Harvard University Press.
Rothbard, M.N. (1982). *The Ethics of Liberty*. Atlantic Highlands, NJ: Humanities Press.

Schumpeter, J.A. (1934). *The Theory of Economic Development*. Cambridge, MA: Harvard University Press.

Sen, A. (1985). *Commodities and Capabilities*. New York, NY: North-Holland.

Sherk, J. and T. Zywicki (2012). "Auto Bailout or UAW Bailout? Taxpayer Losses Came from Subsidizing Union Compensation," Heritage Foundation *Backgrounder* #2700.

Stiglitz, J.E. (2012). *The Price of Inequality: How Today's Divided Society Endangers the Future*. New York, NY: W.W. Norton.

Stockman, D.A. (2013). *The Great Deformation: The Corruption of Capitalism in America*. New York, NY: Public Affairs Press.

Taylor, J.B. (2014). "The Role of Policy in the Great Recession and the Weak Recovery," *American Economic Review* 104:1, 61–66.

White, R. (2011). *Railroaded: The Transcontinentals and the Making of Modern America*. New York, NY: W.W. Norton.

Part VI
Roles and responsibilities within the firm

Introduction

As organizational structures, firms are systems of integrated components in which individuals bear specified roles and corresponding responsibilities. Viewed from the "inside," organizational positions—"offices"—are filled by people who must perform the tasks and responsibilities assigned to them by virtue of their positions as managers, employees, or directors. Viewed from the "outside," the firm itself may have duties and responsibilities toward employees, shareholders, consumers or society. The chapters in this section not only discuss how or by whom firms are, or ought to be, guided or controlled, but take up in addition the theory and practice of management ethics, the moral challenges of workplace leadership, as well as issues of employment, labor, marketing and advertising, and accounting.

In Chapter 24, **Corporate governance**, the late **Ann K. Buchholtz** points out that business ethics studies have enriched the purview of corporate governance by moving beyond the aim of maximizing shareholder wealth to include attention to a broader array of stakeholders. Buchholtz describes the so-called primacy debate regarding the contest of power between shareholders and board directors and chronicles the current push for shareholder empowerment ("shareholder democracy"). However, she draws our attention to the other side of the coin, shareholder responsibilities, which remain relatively ignored in the literature. She also examines other issues of moral responsibility including the performance and effectiveness of corporate boards and board members, as well as the role of the company CEO. Buchholtz reminds us of the crucial point that corporate governance raises questions that should be answered only after settling the logically prior (yet contested) issues of what a corporation is and what its purpose should be.

Valérie Petit and Sarah E. Saint-Michel introduce, in Chapter 25, **Leadership and business ethics: are leaders wolves for business ethics?**, the burgeoning field of leadership studies. After defining "leadership" and confronting the attendant question of whether the very idea of leadership must be linked to ethics, they turn to the normative conception of the leader and canvas a number of theories of "moral leadership." The character traits of the moral leader—personal, ethical, and cognitive—are delineated and then compared with the qualities of "negative" or unethical leadership. Petit and Saint-Michel indicate further how corporate leadership plays a central role in realizing current aims of corporate social responsibility, including those of diversity. The authors conclude by stressing the need for intellectual bridges between empirical and theoretical studies on business ethics and leadership.

In the following Chapter (26), **Theoretical issues in management ethics**, **Joseph A. Petrick** confronts the central theoretical issues in management ethics. As he points out, managers may think, mistakenly, that they are unaffected by ethical theories even as their conduct suggests a tacit acceptance of a specific perspective. Clearing up theoretical muddles in management ethics may contribute to enhancing a manager's awareness of moral responsibilities. Outlining major management theories, Petrick underscores the close relationship between the descriptive and normative dimensions of management—a relationship also encountered in the preceding two chapters. He reminds us how these theories of management may relate to debates over shareholder versus stakeholder responsibility. Summarizing the major schools of moral philosophy, Petrick focuses first on the relationship between the theoretical perspectives on ethics and management theories, and then on a more fundamental question: To what extent can theory guide conduct?

In Chapter 27, **The ethics of managers and employees**, **Linda Klebe Treviño** presents a social-scientific approach to the lived conduct of managers and employees. Distinct from a theoretical approach to ethics that asks "What ought to be done?" the social-scientific approach places a premium on resolving the ethical problems, dilemmas, and challenges of the workplace. Focusing first on the practical conditions of ethical decision-making, including ethical awareness, motivation and judgment, Treviño turns subsequently to management compliance programs, contrasting them with the so-called "ethical culture" policies introduced into organizations and featuring role models, codes of conduct, performance management systems, authority structures, and norms and rituals.

Within the business ethics literature, there is significant emphasis on employers' duties towards employees. In Chapter 28, **Employee ethics and rights**, **Jeffrey Moriarty** follows this norm to a certain extent, but he also engages the duties of employees to employers as these occur in hiring and firing, just pay, meaningful work and workplace democracy, employee privacy, and whistleblowing. Moving beyond the strictly legal or contractual model of employment rights and duties, Moriarty presents the complexity of the ethical issues as these arise in employment and discusses critically the relevant and contrasting arguments.

In Chapter 29, **Exploitation and labor**, **Benjamin Ferguson** examines the notion of labor exploitation, focusing on three questions: How may a laborer be wronged? What do firms owe employees? Who is responsible when a worker receives low compensation? Ferguson characterizes the complexities of defining "exploitation" and its causes (e.g., unjust wages or working conditions), as well as the fact that some would argue that firms owe nothing to their employees apart from honoring the contractual agreement to which both parties agreed. The author sifts critically some of the proposals seeking to specify and vindicate additional duties beyond adherence to contract. Even if there are such additional duties, these must be weighed against any fiduciary duties the firm bears to its shareholders.

Minette Drumwright addresses in Chapter 30, **Ethical issues in marketing, advertising, and sales**, the various criticisms voiced against marketing (to include advertising and sales)—that it is unfair, manipulative, intrusive, wasteful, or that it fosters false values. Drumwright confronts and clarifies these indictments and characterizes some of the solutions proposed in recent scholarship: ethical checklists for marketing practitioners, organizational changes that enhance moral awareness on the part of marketers and advertisers, or consultation with stakeholders on marketing strategies. Drumright's verdict is that research on marketing ethics has not been commensurate to its importance.

Part VI concludes with Chapter 31, **The accounting profession, the public interest, and human rights**. Examining the ethics of professional accounting, **Ken McPhail** focuses on contemporary scholarship and assesses its possible future development. Taking exception to the unjustified neglect of accounting's societal importance, the author situates the accounting profession within a larger political and moral outlook. McPhail sketches accounting ethics, but introduces a sociological analysis of professions in general, and of accountants in particular, bringing forth the relation of accounting to the public interest. After characterizing various notions of public interest in relation to accounting, McPhail proposes that human rights discourse should be linked to accounting ethics so as to highlight the close relationship of accounting and accountability. Connecting human rights to the duties of accountancy not only underlines the social function of accounting but extends rights-based responsibilities from business to global accounting and financial institutions.

Byron Kaldis

24
Corporate governance

Ann K. Buchholtz*

Corporate governance is in crisis mode. For over a decade, a surge of financial scandals and management failures have led to a record number of bankruptcies filed, billions of dollars of wealth destroyed, and countless jobs lost. Not surprisingly, these failures have eroded the public's trust in corporate governance, "every one of the mechanisms set up to provide checks and balances failed at the same time," declared Robert Monks and Nell Minow (2008: 3). Corporate governance should be able to steer companies away from such failures and toward sustainable success so that the considerable resources entrusted to business are put to good use. As Guhan Subramanian (2015) noted, "with trillions of dollars of wealth governed by these rules of the games, we must do better" (Subramanian 2015: 98).

The word *governance* is derived from the Greek word for steering and, as such, means not only to control but also to provide direction (Lafferty 2006). Corporate governance involves prescribing what a firm *ought* to do and then steering the firm in that direction. To fully answer the *ought* question, it is important to be clear about the identity and purpose of the for-profit corporation (Donaldson 2012). Historically, corporate governance has been dominated by a strongly held assumption that shareholder value (i.e., wealth) maximization is the purpose of the corporation: This has led to an unquestioning empirical approach to corporate governance research (Daily et al. 2003). In this view of the corporation, shareholders held primacy and so the ultimate goal of corporate governance, and indicator of firm success, was shareholder value maximization, with value being defined as monetary wealth, as measured by share price and market value. Business ethicists have played an important role in expanding our conception of a corporation by examining the normative implications of a focus on shareholder value maximization as the ultimate purpose of the corporation (Donaldson 2015), while also studying the corporation's many stakeholders as well as the relative responsibility the corporation has to their welfare maximization (Freeman 1984; Donaldson and Preston 1995). In the process, business ethics scholars have drawn on both positivist and normative analyses to study shareholder value maximization and its alternatives (Jones and Felps 2013). This has led corporate governance scholars to reconsider the widely accepted corporate objective of maximizing shareholder value, coupled with the prevailing model of corporate governance that had shareholders as the principals and boards as their representatives. This reconsideration of the role that shareholders and stakeholders play in the corporation and the relative responsibilities the corporation has to them places corporate governance at a crossroads in which long-held assumptions are being questioned in an effort to move the field of corporate governance forward. The first step in moving forward is to answer the *ought* question posed by Donald Hambrick, Axel Werder, and Edward Zajac (2008: 383). "Who runs, and who should run, the company?"

The development of a global market along with the increased mobility of capital has increased the communication among corporate governance models in different regions of the world (Rossouw and Sison 2006). Much of the world has converged to an Anglo-American form of corporate governance, although differences remain (Rasheed and Yoshikawa 2012). Corporate governance conversion has been driven by firms seeking to attract investment and governments seeking to attract candidates to privatize previously state-owned operations or services (Ovidiu and Pop 2012). Multinational companies (MNCs) are becoming transnational companies and so they seek governance codes that fit their global scope (van Veen and Elbertsen 2008). Different countries' corporate governance codes and practices differ in areas such as the board independence norm (BIN) and shareholder vs. stakeholder prioritization (Johanson and Østergren 2010; Majumder et al. 2012; Ovidiu and Pop 2012; Harrigan 2014). However, even though their responses differ, many of the issues with which they deal are the same. This chapter will cover those issues that apply broadly, including shareholder/director primacy, shareholder/stakeholder focus, fiduciary duties, shareholder rights and responsibilities, board diversity, conflicts of interest, agency vs. stewardship views, and the theory of the firm.

Corporate governance is "the determination of the broad uses to which organizational resources will be deployed and the resolution of conflicts among the myriad participants in organizations" (Daily et al. 2003: 371). The deployment of vast resources and the resolution of innumerable conflicts raise a host of ethical issues. At their foundation lies a central question: Who should have primacy—the shareholders or the board? This chapter begins with a discussion of the arguments for and against the shareholder primacy and director primacy perspectives, followed by a presentation of the ethical issues surrounding shareholders, boards of directors and CEOs. The chapter then explores the path forward with concluding remarks.

The primacy debate

The primacy debate is central to any discussion of ethics and corporate governance. Although countries vary in their practices and perspectives, the balance between shareholder and board power is a source of rising tensions throughout the common law world (Hill 2010). Creating long-term sustainable value is the goal of corporate governance (Monks and Minow 2011); however, for whom that value is created remains a controversial question. A key argument for the special status of shareholders is that they take on substantial risk that leaves them vulnerable to the vagaries of firm management because their investments are not protected by contracts (Maitland 1994) or firm assets (Williamson 1985). In sum, shareholders get what remains after the contractual obligations owed to various stakeholders have been satisfied (Fama and Jensen 1983). Shareholder primacy has served as the commonly accepted foundation of Anglo-American corporate governance policy and research (Dalton et al. 1998). From this perspective, the corporate objective is to maximize the wealth of shareholders. Shareholder primacy draws on agency theory to suggest that the board of directors has a fiduciary duty to protect shareholder wealth by monitoring, advising, and controlling top managers to assure they place the interests of shareholders above their own and those of other stakeholders. A key concern in the shareholder primacy model is that the separation of ownership and control, along with dispersion of shareholders, has given managers an opportunity to focus on their self-interest instead of shareholder value maximization. From the agency theory perspective, managers are likely to be self-dealing in the absence of monitoring and control by an effective board (Jensen and Meckling 1976; Fama 1980; Fama and Jensen 1983). Boards of directors have a variety of available control mechanisms, both internal and external, to align the interests of managers and shareholders, thus curbing the tendency of managers to promote their own interests over those of shareholders (Walsh and Seward 1990).

In the shareholder primacy model, shareholders are the principals of the nexus of contracts that comprise a firm and thus are at the top of the hierarchy with ultimate-decision making and control (Alchian and Demsetz 1972). The top managers serve as their agents and the board sits between management and shareholders, bearing the responsibility for ascertaining that the agents (managers) act in a way that maximizes the shareholders' best interests (Fischel 1992; Shleifer and Vishny 1997). The goal of shareholder value (wealth) maximization has the advantage of providing an easily observable and measurable metric that focuses managerial attention in a clear direction (Sundaram and Inkpen 2004). Moreover, the clarity of the shareholder-value-maximizing goal focuses managerial attention, while the absence of a clear goal creates confusion and affords managers too much freedom to determine corporate direction (Jensen 2001). Shareholder primacy advocates also argue that stakeholders have the option of becoming shareholders, a strategy some activist shareholders have already employed (Tkac 2006). Frank Easterbrook and Daniel Fischel (1996) contend that the apparent conflict between shareholder value maximization and stakeholder welfare maximization represents a false dichotomy because shareholder value maximization leads to a greater good by maximizing total firm value (Sundaram and Inkpen 2004) and social welfare (Jensen 2001). This utilitarian argument is based on the argument that the discipline inherent in shareholder wealth maximization benefits all stakeholders by increasing the likelihood of firm survival through lower costs, lower prices and increased cash flows (Maitland 1994). Of course, this argument only holds true if those stakeholder claims are valued and the stakeholder claims are satisfied.

Board primacy, in contrast, is based on a view of the firm as a team production in which multiple parties (e.g., employees, suppliers, customers, investors, creditors and the community) invest time and effort for output that is nonseparable, i.e., not easily attributed to any particular team member's contribution (Blair and Stout 1999). These team members take on risk because much of the contribution made by team members is firm-specific, in that it only has value within the firm (Becker 1962) and so team members cannot easily take it with them and be rewarded for it elsewhere (Blair and Stout 2001). At the same time, the nonseparability and firm-specificity of team member contributions make it very difficult to design contracts that effectively prevent shirking and award team members for their specific contributions (Blair and Stout 1999). From this perspective, shareholders are members of that team along with other stakeholders (Blair and Stout 1999; Lan and Heracleous 2010).

With board primacy, all team members cede control over firm outputs, as well as their firm-specific inputs to the board (Blair and Stout 1999). From this perspective, the firm is a mediating hierarchy, i.e., a nexus of firm-specific investments (Blair and Stout 1999) rather than the nexus of contracts conceptualized in the shareholder primacy model. Margaret Blair and Lynn Stout (1999: 265) argue that the role of principal is eliminated in the mediating hierarchy. Alternatively, L.L. Lan and Loizos Heracleous (2010) propose a board primacy model in which the principal is the corporation and the board serves as a mediating hierach, i.e., an autonomous fiduciary that acts in the corporation's best interests. Although the specifics of board primacy models might vary, the key shared attribute is that the board sits at the top of the hierarchy, responsible for mediating disputes between all corporate team members and allocating duties and rewards. The board primacy model of the board as a mediating hierach is consistent with (but does not presuppose or entail) effective stakeholder management, for the board is positioned both to "rethink problems so that the needs of a broad group of stakeholders are addressed" (Parmar et al. 2010: 406) and to figure out how to make tradeoffs when interests conflict (Freeman et al. 2007).

Issues surrounding shareholders

The primacy debate discussed above is central to any discussion of shareholders and ethics in corporate governance. In their foundational work, Adolf Berle and Gardiner Means (1932) argued that the property rights that stem from ownership confer not only a right to profits but also a responsibility for management and control. They contended, however, that the dispersion of ownership in the modern corporate form effectively weakened the property rights of shareholders because "The profit motive cannot stimulate the owner of passive property to do anything but speculate" (1932: 1370). Ryan (2000) counters that, if the atom did in fact split, it has now fused, due to a combination of shareholder activism and increased concentration in corporate ownership.

For the past two decades, activist shareholders have embarked on a shareholder empowerment movement that generally receives support from the shareholder primacy perspective but is cause for concern from the board primacy perspective. Shareholder empowerment efforts have put shareholder and boards of directors in a zero-sum game because, as shareholders gain power, boards lose power and vice versa (Fairfax 2008). The umbrella term for these efforts to empower shareholders is *shareholder democracy*, a movement that has grown in Europe (Rose 2012), Canada (Veall 2012) and the United States (Buchholtz and Brown 2015). Of course, shareholder primacy advocates are strongly in favor of greater shareholder power (Bebchuk 2005; Bebchuk and Cohen 2005; Fairfax 2009), while director primacy advocates question the wisdom of increasing shareholder power (Anabtawi 2006; Bainbridge 2006; Stout 2007, 2013). It is important to note that shareholders are not a homogeneous group. Individual and institutional investors vary in their goals (Ryan and Schneider 2002), trust levels (Ryan and Buchholtz 2001), investment horizons (Gaspara et al. 2005), and stakeholder orientations (Ryan and Schneider 2003).

A key battleground has been in the area of corporate voting. Shareholders have been largely disenfranchised with voting systems that render their votes basically moot (Fairfax 2009). However, as Easterbrook and Fischel (1983: 403) argue, only shareholders have the incentive to vote in a way that maximizes the total value of the firm because they "receive most of the marginal gains and incur most of the marginal costs." Efforts to empower shareholders by changing the corporate voting system have focused in three areas: adopting a majority vote system, eliminating staggered boards, and giving shareholders access to the proxy ballot for board member candidate nominations (Fairfax 2008). Another voting-related initiative expands the areas in which shareholders can make their voice heard. The purpose of the "say on pay" (SOP) movement is to give shareholders the opportunity to voice their (non-binding) support or opposition to executive compensation plans.

A key concern of shareholder democracy efforts has been to get corporations to change their bylaws from a pluralist voting model to a majority voting model (Lesser et al. 2006). In a pluralist model, the most common form prior to the recent efforts, the proxy ballots firms sent to shareholders gave only two options for each director candidate, "yes" or "withhold." If a director ran uncontested, as most did, that director only needed one "yes" vote to be elected, even if a large number of voters chose "withhold" (Ryan et al. 2010). In contrast, majority voting typically provides shareholders with the option of voting "yes" or "no" and requires directors to get a majority of "yes" votes to be elected. The fight to institute a majority voting model has been largely successful. Institutional Shareholder Services reported that, as of 2014, nearly

90 percent of the S&P 500, and over half of the S&P 1500, had a majority voting standard (ISS 2015). An analysis of the impact of a change to a majority voting system showed that firms with majority voting were more likely to implement shareholder proposals, enhancing the ability of shareholders to achieve desired governance reforms; however, firms with majority voting exhibited no difference in votes withheld or director turnover (Ertimur et al. 2015).

Shareholder empowerment advocates seek to eradicate staggered boards because staggered boards limit the control shareholders have over the selection and replacement of the board slate (Ganor 2008). With staggered boards, only a subset of directors goes up for election in any given year and board members serve multi-year terms. Thus, it takes multiple years for shareholders to vote out a slate of board members who are underperforming. In contrast, unitary (non-staggered) boards hold elections annually and all directors are elected to one-year terms. With unitary boards, it is possible to replace an entire board at one election. The argument against staggered boards is that they reduce shareholder power, allowing directors to become more entrenched and less responsive to market discipline or shareholders (Bebchuk and Cohen 2005). The arguments for staggered boards are that the longer-term orientation of staggered boards enables decision makers to support investments with longer-term payoffs (Jacobs 1991), such as stakeholder management. Staggered boards can mitigate market-based pressures for short-term results, lead to a longer-term orientation and greater board and managerial autonomy, and thereby increase the attention managers can pay to the firm's non-shareholding stakeholders (Kacperczyk 2009). Staggered boards in large corporations, which have received the lion's share of shareholder activist attention, have declined dramatically (Conference Board 2015).

Proxy access is a shareholder empowerment initiative in the US that allows shareholders to nominate directorial candidates for the firm's proxy statement. Unlike majority voting and destaggering of boards, proxy access has had a rocky road to acceptance. It has become the most sought after mechanism for attaining shareholder democracy (Fairfax 2009) and has both advocates and detractors. Advocates argue that access to the proxy is essential for the voting process to have any meaning and detractors argue that the process will be costly and could possibly fall prey to special interests (Fairfax 2009; Hayden and Bodie 2012). In 2007 the Securities and Exchange Commission (SEC) considered but ultimately rejected a proxy access rule (Fairfax 2009). In 2010 the SEC developed a rule for proxy access that was struck down a year later by the US Court of Appeals for the DC Circuit (Hayden and Bodie 2012). Since then, the proxy access movement has been generating momentum but the progress is still slower than most observers expected (Dearlove and Werrett 2013).

The say on pay (SOP) movement was an effort to empower shareholders to cast their non-binding votes regarding CEO compensation. Advisory SOP votes are now required under the 2010 Dodd-Frank financial law. Studies of the impact of SOP are mixed. Few companies fail the vote (only two percent in 2015), but the good news is that they appear to have learned to avoid actions that spark investor outrage, such as not tying pay to performance and using inappropriate peer group comparisons (Chasan 2015). An analysis of manager, director and shareholder responses to SOP votes did not show the intended effect of improving pay contracts: Excess compensation for previously overcompensated managers was not reduced following low SOP votes (Brunarski et al. 2015). As with other initiatives, SOP has both defenders and detractors. SOP's defenders argue that runaway CEO pay indicates that the board has failed in its responsibility to develop appropriate executive compensation contracts. SOP's detractors counter that shareholders lack the information and the incentives to gather the information required for understanding the complexities of executive compensation. Drawing from Kenneth Arrow's work on decision-making, Bainbridge (2006) argues that shareholders lack both the motivation and the information necessary to make sound business policy decisions. He notes further that the business judgment rule, which refers the executive compensation decision to the board, suggests that "the law finds a value in the board's authority that might be lost if director decisions were routinely subject to review" (Bainbridge 2005: 1658). Unlike shareholders, CEOs are unable to diversify their employment portfolios and so they face considerable risk (Buchholtz and Ribbens 1994). The large paychecks that give rise to shareholder frustration are designed to incentivize CEOs to take on risk that is in the firm's best interests (Kolb 2012). Another argument against SOP initiatives is based on the unintended consequences that can stem from using ex ante incentive contracts. These highly specified pay-for-performance contracts are based on an assumption that people are basically selfish (Stout 2014). They set up a transactional (i.e., quid pro quo) relationship in a situation for which a relational (trust-based) contract is most appropriate (Kidder and Buchholtz 2002). This can reduce motivation, leading to the types of behaviors the contract was intended to prevent.

The hedge fund and private equity industries have energized an already dynamic shareholder activism scene. Hedge funds are characterized by a higher than average level of activism coupled with a lower than usual level of regulation (Schneider and Ryan 2011). This combination raises a host of ethical issues. A key contribution of hedge funds and private equity investors is that they can invest heavily in underperforming firms and work to improve the performance of those firms through working closely with management (Ryan et al. 2010). A major concern is their opacity; they are able to hide information from their investors as well as from the government (Donaldson 2008). As a result, they can act in ways that are harmful to other investors such as purchasing distressed debt and compelling executives to declare bankruptcy, then privatizing the firm, causing some investors to lose their equity (Ryan et al. 2010). The ethical issues surrounding hedge funds and private equity firms are complex and require significant attention from scholars and practitioners to approach resolution.

The discussion so far has focused on shareholder rights and ways in which they might be protected. Every right, however, implies a responsibility and so shareholder responsibilities merit discussion as well. This area remains relatively ignored in the corporate governance and business ethics literatures. Iman Anabtawi and Lynn Stout (2008) argue that shareholder empowerment efforts and the increased shareholder power that has resulted create the need for a concomitant increase in shareholder responsibility. They contend the shareholders are no less likely than CEOs to fall prey to the forces of self-interest and greed and they note instances in which shareholders, especially but not exclusively those of hedge funds, have taken actions that benefit their own self-interest to the detriment of other shareholders, stakeholders, and the firm as a whole. Given this, they recommend that the rules of fiduciary duty be extended to apply to activist minority shareholders.

Issues surrounding boards of directors

An effective board is essential for firm success from both the shareholder primacy and board primacy perspective; the power and focus of the board might vary between these perspectives but the importance of a well-functioning board is a constant. Whether the board is focusing on making certain managers maximize shareholder wealth or focusing on mediating diverse stakeholder interests, it is important that the board be independent and effective. Corporate governance scholars have focused for years on improving board performance by specifying optimal board structure and composition. The number of outsiders on the board, board stock holdings, board size, and CEO duality, i.e., the "usual suspects" (Finkelstein and Mooney 2003: 101) have often been examined but neither research nor practice has demonstrated a consistent connection between these factors and board performance (Ryan et al. 2010).

More recently, scholars have turned to board diversity to determine how the composition of a board influences its functioning. Boards can be diverse on a variety of dimensions, including age, education, ethnicity, functional background, nationality, religion, and gender. As corporations become transnational, national diversity on the board becomes increasingly important (van Veen and Elbertsen 2008). A particular concern of corporate policy makers as well as scholars worldwide has been board demographic diversity in general and board gender diversity in particular. Board gender diversity has also been promoted by shareholder activists, institutions, and legislators (Perrault 2015). As of 2015, fourteen countries had gender quotas for boards and sixteen countries had governance codes concerned with gender parity (Adams et al. 2015). Quotas are highly effective at creating board diversity but their use is controversial because they can undermine the achievement of female board members (Kakabadse et al. 2015). Even though female directors have been shown to have backgrounds comparable with male directors (Singh et al. 2008), quotas can create the perception that the women gained their seats for reasons other than merit (Kakabadse et al. 2015). Arguments for board gender diversity encompass both the input into diversity, i.e., fairness and inclusion for directors (Kakabadse et al. 2015) and the output of diversity, i.e., the outcomes associated with having a diverse board (Adams et al. 2015). Some scholars have found that women are more moral when faced with ethical compromise (Kennedy and Kray 2014), and so some corporate governance scholars argue that boards with more female directors are likely to make more moral decisions (Hillman 2015).

Because firm performance is central to the board's responsibility, scholars have devoted considerable attention to analyzing the effects of gender diversity on firm performance, with some studies finding a positive relationship (e.g., García-Meca et al. 2015), others finding a negative relationship (e.g., Adams and Ferreira 2009), and still others finding no relationship between gender diversity and firm performance (e.g., Chapple and Humphrey 2014). Post and Byron (2015) undertook to reconcile the mixed findings through a meta-analysis of female board representation and firm performance. They found a positive relationship between female board representation and accounting returns in general: In countries that have stronger shareholder protections, the relationship they found was even more positive. Post and Byron (2015) found that the relationship between female board representation and market performance depended on the gender parity in the country. In countries with greater gender parity, female board representation was positively associated with market performance, but in countries with lower gender parity, the relationship between female board representation and market performance was negative (Post and Byron 2015).

Other scholars have gone beyond firm performance to explore board diversity outcomes such as board functioning (Veltrop et al. 2015), strategic change (Tarus and Aime 2014), strategic control (Torchia et al. 2011), innovation (Miller and del Carmen Triana 2009), reputation (Brammer et al. 2009), corporate philanthropy (Williams 2003) and corporate social performance (Boulouta 2013). Scholars have also found that having a greater proportion of women on the board increases the likelihood that a woman will be selected as CEO, but only when one of the directors is selected as CEO (Gupta and Raman 2014). Renée Adams, Amir Licht and Lilach Sagiv (2011) found that personal values play an important part in director decision and that women tend to have a greater stakeholder orientation, suggesting that firms with a greater proportion of female board members will have a greater stakeholder orientation. However, if diversity results from new members coming as representatives of factional subgroups instead of as independents, negative outcomes such as increased cognitive conflict can result (Veltrop et al. 2015).

The role of the board gives rise to a host of potential conflicts of interest. As previously discussed, the relative prioritization of shareholders and stakeholders presents ethical challenges that are not easily resolved. The resolution of conflicts of interest is something that is most often handled individually by each board member. Board members differ markedly in that regard. They differ in their primary identification, i.e., whether it is with the organization, with being a CEO, with shareholders, or with certain stakeholders (Hillman et al. 2008). These multiple identities affect their provision of resources and their resolution of conflicts. For example, board members who are former CEOs tend to grant their executives higher pay (Andres et al. 2014). Board pay presents conflicts of interest in that board members determine and set their own compensation: This problem becomes even more pronounced with stock-based compensation (Dalton and Daily 2001). When a security analyst's brokerage firm has a board member who is either a director or upper manager of a firm, the affiliated analysts tend to provide more pessimistic forecasts, making it easier for the firm to best earnings expectations (Mathew and Yildirim 2015). The market for corporate control also presents challenges that lead to conflicts of interest. Trevis Certo and colleagues (2008) found that board members of acquiring firms were paid significantly more than board members in a control group and wondered whether the board members were seeking growth through acquisition as a way of increasing their own pay. When directors are also creditors they are more likely to opt for acquisitions that favor creditors over shareholders (Hilscher and Şişli-Ciamarra 2013). Takeovers also present conflicts of interest between target shareholders, who typically profit, and target board members, who typically lose their board seats. Tompkins and Hendershott (2012) found that older directors, those closer to retirement and thus less likely to fear the loss of a seat, were more willing to take actions that benefitted target shareholders even though that meant they were likely to lose a board seat. Given these conflicts of interest that are inherent in board positions, it is important that corporate governance scholars move from studying boards at the group level of analysis to studying the processes and motivations of individual board members. One important question about board member motivation is why a person would have any interest in joining a board (Finkelstein and Hambrick 1996; Hambrick et al. 2008; Ryan et al. 2010). Board members have only indirect control of firm operations. They receive little credit for a firm's successes (Ryan et al. 2010), yet they are blamed when the firm performs poorly, leading to stigmatization and devaluation (Wiesenfeld et al. 2008). A better understanding of the motivations of individual board members will help corporate governance scholars and practitioners to better prepare boards for ethical challenges that arise.

The nature and role of the CEO

The CEO plays an important part in corporate governance as the target of the board's monitoring and controlling. Ethical challenge and conflicts of interest abound in the CEO/shareholder and CEO/board relationships. The ethical nature of the CEO is an important issue because it determines the manner in which the CEO will be monitored. Traditional corporate governance prescriptions are rooted in agency theory's view of the CEO as *homo economicus*, a rational self-interest utility maximizer (Daily et al. 2003). From this perspective, the CEO will maximize self-interest unless he or she is "frightened or incentivized into taking account of the interests of others" (Collier and Roberts 2001: 68). In contrast, stewardship theory presents a view of the CEO as a person of goodwill, who will maximize the best interests of the firm, its shareholders, and its stakeholders. The stewardship theory view of the CEO is someone intrinsically motivated to do the right thing. While the CEO depicted in agency theory requires strong extrinsic controls to forego self-interest maximization, the CEO depicted in stewardship theory is other-oriented and not prone to self-interest maximization. With agency theory as the foundation for most corporate governance prescriptions (Dalton et al. 1998), the traditional emphasis has been on creating structures that exert strong control. This approach leaves little room for concern about CEO ethics as the extrinsic controls are designed to constrain the CEO from failing to use ethical judgment (Collier and Roberts 2001; Grant and McGhee 2014). Nevertheless, the ethics of a CEO and other top managers remain at the heart of corporate governance and the relative lack of research on executive ethics is a significant loss for corporate governance research (Ryan et al. 2010). This is critical because the greater the intrinsic motivation a person has, the less that person needs external control (Eccles and Wigfield 2002). Furthermore, the use of external incentives and pressure can undermine a person's intrinsic motivation (Deci and Ryan 1985).

Shareholders are vulnerable to CEOs: They hand over their assets knowing that they do not have full information about the firm's operations (Marcoux 2003). The CEO's fiduciary duties come with responsibilities of loyalty, candor, and care (Goodpaster 1991). These responsibilities are abandoned if and when the CEO exploits CEO/shareholder information asymmetries for personal gain (Williams and Ryan 2007). CEOs can and have manipulated the stock market by making symbolic, rather than substantive, actions, such as signaling adoption of CEO long-term incentive plans (LTIPs) but not following through (Westphal and Zajac 1994, 1998). CEOs can also use interpersonal and social influence tactics to deter powerful institutional investors from forcing governance changes (Westphal and Bednar 2008) and motivate security analysts to issue positive reports (Westphal and Clement 2008). CEOs have also used impression management to respond to negative security analyst reports by increasing the formal (but not the social) level of board independence and attesting to an increase in board control: As a result, subsequent appraisals were more positive even though there was no actual increase in board control (Westphal and Graebner 2010). This is a betrayal of the CEO's fiduciary responsibility to treat shareholders with loyalty, candor, and care and to treat all shareholders fairly. To that end, Williams and Ryan (2007) note the ethical issues involved when CEOs "court" a preferred type of shareholder, while withholding or limiting information to a type of shareholder that is less desired.

CEOs also can use information asymmetry and interpersonal influence to manipulate the board of directors. This problem is exacerbated when the CEO also serves as the chair of the board, a practice that is disallowed by some country's corporate governance codes (Majumder et al. 2012). CEO compensation creates conflicts of interest that exacerbate the temptation for CEOs to pursue their own interests to the detriment of the firm and its shareholders. The size of CEO compensation is one ethical question on which there is much disagreement (Moriarty 2005, 2011; Kolb 2011). Stock-based compensation also creates ethical challenges. For example, CEOs are more likely to engage in earnings manipulation when their options are underwater (Zhang et al. 2008). In the aggregate, CEO incentive pay and the temptations it creates has been blamed for contributing to recent financial scandals and, at the individual level, incentive pay has been accused of killing CEO conscience (Stout 2014). Clearly, more attention must be paid to the unintended consequences of current corporate governance practices and the impacts they have on organizational and individual ethics.

Concluding remarks

This chapter began with the question: Who should run the corporation? To address ethics and corporate governance, it is important to step even further back and ask: What is a corporation and to what end should it be run? The question of corporate identity has triggered considerable debate among corporate governance scholars: Some see it as a person, which raises questions about a corporation's rights and duties as well as how it should be treated and how it should treat others (Ripken 2009). Other conceptions of the firm include a nexus of contracts (Coase 1937), a social entity (Lawson 2015), and the assets it owns or controls (Grossman and Hart 1986).

Lan and Heracleous (2010) propose three dominant theories of the nature of the corporation. They are: 1) concession/fiction theory, which conceptualizes the corporation as a legal fiction that exists only in law; 2) contractual/aggregate theory, which conceptualizes the corporation as the sum of its human parts and nothing more; and 3) realist/organic theory, which conceptualizes the corporation as a real entity that can act in the way that a natural person can act. Each of these conceptions of the nature of a firm raises questions about corporate governance ethics and suggest different optimal models of corporate governance (Koslowski 2009).

Along with questions about the nature of the corporation come questions regarding the purpose of the corporation—in the words of Charles Handy (2002: 49), "What's a business for?" This question should be front and center for corporate governance scholars. A reliance on scientific approaches and economic models, however, has left little room for consideration of ethics and moral responsibility. Causal determinism and negative assumptions about people have crowded out consideration of teleological explanations and free will (Ghoshal 2005). As Handy (2002: 54) wrote, we need to "raise our sights above the purely pragmatic." The generally accepted purpose of business is wealth creation, but our limited understanding of *wealth* may limit our understanding of business's purpose. Wealth has a deeper meaning than the economic definition of worldly riches. Wealth has its roots in the Middle English word *wele* meaning well-being (OED Online 2015). The Oxford English Dictionary (2015) defines *wealth* as well-being, as well as the condition of being happy and prosperous. Wealth refers not only to a person but also to a community, i.e., common or public welfare. Business is in a unique position to make the world a better place. Business can and should create wealth in all its forms.

Essential readings

An important reading on the shareholder/director primacy debate and the range of extant theories of the firm and corporate governance models is L.L. Lan and Lozios Heracleous's essay, "Rethinking Agency Theory: The View from Law" (2010). Essential works on the director primacy perspective include Lynn Stout, *The Shareholder Value Myth: How Putting Shareholders First Harms Investors, Corporations, and the Public* (2012) and Margaret M. Blair and Lynn A. Stout's essay, "A Team Production Theory of Corporate Law" (1999). Essential works on the shareholder primacy perspective include Michael C. Jensen and William H. Meckling's "Theory of the Firm: Managerial Behavior, Agency Costs and Ownership Structure" (1976) and Frank H. Easterbrook and Daniel R. Fischel, *The Economic Structure of Corporate Law* (1996). For an overview of all aspects of corporate governance, see Robert A.G. Monks and Nelson Minow *Corporate Governance* (2011, 5th edition).

For further reading in this volume on the nature of business firms, see Chapter 13, What is business? On the nature and identity of corporations, see Chapter 14, The corporation: genesis, identity, agency. On alternative conceptions of corporations, see Chapter 15, Alternative business organizations and social enterprise. On the doctrine of shareholder primacy, see Chapter 11, Stakeholder thinking. For a discussion of kinds of corporate leadership, see Chapter 25, Leadership and business ethics. On the role of governance in sub-Saharan Africa, see Chapter 37, Business ethics in Africa.

Note

* Ann Buchholtz died in September of 2015, just a few months after submitting her chapter to the editors. The version of the chapter printed here reflects her revisions to that initial draft, as well as a few minor changes initiated by the editors.

References

Adams, R.B. and D. Ferreira (2009). "Women in the Boardroom and Their Impact on Governance and Performance," *Journal of Financial Economics* 94:2, 291–309.

Adams, R.B., J. Haan, S. Terjesen and H. Ees (2015). "Board Diversity: Moving the Field Forward," *Corporate Governance: An International Review* 23, 77–82.

Adams, R.B., A.N. Licht and L. Sagiv (2011). "Shareholders and Stakeholders: How Do Directors Decide?" *Strategic Management Journal* 32:12, 1331–1355.

Alchian, A.A. and H. Demsetz (1972). "Production, Information Costs, and Economic Organization," *American Economic Review* 62:5, 777–795.

Anabtawi, I. (2006). "Some Skepticism About Increasing Shareholder Power," *UCLA Law Review* 53 (February), 561–599.

Anabtawi, I. and L. Stout (2008). "Fiduciary Duties for Activist Shareholders," *Stanford Law Review* 60, 1255–1308.

Andres, C., E. Fernau and E. Theissen (2014). "Should I Stay or Should I Go? Former CEOs as Monitors," *Journal of Corporate Finance* 28, 26–47.

Bainbridge, S.M. (2005). "Executive Compensation: Who Decides?," *Texas Law Review* 83, 1615–1662.

Bainbridge, S.M. (2006). "Director Primacy and Shareholder Disempowerment," *Harvard Law Review* 119:6, 1735–1758.

Bebchuk, L.A. (2005). "The Case for Increasing Shareholder Power," *Harvard Law Review* 118:3, 835–914.

Bebchuk, L.A. and A. Cohen (2005). "The Costs of Entrenched Boards," *Journal of Financial Economics* 78, 409–433.

Becker, G.S. (1962). "Investment in Human Capital: A Theoretical Analysis," *Journal of Political Economy* 70, 7–44.

Berle, A.A. and G.C. Means (1932). *The Modern Corporation and Private Property.* New York, NY: Macmillan.

Blair, M.M. and L. Stout (1999). "A Team Production Theory of Corporate Law," *Journal of Corporation Law* 24:4, 751.

Blair, M.M. and L. Stout (2001). "Corporate Accountability: Director Accountability and the Mediating Role of the Corporate Board," *Washington Law Review* 79, 403–447.

Boulouta, I. (2013). "Hidden Connections: The Link between Board Gender Diversity and Corporate Social Performance," *Journal of Business Ethics* 113:2, 185–197.

Brammer, S., A. Millington and S. Pavelin (2009). "Corporate Reputation and Women on the Board," *British Journal of Management* 20:1, 17–29.

Brunarski, K.R., T.C. Campbell and Y.S. Harman (2015). "Evidence on the Outcome of Say-on-Pay Votes: How Managers, Directors, and Shareholders Respond," *Journal of Corporate Finance* 30, 132–149.

Buchholtz, A. and J. Brown (2015). "Shareholder Democracy as a Misbegottten Metaphor," in M. Goranova and L.V. Ryan (eds), *Shareholder Empowerment.* New York, NY: Palgrave Macmillan.

Buchholtz, A.K. and B.A. Ribbens (1994). "Role of Chief Executive Officers in Takeover Resistance: Effects of CEO Incentives and Individual Characteristics," *Academy of Management Journal* 37:3, 554–579.

Certo, S., C. Dalton, D. Dalton and R. Lester (2008). "Boards of Directors' Self Interest: Expanding for Pay in Corporate Acquisitions?" Technical Report 01674544.

Chapple, L. and J. Humphrey (2014). "Does Board Gender Diversity Have a Financial Impact? Evidence Using Stock Portfolio Performance," *Journal of Business Ethics* 122:4, 709–723.

Chasan, E. (2015). "Say-on-Pay Vote Failures Remain Rare," *The Wall Street Journal* (May 19).

Coase, R. (1937). "The Nature of the Firm," *Economica* 4, 386–405.

Collier, J. and J. Roberts (2001). "An Ethic for Corporate Governance?" *Business Ethics Quarterly* 11:1, 67–71.

Conference Board (2015). "Proxy Voting Analytics (2010-2014)." Available at: www.conference-board.org/.

Daily, C.M., D.R. Dalton and A.A. Cannella, Jr. (2003). "Corporate Governance: Decades of Dialogue and Data," *Academy of Management Review* 28:3, 371–382.

Dalton, D.R. and C.M. Daily (2001). "Director Stock Compensation: An Invitation to a Conspicuous Conflict of Interests?" *Business Ethics Quarterly* 11:1, 89–108.

Dalton, D.R., C.M. Daily, A.A. Ellstrand and J.L. Johnson (1998). "Meta-Analytic Reviews of Board Composition, Leadership Structure, and Financial Performance," *Strategic Management Journal* 19:3, 269–290.

Dearlove, C.G. and A.J. Werrett (2013). "Proxy Access by Private Ordering: A Review of the 2012 and 2013 Proxy Seasons," *Business Lawyer* 69:1, 155–182.
Deci, E.L. and R.M. Ryan (1985). *Intrinsic Motivation and Self-Determination in Human Behavior*. New York, NY: Plenum.
Donaldson, T. (2008). "Hedge Fund Ethics," *Business Ethics Quarterly* 18:3, 405–416.
Donaldson, T. (2012). "The Epistemic Fault Line in Corporate Governance," *Academy of Management Review* 37:2, 256–271.
Donaldson, T. (2015). "Where the Facts End: Richard De George and the Rise of Business Ethics," *Journal of Business Ethics* 127, 783–787.
Donaldson, T. and L.E. Preston (1995). "The Stakeholder Theory of the Corporation: Concepts, Evidence, and Implications," *Academy of Management Review* 20:1, 65–91.
Easterbrook, F.H. and D.R. Fischel (1983). "Voting in Corporate Law," *Journal of Law and Economics* 26, 395–427.
Easterbrook, F.H. and D.R. Fischel (1996). *The Economic Structure of Corporate Law*. Cambridge, MA: Harvard University Press.
Eccles, J.S. and A. Wigfield (2002). "Motivational Beliefs, Values, and Goals," *Annual Review of Psychology* 53:1, 109.
Ertimur, Y., F. Ferri and D. Oesch (2015). "Does the Director Election System Matter? Evidence from Majority Voting," *Review of Accounting Studies* 20:1, 1–41.
Fairfax, L.M. (2008). "Making the Corporation Safe for Shareholder Democracy," *Ohio State Law Journal* 69, 53–107.
Fairfax, L.M. (2009). "The Future of Shareholder Democracy," *Indiana Law Journal* 84:4, 1259–1308.
Fama, E. and M. Jensen (1983). "Separation of Ownership and Control," *Journal of Law and Economics* 26:6, 301–325.
Fama, E.F. (1980). "Agency Problems and the Theory of the Firm," *Journal of Political Economy* 88:2, 288–307.
Finkelstein, S. and A.C. Mooney (2003). "Not the Usual Suspects: How to Use Board Process to Make Boards Better," *Academy of Management Executive* 17:2, 101–113.
Finkelstein, S. and D.C. Hambrick (1996). *Strategic Leadership: Top Executives and Their Effect on Organizations*. St Paul, MN: West Publishing Co.
Fischel, D. (1992). "The Corporate Governance Movement," *Vanderbilt Law Review* 35, 1259–1292.
Freeman, R.E. (1984). *Strategic Management: A Stakeholder Approach*. Boston, MA: Pitman.
Freeman, R.E., J.S. Harrison and A. Wicks (2007). *Managing for Stakeholders: Survival, Reputation, and Success*. New Haven, CT: Yale University Press.
Freeman, R.E., A.C. Wicks, and B. Parmar (2004). "Stakeholder Theory and "the Corporate Objective Revisited," *Organization Science* 15:3, 364–369.
Ganor, M. (2008). "Why Do Managers Dismantle Staggered Boards?" *Delaware Journal of Corporate Law* 33:1, 149–199.
García-Meca, E., I.-M. García-Sánchez and J. Martínez-Ferrero (2015). "Board Diversity and Its Effects on Bank Performance: An International Analysis," *Journal of Banking & Finance* 53, 202–214.
Gaspara, J.-M., M. Massa and P. Matos (2005). "Shareholder Investment Horizons and the Market for Corporate Control," *Journal of Financial Economics* 76:1, 135–165.
Ghoshal, S. (2005). "Bad Management Theories Are Destroying Good Management Practices," *Academy of Management Learning & Education*, 4:1, 75–91.
Goodpaster, K.E. (1991). "Business Ethics and Stakeholder Analysis," *Business Ethics Quarterly* 1:1, 53–73.
Grant, P. and P. McGhee (2014). "Corporate Governance Reform: Character-Building Structures," *Business Ethics: A European Review* 23:2, 125–138.
Grossman, S.J. and O.D. Hart (1986). "The Costs and Benefits of Ownership: A Theory of Vertical and Lateral Integration," *Journal of Political Economy* 94:4, 691–719.
Gupta, A. and K. Raman (2014). "Board Diversity and CEO Selection," *Journal of Financial Research* 37:4, 495–518.
Hambrick, D.C., A. v. Werder and E.J. Zajac (2008). "New Directions in Corporate Governance Research," *Organization Science* 19:3, 381–385.
Handy, C. (2002). "What's a Business For?" *Harvard Business Review* 80:12, 49–56.
Harrigan, K. (2014). "Comparing Corporate Governance Practices and Exit Decisions between Us and Japanese Firms," *Journal of Management & Governance* 18:4, 975–988.

Hayden, G.M. and M.T. Bodie (2012). "The Bizarre Law and Economics of Business Roundtable V. Sec," *Journal of Corporation Law* 38:1, 101–137.

Hill, J.G. (2010). "The Rising Tension between Shareholder and Director Power in the Common Law World," *Corporate Governance: An International Review* 18:4, 344–359.

Hillman, A.J. (2015). "Board Diversity: Beginning to Unpeel the Onion," *Corporate Governance: An International Review* 23:2, 104–107.

Hillman, A.J., G. Nicholson and C. Shropshire (2008). "Directors' Multiple Identities, Identification, and Board Monitoring and Resource Provision," *Organization Science* 19:3, 441–456.

Hilscher, J. and E. Şişli-Ciamarra (2013). "Conflicts of Interest on Corporate Boards: The Effect of Creditor-Directors on Acquisitions," *Journal of Corporate Finance* 19, 140–158.

ISS (2015). "2015 Board Practices Study." Available at: www.issgovernance.com.

Jacobs, M.T. (1991). *Short-Term America: The Causes and Cures of Our Business Myopia*. Boston, MA: Harvard Business School Press.

Jensen, M.C. (2001). "Value Maximisation, Stakeholder Theory, and the Corporate Objective Function," *European Financial Management* 7:3, 297–317.

Jensen, M.C. and W.H. Meckling (1976). "Theory of the Firm: Managerial Behavior, Agency Costs and Ownership Structure," *Journal of Financial Economics* 3:4, 305–360.

Johanson, D. and K. Østergren (2010). "The Movement toward Independent Directors on Boards: A Comparative Analysis of Sweden and the Uk Corporate Governance the Movement toward Independent Directors," *Corporate Governance: An International Review* 18:6, 527–539.

Jones, T.M. and W. Felps (2013). "Shareholder Wealth Maximization and Social Welfare: A Utilitarian Critique," *Business Ethics Quarterly* 23:2, 207–238.

Kacperczyk, A. (2009). "Takeover Protection and Corporate Attention to Stakeholders," *Strategic Managent Journal* 30, 261–185.

Kakabadse, N.K., C. Figueira, K. Nicolopoulou, J.H. Yang, A. Kakabadse and M. Özbilgin (2015). "Gender Diversity and Board Performance: Women's Experiences and Perspectives," *Human Resource Management* 54:2, 265–281.

Kennedy, J.A. and L.J. Kray (2014). "Who Is Willing to Sacrifice Ethical Values for Money and Social Status?: Gender Differences in Reactions to Ethical Compromises," *Social Psychological and Personality Science* 5:1, 52–59.

Kidder, D.L. and A.K. Buchholtz (2002). "Can Excess Bring Success? CEO Compensation and the Psychological Contract," *Human Resource Management Review* 12:4, 599–617.

Kolb, R. (2011). "Must CEOs Be Saints? Contra Moriarty on CEO Abstemiousness," *Business Ethics Quarterly* 21:4, 679–686.

Kolb, R. (2012). *Too Much Is Not Enough: Incentives in Executive Compensation*. New York, NY: Oxford University Press.

Koslowski, P. (2009). "The Ethics of Corporate Governance a Continental European Perspective," *International Journal of Law & Management* 51:1, 27–34.

Lafferty, W.M. (2006). *Governance for Sustainable Development: The Challeng of Adapting Form to Function*. Northampton, MA: Edward Elgar Publishing.

Lan, L.L. and L. Heracleous (2010). "Rethinking Agency Theory: The View from Law," *Academy of Management Review* 35:2, 294–314.

Lawson, T. (2015). "The Nature of the Firm and Peculiarities of the Corporation," *Cambridge Journal of Economics* 39:1, 1–32.

Lesser, H., M.F. Hoffman and W.H. Bromfield (2006). "Majority Voting: Where Are We Now?," *Insights: The Corporate & Securities Law Advisor* 20:6, 10–17.

Maitland, I. (1994). "The Morality of the Corporation: An Empirical or Normative Disagreement?" *Business Ethics Quarterly* 4:4, 445–458.

Majumder, A., S.K. Maiti and S. Banerjea (2012). "Corporate Governance Codes in Brics Nations: A Comparative Study," *Indian Journal of Corporate Governance* 5:2, 149–169.

Marcoux, A.M. (2003). "A Fiduciary Argument against Stakeholder Theory," *Business Ethics Quarterly* 13, 1–24.

Mathew, P.G. and H.S. Yildirim (2015). "Does Director Affiliation Lead to Analyst Bias?," *Applied Economics* 47:3, 272–287.

Miller, T. and M. del Carmen Triana (2009). "Demographic Diversity in the Boardroom: Mediators of the Board Diversity–Firm Performance Relationship," *Journal of Management Studies* 46:5, 755–786.

Monks, R.A.G. and N. Minow (2008). *Corporate Governance*. 4th edition. Chichester: John Wiley and Sons.
Monks, R.A.G. and N. Minow (2011). *Corporate Governance* 5th edition. Chichester: John Wiley and Sons.
Moriarty, J. (2005). "Do CEOs Get Paid Too Much?" *Business Ethics Quarterly* 15:2, 257–281.
Moriarty, J. (2011). "The Sky's the Limit: A Reply to Kolb," *Business Ethics Quarterly* 21:4, 686–691.
OED Online (2015). "wealth, n." *OED Online*: Oxford University Press, June.
Ovidiu, N. and Z.C. Pop (2012). "A Comparative Study of Corporate Governance Issues: The Case of Germany and Romania," *IUP Journal of Corporate Governance* 11:1, 20–35.
Parmar, B.L., R.E. Freeman, J.S. Harrison, A.C. Wicks, L. Purnell and S. de Colle (2010). "Stakeholder Theory: The State of the Art," *The Academy of Management Annals* 4:1, 403–445.
Perrault, E. (2015). "Why Does Board Gender Diversity Matter and How Do We Get There? The Role of Shareholder Activism in Deinstitutionalizing Old Boys' Networks," *Journal of Business Ethics* 128:1, 149–165.
Post, C. and K. Byron (2015). "Women on Boards and Firm Financial Performance: A Meta-Analysis," *Academy of Management Journal* 58:5, 1546–1571.
Rasheed, A. and T. Yoshikawa (2012). *The Convergence of Corporate Governance: Promise and Prospects*. London: Palgrave Macmillan.
Ripken, S.K. (2009). "Corporations Are People Too: A Multi-Dimensional Approach to the Corporate Personhood Puzzle," *Fordham Journal of Corporate & Financial Law* 15:1, 97–177.
Rose, C. (2012). "The New European Shareholder Rights Directive: Removing Barriers and Creating Opportunities for More Shareholder Activism and Democracy," *Journal of Management & Governance* 16:2, 269–284.
Rossouw, G.J. and A.J.G. Sison (2006). *Global Perspectives on Ethics of Corporate Governance*. New York, NY: Palgrave Macmillan.
Ryan, L.V. (2000). "Shareholders and the Atom of Property: Fission or Fusion?," *Business & Society* 39:1, 49.
Ryan, L.V. and A.K. Buchholtz (2001). "Trust, Risk, and Shareholder Decision Making: An Investor Perspective on Corporate Governance," *Business Ethics Quarterly*, 11:1, 177–193.
Ryan, L.V., A.K. Buchholtz and R.W. Kolb (2010). "New Directions in Corporate Governance and Finance: Implications for Business Ethics Research," *Business Ethics Quarterly* 20:4, 673–694.
Ryan, L.V. and M. Schneider (2002). "The Antecedents of Institutional Investor Activism," *Academy of Management Review* 27:4, 554–573.
Ryan, L.V. and M. Schneider (2003). "Institutional Investor Power and Heterogeneity: Implications for Agency and Stakeholder Theories," *Business and Society* 42, 398–429.
Schneider, M. and L.V. Ryan (2011). "A Review of Hedge Funds and Their Investor Activism: Do They Help or Hurt Other Equity Investors?" *Journal of Management & Governance* 15:3, 349–374.
Shleifer, A. and R.W. Vishny (1997). "A Survey of Corporate Governance," *Journal of Finance* 52:2, 737–783.
Singh, V., S. Terjesen and S. Vinnicombe (2008). "Newly Appointed Directors in the Boardroom: How Do Women and Men Differ?" *European Management Journal* 26:1, 48–58.
Stout, L.A. (2007). "The Mythical Benefits of Shareholder Control," *Virginia Law Review* 93:3, 789–809.
Stout, L.A. (2012). *The Shareholder Value Myth: How Putting Shareholders First Harms Investors, Corporations, and the Public*. San Francisco, CA: Berrett-Koehler.
Stout, L.A. (2013). "The Toxic Side Effects of Shareholder Primacy," *University of Pennsylvania Law Review* 161:7, 2003–2023.
Stout, L.A. (2014). "Killing Conscience: The Unintended Behavioral Consequences of "Pay for Performance,"*Journal of Corporation Law* 39:3, 525–561.
Subramanian, G. (2015). "Corporate Governance 2.0," *Harvard Business Review* 93:3, 96–105.
Sundaram, A.K. and A.C. Inkpen (2004). "The Corporate Objective Revisited," *Organization Science*, 15:3 350–363.
Tarus, D.K. and F. Aime (2014). "Board Demographic Diversity, Firm Performance and Strategic Change," *Management Research Review* 37:12, 1110–1136.
Tkac, P. (2006). "One Proxy at a Time: Pursuing Social Change through Shareholder Proposals," *Economic Review* 91:3, 1–20.
Tompkins, J. and R. Hendershott (2012). "Outside Director-Shareholder Agency Conflicts: Evidence from Bank Consolidation," *Corporate Governance: The International Journal of Effective Board Performance* 12:3, 378–391.
Torchia, M., A. Calabrò and M. Huse (2011). "Women Directors on Corporate Boards: From Tokenism to Critical Mass," *Journal of Business Ethics* 102:2, 299–317.

Van Veen, K. and J. Elbertsen (2008). "Governance Regimes and Nationality Diversity in Corporate Boards: A Comparative Study of Germany, the Netherlands and the United Kingdom," *Corporate Governance: An International Review* 16:5, 386–399.

Veall, M.R. (2012). "Top Income Shares in Canada: Recent Trends and Policy Implications," *Canadian Journal of Economics* 45:4, 1247–1272.

Veltrop, D.B., N. Hermes, T.J.B.M. Postma and J. Haan (2015). "A Tale of Two Factions: Why and When Factional Demographic Faultlines Hurt Board Performance," *Corporate Governance: An International Review* 23:2, 145–160.

Walsh, J.P. and J.K. Seward (1990). "On the Efficiency of Internal and External Corporate Control Mechanisms," *Academy of Management Review* 15:3, 421–456.

Westphal, J.D. and M.K. Bednar (2008). "The Pacification of Institutional Investors," *Administrative Science Quarterly*, 53:1, 29–72.

Westphal, J.D. and M.B. Clement (2008). "Sociopolitical Dynamics in Relations between Top Managers and Security Analysts: Favor Rendering, Reciprocity, and Analyst Stock Recommendations," *Academy of Management Journal* 51:5, 873–897.

Westphal, J.D. and M.E. Graebner (2010). "A Matter of Appearances: How Corporate Leaders Manage the Impressions of Financial Analysts About the Conduct of Their Boards," *Academy of Management Journal*, 53:1, 15–44.

Westphal, J.D. and E.J. Zajac (1994). "Substance and Symbolism in CEOs' Long-Term Incentive Plans," *Administrative Science Quarterly* 39:3, 367–390.

Westphal, J.D. and E.J. Zajac (1998). "The Symbolic Management of Stockholders: Corporate Governance Reforms and Shareholder Reactions," *Administrative Science Quarterly* 43:1, 127–153.

Wiesenfeld, B.M., K.A. Wurthmann and D.C. Hambrick (2008). "The Stigmatization and Devaluation of Elites Associated with Corporate Failures: A Process Model," *Academy of Management Review* 33:1, 231–251.

Williams, C.C. and L.V. Ryan (2007). "Courting Shareholders: The Ethical Implications of Altering Corporate Ownership Structures," *Business Ethics Quarterly* 17:4, 669–688.

Williams, R.J. (2003). "Women on Corporate Boards of Directors and Their Influence on Corporate Philanthropy," *Journal of Business Ethics*, 42:1, 1–10.

Williamson, O.E. (1985). *The Economic Institutions of Capitalism : Firms, Markets, Relational Contracting*. New York, NY, London: Free Press, Collier Macmillan.

Zhang, X., K.M. Bartol, K.G. Smith, M.D. Pfarrer and D.M. Khanin (2008). "CEOs on the Edge: Earnings Manipulation and Stock Based Incentive Misalignment," *Academy of Management Journal* 51:2, 241–258.

25

Leadership and business ethics

Are leaders wolves for business ethics?

Valérie Petit and Sarah E. Saint-Michel

In the *Nicomachean Ethics*, Aristotle reminds us that we learn about morality not only in treatises but also, and perhaps above all, by observing and imitating the virtue of others and particularly that of powerful individuals whom we refer to as *leaders* (Aristotle 382–322 BCE; see 1999). In contemporary society, what better medium than the cinema to depict the vices and virtues of the powerful? An archetypal film on leadership and business ethics, *The Wolf of Wall Street* (Scorsese 2013), offers a case study of ethics and leadership in the context of business. Situated in the hurly burly of Wall Street in 1980s America, the film tells the story of the rise, fall, and redemption of a young stockbroker, Jordan Belfort. The story of power, business, and ethics may serve as motif for an exploration of the complexities of business leadership and its ethical (or non-ethical) dimensions.

The Wolf of Wall Street is a well-known story inspired by events during the emergence of the financial capitalism that continues to dominate today's globalized economy. The career of Jordan Belfort (played by Leonardo DiCaprio) begins with the stock market crash of 1987 and the subsequent bankruptcy of the firm where the young stockbroker had started his career. Faced with difficult circumstances, Belfort and an associate set up a stockbroking firm, which enjoys rapid—and undisguised—success. Underpinning this success is their willingness to engage in circumventions of the law, as well as fraudulent practices (such as the "pump and dump" by which clients are manipulated to buy a stock which Belfort then sells at an inflated price). These actions prove effective because of the charisma and influence of Belfort. But the young broker crosses not only a legal line but a moral one: his hubris leads him to indulge in drugs, prostitutes, harassment, and violence (Petit and Bollaert 2012). In sum, Belfort becomes corrupted by power and money, and loses all sense of proportion and values, resulting in his downfall (including prison). *The Wolf of Wall Street* depicts a paradoxical business leader: a dominant figure who is the slave of his own addictions, as fascinating and charismatic as he is pathetic and vile in his appetite for excess.

With this story in mind, this chapter offers a comprehensive introduction to the concepts, theories and approaches to have emerged from leadership studies. The first section explores the relationship between leadership and business ethics, focusing on the question of whether the very idea of leadership should include an ethical component. It turns out that, for many scholars, there is a contested and unresolved debate as to whether leadership may be construed in neutral or in ethical terms. The second section focuses on the main models and theories of "ethical leadership." The third section concentrates on the personal characteristics of leaders—their character and psychology, vices and virtues. The fourth section explores a series of issues related, in a broad sense, to social responsibility, including questions of diversity in corporate leadership.

Theoretical foundations: desperately seeking ethics in leadership

Il n'est pas deux peuples sur la surface du globe qui soient vertueux de la même manière.[1]
Marquis de Sade, Justine ou les malheurs de la vertu

Is Jordan Belfort a leader? One viewer might suggest that, yes, this charismatic, intelligent and self-confident individual is a leader because he managed to get hundreds of employees and clients on board, all willing to believe and do anything for him. However, another might disagree, pointing out that Belfort's very lack of morals, in both his goals and the means he employs to achieve them, disqualify him outright from the category of leader. This second view sees Belfort less as a leader than a manipulator and tyrant. On this view no individual can be considered a leader if that person disregards the law and the moral obligations that should be otherwise linked with the responsibility that comes with exercising power, including running a company. But the first view takes a rather Machiavellian perspective: ethics is no more than an optional facet of leadership, so all that counts is the effectiveness of one's influence. How we describe Belfort, therefore, hinges on a key challenge facing anyone who wants to understand the relationship between leadership and business ethics. Before turning directly to this debate on ethics and leadership, it might be helpful to examine several salient definitions of the very idea of leadership.

Defining leadership

Leadership is a wide-ranging concept and area of research (Bass 2008) that has generated a volume of publications whose enormity may suggest the disproportionate fascination that the subject of power holds for thinkers (Meindl 1995). Nonetheless, the words of James MacGregor Burns remain pertinent: "Leadership is one of the most observed and least understood phenomena on earth" (Burns 1978: 2).

There is now relative consensus in the field as to how to define leadership. One commonly used definition, which nonetheless seems circular, characterizes leadership as, "a multidirectional influence relationship between a leader and followers with the mutual purpose of accomplishing real change" (Rost 1993: 92). A more recent and accurate account defines leadership in terms of, "the process of influencing others to understand and agree about what needs to be done and how to do it, and the process of facilitating individual and collective efforts to accomplish shared objectives" (Yukl 2010: 26). The second definition reminds us that leadership is a relational and interpersonal phenomenon manifest in the reciprocal (though distinct) influences between a leader (or several when it is shared) and his followers as they act together toward some shared ends.

The influence of the leader is drawn mainly from the representations (beliefs), desires, and behavior of actors rather than on coercive or manipulative means. In this vein, researchers view leadership as rooted chiefly in the behavior of and relationships among actors rather than as derivative simply from the position, status, power, or expertise of the leader. Many academics draw a distinction between power (an individual's capacity to act) and leadership, a form of influence drawn from an individual's capacity to get other individuals to do what he wants without resorting to coercion, manipulation, or constraint. However, leadership must be distinguished from another kind of influence, social influence, which relies not on the beliefs and consent of actors but on group norms and group pressure. In sum, leadership is the result of a process in which followers freely and voluntarily recognize an individual's leadership (leadership attribution). Recognition leads to commitment and obedience.

Since the interpersonal influence of leadership can draw strength from various behaviors and triggers (whether rational, emotional, or value-based), it is possible to explain the diversity found in leadership styles and in leaders themselves. Similarly, while the goals of leadership are always common goals, they can reflect diverse aspirations: economic performance, change, perhaps general well-being, even the preservation of the status quo. Given that leadership forms are extremely diverse, one question that has occupied researchers since the 1980s has less to do with identifying the characteristics of the "good leader" than in understanding this changing phenomenon and the harmony between leadership style and the circumstances of an organization. Such harmony is an important factor in leadership performance and can ensure its positive impact; nevertheless, beyond this consensus about the nature of leadership, many issues remains unresolved.

Among these questions is, as noted at the beginning of this section, whether leadership is always moral. In so far as Joseph Rost specifies that leadership aims towards "real change," then one may infer that his definition locates ethics—the idea of a real, positive, or beneficial change—at the heart of leadership. Yet Gary Yukl's definition, which appeals to influence, understanding, and "shared objectives," does not seem to mention ethics. Is leadership *qua* leadership inherently ethical? Or, alternatively, is *effective* leadership ethical?

Articulating leadership and ethics

Most research studies on leadership have long concentrated on explaining leadership in terms of effectiveness. Whereas explicit definitions of leadership maintained this task-oriented and morally neutral approach, a moral dimension, like a return of the repressed, has been re-introduced to rework the theories and models of leadership, perhaps spurred by the academic hope of finding *the* answer to *the* question raised by philosophers about power: "Implicit in all these theories . . . is an ethical question. Are leaders more effective when they are nice to people, or are leaders more effective when they use certain techniques for structuring and ordering tasks?" (Ciulla 1995: 14).

By articulating this implicit question, Joanne Ciulla not only clarifies (1995) the crux of the relationship between leadership and business ethics but indicates why so many theories try to empirically demonstrate that the *good* leader not only achieves goals but also demonstrates consideration for people. This desire to understand not just effective leadership but "good effective leadership" explains why ethics specialists describe most leadership theories as "normative" (Ciulla 2013). This normative issue has consequence on the conceptual articulation of leadership and ethics: Ciulla distinguishes between two different ways of combining these two concepts: either ethics is a contingent modality, dimension or consequence of leadership, though not essential to the concept itself, or one speaks of leadership as inherently ethical. For example, Ciulla asks, "How do you answer the question, 'Is Hitler a leader?'" (1995: 13). If leadership is inherently ethical, then Hitler was not simply a bad leader but no leader at all. On the other hand, based on the non-moral criterion of effectiveness, then one could inquire as to whether Hitler was an effective leader in achieving his aims and those of his followers. As these two perspectives reveal, the articulation between ethics and leadership remains ambiguous. As noted by Ciulla, beyond the ambivalence of scholars themselves, we have to deal with the paradoxical nature of power and leadership: "Power is one source of immorality for leaders and morality is one source of power for leaders" (2005: 327).

But why is this discussion about a normative foundation to leadership theories so important? The term *leader* in contemporary society is one that is highly valued and valuable. The fact that it can be used to describe individuals who are indiscriminately immoral seems problematic, especially if the criterion of leadership is the chief basis on which we select and evaluate our future corporate leaders. In the following sections we explore some contemporary work on business ethics and leadership, even as many of these inquiries do not distinguish adequately the ambiguity at the heart of leadership and ethics (Smith and Lewis 2011).

The moral manager: navigating ethical leadership

> Like pornography, we only recognize moral leadership when we see it. The problem is, we so rarely see it.
>
> (Gini 2004: 40)

At what point does the sight of Jordan Belfort's behavior begin to put us ill at ease? Is it his initial lies as he begins to win over naive clients? The scenes of sexual orgies and cocaine consumption on company premises? Or his insider trading, tax fraud, and blind disregard for the consequences of his behavior for his colleagues? Or perhaps we need to wait for the reaction of the tax authorities before suddenly overcoming our fascination for this charismatic leader and discovering with horror the extent of his depravations? In many respects, the history of theories about ethical leadership is also a story about a delayed and horrified response from leadership and management academics as they observed scandalous behavior among some business leaders and realised that it was widespread at the highest level in companies. In the realm of business, most theories describe a virtuous model of leadership and contrast it with unethical behavior. The authors seek to show, with varying degrees of awareness, that their models of moral leadership also prove economically effective. Clearly most of these theories are normative, at least in the sense that they attach, contingently if not essentially, a notion of ethics to their definitions of leadership (Ciulla et al. 2013). The ethical conceptions reflect, typically, the implicit moral norms of the authors or the period and culture in which they live.

Servant leadership: the spiritual approach

The theory of servant leadership is often presented as one of the oldest theories of ethical leadership in the field of leadership studies (Parris and Peachey 2013). Developed in the United States in the late 1970s by Robert Greenleaf, a former manager of research at AT&T, the servant leadership theory breaks with the traditional vision of the leader (Greenleaf 1977). Greenleaf has defended the idea that leaders must put the needs of followers before their own needs, thereby upholding the moral obligation to serve others. "The servant leader . . . begins with the natural feeling that one wants to serve, to serve first. Then conscious choice brings one to aspire to lead" (Greenleaf 1977: 13–14).

More recently researchers have proposed a scale to measure servant leadership that includes five dimensions: altruism, egalitarianism, community-building, interpersonal support, and moral integrity (Liden et al. 2008; Reed et al. 2011). Some empirical studies show the positive effects of servant leadership on the performance and ethics of staff and organizations: a servant-led organization enhances leader trust and organizational trust (Joseph and Winston 2005); organizational citizenship behavior, procedural justice (Ehrhart 2004; Walumbwa et al. 2010); prosocial and altruistic behavior (Ebener and O'Connell 2010; Hu and Liden 2011; Ehrhart 2004; Walumbwa et al. 2010); and team and leader effectiveness (Mayer et al. 2009; Schaubroeck et al. 2012).

But, beyond its popularity and its positive effects on organizations and companies in particular, the servant leadership theory illustrates not only a critique of then existing models of leadership but, above all, the explicit and conscious return of morality to the heart of leadership. The originality of servant leadership rests in its use of spirituality (Fry 2003), especially Christian spirituality, to bring about this return of morality. The apostle Mark wrote that Jesus told his disciples: "whoever wants to become great among you must be your servant, and whoever wants to be first must be slave of all" (Mark 10: 43–44). But Greenleaf added that he had been inspired by reading *Journey to the East*, the spiritual novel by Herman Hesse (2013), whose character of Leo exemplifies the servant leader *par excellence* yet whose leadership became apparent only after his death (Greenleaf 1977). Recent studies have also emphasised the link between servant leadership and the individual's beliefs and spiritual practices (Fry 2003; Reave 2005; Freeman and Auster 2011). Yet in its operational details the servant leader also manifests the values of care—loving others, self-sacrifice, trusting others.

While the servant leadership theory follows a spiritual path to resituate morality at the heart of leadership, it also offers a critique of the dominant model of leadership and of the managerial culture in contemporary businesses. Here, the leader is in the unusual position of stewardship: he acts on behalf of others rather than on his own behalf. By respecting others and by ensuring sound relationships within the group, he makes certain the common good can be served by everyone collectively. Furthermore, the servant leader takes an egalitarian view of the leadership relationship, conceived more as a partnership that is based on the empowerment of others. The moral scope of this model is clear when one compares the servant leader with the abuses of power or the self-serving behavior of other leaders.

Transformational leadership: the ideals or value-based approach

The transformational leadership model is also regularly considered as an ethical model, even though, unlike servant leadership, its advocates do not explicitly emphasise this aspect (Bass and Stodgdill 2009). Unlike the servant approach, the transformational model emphasizes the actual transformation of the followers or of society and focuses on the more idealized, charismatic, and visionary qualities in a leader.

The origins of the transformational leadership model, as defined by Bernard Bass (Bass 1985), a psychology researcher, can be traced to the political science research of James MacGregor Burns (1978). Burns drew a distinction between the transactional and transformational styles. He considered the former to be the traditional form of leadership, focused on the exchange of resources (material or psychological) that occurs between a leader (who receives obedience) and followers (who receive material goods). The transformational approach looks to more elevated needs (self-fulfilment, pursuit of an idealised goal) and seeks to achieve the positive transformation of followers and ultimately of their environment. Drawing on Burns, Bruce J. Avolio and Bernard Bass (1991) set about describing the behavior of these transformational leaders, including those in business. They suggested that four behaviors contribute to the establishment of transformational leadership: idealised influence—the leader acts as a model of identification and projection for his followers, generates trust and admiration, and displays conduct consistent with the values he promotes; inspirational motivation—the leader motivates others by offering a vision that is full of meaning and generates enthusiasm and optimism; intellectual stimulation—the leader stimulates creativity and encourages his followers to change perspective without judging them; and individualized consideration—the leader plays a role as personal development coach, listens to and deals with each individual according to his or her uniqueness or talents.

A number of empirical findings suggest that the transformational style is more effective in terms of followers' work involvement (Meyer et al. 2002) and goal achievement than the transactional style and has a positive affect on these features: the psychological well being of followers (Meyer et al. 2002), self-efficacy (Dvir et al. 2002), psychological empowerment (Avolio et al. 2004), creativity (Hoyt and Blascowitch 2003), citizenship behavior (Podsakoff et al. 1996), and group cohesion (Bass et al. 2003). However, most likely due to its predominance, this model has been the subject of fierce debate when it comes to the importance it places on ethics.

In its original form, Bass's model makes no mention of ethics or morality and thereby appears to break away from its two main sources of inspiration—Max Weber and J.M. Burns. The great German sociologist described the charismatic leader as belonging to a romantic and idealistic tradition in which the leader not only prophesises a *better* world but rattles the existing order with the strength of his conviction and values (Weber 1947; Petit 2012). The charismatic leader embodies the force of an ideal and proves to be a master at mobilising followers. Bass also seems to break from Burns, who had placed the moral commitment of the leader at the heart of transformational leadership: "such leadership occurs when one or more persons engage with others in such a way that leaders and followers raise one another to higher levels of motivation and morality" (Burns 1978: 2).

In reality, however, there was no split from either Weber or Burns: subsequent research and discussions on transformational leadership reveal the profoundly normative and moral nature of Bass's model. Terry L. Price (2003) and Ciulla (2005) highlight the moral ambivalence of transformational leadership, suggesting that, yes, if we strictly adhere to Bass's definition then we could argue that Hitler, based on his charisma, was at once a transformational and immoral leader who manipulated negative ideals and values and brought about a nightmarish transformation of Germany and Europe. However, when Bass was questioned about the place of morality in his model, he responded that truly transformational leadership is always moral and its means and its aims are guided by positive values; otherwise, the leader is pseudo-transformational (Bass and Steidlmeier 1999).

Authentic leadership and the virtue-based approach

Although servant leadership and transformational leadership are currently the two most studied ethical leadership models, others are emerging. The virtue-based approach and the ethics of care (which some categorise as part of virtue ethics; see Halwani 2003) is currently enjoying renewed interest (Crossan et al. 2013; Flynn 2008; Palanski and Yammarino 2007), and thus Aristotle and Confucius are invoked in studies of the foundations of leadership and the conduct of leaders.

One particular and very contemporary instance of the virtue-based approach is that of "authentic leadership," as developed in the United States since 2000 (Gardner et al. 2011). The notion of authentic leadership was developed both by academics and professional leadership figures such as Bill George, former CEO of Medtronic (George and Sims 2007). In his book, co-written with Peter Sims and entitled *True North: Discover Your Authentic Leadership*, the authors unearthed the ancient notion of authenticity, or at least an ancient notion as reworked by latter day psychologists. Susan Harter, who embraces "positive psychology" (with its emphasis on the qualities that enable meaningful living), defines authenticity in terms of "owning one's personal experiences, be they thoughts, emotions, needs, preferences or beliefs" and as desiring to know oneself and behave in a manner that is consistent with one's values and personal opinions (Harter 2002: 382). Authentic leadership can be defined as "a pattern of leader behavior that draws upon and promotes both positive psychological capacities and a positive ethical climate, to foster greater self-awareness, an internalized moral perspective, balanced processing of information, and relational transparency on the part of leaders working with followers, fostering positive self-development" (Walumbwa et al. 2008: 94). Of course, these positive attributes, so generally phrased, could play a role just about everywhere in life, so it is incumbent on the defenders of authentic leadership to explain what is particularly distinct in their characterizations. Some have contended that authenticity requires a deep self-knowledge: To display authentic leadership, we must understand our true nature, what we believe and value, and act transparently towards our followers (Avolio et al. 2004).

To assess authenticity in leadership some measurement scales have been developed (Walumbwa et al. 2008), the most commonly used being the Authentic Leadership Questionnaire (ALQ). This scale measures four dimensions: self-awareness (the individual can describe exactly who he is, his strengths, weaknesses and values), relational transparency (the person is transparent and honest), balanced processing (the person is objective yet open towards other opinions), and moral consistency (the individual acts in accordance with the values he promotes). The personal traits that provide the bases for authentic leadership include optimism, hope, resilience, and self-monitoring (Jensen and Luthans 2006), while its outcomes include satisfaction, motivation, commitment, civic mindedness, happiness among followers, along with a negative consequence of fatigue or "burnout" (Wong and Cummings 2009; Walumbwa et al. 2008; Jensen and Luthans 2006).

The theory of authenticity is closely linked to that of transformational leadership: it is an extension thereof and a response to criticisms of the moral ambivalence attached to the transformational leader. Even so, Ciulla's objection (2013) continues to hold: the starting definition of authenticity is *normative*, yet it seems plausible that an individual could be both authentic and authentically tyrannical, driven by negative values and immoral goals.

Beyond the model of authentic leadership, a number of studies on *virtuous* leaders have flourished since the 2000s, perhaps inspired by positive psychology. Kim S. Cameron (2011: 25) summarizes the virtuous (or responsible) leader in three ways: "as being accountable for performance and being dependable in achieving promised performance"; as someone who has a certain amount of room for manoeuvre and a willingness to act with authority (Salancik and Meindl 1984); and as someone who has commitments towards different stakeholders within the organization (Maak and Pless 2006). Cameron argues that one central element has been overlooked—virtuousness—which he carefully distinguishes from virtue. He defines virtuousness as, "the most ennobling behaviours and outcomes, the excellence and essence of humankind, the best of the human condition, and the highest aspirations of humanity" (2011: 28).

Examples of virtuous leadership might be illustrated by the senior leaders at Prudential's Relocation Company contacting senior executives at BP Oil Company shortly after the Gulf of Mexico oil spill. They offered to provide free relocation services from the UK to the US until the spill was cleaned up. The rationale: we want to help, and we think that it is the right thing to do (2011: 27).

Cameron suggests that virtuousness acts as a fixed point, as a reference for leaders. He thereby clearly accepts the normative dimension of his model and specifies the three assumptions that underpin it: a eudaemonic assumption that there is an inclination towards good in all humans; an inherent value assumption that virtuous action has no goal other than virtuousness, an end in itself; and an amplification assumption that virtuousness generates and sustains or amplifies positive energy. In conclusion, Cameron emphasises that responsible leadership with virtuousness helps identify a universally accepted standard for what leaders can consider the best for individuals and their organizations: "Virtuousness represents the best of what humankind aspires to achieve, and responsible leadership in pursuit of the highest good is a worthy aspiration" (Cameron 2011: 32).

The moral person: exploring the character of business leaders

> I want you to back yourself into a corner. Give yourself no choice but to succeed. Let the consequences of failure become so dire and so unthinkable that you'll have no choice but to do whatever it takes to succeed.
>
> *Jordan Belfort*, The Wolf of Wall Street

The story of Jordan Belfort reminds us of the negative way in which many of us perceive the lack of morality among some corporate leaders, whether we attribute the cause of this ethical weakness to the character of the individual (rotten apples theory) or to the power system that corrupts them (dirty hands theory). In this section we review relevant work dedicated to the qualities, personal or moral, of ethical and unethical leaders.

Ethical leaders

There are various ways of characterising the personality or character of ethical leaders. Some key aspects are highlighted below, including moral development, as well as particular virtues. A first question to ask is whether ethical leaders manifest a higher stage of moral development.

Cognitive moral development might seem crucial in manifesting ethical leadership. Al Gini (2004) suggests that ethical leaders have developed a higher stage of cognitive moral development, which itself refers to how a leader thinks about what is right or wrong and his or her capacity of principled reasoning (Kohlberg 1984). Notably, Lawrence Kohlberg's model (1984) of development emphasises the individual's path from family acceptance to social norms to a final stage at which one acts on self-chosen but universal moral rules. Individuals who have reached the final stage of moral development are more likely to manifest ethical behavior, i.e., integrity, honesty and high moral values (Gini 2004).

Similarly, the notion of morality, and moral identity in particular, is a key aspect in the personality of ethical leaders. Moral identity has been defined as "a self-conception organized around a set of moral traits [e.g., honesty, care, compassion]" (Aquino and Reed 2002: 1424). But not all individuals will possess such a self-conception and these individuals cannot, therefore, be ethical leaders. Leaders with a high moral identity are more likely to manifest behaviors in line with morality and ethics and to make strong efforts to find the best solution and carefully examine ethical perspectives (Mayer et al. 2012).

A second question regarding ethical leaders is whether these individuals possess special virtues or character strengths? One study (Peterson and Seligman 2004) identifies six traditional virtues (courage, temperance, justice, prudence, humanity, and transcendence) and twenty-four character traits that, typically, serve to enable ethical leadership. Subsequent work (Neubert et al. 2009) also suggests that these six virtues are powerful determinants for the characterization of ethical leaders. Acting ethically requires wisdom and knowledge to transmit new viewpoints, courage to take on established views, justice to put in place and sustain procedures that are equitable and fair for all, temperance to act with self-control and reflection, and lastly transcendence to offer a positive and enthusiastic vision of the future.

Unethical leaders

As a counterpoint to portraits of virtuous leaders, authors like Barbara Kellerman (2004) and Jean Lipman-Blumen (2006) offer a profile of "negative" leaders. They identify seven types of negative leaders and negative motivations: the incompetent, who have neither the motivation nor the ability to sustain effective action; the rigid, who can be competent but are unyielding and unable to accept new ideas; the intemperate, who lack self-control and are enabled by followers who either do not want to or cannot intervene; the callous, who are uncaring or unkind, ignoring the needs of followers; the corrupt, who lie, cheat and steal; the insular, who draw a clear boundary between the welfare of their immediate group and that of outsiders; and the evil, who commit atrocities, using their power to inflict severe physical or psychological harm. This classification has not been empirically validated but enables us to debate what we mean by the term *negative leader*. For Kellerman, a negative leader is unethical and has non-beneficial effects on those around him or her. But this impact is not only due to a lack of personal morality; it can also stem from two other deficits, which Kellerman does not address.

One deficit may be cognitive: a leader causes harm due to his inability to correctly analyze the situation (Price 2003). The debate on this is open but requires development. Lamentably, the question of the cognitive capabilities of leaders is currently almost as taboo as that of their addictions, yet it is of critical importance in a world in which the amount of information and the speed with which it circulates are increasing exponentially.

Another deficit may arise from a personality disorder such as narcissism. This subject also needs careful consideration, especially in light of recent studies on narcissism in companies (see, for a review, Bollaert and Petit 2010). As early as the 1970s, Christopher Lasch (1979) highlighted the "culture of narcissism" in contemporary society. More recent research has revealed that narcissistic personalities progress more quickly and receive higher levels of recognition in companies (Spurk et al. 2016; see also Maccoby 2000). On the other hand, several studies in the fields of finance and behavioral strategy have shown that the hubris of corporate leaders has negative implications on company performance and organizational ethics (Petit and Bollaert 2012). However, few studies have focused on the antecedents of hubris, and in particular on the importance of individual and contextual factors that may encourage or discourage it (Owen and Davidson 2009).

Ethical leadership in the age of corporate social responsibility

> Power is one source of immorality for leaders and morality is one source of power for leaders.
> *(Ciulla 2005: 327)*

The story of Jordan Belfort exists alongside the rise of efforts to encourage corporate social responsibility (CSR). The misuse of leadership and the misbehavior of leaders has fueled an awareness within societies and companies of the necessity of responsible leadership. But what is leadership in the age of CSR? How might the corporate realm prevent the rise of a Jordan Belfort, James Cayne or Ken Lay? In this section we offer a broad approach to responsible leadership, which emphasises three challenges for responsible leaders: two of these pivot around power and its consequences, the third turns on new manifestations of diversity.

Preventing the intoxication of power

Corporate leadership gives a business leader great discretion and impact on his or her surroundings. Beyond the legitimacy they enjoy because of their position within a hierarchy, high-level managers are perceived as role models (Bandura 1977). The special power bestowed by their status raises two important questions.

The first concerns the possibility of negative consequences that might ensue for the leader and follower relationship. The reports on the Milgram experiment (1963) described the loss of agency that may occur among those who follow orders and no longer question the morality of a leader's decision or their own conduct. Other studies of charismatic but particularly powerful leaders (Avolio and Yammarino 2002) reveal the risks of such an influence on followers (stress, burnout, lack of objectivity).

A second issue is the ethics of the leader and his or her ability to resist the intoxicating appeals of power. The rise and fall of Jordan Belfort illuminates how a leader's psyche and conduct can be affected by power. The intoxicating effects of power are captured in the classical Greek notion of hubris. As explained by Petit and Bollaert: "Hubris describes a sense of overweening pride, a defiance of the gods, which was then punished through the intervention of Nemesis, who wrought various forms of death and destruction on the hubristic hero and the general population" (2012: 23). The authors define hubris, in the context of business, as a consequence of great power given to an individual in a context of low regulation and few constraints on the leader's behavior. They identify five species of conduct or belief that manifest business hubris: a grandiose sense of self; an overestimation of one's abilities and likelihood of success; a sense of uniqueness; the belief that one is set above others; and the belief that neither the law or a higher power (God) should constrain one. The authors appeal to both corporate governance and culture, as well as leadership authenticity to counter the temptations of power.

There are many different ways of approaching such solutions but most research in this area has focused on the notion of ethical climate (Victor and Cullen 1988) or ethical culture (Treviño 1990)—the characteristics of the organization which do or do not support ethical behavior and attitudes among employees (Treviño et al. 1998). Drawing on social learning theory, Michael E. Brown and Linda K. Treviño (2006) suggest that a reward system that supports ethical conduct, the fair treatment of employees, and the infusion of ethical concerns into daily organizational decision-making should support ethical leadership over time. In this type of environment, ethical leadership is viewed as desirable, so leaders develop and maintain conduct that exemplifies, and conduces others to, ethical leadership. Similarly, the members of such organizations develop an acute sense of what constitutes ethical and fair behavior, have a heightened understanding of ethical problems, and avoid unethical behavior by discouraging undesirable conduct (Treviño 1986). The expectations associated with ethical leaders should take root in an ethical culture shared and understood by all members of their units, so that ethical leadership and ethical cognition and behavior become reinforcing (see Schaubroeck et al. 2012).

It is partly because the image of the trader had become one of decadence and cynicism that Jordan Belfort was able to model his behavior so that it coincided with this stereotypical image. Scorsese's film is an illustration of the importance for Belfort at the beginning of his career of conforming to a model, which he felt was symbolic of traders. Inspired by these models, he adopted the attributes he perceived as typical of traders: disproportionate self-esteem, drug and alcohol consumption and cynicism. The model—and representation—of traders thereby shaped his behavior.

With this example in mind, let us now consider the effects of leadership expectations on leaders and leadership. The ultimate aim of implicit leadership theories is to explore how each individual defines what a leader is or should be (Lord et al. 1984). Individuals develop cognitive structures containing the character traits and behavior they expect in leaders (Lord et al. 1984). Followers categorise leaders based on a process of comparison against the prototype of an ideal category. Because leadership represents the phenomenon of influence, studies have correlated a leader's behavior and the expectations of his followers (Lord and Maher 1993). So when a disparity arises between the expectations of followers and their appreciation of the behavior actually displayed by their leader, the followers tend to lose trust in him and even devalue his abilities, leading to the failure of the leadership process (Epitropaki and Martin 2005).

Studies of the representations of leadership suggest that the loss of trust can be particularly harmful when leaders do not have the traditional characteristics of a leader, i.e., a man with qualities such as assertiveness, mastery, and combativeness (Eagly 1987; Eagly and Karau 2002). This is backed up by the metaphor "*Think leader—Think male*," highlighted by Virginia Schein (1973, 1975). Studies have shown that followers devalue the leadership behavior of those (including females, blacks, or disabled persons) who do not conform to their expectations of their prototype of a leader (Heilman 2001). From this perspective we understand that some misconduct may also result from stereotyped expectations on the part of stakeholders and conformism on the part of leaders. As in *The Wolf of Wall Street*, representations of leadership in the case of traders can encourage leaders to behave in a way that is not necessarily natural for them. Brutality and decadence symbolised the image of the trader, and so Jordan Belfort sought to fashion his behavior in conformity with this representation.

Leadership and CSR: diversity, gender, cross-cultural management

As organizations become globalized, so too do their workforces. Workforce diversity refers to the composition of work units in terms of the cultural or demographic characteristics that are salient and symbolically meaningful in relationships among group members (DiTomaso et al. 2007: 474). Researchers have addressed a range of categorical differences, such as race (Dovidio et al. 2002), ethnicity (Portes and Rumbaut 1996), gender (Heilman 2012), sexual orientation (Ragins et al. 2003), physical ability (Colella and Varma 2001), and religion (Islam and Hewstone 1993). Through social categorisation (Turner and Tajfel 1986), individuals may be victims of inequality, stereotypes, and prejudices that lead to direct or indirect discrimination (Dipboye and Colella 2005), and thus find it difficult to access positions of power or leadership (DiTomaso et al. 2007).

However, the studies conducted on leadership are based, typically, on models that exclude all notions of diversity (Eagly and Chin 2010). The result of this omission is that a) researchers have not questioned the limited access of some individuals to leadership roles, and b) there has been a failure to identify the potential pool of available talent that could provide effective leadership but was historically excluded from leadership roles as it did not match the traditional vision thereof (Eagly and Chin 2010). Faced with these contemporary problems (Werhane 2007), the ethical leader cannot remain indifferent and should seek to raise awareness among those around him of these issues, either by informing or training his colleagues (Treviño et al. 2003). The consequences of discrimination may include less committed employees, increased staff turnover, and reputational damage (Goldman et al. 2006). Organizations must therefore rely on their leaders to push forward fair and ethical practices at an organizational level that allow for the inclusion of all employees without distinction. By putting in place such practices for all of their followers, ethical leaders can be perceived as role models who establish an inclusive work environment for all staff members (Shore et al. 2011).

Gender is a major element of diversity. Given that 39.6 percent of the world's labor market are women (WorldBank 2014), and just 12 percent of board positions are held by women (Catalyst 2016), a more balanced representation of the two genders in positions of leadership seems important. Despite progress on the role of women in organizations, it remains strikingly clear that women are under-represented in leadership positions. What might explain this status quo? What role can ethical leaders play in moving forward?

Two main theories offer a framework that emphasizes the conflicting relationships between gender and leadership. Madeline Heilman (2001) articulated the lack of fit between women's attributes (e.g., communal characteristics) and those required to succeed in a leadership role.

Alice Eagly and Steven Karau (2002) also promoted this idea in their role congruity theory; the mismatch between women's typified gender role (e.g., communal characteristics) and the leader's expected role (e.g., independent decision-making, for example) produces biased evaluations. Therefore, both the lack-of-fit model and the role congruity theory suggest that expectations about female attributes induce two kinds of norms: *descriptive* beliefs designate what women and men *are* like—the consensual expectations about what member groups do (Heilman 2012); and *prescriptive* beliefs designate injunctive norms about what women and men should be—the consensual expectations about what group members should ideally do (Cialdini and Trost 1998). Therefore, women in leadership positions are the targets of two forms of prejudice (Eagly and Karau 2002): 1) less favourable evaluations of their potential to carry out leadership functions, compared with their male counterparts; and 2) less favourable evaluations of their actual leadership behavior because independent agency is perceived as less desirable in women than men. Followers devalue the leadership behavior of women as it does not correspond to the prototype of the ideal leader (Heilman 2001). Ethical leaders have a critical role to play in transforming the mentality of their stakeholders by making them aware of the values of morality, ethics and justice.

A third element of diversity is cultural. Does ethical leadership vary from one culture to another? Is there a universal form of ethical leadership that transcends culture? Several studies have provided empirical evidence that there is both convergence and divergence in the meaning and importance of ethical leadership across cultures. For example, drawing on the Global Leadership and Organizational Behavior Effectiveness study (or GLOBE), Christian Resick et al. (2006) measured four dimensions of an ethical leader: integrity, altruism, collective motivation, and empowerment. They conclude that these dimensions are common to all six of the countries studied (China, Hong Kong, Taiwan, United States, Ireland and Germany). However, the extent to which each dimension is valued varies from one society to the next. The authors surmise that the concept of ethical leadership appears universal but key dimensions of leadership differ across cultures. These results were later corroborated by a qualitative study (Resick et al. 2011) examining the differences and similarities in the notion of ethical/unethical leadership in the same six countries. Even if "ethical leadership is likely to be represented by similar categories of attributes and behaviours across cultures" (Resick et al. 2011: 451), the scope and priority of the categories may vary from one culture to the next, with managers in Ireland, the US, and Taiwan emphasizing character and accountability, managers in Germany, Hong Kong and China focusing on consideration and respect for others.

Concluding remarks

In the example of Jordan Belfort in *The Wolf of Wall Street* we locate some of the complex and paradoxical links between ethics and business leadership. In current leadership studies the concept of ethics remains crucial, even if its invocation is sometimes less than fully or clearly articulated. In this sense, business ethicists have additional work to do in articulating the nature of leadership and business leadership in particular. There are at least two avenues for further development, one theoretical the other empirical. Scholars of leadership and of business ethics should bridge their efforts in order to clarify the moral foundations of business leadership and they should develop more empirical research on leadership more closely attuned to the challenges of CSR and business.

Essential readings

The best reference or overview of leadership theories is that of Bernard M. Bass and Ralph Stodgdill *The Bass Handbook of Leadership* (2009). The most recent and comprehensive collection of contributions on leadership and ethics is that of Joanne B. Ciulla, Mary Uhl-Bien and Patricia H. Werhane, *Leadership Ethics* (2013). Two thoughtful essays on the ambivalence and the challenges of bridging leadership and business ethics are Linda K. Treviño, Laura P. Hartman and Michael Brown's "Moral Person and Moral Manager" (2000) and Joanne B. Ciulla's, "The State of Leadership Ethics and the Work that Lies before Us" (2005). For a review of the work done on the "dark side" of business leaders, see Helen Bollaert and Valérie Petit, "Beyond the Dark Side of Executive Psychology" (2010).

For further reading in this volume on the ethical and psychological qualities of entrepreneurial leaders, see Chapter 16, The ethics of entrepreneurship. On virtue and character, see Chapter 7, Can profit seekers be virtuous? On various theoretical perspectives on management, see Chapter 26, Theoretical issues in management ethics. On the responsibilities of governance officers and corporate leadership, see Chapter 24, Corporate governance. For a discussion of ethical climate in business organizations, see Chapter 27, The ethics of managers and employees. A consideration of moral blindness and self-deception may be found in Chapter 4, Teaching business ethics: current practice and future directions. On issues of leadership and a diverse workforce, see Chapter 8, Feminist ethics and business ethics. For a discussion of business leaders as *trustees*, see Chapter 36, Business ethics in South Asia: Gandhian trusteeship and its relevance for the twenty-first century.

Note

1 There are not two populations on the surface of the globe who are virtuous in the same way.

References

Aquino, K. and A. Reed (2002). "The Self-Importance of Moral Identity," *Journal of Personality and Social Psychology* 83:6, 1423–1440.

Aristotle (1999). *Nicomachean Ethics*, Terence Irwin (trans.), 2nd edition. Indianapolis, IN: Hackett Publishing.

Avolio, B.J. and B.M. Bass (1991). *The Full-Range Leadership Development Programs*. Binghamton, NY: Bass, Avolio & Associates.

Avolio B.J. and F.J. Yammarino (2002). *Transformational and Charismatic Leadership: The Road Ahead*. Greenwich, CT: JAI Press.

Avolio, B.J., W.L. Gardner, F.O. Walumbwa, F. Luthans and D.R. May (2004). "Unlocking the Mask: a Look at the Process by which Authentic Leaders Impact Follower Attitudes and Behaviors," *The Leadership Quarterly* 15:6, 801–823.

Bandura, A. (1977). *Social Learning Theory*. Englewood-Cliffs, NY: Prentice-Hall.

Bass, B.M. (1985). *Leadership and Performance Beyond Expectations*. New York, NY: Free Press.

Bass, B.M., B.J. Avolio, D.I. Jung and Y. Berson (2003). "Predicting Unit Performance by Assessing Transformational and Transactional Leadership," *Journal of Applied Psychology* 88:2, 207–218.

Bass, B.M., R. Bass and R.M. Stogdill (1974). *The Bass Handbook of Leadership: Theory, Research, and Managerial Applications*. New York, NY: Free Press.

Bass, B.M. and P. Steidlmeier (1999). "Ethics, Character, and Authentic Transformational Leadership Behavior," *The Leadership Quarterly* 10:2, 181–217.

Bass, B.M. and R. Stogdill (2009). *The Bass Handbook of Leadership: Theory, Research, and Managerial Applications*. New York, NY: Simon and Schuster.

Bollaert, H. and V. Petit (2010). "Beyond the Dark Side of Executive Psychology: Current Research and New Directions," *European Management Journal* 28:5, 362–373.

Brown, M.E. and L.K. Treviño (2006). "Ethical Leadership: A Review and Future Directions," *The Leadership Quarterly* 17:6, 595–616.

Burns, J.M. (1978). *Leadership*. New York, NY: Harper & Row.

Cameron, K. (2011). "Responsible Leadership as Virtuous Leadership," *Journal of Business Ethics* 98, Supplemental Volume, 25–35.

Catalyst (2016). "Statistical Overview of Women in the Workforce." Available at: www.catalyst.org/knowledge/statistical-overview-women-workforce.
Cialdini, R.B. and M.R. Trost (1998). "Social Influence: Social Norms, Conformity, and Compliance," in D. T. Gilbert, S.T. Fiske and G. Lindzey (eds), *The Handbook of Social Psychology*. Boston, MA: McGraw-Hill, 151–192.
Ciulla, J.B. (1995). "Leadership Ethics: Mapping the Territory," *The Business Ethics Quarterly* 5:1, 5–24.
Ciulla, J.B. (2005). "The State of Leadership Ethics and the Work that Lies Before Us," *Business Ethics: A European Review* 14:4, 323–335.
Ciulla, J.B. (2009). "Leadership and the Ethics of Care," *Journal of Business Ethics* 88:1, 3–4.
Ciulla, J.B. (2013). "Searching for Mandela: The Saint as a Sinner Who Keeps on Trying," in D. Ladkin and C. Spiller (eds), *Authentic Leadership: Clashes, Convergences and Coalescences*. Cheltenham, UK: Edward Elgar, 152–175.
Ciulla, J.B., M. Uhl-Bien and P.J. Werhane (2013). *Leadership Ethics*. Los Angeles, CA: Sage.
Ciulla, J.B., T.L. Price and S.E. Murphy (2005). *The Quest for Moral Leaders: Essays on Leadership Ethics*. Northampton, UK: Edward Elgar.
Colella, A. and A. Varma (2001). "The Impact of Subordinate Disability on Leader-Member-Exchange Relationships," *Academy of Management Journal* 44, 304–315.
Crossan, M., D. Mazutis and G. Seijts (2013). "In Search of Virtue: The Role of Virtues, Values and Character Strengths in Ethical Decision Making," *Journal of Business Ethics* 113:4, 567–581.
Dipboye, R.L. and A. Colella (2005). *Discrimination at Work: The Psychological and Organizational Bases*. Hillsdale, NJ: Lawrence Erlbaum.
DiTomaso, N., C. Post and R. Parks-Yancy (2007). "Workforce Diversity and Inequality: Power, Status, and Numbers," *Annual Review of Sociology* 33:1, 473–501.
Dovidio, J.F., K. Kawakami and S.L. Gaertner (2002). "Implicit and Explicit Prejudice and Interracial Interaction," *Journal of Personality and Social Psychology* 82:1, 62–68.
Dvir, T., D. Eden, B. J. Avolio and B. Shamir (2002). "Impact of Transformational Leadership on Follower Development and Performance: A Field Experiment," *Academy of Management Journal* 45:4, 735–744.
Eagly, A.H. (1987). *Sex Differences in Social Behavior: A Social-Role Interpretation*. Hillsdale, NJ: Lawrence Erlbaum.
Eagly, A.H. and J.L. Chin (2010). "Diversity and Leadership in a Changing World," *American Psychologist* 65:3, 216–224.
Eagly, A.H. and S.J. Karau (2002). "Role Congruity Theory of Prejudice toward Female Leaders," *Psychological Review* 109:3, 573–598.
Ebener, D.R. and D.J. O'Connell (2010). "How Might Servant Leadership Work?" *Nonprofit Management and Leadership* 20:3, 315–335.
Ehrhart, M.G. (2004). "Leadership and Procedural Justice Climate as Antecedents of Unit-level Organizational Citizenship Behavior," *Personnel Psychology* 57:61–94.
Ehrhart, M.G. and S.E. Naumann (2004). "Organizational Citizenship Behavior in Work Groups: A Group Norms Approach," *Journal of Applied Psychology* 89:6, 960–974.
Eisenbeiss, S.A. (2012). "Re-thinking Ethical Leadership: An Interdisciplinary Integrative Approach," *The Leadership Quarterly* 23:5, 791–808.
Epitropaki, O. and R. Martin (2005). "From Ideal to Real: a Longitudinal Study of the Role of Implicit Leadership Theories on Leader-Member Exchanges and Employee Outcomes," *Journal of Applied Psychology* 90:4, 659–676.
Flynn, G. (2008). "The Virtuous Manager: A Vision for Leadership in Business," *Journal of Business Ethics* 78:3, 359–372.
Freeman, R.E. and E.R. Auster (2011). "Values, Authenticity, and Responsible Leadership," *Journal of Business Ethics* 98:1, 15–23.
Fry, L.W. (2003). "Toward a Theory of Spiritual Leadership," *The Leadership Quarterly* 14:6, 693–727.
Gardner, W.L., C.C. Cogliser, K.M. Davis, and M.P. Dickens (2011). "Authentic Leadership: A Review of the Literature and Research Agenda," *The Leadership Quarterly* 22:6, 1120–1145.
George, B. and P. Sims (2007). *True North: Discover your Authentic Leadership*. San Francisco, CA: John Wiley and Sons.
Gini, A. (2004). "Business, Ethics, and Leadership in a Post Enron Era," *Journal of Leadership & Organizational Studies* 11:1, 9–15.
Goldman, B.M., B.A. Gutek, J.H. Stein and K. Lewis (2006). "Employment Discrimination in Organizations: Antecedents and Consequences," *Journal of Management* 32:6, 786–830.

Greenleaf, R.K. (1977). *Servant Leadership: A Journey into the Nature of Legitimate Power and Greatness.* New York, NY: Paulist Press.

Halwani, R. (2003). "Care Ethics and Virtue Ethics," *Hypatia* 18:3, 161–192.

Harter, S. (2002). "Authenticity," in C.R. Snyder and S. Lopez (eds), *Handbook of Positive Psychology.* New York, NY: Oxford University Press, 382–394.

Heilman, M.E. (2001). "Description and Prescription: How Gender Stereotypes Prevent Women's Ascent Up the Organizational Ladder," *Journal of Social Issues* 57:4, 657–674.

Heilman, M.E. (2012). "Gender Stereotypes and Workplace Bias," *Research in Organizational Behavior* 32, 113–135.

Hesse, H. (2013). *The Journey to the East: A Novel.* New York, NY: Macmillan.

Hoyt, C.L. and J. Blascovich (2003). "Transformational and Transactional Leadership in Virtual and Physical Environments," *Small Group Research* 34:6, 678–715.

Hu, J. and R.C. Liden (2011). "Antecedents of Team Potency and Team Effectiveness: an Examination of Goal and Process Clarity and Servant Leadership," *Journal of Applied Psychology* 96:4, 851–862.

Islam, M.R. and M. Hewstone (1993). "Intergroup Attitudes and Affective Consequences in Majority and Minority Groups," *Journal of Personality and Social Psychology* 64, 936–950.

Jensen, S.M. and F. Luthans (2006). "Relationship Between Entrepreneurs' Psychological Capital and their Authentic Leadership," *Journal of Managerial Issues* 2:18, 254–273.

Joseph, E.E. and B.E. Winston (2005). "A Correlation of Servant Leadership, Leader Trust, and Organizational Trust," *Leadership & Organization Development Journal* 26:1, 6–22.

Kellerman, B. (2004). *Bad Leadership: What it is, How it Happens, Why it Matters.* Boston, MA: Harvard Business Press.

Kohlberg, L. (1984). *Essays on Moral Development: The Nature and Validity of Moral Stages.* San Franscisco, CA: Harper & Row.

Lasch, C. (1979). *The Culture of Narcissism: American Life in an Age of Diminishing Expectations.* New York, NY: Warner Books.

Liden, R.C. and J. Antonakis (2009). "Considering Context in Psychological Leadership Research," *Human Relations* 62:11, 1587–1605.

Liden, R.C., S.J. Wayne, H. Zhao and D. Henderson (2008). "Servant Leadership: Development of a Multidimensional Measure and Multi-Level Assessment," *Leadership Quarterly* 19:2 161–177.

Lipman-Blumen, J. (2006). *The Allure of Toxic Leaders: Why We Follow Destructive Bosses and Corrupt Politicians—and How We Can Survive Them.* New York, NY: Oxford University Press.

Lord, R.G., R.J. Foti and C.L. DeVader (1984). "A Test of Leadership Categorization Theory: Internal Structure, Information Processing, and Leadership Perceptions," *Organizational Behavior and Human Decision Performance* 34:3, 343–378.

Lord, R.G. and K.J. Maher (1993). *Leadership and Information Processing: Linking Perceptions and Performance.* New York, NY: Routledge.

Maak, T. and N.M. Pless (2006). *Responsible Leadership.* London: Routledge.

Maccoby, M. (2000). "Narcissistic Leaders: The Incredible Pros, the Inevitable Cons," *Harvard Business Review* 78:1, 68–78.

Mayer, D.M., K. Aquino, R.L. Greenbaum and M. Kuenzi (2012). "Who Displays Ethical Leadership, and Why Does It Matter? An Examination of Antecedents and Consequences of Ethical Leadership," *Academy of Management Journal* 55:1, 151–171.

Mayer, D.M., M. Kuenzi, R. Greenbaum, M. Bardes and R. Salvador (2009). "How Low Does Ethical Leadership Flow? Test of a Trickle-Down Model," *Organizational Behavior and Human Decision Processes* 108:1, 1–13.

Meindl, J.R. (1995). "The Romance of Leadership as a Follower-Centric Theory: A Social Constructionist Approach," *The Leadership Quarterly* 6:3, 329–341.

Meyer, J.P., D.J. Stanley, L. Herscovitch and L. Topolnytsky (2002). "Affective, Continuance and Normative Commitment to the Organization: A Meta-Analysis of Antecedents, Correlates, and Consequences," *Journal of Vocational Behavior* 61:1, 20–52.

Neubert, M.J., D.S. Carlson, K.M. Kacmar, J.A. Roberts and L.B. Chonko (2009). "The Virtuous Influence of Ethical Leadership Behavior: Evidence From the Field," *Journal of Business Ethics* 90:2, 157–170.

Owen, D. and J. Davidson (2009). "Hubris Syndrome: An Acquired Personality Disorder? A Study of US Presidents and UK Prime Ministers Over The Last 100 Years," *Brain* 132:5, 1396–1406.

Palanski, M.E. and F.J. Yammarino (2007). "Integrity and Leadership: Clearing the Conceptual Confusion," *European Management Journal* 25:3, 171–184.

Parris, D.L. and J.W. Peachey (2013). "A Systematic Literature Review of Servant Leadership Theory in Organizational Contexts," *Journal of Business Ethics* 113:3, 377–393.

Peterson, C. and M.E. Seligman (2004). *Character Strengths and Virtues: A Handbook and Classification.* New York, NY: Oxford University Press.

Petit, V. (2012). "Like a Phoenix from the Ashes. A Weberian Analysis of the Charismatic CEO Routinization," *European Management Journal* 30:6, 510–522.

Petit, V. and H. Bollaert (2012). "Flying Too Close to the Sun: Hubris Among CEOs and How to Prevent It," *Journal of Business Ethics* 108:3, 265–283.

Podsakoff, P.M., S.B. MacKenzie and W.H. Bommer (1996). "Transformational Leader Behaviors and Substitutes for Leadership as Determinants of Employee Satisfaction, Commitment, Trust, and Organizational Citizenship Behaviors," *Journal of Management* 22:2, 259–298.

Portes, A. and R.G. Rumbaut (1996). *Immigrant America: A Portrait.* Berkeley, CA: California Press.

Price, T.L. (2003). "The Ethics of Authentic Transformational Leadership," *The Leadership Quarterly* 14:1, 67–81.

Ragins, B.R., J. Cornwell and J.S. Miller (2003). "Heterosexism in the Workplace: Do Race and Gender Matter?" *Group & Organization Management* 28:1, 45–74.

Reave, L. (2005). "Spiritual Values and Practices Related to Leadership Effectiveness," *The Leadership Quarterly* 16:5, 655–687.

Reed, L.L., D. Vidaver-Cohen and S.R. Colwell (2011). "A New Scale to Measure Executive Servant Leadership: Development, Analysis, and Implications for Research," *Journal of Business Ethics* 101:3, 415–434.

Resick, C.J., G.S. Martin, M.A. Keating, M.W. Dickson, H.K. Kwan and C. Peng (2011). "What Ethical Leadership Means to Me: Asian, American, and European perspectives," *Journal of Business Ethics* 101:3, 435–457.

Resick, C.J., P.J. Hanges, M.W. Dickson and J.K. Mitchelson (2006). "A Cross-Cultural Examination of the Endorsement of Ethical Leadership," *Journal of Business Ethics* 63:4, 345–359.

Rost, J. (1991). *Leadership for the Twenty-First Century.* New York, NY: Praeger.

Rost, J. (1993). "Leadership Development in the New Millennium," *The Journal of Leadership Studies* 1:1, 91–110.

Salancik, G.R. and J.R. Meindl (1984). "Corporate Attributions as Strategic Illusions of Management Control," *Administrative Science Quarterly* 29:1, 238–254.

Schaubroeck, J., S.T. Hannah, B.J. Avolio, S.W.J. Kozlowski, R.G. Lord, L.K. Treviño and A.C. Peng (2012). "Embedding Ethical Leadership Within and Across Organizational Levels," *Academy of Management Review* 55:5, 1053–1078.

Schein, V.E. (1973). "The Relationship Between Sex Role Stereotypes and Requisite Management Characteristics," *Journal of Applied Psychology* 57, 95–100.

Schein, V.E. (1975). "The Relationship Between Sex Role Stereotypes and Requisite Management Characteristics Among Female Managers," *Journal of Applied Psychology* 60, 340–344.

Schyns, B. and J.R. Meindl (2005). *Implicit Leadership Theories. Essays and Explorations.* Greenwich, CT: Information Age Publishing.

Shore, L.M., A.E. Randel, B.G. Chung, M.A. Dean, K.H. Ehrhart and G. Singh (2011). "Inclusion and Diversity in Work Groups: A Review and Model for Future Research," *Journal of Management* 37:4, 1262–1289.

Sims Jr., H.P. and P. Lorenzi (1992). *The New Leadership Paradigm: Social Learning and Cognition in Organizations.* Thousand Oaks, CA: Sage.

Smith, W.K. and M.W. Lewis (2011). "Toward a Theory of Paradox: A Dynamic Equilibrium Model of Organizing," *Academy of Management Review* 36:2, 381–403.

Spurk, D., A.C. Keller and A. Hirschi (2016). "Do Bad Guys Get Ahead or Fall Behind? Relationships of the Dark Triad of Personality With Objective and Subjective Career Success," *Social Psychological and Personality Science* 7:2, 113–121.

Treviño, L.K. (1986). "Ethical Decision Making in Organizations: A Person-Situation Interactionist Model," *Academy of Management Review* 11:3, 601–617.

Treviño, L.K. (1990). "A Cultural Perspective on Changing and Developing Organizational Ethics," *Research in Organizational Change and Development* 4:4, 195–230.

Treviño, L.K., K.D. Butterfield and D.M. McCabe (1998). "The Ethical Context In Organizations: Influences on Employee Attitudes and Behaviors," *Business Ethics Quarterly* 8:3, 447–476.

Treviño, L.K., L.P. Hartman and M. Brown (2000). "Moral Person and Moral Manager: How Executives Develop a Reputation for Ethical Leadership," *California Management Review* 42:4, 128–142.

Treviño, L.K., M. Brown and L.P. Hartman (2003). "A Qualitative Investigation of Perceived Executive Ethical Leadership: Perceptions from Inside and Outside the Executive Suite," *Human Relations* 56:1, 5–37.

Turner, J.C. and H. Tajfel (1986). "The Social Identity Theory of Intergroup Behavior," *Psychology of Intergroup Relations* 5, 7–24.

Victor, B. and J.B. Cullen (1988). "The Organizational Bases of Ethical Work Climates," *Administrative Science Quarterly* 33:1, 101–125.

Walumbwa, F.O., B.J. Avolio, W.L. Gardner, T.S. Wernsing and S.J. Peterson (2008). "Authentic Leadership: Development and Validation of a Theory-Based Measure," *Journal of Management* 34:1, 89–126.

Walumbwa, F.O., C.A. Hartnell and A. Oke (2010). "Servant Leadership, Procedural Justice Climate, Service Climate, Employee Attitudes, and Organizational Citizenship Behavior: A Cross-Level Investigation," *Journal of Applied Psychology* 95:3, 517–529.

Walumbwa, F.O. and J. Schaubroeck (2009). "Leader Personality Traits and Employee Voice Behavior: Mediating Roles of Ethical Leadership and Work Group Psychological Safety," *Journal of Applied Psychology* 94:5, 1275–1286.

Weber, M. (1947). *The Theory of Social and Economic Organization*, A.M. Henderson and T. Parsons (trans.). New York, NY: The Free Press.

Werhane, P.H. (2007). "Women Leaders in a Globalized World," *Journal of Business Ethics* 74:4, 425–435.

Wong, C. and G. Cummings (2009). "Authentic Leadership: A New Theory for Nursing or Back to Basics?" *Journal of Health Organization and Management* 23:5, 522–538.

WorldBank (2014). Labor Force Participation Rate. Available at: http://data.worldbank.org/indicator/SL.TLF.CACT.FE.ZS.

Yukl, G. (2010). *Leadership in Organizations*. Upper Saddle River, NJ: Prentice Hall.

# 26

Theoretical issues in management ethics

Joseph A. Petrick

Within the field of management ethics, one finds at least two broad types of theories: theories of management and theories of ethics. For the management ethicist, these theories may intersect or be used independently of one another. For the practicing manager, these theories may have an explicit or tacit influence. For example, a manager of a pharmaceutical firm may implement an advertising strategy in a developing country whose effect will be to encourage unsuspecting consumers to medicate with drugs that are outlawed in more economically prosperous nations. This type of action could be based on the assumption that such a strategy is justified because it promises an increase in short-term profit. Indeed, this manager might seek to defend this initiative on the basis of either a management theory or a particular theory of ethical action (or both). Whether explicit or implicit, theoretical assumptions are often embedded in managerial moral performance; it is, therefore, critical for both practicing managers and management theorists to understand these theoretical assumptions if managerial performance is to be both productive and ethical.

On the assumption that increased awareness of and engagement with alternative management and ethics theories can lead to more responsible managerial decisions and improved moral performance, this chapter offers a broad overview of such theories. The first section of the chapter summarizes, schematically, several of the outstanding theories of management. The second section draws some distinctions between various theories of normative ethics. The third section addresses two topics at the theoretical intersection of management and ethics: moral monism versus moral pluralism, and the degree to which management conduct (or conduct more generally) is guided by considerations of rationalized theories.

Major management theories

According to most major management theorists optimal business management entails effectiveness (competing to achieve goals fast), efficiency (controlling to do things right and not waste resources in the process), innovation (creating new products and techniques, continually improving outputs and processes), responsiveness (collaborating to do things together to address multiple stakeholder interests), sound decision-making (relying on evidence-based judgments), and the avoidance of harm or exploitation (critically evaluating management practices).

Suboptimal business management performance occurs when managers neglect or inadequately operationalize some or all of the above expectations. To explain (and to guide) these features of optimal management, writers and scholars have articulated theories of optimal business management practice (Quinn et al. 2015). Most of these theories operate at both a descriptive and normative level: in other words, the theories not only *explain* certain features of management practice but *encourage* specific emphases as essential to moral and business success. In the following discussion, these theories are schematically summarized, noting salient strengths and limitations.

The *rational goal theory* of management stresses the importance of performance effectiveness, as achievable through setting goals, speeding productivity, and increasing profits faster than external competitors. To realize these measures, the manager may use time-and-motion studies, financial incentives, or technological power to maximize output (Taylor 1911). The strength of this theory is that it accounts for managers providing structure to the activities of the firm and it emphasizes the significance of management initiative and leadership. Such a theory can be misused if it imposes demands on employees that cannot be sustained. The theory may allow or encourage a neglect of individual psychosocial needs in the pursuit of economic returns, thereby affecting individuals negatively and destroying the cohesion necessary to attain the desired goals.

The *internal process theory* of management stresses the importance of operational efficiency as achieved through information management, documentation control, and coordinated processes. Such a theory emphasizes process measurement, the smooth functioning of organizational operations, and the maintenance of structural order. Henri Fayol (1916), the earliest originator of this type of theory, described the five functions of management as planning, organizing, commanding, coordinating, and controlling, and he outlined fourteen principles of good administration, with the most important elements being specialization of labor, unity and chain of command, and the routine exercise of authority to ensure internal control. The strength of this theory is that it accounts for managers' maintaining structure and collecting information. A cautionary note would point out that an exclusive emphasis on processes and structures may neglect new products and techniques, thereby stifling overall progress.

The *human relations theory* of management stresses the importance of stakeholder responsiveness achieved by showing managerial consideration for employees' psychosocial needs to belong, fostering informal group collaboration, and providing recognition at work. This theory also encourages managerial social responsibility and humane community building in society (Mayo 1933). The particular strength of this theory is its encouragement of managerial and employee relationships, as well as the importance of managerial leadership to sustain supportive interaction with stakeholders beyond the firm. Of course, to the extent that a manager becomes concerned only with the development of human relationships, then so does that manager create the risk of slowing production at work and abdicating decision-making authority.

The *open systems theory* of management stresses the importance of sustainable innovation. Positive changes are to be achieved by cultivating organizational learning cultures, developing cross-functional organizational competencies, and respecting quality and ecological system limits (while negotiating for external resource acquisition), building sustainable entrepreneurial networks, and enabling creative system improvement (Lawrence and Lorsch 1967). One positive feature of this theory is that it accounts for managers envisioning improvements and acquiring resources for sustainable system development. However, the implementation of the theory may risk a disruption of established operational procedures and may lead to projects of innovation that do not succeed.

The *evidence-based theory* of management (EBM) contends that managerial decisions and organizational practices be informed by the best available scientific evidence. The theory focuses, therefore, on fact gathering, examining issues from multiple perspectives, analyzing cause–effect connections, and utilizing communities of knowledge—activities essential to arriving at effective management decisions or policies (Rousseau 2014). Evidence-based management assumes that the integration of scientific analysis with critical reasoning enhances both management education and management performance, as it has done for medical education and medical performance. The strength of this theory is that a science-based practice of management not only encourages in the manager an attitude of serious and realistic assessment, but it also promises to deliver better outcomes now and in the future by promoting knowledge-building relationships among management scholars, educators and practitioners. One challenge for this theory is that managers may find that there is no easy access to current aggregated, evaluated, and applicable research that could be employed to improve managerial performance.

Critical management studies (CMS) is less a discrete and univocal theory of management than it is a neo-Marxist critique of traditional management theory and practice and its accommodation to capitalist societies or its seeming legitimization of exploitative business practices. This neo-Marxist critique is pursued by left-wing scholars informed by a variety of theoretical orientations, "including anarchism, critical theory, feminism, Marxism, post-structuralism, postmodernism, postcolonialism and psychoanalysis, representing a pluralistic, multidisciplinary field" (www.criticalmanagement.org/content/about-cms). The aim of CMS is to radically decrease the socio-economic domination of capitalism by critiquing existing relations of power and control and by proposing alternative non-capitalist forms of organizing work and life, thereby liberating human beings from class, racial, and gender discrimination (Alvesson et al. 2011). A theoretical orientation such as this provides a robust challenge to traditional business practice, and such a perspective may prove salutary even if it is not accepted. The viability of constructive yet non-capitalist forms of production remains less than clear, however. And the appeal to various forms of domination are often more assumed than explained or justified.

These theories of management exist alongside another kind of theory, a theory of fiduciary responsibility: Does a manager (or a corporate board) have a primary fiduciary responsibility to stockholders or to stakeholders? Some consider Milton Friedman (1962, 1970) to be advocating the shareholder view but, whatever the case, the shareholder perspective does *not* entail that a manager has *no* duties except to the shareholder (Norman 2013), only that the manager (or the corporate board) has a fiduciary duty to manage the firm in the interests of shareholders. The stakeholder paradigm suggests, in various guises, that management should run the firm with a respect or concern for the interests and views of multiple constituencies such as employees, investors, customers, suppliers, creditors and the public at large (Freeman et al. 2007; Ghoshal 2005).

In principle, each of the above theories of management is compatible with either shareholder or stakeholder responsibility. Some of these theories do suggest that the manager bears responsibilities to stakeholders but that suggestion need not entail that a manager or a board has any fiduciary responsibility to these stakeholders, or a duty that is either equivalent or similar to the responsibility to shareholders. Across almost all of the theories sketched previously, it could be said that a manager may bear special formal and informal contractual relationships as agents to a principal (such as a shareholder), or as stakeholder trustees or as property stewards or as employee supervisors; these relationships may entail additional moral and legal contractual obligations (Mitnick 2008). These contractual relationships differ in terms of their prioritized responsibilities: for example, to advance the interests of the principal or stockholders, to advance the aggregate interests of all stakeholders, to protect and maintain property, or to use supervisory authority to facilitate mutually beneficial cooperation among employees. As an agent of a principal/owner, a manager has the duties to act on behalf of the interests of the principal/owner, to obey the reasonable directions of the principal/owner, and never to act contrary to the interests of the principal/owner. At times, however, when a manager as an agent has more expertise in a specific area than the principal/owner, he is prohibited by his professional ethics to exploit his informational asymmetry advantage and may abridge the normal agency duty to obey the principal/owner if in his professional judgment the principal/owner is about to do something extremely foolish against his (the principal/owner's) interests. On the other hand, a manager who counts himself as a stakeholder trustee could have a duty to protect or advance the interests of all routinely affected groups as he had with protecting and advancing the interests of shareholders, without violating the rights of people who fall outside the stakeholder realm.

A management theory, whether a theory about managerial activity or about managerial fiduciary responsibility, has both immediate and long range consequences. However, theoretical issues may arise not only in the choice of a management theory but in how that theory may align with a theory of ethics more generally. The formation of a managerial judgment may require not only a choice among management theories but a choice of ethical theory as well. The implication of one management theory may prove incompatible with the conclusion of an ethical theory or vice versa. To illuminate this more fully, some of the major ethical theories are sketched in the next section.

Major ethics theories

The following major ethics theories have been utilized to explain dimensions of optimal ethical business management practice (Hosmer 2010; Bowie and Werhane 2004). Major ethics theories can be divided into consequentialist and non-consequentialist categories but each theory has strengths and limitations (Timmons 2012).

A *consequentialist* ethics theory holds that the moral status of an action is determined by the impartially reckoned overall goodness of its consequences (Darwall 2003). This means that when a business manager keeps his promise to employees to raise their annual wages by 2 percent, that act is made morally obligatory and commendable by its good consequences or by the hypothetical good consequences of people accepting a rule that requires it (such as a rule requiring promise keeping).

The varieties of consequentialist ethics theories include ethical egoism and act and rule utilitarianism. Ethical egoism is the personal consequentialist position that maintains that one ought to act out of informed prudent selfishness to satisfy one's desires or to get what one wants (Machan 2003). Ethical egoist managers, however, who become exclusively driven by personal long-term career success may so neglect the interests of others that they provoke a backlash or harm others.

Utilitarianism maintains that managerial actions are good if they are expected to produce the greatest quantity and quality of well-being for the largest number of those affected by the actions (Mill 1861). There are different variations of utilitarianism. Act utilitarianism maintains that the values of the consequences of concrete specific actions determine the moral status of actions. An action is good if it brings about at least as much net well-being as any other action the agent could have performed. Rule utilitarianism maintains that an action is good if and only if it is allowed by a rule with as high a utility as any other alternative rule applying to the situation. A manager who is a rule utilitarian asks what set of rules or moral codes a society should accept so as to maximize human well-being in the long run. So, individual actions of breaking promises or unequally distributing benefits and burdens in society may, in the short run, maximize utility, but are morally objectionable from the rule utilitarian view but not necessarily from the act utilitarian view. Managerial proponents of the market system (as constituted by rules of various sorts), for instance, regard the free market as a powerful mechanism for maximizing economic utility since it provides goods and services at prices that allow individuals and societies to satisfy efficiently their desires, preferences and expectations.

A *non-consequentialist* ethics theory holds that the moral status of an action is not determined by the impartially reckoned overall goodness of its consequences but entails consideration of moral constraint, character, or context. There are different varieties of non-consequentialist ethics theories including: moral duty theories, contractarian moral theory, virtue ethics theory and contextual ethics theory.

There are two major moral duty theories: Kantian ethical theory (Kant 1785/1993) and Ross's common sense moral theory (Ross 2003). Kantian ethics is preeminently an absolute deontological (duty-based) theory focused on right conduct. From Kant's point of view, an action has moral worth (and thus a business management decision has moral worth) only if performed by an agent of "good will"—in other words, only if the motive for the decision and the action is moral obligation. The main moral obligation for Kant was to act in accord with the categorical imperative, an absolutely binding duty, variously formulated as a deep respect for universal moral law and persons. Kant argued that one's duties could be ascertained by considering whether the maxim of one's action could be willed to be universal moral law. Consistent with this notion is the idea that individuals (thus, managers) must not treat people exclusively as a means to their ends because every person has rational autonomy deserving of moral respect. In sum, Kant expected individuals to make the right decision for the right reasons.

Kantian ethical theory has been criticized for its overemphasis on duty since people can do the right thing for a variety of commendable prudential and sympathetic reasons. In addition, Kantian ethical theory has difficulty providing a correct decision procedure because, given the multiplicity of relevant maxims associated with any action, one can use Kant's proposed maxims to derive inconsistent moral verdicts about the same action.

W.D. Ross's common sense moral theory maintains that while there are no absolute moral duties there are common prima facie obligations that must be acted upon by managers unless they conflict on a particular occasion with an equal or stronger obligation (Ross 2003). These duties include beneficence, fidelity to one's promises, gratitude, justice, non-maleficence, reparation, and self-improvement. On this view, every manager would have an unconditional contractual moral obligation and duty to prioritize these prima facie duties. When prima facie duties conflict, the preponderance of evidence and argumentation will determine the relative priority of each duty. Although Ross's common sense theory has been praised for its intuitive appeal and ability to achieve the same ends as Kantian ethical theory without relying on the latter's absolute inflexibility of moral standards, the theory seems to entail that in cases of multiple duty conflicts there may not be a single right action because there would be no way to determine a moral verdict between two or more actions of equal moral weight in the circumstances.

Contractarian moral theory maintains that morality is to be based upon a formal or informal agreement made between parties such that each party will agree to refrain from inflicting harm or damage to other parties provided that the other parties agree to do likewise and that they will keep whatever agreements they voluntarily make now and in the future (Gauthier 1986). Although the general theory is praised for its open-ended moral inclusiveness, since any party at any time can make a contractual agreement to improve a situation, it is difficult and risky to determine whether the party one is about to contract with will or will not prove to be a fellow cooperator. Moreover, in the case of a notable application to business ethics (Donaldson and Dunfee 1999), the contractarian element seems weakly justified and it is not clear how diverse individuals are to discern the overarching agreements (or "hypernorms") enshrined in the particular application.

Virtue ethics theory maintains that regular cultivation of the acquired disposition to think, feel and act ethically determines the moral value of persons. For the virtue ethicist, building character—the sum of individual virtues and vices that indicate the degree of readiness to act ethically—the habitual development of virtues is what life and managing ethically is all about (Sison 2017). Virtue ethics theory is agent-centered, not act-centered or consequence-centered; it is concerned with being rather than doing and attempts to answer the question, "What sort of person should I be?" rather than "What should I do?"

Aristotle argued that cultivation of the classic cardinal virtues of wisdom, courage, temperance and justice was essential to achieve happiness, which he regarded as the natural quality of a whole human life characterized by the degree to which the following goods were secured and maintained: health, wealth, knowledge, friendship, good luck and virtue (Aristotle 350BC/1985). He maintained that there was a difference between having a good time (maximizing pleasurable utility) and leading a good life (maximizing happiness) and that the latter outcome was to be morally preferred to the former (Sison 2016). To this list of virtues, contemporary feminist virtue theorists have added the virtue of care as exemplified in relationships that may be unchosen, intimate and among unequals (Gilligan 1982). There have been other categories of virtues, some of which have been applied to business managers including competence, toughness, resilience, and resourcefulness among others, but ultimately a business manager's character is judged on overall trustworthiness (Solomon 1999). More recently, Deirdre McCloskey has offered a robust narrative of the ways in which the virtues render commercial life possible and ethically successful (McCloskey 2006). One example of a step toward developing managerial character, though hardly emblematic of the kind of ethical habituation embraced by Aristotle or other ethics theorists, is that taken by some business school faculty and graduate students who have expressed their strong moral expectations for future higher professional, social and environmental responsibility standards for business managers by publicly endorsing and signing an MBA oath (Anderson and Escher 2010).

Virtue ethics theory has been criticized for its indeterminacy since a virtuous agent possesses a range of virtues with no absolute rank ordering that determines what the virtuous agent should do. Moreover, some contend that what is recognized and commended as virtuous may be relative to a culture or epoch.

The choice of ethics theories may make a critical difference in moral performance. For example, a corporate manager who endorses ethical egoism may unilaterally shortchange the company pension plan in order to make the company appear to be more profitable than it is, thereby inflating the value of the company stock and his stock options. When at a later date the pension funding falls short and the workers get less than what they were due (or the taxpayers have to make up the part of the shortfall), the ethical egoist manager can move on to another company and still benefit at the expense of others. By contrast, another corporate manager in the same company who endorses contractarian moral theory would object to the deliberate shortchanging of the company pension plan and would fully fund it on the grounds of the importance of honoring contractual promises.

Selected theoretical issues in management ethics

In this section we take up two theoretical issues of management ethics. The first of these focuses on the conceptual relationship between management theories and ethics theories: Should a single moral theory be allied to a specific management theory? Or does moral and efficacious management require a pluralistic view of ethics and management? Moral monism suggests the former, pluralism the latter. A second theoretical concern probes a more fundamental question:

Theoretical issues in management ethics

To what extent can *theory*, whether managerial or normatively ethical, guide *conduct*? We shall sketch some of the positions one might adopt in relation to these questions.

Monism versus pluralism

One theoretical issue of management ethics is the difference between moral monism and limited moral pluralism. Moral monism maintains that moral conduct is and ought to be determined on the basis of a single management theory *linked* to a single ethics theory. For example, a manager who is a Kantian might rely on rational goal management theory on the assumption that the manager has a clear duty to lead the firm in the optimal way. Or a utilitarian might manage a corporation in accordance with human relations theory, perhaps on the assumption that the encouragement and maintenance of employee morale, as well as attention to external stakeholders, is the overall key to success. In these cases, one would need a theoretical justification not only for the normative theory but for the management theory as well. Then a third justification would be required to show that either the normative moral theory entailed the management theory or that the management theory was not inconsistent with the normative theory. This sort of perspective assumes that one theory of morals and one theory of management can be allied to provide clear guidance to a manager.

The thesis of limited moral pluralism is that the complexities of management require input from a plural (but limited) number of management and ethics theories. Simply enough, these theories combine the pluralistic perspectives of distinct management theories along with pluralistic perspectives of distinct moral theories. One form of limited moral pluralism is the combination of a competing values management framework (Quinn et al. 2015) with the integrity capacity moral framework (Petrick 2008; Petrick and Quinn 2001).

From the competing values framework, core managerial role performance is the outcome of efforts to compete (organizational effectiveness), control (operational efficiency), collaborate (stakeholder engagement), and create (continual innovation as well as adaptation to opportunity), all in a dynamic setting of supply and demand (Cameron et al. 2007). For heuristic purposes (Gigerenzer and Hertwig 2015), these are sometimes referred to as the *four Cs* (see Figure 26.1) of management competence: competing, controlling, collaborating, and creating.

This framework incorporates four major theories of management. The four management theories and their emphases (in italics) are designated outside the circle in their appropriate quadrants of emphasis: the rational goal theory emphasizes competing effectively in the external market, the internal process theory emphasizes controlling efficiently within the organization, the human relations theory emphasizes collaborating with employees and other stakeholders, and the open systems theory emphasizes creating new products or environments and accessing external resources.

Each management theory is typified as having an *opposite*: for example, the human relations theory stands opposed to the rational goal theory and the open systems theory runs counter to the internal process theory. Although an open systems manager is concerned with adapting to the continuous changes in the environment, the internal process manager is concerned with maintaining stability and continuity within the system. In addition, complementary parallels among the theories are important. The rational goal and internal process theories share an emphasis on control. The open systems and rational goal theories share an emphasis on external focus outside the firm. The internal process and human relations theories share an internal focus. And the human relations and open systems theories share an emphasis on flexibility. The overarching idea of this framework is that managerial excellence reflects a balance among these four competing and complementary theories.

Joseph A. Petrick

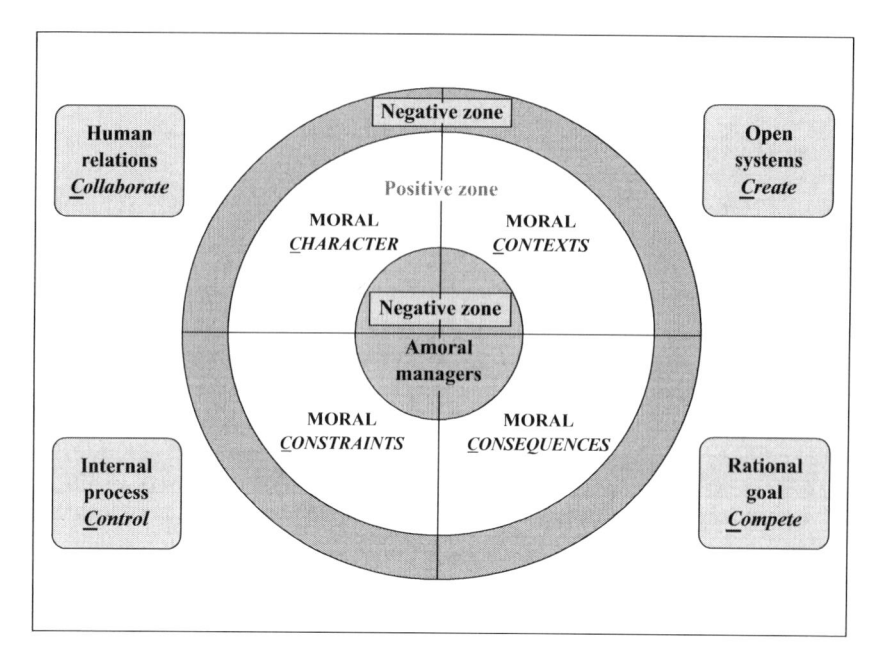

Figure 26.1 Managerial competing values and integrity capacity framework.

Source: From: Encyclopedia of Business and Finance, 3rd edition © 2014 Gale, a part of Cengage, Inc., reproduced with permission: www.cengage.com/permissions.

The relationship of the four core major theories of management (Figure 26.1) is organized in terms of two axes, as long as economic exploitation is avoided and reliance on evidence-based decision-making is the norm. The vertical axis ranges from individual and collective flexibility at the top to control at the bottom. The horizontal axis ranges from an internal organizational focus at the left to an external focus at the right. Each major management theory fits into one of the four quadrants of emphases formed by the intersection of the two axes. Furthermore, the negative zones of managerial quadrant competence are indicated by the central bullseye circle that represents defective performance (amoral management) and the outer ring that represents excessive overemphasis.

From the ethics perspective, integrity capacity is regarded as the intangible strategic asset for which managers are held accountable and is composed of the aggregate individual and collective capability for repeated process alignment of moral awareness, deliberation, character and conduct that demonstrates sound balanced judgment, cultivates moral development and promotes supportive systems for ongoing moral decision making (Petrick and Quinn 2001). Judgment is one key dimension of integrity capacity that requires the balancing of moral consequences, moral constraints, moral character and moral contexts. Three normative ethics theories (Figure 26.1) are designated inside the positive zone of the circle in their appropriate quadrants of emphasis. These three theories are joined by a fourth theory that is less normative than contextual or organizational.

This fourth theory, *contextual ethics*, is invoked to point out how organizational and extra-organizational conditions and circumstances of decision-making and behavior may shape and influence the moral judgment and conduct of individuals. A supportive organizational and extra-organizational moral environment is more likely than a corrupt one to elicit managerial moral performance. For instance, managers can design and institutionalize the context of the organizational work culture to either support or inhibit moral judgment and conduct. Ethical managers design and institutionalize ethical work cultures that not only prevent criminal misconduct but also enable responsible conduct and collective commitment to moral behavior by organizational stakeholders (Collins 2012). Such an ethical work culture has been described as consisting of processes and norms that in the aggregate contextually promote the moral and effective functioning of the organization. The organizational features that might promote ethical conduct include, for example, codes of conduct, ethical audits (Petrick and Quinn 1997) and the promotion of ethical leadership (Laasch and Conaway 2014), among others. Well designed and robust ethical cultures help incentivize and reinforce morally commendable conduct prescribed by ethical theories and traditions.

On the pluralist view each ethical theory, along with the contextual considerations, is critical to the analysis and resolution of management ethics issues. Moreover, the way people in fact manage may suggest, implicitly or explicitly, their accustomed moral value priorities and emphases: for example, a rational goal "bottom line" manager may be inclined to emphasize consequential ethics.

From this limited moral pluralism perspective, improving ethical managerial performance requires that managers move out of their intuitive moral comfort zones and engage in structured dialogue and discourse to elicit and consider the most compelling evidence and soundest arguments (and structures) for a course of action. After critically evaluating these inputs from the core moral and contextual theories, the manager must make a decision on the basis of the preponderance of evidence (Petrick 2014). For example, a rational goal manager, reared and educated in secular and liberal institutions, may be predisposed *not* to hire an employee who is an evangelical or fundamentalist Christian. Yet, if he opens his mind to the inputs (evidence and arguments) of ethics theories, not to mention the obvious constraint of a federal government that guarantees a right to non-discriminatory treatment, then he may make a more balanced ethical decision that will be better in the long run for him and his business. Now it is true that some of these additional moral theory inputs may be accorded different weights, but the switch from the moral monism of a possible short term, perhaps utility-based, discrimination decision to a reflective, mindful non-discrimination moral decision is the foundation for ethical management performance from the limited moral pluralism perspective.

A choice between the monistic or pluralistic perspective requires an estimate of each moral theory and their contextual requirements, as well as a consideration as to whether a balancing of theories and contexts can be rendered clear. If there is some need for balancing then there must also be a justification for the inclusion of specific management theories, as well as specific ethical theories (and their contextual implications or requirements). It is true that the limited moral pluralism model allows broader, more adequate consideration of multiple voices in policy decisions, but it also leaves decision-makers without much of a standard. Indeed, the framework may be criticized because it offers a high level of complexity, demands intense moral discourse from and among managers, and the structural architecture may take on a life of its own that is less than relevant to practical moral decision making. The question of *how* a manager makes ethical decisions leads to a second kind of theoretical question.

Theory and practice

A second theoretical concern pivots on this point: to what extent should theory affect business practice, at least in the moral realm? One motivation for this concern rests in a fundamental question about the role of theory in guiding or directing conduct. One way to approach this question is to return to philosophical examinations of the place of theory in everyday conduct (Oakeshott 1991) or the role of business ethics and businesspersons (Crisp 2003).

Joseph A. Petrick

A potential conflict between theory and practice is suggested by recent work in psychology. Consider that many might think that individuals can derive sound normative moral principles through the structured development of reason alone (Gewirth 1980; Singer 2003). An individual can overcome unconscious psycho-social moral biases, consciously reflect critically on moral reasons, distinguish ethically relevant facts, logically evaluate moral theories and their alternative resolutions, engage in rational moral dialogue, and finally make a rationally responsible moral decision (Gewirth 1980). This is an appealing picture of the power of autonomous reason.

However, in a recent study Jonathan Haidt casts doubt on the power of reason (and grand theories) to guide conduct (Haidt 2012). Against the perspective of moral rationality, Haidt posits a theory of moral foundations. Moral foundations theory emerges from evolutionary psychology and maintains that individuals are unconsciously psycho-socially biased in the extent and degree to which in making moral decisions they intuitively gravitate to six moral foundation polarities: care/harm, liberty/oppression, fairness/cheating, loyalty/betrayal, authority/subversion, and sanctity/degradation. His work suggests that morality entails the sublimation of individual conscience into the broader collective emotions of a tribe or organization, all in order to feel the power of group righteousness.

According to Haidt, these six innate moral intuitions serve unconsciously to differentiate politically liberal managers from politically conservative managers. Unlike the conservative managers who address all six polarities, liberals tend to focus only on three moral polarities (care/harm, liberty/oppression, fairness/cheating). These differences in unconscious moral priorities affect directly managerial decision making and performance, and the reduced focus of liberal managers leave them at a career disadvantage, at least in institutional contexts that reward group cohesion and teamwork.

Such research findings help to explain the compliance engendered and expected by managers who seek to address all six polarities. The task of management ethics, however, is to be able to critically challenge personal moral biases and to enlarge the scope of factors considered in moral decision making and performance. Whether contemporary business managers will rise to the challenge to rationally resolve theoretical issues in management ethics or will simply conform to institutional expectations will determine the quality of future managerial moral performance.

Concluding remarks

The focus of this chapter has been on treating the state of the discipline regarding the critical importance of understanding the organized complexity of theoretical issues in management ethics. The spotlight has shown on three areas: 1) major management theories and their strengths and limitations; 2) major ethics theories and their strengths and limitations; and 3) two selected theoretical issues in management ethics. What makes an issue in management ethics theoretical has to do with how the conceptual relationship between management theories and ethics theories is interpreted to relate to managerial moral performance. Management and ethics theories matter to managerial moral performance. Increased awareness of the opportunities and challenges presented by theoretical issues in management ethics can contribute to improved managerial moral performance in the future.[1]

Essential readings

The essential works on theoretical issues in management ethics include LaRue Hosmer, *The Ethics of Management* (2010), Norman Bowie and Patricia Werhane *Management Ethics* (2004), and Joseph Petrick and John Quinn *Management Ethics: Integrity at Work* (1997). For a comprehensive and critically foundational perspective on managerial competence see Robert Quinn, David Bright, Sue Faerman, Michael Thompson, and Michael McGrath, *Becoming a Master Manager: A Competing Values Approach* (2015), for international expectations for management ethics performance, see Oliver Laasch and Roger Conaway (2014) *Principles of Responsible Management: Global Sustainability, Responsibility, and Ethics*, and for more on moral theory see Mark Timmons *Moral Theory* (2012).

For further reading in this volume on the practical questions of management ethics, see Chapter 27, The ethics of managers and employees. Since the very nature of a business is relevant to theoretical considerations of management, see Chapter 13, What is business? On theoretical issues in marketing ethics, see Chapter 30, Ethical issues in marketing, advertising, and sales. An enlarged discussion of theories of normative ethics may be found in Chapter 5, Consequentialism and non-consequentialism. On moral pluralism as relevant to the ethics of entrepreneurship, see Chapter 16, The ethics of entrepreneurship. On the issues of theory and practice in business ethics, see Chapter 3, Theory and method in business ethics.

Note

1 A few of the ideas expressed in this chapter, along with Figure 26.1, received a preliminary expression in Petrick (2017).

References

Alvesson, M., T. Bridgman and H. Wilmott (eds) (2011). *The Oxford Handbook of Critical Management Studies*. Oxford: Oxford University Press.
Anderson, M. and P. Escher (2010). *The MBA Oath: Setting a Higher Standard for Business Leaders*. New York: Penguin.
Aristotle (1985 [4th century BCE]). *Nicomachean Ethics*. T. Irwin (trans.). Indianapolis, IN: Hackett.
Bowie, N. and P. Werhane (2004). *Management Ethics*. New York, NY: Wiley-Blackwell.
Bowie, N. (1999). *Business Ethics: A Kantian Perspective*. Malden, MA: Blackwell.
Cameron, K., R. Quinn, J. DeGraff and A. Thakor (2007). *Competing Values Leadership: Creating Value in Organizations*. New York, NY: Edward Elgar.
Collins, D. (2012). *Business Ethics: How to Design and Manage Ethical Organizations*. New York, NY: John Wiley and Sons.
Crisp, R. (2003). "A Defence of Philosophical Business Ethics," in William Shaw (ed.), *Ethics at Work: Basic Readings in Business Ethics*. New York, NY: Oxford University Press, 1–14.
Darwall, S. (ed.) (2003). *Consequentialism*. Malden, MA: Blackwell.
Donaldson, T. and T. Dunfee (1999). *Ties that Bind: A Social Contracts Approach to Business Ethics*. Cambridge, MA: Harvard Business School Press.
Fayol, H. (1916). *General and Industrial Management*. London: Pittman.
Freeman, E., J. Harrison and A. Wicks (2007). *Managing for Stakeholders: Survival, Reputation and Success*. New Haven, CT: Yale University Press.
Friedman, M. (1962). *Capitalism and Freedom*. Chicago, IL: University of Chicago Press.
Friedman, M. (1970). "The Social Responsibility of Business Is to Increase Its Profits," *New York Times Magazine* (September 13), 32–33 and 123–126.
Gauthier, D. (1986). *Morals by Agreement*. New York, NY: Oxford University Press.
Gewirth, A. (1980). *Reason and Morality*. Chicago, IL: University of Chicago Press.
Ghoshal, S. (2005). "Bad Management Theories are Destroying Good Management Practices," *Academy of Management Learning & Education*, 4:1, 75–91.
Gigerenzer, G. and R. Hertwig (2015). *Heuristics: The Foundations of Adaptive Behavior*. New York, NY: Oxford University Press.
Gilligan, C. (1982). *In a Different Voice: Psychological Theory and Women's Development*. Cambridge, MA: Harvard University Press.
Haidt, J. (2012). *The Righteous Mind*. New York, NY: Pantheon.

Hosmer, L. (2010). *The Ethics of Management*, 7th edition. New York, NY: McGraw-Hill/Irwin.
Kant, I. (1993 [1785]). *Grounding for the Metaphysics of Morals*, James W. Ellington (trans.), 3rd edition. Indianapolis, IN: Hackett.
Laasch, O. and R. Conaway (2014). *Principles of Responsible Management: Global Sustainability, Responsibility, and Ethics*. Mason, OH: Cengage Learning.
Lawrence, A. and J. Weber (2017). *Business and Society: Stakeholders, Ethics and Public Policy*, 15th edition. New York, NY: McGraw-Hill.
Lawrence, P. and P. Lorsch (1967). *Organization and Environment: Managing Differentiation and Integration*. Cambridge, MA: Harvard University Press.
Machan, T. (2003). *The Passion for Liberty*. Lanham, MD: Rowman and Littlefield.
Mayo, E. (1933). *The Human Problems of an Industrial Civilization*. New York, NY: Macmillan.
McCloskey, D. (2006). *The Bourgeois Virtues*. Chicago, IL: University of Chicago Press.
Mill, J.S. (1861). *Utilitarianism*. London: Routledge and Kegan Paul.
Mitnick, B. (2008). "Theory of Agency," in R. Kolb (ed.), *Encyclopedia of Business Ethics and Society*. 5 vols. Thousand Oaks, CA: Sage, vol. 1, 42–48.
Norman, W. (2013). "Stakeholder Theory," in Hugh LaFollette (ed.), *The International Encyclopedia of Ethics*. Malden, MA: John Wiley and Sons.
Oakeshott, M. (1991 [1948]). "The Tower of Babel," in *Rationalism in Politics and Other Essays*, new and expanded edition. Indianapolis, IL: Liberty Fund, 465–487.
Petrick, J. (2008). "Using the Business Integrity Capacity Model to Advance Business Ethics Education," in D. Swanson and D. Fisher (eds), *Advancing Business Ethics Education*. Charlotte, NC: Information Age Publishing, 103–124.
Petrick, J. (2014). "Strengthening Moral Competencies at Work through Integrity Capacity Cultivation," in L. Sekerka (ed.), *Ethics Training in Action*. Charlotte, NC: Information Age, 207–228.
Petrick, J. (2017). "Theoretical Issues in Management Ethics and Moral Performance," *Journal of International Management Studies* 12:1, 47–54.
Petrick, J. and J. Quinn (1997). *Management Ethics: Integrity at Work*. Thousand Oaks, CA: Sage.
Petrick, J. and J. Quinn (2001). "The Challenge of Leadership Accountability for Integrity Capacity as a Strategic Asset," *Journal of Business Ethics* 34:331–343.
Quinn, R., D. Bright, S. Faerman, M. Thompson and M. McGrath (2015). *Becoming a Master Manager: A Competing Values Approach*, 6th edition. New York, NY: John Wiley and Sons.
Ross, W.D. (2003). *The Right and the Good*. London: Clarendon Press.
Rousseau, D. (ed.) (2014). *The Oxford Handbook of Evidence-Based Management*. Oxford: Oxford University Press.
Scarre, G. (1996). *Utilitarianism*. London: Routledge.
Singer, M. (2003). *The Ideal of a Rational Morality*. Oxford: Clarendon Press.
Sison, A. (2016). *Happiness and Virtue Ethics in Business*. London: Cambridge University Press.
Sison, A. (ed.) (2017). *Handbook on Virtue Ethics in Business and Management*. London: Springer.
Solomon, R. (1999). *A Better Way to Think About Business: How Values Become Virtues*. Oxford: Oxford University Press.
Taylor, F. (1911). *The Principles of Scientific Management*. New York, NY: Harper.
Timmons, M. (2012). *Moral Theory: An Introduction*. New York, NY: Rowman & Littlefield.

27

The ethics of managers and employees

Linda Klebe Treviño

How can managers understand how people actually think and behave in ethically-charged situations and how can such knowledge help them to manage their own ethical conduct and the conduct of their employees? This sort of question approaches employee conduct (and misconduct) as a management challenge that can be successfully addressed if one understands more about human thoughts, feelings, and behaviors in the realm of ethical and unethical conduct in organizations. In other words, this perspective approaches management ethics less as an abstract normative query (e.g., "what is the right thing to do?") than as a practical, social scientifically based, endeavor. This chapter focuses, in particular, on how employees and managers face and respond to ethical dilemmas and problems in the workplace.

Ethical dilemmas are situations where (two or more "right") values are in conflict. For example, a manager may face a dilemma about whether to share information with a close friend about an upcoming layoff that is likely to affect the friend, information that the manager has agreed to keep secret. This dilemma pits loyalty to a friend against promise-keeping and loyalty to the organization. Daily work life is rife with these types of dilemmas but work life also manifests challenges that do not necessarily exemplify ethical dilemmas. Sometimes a manager needs to ensure that employees recognize that a moral value is at stake; on other occasions, a manager may need to encourage adherence to what individuals already recognize as morally important. Normative ethical theories provide multiple frameworks that can help answer the "what should I do" question. However, a social scientific approach raises somewhat different questions. For example, perhaps an employee knows a manager is falsifying expense reports; the employee believes that the incident should be reported but he fears that, if he does so and if his cheating manager learns that he was the reporter, then he will lose his job. Does this employee trust higher-level managers in the organization to protect his identity or to protect him if his identity is learned? These are questions about what it means to be an employee in an authority structure and organizational culture, and about employees' thoughts, feelings, and behaviors in response to ethically problematic situations that arise within these authority structures and cultures.

This chapter focuses chiefly on what we know about managing the ethics of employees through the ethical structures and contexts within the organization (e.g., ethics and compliance programs, ethical climates and cultures, ethical leadership). The first section addresses ethical awareness as a basic precondition of moral action. The subsequent section considers the use of ethics and compliance programs, followed by a third section that examines some of the chief ways in which an ethical culture may be encouraged and sustained. The concluding section offers summary remarks on how one might think about the management of ethical crises.

Ethical awareness, judgment, motivation, and action

Based upon early work on ethical decision making by James R. Rest (1986), many traditional ethical decision making models suggested that we need to better understand what drives individuals' ethical awareness, judgment, motivation, and action. Although awareness is the first stage of Rest's early ethical decision making model, for a long time moral psychology research and behavioral ethics research focused primarily on ethical judgment and its relation to action. Judgment was understood primarily via Lawrence Kohlberg's model of cognitive moral development (1969), which argued that individuals develop from childhood to adulthood through multiple stages of cognitive moral development. The first two stages are referred to as the pre-conventional (and most self-centered) level. At the first stage, individuals understand what is right in terms of obedience to authority and the possibility of punishment for misconduct. If the authority figure says something is wrong and will punish the person for doing it, then it is thought to be wrong. At the next stage, the individual begins to look outside the self, understanding the idea of reciprocity. For example, at some point, most children learn that sharing must be good because sharing means that the recipient will reciprocate. Unfortunately, some adults remain stuck at this very self-centered level of moral development. The next two stages comprise the conventional level, where we find most adults. At stage 3, the individual looks around and decides what is right based upon what peers and significant others (including leaders) think. At stage 4, people begin to look beyond significant others to codes, rules, and the law, understanding that the system exists for a purpose. Therefore, a person at stage 4 doesn't obey traffic signals just because she or he fears getting caught by police but because of an understanding that reduced speed limits in school zones serve an important purpose. At the principled (or post-conventional) level, the person is an autonomous thinker who thinks much like a philosopher about the action that would be most fair (or just) and in service of the greater good. However, only a small percentage of adults reach that level. Therefore, it makes sense for managers to work to influence the ethical thinking and action of those in their charge, most of whom are looking outside of themselves for ethical guidance.

The relationship between a particular cognitive moral development stage and action has been found to be a modest one, leaving open questions about what other variables might be needed to explain moral motivation and action (Blasi 1980). In 1986, Treviño proposed a model that put forward the idea that, if most adults are at the conventional level of cognitive moral development, they are open to influence by contextual factors such as reward systems, leaders, and organizational cultures. Therefore, she proposed a person, situation, interactionist model, arguing that action could be explained as a result of person factors, situational factors, and the interaction between the two. A meta-analysis (Kish-Gephart et al. 2010) of behavioral ethics research provided support for the idea of the importance of personal (e.g., cognitive moral development, locus of control, Machiavellianism) and situational factors (e.g., reward systems, ethical climates) as influences on unethical behavior. But, not enough research has been conducted on the interaction effects proposed in the 1986 model to conduct meta-analytic tests (see Greenberg 2002; Treviño and Youngblood 1990; Ashkanasy et al. 2006 for exceptions). More research on these interactive effects is clearly needed.

More recently, researchers have focused attention on the importance of ethical *awareness* in an unfolding ethical decision making process. Although Rest's (1986) model included moral awareness as a conscious first step in the ethical decision making process, that step had mostly been taken for granted and had rarely been studied directly, especially in the organizational ethics arena. In behavioral ethics, as it turned out, the earlier assumption that ethical judgment was the first step in the ethical decision making process was unwarranted: prior to a judgment individuals must first recognize that they are facing a decision with ethical overtones. Without that recognition or awareness, it is fair to say that ethical considerations will simply not be invoked. Rather, the decision may be treated as a "business" or "financial" decision with little thought to ethical concerns.

Some early behavioral ethics research investigated the importance of ethical awareness (Butterfield et al. 2000), finding that information about harm to other people, the use of charged ethical language, and social consensus in the social environment that something is right or wrong can increase ethical awareness. By contrast, the use of euphemistic language could mute ethical awareness. Much more attention is being paid to this idea in recent years, including the idea put forward by Scott J. Reynolds (2008) that some people are chronically more prone to perceive the ethical nature of a situation. In addition, the publication of a popular book entitled *Blind Spots* (Bazerman and Tenbrunsel 2011) put forward the thesis that people often make unethical decisions without conscious awareness that they are operating in the ethical realm. In the authors' words, the ethical characteristics of a situation simply "fade" from view (in a process known as ethical fading) and the person makes the decision without conscious attention to ethical considerations. One way to address ethical fading is through careful framing of the situation as one with ethical overtones.

Yet another strain of related research refers to the process of moral disengagement, a notion developed by Albert Bandura (Bandura et al. 1996). Bandura proposed that humans are self-regulating with internalized norms and standards that generally keep behavior in line because of anticipated guilt if the individual were to breach those internalized standards. However, it is possible for this self-regulatory process to be disengaged through eight theorized mechanisms (e.g., advantageous comparison, diffusion of responsibility, displacement of responsibility, distortion of consequences, moral justification, attribution of blame, dehumanization, euphemistic labeling) and some individuals have been shown to be more prone to moral disengagement than others. Bandura's research was conducted mostly on children and young adults. Behavioral ethics researchers have become interested in the topic. Moral disengagement mechanisms that are particularly relevant to organizational life include euphemistic labeling (talking about "right-sizing" vs. layoffs or "collateral damage" vs. civilian casualties), displacement of responsibility (my boss made me do it), diffusion of responsibility (it's not my job, it was a group decision), attribution of blame (it's their own fault), and advantageous comparison (it's not as bad as what others are doing). With other scholars, Celia Moore created an eight-item reliable measure of moral disengagement for adults (Moore et al. 2012) that has been shown to predict a variety of types of unethical behavior and that has since been used in other research. It is also available for organizations to use.

Much of the work associated with the view that awareness is important focuses on a less conscious, less rational, and more emotional ethical decision making process. Moral psychologist Jonathan Haidt (2001) is a major contributor to a more intuitive, emotional view of ethical decision making. He proposed a social intuitionist model in which individuals react impulsively and automatically to ethical situations, often with evaluative emotional responses such as the visceral emotion of disgust, which they cannot explain in rational terms, but will attempt to justify post hoc. This phenomenon has been referred to as "moral dumbfounding" (Haidt 2001). People evaluate something as "bad" ("that's disgusting") without being able to explain why in rational terms, but they stick to the evaluation nevertheless. Thus, the intuitive judgment precedes the more rational deliberative judgment. In one of the dilemmas he presented to research subjects, Haidt (2001) presented subjects with a story about a brother and sister who vacationed together and decided that it would be interesting to have sex. The woman was on birth control and they used a condom for extra safety. Afterward, although they enjoyed it, they decided they wouldn't repeat it or tell anyone about it. Subjects had the expected "that's disgusting and immoral" response although they had trouble logically explaining why (beyond the fact that incest is deemed to be wrong in the Bible and in society). As a result of this and related work, researchers became even more interested in understanding the circumstances under which decisions are more automatic than deliberative. Joshua D. Greene and colleagues (Greene et al. 2001) have found that decisions are more emotional and more automatic when the decision is a more personal one that involves potential harm to others (cf., Moore and Gino 2015). If emotions are so important to ethical decision making, then the muting of moral emotions is likely to dampen ethical concerns. For example, psychopaths have been found to react with less empathy to the distress of others. Moore and Gino (2014) provide an excellent review of the research in this realm.

Managing ethical conduct through ethics and compliance programs

Managing ethics and compliance has become a significant activity in many organizations. These activities are structured in a variety of ways and have different emphases. Some are focused broadly on risk assessment in order to evaluate the organization's work and where it is likely to be at risk of non-compliance with laws or other potential bases for scandal or negative attention. The primary emphasis of a risk assessment approach appears to be on compliance with the law and regulations, largely because of the growing number of laws and regulations that apply to organizations. This emphasis on legal compliance was heavily influenced in the US in the early 1990s by the US Sentencing Commission's institution of sentencing guidelines for organizations that were caught breaking the law. The guidelines are based upon a carrot and stick approach to organizational sentencing whereby organizations that can demonstrate that they have followed the guidelines and made a good faith effort to manage misconduct can see their fines and other penalties reduced considerably. The seven guidelines include the following:

1 establish conduct standards that can prevent illegal behavior
2 put a high level person in charge of the standards;
3 avoid giving discretionary authority to persons with the propensity to break the law;
4 communicate the standards to all employees;
5 set up monitoring, auditing and other systems to detect misconduct (to include a retribution-free reporting system);
6 discipline those who break the conduct standards as well as those who should have but did not detect the offense;
7 once misconduct has occurred, take steps to prevent future occurrences.

These guidelines stimulated many organizations to develop ethics and compliance "programs," and a whole new profession (the ethics/compliance officer or variations on the title) was developed in response. These programs responded to the elements discussed in the guidelines. They established standards (codes of conduct), put a high-level person in charge (usually an ethics/compliance officer or sometimes the chief legal counsel), communicated standards (through communication and training devices), set up reporting systems (helplines or hotlines), and took action to discipline misconduct when it occurred and to take steps to prevent future misconduct. These programs varied greatly in effectiveness depending upon their perceived orientation toward values or legal compliance (Weaver and Treviño 1999), the extent to which all of the guidelines were followed, and the extent to which they were integrated into the daily life of the organization (Treviño et al. 1999) versus being decoupled from daily organizational life (MacLean and Benham 2010). A good source of current information about ethics and compliance programs can be found in the National Business Ethics Survey reports published by the Ethics Research Center (located at www.ethics.org/research/eci-research/nbes).

In 2004, revisions to the guidelines stipulated that the board of directors oversee compliance; the result of this stipulation meant that most boards set up oversight committees, with the further outcome that ethics/compliance officers in the US now regularly report directly to the corporate board about compliance issues. Many such officials have a direct or dotted line reporting relationship to the board. The idea of ethical culture also began to garner attention in the world of organizations with this 2004 revision because the Sentencing Commission noted that an ethics/compliance program, to be effective, must be seen as an integral part of the organization's culture rather than just a check-the-box "program" that can easily be decoupled from the organization's daily life (MacLean and Benham 2010). Although the guidelines are only advisory, they have had a profound impact on US businesses' efforts toward ethics and legal compliance. Other types of organizations, including universities, are jumping on the bandwagon, albeit a bit late compared with corporations. Other regulatory agencies such as the US Securities and Exchange Commission have also become interested in organizations' ethical cultures, adding to the focus.

Ethical culture

A focus on culture has left many ethics and compliance officers scratching their heads because the Sentencing Commission did not explain what it meant by "ethical culture." One framework for thinking about ethical culture builds on the more general organizational culture work of Schein (1985) and the more specific ethical culture work of Treviño (Treviño 1986, 1990; Treviño and Nelson 2014). We can think of ethical culture as a combination of formal and informal systems. Formal ethical culture systems include official leader communication, systems (and criteria) for employee selection, values statements and codes of ethics, orientation and training programs, performance management systems, and formal decision making processes. Informal ethical culture systems include the role models and heroes, the norms of daily behavior, the organization's rituals, and the language that is used in the organization.

Leadership and role models

When we focus on the ethics of managers, we are really talking about the ethics of leaders in the organization—leaders at all levels. Leadership has long been important to those interested in business ethics and ethical culture. We have known, for example, that a leader's honesty and integrity were related to others' perceptions of effective leadership. Other well-researched leadership fields such as transformational and socialized charismatic leadership have emphasized the importance of leader values and altruistic motivation. But, until around 2000, we could not point to a body of literature that was dedicated to understanding "ethical leadership" as a separate construct. Michael E. Brown and colleagues defined ethical leadership as "the demonstration of normatively appropriate conduct through personal actions and interpersonal relationships, and the promotion of such conduct to followers through two-way communication, reinforcement, and decision making" (Brown et al. 2005: 120). They used a social learning framework to explain the expected effects. Ethical leaders, because of their behavior and leadership on ethics, are legitimate role models who have a positive influence on followers who wish to mimic the leader's normatively appropriate behavior. Followers also learn about the consequences of right and wrong behavior from ethical leaders who set standards and hold followers accountable to them. The ethical leadership literature has developed substantially since publication of the 2005 article, demonstrating how important leaders are at every level of the organization. With ethical leadership, we see greater prosocial behavior, reduced deviance and unethical behavior, more voice, and better performance (see Treviño and Brown 2014 for a review). Scholars and practitioners have long talked about "tone at the top." Indeed, senior leaders matter a lot because they set the tone for the organization, communicate the importance of ethics (or not), and provide resources (or not) for those whose job it is to keep ethics in the forefront of people's minds (e.g., ethics and compliance officers). Evidence also exists that ethical leadership at the top level "trickles down" to supervisors in the organization (Mayer et al. 2009) and that these supervisors create ethical "unit" cultures with a large impact on ethical/unethical behavior outcomes (Schaubroeck et al. 2012). Therefore, executive leadership is extraordinarily important to planting and sustaining the seeds of an ethical culture. However, research also tells us that executive leaders are often uninformed about the ethical cultures in their organizations. Perceptions of ethics tend to be rosier the higher you go in the organization. So, these leaders must do their best to keep in touch with the ethical culture, especially perceptions of employees at lower levels (Treviño et al. 2008).

Equally if not more important than senior executives are the managers who are on the front lines, leading employees every day. These are the managers who interact with employees regularly, conduct their performance evaluations, and make important decisions about pay and promotion. Especially in organizations with a strong emphasis on bottom line performance, ethical leaders focus attention at least equally on the importance of using ethical means to achieve bottom line goals. Importantly, they also demonstrate that they care about their employees, lead their personal and professional lives in an ethical manner (demonstrating integrity or wholeness), make principled and fair decisions, and are trustworthy. They set an obvious example by role modeling ethical behavior, setting and communicating high ethical standards and using reinforcement mechanisms to hold everyone accountable to those standards. Most of the research on ethical leadership and its effects has been conducted at the supervisory level and, as noted above, ethical leadership at that level is associated with important positive outcomes, including the creation of an ethical culture at the unit level.

Less work has been conducted on the negative side of leadership, although a robust literature exists on the topic of abusive supervision. Abusive supervisors are hostile and aggressive and have been found to have profound negative effects on employee outcomes, including ethics-related outcomes (for a review, see Tepper 2007).

Values statements and codes of conduct

Values and mission statements are broad statements of the organization's identity; they express what the organization stands for and cares about. Nonetheless, they are often the butt of jokes (see Dilbert comics for examples) because cynical observers see them as words on a poster that do not reflect the identity and daily behavior of the actual organization. But, in some organizations, values statements reflect the true identity of the organization (sometimes the founder's mission for creating the organization in the first place) and serve as a compass that directs the actions of the organization and its employees. In order to be effective, values statements should reflect the organization's unique identity and should guide organization members' behavior every day. For example, Johnson & Johnson's Credo states that the organization's first responsibility is to doctors, nurses, and patients, followed by employees, and then shareholders, The Credo is credited with guiding the organization's behavior in the famous Tylenol poisoning crisis in the 1980s when the organization initiated an expensive recall of all Tylenol products and created the tamper-proof packaging that is now so familiar to all of us. Some observers question the continuing relevance of the Credo in today's large decentralized Johnson & Johnson organization that appears to have lost its way in a number of ethical mishaps in recent years. But, this only helps to highlight the complexity of building and sustaining an ethical culture with its many systems that must work together seamlessly in order to succeed. A Credo alone is clearly not sufficient. All of the cultural systems must be aligned to support ethical conduct.

Values statements often are accompanied by codes of conduct that provide much more specific guidance about the behavior that the organization expects of its employees. Codes often include guidelines regarding the giving or receiving of gifts, participating in social media, and conducting business legally overseas or with government contractors, and much more. Many organizations post their values statements and/or codes of conduct on their public websites, and many require that their employees take training each year to ensure familiarity with and agreement to the code's contents. Some organizations are also now requiring that multiple exchange partners (e.g., suppliers, contractors) agree to comply with the firm's conduct codes because companies are increasingly being held responsible for the behavior of exchange partners in their supply chains.

Selection systems

Once the values are established, an important way that organizations create and sustain ethical cultures is by attempting to select employees who share the organization's values. The organization that cares about the ethics of recruits can address this in a number of ways. It can make its values and ethical standards clear in recruiting materials so that it attracts those who share them. It can ask values and ethics-based questions in interviews or when checking references in an attempt to find those who will fit the organization's ethical culture. It can use internships to bring potential employees into the organization for a trial run so that they can be vetted. It can also attempt to insure that those applicants who definitely will not fit the ethical culture are weeded out. For example, the organization can conduct background checks on potential employees, check their social media profiles, check references, etc. Finally, once employees are hired, organizations can use provisional periods to observe new employees in action and ensure a good values fit. Those who don't fit can be asked to leave. An advantage of selecting those who share the organization's values is that the organization is more likely to have a strong culture where behavior is consistent across members. But a potential downside is that too much homogeneity may reduce the expression of dissent and new ideas (see Benjamin Schneider's work, 2008, on the attraction, selection, attrition—ASA—model).

Orientation and training

Once employees are selected, the organization that cares about creating and sustaining an ethical culture will orient new employees to the values and ethical expectations of the organization. In the best case scenario, the CEO or a surrogate will show up at these orientation sessions to demonstrate commitment to the values and culture from the top of the organization, perhaps taking the trainees through a real ethical dilemma and role modeling good values and ethical decision making. Preferably, supervisors and coworkers are also on board and will reinforce those values outside of the orientation program. Most employers of any significant size today also require ethics/compliance training, usually annually. Minimally, this training focuses on insuring that employees know the rules and laws that are applicable to their jobs. The best training is probably face-to-face with managers in the room and will focus on gray areas, providing guidance about the ethical dilemmas that are likely to face employees in their industry, organization, or work. Most large organizations require some sort of ethics or compliance training today. But, unfortunately, we have little research evidence about training effectiveness. The consensus seems to be that every employee should be trained annually. This is mostly because the Sentencing Guidelines say that employees should be trained on the company standards (although no time interval is noted). This particular guideline has led most large organizations to implement annual on-line ethics training that allows the organization to "check the box" that says every employee has been trained annually. Yet, as noted above, this training may or may not be effective. We just don't know. If it leads to cynicism among employees who believe that they are "wasting time," or believe that they already know the content, it could actually backfire, leading employees to perceive a "check the box" culture rather than one that truly supports ethics.

Performance management systems

One of the most significant ethical culture components is the performance management system. Organizational members pay close attention to what is measured and rewarded (or punished) in the organization. Most will try to do what is rewarded and to avoid doing what is disciplined. Therefore, in order to sustain an ethical culture, the formal performance management system should hold organizational members accountable to do their work in a way that upholds the organization's values and ethical standards. For example, if respect for others is a value, then the performance evaluation should include something like "treats others with respect." Those with whom the person works should be given the opportunity to evaluate him or her via peer evaluation (and in other cases, leaders should be evaluated by subordinates). If integrity is a value, the performance evaluation should consider whether the employee is thought to be honest and trustworthy by coworkers, supervisees and customers. Many organizations still emphasize more easily measurable bottom-line outcomes such as sales in their decisions about pay and promotion. But, for an ethical culture to be effective, the performance management system must attend at least as much to the means for achieving outcomes, and count those at least as much in important decisions about compensation and promotion. So, an important question to ask is this: do employees perceive that one can be promoted or get a raise if the individual is not achieving goals in a way that is consistent with the organization's stated values? If the answer is *no*, the message to employees is clear that the organization means what it says about its values. But, if the answer is yes, there is little the organization can do to convince employees that it means what it says until it changes the performance management system. It will be clear to employees that only the bottom line matters and how one gets there does not.

Authority structures and reporting systems

Organizations are authority structures and managers are in a position to strongly influence followers because most people are going to do what an authority figure tells them to do (Milgram 1974). However, organizations also differ in terms of the messages they send about whether it's all right or even expected that their members question authority. Deference to authority helps the organization to run smoothly, but it also allows followers to avoid feeling responsible for ethics-related outcomes. Thus, unethical behavior is more likely. Because of the human inclination to defer to authority, without a strong message to the contrary, most employees will assume that obedience is expected. As a result they will be hesitant to speak up. In fact, some have argued that silence is the default mode among organization members (Kish-Gephart et al. 2010) and that it takes great effort to overcome this default mode. Employees are reluctant to speak up even about routine concerns. But, when the concern is an ethical concern, that reluctance generally becomes complete silence unless the organization has worked especially hard to convince employees that speaking up about ethical concerns is not only safe but expected. Convincing employees that it's safe is a tall order because "whistleblowers" tend to fare poorly. At least those are the stories we hear the most. Because of government requirements, most organizations have some kind of formal reporting system (such as a hotline that is answered by an outside contractor) for employees to report ethical or legal violations. The reports can be anonymous or not. Generally, the person is given a case number and is contacted (if not anonymous) or (using the case number) can check back for an update on the investigation. Protecting the reporter from retaliation is extremely important and some organizations even track the person's career over time to be sure that the reporter has not been retaliated against. The two most powerful reasons that people don't report wrongdoing is because they fear retaliation or expect nothing to come of their report. Therefore, protecting reporters and letting them know that the report was taken seriously, investigated, and acted upon represents the best of an ethical culture. In addition, research tells us that employees are more likely to report misconduct if they feel supported by their leader and coworkers (Mayer et al. 2013).

Decision-making processes

Many organizations have formal decision-making processes and standard operating procedures to guide organization members in the process of making important decisions. If ethical considerations are a routine part of important decisions, employees learn that the organization really does care about the impacts of its decisions. For example, evaluating impacts on the community is more common today than it was a few decades ago. Many organizations have also committed to sustainability goals. Therefore, considering whether a new product or plant contributes to those goals may be required before a final decision to move forward can be made. Some organizations may invite the Ethics/Compliance Officer and or Sustainability Officer to participate in high-level meetings about important decisions as a way to insure that ethical considerations are taken into account. The opposite situation exists when employees perceive that only the bottom-line counts and that, despite what the organization might say in formal documents, they should make decisions with only the bottom line in mind.

Role models

On the more informal side, every organization has people who are looked to as heroes or role models. In a strong ethical culture, the heroes and role models are people who are known for doing the right thing even when it's hard to do. They are people of integrity who not only care about others but are trustworthy, fair, respectful, humble and principled. There may be stories about them or they may be held up as exemplars at important events. By contrast, if the role models are those who get ahead by stepping on others, or by lying to and cheating customers, the message is clear that the people who employees are looking to mimic are models of unethical behavior not ethical behavior.

Norms of daily behavior

Norms are the standards that guide conduct every day. Most employees (who are at the conventional level of cognitive moral development) look around and see what their leaders and coworkers are actually doing and they tend to follow and do the same. It doesn't matter what the values state or what the code of conduct says. So, to understand an organization's culture, it is more important to ask what people are actually saying and doing every day. Do they behave as if ethics matters? Or, do they behave as if only financials matter and ethics is relegated to annual ethics training and dismissed missives from the CEO?

Rituals

Organizations have rituals that demonstrate what they value. Like an anthropologist, one can learn much about an organization's culture by studying the organization's rituals. Is integrity celebrated at those rituals or is only financial performance the focus? For example, many organizations have annual sales meetings. Who at these meetings is given sales awards at the ritual dinner? Is it the salesperson who lied to and cheated customers and stepped on colleagues to get ahead? Or, is it the salesperson who turned down a request for a bribe by a foreign customer? Other rituals may be more mundane but send important signals about what the company stands for. For example, if on-site child care is provided, does one routinely see employees having lunch with their children in the cafeteria? If so, that's a ritual that sends a powerful message that taking time to spend with your child during the day is supported and celebrated. Or, is going out for a ritual happy hour the expectation, so that a colleague who skips happy hour to pick up children at day care is ostracized from the group or denied the knowledge that is shared at such events? Employees pay very close attention to the signals and symbols represented by these rituals.

Language

We said earlier that the use of ethical language increases ethical awareness and that framing decisions as "ethical" decisions makes ethical fading less likely. Therefore, the question becomes, is the organization one where ethical language is not only accepted but expected and even celebrated—where one is expected to ask questions such as "is this proposal the ethical thing to do?" or to ask whether potential harm to stakeholders has been adequately considered before a decision is made. On the other hand, is organizational talk full of euphemistic language that mutes ethical awareness? As one example, "collateral damage" is a euphemistic term used by military and government officials to refer to civilian casualties in war. One's ethical antennae are much more likely to be stimulated by talk about civilian deaths than by talk about collateral damage. It's important for managers to understand the muting effect of euphemistic language and to search for euphemisms in their own organization.

Alignment of formal and informal systems

In order to have a strong ethical culture the many cultural components outlined above should be fully aligned with each other. They all need to be pulling and pushing behavior in the same direction. For example, the performance management system must support the values and ethical standards, and the norms of daily behavior should align with what employees are taught in training. If the culture components are misaligned, employees will get mixed messages and they may infer, plausibly, that the organization doesn't mean what it says about ethics.

Ethical climate

At around the same time that Treviño began discussing ethical culture, Victor and Cullen (1988) introduced the construct of ethical climate as the shared perceptions of the organization's orientation toward ethics that could orient and guide employees' attitudes and behaviors. The authors originally proposed nine theoretical climates. However, subsequent research based upon their survey measure tended to support fewer of these. For example: 1) an instrumental climate based upon self-interest; 2) a caring climate grounded in benevolence; 3) an independence climate based on individual decision-making; 4) a rules climate based upon following organizational rules and policies; 5) a law and code climate reliant on society's laws and regulations to guide decision making. Kelly D. Martin and John B. Cullen (2006) published a meta-analytic review of the ethical climate research. They found the largest and most consistent support for positive relationships between a caring (benevolent) climate and positive employee work attitudes as well as lower unethical behavior; they found the opposite for instrumental climates—in a more self-interested climate employee attitudes are more negative and unethical behavior is higher. Similarly, in their meta-analysis Jennifer J. Kish-Gephart and colleagues (2010) found that egoistic (or self-interest) climates were positively associated with unethical choice while benevolent and principled climates were positively associated with ethical choice. Anke Arnaud and Marshall Schminke (2012) also followed this reduction of ethical climate to these two dimensions (self-interest vs. benevolence climates), suggesting that future work on climate is likely to focus on these two dimensions alone. They suggested that a collective moral emotion and moral efficacy are an important part of the ethical context and serve to moderate the influence of ethical climate on outcomes. They also created a shorter, more usable measure of ethical climate that can be used in future research. Indeed, they found that ethical climate had a significantly stronger effect on outcomes when employees shared concern for stakeholders (collective emotion) and felt that they could do something about ethical issues (collective efficacy). Their approach explained twice as much variance in unethical behavior as we typically find with traditional measures of ethical climate alone. These findings suggest that future research should focus on the complexities of ethical contexts and their relations to outcomes. Treviño, Butterfield, and McCabe (1988) found that ethical culture and climate were highly correlated and had similar relationships with attitudinal and behavioral outcome measures. Kish-Gephart and colleagues' (2010) meta-analysis found similar results. So, there is work yet to do to determine how best to measure the ethical context in organizations.

Finally, in addition to thinking about the ethical climate or culture of the entire organization, research suggests that subunits also have climates and cultures. John M. Schaubroeck and colleagues (2012) found that ethical leaders influence unethical behavior through their influence on creating unit ethical culture. More work will also be required to understand how one creates subunit culture and how subunit cultures relate to organizational cultures.

Assessment—conducting an ethical culture audit

Given the features listed above, how does one get to know and understand an organization's ethical culture? After reading about the complexities of ethical culture, it should be clear that this is not a simple task. The best way to fully understand an ethical culture is to conduct an ethical culture audit. A thorough audit would generally involve interviews, focus groups, and surveys that attempt to capture employee perceptions of the realities of organizational life and the ethical culture of the organization. One would need to assess each culture component as well as whether these are aligned with each other to support ethical behavior or unethical behavior—or, whether these components send mixed messages about what the organization really wants and stands for. In response to mixed messages, employees generally presume that bottom line outcomes matter more than ethics; as a result, ethical culture is compromised. Organizations that are willing to commit the time and resources to assessing their ethical cultures can learn extraordinarily important things about daily life in their organizations, information that is often a shock to senior managers for whom the ethical culture is always "rosier" than it is for those lower down the hierarchy (Treviño et al. 2008). Beyond these more traditional methods for assessing culture, we are likely to see efforts to harness "big data" to track things such as the words (perhaps euphemisms) in employee emails, employee comings and goings, and other actions. These new methods come with substantial privacy concerns and must be handled cautiously lest they send the message to employees that they are not trusted.

Assessment is just the first step in creating and sustaining an ethical culture, which is a complex task that requires ongoing commitment, resources, and management support. An ethical culture can easily be undermined if this commitment to ongoing support disappears (Gehman et al. 2013).

Concluding remarks

Understanding individuals' ethical actions in the context of organizations can help us to understand ethical crises and their management. For example, we discovered in 2015 that Volkswagen engineers created a software program to deceive emissions testing devices. Our inclination might be to focus on those individual engineers and their faulty normative ethical decision making. However, a management perspective focuses our attention on the culture that created a context within which those engineers thought that what they did was the "right" thing to do or, at minimum, it was what they were supposed to do or perhaps had to do in order to keep their jobs. What we know thus far is that the CEO at the time had set tough (if not impossible to achieve) emissions goals for "clean" diesel cars that were going to be sold in the US where emissions requirements are tougher than they are in Europe. The company had set challenging goals for itself in terms of sales of these "clean" diesels in the US. We know that goals are highly motivating and engineers tried all kinds of things in their attempts to meet the expectations. However, they found it difficult to achieve those goals in a legitimate manner and turned instead to the deceptive software. There was something about the culture at Volkswagen that created a context within which this could occur and remain hidden (perhaps even from senior management) for years. An ethics and compliance "program" will not solve Volkswagen's problem although it could be a part of a culture overhaul. The only solution will be a thorough ethical culture audit followed by an overhaul of the culture with constant follow-up in ensuing years to insure that the old ways have not returned.

In the past few decades we have learned a great deal about the management of ethics in organizational context. We now know that we can't take ethical awareness for granted; we have to work to ensure that employees recognize and are attentive to ethical issues when they arise. We also know that managers who are interested in driving ethical behavior in their organizations must create ethical climates and cultures that support and encourage doing the right thing. These go beyond the mentality of some organizations that follow the US Sentencing Guidelines in order to "check the box." Employees are quick to recognize the difference between authenticity and hypocrisy. Also, as noted above, ethical culture is a complex phenomenon composed of multiple formal and informal ethical culture systems that must all work together. Mixed messages suggest hypocrisy. Therefore, an authentic ethical culture or climate can do much to produce positive attitudes and behaviors in employees. However, one that is seen as hypocritical

The ethics of managers and employees

is quickly and easily dismissed as a façade. It isn't easy to create and sustain an ethical context in an organization over time. This is something that must be regularly assessed and the organization must be ready to tackle changes when ethical culture audits reveal problems.

Essential readings

Much of the research on managing the ethics of employees is summarized in Linda Klebe Treviño and Kate Nelson's *Managing Business Ethics: Straight Talk about How to Do it Right* (2014) which reviews the literature on ethical culture and climate (Chapter 5), and ethics programs (Chapter 6) and much more. To understand the foundation of research on moral reasoning, see the discussion in Lawrence Kohlberg, "Stage and Sequence: The Cognitive Developmental Approach to Socialization" (1969) and the more recent work of James R. Rest, *Moral Development* (1986). For an update on moral reasoning that includes the social intuitionist approach, see Jonathan Haidt's study, "The Emotional Dog and its Rational Tail" (2001). For reviews and meta-analyses of literatures more broadly related to the management of ethics in organizations, see the following: Jennifer Kish-Gephart, David Harrison, and Linda Klebe Treviño, "Bad Apples, Bad Cases, and Bad Barrels" (2010); Kelly D. Martin and J. Cullen, "Continuities and Extensions of Ethical Climate Research" (2006); Linda Klebe Treviño, Niki den Niewenboer, and Jennifer Kish-Gephart, "(Un)ethical Behavior in Organizations" (2014); Linda Klebe Treviño, Gary Weaver, and Scott Reynolds "Behavior Ethics in Organizations: A Review" (2006); and Celia Moore and Francesca Gino, "Approach, Ability, Aftermath: A Psychological Process Framework of Unethical Behavior at Work" (2015). For an understanding of what works and what doesn't in ethics and legal compliance in organizations, see Linda Klebe Treviño, Gary Weaver, David Gibson, and Barbara Toffler, "Managing Ethics and Legal Compliance: What Works and What Hurts" (1999), as well as research reports from the Ethics and Compliance Initiative based upon the National Business Ethics Survey (see ethics.org).

For further reading in this volume on management ethics (including intuitive moral judgment), see Chapter 26, Theoretical issues in management ethics. On the notion of ethical climate (or culture) and business leadership, see Chapter 25, Leadership and business ethics: are leaders wolves in business ethics? On some of the ways in which business ethics education may assist moral awareness (or alleviate moral blindness), see Chapter 4, Teaching business ethics: current practice and future directions. On management and corporate governance, see Chapter 24, Corporate governance. On relations between managers and employees, see Chapter 28, Employee ethics and rights. For a discussion of the ways that marketing may prove unethical, see Chapter 30, Ethical issues in marketing, advertising, and sales. On the emphasis on *compliance* in global ethics programs, see Chapter 32, The globalization of business ethics. A discussion of theoretical perspectives in international management may be found in Chapter 33, Cross-cultural management ethics in multinational commerce.

References

Arnaud, A. and M. Schminke (2012). "Ethical Climate and Context of Organizations: A Comprehensive Model," *Organization Science* 23:6, 1767–1780.

Ashkanasy, N.M., C.A. Windsor and L.K. Treviño (2006). "Bad Apples in Bad Barrels Revisited: Cognitive Moral Development, Just World Beliefs, Rewards, and Ethical Decision Making," *Business Ethics Quarterly* 16, 449–47.

Bandura, A., C. Barbaranelli, G.V. Caprara and C. Pastorelli (1996). "Mechanisms of Moral Disengagement in the Exercise of Moral Agency," *Journal of Personality and Social Psychology* 71, 364–374.

Bazerman, M.H. and A.E. Tenbrunsel (2011). *Blind Spots*. Princeton, NJ: Princeton University Press.

Blasi, A. (1980). "Bridging Moral Cognition and Moral Action: A Critical Review of the Literature," *Psychological Bulletin*: 88, 1–45.

Brown, M., L.K. Treviño and D. Harrison (2005). "Ethical Leadership: A Social Learning Perspective for Construct Development and Testing," *Organizational Behavior and Human Decision Processes* 97, 117–134.

Butterfield, K., L.K. Treviño and G.R. Weaver (2000). "Moral Awareness in Business Organizations: Influences of Issue-related and Social Context Factors," *Human Relations* 53:7, 981–1018.

Gehman, J., L.K. Treviño and R. Garud (2013). "Values Work: A Process Study of the Emergence and Performance of Organizational Values Practices," *Academy of Management Journal* 56, 84–112.

Greenberg, J. (2002). "Who Stole the Money and When? Individual and Situational Determinants of Employee Theft," *Organizational Behavior and Human Decision Processes* 89, 985–1003.

Greene, J., D. Somerville, B. Nystrom, J. Darley and J.D. Cohen (2001). "An fMRI Investigation of Emotional Engagement in Moral Judgment," *Science*, 293, 5537.

Haidt, J. (2001). "The Emotional Dog and Its Rational Tail: A Social Intuitionist Approach to Moral Judgment," *Psychological Review* 108, 814–834.

Kish-Gephart, J., D. Harrison and L.K. Treviño (2010). "Bad Apples, Bad Cases, and Bad Barrels: Meta-analytic Evidence about Sources of Unethical Decisions at Work: Understanding Calculated and Impulsive Pathways," *Journal of Applied Psychology* 95, 1–31.

Kish-Gephart, J., J. Detert, L.K. Treviño and A. Edmondson (2010). "Silenced by Fear: The Nature, Sources, and Consequences of Fear at Work," *Research in Organizational Behavior* 29, 163–193.

Kohlberg, L. (1969). "Stage and Sequence: The Cognitive Developmental Approach to Socialization," in D.A. Goslin, (ed.), *Handbook of Socialization Theory*. Chicago, IL: Rand McNally, 347–480.

MacLean, T.L. and M. Behnam (2010). "The Dangers of Decoupling: The Relationship Between Compliance Programs, Legitimacy Perceptions, and Institutionalized Misconduct," *Academy of Management Journal* 5, 1499–1520.

Martin, K.D. and J. Cullen (2006). "Continuities and Extensions of Ethical Climate Research: A Meta-analytic Review," *Journal of Business Ethics* 69, 179–194.

Mayer, D.M., M. Kuenzi, R. Greenbaum, M. Bardes and R. Salvador (2009). "How Low Does Ethical Leadership Flow? Test of a Trickle Down Model," *Organizational Behavior and Human Decision Processes* 108, 1–13.

Mayer, D., S. Nurmohamed, L.K. Treviño, D. L. Shapiro and M. Schminke (2013). "Encouraging Employees to Report Unethical Conduct Internally: It Takes a Village," *Organizational Behavior and Human Decision Processes* 121, 89–103.

Milgram, S. (1974). *Obedience to Authority: An Experimental View*. New York, NY: Harper & Row.

Moore, C., J.R. Detert, L.K. Treviño, V. Baker and D. Mayer (2012). "Why Employees Do Bad Things: Moral Disengagement and Unethical Organizational Behavior," *Personnel Psychology* 65, 1–48.

Moore C. and F. Gino (2015). "Approach, Ability, Aftermath: A Psychological Process Framework of Unethical Behavior at Work," *Academy of Management Annals* 9, 235–289.

Rest, J.R. (1986). *Moral Development: Advances in Research and Theory*. New York, NY: Praeger

Reynolds, S.J. (2008). "Moral Attentiveness: Who Pays Attention to the Moral Aspects of Life?" *Journal of Applied Psychology* 93, 1027–1041.

Schaubroeck, J., S. Hannah, B. Avolio, S. Kozlowski, R. Lord, L.K. Treviño, N. Dimotakis and C. Peng (2012). "Embedding Ethical Leadership Within and Across Organization Levels," *Academy of Management Journal* 55, 1053–1078.

Schein, E.H. (1985). *Organizational Culture and Leadership*. San Francisco, CA: Jossey Bass.

Schneider, B. (2008). "The People Still Make the Place," in D. Brent Smith (ed.), *The People Make the Place: Dynamic Linkages Between Individuals and Organizations*. New York, NY: Taylor & Francis/Erlbaum.

Tepper, B.J. (2007). "Abusive Supervision in Work Organizations: Review, Synthesis, and Research Agenda," *Journal of Management* 33, 261–289

Treviño, L.K. (1986). "Ethical Decision Making in Organizations: A Person-Situation Interactionist Model," *Academy of Management Review* 11:3, 601–617.

Treviño, L.K. (1990). "A Cultural Perspective on Changing and Developing Organizational Ethics," in R. Woodman and W. Passmore (eds), *Research in Organizational Change and Development*. Greenwich, CT: JAI Press, 195–230.

Treviño, L.K. and K. Nelson (2014). Managing Business Ethics: Straight Talk About How To Do It Right, 6th edition. New York, NY: John Wiley and Sons.

Treviño, L.K. and M.B. Brown (2014). "Ethical Leadership," chapter in D. Day (ed.), *Oxford Handbook of Leadership and Organizations*,. New York, NY: Oxford University Press, 524–538.

Treviño, L.K. and S.A. Youngblood (1990). "Bad Apples in Bad Barrels; A Causal Analysis of Ethical Decision-making Behavior," Journal of Applied Psychology 75, 378–385.

Treviño, L.K., K. Butterfield and D. McKabe (1998). "The Ethical Context in Organizations: Influences on Employee Attitudes and Behaviors," *Business Ethics Quarterly* 8:3, 447–476.

Treviño, L.K., G. Weaver and M.E. Brown (2008). "It's Lovely at the Top: Hierarchical Levels, Identities, and Perceptions of Organizational Ethics," Business Ethics Quarterly 18:2, 233–252.

Treviño, L.K., G.R. Weaver and S. Reynolds (2006). "Behavioral Ethics in Organizations: A Review," Journal of Management 32, 1–40.

Treviño, L.K., N.A. den Nieuwenboer and J.J. Kish-Gephart (2014). "(Un)ethical Behavior in Organizations," *Annual Review of Psychology*, 65, 635–660.

Treviño, L.K., G. Weaver, D. Gibson and B. Toffler (1999). "Managing Ethics and Legal Compliance: What Works and What Hurts," *California Management Review* 41:2, 131–151.

Victor, B. and J.B. Cullen (1988). "The Organizational Bases of Ethical Work Climates," *Administrative Science Quarterly* 33, 101–124.

Weaver, G.R. and L.K. Treviño (1999). "Compliance and Values Oriented Ethics Programs:Influences on Employees' Attitudes and behavior," *Business Ethics Quarterly* 9:2, 325–345.

28
Employee ethics and rights

*Jeffrey Moriarty**

Employment relationships can be among the most significant relationships in a person's life. For many people, work requires a major commitment of time and effort, offers a source of purpose, identity, and self-esteem, and provides the material resources needed to live a decent life. But the moral contours of the employment relationship are still not well understood. This chapter advances our understanding of them by considering two general questions. What obligations do employers have toward their employees? What obligations do employees have toward their employers? I approach these questions from a moral rather than a legal perspective. Although I discuss relevant laws, I focus on what employers and employees owe to each other morally. There has been considerably more focus on what duties employers have to employees than the reverse. This is because employers usually have more power than employees, and so are able to impose their will on employees in potentially morally problematic ways. This chapter reflects that focus, while also highlighting certain duties that employees have to employers. There are many more topics in employee ethics and rights than can be discussed here. I focus on ethical issues in five important areas: 1) hiring and firing, 2) compensation, 3) the nature of work, 4) privacy, and 5) whistleblowing. I begin with some reflections about the source of moral obligations in employment.

Freedom of contract: Lochner's shadow

To the questions "What obligations do employers have toward their employees?" and "What obligations do employees have toward their employers?" one might answer: none, other than ones that they have explicitly taken on. That is, we might understand employer–employee obligations exclusively in terms of agreements or contracts. When you agree to work for an employer—suppose it's me—you do so under certain conditions (e.g., that you receive $10 per hour, work 40 hours per week, and so on). We might think that my duties to you, and your duties to me, in the context of the employment relationship, are fully accounted for by these conditions. I have a duty to fulfill "my side" of the agreement, and you have a duty to fulfill "your side" of the agreement, and that's it.

Of course, on this view, we would still have certain *other* duties to each other. For example, I would still have a duty not to kill you or steal from you, and you would still have a duty not to kill me or steal from me. But these are duties that we owe to each other as private citizens, not as employer and employee. On this view, then, "employee ethics and rights" can be reduced to a study of the agreements that employers and employees enter into.

Something close to this view was encoded in law in the US during the "Lochner Era," which lasted from 1905–1937. In 1901, Joseph Lochner, a baker, permitted an employee of his to work 60 hours per week. Although both Lochner and the employee agreed to this arrangement, it violated New York State's law regarding the maximum length of working days, so Lochner was fined. Lower courts upheld the penalty but, on appeal in 1905, the US Supreme Court held this law to be an unconstitutional abridgment of freedom. Thus began the Lochner Era, in which many similar regulations of working conditions were struck down. It was a time of relatively unfettered freedom of contract in the US. The Lochner Era came to a close in 1937 in *West Coast Hotel Co.* v. *Parrish*. Elsie Parrish sued West Coast Hotel for paying her less than the state-mandated minimum wage. In this case, the Supreme Court found for Parrish, not accepting as a justification of her wage that it was freely accepted by both parties. The Court granted that minimum wage rules are abridgments of freedom, but concluded that it was not unconstitutional for states to limit freedom in this way.

As mentioned, this chapter is not primarily about employment law. My goal is not to identify the legal obligations of employers and employees, or to trace the development of employment law over time. But it can be useful to consider employment law because (like other areas of law) it is informed by, and reflects, people's moral judgments. Thus *Lochner* is important because it highlights a moral consideration that is present in many discussions of employment ethics: freedom. It is good, other things equal, if employers and employees are able to arrange their relationships in a way that is mutually agreeable. Any such agreement, presumably, reflects the freedom of each party to accept or reject the proposed arrangement. But many think that there is more to employee ethics and rights than whatever is mutually agreed to by the parties involved. This may be because employers and employees have unequal bargaining power, so one side's agreement (typically, that of employees) is less voluntary—and so has less moral force—than the other side's (typically, that of employers). Or it may be because freedom, while important, is not all that matters. We might think that employers shouldn't treat employees, and employees shouldn't treat employers, in a way that is disrespectful or vicious, even if the party upon whom the disrespectful or vicious treatment is inflicted consented to it. Or it may be because freedom comes in different forms, so that giving employers and employees unfettered freedom to contract may reduce their effective freedom in other ways (as giving people the freedom to sell themselves into slavery would reduce the freedom of those who took this option). These and other considerations come to the fore in our discussion of particular ethical issues in the employment relationship.

Starting and terminating the employment relationship

Ethical issues attend the beginning and end of employment relationships. I begin by highlighting some ethical issues in hiring, then consider issues in firing.

Starting employment: hiring

Suppose a firm needs to hire a worker. It has advertised the position and now has a pool of applicants. Who should it hire? We might think: whomever it wants. We might understand a job as an ongoing exchange of property. When person P takes a job with firm F, F agrees to exchange some of what it owns (viz., money) for some of what P owns (viz., labor). Firm F is not obligated to enter into an exchange at all. So, it might be thought, if F does decide to enter into an exchange, it can do so with whoever it wants.

Most would reject this view, however. It implies that it is not morally wrong for employers to discriminate in hiring on the basis of characteristics such as race and sex. But most think that this practice is morally wrong (Hellman 2008; Lippert-Rasmussen 2014; cf. Epstein 1992). According to Deborah Hellman (2008), discrimination against groups such as black people and women is wrong because it is demeaning. It treats certain people as if they had lesser worth than others. According to Kasper Lippert-Rasmussen (2014), discrimination of this sort is wrong because of the harm it causes, including stigmatization and the loss of opportunity.

An employer engages in discrimination of a sort when she chooses one from among several applicants based on certain facts about her, such as her experience or education. There is nothing wrong with this. But discrimination is wrong when it is based on certain *other* facts about applicants, such as their race or sex. It is not always easy to determine where to draw the line between facts that can and cannot be considered, and thus between morally permissible and morally impermissible discrimination. So-called "reaction qualifications" are a difficult case (Lippert-Rasmussen 2014). A firm might want to select an especially attractive person as a sales representative or a receptionist, on the ground that customers prefer to interact with attractive people. This has the effect of excluding ugly people from the applicant pool. It is not clear that excluding applicants from consideration based on their attractiveness is any worse than excluding applicants based on their race or sex.

A preliminary conclusion we might draw is that, while an employer is not required to hire anyone, if she decides to do so then certain facts should not enter into her deliberations (though there may be disagreement about which facts should be excluded). But some have argued that firms must do more than simply *not* hire people for certain reasons; they have argued that firms should hire the most qualified applicant (Sher 1987). The claim that the most qualified applicant should be hired is sometimes given as a reason why programs of preferential treatment are wrong. In an effort to increase diversity in its ranks, a firm might give preference in hiring to members of traditionally underrepresented groups. The effect of such programs may be to give jobs to less qualified over more qualified applicants, where qualifications are measured in terms of experience, education, training, and the like. But it is not clear that there is an independent obligation to hire the best applicant. We might think that, if those who have a right to control the firm (e.g., shareholders) *want* to hire the best qualified applicants, and they direct their agents (e.g., managers) to satisfy this want, then their agents have an obligation to do so. This may explain why government agencies should hire the most qualified applicants: the public wants them to do so. But we might not think that the government or any other employer has this obligation independently of the will of those who have the ultimate right to determine hiring policy within the organization. Moreover, what makes an applicant "best" for a particular position will be difficult to specify in many cases, and so difficult to codify in law or regulation. At most, this will be a moral obligation for individual employers.

Terminating employment: firing and quitting

Business ethicists have written extensively about the conditions under which employees may be terminated by employers. In the US, the current law in almost all jurisdictions is "employment-at-will" (EAW). Employment-at-will was originally the view that an employer (or employee) may terminate the employment relationship for "good reason, bad reason, or no reason at all." An employer might decide to terminate a worker's employment because the worker is incompetent, or because the worker won't commit a crime for the employer, or just because the employer feels like it. Over time, however, various exceptions to EAW have been carved out, both by courts and legislatures (Twomey 2013). Employers cannot now fire workers because they refuse to commit crimes, among other "bad" reasons.

The main alternative to EAW is "just cause" dismissal rules. On this alternative, employers must have a good reason to terminate employees. Usually these are reasons related to employees' job performance. (Employers may let employees go if the business has financial difficulties, but these are best described as layoffs, not terminations.) So an employer could fire an employee for incompetence or excessive absenteeism, but not because he belongs to a political party the employer does not like.

In sum, in an EAW scheme, as it now works, employers are allowed to fire workers for any reason except for certain ones. By contrast, in a just cause scheme, employers are allowed to fire workers only for certain reasons. In theory, the set of reasons that remain as legitimate reasons to terminate an employee after an EAW scheme eliminates the illegitimate ones could be the same as the set of reasons designated as legitimate by a just cause scheme. In practice, however, these schemes are quite different. This is because most EAW systems leave it open for employers to terminate workers' employment for non-job-related reasons. In some jurisdictions, it would be permissible for an employer to terminate a worker's employment upon discovering that is he a homosexual, or because he engages in risky activities outside of work (e.g., smoking), or because he is found using a competitor's products. No proponent of just cause dismissal rules would countenance these among the legitimate reasons for a worker to be terminated.

Which is ethically superior: EAW or just cause? Those who favor EAW often emphasize the value of freedom. To demand that employers terminate employment relationships only for certain reasons, they say, is an unwarranted diminution of employers' freedom (Epstein 1992). Defenders of just cause have replied that employers' exercising—or even simply having—a robust freedom to fire workers is an unwarranted diminution of *workers'* freedom. To be free is to be able to live your life as you choose. If your employer can deprive you of your livelihood for arbitrary reasons, they say, then you are to that extent unfree (Hsieh 2005; Werhane et al. 2004). Another important consideration is social welfare. Many writers believe that Europe's persistently high unemployment rate relative to the US is explained by the fact that most of Europe uses just cause dismissal rules while the US uses EAW (Maitland 1989). The harder it is for employers to fire employees, the more reluctant they will be to hire them. Just cause may protect workers' jobs at the cost of creating a sclerotic labor market overall. Indeed, even if individual workers prefer strong job protections (and hence just cause), workers as a whole may prefer a healthier labor market (and hence EAW).

We have been considering the question of when an employment relationship may be terminated from the perspective of the employer. But we can also ask this question from the perspective of the employee. That is, we can ask: under what conditions can an employee terminate her relationship with her employer? Can the employee quit for "good reason, bad reason, or no reason at all"? Or must she have a good reason? Business ethicists have paid scant attention to this question (cf. Werhane et al. 2004). But many of the arguments that are deployed in the EAW vs. just cause debate can be deployed here as well. We might say that it is important for employees' freedom to be able to quit when they want to, even if it's not for an objectively good reason. But if employees' freedom is constrained by being terminated by their employers, especially for arbitrary reasons, then employers' freedom is likewise constrained by their employees quitting, especially for arbitrary reasons. Arguments about social welfare are relevant here too. If employees believe that they will be locked into jobs unless they have good reasons to leave, then they will be less likely to take them. Here again, even if individual employers would prefer to be able to keep talented workers, employers as a whole may prefer that employees have the freedom to leave.

I suspect that many business ethicists would say that there is a difference between employers' and employees' obligations with respect to terminating the employment relationship. This is because, they would further say, losing a job is typically more damaging to the employee than an employer's losing an employee is to the employer. In the US, approximately 80 percent of employees work in firms that employ 20 or more people (50 percent work in firms that employ 500 or more and 33 percent work in firms that employ 5,000 or more).[1] On average, it seems easier for a firm of this size to manage in the worker's absence, and find a replacement for the worker, than it is for the worker to find a new job. But we should not conclude that an employee's terminating an employment relationship is always a trivial matter. Some employees may be as important to their firms as those firms are to most employees. This may be the case in the 20 percent of US firms that employ 20 or fewer workers, and especially in the 11 percent of firms that employ 9 or fewer workers. If arguments for just cause are sound, they require at least that, when employees terminate employment relationships, they do so thoughtfully. Their pursuit of new opportunities for themselves should be tempered by a concern for the damage they do to their current employers and co-workers.

Compensation

Pay has been studied extensively by social scientists, including economists and strategists. They are typically concerned with the causes and effects of compensation schemes. That is, they ask: why do certain firms adopt certain pay schemes, and what are the effects of their doing so, especially on worker productivity? The compensation of CEOs has been a particular area of interest. This is because CEO pay is thought to be more than merely pay. It is thought to be a vital tool of corporate governance and, in particular, a way of aligning the CEO's and the firm's interests (Bebchuk and Fried 2004; Kolb 2012). Normative theorists have paid much less attention to compensation. When they have studied it, they have focused on compensation at the "extremes," i.e., CEO compensation and the pay of workers in overseas sweatshops. But it matters to employees generally how much they are paid. And employees think about their pay in moral terms: as fair or unfair, just or unjust (Greenberg and Colquitt 2005). This is an area of inquiry that deserves greater attention.

In the existing discussion of ethical issues in compensation, two views are prominent (Moriarty 2014a). The first can be called the "agreement view." According to this view, the just wage is whatever wage the employer and employee agree to without force or fraud. This view is often justified by appeal to property rights and freedom. Thus John Boatright says that "each person has a right to whatever he or she gains by exchanging his or her property through voluntary transactions" (Boatright 2010: 172; see also Machan and Chesher 2002). The idea is this: I own my money, and you own your labor. I should be free to offer you whatever amount of my money I want for your labor, and you should be free to accept or reject that offer, as you choose. And vice-versa.

The agreement view fits nicely with the "Lochnerian view" of employment ethics: ethics in pay is solely a matter of what is agreed to, assuming the parties are not forced to agree and know what they are agreeing to. But this view will strike many as overly permissive. Suppose that an employer offers a certain amount of money to a man, and a different, smaller, amount of money to an equally qualified woman for doing the same work equally well. Suppose that both the man and the woman voluntarily accept their offers. The result is discrimination in compensation, which many would say is morally wrong (Hellman 2008; Lippert-Rasmussen 2014). But the agreement view finds nothing wrong with this result.

A second prominent view of ethics in compensation can be called the "contribution view." On this view, employees should be paid in accordance with their contributions. This view comes in two versions. On the absolute version, an employee should receive from his employer an amount of money that equals the value of his contribution, perhaps as estimated by his marginal revenue product. If an employee's contribution is worth $60,000, then he should be paid $60,000 (Miller 1999). On the comparative version of this view, employees should be paid in proportion to their contributions, given what others contribute and are paid (Sternberg 2000). So if an employee contributes $60,000 and is paid $40,000, then an employee who contributes $120,000 should be paid $80,000. The contribution view will seem attractive to those who see pay as a reward for work. We might think that, just as the severity of punishments should be proportionate to the seriousness of crimes, so the value of employees' pay should be proportionate to the value of their work.

But if the agreement view seems overly permissive, the contribution view may seem overly restrictive. Suppose that a firm decides to pay the workers at the bottom of the organizational hierarchy more than the value of their contributions and those at the top of the organizational hierarchy less than the value of their contributions. It might do this because it wants to create a more cooperative work environment, or because its owners are committed to egalitarian ideals. Suppose, moreover, that everyone in the firm accepts this arrangement; indeed, they claim to prefer it to alternative arrangements. In this case, we might doubt that there is anything wrong about the firm's paying its employees in this way.

It might be said that the above case—in which the wages that are agreed to by employers and employees do not match employees' contributions—won't occur in the real world (Boatright 2010). For it might be thought that, in a competitive market, employers will *have* to pay workers according to their contributions. If an employer pays a worker less than he contributes, then the worker will be poached by another firm who will make him a better offer. And if an employer pays a worker more than he contributes, then the employer bears an unnecessary cost that puts him at a competitive disadvantage in the market. Either way, market forces will pressure employers and employees to enter into agreements in which employees' pay matches their contributions. If so, then perhaps we do not have to choose between the agreement and contribution views.

This is mistaken. First, the claim that workers will be paid according to their contributions—and hence that employers' wage offers will match employees' contributions—only holds true given a certain simplified view of the labor market, and even then, only in a perfectly competitive market at equilibrium. But actual markets are imperfect. In particular, significant informational deficits attend attempts to discover the value of employees' contributions, especially since their pay is often kept secret (Danziger and Katz 1997). Second, there is empirical evidence that workers do not get paid according to their contributions (Frank 1984). Workers with similar qualifications, performing similar tasks, at similar firms, get paid differently. To take a familiar example, Costco pays its workers a lot more than Wal-Mart's Sam's Club pays its workers, despite the fact that they perform similar jobs (Cascio 2006; cf. McArdle 2013). Third, employers often have good business reasons for using compensation schemes that have the effect of paying workers more or less than their contributions. "Egalitarian" schemes may work best in firms in which teamwork is important (Bloom 1999); "inegalitarian" or "tournament" schemes may work best in firms in which individual effort matters more (Gerhart and Rynes 2003). (The mere fact that different firms use different compensation systems suggests that they have some choice about what to pay their employees. They are not bound to pay them in accordance with their contributions.) To be clear, a firm cannot get away with paying its workers vastly more or vastly less than their contributions, at least for long. But the evidence suggests that firms have some flexibility when it comes to compensation. As for what, in the final analysis, firms should pay employees: there may be compensation systems that are morally problematic, but there may be no morally best one. Or rather, the system that is morally best may differ from firm to firm, and depend on the kind of firm it is.

The nature of work: meaningful work and workplace democracy

It matters how the labor process is organized, and who organizes it. Some argue that workers should have, or at least should have access to, meaningful work (Rawls 1971; Schwartz 1982). And some argue that workers should have a democratic say over how the labor process is organized (Brenkert 1992; McCall 2001). These outcomes need not occur together. Workers may decide through a democratic process to divide the labor process into meaningless tasks. And an autocratic manager may divide the labor process into meaningful tasks. But these topics are often treated together, as arguments for and against meaningful work and workplace democracy draw on similar considerations (Hsieh 2008).

Meaningful work

What is meaningful work? According to Richard Arneson, it is "work that is interesting, that calls for intelligence and initiative, and that is attached to a job that gives the worker considerable freedom to decide how the work is to be done" (1987: 522). For Adina Schwartz, meaningful work is work that allows the worker to act autonomously, work that "abolishes the distinction between those who decide and those who execute others' decisions" (1982: 641). As these definitions make clear, when it is argued that workers should have meaningful work, the claim is not that they should have "important" work, or work that advances a worthy cause. Bolting wheels onto cars is important, because cars are important, but it is not meaningful in the sense under consideration. Nor must meaningful work *feel* meaningful or fulfilling to the worker to qualify as meaningful (cf. Michaelson et al. 2014). Rather, the work must challenge the worker, in particular, by calling upon him both to design and to execute significant tasks.

What reason is there for workers to have meaningful work, understood in this way? One might observe that workers often *want* meaningful work; they often prefer it to meaningless work (Arneson 1987). Other things equal, there is reason for people to have what they want. So there is reason for workers to have meaningful work. This analysis understands meaningful work as a job amenity like paid vacation or free coffee. Seen this way, it is not clear why businesses ethicists—or businesses themselves—should be more concerned about the provision of meaningful work than any other job amenity.

Some reply that meaningful work is different because it is unlikely to be provided in the quantities that workers want in a competitive market (Werhane 1985). A possible explanation for this claim goes back to Adam Smith. A labor process (e.g., pin making) will be more efficient if each worker performs just one or two steps of it repeatedly than if each worker performs all of the steps. In a competitive market, there is pressure to make labor processes as efficient as possible. So there is pressure to assign workers just one or two tasks, i.e., to make work meaningless.

This is true, but it is a mistake to suppose that it will lead inexorably to the elimination of meaningful work. Just as there is a market for consumer goods, there is a market for labor. Firms have an incentive to respond to workers' preferences regarding the nature of their work just as they have an incentive to respond to consumers' preferences regarding the nature of the goods they buy (Maitland 1989). If workers really want meaningful work, then they will trade higher wages, or some other desirable feature of their work, for more meaning (Nozick 1974).

To take an example from university life: professors of accounting could easily double their salaries by becoming auditors in private industry. But they trade money for what they regard as more interesting work as researchers and teachers. We have no more reason to think that competition will make meaningfulness disappear than we have to think that competition will make paid vacation, free coffee, or any other job amenity disappear.

Others see meaningful work not as an optional amenity but as a moral requirement. One argument for this conclusion appeals to autonomy (Bowie and Werhane 2005; Schwartz 1982). Meaningful work requires workers to exercise their autonomy in that it requires them to both design and execute tasks, as opposed to mindlessly following plans laid out for them by others. We might think, following Kant, that autonomy should be respected, and that this requires employers to offer employees meaningful work and employees to accept those offers (Moriarty 2009). In response, we might wonder whether employees can autonomously choose work that does not itself require autonomous choice. It is not clear that it is always disrespectful—to others or oneself—to engage in "mindless" activity. A second argument for thinking of meaningful work as a moral requirement begins with the idea that work has "formative power" (Arnold 2012). People's characters, in particular, can be damaged by their work. Smith puts this colorfully:

> The man whose whole life is spent in performing a few simple operations . . . has no occasion to exert his understanding . . . and generally becomes as stupid and ignorant as it is possible for a human creature to become . . . His dexterity at his own particular trade seems . . . to be acquired at the expense of his intellectual, social, and martial virtues.
>
> *(1976/1776, V.1.178)*

We might conclude that labor processes should be divided into meaningful tasks to prevent this damage. A burden that this argument must meet is showing why character development should be a concern of anyone besides the person whose character it is (at least once this person reaches maturity).

If workers should have meaningful work, a further question is: who should provide it? In an economy dominated by private firms, the locus of meaningful work—where it happens, so to speak—must be those firms. But this leaves open whether the costs of providing meaningful work, if indeed there are costs, should be borne entirely by private firms, or whether the state should bear some of them, perhaps in the form of subsidies for firms to arrange their labor processes into meaningful segments.

Workplace democracy

As noted, a worker having work that is meaningful does not guarantee that his workplace is managed democratically, or vice-versa. But the topics of meaningful work and workplace democracy are often treated together. Both can be seen as ways of giving workers more control over their life at work, and arguments for both appeal to similar ideals.

A hallmark of workplace democracy is control of the firm by workers.[2] But this control can take different forms. Some argue that firms should be controlled exclusively by their workers (Archer 1996; Dahl 1985). Others argue that workers should share control with shareholders (Brenkert 1992; McCall 2001; McMahon 2013). A fully articulated account of workplace democracy must, in addition to defending one of these alternatives, specify the types of decisions within the firm over which workers should have control. We might think that workers should have control over shop floor issues such as work schedules, but not seats on the board.

Workplace democracy is often defended, as is meaningful work, in terms of autonomy or freedom. According to George Brenkert, employees "have a right to freedom, just like other individuals or genuine agents" (1992: 262) In social institutions such as firms, he says, "such a right requires participation, or at least, representation" in bodies that make decisions about what the firm does and how it does it (1992: 262). Similarly, Robin Archer argues that the "basic regulatory principle" of freedom is that "my actions should be governed . . . by my choices" (1996: 17). Unless workers control the firm, Archer says, their actions are determined for them by others. So workplace democracy is necessary to preserve worker freedom (see also Hsieh 2005).

Workplace democracy is also defended by appealing to workers' interests. Thus John McCall says that employees' important interests can be significantly affected by their firms' decisions, and giving employees control over those decisions gives them "greater guarantees that their interests will be considered fairly" (2001: 206). Similarly, Brenkert says that employees require protection from abuses of power by firms, "for employees' lives and futures, in short, their basic interests . . . are directly at stake" (1992: 260).[3] According to McCall and Brenkert, control provides this protection.

Most workers, however, do not labor in organizations that they democratically manage. In most cases, capital hires labor. As a result, providers of capital, or their agents, have ultimate control over the firm. When we reflect on why that is, we see that considerations of freedom and welfare can be used to defend this arrangement too.

The first thing to observe is that there is no legal prohibition on workplace democracy. Labor can hire—and in some cases has hired—capital (Hansmann 1996). So we might conclude that the status quo reflects the free choices of the various stakeholders in the firm (Bainbridge 2008; Macey 1999). In defense of this, note that most stakeholders, including workers, are promised a specific benefit for their contribution. But shareholders are the "residual claimants": they get what is left over. We might see control as the demand that shareholders make to become residual claimants—a position that maximizes the probability that there will be a residual to claim. And we might see stakeholders as agreeing to this demand to attract shareholders' capital to the firm at a reasonable rate. If this story is right, then considerations of freedom tell against greater workplace democracy (cf. Boatright 1994).

Another argument for the status quo appeals to welfare. According to this argument, firms that are controlled by shareholders are more efficient than firms that are controlled by workers. Jensen says that "200 years' worth of work in economics and finance indicate that social welfare is maximized when all firms in an economy maximize total firm value" (2002: 239; see also Boatright 1994). If this is right, it challenges the justification of workplace democracy that appeals to workers' interests. Other things equal, workers may prefer to work in worker-controlled firms. But other things may not be equal: the price of worker control may be a significant decline in firm efficiency and social welfare. If so, workers may prefer an economic system in which they have more welfare to a system in which they have more control over firms. A key lesson of this section is that the debate about meaningful work and workplace democracy depends on empirical questions: on the formative effects of work, the relative efficiency of worker-managed enterprises, and so on.

Privacy

Most people want to keep certain information, including information about who they are and what they do, private from certain other people. In particular, most employees want to keep certain information private from their employers. But employers may have an interest in knowing some of that information. Employees may want to keep their employers from finding out that, while at work, they send personal emails or check their Facebook pages. Employees may also want to keep their employers from finding out that they engage in certain activities outside of work, such as using illegal drugs or having sex with partners of the same sex, or other general facts about them, such as that they are thinking about having children or are at high risk for certain diseases. Employers may have an interest in knowing all of this information. This gives rise to two questions: What information do employers have a right to know? And what methods can they use to discover it?

Informational privacy can be understood in terms of *control* and *access*. Roughly, person P has informational privacy with respect to information N just in case P has control over who has access to N (Tavani and Moor 2001).

Almost everyone agrees that individuals should have privacy with respect to *some* information. Elaborate precautions are taken to protect people's medical and educational records, for example. To determine what other information deserves protection, we need to think in general about why informational privacy is important. One popular justification appeals to intimacy (Cohen 2002). Part of what it is to be close to another person is to have that person, and not others, know certain facts about you (e.g., that you are an atheist). This requires your having control over who has access to those facts. Another, more important, justification for informational privacy appeals to autonomy. Privacy promotes autonomy in two ways. First, the autonomous person acts according to her own plans. If you cannot control who has access to information about you, you may be tempted to "edit" your plans according to society's expectations (Spinello 2010). You may decide not to indulge your atypical political or sexual proclivities, for example, out of fear of others' judgment. Second, the autonomous person presents herself in public according to her own conception of who she is. An inability to conceal certain aspects of your life (e.g., your desire to have a family) may hamper your ability to present yourself in certain ways (e.g., as an ambitious and committed corporate executive) (Shoemaker 2010).

Yet surely employers have a right to know *some* information about employees. For example, employers are entitled to know whether prospective employees have the skills and experience necessary to perform the jobs for which they are being hired, even if employers knowing that information compromises prospective employees' intimacy and autonomy to some degree. More precisely, employers are entitled to ask prospective employees questions about their skills and experience, and make employment conditional upon their answering truthfully.[4] We need a way, then, of distinguishing information that employers are entitled to know from information that they are not entitled to know. A natural suggestion is "job relevance" (DesJardins and Duska 1987). So it might be claimed that employers are entitled to know information that is relevant to employees' jobs, but not information that is not relevant. A problem with this suggestion is that it is not always clear what information is job relevant. Whether a person is politically liberal or a conservative is, in most cases, not job relevant. But what if the prospective employee is thinking of having children? What if he is a smoker? These traits do not directly affect job performance, but they are associated with higher employment costs that an employer may not wish to bear.

The question of what behaviors are and are not job relevant was at the center of a lively debate about the ethics of drug testing in the 1980s and 1990s (Brenkert 1981; Cranford 1998; DesJardins and Duska 1987). Whether an employee is performing his job poorly is clearly job relevant information, and heavy drug use may lead to poor job performance. So, some argued, employers have a right to know whether their employees are using drugs (Cranford 1998). But others argued that, while *the fact that* an employee is performing poorly is job relevant information, *the reason why* he is performing poorly is not. According to these writers, an employer is no more justified in testing an employee for drug use than she would be in "testing" the health of the employee's marriage, on the ground that this too may cause poor job performance. While accepting this as a general rule, we might make exceptions for employees who perform jobs that pose a serious risk of harm to others, such as flying an airplane, driving a bus, or performing surgery (DesJardins and Duska 1987).

Ethical questions about privacy are not exhausted by a determination of *what* employers have a right to know. There are also questions about *how* they can come to know it. Thus, even if employers have a right to know whether their employees are using drugs, they would not be justified in having their employees followed 24 hours a day to see what substances they put into their bodies. To use a different example: an employer has a right to know whether her employees are stealing from her. But she would not be justified in installing cameras in all areas of the workplace, including in its bathrooms, to determine whether employees are stealing from her. And she would not be justified in performing strip searches on employees. In a difficult labor market, an employer might be able to get employees to agree to intrusions of these kinds, but this would not eliminate their moral wrongness.

Questions about privacy are likely to grow in importance in the coming years, as new technology allows employers to collect increasing amounts and kinds of information on employees, and to do so in subtle and unexpected ways. Business ethicists have paid some attention to these issues (DeGeorge 2002), but there is a great deal more work to do.

Whistleblowing

There are many different definitions of "whistleblowing" in existence (Brenkert 2010; Davis 2003; DeGeorge 2009). Based on these definitions, a whistleblower is typically 1) an employee or other person with access to non-public information about an organization, 2) who reports information about activity in that organization that he perceives to be unethical or illegal, 3) outside of the normal reporting channels within that organization, and 4) in particular, to a person or entity that he perceives to have the power to do something to stop the activity. Jeffrey Wigand is thought to have engaged in whistleblowing when he gave an interview to *60 Minutes* in 1996 about the ingredients in Brown & Williamson's cigarettes. As a former high-ranking executive at Brown & Williamson, Wigand 1) had access to non-public information about the ingredients in its cigarettes. He further 2) thought that these ingredients were unusually dangerous. Wigand 3) reported this information to *60 Minutes*, because 4) he thought the public attention would cause Brown & Williamson to stop.

Two questions traditionally asked about the ethics of whistleblowing are: When is whistleblowing permitted? And when is it required?

Perhaps the most popular justification of whistleblowing is due to Richard DeGeorge (2009). On his account, an employee is *permitted* to blow the whistle on his organization when it is about to do something that will harm the public, and the employee has tried without success through normal reporting channels to get the organization not to do it. The employee is *obligated* to blow the whistle when he has good reason to believe that his blowing the whistle will be successful in preventing the harm (because, among other things, he has good evidence that the organization is about to do something harmful). The extra condition for obligation compared with permission is motivated in part by the fact that whistleblowing, due to humans' tribal nature, is typically costly for the whistleblower (Brenkert 2010; DeGeorge 2009). After blowing the whistle, Wigand never worked in corporate America again; he and his wife divorced; he claimed to have been harassed and threatened. DeGeorge's account sensibly implies that one does not have to blow the whistle when it is unlikely to do any good.

A different justification of whistleblowing, due to Michael Davis (2003), appeals to complicity in wrongdoing. He says that an employee is required to blow the whistle on her organization's activities when she (truly and reasonably) believes that it is "engaged in a serious moral wrong" and "[her] work for that organization will contribute . . . to the wrong if . . . [she] [does] not publicly reveal what [she knows]" (2003: 550). While DeGeorge's justification of whistleblowing focuses on the harm that the whistleblower can prevent, Davis's focuses on the harm that the whistleblower herself would otherwise do. As a result, Davis's account is curiously narrow. On it, Wigand did not engage in whistleblowing. For *he* was not responsible for the (alleged) decision to put unusually dangerous chemicals in Brown & Williamson's cigarettes. At the time Wigand blew the whistle he did not even work for the firm. Whatever the merits of Davis's account, then, it cannot be used to justify the actions of a large number of individuals normally classified as whistleblowers.

Recently, Brenkert (2010) had advanced a justification of whistleblowing that incorporates elements of the above two accounts. According to his "Principle of Positional Responsibility" (PPR), people are morally obliged to

> report wrongdoings to those who might prevent or rectify them, when the wrongdoings are of a significant nature . . ., when one has special knowledge due to one's circumstances that others lack, when one has a privileged relationship with the organization . . ., and when others are not attempting to correct the wrongdoing.
>
> *(2010: 582)*

Brenkert offers the PPR as a *pro tanto* and not an absolute rule. *Other things equal*, one ought to report corporate wrongdoing in the conditions he identifies, but if, for example, "the chance of success is limited" or if the whistleblower "will be dramatically injured as a result," then one need not (2010: 588). Interestingly, Brenkert seems to think that how much weight the PPR should have in an individual's deliberations depends on the extent to which he is personally committed to the PPR. "The decision one makes on implementing the Principle of Positional Responsibility," Brenkert says, "will be a decision regarding one's integrity as one decides what one justifiably stands for" (2010: 589). So, if Wigand had decided that he "stood for" making a lot of money as an executive in a major American tobacco corporation, then would it have been permissible for him not to blow the whistle? Or is standing for making a lot of money not "justifiable"? Brenkert does not provide answers to these questions.

The importance of the topic of whistleblowing is reinforced at least every decade, as serious corporate and government wrongdoing comes to light through the actions of whistleblowers (e.g., Roger Boisjoly at Morton Thiokol in the 1980s, Jeffrey Wigand at Brown & Williamson in the 1990s, Sherron Watkins at Enron in the 2000s, Edward Snowden at the National Security Agency in the 2010s). Business ethicists have articulated thoughtful accounts of when whistleblowing might be justified, in the sense of being permissible or required. In my view, however, not enough attention has been paid to the prior question of whether whistleblowing needs a justification at all. The reason typically given for why whistleblowing requires justification, and hence is wrong, all else being equal, is that it is an act of disloyalty (Boatright 2009). By definition, the whistleblower is a person—often an employee or other individual with close ties to the organization—who shares inside information about wrongdoing in the organization with outsiders. She "rats the organization out." But why should people be loyal to their organizations (Duska 2000)? It's not hard to see, of course, why organizations would encourage employees to *think* that they should be loyal. Loyal employees are in many ways better employees than non-loyal ones (Meyer and Allen 1997). However, it is not clear that employees should believe their organizations. Suppose you are operating a meth lab in your house and I report this information to the police. It's not clear that there is *any* sense in which my reporting this information to the police is wrong, even if I am helping you to operate the lab. But this is precisely what those who offer justifications of whistleblowing assume. At the very least, it seems, what is needed is an account of the conditions under which employees have a duty of loyalty to organizations. This may give us a clearer sense of when whistleblowing, as a putative act of disloyalty, is justified.

Concluding remarks

This chapter considered recent research on employee ethics and rights. In particular, it considered ethical issues in: 1) hiring and firing, 2) compensation, 3) the nature of work, 4) privacy, and 5) whistleblowing. While these are not the only ethical issues that attend the employment relationship, they are among the most important.

A recurring theme in this chapter is that freedom matters. But freedom is a complicated concept: it is not always clear what freedom requires in employment. Moreover, freedom is not all that matters: in some cases, other values should prevail. "Lochnerians" may think that it is best if there are few if any restrictions on the content of employment agreements. On their view, employers should propose whatever terms they want to employees, and employees should propose whatever terms they want to employers, and the results are morally acceptable just in case they are voluntarily agreed to by both sides. But our consideration of specific issues within employment ethics reveals that, according to many writers, this view is too spare. First, a robust freedom to contract may be secured at the expense of other values, such as merit. For example, if wages are settled through bargaining only, workers may not be paid in accordance with their contributions. Second, contractual freedom may come at the expense of other kinds of freedom. If workers have the freedom to select meaningless work, they may damage their capacities for autonomous choice.

For the past few decades most researchers in business ethics have looked "outward," investigating issues at the intersection of business and society. They have considered, for example, what the responsibilities of businesses are to address major social ills such as poverty and climate change. These are important issues to be sure. But equally important, albeit less glamorous, are the ethical issues that arise "inside" the organization, between employers and employees. The responsibilities that employers have toward their employees, and that employees have toward their employers, deserve greater attention.

Essential readings

Ian Maitland presents a case for a robust freedom of contract in his classic article, "Rights in the Workplace: A Nozickian Argument" (1989). Jeffrey Moriarty critically discusses work on compensation ethics in "Compensation Ethics and Organizational Commitment" (2014a). For an excellent survey of recent research on meaningful work and workplace democracy, see Nien-hê Hsieh, "Survey Article: Justice in Production" (2008). George Brenkert summarizes the state of the debate about whistleblowing, and advances it significantly, in "Whistle-Blowing, Moral Integrity, and Organizational Ethics" (2010). Richard DeGeorge considers informational privacy and other issues complicated by emerging technologies in *Ethics and Information Technology* (2002). For a general survey of issues in employment and employee ethics, see Patricia Werhane and Tara Radin (with Norman Bowie), *Employment and Employee Rights* (2004).

For further reading in this volume on contract and business see Chapter 13, What is business? On the rights of owners, see Chapter 18, Property and business. On the obligations of firms to employees, see Chapter 29, Exploitation and labor. On moral awareness and the responsibility of the manager, see Chapter 27, The ethics of managers and employees.

Notes

* For detailed and perceptive comments on this chapter, I thank Eugene Heath and Alexei Marcoux.
1 These data are drawn from the US census bureau, accessible here: www.census.gov/econ/smallbus.html.
2 Early versions of stakeholder theory called for workplace democracy of a different kind. They called for control of the firm by boards composed of representatives of *all* of the major stakeholder groups, including workers and shareholders, but also members of the community, suppliers, and consumers. For a discussion and evaluation of this feature of stakeholder theory, see Moriarty (2014b).
3 A third type of argument for workplace democracy is the so-called "parallel case" argument (Dahl 1985). According to this argument, states should be governed democratically by those who are subject to their rules, viz., states' citizens. Since firms are like states, firms should be governed democratically by those who are subject to their rules, viz., firms' workers. This argument does not attempt to supply a normative ground for democratic rule in either the state or firm. Indeed, insofar as the basis is autonomy or interest-protection, the parallel case argument can be reduced to one of the two arguments discussed in the text.
4 It might be said that, even if an employer has a right to know certain information about you—in the sense that the employer has a right to ask you certain questions and make your (continued) employment conditional upon answering them truthfully—your informational privacy with respect to that information is uncompromised. You can always refuse to answer. But this is questionable. If an employer can impose a loss on you for refusing to answer certain questions, then your control over your employer's access to that information is compromised to an extent. Similarly, if a mugger says to you, "your money or your life," and you hand over your money in response, then even though your decision to do so is in some sense yours, the mugger exercised a great deal of control over it by threatening to impose a loss on you if you didn't. Much depends, of course, on how much of a loss the employer is able to impose on you for failing to answer her questions. Being denied a certain job, or continued employment in that job, may be a significant loss in some circumstances, but an insignificant one in others.

References

Archer, R. (1996). "The Philosophical Case for Economic Democracy," in U. Pagano and B. Rowthorn (eds), *Democracy and Efficiency in the Economic Enterprise*. New York, NY: Routledge, 13–35.
Arneson, R.J. (1987). "Meaningful Work and Market Socialism," *Ethics* 97:3, 517–545.
Arnold, S. (2012). "The Difference Principle at Work," *Journal of Political Philosophy* 20:1, 94–118.
Bainbridge, S.M. (2008). *The New Corporate Governance in Theory and Practice*. New York, NY: Oxford University Press.
Bebchuk, L. and J. Fried (2004). *Pay Without Performance: The Unfulfilled Promise of Executive Compensation*. Cambridge, MA: Harvard University Press.
Bloom, M. (1999). "The Performance Effects of Pay Dispersion on Individuals and Organizations," *Academy of Management Journal* 42:1, 25–40.
Boatright, J.R. (1994). "Fiduciary Duties and the Shareholder-Management Relation: Or, What's So Special about Shareholders?" *Business Ethics Quarterly* 4:4, 393–407.
Boatright, J.R. (2009). *Ethics and the Conduct of Business*, 6th edition. Upper Saddle River, NJ: Pearson Prentice Hall.
Boatright, J.R. (2010). "Executive Compensation: Unjust or Just Right?" in G.G. Brenkert and T.L. Beauchamp (eds), *Oxford Handbook of Business Ethics*. New York, NY: Oxford University Press, 161–201.
Bowie, N.E. and P.H. Werhane (2005). *Management Ethics*. Malden, MA: Blackwell.
Brenkert, G.G. (1981). "Privacy, Polygraphs, and Work," *Business & Professional Ethics Journal* 1:1, 19–35.
Brenkert, G.G. (1992). "Freedom, Participation, and Corporations: The Issue of Corporate (Economic) Democracy," *Business Ethics Quarterly* 2:3, 251–269.
Brenkert, G.G. (2010). "Whistle-Blowing, Moral Integrity, and Organizational Ethics," in G.G. Brenkert and T.L. Beauchamp (eds), *Oxford Handbook of Business Ethics*. New York, NY: Oxford University Press, 563–601.

Cascio, W.F. (2006). "Decency Means More than 'Always Low Prices': A Comparison of Costco to Wal-Mart's Sam's Club," *Academy of Management Perspectives* 20:3, 26–37.

Cohen, J.L. (2002). *Regulating Intimacy: A New Legal Paradigm.* Princeton, NJ: Princeton University Press.

Cranford, M. (1998). "Drug Testing and the Right to Privacy: Arguing the Ethics of Workplace Drug Testing," *Journal of Business Ethics* 17:16, 1805–1815.

Dahl, R.A. (1985). *A Preface to Economic Democracy.* Berkeley, CA: University of California Press.

Danziger, L. and E. Katz (1997). "Wage Secrecy as a Social Convention," *Economic Inquiry* 35, 59–69.

Davis, M. (2003). "Whistleblowing," in H. LaFollette (ed.), *Oxford Handbook of Practical Ethics.* New York, NY: Oxford University Press, 539–563.

DeGeorge, R.T. (2002). *The Ethics of Information Technology and Business.* Malden, MA: Blackwell.

DeGeorge, R.T. (2009). *Business Ethics,* 7th edition. Upper Saddle River, NJ: Pearson.

DesJardins, J. and R. Duska (1987). "Drug Testing in Employment," *Business & Professional Ethics Journal* 6:3, 3–21.

Duska, R. (2000). "Whistleblowing and Employee Loyalty," in J.R. Desjardins and J.J. McCall (eds), *Contemporary Issues in Business Ethics,* 4th edition. Belmont, CA: Wadsworth, 167–172.

Epstein, R.A. (1992). *Forbidden Grounds: The Case Against Employment Discrimination Laws.* Cambridge, MA: Harvard University Press.

Frank, R.H. (1984). "Are Workers Paid Their Marginal Products?" *American Economic Review* 74:4, 549–571.

Gerhart, B.A. and S. Rynes (2003). *Compensation: Theory, Evidence, and Strategic Implications.* Thousand Oaks, CA: Sage.

Greenberg, J. and J.A. Colquitt (2005). *Handbook of Organizational Justice.* Mahwah, NJ: Lawrence Erlbaum Associates.

Hansmann, H. (1996). *The Ownership of Enterprise.* Cambridge, MA: Harvard University Press.

Hellman, D. (2008). *When is Discrimination Wrong?* Cambridge, MA: Harvard University Press.

Hsieh, N.-h. (2005). "Rawlsian Justice and Workplace Republicanism," *Social Theory & Practice* 31:1, 115–142.

Hsieh, N.-h. (2008). "Survey Article: Justice in Production," *Journal of Political Philosophy* 16:1, 72–100.

Jensen, M.C. (2002). "Value Maximization, Stakeholder Theory, and the Corporate Objective Function," *Business Ethics Quarterly* 12:2, 235–256.

Kolb, R.W. (2012). *Too Much is Not Enough: Incentives in Executive Compensation.* New York, NY: Oxford University Press.

Lippert-Rasmussen, K. (2014). *Born Free and Equal? A Philosophical Inquiry into the Nature of Discrimination.* New York, NY: Oxford University Press.

Macey, J.R. (1999). "Fiduciary Duties as Residual Claims: Obligations to Nonshareholder Constituencies from a Theory of the Firm Perspective," *Cornell Law Review* 84:5, 1266–1281.

Machan, T.R. and J. Chesher (2002). *A Primer on Business Ethics.* Lanham, MD: Rowman & Littlefield.

Maitland, I. (1989). "Rights in the Workplace: A Nozickian Argument," *Journal of Business Ethics* 8:12, 951–954.

McArdle, M. (2013). "Why Wal-Mart Will Never Pay Like Costco," *Bloomberg Business,* August 27. Available at: www.bloomberg.com/news/2013-08-27/why-walmart-will-never-pay-like-costco.html/.

McCall, J.J. (2001). "Employee Voice in Corporate Governance: A Defense of Strong Participation Rights," *Business Ethics Quarterly* 11:1, 195–213.

McMahon, C. (2013). *Public Capitalism: The Political Authority of Corporate Executives.* Philadelphia, PA: University of Pennsylvania Press.

Meyer, J.P. and N.J. Allen (1997). *Commitment in the Workplace: Theory, Research, and Application.* Thousand Oaks, CA: Sage.

Michaelson, C., M.G. Pratt, A.M. Grant and C.P. Dunn (2014). "Meaningful Work: Connecting Business Ethics and Organization Studies," *Journal of Business Ethics* 121:1, 77–90.

Miller, D. (1999). *Principles of Social Justice.* Cambridge, MA: Harvard University Press.

Moriarty, J. (2009). "Rawls, Self-Respect, and the Opportunity for Meaningful Work," *Social Theory & Practice* 35:3, 441–459.

Moriarty, J. (2014a). "Compensation Ethics and Organizational Commitment," *Business Ethics Quarterly* 24:1, 31–53.

Moriarty, J. (2014b). "The Connection Between Stakeholder Theory and Stakeholder Democracy: An Excavation and Defense," *Business & Society* 53:6, 820–852.

Nozick, R. (1974). *Anarchy, State, and Utopia*. New York, NY: Basic Books.
Rawls, J. (1971). *A Theory of Justice*. Cambridge, MA: Harvard University Press.
Schwartz, A. (1982). "Meaningful Work," *Ethics* 92:4, 634–646.
Sher, G. (1987). *Desert*. Princeton, NJ: Princeton University Press.
Shoemaker, D.W. (2010). "Self-Exposure and the Exposure of the Self: Informational Privacy and the Presentation of Identity," *Ethics and Information Technology* 12:1, 3–15.
Smith, A. (1976/1776). *An Inquiry into the Nature and Causes of the Wealth of Nations*. Chicago, IL: University of Chicago Press.
Spinello, R. (2010). "Informational Privacy," in G.G. Brenkert and T.L. Beauchamp (eds), *Oxford Handbook of Business Ethics*. New York, NY: Oxford University Press, 366–387.
Sternberg, E. (2000). *Just Business: Business Ethics in Action*, 2nd edition. New York, NY: Oxford University Press.
Tavani, H.T. and J.H. Moor (2001). "Privacy Protection, Control of Information, and Privacy-Enhancing Technologies," *Computers and Society* 31:1, 6–11.
Twomey, D.P. (2013). *Labor & Employment Law: Text and Cases*, 15th edition. Mason, OH: South-Western, Cengage Learning.
Werhane, P.H. (1985). *Persons, Rights, and Corporations*. Englewood Cliffs, NJ: Prentice-Hall.
Werhane, P.H., T.J. Radin and N.E. Bowie (2004). *Employment and Employee Rights*. Malden, MA: Blackwell Publishing.

29

Exploitation and labor

Benjamin Ferguson

Consumers confront many ethical choices. The purchase of consumer goods in a globalized economy often has far-reaching consequences. Sometimes we are unaware of the ethical implications of our consumer behavior, or choose not to think very hard about such choices, but even when we are ethically motivated to "do the right thing," it often seems that figuring out just what the "right thing" involves is a rather complex matter. One part of this complexity involves the ethical evaluation of the businesses with which we interact.

Suppose you would like to buy a new smartphone and, faced with the large number of options on the market, you ask a friend to help you choose one. As it happens, you think the latest model from brand X is a good option, but your friend disagrees. "Sure," she says, "it has great features and a low price, but brand X exploits the workers who produce the phone. You should not buy it." When you ask what she means by exploitation, she cites the low pay of the employees. But, you ask, aren't the wages in the factories where the phones are produced often higher than those available elsewhere? She acknowledges that this may be true in some cases, but, she counters, "the problem is not with the amount they are paid, but with the *proportion* of the profits the workers receive—they are paid pennies for producing phones that sell for hundreds of dollars." "Besides," she continues, "exploitation is not only about money, but also about the *quality of work*." "The factories," she claims, "hire underage laborers, who they harass and force to work long hours in physically and psychologically unsafe conditions."

You agree that her list of objections concerns you, but something seems odd. If the conditions are horrible, then why don't the workers simply quit? Well, your friend responds, "sometimes the workers are *forced* to labor, but in many other cases, these jobs, though horrible, represent the best options for the workers." While you do not dispute the facts your friend presents, you are unsure whether she has reached the right *normative* conclusion: if these jobs—despite the low pay and harmful conditions—really are the best thing going for poor workers, it seems odd to conclude that we should refuse to buy brand X phones. After all, if we asked, wouldn't the workers *themselves* claim they would rather work in factories producing phones for brand X than not? This line of reasoning is neatly summarized by Joan Robinson's claim that "the misery of being exploited by capitalists is nothing compared to the misery of not being exploited at all" (Robinson 1962: 45).

This imagined conversation references many—but not all—of the confusing features that complicate our ethical judgements about fair wages and working conditions experienced by the poorest of laborers. It also highlights an important tension in our thinking about these kinds of cases: on the one hand, because there appears to be something wrong with these kinds of labor environments, it seems like they should be abolished; on the other hand, it seems that doing so would be even worse for the very people we are trying to help. An important part of understanding this tension involves determining whether and how firms can wrong their employees. A related issue concerns how consumers should respond to firms when firms do wrong their employees. Both issues are interesting and important, but in the chapter that follows I will focus my attention on the behavior of the firm. In the first two sections I address questions related to what we might broadly call the exploitation of labor: "How are laborers wronged?" and "What do firms owe their employees?" Having addressed these questions, I focus on responsibility in the third section, asking "Who is responsible when workers *are* wronged?"

How are laborers wronged?

It is common to say that firms can wrong their employees by exploiting them. But what do we mean by "exploitation"? Philosophers and economists have long quibbled about the details, but most agree that exploitation broadly involves "taking unfair advantage." While this definition seems correct, it doesn't tell us very much. We still need to know what it means to "take advantage of" someone and what it means to treat them "fairly." Rather than focusing on philosophical definitions of exploitation, we might make a better start by simply considering the particular ways in which workers can be wronged before revisiting the exploitation question at the end of the chapter.[1]

There are many unique ways that people can be wronged, but the ways in which they can be wronged *as a laborer* fall into two broad categories. Laborers may be inappropriately compensated for their work, or they may work in unacceptable conditions. So, while workers might be cheated by their employers, paid unfairly low wages, denied benefits or wages to which they are entitled, and even enslaved, each of these wrongs involves an extraction of labor from the employee that is not appropriately compensated. Workers may also be subject to physical and psychological abuse, unreasonably dangerous or uncomfortable production processes, forced to work long hours, and exposed to dangerous chemicals. Each of these represents a potentially morally unacceptable working condition. Let's consider each source of wrong in turn.

Unjust wages

There is significant disagreement about what counts as appropriate compensation, but various theories about fair wages often take one of two broad approaches. According to "distributive" theories, laborers are paid enough when they receive a certain proportion of the mutual gains that are created by the combination of their labor and the firm's capital. So, for example, a distributive theory might claim that if Alice employs Bob to work in her factory and pays him 10 percent of the gains while keeping 90 percent for herself, Alice wrongs Bob by unfairly distributing the gains. Various distributive approaches offer different criteria for what counts as a fair division of gains. Some claim a fair division is an equal division. Others that a fair division is proportional to the individuals' efforts or contributions. Still others that *any* division is fair, provided the ways in which the parties bargain for their shares do not violate certain procedural requirements. For example, proponents of this last approach may claim that distributions compromised by fraud and coercion are unfair.[2]

A second approach to just wages can be called an "absolute" approach. According to these theories, Alice ought to ensure that Bob is paid a certain absolute amount, regardless of the total profit amount. Often these theories describe this amount as a living wage, or an amount compatible with human flourishing. As with distributive accounts, absolute accounts provide many different criteria for what counts as a living wage.[3]

Finally, these two broad approaches may also be combined in a "hybrid" account. For example, a hybrid account might claim that Alice is normally required to pay Bob a living wage, but if the firm's profits are too low to support this wage without it going out of business, then Alice must at least provide Bob with a fair distribution of the firm's profits. This kind of hybrid account prioritizes an absolute level of pay and uses a distributive criterion only when the absolute requirement cannot be satisfied. Alternatively, a hybrid account may prioritize distributive criteria by requiring Alice to pay Bob a certain proportion of the profits but never less than a living wage.

Unjust conditions

Laborers may also be wronged if the labor environment is unacceptably hazardous. Workplace hazards may be necessary features of the work itself, or they may be caused by the firms and managers (though, as we will see, this distinction is not always sharp). Certain jobs—oil rigging, crab fishing, and mining, for example—are hazardous because of the activities they require and the risks to which they expose laborers. Although firms can implement risk management procedures to mitigate these hazards, given current technological constraints, the tasks required for some jobs mean that their hazards are "necessary hazards" and cannot be completely removed.

Other jobs may be harmful to workers not because of the nature of the work, but because of the actions of firms or managers. For example, workers may be exposed to physical and psychological abuse, or unsafe working conditions may be introduced through managerial negligence. These are "unnecessary" hazards because they are not caused by the nature of the work.

Although distinguishing these two sources of hazard is a helpful heuristic, many of the real-world risks to which laborers are exposed involve a combination of both. Consider leather tanning, which involves the use of many dangerous substances. The most popular method of tanning uses chromium (CrO_2 and Cr_2O_3), which causes chronic health problems and leads to a significantly elevated risk of cancer (EPA 1998). Overall, tanners exposed to chromium are twice as likely to suffer some form of morbidity than persons with similar demographic traits that do not work in leather tanning (Rastogi et al. 2008). While chromium is necessary for tanning many kinds of leather, contact with chromium is avoidable (and so unnecessary). In high-income countries industry regulation significantly limits exposure to chromium, reducing the risks associated with leather tanning. However, these controls are expensive and are rarely utilized by tanners in low-income markets. So, although some of the hazards to which workers are exposed are simply necessary hazards of the job; others are unnecessarily introduced. In many—and perhaps most—cases, the nature of the work involves hazards that, once necessary, are now removable, albeit for a cost. Such hazards, while not *needlessly* introduced by managers, are still avoidable and so fall somewhere between purely necessary and unnecessary hazards.

So, laborers may be wronged while working either because they are not paid appropriately, or because the conditions in which they labor are unacceptably harmful. Furthermore, wages may be too low in either an absolute or a distributive sense. Hazardous working conditions may be necessary because of the nature of the work, or unnecessary because they are needlessly introduced by the firm. However, these latter two distinctions are not without exception.

Some hybrid accounts of fair wages combine both absolute and distributive criteria and some workplace hazards are necessary aspects of the job, but the level of risk can be mitigated at a cost.

Some philosophers and economists also challenge the very first distinction between wages and working conditions. While accepting that pay can be *distinguished from* working conditions, they argue that there is no meaningful *moral* difference between the two because workers can make trade-offs between both kinds of goods. Standard economic theory endorses the following:

> **Fungibility thesis**. Working conditions, monetary wages, and other employment benefits are *fungible* goods that can always be traded off against one another: increases or decreases in the amount of one of these goods can be compensated for by increases or decreases in the amount of another.

According to standard economic theory, rational laborers select a compensation bundle—a mix of these goods—that provides them with a combination of benefits, working conditions, and wages that maximizes their overall utility. For example, offshore oil rig engineers have higher average salaries than similarly skilled laborers in other industries. This differential is explained by the high risks associated with the work: the offshore workers are compensated for their hazardous work environment with higher pay. Those who choose this work prefer lower safety and higher pay to higher safety and lower pay.

If these goods really are fungible, then the proper subject of moral evaluation is the *bundle* that workers consume. Rather than looking at pay, benefits, and working conditions separately, we should evaluate the total package that workers receive from employers. This does not mean that we no longer need to consider both working conditions and wages; after all, we need to know the level of each to calculate workers' total compensation bundles. But it does mean that we cannot conclude employees are mistreated simply from the fact that their compensation in *one* of these dimensions is low, for they may be highly compensated in another dimension and, consequently, sufficiently compensated overall. Although this taxonomy answers the question of *how* workers can be wronged, it does not answer the more pressing question of what levels of these goods firms owe employees.[4]

What do firms owe their employees?

The discussion so far has supposed that firms owe their employees *something*; that certain working conditions and wage rates are morally unacceptable. However, before considering what acceptable conditions and wages might be, it is worth considering the radical—yet rather widespread—claim that firms owe their employees *nothing*.

The laissez faire approach

More carefully stated, the claim is that if a laborer's association with a firm is *voluntary*, then the firm is not required to ensure that the employee works under any specific working conditions or receives any particular distribution (or absolute level) of pay.[5] This *laissez faire* approach claims that voluntary association is both necessary *and* sufficient for permissible labor contracts. The approach comes with two important caveats. The first is that while there may be no restrictions on the content of voluntary contracts that firms and laborers can enter into, once a contract has been established, then firms *are* morally and legally obliged to respect the terms of the contract. The second is contained in the conditional statement above: the laborer's association must really be voluntary. While the first condition is relatively straightforward to understand, the second requires some unpacking.[6]

There is disagreement about what features must be present in order for a contract to be voluntary. On the "minimal understanding," a laborer's association is voluntary when he or she "tokens consent," that is, when the person ostensibly expresses consent to the contract. The minimal understanding of voluntariness is not very attractive since it would allow, *inter alia*, fraudulent contracts and contracts with mentally incapacitated persons. Not only do many philosophers reject the minimal account, but there is a strong legal precedent that contracts made with those who lack sufficient mental capacities, or which are predicated on deceit, are unenforceable.

A broader notion of voluntariness requires "informed consent": contractees must not only token consent, but this consent itself must also be "informed." The conditions of informed consent vary, but it is generally taken to require that the contractee is mentally competent, informed of the relevant facts, risks, and consequences of the contract, and that she understands these elements.

Although the informed consent understanding prohibits many intuitively undesirable contracts, it still permits contracts made under coercion. Suppose Bob threatens to kill Alice unless she agrees to pay him 70 percent of her future earnings. Even if Alice tokens consent to Bob's offer and fully understands its terms and implications—that is, even if she tokens her informed consent—few would call her agreement voluntary. So perhaps voluntariness is "informed consent without coercion." What qualifies as coercion varies under different accounts, but almost all accounts accept that coercion includes imminent threats to wrongfully harm the contractee by the person offering the contract.[7] In order for the *laissez faire* approach to be plausible, it seems it should adopt an understanding of voluntariness that equates it to informed consent without coercion, as outlined above. Narrower understandings would allow, for example, contracts for slavery signed under a threat of death, introduced by the other party. Such contracts are clearly impermissible. If we take this approach, the *laissez faire* approach makes the following claim:

> **Laissez faire duties**. A firm's *only* duty to employees is to honor voluntary contracts made with these persons. Contracts are voluntary if and only if they are made with the uncoerced informed consent of all parties.

Whether this account is true depends on whether there are plausible accounts of *additional* duties that firms have towards their employees. This brings us to accounts that argue firms have more substantive duties towards their employees than simply honoring voluntary agreements.

Substantive duties

While those who endorse the claim that firms have more substantive duties toward their employees agree that voluntariness is necessary for contracts to be morally permissible, they do not think it is *sufficient* for permissible contracts. Instead they argue that firms must provide minimally acceptable working conditions, or minimal levels of remuneration, or both. If the fungibility thesis outlined in the previous section is true, then provided firms do have substantive duties, they must provide workers with an overall bundle that satisfies a certain criterion of fair compensation.

The details of firms' specific substantive obligations will, in theory, depend on the truth of the fungibility thesis. However, in practice, the thesis applies primarily to those who either earn very high salaries, but work in very hazardous conditions, or who work in excellent conditions, but are paid very little. Sweatshop workers, whose situations motivate charges of exploitation, are paid little *and* work in poor conditions. The form of firms' substantive duties towards these workers is likely to be little affected by the truth of the fungibility thesis, since both components of their compensation package are low. Since the primary focus of the chapter is on severely disadvantaged workers, I shall consider firms' possible substantive duties under the simplifying assumption that the fungibility thesis is true.

If firms' duties to their employees extend beyond honoring voluntary contracts and include a duty to provide a minimally acceptable compensation bundle, then what exactly *is* a minimally acceptable bundle? The assumption that the fungibility thesis is true means that we can focus directly on monetary compensation, since any workplace hazards can be traded off for higher pay. As we saw in the previous section, there are two general approaches to fair pay. According to the absolute approach, workers are paid fairly when their compensation is equal to or exceeds an absolute level, usually defined as a "living wage"; on the distributive approach, they are paid fairly when the benefits produced by their work are fairly distributed between the firm and the employee. Also, of course, these two approaches may be combined in a hybrid account.

Absolute criteria for fairness

Ruth Sample argues that firms are obliged to honor a person's value when they engage in mutually beneficial cooperation. She claims firms can fail to honor a person's value by, *inter alia*, "neglecting what is necessary for that person's well-being or flourishing" (Sample 2003; see also Snyder 2008 and Arnold and Bowie 2003). Sample's appeal to basic needs makes hers an absolute account of fair compensation. The basic needs approach makes the following claim:

> **Basic needs duties.** In addition to respecting voluntary contracts, firms must also ensure that the contracts they make with their employees provide wages that are sufficient to meet employees' basic needs.

Although this account is intuitively attractive—we all want to flourish and have our basic needs met—an appeal to basic needs appears neither necessary nor sufficient for fair compensation.

It is not sufficient because it seems that transactions between two persons who have their basic needs met may still be unfair. If meeting basic needs were sufficient for fair compensation, then any wage that met basic needs (and satisfied the *laissez faire* duties) would be fair. Yet, it seems possible that middle-class managers may still be paid unfairly despite the fact that their basic needs are met. Meeting basic needs is also not necessary for a transaction to be fair. In some cases firms cannot afford to pay a wage that meets their employees' basic needs. Of course, what exactly firms can and cannot "afford," is a contentious issue. But Sample herself includes this caveat: "if the only mutually beneficial transaction possible is one in which [basic] needs cannot be satisfied, then such interaction is not exploitative" (Sample 2003: 75).

A final (relatively minor) problem for such accounts is that they are not easily applied to specific transactions. Suppose that in Alice and Bob's community basic needs can be met by $10,000 per year. If Alice buys an apple from Bob, surely she does not need to pay him $10,000 in that single transaction. But how much *should* she pay him? Perhaps she should pay him $10,000 divided by the number of apples Bob can sell in a year. But what if Bob sells few apples? What if he sells many? These issues do not directly undermine the flourishing account. It can still be applied to employees' monthly or yearly salaries, since there we may be more interested in the aggregate amounts. But it does mean it may not be useful as a *general* theory of fair transaction.

Benjamin Ferguson

Should we abandon basic needs or flourishing accounts in favor of some other absolute criterion of fair compensation? It is not clear this will help. Not only will alternative absolute accounts inherit many of the above problems, they must also justify any new threshold levels of compensation they claim are essential to fair compensation. However, unlike the claim that we should meet persons' basic needs, other absolute levels of compensation do not have intuitive appeal. In place of absolute accounts, let us consider the distributive alternative.

Distributive accounts of fairness

Distributive accounts of fair compensation do not claim that firms must provide their workers with any *particular* level of compensation, but rather that they must distribute the mutual benefits of the worker's labor. Perhaps the most (in)famous distributive account was championed by Karl Marx, but many other criteria of fair distribution also exist. Here I will outline four: Marx's account, based on the labor theory of value; an egalitarian distribution; Alan Wertheimer's (Wertheimer 1996) hypothetical market approach; and Hillel Steiner's liberal account (Steiner 1984; Steiner 1987; Steiner 2010).

Marx (1887) claims that workers are exploited (and thus unfairly compensated) when the pay that they receive embodies less labor than is embodied in the goods they can consume with their wages. Or, in other words, firms must pay workers an amount of labor *equal* to what workers provide firms. Marx claimed that the value of a good is determined by the amount of labor required to produce it. So, if it takes Alice five hours to produce a chair, the chair "embodies" five hours of labor. A fair price for her chair is one in which Alice receives either material goods that also embody five hours of labor, or enough money to buy such goods.

The labor theory of value has prima facie appeal: goods that take more time to produce do seem to have greater value—the labor theory of value can explain why a handmade Rolls Royce costs more than a mass produced Honda. Furthermore, Marx's criterion captures two common intuitions about fairness. First, it is *egalitarian*, because it requires an equal exchange of labor. Equality is tightly linked with fairness: in a straightforward sense a fair division of cake would suggest an *equal* division of cake. Second, it incorporates a notion of desert because it claims that persons should be compensated for the work they do. So, some may object to the equal cake example, claiming that it is not compelling in cases where Bob contributes only half as much time to the cake's production as Alice. Yet, Marx agrees that in such cases the producers' compensation should reflect their differential inputs. He would claim the cake's fair price is three units of labor, two are owed to Alice and one to Bob. According to Marx, then, firms have the following duties towards their employees:

> **Marxist duties**. In addition to respecting voluntary contracts, firms must also ensure that the contracts they make with their employees provide wages that can be used to buy goods that embody an amount of labor *equal* to that expended by the employee.

One interesting aspect of Marx's account is that it applies to both laborers and firms: while firms pay employees unfairly when they fail to discharge their Marxist duties, *employees* receive an unfairly high wage if they provide less labor than is embodied in their wages. In contrast, the basic needs approach does not imply that workers act inappropriately when they receive wages that are greater than those required to meet their basic needs.

Although the labor theory of value captures intuitions about equality and desert, it faces some significant challenges. Robert Nozick famously listed many exceptions to the labor theory of value:

found natural objects (valued above the labor necessary to get them); rare goods . . . that cannot be reproduced in unlimited quantities; differences in value between identical objects at different places; differences skilled labor makes; changes caused by fluctuation in supply and demand; aged objects whose producing requires much time to pass . . . and so on.

(Nozick 1974: 258)

The labor theory of value faces both normative and descriptive problems. Normatively there seem to be examples of goods, like those in Nozick's list, that we think *are* of greater value than others, but which embody less labor. The causes of this divergence are varied, but the general problem is that the labor theory does not always map onto our intuitions about what really does (or ought to) have value.

Descriptively, the labor theory of value has a hard time explaining why the *prices* that goods command on the market diverge from their labor values. Although numerous attempts have been made to solve this "transformation problem," none has been successful (see Samuelson 1971). These and many other problems have led most economists to reject the labor theory of value and, with it, Marx's criterion of fair exchange.[8]

In place of Marx's labor theory of value, contemporary neoclassical economics uses a subjective theory of value, according to which the values of goods and services are determined by individuals' preferences. In short, the theory claims that goods are simply worth whatever people are willing to pay for them. While the subjective value theory faces some difficulties, it generally does a better job not only of capturing our normative intuitions about what has value, but also of accurately describing the relationship between prices and values. A second distributive criterion combines Marx's egalitarian insight with the subjective theory of value:

> **Subjective egalitarian duties**. In addition to respecting voluntary contracts, firms must also ensure that the contracts they make with their employees equally divide the benefits of the employment between the firm and the worker.

In order to understand this duty, we must take a step back to distinguish two concepts central to distributive fairness: the "distribuendum," and the "fairness criterion." The distribuendum is the *object* of distribution, the thing being distributed. On the Marxist approach, the distribuendum is labor time; on the subjective egalitarian approach, it is "benefits."

The fairness criterion tells us *how* the distribuendum should be allocated. Although the Marxist and the subjective egalitarian approaches offer different accounts of *what* is being distributed, they both claim that what is being distributed should be distributed equally. So, the Marxist and subjective egalitarian approaches use the same fairness criterion, but different distribuenda. The Marxist approach fails because its distribuendum, labor time, is problematic. But how, exactly, are we to think about the subjective egalitarian distribuendum of benefits?

The best way to think about how someone benefits from a transaction is to consider the difference between the terms of the actual transaction and the person's "reservation price." For example, suppose that Alice wants to buy an apple from Bob. The most Alice is willing to pay for an apple is $2—at any higher price she'd rather keep her money. This means $2 is Alice's reservation price. Alice is indifferent between buying the apple and not buying the apple at $2; she *benefits* when she buys the apple for less than $2, and the cheaper the price, the greater her benefit. Bob, on the other hand, would like to sell the apple for as much as possible. Suppose that the least Bob is willing to accept for his apple is $1. This is Bob's reservation price. Anything less and he'd rather keep the apple. Bob benefits when the apple sells for more than $1 and the greater the price of the apple, the more he benefits. If Bob's reservation price is $1 and Alice's is

$2, then the only *mutually beneficial* transactions that are possible are at prices between $1 and $2. At any price outside this range one or the other of the traders would prefer to walk away without transacting. There are many distributions of benefits between $1 and $2. If the price is $1.10 Alice receives 90 percent of the benefits; if it is $1.55 Bob receives 55 percent of the benefits.

The subjective egalitarian fairness approach claims that the distribuendum—*what* is being distributed—are the benefits each receives over her or his reservation price. Its fairness criterion—*how* things should be distributed—is egalitarian. In the apple case, the subjective egalitarian criterion claims that the fair price is $1.50. This appeal to equality makes the approach attractive. Unfortunately, it also faces a serious problem.

Consider a case where Alice's car breaks down on her way to an important interview for a lucrative job, one she is likely to be offered. The high probability of years of highly paid work is quite desirable for Alice. Suppose that in order to make it to the interview she would be willing to pay up to $20,000 to have her car repaired. Suppose that Bob, the auto mechanic, discovers that the repair is simple to perform—the problem is a broken fan belt. Bob normally charges $150 to repair the fan belt and his reservation price is $50. In this case, both Alice and Bob benefit at any price between $50 and $20,000. According to the subjective egalitarian criterion, the fair price for the repair is $9,975.[9] This seems unfair. The problem generalizes to a wide number of cases. Whenever one transactor attaches extreme importance to the transaction's occurrence, and consequently has an atypically high (or low) reservation price, the subjective egalitarian criterion delivers counterintuitive results.

There is good reason to believe that any plausible fairness criterion *must* at least select a fair transaction point (or range) that is mutually beneficial. To see why this is so, consider a fairness criterion that places the fair division point *outside* the interval of mutually beneficial transactions. Suppose that the "fair" price for the apple in the prior example was $0.50, which is below Bob's reservation price of $1. Suppose Bob is both rational and morally motivated in the sense that he wants to avoid acting wrongly. Bob has two options that involve no wrongdoing. He can either transact fairly, or he can refrain from transacting at all. There is, after all, no reason to think he is *obliged* to transact. Given a choice between transacting at $0.50 and not transacting, Bob will not transact. The $0.50 price is below his reservation price and will make him worse off. A fairness criterion that requires either harm to one party or no transaction at all seems absurd; after all, there are many possible transactions between the reservation prices that would be better for *both* Alice and Bob. Yet, these would be prohibited if the fair division point lies outside the mutually beneficial interval. In the case of sweatshop workers, part of our concern is that they are treated unfairly, but a large portion of our worry also stems from the fact that they are very poor. Surely we should avoid fairness criteria that may incentivise non-transactions and, in so doing, leave these vulnerable persons even worse off than they would have been if they had traded. Thus, any plausible fair division point must lie between the transactors' reservation prices (see also Ferguson and Steiner 2018).

If a fair transaction is one in which the joint benefits from transacting are fairly distributed and the most obvious fair division point—an equal division of benefits—is not always plausible, then what *is* a fair division of benefits? And why does the egalitarian division give odd results in certain cases? One problem for the egalitarian division is that although it takes into account individuals' demands for a particular good or service, it is insensitive to how rare these goods are, or how many other persons would also like to have them. The approach is sensitive to the demand for goods, but not the *supply*.

Alan Wertheimer's fair market value (FMV) fairness criterion addresses this problem by claiming that fair transactions and, by extension, fair employment contracts, are those that fulfill the following duties:

FMV duties. In addition to respecting voluntary contracts, firms must also ensure that the contracts they make with their employees provide wages that are equivalent to those the worker would receive in a hypothetical fair market environment.

Markets incorporate information about both supply and demand. Wertheimer claims that fair transactions are those that take place at the "fair market value . . . the price that an informed and unpressured seller would receive from an informed and unpressured buyer if the [good] were sold on the market" (Wertheimer 1996: 230). At such prices, he claims, neither party "takes *special* unfair advantage of particular defects in the other party's decision-making capacity or special vulnerabilities in the other party's situation" (Wertheimer 1996: 232).

Wertheimer's appeal to the market is compelling. The fair price for goods and services depends both on how rare they are and how much others desire them: if everyone really wants something that is relatively rare, then it is only fair that the person who receives that thing should give up many other goods in order to get it. Furthermore, FMV avoids the problems of the subjective egalitarian approach because it abstracts from individual desires and circumstances to appeal to *aggregate* demand (and supply). So, in the interview example, Alice's circumstance-driven preferences mean she has a very high reservation price and, consequently, that the fair price for repairing her fan belt is $9,975. The story also mentions that Bob "usually" charges $150 to replace a fan belt. Assuming that this is the price Alice would have to pay in a hypothetical market environment, then, according to FMV, the fair price for repairing the fan belt is $150. Not only is this a more intuitively plausible fair price, it is a price at which Bob does not take "special advantage" of Alice's vulnerability. Despite its attractiveness, FMV also faces problems.

It is unclear how the fair market value is to be determined. The most obvious hypothetical market environment is a perfectly competitive market, characterized, *inter alia*, by an infinite number of buyers and sellers, perfect information, and an absence of externalities and barriers to entry. While these idealized features make perfectly competitive markets useful for economic theory, they also mean that idealized markets differ significantly from real world markets. This difference is so stark that many situations we would like to evaluate with the FMV criterion simply would not exist in perfect competition. Indeed, the very idea of a fair division of benefits cannot arise in perfectly competitive markets, because in perfect competition all agents are "price takers" and there is no room for bargaining. In other words, all transactions that occur are those in which the most Alice is willing to pay is exactly equal to the least Bob is willing to accept and thus there are no benefits to divide. So it seems Wertheimer's approach cannot appeal to hypothetical markets. Nor can it appeal to *actual* markets. Using actual markets as the fairness baseline would preclude criticism of existing market prices because the fair price would also be the actual market price. If Wertheimer's hypothetical markets are neither actual markets, nor perfectly competitive markets, then what are they?

Wertheimer's claim that the fair market value is a price that *informed* and *unpressured* agents would receive suggests his hypothetical markets would be similar to actual markets, but would exclude intuitively unfair circumstances, such as personal duress and price gouging during disasters. It is the influence of these kinds of features more than the influence of perfect information or barriers to entry that Wertheimer wants to prohibit from effecting the market price. But what circumstances that influence *actual* market prices should be excluded when we calculate the fair *hypothetical* market prices? Unfortunately, Wertheimer does not tell us.

One plausible answer to this question is provided by Hillel Steiner's liberal account of distributive fairness. According to Steiner, prices are unfair when one party benefits less and the other party benefits more "than they would each have gained had a *prior injustice* not occurred"

(Ferguson and Steiner 2018). This claim implies that employers have the following liberal duties towards their employees:

> **Liberal duties**. In addition to respecting voluntary contracts, firms must also ensure the distribution of benefits in the contracts they make with their employees do not reflect prior injustices.

The liberal duties account is similar to Wertheimer's claim that the fair price should exclude certain kinds of influence. Also, like both the FMV and subjective egalitarian accounts, the liberal duties account retains benefits as the distribuendum. But it also adds a crucial reference to justice, claiming the features that should be excluded from influencing the price in the hypothetical market are just those that a given theory of justice claims are unjust. Thus, what counts as a fair price depends crucially on the theory of justice that we adopt.

Different theories of justice make different claims about what counts as an injustice. This, in turn, means that different theories will also deliver different criteria of distributive fairness in transactions. The dependence of a theory of fair distribution on a prior, and more general, theory of justice means that Steiner's account can explain why there are so many different intuitions about what counts as a fair price: these disagreements are often caused by prior disagreements about justice. Nevertheless, there is widespread agreement about the injustice of certain acts, such as murder or theft. Also, in many cases of sweatshop labor it does seem that those whom we would describe as exploited are, in fact, clear victims of prior distributive injustice. However, two important questions remain for the liberal duties account.

The first concerns the scope of unfairness. As Steven Walt points out, nearly everyone's position has been affected in some way by prior injustice. If unfair transactions result from these unfair starting points, then nearly all transactions are unfair: "But this is implausible. The presence of exploitation is unquestionable. Its *omnipresence* is questionable" (Walt 1984). Moreover, liberal duties cannot explain what is *particularly* upsetting about sweatshop labor, compared with, say, my purchase of an apple in the market. Both the sweatshop worker's wage and my purchase of the apple may be affected by prior injustice but, unlike the sweatshop case, the apple purchase does not seem to be unfair.

The second question concerns how the fair price is to be calculated. Although the liberal duties approach tells us that a fair wage should exclude the influence of prior injustices, it does not provide specific instructions for how to determine what that wage *would have been*. This question is further complicated by the fact that absent prior injustices mean that many transactions simply would not take place. For example, suppose Alice's car is stolen and she needs to rent a car from Bob to use while her old one is replaced. The liberal duties account tells us that Bob should not take advantage of this injustice to gain more than he would have from Alice had her car not been stolen—yet, had Alice's car not been stolen she would not transact with Bob in the first place. This problem cannot be solved by simply claiming Bob should not charge Alice anything for the car. Not only is this implausible, but this price is ruled out by the liberal account. If Bob were to let Alice have the car for free, then Bob, not Alice, would get less than he would have received from a transaction because of a prior injustice, for presumably Bob could have sold the car to someone else for a price greater than $0.[10]

It is time to take stock. I began this section by considering whether firms had any obligations beyond the minimal requirement that they respect voluntary contracts with their employees. The *laissez faire* duties approach denies that firms have any stronger substantive duties to their employees. Since the truth of this negative claim depends on the plausibility of any more substantive duties, I then considered substantive accounts to see whether they could offer convincing rebuttals. Significant problems surfaced with each account. Although these problems do not necessarily mean the *laissez faire* approach is correct, they do reveal that more work must be done if one wants to claim that it is false.

Who is responsible when workers are wronged?

The idea that firms *do* owe their employees more than merely the respect of voluntary contracts has a great deal of intuitive traction. Surely, we might think, there must be *some* way to ground more substantive duties. Unfortunately, for advocates of substantive accounts, even if we suppose that a plausible substantive account can be developed, another potential problem looms.

Are firms tied by invisible hands?

When workers are wronged because their compensation bundles are too low, who is responsible for this wrong? At first the answer seems obvious. Surely *firms* are responsible. In a causal sense, this answer is correct. Yet, when we expand our view to consider the broader regulatory and market environments the claim that firms are *morally* responsible is no longer as compelling. Firms may argue that they are merely middlemen in an economic chain that connects their investors to consumers. Thus, even if there are substantial obligations to provide workers with a certain compensation bundle, firms may not bear any responsibility for failing to discharge this duty. The argument is similar to the *laissez faire* duties claim, but it differs in an important way. Rather than attempting to establish that there are *no* substantive duties to workers, this argument claims that even if such duties *do* exist, firms are not responsible for fulfilling them.

> **The fiduciary argument**. Firms have a fiduciary duty to their investors which dictates that firms maximize profits, subject to legal constraints. This duty trumps all other duties. Firms' profits are primarily dictated by a) the regulatory environment in which they operate, b) the price of inputs used to produce their product, and c) consumers' demand for their product. Thus, firms exercise control only over the efficient conversion of inputs to finished products: both the price of finished products and the price of inputs are dictated by the market. Any substantive duty firms might have to pay their workers more is either superfluous, or trumped by fiduciary duties.

The argument claims that because firms cannot control input prices or output prices, they exercise free choice only over the conversion of inputs to outputs. Yet, their fiduciary obligations dictate that this conversion must be done in a profit maximizing (and legal) way. Thus, firms have no room to set wage rates. If we assume that what one ought to do is constrained by what one can do, then firms cannot be held responsible for failing to discharge substantive duties because they *can* do only one thing: maximize profits to fulfill their fiduciary obligation. If workers ought to be paid more, as defenders of substantive duties claim, then wage increases must come from a change in one of the other variables: input costs, the regulatory environment, or consumer preferences. This means that if substantive duties do exist, the responsibility for fulfilling them lies with consumers, shareholders, and politicians (on this point, see also Powell and Zwolinski 2011).

The argument is compelling and forceful. However, it makes a number of questionable assumptions. First, although firms have limited choices in perfectly competitive markets, existing markets are not perfectly competitive. Firms may have greater latitude for choice in the conversion of inputs to outputs than the argument admits. Second, since real-world firms operate outside perfectly competitive markets, they can, at times, influence input costs and sales price through supply chain integration and advertising. Nevertheless, even when firms *can* influence these factors, the claim that firms have an overriding fiduciary obligation to maximize profits dictates that any gains from the choices that are available to them should be passed on to the investor. Thus, the premise that does the real work in the argument is the claim that firms' fiduciary duties are overriding.

Perhaps the most famous defense of this crucial premise is Milton Friedman's claim that "the social responsibility of business is to increase its profits"—to do otherwise, he argues, is tantamount to "spending someone else's money for a general social interest" (1970: 33). Friedman allows few constraints on this responsibility, claiming a firm must maximize profits "so long as it stays within the rules of the game, which is to say, engages in open and free competition without deception or fraud" (Friedman 1962: 133). Elsewhere he makes the more substantial concession that profit maximization should be constrained not only by law but also by rules "embodied in ethical custom" (Friedman 1970: 33).[11] Though intended as mere qualifying caveats, these comments are important, for they show that fiduciary obligations are secondary to at least *some* moral considerations.

As noted, the core of the question is whether fiduciary duties outweigh (potential) substantive duties. If fiduciary duties are overriding, then firms' first obligation is to shareholders. If they are not overriding, then there is room for substantive duties towards employees. There is a tension in Friedman's claims. On one hand, he asserts "the manager is the agent of the individuals who own the corporation . . . and his *primary* responsibility is to them" (Friedman 1970: 33). On the other hand, he allows that this responsibility is subject to the aforementioned constraints. If fiduciary obligations are subject to other moral constraints, then fiduciary obligations cannot be primary, for other moral constraints will "kick in" first. But if fiduciary obligations *are* truly primary, then they will outweigh any potential moral side constraints, making the latter superfluous.

One way to make sense of Friedman is to see him as distinguishing two kinds of moral considerations: those that are prior to fiduciary obligations (laws and ethical customs) and those that are not (social responsibilities). Consider two possible acts: murder and a donation to environmental causes. It seems Friedman would claim that managers' duty to maximize profits falls "between" these acts. That is, profit maximization is subject to a constraint not to murder, but outweighs donation to environmental causes.

The idea that certain moral considerations outweigh fiduciary obligations and certain moral considerations do not is plausible. Consider a similar case: Alice promises to return Bob's library book for him by the end of the day. Surely Alice should *not* return the book if somehow by doing so she were to cause serious injury to another person. This injury would outweigh her promise to Bob. And it is just as reasonable to say that she is not permitted to break her promise to Bob in order to have a coffee with a friend. Although socializing over coffee is a good thing, unlike serious injury it does not override her obligation to return the book. Similarly, then, Friedman may claim fiduciary duties are outweighed by some moral considerations and not others.

However, this means that the fiduciary argument cannot simply assume that potential substantive duties are indeed trumped by fiduciary obligations. Rather, this claim must be defended. Without additional premises, the fiduciary argument cannot show that fiduciary obligations excuse firms from fulfilling substantive duties to their employees.

Of course, as we have seen, the existence of substantive duties has yet to be fully established. This criticism of the fiduciary argument shows that *if* substantive duties do exist, then firms are not necessarily excused for failing to fulfill these duties by their fiduciary obligations. While the fiduciary argument fails to establish its strong conclusion, it does draw our attention to the fact that firms are not the only parties with some control over remuneration. Consumer demand and market prices for inputs also shape employee compensation.

Concluding remarks

So, should you refrain from buying a brand X phone? Can we make sense of the idea that a corporation's production of brand X wrongs its workers? In an attempt to answer these questions I considered first the ways in which workers might be wronged; second what firms owe their employees; and, finally, whether firms are responsible when employees are wronged.

In the first section I noted employees may be wronged when their working conditions are wrongfully harmful or when their wages are unfairly low. Furthermore, if the fungibility thesis is true, we can combine these concerns to say that employees are wronged when their compensation bundles are too low.

In the second section I considered how a compensation bundle could be "too low." There I canvassed a number of possibilities. The *laissez faire* approach maintains that there should be no restrictions on the contracts firms offer their employees, provided they are made voluntarily; firms wrong their employees only when they fail to honor their contracts. I also considered various substantive approaches including basic needs, Marxist, and subjective egalitarian duties. Unfortunately, each of these faces serious challenges. Though two nuanced approaches—Wertheimer's hypothetical market account and Steiner's liberal account—fare better, they both have trouble specifying the fairness baseline. So, while there are no strong arguments against the theoretical possibility of substantive duties, none of the accounts we surveyed escaped unscathed.

In the final section I considered a question about responsibilities: if substantive duties do exist, are firms responsible for fulfilling them? The fiduciary argument claims they are not. However, in order for the fiduciary argument to work it must show that fiduciary obligations specifically trump potential substantive duties. Thus, it is not clear that firms can escape responsibility for fulfilling these duties, should they be shown to exist.

So, what about exploitation? Exploitation involves taking unfair advantage. Yet without a plausible account of substantive duties, it is difficult to show that firms actually treat their employees unfairly. And if we cannot show firms treat their employees unfairly, we cannot show that they exploit them. Nevertheless, many people, myself included, have the intuition that some firms do exploit their workers. The task still at hand is to offer a plausible account of substantive duties that underlie this intuition in order to show convincingly that workers' wages or working conditions are exploitative.

Essential readings

The most sophisticated *defenses* of labor conditions commonly described as sweatshops have been written by Matt Zwolinski. In two articles "Sweatshops, Choice, and Exploitation" (2007) and "The Ethical and Economic Case Against Sweatshop Labor: A Critical Assessment" (2011), written with Benjamin Powell, one encounters a strong case for the *laissez faire* approach. For discussion of how we could wrong persons even as we benefit them see my article "The Paradox of Exploitation" (Ferguson 2016). Helpful discussions of Kantian approaches to fair wages and exploitation can be found in Denis Arnold and Norman Bowie's article "Sweatshops and Respect for Persons" (2003), as well as Ruth Sample's book *Exploitation: What it is and Why it is Wrong* (2003). The core of Karl Marx's theory of exploitation can be found in his *Capital, volume I*, Chapter 9, Section 1 (1887). Important discussions of the Marxist theory are provided in John Roemer's book, *A General Theory of Exploitation and Class* (1982), and in G.A. Cohen's article "The Labour Theory of Value and the Concept of Exploitation" (1979). An interesting but often overlooked article that relates the Marxist and Kantian approaches is Jonathan Wolff's "Marx and Exploitation" (1999). Perhaps the most prominent contemporary discussion of exploitation is Alan Wertheimer's book *Exploitation* (1996). An excellent anthology comprising contemporary and historical accounts of this subject is *Modern Theories of Exploitation*, edited by Andrew Reeve (1987).

For further reading in this volume on the obligations of owner and managers to employees, see Chapter 28, Employee ethics and rights. On property relations in general, see Chapter 18, Property and business. For an account of business ethics that prioritizes open and free communication as a basis for just practices, see Chapter 12, Integrative Economic Ethics: concept and critique. On the fiduciary duties of managers to shareholders, see Chapter 11, Stakeholder thinking. On the practical ethics of management, see Chapter 27, The ethics of managers and employees.

Notes

1 Two anthologies with many articles on theories of exploitation are Reeve (1987) and Neilson and Ware (1997).
2 Distributive accounts based on equal division are endorsed by Marx (1887), Roemer (1982), Moore (1973) and Levine (1988). Purely procedural distributive accounts are defended by Nozick (1974) and Steiner (1984, 1987). A bargaining-based distributive account is defended in Ferguson (2013). A discussion of distributive accounts can be found in Wertheimer (1996).
3 Many absolute accounts exist, but three that explicitly reference labor and exploitation issues are Goodin 1987, Sample 2003 and Arnold and Bowie 2003.
4 Both Maitland (1996) and Arnold (2010) provide helpful overviews of some of the empirical aspects of sweatshop working conditions, as well as discussions of their normative importance.
5 See Zwolinski (2007) for an elegant defense of the *laissez faire* approach.
6 For an extended discussion of voluntariness see Olsaretti (2004). Wertheimer (2003) contains a helpful discussion of consent.
7 Detailed discussions of coercion can be found in Nozick (1969), Wertheimer (1987), and van der Rijt (2011).
8 Many "equal exchange" accounts are Marxist in spirit, yet independent from the labor theory of value, as in Roemer (1982) and Veneziani (2013). Cohen (1979) argues the labor theory of value is unnecessary for Marxist accounts. The relationship between Kantian and Marxist accounts is discussed in Wolff (1999). Reiff (2013) defends a cost of production account.
9 Any transaction in the interval $50 to $20,000 is mutually beneficial; the midpoint of this interval is ($20,000-$50) / 2 = $9,975.
10 Ferguson (2013) suggests Steiner's problems can be mitigated by focusing on awareness of prior injustice and counterfactual bargain power.
11 This remark about ethical custom is odd since constraints based on ethical custom seem to open the door to the social interests he wishes to exclude.

References

Arnold, D. (2010). "Working Conditions: Safety and Sweatshops," in G. Brenkert and T. Beauchamp (eds), *The Oxford Handbook of Business Ethics*. New York, NY: Oxford University Press, 628–653.
Arnold, D. and N. Bowie (2003). "Sweatshops and Respect for Persons," *Business Ethics Quarterly* 13:2, 221–242.
Cohen, G. (1979). "The Labour Theory of Value and the Concept of Exploitation," *Philosophy & Public Affairs* 8:4, 338–60.
Environmental Protection Agency (EPA) (1998). "Toxicological Review of Hexavalent Chromium," *Summary Information on the Integrated Risk Information System*, CAS No. (18540-29-9). Washington, DC: US Environmental Protection Agency.

Ferguson, B. (2013). "The Paradox of Exploitation: A New Solution." PhD thesis, London School of Economics and Political Science.
Ferguson, B. (2016). "The Paradox of Exploitation," *Erkenntnis* 81:5, 951–972.
Ferguson, B. and H. Steiner (2018). "Exploitation," in S. Olsaretti (ed.), *The Oxford Handbook of Distributive Justice*. Oxford: Oxford University Press.
Friedman, M. (1962). *Capitalism and Freedom*. Chicago, IL: University of Chicago Press.
Friedman, M. (1970). "The Social Responsibility of Business is to Increase its Profits," *The New York Times Magazine* Sept. 13, 1970, 32–33, 122–126.
Goodin, R. (1987). "Exploiting a Situation and Exploiting a Person," in A. Reeve (ed.), *Modern Theories of Exploitation*. London: Sage, 166–97.
Levine, A. (1988). *Arguing for Socialism*. London: Verso.
Maitland, I. (1996). "The Great Non-Debate over International Sweatshops," in T. Beauchamp and N. Bowie (eds), *Ethical Theory and Business*. British Academy of Management Annual Conference Proceedings. Englewood Cliffs: Prentice Hall, 593–605.
Marx, K. (1887). *Capital: A Critique of Political Economy*. Moscow: Progress Publishers.
Moore, B. (1973). *Reflections on the Causes of Human Misery*. Boston, MA: Beacon Press.
Neilson, K. and R. Ware (eds) (1997). *Exploitation*. New York, NY: Humanities Press.
Nozick, R. (1969). "Coercion," in S. Morgenbesser, P. Suppes and M. White (eds), *Philosophy, Science, and Method: Essays in Honor of Ernest Nagel*. New York, NY: St. Martin's Press, 440–472.
Nozick, R. (1974). *Anarchy, State, and Utopia*. New York, NY: Basic Books.
Olsaretti, S. (2004). *Liberty, Desert and the Market*. Cambridge: Cambridge University Press.
Otsuka, M. (2003). *Libertarianism Without Inequality*. Oxford: Oxford University Press.
Powell, B. and M. Zwolinski (2011). "The Ethical and Economic Case Against Sweatshop Labor: A Critical Assessment," *Journal of Business Ethics* 107:4, 449–472.
Rastogi, S., A. Pandey and S. Tripathi (2008). "Occupational Health Risks Among the Workers Employed in Leather Tanneries at Kanpur," *Indian Journal of Occupational & Environmental Medicine* 12:3, 132–135.
Reeve, A. (ed.) (1987). *Modern Theories of Exploitation*. London: Sage.
Reiff, M. (2013). *Exploitation and Economic Justice in the Liberal Capitalist State*. Oxford: Oxford University Press.
Robinson, J. (1962). *Economic Philosophy*. London: Transaction.
Roemer, J. (1982). *A General Theory of Exploitation and Class*. Cambridge, MA: Harvard University Press.
Sample, R. (2003). *Exploitation: What it is and Why it's Wrong*. Lanham, MD: Rowman & Littlefield.
Samuelson, P. (1971). "Understanding the Marxian Notion of Exploitation," *Journal of Economic Literature* 9:2, 399–431.
Sandel, M. (1998). "What Money Can't Buy: The Moral Limits of Markets," in *The Tanner Lectures on Human Values*. Oxford University: May 11–12.
Satz, D. (2010). *Why Some Things Should Not Be For Sale: The Moral Limits of Markets*. Oxford: Oxford University Press.
Snyder, J. (2008). "Needs Exploitation," *Ethical Theory and Moral Practice* 11:4, 389–405.
Steiner, H. (1984). "A Liberal Theory of Exploitation," *Ethics* 94:2, 225–41.
Steiner, H. (1987). "Exploitation: A Liberal Theory Amended, Defended and Extended," in A. Reeve (ed.), *Modern Theories of Exploitation*. London: Sage, 132–48.
Steiner, H. (2010). "Exploitation Takes Time," in J. Vint, J.S. Metcalfe, H.D. Kurz, N. Salvadori and P.A. Samuelson (eds). *Economic Theory and Economic Thought: Essays in Honour of Ian Steedman*. London: Routledge, 20–29.
van der Rijt, J. (2011). *The Importance of Assent: A Theory of Coercion and Dignity*. Dordrecht: Springer.
Veneziani, R. (2013). "Exploitation, Inequality, and Power," *The Journal of Theoretical Politics* 25:4, 526–545.
Walt, S. (1984). "Comment on Steiner's 'A Liberal Theory of Exploitation,'" *Ethics* 94:2, 242–47.
Wertheimer, A. (1987). *Coercion*. Princeton, NJ: Princeton University Press.
Wertheimer, A. (1996). *Exploitation*. Princeton, NJ: Princeton University Press.
Wertheimer, A. (2003). *Consent to Sexual Relations*. Cambridge: Cambridge University Press.
Wolff, J. (1999). "Marx and Exploitation," *The Journal of Ethics* 3:2, 105–20.
Zwolinski, M. (2007). "Sweatshops, Choice, and Exploitation," *Business Ethics Quarterly* 17:4, 689–727.

30

Ethical issues in marketing, advertising, and sales

Minette Drumwright

Marketing. The word is often used derisively even though it describes one of the primary fields of business. Marketing is perhaps the most visible and most criticized aspect of business. Some have argued that criticisms of marketing—especially its most visible component, advertising—are in fact criticisms of capitalism and the market system itself (Phillips 1997). Many sarcastically say "marketing ethics" is an oxymoron, and advertising ethics has been referred to as the "ultimate oxymoron" (Beltramini 2003). Delving into ethical questions is difficult for any profession because it raises complex, debatable, and often uncomfortable issues. However, such an analysis is vital to the responsible, ethical practice of marketing, and it is fundamental to understanding marketing and business more generally as a profession whose managers are "agents of society's interest" (Khurana and Nohria 2008: 76).

This chapter begins with definitions of marketing and marketing ethics and then, in the second section, examines key criticisms of marketing, especially those related to advertising and personal selling. A third section proceeds to discuss concepts and frameworks helpful in understanding why ethical behavior in marketing is challenging and then suggests ways to encourage responsible, ethical marketing.

Marketing, ethics, and marketing ethics

The American Marketing Association defines marketing as "the activity, set of institutions, and processes for creating, communicating, delivering, and exchanging offerings that have value for customers, clients, partners, and society at large" (American Marketing Association 2013). Marketing refers to "everything done to promote a brand, e.g., creating the product, pricing it, placing it where it can be bought, and promoting it" (Thornson and Rodgers 2012: 4). These activities are generally referred to as the "4 Ps: product, price, place, and promotion" (Kotler and Keller 2012; Thornson and Rodgers 2012). Advertising and personal selling are subfields of the fourth "P," promotion.

Advertising traditionally has been defined as paid messages from an identified sponsor using mass media to persuade an audience (Thornson and Rodgers 2012). However, digital media have broadened and blurred the definition of advertising. Companies typically do not pay for advertising messages sent through social media platforms, and digital media provide opportunities to customize messages in ways that traditional mass media do not. On the other hand, personal selling involves face-to-face persuasion to sell a product (Anderson et al. 2007). Promotion also encompasses a variety of other communication approaches such as public relations and sales promotions. Public relations encompasses management and communication activities designed to enhance long-term mutual understanding, good will, and support between a company and its publics (Smith 2002), while sales promotions are incentives that organizations use to change temporarily the perceived value of a market offering (e.g., coupons, contests, price discounts) (Shultz, Robinson, and Petrison 1998). The various aspects of the fourth "P," promotion, are the most visible and most criticized aspects of marketing.

The other three "Ps"—product, price, and place (or distribution)—also raise many ethical issues. Moreover, marketing typically involves strategies integrating the "4 Ps" in a variety of ways depending on the objective, the target audience, and the context. A practice that might seem neutral on its face and unproblematic in one context might be unethical and highly problematic in another. Marketing can have unintended consequences. The complexity of marketing can make it difficult to draw the line between responsible ethical marketing conduct and irresponsible unethical marketing conduct. Drawing such a line sometimes depends upon one's prior beliefs about responsibility.

The focus of this chapter is on identifying and understanding potential criticisms of marketing and the related ethical issues with the hope of encouraging responsible ethical marketing practices that can mitigate marketing's potentially negative effects. However, one should note that marketing makes, or at least has the potential to make, many positive contributions to consumers and to the larger economic system (Wilke and Moore 1999, 2014). Benefits to consumers are intertwined with the notion of "customer focus" or "customer orientation," which is the heart of effective marketing. "Customer focus" is premised on defining an organization's strategic vision broadly in terms of customer needs rather than narrowly in terms of product attributes (Levitt 1960). As such, marketing can provide consumers with quality products and services that they need and want that are priced appropriately (Wilke and Moore 1999, 2014). Marketing also provides consumers with information about those products and services and makes them available for purchase in places consumers find convenient. Marketing's potential benefits to the overall economic system are numerous and integral to a society's economic prosperity (Wilke and Moore 1999, 2014). Along with providing employment and incomes for many people, marketing fosters innovation and plays a key role in enhancing the overall standard of living. Internationally, marketing contributes to a nation's balance of trade, and, in seeking new markets, marketing can be a force for international development. However, the fact that marketing can be a profound force for good does not lessen the importance of examining it critically with an eye to potential ethical problems and ways to mitigate them.

Marketing ethics is the "systematic study of how moral standards are applied to marketing decisions, behaviors, and institutions" (Laczniak and Murphy 1993: x). One definition of ethical marketing refers to "practices that emphasize transparent, trustworthy, and responsible personal and/or organizational marketing policies and actions that exhibit integrity as well as fairness to consumers and other stakeholders" (Murphy et al. 2012: 4). A fundamental mistake is to assume that because something is legal, it is ethical, or that if something is unethical, it will be made illegal (Drumwright 1993). Too often ethics and law are blended, and the latter comes to define the former. The relationship between law and ethics requires clarification. Although laws ultimately reflect ethical judgments, and societies often make illegal what they consider most unethical, ethics often involves judgments about issues that have not been addressed in law. Marketing law is a subset of marketing ethics. It does not and cannot encompass all of marketing ethics. Ivan L. Preston observed that for marketers who believe the law is sufficient, "ethics never really starts" (1994: 128).

Minette Drumwright

Criticisms of marketing

Many of the general criticisms of marketing are primarily criticisms of the fourth "P," promotion (or marketing communication). Criticisms of the other three "Ps"—product, price, place—often involve their intersection with promotion. For example, the ethical issues related to marketers' primary responsibilities for the first "P"—product—often revolve around whether marketing communications truthfully portray the product's features and benefits (Chonko 1995) and whether salespeople provide truthful information about the product and adequate instruction concerning correct usage of the product (Boedecker et al. 1991).[1] Regarding the second "P"—price—marketers' responsibilities intersect with communication around issues related to whether prices and any other customer costs are clearly, fully, and accurately conveyed in marketing communication.[2] Ethical issues related to the third "P"—place (or distribution)—typically involve the manner in which a sales force interacts with and sells to various members of the distribution channel. Since other ethical issues related to distribution are often influenced or controlled by other members of the distribution channel, this chapter focuses primarily on general criticisms of marketing tied to marketing communications—particularly advertising and personal selling. An analysis of decades of criticism reveals some common themes, some of which are reviewed below. Themes sometimes overlap with one another, but each has been raised as a distinct criticism of marketing.

Marketing is deceptive

One of the most obvious criticisms is that marketing can be deceptive—that marketers "lie, do not fully disclose relevant information, and are guilty of . . . extreme embellishment" (Murphy and Bloom 1990: 73). As such, marketing communication is the focus of much legal regulation. However, regulations are frequently vague and subject to interpretation, and they are often under-enforced because of regulatory constraints or regulators who disagree with their content. In any event, regulations set only the moral minimum with regard to ethical questions. Most regulation of commercial speech in the US focuses on ensuring that advertising messages are not deceptive or misleading. Advertising claims must be truthful and substantiated, which means that the marketer must have proof that the claims are true. Marketing law scholars Rebecca Tushnet and Eric Goldman state the essence of advertising law:

> No matter who the challenger is and no matter what the forum, the basic target of false advertising law is the same: deception that tends to make consumers more likely to buy what the advertiser is selling (or less likely to buy the competitors' products or services).
>
> *(2012: 160–161)*

Providing consumers with truthful information upon which to make sound purchasing decisions is not the only rationale for regulation of commercial speech. Assuring that companies compete on the basis of truthful information also contributes to a level playing field for competitors in which responsible ethical marketers who provide truthful information are not penalized. Unethical competitors who falsely claim product benefits in their advertising typically have an advantage, at least in the short term, over truthful marketers. To some degree, the playing field is leveled by having a criterion, such as truthfulness, to which all must adhere.

Determining what is ethical is usually more complicated than determining what is legal, and this is true for marketing. However, in marketing, even determining what is legal can be quite complicated and making responsible, ethical behavior difficult. As such, it is important first to understand the legal aspects of marketing. In determining whether a commercial message is misleading, regulatory agencies (e.g., the Federal Trade Commission, the Food and Drug Administration) and courts typically consider whether the "overall effect" or the "net impression" of an advertisement conveys a material fact in a manner that would mislead a reasonable consumer (Tushnet and Goldman 2012). A material fact is one that matters in the decision to purchase the product or service. A misleading portrayal of a material fact may be an explicit statement, or it may be implied by text, visuals, or a combination of the two. It may be misleading by what is omitted as well as by what is stated. As such, it is possible for a statement that is technically true to be misleading (e.g., something important is omitted). It is also possible that a false statement may not mislead (e.g., a reasonable person would not believe it, or it might not matter in purchasing). The "reasonable-person" standard takes into account the sophistication of the audience. For example, a doctor or nurse might not be misled by information that would mislead patients. Puffery represents the prototypical case of a false statement that is not deceptive because it does not state a fact that a reasonable person would believe (e.g., buy this pillow because it is as soft as a cloud). Puffery, which is legal, is defined as "advertising or other sales presentations that praise the product or service with subjective opinions, superlatives, or exaggerations, vaguely and generally, stating no specific facts" (Preston 1975: 17). According to the law, puffery is not deceptive because of one or more of the following characteristics: it is general and vague, subjective, impossible to measure or verify, or exaggerates in a way that no reasonable consumer would believe (Tushnet and Goldman 2012). Note that US advertising law regulates facts—not opinions. However, some scholars argue that puffery, nonetheless, makes misleading promises (e.g., Preston 1975, 1994; Prosser 1971). Ivan Preston (1975: 29) referred to puffery as "soft core" deception whose "continued existence in the mass media shows that advertisers think it effective with a substantial portion of the public in obtaining reliance and altering purchase decisions." Marketers, no doubt, have a legal and an ethical obligation to be truthful. This is especially important because companies oftentimes have information about the quality of products that consumers do not have. As one can see, however, truthfulness is legally complex. The ethical marketer cannot assume that the law will be sufficient in determining responsible ethical behavior in marketing.

Marketing is unfair

United States law requires marketing and advertising to be non-deceptive and non-misleading, but fair marketing and advertising typically go beyond the law and require ethical and responsible behavior by marketers. A broad concept, "fairness" encompasses behavior that is just and equitable. Marketers often have more information about product quality and more power in the exchange relationship than individual customers, which is referred to as the asymmetric power of marketing (Wilke and Moore 1999, 2014). To be "fair" also involves refraining from abusing power. Fair marketing is in opposition to a perspective known as *caveat emptor* ("let the buyer beware"). *Caveat emptor* puts the burden on consumers to be cautious rather than on marketers to be responsible. Fair marketing compels marketers to be forthright about any trade-offs, risks, or uncertainties involved in the products and services that they are promoting. Fair marketing prompts marketers to take into account any vulnerabilities of their target consumers that would hinder those consumers in making independent, competent, and informed decisions, and to refrain from appeals that would have detrimental effects on a target. In certain circumstances, some consumers (e.g., children, the elderly, the illiterate, the poor) may not have the skills, the capabilities, or the dispositions to make choices about products and services, particularly those that might be harmful. For example, is it fair for a state lottery to target low-income consumers, who can be easily lured by high dollar payouts, rather than affluent consumers for whom the price is trivial? Is it fair to target a less educated group who may not understand the odds of winning? Is it fair for a company with high sugar, high fat food products to target young children? At times, the problem may not be so much with a single ad or marketing campaign, but with the aggregate effects of many ads that differentially target a potentially vulnerable group. As an example, in Baltimore, 76 percent of the billboards in low-income areas advertised alcohol and cigarettes as compared with 20 percent in middle and upper income areas (Brenkert 1998). Determining what is fair may involve both examining individual marketing initiatives and assessing the aggregate effects of marketing.

New media raise novel questions about fair marketing, and many of these questions are intertwined with issues of consumer autonomy; the ability of consumers to make independent informed decisions without undue influence or excessive power exerted by the marketer. For example, is it fair for marketers to target children with "advergames"—videogames designed specifically with the objective of promoting a brand or product (Cicchirillo 2014)—on websites? Advergames often incorporate elements designed to prompt children to play them for extended periods of time. As a result, children may be exposed to promotional messages in advergames for ten to fifteen minutes—creating a much more intense marketing exposure than a 30-second television commercial. Advergames affect product awareness, product attitudes, and product choice (Hernandez and Chapa 2010; Moore and Rideout 2007). Moreover, research has demonstrated that children often cannot distinguish entertainment from persuasion in advergames or in other forms of online marketing such as websites and viral marketing (Cicchirillo 2014; Eastin et al. 2006). Monica Hernandez and Sindy Chapa (2010) found that the emotional aspects of playing advergames positively affected the product attitudes and snack choices of adolescents. Fair marketing should take into account the limitations of children and adolescents and the potentially problematic characteristics of the medium that can diminish the autonomy of young consumers.

Other issues of fairness revolve around whether the marketer is clearly identified as the sponsor of a commercial message, and these also raise questions of consumer autonomy. For example, native advertising is an emerging form of digital advertising that looks as if it is content originating from digital publishers, but it actually comes from and is controlled by advertisers. The underlying premise of native advertising (perhaps more appropriately named "camouflaged advertising") is that online readers will be more likely to respond positively to digital marketing tactics that mimic content rather than appear as advertising. Typically, great care is taken by advertisers to camouflage native advertising so that it truly looks "native." Such tactics are problematic from a fairness perspective in that they compromise consumer autonomy by obscuring the commercial nature of the message. A defense of advertising has long been that people know that a message is advertising and can take the commercial nature of the message into consideration in evaluating the claims.

"Stealth marketing" or "undercover marketing" is another technique in which products are marketed to people who are unaware that they are the target of marketing. As with native advertising, these tactics are unfair in that they compromise consumer autonomy by concealing the commercial nature of the interaction. For example, in introducing the Ford Focus, Ford gave opinion leaders in some markets free cars with the understanding that they could use the cars for six months provided that they would promote them to their friends and acquaintances without revealing their agreement and relationship with Ford (Murphy et al. 2005). As another example, Sony Ericsson, in an effort to market its phone camera, hired actors to pose as tourists who demonstrated the camera and generated interest among other unsuspecting tourists (Vranica 2002). Similarly, while serving as Wal-Mart's public relations counsel, Edelman

Public Relations retained a retired couple to roam the country in an RV and park overnight in Wal-Mart parking lots (Gogoi 2006). All through their travels they created highly favorable videos about Wal-Mart, which they posted online on a blog without disclosing their relationship to Edelman or Wal-Mart. As this example illustrates, stealth marketing occurs online as well as through in-person contacts; irrespective of the context, non-disclosure results in both unfairness and a lack of respect for consumer autonomy. The couple appeared to be a part of an online grassroots movement called "Working Families for Wal-Mart," which was created by Edelman. When companies hire people to pose as consumers who are a part of a grassroots movement, the technique is referred to as "astroturfing," indicating that it is a fake grassroots movement (Bienkov 2012). This relates to the more general problem of fake online reviews. In 2013, New York Attorney General Eric Schneiderman announced that nineteen companies had been fined more than $350,000 and had agreed to stop posting fake online reviews of their products and services (Streitfeld 2013).

Within the United States, the Federal Trade Commission (FTC) has long held that consumers have a right to know the sponsor of a commercial message. As an example, a 1968 FTC advisory demanded that "advertorials," print ads that were designed to look like editorials, must clearly disclose that they were advertising, not editorial (Federal Trade Commission 2013). Likewise, the FTC opposed door-to-door salespeople who posed as pollsters to get a foot in the door and an audience with consumers. The FTC has recently clarified that advertisers, whether online or not, have an obligation to tell readers that a message is promotional and that a speaker has a connection to the promoted brand (Friel and Bohorquez 2015).

Another issue of fairness involves disclosing conflicts of interest. This issue is especially relevant in personal selling. Fair marketers try to avoid even the appearance of a conflict of interest, and when one exists, they should disclose it. Issues related to disclosing conflicts of interest have been highlighted recently in drug and medical device industries in which doctors, who are called "key opinion leaders," have been paid by companies to promote drugs and medical device products to other doctors through a variety of marketing techniques without sufficient disclosures (Dhillon 2015).

Marketing is manipulative

Manipulation, like unfairness, is largely not regulated by law. Marketing has long been criticized for manipulating consumers and persuading them to buy products that have detrimental effects (e.g., cigarettes, alcohol, junk food) or things that they do not need (e.g., luxurious automobiles, expensive designer clothing, lavish homes) (Murphy and Bloom 1990). Manipulation and unfairness are distinct criticisms, yet they remain conceptually similar since both undermine consumer autonomy. At the heart of the criticism related to manipulation is concern about the inappropriate use of persuasion. Though it may be difficult to differentiate the informative and the persuasive, marketing scholars often adopt such a distinction arguing that a marketing message that informs with facts is generally not controversial. However, the appropriateness of persuasive tactics—e.g., emotional appeals, certain types of visual images—is debated. Some scholars have gone so far as to claim that all informative marketing messages are ethical, and all persuasive marketing messages are unethical (e.g., Santilli 1983). The premise is that persuasive marketing undermines the rational cognitive processes through which people determine what their needs and desires are and actually creates needs and desires (Galbraith 1958, 1967; Braybrooke 1969). Persuasive advertising prompts consumers to act upon desires that are not their own, and it undermines their ability to recognize and neutralize marketing's manipulative power (Nwachukwu et al. 1997). For example, ads using emotion to play excessively on the anxieties and fears of consumers (e.g., ads targeting a vulnerable audience with scare tactics based on non-rational appeals) have been resoundingly criticized for undermining consumer autonomy (Hyman and Tansey 1990).

Others have insisted that marketing does not undermine consumer autonomy in any significant way (e.g., Bishop 2000; Hayek 1961). For example, in response to John Kenneth Galbraith's (1958) claim that marketing creates needs and desires, F.A. Hayek (1961: 346) asserted "that a great part of the wants which are still unsatisfied in modern society are not wants which would be experienced spontaneously by the individual left to himself, but are wants which are created by the process by which they are satisfied." He suggested further that few needs are independent of the social environment, and most needs, including "probably all our esthetic feelings" for things like literature, are "acquired tastes" (346). As such, the fact that needs and desires are stimulated by marketing does not mean that they are not important or legitimate. As another example, with respect to advertising, John Bishop (2000) asserted that consumers have choice regarding their exposure to image ads, that they are free to accept or reject the images in the ads, and free to choose whether or not to buy the product. According to Bishop, any desires that image ads might create are not unconscious or irrational, and, as such, consumer autonomy is not undermined. Bishop's argument represents a typical defense of marketing and advertising—"that consumers knowingly interpret visual or text-based messages, selectively choose meanings and resist rhetorical persuasion" (Borgerson and Schroeder 2005: 258). There is some evidence that individuals often believe that they personally are immune to marketing even when they believe that others are influenced by it. For example, in a survey of physicians, M. A. Steinman et al. (2001) found that a majority of respondents (61 percent) said that pharmaceutical marketing did not influence their own prescribing, but only 16 percent felt that other physicians were similarly unaffected (see also Orlowski and Wateska 1992; Schulz et al. 2013). As such, some scholars have referred to individuals' claims that they are beyond influence by marketing as the myth of immunity to persuasion (Pollay 1986).

However one comes out on this theoretical debate, from a practical perspective the stance *against* persuasion is problematic for multiple reasons. First, distinguishing between information and persuasion can be difficult, and most ads are a combination of both. In fact, one could argue that it is often necessary to use a form of persuasion (e.g., appealing to a desire or pleasure) to catch a viewer's attention in order to then impart information. Second, persuasion is often needed in advertising and marketing of social causes (i.e., social marketing) to motivate people to change their behavior (e.g., to refrain from texting and driving, to recycle, to avoid drinking and driving). Would we want to deny social marketers the use of persuasion? Few ethicists would likely say "yes." As such, it is difficult to condemn persuasion in and of itself. In marketing, one must ask, "When does persuasion become ethically problematic?" Is it the target (e.g., children vs. adults), or the type of message strategy (e.g., fear and anxiety vs. hope and optimism), or the media (e.g., mass media vs. personal selling vs. direct mail), or whether the sponsor is clearly identified (native advertising in digital media vs. traditional mass-media advertising), or perhaps even the product (potentially harmful products, services, or ideas vs. unobjectionable products, services, or ideas)?

Marketing is intrusive

Issues of intrusiveness in marketing typically involve invasion of personal privacy. One definition of privacy is "the right to be let alone, or freedom from interference or intrusion," and information privacy is defined as the "right to have some control over how your personal information is collected and used" (International Association of Privacy Professionals). As stated, concerns about privacy, particularly in the digital age, are wide ranging, and marketing is germane to only a part of the concerns, but it is not a trivial part. Marketing's potential to intrude on privacy has increased exponentially as media and messages have proliferated and become more tailored to individuals (e.g., telemarketing, internet-based advertising, email marketing, social media). Technological advancements enabling behavioral targeting have exacerbated concerns about invading consumers' privacy. Behavioral targeting allows electronic publishers and marketers to collect a wide range of personal information from consumers' online activities. Marketers buy these data and use them in identifying target markets for their campaigns. Invasions of privacy occur when consumers' personal data are collected (i.e., "mined") or sold without their knowledge. In a sense, these concerns are not new. Point-of-sale data have long been gathered from physical transactions, and magazines have long sold their subscribers' addresses to other marketers. However, some scholars have asserted that privacy issues in the online environment are fundamentally different in nature and scope from privacy issues in traditional environments (Ashworth and Free 2006). For example, cookies, spyware, adware, and online forums enable marketers to access a richer and more personal set of information (on consumers' browsing patterns, purchases, dates and times of activities, even keystroke behavior) than what would be available through traditional point-of-sale data. In addition, online data can be collected without consumers knowing or being able to avoid the data collection.

In the US, for example, FTC Chairwoman Edith Ramirez recently called for "an effective and meaningful" system "that would let consumers signal with their browsers . . . that they do not want their online behavior monitored for marketing purposes" (Guynn 2013). There have been some industry attempts at self-regulation that have fallen short. The FTC also has urged the mobile industry to include "do not track" features in software and apps on smartphones and tablets because consumers increasingly access the Internet through these devices (Wyatt 2013). The Children's Online Privacy Protection Act regulates behavioral tracking of children under 13 years of age. Marketers must secure parental permission to collect a child's personal information and must disclose how the information will be used. Most people would agree that marketers have an ethical obligation to permit consumers to opt out of data collection, secure their permission before collecting data, and inform them of the uses of the data. The debate and the problem begin with the implementation. For example, are the conditions and uses of data stated in clear and understandable terms, and are consumers' identities protected when they permit their data to be collected? Most consumers know that this is not easily accomplished. Who reads all the warnings; and if one does, does one truly understand them, or have confidence that the conditions agreed to will be honored?

Despite strong concerns on the part of privacy experts and regulators, there is some evidence that consumers are relatively unconcerned about privacy. For example, Sableman et al. (2013) found that consumers in the US were willing to trade-off or ignore concerns about privacy in digital media in order to have ad content that was personally relevant. Likewise, advertising practitioners in the Middle East and North Africa reported that consumers in their markets were largely unconcerned about privacy issues and "drunk on their new found power to express their sentiments" with digital media (Drumwright and Kamal 2015: 11). These findings are in keeping with reports that consumers from both less and more affluent countries were generally inclined to set aside privacy concerns in order "to get a good product for a good price" (Belk et al. 2005: 282). That said, we do not always defer to consumers' concerns (or lack thereof) as the sole arbiter of whether there should be regulations or standards of ethics.

Marketing also has the potential for troubling environmental impacts. It can intrude upon the natural environment with excessive use of outdoor media. It can also clutter the airwaves and electronic media. The shift from traditional to electronic media highlights the increased opportunities that today's marketers have to spam and create excessive electronic advertising clutter now more than ever before. Technology has provided some market solutions such as ad-blocking software, but, as digital media platforms evolve, new opportunities arise for marketers to create electronic clutter.

Marketing is wasteful

Charges that marketing communication is wasteful typically involve two topics: the sheer volume of money that companies spend on marketing to differentiate their offerings and communicate persuasive messages in a competitive marketplace, and, second, marketing's impact on the natural environment. Companies have been called to task for spending money on marketing that perhaps would be better spent on other things such as research and development. As an example, in 2013, nine out of the ten largest pharmaceutical companies spent more on marketing than on research and development (Swanson 2015). The drug companies spent $24 billion on marketing to doctors, in which personal selling expenditures dominated, and $3 billion marketing to consumers largely through direct-to-consumer advertising. In response, some scholars argue that marketing is necessary to provide product knowledge, enlarge the market, and engender acceptance for new products and services (Wilke and Moore 1999, 2014). They also point to the potential benefits of an enlarged market such as lower prices and reduced distribution costs.

Marketing's effect on the natural environment is dramatic and involves a wide range of issues from excessive product packaging to planned obsolescence. Excessive product packaging wastes natural resources and unduly contributes to landfills. "Planned obsolescence" is a strategy for reducing the time between product purchases by prompting consumers to replace functioning products with newer, more fashionable versions of the product. This criticism has been made of a wide range of products from fashion clothing to technology products such as the Apple iPhone, whose new versions sometimes require consumers to buy a new set of accessories. Planned obsolescence contributes to landfills as consumers discard functioning products. It also contributes to consumerism and the related false values that are discussed in more detail below. Defenders of marketing point to its role in the continued improvement of products and in enhancing the quality of product benefit bundles (Wilke and Moore 1999, 2014).

Marketing creates and perpetuates false values

Marketing's power to create false values is premised on marketing's ability not only to persuade but also to influence culture, and it typically results from the aggregate effects of many marketing messages and campaigns. There have been a host of specific criticisms, but one of the most prevalent involves marketing's role in creating excessive materialism among consumers. These charges typically are tied to marketing's role in molding what is referred to as a "consumer culture" or "consumerism," a perspective that encourages the acquisition of goods and services in ever-increasing and seemingly unending amounts (Swagler 1994). Marketing, and especially mass-media advertising, have been accused of contributing to consumerism by elevating consumption over other social values, socializing individuals as consumers rather than citizens, and using products and services to fulfill social needs such as friendship. Excessive materialism has been identified as the source of many negative effects not only on culture but also on consumers: an unending treadmill of working and spending, a general dissatisfaction with their lives, and a state of what has been termed "affluenza"—a painful, contagious, socially transmitted condition of overload, debt, anxiety, and waste resulting from the dogged pursuit of more

Ethical issues in marketing, advertising, and sales

(deGraff et al. 2001). Consumerism is controversial enough in the US and in other countries with similar cultural values. It becomes even more problematic in societies with different cultural values in which it is seen as an assault on their values (Drumwright and Kamal 2015).

A number of charges revolve around marketing's, and especially advertising's, ability to create, or at least reinforce, problematic stereotypes. Through the manner in which various groups are portrayed, marketing and advertising can selectively reinforce stereotypes about sex, gender, race, age, occupation, or groups such as people with disabilities in a manner that is harmful to the group. This argument hinges on the "gross imbalance of the images presented" (Bishop 2000: 381). Often, the most disadvantaged and marginalized groups have been the victims of stereotyping. For example, in the first half of the twentieth century, African Americans were portrayed in ads and other marketing materials as domestic servants (e.g., Aunt Jemima, Uncle Ben) (Sheehan 2014). Stereotypes do not need to be negative to be problematic. In a study of magazine advertising, Charles Taylor et al. (2005) found that Asian Americans were portrayed as the stereotype of the "model minority"—successful, serious, hardworking, and technologically sophisticated. The authors pointed to the manner in which even a positive stereotype can do a disservice to group members and have harmful effects, including damaging the self esteem of group members, limiting their opportunities, furthering their marginalization, and reinforcing and perpetuating stereotypes. In addition, the underrepresentation or invisibility of a group in advertising can contribute to feelings of marginalization and cause group members to view themselves as cultural outsiders (Sheehan 2014).

Debate and commentary about advertising's aggregate effects on cultural values have a long history and cut across academic disciplines (e.g., Bishop 1949; Galbraith 1958, 1967; Leiser 1979; Pontifical Council for Social Communications 1997; Sheehan 2014). Pollay (1986) characterized this scholarship as "a major indictment of advertising" (31) that was "shocking" in its "veritable absence of perceived positive influence" of advertising (19). Beyond academic debate, marketing practitioners often have difficulty taking these concerns about the aggregate effects of marketing seriously (Lantos 1987; Drumwright and Murphy 2004). For example, Drumwright and Murphy (2004) found that the advertising practitioners in their sample were least likely to recognize societal-level ethical issues. The real culprits responsible for these effects are other parties—peers, parents, regulators, media (Lantos 1987). Others have asserted that marketing influences values even if only by choosing to reinforce some images rather than others (Drumwright 2007).[3]

Conceptual and theoretical perspectives on marketing ethics

Having considered the major criticisms of marketing, we now turn to scholarship that focuses on these topics in a more general way and provides insights into both problems and solutions.

Behavioral ethics and moral myopia

A relatively new field of research called behavioral ethics focuses on understanding why people make the unethical and ethical decisions that they do (Bazerman and Tenbrunsel 2011; Gino 2013; Prentice 2014; Drumwright et al. 2015). Drawing on research that cuts across contexts, it focuses on the cognitive limitations, social and organizational pressures, and situational factors that can make it difficult for even well intentioned people to act as ethically as they would like. Specific to marketing, Drumwright and Murphy (2004) found that advertising practitioners can fall prey to "moral myopia." If advertising practitioners cannot see ethical issues clearly, or at all, it is hard to avoid ethical problems. Moral myopia is often reinforced and perpetuated by moral muteness, the unwillingness to talk about ethical issues. Moral myopia and moral muteness are often caused by a variety of rationalizations: "the client is always right," "what is legal, is moral," and "consumers are smart" (therefore, we could not mislead them if we tried). Marketing practitioners can also develop what Drumwright and Kamal (2015) referred to as "moral immunities" in which experienced practitioners become accustomed to unethical behavior over time to the point that it does not bother them and they accept it as status quo. As such, they continue to role-model unethical behavior, which serves to influence others, especially more junior workers, to engage in unethical behavior. Factors related to behavioral ethics hinder moral awareness and moral decision making. Marketers who are aware of these factors and their vulnerabilities to them are more likely to live in sync with their ethical values.

Consumer sovereignty and ethical checks

With regard to the problems of consumer autonomy, Smith (1995) proposed a consumer sovereignty test that individual marketing practitioners can use in assessing their campaigns. It prompts a marketer to ask three questions about the campaign in question:

1. Do consumers have the capability to make an independent and competent decision, or do they have vulnerabilities that limit their capacities (e.g., age, education, income)?
2. Do consumers have sufficient information to make a competent, independent decision?
3. Do consumers have a choice and the opportunity to change their minds without excessive switching costs?

If the answer to any of the above questions is *no*, then marketers must rethink their plans. The consumer sovereignty test is helpful in identifying consumer limitations and vulnerabilities and serving as an antidote to a marketer's tendency toward an attitude of *caveat emptor* (let the buyer beware).

Other scholars have suggested checklists as well. Some have recommended that marketing practitioners use a checklist of ethical questions based on comprehensive ethical theories. For example, Patrick Murphy et al. (2005) proposed a set of questions that test the ethics of a marketing campaign. For example, will major damages to people or organizations result from the action (the consequences test)? Is the action contrary to widely accepted moral obligations (e.g., duties of fidelity, duties of gratitude, duties of justice)? While it is helpful to analyze how ethical theories would play out in a given situation, using ethical theories does not necessarily resolve all ethical issues. For example, how does one know which ethical theory to use in a given situation? What should one do when different ethical theories lead to different actions?

Stakeholder marketing

Craig Smith, Minette Drumwright, and Mary Gentile (2010) have argued that marketers have learned the lesson of customer orientation so well that they have created a whole new set of problems. They pointed out that marketers tend to have 1) a single-minded focus on the customer to the exclusion of other stakeholders; 2) an overly narrow definition of the customer and his or her needs; and 3) a failure to recognize the changed societal context of business in which companies must consider multiple stakeholders to thrive. As such, some marketers view the customer only as a "consumer"—a commercial entity seeking to satisfy short-term material needs via consumption behaviors. The authors asserted that some companies are myopic in that they do not view customers as citizens, parents, employees, community members, or people who have a long-term stake in the future of the planet.

The authors cited also argued for embedding stakeholder management in marketing practice. Such practice calls for a more sophisticated understanding of consumption that takes into consideration a wider set of stakeholders, including groups that managers often see as adversaries (activists, scientists, politicians, and the local community) (Freeman et al. 2007). Collaborating with these stakeholders potentially could help marketers develop foresight regarding future market trends, and it could prompt innovation. For example, rather than initially resisting their critics, what if food manufacturers and fast food retailers had responded to their critics by leading the way in providing new healthy food options? Smith et al. (2010) recommended that marketers map stakeholders, determine their salience or importance, research stakeholder issues and expectations, engage stakeholders, measure impact, and embed a stakeholder orientation in marketing practice. Stakeholder marketing involves far more than market research: it encompasses interacting with stakeholders, listening to them, and collaborating with them to generate mutually beneficial solutions.

Another approach that prompts companies to think about multiple stakeholders is referred to as the "quadruple bottom line" (Drumwright 2007). It augments and expands the "triple bottom line," which advocates of corporate social responsibility have long recommended. The triple bottom line encompasses 1) the traditional financial bottom line, 2) a social bottom line that focuses on stakeholder relationships with the immediate community, and 3) an environmental bottom line that involves assessing the business's impact on the natural environment. The fourth bottom line is cultural, and it assesses a firm's impact on the culture or cultures within which it operates. For example, in one study, advertising practitioners in the Middle East and North Africa expressed concern about the effect of marketing campaigns imported from other parts of the world and adapted by expatriate workers who had little understanding of the local culture (Drumwright and Kamal 2015). They perceived that these campaigns were diluting the indigenous culture. The quadruple-bottom-line approach seems especially relevant for marketers in that it puts social issues related to criticisms of marketing (e.g., creating false values) on the agenda.

The notion of alternative bottom lines has been criticized for being vague and for dealing with dimensions that cannot be aggregated in the same way as a financial bottom line (Norman and MacDonald 2004). For example, the social bottom line typically encompasses information such as employee turnover and satisfaction, customer satisfaction, and pending law suits by employees or other stakeholders. These diverse measures cannot be aggregated into a single standard indicator that can be compared across companies. Furthermore, Wayne Norman and Chris MacDonald (2004: 249) asserted that "it would be impossible to formulate a sound and relatively uncontroversial methodology to calculate a social bottom line." Despite these doubts about the coherency of "alternative bottom lines," many scholars still invoke these notions as a means of elevating aspects of company performance other than the financial dimension.

Concluding remarks

Marketing often pushes the boundaries of what is familiar and acceptable. That is often what makes it work. In such a context, however, making ethical judgments can be particularly challenging. Scholarship on marketing ethics also faces challenges. Its difficulties range from framing normative judgments to defining the object and scope of investigation. The amount of academic research on marketing ethics has not been commensurate with its importance. The scope of ethics in marketing is so broad and encompassing that research is thin and inconclusive in important areas, and some areas have received far greater attention than others. Research on marketing ethics has been investigated largely through a micro-macro approach

(Drumwright 2007). Much of the micro-level research is descriptive and focuses on consumers' perceptions of whether individual ads, campaigns, or specific advertising techniques are ethical. While consumers' perceptions can certainly be informative, one has to wonder if consumer perceptions are sufficient to illuminate the ethics that should guide marketers' actions and if it is sufficient to focus on perceptions of individual ads, campaigns, and techniques without considering their aggregate effects. Much of the research on macro issues in marketing has consisted of commentary and debate regarding marketing's impact on society. There is a need for more empirical research using expanded multidisciplinary research approaches to capture longitudinal effects that may not be directly observable. The intermediate or meso level of organizations or groups of organizations generates its own issues such as organizational culture, climate, systems, policies, and practices and their effects on marketing ethics. These topics have been generally under researched.

Practice and research related to marketing ethics must encompass an awareness of all three levels.[4] It is often not enough to analyze the ethics of an individual ad, selling technique, or campaign at the micro level of a single marketing initiative. A marketing initiative must also be assessed in terms of the impact of many similar campaigns targeting the same group or groups. The meso level is particularly important in that it shapes behavior at the micro level, and without meso-level collaboration of groups of organizations, it is impossible to influence macro-level criticisms of marketing.

Marketing professionals, scholars, critics, and ethicists may disagree about what constitutes responsible, ethical marketing and where to draw the line between responsible, ethical marketing and irresponsible, unethical marketing. Disagreement is not the problem; failure to recognize the ethical questions that marketing raises is.

Essential readings

For an examination of ethical marketing as it applies to the four "Ps," see Patrick E. Murphy, Gene R. Laczniak, Norman E. Bowie, and Thomas A. Klein, *Ethical Marketing: Basic Ethics in Action* (2005). Comprehensive models of ethical decision making in marketing are presented by Shelby D. Hunt and Scott Vitell, "A General Theory of Marketing Ethics: A Revision and Three Questions" (2006) and O.C. Ferrell, "A Framework for Understanding Organizational Ethics" (2005). For a classic debate regarding the criticisms of advertising, see Richard W. Pollay, "The Distorted Mirror: Reflections on the Unintended Consequences of Advertising" (1986) and Morris B. Holbrook, "Mirror, Mirror on the Wall, What's Unfair in the Reflections on Advertising?" (1987). For an understanding of behavioral ethics and advertising, see Minette Drumwright and Patrick E. Murphy, "How Advertising Practitioners View Ethics: Moral Muteness, Moral Myopia, and Moral Imagination" (2004) and Minette E. Drumwright and Sara Kamal "Habitus, Doxa, and Ethics: Insights from Advertising in Emerging Markets in the Middle East and North Africa" (2015). For international perspectives on marketing ethics, see Patrick E. Murphy, Gene R. Laczniak, and Andrea Prothero, *Ethics in Marketing: International Cases and Perspectives* (2012).

For further reading in this volume on complementary considerations in management ethics, see Chapter 26, Theoretical issues in management ethics. On the topic of "moral myopia," one may consult the discussion of moral blindness in Chapter 4, Teaching business ethics: current practice and future directions, and that on moral awareness in Chapter 27, The ethics of managers and employees. A critical assessment of ethical expertise is offered in Chapter 3, Theory and method in business ethics. For further reading on the conceptual issues of regulation and business activity, see Chapter 21, Regulation, rent seeking, and business ethics. For a wide-ranging examination of market innovation, see Chapter 19, Creativity, innovation, and the production of wealth. On questions of norms in and across divergent cultures, see Chapter 33, Cross-cultural management ethics in multinational commerce.

Notes

1 Marketers' responsibilities for product issues that do not intersect with promotion, such as product safety, are typically in collaboration with other business functions, such as product design and engineering.
2 Marketers' responsibilities for pricing issues such as dynamic pricing (e.g., peak load or surge pricing) or price gouging are often in collaboration with business functions such as finance or accounting, or they may actually be controlled by other members of the distribution channel.
3 For an examination of the role that marketing played in reinforcing racism, see the video produced by the Jim Crow Museum (www.youtube.com/watch?v=yf7jAF2Tk40).
4 For models of ethical decision making that portray the three levels, see Ferrell and Gresham (1985), Hunt and Vitell (1986, 2006), Ferrell, Gresham, and Fraedrich (1989) and Ferrell (2005).

References

American Marketing Association (2013). "Definition of Marketing." Available at: www.ama.org/AboutAMA/Pages/Definition-of-Marketing.aspx.
Anderson, R.E., A.J. Dukinsky and R. Mehta (2007). *Personal Selling: Building Customer Relationships and Partnerships*, 2nd edition. Boston, MA: Houghton Mifflin Harcourt.
Ashworth, L. and C. Free (2006). "Marketing Dataveillance and Digital Privacy: Using Theories of Justice to Understand Consumers' Online Privacy Concerns," *Journal of Business Ethics* 67, 107–123.
Bazerman, M. and A. Tenbrunsel (2011). *Blind Spots*. Princeton, NJ: Princeton University Press.
Belk, R.W., T. Devinney and G. Eckhardt (2005). "Consumer Ethics Across Culture," *Consumption Markets & Culture* 8:3, 275–289.
Beltramini, R.F. (2003). "Advertising Ethics: The Ultimate Oxymoron?" *Journal of Business Ethics* 48 (December), 215–216.
Bienkov, A. (2012). "Astroturfing: What Is It and Why Does It Matter," *The Guardian*, Feb. 8. Available at: www.nbcnews.com/id/15319926/ns/business-us_business/t/wal-mart-vs-blogosphere/#.VretGcekUlZ.
Bishop, J.D. (2000). "Is Self-Identity Image Advertising Ethical?" *Business Ethics Quarterly* 10:2, 371–398.
Bishop, F.P (1949). *The Ethics of Advertising*. Bedford Square: Robert Hale Limited.
Boedecker, K.A., F.W. Morgan and J.J. Stoltman (1991). "Legal Dimensions of Salespersons' Statements: A Review and Managerial Suggestions," *Journal of Marketing* 55: (January), 70–80.
Borgerson, J.L. and J.E. Schroeder (2005). "Identity in Marketing Communications: An Ethics of Visual Representation," in A.J. Kimmel (ed.), *Marketing Communication: New Approaches, Technologies and Styles*. New York, NY: Oxford University Press, 256–277.
Braybrooke, D. (1969). "Skepticism of Wants, and Certain Subversive Effects of Corporations on American Values," in S. Hook (ed.), *Human Values and Economic Policy*. New York, NY: New York University Press, 502–508.
Brenkert, G.G. (1998). "Marketing to Inner-city Blacks: Powermaster and Moral Responsibility," *Business Ethics Quarterly* 8:1, 1–18.
Chonko, L.B. (1995). *Ethical Decision Making in Marketing*. Thousand Oaks, CA: Sage
Cicchirillo, V. (2014). "Ethics and Advergaming: Concerns of Marketing to Youth," in M.E. Drumwright (ed.), *Ethical Issues in Communication Professions: New Agendas in Communication*. New York, NY: Routledge, 85–106.
de Graff, J., D. Wann and T.H. Naylor (2001). *Affluenza: The All-Consuming Epidemic*. San Francisco, CA: Berrett-Koehler.
Dhillon, K.S. (2015). "Conflicts of Interest in Orthopaedic Surgery: The Intertwining of Orthopaedic Surgery, Peer Review Publications and Corporate Sponsorship," *Malaysian Orthopaedic Journal* 9:1, 47–59.

Drumwright, M.E. (1993). "Ethical Issues in Advertising and Promotion," in N.C. Smith and J. Quech (eds), *Ethics in Marketing*. Homewood, IL: Irwin, 607–625.

Drumwright, M.E. (2007). "Advertising Ethics: A Multi-level Theory Approach," in G.J. Tellis and T. Ambler (eds), *The Handbook of Advertising*. London: Sage, 398–415.

Drumwright, M.E. and P.E. Murphy (2004). "How Advertising Practitioners View Ethics: Moral Muteness, Moral Myopia, and Moral Imagination," *Journal of Advertising* 33:2, 7–24.Drumwright, M.E. and S. Kamal (2015). "Habitus, Doxa, and Ethics: Insights from Advertising in Emerging Markets in the Middle East and North Africa," *Consumption Markets & Culture*, DOI: 10.1080/10253866.2015.1080165.

Drumwright, M.E., R. Prentice and C. Biasucci (2015). "Behavioral Ethics and Teaching Ethical Decision Making," *Decision Sciences Journal of Innovative Education* 13:3, 431–458.

Eastin, M.S., M.S. Yang and A.I. Nathanson (2006). "Children of the Net: An Empirical Exploration into the Evaluation of Internet Content," *Journal of Broadcasting & Electronic Media* 50:2, 211–230.

Federal Trade Commission (2013). Transcript of "Blurred Lines: Advertising or Content? *An FTC Workshop on Native Advertising."* Available at: www.ftc.gov/system/files/documents/public_events/171321/final_transcript_1.pdf.

Ferrell, O.C. (2005). "A Framework for Understanding Organizational Ethics," in R.A. Peterson and O.C. Ferrell (eds), *Business Ethics: New Challenges for Business Schools and Corporate Leaders*. Armonk, NY: M.E. Sharpe, 3–17.

Ferrell, O.C. and L.G. Gresham (1985). "A Contingency Framework for Understanding Ethical Decision Making in Marketing," *Journal of Marketing* 49:3, 87–96.

Ferrell, O.C., L.G. Gresham and J. Fraedrich (1989). "A Synthesis of Ethical Decision Models for Marketing," *Journal of Macromarketing* 9:2, 55–64.

Freeman, R.E., J.S. Harrison and A.C. Wicks (2007). *Managing for Stakeholders: Survival, Reputation and Success*. New Haven, CT: Yale University Press.

Friel, A.L. and F.A. Bohorquez, Jr. (2015). "FTC Clarifies Native and Online Ad Obligations," *Data Privacy Monitor*. Available at: www.dataprivacymonitor.com/social-media/ftc-clarifies-native-and-online-ad-obligations/ [accessed 27 November 2015].

Galbraith, J.K. (1958). *The Affluent Society*. Boston, MA: Houghton Mifflin.

Galbraith, J.K. (1967). *The New Industrial State*. Boston, MA: Houghton Mifflin.

Gino, F. (2013). *Sidetracked*. Boston, MA: Harvard Business Review Press.

Gogoi, P. (2006). "Wal-Mart vs. the Blogosphere," *Bloomberg Businessweek*, Oct. 18. Available at: www.nbcnews.com/id/15319926/ns/business-us_business/t/wal-mart-vs-blogosphere/#.VretGcekUlZ.

Guynn, J. (2013). "FTC Calls on Online Ad Industry to Agree to Do-not-track Standards." Available at: http://articles.latimes.com/2013/apr/17/business/la-fi-tn-ftc-online-ad-industry-do-not-track-20130417.

Hayek, F.A. (1961). "The Non Sequitur of the 'Dependence Effect,'" *Southern Economic Journal* 27:4, 346–348.

Hernandez, M.D. and S. Chapa (2010). "Adolescents, Advergames and Snack Foods: Effects of Positive Affect and Experience on Memory and Choice," *Journal of Marketing Communications* 16, 59–68.

Holbrook, M.B. (1987). "Mirror, Mirror on the Wall, What's Unfair in the Reflections on Advertising?" *Journal of Marketing* 51:3, 95–103.

Hunt, S.D. and S. Vitell (1986). "A General Theory of Marketing Ethics," *Journal of Macromarketing*. 6:1, 5–16.

Hunt, S.D. and S.J. Vitell (2006). "The General Theory of Marketing Ethics: A Revision and Three Questions," *Journal of Macromarketing* 26:2, 143–153.

Hyman, M.R. and R. Tansey (1990). "The Ethics of Psychoactive Ads," *Journal of Business Ethics* 9 (February), 105–114.

International Association of Privacy Professionals. "What Does Privacy Mean?" Available at: https://iapp.org/about/what-is-privacy/ [accessed 20 July 2016].

Khurana, R. and N. Nohria (2008). "It's Time to Make Management a True Profession," *Harvard Business Review* 86:10 (October), 70–77.

Kotler, P. and K.L. Keller (2012). *A Framework for Marketing Management*, 5th edition. Upper Saddle River, NJ: Pearson Education, Inc.

Laczniak, G.R. and P.E. Murphy (1993). *Ethical Marketing Decisions: The Higher Road*. Needham Heights, MA: Allyn & Bacon.

Lantos, G.P. (1987). "Advertising: Looking Glass or Molder of Masses?" *Journal of Public Policy and Marketing* 6:1, 104–128.

Leiser, B. (1979). "Beyond Fraud and Deception: The Moral Uses of Advertising," in T. Donaldson and P. Werhane (eds), *Ethical Issues in Business*. Englewood Cliffs, NJ: Prentice-Hall, 59–66.
Levitt, T. (1960). "Marketing Myopia," *Harvard Business Review* 38:4 (July/August), 57–66.
Moore, E.S. and V.J. Rideout (2007). "The Online Marketing of Food to Children: Is It Just Fun and Games?" *Journal of Public Policy & Marketing* 28:2, 202–220.
Murphy, P.E. and P.N. Bloom (1990). "Ethical Issues in Social Marketing," in S. Fine (ed.), *Social Marketing: Promoting the Causes of Public and Nonprofit Agencies*. Boston, MA: Allyn and Bacon, 68–78.
Murphy, P.E., G.R. Laczniak and A. Prothero (2012). Ethics in Marketing: International Cases and Perspectives. London: Routledge.Murphy, P.E., G.R. Laczniak, N.E. Bowie and T.A. Klein (2005). *Ethical Marketing: Basic Ethics in Action*. Upper Saddle River, NJ: Pearson Education, Inc.
Norman, W. and C. MacDonald (2004). "Getting to the Bottom of 'Triple Bottom Line,'" *Business Ethics Quarterly* 14:2, 243–263.
Nwachukwu, S.L.S., S.J. Vitell, Jr., F.W. Gilbert and J.H. Barnes (1997). "Ethics and Social Responsibility in Marketing: An Examination of the Ethical Evaluation of Advertising Strategies," *Journal of Business Research* 39, 107–118.
Orlowski, J.P. and L. Wateska (1992). "The Effects of Pharmaceutical Firm Enticements on Physician Prescribing Patterns: There's No Such Thing as a Free Lunch," *CHEST* 102:270–273.
Phillips, B.J. (1997). "In Defense of Advertising: A Social Perspective," *Journal of Business Ethics* 16 (February), 109–118.
Pollay, R.W. (1986). "The Distorted Mirror: Reflections on the Unintended Consequences of Advertising," *Journal of Marketing* 50:2, 18–31.
Pontifical Council for Social Communications (1997). *Ethics in Advertising*. Vatican City: Vatican Documents.
Prentice, R. (2014). "Teaching Behavioral Ethics," *Journal of Legal Studies Education* 31:2, 325–365.
Preston, I. (1975). *The Great American Blow-Up: Puffery in Advertising and Selling*. Madison, WI: University of Wisconsin Press.
Preston, I. (1994). *The Tangled Web They Weave*. Madison, WI: The University of Wisconsin Press.
Prosser, W. (1971). *Handbook of the Law of Torts*, 5th edition. St. Paul, MN: West Publishing.
Sableman, M., H. Shoenberger and E. Thorson (2013). "Consumer Attitudes Toward Relevant Online Behavioral Advertising: Crucial Evidence in the Data Privacy Debates," *Media Law Resource Center Bulletin* 1, 93–110.
Santilli, P.C. (1983). "The Informative and Persuasive Functions of Advertising: A Moral Appraisal," *Journal of Business Ethics* 2:February, 27–33.
Schultz, A.P., A. Jonsson, R. Kasch, P. Jettoo and M. Ghandari (2013). "Sources of Information Influencing Decision-Making in Orthopaedic Surgery—An International Online Survey of 1147 Orthopaedic Surgeons," *BMC Musculoskeletal Disorders* 14:96, 1–8.
Schultz, D.E., W.A. Robinson and L.A. Petrison (1998). *Sales Promotion Essentials: The 10 Basic Sales Promotion Techniques. . . and How to Use Them*, 3rd edition. Lincolnwood, IL: NTC Business Books.
Sheehan, K. (2014). *Controversies in Contemporary Advertising*. Thousand Oaks, CA: Sage, Inc.
Smith, N.C. (1995). "Marketing Strategies for the Ethics Era," *Sloan Management Review* 36:4 85–97.
Smith, N.C., M.E. Drumwright and M.C. Gentile (2010). "The New Marketing Myopia," *Journal of Public Policy & Marketing* 29:1, 4–11.
Smith, R.D. (2002). *Strategic Planning for Public Relations*. Mahwah, NJ: Lawrence Erlbaum Associates.
Steinman, M.A., M.G. Shlipak and S.J. McPhee (2001). "Of Principles and Pens: Attitudes and Practices of Medicine Housestaff toward Pharmaceutical Industry Promotions," *American Journal of Medicine* 110:May, 551–557.
Streitfeld, D. (2013). "Give Yourself 5 Stars? Online, It Might Cost You," *New York Times*, Sept. 22. Available at: www.nytimes.com/2013/09/23/technology/give-yourself-4-stars-online-it-might-cost-you.html?_r=0.
Swagler, R. (1994). "Evolution and Applications of the Term Consumerism: Themes and Variations," *Journal of Consumer Affairs* 28:2, 347–360.
Swanson, A. (2015). "Big Pharmaceutical Companies Are Spending Far More on Marketing Than Research," *The Washington Post*, Feb. 11. Available at: www.washingtonpost.com/news/wonkblog/wp/2015/02/11/big-pharmaceutical-companies-are-spending-far-more-on-marketing-than-research/.
Taylor, C.R., S. Landreth and H-K. Bang (2005). "Asian Americans in Magazine Advertising: Portrayals of the 'Model Minority,'" *Journal of Macromarketing* 25 (December), 163–174.

Thornson, E. and S. Rodgers (2012). "What Does 'Theories of Advertising' Mean?" in Rodgers, S. and Thornson, E (eds), *Advertising Theory*. New York, NY: Routledge.
Tushnet, R. and E. Goldman (2012). *Advertising & Marketing Law: Cases and Materials*. Available at: www.scribd.com/doc/99904133/Advertising-and-Marketing-Law-Casebook-July-2012-by-Tushnet-and-Goldman.
Vranica, S. (2002). "Sony Ericsson Campaign Uses Actors to Push Camera-Phone in Real Life," *Wall Street Journal*, July 31. Available at: www.wsj.com/articles/SB1028069195715597440.
Wilke, W.L. and E.S. Moore (1999). "Marketing's Contributions to Society," *Journal of Marketing* 63:4, 198–218.
Wilke, W.L. and E.S. Moore (2014). "A Larger View of Marketing: Marketing's Contributions to Society," in P.E. Murphy and J.F. Sherry, Jr. (eds), *Marketing and the Common Good*. New York, NY: Routledge.
Wyatt, E. (2013). "FTC Suggests Privacy Guidelines for Mobile App." Available at: www.nytimes.com/2013/02/02/technology/ftc-suggests-do-not-track-feature-for-mobile-software-and-apps.html?pagewanted=all&_r=0.

31
The accounting profession, the public interest, and human rights

Ken McPhail

This chapter situates the study of accounting ethics within its broader political and economic context (McPhail 2015) and has two objectives. First, it provides a broad overview of some of the main ways scholars and practitioners have thought ethically about accounting. This synopsis will highlight the changing ethical focus in relation to the accounting profession's moral responsibilities and will be constructed along crude historical lines. Second, the chapter speculates on how the ethics of accounting may develop in the future. Drawing on contemporary developments in relation to corporate responsibility for human rights, the chapter contends that we may be at a turning point in the way we think about the ethics of accounting and the function of the accounting profession in society.

Many books on accounting ethics tend to think about the practice of accounting and its associated ethical challenges in too narrow terms. So, before outlining the structure of the chapter, I want to explain the perspective that underpins it.

The contemporary importance of accounting is not taken seriously enough. Chris Chapman, David Cooper, and Peter Miller, for example, comment,

> Somewhat belatedly, social scientists are beginning to pay increasing attention to the important roles that accounting plays in so many aspects of social and economic life. Accounting is no longer perceived as 'mere' bookkeeping, as a set of records that neutrally records the facts of economic life. Accounting has finally arrived, or, to be precise, arrived *back* on the social science agenda.
>
> *(Chapman et al. 2009: 3, emphasis original)*

Similarly, most books on accounting ethics generally stop short of addressing the fundamental moral and political philosophy that lies at the heart of accounting practice (Fogarty 1995). I want to begin to redress this imbalance by devoting a greater proportion of the chapter to the big moral questions that lie at the heart of accounting ethics. In order to help us do this, the chapter will draw on two ethical notions: *accountability* and the *public interest*.

At its most basic level, ethics is the study of what constitutes the right way to act, a question that maps directly onto both the function of accounting and the practice of individual accountants. Accounting practice is about the giving of an account, it is about *accountability*.

In his wonderful book, *The Reckoning: Accountability and The Making and Breaking of Nations* (2014), Jacob Soll shows how accounting is absolutely key to accountability. His work, which focuses on political accountability, is even more pertinent for the complex relationship between business, accounting and society. Secondly, the accounting profession tacitly assumes that the practice of accounting is ethical through its claim to act in "the public interest" (Dellaportas and Davenport 2008; Sikka et al. 1989). This chapter looks at how professional bodies have historically construed the notion of the public interest and asks whether the emerging focus on the human rights responsibilities of business means that the next stage in the evolution of accounting ethics might be to connect the public interest claims of professional bodies to the discourse of business and human rights.

The chapter is split into four main sections, the first of which provides a broad introduction to accounting ethics and provides the context for the specific focus of the chapter on the public interest claims of the accounting profession. A second section focuses on the professions and the public interest. The subsequent section provides an historical overview of how the notion of the public interest has been construed within the acounting profession. The fourth section outlines the development of the business and human rights agenda and explains some of the current ways human rights obligations are being connected to accounting practice. The chapter concludes with some reflections on areas for further research.

Introducing accounting ethics

The traditional field of accounting ethics is a broad one that covers both the ethics of accountants and the ethics of accounting. Accountants, like other professionals, are faced with their own individual ethical dilemmas related to the tasks and roles they perform. International financial reporting standards require accountants to capture the substance of business transactions, and consequently there is a significant amount of judgment involved in producing a set of company reports, for example, in relation to complex financial instruments where there is no readily available market value for the assets and liabilities they represent. Because a judgment made by an accountant materially affects a company's financial position, the account must negotiate pressure from the client to present the company in the best possible light (Likierman 1989; Smith and Hume 2005). In addition, there is also the temptation to stray beyond the sphere of professional judgment into illegal activity. The Tesco accounting scandal in the UK, where the chief finance officer fraudulently recognized income before it had occurred, and the Enron scandal in the US, which involved the chief auditor shredding audit evidence, are just two cases in a very long list of examples where accountants have failed to do the right thing when faced with an ethical decision.

There is a considerable literature that tries to understand how both the qualities of specific dilemmas and the characteristics of individuals lead to unethical behavior. On the one hand, there is a literature that models the different qualities that contribute towards the size and nature of ethical dilemmas. T. M. Jones (1991), for example, identifies six factors that might contribute towards the "moral intensity" of an ethical dilemma: the magnitude of the consequences of an action; social consensus regarding the ethical issues at stake; the probability that an action will generate specific consequences; when these results will be experienced; the physical proximity of the decision-maker to those affected by an action; and the number of people affected. On the other hand, there is another literature that explores the individual, that person's stage of moral development, and whether it is possible to improve an accountant's individual ethical integrity in responding to these kinds of dilemmas through educational interventions (see, for example, Everett 2007; Ponemon 1990, 1992; Stanga and Turpen 1991).

A second major tranche of literature studies the ethics of accounting practice itself. This body of work focuses, for example, on the moral significance of the act of rendering an account (Arrington and Francis 1993), the ethics of accountability, and the moral obligations on which the entitlement to receive an account are based. While initially this literature focused on the "moral hazard" associated with the separation between the management and ownership of companies from within an agency theory framework, this narrow economic perspective has been supplemented with a broader stakeholder view of corporate accountability and the requirement for corporations to secure their broader license to operate by recognizing the legitimate claims that employees, local communities, customers and so on, have to receive an account of how the corporation impacts their interests. The literature on the ethics of accounting also addresses the role that accounting practice plays in the broader economic system both in terms of allocating scarce economic resources and in relation to distributing the output from that economic activity. For example, Patrick Primeaux and John Steiber comment:

> The neo-classical theory of economic efficiency is rooted in a dual realization: (1) that men and women in business are managers and (2) that managers allocate scarce resources of land, labor-time, capital, and human creativity in a world of unlimited human wants. The success or failure of a manager is measured by the amount of goods or services produced from a given set of scarce resources. Those who produce the most are efficient; those who produce less are inefficient. The human behavior driving this efficiency is prescribed in the paradigm of profit maximization.
> *(Primeaux and Steiber 1994: 289; see also Williams 1987, Lehman 1988)*

Primeaux and Steiber (1994) contend that accounting plays a fundamental role in the allocative efficiency of capital markets, while others extend the analysis to consider notions of distributional justice and whether the distribution of economic returns is fair (Flower 2010).

Introducing professions and the public interest

Since Andrew Abbot's seminal studies (1988, 1983), a large body of literature has explored the sociology of the professions. This literature clearly establishes that accounting, like other elite professions, is a social practice that reflects the social relationships and political context within which it develops. Tim Fogarty (1995) explains that such a sociological perspective opens up the extra-personal aspects of ethical decision making. The accounting profession, like that of law and medicine, is socially constructed and notions of how it should function in society change over time as society changes. Extending this sociological analysis, post-structuralist studies of accounting ethics have tended to focus less on normative arguments about what the responsibilities of individual accountants, or the profession as a whole, should be and more on how power operates to sustain notions of right and wrong (see, for example, Miller and O'Leary 1987; McPhail 1999). The sociological view therefore sees ethics as the result of historical and political forces (Neu and T'Aerien 2000; Fogarty 1995), a view that also creates the rather tantalising possibility that professional accounting bodies can take on new normative roles in society, depending on societal wants or needs (Williams 2004). In other words, professional bodies can be re-engineered to be what we (society) want them to be.

Different authors have proposed different lists of characteristics that distinguish a profession from other groups in society. These traits include, for example, having a professional association, a code of professional ethics, a specific knowledge base, a focus on education as opposed to training, along with disciplinary mechanisms (Downie 1990). In addition, many studies also contend that individual accountants are characterised by a professional attitude. These individual characteristics, it is claimed, include a sense of calling, a belief in altruism, and a belief in public service (Dellaportas and Davenport 2008). Of course, as the sociological perspective outlined above points out, these characteristics change over time, as does what they mean (Fraser 2016).

A common theme that emerges from these studies of professional characteristics is that professional bodies often attempt to secure their legitimacy through a commitment to the public interest (Dellaportas and Davenport 2008; Sikka et al. 1989). In fact, the substantive ethical mandate for professions has historically been based on this commitment (Edwards 2001; Lee 1995; Walker 1991; Macdonald 1984). Steven Dellaportas and Laura Davenport (2008), for example, contend that the public interest is a critical factor in distinguishing professions from other occupational groupings (Briloff 1986; Robson et al. 1994; Sikka and Willmott 1995; Cooper and Robson 2006; Sikka 2008; Suddaby et al. 2009; Canning and O'Dwyer 2001). However, it is difficult to establish exactly what the substance of the public interest might mean (Baker 2014).

Within the UK, groups of experts have secured their professional status by arguing that what they do is in the public interest. The Royal Charter (1948) of the Institute of Chartered Accountants of England and Wales (ICAEW), for example, states, "the furtherance of the aforesaid objects would be facilitated and *the public interest served*," while the American Accounting Association states that they will "act in a way that will *serve the public interest*, honour the public trust and demonstrate commitment to professionalism" (emphases added). Similarly, the American Institute of CPAs' code of professional ethics (1989, available in Claypool et al. 1990) exhorted American Accountants to, "act in a way that will serve the public interest, honour the public trust and demonstrate commitment to professionalism." Of course, there is considerable debate within the literature on the extent to which the accounting profession, and indeed any profession, really does have the public interest at heart (Sikka et al. 1989), with some commentators suggesting that they are just economic pressure groups principally concerned with their own and their members' economic interests (Primeaux and Steiber 1994). The culture of commercialism (Roberts 2001; Willmott and Sikka 1997) within professional firms, allegations of money laundering (Mitchell et al. 1998) and its complicity in corporate collapses like Enron (Cullinan 2004) have caused many commentators to question the authenticity of the accounting profession's claim to be champions of the public interest, and rightly so.

There may indeed be a sense in which the profession is grappling—perhaps out of a sense of altruism or good will—with what the "public interest" means. However, the different historical formulations of the public interest can be clearly understood only if they are set against the broader reality of commercialization and private interests within the professional bodies, as well as broader social and economic pressures. It is also important to note that the struggle of accountants to articulate their relationship with the public is not specific to the accounting profession. The legal, engineering, and medical professions, for example, have similarly struggled to construe, articulate, and practice the public interest.

Clarke E. Cochran offers an initial attempt at classifying four different notions of the public interest: normative, consensualist, process, and abolitionist (Cochran 1974; see also Dellaportas and Davenport 2008). Normative theories focus on the standards by which actions could be judged to be in the public interest. Abolitionist theorists deny the public interest as an ideal, suggesting instead that society is made up of competing groups each pursuing its own interests. Process theorists focus on the means by which different competing interests are changed into policies, while consensualist theorists start from the assumption that the public interest is a vague term without a definitive meaning.

By contrast, this chapter considers four different forms that the idea of the public interest has taken historically within the accounting profession: as individual character; individual competence; individual integrity; and as independence. We will conceptualise this historical trajectory in terms of a shift from ethics towards justice.

Expressions of the public interest

This subsection explores the four historical representations of the public interest, bringing us up to the present.

The public interest as individual character

The literature contains a number of historical studies of the emergence of the accounting profession (see, for example, Edwards 2001; Lee 1995; Walker 1991; Willmott 1986; Neu and T'Aerien 2000). These studies contend that some early notions of the public interest were often construed in terms of individual "character" (Edwards 2001). What constitutes "character" differs in divergent social and professional contexts. Within early formulations of the profession, the idea of character was loosely associated with an individual's class status (Edwards 2001; McPhail et al. 2010). Entrance to the profession depended on candidates' "suitability," with the ability to pay for an indentureship functioning as an important sign of an individual's social standing and ethics (Macdonald 1984; Walker 1988; Lee 1995). In this sense, professionalism was seen as something that was internal to the individual (Neu and T'Aerien 2000), not something that had to be written down in the form of codes of conduct (Cohen, Pant, and Sharp 1992). It was only later when subsequently faced with crisis that professional bodies began to codify professionalism.

The focus on the individual characteristics of the professional accountant as opposed, for example, to the morality of accounting standards or the economic system that accounting facilitates, has been an enduring characteristic of the ethical study of accountants (Neu and T'Aerien 2000). Contemporary studies explore moral character in terms of virtues such as courage or honesty (Melé 2005). Work by Theresa Libby and Linda Thorne (2007), for example, has investigated the impact of partner's behavior on the development of auditor's virtues.

Professionalism as competence

Secondly, the notion of the public interest was grounded in the individual's ability to perform a specific task competently. The notion of competence was closely associated with acquiring a specific body of knowledge as a hurdle to entering the profession. Professional education however focused specifically on the technical, as opposed to the moral or emotional competence of members. Skill in the application of a particular body of knowledge was equated with competence and therefore in the public interest. This notion of competence is related to the magnitude of the consequences that would follow malpractice. Think, for example, of the civil engineer's competence to construct a bridge, or the surgeon's technical ability to perform an operation. The public impact of getting these activities wrong is considerable. Professional bodies hold individuals out to be worthy of trust in performing particularly important tasks. In doing so there is an expectation that professionals possess the requisite competence.

The public interest as integrity

However, in the face of a growing number of scandals, such as the Enron debacle, the accounting profession found itself having to clarify its commitment to the public interest (Parker 2005).

In addition to possessing technical competence, the professional accounting bodies found themselves having to articulate once more what it means for a profession to act in the public interest. Again, the concern here was over the ethics of individual accountants. For example, twenty years ago, A.I.M. Fleming (1996: 207) concluded, "the tendency of the evidence is to suggest, if anything, that accountants either occupy the middle ground or lean towards an amoral ethical position."

There was therefore a subsequent need to provide further clarity to the notion of character that had been associated with class (and the ability to pay) in the early formations of professional accounting practice. One prominent approach was to articulate this commitment in terms of a focus on "Integrity." Professional bodies, along with pan-European organizations such as the Federation of European Accountants, produced numerous discussion papers on "Integrity in Professional Ethics."

During this period, the study of accounting and ethics continued to focus on the ethics of the individual accountant. Some studies modeled integrity in terms of the cognitive moral development of individual accountants (Abdolmohammadi and Baker 2006). A number of well established cognitive development instruments have been used extensively within the literature, for example Rokeach's Values Survey, Rest's Defining Issues Test, or Lawrence Kohlberg's theory of cognitive moral development. These tests have been used to explore whether factors like gender or age influence moral development (Ponemon 1990; Enyon et al. 1997). This literature drew on these standard models of moral development to compare accountants with other cohorts (Stanga and Turpen 1991) and also to test the effects of different educational interventions designed to advance students to higher levels in Kohlberg's stages of moral awareness (Armstrong 1987). This body of work has also explored the impact of external factors like organizational culture (Sims and Brinkman 2003; Schlachter 1990) on the ethics of individual accountants.

Although this body of work has generated significant insights, it has also received a considerable amount of criticism (Fogarty 1995). Sara Ann Reiter (1996), for example, contends that Kohlberg's theory is based on rational masculine notions of ethics, and proposes a more empathetic approach to moral development.

The public interest as independence

Independence has also been an important constituent of the idea of being professional (Claypool et al. 1990; Carmichael and Swieringa 1968). However, Jeanne F. Backof and Charles L. Martin (1991) contend that it was not until 1973 that concepts of independence and objectivity formally entered the codes of conduct for American CPAs. A key function of the accounting profession has been to audit the financial accounts of companies in order to ensure they are trustworthy. Within the context of professional ethics, independence was narrowly construed in terms of ensuring that income from non-audit consultancy services, or the size of a single audit client, did not undermine auditors' objectivity (Likierman 1989).

A narrative of independence developed in response to specific challenges on the profession's ability to deliver an accounting and auditing function that was in the public interest. This discourse was associated with the structure of the profession, the limitation of non-audit services and the rotation of audit partners. However, Prem Sikka and Hugh Willmott (1995) contend that the profession uses the narrative of independence to manage threats to its interests (see also Zeff 1989).

It is therefore possible to see different (although overlapping) moral dialogues around the notion of the public interest in the evolution of accounting's professional narrative: from character and competence, to integrity and independence. The argument is not necessarily that one replaced the other, but rather that it is possible to identify discrete narratives that relate to a grasping after what it means for accounting to function in the public interest. Underlying each narrative is a tacit assumption that the role of accounting in helping capital markets to operate efficiently in the allocation of scarce resources is taken as self-evidently in the public interest.

The remainder of this chapter will speculate on how the notion of the public interest might develop in the future given the shifts in the social and political context within which it is currently operating. Within the business ethics literature, in particular, there has been a shift towards thinking about the social responsibility of business in terms of human rights responsibilities. However, as yet there is little discussion of how this shift might translate into the context of professional bodies and the notion of the public interest.

Accounting and human rights

Over the past decade the United Nations has been promoting the responsibility of corporations to respect human rights. This business and human rights agenda is considered to be one of the most significant developments in Corporate Social Responsibility in decades. The discourse of human rights is emerging as the most credible framework for understanding the social responsibility of business. This section of the chapter begins to make the connection between human rights and the public interest claims of professional accountants. By doing so it begins to explore the function of accounting in society beyond the provision of purely economic information designed to make the market more efficient in its allocation of scarce resources (Williams 1987; see also Lehman 1988).

Introducing rights

The Universal Declaration of Human Rights represents a universal expression of the fundamental rights and freedoms to which each human being across the world should be entitled. The declaration articulates these rights in terms of articles. For example, Article 4 states that "No one shall be held in slavery or servitude; slavery and the slave trade shall be prohibited in all their forms."

As such, the discourse of human rights provides one of the most comprehensive and widely accepted discussions on what the public might be interested in. According to the Universal Declaration, the public is interested in not being held in slavery; not being subject to torture or inhuman treatment; freedom of association, privacy, freedom of movement, owning property (and not to being arbitrarily deprived of it), freedom of speech, and a standard of living adequate for health and well being. In terms of a definition of the public interest, the human rights discourse provides one of the most comprehensive and universally accepted examples that we have.

It is important to note that, while the discussion of the universal declaration within the context of accounting ethics may seem alien, some of its principles lie at the core of conventional accounting practice. Article 17, for example, claims that "Everyone has the right to own property alone as well as in association with others" and that, "No one shall be arbitrarily deprived of his (sic) property." The recognition of property rights is fundamental to the conventional understanding of the practice of accounting. It is this right that provides the basis for shareholder entitlement to receive an account of what has been done with his or her investment.

Ken McPhail

The UN Guiding Principles on Business and Human Rights

More recently, the discussion of the broader rights responsibilities of business was brought to the fore when the United Nations formally endorsed the Guiding Principles on Business and Human Rights in June 2011 (hereinafter, the Guiding Principles). This growing focus on corporate accountability for human rights is reflective of the big political and economic shifts that underlie globalization. The International Business Leaders Initiative on Human Rights (IBLF 2005) comment for example:

> The rights of transnational firms—their ability to operate and expand globally—have increased greatly over the past generation as a result of trade agreements, bilateral investment treaties and domestic liberalisation . . . In light of this transformation in the institutional features of the world economy, it is hardly surprising that the transnational corporate sector—and by extension the entire universe of business—has attracted increased attention by other social actors, including civil society and States themselves.

Although this increased attention from social actors and civil society has highlighted the negative impact that business can have on human rights—for example, in relation to workers' rights in the Rana-Plaza collapse in Bangladesh—there is also increased attention on the positive role that corporations could play in realizing rights. Indeed, post Rana-Plaza, multinational corporations have played a considerable role in improving workers' conditions in Bangladesh where state interventions have proved less effective. A number of studies are beginning to show how corporations are having a positive impact on rights through supply chain management and the introduction of human rights clauses in commercial contracts (Campbell 2006; Backer 2011). Some companies, for example, incorporate a requirement to adhere to specific standards in a supplier's contract. Other studies are also showing how new human rights criteria of investors and lenders are also driving the development of corporate human rights due diligence practices (Missbach 2007; McPhail and Ferguson 2016; Kobrin 2009).

The UN appointed Professor John Ruggie of Harvard as a Special Representative of the UN Secretary-General on Business and Human Rights. In 2008, Prof. Ruggie presented a policy framework of three core principles to the UN Human Rights Council to guide the business and human rights agenda (Ruggie 2008). These principles address the protection of rights, the obligation to respect them, and the significance of remediation or restitution for violation of rights:

1 A sovereign state has the duty to protect against human rights abuses by third parties, including business;
2 Each business bears the responsibility to respect human rights;
3 The victims of rights abuses need effective access to remedies or restitution.

(Ruggie 2008)

In 2011 Ruggie's work culminated in the development of a set of *Guiding Principles on Business and Human Rights* (Ruggie 2011) that were formally ratified by the UN Human Rights Council in June of the same year, an event hailed as one of the most significant contemporary developments in global corporate governance (Taylor 2011). The principles purportedly represent an attempt to move towards more binding corporate responsibility for human rights based in existing international standards (Nolan 2010; Taylor 2011). International human rights rather than national laws are therefore assumed to provide the standard for corporate social responsibility, with some contending that the international human rights treaties should be incorporated into law and corporations should be obliged to obey the law. In any case, as L. C. Backer also notes (2011), the appeal to international human rights represents a significant shift in traditional human rights thinking as it challenges the established idea of the primacy of states in relation to the law that applies to its citizens.

Accounting and the United Nations' Guiding Principles

The Guiding Principles themselves envisage a significant role for accounting in implementing both state and corporate accountability for rights. The commentary to Guiding Principle 5 stipulates,

> As a necessary step, the relevant service contracts or enabling legislation should clarify the State's expectations that these enterprises respect human rights. States should ensure that they can effectively oversee the enterprises' activities, including through the provision of adequate independent monitoring and accountability mechanisms.
>
> (Guiding Principles, *Principle 5 Commentary*)

As indicated above, the relationship between accounting and accountability lies at the heart of any discussion of the ethics of accounting. The reason why the Guiding Principles are so important is because they suggest that the relationship between what we are asked to account for and the information (numbers and narrative) that we capture and report through accounting practice needs to change quite significantly. The implication is that accounting practice can be more ethical.

At a fundamental level the business and human rights agenda affects our conceptions of accounting, accountability, and corporate governance more broadly (Soll 2014). The Guiding Principles, for example, comment on how the mechanisms it enumerates should "provide for accountability and help enable the remediation of adverse human rights impacts." The idea of accountability has been the subject of much analysis within the accounting literature. William Schweiker (1993), for example, discusses the morally constitutive act of rendering an account, while Jerry L. Mashaw (2007) explores the different constitutive elements of an accountability relationship: for example, who, to whom, for what, through what process, by what standard, and with what effect. Introducing a responsibility for rights into our understanding of what corporations should be accountable for and adding a requirement to provide non-judicial forms of remedy, fundamentally reconstitute the moral identity of the corporation. Whether the implementation of the Guiding Principles will result in new forms of governance and accountability remains to be seen.

In addition to challenging our notion of accountability, the business and human rights agenda also affects accounting measurement. Guiding Principle 20, for example, comments on how a corporation's responsibility to respect human rights needs to be "based on appropriate qualitative and quantitative indicators." There is also an expectation that human rights due diligence (the continual assessment of any adverse impact on human rights) will be integrated into existing measurement and reporting processes. The UN Human Rights Council, for example, comments, "Financial reporting requirements should clarify that human rights impacts in some instances may be 'material' or 'significant' to the economic performance of the business enterprise" (UN Human Rights Council 2011: 9). Backer concludes:

> There is an expectation that data will be harvested from all phases of the human rights due diligence process and all contacts with affected stakeholders. The Commentary urges integration into relevant reporting processes with a cross-reference to the corporation's remediation obligations.
>
> (Backer 2011: 135)

While these expectations may seem far removed from traditional accounting practice, it is important to remember that much of what we now take for granted as standard aspects of corporate reporting, for example in relation to complex financial instruments, accounting for brands and brand revaluation, or the disclosure of the gendered composition of boards, would have similarly seemed alien to accountants a few decades ago.

The Guiding Principles are beginning to affect new forms of financial reporting practice. For example, the accounting firm Mazars, in collaboration with the NGO "Shift," launched "The Human Rights Reporting and Assurance Frameworks Initiative" (RAFI) in February 2015. The framework provides guidance on how companies can report on their human rights performance in accordance with the Guiding Principles, specifically in relation to managing risk, undertaking due diligence and reporting to stakeholders (Mazars 2015; Shift 2012). The Framework advocates, amongst other things, a statement on salient human rights issues along with disclosure on how these issues are managed through policies, stakeholder engagement and tracking performance. A second phase of the RAFI project will focus on the development of a framework for the assurance of human rights reporting.

The impact of the Guiding Principles is being compounded by other policy and regulatory developments. For example, the European Union (EU) Accounting Directive now requires public interest entities with more than 500 employees to disclose non-financial information related to social, environmental, and human rights issues. Additionally, the introduction of the UK's Modern Slavery Act in October 2015 requires companies with turnover in excess of £38 million to ensure that slavery is not present in their business and supply chains. Disclosure is recommended to cover the following six areas: business organization structure and supply chains; policies; due diligence; risk assessment; performance indicators and training.

In 2016 the Chartered Institute of Management Accountants (CIMA) in collaboration with the American Institute of CPAs produced guidance for management accountants on assessing and protecting human rights (CIMA 2016). The introduction to the guidance begins, "This briefing is a call to action for CGMAs [Chartered Global Management Accountants] and provides a roadmap showcasing how they can pursue their *new professional responsibilities*" (CIMA 2016: 2, emphasis added). The guidance bases these new human rights responsibilities for management accountants in their technical competence but also their professional identity. The Chartered Institute of Management Accountants comments:

> As qualified accountants, CGMA designation holders recognise their ethical and professional responsibilities, both to the codes of their professional bodies and particularly in relation to delivering objectivity, independence and integrity. Using this lens, they are well placed to review human rights impacts and determine how prepared their organisations are in terms of applying the Guiding Principles.
>
> *(CIMA 2016: 6)*

The guidance outlines a role for management accountants in relation to contracting and procurement; assessing human rights risk around mergers and acquisitions; risk management; the development of new key performance indicators and human rights impact assessments.

Unilever was one of the first multinationals to produce a stand alone Business and Human Rights Report in 2015. The company uses a business and human rights framework to assess the risks associated with its business structure and operational model. The company, which has 76,000 suppliers and sales in 190 countries, has identified a number of salient human rights risks across this value chain, for example: health and safety; harassment; forced, child and trafficked labor; and land rights. New internal information systems are being used to assess non-compliance with these rights per country by supply chain.

While the discourse of human rights is beginning to impact accounting practice, there is still a lot of work to be done on developing new accounting measures. For example, Unilever comments in their 2015 Business and Human Rights Report,

> One of the gaps we constantly came across was the need for better metrics for progress and impacts reporting. Social impact measurement is inherently more complex than environmental. To shift toward best practices on disclosure and transparency, we must work together as a business community, and create consensus around measurement and reporting, sharing lessons and challenges along the way. More attention needs to be given to measuring social profit and loss.
>
> *(Unilever 2015: 61)*

There is some evidence that the language of human rights is beginning to affect the way some professional accounting firms construe their public interest commitments. For example, the accounting firm KPMG published its own human rights policy at the beginning of 2013 affirming,

In following the Guiding Principles, KPMG International and KPMG member firms:

(I) undertake to avoid causing or contributing to adverse human rights impacts through their own activities, and address such impacts when they occur and
(II) seek to prevent or mitigate adverse human rights impacts that are directly related to their operations, products or services through their business relationships.

(KPMG 2017)

In addition to the role of accounting in the Guiding Principles and the emergent discussion of accounting firms' human rights responsibilities, there is the nascent discussion of the human rights responsibilities of global accounting organizations. McPhail et al. (2016), for example, explore whether the responsibilities of the International Accounting Standards Board (IASB) could be construed in human rights terms. Their argument builds on attempts that have been made to extend the logic of the Guiding Principles from business to other global financial institutions that exercise considerable political power. For example, Wouter Vandenhole states,

> Given the multiplicity of State and non-state actors with varying degrees of power and importance, human rights law needs to be adapted, so that new duty-bearers such as foreign States, transnational corporations *and international organizations* can be integrated into the human rights legal regime.
>
> *(Vandenhole 2012: 2, emphasis added)*

Like national professional bodies, the IASB contends that what it does is in the public interest. The IASB explains its objective as being: "to develop, in the public interest, a single set of high quality, understandable, enforceable and globally accepted financial reporting standards based upon clearly articulated principles" (IFRS Foundation 2013: 5). However, McPhail et al. (2016) argue that discussions of the *public interest* responsibilities of the profession of accounting should not be dissociated from an understanding of the ways in which it exercises *public power*. They argue that given that accounting standards affect the lived experience of rights, it is entirely appropriate to construe the responsibilities of the IASB in terms of human rights obligations. Indeed, they point out that there has been growing demands for the IASB to be more publicly accountable in light of the growing awareness of its public functions and powers.

Although we may be quite some distance away from the professional bodies framing their public interest commitments in terms of human rights responsibilities, the emerging discourse of business and human rights certainly opens up the possibility that this could happen. There is a hint that the language of human rights is beginning to enter into our understanding of the practice of accounting and the responsibilities of accounting firms. However, the literature also cautions against assuming that this is necessarily a positive development. After all, the ubiquity of accounting technologies and their propensity to dehumanize, colonize, and technologize (Power 1991; McPhail 2001) has been discussed extensively within the literature (Power 1997; Kamuf 2007; McKernan and McPhail 2012; Li and McKernan 2016).

One of the most confronting examples of the ability of accounting to denude individuals of their humanity is found in Zygmunt Bauman's celebrated work *Modernity and the Holocaust*. Bauman identifies accountancy as being particularly culpable. He says, "Industry's influence was felt in the great emphasis upon accounting, penny saving, and salvage, as well as in the factory like efficiency of the killing centres" (Bauman 2013: 14).

Bauman argues that managerial techniques like accounting diminish moral sympathy for other human beings because they dehumanize individuals by categorizing them and ascribing them a number. More mundane examples would be the way in which accounting frames individuals as labor and production costs, the very expenses that business generally try to reduce.

Concluding remarks

This chapter has explored the ethics of professional accounting. It has provided an overview of how professional bodies have historically construed the notion of the public interest. It is possible to identify in the historical development of the profession four discrete conceptualisations of the public interest: as individual character, individual competence, individual integrity, and as independence. The chapter has also examined the emerging focus on the human rights responsibilities of business and has proposed the possibility that the next stage in the evolution of accounting ethics might be to connect the public interest claims of professional accounting organizations to the discourse of business and human rights.

As outlined in the introduction, the question of what it means to act in the public interest is a broad one that lies at the heart of ethics. While the majority of books on accounting ethics tend to focus on the ethics of individual accountants and professional codes of practice, the balance of this chapter has focused on the broader conceptions of how we might think about accounting as something that is good in itself. This is important, for as Zygmunt Bauman (2013) suggests, it might be possible to carry out a task with both competence and integrity, but doing so says nothing of whether the task itself should or should not be undertaken.

The philosopher Thomas Nagel comments,

> We do not live in a just world. This may be the least controversial claim one could make in political theory. But it is much less clear what, if anything, justice on a world scale might mean, or what the hope for justice should lead us to want in the domain of international or global institutions, and in the policies of states that are in a position to affect the world order.
>
> *(Nagel 2005: 113)*

By inference, Nagel casts the question of the public interest in terms of "justice on a world scale." As I commented in the introduction, the role of accounting in society is becoming more significant. The possibility of a shift in the understanding of "the public interest" comes at a time when corporations are playing an increasingly important role in society while concerns over the extent to which market forces are working in the interests of everyone is being questioned. Partly as a consequence, a greater understanding of the potential role of accounting and accountability systems in steering corporations in line with societal interests is becoming more necessary.

The shift in public interest focus from a concern with the character, competence and integrity of individual accountants, to a concern with the goal of the practice of accounting charted in this chapter, can be summed up in a distinction that the philosopher Thomas Pogge drew between what he calls *interactional* and *institutional* frameworks for reflecting on moral and political responsibilities. An interactional perspective assesses the morality of an action based on interactions between individuals. Pogge explains that this is a question of how individuals ought to behave—a matter of *ethics*. The institutional view, however, assesses the overall legitimacy of social or institutional systems. According to Pogge, this is a matter of *justice*: "In order to determine how agents ought to act within some given institutional framework, we must first assess how just this framework is and whether there are feasible avenues of institutional reform" (Pogge 1992: 90–91).

I tend to agree with Nagel. It is obvious that we do not live in a just world. I also agree with Bauman. Injustice has happened despite the fact that the majority of accountants have acted with competence and integrity. While the individual morality of accountants is important, we need to develop a much broader conception of what the ethics of accounting entails. We require much more scholarship on whether the public interest claims of professional accounting bodies could be framed in terms of human rights responsibilities and what that would mean for accounting practice (Sikka 2011; Gallhofer et al. 2011; Gray and Gray 2011; Li and McKernan 2016). If, as Abbott contends (1988), professional bodies are our creations, then Zygmunt Bauman's response to the question "why do you write books" seems to me to be a particularly challenging way to conclude the chapter. He said, "because things could be different, they could be made better" (Bunting 2003). The ethical question posed by this chapter is precisely that: how could accounting be different and how could a different kind of accounting lead to more justice in the world? Maybe this is the only ethical question worth asking.

Essential reading

Seminal work that focuses on the moral reasoning of individual accountants includes Lawrence Ponemon's essay "Ethical Reasoning and Selection—Socialization in Accounting" (1992) and Keith Stanga and Richard Turpen, "Ethical Judgments on Selected Accounting Issues: An Empirical Study" (1991). An influential piece of work that explores the fundamentally moral nature of giving an account is William Schweiker, "Accounting for Ourselves: Accounting Practice and the Discourse of Ethics" (1993). Tim Fogarty's important paper "Accountant Ethics: A Brief Examination of Neglected Sociological Dimensions" (1995) shifts the focus of accounting ethics away from the individual accountant. Important work on professions and the public interest include Ed Arrington's essay, "Intellectual Tyranny and the Public Interest: The Quest for the Grail and the Quality of Life" (1989) and that of Prem Sikka, Hugh Willmot and Tony Lowe, "Guardians of Knowledge and Public Interest: Evidence and Issues of Accountability in the UK Accounting Profession," (1989). Rob Gray, Jan Bebbington and Ken McPhail study the potential for accounting education to contribute towards the ethical development of accounting students in, "Teaching Ethics in Accounting and The Ethics Of Accounting Teaching" (1994). Essential work on the application of virtue ethics to accounting includes Jere Francis, "After Virtue? Accounting as a Moral and Discursive Practice" (1990). Essential reading on accounting and human rights include the papers by Ken McPhail and John Ferguson "The Past, the Present and the Future of Accounting for Human Rights" (2016) and Yingru Li and John McKernan "Human Rights, Accounting, and the Dialectic of Equality and Inequality" (2016).

For further reading in this volume on accounting as essential to the activity of business, see Chapter 13, What is business? On the topic of property rights, see Chapter 18, Property and business. The notion of a social end or mission for corporations is taken up in Chapter 15, Alternative business organizations and social enterprise. On the topic of business and human rights, see Chapter 10, Social responsibility. On corruption in transnational commerce, see Chapter 34, Corruption, bribery, and moral norms across national boundaries. On the prospects of a globalized ethics (including the United Nations' Guiding Principles on Business and Human Rights) see Chapter 32, The globalization of business ethics.

References

Abbott, A. (1988). *The System of Professions: An Essay on the Division of Expert Labour*. Chicago, IL: University of Chicago Press.

Abbott, A. (1983). "Professional Ethics," *American Journal of Sociology* 88:5, 855–885.

Abdolmohammadi, M.J. and R. Baker (2006). "Value Preferences and Moral Reasoning of Graduate Accounting Students," *Journal of Business Ethics* 69, 11–25.

Armstrong, M.B. (1987). "Moral Development and Accounting Education," *Journal of Accounting Education* 5 (Spring), 27–43.

Arrington, E. (1989). "Intellectual Tyranny and the Public Interest: The Quest for the Grail and the Quality of Life," *Advances in Public Interest Accounting* [annual] 1–15.

Arrington, C.E. and J.R. Francis (1993). "Accounting as a Human Practice: The Appeal of Other Voices," *Accounting, Organizations and Society* 18:2/3, 105–106.

Backer, L. (2011). "From Institutional Misalignment to Socially Sustainable Governance: the Guiding Principles for the Implementation of the United Nation's 'Protect, Respect and Remedy' and the Construction of Inter-systemic Global Governance," *Pacific McGregor Global Business and Development Law Journal*. Available at: http://ssrn.com/abstract=1922953 [Accessed 17 April 2017].

Backof, J.F and C.L. Martin (1991). "Historical Perspectives: Development of the Codes of Ethics in the Legal, Medical and Accounting Professions," *Journal of Business Ethics* 10:2, 99–110.

Baker, R.C. (2014). "An Examination of the Ethical Discourse of the U.S. Public Accounting Profession from a Foucaultian Perspective," *Journal of Accounting & Organizational Change* 10:2, 216–228.

Bauman, Z. (2013). *Modernity and the Holocaust*, revised edition. Cambridge: Polity.

Briloff, A.J. (1986). "Accountancy and the Public Interest," *Advances in Public Interest Accounting* 1, 1–14.

Briloff, A.J. (1990). "Accountancy and Society: A Covenant Desecrated," *Critical Perspectives on Accounting* 1:1, 5–30.

Bunting, M. (2003). "Passion and Pessimism," *The Guardian* Friday 4 April. Available at: www.theguardian.com/books/2003/apr/05/society.

Campbell, T. (2006). "A Human Rights Approach to Developing Voluntary Codes of Conduct for Multinational Corporations," *Business Ethics Quarterly* 16:2, 255–269.

Canning, M. and B. O'Dwyer (2001). "Professional Accounting Bodies' Disciplinary Procedures: Accountable, Transparent and in the Public Interest?" *European Accounting Review* 10:4, 725–49.

Carmichael, D.R. and R.J. Swieringa (1968). "The Compatibility of Audit Independence and Management Services—An Identification of Issues," *The Accounting Review* 43:4, 697–705.

Chapman, C., D. Cooper and P. Miller (2009). "Linking Accounting, Organizations, and Institutions," in C. Chapman, D. Cooper and P. Miller (eds), *Accounting, Organizations, and Institutions: Essays in Honour of Anthony Hopwood*. Oxford: Oxford University Press, 1–30.

Chartered Institute of Management Accountants (CIMA) (2016). *Business & Human Rights: Evolution and Acceptance. GCMA Guidance for Assessing and Protecting Human Rights*. London: CIMA.

Claypool, G.A., D.F. Fetyko and M.A. Pearson (1990). "Reactions to Ethical Dilemmas: A Study Pertaining to Certified Public Accountants," *Journal of Business Ethics* 9, 699–706.

Cochran, C.E. (1974). "Political Science and 'The Public Interest,'" *The Journal of Politics* 36:2, 327–355.

Cohen J.R. and L.W. Pant (1991). "Beyond Bean Counting: Establishing High Ethical Standards in the Public Accounting Profession," *Journal of Business Ethics* 10:1, 45–56.

Cohen J.R., L.W. Pant and D.J. Sharp (1992). "Cultural and Socioeconomic Constraints on International Codes of Ethics: Lessons from Accounting," *Journal of Business Ethics* 11, 687–700.

Cooper, D.J. and K. Robson (2006). "Accounting, Professions, and Regulation: Locating the Sites of Professionalization," *Accounting, Organizations, and Society* 31:4–5, 415–444.

Cullinan, C. (2004). "Enron as a Symptom of Audit Process Breakdown: Can the Sarbanes-Oxley Act Cure the Disease?" *Critical Perspectives on Accounting* 15:6–7, 853–864.

Dellaportas, S. and L. Davenport (2008). "Reflections on the Public Interest in Accounting," *Critical Perspectives on Accounting* 19:7, 1080–1098.

Downie, R.S. (1990). "Professions and Professionalism," *Journal of Philosophy of Education* 24:2, 147–159.

Edwards, J.R. (2001). "Accounting Regulation and the Professionalisation Process: An Historical Essay Concerning the Significance of P.H. Abbott," *Critical Perspectives on Accounting* 12:6, 675–696.

Everett, J.S. (2007). "Ethics Education and the Role of the Symbolic Market," *Journal of Business Ethics* 76, 253–267.

Eynon, G.N., T. Hill and K.T. Stevens (1997). "Factors That Influence the Moral Reasoning Abilities of Accountants: Implications for Universities and the Profession," *Journal of Business Ethics* 16, 1297–1309.

Fleming, A.I.M. (1996). "Ethics and accounting education in the UK—a professional approach?" *Accounting Education* 5:3, 207–217.

Flower, J. (2010). *Accounting & Distributive Justice*. London: Routledge.

Fogarty, T.J. (1995). "Accountant Ethics: A Brief Examination of Neglected Sociological Dimensions," *Journal of Business Ethics* 14:2, 103–115.

Francis, J.R. (1990). "After Virtue? Accounting as a Moral and Discursive Practice," *Accounting Auditing and Accountability Journal* 3:3, 5–17.

Fraser, J.A. (2016). "How Many Accountants Does It Take to Change an Industry?" *Inc.* Magazine Available at: www.inc.com/magazine/19970401/1210.html [accessed 17 April 2017].

Gallhofer, S., J. Haslam and S. van der Walt (2011). "Accountability and Transparency in Relation to Human Rights: A Critical Perspective Reflecting upon Accounting, Corporate Responsibility and Ways Forward in the Context of Globalization," *Critical Perspectives on Accounting* 22:8, 765–780.

Gray, S. and R. Gray (2011). "Accounting and Human Rights: A Tentative Exploration and Commentary," *Critical Perspectives on Accounting* 22:8, 781–789.

Gray, R., J. Bebbington and K. McPhail (1994). "Teaching Ethics in Accounting and the Ethics of Accounting Teaching: Educating for Immorality and a Possible Case for Social and Environmental Accounting Education," *Accounting Education* 3:1, 51–75.

IBLF (2005). "Human Rights. It's your Business. The Case for Corporate Engagement," The International Business Leaders Forum. Available at: www.iblf.org/humanrights/ [accessed 17 April 2017].

IFRS Foundation (2013). *IFRS Foundation Constitution*. London: IFRS Foundation Publications Department.

Institute of Chartered Accountants of England and Wales (1948). "Supplemental Charter of the 21st December 1948." Available at: www.icaew.com/-/media/corporate/files/about-icaew/who-we-are/charters-bye-laws/supplemental-charter-of-the-21st-december-1948.ashx?la=en [accessed 17 April 2017].

Jones, T.M. (1991). "Ethical Decision Making by Individuals in Organisations: An Issue-Contingent Model," *Academy of Management Review* 16:2, 366–395.

Kamuf, P. (2007). "Accounterability," *Textual Practice* 21:2, 251–266.

Kobrin, S.J. (2009). "Private Political Authority and Public Responsibility: Transnational Polities, Transnational Firms, and Human Rights," *Business Ethics Quarterly* 19:3, 349–374.

KPMG (2017). "Business and Human Rights Statement." Available at: https://home.kpmg.com/ye/en/home/about/citizenship/human-rights-statement.html [accessed 17 April 2017].

Lee, T. (1995). "The Professionalisation of Accountancy: A History of Protecting Public Interest in a Self-interested Way," *Accounting Auditing and Accountability Journal* 8:4, 48–69.

Lehman, C.R. (1988). "Accounting Ethics: Surviving Survival of the Fittest," *Advances in Public Interest Accounting* 2, 71–82.

Li, Y. and J. McKernan (2016). "Human Rights, Accounting, and the Dialectic of Equality and Inequality," *Accounting, Auditing and Accountability Journal* 29:4, 568–593.

Libby, T. and L. Thorne (2007). "The Development of a Measure of Auditors' Virtue," *Journal of Business Ethics* 71:1, 89–99.

Likierman, A. (1989). "Ethical Dilemmas for Accountants: A United Kingdom Perspective," *Journal of Business Ethics* 8, 617–629.
Macdonald, K.M. (1984). "Professional Formation: The Case of Scottish Accountants," *The British Journal Of Sociology* 35:2, 174–189.
Mashaw, J.L. (2007). "Accountability and Institutional Design: Some Thoughts on the Grammar of Governance," Yale Law School, Research Paper No. 116.
Mazars (2015). "Business and Human Rights: UNGP Reporting Framework to launch." Available at: www.mazars.co.uk/Home/Our-Services/Publications/Consulting-publications/Human-Rights-publications/UNGP-Reporting-Framework-to-launch [accessed 17 April 2017].
McCarthy, I.N. (1997). "Professional Ethics Code Conflict Situations: Ethical and Value Orientation of Collegiate Accounting Students," *Journal of Business Ethics* 16:12, 1467–1473.
McKernan J. and K. McPhail (2012). "Accountability and Accounterability," *Critical Perspectives on Accounting* 23:3, 177–182.
McPhail, K. (1999). "The Threat of Ethical Accountants: An Application of Foucault's Concept of Ethics to Accounting Education and Some Thoughts on Ethically Educating For The Other," *Critical Perspectives on Accounting* 10, 833–866.
McPhail, K. (2001). "The Other Objective of Ethics Education: Rehumanising the Accounting Profession: A Study of Ethics Education in Law, Engineering, Medicine and Accountancy," *Journal of Business Ethics* 34:3/4, 279–298.
McPhail, K. (2015). "Accounting, Ethics and Organization: Accounting for Human Rights in a Post-Sovereign World?" in A.Pullen and C.Rhodes (eds), *The Routledge Companion to Ethics, Politics and Organizations*. London: Routledge, 181–197.
McPhail, K. and J. Ferguson (2016). "The Past, the Present and the Future of Accounting for Human Rights," *Accounting, Auditing & Accountability Journal* 29:4, 526–541.
McPhail, K., K. MacDonald and J. Ferguson (2016). "Should the International Accounting Standards Board Have Responsibility for Human Rights?" *Accounting, Auditing and Accountability Journal* 29:4, 594–616.
McPhail, K., C. Paisey and N. Paisey (2010). "Accounting at School: The Impact of Policy, Teachers and Class on the Ethical Construction of Accounting and Business in Scottish Secondary Schools," *International Journal of Critical Accounting* 2:3, 289–318.
Melé, D. (2005). "Ethical Education in Accounting: Integrating Rules, Values and Virtues," *Journal of Business Ethics* 57:1, 97–109.
Miller, P. and T. O'Leary (1987). "Accounting and the Construction of the Governable Person," *Accounting, Organizations and Society* 12:3, 235–265.
Missbach, A. (2007). "Human Rights are Banking Risks," *BankTrack at the Consultation on Human Rights and the Financial Sector*. Geneva Available at: www.banktrack.org/download/human_rights_are_banking_risks/0_070216_presentation_ruggie_andreas_missbach.pdf [accessed 17 April 2017].
Mitchell, A., Sikka, P. and Willmott, H. (1998). "Sweeping it under the Carpet: The Role of Accountancy Firms in Money Laundering," *Accounting, Organizations and Society* 23:4–5, 589–607.
Nagel, T. (2005). "The Problem of Global Justice," *Philosophy and Public Affairs* 33:2, 113–147.
Neu, D. and R. T'Aerien (2000). "Remembering the Past: Ethics and The Canadian Chartered Accounting Profession, 1911–1925," *Critical Perspectives on Accounting* 11:2, 193–212.
Nolan, J. (2010). "The United Nations' Compact with Business: Hindering or Helping the Protection of Human Rights?" *University of New South Wales Faculty of Law Research Series 2010*. Working Article 10. Sydney: Faculty of Law, University of New South Wales.
Parker, L.D. (2005). "Corporate Governance Crisis Down Under: Post-Enron Accounting Education and Research Inertia," *European Accounting Review* 14:2, 383–394.
Pogge T.W. (1992). "Cosmopolitanism and Sovereignty," *Ethics* 103:1, 48–75.
Ponemon, L.A. (1990). "Ethical Judgments in Accounting: A Cognitive-developmental Perspective," *Critical Perspectives on Accounting* 1:2, 191–215.
Ponemon, L.A. (1992). "Ethical Reasoning and Selection-Socialization in Accounting," *Accounting, Organizations and Society* 17:3/4, 239–258.
Posner, M. (2016). "Business & Human Rights: A Commentary from the Inside," *Accounting, Auditing and Accountability Journal* 29:4, 705–711.
Power, M. (1991). "Educating Accountants: Towards a Critical Ethnography." *Accounting, Organizations and Society* 16:4, 333–353.
Power, M. (1997). *The Audit Society*. Oxford: Oxford University Press.

Primeaux, P. and J. Steiber (1994). "Profit Maximization: The Ethical Mandate of Business," *Journal of Business Ethics* 13, 287–94.

Reiter, S.A. (1996). "The Kohlberg–Gilligan Controversy: Lessons for Accounting Ethics Education," *Critical Perspectives on Accounting* 7:1, 33–54.

Roberts, R.W. (2001). "Commercialism and Its Impact on the Integrity of Professional Tax Services in the United States," *Critical Perspectives on Accounting* 12, 589–605.

Robson, K., H. Willmott, D. Cooper and T. Puxty (1994). "The Ideology of Professional Regulation and the Markets for Accounting Labour: Three Episodes in the Recent History of the U.K. Accountancy Profession," *Accounting, Organizations and Society* 19:6, 527–553.

Ruggie, J. (2008). "Protect, Respect and Remedy," *Report of the Special Representative of the Secretary-General on the Issue of Human Rights and Transnational Corporations and other Business Enterprises*. Available at: https://business-humanrights.org/sites/default/files/reports-and-materials/Ruggie-report-7-Apr-2008.pdf [accessed 17 April 2017].

Ruggie, J. (2011). "Guiding Principles on Business and Human Rights: Implementing the United Nations 'Protect, Respect and Remedy' Framework," *Report of the Special Representative of the Secretary-General on the Issue of Human Rights and Transnational Corporations and other Business Enterprises*. Available at: www.ohchr.org/documents/issues/business/A.HRC.17.31.pdf [accessed 17 April 2017].

Schlachter, P.J. (1990). "Organizational Influences on Individual Ethical Behavior in Public Accounting," *Journal of Business Ethics* 9, 839–853.

Schulte, A.A. (1966). "Management Services: A Challenge to Audit Independence?" *The Accounting Review* October, 721–728.

Schweiker, W. (1993). "Accounting for Ourselves: Accounting Practice and the Discourse of Ethics," *Accounting, Organizations and Society* 18:2/3, 231–252.

Shift (2012). "Human Rights Reporting and Assurance Frameworks Initiative—RAFI." Available at: www.shiftproject.org/project/human-rights-reporting-and-assurance-frameworks-initiative-rafi [accessed 17 April 2017].

Sikka, P. (2008) "Enterprise Culture and Accountancy Firms: New Masters of the Universe," *Accounting, Auditing & Accountability Journal* 21:2, 268–295.

Sikka, P. (2011). "Accounting for Human Rights: The Challenge of Globalization and Foreign Investment Agreements." *Critical Perspectives on Accounting* 22:8, 811–827.

Sikka, P. and H. Willmott (1995). "The Power of 'Independence': Defending and Extending the Jurisdiction of Accounting in the United Kingdom," *Accounting, Organizations and Society* 20:6, 547–581.

Sikka, P., H. Willmott and T. Lowe (1989). "Guardians of Knowledge and Public Interest: Evidence and Issues of Accountability in the UK Accountancy Profession," *Accounting, Auditing & Accountability Journal* 2:2, 47–71.

Sims, R.R. and J. Brinkmann (2003). "Enron Ethics (or: Culture Matters More than Codes)," *Journal of Business Ethics* 45:3, 243–256.

Smith, A. and E.C. Hume (2005). "Linking Culture and Ethics: A Comparison of Accountants' Ethical Belief Systems in the Individualism/Collectivism and Power Distance Contexts" *Journal of Business Ethics* 62:3, 209–220.

Soll, J. (2014). *Financial Accountability and The Making and Breaking of Nations*. Harmondsworth, UK: Penguin.

Stanga, K.G. and R.A. Turpen (1991). "Ethical Judgments on Selected Accounting Issues: An Empirical Study," *Journal of Business Ethics* 10, 739–747.

Suddaby, R., Y. Gendron and H. Lam (2009). "The Organizational Context of Professionalism in Accounting," *Accounting Organizations and Society* 34:3–4, 409–427.

Taylor, M.B. (2011). "The Ruggie Framework: Polycentric Regulation and the Implications for Corporate Social Responsibility," *Etikk I praksis: Nordic Journal of Applied Ethics* 5:1, 9–30.

UN Human Rights Council (2011). "Guiding Principles on Business and Human Rights: Implementing the United Nations 'Protect, Respect and Remedy' Framework," A/HRC/17/31. Available at: www.ohchr.org/documents/issues/business/A.HRC.17.31.pdf [accessed November 08 2017].

Unilever (2015). "Human Rights Report: Enhancing Livelihoods, Advancing Human Rights." Available at: www.unilever.com/Images/unilever-human-rights-report-2015_tcm244-437226_en.pdf [accessed 17 April 2017].

Vandenhole, W. (2012). "Emerging Normative Frameworks on Transnational Human Rights Obligations," European University Institute Working Paper RSCAS 2012/17 ISSN 1028-3625.

Walker S. (1988). *The Society of Accountants in Edinburgh, 1854–1914: A Study of Recruitment to a New Profession*. New York, NY: Garland Publishing.

Walker, S.P. (1991). "The Defense of Professional Monopoly: Scottish Chartered Accountants and 'Satallites in the Accounting Firmament' 1854–1914," *Accounting Organizations and Society* 16:3, 257–283.

Williams, P.F. (2004). "Recovering Accounting as a Worthy Endeavor," *Critical Perspectives on Accounting* 15:4/5, 513–517.

Williams, P.F. (1987). "The Legitimate Concern with Fairness," *Accounting, Organizations and Society* 12:2, 169–189.

Willmott, H. (1986). "Organizing the Profession: A Theoretical and Historical Examination of the Development of the Major Accountancy Bodies in the UK," *Accounting Organizations and Society* 22:8, 831–842.

Willmott, H. and P. Sikka (1997). "On the Commercialization of Accountancy Thesis: A Review Essay," *Accounting, Organizations and Society* 22:8, 831–842.

Zeff, S.A. (1989). "Recent Trends in Accounting Education and Research in the USA: Some Implications for UK Academics," *The British Accounting Review* 21:2, 159–176.

Part VII
Multinational corporations and globalization

Introduction

Globalization involves the spread of commerce and trade among nations, the movement of peoples across borders, and the communication of ideas throughout the world. Many companies have been transformed from national to multinational corporations and even to transnational ones. Even before the trends of a globalized world economy became visible, the increasing presence and operation of corporations in more than one country—and, more often than not, in different cultures and political or legal systems—raised questions about whether the approaches to moral issues in management dominant in the West should be exported beyond Western borders. Does a globalized economic system demand a universal or globalized business ethics? Or should cultural or other differences require a contextual approach to business ethics? Should a manager of a corporation from Europe or North America adhere to Western notions of moral management? What if the conditions of conducting business involve the bribery of public officials?

In Chapter 32, **The globalization of business ethics**, **Kirk O. Hanson** illuminates how the study and practice of business ethics has turned into a global phenomenon in the last half century. Following on the globalization of markets and the rise of so-called global enterprises, both managers and academics felt the need for a kind of "global ethics" in theory and practice. Hanson traces the development of business ethics from its early origins, in the 1970s, in the United States, to its growth in business schools and corporations. In the following decades, business ethics gradually spread across the globe as a result of various factors: growing religious concerns, fighting apartheid and economic injustice, and the emerging social-investor movements, not to mention a growing academic interest in the field. An increasingly globalized economy proved to be the next catalyst for a globalized business ethics. Hanson proceeds to examine the theoretical and practical challenges involved in defining a globalized ethics program suitable for businesses operating worldwide.

In Chapter 33, **Cross-cultural management ethics in multinational commerce**, **Terence Jackson** introduces the subject of cross-cultural management ethics in multinational commerce. Summarizing prominent descriptive theories of values across cultures and nations, as well as their tentative steps toward a critique of supposedly universal or international management norms, he points out the conceptual and methodological limitations of these studies, the tacit value judgments hidden in their comparisons, as well as the dubious role played by the notion of "modernization." Jackson examines specific elements involved in shifting from a description of differences in values to the construction of a robust cross-cultural ethics that could effectively guide managers in how they *ought* to act when operating across national and cultural borders.

One of the most important recurring challenges when doing business across national borders is that of corruption, in particular whether a firm should bribe a public official if that is the condition for doing business. These concerns have been further magnified by contemporary economic globalization and the sheer size of multinational and translational corporations. In Chapter 34, **Corruption, bribery, and moral norms across national boundaries**, **Wesley Cragg** analyzes the two notions of corruption and bribery and their subtypes. Focusing on bribery as the salient species of corruption, he discusses definitions of bribery and specifies its typical features, including the negative effects that are morally blameworthy. Cragg examines bribery as a complex social, economic and political phenomenon in order to explain the widespread contradiction that, while bribery is considered wrong and punishable in one's country, it may be justified as excusable when doing business abroad—especially in less developed countries. Although legal measures are one way to combat this phenomenon, Cragg underlines in addition the roles of transparency and accountability and offers two key corporate reforms needed for this to succeed.

Byron Kaldis

32

The globalization of business ethics

Kirk O. Hanson

Between 1975 and 2015, the study and practice of business ethics became a truly global phenomenon. Its development paralleled the growth and integration of markets in both the developed and developing world. The study and practice of business ethics became global as markets became global.

During this same period, multinational firms from developed Western countries, and increasingly from developing countries, became "global enterprises." Global companies, operating in countries around the world, needed to meet the ethical expectations of their home countries, but also the ethical expectations of the growing number of countries in which they now operated. In developing countries, where oligarchies often controlled key elements of the economy, a new awareness of the costs of corruption and other questionable behaviors led to a growing demand for ethical behavior by local leaders in both business and civil society.

These developments led to a growing desire for what came to be known as "global ethics," a common global standard of behavior for businesses, for non-governmental organizations (NGOs), and for governments themselves. In addition to the search for a global ethic among intellectuals and managers, there was an explosion of organizations creating and promoting specific standards of global ethical business behavior. Companies were asked, and frequently pressured, to pledge to follow these multiple standards. At times, executives of these companies felt besieged by requests to provide detailed information on their operations in anticipation of or as a result of their decision to join these "voluntary" organizations.

Academic scholars followed these developments, chronicling the growing interest in global business ethics and making some significant contributions to its progress. But interest in and the study of business ethics had first emerged in the United States and in US graduate schools of business.

This chapter describes how the concept of business ethics emerged in the United States in the 1970s and 1980s, in business schools and then in corporate practice; how in the 1980s and 1990s the concept then spread beyond the United States to other parts of the world; how the globalization of the world economy changed the debate over business ethics; and how corporate programs to implement a global commitment to business ethics developed. The chapter ends with a discussion of the challenges faced in defining and implementing a commitment to global business ethics.

Kirk O. Hanson

Business ethics emerges in US business schools

Business ethics first emerged as a management concern and as an academic subject in the United States in the late 1970s. Two specific episodes drove this development, though the general context was the dramatic growth of global trade.

A significant number of American business leaders and their firms made illegal campaign contributions to the reelection of US President Richard Nixon in 1972. Simultaneously, the leaders of these increasingly multinational US enterprises made payments or bribes to politicians and government officials in numerous countries to win business. During the mid and late 1970s, over 100 major US companies admitted publicly that they had made the illegal campaign contributions and more than 200 admitted to bribery of foreign officials, which some euphemistically called "unusual payments abroad." The Lockheed Corporation's bribery of Japanese officials and Diet members to secure the sale of L1011 commercial aircraft to Al Nippon Airways was the iconic bribery case of the era, but was simply a well-documented example of a much broader problem.

The immediate impacts of these scandals were laws that imposed stronger penalties on companies and their leaders. United States legislation passed shortly after President Nixon's forced resignation from office restricted corporate political meddling (though subsequent court cases weakened the constraints). Cases of overseas bribery led to the adoption in 1978 of the US Foreign Corrupt Practices Act (FCPA), which made it explicitly illegal for a representative of a US company to bribe an official of a foreign government. Almost forty years later, the FCPA is still a major concern of American companies as they operate more and more outside the United States. Among most observers, the FCPA is regarded as an effective vehicle in the campaign against corruption (see, for example, Urofsky et al. 2012). Companies have major anti-bribery programs for their own employees, sometimes focusing on the special problems of doing business with state-owned enterprises whose managers fit FCPA definitions of public officials.

One impact of these two scandals was a call for an emphasis on business ethics in leading schools of business. How could respected US business leaders, some asked, have engaged in these behaviors? As many were graduates of the country's major business schools, attention focused first on the development of business school courses that could "teach" ethics to the next generation of business leaders. In the 1978–1980 period, the major United States business schools hired their first dedicated business ethics faculty. Harvard, Stanford and Wharton business schools created elective courses, and academic conferences on business ethics proliferated. Prior to 1978, a few academics had studied business ethics, but they tended to be located in Catholic, often Jesuit, colleges and universities.

Over the next 20 years, elective and then required courses on business ethics became the norm at most major American business schools, encouraged by accrediting standards that all but required such attention (AACSB 2013). Two professional associations of faculty emerged. The Social Issues Division of the Academy of Management, which had been launched in 1971 by business school professors, increasingly focused during the 1980s on business ethics as well as on the "social responsibility of business." The Society for Business Ethics, launched in 1980 by philosophy professors who studied the applied field of business ethics, grew gradually over the 1980s through the 2010s. After 2000, membership in the two associations increasingly overlapped and the organizations' professional meetings were held back-to-back in the city where the Academy of Management had held its annual national conference.

A focus on business ethics emerges in US corporations

Attention to business ethics in US corporations was generally limited to legal compliance with explicit laws and regulations such as the FCPA and with increasingly numerous consumer and clean air and water regulations adopted in the 1960s and 1970s. Only in 1983 did explicit corporate attention to business ethics emerge, first with a few top management seminars and then with ethics training for all employees at two defense firms: McDonnell Douglas pioneered company-wide training on ethics, followed quickly by General Dynamics in the aftermath of the emerging defense industry scandals of the mid-1980s.

The US defense industry scandals of the 1980s, in which virtually all twenty major defense contractors were found to be mischarging the Defense department for products and for research time, was instrumental in launching formal corporate attention to the management of corporate ethics. The scandal led to the formation of The President's Blue Ribbon Commission on Defense Management, headed by David Packard, then Hewlett-Packard CEO and a former Deputy Defense Secretary. On the day that the Commission issued its final report, GE CEO Jack Welch announced that twelve major defense contractors were forming the voluntary Defense Industry Initiative on Ethics and Compliance (DII) to establish standards for the management of ethical behavior and measure their progress toward that objective. This step was the beginning of expanded corporate attention to business ethics, initially in the defense industry and later in the financial services industry, engulfed by the first of several scandals in the late 1980s.

At this point, however, attention to business ethics was almost exclusively an American concern and was generally ignored by companies in other countries. Critics of the emphasis on ethics at the time said Americans were tying one hand behind their backs in competing internationally with European firms who did not hold to similar ethical standards. They argued that American firms would also lose out to local companies in many countries where corruption and payoffs were common. Predictions were that the American concern for business ethics would hinder the global economic success of US firms.

Academic research and publication developed several core concepts that undergirded the development of business ethics. Among the most widely studied were the "interpenetrating systems" model of business–government and business–society interaction developed by Lee E. Preston and James E. Post in 1975 (Preston and Post 1975). Wharton professors Thomas Donaldson and Thomas Dunfee expanded on existing notions of social contract theory to describe how global companies contracted with multiple countries and multiple stakeholders (Donaldson and Dunfee 1999). University of Virginia professor R. Edward Freeman and a succession of co-authors developed various versions of "stakeholder theory," which modeled forces influencing the firm's freedom to operate and encouraged the firm, either through governance or management, to take into account the interests of these forces or "stakeholders" (Freeman 1984; Freeman et al. 2010). In addition, University of California Berkeley professor David Vogel wrote a series of books employing political theory to explain how companies and society interacted and reached policy if not value consensus (Vogel 1995, 2005; Vogel and Ansell 2006).

Interest in business ethics beyond the United States

Interest in business ethics outside the United States was initially evident in religiously based circles. Beginning in 1892, Roman Catholic popes had issued what were known as social encyclicals or letters that addressed the moral issues in society, including how business operated. Pope Leo XIII issued the first of these encyclicals called *Rerum Novarum* (Leo XIII 1892). It focused in part on the rights of labor. In 1991, Pope John Paul II summarized a century of papal social teaching in Centesimus Annus (John Paul II 1991). And in 2013 and 2015, Pope Francis promulgated the most extensive papal commentary on global business behavior in two documents, an apostolic exhortation *Evangelii Gaudium* (Francis 2013) and his encyclical *Laudato Si*, the first papal document to address moral responsibility for the environment (Francis 2015).

Since the mid twentieth century, Christian (particularly Catholic) associations of businessmen held conferences and pledged adherence to religious values embodied in the Christian gospels and in Catholic social teaching embodied in the social encyclicals. One of these associations, the International Christian Union of Business Executives, known as UNIAPAC, was created in 1931 and has championed intellectual and practical inquiries into how business activity can serve the common good. In the United Kingdom, in the 1970s, the Institute for Business Ethics, which grew from a religious movement known as Moral Rearmament, campaigned for higher standards of business behavior and assisted companies that wanted to adopt business ethics programs.

In the 1980s, the teaching of business ethics by major American business schools also led major European business schools, particularly London Business School, INSEAD in Fontainebleau and IMEDE in Lausanne, Switzerland, to consider incorporating business ethics into their curricula. By the 1990s, the accrediting body for business schools, the American Association of Collegiate Schools of Business, adopted its first accrediting standard that required some attention to business ethics (AACSB 2013). This led business schools worldwide, seeking to emulate American business education, to take notice and launch attempts to integrate business ethics into their curricula. The 2013 Standards, the latest adopted by AACSB, require attention to ethical reasoning but do not specify how the topic is to be addressed, whether in a separate course or integrated into other courses. Some critics believe the AACSB standards should be more explicit about the attention to ethics required in a business or management program (see, for example, Swanson and Fisher 2011, and Franks and Spalding 2013)

In the 1980s, a small group of European academics created the European Business Ethics Network and began holding an annual conference. Nationally based networks also sprang up, notably the Italian Business Ethics Network that was particularly active. Academics in the US and Europe formed the International Society of Business, Ethics and Economics (ISBEE), which holds a world congress every four years. In 1990, a group of younger academics from Europe and the United States formed the International Association for Business and Society (IABS), which meets in alternate years in Europe and the United States.

There had been, for several decades in the mid-twentieth century, a concern for the behavior of multi-national companies (MNCs). This concern increased significantly after World War II as many companies developed more international trade, often with their former colonies. However, these companies were accurately described as transnational or multi-national rather than global. They might source raw materials in one country to supply manufacturing and consumption in a home market. They might expand their sales effort to one or more neighboring countries, but were not yet engaged in what we now call "global trade." The MNCs often dwarfed the governments of countries they sourced from or operated in and therefore could force or bribe officials in those countries to permit the MNCs to operate with few constraints. These companies frequently paid little attention to ethics or to the interests of the host countries. Professor Raymond Vernon of the Harvard Business School was one of few who wrote extensively on the power and responsibility of MNCs (Vernon 1977).

The global attention to corruption and bribery in the late 1970s changed the discussion significantly, leading to the FCPA in the United States, and to a growing pressure in some countries, to root out corruption, particularly among government officials. In the 1980s, the Organization for Economic Cooperation and Development (OECD), composed of leading developed nations, adopted a code of corporate behavior that was enhanced several times over succeeding years. Its strongest statement about corporate bribery was adopted in 1997 in the *Convention on Combating Bribery of Foreign Public Officials in International Business Transactions* (OECD 1997). In 1993, Transparency International, a Berlin-based NGO, was founded to create locally-based associations in many countries dedicated to reducing business corruption.

Two other developments in the 1970s and 1980s hastened the global spread of concern for business ethics. One was the persistence of the apartheid regime in South Africa, which by law restricted the work, residential, and citizenship rights of black and colored (mixed race) people. While activist pressure was particularly focused on US companies operating in South Africa, urging them to challenge and disobey the government's racial exclusion laws, pressure was also applied to European companies operating there. Led by a charismatic US Baptist minister Leon Sullivan, who served on the board of directors of General Motors, the Sullivan Principles movement was created and pressured companies to follow a set of equal working rights principles—or leave South Africa. When General Motors was stopped by the Apartheid government from following the Sullivan Principles, the company sold its South African operations to its local managers and departed. Other companies, including Hewlett-Packard, departed when government and private buyers of computers in the United States declared that any company that still operated in South Africa was ineligible to bid on large computer contracts.

The other development was the growing social investor movement in the United States. Activists acquired shares in companies in order to present shareholder resolutions requesting or demanding changes in corporate behavior. In 1970 an organization called "Campaign GM" submitted what is considered the first "social proxy resolution" to the shareholders of the world's largest corporation, General Motors. The resolutions in 1970 and 1971 demanded the appointment of minority and consumer representatives to the board of directors, and attention to vehicle safety and environmental impacts. These resolutions, like most social resolutions to other companies that followed in the 1970s through 1990s, failed to win more than a token vote, but occasionally led to voluntary action by companies to implement ethical and social initiatives articulated in the resolutions. For example, General Motors, presented with a resolution to add racial minorities to its board, elected Rev. Leon Sullivan, an African American, and he subsequently launched the Sullivan Principles that General Motors endorsed.

All of these developments—the spread of business ethics courses in American and European business schools, the debate over fundamental human rights in South Africa, increasing attention to the problem of corruption and bribery, the emerging social investment movement, and the growth of nonprofit global organizations interested in business ethics—made the ethical behavior of businesses outside the United States a topic of growing concern.

Globalization becomes an economic reality

During the 1980s and 1990s it became apparent how truly global business had become. By 2005, when Thomas Friedman's *The World is Flat* was published, global trade had increased dramatically from the end of World War II (Friedman 2005). By one index, global trade multiplied more than 25 times in real dollars from 1950 to 2005, and by 33 times by the economic crisis of 2008 (Ortiz-Ospina and Roser 2017). Large and even medium-sized and small companies had supply chains that reached across the globe to manufacturing firms in China, Pakistan, and Vietnam. For a time Japanese companies and manufacturing reigned supreme, and economists were touting the success of the "four tigers" (South Korea, Taiwan, Singapore, and Hong Kong) that were building global enterprises that served the world, and set their countries on the path of rapid development.

As globalization spread rapidly during the 1980–2010 period, so also did concerns for the ethics of these increasingly powerful entities called "global corporations." The business and popular press published thousands of articles about the behavior of corporations, particularly in less developed countries.

The growing concern for the ethical behavior of global corporations led a growing number of NGOs to follow the example set by the Sullivan Principles organization and prepare a set of principles or standards of conduct that they promoted, pressuring global corporations to sign on to these regimes or be embarrassed for not doing so. Among these were the McBride Principles on corporate operations in Northern Ireland during the "troubles" between Catholics and Protestants (see McManus 2001), as well as the conflict minerals campaign, aimed at restricting corporate purchase of minerals from warring parties in conflict zones, thereby funding the conflicts. Many NGOs were active in this campaign and, in the United States, the 2010 Dodd-Frank Act required corporate reports on the use of conflict minerals.

Perhaps the most powerful of these social movements for global ethical practice was the campaign for "responsible" supply chains. Touched off by a growing unease about the conditions under which workers made many of the products marketed in the developed world, multiple campaigns promoted standards of behavior for workplace practices, human rights, and environmental management. Impelled by the voluntary adoption of supply chain standards by Levi Strauss & Co in 1991 and by criticism of the practices of Nike Corporation, by the first decade of the new millennium, the movement had assisted in bringing about detailed standards of behavior and extensive auditing regimes (see Berliner et al. 2015).

While much progress has arguably been made in policing the working conditions and environmental impacts of global supply chains, criticisms continue to be heard. In 2013 the collapse of a poorly designed and maintained multistory building at Rana Plaza in Dhaka, Bangladesh, killed more than 1,000 workers, many producing goods for American companies and the American market. In 2014, Apple was heavily criticized for conditions in factories in China run by Foxconn, the world's largest contract manufacturer. Critics cited worker suicides, which they claimed were due to the oppressive conditions in FoxConn's facilities. By 2017, most global corporations had adopted supply chain standards and spent substantial sums policing their independent supply chains and conducting independent audits to convince the public that workers and the environment were well treated.

In 1999 UN General Secretary Kofi Annan delivered a speech at the World Economic Forum in Davos calling for companies to adopt sustainable and socially responsible policies and report on their implementation. In 2000 Annan's speech led the United Nations to establish the Global Compact to promote a code of nine principles for responsible corporate behavior (see United Nations 2017). Like many other moderates, Annan believed the benefits of global trade were threatened if corporate behavior outraged groups around the world and corporations acted as if they were above or outside the law. The Global Compact Principles, which later grew to ten with the addition of an anti-corruption principle, were promoted to businesses worldwide. Interestingly, the Global Compact, which at first did not require an audit of a company's behavior, spread rapidly in all parts of the world except the United States. United States companies were wary of incurring legal obligations by becoming signatories, though that concern faded over time. In its first ten years, the Global Compact came to require annual reports and a modest form of auditing, and disqualified hundreds of companies from membership when they did not adopt these practices. Perhaps most importantly, the Global Compact organization conducted conferences on best practices in many areas of corporate operations and ethical behavior.

The growth of corporate global ethics programs

The development of the first corporate ethics programs in the wake of the defense industry scandals of the mid 1980s led to the development of a class of corporate managers charged with managing these programs. Dubbed "ethics officers," these managers were drawn from diverse backgrounds in human resources, organizational development, and law. Some companies, uncertain what the real responsibilities of these managers were, turned to outsiders from nonprofit or even religious backgrounds to implement these programs.

In 1991 a group of corporate ethics officers, who had met at meetings organized by the Defense Industry Initiative on Business Ethics and Conduct and by Bentley College's Center for Business Ethics, created the Ethics Officers Association to be their professional society. Initially housed at Bentley, the society became fully independent and was located until 2016 in the Boston area.

The appointment of ethics officers by large corporations was accelerated by the 1991 adoption of the US Sentencing Guidelines, a set of standards by which judges sentence individuals and organizations convicted of federal crimes, including violation of the many regulatory standards governing corporate behavior. These guidelines, notably, gave "credit" to companies who, though now convicted of federal crimes, had earlier implemented ethics programs. Not surprisingly, companies rushed to establish ethics programs led by ethics officers, thereby satisfying the language of the Sentencing Guidelines.

Between 1991 and 2016 the language of the Sentencing Guidelines (US Sentencing Commission 2017) became more and more explicit regarding what was considered an adequate corporate ethics program. Initial emphasis on having a code of conduct and conducting annual employee training was expanded to include emphasis on anonymous reporting systems for employees to report misbehavior, prompt and thorough investigation of complaints, top management support for ethics, the development of a culture that encouraged ethical behavior, and oversight of the company's "ethics system" by the board of directors. A parallel effort by the Department of Justice to give guidance to prosecutors deciding whether to bring charges against corporate entities stipulated that leniency could be granted if a company had an effective ethics program. The latest version, authored by Deputy Attorney General Sally Yates, was released in 2015 (Yates 2015). Given these two incentives, corporate general counsels encouraged their firms to create ethics programs to meet the standards of both documents.

Unfortunately, a legal mindset developed in many corporations that the ethics program was aimed primarily at compliance with laws and regulations not at a broader but less defined standard of "business ethics." Many corporate programs became "check the boxes" exercises more than an effort to create a truly effective program for motivating ethical behavior. When such programs did focus on behavior, the concerns were frequently limited to compliance and not with the broader concept. In 2005 the Ethics Officers Association, recognizing that their membership had become increasingly dominated by lawyers, renamed itself the Ethics and Compliance Officers Association. A second professional society, the Society for Corporate Compliance and Ethics, which catered initially to small and mid-sized firms and to compliance officers in government, universities, and other types of organizations, was even more compliance oriented.

While US-based companies implemented ethics programs to meet the expectations of the US legal system and its public, they also became increasingly concerned about how compliance and ethics was managed in their operations outside the US. There were two primary reasons for this increasing emphasis. First, an increasing number of US laws and regulations were applied "extraterritorially" to operations outside the US borders. An employee of a US firm located in Asia or Africa might engage in bribery that violated the domestic FCPA. The manipulation of financial accounts in a small division in another country could be prosecuted in the US as if it had occurred at the US headquarters. The second reason was that an increasing number of foreign countries had begun to adopt and enforce laws similar to some in the US, particularly in the fields of bribery and corruption. Most notably, the United Kingdom in 2010 adopted the Anti-Bribery Act, which made any firm that operated in the UK liable for bribery that occurred anywhere in the world. The extraterritorial reach of the UK anti-bribery law was even more extensive than the US FCPA.

Efforts by US corporations to spread their own codes of conduct globally began feebly, often by shipping copies of the ethics code (frequently only in English) to country managers with written instructions to implement the codes. When this proved insufficient, companies tried other techniques, such as bringing foreign managers to the US for training in how to present the corporation's ethics commitments in the managers' own countries. Eventually, companies began to translate their codes into local languages. When ethical scandals persisted abroad, many companies adopted a "best practice" of having a lawyer or ethics officer from the US visit every international operation annually to conduct standardized training at least for the senior management team. Violations often persisted, and some questioned the ability of a US-based official to communicate effectively the values and standards by which the local operation with a different culture is to function. A few pioneering experiments are being conducted in 2017 to produce training programs that are both culturally sensitive to each national setting, and can be delivered by local managers with more credibility than a US-based traveling manager. One of these experiments, initiated by a Silicon Valley high tech company, combines insights from Chinese and Western ethical theory to present the company's commitment to ethical behavior.

In general, non-US global firms have lagged in developing management systems for ethical behavior. However, as more non-US firms set up sizable US operations, they have been exposed to how US firms have proceeded and are bound themselves by the standards of the US Sentencing Guidelines. Notable scandals involving non-US global firms, including a major bribery scandal involving the German firm Siemens, and illegal marketing practices of several European pharmaceutical firms, have led to growing interest among such firms in "best practices" in managing ethics (see, for example, Watson 2013 and Barboza 2016).

Defining a global ethic for business: challenges

One of the major barriers to the further development of global business ethics has been a lack of agreement on what ethical standards should be observed worldwide. Do the same standards of ethical behavior hold everywhere in the world? Also, more practically for companies, do we operate by a single global ethical standard, or do we adapt policies to local markets?

One approach focuses chiefly if not wholly on compliance: a company's "ethical" standards are determined explicitly by the laws and regulations the firm is obliged to follow; these would include both those of the corporation's home country and those set forth by any government entity in which the corporation operates. This approach, which uses the concept of *ethics* less frequently than that of *compliance*, has considerable attraction for companies that find it difficult to define the concept of ethics, particularly global ethics. But the emphasis on compliance can lead to problems, especially when employees and managers interpret this focus as encouragement to meet legal requirements but nothing more. In some companies, this approach has led employees or managers to interpret the company's wish to be, "don't get caught violating the law."

A second approach has been to emphasize the "traditional values" of the company from its history and seek to implement those consistently throughout its operations. This approach seeks to ground the company's global ethics in the company's traditions, which themselves may be reflective of the corporation's home country. A third approach is to have a minimum set of global standards and let the local country managers interpret what the local cultural and business standards require. This "local adaptation" approach has backfired in some countries as local managers game the system to justify almost any practice.

Since the early 1980s there has been a substantial body of intellectual and academic work directed at defining what standards a company ought to follow and what might constitute a global business ethic that could be said to apply to all firms. As noted earlier, the problem is that different cultures define ethics in different ways. The diversity of religious traditions and teachings also make the definition of a single global ethic difficult. In 1996 Thomas Donaldson published an essay in the *Harvard Business Review* entitled "Values in Tension: Ethics Away from Home," arguing for a core of universal ethical values, plus a zone of "moral free space" or discretion where local cultural norms could be accommodated (Donaldson 1996). A substantial body of writings by academics, corporate executives, and NGO leaders on specific types of global corporate behavior have appeared since the 1990s. David Vogel, for example, has published analyses of consumer and environmental regulation in the global economy (Vogel 1995) and essays on food safety regulation in European countries (Vogel and Ansell 2006). Others have addressed such areas as human rights, supply chain, product safety, environmental sustainability, and relationships with governments.

The search for a single definition of global ethics began immediately after World War II. In 1948, the United Nations, traumatized by the inhumanity witnessed during the war, sought to define universally recognized human rights as one of its first priorities. A commission chaired by former US First Lady Eleanor Roosevelt produced the UN Universal Declaration of Human Rights (United Nations 1948). This document has had an outsized impact on all future discussion of global ethics. The document emphasizes so-called negative rights, that is the right to be left alone and not oppressed, but it also mentions positive rights such as education, health care, and economic security. Admittedly, these were more an aspiration than a real possibility when the declaration was first adopted. The principles and concepts in this document have been the most important and influential in the past 70 years. Succeeding United Nations documents have been designed to extend and implement the concepts in the Declaration. An extensive body of what is now called "international law" is built on the Declaration.

As noted earlier, individual religions had spoken on ethical standards with the intent that they be applicable to all, not just to the religion's adherents. Attempts at an interfaith religious dialogue to define a single global ethic have occurred intermittently over the past 125 years. In 1893, the first Parliament of World Religions met at the Chicago World's Fair and set a goal to encourage a dialogue among religions toward the betterment of the world. In 1993, the Parliament met for a second time, considered and adopted a declaration "Toward a Global Ethics," primarily authored by Professor Hans Küng, a Roman Catholic theologian and ethicist (Parliament of World Religions 1993). Küng has continued to champion an interfaith global ethic through his Global Ethic Foundation. Among the successor documents is the proposed *Universal Declaration of Human Responsibility*, again authored primarily by Küng, and adopted and promoted by the InterAction Council, a global assembly of former heads of state and government (InterAction Council 1997).

As noted earlier, UN General Secretary Kofi Annan launched the Global Compact in 1999 to encourage companies to adopt a common set of ethics principles. Within the UN, the topic of corporate behavior became the concern of many branches and initiatives. Among the most important was an effort by the UN High Commissioner for Human Rights to define business's role in helping governments to "respect, protect and fulfill human rights and fundamental freedom" of its citizens. The inquiry produced the *Guiding Principles on Business and Human Rights* (United Nations 2011). Known as the Ruggie Principles after its principle author, UN Special Representative John Ruggie, the principles call for governments to prevent companies from violating the human rights of citizens, and for companies themselves to respect the human rights of all whose lives they impact.

We have identified two significant barriers to the further development of a global ethics commitment by companies. The first is the difficulty in defining what behavior global ethics requires of companies. Is there a single global ethic or just a series of local ethics? The second barrier is the strong practical tendency to default to compliance with multiple laws and regulations rather than adopt a broader standard of ethical behavior.

The development of a global business ethics will continue, but its advocates will have to contend with these and several other practical barriers to its evolution. Among them are:

1. *An exclusive belief in free markets and the profit motive.* The advocates of a global business ethics must contend with a strong ideological belief among some that markets and companies that operate in them should be free from regulation and constraints. By an "invisible hand," the most beneficial outcome will result from the pursuit of self-interest. For those with such beliefs, the adoption of ethical standards is sometimes abhorrent. It diverts the proper functioning of the market system and can run the risk that the unrepresentative ethical views of some wealthy industrialists may have undue influence. Other advocates of free markets, however, embrace a minimum standard of ethics that eschews deceptive transactions.
2. *A willingness in some countries to permit the exploitation of workers or the natural environment, perhaps coupled with an unwillingness to adopt or to enforce consistently (and impartially) protective laws and regulations.* Not all countries are run by benevolent leaders, and some permit or even encourage exploitation by local and global businesses. In some of these countries, there is little "rule of law." In others, payoffs to the governmental leaders can even create the legal authority to engage in unethical practices, for all business people or for selected elites. These can be difficult places for ethical companies to operate.
3. *Competition from global and local enterprises less committed to ethical practice.* Whereas an increasing number of global ethics standards are being embodied in US and UK law, there are still many global enterprises willing to engage in corruption and exploit workers and the environment in ways that violate local laws and global ethics standards. Competing against these enterprises can be difficult. Global companies argue for a "level playing field" either by loosening the ethics standards they must follow, or by finding ways to impose ethics standards on other companies.
4. *A persistent belief in some parts of the developing world that the campaign for ethical behavior in business is an imperialist campaign by the West.* Because attention to business ethics developed first in the United States and then in Europe, some leaders in the developing world believe an emphasis on ethics is a Western notion only. Resistance to global business ethics standards in developing countries often invokes this argument. However, as the ethical foundations of Islam, Confucianism, and other belief systems are studied and applied to commercial interaction so do many in developing societies recognize the "cost" of corruption, thereby weakening some of the initial resistance.
5. *Practical problems implementing a single corporate standard of ethics in a dispersed global corporation.* Global companies have not yet solved the problems of communicating ethical commitments effectively, holding employees and managers to account for their ethical performance, and, more difficult yet, defining the sorts of conduct that are to be valued and those that are to be discouraged or prohibited. While some progress has been made, innovation in leadership and control systems is still badly needed.

Concluding remarks

The enterprise of global business ethics, stimulated by the dramatic growth of global trade since 1950, has made significant inroads into the practice of global management and to the teaching of business management world-wide. Colleges in India, Kenya, and Columbia have joined those in the United States and Europe in adding courses on business ethics. Even companies with little international engagement are confronting the challenges of global business ethics as they deal with companies who do trade globally.

The success of the global business ethics effort depends on three developments. They are progress in clarifying global standards of ethics, the development of effective management systems to implement ethics commitments, and strengthening the willingness of corporate executive teams and boards to make ethics a priority.

This last factor, as of 2017, is the most troubling. There is evidence that the management of even the largest global enterprises may be willing to put aside concern for ethics when profits beckon. Three contemporary examples are particularly discouraging. The management of Volkswagen, a distinguished and successful German company, created and deployed a "defeat device" in its small diesel engines to falsify results on emissions tests conducted in the United States, and possibly in Europe. The American financial firm Wells Fargo Bank created an incentive program so manipulative that over 5,000 sales employees created fake customer accounts, often costing other customers hundreds and even thousands of dollars. Even more distressing, senior Wells Fargo executives and board members did not intervene for several years despite reports of widespread misbehavior. Finally, Takata, producer of the air bags used in most American-made automobiles, delayed revealing dangerous flaws in their product for months and even years. In a portion of air-bag deployments, the Takata product sprayed metal fragments that injured or even killed occupants. It is even alleged that some American car executives knew about the defect and failed to act to protect their customers. In each case, these scandals will cost the companies millions and even billions of dollars, damaging their reputations for years to come. The global business ethics enterprise does indeed have work to do.

Essential reading

There are several conceptual treatments of global business ethics as mentioned in this chapter. However, there is no single comprehensive treatment of best practices in the corporate implementation of global business ethics, though the reader will find dozens of short articles by consultants and commentators on the topic. Other essential documents of global business ethics include the codes of conduct outlined in the United Nations *Global Compact Principles* (United Nations 2017) and the United Nations *Guiding Principles on Business and Human Rights* (United Nations 2011). The writings of Pope Francis, particularly in his encyclical *Laudato Si* (2015), include the most extensive religious treatment of the obligations of business toward employees, customers, and the environment. For the reader who would like to explore the historical themes in this chapter in greater depth, there are three books worth consulting. William Sullivan and Will Kymlicka have edited *The Globalization of Ethics: Religious and Secular Perspectives* (2007). Frederick Bird and coauthors have produced *The Practices of Global Ethics: Historical Backgrounds, Current Issues and Future Prospects* (2016). Chronicling the history of corporate social responsibility and business ethics from an American experience, Kenneth Goodpaster and colleagues have written *Corporate Responsibility: The American Experience* (2012).

For further reading in this volume on the history of business ethics, see Chapter 1, The history of business ethics and Chapter 3, Theory and method in business ethics. On the prospects for a business ethics reflective of traditions of non-Western cultures and regions, see the chapters in Part VIII that focus on business ethics in China (Chapter 35), South Asia (Chapter 36), and Africa (Chapter 37). On the work of religious groups in civil society, see the discussion in Chapter 38, Business ethics in Latin America. On the spread of Western business ethics to nations that were once communist, see Chapter 39, Business ethics in transition: communism to commerce in Central Europe and Russia. On the work of global organizations to combat corruption and bribery, see Chapter 34, Corruption, bribery, and moral norms across national boundaries. For an examination of the Brundtland Report (United Nations) and its recommendations for a global policy on sustainability, see Chapter 22, Business, nature, and environmental sustainability. On developments in accounting and international human rights, see Chapter 31, The accounting profession, the public interest, and human rights. On the subject of norms across national boundaries, see Chapter 33, Cross-cultural management ethics in multinational commerce. On leadership and diverse groups, see Chapter 25, Leadership and business ethics. On ethics programs within the corporation (with a focus on the US) see Chapter 27, The ethics of managers and employees. On the nature of exploitation in labor relationships, see Chapter 29, Exploitation and labor.

References

AACSB (2013). *AACSB Accreditation Standards*. Available at: www.aacsb.edu/accreditation/standards [accessed 20 March 2017].

Barboza, D. (2016). "Drug Giant Faced a Reckoning as China Took Aim at Bribery," *New York Times*, November 1. Available at: www.nytimes.com/2016/11/02/business/international/china-rules-glaxo-bribes-sex-tape-whistleblower-cautionary-tale.html [accessed 24 April 2017].

Berliner, D., A.R. Greenleaf, M. Lake, M. Levi and J. Noveck (2015). *Labor Standards in International Supply Chains: Aligning Rights and Incentives*. Cheltenham, UK: Edward Elgar.

Bird, F., S. Twiss, K. Pedersen, C. Miller and B. Grelle (2016). *The Practices of Global Ethics: Historical Backgrounds, Current Issues and Future Prospects*. Edinburgh: Edinburgh University Press.

DeGeorge, R. (2010). *Business Ethics*, 7th edition. Englewood Cliffs, NJ: Prentice Hall.

Donaldson, T. (1996). "Values in Tension: Ethics Away from Home," in *Harvard Business Review*, Sept-Oct, 48–62.

Donaldson, T. and T. Dunfee (1999). *Ties That Bind: A Social Contracts Approach to Business Ethics*. Boston, MA: Harvard Business School Press.

Francis, Pope (2013). *Evangelii Gaudium*. Vatican: Holy See. Available at: http://w2.vatican.va/content/vatican/en.html [accessed 20 March 2017].

Francis, Pope (2015). *Laudato Si*. Vatican: Holy See. Available at: http://w2.vatican.va/content/vatican/en.html [accessed 20 March 2017].

Franks, R. and A. Spalding (2013). "Business Ethics as an Accreditation Requirement: A Knowledge Mapping Approach," *Business Education & Accreditation* 5:1, 17–30.

Freeman, R.E. (1984). *Strategic Management: A Stakeholder Approach*, reprinted in 2010. New York, NY: Cambridge University Press.

Freeman, R.E., J.S. Harrison, A.C. Wicks, B.L. Pamar and S. de Colle (2010). *Stakeholder Theory: The State of the Art*. New York, NY: Cambridge University Press.

Friedman, T. (2005). *The World is Flat: A Brief History of the Twenty-First Century*. New York, NY: Farrar, Straus and Giroux.

Goodpaster, K., A. Carroll, K. Lipartito, J. Post and P. Werhane (2012). *Corporate Responsibility: The American Experience*. Cambridge: Cambridge University Press.

Hartman, L. and J. DesJardins (2014). *Business Ethics: Decision Making for Personal Integrity and Social Responsibility*. New York, NY: McGraw Hill Irwin.

InterAction Council (1997). *A Universal Declaration of Human Responsibilities*. Available at: http://interactioncouncil.org/universal-declaration-human-responsibilities [accessed 20 March 2017].

John Paul II (1991). *Centesimus Annus*. Vatican: Holy See. Available at: http://w2.vatican.va/content/vatican/en.html [accessed 20 March 2017].

Leo XIII (1892). *Rerum Novarum*. Vatican: Holy See. Available at: http://w2.vatican.va/content/vatican/en.html [accessed 20 March 2017].

McManus, S. (2001). "The MacBride Principles: The Essence," *Irish National Caucus*. Available at: www.irishnationalcaucus.org/principle/the-macbride-principles-the-essence/ [accessed 24 April 2017].

OECD (1997). *Convention on Combating Bribery of Foreign Public Officials in International Business Transactions.* Available at: www.oecd.org/corruption/oecdantibriberyconvention.htm [accessed 20 March 2017].

Ortiz-Ospina, E. and M. Roser (2017). "International Trade," on *Our World in Data* website. Available at: https://ourworldindata.org/international-trade [accessed 20 March 2017].

Parliament of World Religions (1993). *Toward a Global Ethic.* Chicago, IL: Parliament of World Religions. Available at: https://parliamentofreligions.org/content/toward-global-ethic-initial-declaration [accessed 20 March 2017].

Preston, L.E. and J.E. Post (1975). *Private Management and Public Policy: The Principle of Public Responsibility*, republished in 2013. Stanford, CA: Stanford University Press.

Sullivan, W. and W. Kymlicka (2007). *The Globalization of Ethics: Religious and Secular Perspectives.* Cambridge: Cambridge University Press.

Swanson, D. and D. Fisher (eds) (2011). *Toward Assessing Business Ethics Education.* Charlotte, NC: Information Age Publishing.

United Nations (1948). *Universal Declaration of Human Rights.* Available at: www.un.org/en/universal-declaration-human-rights/ [accessed 20 March 2017].

United Nations (2011). *Guiding Principles on Business and Human Rights.* Available at: www.ohchr.org/Documents/Publications/GuidingPrinciplesBusinessHR_EN.pdf [accessed 20 March 2017].

United Nations (2017). *Global Compact Principles.* Available at: www.unglobalcompact.org/what-is-gc/mission/principles [accessed 20 March 2017] (first published in 2000).

United States Sentencing Commission (2017). *U.S. Sentencing Guidelines.* Washington, DC. Available at: www.ussc.gov/guidelines [accessed 24 April 2017].

Urofsky, P., H. Moon and J. Rimm (2012). "How Should We Measure the Effectiveness of the Foreign Corrupt Practices Act," *Ohio State Law Journal* 73:5, 1145–1179.

Velasquez, M. (2011). *Business Ethics: Concepts and Cases*, 7th edition. Englewood Cliffs, NJ: Prentice Hall.

Vernon, R. (1977). *Storm Over the Multinationals: The Real Issues.* Boston, MA: Harvard University Press.

Vogel, D. (1995). *Consumer and Environmental Regulation in the Global Economy.* Boston, MA: Harvard University Press.

Vogel, D. (2005). *The Market for Virtue: The Potential and Limits of Corporate Social Responsibility.* Washington, DC: Brookings Institution.

Vogel, D. and C. Ansel (eds) (2006). *Where's the Beef? The Contested Governance of European Food Safety.* Cambridge, MA: MIT Press.

Watson, B. (2013). "Siemens and the Battle Against Bribery and Corruption," *The Guardian*, 18 September. Available at: www.theguardian.com/sustainable-business/siemens-solmssen-bribery-corruption [accessed 24 April 2017].

Yates, S. (2015). *Individual Accountability for Corporate Wrongdoing.* Washington, DC: US Department of Justice. Available at: www.justice.gov/archives/dag/file/769036 [accessed 24 April 2017].

33
Cross-cultural management ethics in multinational commerce

Terence Jackson

Despite the fact that the foundations of extant cross-cultural management studies have been based on concepts of national values, little of the theory developed has been translated into an understanding of ethics across different cultures. Where the step from descriptive values to normative ethics has been taken, this is often in an uncritical way. Much of the foundation of cross-cultural management studies based on differences in values has been criticized over the last few years, with Geert Hofstede's (1980a) seminal work receiving particular attention. Despite a number of studies that have sought to offer alternatives or updates to Hofstede's now ageing study, there remain questions about the conceptual foundations of such an approach. The current chapter seeks to review the work in this area, discussing the relevance to a consideration of differences in ethicality, or an appreciation of what is ethical or not ethical across cultural contexts in multinational commerce, and to provide an appraisal of what is missing from a critical theory of management ethics across countries and the future of research in this area.

The current chapter seeks to make the transition from a purely descriptive account of cultural values, that suggests ethical issues in working across cultures, to a normative one that may guide ethical management across cultures. The chapter first focuses on cultural comparison studies (and their shortcomings), chiefly those by Hofstede (1980a; Hofstede et al. 2010). A second section examines studies that have built on Hofstede's work, including the GLOBE study, as well as revisions to the work of Fons Trompenaars (1993). The third section takes up the World Values Survey and examines the role of modernization theory that appears to implicitly inform this and the other comparative studies. Each professes to be descriptive yet hides value judgments that appear to favor some values (such as individualism) over other values (such as collectivism). The last section of the chapter focuses on theories that seek to advise or assist those who manage across cultural contexts when faced with conflicting cultural values.

Foundations: Hofstede's cultural values approach in international management studies

In his cultural values approach to comparing nations, Geert Hofstede (1980a) made a significant contribution to international management studies. His early work has attracted a number of studies based on his theories, replications (Hofstede 1980a) and conceptual and empirical updates (Hofstede et al. 2010). He provided a critique of the universal nature of management knowledge, policies and practices. Hofstede (1980b) questioned whether American management practices, such as participative management, are appropriate in countries that have cultural values that are distinct from those of the Anglo-American cultures. In doing so, he opened the possibility of critically examining aspects of management values, such as what is regarded as ethical or not across different national environments. From the point of view of businesses and organizations operating across national borders, it is important for managers to understand the meaning of ethicality (what is regarded as ethical) in different cultural contexts.

Yet Hofstede's work itself is limited in this aspect in two different ways. First, he did not go on to examine ethics specifically, refraining from taking the jump from cultural values to cross-cultural ethics, although it could be argued that he offered the basis for such an analysis. Second, work that simply compares nations on the basis of value differences remains purely descriptive and lacks a basis for managers and staff to make a judgment about what they should do. So, it is limited in its utility to managers working across cultural contexts, even as it forces this question: what should managers do when there are ethical differences between the home country and the host country, as based on the cultural values that Hofstede is describing?

Conceptually Hofstede's work is rooted in the positivist paradigm. Although other studies have continued in this tradition (Trompenaars 1993; Smith et al. 1996; House et al. 2004, 2014; Trompenaars and Hampden-Turner 2012), there are additional analyses, typically undertaken outside management studies, that have related more generally to wider societal values rather than organisational and management values (Inglehart et al. 1998; Basanez 2016; Schwartz 1999; Fischer et al. 2010). These works discuss values in management and organization and they tend to represent values at different macro, meso, or micro levels. Jackson (2002) pointed out that Shalom H. Schwartz's (1994) data on the former West and East Germanys indicate similarities of wider societal values, suggesting that the prevailing cultural values of the two Germanys were more similar and pervasive during the Iron Curtain years than is suggested by data from studies of organizational employees and managers (such as Trompenaars 1993), that appear to point to differences in management values only.

In the case of former soviet and former colonial countries some work organizations fail to reflect the wider values of the societies within which they exist (Jackson 2004). Yet, there are also connections between organizational values and societal values. Hence such studies of wider societal values can be used to indicate the degree of fit with organizational values.

Understanding the values of the wider (macro) society within which organizations evolve or are imposed is important. First, Western countries such as Britain, France and the USA do business abroad with a set of cultural values that often are not manifest or explicit but are assumed to be universal (Jackson 2011a). This has been one of the major critical purposes of cross-cultural studies: to question whether management practices used in the home country are appropriate in other countries. It is important to understand the values from which management systems, or sets of policies and implicit rules used in organizations, are derived, and how they influence the way organizations are managed in other countries.

From values to ethics

Geert Hofstede (originally in 1980a, later revised in 2003) was one of the first to attempt to develop a universal framework for understanding cultural differences in managers' and employees' values based on a world-wide survey within the company that employed him at the time: IBM. Hofstede's work focuses on "value systems" of national cultures that were originally represented by four dimensions, discussed below. His descriptions of value dimensions are suggestive of differences in ethicality across cultural contexts.

Power distance

This is the extent to which inequalities among people are perceived as normal. This dimension stretches from equal relations being seen as normal to wide inequalities being viewed as normal. According to Hofstede, power distance is polarized into small and large power distance and comprises attitudes that people within the culture have about the acceptable inequalities between people in the society or organization.

Power distance offers some explanation for the justification of autocratic management styles and high hierarchies in organizations as well as inequalities of wealth in the wider society. For example, in large power distant cultures, differences in rank or authority are expected and viewed as right and proper.

Yet, from a critical perspective, in terms of considering differences in ethicality, this value dimension, which is presented as descriptive, has certain issues. The first could be viewed as an implied Western-centric value judgment that low power distance is to be preferred over high power distance. Thus, democracy is to be preferred over autocracy, participatory management over autocratic non-participative management. This perspective could be applied over all Hofstede's and others' conceptualization of national value judgments, and could be seen as accompanying a modernization ethos within international management studies where the Western model of industrialization and modernization is valued, implicitly or explicitly. This perspective is also assumed in the World Values Survey literature (e.g., Inglehart 1997), discussed below.

A second problem, which could be seen as the other side of the coin, is that of a lack of normative perspective in a theory that concerns values. If we are guided by Hofstede's description that Belgium is higher in power distance than the Netherlands, what do managers from the Netherlands do when they go to manage a company in Belgium? This question might seem contradictory to the assertion above of an implied value judgment (that low power distance is best), but it is not: the implied judgment rests tacitly *within* the theory but the question reflects the sort of concern that the manager might entertain. It is necessary to turn to other bodies of theory to understand these two issues. For the first problem outlined above we need to turn to critical theory such as postcolonial theory, and for the second problem we need to turn to theories of ethical relativism and its alternatives. These will be revisited later.

Uncertainty avoidance

This refers to a preference for structured situations versus unstructured situations. This dimension runs from being comfortable with flexibility and ambiguity to a need for extreme rigidity and situations with a high degree of certainty. Weak uncertainty avoidance cultures, according to Hofstede, accept uncertainty as a feature of everyday life, there is generally low stress and people feel comfortable in ambiguous situations. Strong uncertainty avoidance is characterized by the threat of uncertainty that is always present but must be fought. It is characterized by high stress and a fear of ambiguous situations and unfamiliar risk.

This value dimension appears to have implications for the ethicality of imposing fixed and rigid rules in a workplace as opposed to flexibility and room for individual expression. Again, there may be a Western-centric implication that the latter is to be preferred. Management textbooks appear to be written from the implicit assumption that staff are able to cope with higher levels of ambiguity as the following example seeks to illustrate.

The process of "change management," as featured in Western management textbooks, assumes a need to openly communicate and discuss the change throughout hierarchical levels, to get staff to take ownership of the change, to make suggestions, to be involved from start to finish in the change process. Yet Jackson (2011a) has pointed out that although this may work well in a low power distance and low uncertainty avoidance cultural context, this may be quite inappropriate in a high power distance context ("you are the boss, why aren't you managing?") and a high uncertainty avoidance context. Change is a highly uncertain process, making staff uneasy even in a low uncertainty avoidance context. By treating the process in a way that places responsibility on staff creates more uncertainty in a high uncertainty avoidance context and may be entirely inappropriate.

The concept of *appropriateness* is a very important concept in cross-cultural management theory (Jackson 2011b). It implies issues of ethicality, yet rarely within this field of theory is this connection made explicitly. Is it appropriate for managers to adopt a more democratic style of managing in a high power distance culture, or should they adopt a more autocratic style? Is it right or wrong? These are issues of appropriateness that Hofstede (1980b) touched on in his landmark article that examined whether American management principles can be applied abroad, but he never explored the ethical implications. Once one starts to ask if something is right or wrong, then the territory of normative ethics is entered. Once one moves across different cultural contexts in international management and multinational commerce, the question of right and wrong becomes more complex and, for scholars, more interesting.

Collectivism–individualism

The polarity of collective and individual looks at whether individuals are accustomed to acting as individuals or as part of cohesive groups, perhaps based on the family (which is more the case with Chinese societies) or the corporation (as may be the case in Japan).

As with low uncertainty avoidance and low power distance, individualism could be seen as implied as the Western-centric norm. To give an example, the area of conduct that Western observers call nepotism illustrates what Western managers often encounter in Eastern countries (if one can forgive the wide generalization in this statement). The nepotism may include, let us say, Chinese or Nigerian managers who recruit staff based on whom they know (rather than from a stock of applicants arising from advertisements placed in local newspapers who have been interviewed and perhaps vetted through various assessment centres), but the Western manager will frown upon practices such as these. However, from the Nigerian manager's perspective, it is inept to recruit a complete stranger whom one does not know, and with whom one has no mutual obligation, whose family and background is unknown. How much better to recruit someone from the same in-group (village, community, family) where there are mutual obligations existing, where pressure can be exerted if they do not perform, whose family can be approached to pull them back into line. From the perspective of the Chinese manager—already facing difficulties in recruiting good Chinese staff for a foreign private company because the best are retained by state-owned enterprises—it is impractical to look for staff on the open market. One has to go through personal networks (*guanxi*), for otherwise the company will end up with employees who cannot get a job anywhere else.

Hence "nepotism," which is seen as unethical in Western countries, may be seen as good practice and common sense in many non-Western countries. A concept of collectivism–individualism helps us to understand this, if thought through logically, yet is not without its issues, particularly from a Western perspective. In-group favoritism can be a problem even where this may be seen as common sense in, for example, an African country where many companies can be dominated by a particular cultural/ethnic/linguistic group (Jackson 2004).

Masculinity–femininity

Hofstede distinguishes "hard values" such as assertiveness and competition, and the "soft" or "feminine" values of personal relations, quality of life and caring about others. In a masculine society gender role differentiation is emphasized.

There appears to be two aspects of Hofstede's dimension. The first concerns the prominence of "feminine" values across the genders, as opposed to the differentiation between male values and female values in countries that score high on masculinity. The latter leads to the second aspect, which is the dominance of males in, for example, managerial jobs (e.g., Japan) and a lack of equality between male and female. The distinct values of femininity and masculinity offer justification for gender inequalities, but may also be connected with the levels of achievement orientation in society, including the centrality of work outside the home and the work-life balance, with its implications for levels of women in the workforce, childcare provision, and imposition of corporations on the wider life-space of individuals. Not only do the values of femininity and masculinity bear implications for the perceived ethicality of gender inequality but they also suggest a cultural justification for workplace discrimination. This aside, there still appears to be an implied Western-centric value judgment that masculinity may be the preferred pole of the dimension with links being made from assertiveness to competition, achievement societies and successful economies, with Hofstede (1991) himself linking his masculinity pole with high achievement motivation societies, as noted in David C. McClelland's studies (1961/1987). This association is also reflected in the international proliferation through management education and by multinational enterprises of results-oriented human resource management systems that connect pay and promotion directly to results (Sparrow et al. 2017).

Adding a fifth dimension: Confucian dynamism

To his original four dimensions Hofstede added a fifth, which was developed through the Chinese Cultural Connection study (CCC 1987) and justified, in part, by Hofstede's warning of the dangers of developing constructs from a Western point of view. The Chinese Cultural Connection was an attempt to counter this by introducing an Eastern perspective and values. Nonetheless, the study reinforced three out of the four dimensions in Hofstede's original study: the Chinese dimension of "human-heartedness," which incorporates values such as kindness, courtesy and social consciousness, correlates negatively with masculinity; "integration," which encompasses the cultivation of trust, tolerance and friendship, correlates negatively with power distance; "moral discipline," including values of group responsiveness, moderation, adaptability and prudent behavior, correlates negatively with individualism.

None of the new dimensions correlated with uncertainty avoidance, but a new dimension was added, termed Confucian dynamism and then long term orientation, with values of persistence and perseverance, ordering relationships by status and observing order, thrift and having a sense of shame. Uncertainty avoidance is concerned with absolute *truth*, which may not be a relevant value in Chinese society and other Eastern cultures that are more concerned with *virtue*. Of particular relevance is the virtue of working hard and acquiring skills and traits such as thrift, patience and perseverance, all values connected with this fifth dimension that may replace uncertainty avoidance as a relevant Eastern concept. Truth and the value of truth is an important concept in Western ethics. The value of this fifth dimension is that it points to the culturally relative nature of truth, particularly in the account above of the importance of virtue, and maintaining "face" rather than a belief in any absolute truth. Western-centric implicit assumptions also appear not to be present to the same extent as the other four dimensions, with a deliberate attempt on Hofstede's part in being Eastern-centric.

Building on Hofstede's foundations

The GLOBE study

The main successor to Hofstede's study is GLOBE (Global Leadership and Organizational Behavior Effectiveness Research Program), a more recent cross-national study undertaken by Robert House and a team of 170 researchers across 62 societies (House et al. 2004; House et al. 2014). The GLOBE project findings reflect many of the cultural dimensions proffered in earlier studies, and, as such, do not add conceptually to a descriptive understanding of ethical values across cultures. These findings do, however, provide more current information that is perhaps more rigorously validated, covers more countries than previous studies did, and distinguish between "values" (what should be) and "practices" (what is seen to be done). For example, the GLOBE study covers some six African countries and six post-soviet countries. Many of the dimensions correlate with Hofstede's dimensions.

The main value of the GLOBE study appears to be in updating Hofstede's empirical base and providing more current descriptive information on values held in organizations. In terms of future research comparing national values to ethical beliefs and practices, scholars would benefit from referring to this more recent study.

Trompenaars reanalyzed

The other study that is often cited in the cross-cultural management literature (although little work directly links this to an analysis of ethics across cultural contexts) is that of Fons Trompenaars (Trompenaars 1993; Trompenaars and Hampden Turner 2012). Although this study has severe methodological issues and lacks academic rigour, it does have relevance to an understanding of ethics in multinational commerce, but only in the form of the data's rigorous reanalysis by Peter Smith, Shaun Dugan, and Fons Trompenaars (1996).

The original work identified the following value dimensions: regard for rules or relations (universalism–particularism), individualism–collectivism, neutral–affective expression of emotions, low and high context societies (specific–diffuse) and the way status is accorded (achievement–ascription). Smith, Dugan and Trompenaars (1996) performed a statistical reanalysis through multidimensional scaling of Trompenaars' extensive international database. This reanalysis provided two major cultural value dimensions: conservatism–egalitarianism and utilitarian involvement–loyal involvement. Conservatism comprises items that represent ascribed status, particularist/paternalistic employers and formalized hierarchies, and represents an external locus of control. It correlates with Hofstede's collectivism and power distance. Egalitarian commitment comprises achieved status, universalistic and non-paternalistic values, as well as functional hierarchy and internal locus of control, and correlates with Hofstede's individualism and low power distance. Utilitarian involvement comprises aspects of individualism that emphasize individual credit and responsibility. It correlates with Hofstede's individualism and low power distance. Loyal involvement comprises aspects of collectivism that stress loyalty and obligation to the group, as well as corporate loyalty and obligation. It correlates with Hofstede's collectivism and high power distance.

Incorporated within the conservatism–egalitarian commitment, Trompenaars' (1993) dimensions of universalism–particularism, achievement–ascription and locus of control are the most relevant to a discussion of ethics across cultural contexts, and provide more refinement to the ethical implications of Hofstede's dimensions. In some cultural contexts people see rules and regulations as applying universally to everyone, regardless of who they are. In cultures that are more particularist, people see relationships as more important than applying rules the same way for everyone. There is an inclination to apply the rules according to friendship and kinship relations. This tendency has implications for recruitment and promotion policies in organizations in, for example, some Asian countries, whose policies may be at variance with practices in countries such as the United States and Britain where, as discussed above, such practices might be deemed to exemplify "nepotism," and be regarded as ethically suspect. However, there are differences in European countries. Greece, Spain and France are seen as more particularist, and Sweden, former West Germany and Britain as more universalist.

Also within the conservatism–egalitarian commitment construct is Trompenaars' concept of achievement–ascription. Status is accorded to people on the basis of what they accomplish in their jobs and their lives (achievement) or, alternatively, on the basis of who they are and where they come from, such as family background, school, or some other prior factor (ascription). Quite often more traditional societies attribute status according to ascription. Again, this may influence recruitment and promotion policies that may be at variance to practices in some (but not all) Western cultures, and again may raise ethical issues. On some measures Austria, Belgium, Spain and Italy are more ascription oriented, and Denmark, Britain and Sweden more achievement oriented.

Locus of control is another concept that is subsumed within the conservatism–egalitarian commitment construct. People tend to believe that what happens to them in life is their own doing (internal locus of control), or they have no or little control over what happens to them (external locus of control), the causes of which are external to them. Locus of control raises issues about how people relate to their environment, and the level of control they believe they have over the natural world. This may have implications for the nature of interaction with the natural and social world, and raises ethical questions about power (in the social sphere) and environment controls (in the natural sphere). It also may have implications for the nature of management control in organizations. For example, setting targets may be inappropriate as a form of management control in a society that culturally has an external locus of control.

Paternalism is also an important concept in cross-cultural management research and is captured in part by Trompenaars' concept of specific–diffuse, which contains questionnaire items such as "should the company provide housing." The specific–diffuse dimension—which involves the extent to which relationships at work, particularly with the boss, are carried through to other aspects of one's life—is subsumed within the construct of conservatism, and may have ethical implications for the regard for interference/protection in one's life by the corporation. Paternalism is a construct that is often seen as negative from a Western-centric perspective. Yet Zeynep Aycan (2006) has done much to disabuse this image, seeing paternalism as protection of those under the patronage of a caring boss.

The dimension of utilitarian involvement–loyal involvement (Smith et al. 1996), though allied to Hofstede's individual–collectivism and power distance, also reflects the nature of loyalty of the individual to the group and corporation. Individuals may have a contractual relationship with the organization within the utilitarian involvement construct, yet members of a group or corporation also have relations with the wider collective that involve obligation and reciprocity. Such obligation and reciprocity may reflect the extent to which loyalty issues are regarded ethically. For example, whistleblowing may be regarded quite differently by societies whose culture is at two different poles of this dimension. A lack of loyalty (as well as what constitutes loyalty) may be an ethical issue in a society that reflects more the loyal involvement side of the pole.

What each of the GLOBE and Hofstede's theory lacks is any comparison with wider societal values. Yet the World Values Survey (WVS), or at least its interpretation, appears to explicitly accept the "modernization project"—the notion that societal progress inevitably will, and should, follow a Western model of development in the industrial and postindustrial eras.

World Values Survey and modernization theory

Modernization theory makes assumptions of societal progress. Management studies as a subject area appears often implicitly to support this worldview. As this author has noted in a recent article, "'Autocracy is better than democracy.' How many cross-cultural management scholars would agree with this? Yet why should democracy be an aim of modern societies? Are there not other routes to societal development?" (Jackson 2015: 131). A salient illustration of the tacit assumption of modernization is provided in one article on women in leadership positions in the Arab Gulf countries: "Many countries and regions around the world have made *progress* in past decades in terms of women holding senior management positions." The authors add, "although *progress* has been made, women are still underrepresented in senior positions particularly within business across the world" (Kemp et al. 2015: 216, emphasis added).

Hofstede, as noted above, has been taken to task about the value judgments his cultural dimensions seem to engender (Human 1996) as being far from dispassionate descriptors. Indeed, Hofstede (1980a) showed a 0.82 correlation between individualism and economic development, although Çiğdem Kağıtçıbaşi (1997) noted a challenge to this by the rapid industrialization of collectivist Asian countries. This challenge may go far deeper today with developments in the Chinese economy. The development path of China has certainly been different from that of Western economies, with what many Western commentators would see as a subjugation of individual human rights (Jackson 2011a). Critical theory should challenge these underlying assumptions as these have fundamental implications for what is seen as ethical. Hence if Western-style democracy is seen as a goal to aim for in "developing" countries, those systems of government that are seen as non-democratic may be perceived as acting less ethically towards their citizens.

Yet if the assumptions of modernization are implicit in Hofstede's work, they are quite explicit in Ronald Inglehart's own interpretation of his data from the WVS.

> The World Values Survey data show us that the world views of people of rich societies differ systematically from those of low-income societies across a wide range of political, social, and religious norms and beliefs. The two most significant dimensions that emerge reflected, first, a polarization between *traditional* and *secular-rational* orientations towards authority and, second, a polarization between *survival* and *self-expression* values. By *traditional* we mean those societies that are relatively authoritarian, place strong emphasis on religion, and exhibit a mainstream version of preindustrial values such as an emphasis on male dominance in economic and political life, respect for authority, and relatively low levels of tolerance for abortion and divorce. Advanced societies, or *secular-rational*, tend to have the opposite characteristics.
>
> A central component of the survival vs. self-expression dimension involves the polarization between materialist and postmaterialist values. Massive evidence indicates that cultural shift throughout advanced industrial society is emerging among generations who have grown up taking survival for granted. Values among this group [self-expression, for example] emphasize environmental protection, the women's movement, and rising demand for

participation in decision making in economic and political life. During the past 25 years, these values have become increasingly widespread in almost all advanced industrial societies for which extensive time-series evidence is available.

(Inglehart and Baker 2000: 16–17)

When linking such cultural dimensions to measures of economic development and prosperity, as indeed, for example, Hofstede (1980a) and Ingelhart (1997) do, there does appear to be a value judgment in terms of a correlation between economic and social development and cultural values that can lead to judgments of ethicality: one society being less ethical than another. Hence, developed countries are individualistic, low in power distance, and high on self-expression. Developing countries are seen as not living up to these values and suffer from in-group favoritism, or nepotism, autocracy and low regard for environmental protection and individual rights. Inglehart's studies are longitudinal. This is their advantage, and also their disadvantage, as Inglehart appears to surmise from this that less industrialized societies are gradually catching up with industrialized societies and moving towards modernization; yet industrialized societies are now moving to postmodernization, so less industrialized societies have even further to go in following the path of the more advanced countries. In addition, the move towards greater "individual autonomy" appears to reflect a shift towards more individuality and away from collectivism and communalism. Inglehart sees modernization as emphasizing economic efficiency, bureaucratic authority and scientific rationality; and the move towards postmodernization as moving towards "a more human society with more room for individual autonomy, diversity and self expression" (Inglehart 1997:12).

One of Inglehart's main collaborators, Miguel Basáñez (2016), reflects this view twenty years on when he derives three main "cultures" from the WVS data. Cultures of honor that emphasize political authority; cultures of achievement priotizing economic advancement; and cultures of joy that focus on social interactions. He asserts that these cultures evolve chronologically and mirror the development of agrarian, industrial and service societies.

Such judgments about what ought to be are within the realms of ethical theory, but in the case of Inglehart's and Basáñez's interpretations of the WVS data this is not explicit. It is not within the scope of this chapter to recount in detail this interpretation, but to mention some of the ethical implications coming out of this study.

It can be seen therefore that studies involving cultural value dimensions have implications for the way ethicality is perceived in different cultural contexts, yet authors of these studies have generally not drawn these conclusions. A more critical reading of these studies also suggests that there are implicit value assumptions within these studies, which generally are not openly stated or incorporated in, or controlled for, within the studies. Hence, modernization theory appears implicit within these studies, and is made most apparent in Inglehart's interpretation of the WVS data. If it is assumed that the aim of so-called developing economies is to develop towards the modern economies of the West, and then towards the post-modern advanced economies of what many Western economies have become, then this assumption has serious ethical implications when such developing economies do not develop in this way, or do not in fact follow this developmental path. Susanne Schech and Jane Haggis (2000: 161), for example, demonstrate through documentary and press evidence the contrasting perceptions of human rights between the United States and China. Perceptions from the USA see China as infringing individual human rights by cracking down on political dissent and controlling the number of children couples have; while the perception from China is that the United States abuses the human rights of the poor and blacks, have a huge prison population, low voter turn outs and massive inequalities of wealth. The path to development of China has been quite different from that of the United States.

Yet, despite these implicit assumptions, studies remain descriptive instead of openly dealing with or taking advantage of what Bent Flyvbjerg (2001: 167) has described as the main strength of the social sciences: an ability to deal with what ought to be. He contends that: "the purpose of social science is not to develop theory, but to contribute to society's practical rationality in elucidating where we are, where we want to go, and what is desirable according to diverse sets of values and interests." The positivist paradigm, which underpins the cultural comparative studies outlined above, prevents these issues being addressed. However, these are exactly the issues that have to be addressed on a day-to-day basis by managers involved in multinational commerce, and who have to manage within international and cross-cultural contexts.

Ethical judgments, algorithms, and codes of ethics

Studies such as Hofstede's and the others considered in this chapter provide an explanation of why ideas of ethicality may differ across the globe. Power distance, for example, may explain why inequality is seen as right and proper in one society and deplored in another. Value judgments about what is right or fair are made, at least in part, from our cultural perspective: the way we have been brought up, socialized, educated. Yet culture is more complex than four or five dimensions representing the collective values of some 50 nations, where socialization may be quite different within a society among different socio-ethnic groups and by class or socioeconomic groupings. The critical cross-cultural literature on these issues appears to be lacking.

Making ethical judgments

The weakness of cultural values studies is their descriptive nature. They do not offer guidance on what to do. For example, consider a manager from a low power distance country who goes to a high power distance country: in terms of adapting to the high power distance culture or trying to encourage a more democratic working, how is this manager to make ethical judgments? To answer this we have to look elsewhere in the literature where the basis for ethical judgments seems logically to fit into two broad perspectives:

> judgments based on consequential considerations (teleology); and,
>
> judgments based on non-consequential considerations (deontology).

Consequential judgments are based on the expectation that an action, policy, or rule will, if generally enacted, have a result that on balance is good for the majority of persons or stakeholders (as in utilitarianism), or in the overall interests of the person making the decision or those with whom he or she identifies, such as the company (as in egoism). Non-consequential judgments are based on prior considerations of an explicit or implicit set of rules or principles whose rightness seems inherent to the rule or principle (assumed to be universal) and not derivative of anticipated results or effects (deontology).

However, it is unlikely that the bases for these different types of judgment are "pure" (Hunt and Vitell 1986) or that we rely solely on one to the exclusion of the other (Brady 1990) to make an ethical judgment. Hence, we may make a judgment on prior considerations of what we believe to be "fair" to all concerned (justice). However, ideas of fairness may be based on perceptions of the outcome of a decision providing to each the greatest amount of liberty which is compatible with a like liberty for all, but these may also imply judgments of the extent to which such rewards and opportunities should be distributed unequally (Rawls 1971), or as in Hofstede's (1980a/2003) concept of power distance. We may also make ethical judgments based on what we believe is acceptable to us as a member of a family, to other groups which influence us, and as a member of a cultural group or society (ethical relativism).

It is also unlikely that these principles are invariable across cultures, and across different contexts. In a sense, ethical relativism is the only theory that addresses this issue, if not by explaining or justifying it, but simply by acknowledging it.

Although the cross-cultural literature focuses more on the content of ethical decisions, there is some evidence that the way judgments are made may vary among different cultural groups, although this has mainly focused on differences between Asian and non-Asian cultures. David A. Ralston et al. (1994), for example, discussed differences between the seemingly self-serving attitudes of Hong Kong Chinese managers compared with American managers, which may be explained by differences in the Western view of ethical behavior as an absolute that applies universally, and is in line with Hofstede's fifth dimension of Confucian dynamism and the difference between truth and virtue discussed above. In the East "face" is important and ethical behavior depends on the situation. This situationalism was also seen in M. M. Dolecheck and C. C. Dolecheck's (1987) study, which found that Hong Kong managers equate ethics to acting within the law, compared with American managers who see ethics as going beyond keeping to the letter of the law. Anusorn Singhapakdi et al. (1994) also found that Thai managers rely more on the nature of the ethical issue or circumstance and less on universal moral principles when making ethical judgments, at least as compared with their American counterparts. This conclusion may provide some (though not conclusive) support for assuming that Asian ethical judgment may be more relativistic in structure, and that the way judgments are made may vary from one situation to the other. Ethical judgments of Western managers may be based more on the application of universal principles of ethical behavior.

More specifically, a study by Gael McDonald and Patrick Pak (1997) set out to investigate cross-cultural differences in "cognitive philosophies" among managers from Hong Kong, Malaysia, New Zealand and Canada. Their findings suggested that self-interest is important in ethical decision making for Hong Kong managers, but that "duty" (a deontological consideration) is important to all these national groups. Justice, or considerations of fairness, is also important to all national groups. Utilitarian considerations are shown to be less important, but more important relatively for the Malaysian group. This study, as others that focus on the way ethical judgments are made (Reidenbach and Robin 1988, 1990), indicated that judgments are made using multiple criteria rather than relying on one specific basis of ethical decision making. It is the combination of multiple criteria that constitutes the way in which ethical judgments are made.

Specific studies of management ethics in Japan suggest that Japanese managers' ethical decisions tend to be situational (Nakano 1997), although the development of Japanese "moralogy" (Taka and Dunfee 1997) may be indicative of a deontological emphasis in ethical decision making. American managers may look to industrial norms and what their company expects when making an ethical decision (Posner and Schmidt 1987). Although this runs counter-intuitively to the perceptions of the USA as an achievement-oriented society, this apparent deontological orientation may be the basis of the rise of codes of ethics among US corporations, and their spread by US multi-national enterprises across the globe. We discuss research below that runs contrary to this finding.

Consequential considerations of organizational efficiency figured lower for American than for Australian and Hong Kong managers in a comparative study of organizational values by Robert Westwood and Barry Posner (1997). In this study organizational stability was seen as significantly more important by the American than by the Australian and Hong Kong managers. A comparative study by D. S. Elenkov (1997) of managers in the United States and Russia suggested that Russian managers display higher levels of Machiavellianism than those in the

United States, as well as being as competitively oriented as the American group and equally non-dogmatic. This may indicate a tendency to employ self-seeking criteria in ethical decision making, or at least employing utilitarian criteria among Russian managers.

However, George Neimanis (1997) suggested the Soviet system militated against people making their own decisions, but had the effect of justifying the interests of the state, the corporation, or the party as superseding any ethical considerations. This may have encouraged an egoism based on the best interests of the corporation, and more latterly based on self-interest with a move towards a free market economy (see also Apressyan 1997). However, it may also have encouraged a reference to rules and principles in order to avoid the consequences (punishment) of making a wrong decision. Principle-based decision making of managers and negotiators in the former Soviet Union is well documented (see, for example, Glenn et al. 1977, in relation to negotiation style), and the more recent Russian (and other post-Soviet countries) ethical judgment structure may be a complex of historical and current influences (Apressyan 1997).

Jackson et al. (2000) set out to study these possible differences in the way ethical judgments are made using the Reidenbach-Robin multidimensional scale (Reidenbach and Robin 1988, 1990). It provides an instrument that is purported to measure the ethical decision-making process by anchoring items to ethical philosophies, namely: justice, relativism, egoism, utilitarianism, deontology (Reidenbach and Robin 1990). Jackson et al.'s (2000) study focused on internal stakeholders, concerning corporate loyalty to employees, loyalty to company and loyalty to one's group, and uses three vignettes to represent each of these aspects. The study included managers in the Anglo-Saxon countries of the United States and Australia; the East Asian "tiger" countries of Japan, Korea and the economic region of Hong Kong; and managers in the "transitional" countries of Russia (albeit in the Asiatic region) and Poland, and drew the following conclusions. Managers from the "Anglo-Saxon" countries seem to look more to the consequences of their decisions in order to judge whether a decision is ethical, while managers from East Asian countries employ a social referencing to guide their judgments, and Russian managers employ more principled or deontological considerations. Although all groups tend to use multiple criteria, the study indicates differences in emphasis among different cultures or countries.

This different emphasis on different decision criteria among managers from different cultures has implications for the way organizations attempt to influence the ethical decision-making of its managers. There is little direct relevance of employee codes of ethics if managers are employing predominantly consequential criteria, as in the case of the managers from Anglo-Saxon countries. This may be more directly pertinent to managers in Russia to whom deontological considerations are more relevant. Intervention in group processes may be more applicable to East Asian managers, and to a certain extent to Australian managers who employ socially referenced criteria alongside consequential considerations. For those managers such as the Americans, who employ predominantly consequential considerations (contrary to Posner and Schmidt's 1987 findings above), discussion groups within organizations (which address the issues of the consequences of management decisions) may be more applicable in guiding ethical choice than managerial decision alone.

Decision algorithms

Although the way ethical judgments are made may differ across cultural contexts, this still does not provide guidance to international managers making decisions across these different contexts. Decision algorithms provide a means of making judgments that transcend either applying a cultural relativist position, or simply imposing inappropriate judgments from the home country of an MNE onto a host country organization and staff. A classic view of this is presented by Thomas Donaldson (1989: 16) who suggests that the idea of cultural relativism in ethical decision-making is common (perhaps more common in practice than in conceptualization). As Donaldson reports, the idea goes something like this. All cultures are different and no culture is any better or worse than any other, they are simply different. It is therefore correct to accept a culture, and its values, for what they are, and not to be judgmental. Therefore, if the value system within one culture allows for corporate bribery, then this should be acceptable. Donaldson (1989) believes this position to be untenable, suggesting that people mistakenly endorse cultural relativism, confusing it with cultural tolerance.

Hence, although Donaldson (1989: 104) rejects the international arena as a moral free-for-all, neither does he accept that moral values from one country such as the United States can be applied in another country. This tension makes it difficult to establish a universal moral objectivity applicable throughout the world. Donaldson's solution is to propose an "ethical algorithm" to be used as a guideline in answering the question, "Is the practice permissible for the multinational company when it is morally and/or legally permitted in the host country, but not in the home country?" He first identifies two types of conflict.

> Type 1 conflict: The reason why the host country's view is different is related to its level of development (e.g., levels of pollution);
>
> Type 2 conflict: The reasons why the host country's view is different are independent of its economic level of development.

The former occurs when the host country's view is related to the level of its economic development. For example, this may be the case where regulations relating to levels of pollution may be more lax. The resolution of the conflict is then based on the principle that the practice is permissible if under similar economic circumstances the home country would regard the practice as permissible. Type 2 conflicts occur when the host country's view is independent of its economic level of development. Whether or not nepotism is a useful example may be questioned in view of the discussions above in relation to cultural values and the relationship to collectivism and modernization assumptions. Similarly, bribery may provide another example in this context.

In Donaldson's algorithm the question must be asked: Is it possible to conduct business successfully in the host country without undertaking this particular practice? If the answer is no, the next question is: Is the practice a clear violation of fundamental international human rights? If the answer is no, then if the practice is necessary to conduct business in the host country and it does not violate fundamental human rights, but if it does go against basic moral principles of the home country, then managers in the multinational corporation should speak against it.

However, in a cross-cultural context this approach may now be regarded as simplistic, but for managers working across countries, where companies have tended to rely almost exclusively on codes of ethical conduct to which managers are expected to adhere, following such an algorithm may run contrary to following one's company's code of ethics. Yet findings presented by Jackson (2000) from a study across six countries suggest that corporate policy has little influence on managers' ethical attitudes and decision-making, with little variation across the countries studied, and that codes of ethics may be useful only as policy statements for external stakeholders, to enable corporations to comply with legislation, and probably only in countries such as the UK and USA that have less regulated economies. The study found that ethical attitudes and behaviors of peers were far more important than trying to legislate for ethical behavior.

Implications for managers working in multinational commerce

It is evident from this study that far more should be done by corporations for their managers working across international boundaries. Jackson has recommended that the following measures be taken in companies.

> Peer discussion groups to address issues such as pilfering, taking gifts and reporting others' violations of company policies, in order to gain some consensus and to make explicit commonly held views in these areas, particularly bearing in mind that attitudes and behaviors may differ among national cultures;
>
> Regular or ad hoc stakeholders' discussion groups including suppliers and key customers as well as internal stakeholders including top managers, and home-country and host-country managers, to gain valuable input and to take ownership of output;
>
> Appropriate information and decision making systems which facilitate decision making in line with the output of discussion groups;
>
> Training for managers in necessary ethical decision making competences including sensitivity to cross-cultural differences in these areas.
>
> (Jackson 2000: 367–8)

Concluding remarks

From the above discussion it is apparent that there are data from extensive cross-border studies of values dimensions that may be useful for understanding the nature of ethicality and its interpretation in different cultural contexts. Yet there are weaknesses that prevent these studies being used for this purpose. The first is the positivistic methodologies behind such studies that focus on description, rather than dealing with what ought to be, which is the domain of ethics, and, according to Flyvbjerg, the main strength of the social sciences. Future research should aim to integrate ideas of what should be done, or how decisions can be made by managers working across cultural contexts, into wider cross-cultural studies. It could be argued that it is not the purpose of these studies to do anything other than describe cultural differences in a dispassionate, scientific, way. Yet this argument is somewhat countered by the other main weakness of these studies.

Secondly, as in much of international management studies, these studies appear to reflect a modernization theory that in itself makes judgments about what ought to be. Yet these judgments are held implicitly and do not form part of the methodology of such studies. Critical studies of modernization theory, such as Postcolonial Theory (e.g., Said 1978/1995), may provide a means for future research to critique such Western-centric assumptions, and may be a fruitful area to investigate. It is only when these implicit assumptions are made apparent, and either integrated or controlled for within the methodology, that an argument for their being "objective" can be made.

Yet, from the discussion in this chapter, such broad studies can be seen to be useful to understanding why concepts of ethicality differ across borders, and why a practice may be appropriate in one country and not in another. This is useful information for managers in multinational commerce, but does not answer questions about what these managers should do when confronted with such difference. Codes of ethics, a solution offered by many multinational companies, appear largely ineffective. Decision algorithms may be more useful, but also have their limitations. Yet, the way such decisions are made themselves vary across borders. The effectiveness of different methods that companies use may therefore vary across different countries, and more research needs to be undertaken in this area.

Essential readings

A useful and thorough examination of cross-cultural theory from the perspective of cultural values comparison can be found in M. Minkov and Geert Hofstede, *Cross-cultural Analysis: The Science and Art of Comparing the World's Modern Societies and their Cultures* (2012). A more critical analysis connecting cultural comparative theory with an ethical approach may be found in Terence Jackson, *International Management Ethics: A Critical, Cross-cultural Perspective* (2011a).

For further reading in this volume on business and business ethics in various nations and cultures, see the selection of chapters in Part VIII: Business ethics across the globe. For further reading on issues of globalization and the West, see Chapter 32, The globalization of business ethics. On the topic of international agreement in norms, see the discussion of the social contract theory of Thomas Donaldson and Thomas Dunfee in Chapter 6, Social contract theories. On theoretical perspectives in management theory, see Chapter 26, Theoretical issues in management ethics. For a critical assessment of relativism in pedagogy, see Chapter 4, Teaching business ethics: current practice and future directions. For a view of business ethics that counsels the explication of practices, including tacit norms, see Chapter 3, Theory and method in business ethics.

References

Apressyan, R.G. (1997). "Business Ethics in Russia," *Journal of Business Ethics* 16, 1561–70.
Aycan, Z. (2006). "Paternalism: Towards Conceptual Refinement and Operationalization," in K.S. Yang, K. K. Hwang and U. Kim (eds), *Scientific Advances in Indigenous Psychologies: Empirical, Philosophical and Cultural Contributions*. Cambridge: Cambridge University Press, 206, 445–66.
Basáñez M.E. (2016). *A World of Three Cultures*. Oxford: Oxford University Press.
Brady, F.N. (1990). *Ethical Management: Rules and Results*. London: Macmillan.
CCC (Chinese Cultural Connection) (1987). "Chinese Values and the Search for Culture-Free Dimensions of Culture," *Journal of Cross-Cultural Psychology* 18, 143–64.
Dolecheck, M.M. and C.C. Dolecheck (1987). "Business Ethics: a Comparison of Attitudes of Managers in Hong Kong and the United States," *Hong Kong Managers* 1, 28–43.
Donaldson, T. (1989). *The Ethics of International Business*. New York, NY: Oxford University Press.
Elenkov, D.S. (1997). "Differences and Similarities in Managerial Values between U.S. and Russia Managers," *International Studies of Management and Organization* 27 (1), 85–106.
Fischer, R., C.M. Vauclair, J.R.J. Fontaine and S.H. Schwartz (2010). "Are Individual-Level and Country-Level Value Structures Different? Testing Hofstede's Legacy With the Schwartz Value Survey," *Journal of Cross-Cultural Psychology* 41, 135–51.
Flyvbjerg, B. (2001). *Making Social Science Matter*. Cambridge: Cambridge University Press.
Gatley, S., R. Lessem and Y. Altman (1996). *Comparative Management: A Transcultural Odyssey*. London: McGraw-Hill.
Glenn, E.S., D. Witmeyer and K.A. Stevenson (1977). "Cultural Styles of Persuasion," *International Journal of Intercultural Relations* 1:3, 52–66.
Hofstede, G. (1980a/2003). *Culture's Consequences: International Differences in Work Related Values*. Beverly Hills, CA: Sage.
Hofstede, G. (1980b). "Motivation, Leadership and Organization: Do American Theories Apply Abroad?" *Organizational Dynamics*, Summer, 42–63.
Hofstede, G. (1991). *Cultures and Organizations: Software of the Mind*. London: McGraw-Hill.
Hofstede, G., G.J. Hofstede and M. Minkov (2010). *Cultures and Organizations: Software of the Mind*, revised and expanded 3rd edition. New York, NY: McGraw-Hill.
House, R., P.J. Hanges, M. Javidan and P.W. Dorfman (2004). *Leadership, Culture and Organizations: The GLOBE Study of 62 Societies*. Thousand Oaks, CA: Sage.
House, R., P.W. Dorfman, M. Javidan, P.J. Hanges and M. Sully de Luque (2014). *Strategic Leadership Across Cultures: GLOBE Study of CEO Leadership Behavior and Effectiveness in 24 Countries*. Los Angeles, CA: Sage.

Human, L. (1996). *Contemporary Conversations*. Dakar, Senegal: The Goree Institute.
Hunt, S.D. and S.J. Vitell (1986). "A General Theory of Marketing Ethics," *Journal of Macromarketing* 6, 5–16.
Inglehart, R., M. Basanez and A. Moreno (1998). *Human Values and Beliefs: A Cross-cultural Sourcebook*. Ann Arbor, MI: The University of Michigan Press.
Inglehart, R. (1997). *Modernization and Postmodernization: Cultural, Economic, and Political Change in 43 Societies*. Princeton, NJ: Princeton University Press.
Inglehart, R. and W.E. Baker (2000). "Modernization, Cultural Change, and Persistence of Traditional Values," *American Sociological Review* 65 (February), 19–51.
Jackson, T., et al. (+ 11 authors) (2000). "Making Ethical Judgements: A Cross-cultural Management Study," *Asia Pacific Journal of Management* 17:3, 443–72.
Jackson, T. (2000). "Management Ethics and Corporate Policy: a Cross Cultural Comparison," *Journal of Management Studies* 37:3, 349–69.
Jackson, T. (2002a). *International HRM: A Cross-cultural Approach*. London: Sage.
Jackson, T. (2004). *Management and Change in Africa: A Cross-cultural Perspective*. London: Routledge.
Jackson, T. (2011a). *International Management Ethics: A Critical, Cross-cultural Perspective*. Cambridge: Cambridge University Press.
Jackson, T. (2011b). "From Cultural Values to Cross-cultural Interfaces: Hofstede Goes to Africa," *Journal of Organization Change Management* 24:4, 532–58.
Jackson, T. (2015). "Modernization Theory in International Management Studies and the Role of Cross-cultural Management Scholarship," *International Journal of Cross Cultural Management* 15:2, 131–3.
Kağıtçibaşi, C. (1997). "Individualism and Collectivism," Chapter one in J.W. Berry, M.H. Segall and C. Kağıtçibaşi (eds), *Handbook of Cross-Cultural Psychology*, Vol. 3, *Social Behavior and Appplication*, 2nd edition. Boston, MA: Allyn and Bacon, 1–50.
Kemp, L., S. Madsen and J. Davis (2015). "Women in Business Leadership: A Comparative Study of Countries in the Arab Gulf States," *International Journal of Cross Cultural Management* 15:2, 215–33.
McClelland, D.C. (1961/1987). *Human Motivation*. Cambridge: Cambridge University Press.
McDonald, G.M. and C.K. Pak (1997). "Ethical Perceptions of Expatriates and Local Managers in Hong Kong," *Journal of Business Ethics* 16, 1605–23.
Minkov, M. and G. Hofstede (2012). *Cross-cultural Analysis: The Science and Art of Comparing the World's Modern Societies and their Cultures*. Los Angeles, CA: Sage.
Moreno, A. (2003). "Corruption and Democracy: A Cultural Assessment," in R. Inglehart (ed.), *Human Values and Social Change: Findings from the Values Surveys*. Leiden, The Netherlands: Brill, 265–278.
Nakano, C. (1997). "A Survey Study on Japanese Managers' Views of Business Ethics," *Journal of Business Ethics* 16, 1737–51.
Neimanis, G.J. (1997). "Business Ethics in the Former Soviet Union: a Report," *Journal of Business Ethics* 16, 357–62.
Posner, B.Z. and W.H. Schmidt (1987). "Ethics in American Companies: A Managerial Perspective," *Journal of Business Ethics* 6, 383–91.
Ralston, D.A., R.A. Gaicalone and R.H. Terpstra (1994). "Ethical Perceptions of Organizational Politics: a Comparative Evaluation of American and Hong Kong Managers," *Journal of Business Ethics* 13, 989–99.
Rawls, J. (1971). *A Theory of Justice*. Cambridge, MA: Harvard University Press.
Reidenbach, R.E. and D.P. Robin (1988). "Some Initial Steps Towards Improving the Measurement of Ethical Evaluation of Marketing Activities," *Journal of Business Ethics* 7, 871–9.
Reidenbach, R.E. and D.P. Robin (1990). "Towards the Development of a Multidimensional Scale for Improving Evaluations of Business Ethics," *Journal of Business Ethics* 9:8, 639–53.
Said, E. (1978/1995). *Orientalism*. London: Penguin.
Schech, S. and J. Haggis (2000). *Culture and Development: A Critical Introduction*. Oxford: Blackwell.
Schwartz, S. (1994). "Beyond Individualism/Collectivism: New Cultural Dimensions of Values," in U. Kim, H.C. Triandis, Ç. Kağıtçibaşi, S-C. Choi and G. Yoon (eds), *Individualism and Collectivism: Theory, Method and Application*. Los Angeles, CA: Sage, 85–119.
Schwartz, S.H. (1999). "A Theory of Cultural Values and Some Implications for Work," *Applied Psychology: An International Review* 48:1, 23–47.
Singhapakdi, A., S.J. Vitell and O. Leelakulthanit (1994). "A Cross-Cultural Study of Moral Philosophies, Ethical Perceptions and Judgements: a Comparison of American and Thai Marketers," *International Marketing Review* 11:6, 65–78.

Smith, P.B., S. Dugan and F. Trompenaars (1996). "National Culture and the Values of Organizational Employees: a Dimensional Analysis Across 43 Nations," *Journal of Cross-Cultural Psychology* 27:2, 231–64.
Sparrow, P., C. Brewster and C. Chung (2017). *Globalizing Human Resource Management*. London: Routledge.
Taka, I. and T.W. Dunfee (1997). "Japanese Moralogy as Business Ethics," *Journal of Business Ethics* 16, 507–19.
Trompenaars, F. (1993). *Riding the Waves of Culture: Understanding Cultural Diversity in Business*. London: Nicholas Brealey.
Trompenaars, F. and C. Hampden-Turner (2012). *Riding the Waves of Culture: Understanding Diversity in Global Business*. New York, NY: McGraw-Hill.
Westwood, R.J. and B.Z. Posner (1997). "Managerial Values Across Cultures: Australia, Hong Kong and the United States," *Asia Pacific Journal of Management* 14, 31–66.

34

Corruption, bribery, and moral norms across national boundaries*

Wesley Cragg

There are few issues in business ethics that are more clearly on the public agenda than that of corruption and bribery. Neither are there many topics to which both business and government have given more attention over the past two decades. Corruption in the world of business is of course not an exclusively modern or contemporary phenomenon. Evidence of its moral and ethical significance can be found in the Hebrew Bible/Christian Old Testament (e.g., Leviticus 19:35 ff.) and the code of Hammurabi (e.g., the Oman Tablets), both of which prohibit the use of false weights, lying and other forms of dishonesty in business dealings. The contemporary significance of corrupt or unethical conduct has been magnified, however, by globalization accompanied by the sheer size and reach of today's multinational corporations. The result is that corporate corruption can have devastating economic consequences for individuals, organizations, and national and international economies. The Enron scandal, which illustrates this development, destroyed careers, eliminated the pension savings of hundreds, perhaps thousands of people, impoverished many investors, led to the demise of one of the world's leading accounting and auditing firms, Arthur Anderson, undermined confidence in the stock market and contributed to an energy crisis in California (Eichenwald 2005; McLean and Elkind 2003). Had the Enron scandal been a one-off event, it might warrant a footnote in business history. However, it proved to be just one in a series of scandals that have shaken confidence in business leadership in the industrialized world. More recently, the financial crisis of 2008, in which corrupt business practices, for example in housing and mortgage markets, contributed to a serious recession, has generated global repercussions, and many national economies, as of the time of writing, have yet to recover. The Siemens' bribery scandal, Volkswagen's manipulation of emissions testing and on-going evidence of corruption in financial services, for example the Libor scandal, all provide persuasive evidence that corruption is deeply embedded in the contemporary global economy (Kansas 2009; Santoro and Strauss 2012; Schubert and Miller 2008; Manacorda et al. 2014; Hotten 2015; McBride 2016).

The Oxford English Dictionary defines the word "corrupt" as "rotten; depraved; wicked." Corruption is defined as decomposition and moral deterioration. Corruption construed this way is broadly synonymous with "unethical," "immoral" or, as some sources put it, "ethically depraved." The discussion of political corruption in Wikipedia ("Corruption") describes political corruption as the use of power by government officials for illegitimate private gain.

It goes on to catalog the various forms of corruption as including bribery, extortion, cronyism, nepotism, patronage, influence peddling, graft, and embezzlement. Although the focus in the Wikipedia account is political corruption, it gets us closer to our topic inasmuch as corruption as it relates to business is frequently closely associated with political corruption. This is particularly true of bribery as widely understood and commonly defined, as we shall see.

Three features of corruption are significant for what follows. First, the definitions of "corrupt" and "corruption" just set out, together with the catalog of forms of political corruption, encapsulate virtually the whole range of unethical business conduct. Defined this way, we could say the antonym of "corruption" is "integrity." A second feature of corruption as commonly defined is how closely corruption is associated with bribery. *The Oxford English Dictionary*, for example, includes in its definition of the word "corrupt," "influenced by bribery." Wikipedia utilizes the work of economist Ian Senior and defines economic corruption as "an action to (a) secretly provide (b) a good or a service to a third party (c) so that he or she can influence certain actions which (d) benefit the corrupt, a third party, or both (e) in which the corrupt agent has authority" (see the original definition in Senior 2006: 27). This is, in fact, virtually a definition of bribery. Transparency International, a global anticorruption coalition, also uses the terms "bribery" and "corruption" virtually interchangeably (Eigen 2003). Third, and finally, definitions of corruption typically point out that what the law defines as corruption can and does vary from country to country, a claim which, taken by itself, is indisputable. This is in turn a fact that is often thought to imply the more general and unconditional moral claim that what counts as corruption varies from country to country, or society to society, or culture to culture. Analysing and evaluating that view is a central topic for this chapter.

While the broad theme of the chapter is corruption, the form of corruption on which discussion will largely focus is bribery. The scope and impact of bribery on economic development, particularly in the developing and underdeveloped world, has emerged since World War II as both troubling and contentious (Kaufmann 1997; Linn 2000). As a result, bribery has captured the attention of business, government, and standard-setting international business associations and institutions like the Organisation for Economic Co-Operation and Development (OECD), the World Bank, the International Monetary Fund and the United Nations. Each has responded to the phenomenon of bribery with charters, conventions and codes of ethics that define bribery as morally unacceptable. This is not to say that other forms of corruption are ethically speaking less significant. It is to say, however, that while behaviors like extortion, cronyism, nepotism, patronage, influence peddling, graft, and embezzlement can and do have significant damaging impacts, their ethically suspect character is as a rule more easily and less controversially identified and therefore more easily addressed from an ethical and public policy perspective. Reasons for this will emerge in the discussion that follows.

With regard to the third element, does the understanding of corruption vary across national boundaries? The answer is undeniably "yes" for legal definitions of corruption. For example, what is prohibited as nepotism or cronyism in some legal systems is legally permitted in others. Until 1996, while the bribery of public officials in the country in which a company was headquartered was contrary to law throughout Europe, the bribery of foreign public officials was accepted by those same countries as a legitimate business practice and bribes directed to foreign public officials were regarded as legitimate business expenses for tax purposes. These examples focus on corruption as legally defined. Ethics and law, however, are not co-extensive. That some forms of unethical behavior are legally permitted is a common feature of legal systems generally. However, the fact that cultural and societal norms do vary from society to society and culture to culture, together with the fact that bribery is commonplace in many parts of the world, does raise questions about whether moral or ethical norms governing bribery have global or what is more typically described as universal validity.

In what follows, we consider first the concept of bribery and distinguish it from gift giving. We then identify in the second section the inherent features of bribery and its typical effects. In section three we look at bribery as a complex social phenomenon and confront the paradox that although bribery is almost universally condemned, its practice is widespread. The fourth section points out some of the legal measures undertaken to discourage bribery and corruption more generally, emphasizing in particular the roles of international organizations and global conventions. The fifth section explores the roles of transparency and accountability in combating bribery across borders and sets out two steps that need to be taken to curb bribery and corruption as both local and global phenomena. The discussion ends with a brief overview of the moral character of the different forms of corruption and summarizes the conclusions following from the discussion.

Bribery and gifts

John Noonan, in one of the seminal explorations of the subject, defines bribery as "an inducement improperly influencing the performance of a public function meant to be gratuitously exercised" (Noonan 1984: xi). In the introduction to his study, Noonan (xx ff.) observes that:

- bribery has been an element of public life virtually since the dawn of organized social life;
- views about the moral character of bribes have evolved over a long period of time;
- the distinction between a bribe and a gift is fundamental to understanding both the nature of bribery and the difficulty societies have had throughout history in identifying its problematic character;
- the connection between reciprocity and gift giving makes differentiating between bribes and gifts complex; and
- bribes today are disapproved of by virtually every culture.

Perhaps the most interesting thing about the history of the idea of bribery is the difficulty that cultures and societies have had, and in many cases continue to have, first differentiating between gifts and bribes, second clarifying what makes bribes morally problematic, and consequently identifying the conditions under which gifts or favours become bribes. Exploring the nature of this challenge is where our discussion begins.

Gifts and the challenge of reciprocity

What is it then about gift giving and reciprocity that complicates efforts to identify clearly what bribes are and why they are morally or ethically problematic[1] Gifts mark and acknowledge friendships and family bonds. Gifts are frequently offered as a way of building or indicating a desire to build a relationship or a friendship. They are by their nature informal and voluntary. They cannot be coerced. They are a feature of social behavior in virtually all cultures. They play an integral role in building business relationships historically and in today's world. Perhaps most importantly for our purposes, the exchange of favours in business as in other social settings is often governed by the norms of reciprocity. A favor may be given with the intention of generating an obligation on the part of the recipient to return the favor, though what is expected in return may be unspoken and unspecified (Nguyen and Cragg 2012).

Offering and accepting gifts historically therefore has carried, expressed and generated reciprocal obligations. It would be surprising, therefore, *not* to find these patterns reflected in relations with those in positions of power or influence. Establishing good will and attempting to ensure that one's business proposition or case or petition was favourably received by offering a gift could be seen from this perspective as simply another expression of a basic social pattern serving to establish and shape social relationships.

We might say, then, that the story of bribery is a story of the struggle to differentiate gifts from bribes.

Distinguishing gifts and bribes

Historically, the distinction between bribes and gifts emerged out of reflections, frequently set in a religious context, of the role, duties and obligations of judges. Justice was seen as a divine attribute. Gradually, the realization emerged that God's judgment could not be swayed by gifts designed to curry favor. Divine justice did not respond to wealth and did not discriminate against the weak or poor or the powerless. Notions of divine justice began to shape understandings of the obligations of human judges called on to settle disputes and impose penalties and punishments on wrong doers. We find in the Old Testament, for example, evidence of an emerging realization that human judges had an obligation to follow the divine pattern, which in turn required that they reject gifts designed to sway their judgment and commit to rendering impartial judgments (Noonan 1984: 14–30). With what is essentially a moral insight, the charting of the moral contours of bribery could take place.

It is not surprising that the moral significance of impartiality should emerge in understandings of the roles and obligations of judges. Justice requires that the law be applied impartially without fear or favor. Impartiality requires cases to be judged on their merits, set against the laws relevant to the case being tried. What that means and what it requires then becomes a key element in the evolution of law and judicial systems (Pepys 2007). As a result, notions of impartiality are deeply imbedded in modern legal systems, with the result that gift giving involving judges is today uncontroversially acknowledged and recognized to be morally and legally unacceptable.

Historically, applying similar distinctions and concepts to the roles and obligations of other public officials has proven more difficult. Public policy does not treat everyone equally. Taxes vary across different groups of taxpayers. Welfare systems and policies differentiate between and among welfare recipients. Economic development policies treat different categories of economic activity differentially. Nonetheless, justice and fairness require the capacity to differentiate when and where gift giving is morally inappropriate. The key principle in the administration of public policy is the impartial determination of merit. Public policy and the laws and regulations put in place to guide its application establish criteria that identify how and to whom a given policy applies. What is key, morally speaking, is that the criteria be administered fairly, which in this case means impartially. What impartiality requires is that those who benefit are entitled to the benefits received and those who do not benefit are excluded because they are not entitled under the policy in question to benefit, as set against the criteria the decision maker has an ethical responsibility to apply in making the decision (Noonan 1984: 30–41).

For law makers, for example politicians, distinguishing between gifts and bribes is still very much in contention and the application of concepts such as fairness and impartiality remain matters that are widely debated. What is not disputed, however, is that gifts designed to influence policymakers to use their power to advance the interests of the gift giver in ways inconsistent with their responsibilities as decision makers are morally inappropriate.

These same considerations apply also in the realm of business and in interactions between business and government. In business, those in positions of responsibility have an obligation to advance the interests of the firm or business for which they have decision-making responsibilities. But they must do so in ways that acknowledge and respect obligations to clients and other stakeholders (Hess and Dunfee 2008). Doing so well is the core challenge of management. Gift giving designed to curry favor and influence inappropriately how decisions are made is as morally inappropriate in business as it is in government and the public sector (Nguyen and Cragg 2012).

Bribery: inherent characteristics

Like gifts, bribes in the world of business are voluntary. They involve a voluntary exchange between two parties, a giver and a recipient. They are also informal. Their purpose is:

- to influence a decision maker who holds a position of responsibility in a public, private or voluntary sector organization;
- through the use of a financial or other inducement designed to advance the decision makers' interests or those of another person or group to which the decision maker is linked through personal, professional or group loyalties, relationships, commitments or obligations;
- to make a decision or recommendation designed to benefit the bribe giver or another person or group to which the bribe giver is linked through personal, professional or group loyalties, relationships, commitments or obligations;
- on grounds or for reasons *other* than those the decision maker is ethically required to apply by virtue of the decision maker's position of responsibility.

What this definition makes clear is that bribery is possible wherever there are decision makers in positions of responsibility. Bribes are always directed at *individuals* because their purpose is to persuade either an individual or a group of individuals in positions of authority to make a decision or engage in an action that is inconsistent with their responsibilities. On the other hand, both individuals *and* organizations can offer bribes, though for organizations this requires the complicity of one or more of their employees or agents.

With this account, we have the foundations for an explanation of why, as Noonan points out, for all cultures, societies and countries, bribery is unethical (Noonan 1984: 702).

1. Bribery requires deliberate deception. This fundamental characteristic is one reason why bribery, when revealed, is followed by public condemnation. Though bribery is common in many parts of the world today, no company has a line item in their audited statements labelled "bribes" (even where the bribery of foreign public officials is allowed by countries for income tax purposes), just because bribery is universally condemned. If this were not the case, it would not be necessary to conceal bribes behind a veil of secrecy. They would simply be reported as such on balance sheets and in audited statements.
2. Bribery generates unfairness and injustice. In competitive business environments, bribes override the rules governing competition with the result that decision-making processes are corrupted.
3. Bribery corrupts moral character. One of the morally perverse characteristics of bribery is that it tempts people in positions of responsibility to put their own interests ahead of the duties and responsibilities that flow from the positions of responsibility they hold.
4. Bribery is infectious. As numerous empirical studies have shown, it is much more difficult to resist a bribe or to avoid offering one if one is doing business in an environment where it is believed that fellow workers or fellow competitors are actively engaged in bribery (Dass et al. 2014; Zoido and Chavis 2004).

5 Bribery when exposed both damages and destroys reputations. This is both a sign and a consequence of its unethical character. However, the damage it causes, while it may be deserved in part, almost always affects innocent third parties. Although the bribery in question may be the result of the actions of an individual or group acting quite independently of the organization in which they hold positions of responsibility, the reputational damage may well be felt across the organization, with harmful consequences for innocent employees and their dependents and also for the organization itself and its many stakeholders. Where the bribery is carried out with organizational complicity, support or active engagement, the resulting reputational damage, on detection, is likely to extend beyond the organization and its immediate stakeholders to other organizations and firms engaged in the same field of activity and even to whole industries and countries. The passage of the American Foreign Corrupt Practices Act was motivated in part by fears on the part of the American Congress that revelations that the bribery of foreign governments by American companies was widespread were damaging the reputation of American companies generally as well as the reputation and moral standing of the American government (Woof and Cragg 2005: 134).

6 Where bribery is widespread, accusations of bribery take on increased credibility, whether or not they are grounded in fact. Hence accusations of bribery become weapons whose target is as likely to be the honest as the dishonest.

7 Bribery involving public officials undermines the proper functioning of the democratic process. Since the purpose of a bribe is to persuade someone in a position of authority to do something that is not consistent with his or her responsibilities, bribery undermines the proper functioning of elections, legislatures, and law enforcement in all its aspects. As a result, bribery has political significance in today's world where democratic institutions are thought to play a central role in protecting and advancing important values like human rights, personal development, fairer distribution of economic wealth and environmental sustainability (Rose-Ackerman 1999a: 363–378).

8 Bribery conflicts with values central to the operation of a free and competitive marketplace. Markets allow buyers to make the most efficient use of their material resources in acquiring the goods and services that they need and want. And they allow sellers to compete for their business. Markets can function only if buyers and sellers are able to evaluate what is being offered on its merits. Bribery short circuits this process. It rewards expertise in reading patterns of corruption and bribing the "right" decision makers rather than those who have acquired the skills and competence to provide the desired quality of goods and services at the most competitive prices. Although market theorists differ widely about the rules that are required to ensure that markets operate efficiently, what Milton Friedman calls "the rules of the game," there is general agreement that deception subverts free and open competition (Friedman 1970: 133).

9 Bribery undermines economic development and worthwhile public and private sector initiatives. Where bribery leads to higher costs or poorer quality for schools or hospitals or roads, to cite just a few examples, then resources are being used inefficiently and resources that could otherwise be used to provide needed goods and services are no longer available (Lambsdorff 2004; Kaufmann 1997).

10 Bribery can be used to rationalize and excuse failure. This is one of the debilitating aspects of bribery seen particularly from the perspective of business. Where bribery is thought to be common, failure to win contracts or attract buyers or build competitive goods or provide services at competitive prices can be blamed on bribery. Since bribery is by its nature covert, it is very difficult to verify rationalizations of this variety (Woof and Cragg 2005).

Bribery: a complex social, economic, and political reality

On the account given, bribery is by its nature morally problematic. Yet the research and findings of organizations like Transparency International suggest that bribery is commonplace and indeed endemic in many parts of the world (see Transparency International 2004). A casual observer might be tempted to assume from this account that the fact that bribery is widespread demonstrates that ethics is of little concern in the conduct of business that crosses borders. However, this conclusion is premature. Paradoxically, there are also strong ethical imperatives that would appear to justify the use of bribery as a business strategy.

Shareholder-owned corporations have both legal and moral obligations to their shareholders. The shares of most multinational corporations are widely held and are likely to include as shareholders pension funds, pensioners, insurance companies and the many others whose material welfare may well be directly dependent on corporate earnings. Corporations are also widely argued to have obligations to other stakeholders as well such as, for example, their employees and their families, their suppliers, their clients and customers and the communities in which they do business. A corporation that fails to "play the game" of bribery may lose business with a consequent fall in share value, the loss of jobs both on the part of employees and suppliers of goods and services, the loss of tax revenues for dependent communities and so on. The dilemma faced by Carl Kotchian, president of Lockheed Aircraft Corporation in the early 1970s, offers a classic example of the morally ambiguous character of bribery (see Woof and Cragg 2005: 118; Boatright 1997: 27ff). The company was on the edge of bankruptcy. Winning a contract to supply passenger jets to All Nippon Airways was vital to the survival of the company. Bribes in excess of $12 million secured contracts for planes and ensured the company's survival.

Bribery is thus a significantly more complex moral phenomenon than might at first seem to be the case. This may help to explain why a business strategy that is, from one perspective, uncontroversially unethical has nonetheless become so widespread. Examining this paradoxical state of affairs is our next task.

Bribery, particularly the bribery of public officials, is identified as a criminal offence in virtually all modern legal systems. Equally important, respect for the law is an acknowledged obligation of managers in virtually all modern management systems and theories of management. So too do virtually all companies doing business nationally or internationally regard the acceptance of bribes by their own employees to be an offence justifying dismissal. Yet, paradoxically, as already noted, even as corporations profess an obligation to obey the law and regard the acceptance of bribes by their own employees to be unacceptable, bribery is nonetheless for many of those same corporations accepted as a strategy for gaining or retaining business. It is striking and equally paradoxical that, until the late 1990s, most governments in the industrialized world, with the exception of the United States, allowed bribery as a legitimate business expense for tax purposes but only where it involved the bribery of foreign public officials.

What is to explain this paradox? Both the theory and the practice of modern management pay unambiguous homage to obeying the law. However, law is a national phenomenon. Furthermore, the theory and practice of sovereignty generally restrict the reach of legal systems to the geographical territory of the nation state. Since the preponderance of bribes are paid by corporations headquartered in industrialized countries and the preponderance of recipients are in developing or underdeveloped countries, head offices can (or rather could until very recently) claim correctly, as the president of Lockheed did in 1972, that they were not breaking their country's laws by offering bribes to public officials in other countries.[2] Further, if the obligation of corporations to obey the law is understood to extend only to laws that are actively enforced or laws whose breach carries a reasonable risk of detection and punishment, then, in many countries in the developing and underdeveloped world, bribery could also be said, in effect, not to be against the law, and therefore to be a legitimate business option: "when in Rome, do as the Romans do."

It is the intersection of these two value judgments—that bribery is morally unacceptable and worthy of criminal sanctions in one's own country, yet justified or excusable as a requirement for doing business in other countries in which one does business (particularly in less developed nations)—that gives bribery an ethically paradoxical and ambiguous character. Furthermore, evidence of clashing value systems that seem to judge bribery as acceptable in some contexts but not in others, together with the fact that in some parts of the world bribery is widely accepted as a business reality, may appear to give credence to the view that bribery is a culturally relative ethical norm. Previous discussion provides convincing reasons for rejecting that conclusion. However, it also points to a serious ethical tension in response to the phenomenon of bribery in the contemporary world of business.

Addressing the paradox of bribery through legal reform

Bribery as a twentieth-century moral and economic issue emerged in the first instance as an American phenomenon driven by American governance institutions and American multinational corporations. The first reports of serious wrongdoing by American firms surfaced when it was discovered that the International Telephone and Telegraph Corporation (ITT) had offered the US Central Intelligence Agency (CIA) $1 million in 1970 to block the election of Chilean presidential candidate Salvador Allende. The CIA, as it turned out, declined the offer. Subsequent investigations also concluded that that ITT had not broken any American laws (see the US Senate Report, Committee on Foreign Relations, 1973). What did emerge, however, was that the ITT incident was not an isolated event. Senate investigations concurrent with the Watergate scandal subsequently identified over 400 US corporations that admitted making bribery-related payments totaling more than $300 million (see the account, FBI 2010).

Revelations emerging from the Watergate investigations raised serious concerns about financial reporting of American corporations on the part of the Securities and Exchange Commission (the SEC) and the implication of the bribery of foreign public officials for American foreign policy and international relations. The result was passage of the US Foreign Corrupt Practices Act (FCPA) in 1977. The Act prohibited payments made directly or through an intermediary with a view to influencing a foreign official in the performance of authorized duties and functions in exchange for unwarranted benefits or considerations. Prohibited bribe recipients included foreign government officials and all foreign political parties and candidates as well as all intermediaries for people in these positions.

The Impact of the FCPA

The passage of the Foreign Corrupt Practices Act (FCPA) by the US government in 1977 was a watershed event in the fight against bribery in the post-war era for two key reasons. First, it brought to light the threat that bribery posed for integrity in government. Second, it put the role of law and regulation in combating corruption on the international agenda. Nonetheless, two decades were to pass before any other national governments followed suit.[3] There were several reasons for this. One was a fear on the part of governments in the industrialized world that prohibiting the bribery of foreign public officers would put their own business sector at a competitive disadvantage in international markets (Woof and Cragg 2005: 114; Koehler 2012: 975). Further, the very limited available economic research into the impact of corruption on economic development was interpreted to suggest that bribery, particularly in the developing and underdeveloped world, greased economic activity in the face of dysfunctional public regulatory institutions and laws (see Kaufmann 1997).

However, for a variety of reasons, attitudes in the 1990s began to evolve. The fall of the iron curtain was certainly an important factor. The Soviet Union, long a strong international opponent of anti-bribery initiatives by international institutions such as the World Bank, argued that any international initiatives would constitute unacceptable interference in the domestic affairs of sovereign countries. With that obstacle removed, the economic impacts of bribery came under closer scrutiny and a serious well-financed research agenda emerged that pointed to a decisive negative impact of bribery on economic development (Rose Ackermann 1999b; Kaufmann 1997).

A second factor was the birth of Transparency International (TI) in 1993. Headquartered in Berlin, Germany, Transparency International was born out of frustration on the part of a small group of World Bank senior middle management who could see the ravages of corruption in those areas of the world for which they were specifically responsible. Africa was a particular focus of concern. One of the first actions of TI was to research and publish the *Corruption Perception Index* (CPI). This index, first published in 1995, ranked countries by reference to perceived levels of corruption. Its effect was to make corruption and bribery a high profile public policy issue. The countries identified as the most corrupt by the CPI, however, were all in the developing or underdeveloped world. Transparency International was accused of biased and imperialistically motivated studies that identified bribery as a third-world problem and a reflection on third-world moral standards. Transparency International's response was to commission a second study designed to rank countries by reference to the perceived propensity of their companies to offer bribes to foreign officials in the pursuit of business opportunities. The result of this study was the *Bribe Payers Index*, first published in 1999. All of the countries in this index were located in the industrialized north.

In 1994, the OECD issued a statement calling on member countries to combat corruption. In 1996, the OECD called on member countries to discontinue the practice of allowing bribes to be deducted as legitimate business expenses for tax purposes. In 1997, the OECD adopted an anticorruption convention calling for signatories to criminalize the bribery of foreign public officials by companies under their jurisdiction (for the full text see *OECD Convention* 1999).

The OECD *Anti-Bribery Convention* took effect in 1999. It was significant not just for its stand on bribery but also because of its rules of implementation. The convention required, first, that signatories submit their legislation implementing the convention for peer review to ensure that it met convention standards and could be seen by participating countries to create a level playing field for companies competing in the international market place. Even more significantly, the convention required that the enforcement efforts of signatory countries be monitored by the OECD and therefore indirectly by other countries party to the OECD anti-corruption convention (see "Country Monitoring Reports," OECD). Both these requirements were groundbreaking.

As of the time of writing (2016), all OECD countries and a number of others as well have signed the convention and have put enabling legislation in place.

Other international developments

Not surprisingly, concern with the impact of bribery has not been confined to the OECD. The position of the World Bank too has changed quite dramatically over the past three decades. Serious study, much of it now funded by the World Bank, has now confirmed what has been evident to some observers for several decades, namely that the bribery of government officials constitutes a serious impediment to economic growth. The World Bank now has in place guidelines on procurement and consulting and a legal framework for enforcing its policies and for sanctioning firms on World-Bank-financed projects that fail to comply with these policies. Companies that engage in bribery on projects financed by the World Bank can now find themselves blacklisted and cut off from World-Bank-funded projects. Two important recent examples of leading multinational firms that have been fined and sanctioned include Siemens, headquartered in Germany, and SNC Lavalin, an international engineering firm headquartered in Canada.[4]

The International Monetary Fund (IMF) has followed with strong anti-corruption policies and regulations that it links closely to good governance (see IMF 2016, *Factsheet*). Further, the International Standards Association is preparing an anti-bribery management systems standard, ISO 37001, which "is designed to help large, medium and small public, private and voluntary sector organizations prevent bribery and promote an ethical business culture" (ISO 2015). The standard is expected to be in place by 2017.

The World Trade Organization has moved more slowly. It has had the topic on its agenda for several years and is currently considering proposals to build transparency requirements into government procurement trade policies (Wolfe 2013).

Perhaps the most significant anti-corruption event in this century is the entry into force in December 2005 of the United Nations Convention Against Corruption and with it the emergence of a global cross-cultural norm recognized as central to economic development, the eradication of poverty, combatting climate change, preservation of the natural environment and biodiversity, and the protection and enhancement of human rights (see United Nations, undated).

The pursuit of integrity in business and government: lessons and challenges

The developments described in the previous sections may be seen as attempts to address what I have described as the paradox of corruption. Yet bribery and other forms of corruption continue to be disconcertingly common. What then does the future hold? This question is complex and a comprehensive answer is beyond the scope of this chapter. However, there are some general conclusions that emerge from efforts to curb corruption in global markets that are significant and point the way forward.

One conclusion that emerges from the criminalization of the bribery of foreign public officials is that criminalization itself is not sufficient to curb corruption in its various forms nationally or internationally. This is not to say that the criminalization of the bribery of foreign public officials and other forms of corruption is and has been of no value. In the case of bribery, for example, if nothing else, it has raised the profile of the issue locally and globally. It has also generated research that has provided and continues to provide important insights on the phenomenon and its social, cultural, political, environmental and economic impacts locally and globally (Seitzinger 2012). Finally, it has shaped the structures and the policies of important international institutions such as the United Nations and its various agencies, international financial institutions, for example the World Bank, and national export development agencies created to encourage and support the export of goods and services by national firms. It has also had a significant impact on the conduct of virtually all multinational companies, international industry, and private sector associations and voluntary sector organizations such as the International Standards Association and the Global Reporting Initiative.

A second outcome is the realization that both transparency and accountability are key to curbing not just bribery but corruption more generally. Corruption in all its forms, including bribery, is by its nature covert, for which the now widely prescribed antidote is financial transparency on the part of business and government. If financial transactions are publically visible then the second principle, accountability, can be brought to bear and those responsible for the administration of corporate and government finances held accountable.

An example of these principles at work is the Extractive Industries Transparency Initiative, which was inspired by a movement to require corporations to "publish what you pay." The goal of this movement is to combat both bribery and corruption more generally by making the flow of money, between mining and oil and gas firms on the one hand, and governments in the countries in which they are active on the other, a matter of the public record. Transparency is achieved by ensuring: 1) that all funds paid for the privilege of extracting natural resources in a country party to the EITI agreement are publicly reported; and 2) all moneys received by the government in question are reported by that government. What this is designed to ensure is that financial transactions between resource extraction companies and the governments of the countries in which they propose to extract natural resources are fully transparent.

Transparency is a key to eliminating bribery where effective legislation is in place. This in turn opens the door to accountability. If funds available to a government from resource extraction are public knowledge, government officials can then be held accountable for how that money is spent. The goal here is to prevent corruption in the allocation of public resources on the part of public officials.[5] The focus on resource extraction is particularly significant in as much as, historically, corruption has meant that countries and their citizens in the developing and underdeveloped world have, as a rule, experienced heavy costs and meager benefits from the exploitation of their natural resources, a phenomenon sometimes referred to as "the resource curse" (see "Extractive . . . " and consider the report on "publish what you pay" in van Orange and Parham 2009). Virtually all proposals and policy recommendations designed to curb corruption incorporate these two principles either directly or indirectly.

What then remains to be done? One commonly heard response is more and more effective enforcement. However, enforcement patterns in any country are governed by prevailing governance values and institutional capacity. As a consequence, a great deal of attention has shifted from a relatively exclusive focus on corruption to a focus on good governance. The policies and practices of the World Bank illustrate this development. Further, since good governance is both a private sector and a public sector issue, the proposal that good governance holds the key to curbing corruption implies the need for improved standards of governance in both the public and the private sectors. The effect has been a shared acknowledgment that both the private and public sectors share responsibility for combatting bribery and corruption in business transactions. This in turn opens the door wider to understanding the drivers of corruption on both the demand and the supply sides and what is required on the part of both government and business to curb corruption (Rose-Ackerman 1999b: 4).

Two key *corporate* governance reforms are needed if this goal is to be achieved. The first reform is required of companies already committed to high anti-corruption standards in their strategic planning and day-to-day operations. These companies have strong ethics codes and business ethics training programs, publish regular corporate social responsibility reports in accordance with best practice standards, for example those set out by the Global Reporting Initiative, and advocate for high standards in their respective business organizations (see GRI undated). What is systematically lacking, however, is arm's length monitoring of their operations designed to determine whether corporations are actually living up to the values and principles set out in their ethics codes and related strategic and operational policies. The insistence on effective arms-length monitoring of countries that have signed the OECD anti-corruption convention by the OECD speaks eloquently to the need to address this lacuna on the private sector side as well. Effective monitoring helps to ensure that the companies headquartered in countries that are serious about prohibiting the bribery of foreign public officers are not put at a serious competitive disadvantage because the anti-corruption standards they must live with are effectively enforced. Requiring effective independent monitoring of the implementation of corporate ethics codes and policies is therefore a key reform required to curb corporate corruption.

The second reform is also company focused. In market economies, profitability is a business requirement. Profits generate the capital that keeps a business in business. A particularly significant management theory, advanced by the Chicago School of Economics in the 1960s and 70s and popularized by Milton Friedman in a now famous article in the *New York Times Magazine* (1970), however, added a significant embellishment to this fundamental characteristic of market-driven economic systems. The primary obligation of management, Friedman argued, was not simply to ensure profitability but rather to maximize profitability for owners and shareholders. About a decade later, the grip of this view of the purpose of private sector shareholder-owned corporations on corporate governance was significantly tightened by the development and application of agency theory (Jensen and Meckling 1976). If the purpose of the firm is to maximize profits for the benefit of owners and shareholders, then a fundamental responsibility of corporate boards is to motivate senior management to maximize profits. Agency theory provided a framework for accomplishing this corporate goal (an extended discussion is in Cragg et al. 2009: xiv–xxxiii).

Agency theory assumes that managers are motivated largely by self-interest. It provides a model for designing financial incentives that will motivate managers to maximize profits for the benefit of shareholders and owners. It is an approach to corporate governance and management that is today deeply embedded in corporate governance in the industrialized world.

Research is making it increasingly clear that the focus on profit maximization is a key factor driving what could be described as a corruption epidemic in global markets. Roger Martin, the former Dean of the University of Toronto Rotman School of Business, in his analysis of the 2007–2008 financial crisis, argues that the thesis that profit maximization is the overriding purpose of business has "the ability to destroy our economy and rot out the core of American capitalism." What is his evidence for this view? The answer is "three massive, blowout scandals involving hundreds of executives each: the accounting scandals (2001–2002), the options backdating scandal (2005–2006), and the subprime mortgage scandal (2008–2009)" (Martin 2011: 93). Other examples include the case of Philip Condit, former CEO of Boeing who "in the interests of maximizing value among other things engaged in procurement corruption and industrial espionage" (Martin 2011: 113). Denis Arnold (2016) points out that "the relentless pursuit of profit advocated by the shareholder ideology implicitly advocates illegal activity where such activity is profitable and governments are unable to enforce existing regulations." The global bribery epidemic,[6] the erosion of ethical standards in the financial services industry (see Waitzer and Sarro 2014) and the history in the first decades of the twenty-first century of corporate misconduct, including, most recently, the Volkswagen emissions and the SNC Lavelin scandals, underscore Arnold's observation. Cable and Vermeulen (2016) point to empirical studies that indicate that paying for performance results in cooked books, false sales reports, and illegal means to performance, all of which is widely evidenced in the world of business.

Neither Milton Friedman nor the advocates of agency theory support falling back on corrupt business practices to maximize profits. However, as is now widely acknowledged and illustrated by the preceding examples, incentives designed to promote profit maximization can and do push managers in the direction of corrupt business practices. Bribery is just one of the consequences. It can win contracts by undercutting the competition. It can bypass environmental and other regulations saving a corporation sometimes large sums of money. It follows that corruption is unlikely to be reduced either locally or globally unless this now dominant view, that the purpose of corporations is to maximize profits or share value and the dominant interest of business management is maximizing personal financial wealth, is significantly modified.

The character of corruption

Our discussion has moved from an overview of corruption and the variety of forms it can take, to an analysis of bribery finally transitioning to a discussion of corruption more generally. What then can we conclude from our discussion of bribery and corruption more generally about specific forms of corruption identified in our introduction such as extortion, cronyism, nepotism, patronage, influence peddling, graft, and embezzlement?

Of this list, extortion is the most closely related to and the most frequently confused with bribery. Extortion like bribery has the form of an exchange between two parties. What distinguishes extortion from bribery, however, is the presence of coercion. Bribery becomes extortion when the reciprocity involved is coerced, for example ransom demands following a kidnapping. Unlike bribery, however, extortion is never morally ambiguous, though determining when the threshold between bribery and extortion has been crossed is not always easy and is inevitably context dependent. Graft and embezzlement also lack any moral ambiguity. There are no social or economic systems in which they pass or could pass as socially acceptable components of economic activity. One thing these forms of corruption have in common with bribery, however, is that they are often driven by narrowly focused financial self-interest, that is to say, the moral vice of greed. Greed, however, is not the only motivation for corruption. Other factors can include such things as strong ideological commitments or family loyalties.

Cronyism and nepotism are different in nature. Each, like bribery, involves using a position of power or authority to advance personal interests. However, neither is necessarily covert or dishonest. Nepotism, for example, in cases of private business ownership, is widely practiced and for the most part lacks moral ambiguity. For privately owned firms, for example those involving family ownership, employing family members and passing ownership from one generation of a family to the next is morally uncontroversial. Nepotism is morally questionable for public shareholder-owned corporations where management has an ethical obligation to operate efficiently and treat its diverse stakeholders fairly and equitably. Cronyism, like nepotism, is morally offensive when it prioritizes business decision makers' social or personal interests or relationships over the efficient pursuit of a firm's business interests and does so in ways that are unfair to firm shareholders or stakeholders and are inconsistent with firm policies and legal obligations. That being the case, the values and principles that determine the ethical status of both nepotism and cronyism are similar across cultures, although, whether specific instances of both are unethical is context dependent in a way that is not true of bribery or the other forms of wrong doing under examination here. When the focus shifts from the private to the public sector, however, the moral character of both nepotism and cronyism is clear and unequivocal. Public office holders, as we saw earlier, have an obligation to serve public interests. Both cronyism and nepotism involve putting private interests ahead of the dispassionate and disinterested implementation of public policy and are therefore unambiguously unethical.

Concluding remarks

In summary, avoiding corruption is a universal moral requirement that is fundamental to the efficient and ethical operation of market economies. Corruption undermines economic development. It subverts efforts to eliminate poverty and to create an improved quality of life on the part of a broad cross section of those living in the developing and underdeveloped world.[7] It opens the door to bribery, encouraging policy makers to focus public expenditures on the purchase of goods and the provision of services for which bribes are most easily and covertly collected by corrupted officials and decision makers. It entrenches ruling elites by diverting public resources to their private use for personal and political ends. It corrodes the quality of public services by draining public funds from the projects they are intended to support to the private uses of the corrupted officials. Finally, it undermines trust in democratic institutions.[8] Understanding the different forms corruption can take and taking action to combat them can be said, therefore, to be a fundamental principle of business ethics and a fundamental obligation of business and business leaders.

Essential readings

Essential scholarly works on corruption and bribery include John Noonan Jr., *Bribes: The Intellectual History of a Moral Idea* (1984) and Susan Rose-Ackerman, "Political Corruption and Democracy" (1999a). For an early and influential post-cold-war study of corruption and its impact see Daniel Kaufmann, "Corruption: The Facts" (Summer 1997). For a study of the impact of the American Foreign Corrupt Practices Act prior to the adoption of a series of international anti-corruption conventions, see William Woof and Wesley Cragg, "The US Foreign Corrupt Practices Act" (2005). Important international anti-corruption conventions include the OECD (1999) *Convention on Combating Bribery of Foreign Public Officials in International Business Transactions*; United Nations (2000) *The United Nations Convention Against Corruption*; and the Global Compact's tenth principle (United Nations 2004). For a historical record of the impact of corruption and efforts to curb corruption, see the annual reports and other publications of Transparency International (2004), available on-line at the website.

For further reading in this volume on a globalized ethics of business, see Chapter 32, The globalization of business ethics. On how the discourse of human rights is affecting the practice of accounting in multinational corporations, see Chapter 31, The accounting profession, the public interest, and human rights. On specific challenges to anti-corruption efforts, see the discussions in Chapter 37, Business ethics in Africa and Chapter 38, Business ethics in Latin America. For an account of corruption in the privatization of state-owned companies, see Chapter 39, Business ethics in transition: communism to commerce in Central Europe and Russia. On the use of political power for private ends, see Chapter 7, Can profit seekers be virtuous? and Chapter 21, Regulation, rent seeking, and business ethics. On the role of interests rather than ethics in political policy-making decisions, see Chapter 23, The economic crisis: causes and considerations.

Notes

* Wesley Cragg died in late August of 2017, just a few months after his chapter had been finalized for inclusion in this volume.

1 For the purposes of the discussion in this chapter, "morality" and "ethics" are treated as synonymous.
2 This claim ceased to be true for American companies in 1977 with the passage of the American Foreign Corrupt Practices Act. It also ceased to be true for corporations headquartered in countries as they have become parties to the 1997 OECD Anti-Bribery Convention and modified their criminal codes to criminalize the bribery of foreign public officials as required by the Convention.

Corruption, bribery, and moral norms across national boundaries

3 Arguably Sweden had similar provisions in its criminal code and was therefore an exception to this generalization.
4 Relevant documents may be found on-line at the World Bank's website. On the impact of corruption on economic development, see *Procurement: World Bank Listing of Ineligible Firms & Individuals (Fraud and Corruption)*, undated, available at: http://web.worldbank.org/external/default/main?theSitePK=84266&contentMDK=64069844&menuPK=116730&pagePK=64148989&piPK=64148984. On World Bank policies and enforcement strategies, see *Law, Justice and Development*, available at: http://web.worldbank.org/WBSITE/EXTERNAL/TOPICS/EXTLAWJUSTICE/0,,contentMDK:23394103~menuPK:9203924~pagePK:148956~piPK:216618~theSitePK:445634,00.html. For a list of debarred firms go to *Procurement: World Bank Listing of Ineligible Firms & Individuals (Fraud and Corruption). Table 1: Debarred and Cross-Debarred Firms & Individuals*, undated, available at: http://web.worldbank.org/external/default/main?theSitePK=84266&contentMDK=64069844&menuPK=116730&pagePK=64148989&piPK=64148984.
5 The argument here is not intended to imply that transparency and accountability are foolproof ways of eliminating corruption. To put it another way, transparency does not guarantee accountability. For the public to hold governments or business entities accountable requires institutional capacity that provides the public with the tools needed to call those with power to account. Thus EITI has not been fully effective in ensuring accountability in those countries where it has been adopted.
6 See, for example, the Transparency International Corruption Perceptions Index.
7 Events unfolding in Brazil as this chapter is being written are an obvious illustration.
8 See Transparency International website for the detailed delineation of these impacts.

References

Arnold, D. (2016). "Corporations and Human Rights Obligations," *Business & Human Rights Journal* 1:2, 255–275.
Boatright, J.R. (1997). *Ethics and the Conduct of Business*, 2nd edition. Upper Saddle River, NJ: Prentice-Hall.
Cable, D. and F. Vermeulen (2016). "Stop Paying Executives for Performance," *Harvard Business Review* (February 23).
Cassidy, J. (2002). "The Greed Cycle: How Corporate America Went Out of Control," *New Yorker* (September 23).
Cragg, W., M. Schwartz and D. Weitzner (2009). *Corporate Social Responsibility*. Farnham: Ashgate.
Dass, N., V. Nanda and S.C. Xiaio (2014). "Firms in Corrupt Environments and the Value of Corporate Governance," 27th Australasian Finance and Banking Conference (Sydney).
Drucker, P. (2001). *The Essential Drucker: The Best of Sixty Years of Peter Drucker's Essential Writings on Management*. New York, NY: Harper.
Duska, R. (2007). *Contemporary Reflections on Business Ethics*. Dordrecht: Springer.
Eichenwald, K. (2005). *Conspiracy of Fools*. New York, NY: Broadway Books.
Eigen, P. (2003). "Introduction," in R. Hodess (ed.), *Transparency International—Global Corruption Report 2003*. Vincenza: Profile Books.
Evans-Pritchard, A. (2015). "'Made in Germany' Lies in the 'Gutter' after Volkswagen Caught Cheating." *The Telegraph* (September 21).
Extractive Industries Transparency Initiative (EITI) (undated). Available at: www.eiti.org.
FBI (Federal Bureau of Investigation) (2010). *Corporate Corruption: A Historic Takedown*, January. Available at: www.fbi.gov/news/stories/2010/january/fcpa_012610.
Friedman, M. (1970). "The Social Responsibility of Business is to Increase its Profits," *New York Times Magazine* (September 13), 32–33 and 122–126.
Ghoshal, S. (2005). "Bad Management Theories are Destroying Good Management Practices," *Academy of Management Learning and Education*. 4:1, 75–91.
Ghoshal, S. (2015). "The Profit Maximization Mantra and the Challenge of Regaining Trust, Humanity and Purpose in an Age of Crisis," in K.J. Ims and J.D. Pederson (eds), *Business and the Greater Good*. Cheltenham: Edward Elgar, 41–64.
Global Reporting Initiative (GRI) (undated). Available at: www.globalreporting.org/resourcelibrary/GRIG4-Part1-Reporting-Principles-and-Standard-Disclosures.pdf.
Hess, D. and T. Dunfee (2008). "Taking Responsibility: The Multinational Corporation's Role in Combatting Corruption," in T.L. Beauchamp, N. Bowie and D.G. Arnold (eds), *Ethical Theory and Business*, 8th edition. Upper Saddle River, NJ: Pearson—Prentice Hall, 624–632.

Hotten, R. (2015). "Volkswagen: The Scandal Explained," *BBC News*. Available at: www.bbc.com/news/business-34324772 (December 10).
International Monetary Fund (2007). *IMF Code of Good Practices on Fiscal Transparency*. Available at: www.imf.org/external/np/fad/trans/code.htm.
International Monetary Fund (2016). *Factsheet: The IMF and Good Governance*. March 16. Available at: www.imf.org/external/np/exr/facts/gov.htm.
ISO (undated). Bribery Standard Website. Available at: www.iso.org/iso/home/news_index/news_archive/news.htm?refid=Ref1916.
ISO (2015). *Progress on Anti-bribery Standard*. May 27. Available at: www.iso.org/iso/home/news_index/news_archive/news.htm?refid=Ref1967.
Jensen, M.C. and W.H. Meckling (1976). "Theory of the Firm: Managerial Behavior, Agency Costs and Ownership Structure." *Journal of Financial Economics* 3:4, 303–431.
Johns, Rev. C.H.W. (1910–1911). "Babylonian Law: The Code of Hammurabi." *Encyclopaedia Britannica*, 11th edition. Available at: www.sacred-texts.com/ane/ham/ham02.htm.
Kansas, D. (2009). *The Wall Street Journal Guide to the End of the World As We Know It*. New York, NY: Harper Business.
Kaufmann, D. (1997). "Corruption: The Facts," *Foreign Policy* 107, 114–131. Available at: www1.worldbank.org/publicsector/anticorrupt/fp_summer97.pdf.
Kaufmann, D. (2006). "Myths and Realities of Governance and Corruption," Chapter 21 (2005) in *The Global Competitiveness Report 2005–2006*. New York, NY: World Economic Forum, Oxford University Press, 81–98. Available at: http://siteresources.worldbank.org/INTWBIGOVANTCOR/Resources/2-1_Governance_and_Corruption_Kaufmann.pdf.
Koehler, M. (2012). "The Story of the Foreign Corrupt Practices Act," *Ohio State Law Journal* 73:5, 929–1013.
Lambsdorff, J.G. (2004). "How Corruption Affects Economic Development," *Transparency International Global Corruption Report 2004*, 310–312.
Linn, J.F. (2000). "Executive Summary," *Anti-Corruption in Transition: A Contribution to the Policy Debate*. Washington, DC: The World Bank, xiii–xxxi.
Manacorda, S., F. Centizone and G. Forti (2014). "Case Studies 18.9.1.—Siemens: Evolution of a Compliance Program," in S. Manacorda, F. Centizone and G. Forti (eds), *Preventing Corporate Corruption: The Anti-Bribery Compliance Model*. New York, NY: Springer, 386–388.
Martin, R.L. (2011). *Fixing the Game: Bubbles, Crashes and What Capitalism Can Learn From the NFL*. Cambridge: Harvard Business Review Press.
McBride, J. (2016). "Understanding the Libor Scandal," Council on Foreign Relations, Updated October 12, 2016. Available at: www.cfr.org/united-kingdom/understanding-libor-scandal/p28729?cid=ppc-Google-grant-libor_scandal&gclid=CO7Lt8LP_c8CFQeQaQodb9AFaQ [accessed 28 October 2016].
McLean, B. and P. Elkind (2003). *The Smartest Guys in the Room: The Amazing Rise and Scandalous Fall of Enron*. New York, NY: Portfolio.
Mintzberg, H. (2000). "Interview," *Ivey Business School Journal* (September/October), Western University, Canada.
Nguyen, A. and A.W. Cragg (2012). "Interorganizational Favour Exchange and the Relationship Between Doing Well and Doing Good," *Journal of Business Ethics* 105:1 (January), 53–68.
Noonan, J.T. (1984). *Bribes: The Intellectual History of a Moral Idea*. New York, NY: Macmillan Publishing Co.
OECD (various). "Country Monitoring Reports," OECD Convention on Combatting Bribery of Foreign Government Officials in International Business Transactions. Available at: www.oecd.org/corruption/oecdantibriberyconvention.htm.
OECD (1999). *OECD Convention on Combatting Bribery of Foreign Public Officials in International Business Transactions*. Minneapolis, MN: University of Minnesota, Human Rights Library. Available at: www1.umn.edu/humanrts/instree/oecdbribery-1999.html.
Pepys, M.N. (2007). "Corruption Within the Judiciary: Causes and Remedies," *Transparency International Global Corruption Report 2007: Corruption in Judicial Systems*. Cambridge: Cambridge University Press, 3–11.
Rose-Ackerman, S. (1999a). "Political Corruption and Democracy," *Connecticut Journal of International Law* 14, 363–378.
Rose-Ackerman, S. (1999b). *Corruption and Government: Causes, Consequences and Reform*. Cambridge: Cambridge University Press.

Santoro, M.A. and R.J. Strauss (2012). *Wall Street Values: Business Ethics and the Global Financial Crisis*. Cambridge: Cambridge University Press.

Schubert, S. and T.C. Miller (2008). "At Siemens, Bribery Was Just a Line Item," *New York Times* (December 20).

Seitzinger, M.V. (2012). (March 15, 2016). "Foreign Corrupt Practices Act (FCPA): Congressional Interest and Executive Enforcement," *Congressional Research Service*. Available at: www.fas.org/sgp/crs/misc/R41466.pdf.

Senior, I. (2006). *Corruption: The World's Big C*. London: Institute of Economic Affairs.

Transparency International (2004). "Executive Summary" (1–5) in *Transparency International: Global Corruption Report 2004*.

United Nations (2000). *United Nations Convention against Corruption*. Available at: www.unodc.org/unodc/en/treaties/CAC.

United Nations (2004). *United Nations Global Compact*, 10th Principle: Anti-Corruption. Available at: www.unglobalcompact.org/what-is-gc/mission/principles/principle-10.

United Nations (undated). Office on Drugs and Crime, *United Nations Convention Against Corruption*. Available at: www.unodc.org/documents/brussels/UN_Convention_Against_Corruption.pdf.

United States Senate (1973). Committee on Foreign Relations, Subcommittee on Multinational Corporations, *The International Telephone and Telegraph Company and Chile, 1970–1971, Report to the Committee by the Subcommittee*, June 21.

van Orange, M. and H. Parham (2009). *Publishing What We Learned: An Assessment of the Publish What You Pay Coalition*. Available at: https://eiti.org/files/Publishing%20What%20We%20Learned.pdf.

Waitzer, E.J. and D. Sarro (2014). "Fiduciary Society Unleashed: The Road Ahead for the Financial Sector," *The Business Lawyer* 69, 1081–1116.

Wikipedia (undated) *Corruption*. Available at: https://en.wikipedia.org/wiki/Corruption.

Wolfe, R. (2013). "Letting the Sun Shine in at the WTO: How Transparency Brings the Trading System to Life," Staff Working Paper ERDS 2013–03. World Trade Organization Economic Research and Statistics Division. Available at: www.wto.org/english/res_e/reser_e/erds201303_e.pdf.

Woof, W. and A.W. Cragg (2005). "The U.S. Foreign Corrupt Practices Act: The Role of Ethics, Law and Self-Regulation in Global Markets," in A.W. Cragg (ed.), *Ethics Codes, Corporations and the Challenge of Globalization*. Cheltenham: Edward Elgar, 112–153.

World Bank (2006). *World Bank Guidelines on Preventing and Combatting Fraud and Corruption in Projects Financed by IBRD Loans and IDA Credits and Grants*. Available at: http://siteresources.worldbank.org/INTOFFEVASUS/Resources/WB_Anti_Corruption_Guidelines_10_2006.pdf.

World Bank (undated). *Procurement: World Bank Listing of Ineligible Firms & Individuals (Fraud and Corruption)*. Available at: http://web.worldbank.org/external/default/main?theSitePK=84266&contentMDK=64069844&menuPK=116730&pagePK=64148989&piPK=64148984.

World Bank (undated). *Law, Justice and Development*. Available at: http://web.worldbank.org/WBSITE/EXTERNAL/TOPICS/EXTLAWJUSTICE/0,,contentMDK:23394103~menuPK:9203924~pagePK:148956~piPK:216618~theSitePK:445634,00.html.

World Bank (undated). *Procurement: World Bank Listing of Ineligible Firms & Individuals (Fraud and Corruption). Table 1: Debarred and Cross-Debarred Firms & Individuals*. Available at: http://web.worldbank.org/external/default/main?theSitePK=84266&contentMDK=64069844&menuPK=116730&pagePK=64148989&piPK=64148984.

Zoido, P. and L. Chavis (2004). "Introduction to Corruption Research," *Transparency International Global Corruption Report 2004*. London: Pluto Press.

Part VIII
Business ethics across the globe

Introduction

Though initially a Western (or more particularly, a North American) product, business ethics, both as theory and practice, has expanded across the world to encompass different economies, political systems and cultures. One might view this expansion, following on Part VII, as triggered by the increasing presence and practice of multinational corporations worldwide. However, the world contains distinct economic and political realities each with distinctive histories and traditions, so the broadened compass of business ethics must confront a diversity of experience. It is therefore natural that different countries or geographical regions will manifest distinct challenges and business ethics may therefore assume distinct profiles, even as some core ideas remain the same. The chapters in this section of the volume cover the theory and practice of business ethics across the non-Western part of the world, particularly in China, South Asia, and Africa, as well as in the nations of Latin America, and Central Europe and Russia.

In Chapter 35, **Business ethics in China**, Yuqiao Xiang tracks the relatively late introduction and gradual growth of business ethics in China as a result of the deliberate adoption of the new economic model of a socialist market economy. Given China's history in the second half of the twentieth century, business ethics could not be anything but a latecomer to business—a welcome consequence of the recent official process of "reform and opening-up" that ushered in China's modern era and replaced the erstwhile centralized economy. Although business ethics is a modern development, some aspects of China's longstanding tradition in moral philosophy may be of relevance today. Tracking the contemporary history of academic business ethics in China, Xiang showcases its major protagonists and brings to the reader's attention novel themes, special concepts, and notable critical stances as developed by contemporary Chinese scholars. An interesting, probably unique, feature of the way business ethics has developed in China is the phenomenon of wealthy businesspersons who are actively engaged in the teaching and practice of business ethics.

S. Ramakrishna Velamuri introduces, in Chapter 36, **Business ethics in South Asia: Gandhian trusteeship and its relevance for the twenty-first century**, the state of business ethics in India and, more generally, South Asia. Reminding us that this populous region, with its fast growing economies, is the birthplace of two of the most important religions,

Velamuri observes the paradox that this part of the world also attains one of the highest corruption scores overall. After reviewing the teaching, research, and practice of business ethics in South Asia, Velamuri introduces, applies, and assesses Mahatma Gandhi's important concept of *trusteeship* as crucial to ethical conduct in contemporary Indian economic affairs—this despite the fact that, as the author is quick to explain, Gandhi himself was disillusioned with free trade and opposed to industrialization as well as to the market economy, consumerism, and commodity exchange in general.

In Chapter 37, **Business ethics in Africa**, Minka Woermann presents an account of business ethics in sub-Saharan Africa. She points out that business ethics as an academic field has been developing in the region since 2000, though quite unevenly within the different countries comprising sub-Saharan Africa. Though business ethics in this region developed first along Western lines, its trajectory arcs across African contexts and traditions. The history of the sub-Saharan nations, their cultural norms, and levels of economic growth have also affected the development of business ethics. Informed by a culturally-inflected type of communitarianism, firms understand their responsibilities and discharge them by way of an inclusive stakeholder model prevalent throughout the region. Woermann discusses three competing theses regarding the relationship between capitalism, African economic development and colonialism. After identifying some of the current challenges to economic development, she advances the possibility of a distinctively African business ethics using the concept of *ubuntu*.

In the following Chapter (38), **Business ethics in Latin America**, Álvaro E. Pezoa illuminates the state of business ethics in Latin America, signaling from the start that the principal moral issue, corruption, arises from the interconnection between the private and the public sphere. Based on factual information culled from recent press publications, he paints a stark picture of corruption's prevalence among private companies, as well as the appearance of widespread tax fraud, environmental damage, and other problems. Pointing out significant differences among the various countries of the region, Pezoa then turns to discuss empirical findings on public corruption. Documenting the state of business ethics research and teaching, he identifies the interesting peculiarity that in Latin America corporate social responsibility has been studied as a subject distinct from business ethics. In the closing section Pezoa presents a number of recent positive developments and initiatives regarding the practice of Latin American business ethics.

Any assessment of the current status of business ethics in the former Soviet Bloc must take into account a communist past inimical to private enterprise and commercial activity. In Chapter 39, **Business ethics in transition: communism to commerce in Central Europe and Russia**, Rodica Milena Zaharia opens her chapter on Central Europe and Russia by reminding her readers of that fact. Taking account of the variance among countries, Zaharia holds that, on the one hand, some elements of their anti-capitalist past are interwoven with the (varied) processes of economic transformation these nations have experienced; on the other hand, factors arising from contemporary economic globalization have proven powerful in shaping business ethics in this region. After chronicling the era of centrally planned economies, in which the very notion of "business ethics" was considered to be a contradictory remnant of bourgeois morality, she delineates how the poorly managed transition to a market economy generated negative effects and sowed the seeds of distrust regarding the ethical standing of capitalist business. Nonetheless, the transition also yielded the birth of business ethics, as a discipline and practice imported from the West. Noting the destruction of civil society during the communist era, Zaharia points out, as well, how differences in economic development among countries may give rise to differences in the ethics of business and differential paths of economic transformation.

Byron Kaldis

35
Business ethics in China

Yuqiao Xiang

China is a country with a long history of ethics and moral governance, but its history of business ethics is akin to a short story. In China, the rise of business ethics, as scholarly pursuit, occurs later than its emergence in most Western developed countries, but the later emergence does not mean that the narrative of China's business ethics is without content or interest. With the rapid increase of China's international economic position, there are many indications that business ethics is now developing rapidly in China. Although business ethics arrived late to China, the ethical concerns are deeply-rooted in the traditional morals of the Chinese people. In this way, the advent of business ethics is not *new* even as the application of ethical ideas to a market economy seems new. Even the classic Chinese thinkers—Kongzi and Mengzi—had something to say about responsibility and wealth, though their legacy shall not be a central feature of this chapter.

Instead, this chapter offers a summary portrait of the emergence of business ethics during the past three decades. In 1978 the Communist Party of China set forth a new policy—literally "reform" and "opening up" (hereinafter, simply "reform")—in which the planned socialist economy would be transformed into a socialist market economy. The Party's declaration made possible the market (and social) conditions that render plausible any genuine ethical consideration of the operations and aims of businesses and markets. With a primary focus on the academic or intellectual consideration of business ethics, rather than actual practice, this chapter will first address the connection between China's business ethics and China's social and political background, especially in relation to the policies since 1978. A second section details some of the main theoretical trends in China's business ethics during the past thirty years. The third section examines some of the possible challenges that China's business ethics will be facing in the future. Throughout the chapter the primary emphasis will be on current scholarship, chiefly that of Chinese rather than Western academics. Much of this scholarly literature has not been translated into English.

The new era in China and the rise of business ethics

In any country, the birth of business ethics usually requires two conditions, one objective and the other subjective. On the one hand, there should be an economic system objectively suitable for the development of business ethics; on the other hand, there should be mature agents of economic activity who subjectively recognize the value of business ethics and feel strongly motivated to establish it as a new branch of learning. After entering the era of reform China satisfies both conditions.

In modern China, three historical events have enormous significance. First, the Xinhai Revolution of 1911 ended the feudal system of China. With the demise of feudalism, the Chinese people began to embrace such modern ideas as liberty, equality, and democracy. Second, the founding of the Republic of China in 1949 not only heralded the birth of a new socialist country in East Asia, but symbolized the beginning of the Chinese nation's real independence and universal emancipation. Thirdly, the reform policy carried out by China's government since 1978 has encouraged the Chinese people to an unprecedented open-mindedness, coupled with a new understanding of the significance of innovation and creativity. In sum, the policy of reform has proved to be a powerful driving force in the recent development of contemporary China.

From 1949 to 1978 the Chinese people lived in a planned socialist economy. As is generally known, the system is characterized by the central government's absolute monopoly over economic activities, with executive edicts being the soul of the national economy. As the single agent of economic activity, the central government had absolute power to devise economic plans and enforce them; meanwhile other market agents, individuals and enterprises, could do nothing but carry out those plans without discussion or hesitation.

If such a planned economy system expressed a fundamental normative implication, it would be the requirement of obedience: one must comply obediently with the executive orders of the central government. During that historical period, the moral requirement for obedience to executive orders was issued and enforced by the central government, yet it was in a sense accepted by people: obedience was thought of as something like a virtue, for its existence did reflect the norms of the planned economy and helped to achieve moral uniformity, if not consensus. However, enforced obedience has the result of becoming blind obedience, for when the economic life of society is wholly governed by the government, then individuals and enterprises are left without any opportunity to exercise moral choice. To be deprived of the right of making moral choices renders individuals and enterprises effectively blind. One comes to perceive what one is told to see and one comes to follow only those paths down which the leaders tell one to walk.

Since the planned economy provided limited space for human moral pursuits, it was unsuitable for the growth of business and thus for business ethics. As Lulu Wang and Jie Wang have described, there was no systematic discourse of business ethics in the 30 years after the founding of New China in 1949, but only some rather narrow or incomplete ethical thoughts related to economy (Wang and Wang 2014: 17). In fact, it is not simply that one was to obey these plans and orders, but that they were valorized and lauded, regardless of their effects. The worship of executive plans and orders means that they remained unchallengeable in economic life. Choice and responsibility was completely borne by the central government. Having been deprived of any decision-making rights, individuals and enterprises lost any sense of autonomy and responsibility. Since they were not treated as autonomous market agents, their actions, whatsoever these were, were non-moral. In the very activities of work that take up so much of everyday life, an individual did not have to consider whether his or her actions were moral or immoral.

Of course, one could assert that the individuals in the planned economy did live lives of moral meaning, for they participated in practical economic activities guided by the moral values of the central government. However, since they were not truly autonomous in their actions or decision-making, they could not be said to have a moral identity that incorporated any notion of choice, autonomy, or responsibility—not even the notion of mutual benefit. In this sense the characters of individuals within the planned economy would prove, in many ways, unsuitable for a market economy.

On December 22 1978, the Communist Party of China held the third session of the Eleventh Central Committee and announced that the nation would replace the planned economy system with a market economy system. Six years later, on October 20 1984, at the third session of the Twelfth Central Committee, the Party declared that China had started carrying out the policy of opening to the outside world (*Documents* 2013: 17). In 1993 the Fourteenth Party Congress declared that China would implement a socialist market economy (*Documents* 2013: 55).

The policy of reform has proven successful and has brought about significant economic and societal changes. The policy has animated a spirit of hope and positive change even as it serves as a reminder that China has various and manifold tasks if it is to develop its economy and society. If one looks to the moral and social effects of the policy, it seems clear that the policy has reasserted the decision-making rights of individuals and enterprises: individuals and firms are no longer seen as followers but as market agents who are worthy of being respected. The other significant effect is the obvious one: a giant leap in the overall productivity of China. As a matter of fact, with the deepening of reform and opening-up, the Chinese people have the opportunity and necessity to learn more and more about the real meaning of the market economy and its operating rules and conventions, including the allocation of resources based on supply and demand and the corollary idea of price fluctuations. There exists a growing recognition of how these features enhance productivity and provide a plausible alternative to an economy of command, control, and obedience.

In the early years of the reform policy the central government was often hesitant or even unwilling to let individuals and firms enjoy the rights of determining methods and products—the very essence of a market allocation of resources. Even as the government initiated the reform its own inherent tendencies (to assume a knowledge of the economy and to exercise control) conflicted with the aims of the policy itself. And for the citizenry, many individuals and enterprises were less than ready to function as self-governing agents in market economy.

An appreciation of market phenomena not only is essential if participants are to make wise choices that will enhance their productivity but it also provides conditions under which ethical choices come to the fore. The policy of reform has encouraged a subjective liberation, a liberation of the mind. But this liberation should not entail an indifference to the public interest, fraudulent practices or products, or any attempt to utilize the market for oneself alone (so that potential or actual competitors are put at a legal or regulatory disadvantage). Clearly this liberation comes with the fact that the advent of a market economy has also generated certain negative social problems: income disparity, money worship, sale of fake commodities, all of which were hardly encountered in the era of the planned economy system. These social problems have ethical import.

It could be concluded, quickly but too easily, that the market economy is an economic system generating ethical problems. If this claim were meant as an indictment of the market economy, then this would be an ill-advised inference. After all, there are ethical problems in the planned economy system too, but in a sense they are much simpler: the planned economy not only puts the central government at the center of economic life but its very aim *is* to simplify, regulate, and control ethical relations (for better or worse!). Specifically speaking, planning reduces the ethical relations of the society to those between the central government and market agents. Having been deprived of economic autonomy, individuals and enterprises actually lose their moral autonomy. With no say in economic decision-making, they lose the sense of moral responsibility regarding the consequences of their decisions. Because the market grants agents their due rights to make moral judgments and economic decisions, the moral space of the market economy is much larger than that of the planned economy.

It is within this moral space that business ethics becomes possible. The rise of business ethics in China, therefore, has much to do with the rapid development of the market economy. Not surprisingly, then, it is in the last decade of the twentieth century that business ethics as a discipline begins to develop in China. In 1993 Xiaoxi Wang, then a young Chinese scholar, published an essay, "The Outline of Business Ethics," in the Chinese journal *Jiangsu Social Sciences* (Wang 1993). This paper turned out to be the first published essay in China dedicated specifically to business ethics. For his Chinese audience, Wang defined the concept of business ethics and discussed its subject matter, yet in many ways the essay was tentative and general. Business ethics was defined as a branch of philosophy focused on the good versus evil value-orientation of human economic activities, but there was little in the way of developed argument or explanation. Nonetheless, this publication marks the starting point of China's business ethics: not only did Wang contend that business ethics was a necessary part of any study of applied ethics but he also predicted that China would witness the rapid development of business ethics with the deepening of its economic reforms.

Shortly thereafter, in 1994, Xiaoxi Wang published a book-length treatise, *China's Business Ethics Seen from Historical and Realistic Perspectives* (Wang 1994). This was the first book-length treatment of business ethics in China. Wang reviewed the history of mankind's ethical thoughts in the field of business and considered whether traditional Confucian ethics and Taoist ethics should be regarded as necessary historical resources for the development of China's business ethics. Here Wang anticipated a debate that would recently arise among business ethicists: to what extent does classical Chinese thought, in particular that of Kongzi (Confucius) or Mengzi (Mencius), provide a conceptual or normative basis for contemporary thought about business? Some have argued, with Wang, that Confucian thinking provides a rich potential (Chan 2008; Zhu and Yao 2008) but others have suggested that classical thought has little relevance, or even a negative one, on ethical business (Ip 2009). The most recent study (Elstein and Tian 2017) is more nuanced and points out how the classic texts do not easily yield normative conclusions.

Along with his defense of the Confucian tradition, Wang contends that the socialist market economy system upholds both a set of moral values, which he identifies with socialism, and the productivity provided by the incentives of markets. While defending the notion of distributive justice, Wang does not identify this with the egalitarianism of the planned economy of communism. Rather, in recognizing that most Chinese have given up strict egalitarianism, Wang defends a principle of fair distribution of income in proportion to the economic worth of one's labor.

Wang remains one of the few Chinese scholars who have conducted research on business ethics as a discipline. His studies, even if preliminary, are nonetheless significant for they have laid down the necessary theoretical preparations for the rise of China's business ethics and brought to mind the importance of constructing a discipline of business ethics in contemporary China. In fact, Wang has sought to establish a business ethics that bears particularly Chinese features. Moreover, he maintains that the socialist market economy of China cannot survive without the support of a strong business ethics culture. In other words, the lived experience of individuals in corporations and firms must be one in which ethics is a valued guide.

During the decade of the 1990s, as only a handful of Chinese ethicists walked cautiously into the field of business ethics, some economists surprised the academic circles of China with systematic investigations into business ethics and market morality. Two well-known economists, Yining Li and Yushi Mao, were the most notable. In his *Ethical Issues in Economics* (1995), Li held that economics could not avoid discussing and investigating ethical issues. Efficiency, he argued, is related to fairness, and the economist must take into account how macroeconomic objectives may affect individual plans, including investment and consumption behavior. Li saw a clear role in economics for both positive and normative analyses. Two years later, another Chinese economist, Yushi Mao, published *The Moral Prospect of the Chinese People* (1997). Mao urged, rightly, that with the transformation from the planned economy to the market, China needed to reconstruct its moral values so that they were more compatible with the requirements of markets. However, Mao also held the mistaken belief that during the era of communist planning, the Chinese had resorted to traditional Confucian values to guide their activities. So, if the traditional values were suitable for the planned society, then new values were necessary for market economy. But the latter could be true without the former being correct. In any case, both Li and Mao are part of the larger debate in China as to whether, how or to what extent market morality conflicts with, complements, or improves traditional morals (see Hanafin 2002 for a discussion of these three perspectives).

These economists' interest in and interventions into ethical issues had a surprising impact upon academic circles in China, especially those which included ethicists. The work of these economists played an important role in motivating Chinese ethicists to further the development of business ethics and to make their own theoretical contributions in this field. Even if the economists' investigations into ethical issues lacked systematic philosophy, the economists' practical experience and knowledge in the field of markets, not to mention their grasp of concrete empirical data, carried their own particular persuasion. Given the nation's overall emphasis on economic development as the core task of the country, it was not unexpected that these declarations from economists would draw attention across society.

With internal pressure from the circle of ethicists and external pressure from the economists, by the turn of the century additional scholars had turned their attention to the field of business ethics. Xiaohe Lu, a professor in the Shanghai Social Sciences Academy, published work in both English (1997) and Chinese (2008). Agreeing that economic reform has enhanced the development of business ethics in China, she encouraged the study of business ethics from three levels: the macro-level of institutions, the medium-level of organizations, and the micro-level of individuals (2008: 67–68). Although this standpoint is borrowed from Western business ethics, it helps the Chinese people to recognize the relations among the types of market actors (government, enterprise, and individual), and it indicates a basic structure to the field. Although the Chinese entered the era of the market economy system thirty years ago, their self-consciousness as market actors has remained inadequate even up to now. Therefore, in instances in which China's business ethics borrows from Western countries, these adoptions have often proven crucial to strengthening the general comprehension of markets and the consciousness of market agency. According to Xiaohe Lu, the chief task of business ethics is to explore the relations between economic value and moral value. In so far as business ethics is a branch of the so-called applied ethics, it must answer two basic questions, namely, which moral or business ethics theory proves to be more suitable (and what the criteria of suitability may be), and how a theory may be applied to economic practice.

In October of 2010 the China Association of Business Ethics (CABE) was founded in Nanjing Normal University with Professor Xiaoxi Wang as the first president (still serving as one). This event marked an important milestone in the development of Chinese business ethics. The association has played an important role in securing academic interest in the study of business ethics and in boosting scholarly work in business ethics. After the founding of the association, business ethics became much more popular among China's academic circles, has attracted an increasing number of Chinese scholars, and has shifted to a stage of quicker development. The CABE holds an annual conference and has more than two hundred members, the majority being scholars from universities and colleges, the rest being businessmen from either public- or private-enterprises.

Since its founding, CABE's president has insisted on compiling and publishing annually, since 2000, *The Yearbook of China's Business Ethics*, intended to gather the scholarly achievements of Chinese scholars working in the field of business ethics. The presence of the yearbook not only helps to sort out the history of China's business ethics, but also helps to expand the impact of China's business ethics. Written in Chinese, it is a good window through which Chinese scholars, as well as those of other nations, may get to know the history and current situation of China's business ethics.

Theoretical trends in Chinese business ethics

The era of reform has generated diversity and innovation in China. Motivated by the ideas of reform and opening to the outside world, the Chinese people have gradually abandoned such moral values as strict egalitarianism and the moral lifestyle that accompanied it, marked by excessive emphasis on obedience. The Chinese have shown great interest in welcoming new moral values. Some advocate the features of markets such as mutual benefit (the mutual benefits of trade), and others emphasize the importance of philanthropy, but there is a genuinely open attitude towards Western moral values such as equality and liberty. In fact, Western moral values have played a role in enriching the content of modern China's values, rendering the moral life of China more diversified. However, the Chinese people have never been ready to merely accept Western moral values without criticism. This tension has created an interesting situation: on the one hand the Chinese mentality rests earnestly on traditional moral values, e.g., Confucian values, while, on the other hand, the modern Chinese exhibit a willingness to engage with new moral values as well.

Of course, the traditional ethics of China did not have an independent branch that could be called business ethics, but it did contain ethical thoughts that could serve as the source of some concepts or ideas of relevance to contemporary Chinese business ethics theories (for a full discussion, see Elstein and Tian 2017). For example, Kongzi talked about the issue of distributive justice in *The Analects* and believed that the citizens of a state were concerned more with the problem of inequality of material wealth than with that of poverty (Kongzi 2015, *Analects*: Chapter 16, para. 6). This Confucian standpoint—which is not opposed to either wealth or to profit (Elstein and Tian 2017: 58)—may aid, to a certain degree, the explorations of business ethicists on the subject of income and wealth disparities.

However, China inherits a long tradition in which it is expected that a person in business, a businessman, would embrace moral values, especially *Confucian* moral values, so the Chinese people have always liked to call excellent businessmen "Confucian Businessmen." This linkage may derive from the fact that one of Kongzi's outstanding students, Zigong, was a successful businessman. As a matter of fact, he was not only a rich but also a virtuous and philanthropic businessman who financed most of Kongzi's academic activities, including his travels from one state to another. He was one of the so-called Confucian businessmen who kept in mind the moral doctrine of Confucianism, as expressed by Mengzi, that when a person was poor himself, he should maintain his moral personality; but when he became rich, he should try his best to help others with his good conduct (Mengzi 2006: Section 13, para. 9).

The implementation of China's reform policy has not only permitted more freedom of thought but it has also yielded a remarkable increase in creativity. After a long period of confinement, there is great interest in theoretical and practical innovation, as evidenced in the interest in technological products for the individual (the ubiquitous cellphone), as well as high-speed rail and an aerospace industry.

Business ethics is no exception. As the economy has expanded so have new ethical issues emerged that warrant attention from the perspective of business ethics. These include the extent to which the market has a negative or positive effect on morals (Hanafin 2002), and it also includes the emerging concern over income inequalities, as well as questions surrounding the pursuit and uses of wealth. Many of these may have been present even under a planned economy but the central government would not encourage their recognition much less their discussion. But every era has its ethical issues, so the current theorizing among China's business ethics community is closely related to the social and economic reality of contemporary China.

It is important to note a positive peculiarity of Chinese business ethics: its scholars have a strong interest in exploring the field from a historical perspective. In their studies, most of them consider it theoretically necessary to find out and explore the historical background of a question or theme. There are at least two reasons to explain this phenomenon. One is the cultural fact that the Chinese enjoy a self-consciously long history of civilization, so they tend to think historically and to rely on historical memory. In this sense, history suggests ways of considering and treating important questions. Some of this tendency is reflected in the general interest among students and scholars in China for the study of disciplinary history. Another and more contemporary reason is that many Chinese scholars, educated in national institutions and universities, have been profoundly influenced by Marxist philosophy, with its emphasis on the methodology of historical materialism. Thus, when Chinese scholars come to consider a question or topic in business ethics, they commonly tend to treat it as a result of history. As an example of this historical emphasis, Xiaohe Lu's work in Chinese, *A Study of Business Ethics* (2008), includes three long chapters that explore the history of business ethics as developed in Western nations. She narrates a version of business ethics as developing or extending from America to the whole world.

A second theoretical trend is that most Chinese scholars working in business ethics attach great importance to the study of basic theoretical issues. Business ethics started relatively late in China, as we have seen, so many Chinese scholars begin their study of the subject by writing textbooks in which they discuss such issues as the definition of business ethics, its disciplinary nature, research goals and tasks, and the practicality and overall value of business ethics. Business ethics is regarded by Chinese scholars as an important branch of applied ethics. Therefore, in these textbook-like treatises, Chinese scholars try to establish a theoretical system for a business ethics that nonetheless bears special Chinese features. These features include, as we describe below, notions of moral capital and conceptions of the relation between the ecological and the economic. In this way, these texts are not simply introducing Western business ethics theories into a Chinese context. The theoretical elements are to help people understand the ethical implication of economic activities; thus the assumption is that the theory will prove practically relevant to those who seek to carry out the moral tasks advocated by business ethics (Wang 2015a: 2).

Thirdly, the issue of moral responsibility remains a primary focus in the Chinese literature on business ethics. The ethical tradition of China has always been marked by an emphasis on moral responsibility. Within this tradition, the concept is often connected to the requirement for people to be responsible for self, to other individuals, and to society as a whole. For example, Confucian ethics requires people to practice self-cultivation, but stresses that the aim of cultivation is to develop the ability to take on moral responsibility of serving society. Taoist ethics calls on people to learn from the virtue of water: "The highest goodness is nothing but the virtue of water" (Lao Tze 1998). What is the virtue of water? It is to keep self and others afloat—to support or shoulder the performance of benevolent actions. Chinese moralists have always believed that moral responsibility is the key element of the moral life: without a sense of responsibility, there would be no morality of any sort at all.

China's business ethicists pay special attention to whether actors within the market economy shoulder moral responsibility. Not only does this concern draw from tradition but it may also reflect a tendency, even today, to wonder how an open economy can function if individuals are not otherwise controlled or directed to specific ends. In the era of the planned economy, China's enterprises and individuals were not able to be morally responsible for what they did because the central government was the sole decision maker. In contrast, Chinese moralists with an interest in business and a strong conviction in business morality seek to find ways to reconcile an appropriate role for government with the imperative to allow market actors, whether enterprises or individuals, to choose for themselves. The appeal to moral responsibility ensures that one may choose even as one must accept the consequences of one's action. In this context, some Chinese scholars said that the responsibilities of government are distinct from the responsibilities of enterprises and individuals (Yu et al. 2015).

A fourth aspect of current business ethics is a focus on the relation between nature and human economic activities. Zeying Wang has argued for an "eco-economic ethics" (Wang 2001) that would extend the concept of business ethics beyond the scope of human economic activities and interpersonal interactions to the relations between human beings and the natural environment. Wang emphasizes that the issue of natural-environmental protection is a topic that Chinese business ethics should not neglect, but he locates the topic less in the standard theoretical positions than within a new field, namely "eco-economic ethics" (Wang 2001: 167). Wang's standpoint has received support from this author whose book, *Eco-Economic Ethics* (Xiang 2004), argues for establishing a standpoint from which to lay out systematic investigations into the ethical relations among man, economy, and nature. According to Xiang, the relations among man, economy, and nature are of ethical significance yet they cannot be reflected adequately in the current language of business ethics. A new concept of eco-economic ethics is required to articulate the moral values to govern those relations (Xiang 2004: 1).

A fifth feature of Chinese business ethics is the subject of economic justice. The development of the socialist market economy has helped China accumulate material wealth, but it appears to have led to a widening gap between rich and poor too. This gap has occurred across regions as well as individuals. The market economy encourages and rewards enterprises and individuals whose labor and products are highly valued. Inequalities do not arise simply because enterprises and individuals with extra resources or abilities gain relatively more than others as a result of market competition; they also emerge from systematic unfairness, as when firms or individuals with political (or other) relations to government officers or regulators employ these connections to favor themselves or to disfavor others. Therefore, income inequality has a twofold basis, one resulting from the fluctuating values of labor and the other from the misuse of state power to secure non-competitive advantages.

In present-day China the issue of income disparity has caught the attention of many people. The Chinese government has implemented a project called "Precision Poverty Alleviation Project," to run from 2016–2018, that is designed to help people who live below the poverty line enjoy a decent and dignified life. Of course, the issue of the fair distribution of material wealth is very complicated and incorporates philosophic as well as empirical elements. For example, it concerns the relative values of material versus intellectual wealth, the extent to which greater material wealth is a good, along with the empirical ways in which markets rely upon prices and incentives, as well as the various regional differences across China, to mention but a few. The scope of the issue is so important that some Chinese scholars have recognized the need to establish an ethics of wealth. Kailin Tang, one of the most well-known ethicists in contemporary China, has proposed the concept of "wealth ethics" in his essay celebrating the thirtieth anniversary of the journal *China Social Sciences* (Tang 2010). Tang argues that China has arrived at a crisis of development and modernization in which the citizenry has become indifferent, respectively, to both the moral requirements of a market (development) and to any problems associated with it (such as rapid modernization and inequality). Therefore, a *wealth ethics* is urgently needed to help the Chinese people to solve the crisis of development and the dilemma of modernization (Tang 2010: esp. 34–35). Other scholars, including this author, have also taken up the idea of an ethics of wealth (Xiang 2010) and defended a system of moral values (a wealth morality) to guide the production, distribution, exchange, and consumption of material wealth. Xiang emphasizes the necessity of respecting *all* wealth creators, including those who work with their hands (manual labor), and the necessity to respect all forms of productive endeavor, whether intellectual or manual. He thinks that the pride of wealth creators, especially that of those with less education, is not adequately respected in human society, but it is an important ethical issue that should be studied by an ethics of wealth.

On a related note, Xiaoxi Wang, already mentioned as a pioneer of China's business ethics, has argued, over the past two decades, for a controversial concept of *moral capital*. According to Wang, moral capital is a form of spiritual capital that functions to enhance productivity as it sustains the moral outlook that complements property, creativity, and exchange (Wang 2015b: 56). After he set forth this notion in 2000, Wang has made unremitting efforts to publicize and defend it even against scholars who have questioned the very rationality of the concept (see also Wang 2016). Some Chinese scholars (e.g., Yaoming 2012) who think that it is unimaginable to create a concept of moral capital do so by drawing from Karl Marx's theory of capital as relations of production sullied by exploitation. Others contend that if morality is a kind of capital, then so does it become less a norm or standard than an instrument to be used as one wants. Even if Wang's proposal is controversial, it represents a novel direction in China's business ethics. In fact, Wang is one of the few Chinese scholars who have attained international recognition through his scholarly investigations. At the very least his work helps people to think more deeply about the definition and consequences of morality.

A final theme in Chinese business ethics is the idea of philanthropy, the voluntary giving or sharing of wealth. This theme has arisen in large part due to the economic prosperity that the reforms have engendered. In fact, the interest in this theme also comes from actual entrepreneurs, of whom Dezhi Lu, chairman of Hong Kong Life Insurance Co. Ltd., is the most well-known example. Dezhi Lu studied the issue of charity from an ethical point of view as a PhD student (2004–2007) at the Research Institute of Moral Culture of Hunan Normal University. Since receiving his PhD in 2007, Lu has, while managing his insurance company, written several works on philanthropy: *The Spirit of Capital* (2007), *Charities* (2013a), *Toward Sharing* (2013b), *Capital Sharing* (2015), and *The Spirit of Capital and the Collaborative Development of Human Civilization* (2017). According to Dezhi Lu, "sharing" or philanthropic generosity, is a human virtue that mankind has always tried to cultivate, with its most common form of expression found in the sharing of material wealth. Dezhi Lu is a particularly interesting representative of a class of contemporary Chinese entrepreneurs who, armed with strong moral consciousness, are exerting practical influence on the development of China's business ethics.

Philanthropy is an instance of practical business morality made possible by the productive capacity of commerce. Many Chinese enterprises undertake an even greater extension of ethics in business. For example, Haier, a world-famous air-conditioner company, has insisted, since its founding in 1984, on the moral goal of "being faithful to customers forever." Even if this insistence has roots in the firm's desire for profit and the firm's sustainable development, it is the sort of action that also generates its own a moral force independent of any instrumental use. Moreover, examples such as these—philanthropy and customer loyalty—are signs of a maturing of the overall business climate and an indication that Chinese enterprises are now realizing the role that morality can play in economic development.

The future challenges of business ethics in China

It is not unreasonable to think that the scholarly pursuit of business ethics will flourish in the next two decades, for China has an urgent need to support its huge economic machine with a robust business ethics.

As we said before, the era of reform and opening to the outside world has given the Chinese people the opportunity to explore, innovate, and investigate. The Chinese people have relinquished some traditional beliefs and learned to face a lot of new problems and novel challenges. The most crucial problem is that, while experiencing continuous economic growth, China must ensure that its market economy can operate productively and ethically. The operation of the market economy should not conflict with established moral values (equality of opportunity, mutual benefit, and environmental protection) for these provide the long-term basis for further development and for a genuinely lived ethics of business in firms large and small.

China's current social environment is conducive to the further development of business ethics. China is now engaged more deeply in the process of economic globalization, so the ethical perspective of the Chinese people is also becoming increasingly international. In addition, the interest of Chinese scholars in pursuing more innovative work contributes to a favorable climate for the development of China's business ethics. Even so, this development is not automatic or without challenge.

First, there is the need to develop young talent in the field. In the past thirty years a number of Chinese scholars, including Xiaoxi Wang (Nanjing Normal University), Xiaohe Lu (Shanghai Social Sciences Academy), Zhongzhi Zhou (Shanghai Normal University), Zeying Wang (Hunan Normal University), among others, have expended considerable effort to establish the position of business ethics in China. The cultivation of young scholars is indispensable if Chinese business ethics is to grow and flourish into the future.

As things currently stand, most who study business ethics are professors of philosophy, whose areas or primary expertise are distinct from business ethics. This fact has its advantages in that a philosophical preparation is important to the study of business ethics. Yet there is this disadvantage: those whose responsibilities extend beyond the field of business ethics may be less inclined to systematically engage in primary research on business ethics.

Secondly, the academic circles of China's business ethics need to enhance their international contacts. Chinese business ethicists, though few in number, still do not have international influence. One reason is that they do not attend conferences or engage in other channels of international communication. Many are satisfied with the study of business ethics in the context of China. Others do not seem to be mindful of how to disseminate their work to the world. These facts not only limit their research vision, but it also restricts the international influence of China's business ethics. The study of business ethics in China should not be a game of self-enjoyment. Chinese scholars need to learn what the scholars of other countries are doing (and have done), but they should certainly not be confined to this task. Chinese scholars must also globalize China's business ethics so that scholars abroad may know of Chinese contributions to the field.

Thirdly, the development of China's business ethics needs to attain an internal regional balance. At present, the Chinese scholars who study business ethics are mainly concentrated in developed coastal areas, such as Shanghai, the Jiangsu Province, and the Guangdong Province. The number of scholars in other areas of China who come to study business ethics is limited.

The development of the market economy is now spreading throughout the country, so business ethics needs to extend itself to other geographical areas of China too. Other regions of China should have more scholars join in the research teams of business ethics, otherwise the development of China's business ethics will remain limited.

Fourthly, many Chinese scholars who come to study business ethics are not familiar with practical economic activities. These individuals are the so-called "pure scholars" in colleges and universities. Ensconced in colleges and universities, they lack contact with and knowledge of business enterprise and the market economy. This deficit means that their writing is not only not informed by actual business practice but lacks practical relevance. Therefore, when one reads the writings on business ethics by some Chinese scholars, one sometimes has the impression that they have little acquaintance with the operations of firms or markets.

In order to overcome this state of things, the academic circles of China should have the willingness and courage to learn about and to participate in specific market economic activities. Most importantly, they must learn to co-operate with entrepreneurs. This does not mean that business ethicists should enter into business, but it does mean that they should get to know more about business and businesspersons. The business enterprise is the pillar of the modern economy, so if Chinese scholars are not acquainted with the operation of these firms, their research on business ethics is sure to be divorced from reality.

Related to the above challenge is a fifth concern: China's scholars should do more empirical research in the field of business ethics. As noted above, many Chinese scholars are better at theoretical than empirical research. Due to the lack of empirical research, the theoretical writings of the Chinese scholars often receive a less than welcome acceptance from businesses and individuals. China's business ethics should walk forward with both feet, covering thereby the grounds of theoretical contemplation and empirical consideration. Without empirical context or understanding, a business ethics remains definitional and unrealistic. The vitality of China's business ethics lies in both theory and practice, as we have said. It cannot survive with either of the two dimensions left in the shadows.

A sixth and final challenge relates to influence. As Chinese business ethicists advance in their studies, acquiring greater knowledge of business and the workings of markets, so should they do more to influence the decision-making of the Chinese government. At present, those who have great influence on the decision-making of the Chinese government are chiefly economists. They are actually the leaders of China's national economy. Nevertheless, when they make proposals to influence the economic decision-making of the Chinese government, they tend to pay attention to issues such as how to increase GDP, but they seldom, if ever, deliberate on the ethical dimension of the market economy system. Therefore it will be incumbent upon the scholars who study business ethics in China to make more effort to influence the government's economic decision-making. With greater knowledge of business and markets, Chinese business ethicists should be in a position to influence the government knowledgeably and actively.

China's business ethics faces many challenges right now but the most important thing is to establish new pathways for the sustainable development of the discipline of business ethics across China and into the international arena. This development should be based on the ethical wisdom of China's scholars who care deeply about the healthy development of an ethical market economy in their homeland.

Concluding remarks

When we try to find a proper way to achieve the goal of economic development, what we have to consider is that our economic activities should not be in conflict with our moral values.

No matter what economic activities we perform, they must stand the test of certain moral values, which can be found in business ethics. The presence of business ethics in human society helps to ensure that our economic activities do not lack moral value.

China is a developing country with great potentiality and vitality, so what is now happening in the country is witnessed by the world. The fact of becoming the second biggest economic entity not only means that China's international economic position ranks higher than before, but also shows that the international community expects the nation to take on more responsibility, the most fundamental one being to keep its own economy operating on an ethical track. One way to achieve this goal is to encourage citizens to *practice* business ethics and to have scholars who think and write about markets and morals.

Business ethics is now understood and welcome by more and more Chinese people who accept the idea that the operation of the market economy system should be allowed to function yet be based on a concrete ethical foundation. This great change in attitude represents one of the most significant transitions in contemporary China. Like all other nations of the world, the Chinese people hope to have a market economy that is productive and ethical. The development of business ethics in contemporary China testifies to the fact that the Chinese people are embracing a better conception of the market economy and of business ethics.

Essential readings

To learn about the history of China's business ethics, se Xiahe Lu's *A Study of Business Ethics* (2008, in Chinese). On differing view of morals and the market in post-communist China, see John J. Hanafin, "Morality and the Market in China: Some Contemporary Views" (2002). Perhaps the best of the theoretical works on business ethics, and available in English, is Xiaoxi Wang's *On Moral Capital* (2015b). The revisionist view of humans and nature is discussed in Yuqiao Xiang's *Eco-Economic Ethics* (2004, in Chinese). Dezhi Lu's book, *Toward Sharing* (2013b) is an excellent example of the attitude of some Chinese businessmen towards philanthropy.

For further reading in this volume on the transition from communism to markets, see Chapter 39, Business ethics in transition: communism to commerce in Central Europe and Russia. On business ethics developments in South Asia, see Chapter 36, Business ethics in South Asia: Gandhian trusteeship and its relevance for the twenty-first century. On the relations of politics and markets in general, see Chapter 21, Regulation, rent seeking, and business ethics. On the relations of markets and nature, see Chapter 22, Business, nature, and environmental sustainability.

References

Chan, G.K.Y. (2008). "The Relevance and Value of Confucianism in Contemporary Business Ethics," *Journal of Business Ethics* 77:3 34–60.
Documents of the Third Sessions of the Central Committee of the Communist Party of China (2013). Beijing: The People's Publishing House [Chinese].
Elstein, D. and Q. Tian (2017). "Confucian Business Ethics: Possibilities and Challenges" in E. Heath and B. Kaldis (eds), *Wealth, Commerce, and Philosophy: Foundational Thinkers and Business Ethics*. Chicago, IL: University of Chicago Press, 53–73.
Hanafin, J.J. (2002). "Morality and the Market in China: Some Contemporary Views." *Business Ethics Quarterly* 12:1, 1–18.
Ip, P-K. (2009). "Is Confucianism Good for Business Ethics in China?" *Journal of Business Ethics* 88:3 (September), 463–76.
Kongzi (2015). *The Analects*. Beijing: Zhong Hua Book Company [Chinese].

Lao Tze (1998). *Tao Te Ching*. Beijing: The Publishing House of Foreign Languages Teaching and Research [Chinese].
Li, Y. (1995). *Ethical Issues in Economics*. Beijing: Life, Reading, and New Knowledge, a Joint Publishing House [Chinese].
Lu, Dezhi. (2007). *The Spirit of Capital*. Beijing: Dong Fang Press [Chinese].
Lu, Dezhi (2013a). *Charities*. Beijing: Dong Fang Press [Chinese].
Lu, Dezhi (2013b). *Toward Sharing*. Beijing: Dong Fang Press [Chinese].
Lu, Dezhi (2015). *Capital Sharing*. Beijing: Dong Fang Press [Chinese].
Lu, Dezhi (2017). *The Spirit of Capital and the Collaborative Development of Human Civilization*. Beijing: Dong Fang Press [Chinese].
Lu, X. (1997). "Business Ethics in China," *Journal of Business Ethics* 16:14, 1509–1518.
Lu, X. (2008). *A Study of Business Ethics*. Shanghai: Shanghai Social Sciences Academy [Chinese].
Mao, Y. (1997). *The Moral Prospect of the Chinese People*. Guangzhou: Jinan University Press [Chinese].
Mengzi (2006). *Mengzi*. Beijing: Zhong Hua Book Company [Chinese].
Tang, K. (2010). *Enhance the Study of Wealth Ethics*. Beijing: China Social Sciences [Chinese].
Wang, L. and J. Wang (2014). *Economic Ethics*. Beijing: The People's Publishing House [Chinese].
Wang, X. (1993). "The Outline of Business Ethics," *Jiangsu Social Sciences*, [Chinese].
Wang, X. (1994). *China's Business Ethics Seen from Historical and Realistic Perspectives*. China Commercial Publishing House [Chinese].
Wang, X. (2015a). *Business Ethics: The Relationship between Economy and Morality*. Beijing: The People's Press [Chinese].
Wang, X. (2015b). *On Moral Capital*. Berlin: Springer.
Wang, X. (2016). *The Theory of Moral Capital*. Nanjing: Yilin Press [Chinese].
Wang, Z. (2001). *The Essentials of Eco-economic Ethics*, Vol. 2. Nanjing: Jiangsu Social Sciences [Chinese].
Xiang, Y. (2004). *Eco-economic Ethics*. Changsha: Hunan Normal University Press [Chinese].
Xiang, Y. (2010). "The Rise of the Ethics of Wealth," *Studies in Ethics* 6, 8892 [Chinese publication: Moral Culture Research Institute, Hunan Normal University].
Yaoming, G. (2012). "Questioning the Concept of Moral Capital," *Philosophical Trends* 11 [Chinese].
Yu, D., Y. Dai and G. Cheng (2015). *The Development of China's Business Ethics*. Hefei: Hefei University of Technology Press [Chinese].
Zhu, W. and Y. Yao (2008). "On the Value of Traditional Confucian Culture and the Value of Modern Corporate Social Responsibility," *International Journal of Business and Management* 3:2 58–62.

36
Business ethics in South Asia
Gandhian trusteeship and its relevance for the twenty-first century

S. Ramakrishna Velamuri

> Generations to come, it may be, will scarce believe that such a one as this ever in flesh and blood walked upon this earth.
>
> *Albert Einstein on Mahatma Gandhi (Einstein 1950: 240)*

Theories of business ethics are often associated with the moral theories of great thinkers—the virtue ethics of Aristotle, the utilitarianism of John Stuart Mill and Jeremy Bentham, the deontology of Immanuel Kant, or the pragmatism of William James and John Dewey, to name just four mainstream theories. However, religion has also played a role in shaping business ethics practice, and so it is not surprising that there is a growing body of literature on conceptualizations of business ethics consistent with the great religions of the world. Yet much of the research and teaching of business ethics has been dominated by Western thinkers and religions, perhaps because, since World War II the North American and Western European economies have been the largest and most successful and, as a result, these economies have also produced the largest and most successful corporations. The issues these corporations faced provided the earliest impetus to business ethics research.

As the economies of the other regions of the world, such as Asia, have started to grow and produce large and successful corporations, there is increasing interest on the part of scholars to underpin good business practices in local religious and philosophical traditions. Some of these scholars (for example, Sekhar 2001; Lam 2003; Ip 2009; Chan et al. 2010) have been successful in publishing their research in international peer-reviewed journals based in the West, thus bringing novel perspectives into the mainstream literature.

One region that has been under-represented in the business ethics literature is South Asia, in spite of being the birthplace of two great religions: Hinduism and Buddhism. It is home to approximately 1.74 billion people, nearly a quarter of the global population. Eight countries constitute the region: Afghanistan, Bangladesh, Bhutan, India, Maldives, Nepal, Pakistan, and Sri Lanka. In terms of economic activity, the region's combined 2015 nominal Gross Domestic Product (GDP) in current US$ was 2.9 trillion (World Bank 2016a) and in purchasing power parity (PPP) terms was US$9.9 trillion (World Bank 2016b). The region experienced one of the highest growth rates in the world in the ten-year period from 2006 to 2015, with average annual

GDP growth of 6.95 percent (World Bank 2016c). Afghanistan (7.7 percent), Bhutan (7.53 percent) and India (7.42 percent) performed better than the regional average, whereas Pakistan (3.73 percent) and Nepal (4.33 percent) performed significantly worse (World Bank 2016c).

As the region's economies have continued to expand, so has the enterprise activity of both domestic firms and multinational companies. As a result, the ethical conduct of regional businesses has come increasingly under the spotlight. According to Srirak Plipat, Asia Pacific Regional Director of Transparency International, corruption is on the rise in the region, "caused by opaque public institutions, lack of protection for anti-corruption actors and widespread government interference in the work of anti-corruption watchdogs" (Plipat 2014). With the exception of Bhutan, which is ranked 27th out of 168 countries, the countries in the region are ranked between 76th (India) and 166th (Afghanistan) out of 168 countries in Transparency International's 2015 Corruption Perceptions Index survey (Maldives was not ranked in 2015).

Religion plays an important role in the everyday lives of the citizens of South Asian countries, and its influence on businesses should not be underestimated (Uppal 1986). There are four countries with Islam as the dominant religion (Afghanistan, Bangladesh, Maldives and Pakistan), two with Buddhism (Bhutan and Sri Lanka) and two with Hinduism (India and Nepal). India also has one of the largest Muslim populations in the world. South Asia has more than 1 billion Hindus, representing approximately 97 percent of the worldwide Hindu population, approximately 536 million Muslims (about a third of the worldwide Muslim population), approximately 33 million Christians (approximately 1.4 percent of the worldwide Christian population), approximately 23 million Buddhists (approximately 5 percent of the worldwide Buddhist population) and approximately 21.5 million Sikhs (approximately 93 percent of the worldwide Sikh population).

One South Asian thinker whose views on business ethics have only recently started to diffuse in the mainstream business ethics literature is Indian freedom fighter and humanist Mohandas Karamchand Gandhi, also known as Mahatma Gandhi (see, for example, Gopinath 2005; Chakrabarty 2012, 2015; Balakrishnan et al. 2017). Gandhi formulated a conception of *trusteeship* as a significant constituent of an elaborate theory of how the politics, economics and social relations of a country should be structured. Trusteeship rests on multiple building blocks of Gandhi's philosophy: swaraj (self-rule), ahimsa (non-violence), sama bhava (equality or oneness with all), satyagraha (insistence on truth through non-violent resistance), sarvodaya (universal uplift or betterment) and aparigraha (non-possession or non-hoarding). Gandhian trusteeship could be one (but not the only) potentially unique contribution of South Asia to the business ethics literature. In this chapter I shall explore how Gandhi's thinking influenced business ethics in post-independent India and how it can contribute to business ethics beyond South Asia. I shall elaborate both on the theory as it was formulated and the extent to which the theory has been applied in practice.

There are three main reasons for the focus on an Indian political leader and humanist in the context of a discussion of business ethics in South Asia. First, Gandhi's trusteeship concept took shape in the early twentieth century, but several of its core ideas might be relevant to business ethics in the twenty-first century. Whether the theory is applicable today as Gandhi formulated it remains an open question (and one that I deal with in the latter part of this chapter). Second, within the South Asian region, India, Indian leaders, and Indian corporations have been the most written about by management and business ethics scholars; we know relatively little about business ethics in the other South Asian countries. Third, India accounted for nearly 78 percent of South Asia's GDP in current US$ in 2015, and nearly 74 percent of its population (World Bank 2016a).

In the next section, I provide a review of the literature on business ethics in South Asia, after which I explain more fully the trusteeship concept by exploring the building blocks of Gandhian trusteeship and why each of them is critical to the theory. I then conduct an appraisal of trusteeship as envisaged by Gandhi and compare his economic views with the dominant global economic paradigm that started to emerge in the last couple of decades of the twentieth century and that continues to be dominant in the early twenty-first century. In the final section, I provide concluding remarks on the implications of Gandhi's thinking for research and practice of business ethics in India, South Asia and beyond.

Business ethics in South Asia: scholarship, teaching, and practice

It is difficult to find a business ethics theme that is uniquely South Asian and at the same time cuts across all or most of the South Asian countries. The terms "business ethics," "corporate social responsibility" (CSR), "corporate governance," and "sustainability" are becoming more and more widely used in academia and management practice in South Asia, just as they are in other parts of the world. On April 1, 2014, the Indian government introduced new CSR legislation requiring companies with revenues higher than INR 10 billion (approximately US$ 150 million) to spend 2 percent of their net profit on social initiatives such as environmental protection, skill development, hunger eradication, and rural development, among others. Corporations may implement these initiatives on their own or through partnerships with registered non-governmental organizations (NGOs) with a track record of at least three years. This initiative should make CSR even more salient across the social spectrum.

Business ethics teaching, training, and research

There have been a limited number of studies that have looked at business ethics and CSR in South Asia. The terms "business ethics" and "CSR," while not considered synonymous, are often used interchangeably. A recent survey (Srinivasan 2011) canvased twelve countries in South and South East Asia (i.e., Bangladesh, Bhutan, Cambodia, India, Laos, Malaysia, Myanmar, Nepal, Pakistan, Sri Lanka, Thailand, and Vietnam) in order to analyze the state of teaching, training, and research in business ethics, CSR and corporate governance. The results showed that academic institutions in all six South Asian countries covered by the survey offer business ethics either as an elective or a core course. Business ethics courses are offered in both undergraduate and postgraduate programs and in both stand-alone business schools and university-affiliated ones. Short-duration training in ethics, governance, compliance and CSR is also widely offered by business schools, consulting companies, NGOs (such as Building Resources Across Communities (BRAC), based in Bangladesh), industry associations and professional associations (such as the Institute of Chartered Accountants in India). Multinational corporations in particular organize training in these subjects for their employees. Supply chain partners of multinational companies such as garment producers are also recipients of training (Srinivasan 2011).

Research is the weakest among the three activities of teaching, training and research across the region. Chan et al. (2010) examined 4,200 articles in ten leading business ethics journals published between 1999 and 2008. Their results show that scholars affiliated to eight academic institutions from only two South Asian countries—India and Pakistan—were represented out of a total of 1,451 institutions from 66 countries. The articles from these two countries represented just 0.22 percent of the total. In comparison, scholars from 567 academic institutions in the US contributed 52.4 percent of the 4,200 articles. Vasanthi Srinivasan (2011) suggested regional collaborations to tackle the challenge of resource constraints for conducting research.

Business ethics as practice

Firms started to recognize the importance of ethics, particularly in the first decade of the twenty-first century, following scandals at companies such as Enron, Worldcom, Parmalat, AIG, and the New York Stock Exchange. Within the United States, for example, Thomas Donaldson et al. note that the Sarbanes Oxley Act, passed in 2002, is "the most sweeping change in the regulation of business since the creation of the SEC (Securities Exchange Commission) in the 1930s" (Donaldson et al. 2008: xi). In South Asia, corruption is pervasive (see Agarwala 2001 with reference to India), and societal perception of the ethical conduct of businesses is low. For example, "business" in India was ranked fifth out of ten segments of society evaluated for corruption in a *Times of India*-MODE opinion poll, with 76 percent of respondents rating it as corrupt (Chakraborty 1997). In comparison, the "Politicians and Ministers" category was rated corrupt by 98 percent of the respondents, "Teachers" by 43 percent and "Ordinary People" by 38 percent. Scholars have suggested that the highly bureaucratic business ecosystem in India may be the cause of the high incidence of corruption (Dehejia and Dehejia 1993; Agarwala 2001; Sharma 2009; Ardichvili et al. 2012). This is consistent with the seminal work of Anne Krueger (1974), who showed how regulations concentrate discretionary power in the hands of bureaucrats, leading firms to spend significant resources to compete for this discretionary power, which she termed "competitive rent seeking," a concept developed further by Gordon Tullock (1993) and others.

Ron Berger and Ram Herstein (2014) divided the evolution of the practice of business ethics in India into five historical phases. The first phase (Phase 1), which they refer to as *Panchayati Raj*, featured decentralized rule in which villages managed their own affairs through local assemblies. This period extended from the earliest recorded history up to 1700. During the Panchayati Raj traders acted as role models for the trading community through their ethical behavior (Majumdar 2004, as cited in Berger and Herstin 2014: 1080). As a result, business ethics played an important role during Phase 1 in India. Phase 2 (British Raj) went from 1858 to 1947, during which India was controlled by the British. Because of the British colonial rule, the original ethical principles that had been embraced during the Panchayati Raj were replaced by a new ethical system, based on Western practices. As a result, the old traditional ethical system broke down, leading to a decline in ethical conduct in India (Chakraborty 1997, as cited in Berger and Herstein 2014: 1080). Phase 3 went from 1947 to 1990 and is referred to as the License Raj or Permit Raj, meaning that there was a governmental bureaucracy with elaborate rules and regulations that had to be navigated by business people. During this period, India became an independent nation, and the ruling party preferred to continue with Western administrative and economic systems that had been introduced during the British period (Kanagasabapathi 2007, as cited in Berger and Herstein 2014: 1080). The public sector controlled a significant portion of investment and business, and, consequently, the Indian business infrastructure was over-reliant on government-controlled sectors, causing rampant corruption and unethical behavior (Berger and Herstein 2014: 1081). A very brief Phase 4 went from 1990 to 1995 and was referred to as the Invisible Raj. During this period the impact of traditional Hindu and Vedantic ethical thought was further diminished due to pressure from global markets (Kanagasabapathi 2007, as cited in Berger and Herstein 2014: 1081). The economic reforms introduced by Prime Minister Narasimha Rao's government liberalized the Indian economy by significantly reducing governmental interference in how businesses were run and reduced barriers to foreign trade. Free trade and modernization created abundant business opportunities but weak and poorly developed institutions led to more unethical practices entering the Indian business system (Berger and Herstein 2014).

Phase 5, which began in 1995 and continues at the present time, is called the Jugaad Raj ('jugaad' means ingenuity in finding solutions to resource constraints). This period has accentuated the decline in ethical standards in society and the economy. As Berger and Herstein note,

> Indians have had to find a way to run businesses in an unethical, corrupt and competitive business environment with a lack of resources, in the hope of a transformation from indigence to prosperity.
>
> *(Berger and Herstein 2014: 1081)*

As noted, "Jugaad" refers to the ingenuity of Indians to find solutions to problems that require very little resources. Notwithstanding Berger and Herstein's (2014) pessimistic assessment of the situation, there is some evidence that things are improving: Transparency International's Corruption Perceptions Index 2015 ranked India in 76th position, much improved from the 85th position it occupied in 2014.

In the estimate of Berger and Herstein, Indian managers rely more on applying ethical judgment differently to different contextual situations, taking into account (even prioritizing) friendship and kinship relations, whereas Western managers rely more on a universal (i.e., not context dependent) conceptualization of ethics (Berger and Herstein 2014: 1083). Fons Trompenaars and Charles Hampden-Turner (1997) refer to this dimension as particularism versus universalism.

R. S. Ramesh and Punita Goel (2014) go on to state that in order to compete in the global market and manifest positive aspects of business to the Indian public, it is important for India to confront the importance of business ethics from governments to individuals, and to find the right ways to solve ethical problems. The ethical problems that one encounters in the Indian business context are no different from those in other countries: bribery, conflicts of interest, misrepresentation of product characteristics, among others.

As can be seen from the above discussion, the importance of business ethics in India is being acknowledged by scholars and is reflected in more and more academic institutions and business corporations emphasizing teaching and training in business ethics. Between the traditional religious conceptions of India and the more universal principles of Western business ethics, is there an alternative possibility? Can the thought of Mahatma Gandhi offer some new direction for Indian business and society?

Gandhi's trusteeship framework

In 1915, after 21 years campaigning for the rights of Indians in South Africa, Mahatma Gandhi returned to India having earned a reputation for being an Indian nationalist and civil rights activist. Between the time of his return and his assassination in 1948, he led the movement to free India from British colonial rule. During this time he was at his prolific best as a writer, focusing on trusteeship and many other topics. The idea of trusteeship, nestled within Gandhi's larger sociopolitical perspective, does not, as we shall see below, take into account some of the features of markets that many regard as important. For example, he did not mention the efficiency-enhancing properties of a market economy and he equated economic competition to violence. Gandhi also made clear that, in his view, production was primarily for local consumption rather than for exchange. One might well wonder, therefore, how or whether this sort of view might contribute anything important to an ethical understanding of business.

One reason for Gandhi's lack of acknowledgment of the virtues of the competitive market economy and international trade may be due to the fact that some of the most significant work in these areas was done only towards the end of his life and after his death. For example, the influential work of Joseph Schumpeter, *Capitalism, Socialism and Democracy*, in which he dwelt on how the capitalist system enhanced the welfare of workers, was only published in 1932 (Schumpeter 2013 [1932]). Friedrich Hayek's influential works, such as his popular book *The Road to Serfdom* (1944), as well as his scholarly essays published in the mid-1930s and 40s, including his influential article "The Use of Knowledge in Society" (published in 1945 and then again in a collection in 1948), which discussed the informational efficiency of the market economy, were all published just a few years before Gandhi's death. Although David Ricardo's nineteenth-century treatise on the benefits of free trade (*On the Principles of Political Economy and Taxation* 2009[1821]) was well known during Gandhi's lifetime, Gandhi was most probably disillusioned with what he saw of free trade, i.e., the entry into India of the British East India Company followed by the British Crown, which led to the export of cheap raw materials from India to the factories of Britain and the import of expensive finished goods.

Another reason for the absence, in Gandhi's writings, of any acknowledgment of the virtues of the market economy could be that he viewed trusteeship as a humanistic framework that was based on a spiritual foundation. Thus, he did not really see the need to justify it based on its ability to enhance the economic welfare of society, in the same way as this is understood in modern economics.[1] He had fundamental ethical reservations about the market economy and its many accompanying characteristics, such as consumerism, industrialization, urbanization, competition, etc, as I will show later in this chapter. His concerns would not have been mitigated by the efficiency properties of the market system.

The fundamental idea behind trusteeship is that individuals who accumulate wealth should consider as their own only what they need for comfortable living; the remainder should go to the benefit of society. In essence, they should act as trustees of the part of their wealth that is beyond their needs. Bidyut Chakrabarty (2015) traces the roots of Gandhi's trusteeship concept to four sources: i) the Hindu religion, ii) John Ruskin (1901), iii) English law, and as a fourth possible source, iv) Andrew Carnegie.

First, Gandhi drew on ancient Hindu texts such as the Isopanishad and the Bhagavad Gita (see also Rolnick 1962; Gopinath 2005; Chakrabarty 2015). The first mantra of the Isopanishad states:

> Everything animate or inanimate that is within the universe is controlled and owned by the Lord. One should therefore accept only those things necessary for himself, which are set aside as his quota, and one should not accept other things, knowing well to whom they belong.
>
> *(Bhaktivedanta Database)*

Gandhi integrated into his trusteeship theory the concepts of Swaraj (self-rule), swadeshi (self-sufficiency), ahimsa (non-violence), sama bhava (oneness with all), aparigraha (non-possession or non-hoarding), satyagraha (insistence on truth through non-violence) and sarvodaya (betterment or upliftment for all) (see Gopinath 2005; Chakrabarty 2015).

Swaraj (self-rule): By Swaraj, Gandhi referred not just to the governance of India by Indians (i.e., freedom from colonial rule) but freedom of the individual from state rule. This second aspect of Swaraj is critical to understanding Gandhi's ideal socio-political and economic structure. He called the state a "soulless machine," which has the potential to cause great harm to mankind (see Jesudasan 1984). Gandhi elaborated that every village had to be self-sustaining both economically and politically (Murthy 1987).

Such was Gandhi's distrust of the state that, according to Woodcock (1982), Gandhi even identified himself as an anarchist. The decentralization of political power to individuals through closely-knit village-based communities is a central characteristic that underpinned his trusteeship theory. Interestingly, Gandhi argued for the decentralization of political power not so much for individual freedoms but for the freedom and self-sufficiency of small (village-based) communities. The concept of *swadeshi* (self-sufficiency) was a derivative of Swaraj. Initially, swadeshi was integral to India's fight for independence from British rule and was manifested in the boycott of British-made goods (many of which were made with raw materials procured cheaply from India). After independence, swadeshi was one of the few components of Gandhi's economic model adopted by Nehru, which became reflected in India's protectionist policies that were implemented through the erection of high barriers to international trade and her insistence on manufacturing as many products domestically as possible.

Ahimsa (non-violence): According to Bhaneja (2007), for Gandhi there was no other God than Truth, and the only means of realizing Truth was through Ahimsa, which he defined as non-violence in thought, word and deed. Gandhi considered the state to be a manifestation of violence, which is why he advocated a society in which individuals were governed the least. Gandhi also repeatedly invoked non-violence to justify his stance that a rich person's wealth should not be forcibly taken away.

> That is where I disagree with the Communist... With me the ultimate test is non-violence... You may argue that a man who surrenders by compulsion today will voluntarily accept the position tomorrow. That, to my mind, is a remote possibility on which I should not care to build much. What is certain is that if I use violence today, I shall be doubtless faced with greater violence. With non-violence as the rule, life will no doubt be a series of compromises. But it is better than an endless series of clashes.
>
> *(As quoted in Kelekar 2013:10)*

Samabhava and aparigraha: Several scholars (see, for example, Gopinath 2005; Chakrabarty 2015) have characterized two concepts—samabhava (equality or oneness with all) and aparigraha (non-possession or non-hoarding)—that Gandhi espoused and that were central to his trusteeship theory as originating in the Bhagavad Gita. However, as Kees W. Bolle (1989) points out, there is no mention of either term in the Gita. Gandhi himself may have contributed to this confusion in Part 4, Section 5 of his autobiography: "What effect this reading of the Gita had on my friends only they can say, but to me the Gita became an infallible guide of conduct... Words like *aparigraha* (non-possession) and *samabhava* (equability) gripped me" (Gandhi 1948: 318).

The sacred text does contain many themes that are very similar to the two mentioned by Gandhi. Whether or not they originated in the Gita, it is undeniable that they constitute important building blocks of trusteeship. Samabhava has been translated as equality and oneness with all. In his *Essays on the Gita*, Sri Aurobindo explains equality: "For an equal and all-equalising spirit is that Oneness in the midst of the million differences and inequalities of the world; and equality of the spirit is the sole real equality" (Aurobindo 2013: 188). In Gandhi's view, samabhava allows an individual to relate to fellow human beings as equals irrespective of their nationality, race or socio-economic status. It is a universal consciousness that leads an individual to empathize with the dispossessed and downtrodden, even if the individual has no friendship or kinship with them. Samabhava is thus a key antecedent for a wealthy individual to adopt the role of trustee in society.

Aparigraha, translated as non-possession or non-hoarding, was based on Gandhi's belief that India could not and should not follow the Western economic model. He opined that the distinguishing characteristic of modern civilization is an indefinite multiplicity of wants.... I whole-heartedly detest this mad desire to destroy distance and time, to increase animal appetites and go to the ends of the earth in search of their satisfaction. If modern civilization stands for all this, and I have understood it to do so, I call it satanic and with it the present system of Government, its best exponent.

(Gandhi 1927: 483)

He added:

I suggest that we are thieves in a way. If I take anything that I do not need for my own immediate use, and keep it, I thieve it from somebody else. I venture to suggest that it is the fundamental law of Nature, without exception, that Nature produces enough for our wants from day to day, and if only everybody took enough for himself and nothing more, there would be no pauperism in this world, there would be no man dying of starvation in this world.

(Kelekar 2013: 5)

From the above quotations, one may glean how Gandhi clearly believed that: i) while there was a limit to resources, especially natural resources, there was enough for everybody as long as no one took more than what he or she needed; ii) curtailment of consumption on the part of individuals was a good thing, both for the individual and for the community; and iii) such curtailment would not negatively impact the motivation of individuals to continue to produce wealth.

Satyagraha: For Gandhi, this meant insistence on truth through non-violent protest, and was a key weapon in his fight for independence against the British. In 1920, Gandhi distinguished between passive resistance and satyagraha, terms that he had until then used synonymously.

I often used passive resistance and satyagraha as synonymous terms: but as the doctrine of satyagraha developed, the expression passive resistance ceases even to be synonymous, as passive resistance has admitted of violence as in the case of suffragettes and has been universally acknowledged to be a weapon of the weak. Moreover passive resistance does not necessarily involve complete adherence to truth under every circumstance. Therefore it is different from satyagraha in three essentials: satyagraha is a weapon of the strong; it admits of no violence under any circumstance whatever; and it ever insists upon truth. I think I have now made the distinction perfectly clear.

(Gandhi 1920b: 350)

Satyagraha is important for Gandhi's trusteeship theory; he recommended that workers adopt this approach if they were not well treated by their employers rather than adopt violent methods. Gandhi believed that satyagraha would lead the person responsible for the misconduct to reform himself or herself and thus leave no bitterness in the subsequent relationship.

Sarvodaya: This term was used as early as the 2nd century AD (Upadhye 2000) and is translated as universal betterment or well-being for all. On this facet of trusteeship, Gandhi was deeply influenced by the thinking of John Ruskin, especially the ideas expressed in his book *Unto This Last* (Ruskin 1901[1860]). Gandhi discovered this book in South Africa in 1904, and read it on a train journey from Johannesburg to Durban. He was so impressed by the ideas contained therein that he decided to live his life in accordance with them. In 1908, Gandhi translated the book into his mother tongue, Gujarati, under the title "Sarvodaya." In his autobiography, he summarized Ruskin's impact on his thinking as follows:

> I believe that I discovered some of my deepest convictions reflected in this great book of Ruskin, and that is why it so captured me and made me transform my life. A poet is one who can call forth the good latent in the human breast. Poets do not influence all alike, for everyone is not evolved in an equal measure.
>
> The teaching of *Unto This Last* I understood to be:
>
> 1. That the good of the individual is contained in the good of all.
> 2. That a lawyer's work has the same value as the barber's inasmuch as all have the same right of earning their livelihood from their work.
> 3. That a life of labor, i.e., the life of the tiller of the soil and the handicraftsman, is the life worth living.
>
> The first of these I knew. The second I had dimly realized. The third had never occurred to me. *Unto This Last* made it as clear as daylight for me that the second and the third were contained in the first. I arose with the dawn, ready to reduce these principles to practice.
>
> *(Gandhi 1948: 360)*

When Gandhi accepted Ruskin's view that the work of all workers was equally valuable, did he mean that everyone's work is equally valuable from an economic (or market) perspective? We understand labor markets well enough today to reject such a notion. Indeed, Gandhi himself stated explicitly that business owners possess intelligence and skills, which are scarce in society, for the creation and preservation of wealth. What Gandhi may have meant is that everyone's work is equally valuable from the moral and spiritual standpoints because everyone has a right to earn a living through their labor. Gandhi added that the business owner who employs the laborer has, in his role as trustee, the moral obligation to pay a wage that is sufficient for the worker to make a living.

Chakrabarty (2015) posits that Gandhi *could* also have been influenced by Andrew Carnegie's *The Gospel of Wealth*, in which Carnegie urged wealthy individuals to adopt the principle of trusteeship.

> To set an example of modest, unostentatious living, shunning display of extravagance; to provide moderately for the legitimate wants of those dependent upon him; and, after doing so, to consider all surplus revenues which come to him simply as trust funds, which he is called upon to administer . . . [T]he man of wealth thus becoming the mere trustee and agent for his poorer brethren, bringing to their service his superior wisdom, experience, and ability to administer, doing for them better than what they would or could do for themselves.
>
> *(Carnegie 1889: 48)*

Finally, as George Goyder suggests, Gandhi may also have absorbed ideas from English law, which he studied in London from 1888 to 1891.

> No doubt Gandhi studied the English trust when a law student in London and became familiar with the concept of trust as understood in English law. Yet Gandhi appears to have been more concerned with trust as a moral obligation than as a legal form. The two are, of course, closely related, for moral obligation must be definable before its breach can become actionable, while the objective of trusteeship as understood and expounded by Gandhi is the willing acceptance of moral responsibility by owners of companies and inheritors of wealth together with self denial amounting ideally to self abdication.
>
> *(Goyder 1979a: 53)*

Trusteeship: a critical appraisal

As has been described in the previous section, Gandhi's trusteeship theory is one part of his socio-political and economic model, which has several distinguishing characteristics that militate against the dominant economic ideas, which have almost attained the status of axioms as of the early twenty-first century. The first is his opposition to state rule, as elaborated in the previous section. "The state represents violence in a concentrated and organized form" (in Kelekar 2013: 23). Although free market theorists have always argued for a minimal role for the state, they have always considered its role as crucial in the functioning of the market. For example, in his great treatise, *The Wealth of Nations*, Adam Smith writes:

> Commerce and manufactures can seldom flourish long in any state which does not enjoy a regular administration of justice, in which the people do not feel themselves secure in the possession of their property, in which the faith of contracts is not supported by law, and in which the authority of the state is not supposed to be regularly employed in enforcing the payment of debts from all those who are able to pay. Commerce and manufactures, in short, can seldom flourish in any state in which there is not a certain degree of confidence in the justice of government.
>
> *(Smith 1981 [1976]: V.iii.7)*

This early view of Adam Smith has been reinforced in the more recent work of economists who emphasize the critical role played by institutions in the efficient functioning of markets (see, for example, Acemoglu and Robinson 2012). To the extent that institutions, such as laws, require state action, this contemporary view also underscores the important role of the state.

The second is his opposition to individual property rights. He tolerated stewardship of businesses by industrialists only insofar as it contributed to societal well-being. Several of Gandhi's followers drafted a document titled "Practical Trusteeship Formula," which contained six points. Gandhi approved it after making some changes. The second point in the document states: "It (trusteeship) does not recognize any right of private ownership of property except so far as it may be permitted by society for its own welfare" (in Kelekar 2013: 39). As further explained by Kelekar,

> They would be allowed to retain the stewardship of their possessions and to use their talent to increase the wealth, not for their own sakes, but for the sake of the nation and, therefore, without exploitation. The State would regulate the rate of commission which they would get commensurate with the service rendered and its value to society. Their children would inherit the stewardship only if they proved their fitness for it.
>
> *(2013: 9)*

Notwithstanding his suspicion of the State, Gandhi seemed to be comfortable with the State determining the profit that entrepreneurs would make in return for improving societal welfare through the productive use of property. Such a view might be analogous to a utilitarian defense of private property ownership, though it is not clear that this was part of Gandhi's intention.

Third, Gandhi was opposed to both socialism/communism and capitalism. He had a genuine concern for laborers, and was involved in industrial labor issues even during his time in South Africa (1893–1914). Indeed, V.V. Giri, a well-known trade unionist who would later become the President of India, referred to Gandhi as the "founder of the modern trade union movement in India" (Giri 1959: 188). However, Gandhi did not see the need for class conflict at all

(Chatterjee 1970: 217). He was strongly opposed to militancy on the part of workers, as he was to the politicization of workers' unions.

With regard to business owners, Gandhi sought to draw a distinction between capitalism and capitalists.

> By the non-violent method we seek not to destroy the capitalists, we seek to destroy capitalism. We invite the capitalist to regard himself a trustee for those on whom he depends for the making, the retention and the increase of his capital. Nor need the workers wait for his conversion. Immediately the worker realizes his strength, he is in a position to become a co-sharer of the capitalist instead of remaining his slave.
>
> *(Gandhi 1931: 296)*

Thus, Gandhi believed that employers and workers should build a harmonious relationship with one another. His attempt to reconcile the interests of the workers with those of the capitalists needs to be understood in the wider context of Gandhi's principal endeavor, which was to achieve freedom for India from British colonial rule. In this regard, Chakrabarty (2015) notes that Gandhi was pursuing a political agenda, which consisted of mobilizing the masses on the one hand, of which the workers formed a key constituency, and seeking funding for the freedom movement from the business owners on the other. Two Indian industrialists—Jamnalal Bajaj and G.D. Birla—provided considerable financial support to Gandhi, to the point that several of his colleagues expressed discomfort at the closeness of his relationship with the industrialists (Chakrabarty 2015). They believed that he was compromising the interests of the workers by turning a blind eye to their poor working conditions.

Gandhi's opposition to capitalism also stemmed from his distrust of the market and of competition, which he deemed to be a manifestation of violence. Parmeshwari Dayal explains: "According to Gandhi the concept of competition glorifies the tendencies of selfishness, greed, rivalry, jealousy, hatred and violence. The values of equality, trust, love, cooperation and truth stand discounted in any society based on this principle" (Dayal 2006: 121–122). In his view, one way of curtailing this violence was to ensure that production of goods was mainly for local (i.e., village level) consumption and exchange.

Fourth, Gandhi was opposed to industrialization, because he believed in decentralized village-based production primarily for local consumption. One reason for Gandhi's opposition to industrialization was an environmental one. Ramachandra Guha makes the point that Gandhi was one of the earliest environmentalists, having highlighted his concerns approximately fifty years before the German Green Party was formed (Guha 2003). Gandhi noted:

> God forbid that India should ever take to industrialization after the manner of the West. The economic imperialism of a single tiny island kingdom (England) is today keeping the world in chains. If an entire nation of 300 million took to similar economic exploitation, it would strip the world bare like locusts.
>
> *(Gandhi 1928: 412–413)*

It follows from his opposition to industrialization that he was also opposed to urbanization, which involves the migration of large masses of people from the rural to the urban areas seeking employment.

Fifth, Gandhi abhorred consumerism—"High thinking is inconsistent with a complicated material life based on high speed and imposed on us by mammon worship." This position contrasts with the emphasis today on economic growth, which requires more and more consumption on the part of economic agents, as explained eloquently by Victor Lebow over five decades ago:

> Our enormously productive economy demands that we make consumption our way of life, that we convert the buying and use of goods into rituals, that we seek our spiritual satisfaction and our ego satisfaction in consumption. We need things consumed, burned up, worn out, replaced and discarded at an ever-increasing rate.
> *(Lebow 1955: 7)*

Finally, there is an element of paternalism in the trusteeship system, which arose from Gandhi's confidence in the ability of the capitalists to grow and manage wealth for the benefit of the workers. He believed that the workers were incapable of looking after themselves.

> [W]hen labour comes fully to realize its strength, I know it can become more tyrannical than capital. The mill-owners will have to work, dictated by labour if the latter could command the intelligence of the former. It is clear however that labour will never attain to that intelligence. If it does, labour will cease to be labour and become itself the master. The capitalists do not fight on the strength of money alone. They do possess intelligence and tact.
> *(Gandhi 1920c: 387)*

Nobel laureate economist Gunnar Myrdal remarked that "the trusteeship idea is fundamentally a concept that fits into a paternalistic, feudal, pre-democratic society [because] it is so flexible that it can serve as a justification for inequality" (Myrdal 1968: 755). This paternalism contradicts a very strong building block of the free market economy, which is the assumption that economic agents who participate in the market system are free, rational and autonomous decision makers.

Gandhi's trusteeship theory was met with incredulity, most notably from Jawaharlal Nehru, who considered himself Gandhi's disciple. Nehru stated:

> Is it reasonable to believe in the theory of trusteeship—to give unchecked power and wealth to an individual and to expect him to use [it] entirely for the public good? Are the best of us so perfect as to be trusted in this way? Even Plato's philosopher-kings could hardly have borne this burden worthily. And is it good for the others to have even these benevolent supermen over them? But there are no supermen or philosopher-kings: there are only frail human beings who cannot help thinking that their own personal good or advancement of their own ideas is identical with the public good. The snobbery of birth, position and economic power is perpetuated, and the consequences in many ways are disastrous.
> *(Nehru 1941: 52)*

Gandhi was aware of the skepticism but was adamant in defense of his theory. In his *Constructive Programme: Its Meaning and Place* (1941) he maintained, "I adhere to my doctrine of trusteeship in spite of the ridicule that has been poured upon it. It is true that it is difficult to reach. So is non-violence difficult to attain. But we made up our minds in 1920 to negotiate that steep ascent. We have found it worth the effort" (as excerpted Kelekar 2013: 4).

Applicability of Gandhian trusteeship in the twenty-first century

Clearly, the world and even India have followed a developmental model that differs radically from the integrated socio-political and economic model that Gandhi envisaged, of which trusteeship was but one component. The mainstream economic views of the late twentieth century were perhaps best captured by James Williamson in what he termed the "Washington Consensus" (Williamson 1990). The Washington Consensus consists of a set of 10 policy instruments for the efficient management of an economy: fiscal discipline, reduction of public deficits, tax reform consisting of a widening of the tax base and a lowering of marginal rates, market-driven interest rates, market-driven exchange rates, liberalized trade policy, openness to foreign direct investment, private ownership of business assets, deregulation of the economy as a means of promoting competition, and protection of property rights. In 2004, Joshua Cooper Ramo introduced a rival economic framework based on China's development, which he termed the Beijing Consensus (Ramo 2004). There is less agreement, relative to the Washington Consensus, on what the Beijing Consensus stands for (see Huang 2011 for a counterview to the Beijing Consensus). It is beyond the scope of this chapter to analyze the merits and demerits of the Washington or the Beijing Consensus. Suffice it to say that they *both* stand in sharp contrast to what Gandhi advocated, because neither model questions the merits of industrialization, urbanization, competitive market economy, international trade, property rights or consumerism. On the face of it, the Third Way political movement, with which Bill and Hillary Clinton, Tony Blair, and industrialist Ernest Bader, among many others, are sometimes identified, and which combines commitment to a market economy with strong social protection, might seem more amenable to comparison with Gandhi's trusteeship. After all, Gandhi recognized the wealth-creating potential of entrepreneurs and at the same time was highly sensitive to the needs of the workers and the larger community. However, this superficial similarity does not withstand much scrutiny, since Gandhi repudiated the market economy in the strongest of terms. The advent of stockholder capitalism, manifested in the appearance of large business corporations with diffuse ownership (see Berle and Means 1932), in which there is a separation between the owners and managers, further complicates the application of Gandhi's trusteeship theory today.

One could argue that Gandhi's economic views are so much at odds with modern-day conceptions of trade and exchange that they represent an indictment of the very moral foundations of business rather than being an alternative approach to conducting business.[2] It is clear that Gandhi proposed a radically different socio-economic and political model. For this reason, unless there is a sea change in mainstream economic thinking, it is infeasible and impractical to hope that there is any likelihood of an integrated Gandhian socio-political and economic model being implemented in any country in the foreseeable future.

Post-independent India, which, under Jawaharlal Nehru, quickly abandoned every element of Gandhi's developmental model except swadeshi (self-sufficiency), has diverged even further since the 1991 economic reforms, leading it to embrace a liberalized economic system that is moving ever closer to the Washington Consensus. According to Subratesh Ghosh:

> Though Gandhiji is adored by his countrymen as the Father of the Nation, his teachings and beliefs appear to hardly inform the policies of the Government, or the behavior of the people he died for. The fate of his trusteeship theory well illustrates this point.
>
> *(Ghosh 1989: 35)*

Even if trusteeship as Gandhi conceived it is impractical today, the basic idea that the wealthy should dedicate the majority of their wealth to serve the poor is a noble one and highly relevant in today's world. Clearly, this is a voluntary decision for enlightened individuals and families to make and cannot be imposed through policies formulated by governments. Educational efforts provide a good mechanism to emphasize how a philanthropic trusteeship may provide psychic benefits to the givers as well as benefits to society more generally.

There are companies that over the course of the last 100 years have been governed with the interests of stakeholders other than investors in mind. George Goyder mentions some examples of companies that have given primacy to the interests of employees, to the point of making them significant shareholders, such as Scott Bader (founded by Ernest Bader), the John Lewis Partnership (founded by John Lewis and given away to workers by his son John Spedan Lewis), and Airflow (founded by Connor Wilson) (Goyder 1979b: 5). Making employees the owners of the companies they work in is of course not the only mechanism of practicing trusteeship. It is possible for ownership of the firm to be substantially concentrated in a trust, which uses this stake to further the welfare of all the stakeholders. One such example is the Indian conglomerate, the Tata Group.

In fact, the Tata Group may serve as an example of a limited application in India of Gandhi's trusteeship theory. Founded by Jamsetji Nusserwanji Tata in 1868, the group today consists of more than 100 operating companies (of which 29 are listed on the Indian stock markets) operating in more than 100 countries in six continents. The group revenues for the fiscal year from April 1, 2015 to March 31, 2016 were US$ 103 billion (more than two-thirds coming from outside India), with a workforce of approximately 660,000. The operating companies function independently of one another, guided and monitored by their Boards of Directors. The market capitalization of the 29 listed companies was US$ 116 billion as of March 31, 2016. Many Tata companies such as Tata Steel, Tata Motors, Tata Consultancy Services, Tata Chemicals, Tata Communications, and Indian Hotels have acquired significant scale. Many of them are also the largest in their respective industry sectors.

Clearly, the Tata companies are highly competitive, judging by the market positions they have achieved and sustained over time. They act as full-fledged participants in the market economies of the countries in which they operate, providing all their stakeholders with compelling business value—attractive products, competitive compensation and benefits to employees, and attractive returns to investors. At the same time, the Tata Group is well known for conducting business in accordance with the highest standards of ethical behavior. Group companies have also been pioneers in introducing benefits for employees and the community, in many cases years before these benefits became mandated by Indian law (see Hughes et al. 2004; Deshmukh and Adhikari 2010; Nohria et al. 2006). The Tata group companies do not conform to Gandhi's ideal corporation because they are large, have a global presence and operate themselves in accordance with the rules of the market economy.

However, the founding family of the group, the Tata family, comes closer to meeting the definition of trustee that Gandhi had in mind. The principal holding company of the Tata Group is Tata Sons, which is privately held. As Steen Thomsen (2011) points out, the ownership structure of the group is unique in that approximately 66 percent of the Tata Sons' shares are owned by charitable trusts, of which the Sir Dorabji Tata Trust and the Sir Ratan Tata Trust are the largest, owning between them just over 51.5 percent of the holding company. The Tata Trusts have helped create several iconic institutions in healthcare, education, research and the arts, such as the Tata Memorial Hospital, the Indian Institute of Science, the Tata Institute of Fundamental Research, and the National Center for the Performing Arts, to name just a few. According to Thomsen (2011), the Tata group and the Tata Trusts spend between 3 and 6 percent of the group's profits on philanthropic activities every year. The trustees, i.e., the eminent individuals who serve on the boards of the Trusts, receive a very small annual compensation (about US$ 15 to 20). Thomsen (2011) suggests that Tata Sons' ownership structure might be one reason that the listed Tata companies significantly outperformed the Indian stock market between 2004 and 2011.

In structuring its activities in this way the Tata family has chosen to take a different path from the one taken by Bill Gates and Warren Buffett, who have also dedicated the vast majority of their personal wealth to philanthropy. However, there is no doubt that Gates and Buffett are also behaving as trustees of their wealth, in accordance with Gandhi's definition of trustees. In the case of Gates, he first acquired great personal wealth through his business activities as the co-founder, CEO and later Chairman of Microsoft and then decided to establish the Bill and Melinda Gates Foundation through which to channel his philanthropic activities. Therefore, Gates first reaped the financial benefits of being a shareholder of Microsoft and then, in his individual capacity, set up a foundation to help the needy. In contrast, the Tata Sons' ownership structure means that the ownership of the businesses is held directly by charitable trusts, with the Tata family owning a minority of the holding company.

Concluding remarks

In 1973, a quarter of a century after Gandhi was assassinated, E.F. Schumacher, the British economist who wrote the influential book *Small is Beautiful* (Schumacher 1973) stated in his Gandhi Memorial Lecture that Gandhi was the greatest "people's economist," whose thinking was compatible with spirituality as opposed to materialism. In this second decade of the twenty-first century, we may ask under what conditions would the world pay more attention to Gandhi's socio-political and economic framework? Confident of his theory, in 1939, in his newspaper *Harijan*, Gandhi expressed how, "My theory of trusteeship is no makeshift, certainly no camouflage. I am confident that it will survive all other theories. It has the sanction of philosophy and religion behind it. . . . No other theory is compatible with non-violence" (Kelekar 2013: 4).

There are several problems that the world faces today that may prompt a revival of Gandhian economics: global warming, income inequality that in many countries seems to become more accentuated with economic growth, and jobless growth due to increasing levels of automation, to name just a few. Even if this revival does not happen, we are fortunate to have role models who have acted as true trustees: for example, Andrew Carnegie, the Tatas, Bill and Melinda Gates, Warren Buffett, and Mark Zuckerberg, who all decided to dedicate the vast majority of their personal wealth for the benefit of others.

Essential readings

Gandhi was prolific in documenting his ideas in writing. The Publications Division of the Government of India has made available all his works online: *Collected Works of Mahatma Gandhi*, available at: www.gandhiserve.org/e/cwmg/cwmg.htm. To my knowledge, the first essay on Gandhian trusteeship to appear in an international peer-reviewed business journal is that of C. Gopinath, "Trusteeship as a Moral Foundation for Business" (2005). For a recent and comprehensive description and assessment of Gandhi's trusteeship, see Bidyut Chakrabarty, "Universal Benefit: Gandhi's Doctrine of Trusteeship: A Review Article" (2015). The essential writings of Gandhi on trusteeship have been compiled by Ravindra Kelekar in *Trusteeship by M.K. Gandhi* (2013).

For further reading in this volume on religion and business ethics, see Chapter 9, Business ethics and religious belief. Since the concept of trusteeship relates to corporate governance and leadership, one may read further on governance in Chapter 24, Corporate governance and on the notion of "servant leadership" in Chapter 25, Leadership and business ethics: are leaders wolves for business ethics? On the problem of corruption across the globe, see Chapter 34, Corruption, bribery, and moral norms across national boundaries. For a consideration of how modernization incorporates Western values, see Chapter 33, Cross-cultural management ethics in multinational commerce. On conceptualizations of property, see Chapter 18, Property and business.

Notes

1 I am grateful to C. Gopinath for this perspective.
2 I am grateful to Eugene Heath for this insight.

References

Acemoglu, D. and J. Robinson (2012). *Why Nations Fail*. New York, NY: Crown Business.
Agarwala, N. (2001). *A Comprehensive History of Business in India—from 3000BC to 2000AD*. New Delhi: Tata McGraw-Hill.
Ardichvili, A., D. Jondle, B. Kowske, E. Cornachione, J. Li and T. Thakadipuram (2012). "Ethical Cultures in Large Business Organizations in Brazil, Russia, India, and China," *Journal of Business Ethics* 105:4, 415–428.
Aurobindo, S. (2013). *Essays on the Gita*, 9th edition, Seventh Impression. Pondicherry, India: Sri Aurobindo Ashram Trust.
Balakrishnan, J., A. Malhotra and L. Falkenberg (2017). "Multi-Level Corporate Responsibility: A Comparison of Gandhi's Trusteeship with Stakeholder and Stewardship Frameworks," *Journal of Business Ethics* 141:1, 133–150.
Berger, R. and R. Herstein (2014). "The Evolution of Business Ethics in India," *International Journal of Social Economics* 41:11, 1073–1086.
Berle, A.A. and G.C. Means (1932). *The Modern Corporation and Private Property*. New York, NY: Macmillan.
Bhaktivedanta Database. Available at: www.vedabase.com/en/iso/1 [accessed 07 November, 2016].
Bhaneja, B. (2007). "Understanding Gandhi's Ahimsa (Non-violence)," *Asteriskos* 3/4, 215–224.
Birtchell, T. (2011). "Jugaad as Systematic Risk and Disruptive Innovation in India," *Contemporary South Asia* 19:4, 357–372.
Bolle, K.W. (1989). "Gandhi's Interpretation of the Bhagavad Gita," in Hick, J. and Hempel, L.C. (eds), *Gandhi's Significance for Today* Basingstoke, UK: Macmillan Press, 137–151.
Carnegie, A. (1889). *The Gospel of Wealth*. Available at: www.carnegie.org/about/our-history/gospel ofwealth/ [accessed on 08 November, 2016].
Chakrabarty, B. (2012). *Corporate Social Responsibility in India*. Abingdon, UK: Routledge.
Chakrabarty, B. (2015). "Universal Benefit: Gandhi's Doctrine of Trusteeship: A Review Article," *Modern Asian Studies* 49:2, 572–608.
Chakraborty, S.K. (1997). "Business Ethics in India," *Journal of Business Ethics* 16:14, 1529–1538.
Chan, K.C., H.G. Fung and J. Yau (2010). "Business Ethics Research: A Global Perspective," *Journal of Business Ethics* 95:1, 39–53.
Chatterjee, N.N. (1970). "Mahatma Gandhi and the Industrial Worker," *International Labour Review* 101:3, 215–228.
Dayal, P. (2006). *Gandhian Theory of Social Reconstruction*. New Delhi: Atlantic Publishers & Distributors.
Dehejia, R. and V. Dehejia (1993). "Religion and Economic Activity in India: An Historical Perspective," *American Journal of Economics and Sociology* 52:2, 145–153.
Deshmukh, R. and Adhikari, A. (2010). *Tata Power: Corporate Social Responsibility and Sustainability*. Western University, Richard Ivey School of Business Case, 910M13. London: Ontario.
Donaldson, T., P.H. Werhane and J. Van Zandt, (eds), (2008). *Ethical Issues in Business: A Philosophical Approach*. Upper Saddle River, NJ: Prentice Hall.
Einstein, A. (1950). *Out of My Later Years*. New York, NY: Philosophical Library.
Gandhi, M.K. (1920a). *Collected Works of Mahatma Gandhi (CWMG)*, Vol. 19. Publications Division Government of India, New Delhi.
Gandhi, M.K. (1920b). "Letter to Someone in Madanpalli," January 25, in *Collected Works of Mahatma Gandhi (CWMG)*, Vol. 19, p. 350. New Delhi: Publications Division Government of India.
Gandhi, M.K. (1920c). "Conditions of Labour," in *Navajivan*, February 8, *Collected Works of Mahatma Gandhi (CWMG)*, Vol. 19. New Delhi: Publications Division Government of India, 386–388.
Gandhi, M.K. (1927). "Choice Before Us," in *Young India*, June 2, *Collected Works of Mahatma Gandhi*, Vol. 38. New Delhi: Publications Division, Government of India, 482–484.
Gandhi, M.K. (1928). "Discussion with a Capitalist," in *Young India*, December 20, *Collected Works of Mahatma Gandhi*, Vol. 43. New Dehli: Publications Division Government of India, 412–413.
Gandhi, M.K. (1931). "Can You Avoid Class War?" in *Young India*, March 26, *Collected Works of Mahatma Gandhi*, Vol. 51, p. 296. New Dehli: Publications Division Government of India.

Gandhi, M.K. (1941). *Constructive Programme: Its Meaning and Place*. Ahmedabad: Navajivan Publishing House.
Gandhi, M.K. (1948). *Autobiography: The Story of my Experiments with Truth*. New York, NY: Dover Publications.
Ghosh, S. (1989). "Trusteeship in Industry: Gandhiji's Dream and Contemporary Reality," *Indian Journal of Industrial Relations* 25:1, 35–44.
Giri, V.V. (1959). *Labor Problems in Indian Industry*, 2nd edition. London: Asia Publishing House.
Gopinath, C. (2005). "Trusteeship as a Moral Foundation for Business," *Business and Society Review* 110:3, 331–344.
Goyder, G. (1979a). "Introduction," in G. Goyder (ed.), *Trusteeship: A Possible Solution to Problems of Power, Exploitation, Conflict and Alienation*. Mumbai: Leslie Sawhny Programme of Training for Democracy, 3–6.
Goyder, G. (1979b). "The Responsible Company," in G. Goyder (ed.), *Trusteeship: A Possible Solution to Problems of Power, Exploitation, Conflict and Alienation*. Mumbai: Leslie Sawhny Programme of Training for Democracy, 52–5.
Guha, R. (2003). "How Much Should a Person Consume?" *Vikalpa* 28:2, 1–11.
Hayek, F.A. (1944). *The Road to Serfdom*. Chicago, IL: The University of Chicago Press.
Hayek, F.A. (1945). "The Use of Knowledge in Society," *The American Economic Review* 35:4, 519–530.
Hayek, F.A. (1948). *Individualism and Economic Order*. Chicago, IL: University of Chicago Press.
Huang, Y. (2011). "Rethinking the Beijing Consensus," *Asia Policy* 11:1, 1–26.
Hughes, K., J-F. Manzoni and V. Tibrewala (2004). *Tata Steel: A Century of Corporate Social Responsibility*. INSEAD Business School Case, number INS646. Available at: https://cases.insead.edu.
Ip, P.K. (2009). "Is Confucianism Good for Business Ethics in China?" *Journal of Business Ethics* 88:3, 463–476.
Jesudasan, I. (1984). *A Gandhian Theology of Liberation*. Maryknoll, NY: Orbis Books.
Kanagasabapathi, K. (2007). "Ethics and Values in Indian Economy and Business," *International Journal of Social Economics* 34:9, 577–585.
Kelekar, R. (2013). *Trusteeship by M. K. Gandhi*, compiled by R. Kelekar, 9th Reprint, Ahmedabad, India; Navjivan Publishing House.
Krueger, A.O. (1974). "The Political Economy of the Rent-seeking Society," *The American Economic Review* 64:3, 291–303.
Lam, K.C.J. (2003). "Confucian Business Ethics and the Economy," *Journal of Business Ethics* 43:1–2, 153–162.
Lebow, V. (1955). "The Real Meaning of Consumer Demand," *Journal of Retailing* 31:1, 5–10.
Majumdar, S.K. (2004). "The Hidden Hand and the License Raj to an Evaluation of the Relationship between Age and the Growth of Firms in India," *Journal of Business Venturing* 19:1, 107–125.
Murthy, B.S. (ed.) (1987). *Mahatma Gandhi and Leo Tolstoy Letters*. Long Beach, CA: Long Beach Publications.
Myrdal, G. (1968). *Asian Drama* (Vol. II). New York, NY: Pantheon.
Nehru, J. (1941). *An Autobiography: With Musings on Recent Events in India*. London: John Lane.
Nohria, N., A.J. Mayo and M. Benson (2006). *J.R.D. Tata*. Harvard Business School Case, number 9-407-061. Available at: https://cb.hbsp.harvard.edu.
Plipat, S. (2014). "South Asia's Corruption Watchdogs Need Sharper Teeth," Transparency International Secretariat. Available at: www.transparency.org/news/pressrelease/south_asias_corruption_watchdogs_need_sharper_teeth [accessed 06 November, 2016].
Ramesh, R.S. and P. Goel (2014). "Attitude and Perception of Public Towards Business Ethics: Evidence from Select Seven States of India," *Indian Journal of Commerce and Management Studies* 5:1, 47–53.
Ramo, J.C. (2004). *The Beijing Consensus*. London: Foreign Policy Centre.
Ricardo, D. (2009 [1821]). *On the Principles of Political Economy and Taxation*. Whitefish, MT: Kessinger Publishing.
Rolnick, P.J. (1962). "Charity, Trusteeship, and Social Change in India," *World Politics* 14:3, 439–460.
Ruskin, J. (1901[1860]). *Unto This Last: Four Essays on the First Principles of Political Economy*. London: George Allen.
Schumacher, E.F. (1973). *Small is Beautiful: A Study of Economics as if People Mattered*. London: Blond & Briggs.
Schumpeter, J.A. (2013[1942]). *Capitalism, Socialism and Democracy*. London: Routledge.
Sekhar, R.C. (2001). "Trends in Ethics and Styles of Leadership in India," *Business Ethics: A European Review* 10:4, 360–363.

Sharma, D. (2009). *China and India in the Age of Globalization.* New York, NY: Cambridge University Press.

Smith, A. (1981 [1976]). *An Inquiry into the Nature and Causes of the Wealth of Nations*, 2 vols, R.H. Campbell and A.S. Skinner (eds), textual editor W.B. Todd. Indianapolis, IN: Liberty Fund.

Srinivasan, V. (2011). "Business Ethics in the South and South East Asia," *Journal of Business Ethics* 104:1, 73–81.

Thomsen, S. (2011). "Trust Ownership of the Tata Group," December 22, Paper 1976958. *Social Sciences Research Network.* Available at: www.srn.com.

Trompenaars, F. and C. Hampden-Turner (1997). *Riding the Waves of Culture: Understanding Cultural Diversity in Business.* London: Nicholas Brealey.

Tullock, G. (1993). *Rent Seeking.* Brookfield, VT: Edward Elgar.

Upadhye, A.N. (2000). *Mahavira, His Times and His Philosophy of Life.* New Delhi: Bharatiya Jnanpith.

Uppal, J.S. (1986). "Hinduism and Economic Development in South Asia," *International Journal of Social Economics* 13:3, 20–33.

Williamson, J. (1990). "What Washington Means by Policy Reform," *Latin American Adjustment: How Much Has Happened?* Washington, DC: Peterson Institute for International Economics.

Woodcock, G. (1982). *Letter to the Past: An Autobiography* (Vol. 1). Toronto: Fitzhenry & Whiteside.

World Bank (2016a). South Asia GDP at current $. Available at: http://data.worldbank.org/indicator/NY.GDP.MKTP.CD?locations=8S [accessed 01 November 2016].

World Bank (2016b). South Asia GDP at PPP. Available at: http://data.worldbank.org/indicator/NY.GDP.MKTP.PP.CD?locations=8S [accessed 01 November 2016].

World Bank (2016c). South Asia GDP growth rates. Available at: http://data.worldbank.org/indicator/NY.GDP.MKTP.KD.ZG?locations=8S [accessed 05 January 2016].

37
Business ethics in Africa

Minka Woermann

Since the beginning of the twenty-first century, a number of developments pertaining to business ethics as both academic enterprise and practice have taken place on the African continent. To address properly the theme of business ethics in Africa, one should bear in mind the great social, political, geographical, and religious heterogeneity that characterizes the fifty-three countries that constitute the continent (Sheeran 2008, esp. 38). As such, this chapter presents a systematic consideration of business ethics within Africa. Taking into account that business ethics is both an academic enterprise and a matter of practical conduct, the presentation also draws attention to pertinent historical, cultural, and institutional considerations that serve to complicate such analysis.

Apart from heterogeneity, a second challenge to writing on business ethics in Africa is "that scholars have largely ignored Africa," as revealed by a review (Parboteeah et al. 2013: 979) of leading business ethics and management journals. Praveen Parboteeah and colleagues argue that the lack of scholarship on Africa is "surprising given the growing importance of the [African] region in terms of global trade" (980). The dearth of literature on business ethics in Africa is most dire in the case of North Africa. For practical reasons, the focus of this chapter will thus be on the forty-four countries of sub-Saharan Africa (SSA), which is further divided into West Africa, Southern Africa, East Africa, and Central and Francophone Africa.

That there is little in the way of scholarly literature on business ethics in the African continent need not, however, imply that there is little in the way of practical business ethics or that there are not strong African traditions that may sustain a business ethics. Therefore, to provide a comprehensive overview of the topic at hand, three perspectives on the topic are explored.

The first and obvious approach (forwarded in the first section) constitutes a predominantly descriptive report on developments in business ethics in the different regions of SSA. Another frame of reference, undertaken in the second section, scans the development of business in Africa with specific reference to traditional African and Western influences. Despite the fact that Africa has inherited the business ethics language and tools from the West, the issues affecting the practice of business ethics in Africa cannot be separated from their unique contexts, which, in part, are shaped by historical forces. A third and final perspective delineates a normative response to African business ethics, premised on African culture, values, and business practices. As Augustine Shutte notes:

there exists a characteristic indigenous ethical tradition or set of traditions in sub-Saharan Africa that has certain common characteristics . . . [and that] embodies ethical insights that are both true and important in themselves, and are also significantly lacking in the dominant ethical thinking in the global community.

(2008: 16)

This uniquely African ethical tradition is commonly referred to as *Ubuntu*. In the third section, the question of whether, and to what extent, Ubuntu could inform thinking on business ethics on the continent, as well as contribute to the formulation of global norms, is investigated.

Business ethics developments in Sub-Saharan Africa

Findings from the Global Survey on Business Ethics

In terms of academic business ethics, the first comprehensive and valid baseline study for Sub-Saharan Africa (SSA) was published in 2000 (Barkhuysen and Rossouw 2000). This study reveals that, at the time, business ethics was taught in six African countries, and that a total number of 167 publications on business ethics in Africa existed (of which 130 were articles and 37 were books or unpublished dissertations). In both teaching and research, the bulk of activity originated in South Africa, the focus of activities was on the micro and meso-economic levels,[1] and the approach to business ethics was mostly descriptive or prescriptive.

When compared with this study, the report on Africa (Rossouw 2012) in "Global Survey of Business Ethics in Teaching, Training, and Research"[2] (Rossouw and Stückelberger 2012) reveals that significant—if uneven—strides have been made by countries in the development of business ethics as an academic field in SSA since 2000. By 2010, there was evidence of business ethics-related academic activities in 20 Sub-Saharan African countries.[3] A total number of 145 university courses,[4] in which business ethics was taught at undergraduate level and postgraduate level, were identified, and the number of research publications[5] for the period under review totaled 218.

The bulk of activity was reported in East Africa and Southern Africa. In Southern Africa, activity continued to be almost exclusively concentrated in South Africa, whereas East Africa was identified as the region in which business ethics-related activities were the most evenly dispersed across countries. In South Africa, business ethics is now an established field in higher education; whereas in East Africa, business ethics is finding traction in younger faith-based universities (where curricular reform is less onerous than in well-established universities), and the focus tends to be on ethics and civic education rather than on business ethics as such. This latter focus is mostly due to the fact that some states play a prominent role in promoting business ethics. The Ethiopian government, for example, has a Federal Ethics and Anti-corruption Commission (FEAC), which is heavily involved in business ethics teaching and training[6] at both secondary and tertiary education levels.

Little activity in the field of business ethics was reported for West Africa and Francophone Africa. However, there is evidence that the discipline is beginning to develop more rapidly. The current emphasis in these regions is on strong advocacy[7] in business ethics and good governance. The primary activity identified in these regions was that of research, as opposed to training and teaching (publications included non-academic documentation, possibly connected to the promotion of ethics and governance in the regions). Faith-based organizations (including NGOs and universities) again play a prevalent role in advancing the business ethics agenda.

In terms of prevalent themes addressed in training, teaching, and research, Deon Rossouw notes that the emphasis continued to be on the meso- and micro-economic levels in SAA,[8] and that a possible reason for this is that the high levels of corruption and corporate misconduct at all levels in SSA serve to focus the attention on issues of ethical management and leadership (including the subthemes of corporate governance and the prevention of corruption and corporate malpractice within organizations). This was particularly true of training in business ethics. In contrast, academic teaching (specifically at the undergraduate level) tended to be more focused on the theoretical frameworks that can guide ethical decision-making.

The strong focus on corruption and corporate misconduct also relates to the manner in which business ethics terminology is used. A peculiar feature regarding the usage of the term "business ethics" in SSA is that it implies the "business" of both the private and the public sectors (which, as previously mentioned, clarifies why the term "civic education," as used in Ethiopia for example, is sometimes viewed as synonymous with business ethics). A first possible explanation, forwarded in the Survey by Rossouw, for this usage is that the state remains a key player in many African economies due to the high prevalence of state-owned enterprises. State enterprise is thus identified with market enterprises and so—in many instances—business ethics is a matter of state rather than private firms. In this sense business ethics offers a description and evaluation of current organizations, rather than a reflection on how private for-profit entities ought to conduct themselves. A second reason is that business ethics activities in SSA are closely associated with anti-corruption initiatives (such as corporate governance reform) and the improvement of ethical standards in both the private and the public sector. As argued below, governance reform is viewed as critical to conducting ethical business in Africa, and attention accorded to governance reform in both the private and public sectors points to a mutual "business" ethics agenda, despite the obvious differences between these sectors.

Governance reform in Sub-Saharan Africa

The academic business ethics agenda is closely related to governance considerations due to the manner in which the role of business enterprise is articulated in many governance regimes in SSA. The role of the firm is understood in terms of attending to a broad array of stakeholder concerns and interests, as opposed to being viewed primarily in terms of shareholder interests (as in the United States). Rossouw (2009) offers two hypotheses for why this may be the case: first, corporate governance regimes are embedded in larger socio-cultural systems, and, as such, reflect the values and norms of these systems. In Africa, the cultural and societal norms are more communitarian-orientated than is the case in the West, so the purpose of the firm is seen as extending beyond the interests of individual shareholders.[9] Second (and as noted above), the socio-political environment plays a role in defining the purpose of the firm. In Africa most states have an active stake in enterprises, so the state's socio-political priorities also influence the firm's agenda. As such, African businesses operating in a post-apartheid or post-colonial context are expected to contribute to socio-political reform and development. As a consequence, the values according to which business ought to be conducted, and the interests that business ought to serve, cannot be isolated from the larger environment in which business operates or from the corporate governance regime underpinning that environment.

Apart from these normative considerations, it is also important to note that the goal of governance reform is to affect change in the economic (and political) environment(s). For this reason, governance reports and codes also provide concrete measures and guidelines for realizing ethical considerations, including defining the duties and responsibilities of the board and suggesting or prescribing measures for the active management of a company's ethical performance.

As such, governance concerns transcend the more specific normative and descriptive focus of academia by focusing on the operational dimensions of ethical business.

South Africa's corporate governance regime is representative of corporate governance on the African continent as a whole. South Africa's corporate governance stance is set forth in the King Reports on Corporate Governance in South Africa. These reports constitute a set of corporate governance guidelines for South Africa. King I, specifically, represented an attempt "to reinforce the fundamentals of a capitalist corporate system . . . and a means of aligning the economy with international trends and imperatives" (West 2009: 11). The post-apartheid corporate environment was, therefore, modelled on the Anglo-American shareholder-centered model. Yet, even at this early stage, the state's socio-political priorities served to temper businesses' focus on shareholder interests in that several legislative statutes applicable to business,[10] and passed in the 1990s and the subsequent decade (West 2009), are aimed directly at redressing economic inequalities stemming from apartheid.

Apart from these legislative statutes, the orientation of the King Reports serves to challenge the primacy of shareholders. The governance model promulgated in these Reports is an inclusive, stakeholder-centered model, which "considers, weighs and promotes the interests of all the company's stakeholders" (IoD RSA 2009: 1.11). Andrew West (2009) concludes that South Africa's corporate governance environment is most aptly described as "a modified Anglo-American model" (12): the orientation is broadly capitalistic but stakeholder interests and socio-political and socio-economic imperatives are also considered.

The inclusive stakeholder model is prevalent throughout SSA. Indeed, the only Sub-Saharan African country not to have initially followed the stakeholder model was Nigeria. However, in the 2011 revision of their 2003 governance code, emphasis was placed on management's responsibilities towards employees and other stakeholders (SEC Nigeria 2011: 2.2.). Furthermore, and again following the example of South Africa, all the governance codes in SSA advocate a unitary board model[11] and a self-regulatory approach, where companies are encouraged to treat their national corporate governance code or report as a guideline for ethical behavior (the "comply or explain" or "apply or explain" approach), as opposed to a set of legislated rules (the "comply or else" approach).

Although South Africa's governance reports are heralded as world-class, James Khomba and Frans Vermaak (2012) question the appropriateness of using the King Reports as the model for governance regimes in the wider African context. In particular, they argue that corporate citizenship (as reflected in social and environmental corporate responsibilities) is often not fully embedded in the structures and systems of organizations or adequately represented at board level, stakeholder interests are not sufficiently accounted for, and power differentials and conflict is not considered. These issues lead the authors to conclude that "[g]enerally, corporate governance issues in Africa are in their infancy and are, therefore, transitional" (3513).

Apart from the practical problems pertaining to the inclusive stakeholder-centered approach, scholars also argue that the modified Anglo-American corporate governance model (that characterizes South Africa's governance regime) may not be suited to other African countries, since these countries often do not reflect South Africa's level of economic development. In this regard, West argues that:

> many African countries do not have the size and sophistication of markets, or regulatory frameworks, for the concept of [regional] convergence to be meaningful. For many, the need for economic growth overshadows considerations of governance, and it is likely that the biggest influence on corporate governance in individual African countries will be their partners in trade and investment.

(2009: 15)

The foregoing demonstrates that both practitioners and business ethicists need to take cognizance of the history and level of economic development and accepted cultural norms in order to ensure that business ethics teaching and governance interventions resonate with African contexts and the experiences of African people.

Business in Africa: contextual considerations and challenges

A consideration of the historical and economic context does not yield unique and incontrovertible conclusions. In this section, three competing theses on the link between business ethics and the development of capitalism in Africa are set forth, followed by an overview of current challenges affecting business and the business ethics agenda.

The development of capitalism in Africa

The three theses can be summarized as follows: The first holds that the values underpinning Western capitalism are fundamentally incompatible with African (economic) values, with the result that capitalism has not led to the economic successes witnessed in the West. The second thesis is that Africa inherited a dysfunctional form of capitalism from the West with the consequence that ethical business values are largely lacking in the post-colonial African context. The third thesis postulates that Africa's current-day business ethics challenges are the result of a dysfunctional post-colonial political system, partly kept in place by Western aid.

Western economic liberalism arrived in Africa via several sources—colonialism, Islam, and Christianity. With that in mind, Munyaradzi Felix Murove (2005, 2009) explores the first and second of the above theses. In contending that economic liberalism is incompatible with African values, Murove draws on the work of John Iliffe (1983) and Paul Kennedy (1988). Iliffe's (1983) argument is that economic liberalism is a consequence of the Christian influence, in that Christianity (particularly Protestantism) stresses individual as opposed to community salvation, and thus provides the genesis for the individualism that undergirds capitalism. Iliffe maintains that this emphasis on the ethics of individualism is foreign to traditional African societies and that, as such, "[t]here is very little indication that indigenous institutions aided the emerging capitalist" (52). Similarly, Kennedy (1988) argues that the entrepreneurial spirit, which is so central to the development of capitalism, is missing in Africa, in which the collective is prized over individual achievement. Like Iliffe, Kennedy also stresses the role of religion in sanctioning Western economic liberalism.

Although the strong liberal underpinnings of modern capitalism was absent in traditional African societies, George Ayittey, in contrast, argues that capitalism is "as African as the sunset on the savannah" (2009: 41). He states that in pre-colonial African capitalism the means of production were privately owned, but—unlike in the West—the basic economic and social unit was the extended family, as opposed to the individual. Ayittey offers the following description of traditional African economic life:

> The family pools the resources of its members to produce agricultural products, the surpluses of which are sold on free markets at the village and regional levels. Here prices are determined by bargaining; they are not fixed by tribal chiefs or anyone else . . . Africans generally went about their economic activities on their own initiative and free will . . . In modern parlance, such people are called free enterprisers.

(2009: 40)

Christine Gichure's research affirms Ayittey's account of traditional African capitalism. She notes that "[l]ocal trade was part and parcel of the social and food production systems that evolved amongst communities" (2006: 42). The manner in which local trade functioned curbed unethical behavior in that the continual need to barter for essentials, as well as social patterns and mores, limited groups and individuals from amassing large quantities of wealth at the expense of others; the payment of goods and services was determined by local customs; local trade facilitated the integrity of, and the interdependence between, groups; and wealth (in the form of livestock, wives and children, land, drums, trinkets) was on open display, which limited fraud and embezzlement.

Both Ayittey's and Gichure's accounts provide a challenge to the thesis that traditional African economics did not provide fertile soil for the development of capitalism (albeit that the particular Western flavor of individual liberalism does not have a good base in Africa). Furthermore, Gichure's description of the social organization and norms structuring pre-colonial economic activities also provides a partial challenge to the second thesis, which holds that Africa's current business ethical challenges stem from the fact that Africa inherited a dysfunctional form of capitalism from the West. This argument presumes that business (and the norms guiding business conduct) did not exist before the arrival of colonialism, which—as demonstrated above—is a contested claim. Nevertheless, there is no denying the fact that colonialism had an impact on Africa's socio-economic landscape, and, as such, the second thesis—warrants investigation.

With reference to the second thesis, Murove (2009, 2005) argues that the Protestant work ethic did not find traction in post-colonial Africa, and, as a result, modern-day capitalism is all too often associated with "'ostentatious consumption' without production" (344). Yet scholars like Ali Mazrui (1986) lay the blame squarely at the feet of the colonialists, arguing that these early capitalists were responsible for severing the connection between commerce and ethics. He contextualizes this point as follows:

> The aristocratic legacy of masters and servants had its adverse consequences for the work ethic in post-colonial Africa . . . White masters in Africa drinking their gin and tonic leisurely while their servants pulled off their boots—this was the colonial caste which transformed physical labour into a burden of servitude.
>
> *(233)*[12]

Based on the above, Murove (2009: 225) concludes that post-colonial Africa inherited "the economic ethic of looting" from Western colonialists. Like Murove, Wayne Nafziger (1990) also draws attention to the negative socio-economic consequences of colonial capitalism, including general oppression and the destruction of indigenous institutions, religions, and cultures. Although colonialism paved the way to new sources of wealth creation and economic development, Nafziger notes that the majority of colonial investment was in infrastructure designed to promote trade with the colonizing country (mostly in mineral-related industries), that colonial expenditures were generally meager, and that the colonial legacy contributed to agricultural underdevelopment in the post-colonial period. Nafziger contends that as a result of rule by the West, forms of post-colonial capitalism are also still largely contingent on "the dependence of ruling classes on M.N.C.s, foreign aid and western military support" (150).

Ayittey downplays Africa's colonial legacy in favor of an interpretation centered on the exploitation of the state by the ruling elite, coupled with misdirected development aid from the West. In this regard Ayittey writes that Africa "is not poor because of the residue of colonialism . . . [but]

because its dysfunctional, kleptocratic politics have disorganized its societies, and Western countries and their aid vehicles have been unwittingly complicit in this" (2009: 37). On the questions of economic development one should consult also the work of William Easterly (2006), as well as the earlier and important studies of P.T. Bauer (1972, 1981).

In elaborating on this third thesis, Ayittey argues that in failing to consider history and context, the global development elite have largely ignored the fact that African economies consist of three sectors operating according to distinct principles: namely the traditional sector, the modern or formal sector, and a transitional or informal sector. Even though the majority of Africa's wealth is generated in the traditional and transitional sectors, development projects have focused almost exclusively on the formal sector, i.e., the regulated sector, in which companies are legally registered and (crucially) contribute to the tax base. Ayittey argues that this emphasis, coupled with corrupt political leadership, has strengthened what he calls "the artificial, parasitic African vampire state . . . [in which] Western-funded state enterprises became towering edifices of gross inefficiency, waste and graft" (2009: 39, 42). This enabled the ruling-elite—whom Ayittey depicts as "a gang of unrepentant bandits and vagabonds in Ray-Ban sunglasses and Italian suits" (42)—to enrich themselves and their tribes at the expense of their countrymen, sediment their positions of power, and lock out rivals, with the effect that a new system of economic apartheid has established itself in Africa. This system of economic apartheid has thwarted both local and foreign enterprise because the market cannot function properly in a context marred by unfair competition, opportunism, cronyism, rent seeking, and corruption.

Current-day challenges to business ethics in Africa

The foregoing discussion of some of the developments of capitalism in Africa already points to a number of structural features that mark the African business landscape as fundamentally different from that of the developed world (particularly the West). Consequently (and as demonstrated in the discussion on corporate governance regimes), the prevailing norms and issues that should be prioritized in African contexts may also be different from those of the developed world.

Although space does not permit an exhaustive analysis of pertinent issues or how and where they manifest themselves, an overview of the extant literature reveals that corruption and weak institutions, ethnic diversity, and economic pressures (which partly stem from Africa's history of economic development) pose significant challenges to sound business ethics practices in much of Africa.

Corruption and weak institutions

Corruption is often seen as Africa's number one problem, and the 2014 Corruption Perception Index conducted by Transparency International (TI) indicates that "the majority of [Sub-Saharan] African countries still have a score of less than 50 per cent, which . . . depicts a situation of endemic corruption" (Uwimana 2014: para. 1). Chantal Uwimana reports that the persistence of widespread corruption is one of the central features that prevent "the transformation of economic growth into development dividends for all citizens" (para. 2).

Opportunities for corrupt activity exist when a country's macro-level institutional infrastructure is weak. This infrastructure is required for the enforcement of legitimate property rights (e.g., in some developing nations the poor cannot get a document of ownership), freedom of entry and exit into enterprises, non-confiscatory tax laws, predictable and non-onerous regulation, an impartial judiciary, and a sound currency—all of which contribute to sustainable business practices. When these macro-institutions are either non-existent, weakly enforced, or marred by corruption, business is weakened, which both undermines investment potential and reinforces the perception that it is impossible to do (clean) business in Africa. This point is widely recognized and, as a result, a number of Sub-Saharan African countries, including Nigeria, South Africa, Tanzania, and Uganda, have amended their anti-corruption legislation (TI, 2009).

Strong macro-level institutional infrastructure not only safeguards business but also public interests. In Transparency International's *Global Corruption Report 2009: Corruption and the Private Sector*,[13] Jomo Kwame Sundaram (TI 2009: xx) notes that "[i]t is not uncommon for domestic firms and multinationals to pay bribes in order to secure public procurement contracts, nor unusual to learn of powerful corporate entities exerting undue pressure so as to capture institutions and influence regulations to elicit favourable investment conditions." Corruption may extend beyond the practice of simple bribery and may include the taking of "*any* undue advantage, irrespective of value, results, perception of local custom, tolerance or alleged necessity" (TI 2009: 1119). Narayana Murthy (TI 2009: xix) further notes that in instances where corruption is rife, "[the] public trust in the beneficial partnership between business and society is gradually undone."

In order to address private sector corruption, two elements are crucial: "the commitment and compliance systems of *companies*; and the rules, regulations and enforcements of *governments*" (TI 2009: 8). Enforcing good governance within companies (i.e., at the micro-level) ensures both that the risks associated with corruption within the organization are identified and addressed by corporate management, and that business responds effectively to the stakeholder networks that constitute the social and reputational contexts within which businesses operate at the meso-level. The responsibility of ensuring that the laws and institutions that constitute the macro-level business environment are legitimate, credible, and fair rests primarily with law makers and government regulators. The findings of the *Global Survey* (Rossouw and Stückelberger 2012) regarding the anticipated future focus of business ethics in SSA confirm that there is an increasing awareness amongst business ethicists of the significance of the macro-level business environment. As such, this environment is likely to constitute an increasingly important focus area for academic business ethics.

Ethnic diversity

Another challenge to general and equitable development has arisen, say some scholars, from the factionalization linked to ethnic groups. The problem or challenge is less one of ethnic diversity than of how ethnic identities have been used by colonialists and by current leaders to reward some and punish others. Praveen Parboteeah et al. report that misuse of ethnic diversity also has had "[a] dramatic impact on . . . economic development" (2013: 983), primarily through influencing national and business climates. According to Parboteeah et al., the political uses of ethnic diversity can be traced back to the "scramble for Africa," during which time informal indigenous political systems were upended and spheres of influences were determined by colonial rulers. Often colonial rulers pitted different ethnicities against one another, and ethnic groups became competitive rather than cooperative.

In post-colonial Africa, this competitive behavior continues, and Parboteeah et al. (2013: 984) note that the perception too often exists that "only when a particular ethnic group has its own kind in political or organizational power, can it benefit from the nation's or organization's resources, hence increasing the phenomenon of ethnic identity." There, thus, seems to be a connection between the valorization of ethnicity and cronyism. The widespread occurrence of ethnically-mediated cronyism in contemporary African politics confirms that this perception, however general, is not unfounded. Furthermore, others have noted that a strong emphasis on ethnic identity fuels "despotism, repression, state terrorism and manipulated ethnic hatred" (Ayittey 2009: 42), as well as xenophobic violence—all of which undermine economic stability and success.

In their research on the ethical climates of companies in Africa, Parboteeah et al. (2013) further found that ethnic valorization is positively correlated with business climates in which "company norms support the satisfaction of self-interest at the expense of or with disregard to others" (981). Parboteeah et al. found that very few young people entering the labor force in Africa have faith that employment opportunities in the public and private sector will be allocated on merit rather than ethnic identity. This reinforces a corrupt business climate wherein *who* you know is more important than *what* you know.

Economic pressures

As developing nations, the countries of Sub-Saharan Africa are marked by widespread poverty and high levels of unemployment. Economic interests are thus paramount. Wayne Visser (2006) argues that due to the centrality accorded to economic interests in SSA, the social impact of business is primarily assessed in terms of business's economic contribution. For this reason, and with reference to Archie Carroll's (1991) influential CSR pyramid, Visser (2006) argues that in Africa, economic responsibilities trump all other responsibilities, and are highly prized by society. In order to discuss the extent to which these economic obligations are accepted by business, it is necessary to compare the trajectories of large formal enterprises with those of smaller firms and more informal modes of doing business.

In defining the scope of economic responsibilities, Visser notes that—as in Europe—the economic contributions of companies operating in Africa are more widely defined than is the case in North America, where the focus is on profitability and return to shareholders. In a 2014 policy briefing on governance in Africa, Terence Corrigan states that, in terms of governance, "[a] major African contribution to corporate governance thinking has been to entrench considerations of stakeholders' interests in business operations" (2014: 2). However, the degree to which stakeholders (and their economic interests) are considered is contingent upon the depth of understanding of CSR practices. In this regard, Corrigan draws on economist and management expert Simon Zadek and his conceptions of three generations of CSR (2001). Corrigan summarizes the three notions as follows:

> The first . . . [is] a form of philanthropy, sometimes ad hoc, dealing with social issues. The second involves a greater professionalism and the systematisation of initiatives—targets are set and progress reported, and CSR is integrated into planning. A third would see businesses taking a more active role in partnering with other elements in society to deal with overarching social problems such as poverty and environmental sustainability.
>
> *(2014: 2)*

If Visser is correct in arguing that the social impact of business in Africa is primarily measured in terms of economic development (and, more specifically, in terms of "'economic multipliers'" (2006: 38), including generative investment and income, safe products and services, job creation, human capital investment, local business linkages, the uptake of international business standards, technology transfer, and physical and institutional infrastructure development), then one could hypothesize that we are likely to witness a move towards second and (especially) third generation CSR, where business takes an active role in addressing overarching problems (including issues pertaining to socio-economic and equitable development).

As previously argued, this broad stance to CSR is reflected in South Africa's King Reports. However, drawing on research conducted in six Southern African countries (Lesotho, Mauritius, Mozambique, South Africa, Tanzania, and Zambia), Corrigan concludes that although "[i]n conception, Africa's expectations of CSR are expansive . . . small, 'first-generation' activities may be all that is feasible for emerging businesses" (2014: 2, 4). It thus seems that, in many cases, economic benefits are merely incidental, and are not actively conceptualized in terms of corporate responsibilities, even though—in theory—the need to "reconcile economic growth with developmental benefits . . . is a growing strategic issue" (2014: 2).

Both the small and medium-sized enterprises (SME) and informal business sectors make up a significant part of the economic landscape in SSA, and, as such, the (potential) economic contributions of these sectors warrant investigation. Emmanuelle Lavallée and François Roubaud note that "operating in the informal sector is the rule rather than the exception [in SSA] and is not the result of recent systemic changes" (TI 2009: 412). They reference a 2002 World Bank discussion paper in which it is stated that Africa's informal sector "is estimated to account on average 42 per cent of GDP in Africa in 2000" (Schneider 2002), although they also note that the size of the informal sector varies radically between countries. It stands to reason that factors that prevent the formal institutionalization of business also directly undermine CSR (defined in terms of economic imperatives) because many economic benefits—including taxation, investment, and safe products and services—are contingent on the registration and regulation of business.

Lavallée and Roubaud postulate that corruption may be one factor that perpetuates Africa's informal sector. Yet, despite the size of this sector, Lavallée and Roubaud state that, to date, little comprehensive empirical research on the link between corruption and the informal sector has been undertaken. In order to generate some data on this link, the authors conducted a study of the informal sector in seven major cities in the Western African Economic and Monetary Unit. Their findings reveal that non-compliance in terms of legal registration of businesses has more to do with ignorance of the law and ineffective enforcement of registration requirements than with corruption (although Lavallée and Roubaud (TI 2009: 414) also report that paying bribes for non-compliance "is a significant means for settling disputes with public agents").

As with the informal sector, SMEs also play an important role in SSA and, as such, it is worthwhile to investigate the extent to which they embrace CSR. Mollie Painter-Morland and Kris Dobie's research indicates that these businesses are perceived by many as the "engine of the economy" (2009: 9), and are generally viewed as being in a much closer relationship to their communities than is the case with big business. However, Painter-Morland and Dobie also note that many SMEs believe themselves to be operating in survival mode. This perceived business pressure, coupled with the existence of systemic corruption, means that SMEs often "'cut corners,' reduce product quality, and overpromise or over commit, which eventually impacts negatively on the sustainability of these operations" (2009: 9).

What is clear, even from the above summary discussion, is that both the informal sector and SMEs pose significant opportunities for economic development in SSA, and that—as such—it is important to define, harness, and identify threats to these opportunities. Ayittey writes that "the stark truth is that meaningful development and poverty reduction cannot occur by ignoring Africa's traditional and transitional sectors, nor can these sectors be developed without an operational understanding of the institutions supporting them" (2009: 39). This point is particularly important from the perspective of future business ethics research, since—to date—the paradigm case for most conceptual and empirical studies has been big business. In SSA, SMEs and the informal sector (as well as their links with other economic sectors and actors, and with government) should also be considered if we truly wish to develop business as a vehicle for socio-economic development.

Towards an African business ethics

Much of the analysis thus far has dealt with the macro-economic landscape, and how it supports or undermines business and business ethics. However, this third and final section investigates the extent to which an indigenous African ethics can contribute to the normative basis of business ethics.

Ubuntu: a uniquely African ethics?

One should be loath to speak of *an* African ethics in the singular. However, there is evidence that the concept of *Ubuntu*—a Nguni Bantu term frequently explained with reference to the aphorism "*umuntu ngumuntu ngabantu*" or, loosely put, "a person is a person through other people" or "I am because we are"—is widely accepted across much of SSA as a normative standard of conduct. Ubuntu is typically construed as conveying a communitarian ethic distinct from the more individualistic emphases of the West. Thaddeus Metz (2007), who has done extensive work clarifying the concept, notes that the Ubuntu maxim has both descriptive and prescriptive meaning. Ubuntu signifies that one's personhood or identity *is* inextricably bound up (in both a causal and metaphysical sense) with the identity of others. Yet Ubuntu also *obliges* us to morally support one another.

Empirically there is evidence that an African ethics is widely referenced across SSA (see Newenham-Kahindi 2009). The widespread occurrence of Ubuntu terminology, however, is not sufficient evidence for the claim that Ubuntu signifies a uniquely African ethics. If, however, it can be shown that the notion of Ubuntu is rich enough to inform a normative theory of right action, then the idea of an African ethical theory—representative of moral reasoning across the continent—need not be at odds with Africa's heterogeneity. The reason for this is that, when formulated in terms of an ethical theory, Ubuntu would not be contingent on contextually-determined norms, but would rather signify a "general principle grounding particular duties that is informed by such values and that could be compared to dominant Western theories such as Hobbesian egoism or Kantian respect for persons" (Metz 2007: 321). Furthermore, if such an ethics truly does present an alternative to the Western ethical canon, then we also find support for the claim that Ubuntu can make a unique contribution to the global debate on business ethics.

A number of introductions to, and applications of, Ubuntu to the field of business ethics appear in the scholarly literature.[14] West (2014) notes that these contributions are generally based on two strands of argument, both of which presume that Ubuntu constitutes a true alternative to Western ethical theories. The first argument is that African economic systems should reflect African values and that Ubuntu values should thus form the cornerstone of business in Africa (Murove 2005, 2009); whereas the second argument is that, because of its distinctive nature, African ethics can contribute to the development of a global business ethics (Shutte 2008; Visser 2004).

Andrew West (2014) is critical of both of these lines of argumentation, for the reason that it is not clear that Ubuntu values differ significantly from Western values.[15] If West is correct, then the appeal to Ubuntu as a uniquely African business ethics is undermined. As concerns the first argument, West states that the claim that Ubuntu values differ from Western values is often simply assumed rather than supported by empirical evidence. In cases where empirical evidence is provided, it tends to be anecdotal. As such, he concludes that there is simply not enough proof in the literature to support this argument. This conclusion also holds implications for the second argument: if the distinctiveness of Ubuntu cannot be proven—in other words, if the language of Ubuntu resonates with Western ideas—it is not clear what unique contribution African ethics can make to the development of a global business ethic. Compounding this issue is the fact that there are many ambiguities and differences of opinion as to what the distinctive features of Ubuntu are.

Given the above, West argues that there is a need to undertake comparative empirical studies, aimed at determining both whether there are variations in the value systems of different African countries and cultures, and whether there are significant value differences between Africans and non-Africans. West further notes that additional research aimed at clarifying the meaning of Ubuntu (and its relation to other ethical systems) is required if Ubuntu is to move beyond being a vague communitarian philosophy (that encompasses a number of virtues), to become a robust normative position capable of promoting a just and equitable society, and capable of being fruitfully applied to various disciplines.

Towards a general principle of Ubuntu

Some of the more recent scholarship on Ubuntu centers on the attempt to extract a principle from a plethora of different meanings associated with the term. Of particular influence is the work of Metz who has attempted to develop an Ubuntu principle to ground a normative ethical theory that can serve as an alternative to the normative principles espoused in the Western canon. As a standard to guide right action, Metz formulates the following principle:

> An action is right just insofar as it promotes shared identity among people grounded on good-will; an act is wrong to the extent that it fails to do so and tends to encourage the opposites of division and ill-will.
>
> *(2007: 338)*

Metz's methodology for deriving this principle was to identify two sets of moral judgements, namely those viewed as uncontroversial by both Africans and Westerners, and those deemed to be more uncontroversial by Africans than by Westerners. In terms of the former, shared moral judgements include prohibitions against killing, raping, lying, stealing, breaking promises, and discriminating. In terms of the latter, moral intuitions associated more strongly with Africans include beliefs that the following are wrong: retributive punishment, decision-making in the face of dissensus, fiercely competitive economics, a rights-based allocation of wealth, isolation from a community's way of life, and failure to procreate through marriage.

Having identified these sets, Metz then attempts to develop an integrating principle that accounts for the moral judgements in both sets. On this basis, he generates six competing principles, of which the above formulation constitutes the most promising theoretical foundation of an African ethic. Metz argues that the combination of shared selfhood (or personhood) and good-will (understood in terms of the search for the good of others) espoused in the above definition promotes social harmony and togetherness, which Bishop Desmond Tutu (1999: 35) defines as both the crux of Ubuntu and "the *summum bonum*—the greatest good." Furthermore, these characteristics best accommodate both the moral intuitions shared by Africans and Westerners, and the moral intuitions that are more common in Africa.

Metz (2007) notes that this project leaves some unanswered questions, primarily related to the promotion of harmony. Nevertheless, despite these unanswered questions, Metz is of the opinion that the above formulation represents the best "fundamental and general principle prescribing right actions that is epistemically justified relative to the circumscribed set of African competitors that could in future work be paired up against Western moral theories" (322–333).

Applying Ubuntu

In order to operationalize Ubuntu, it must find significant traction in the fields of moral philosophy and business ethics.[16] Three factors currently impede the incorporation of Ubuntu in business ethics: Firstly, Ubuntu concepts are vague, abstract, and difficult to operationalize (Metz's project of systematizing Ubuntu principles in a coherent normative ethical theory is important in overcoming this problem). Secondly, current scholarship is unlikely to culminate in one overarching theory of Ubuntu. The heterogeneity of the term could undermine its uptake in the global ethics community, yet West (2014) argues that this need not mean that Ubuntu could not have a profound impact on certain local contexts.[17] Thirdly, Ubuntu shares distinctive features with Western ethical thought (particularly with communitarian positions) and it is also not clear that the moral judgements that feature more strongly in African moral reasoning could not be sufficiently accommodated in existing ethical frameworks.

Apart from these structural challenges to operationalizing Ubuntu, the uptake of Ubuntu in the business community has also been the subject of criticism. David McDonald, for example, views the marketization of Ubuntu values in South Africa over the last two decades as an exercise in window-dressing. He argues that "there is little to suggest that *ubuntu* rhetoric has done anything to change corporate practice in [South Africa]" (2010: 147). To the contrary, the marketization of Ubuntu has allowed South African business to profess values such as putting communal interests ahead of the individual and strengthening social relations, whilst—for the most part—pursuing business as usual. McDonald argues that governance and corporate responsibility practices in South Africa rather seem to be shaped by international norms and markets (which are becoming increasingly homogenized), than by "any abstract notion of an African *ubuntu* 'cosmos'" (2010: 147). As such, he concludes that, to date, the value of the Ubuntu discourse has not been its transformative impact, but its ability to convince "South Africans that market reforms are democratic and egalitarian, while at the same time serving to defuse opposition to underlying neoliberal change" (2010: 140).

To what extent Ubuntu could find traction in business ethics scholarship and practice remains to be seen. However, the emergence and proliferation of high-quality scholarship on Ubuntu in recent years (particularly in the philosophical literature) is a positive development.

Concluding remarks

This chapter has sought to situate and contextualize the study and practice of business ethics in Africa and to suggest, thereby, some avenues for further exploration. It should however be noted that a meta-analysis of the kind undertaken here cannot do proper homage to the plethora of unique socio-economic and scholarly environments in which the subject of business ethics in Africa should be interpreted, evaluated, and operationalized. Yet, the hope is that, in showing how historical, institutional, and cultural contingencies both affect and complicate questions related to the development of business ethics, this research provides an illustration of the type of considerations that should inform any serious reflection on business ethics, whether it be in the African or any other context.

In most of Africa, business ethics is not yet properly institutionalized (both as a practice and as an academic field), and there are many challenges related to its institutionalization. However, the fact that the discipline is still in its infancy also provides exciting opportunities for those working in the field. Business and business ethics practices have the potential to make a big contribution in Africa, particularly because the public sector in many countries is lacking in institutional capacity. Practical contributions should resonate with local realities, and, in this regard, those working in the field should concentrate on developing culturally-sensitive solutions to the identified challenges.

In light of this analysis, the following were identified as important focus areas for the future: With regard to academic business ethics and governance reform initiatives, research initiatives should be aimed at identifying salient contextual factors that may affect (either positively or negatively) the efficacy of current and future programs, policies, and guidelines. In terms of addressing significant current-day challenges to ethical business and sustainable economic development, focus needs to be placed on the macro-environment in which business operates (and which all too often prevents, thwarts, or renders difficult the development of sustainable enterprise), as well as on SMEs and Africa's informal sector. With regard to developing business ethics tools for dealing with African problems, a three-pronged approach is forwarded: indigenous governance, political, and economic structures should be investigated with the goal of harnessing and redefining traditional knowledge for modern business; influential Western business ethics theories should be reinterpreted in light of the African context; and, the current scholarship on an Ubuntu ethic, and its potential application to the field of business ethics, should be further explored.

Essential reading

For region and country-specific information on business ethics developments in sub-Saharan Africa see Deon Rossouw and Christoph Stückelberger, *Global Survey of Business Ethics in Teaching, Training, and Research* (2012). For information on current developmental challenges and opportunities in Africa, see George Ayittey, *Africa Unchained: The Blueprint for Africa's Future* (2005). For scholarship on African ethics and its applications, see Munyaradzi Felix Murove (ed.), *African Ethics: An Anthology of Comparative and Applied Ethics* (2009), and Thaddeus Metz's forthcoming monograph, titled *A Relational Moral Theory: African Contributions to Global Ethics*. The *African Journal of Business Ethics* (available online at http://ajobe.journals.ac.za/pub) is also a good resource on business ethics developments in Africa.

For further reading in this volume on the international extension of Western notions of business ethics, see Chapter 32, The globalization of business ethics. For a general discussion of the question of values across cultures, see Chapter 33, Cross-cultural management ethics in multinational commerce. A discussion of corruption and bribery can be found in Chapter 34, Corruption, bribery, and moral norms across national boundaries. On general issues of corporate governance, see Chapter 24, Corporate governance. On stakeholder theory, see Chapter 11, Stakeholder thinking. For a consideration of the conditions of economic development and innovation, see Chapter 19, Creativity, innovation, and the production of wealth.

Notes

1 The micro-economic or intra-organizational level "focuses on economic activity within business organizations. It concentrates on the moral dimension of business practices, policies, behavior and decisions that occurs within business" (Kretzschmar et al. 2012: 22). The meso-economic or organisational level "refers to the level at which the impact of business on broader society is evaluated" (282) and pertinent themes include corporate responsibility and corporate citizenship. The macro-economic level or economic systems level is the "level at which economic systems or macro-economic policies and trade agreements are scrutinised to see that they are equitable and fair" (280). Here the focus is on economic ethics and sustainability.
2 The Global Survey was commissioned by Globethics.net in 2009 and tracks business ethics developments between 1995 and 2010.

3 The countries are South Africa, Botswana, Zimbabwe, Angola, Mozambique (Southern Africa); Uganda, Kenya, Tanzania, Ethiopia, Somalia (Eastern Africa); Nigeria, Ghana, Cameroon, Benin Republic, and Togo (Western Africa); and, Ivory Coast, Burundi, Senegal, Rwanda, and the Democratic Republic of the Congo (Central and Francophone Africa).
4 The Survey, in fact, refers to "modules" but without any definition. However, the term is typically used to refer to a university course that runs either over one term (i.e., a quarter of an academic year) or over one semester (i.e., half of an academic year).
5 For the purposes of this survey, the term "publication" was widely interpreted to include academic research, educational publications, corporate reports, and public documents dealing with business and economic ethics research (Rossouw and Stückelberger 2012).
6 For the purposes of this chapter, training programs focusing on business and economic ethics, and taught by universities, professional organisations, and anti-corruption agencies, are distinguished from teaching programs, understood in terms of formal academic courses on business and economic ethics (Rossouw and Stückelberger 2012).
7 Advocacy typically means that the need for, and commitment to, ethical business is affirmed by key stakeholders in business, government, and academia; and this commitment is often expressed by establishing networks and special interest groups centered on the promotion of ethical business.
8 Interestingly, Francophone Africa currently exhibits a much stronger focus on development and economic ethics, when compared with the other regions (Rossouw 2012). The macro context also featured more strongly in the research outputs of Francophone and West Africa than in the other regions. Rossouw offers two possible reasons for this, namely that in these regions business ethics problems are seen as structural rather than functional, and that faith-based institutions involved in the production of most of the research in these areas tend to focus on the macro, as opposed to the meso or micro, context.
9 Rossouw (2009) notes that the interesting exception to this hypothesis is Europe. Despite the fact that individualism and personal autonomy are viewed as paramount, most European countries follow a stakeholder-orientation with regard to governance.
10 These statutes included the Labour Relations Act of 1995, the Basic Conditions of Employment Act of 1997, the Employment Equity Act of 1998 (which, in part, promotes the inclusion of black labor in the formal economy), and the Broad-based Black Economic Empowerment Act of 2003.
11 A unitary board refers to a single-tiered board model, where executive and non-executive board members have an equal legal responsibility for the management and performance of the company.
12 This bleak picture also provides an apt description of the policy (and culture) of apartheid in South Africa, in which people of color were viewed and treated as subservient to white people. Apartheid was kept in place from 1949–1994 by the National Party Government who, through a process of state engineering, artificially segregated the races and provided inferior education to the black population.
13 This report, which can be downloaded from www.transparency.org/whatwedo/publication/global_corruption_report_2009, also provides data and information on private sector corruption in the following sub-Saharan countries: Burundi, Cameroon, Ethiopia, Ghana, Kenya, Nigeria, Rwanda, and Zimbabwe.
14 Beyond the scholarly literature, it is interesting to note that Ubuntu values have also been included in the King Reports. This inclusion bears testimony to the fact that the South African business community believes that Ubuntu can be profitably applied to business, as a means "to better corporate governance and social responsibility while at the same time improving the bottom line and safeguarding the market economy" (McDonald 2010: 143).
15 Many philosophers argue that beneath the apparently different moral norms that exist between cultures, there lies a more abstract agreement on ultimate values. What accounts for these seemingly different moral norms are different backgrounds and non-moral beliefs about the way in which the world works (see, for example, the discussion of cultural relativism in Chapter two of Rachels and Rachels 2007).
16 See Barbara Nussbaum (2009, esp. 249–250) for a discussion on an Ubuntu-infused capitalism.
17 A case in point is South Africa: the smooth transition to a post-apartheid South Africa was facilitated by both Nelson Mandela's notion of a "Rainbow Nation," and Bishop Tutu's reference to Ubuntu during the Truth and Reconciliation Commission hearings. In this context, the Ubuntu rhetoric was instrumental in building a new national identity, thereby straddling the divide between races and facilitating moral regeneration (West 2014).

References

Ayittey, G. (2009). "Misleading Africa," *The American Interest* Spring (March/April), 37–45.
Ayittey, G. (2005). *Africa Unchained: The Blueprint for Africa's Future*. London: Palgrave Macmillan.
Barkhuysen, B. and G.J. Rossouw (2000). "Business Ethics as an Academic Field in Africa: Its Current Status," *Business Ethics: A European Review* 9:4, 229–235.
Bauer, P.T. (1972). *Dissent on Development*. Cambridge, MA: Harvard University Press.
Bauer, P.T. (1981). *Equality, the Third World, and Economic Delusion*. Cambridge, MA: Harvard University Press.
Carroll, A.B. (1991). "The Pyramid of Corporate Social Responsibility: Toward the Moral Management of Organizational Stakeholders," *Business Horizons* 34, 39–48.
Corrigan, T. (2014). "'Good Citizens': Corporate Social Responsibility in Africa," in *SAIIA, Policy Briefing 103: Governance and APRM Programme*. SAIIA, September.
Easterly, W. (2006). *The White Man's Burden: Why the West's Efforts to Aid the Rest have Done So Much Ill and So Little Good*. New York, NY: Penguin.
Gichure, C.W. (2006). "Teaching Business Ethics in Africa: What Ethical Orientation? The Case of East and Central Africa," *Journal of Business Ethics* 63:1, 39–52.
Iliffe, J. (1983). *The Emergence of African Capitalism*. London: Macmillan.
Institute of Directors (IoD) Southern Africa, Republic of South Africa (2009). *King Report on Governance for South Africa (King III)*. Johannesburg: Institute of Directors.
Kennedy, P. (1988). *African Capitalism: The Struggle for Ascendancy*. Cambridge: Cambridge University Press.
Khomba, J.K. and F.N.S. Vermaak (2012). "Business Ethics and Corporate Governance: An African Socio-Cultural Framework," *African Journal of Business Management* 6:9, 3510–3518.
Kretzschmar, L., F. Prinsloo, M. Prozesky, G.J. Rossouw, S. Korien, J. Siebrits and M. Woermann (2012). *Ethics for Accountants and Auditors*. Cape Town: Oxford University Press Southern Africa.
Mazrui, A.A. (1986). *The Africans: A Triple Heritage*. London: BBC Publications.
McDonald, D.A. (2010). "*Ubuntu* Bashing: The Marketisation of 'African Values' in South Africa," *Review of African Political Economy* 37:124, 139–152.
Metz. T. (forthcoming 2018). *A Relational Moral Theory: African Contributions to Global Ethics*. Oxford: Oxford University Press.
Metz, T. (2007). "Toward an African Moral Theory," *Journal of Political Philosophy* 15:3, 321–341.
Murove, M.F. (ed.) (2009). *African Ethics: An Anthology of Comparative and Applied Ethics*. Scottsville: University of KwaZulu Natal Press.
Murove, M.F. (2009). 'The Incarnation of Max Weber's *Protestant Ethic and the Spirit of Capitalism* in Post-Colonial African Economic Discourse: The Quest for an African Economic Ethic," in M.F. Murove (ed.), *African Ethics: An Anthology of Comparative and Applied Ethics*. Scottsville: University of KwaZulu Natal Press, 221–237.
Murove, M.F. (2005). "The Voice from the Periphery: Towards an African Business Ethics Beyond the Western Heritage," *South African Journal of Economic and Management Sciences* 8:3, 339–347.
Nafziger, E.W. (1990). "African Capitalism, State Power, and Economic Development," *The Journal of Modern African Studies* 28:1, 141–150.
Newenham-Kahindi, A. (2009). "The Transfer of Ubuntu and Indaba Business Models Abroad: A Case of South African Multinational Banks and Telecommunication Services in Tanzania," *International Journal of Cross Cultural Management* 9:1, 87–105.
Nussbaum, B. (2009). "Ubuntu and Business: Reflections and Questions," in M.F. Murove (ed.), *African Ethics: An Anthology of Comparative and Applied Ethics*. Scottsville: University of KwaZulu Natal Press, 238–255.
Painter-Morland, M. and K. Dobie (2009). "Ethics and Sustainability within SMEs in sub-Saharan Africa: Enabling, Constraining and Contaminating Relationships," *African Journal of Business Ethics* 4:2, 7–19.
Parboteeah, K.P., H.T. Seriki and M. Hoegl (2013). "Ethnic Diversity, Corruption and Ethical Climates in sub-Saharan Africa: Recognizing the Significance of Human Resource Management," *The International Journal of Human Resource Management* 25:7, 979–1001.
Rachels, J. and S. Rachels (2007). *The Elements of Moral Philosophy*, 5th edition. New York, NY: McGraw-Hill.
Rossouw, G.J. (2012). "Africa," in G.J. Rossouw and C. Stückelberger (eds), *Global Survey of Business Ethics in Teaching, Training, and Research (Globethics.net Global No. 5)*. Geneva: Globethics.net, 127–142.

Rossouw, G.J. (2009). "The Ethics of Corporate Governance: Global Convergence or Divergence?" *International Journal of Law and Management* 51:1, 43–51.

Rossouw, G.J. and C. Stückelberger (eds) (2012). *Global Survey of Business Ethics in Teaching, Training, and Research (Globethics.net Global No. 5)*. Geneva: Globethics.net.

Schneider, F. (2002). *Size and Measurement of the Informal Economy in 110 Countries around the World*, discussion paper. Washington DC: Washington.

Security and Exchange Commission Nigeria (2011). *Code of Corporate Governance for Public Companies in Nigeria*.

Sheeran, P.D. (2008). "African Business Ethics," in R.W. Kolb (ed.), *Encyclopaedia of Business Ethics and Society*. Thousand Oaks, CA: Sage, 37–39.

Shutte, A. (2008). "African Ethics in a Globalising World," in R. Nicolson (ed.), *Persons in Community: African Ethics in a Global Culture*. KwaZulu-Natal: University of KwaZulu Natal Press, 15–34.

Transparency International (TI) (2009). *Global Corruption Report 2009: Corruption and the Private Sector*. New York, NY: Cambridge University Press.

Tutu, D. (1999). *No Future without Forgiveness*. New York, NY: Random House.

Uwimana, C. (2014). "Sub-Saharan Africa: Corruption Still Hurts Daily Lives," *Transparency International* 3, December.

Visser, W. (2004). "The Notion of Ubuntu and Communalism in African Educational Discourse," *Urban Studies* 45:12, 2565–2593.

Visser, W. (2006). "Revisiting Carroll's CSR pyramid: An African Perspective," in M. Huniche and E.R. Pedersen (eds), *Corporate Citizenship in Developing Countries: New Partnership Perspectives*. Copenhagen: Copenhagen Business School Press, 29–56.

West, A. (2014). "*Ubuntu* and Business Ethics: Problems, Perspectives and Prospects," *Journal of Business Ethics* 121, 47–61.

West, A. (2009). "The Ethics of Corporate Governance," *International Journal of Law and Management* 51:1, 17–26.

Zadek, S. (2001). *The Civil Corporation: The New Economy of Corporate Citizenship*. London: Earthscan.

38
Business ethics in Latin America

Álvaro E. Pezoa

For the nations of Latin America, corruption is and will remain the largest political and economic concern. With few exceptions, it is deeply entrenched and reaches into both politics and business and the relations between them. Among the citizens of the continent, the common perception is that a significant level of ethical failures exist in Latin American business activity, albeit with relevant differences among distinct countries. Is there any basis for this perception? Within too many nations there is a corruption of the public political sphere, sometimes involving private or corporate actions. The media tend to focus on this sort of public corruption, especially since the ethical violations committed between and among private individuals, firms, and corporations are often relegated to less important pages in the print media.

A consideration of business ethics in Latin America must take into account both the private realm and the public, as well as the status of the academic study of business ethics, and the role of non-profit and non-governmental organizations (NGOs). This chapter seeks to provide such an overview. It addresses the question of private corruption by summarizing information in the press over the five years spanning 2011 to 2015. In the next section, the chapter offers a comparative assessment of public (governmental) corruption in Latin America in relation to other nations throughout the world. The third section shifts from the practical to the academic and addresses business ethics in terms of pedagogy and research. A final section sheds light on the efforts of NGOs as well as corporations and governments to confront corruption.

Business ethics in Latin America: an approach to reality through the press

It is not easy to gain a view on the status of business ethics as a matter of practice rather than academic study. Within Latin America, few studies chronicle the state of conduct within commerce. This paucity of academic studies on actual business ethics suggested to this author the necessity of an investigation as to the extent and kinds of ethical problems experienced within business in Latin America (Pezoa 2016). The sources of this study were cases reported in the press, mainly during the five years from 2011 to 2015, for six selected countries: Argentina, Brazil, Chile, Colombia, Mexico and Peru. This study, which offers an up-to-date, panoramic, and representative vision of the state of business ethics in the region, is the foundation for the remarks that follow.

Álvaro E. Pezoa

The study assumes that the news reports of ethical problems, as published in articles and columns, provide a picture about the everyday morality of business conduct. Such a picture, or panorama, is not exact and reflects a qualitative rather than quantitative assessment. The media chosen for the study were business newspapers or business sections of the main newspapers in each of six countries (Argentina, Brazil, Chile, Colombia, Mexico, and Peru). These media had to meet two minimal characteristics: each had to be representative of the business journalism in that country and each must allow an easy access to complete information (e.g., through public access of web pages). Moreover, the study surveyed *all* articles about business ethics that appeared within the pages of these media during the defined period. Even as a qualitative assessment, this study has two additional limitations: first, it does not capture information that has not become public knowledge; second, it almost certainly *exaggerates* the dominance of ethical lapses, since there are virtually no references in the media during the five-year period that describe positive or ethically uplifting news, quite possibly because these stories are not attractive for newspapers editors or readers.

As conducted, the study intentionally omitted any information related to corruption cases having to do with collusion *between* political powers and business, a subject we leave for the next section. Ethical failures of this nature—sometimes referred to as influence trafficking, bribery, rent seeking—are recurrent in the countries of the region and normally attract the most attention of the media and public opinion today. This so-called "public–private" corruption is intimately related to the funding of political parties (and their candidates) with money from private businesses; such corruption is not simply due to the improper use of political power more generally. In many cases corruption also takes place between the public–governmental sector and state enterprises. As an example of the latter, the worldwide scandal that recently came to light between the Brazilian government and Petrobras, the giant Brazilian state oil company, comes to mind. This affair led to the impeachment and ultimate removal of President Dilma Rousseff by Congress in 2016.

Beyond news reporting dedicated to the cases mentioned in the previous paragraph—of which cases there were many—the focus of the investigation was the information in the press associated with ethical issues surrounding business conducted by and between private individuals and firms (whether corporations or not). In light of the aforementioned, the main findings can be summarized as follows.[1]

1   In the countries under consideration, the ethical transgressions most frequently reported exemplify cartels, collusion, abuse of dominant positions, unfair competition and violations of free competition.

   In the spring of 2016 the Argentine government decided to analyze whether there is a dominant firm in eleven distinct economic sectors. The justification for the inquiry is that a dominant firm could violate free competition. Only two months prior to the start of this inquiry, the head of the Argentine Chamber of Meat Industry and Trade (CICCRA) reported that supermarkets were very eager to maximize profits, charging a very high 50 percent margin on the price of meat. Meanwhile, in Chile, in late 2015, a case of collusion in the "tissue paper" market was brought to light between Compañía Manufacturera de Papeles y Cartones (CMPC) and the Swedish firm Svenska Cellulosa (or SCA, which itself had previously acquired a Chilean firm, PISA). This revelation followed the voluntary admission of collusion by officials of CMPC. Three years earlier, the chicken market (in Chile) was the object of controversy as the result of the accusation, launched by the National Economic Prosecutor (FNE), of collusion among the Agrosuper, Ariztía and Don Pollo companies; previously three large pharmacy chains were in the news for similar reasons. Other industries that have been investigated for such malfeasances, but without receiving convictions or sanctions, include supermarkets, airlines, buses, and the fishing industry. Of course, the fact of an investigation does not entail guilt and in some of these cases there were, in fact, no findings of ethical or legal improprieties. In Colombia, the situation of the so-called "toilet paper" cartel merits a highlight: commencing as early as 1998, there appears to have been a restrictive and continuous agreement, until 2013, among the companies and economic groups of Kimberly, Familia, Risaralda Cardboard and Paper, and National Paper to set the price for napkins, paper hand towels, kitchen roll paper and toilet paper. The result was to imperil competition and to force Colombians to pay more for these soft paper products. In Peru, the so-called "sugar" cartel found itself paying a fine levied by the Superintendency of Industry and Commerce (SIC) against a trade union, fourteen companies and an equal number of executives working within the sugar sector. Similarly, abuses of economic power and acts in violation of free trade were observed in the television, mobile telephone, and engineering industries, and prior to these, in the power utilities. In Mexico, meanwhile, the companies that sell corn tortillas, along with the telecommunications sector, pharmaceutical laboratories, and the chief producer of cement, among others, have made news for their monopolistic practices. In Peru, the phone industry has been exposed to allegations of anti-competitive practices, as well as the cement and freight sectors. Most of these cases have resulted in the companies having to pay fines for their acts.

2 Cases of major tax fraud have received significant press coverage, though less than the cases of collusion. Argentina, Brazil, Mexico, and Peru all provide instances of documented cases in the media on this matter.

In Argentina the international company Procter & Gamble (P&G) was subject to a suspension of operations by the Federal Public Revenue Administration (AFIP) for an alleged tax fraud relating to imports from Brazil invoiced through a subsidiary based in Switzerland. Previously, in 2014, P&G faced investigations by the Mexican authorities for alleged tax evasion. Another international company, the Spanish firm Telefónica, faced challenges in Brazil in relation to the value added tax levied on telecommunications services, while also having to deal with tax disputes in Peru. Additionally, companies and business leaders in the mining sector caught the attention of Brazilian news agencies for tax fraud. In Mexico, anomalies were found in the tax returns of two large tobacco companies, Philip Morris and British American Tobacco, and the semi-public company, Pemex. In Peru, Telefónica was the focus of special interest in tax disputes, while various economic and business sectors were placed under special monitoring by the tax regulator.

3 Consumer scams and unfair business practices (Brazil, Chile, Mexico, Peru) as well as cases of misleading advertising (Peru), also appear among the most frequently mentioned potential ethical failures.

Of particular relevance for its size and scope was the financial scandal of La Polar, a Chilean retailer implicated for abusive lending practices in which hundreds of thousands of customers were subject to changes in the conditions of their loans without due notice. Moreover, in the case of Peru, it is noteworthy how often companies in the telecommunications sector are mentioned for actions that seem to damage their customers.

4 The occurrence of environmental damage also catches the attention of news agencies, not only for the significant harms to the ecosystem but also due to the frequency of the incidents, especially notable in the cases of major mining companies. News of such harm has been published in Brazil, Chile, and Peru. To measure the importance of the damage generated by spillage, one may read, for example, of the situation in which Chevron spilled

crude oil off the coast of Brazil twice in five months; in another instance, Vale—the iron giant of southern Brazil—produced the greatest environmental damage in Brazilian history through the so-called "tsunami of toxic mud" that poured into the valleys surrounding its mining operations.

5   Ethical failures related to working conditions are relatively common in Latin America. However, the review of the press on this front seems to have produced few news stories, perhaps because these conditions are already widely known and even accepted. Nonetheless, some reports mention unhealthy workplaces or work environments that undermine health (Brazil), not to mention the work of minors (Peru) and the nonpayment of wages (Mexico, Peru).
6   The perpetration of fraud within companies (Argentina, Brazil) is a type of moral failure that also appears only infrequently in the news, but is probably more common than the news reports would suggest. It may be that, except for very high profile situations, it is not of interest to the media or does not go beyond the affected companies.
7   The above forms of misconduct are followed closely in occurrence by financial fraud (Colombia, Mexico), and diversion of resources and money laundering.
8   Another form of malfeasance involves the omission or misrepresentation of information, or an intentional lack of transparency (Chile, Mexico), even the use of insider information. Sometimes the omission or misrepresentation occurs precisely in order to hide one of the lapses noted above, such as collusion or tax fraud.
9   Taking imprudent risks in the stock market (Colombia), filing fraudulent bankruptcy claims (Mexico), along with conflicts of interest and irregularities in the awarding of contracts (Colombia) form part of the group of unethical actions that have relatively fewer appearances in the media than other types of malfeasance.
10 Bribes and extortion, including organized criminal behavior (Mexico), are addressed in the news with some recurrence, but these often take place within relationships between the public and private sectors. Even though this sort of conduct, whether occurring in the public or private realm, is widely reported, the everyday perception is that the frequency of events of this nature is even *more* common than might appear in the media.

Overall, the impression remains that there is a high level of unethical behavior in the private business practices of Latin America; however, at the same time, significant differences can be detected among various countries of the region. Among the six major Latin American economies, that of Chile arguably gives evidence of a comparatively better ethical climate, although people perceive a deterioration to have taken place in recent years. Moreover, public corruption and its relationship with the private sector is high throughout the region and in some countries accounts for the bulk of the media stories regarding corruption. This would seem to be the situation in Argentina, Brazil and Mexico. Even if private ethical failures are still overshadowed by the enormous importance that public corruption has acquired, it does not seem wise to infer that private lapses are necessarily infrequent or of minor importance. Nonetheless, the extent of public corruption looms large, as we see in the next section.

Comparative data on public corruption

In what follows, comparative data on public (governmental) corruption among the countries of the region is presented. This exposition of the ethical vagaries of the public sector should complement the information in the previous section on corruption in the private sector. We shall utilize the most recent (2013) *Global Corruption Barometer* (GCB) developed and published by Transparency International, the global organization leading the fight against corruption. This report examines how corruption features in people's lives around the world. The Transparency International survey of more than 114,000 respondents in 107 countries addresses people's direct experiences with bribery and details their views on corruption in the main public institutions in their countries.

The Transparency International report provides evidence of the overall picture of corruption in the world and allows us to contrast the Latin American nations with the rest of the world. The 2013 *Global Corruption Barometer* concludes, "Bribery worldwide is widespread: overall, more than one in four people (27 per cent) report having paid a bribe in the last 12 months when interacting with key public institutions and services" (Transparency International 2013 GCB: 3). When the data are broken down according to the percentage of people who, over the past twelve months, have paid bribes (when interacting with public officials or institutions), the following distribution is observed: less than 10 percent—Uruguay; 10–14.9 percent—Argentina, Chile, El Salvador and Jamaica; 20–29.9 percent—Colombia, Paraguay, Peru and Venezuela; and 30–39.9 percent—Bolivia and Mexico (these are the countries of Latin America included in the study).

The Latin American nations together show a dispersion in terms of a declared practice of paying bribes. For example, if the percentages obtained by Uruguay, as opposed to those of Bolivia or Mexico, are compared with the scores of most European and North American nations, then Uruguay clearly performs better in terms of honesty (GCB: 10). Considered on average, the Uruguayan results are also better than many Asian, and especially African states, where, according to the survey, the declared payment of bribes by citizens reaches its highest levels (GCB: 10).

Data from across the globe, including Latin America, suggests that, "Governments are not thought to be doing enough to hold the corrupt to account: the majority of people around the world believe that their government is ineffective at fighting corruption and corruption in their country is getting worse" (GCB: 3). It is interesting to know the public's views on whether corruption in their country has increased, stayed the same or decreased over the last two years at the time of responding. But when asked, "Do you think that corruption has increased in your country?" it was found that all Latin American countries included in the field research conducted for the 2013 *Global Corruption Barometer* are without exception among those that believed corruption had increased over the past two years, regardless of the level of corruption perceived in each country compared to the group of countries included in the study.

In Latin America, as throughout the world, "The democratic pillars of societies are viewed as the most corrupt . . . institutions" (GCB: 3). It is striking that the study found that the sector of society considered most corrupt is the public sphere—political parties, congress or parliament, police and judicial system. The private business sector is perceived as less corrupt than the public sphere. Although a wide variability of percentages is evidenced—following the trajectory of results produced by successive *Global Corruption Barometers* from 2003 to 2013—this hierarchy is consistent with a relatively homogeneous trend among countries and regions, including Latin America, as well as over time: a tendency towards an increasingly stronger perception of private–business corruption, yet still below the perception of public corruption. One could argue tentatively, therefore, that "political ethics" is evaluated as worse than "business ethics," a conclusion that would in no case mean that serious moral flaws are not recognized in the sphere of business.

Throughout the world, "Personal connections are seen as corrupting the public administration: . . . almost two out of three people believe that personal contacts and relationships help to get things done in the public sector in their country" (GCB: 3–4); in addition, it is held that "powerful groups rather than the public good are . . . driving government actions: more than one in two people (54 per cent) think their government is largely or entirely run by groups acting in their own interests rather than for the benefit of the citizens" (GCB: 4). These last two findings—relating the power of personal relationships and group interests—suggest that people believe that particular factions of society have a decisive influence on the decisions made within the public sphere, all to the detriment of the common good of society. These findings should lead to a greater understanding of the complex interrelationship between the actions of those in the limelight in the public sector (politicians and senior public administration officers) and members of the private sector (business owners and senior managers of businesses). Social corruption would have its source primarily in political agents willing to sacrifice the public for their private good and, to a lesser extent, in business persons, all of whom conduct themselves as role models for ordinary citizens who then practice their own forms of so-called "petty corruption."

Connected to the above findings are the responses to this question, "To what extent is this country's government run by a few big interests looking out for themselves?" Among the respondents in the Latin American countries belonging to the relatively exclusive group of OECD nations and included in the 2013 GCB survey—Mexico and Chile—one finds the following statistics: that 62 percent of Mexican and 63 percent of Chilean respondents believe that their governments are oriented towards satisfying a few big interests rather than serving the public good. However, and interestingly enough, nations as developed as the United States (64 percent), Spain (66 percent), Belgium (70 percent), and Italy (70 percent) receive even worse evaluations on this item than Mexico or Chile, a fact that does not detract from the seriousness of the situation in these countries, but highlights the great difficulties that still exist for governments to truly be guided by the search for the common good and not to give in to the particular interests of groups exercising power or influence, including large business corporations.

Is reform possible? "People [worldwide] state they are ready to change this *status-quo* [levels of corruption]: nearly 9 in 10 surveyed say they would act against corruption" (GCB: 4). Moreover, a significant percentage (54 percent) of respondents declared to be willing to pay a premium for a product from a company whose ethical conduct is upright. Obviously, this is a declaration of intent and not of actual behavior. However, it does reflect the importance that individuals place on political reform and on business ethics, and it reflects how a genuine ethics of commercial conduct produces respect.

In the absence of the publication of a *Global Corruption Barometer* since 2013, it is helpful to emphasize that the most recent (2014) *Corruption Perceptions Index*, a measurement instrument created in 1995 by Transparency International to register "expert" opinion on corruption in the public sector, also shows no significant movement in the scores of the countries in the Americas. A country or territory's score, from 0 (highly corrupt) to 100 (very clean), demonstrates a perceived level of public sector corruption. The 2014 *Index* included 175 countries and territories.

In an article (2014) on corruption in the Americas, Alejandro Salas comments on the degree of continuity in the level of corruption assigned by experts to Latin American countries in the *Corruption Perceptions Index*.[2] He notes,

> For the more cynical among us, this [continuity] is a good sign as there is always the possibility of worsening. But the reality is that stagnation is not good news. Each year that passes without things improving is a lost year for the process of strengthening state institutions and the improvement of quality of life of people. This is well exemplified by Brazil (score of 43 . . .) and Mexico (35). The case of Petrobras in Brazil, where corrupt officials and their private sector cronies siphoned billions of dollars from the country's largest company into political parties' coffers and private hands . . . [is just a recent example that serves as a reminder of the lack of significant progress in the region].
>
> *(Salas 2014)*

These two countries—instead of making positive use of their influence as geopolitical leaders—show signs of stagnation and even retrogression by allowing the abuse of power and the looting of the citizens' resources for the benefit of the few.

The case of Chile, a nation that (along with Uruguay) remains one of the Latin American societies that has consistently demonstrated a greater degree of rectitude in the conduct of its public officials, also provides new examples of ethical decadence in the political and business classes. In the three-year period of 2014–2016, Chile has endured an escalation of moral scandals that have reached into the government and have implicated politicians of all stripes, as well as recognized members of the business community. Things have developed to the point that the president of Chile entered the international arena to remind other nations that, "we are not a country worthy of little respect; we are not populists." The president added subsequently that reforms would be necessary to eradicate ethical malfeasance in politics between business enterprises.[3]

Teaching and research

Turning from the practices of politics and business to the province of academe, one encounters another crucial yet underdeveloped aspect of business ethics in Latin America: teaching and research. A previous study (Pezoa and Riumalló 2012a), which has subsequently appeared in a shortened version (Pezoa and Riumalló 2012b), may serve as a starting point. (Prior to this study, there was but one investigation on the status of business ethics in Latin America: Arruda and Enderle 2006.) Based on a survey of academics and professionals, the study reveals that both inquiry and activity are growing in the areas of teaching, training, and research.

In the universities, courses and academic programs are still aimed almost exclusively at undergraduate and postgraduate students in business administration (specifically MBA students) and, in some instances, to the education of executives and managers in the corporate world. Almost no other university disciplines include business ethics courses, though such areas of study as engineering, accounting, or economics could also include them in their curricula. In university curricula, the field of business ethics remains underdeveloped. There are but a small number of individuals and institutions, including business schools, dedicated to this subject.

There exists, therefore, a need for more business schools (or NGOs) with dedication to supporting and funding business ethics courses or programs. Throughout the continent the need is glaring and the opportunities enormous. One means of encouraging a more robust study of business ethics is by developing stronger networks of academics and business professionals both within Latin America and with the wider world. One aid to the development of such networks would be systematized information on the teaching of business ethics. However, since the study noted above (Pezoa and Riumalló 2012a) there is little systematized information on teaching business ethics in the universities of the region. However, the author's informal consultation among Latin American professors recognized as experts in the field[4] seems to indicate that no substantial changes have occurred since the publication of the study noted above (Pezoa and Riumalló 2012a). With that said, there is one obvious difference among the nations of Latin America. Without doubt, Brazil is, comparatively speaking, the country in which business ethics is more developed: The nation of Brazil has a larger cohort of academics who study business ethics and who publish their research. Even so, there is still room in Brazil and the rest of Latin America for growth and diversification in education and, as we see below, scholarly research.

Most of the research on business ethics is local and not of the most rigorous quality. The studies that manifest high academic standards are published in national journals or in books published in the countries of origin, and almost always in the native language (Spanish or Portuguese). There has been little scholarly work published in prestigious international journals or by publishers with worldwide coverage and recognition. For example, during the period 2011–2015, articles on business ethics published in various non-specialized academic journals within the continent have been few but of very diverse nature (Pezoa and Pezoa 2015). A recent search of the databases of major international journals devoted to business ethics gives evidence of the persistence of the trend first shown in the study noted above (Pezoa and Riumalló 2012a) that publications in these journals by Latin American authors remain scarce. With that said, however, there is an emergent trend to push university scholars to engage in more formal academic research, with publications in recognized international journals or chapters in books published in English and available to a broader audience. Within the context of academic production, it is worth pointing out that one positive contribution has emerged from the periodic conferences held by the Latin American Association of Ethics, Business and Economics (ALENE: see the website www.alene.org), an organization that brings together (mainly) professors but also business leaders from the region interested in promoting ethical values in business.

There are interesting developments in the study of topics *related* to business ethics. These include various investigations that can plausibly be included in a broad category that could be called business and society (Ogliastri and Reficco 2009). In addition, a variety of studies have appeared on the balance between work and family (Las Heras 2010; Destéfano 2011; Pezoa et al. 2011; Bosch and Riumalló 2012; Debeljuh and Destéfano 2013; Estol 2011; Destéfano 2013; Bosch et al. 2015).

The new developments also include scholarly work on corporate social responsibility (Cardoso et al. 2010). For many readers, it might be assumed that a study on corporate social responsibility lies at the heart of business ethics. However, within Latin America the theme of "corporate social responsibility" is traditionally treated as a field of action and research *distinct* from business ethics, even though it bears a relation to it. Corporate social responsibility has been seen as an area concerned, theoretically and practically, with the social activities that companies must consider and manage, as well as with the firm's relations with its stakeholders. These subjects have often been treated without consideration of the way in which ethics, or business ethics, might be involved in such activities and relations. In this way, the study of business ethics and corporate social responsibility have been running along parallel rails. Although this distinction has been well-entrenched in Latin America, there have always been a minority of academics and practitioners who understood that corporate social responsibility had ethical roots and constituted a social ethics dimension of business.

Corporate practices, Non-Governmental Organizations (NGOs) and government initiatives

In the twenty-first century, with the globalization of business, there has been an increasing demand for corporate transparency and corporate involvement in society. These global developments, along with the high levels of public–private corruption existing in most Latin American countries, have brought about new endeavors to encourage good business practices, greater corporate social responsibility, and attention to environmental sustainability. The positive effects are starting to be visible and may be greater in the near future. These endeavors include the establishment of declarations of business principles, codes of company ethics, and the distribution of manuals of good moral practices—all of these have become more common during the past decade. In addition, the number of companies that have established departments of ethics and corporate compliance have been increasing, along with the announcements of strategies and concrete actions to fulfill corporate social responsibility.

Similar to what has been happening with business activity, the last fifteen to twenty years have been marked by the founding of NGOs and voluntary associations of different types whose explicit purpose is to promote initiatives in corporate ethics. In general, they have performed an important task by putting these issues on the public agenda, raising the consciousness of society, and increasing the felt urgency within the business firms themselves. Some of these organizations have also focused on generating various indices and other support material to help businesses carry out their own programs and actions for improving corporate ethics. Organizations associated with the Latin American chapter of the International Christian Union of Business Executives (*Union Internationale des Associations Patronales Catholiques*—UNIAPAC) deserve special mention in this area. Their active presence in ten countries on the continent helps to spread the ideas associated with Catholic social teaching on economic and business life and, for a significant number of business leaders, has inspired an ethic of social responsibility founded on Christian principles. In fact, in recent years this group has made a concerted effort to put into the hands of business leaders a document prepared by the Pontifical Council for Justice and Peace, *The Vocation of the Business Leader, A Reflection* (Pontificio Consejo Justicia y Paz 2014). In like fashion, and whether motivated by religious, humanistic or pragmatic-professional aspirations, institutions of various stripes[5] have deployed in each country to convey to business leaders the importance of the moral dimension in all commercial work and the responsibilities to society that all of us share. These groups often share common goals—such as the promotion of moral values, sustainable development, and the social and ecological management of businesses—but they also formulate their research and programs in accordance with local and regional circumstances and concerns.

It is notable that there are virtually no government initiatives worthy of mention that seek to improve the ethics of commercial life. Of course, there are the ad hoc committees, created or sponsored by legislative bodies, to study how to reduce corruption and its consequences. Sometimes there is an enactment of legal regulations to combat and ensure ethical behavior, especially within the public sector. In a number of countries of the region initiatives of greater or lesser scope have been carried out in this regard. The fate of these projects has been irregular, although in most cases the results have been meager. These initiatives have pertained more to the political and legal order, a fact which, at the least, helps to increase awareness among the population (and between companies and their managers) of the social and economic value of ethical behavior in economic affairs. Moreover, if such commissions and standards prove effective, then, given the punitive character that laws possess, they may manage to have a deterrent effect on bad moral conduct in business. However, many such measures fall more within the framework of compliance to law and regulation than to an ethical outlook per se.

Concluding remarks

An analysis of information in the press for the five-year period of 2011 to 2015 in the six major economies of Latin America (Argentina, Brazil, Chile, Colombia, Mexico, and Peru) demonstrates a high degree of ethical failures in Latin American business activity (even taking into account significant differences among countries). As a whole, the misconduct associated with collusion, cartels and unfair competition are the first to stand out, followed by tax fraud, and, third, consumer scams and fraud. Public corruption, and its various effects on and links with the private sector, seems predominant in many nations—Argentina, Brazil and Mexico, in particular.

There is some consensus among Latin American academicians that corruption seems to be the major concern for the near future. Both the opinion of citizens in everyday life as well as existing studies provide ample evidence that the view of academics is a fair assessment of the situation. Research also shows that corruption has become stabilized, even established and expected, within society, a fact that should be of serious concern to all citizens. Even a country such as Chile, usually known for its trustworthiness and high levels of upright behavior, has in recent years experienced several notable cases of moral misconduct, both among the political class as well as certain business sectors (and in the relations between the two). The use of political power for private gain remains the most common form of corruption in Latin America.

Academic research in business ethics remains scarce and, in general, lacking in rigor. Consequently, the number of publications is few and most are published in local academic journals of limited reach and impact. It follows that there is ample room for research and publication in the field of business ethics focused on the Latin American context. The discipline is still in a stage of early development, which provides the opportunity for new scholars to form part of its development, and for those already involved to deepen the work done so far. Other possible initiatives might include strengthening the work of the organization ALENE, and establishing a specialized journal on business ethics in Latin America. Similarly, the teaching of business ethics is mostly concentrated in a few business schools and universities in each country. The impression remains that there is, at times, no real willingness to increase business ethics course offerings; in some instances there are not enough professors able to teach the corresponding courses. For a real improvement in business ethics in Latin America it would seem essential to promote ethics education among university (and secondary) students, which requires, in turn, the determined will of educational institutions and the training of the professors.

There is a lack of research results, inter alia, and an almost complete absence of studies on the activities and level of progress achieved by businesses (via codes, compliance offices, training programs) and NGOs (programs on business ethics and their social impacts). The information available is piecemeal, anecdotal, and undeveloped. All said, it is strange that the various existing institutions are not more connected with each other than they are. A tremendous opportunity exists for collaboration between organizations in order to achieve increased positive influence in their societies and in the region.

Governments in the region have not carried out properly conceived initiatives on ethics, but have rather limited their efforts to those of a normative legal order, chiefly with an eye to greater integrity in the public sector. Yet the laws in this area have not translated into substantive improvements in the behavior of the groups or officials who are, ostensibly, the target of these laws. It is not unreasonable to speculate why this might be the case: Since the very persons who draft and enact these laws are the same persons who are the focus of these laws, they have little incentive to make or to enforce a law which might, so to speak, put them "out of business." This sad conclusion at least points to the need to create separate agencies equipped with enough power to deal with bad ethical practices, at least from a legal/regulatory perspective.

The final conclusion is the obvious one: From either a practical or theoretical point of view, there is plenty of room for action or for reform. This fact should arouse the motivation and sense of responsibility of researchers, professors, officials of NGOs, business and political leaders, and all citizens. The strong impression remains that there is much good at stake for the countries of the region or, at the very least, the avoidance of abundant evil in the future.

Essential readings

There exist few published studies on business ethics in Latin America. The unpublished study by María C. Arruda and Georges Enderle, "Is Corporate Ethics in Latin America becoming More Articulated? Views from Experts in the Field" (2006), remains quite valuable. The published study of Álvaro E. Pezoa and María P. Riumalló, "Survey of Teaching, Training and Research in the Field of Economics and Business Ethics in Latin America," has both a long version (2012a) and a short one (2012b).

For further reading in this volume on the global problems of corruption and bribery, see Chapter 34, Corruption, bribery, and moral norms across national boundaries. On problems of rent seeking and public corruption, see Chapter 7, Can profit seekers be virtuous? and Chapter 21, Regulation, rent seeking, and business ethics. On globalization and business ethics, see Chapter 32, The globalization of business ethics. On business ethics in the North American context, see Chapter 4, Teaching business ethics: current practice and future directions.

Notes

1 The relevant citations for these summary remarks are in the appendix to this chapter. Citations are grouped in accordance with the number of the summary remarks (e.g. 1, 2, 3, and so on); within these groupings, citations for distinct themes or types of claims are separated by a two parallel lines ("//").
2 A survey on business ethics called the Barometer of Values and Ethics, conducted annually by the Fundación Generación Empresarial (Business Generation Foundation) among employees of various Chilean companies, reveals results that point in the same direction as those of studies on corruption carried out by Transparency International for Latin America. The state of ethics in companies operating in Chile would seem to be characterized by stagnation, without experiencing statistically significant variations over the last three years (2011–2013).
3 The first statement occurred at a meeting between President Michelle Bachelet and French businessmen: M.E. Alvarez, "Michelle Bachelet en encuentro con empresarios franceses: 'No somos un país poco serio, no somos populistas,'" June 9, 2015, online at: www.latercera.com/noticia/politica/2015/06/674-633467-9-bachelet-en-encuentro-con-empresarios-franceses-no-somos-un-pais-poco-serio-no.shtml. The second quotation may be found in the same newspaper on the same date: see R. Alvarez and M.E. Alvarez, "Bachelet aborda corrupción en discurso frente a la OCDE" online at www.latercera.com/noticia/politica/2015/06/674-633479-9-bachelet-aborda-corrupcion-en-discurso-frente-a-la-ocde.shtml, June 9, 2015.
4 María Cecilia Arruda (Emeritus Professor EAESP—FGV, Brazil), Patricia Debeljuh (Professor IAE Business School, Universidad Austral, Argentina) and Javier I. Pinto (Professor College of Business Administration, Universidad de los Andes, Chile).
5 By way of example, the following can be highlighted: the Argentine Institute of Corporate Social Responsibility (IARSE); the Ethos and Social Balance Indicators Institute (IBASE) in Brazil; Acción RSE, Business Generation and ProHumana in Chile; the Colombian Center for Social Responsibility (CCR); and the Business Foundation for Social Action (FUNDEMAS) in El Salvador, among others.

References

Arruda, M. and G. Enderle (2006). "Is Corporate Ethics in Latin America Becoming More Articulated? Views from Experts in the Field." Presentation at the Academy of Management. Atlanta, GA.
Bosch, M. and M. Riumalló (2012). *Índice de Entornos de Responsabilidad Familiar Corporativa*. Santiago de Chile: ESE Business School, Universidad de los Andes.
Bosch, M., M. Riumalló and R. Capelli (2015). *Conciliación Trabajo y Familia: Guía de Buenas Prácticas*. Santiago de Chile: Editorial Valente.
Cardoso, M., I. Font, P. Gudiño, C. Medina and A. Sánchez (2010). "Responsabilidad Social Empresarial en América Latina: un Panorama General," *Administración y Organización*. México: UAM Azcapotzalco, 57–73.
Debeljuh, P. and Á. Destéfano (2013). *Hacia la Responsabilidad Familiar Corporativa: Guía de Buenas Prácticas*. Buenos Aires: IAE Publishing.
Destéfano, Á. (ed.) (2011). *Hacia una Empresa Familiarmente Responsable*. Buenos Aires: sin editorial.
Destéfano, Á. (ed.) (2013). *Hacia la Responsabilidad Familiar Corporativa*. Buenos Aires: sin editorial.
Estol, C. (ed.) (2011). *Varón + Mujer = Complementariedad*. Buenos Aires: LID Editorial.
Generación Empresarial (2014). *VII Barómetro de Valores y Ética Empresarial*. Santiago de Chile: Fundación Generación Empresarial.
La Tercera (2015). Available at: www.latercera.com, Santiago de Chile, June 9.

Las Heras, M. (ed.) (2010). *Mujer y Liderazgo: Construyendo Desde la Complementariedad*. México: LID Editorial.

Ogliastri, E. and E. Reficco (eds) (2009). *Empresa y Sociedad en América Latina/Business and Society in Latin America. Academia*. Bogotá: CLADEA.

Pezoa, Á.E. (2016). *Recopilación de Información en Prensa Sobre la Ética Empresarial en América Latina para el Periodo 2011/ 2105: Argentina, Brasil, Chile, Colombia, México y Perú*. Working Paper. Santiago de Chile: ESE Business School, Universidad de los Andes.

Pezoa, Á.E. and, Á.A. Pezoa. (2015). *Recopilación Bibliográfica Sobre la Ética Empresarial en América Latina*. Working Paper. Santiago de Chile: ESE Business School, Universidad de los Andes.

Pezoa, Á.E. and M. Riumalló (2012a). "Survey of Teaching, Training and Research in the Field of Economics and Business Ethics in Latin America," in D. Rossouw and C. Stückelberger, (eds), *Global Survey of Economics and Business Ethics in Teaching, Training and Research*. Geneva: Globethics.net Global, 19–91.

Pezoa, Á.E. and M. Riumalló (2012b). "Survey of Teaching, Training, and Research in the Field of Economic and Business Ethics in Latin America," in *Journal of Business Ethics*, vol. 107, supplement 1, 43–50.

Pezoa, Á.E., M. Riumalló and K. Becker, K. (2011). *Conciliación Familia-Trabajo en Chile*. Santiago de Chile: ESE Business School—Grupo Security.

Pontificio Consejo Justicia y Paz (ed.) Unión Social de Empresarios Cristianos (USEC) (co-ed.) (2014). *La Vocación del Líder Empresarial, una Reflexión*. Città dell Vaticano—Santiago de Chile: USEC.

Rossouw, D. and C. Stückelberger, (eds) (2012). *Global Survey of Economics and Business Ethics in Teaching, Training and Research*. Geneva: Globethics.net Global.

Salas, A. (2014). "Corruption in the Americas: the Good, the Bad and the Ugly." Available at: www.transparencyinternational.org, miscellaneous section, December 3.

Transparency International (2013). *Global Corruption Barometer*. Berlin: Transparency International.

Transparency International (2014). *Global Corruption Index*. Berlin: Transparency International.

Appendix: press citations

1. Notes for cartels, collusion, abuse of dominant position

"El Gobierno analizará si hay posición dominante en 11 sectores," *ieco.clarin.com*, Economy section, April 2, 2016. // "Precio de la carne: acusan a los supermercados," *ieco.clarin.com*, Economy section, February 10, 2016. // "Cinco ejecutivos ya han ido a declarar por el caso de colusión," *diario.latercera.com*, Business section, December, 2015. // "Estudio de Dictuc rebate acusación de FNE sobre colusión en el mercado del pollo," *diario.latercera.com*, Business section, July 10, 2013; "FNE pide aumentar multas a Don Pollo y la APA por colusión," *diario.latercera.com*, Business section, October 10, 2014. // "El caso farmacias es el más sensible de los que estoy heredando," *diario.latercera.com*, Business section, April 2, 2010; "Los últimos argumentos de la FNE y las farmacias al cierre del caso colusión," *diario.latercera.com*, Business section, August 29, 2011; "TDLC aplica multa histórica a farmacias y fallo será base para la arista penal," *diario.latercera.com*, Business section, February 1, 2012; "Salcobrand y Cruz Verde niegan colusión y acudirán a Suprema," *diario.latercera.com*, Business section, February 1, 2012; "Fiscalía pedirá penas de cárcel para 10 ejecutivos por alterar precios de los remedios," *diario.latercera.com*, July 11, 2012. // "Los secretos del cartel del papel higiénico," *ElEspectador.com*, Economy section, April 6, 2016.

See also, "Grupo Familia suspende gerente general por cartel del papel higiénico," *elcolombiano.com*, Business section, April 13, 2016. // "La SIC multó al cartel del azúcar," *elcolombiano.com*, Business section, October 8, 2015. // "Une alerta monopolio en T.V.," *elcolombiano.com*, Historical section, February 4, 2014. // "Multa histórica de la SIC a Claro: $87.750 millones," *elcolombiano.com*, Historical section, September 4, 2013; "La SIC pone lupa en operadores móviles," *elcolombiano.com*, November 18, 2013; "Ratifican multa por 45 millones de dólares contra Claro en Colombia," *elcolombiano.com*, Historical section, November 20, 2013. // "Cuatro empresas de ingeniería fueron sancionadas por cartelización," *elcolombiano.com*, Colombia section, January 19, 2015. // "Hay abusos con precios de energía: Superservicios," *elcolombiano.com*, Historical section, October 28, 2009. // "Denunciarán a empresas por prácticas monopólicas," *jornada.unam.mx*, Economy section, March 24, 2011. // "Demandarán 25 empresas a Telmex y Telcel," *jornada.unam.mx*, Economy section, March 7, 2011; "La sanción a Telcel, 18 veces mayor al total de las multas que aplicó la CFC desde 2007," *jornada.unam.mx*, Economy section, April 18, 2011; "Decidió competencia sobre multa por $12 mil millones a Telcel," *jornada.unam.mx*, Economy section, May 1, 2012; "Multa Ifetel a Telmex con $ 50 millones por una práctica monopólica relativa," *jornada.unam.mx*, Economy section, October 1, 2014. // "Multa la CFC a seis laboratorios por elevar artificialmente precios IMSS," *jornada.unam.mx*, Economy section, February 24, 2010. // "Sanciona competencia a Cemex por boicotear importadora de cemento," *jornada.unam.mx*, February 21, 2012. // "Admiten denuncia contra Telefónica," *gestión.pe*, Business section, June 22, 2012. // "Indecopi multa con S/. 5.7 millones a Cementos Lima por faltar a la libre competencia," *gestión.pe*, Business section, February 6, 2013. // "Indecopi multa con S/. 2.71 millones a 72 transportistas de carga de Ancash," *gestión.pe*, Business section, January 30, 2014.

2. Tax fraud

"P&G detiene operaciones e inicia diálogo con Argentina sobre evasión fiscal," *gestión.pe*, Business section, November 4, 2014. // "Los litigios fiscales de Telefónica en Brasil suman ya 2.038 millones sin provisionar," *economía.elpais.com*, Economy section, February 28, 2014. // "MMX niega multas del Servicio de Impuestos Internos," *Valor*, January 9, 2013; "Tribunal Federal condena a Valério por evasión de impuestos y falsificación," *Valor*, February 15, 2012. // "Hallan anomalías en declaración de impuestos de 2 grandes tabacaleras," *jornada.unam.mx*, Economy section, February 25, 2013. // "Afronta Pemex más de 20 mil juicios que le costarán $ 44 mil millones," *jornada.unam.mx*, Economy section, March 7, 2010. // "Telefónica: deuda tributaria aún deberá ser resuelta por el poder judicial," *gestión.pe*, Business section, March 27, 2015; "Telefónica del Perú pierde litigio y deberá pagar más de S/. 1,500 millones," *gestión.pe*, Economy section, March 27, 2015. // "Se aumentará la fiscalización de los gastos de las empresas," *gestión.pe*, Business section, April 25, 2012; "Deudas tributarias por más de S/. 10 millones," *gestión.pe*, Business section, March 24, 2013; "Embargo al Grupo Santo Domingo fue aprobado por Tribunal Fiscal, afirma la Sunat," *gestión.pe*, Business section, April 11, 2014; "Rústica espera resultados de investigación tributaria de Sunat en 45 días," *gestión.pe*, Business section, January 14, 2015.

3. Consumer scams and unfair business practices

"Gobierno investiga las quejas contra los bancos," *Valor*, January 4, 2013; "Unicel desaparece, pero deja las deudas y créditos," *Valor*, September 21, 2011. // "Sernac demanda a Presto por clientes en Dicom y empresa niega acusación," *diario.latercera.com*, Business section, June 20, 2011; "El precedente que dejó el fallo de la Corte Suprema contra Cencosud," *diario.latercera.com*, Business section, May 7, 2013. // "Desatada, la especulación en la venta de alimentos en el país," *jornada.unam.mx*, Economy section, January 24, 2010; "Consumidores cautivos de monopolios son base de fortunas," *jornada.unam.mx*, Economy section,

March 16, 2010; "Por prácticas comerciales abusivas sanciona Profeco 15 hoteles del DF," *jornada.unam.mx*, Economy section, July 25, 2013; "Aumentaron 129 percent los reclamos por tarjetas de crédito no solicitadas," *jornada.unam.mx*, Economy section, July 30, 2013; "Alto costo del limón hace meses, por 'práctica comercial desleal,'" *jornada.unam.mx*, Economy section, October 14, 2014; "Alerta Condusef sobre fraudes de las empresas que otorgan 'créditos exprés,'" *jornada.unam.mx*, Economy section, May 13, 2015. // "Osiptel multó a Nextel del Perú con S/.255,000," *gestión.pe*, Business section, August 20, 2012; "Osiptel sancionó a Telefónica con 83 UIT por infracción grave a prestación de servicios," *gestión.pe*, Business section, March 16, 2013; "Indecopi sancionará a unas 100 framacias por no exhibir precios," *gestión.pe*, Business section, May 2, 2013; "Osiptel multó a Telefónica con más de S/. 1.4 millones," *gestión.pe*, Business section, June 28, 2013; "Indescopi sancionó a Telefónica con S/. 11,100 por no entregar vuelto completo en Cusco," *gestión.pe*, Business section, December 13, 2013; "Indecopi sancionó al BCP por reportar indebidamente a consumidora ante la central de riesgos de la SBS," *gestión.pe*, Business section, December 13, 2013; "Osiptel multa a Telefónica con más de S/. 714,000 por mal servicio," *gestión.pe*, Business section, March 1, 2014; "SMV clausuró empresas que operaban sin autorización," *gestión.pe*, Business section, February 5, 2015. // "Indecopi investiga a tres empresas por publicidad engañosa," *gestión.pe*, Business section, November 28, 2013; "Indecopi sanciona academias preuniversitarias por publicidad engañosa," *gestión.pe*, Business section, September 19, 2014. // "Escándalo financiero en La Polar golpea a la Bolsa y AFP ven pasos legales," *diario.latercera.com*, Business section, June 10, 2011; "Firma ofrecerá a clientes repactados mantener la deuda original," *diario.latercera.com*, Business section, June 16, 2011; "Servicio de Impuestos Internos evalúa situación tributaria del caso La Polar," *diario.latercera.com*, Business section, June 16, 2011; "Coloma dice que las sanciones por caso La Polar pueden llegar a 15.000 UF," *diario.latercera.com*, Business section, June 23, 2011; "SVS alista cargos en caso La Polar y fiscalía refuerza equipo," *diario.latercera.com*, Business section, July 1, 2011; "Reclamos al Sernac aumentan 75 percent entre junio y septiembre por La Polar," *diario.latercera.com*, Business section, September 28, 2011; "Tribunal ordena prisión contra el ex presidente y dos ex gerentes de La Polar," *diario.latercera.com*, Business section, December 16, 2011.

4. Environmental damage

"Chevron derrama crudo en la costa de Brasil por segunda vez en cinco meses," *elpais.com*, Society section, March 16, 2012; "El miedo se instala en la región brasileña de Mariana," *elpais.com*, International section, November 10, 2015; "Vale, el gigante de hierro del sur," *elpais.com*, Economy section, December 20, 2015; "El tsunami de barro tóxico, el mayor desastre medioambiental de Brasil," *elpais.com*, December 31, 2015. // "Pascua Lama arriesga permiso ambiental tras reconocer que incumplió exigencias," *diario.latercera.com*, Business section, May 7, 2013; "Fallo del Tribunal Ambiental complica a Pascua Lama y a la SMA," *diario.latercera.com*, Business section, March 4, 2014. // "Ninguna empresa paga multas ambientales impuestas por OEFA," *gestión.pe*, Economy section, April 20, 2012; "Más del 50 percent de la industria no cuenta con regulación ambiental," *gestión.pe*, Economy section, May 29, 2012; "Yanacocha acepta pagar la multa del OEFA, pero niega impacto negativo al medio ambiente," *gestión.pe*, Business section, November 8, 2012; "El OEFA multó a minera en S/. 235,600," *gestión.pe*, Business section, January 2, 2014; "El OEFA ordena a siete empresas detener el vertimiento de efluentes al mar en Piura," *gestión.pe*, Business section, May 8, 2016.

5. Working conditions

"Doencas do trabalho oneram mais o INSS," *Valor*, January 14, 2013. // "Petroperú niega contratación de menores de edad para limpiar derrame de petróleo," *gestión.pe*, Business section, July 21, 2014. // "Mexicana, Click y Link suspenden pago de salarios," *jornada.unam.mx*, Economy section, August 10, 2010. // "Doe Run Perú niega incumplimiento en pago de sueldos a personal de La Oroya," *gestión.pe*, July 11, 2014.

6. Fraud within companies

"Las empresas prevén una suba en los fraudes durante el año," *clarín.com*, Politics section, July 5, 2014. // "Un creciente número de fraude realizado por los empleados," *Valor*, January 23, 2012.

7. Financial fraud

"Claves para entender la crisis de Saludcoop," *eltiempo.com*, Lifestyle and Health section, August 8, 2015; "Saludcoop: lo que fue y lo que está por venir," *elespectador.com*, Investigation section, November 28, 2015; "Saludcoop, el desfalco de la historia," *semana.com*, National section, May 8, 2016. // "Caso Ficrea: sin solución, reunión entre defraudados y autoridades," *jornada.unam.mx*, Economy section, December 23, 2014; "Caso Ficrea elevó reclamos ante Condusef," *jornada.unam.mx*, Economy section, January 23, 2015; "Alerta Condusef sobre fraude de las empresas que otorgan 'créditos exprés,'" *jornada.unam.mx*, Economy section, May 13, 2015. // "Se duplican operaciones *sospechosas* de lavado en el sector financiero," *jornada.unam.mx*, Economy section, September 19, 2010; "Subieron 24 percent las operaciones financieras inusuales," *jornada.unam.mx*, Economy section, July 19, 2013; "Autoridades financieras intervienen Ficrea por posible lavado de dinero," *jornada.unam.mx*, Economy section, November 8, 2014.

8. Information and lack of transparency

"SVS sanciona a gerente general de Larraín Vial," *diario.latercera.com*, Business section, January 5, 2010; "Por qué la SVS no aplicó a Larraín Vial la sanción máxima," *diario.latercera.com*, Business section, September 5, 2014; "Iusacell demandará a Pérez Motta por 'difundir información confidencial,'" *jornada.unam.mx*, Economy section, January 20, 2012.

9. Risks, fraudulent bankruptcy and conflicts of interest

"Interbolsa, la historia de un desplome," *elespectador.com*, Economy section, November 8, 2012; "Condenan a Tomás Jaramillo y Juan Carlos Ortiz por desfalco de Interbolsa," *elpais.com.co*, Economy section, April 28, 2016; "La verdad sobre la comisionista Interbolsa," *semana.com*, National section, May 8, 2016. // "La quiebra de Mexicana, fraude maquinado, acusa diputado," *jornada.unam.mx*, Economy section, August 6, 2010; "Fraude maquinado por sus dueños: PRI y PRD," *jornada.unam.mx*, Economy section, August 13, 2010. // "Por el carrusel de contratación imputan otro delito a Federico Gaviria," *elpais.com.co*, July 11, 2011; "Por carrusel de contratación, a la cárcel concejal de Bogotá José Juan Rodríguez," *elpais.com.co*, May 23, 2013; "Condenan a diez años de cárcel a Julio Gómez por el carrusel de contratación," *elpais.com.co*, July 14, 2014; "Así fue como quebraron a Saludcoop," *elpais.com.co*, November 29, 2015. // "Mexicanos guardan en paraísos fiscales más del doble de la reserva de divisas del país," *jornada.unam.mx*, Economy section, February 12, 2015.

10. Bribes and extortion

"El pago de sobornos se lleva hasta 20 percent de ingresos," *jornada.unam.mx*, Economy section, April 14, 2010; "Difusión de supuestos sobornos para desprestigiar: OHL México," *jornada.unam.mx*, Economy section, June 2, 2015; "Ni autoridades ni empresarios enfrentan a mafias en la industria de la construcción," *jornada.unam.mx*, Economy section, July 4, 2014.

39

Business ethics in transition

Communism to commerce in Central Europe and Russia

*Rodica Milena Zaharia**

For most of the twentieth century the nations of Central Europe and Russia were ruled by communist governments for whom the very idea of commercial activity, free enterprise, or business was anathema. Not only have these societies faced significant challenges since the demise of the communist empire, but so too has the very possibility and public conception of ethical business. This chapter offers an overview of the challenges to business ethics (understood chiefly as practical conduct but also as an academic discipline) during the transition process in Central Europe and Russia during the twenty-five years since the fall of communism. These challenges reveal critical issues for business conduct in these countries. The ethics of everyday business life remains in an evolution shaped by the ideological, cultural, and religious heritages of the former communist nations, as well as by the complex transformations these countries have experienced. Nonetheless, as the chapter concludes, business ethics in Central Europe and Russia is affected less by internal than external factors: the globalization of business and the European integration process. These elements may prove more powerful factors in shaping business ethics in these countries than any local vision about how business may be conducted ethically.

The countries analyzed in this chapter are mentioned in the literature under many appellations: "Central European countries," "Central and Eastern Europe," and "former communist countries" are typical terms. Because of the various referents of these appellations, from geographical to economic, cultural to political, there is ongoing discussion about what countries should be included in "Central Europe." Opinions vary from the narrow (the four countries within the Vishegrad Group: Czech Republic, Slovakia, Hungary, and Poland) to the expansive (the Vishegrad Group, plus Slovenia, Croatia, Romania, and Bulgaria). Under the influence of an expanded European Union (EU) and NATO, the term "Central Europe" has become a fluid concept (*The Economist* 2000). With an embrace of the expansive notion of Central Europe, this chapter ranges over Central and Eastern European countries (specifically, Czech Republic, Slovakia, Hungary, Poland, Slovenia, Croatia, Romania, Bulgaria, other former Yugoslav Republics, and the Baltic nations), as well as Russia and Ukraine.

Prior to 1989, many communist countries were regarded, often without justification, as similar. They did share common ideological values (i.e., a centrally planned economy), but these were typically imposed rather than indigenous. Nonetheless, these imposed values also influenced attitudes toward business ethics. Indeed, the transition towards something akin to a capitalist economy disclosed many similarities across these countries (Lewicka-Strzalecka 2006; Estrin et al. 2006; Čiegis et al. 2008; Kuznetsov and Kuznetsova 2012). However, important differences existed among these nations before the arrival of communism and after its demise, with these differences also affecting the ensuing transformation from centrally planned to market economy. The distinct histories of each nation, their particular encounters with communism, and their varied transitions towards market economies has influenced the actual practice of business conduct (practical business ethics) and the academic domain of business ethics (Bohata 1997; Katchanovski 2000; Kronenberg and Bergier 2012).

In practical terms, the ethics of everyday business in the former communist countries lag behind those of developed countries (Tsalikis and Seaton 2007). Communist rule encouraged a marked disregard towards business as a profession, and a corresponding lack of concern about business ethics. As a result, the development of business ethics has been mostly a consequence of external factors such as the business ethics practices implemented by large foreign corporations or encouraged by the EU. Thus, business ethics' evolution in the former communist countries has been more a replication or adaptation of business ethics from advanced countries (mostly the EU and USA) than an indigenous process of building a new model of business ethics.

This chapter examines how business ethics manifested itself in the commercial landscape after communism's collapse in Central Europe: how did the field, as practice or academic enterprise, emerge and evolve? The first section of the chapter explains the difficulties in analyzing business ethics in former communist countries. In these countries the very concept of *business* renders a first challenge to any attempt to define *business ethics*. The problem is not simply that "business" was considered a capitalist term, burdened with a "bad" connotation, but in the Slavonic languages, for example, there is no equivalent for "business" (Bohata 1997). In the subsequent sections of this chapter we focus on the transition from communism to markets. One of the most interesting and challenging processes in world history, this was a "giant social experiment" (*The Economist* 2008) influencing not only business, academia, and world politics but the lives of ordinary citizens. We first consider similarities among the former communist nations, and then, in the subsequent section, we take up differences. It is the differences that provide the key to understanding the evolution of business ethics in these transitional economies. The final section addresses, briefly, how the present and future of business ethics in most former communist countries are now linked to the EU.

Business ethics under communism

By the middle of the Cold War business ethics emerged in the capitalist world as an interdisciplinary field of study, bringing together philosophy, law, business theory, sociology, economics and other branches of social science (Shaw 2009). Business ethics gained particular attention in the 1960s, when unethical business conduct (for example, questionable labor practices, bribery, and undesirable moral attitudes) were showcased by the mass media (Lantos 2001). As business ethics came of age in the capitalist world, the communist nations remained committed, in word and often in deed, to the implementation of the doctrines of Marx and Engels, as enriched by Lenin's vision and adapted by different communist rulers to the specific conditions of countries from Eastern Europe, Asia and the Caribbean. Communism in Central Europe and Russia was imposed on its citizens as the most ethical type of society.

The main characteristics of the communist countries of Central Europe and Russia were by some measures similar: the means of production were almost entirely the property of the state, thereby transforming all citizens into owners; decisions influencing all areas of activity were made by the Communist Party; economic initiatives were set forth and implemented by a compulsory plan (what to produce, how much, at what price, and for whom); and, of course, political freedom was suspended. "Business,"[1] as it was understood in capitalism, wasn't a term or an activity that was tolerated in communism. In the first place, communist doctrine rejected the very notion of *profit*, deeming it to be based on the exploitation of the working class. Nonetheless, within their state enterprises the communists did seek a surplus greater than costs, but this was deemed to be a "benefit." Unlike profits, benefits were not gained through exploitation and so these were not for the use of a few. Rather, benefits, it was said, were obtained through equal rights and as a result of the "creative work of the workers" (Constantinescu 1983: 364), undertaken in the interest of the people (who were, of course, the owners). Secondly, since everything was planned, no economic activity could be accepted outside the plan; there was no room for the unforeseen emergence of new forms of business, entrepreneurial efforts, or privately held firms. Given the absence of private property and a centralized economy, private economic initiatives were impossible and managers[2] had mostly a passive and defensive role (Kozminski 1995: 90). The third reason that business was not tolerated under communism was that capitalist firms presuppose private property over the means of production and capital, but such ownership was not possible in communism except under specific and limited conditions (including state control over all production, prices, and distribution).[3] Not surprisingly, the Communist Party's exertion of control exceeded the area of economic and social activity, interfering with the personal lives of the citizens. It would be hard to control the economic and the social without also controlling the personal actions and ambitions of citizens.

Communist society, constructed explicitly on principles deemed scientific (as well as ethical and egalitarian), was proclaimed to be the only society eliminating exploitation and ensuring welfare for all citizens. In such a society there were no reasons for business and certainly no reasons for "business ethics." The very concept of business ethics is an unscientific association for the Marxist: even if there were certain expectations or obligations *within* business societies, these were but the norms of bourgeois commerce; however, the point of communism was to overcome these exploitative practices and usher forth a new society. Thus, business ethics was considered an impossible and irrelevant concept for communism, a way of diverting attention from the systemic iniquities of capitalism (Shaw 2009). How can capitalist business be associated with ethics, when capitalism is exploitative and business practice relies on and sustains greed and inequality? How can capitalist businesses promote ethics when people are guided by self-interest instead of seeking prosperity for all citizens?[4]

Marxist ethics denounced the domination of the proletariat by the bourgeoisie and, thus, the ethics of capitalism. Marx did not introduce a new ethical theory, and some would contend that Marx purported only to engage in science; however, his philosophy did express considerations employing ethical terms such as "good," "bad," and "justice" (Ollman 1976). In this sense, Marxism concentrated on labor ethics and urged, following Marx himself, "the true resolution of the strife . . . between freedom and necessity, between the individual and the species" (Marx 1844: 84). In communist society individuals would labor with conscious intent and pleasure (Condur 2011), remain devoted to the communist cause, and contribute to society as people who were industrious, honest, responsible, self-critical, and committed to self-improvement as a means to social betterment. This is a society in which work is not the means but the purpose of life, where the driving principle is, "From each according to his abilities, to each according to his needs" (Marx 1844: 531). The new society should achieve genuine well-being for each citizen through public property, full employment, a centralized economy, and political power for the working class.

The social and economic context was more complex. In almost all communist countries, trade with (and travel to) the capitalist world was limited and under the strict control of the

Communist Party and Secret Police. The absolute control of society and the isolation of communist countries from the capitalist world lowered overall economic performance, nullified civil rights, and diminished the welfare of their citizens. To keep a discontented population under control, the secret police became omnipresent. Police control over the daily lives of citizens induced fear, elicited distrust in peers and family members, eroded any spirit of voluntarism, and crippled the desire to help one's neighbour. As civil society became debilitated, so did it become less of a guarantor of morality. Moreover, disregard for religion was promoted by communist parties in all countries, further weakening the moral conduct of the people. Under these circumstances, even the strongest society, one traditionally motivated towards ethical behavior, succumbed to distrust and moral indifference.

Ethics in business was perhaps the most illustrative example of such derailment. For example, although property was allegedly owned collectively by all of the citizens, some would appropriate public property.[5] Such acts, practiced on a large scale in many former communist countries, were often rationalized as rectification of an injustice, or even as manifestation of a kind of "dissidence." In other cases, thievery was conceived as no thievery at all: it is not theft if the thief is the owner! The transformation of the working class into owners of the means of production had not only devastated economic efficiency but failed to build a society of morally strong individuals. In many ways the collectivization of property created a "property deficit,"[6] an alienation of workers, as owners, from the means of production, the objects produced, and even the goods that they held outside of work. The state's absolute control over the means of production neutralized any natural manifestation of property rights (via possession, use, agreement, or shareholding) over land, buildings, or resources. Once the people were proclaimed owners of everything (in terms of rights) they regarded themselves as owners of nothing (in terms of responsibilities). Therefore, they acted as owners alienated from their property. This left individuals with little incentive to care for the property even as they felt emboldened to take as much as they could, especially since the everyday person suffered from an ever-present lack of any genuine property to satisfy needs or desires. A Soviet era expression summarized the dismal situation: "If you are not stealing from the state, you are stealing from your family" (Nowak 1996: 323).

Material deprivation and the increased appetite of the communist elite for power, wealth and favours (Matthews 2011) created a huge gap between workers, the majority of the population, and the small ruling class, considered the de facto owners of everything. The pressure of full employment kept wages low, discouraging an interest in pursuing increased productivity[7] (Cerami and Vanhuysse 2009: 23; Romano 2014: 32). Moreover, individuals were not hired or promoted on the basis of merit, a feature of the economy that led many denizens of these nations to the general belief that the communist society was, in fact, unethical and immoral. In many ways the ethics deficits of the economic actors under communism was a combination between the moral shortfalls of the ruling class (communist elite) and the resultant demoralization of workers (who did not identify with their role as owners of the means of production, and treated the state as an exploitative owner).

Similarities among former communist countries

The transition from centrally planned economy to market economy was one of the most interesting, complex and least-predictable processes in recent history. As Peter Boettke (2002: 2) mentions, scholars were neither prepared with a theory to explain the failure of socialist political economy nor able to present a workable theoretical framework for a shift to post-communist political economy. Yet such a shift would affect all aspects of the society—economy, politics, the judiciary—thereby influencing everyday expectations about the conduct of one's fellow citizens. What did the transition mean for business ethics? We can broach this question at three levels: theoretical (the concept and theory of business ethics), educational (business ethics as a discipline in the university curriculum) and practical (business ethics as a lived practice).

Business ethics as theory

Because of the difficulty of even conceiving of "business ethics" within the communist framework, those initiating dialogue on the concept of business ethics in Central Europe were Western scholars. The moral challenges involved in the transition from planning to market freedoms were taken up in meetings of the European Business Ethics Network (London 1992) and of the International Association for Business and Society (Vienna 1995). During the first few years of the 1990s, Central European scholars were open to a global academic discussion about how business ethics would be approached in this new context. The subjects of discussion ranged over the qualities and effects of business transactions: maintaining business relations, responding to the needs of business partners, embracing the development of the community, and advancing the firm's capacity to differentiate its goods and services (Mahoney and Vallance 1992: vii). In addition, these same scholars discussed the theories most relevant for an ethical evaluation of the transformation of public into private property, as well as the necessity of business ethics in a climate of distrust (Sexty 1998). In short order, however, the discussion drew almost wholly from Western ideas and scholars, with their appeals to corporate social responsibility and corporate citizenship. Consequently, the debates were hardly different from those existing in the more flourishing Western democracies. In some cases the conversation was enriched with examples from the transitional economies or otherwise given a particular emphasis on specific *practices*. Moreover, some questions—"is unemployment an unethical matter?" or "is the egalitarian society good or bad?"—proved of particular interest to journalists and to university scholars in the former communist countries. However, business ethics came to be pursued under the same approaches and perspectives utilized by ethicists from Western countries.

Business ethics in the universities

As a discipline of study, business ethics has been influenced significantly by the importation of topics from Western curricula. The emergent pedagogy reflects little of the economic and social realities of the formerly communist nations. Of course, the academic structure inherited from communism didn't include among its disciplines anything related to business ethics. During the communist period, ethics focused on the superiority of Marxist-Leninist ideology and celebrated the egalitarian character of the socialist society. This perspective was considered the only one capable of eliminating exploitation, offering genuine equality and equal opportunities for all members of the society.

After 1990, as academic exchanges developed between West and East, many universities in the formerly communist countries began to adapt their courses to the Western curricula. By 1992 business ethics had its own course at the Economic University of Prague; in that same year a single course devoted to business ethics and engineering ethics was introduced at the Faculty of Management and Economics, Gdansk University of Technology (Nemcova 1993; Popowska 2016: 124). As markets developed and society became freer, so did business ethics and related disciplines begin to appear in the curricula of other universities (Sexty 1998; Matten and Moon 2004).

However, the parallel development of market and society and the advancement of business ethics have occurred without many connections between them. Academic business ethics has tended towards the abstract, focusing on topics such as sustainable development, corporate social responsibility, and corporate governance. Even so, some twenty-five years after communism's fall, business ethics is present in almost all economic and business academic programs in Central Europe and Russia. For the former communist countries that joined (or signed a cooperation agreement with) the EU, an important step in the development of business ethics as an academic discipline was the "Bologna Process." Launched in 1998, this series of accords sought to standardize and enhance the quality of higher education across the EU countries. The adherence of former communist countries to the Bologna accords (European Commission 2015) led to a harmonization in curricula, including business ethics.

Business ethics as practice

During the transition the hardest test for business ethics has been business ethics as a *practice*. Any consolidation of a genuine business ethic, as an expected form of commercial conduct, has been challenged by several factors. There is, first, the factor of *mental attitudes*, the mind-set encouraged and rewarded during the communist regime (for example, a reluctance to undertake risk and a disposition to compliance). Since business was illegal during communism, and regarded as a corrupt and exploitative activity, individuals acquired the belief that a person engaged in business was a mere speculator, using any unfair and unethical activity to gain an advantage (Lewicka-Strzalecka 2006; Čiegis et al. 2008). Although in some studies (Peng 2001) illegal business activities (as defined under communist law) are shown to manifest a version of entrepreneurial skill, the general public tolerated these activities more than they agreed with them. Those engaged in business ("business people") were not necessarily admired for their illegal activities; if these individuals were accepted, even sometimes envied, this was a grudging acknowledgment of their role as providers of scarce goods hardly available otherwise. In terms of the communist ethos and its corresponding ethical attitudes, such activity was not considered ethical.

Unfortunately, the transition process didn't change totally this negative perception of the link between business on the one hand, and, on the other, the enrichment of those whose new-found wealth signaled illicit gains or, at best, social *arrivisme*. The changes occurring in the transition reinforced skepticism about the legitimacy of business and fomented mistrust regarding the conduct of business people (Howard 2002; Kuznetsov and Kuznetsova 2012). In particular, privatization and the new regulatory environment were politicized: those in power in the communist era suddenly emerged as the owners or shareholders of large businesses (Wasilewski 1998). Moreover, these former *apparatchiks* used their power to forge new government policies inimical to free competition. Within their firms these figures also perpetuated the nepotism of the old regimes. Business was now intertwined with political power. Business initiative was still not associated with intelligent, hardworking, innovative people willing to assume economic risks, but with people who had the right political connections, perhaps with some former activist[8] or a representative of the old secret police. On top of these forms of political cronyism, there emerged a new wave of illegal activities—corruption, tax evasion, bank fraud, and money laundering (Estrin et al. 2006).

These troubled associations between politics and business seemed to flourish in the privatization process, one of the biggest challenges for the formerly communist countries. Nonetheless, the privatization of state enterprises was not only a key step in the transformation of an inefficient centrally planned economy into a more productive one but a crucial element in the restoration of the role and position of private property in society. The number and sizes of the enterprises that could be privatized was huge. According to Daniel Kaufmann and Paul Siegelbaum (1997: 419), in the first half of the 1990s more than 500,000 medium- and large-scale enterprises were privatized in former communist countries. The capital required for the purchase of shares had to come from either foreign or domestic sources, but domestic capital was almost non-existent in these countries. The scarcity of domestic capital, the low performance of the communist enterprises, and the desire of all governments to attract foreign investors fueled the instability of the legal and institutional framework, opening the gate for non-transparent agreements between governments and foreign investors. The result was a steady stream of corrupt practices: influence trafficking, bribery of government officials (e.g., to secure state contracts or to promote regulations favorable to some, or to acquire a right to buy resources at subsidized prices), as well as favoritism for large as opposed to small firms, illegal privatization (i.e., without public auction), and unclear rules for the restitution of property to former owners (Ramanadham 2002; see also Corruption Information Exchange 2003).

Privatization illustrates both the corrupting links between politics and business and the lack of a stable, predictable legal framework—the rule of law. Thus, instead of promoting the entrepreneurial spirit or encouraging private initiative, a corrupt process of privatization discredited the business profession (Lewicka-Strzalecka 2006; Čiegis et al. 2008; Kuznetsov and Kuznetsova 2012). After 1989, the means by which some people undertook new businesses, together with a pre-existing distrust in "business people," contributed to businesspeople being held in low esteem. The corruption of the privatization process generated public suspicion about the huge fortunes accumulated, in a short period of time, by some former activists, their friends or relatives, or former directors of state-owned companies. In Russia, for example, rights to operate some monopolies were distributed as political "spoils" to former high government officials and prominent businessmen (Kotchegura 2004: 139). The net result is that almost three-fourths of Russians declared themselves in favor of a reversal, full or partial, of privatization (Kuznetsov and Kuznetsova 2012: 38). In Poland, the businessperson's image fell almost as far: the businessperson was now seen as "less respected socially as [than] a cleaning lady" (Domanski 2004, cited in Lewicka-Strzalecka 2006: 441). In Romania, in a 2015 survey of the public's trust in various institutions (among which were included trade unions, the press, universities, police, non-governmental organizations, journalists, and "business owners"), only 15.5 percent of respondents reported having trust in "business owners," a result that placed business in the twenty-first place out of 24 institutions (INSCOP 2015).

The troubled relations between politics and business indicate a more general problem: the legal framework during the transition permitted serious deviations from ethical conduct and failed to provide the conditions for free and fair competition. In Russia, for example, businesses were guided by unofficial imperatives to withhold information, including to government bodies, except where the information must be disclosed by law.[9] In general, the lack of an appropriate legal framework also incentivized neglect of ethical norms. Large corporations adapted early to a vague and equivocal legal framework. In their home countries these multinational corporations had promoted ethical conduct within the business, but in these transitional economies they tolerated or accepted corruption (including bribery of public officials or lobbying for regulatory favors) as a standard way of doing business, sometimes ignoring the rights of workers, or engaging in fraud or illegal payments (Čiegis et al. 2008).

Another factor contributing to the erosion of the ethical character of business practices was the lack of concern of business (mostly among large foreign corporations) about anything other than profit. Small and medium enterprises (SMEs) felt that the law discriminated against them in favor of large foreign corporations. There are cases in which a large corporation has been granted a legal monopoly for limited periods of time (for example, Romtelecom, a telecommunications company in Romania). The SMEs considered themselves as already exercising social responsibility by providing jobs and paying taxes (Zaharia et al. 2010). Given this context, these same SMEs formed the attitude that any costly new ethical practice should apply to large corporations already privileged by law.

Subsequent to the initial years of privatization, not enough has been written in business ethics journals about the social consequences of privatization and whether large corporations have dealt with any related social problems. For example, once privatized, the newly restructured enterprises received updated technology but instituted a dramatic reduction in workforce. When Renault bought Dacia Pitesti (Romania) in 1999, there were over 20,000 workers in that enterprise; in 2014 there were around 13,500. In the steel plant Sidex Galati (Romania), there were 27,000 employees before privatization in 2001, but only about 7,000 employees in 2013 after acquisition by multinational ArcelorMittal. In other cases, former communist enterprises have been bought by private investors and sold as junk (with physical assets sold as scrap, factories demolished, and the land used for new buildings). There have been few if any concerns about unemployment resulting from privatizations, or about the death of towns dependent on a single major enterprise later privatized, then either closed or demolished, often by a foreign investor. It is, of course, true that the communist dictum of full employment created bloated and inefficient enterprises. It is also correct that, in the long run, a more efficient economy, to be delivered in part through privatizations, would also entail a reconfiguration of industries and their workforces. However, in the context of the transition, the motivation of new investors (many of whom were not, as indicated above, interested in a genuinely free and competitive market) was purely economic: to increase the profit and to do so by taking advantage of weak political leadership and corrupt authorities. New investors seemed to make little effort to identify ways to cooperate with the government or local administrations to develop common programs that would increase the employability of the released personnel or to develop their entrepreneurial or business skills.

Of crucial importance for the practice of business ethics is the power and influence of the civil society. A vibrant civil society—as constituted by non-governmental and non-commercial organizations and activities—not only sets standards and shapes behavior, but helps to monitor and react to human rights violations, abuses of power, corruption and other unethical, unfair, and unjust practices. In almost all former communist countries civil society was severely damaged. Communist regimes repressed all forms of autonomous non-state activity, sabotaging (and ultimately replacing) such spontaneous locally directed organizations and endeavors by forcing them into organizations established and controlled by the Communist Party (Howard 2002: 160). For example, trade unions lost entirely their purpose of supporting members' (employees') interests against the owner's (employer's) interest: trade unions were sanctioned only to control and to indoctrinate those who were not members of the Communist Party. In the larger society, any sort of voluntary work became compulsory ("patriotic work," as it was called in Romania); voluntary organizations were considered unnecessary and the putative need for them was considered nonexistent or fulfilled by the state. For example, there was no necessity for charitable organizations: under communism, people worked for the good of all and lived in happiness. Even organizations for the protection of animals were forbidden. After all, even the dogs and horses were protected by communism!

Differences among former communist countries

Although there are many similarities among Central European countries and Russia, their post-communist evolution and achievements reflect differences. As Fenger (2007: 13) mentions, there exists a wide variety among these countries in terms of institutional characteristics and paths to development. For business ethics, these differences may be assessed indirectly through some of the factors influencing a company's ethical behavior. These factors include the nation's business heritage before communism, as well as the degree to which the implementation of communism allowed some modicum of private property. Along with these two features one must also take into account, both before and during communist rule, the distinct roles of civil society, the divergent levels of economic development, and the role of religion, both institutionally and in the daily lives of individuals (Bageac et al. 2011). In the discussion below, these features are set forth in a general way so as to indicate, albeit indirectly, how post-communist business conduct might reflect different historical features of the nations living under communist rule.

During communist rule in Central Europe and Russia (as opposed to the People's Republic of China) the political ideology was fundamentally the same, but the heritages of those countries before communism were distinct. At the beginning of the twentieth century in the first country to establish communism (1917), many private firms had strong ethical guidelines and a code of ethics, "Seven Principles Governing Business in Russia," was adopted at national level in 1912 and expressed the core values of business, among them being respect for the government, honesty and truth, respect for private property rights, love and respect for one's fellow man, being true to your word (a hand shake is worth more than a formal piece of paper), not living beyond one's means, and being purposeful (IDA-RID 2004: 12). Some authors appreciate that 64 percent of the Russian businessmen (the so called Old Believers) adhered to those ethical principles (Korobkova 2015). After the Red Revolution, any such spirit of ethics in business disappeared, together with business people. By the end of World War II the Russian tradition of ethical business principles had been destroyed and forgotten (Apressyan 1997). Even now, in the decades following the demise of communism, Russia and its businesses remain "unbalanced [and] corruption-ridden" (Puffer and McCarthy 2011: 21).

In the case of countries such as Poland, the Czech Republic, or Slovakia, prior to communism, businesses functioned within the society's traditional ethical and philanthropic practices; in these countries commerce was more embedded within society than in countries with a fragile (Romania) or almost nonexistent (Bulgaria or Albania) class of entrepreneurs or industrialists (on the sociological notion of embeddedness see Granovetter 1985). The implementation of communism in Central Europe was also different from Russia's. In Poland, the Czech Republic, Slovakia, and Yugoslavia private property was not completely abolished. Throughout communist rule, private farms dominated the Polish and Yugoslavian agriculture sector (in terms of both production and land). Liberalization reforms were implemented in Hungary before communism's fall, and Yugoslavia had long granted a certain degree of autonomy to enterprises (Katchanovski 2000: 56, 161). In countries with private land holdings, the shortage of common goods didn't reach the dimensions it did in Romania, for example. In these nations, the continued memory of an ethics of doing business, not to mention the philanthropic actions of former businessmen, helped these countries recover more quickly and adapt more easily to the Western model of business ethics (Bohata 1997). In the Czech Republic, for example, after the collapse of communism, the management principles of famous industrialists, such as Tomasz Bata or Emil Skoda, as well as the practices of ethical commerce (existing prior to communism) eased the transition to a private economy and have ensured that these ideals have been not only recovered but integrated into the training of managers and the teaching of management principles and business ethics (Bohata 1997: 1573).

Closely related to the pre-communist heritage, important differences among former communist countries are exhibited in the role of civil society. Although trust among people was eroded by the repressive instruments of all communist regimes, there existed important differences among communist countries. In Romania, for example, the lack of a participative tradition of voluntarism and an insufficient trust in one's fellow citizens[10] delayed the re-emergence of a strong active civil society. The example of Romania lends evidence to the more general consideration of how conduct and social institutions are affected by the damage done to social relations (see Granovetter 1985: 487). By contrast, in Poland and the Czech Republic a strong tradition of independence and dissidence from authority helped civil society organizations regain their status and functions, thereby supporting and reinvigorating their citizens' latent ethical sense.

Another difference among the Central European nations was overall levels of economic development. The extent of economic development, it is argued, may exert an important influence on business ethics. According to Ronald Inglehart (2008), individuals in wealthy countries are driven by post-materialistic values. By contrast, those in less developed countries, with an economic context of poverty, are governed by self-interest and are willing to accept corruption more readily. Presumably, therefore, there is a stronger orientation toward ethical behavior in developed than in developing countries. If this generalization has merit, it might explain *some* of the difference between business conduct in the formerly communist nations and that of Western European nations. At the beginning of their communist history, the level of development among former communist countries was different. The Czech Republic and Poland were the most advanced industrialized countries in Central and Eastern Europe, followed by Hungary and Slovakia. Romania, by contrast, was largely agrarian with a labor-intensive economy. Bulgaria had almost no industrial infrastructure, producing agricultural goods inefficiently at high cost, mainly due to lack of modern mechanical equipment (Dăian and Manova 2013: 56). Albania was the poorest country in the region. With almost 80 percent of the population illiterate, 80 percent of the population in extreme poverty, and almost no industry (in 1949), Albania implemented one of the most severe versions of communism (Gjonça 2001). If ethical conduct in business tracks levels of economic development, then there should be relevant differences in business conduct among these nations. In fact, some unethical practices (e.g., various forms of corruption, influence trafficking, tax evasion, and disregard for worker rights) seem to be more pronounced in less economically advanced countries of Central Europe (such as Albania or Bulgaria) than in more advanced countries such as the Czech Republic.[11] All the former communist countries suffered from material and spiritual[12] deprivation (Willis 2013), but there were differences among them reflected in the depth and speed of implementing economic reforms (such as laws liberalizing trade or removing price controls) and re-building important institutions (stock markets, political parties, independent judiciaries) after communism's collapse. Some economic achievements during the transition—as in the cases of the Czech Republic or Poland—seem to mirror the degree of actual ethical behavior in business (Woolcock 1998; Foss 2012).

The relationship between religious commitment and business ethics may also prove positive. Some studies have suggested that individuals who recognize religion as important in their own lives also demonstrated higher levels of ethical behavior (Longenecker et al. 2004: 371). We can extend this generalization to former communist countries. Of course, communist governments generally sought to undermine religious institutions, but it remains the case that religion and religious institutions played different roles in different nations. In Poland, the Catholic Church was a symbol of resistance against communism, but the Orthodox Church in Romania and Russia were rather supportive of the Communist Party. In Albania, religion was interdicted by law for more than 20 years, starting with 1967 when Albania became officially the first atheist country in the world (Albania 1992). The Romanian Orthodox Church offered no alternative to communist authority; the Romanian Church was preoccupied, throughout much of its history, with adapting itself to political leaders and serving thereby the Church's pecuniary interests (Stan and Turcescu 2000: 1467). In Russia, the Orthodox Church provided a religious foundation for an autocratic state, helping isolate Russia from Catholic and Protestant Europe's influence (IDA-RID 2004). Ethical behavior in countries where the chief or dominant religious institution has stood as guardian for human values is stronger than in countries where religious authorities collaborated with the communist regime. For example, in Albania or Russia statistics record higher degrees of bribery, money laundering, and fraud than in Poland (Kroll 2015).

Business ethics and the EU

The EU's enlargement to the East is probably, after the collapse of the Berlin Wall in 1989, one of the most important events in the recent history of this region. The EU's 2004 enlargement—including eight former communist countries (Estonia, Latvia, Lithuania, Poland, Czech Republic, Slovakia, Hungary, and Slovenia), continuing in 2007 with another two (Romania and Bulgaria), and in 2013 with one more (Croatia)—brought huge challenges to the EU, as an entity, and to its member states. Although the EU acts as a single market for the movement of capital, labor, goods and services, it remains too extended to encourage a uniform European business ethics model (Habisch et al. 2005). Nonetheless, an "implicit" model of commercial responsibility, specific to Europe, may be identified (Matten and Moon 2008): it embraces a more regulated economic and social environment, common policies, and the existence of supranational bodies (such as the European Commission). However, in many aspects (such as business ethics), the EU remains a group of particular nations, not a single entity. In this sense, issues in business ethics still vary across Europe, from environmental concerns in Northern Europe, to social inclusion and employment issues in Southern Europe, and to employees' rights in Central and Eastern Europe (Furrer et al. 2010). Unfortunately, the former communist countries are not very active in these discussions, neither in promoting business ethics nor implementing successfully some guidelines for ethical business practices. The former communist countries have to overcome their weak societal infrastructure and their debilitated capacity to provide the public goods—e.g., roads, schools, impartial and predictable law—necessary for economic development. Along with a culture of distrust of government bodies and of politicians (Habisch et al. 2005: 3), these factors combine to render difficult any implementation of ethical business practice in the national context (Clark Williams and Seguí-Mas 2010).

Outside the EU, Russia remains a world power whose business enterprises remain intermingled with politics, as manifest by a business oligarchy with strong connections to the former KGB. Even though the practice of commercial ethics is fragile, the business ethics discourse of many business people in Russia is dominated by *rejection* of unethical business practices associated with the corrupt Russian business environment (which includes cooperation with criminals, money laundering, and disrespect for the law). Nonetheless, only a limited number of Russian companies have even started to develop codes of business ethics, so it remains almost impossible to evaluate how well such codes function.

Concluding remarks

The former communist countries offer a unique case for business ethics. They have traversed two ideological regimes, with almost totally opposed values. Within these countries, the current practice of business ethics is fundamentally influenced by the business heritage each nation enjoyed prior to the imposition of centrally planned economies, as well as by the transition to democracy, and, ultimately, by integration (in most of these countries) into the EU. There remain several critical business ethics issues for the future of these countries. These issues are more acute for some than for others. For many of the former communist countries, the

European integration process imposes (additional) rules calling for explicit ethical policies for companies (Matten and Moon 2008). This is a major challenge for SMEs: rules and regulations raise the cost of doing business, and, given the ongoing economic difficulties in many of these nations, EU policies may inhibit growth and expansion (or pose additional barriers to entry into the market). In this way some smaller enterprises may find the appeals to ethics to be so inhibiting that they give these a low priority. Such costs must be taken into account by regulators and policy makers even as the EU's commitment to business ethics through various regulations (including standards of employment, codes of conduct, and environmental constraints) challenges all economic actors to pursue ethical guidelines.

Business ethics is inseparable from the general economic, political, and social environment. A society's moral climate is reflected in its commercial morality. The larger moral dimension is, in general, part of the challenge that confronts practical business ethics (Argandoña 2012: 3). Since this dimension is felt acutely in the former communist nations of Central Europe and Russia, a significant test is to rebuild trust, restore confidence in institutions, diminish moral *anomie*, and, consequently, to decrease the cynical attitudes affecting the motivations and conduct of citizens. Corruption is still high in some countries (such as Romania and Bulgaria—even higher in Russia and Albania) and politics mixes too much with business (mostly, but not only, in Russia). Businesses must be seen less as strategic avenues for gain than as creative, productive organizations whose management and employees act with courage and resolve, treat others with honesty and respect, observe the law, and seek to sustain a culture of freedom in which competition and enterprise are esteemed, cronyism and corruption condemned.

A stable prosperous society encourages a culture of business ethics that supports ethical behavior within and by business firms. Ethical norms, moral guidelines for conducting business, ethical boards specific to different business associations and professions indicate how a mature society commits itself to ethical behavior. In the case of Central European countries and Russia there remains room for improvement. For the moment, mostly large and usually foreign companies are those promoting business ethics codes or ethical policies for conducting business.

Finally, it is not only in politics, but also business, that leadership is of exceptional importance. Among the critical issues in business ethics, the problem of leadership is probably the most acute concern for Central Europe and Russia. In some former communist countries (like the Czech Republic or Poland) examples of moral leaders before communism (and the management principles they promoted in their firms) have been rediscovered and presented as models for future managers. Businesses do not exist outside human relationships. Business action is human action; a company's decisions are its leaders' decisions. The Volkswagen scandal is an example of the necessity of moral leaders. Moral companies are led by moral leaders; and moral leaders are a result of a moral society and of a moral education. Moral leaders have an internal motivation, but they are shaped through education and lived example, each emblematic of the values accepted and rewarded by the society.

Essential readings

A view of life under communism is presented by Jim Willis in *Daily Life Behind the Iron Curtain* (2003). The complex context of politics, sociology, and history in the former Soviet Union and the privileges reserved to its elite are detailed in Mervyn Matthews' book *Privilege in the Soviet Union: A Study of Life-Styles Under Communism* (2011). A detailed presentation of the transition from communism to markets, with a focus on the Soviet (Russian) context, is offered in the collection of essays by Peter Boettke, *Calculation and Coordination: Essays on Socialism and Transitional Political Economy* (2002). For a general view on the political, economic and social changes in former communist countries see the collection of papers in Donnacha Ó. Beacháin, Vera Sheridan and Sabina Stan, *Life in Post-Communist Eastern Europe after EU Membership* (2012). An analysis of business legitimacy and responsibility in Russia is presented in the article by Andrei Kuznetsov and Olga Kuznetsova, "Business Legitimacy and the Margins of Corporate Social Responsibility in the Russian Context" (2012). Those wanting a discussion of business ethics and Marxism should consider William H. Shaw's recent article, "Karl Marx on History, Capitalism, and . . . Business Ethics?" (2017). A general European analysis of business ethics and related concepts may be found in the collection edited by Andre Habisch, Jan Jonker, Martina Wegner and Rene Schmidpeter, *Corporate Social Responsibility across Europe* (2005).

For further reading in this volume on the nature of business as a profit-seeking activity, see Chapter 13, What is business? On the significance of property to markets and business, see Chapter 18, Property and business. A philosophical account of the nature and conditions of exploitation may be found in Chapter 29, Exploitation and labor. For a general discussion of the problem of corruption, see Chapter 34, Corruption, bribery, and moral norms across national boundaries. On the ways in which the political process may influence and alter markets and business, see Chapter 21, Regulation, rent seeking, and business ethics. On the influence of Western conceptions of business ethics, see Chapter 32, The globalization of business ethics. For a relevantly analogous case of the transition from communism to a version of market society, see Chapter 35, Business ethics in China.

Notes

* This research was partially possible thanks to a research grant offered by the United States Fulbright Commission in 2014, at Marywood University, Scranton, Pennsylvania.

1 In many communist countries the preferred term for "business" was "economic activity." For the sake of consistency, "business under communism" should be understood as "economic activity."
2 "Managers" were called "directors." They were appointed by the communist party and supposed to have similar responsibilities as the "managers" of capitalist enterprises: to coordinate, organize, plan and control the activity of the enterprise. However, these duties occurred only under the constraints of central planning and the pressure of communist propaganda. As a result, the directors acted according to the communist party instructions; obedience was the means of keeping one's position.
3 In some countries small private initiatives were permitted (some family businesses existed prior to communism—tailoring, cobblers, small shops). In the context of a controlled market, these private initiatives were severely limited.
4 For the communist these are rhetorical questions, but for others these questions are a mix of normative and empirical assumptions, all of which must be evaluated and sifted. We cannot address these here.
5 Some examples of the theft of public property include stealing from canteens, appropriating medicines from hospitals (for personal use or for resale on the black market), or helping oneself to agricultural goods or production materials (tin, cement, wood) for personal use.
6 The notion of a "property deficit" concept is inspired by the similar concept of a "democratic deficit," as defined by Levinson (2007, 859). A democratic deficit may be characterized in terms of the failure of democratic organizations or institutions to fulfill the principle of democracy in actual practice. In the context of a communist society, a property deficit may be understood as a failure of the natural functioning of the relationship between the owner and the object of his or her property. Under communism the means of production were under public, not individual, control so the relations between the public owners (individuals) and the object of property were altered and compromised.
7 Under communism there was full employment, but this was a kind of mirage that hid low wages, slight wage differentials across skill levels, and inefficiencies in work and production. Unethical hiring practices were encouraged: people well connected to the ruling class were hired in "warm" venues and often given few responsibilities (not to mention five secretaries instead of one, seven accountants instead of three, and so on).
8 An "activist" under the communist regime was a person responsible for distributing communist propaganda in schools, enterprises, and so on.

9 A lack of transparency meant that the public was not informed about who owned what, or even, in the case of privatizations, who was participating in public auctions and on what terms.
10 For example, in Romania, after the demise of communism, the disclosure of documents from the secret police (Securitate) revealed cases in which parents had denounced their children for their intention to flee to the West, husbands or wives had spied on a spouse, priests had disclosed to the Securitate the confessions of parishioners, and doctors and lawyers had divulged their patients or clients' thoughts to the communist regime (Mitran 2013).
11 For three relevant nations, the World Bank data (WB 2014) shows the GDP per capita as follows: Albania $4,256, Bulgaria $7,498 and $19,858 for the Czech Republic.
12 In almost all communist countries there existed a long-standing "Cultural Revolution" (distinct from the sort instituted by Mao Tse-Tung in China) and with this on-going revolution came different degrees of religious interdictions: some authors, considered to be a danger for the new regime, were banned; access to Western literature was limited and under strict control of the Party; the history of the nation was reinterpreted and taught in schools according to the interests of the communist regime. In Albania, for example, there was a complete ban on religion by the Communist Party. In other countries, religious symbols were forbidden or replaced by secular symbols. For example, in Romania, the Santa Claus of Christmas Eve was replaced by *Mos Gerila*, a purely secular version of "Jack Frost" related not to Christmas but to New Year's Eve.

References

Albania (1992). Available at: www.country-data.com/cgi-bin/query/r-170.html.
Apressyan, R.G. (1997). "Business Ethics in Russia," *Journal of Business Ethics* 16:14, 1561–1570.
Argandoña, A. (2012). "Three Ethical Dimensions of the Financial Crisis." Available at: www.iese.edu/research/pdfs/di-0944-e.pdf.
Bageac, D., O. Furrer and E. Reynaud (2011). "Management Students' Attitudes toward Business Ethics: A Comparison between France and Romania," *Journal of Business Ethics* 98:3, 391–406.
Beacháin, D.Ó., V. Sheridan and S. Stan (eds) (2012). *Life in Post-Communist Eastern Europe after EU Membership*. Abingdon, UK: Routledge.
Boettke, P.J. (2002). *Calculation and Coordination: Essays on Socialism and Transitional Political Economy*. Abingdon, UK: Routledge.
Bohata, M. (1997). "Business Ethics in Central and Eastern Europe with Special Focus on the Czech Republic," *Journal of Business Ethics* 16:14, 1571–1577.
Carroll, A.B. (2000). "Ethical Challenges for Business in the New Millennium: Corporate Social Responsibility and Models of Management Morality," *Business Ethics Quarterly* 10:1, 33–42.
Cerami, A. and P. Vanhuysse (eds) (2009). *Post-communist Welfare Pathways*. Basingstoke, UK: Palgrave Macmillan.
Čiegis, R., A. Gavenauskas, N. Petkevičiūte and D. Štreimikiene (2008). "Ethical Values and Sustainable Development: Lithuanian Experience in the Context of Globalisation," *Technological and Economic Development of Economy* 14:1, 29–37.
Clark Williams, C. and E. Seguí-Mas (2010). "Corporate Governance and Business Ethics in the European Union: a Cluster Analysis," *Journal of Global Responsibility* 1:1, 98–126.
Condur, G. (2011). "Avatarurile Omului nou–din Comunism în Postcomunism" [The New Man's Avatars–From Communism to Post-Communism] *Sfera Politicii* 160, 63–71.
Constantinescu, N.N. (coord.) (1983). *Economia Politica a Socialismului* [Political Economy of Socialism]. Editura Didactica si Pedagogica Bucuresti.
Corruption Information Exchange (2003). Available at: http://legacy.fordham.edu/economics/vinod/cie/%5Ceasterneurope.htm.
Dăian, M. and K.B. Manova (2013). *The Veil of Communism: An Analysis of Lifespan, GDP per Capita, Human Capital, and Agricultural Productivity in Eastern Europe*. LAP LAMBERT Academic Publishing.
Dimancea, L. and M. Iordache (2005). "Omar Hayssam a dat bani la PSD," [Omar Hayssam has Given Money to PSD]. Available at: http://jurnalul.ro/special-jurnalul/omar-hayssam-a-dat-bani-la-psd-47897.html [accessed 31 March 2005].
Domanski, H. (2004). "Prestizowa pokojowa" ["Prestigious Cleaning Lady"] (Polish), *Polityka* 48, 24–6.

Enderle, G. (1997). "A Worldwide Survey of Business Ethics in the 1990s," *Journal of Business Ethics* 16:14, 1475–1483.

Estrin, S., K.E. Meyer and M. Bytchkova (2006). "Entrepreneurship in Transition Economies," in M. Casson, B. Yeung; A. and N. Wadeson, (eds), *The Oxford Handbook of Entrepreneurship*. New York, NY: Oxford University Press, 693–725.

European Commission (2015). "The Bologna Process and the European Higher Education Area." Available at: http://ec.europa.eu/education/policy/higher-education/bologna-process_en.htm.

Fenger, H.J.M. (2007). "Welfare Regimes in Central and Eastern Europe: Incorporating Post-Communist Countries in a Welfare Regime Typology," *Contemporary Issues and Ideas in Social Sciences* 3:2, 1–30. Available at: http://hdl.handle.net/1765/34876.

Foss, N.J. (2012). "Linking Ethics and Economic Growth: a Comment on Hunt," *Contemporary Economics* 6:3, 4–9.

Furrer, O., C.P. Egri, D.A. Ralston, W. Danis, E. Reynaud, I. Naoumova, M. Molteni, A. Starkus, F.L. Darder, M. Dabic and A. Furrer-Perrinjaquet (2010). "Attitudes toward Corporate Responsibilities in Western Europe and in Central and East Europe," *Management International Review* 50:3, 379–398.

Gjonça, A. (2001). *Communism, Health and Lifestyle: the Paradox of Mortality Transition in Albania, 1950–1990* (No. 8). Westport, CT: Greenwood Publishing Group.

Granovetter, M. (1985). "Economic Action and Social Structure: the Problem of Embeddedness," *American Journal of Sociology* 91:3, 481–510.

Habisch, A., J. Jonker, M. Wegner and R. Schmidpeter, (eds) (2005). *Corporate Social Responsibility across Europe*. Berlin-Heidelberg: Springer.

Howard, M.M. (2002). "The Weakness of Postcommunist Civil Society," *Journal of Democracy* 13:1, 157–169.

IBRD (2013). *Doing Business 2013*. Available at: www.doingbusiness.org/~/media/GIAWB/Doing%20Business/Documents/Annual-Reports/English/DB13-full-report.pdf.

IDA-RID Guidelines for Russian Companies (2004). Available at: www.ita.doc.gov/goodgovernance/adobe/IDARIDBusEthicsGuidelinesEng.pdf.

IMF (2012). IMF data. Available at: www.imf.org/external/pubs/ft/weo/2012/01/weodata/weoapr2012all.xls.

Inglehart, R. (2008). "Changing Values Among Western Publics From 1970 to 2006," *West European Politics* 31:1–2, 130–146.

INSCOP (2015). In cine au incredere romanii: SRI, peste BNR si ANAF, peste CCR [Who Romanians trust: SRI, above BNR and ANAF and above CCR]—sondaj INSCOP. Available at: www.inscop.ro/wp-content/uploads/2015/05/INSCOP-05.2015.-Incredere-in-institutii.pdf [accessed 19 May 2015].

Katchanovski, I. (2000). "Divergence in Growth in Post-communist Countries," *Journal of Public Policy* 20:1, 55–81.

Kaufmann, D. and P. Siegelbaum (1997). "Privatization and Corruption in Transition Economies," *Journal of International Affairs* 50, 419–458.

Korobkova, Y.E. (2015). "Corporate Culture of the Russian Merchantry as an Example of Socially Oriented Business," *Theoretical and Applied Economics*, 3. Abstract only, available at: http://en.e-notabene.ru/etc/article_15450.html.

Kotchegura, A. (2004). "Reducing Corruption in Post-Communist Countries," *International Public Management Review* 5:1, 138–156.

Kozminski A.K. (1995). "From the Communist Nomenklatura to Transformational Leadership: the Role of Management in the Post-communist Enterprises," in B. Grancelli (ed.), *Social Change and Modernization: Lessons from Eastern Europe*. Berlin, New York, NY: Walter de Gruyter, 83–105.

Kroll (2015). "Global Fraud Report: Vulnerabilities on the Rise," Available at: http://anticorruzione.eu/wp-content/uploads/2015/09/Kroll_Global_Fraud_Report_2015low-copia.pdf.

Kronenberg, J. and T. Bergier (2012). "Sustainable Development in a Transition Economy: Business Case Studies from Poland," *Journal of Cleaner Production* 26, 18–27.

Kuznetsov, A. and O. Kuznetsova (2012). "Business Legitimacy and the Margins of Corporate Social Responsibility in the Russian Context," *International Studies of Management & Organization* 42:3, 35–48.

Lantos, G.P. (2001). "The Boundaries of Strategic Corporate Social Responsibility," *Journal of Consumer Marketing* 18:7, 595–632.

Levinson, S. (2007). "How the United States Constitution Contributes to the Democratic Deficit in America," *Drake Law Review* 55, 859–1057. Available at: https://litigation-essentials.lexisnexis.com/

webcd/app?action=DocumentDisplay&crawlid=1&srctype=smi&srcid=3B15&doctype=cite&docid=55+Drake+L.+Rev.+859&key=1d2f4bc348d6d89e85fccb373f4579c3.
Lewicka-Strzalecka, A. (2006). "Opportunities and Limitations of CSR in the Post-communist Countries: the Polish Case," *Corporate Governance: The International Journal of Business in Society* 6:4, 440–448.
Longenecker, J.G., J.A. McKinney and C.W. Moore (2004). "Religious Intensity, Evangelical Christianity, and Business Ethics: An Empirical Study," *Journal of Business Ethics* 55:4, 371–384.
Mahoney, J. and E. Vallance, (eds) (1992). *Business Ethics in a New Europe*. Dordrecht: Kluwer.
Marx, K. (1844 [1978]). "Economic and Philosophical Manuscripts of 1844," in Robert C. Tucker (ed.), *The Marx–Engels Reader*, 2nd edition. New York, NY: W.W. Norton, 66–125.
Marx, K. (1875 [1978]). "A Critique of the Gotha Program," in Robert C. Tucker (ed.), *The Marx–Engels Reader*, 2nd edition. New York, NY: W.W. Norton, 525–541.
Mather, A. and J.S. Bryden, (eds) (2009). *Area Studies (Regional Sustainable Development Review): Europe*. EOLSS Publications.
Matten, D. and J. Moon (2004). "Corporate Social Responsibility Education in Europe," *Journal of Business Ethics* 54:4, 323–337.
Matten, D. and J. Moon (2008). "'Implicit' and 'Explicit' CSR: A Conceptual Framework for a Comparative Understanding of Corporate Social Responsibility," *Academy of Management Review* 33:2, 404–424.
Matthews, M. (2011). *Privilege in the Soviet Union: a Study of Elite Life-styles under Communism*. Abingdon, UK: Routledge.
Mitran, L. (2013). "Reportaj: Surprize în dosarele CNSAS—soția își turna soțul din gelozie, finul pe nași din invidie" [Surprise in CNSAS files: the wife denunciates husband out of jealousy, the godson denunciates godparents because of envy]. Available at: www.mediafax.ro/social/reportaj-surprize-in-dosarele-cnsas-sotia-isi-turna-sotul-din-gelozie-finul-pe-nasi-din-invidie-11807677.
Nemcova, L. (1993). "Importance of Teaching Business Ethics in Post-communist Czech Republic." Available at: www.friends-partners.org/newfriends/audem/audem93/nemcova.html.
Nowak, R. (1996). "Corruption and Transition Economies," *Science* 48, 321–35.
Ollman, B. (1976). *Alienation: Marx's Conception of Man in a Capitalist Society*. Cambridge: Cambridge University Press.
Peng, M.W. (2001). "How Entrepreneurs Create Wealth in Transition Economies," *The Academy of Management Executive* 15:1, 95–108.
Popowska, M. (2016). "Shaping New Generations of Managers and Consumers: CSR Implementation and Higher Education System in Poland," in D. Turker, C.A. Vural and S.O. Idowu (eds), *Social Responsibility Education Across Europe*. Berlin-Heidelberg: Springer, 115–138.
Puffer, S.M. and D.J. McCarthy (2011). "Two Decades of Russian Business and Management Research: An Institutional Theory Perspective," *The Academy of Management Perspectives* 25:2, 21–36.
Ramanadham, V.V. (ed.) (2002). *Constraints and Impacts of Privatisation*. Abingdon, UK: Routledge.
Romano, S. (2014). *The Political and Social Construction of Poverty: Central and Eastern European Countries in Transition*. Bristol, UK: Policy Press.
Schneider, F., A. Buehn and C.E. Montenegro (2010). "Shadow Economies all over the World: New Estimates for 162 Countries from 1999 to 2007," *World Bank Policy Research Working Paper Series* 5356. Available at: https://openknowledge.worldbank.org/bitstream/handle/10986/3928/WPS5356.txt?sequence=2&isAllowed=y.
Sexty, R.W. (1998). "Teaching Business Ethics in Transitional Economies: Avoiding Ethical Missionary," *Journal of Business Ethics* 17:12, 1311–1317.
Shaw, W.H. (2009). "Marxism, Business Ethics, and Corporate Social Responsibility," *Journal of Business Ethics* 84:4, 565–576.
Shaw, W.H. (2017). "Karl Marx on History, Capitalism, and . . . Business Ethics?" in E. Heath and B. Kaldis (eds), *Wealth, Commerce, and Philosophy: Foundational Thinkers and Business Ethics*. Chicago, IL: University of Chicago Press, 321–339.
Stan, L. and L. Turcescu (2000). "The Romanian Orthodox Church and Post-Communist Democratisation," *Europe-Asia Studies* 52:8, 1467–1488.
The Economist (July 2000). "Where is Central Europe?" July 6. Available at: www.economist.com/node/4711.
The Economist (November 2008). "Twenty Years of Capitalism: Was it Worth it?" Nov 19. Available at: www.economist.com/node/12494500.

The Guardian (2014). "Hewlett-Packard to Pay $108m to Settle Scandal over Bribery of Public Officials," April. Available at: www.theguardian.com/business/2014/apr/09/hewlett-packard-108m-corruption-government-it-us-bribery.

Traicu, A. (2016). "Omar Hayssam este Audiat la DNA în Cazul Privatizării IPRS Băneasa" [Omar Hayssam is Heard by DNA on the Privatization of IPRS Baneasa], March 25. Available at: www.media fax.ro/social/omar-hayssam-este-audiat-la-dna-in-cazul-privatizarii-iprs-baneasa-15149460.

Tsalikis, J. and B. Seaton (2007). "The International Business Ethics Index: European Union," *Journal of Business Ethics* 75:3, 229–238.

Visser, W. (2008). "Corporate Social Responsibility in Developing Countries," in A. Crane, A.A. McWilliams, D. Matten, J. Moon and D. Siegel (eds), *The Oxford Handbook of Corporate Social Responsibility*. Oxford: Oxford University Press, 473–479.

Wasilewski, J. (1998). "Hungary, Poland, and Russia: The Fate of Nomenklatura Elites," in M. Dogan and J. Higley (eds), *Elites, Crises, and the Origins of Regimes*. Boulder, CO: Rowman and Littlefield, 147–167.

Willis, J. (2013). *Daily Life Behind the Iron Curtain*. Santa Barbara, CA: Greenwood/ABC-CLIO.

Woolcock, M. (1998). "Social Capital and Economic Development: Toward a Theoretical Synthesis and Policy Framework," *Theory and Society* 27:2, 151–208.

World Bank (2014). "GDP per capita." Available at: http://data.worldbank.org/indicator/NY.GDP.PCAP.CD/countries.

Zaharia, R.M., A. Stancu, C. Stoian and M. Diaconu (2010). "Commercial Activity Contribution to Sustainable Development by Social Responsibility Actions: a Vision of SMEs," *Amfiteatrul Ecnomic* 27, 84–100.

Index

AACSB *see* American Association of Collegiate Schools of Business
Abbott, Andrew 525, 535
Abend, Gabriel 40
Academy of Management 544
accountability 63–64, 188, 343; accounting 413, 523–524, 525; corruption 583, 587n5; entrepreneurship 277; financial institutions 347, 351; human rights 531; leadership 441; MBA Oath 199, 203; sharing 139; social enterprises 264; Wenger 142–143
accounting 86, 231, 232, 235, 347, 413, 523–540
Acemoglu, Daron 337
achievement orientation 561–562
Ackerman, Bruce 107
act utilitarianism 450
Adams, Renée 421
advergames 510
advertising 506–518, 643
advertorials 511
affirmative action 52
Afghanistan 606, 607
Africa 581, 592, 624–640, 645
agency 239, 248–252
agency theory 226–228, 416–417, 584; accounting 525; corporate governance 422; economics 291, 298–299, 301
aggregate theory 243, 244, 245, 248–249, 252, 254n12, 424
Agle, Bradley R. 6, 60–76, 186
agriculture 388
AIG *see* American International Group
Air New Zealand 250
Airflow 619
Akerlof, George 297
Albania 665, 666–667, 668, 670n11
Alchian, Armen 226–227, 245, 298, 331
Alderson, Wroe 15
ALENE *see* Latin American Association of Ethics, Business and Economics
algorithms 567–568, 569
Allison, John A. 393, 394, 401
alternative business organizations 222, 257–274

altruism 30, 35, 292; accounting 526; Confucianism 161; leadership 441, 463; servant leadership 433; social entrepreneurship 278
Alzola, Miguel 114
American Accounting Association 526
American Association of Collegiate Schools of Business (AACSB) 60, 546
American International Group (AIG) 400, 609
American Marketing Association 506
American Recovery and Reinvestment Act (2009) 402–403
American Research and Development Corporation 125
amoral entity, firm as 362
Anabtawi, Iman 420
analytic philosophy 45, 47, 48
Anderson, A.R. 284
Andreas, Dwayne O. 126
animal rights 192, 380–381, 390
Annan, Kofi 17, 548, 551
Annas, Julia 46
Anscombe, Elizabeth 15, 43, 46, 80
anti-Semitism 10
apartheid 547, 627, 638n12
Apel, Karl-Otto 204
Apple 121, 514, 548
Appley, Lawrence 13, 16
applied philosophy 46
appropriateness 559
Aquinas, St Thomas 5, 9, 26, 151, 153–154; cardinal virtues 10, 154, 155; Catholic social justice 12; entrepreneurial virtue 122, 123; happiness 25; influence of 27; rules 80; virtue ethics 82
Aquino, K. 437
arbitrage 117, 347, 352
Archer-Daniels-Midland Corporation 126
Archer, Robin 482
Argandoña, Antonio 307, 343–358
Argentina 641–644, 645, 649
Aristotelian ethics 9, 43, 148
Aristotle 8, 24–26, 33, 46; character 27; distributive justice 48; fair trade

114–115; friendship 1; influence on Mill 91–92; leadership 430, 435; motivation 85; teleological biology 41; trade 5; virtue ethics 82, 88, 91, 151, 284, 452, 606
Arnaud, Anke 469
Arneson, Richard 480
Arnold, Denis 584
Arrow, Kenneth 299–301, 419
Arthur Anderson 251, 573
artificial person theory 243–244, 248–249
asceticism 41, 42, 157
ascription orientation 561–562
Ashley, A. 278, 283
Asia 17, 159–162, 562, 566, 606; *see also* South Asia
audits 455, 469–470, 548
Augustine, St 11
Aurobindo, Sri 612
Australia 566, 567
Austria 562
authentic leadership 435–436
authoritarianism 563
authority structures 466–467
auto industry bailout 399, 402
autonomy 30, 33, 54; China 594–595; consumer 510, 511, 512, 516; Europe 638n9; feminist ethics 135; informational privacy 483; Integrative Economic Ethics 206; Kantian ethics 86, 451; Lockean liberty narrative 50; meaningful work 481; modernization theory 564; Rousseauean equality narrative 51; self and other 140; social contract theory 104, 108; workplace democracy 482
Avolio, Bruce J. 434
Aycan, Zeynep 562
Ayittey, George 628–630, 632, 633
Ayres, Ian 361

B Corp trademark 262, 265
Backer, L.C. 530–531
Backof, Jeanne F. 528
Bacon, Francis 223
Bader, Ernest 618, 619
Bainbridge, S.M. 419–420
Bajaj, Jamnalal 616
Bakan, Joel 170
Baker, W.E. 563–564
Baldwin, Robert 364
Baltic nations 657
Bandura, Albert 461
Bangladesh 530, 548, 606, 608
bankruptcy: bankruptcy law 402; fraudulent 644, 655–656
banks 345, 346–348, 350; ethical banking 353; financial industry bailout 399–402, 407; mortgage lending 395–398, 403, 404
bargaining problem 108, 234

Barkhuysen, B. 625
Barnard, Chester 200n3
Barnes, Kenneth J. 78, 148–164
Barry, Bruce 233
Basáñez Miguel 564
basic needs duties 495–496
Bass, Bernard 434, 435
Bastiat, Frédéric 118, 120
Bata, Tomasz 665
Bauer, P.T. 630
Bauman, Zygmunt 534, 535
Baumhart, Raymond 12
Baumol, William J. 276, 279, 334–335, 394
Bazerman, Max 71
Bear Stearns 400
Beauchamp, T.L. 359
Becker, G.S. 404
Beekun, Rafik I. 158
behavioral economics 291
behavioral ethics 62, 64, 65, 109; ethical awareness 461; marketing 515–516; moral blindness 71; person and situation factors 460
behavioral targeting 513
Behnam, Michael 105–106, 205
Beijing Consensus 618
Belgium 267, 269, 558, 562, 646
Belk, R.W. 513
beneficence 86–87, 451
benefit corporations 260–263, 264, 265, 270n4, 271n9
benevolence 158, 469
Benhabib, Seyla 139
Bentham, Jeremy 5, 27, 35; consequentialism 80; stakeholder theory 34; utilitarianism 30, 33, 83–84, 93n1, 606
Berger, Ron 609, 610
Berle, Adolf 185, 227, 298, 418
Berlin, Isaiah 284
Beschorner, Thomas 166, 204–219
best practices 550
Betta, Michela 277
Bhagavad Gita 611, 612
Bhaneja, B. 612
Bhutan 606, 607, 608
biases 456
Bible 8, 9, 573; Christianity 151–153, 156; divine justice 576; Hebrew tradition 148–151
biodiversity 389, 582
biomimicry 384
Birla, G.D. 616
Bishop, John 99, 512, 515
Blackstone, William 241
Blaim, Katherine 158–159
Blair, Margaret 245–246, 302, 417
Blair, Tony 618
blame 168
Bloch, Marc 8

Index

bluffing 28, 53, 293, 373n4; *see also* deception
Blumberg, Phillip 243
boards of directors 420–422, 440; CEO role 423; compliance programs 463; primacy debate 416–418; Sentencing Guidelines 549; social investor movement 547; staggered 418, 419; *see also* directors
Boatright, John 64, 104–105, 185–186, 302, 368, 478
Boeing 584
Boettke, Peter 660
Boisjoly, Roger 485
Bolivia 645
Bollaert, H. 439
Bolle, K.W. 612
Bologna Process 662
Bolte, Angela 137
Borgerson, Janet L. 133, 134, 512
Borzaga, C. 266
bounded ethicality 71
Bovard, James 126
Bowen, Howard R. 12, 171
Bowie, Norman 14, 69, 85, 86–87, 227, 366
BP 436
Bragues, Georges 5, 23–37
Braithwaite, John 361
Bratton, W.W. 254n8
Braudel, Fernand 230
Brazil 641–644, 646–647, 649
Brenkert, George 39, 276, 277–278, 279, 359, 482, 485
Brennan, J. 367
bribery 542, 544, 549–550, 573–589; acceptability in foreign environments 574, 579–580; Africa 631, 633; Central Europe and Russia 663, 667; cultural relativism 567–568; definition of 575; gifts and 17, 575–577; *Global Corruption Barometer* 645; India 610; inherent characteristics 577–578; Integrative Economic Ethics 208–209; integrative social contracts theory 105; Latin America 642, 644, 645, 656; multinational companies 546; *see also* corruption
British American Tobacco 643
Brown & Williamson 484, 485
Brown, Michael E. 439, 463–464
Brundtland Commission 17, 381–383, 385, 386, 387–388, 389
Bruton, Samuel V. 70
Bubble Act (1720) 241, 243, 246, 253n3
Bucar, Branko 281
Buchanan, Allen 301
Buchanan, James M. 43, 96, 100–101, 369, 370, 394, 407n1
Buchholz, Ann K. 411, 415–429
Buchholz, R.A. 283
Buddhism 9, 159, 160, 606, 607
Buffett, Warren 619–620

Bulgaria 657, 665, 666–667, 668, 670n11
Burns, James MacGregor 431, 434, 435
Bush, Vannevar 332
business 221, 223–238; as an activity 223, 228–232, 235; Central Europe and Russia 658, 659, 662, 663, 669n1; hostility to 24, 39–41; as an organization 223, 224–228; purpose of 424; stakeholder theory 232–235; *see also* commerce; corporations; firms
business ethics education 6, 18, 60–76, 544, 546, 553; Africa 625, 626; Central Europe and Russia 661–662; content of 63–65; history of 12–15; Latin America 647, 650; moral leaders 668; moral sense and commitment 67–70; opposition to 40; purpose of 55, 62–63; self-deception and moral blindness 70–72; South Asia 608; stakeholder thinking 197–199; stand-alone or integrated 65; teaching methods 66–67; timing of exposure 66; training compared with 60–62; university culture 65–66
Business Roundtable Institute for Corporate Ethics 66
Butterfield, K. 469
Byron, K. 421

CABE *see* China Association of Business Ethics
Cable, D. 584
Cafaggi, F. 266
Calás, Marta 277
Caldwell, Philip 125
Calvin, John 155, 156–157
Cambodia 608
Cameron, Kim S. 436
Canada 281, 418, 566
Cantillon, Richard 276, 279
capabilities 27, 385, 394, 395
Capaldi, Nicholas 5–6, 38–59
capital 124, 241, 242, 482; moral 601; social enterprises 264–265, 269
capitalism: Africa 628–630; business ethics education 64, 65; Calvin 155; Central Europe and Russia 657–658; Creating Shared Value approach 176; critical management studies 449; critics of 10–12, 18; crony 404, 407; early modern 10; feminist ethics 134–135, 143–144; Gandhi 615–616, 617, 618; inequalities 40; lack of moral awareness 62; Marxist critique 32–33, 659; political 308, 405–406, 407; problems of 13–14; Schumpeter 611; self-interest 68; shareholder 339; social contract theory 97; social market economy 214; virtue 138
Card, C. 136
care, ethics of 132, 133–134, 135, 136–137, 143, 452
Carnegie, Andrew 611, 614, 620
Carr, Albert Z. 28, 53, 293, 373n4
Carroll, Archie B. 224, 366, 632

Carson, Rachel 12–13
Carson, Thomas 69–70
cartels 642–643, 649, 652–653
categorical imperative 30–31, 204, 451
Catholic Church 11–12, 18, 40, 157–158, 545–546; Catholic Social Thought 27; Central Europe and Russia 666; Latin America 649; social and human teleology 43; *see also* Christianity
caveat emptor principle 509
Cayne, James 438
CBE *see* contractarian business ethics
Center for Business Ethics 61
Central Europe 592, 657–673
Central Intelligence Agency (CIA) 580
CEOs *see* chief executive officers
Certo, Trevis 422
Chakrabarty, B. 611, 614, 616
Chan, K.C. 608
Chandler, Alfred 334–335, 338–339
change management 559
Chapa, Sindy 510
Chapman, Chris 523
character: accounting 526, 527, 528–529, 535; Aristotle 24, 27; business ethics education 62; corrupted by bribery 577; leaders 437–438; managers 452, 454; profit seekers 125, 126; virtue 114
charities 257, 259, 260, 263, 619–620, 664
Chartered Institute of Management Accountants (CIMA) 532
cheating 71, 227, 438, 456, 459
Chesbrough, Henry 336
Chevron 643–644
chief executive officers (CEOs) 422–423; compensation 419–420, 423, 478; orientation sessions 465; women 421; *see also* leadership
Child, J. 234
child labor 10, 171
children 510, 513
Chile 641–644, 645, 646, 647, 649–650, 651n2
China 547, 591, 593–605; Beijing Consensus 618; Buddhism 160; collectivism 559; Confucian ethics 8, 17, 161–162; human rights 563; leadership 441; Taoism 160–161; *see also* Confucianism
China Association of Business Ethics (CABE) 597–598
Chinese Cultural Connection (CCC) study 560
Christensen, Clayton 335
Christianity 9, 26, 28, 151–158, 159, 337; Africa 628; Aristotelian ethics 148; business associations 546; Central Europe and Russia 666–667; economic justice 383; economic liberalism 628; medieval philosophy 41–42; ordoliberalism 215; servant leadership 434; South Asia 607; *see also* Catholic Church; Protestantism

Chrysler 399, 402
CIA *see* Central Intelligence Agency
Cicero, Marcus Tullius 25, 26, 113, 114
CICs *see* Community Interest Companies
CIMA *see* Chartered Institute of Management Accountants
Ciulla, Joanne 432, 435, 436, 438
civic virtues 210–211
civil society: Central Europe and Russia 664, 665–666; social contract theory 97
class 32, 135–136, 449
classical philosophy 41
climate *see* ethical climate
climate change 18, 327, 582, 620
Clinton, Bill and Hillary 618
clusters of innovation 335–336, 339
CMS *see* critical management studies
Coase, Ronald 225–226, 229, 245, 298
Cochran, Clarke E. 526
codes of ethics/conduct 12, 15, 455, 567; Central Europe and Russia 665, 667; compliance programs 462; decision algorithms 568; ethical culture 463, 465; ineffectiveness of 569; Latin America 648; religious belief 162; Sentencing Guidelines 549; United States 566
cognitive abilities 62
cognitive biases 71
cognitive moral development 460, 528
Coke, Edward 241, 243
collaboration: management theories 447, 448; stakeholder thinking 192, 196, 197, 198; Wenger's theory 144; *see also* cooperation
collectivism 559, 561, 564, 568
Collier, J. 422
Collins, D. 64
Colombia 553, 641–644, 645, 649
colonialism: Africa 628, 629, 631; India 611, 612, 616
commerce 24–27, 35, 40; Central Europe and Russia 665; consequentialism 79; corporations 240; feminist ethics 138, 144; Islam 159; Judaism 150; Kant 31; modern philosophy 43; moral value of 337; norms of 38–39; regulation 44; role of the state 615; *see also* business; corporations; firms
commercial banks 348
commercial society 78, 125–126
common good 192, 196, 197, 198, 199, 434
common resources 314–316, 319
common sense theory 451
communicative action 204, 205, 212–213
communicative ethics 208
communism: Central Europe and Russia 592, 657–669; China 597; Gandhi 612, 615; social market economy 214
Communist Party of China 593, 595

communitarianism 104, 106; Africa 592, 626, 634, 635, 636; Integrative Economic Ethics 210
communities of practice 78, 140, 141, 142–143
community 41–42, 43, 141, 210
Community Interest Companies (CICs) 267–269, 270, 271n12, 271n14
Community Reinvestment Act (CRA) 395–396, 403, 406
compassion 144
compensation 478–480; executive pay 16, 48, 52, 418, 419–420, 422, 423, 478; firms' duties 494–503; pay inequality 131, 132, 135; results-oriented pay 560; standard economic theory 493; unjust wages 491–492, 503; *see also* wages
competence 142–143, 527, 528–529, 534, 535
competing values framework 453–455
competition 120, 121, 292–293, 331; barriers to global business ethics 552; Central Europe and Russia 668; Integrative Economic Ethics 209; lobbying 124; market economies 42, 328; markets 499; masculine cultures 560; undermined by bribery 578; unfair 630, 642, 649
compliance 102–103, 198, 549, 568; barriers to global business ethics 550, 552; economic calculation 362; managing ethical conduct 462–463
comprehensive moral thinking 185, 195–197, 198, 199
concession theory 243, 244, 254n10, 424
Condit, Philip 584
conflict minerals 548
conflicts of interest 63, 347, 418; boards of directors 421–422; CEOs 423; hedge funds 349; India 610; Latin America 644, 655–656; marketing 511
Confucianism 9, 17, 161–162, 596; barriers to global business ethics 552; cross-cultural management ethics 560, 566; hard work 8; self-cultivation 599; traditional values 597, 598
Confucius (Kongzi) 8, 161, 435, 593, 596, 598
conscience: definition of 187; Luther 155; moral foundations theory 456; stakeholder thinking 165–166, 184–185, 187–188, 191, 194, 195, 198
consensus 139
consequentialism 15, 77, 79–81, 83–85, 89–92, 450–451; cultural differences 567; ethical judgments 565; Islam 159; Kantian ethics 87; management ethics 455; punishment 251; stakeholder thinking 192; totality of effects 225; *see also* teleology; utilitarianism
conservationism 381, 382, 383, 387–388, 389
conservatism 561, 562
constitutive contractarian business ethics 97–98, 107–108
consumer demand 385–386

Consumer Product Safety Improvement Act (CPSIA) 225
consumer scams 643, 649, 653–654
consumer sovereignty 516
consumerism 41, 514–515; ethical 47; Gandhi's opposition to 592, 611, 616–617
consumption 23, 613, 617, 629
contextual ethics 454–455
contingency 283
contractarian business ethics (CBE) 96, 97, 99–103, 105, 106–109
contractarianism 77–78, 96–97, 99, 108–109, 451; compliance 102; consequentialism 91; hypernorms 106; limited liability 246; managers 452; non-consequentialism 82, 85, 87–88; "order ethics" 107; *see also* social contract
contracts: corporations 245, 246–248, 302; fair 234; fair market value 498–499; financial institutions 346–347; freedom of contract 474–475, 486; irregularities 644; laissez faire approach 503; nexus-of-contracts theory 243, 245–246, 247, 252, 417, 423; role of the state 615; rules 228; stakeholder theory 233; transaction cost theory 225–226, 227–228; voluntary 493–494; *see also* social contract
conventionalism 317–318
Coombs, Timothy 137
Cooper, David 523
cooperation 101, 115, 316; economics 297, 299; ethic of care 137, 139; Gandhi 616; *see also* collaboration
cooperatives 265–267, 269–270, 271n10
copyright 319
corporate citizenship 16, 176, 207, 208, 209, 257
corporate conscience 184, 185, 187–188, 191, 194, 195, 198
corporate governance 13, 48, 109, 246, 252, 411, 415–429; academic business ethics 662; Africa 626–628, 632; corruption 583–584; definition of 416; issues surrounding boards of directors 420–422; issues surrounding shareholders 418–420; nature and role of the CEO 422–423; primacy debate 416–418; South Asia 608; stakeholder thinking 184, 185–186
corporate moral responsibility 16
Corporate Social Responsibility (CSR) 13, 30, 40–41, 131, 165, 167–183; Africa 632–633, 636; business ethics education 64, 662; context-specific variation 363; definition of 171; environmental issues 376; evolution of social responsibility into 224; feminist ethics 135; human rights 178–179, 529, 530; Integrative Economic Ethics 208–209, 215–216; Latin America 592, 648; leadership 438; Locke/Rousseau narratives 52; Milton's critique 14; philosophy 23; political 177–178; practice 175–176; shared value 176–177;

social and environmental goals 257–258, 269; social contract theory 107; South Asia 608; stakeholder theory 34; sustainability 387; theories 172–174; "triple bottom line" 517; UN Global Compact 17; utilitarianism 91; voluntary regulation 367
corporations 221–222, 239–256, 298, 321, 363; barriers to global business ethics 552; benefit corporations 260–263, 264, 265, 270n4, 271n9; bribery and corruption 579, 583–584, 585; business as the corporation 223, 224–225; Central Europe and Russia 663–664; corporate ethics programs 548–550; corporate law 301–302; emergence of business ethics 544–545; globalization 547–548; innovation 327, 331, 333, 334–335; moral agency 169–171, 248–252; origins of 239–243; social contract theory 98–99, 109; theories of the corporation 243–248, 424; use of the term 239; *see also* employers; firms; multinational companies
Corrigan, Terence 632–633
corruption 131, 542, 544, 546, 573–589; Africa 626, 630–631, 632, 633; barriers to global business ethics 552; Central Europe and Russia 662, 663, 665, 666–667, 668; character of 585; definitions of 573–574; developing countries 543, 666; Integrative Economic Ethics 208–209; Latin America 592, 641, 642, 644–647, 648, 649–650; leaders 438; MBA Oath 203; South Asia 591–592, 607, 609, 610; *see also* bribery
Corruption Perceptions Index 581, 607, 610, 630, 646
Costco 479
courage: Aquinas 154; Aristotle 25; Christianity 158; Judaism 151; leadership 437; Luther 155; moral 62; virtue ethics 82, 138, 452
Cowen, Tyler 338
Cragg, Wesley 542, 573–589
Crane, A. 177
Creating Shared Value (CSV) approach 176–177
"creative destruction" 329, 330, 331
"creative responses" 328–329
creativity 280, 283, 284, 307; China 594, 598; entrepreneurship 279; innovation 326–327, 329, 339; transformational leadership 434, 435
creditors 246–248, 254n11, 402, 422
critical management studies (CMS) 449
Croatia 657, 667
Crockett, C. 284
crony capitalism 404, 407
cronyism 574, 585, 630, 631, 662, 668
cross-cultural management ethics 541–542, 556–572
Crossley, T. 62
CSR *see* Corporate Social Responsibility
Cullen, John B. 469
cultural relativism 88, 567–568

culture: business ethics education 65, 72; Confucianism 161; corporate ethics programs 550; corruption 574; cross-cultural management ethics 541–542, 556–572; ethical relativism 69; global ethics standards 550, 551; innovation 337; leadership 441; transcultural concepts 87–88
cunning 10, 18
customer focus 507
Czech Republic 657, 665, 666–667, 668, 670n11

Dacia Pitesti 664
Daily, C.M. 416
Darden School 66
data collection 513
Davenport, Laura 526
Davis, Michael 485
Day, Theodore 396, 397
Dayal, Parmeshwari 616
De Bruin, Boudewijn 393
De George, Richard 14
De Graaf, Gjalt 97–98, 106, 108
Deaton, Angus 321
Debreu, Gerard 299–300
deception 352, 373n4, 508–509, 577; *see also* bluffing; dishonesty; lying
decision making: bribery influence on 577; business ethics education 62, 67; China 603; Community Interest Companies 268; corporate intentionality 170; cross-cultural management ethics 569; cultural differences 566–567; decision algorithms 567–568, 569; emotional factors 461–462; entrepreneurs 282–283; ethical awareness 460–461; ethical climate 469; ethical culture 463, 467; gender differences 136; management ethics 454, 455; management theories 447, 449–450; moral agency 170; norms 186; reason 456; social enterprises 264; stakeholder theory 233
decision theory 295–296
defense industry scandals 545
DeGeorge, Richard 168–169, 224, 362, 484–485
Delaware 262–263
deliberation 106, 209, 211, 212–213, 215
Dellaportas, Steven 526
dematerialization 384
democracy: Central Europe and Russia 667; China 594; democratic deficit 669n6; participation in decisions 48; undermined by bribery 578, 586; Western-style 563; workplace 480, 481–482, 487n2, 487n3
Dempsey, James A. 252
Demsetz, Harold 226–227, 245, 298
Demuijnk, Geert 69
Denmark 336, 562
Dennett, Daniel 250

679

Index

deontology 77, 81, 85, 162, 293–294, 297; cultural differences 566, 567; ethical judgments 565; Integrative Economic Ethics 208; Islam 159; Kantian ethics 451, 606
deregulation 14, 618
derivatives 349
Derry, Robin 137
Descartes, René 42, 44, 53
DesJardins, Joseph 64, 69, 89, 308, 376–392
developing countries 543, 552, 563–564, 583, 586, 666
deviant behavior 105
Dewey, John 245, 254n8, 606
Dey, P. 283
dharma 9, 160
dialogue 106, 139, 212
digital media 506–507, 513–514
dignity 337, 385; hypernorms 104; Islam 158; Judaism 149, 151; Kant 35, 81–82; MBA Oath 199, 203; Rawls 34; stakeholder thinking 192, 196, 197, 198, 199; utilitarianism 90
Diprose, Rosalyn 131–132
directors 261, 267–268, 418–419; *see also* boards of directors; leadership
discourse ethics 105, 204–205, 206, 210, 211, 212, 216
discourses 8, 18, 207, 212
discretionary authority 225–226
discrimination: compensation 478; critical management studies 449; gender 98, 105, 131, 560; hiring 476; leadership 440; management ethics 455; MBA Oath 203; mortgage lending 396, 397–398, 403, 406, 408n3; utilitarianism 90
disgust 461–462
dishonesty 82, 151; *see also* deception; lying
distributive fairness in compensation 491–492, 496–500
distributive justice 48, 101–102; accounting 525; Aquinas 153–154; China 596, 598; economics 295, 296; property rights 317
diversity: Africa 630, 631–632; boards of directors 421; feminist ethics 132; institutional design 371; leadership 440; Locke/Rousseau narratives 52; medium-sized enterprises 98; utilitarianism 90
dividends 268, 269
division of labor 480, 481
Dobie, Kris 633
Dobson, John 136–137
Dodd, E. Merrick 185, 243, 321
Dodd-Frank Act (2010) 401, 403, 548
Dodge v. Ford 301–302
Dolecheck, M. and C. 566
Donaldson, Thomas: business ethics education 64; decision algorithms 568; influence of Rawls on 46; moral agency 170; Sarbanes-Oxley Act 609; social contract theory 34, 85, 87–88, 96, 98–101, 103–105, 107–109, 165, 173, 545; stakeholder thinking 186, 194–195; universal ethical values 551
Donovan, A. 8, 372n1
Doriot, Georges 125–126
double-entry bookkeeping 230, 231
downsizing 105, 108
Drucker, Peter 39, 178, 187, 188, 275, 276, 278
drug testing 483–484
Drumwright, Minette 412, 506–522
Dubbink, Wim 251–252
due diligence 531, 532
Dugan, Shaun 561
Dunfee, Thomas W.: influence of Rawls on 46; social contract theory 34, 85, 87–88, 96, 98–100, 102–109, 165, 173, 545
Dunham, Laura 277, 279, 284
Duns Scotus, John 80
duties: accounting 413; cultural differences 566; employees and employers 412, 474–475; finance 345, 346, 347, 351; firms 411, 494–503; social contract theory 102; sustainable development 383; Ubuntu 634; *see also* fiduciary duty; obligations
duty 79, 86, 92, 451
Dworkin, Ronald 88

e-money 345–346
Eagly, Alice 441
East Asia 17, 547, 567
Easterbrook, Frank 247, 301–302, 417, 418
Easterly, William 630
EAW *see* employment-at-will
EBM *see* evidence-based theory of management
"eco–economic ethics" 600
eco-efficiency 384
economic citizen virtues 211
economic crisis 308, 393–409; auto industry bailout 399, 402; ethics of policy response 403; financial industry bailout 399–402, 405, 407; housing policy and political interests 404–405; political capitalism 405–406, 407; *see also* financial crisis
economic development/growth 48, 327, 330, 337, 338; Africa 592, 627–628, 630, 631, 632–633; Brundtland Report 382, 383; Central Europe and Russia 592, 666; China 597, 601–602, 603–604; consumerism 616–617; impact of bribery on 578, 580–582, 586; income inequality 620; South Asia 606–607
economic policy 393, 394, 395–399, 402, 403–405
economic theory of regulation 364
economics 32, 42, 394; academic discipline of 221; contribution to business ethics 222, 290–305; evolutionary 335–336; innovation

307, 326, 327–330; Integrative Economic Ethics 166, 204–219; rational choice theory 295–300; social contract theory 99; subjective theory of value 497
Economist Intelligence Unit (EIU) 175
Edelman Public Relations 510–511
Edquist, Charles 336
education 6, 18, 60–76, 544, 546, 553; Africa 625, 626; Central Europe and Russia 661–662; content of business ethics education 63–65; history of business ethics 12–15; Latin America 647, 650; moral leaders 668; moral sense and commitment 67–70; opposition to business education 40; purpose of business education 55, 62–63; self-deception and moral blindness 70–72; South Asia 608; stakeholder thinking 197–199; stand-alone or integrated 65; teaching methods 66–67; timing of exposure 66; training compared with 60–62; university culture 65–66
Eells, Richard 13
effectiveness 447, 448, 453
efficiency: China 596–597; competing values framework 453; cultural differences 566; eco-efficiency 384; financial practices 344; government failure 364; management theories 447, 448; modernization theory 564; neoclassical economics 327, 328, 525; rent seeking 368; shareholder capitalism 339; utilitarianism 89; see also Pareto efficiency
efficiency wages 297
egalitarianism: Central Europe and Russia 661; China 596, 598; compensation 479; labor theory of value 496; servant leadership 434; South Africa 636; subjective egalitarian duties 497–498; Trompenaars 561, 562; see also equality
egoism 28, 68, 82, 85, 292, 450; agency theory 227; consequentialism 80, 83; cultural differences 567; entrepreneurship 281; ethical climate 469; ethical judgments 565; managers 452; Russia 567; social contract theory 102; Ubuntu 634; see also self-interest; selfishness
Einstein, Albert 606
EITI see Extractive Industries Transparency Initiative
El Salvador 645
Elenkov, D.S. 566–567
elimination 45
Eliot, T.S. 199
elites 24, 42; Africa 629–630; Central Europe and Russia 660; corruption 586; economic crisis 404, 405–406, 407
emancipation 277, 279, 280, 283
Emmons, W.R. 398
emotions 461–462, 511–512, 561
employees 412, 459, 470, 474–489; compensation 478–480; ethical culture 463–470; ethics and compliance programs 462–463; exploitation 490–505; firing and quitting 476–478; freedom of contract 474–475; hiring 475–476; management ethics 412, 453; management theories 448, 449; meaningful work 480–481; privacy 482–484; selection 463, 465; as shareholders 619; whistleblowing 484–486; see also labor
employers 32, 45; compliance programs 462–463; employee ethics and rights 412, 474–489; see also corporations; firms
employment-at-will (EAW) 44–45, 476–477
empowerment 139; leadership 435, 441; shareholders 48, 411, 418–420
endangered species 380, 389
Endangered Species Act (1973) 380
energy use 384
Engels, Friedrich 229, 658
England 244, 337; see also United Kingdom
English law 240, 611, 614
Enlightenment 10, 14, 44–45, 339
Enron 362, 485, 524, 526, 527, 573, 609
enterprise association 41, 48, 51
entity shielding 247–248, 252
entity theories 243, 244–246, 248–250, 252, 423, 424
entrepreneurship 39, 116–127, 199, 222, 275–289, 331; conceptions of 276–278; core elements of 279–280; ethical 280–285; innovation 327, 329–330, 334; Locke/Rousseau narratives 52; social 47; virtuous intent 78
environmental determinism 48
environmental issues 308, 376–392; alternative finance 353; barriers to global business ethics 552; business ethics education 64, 65; China 600, 602; concept of sustainability 386–389; concept of the Environment 48; Corporate Social Responsibility 171; Gandhi 616; Latin America 643–644, 654; marketing 513, 514, 517; markets 377–381; sustainable development 381–386; UN Convention Against Corruption 582; utilitarianism 91; see also sustainability
environmentalism 12–13, 32, 382, 388, 616
Epicureans 24–25, 30
Epicurus 84, 91–92
epistemological realism 41
equality: Central Europe and Russia 661; China 594, 602; economics 295; environmental values 381; Gandhi 612, 616; gender 132; innovation 327; Islamic finance 354; Rousseauean equality narrative 49, 50–51, 52; see also egalitarianism
essentialism 131–132, 133
Estonia 667
ethical awareness 62, 460–462, 468, 470
ethical banking 353
ethical climate 439, 460, 469, 632
ethical culture 16, 64, 412, 463–470

681

Index

ethical dilemmas 459, 524; *see also* moral dilemmas
ethical egoism 83; *see also* egoism
ethical fading 71, 461, 468
ethical leadership 16, 64–65, 433, 437, 439, 441, 455, 463–464; *see also* leadership
ethical reasoning 15, 17, 23; AACSB standards 546; business ethics education 63; feminist ethics 135; integrative social contracts theory 105
ethical relativism *see* relativism
EthicalSystems.org 67
ethics 45, 46; categories of economic 206; economic outcomes 394, 403, 406; leadership 431, 432–433, 441; major theories 450–452, 456; training 60–62; *see also* business ethics education; moral philosophy; moral theories; morality
ethics officers 548–549
Ethiopia 625, 626
ethnic diversity 630, 631–632; *see also* race
Europe: business ethics education 546, 553; integration of Central Europe and Russia 657, 667–668; just cause dismissal 477; particularism and universalism 562; shareholder democracy 418; social enterprises 265–269, 271n8; stakeholder-orientation 638n9
European Business Ethics Network 546, 661
European Commission 171
European Union (EU): Accounting Directive 532; anti-market advocates 39; Bologna Process 662; company forms 265; gender equality 132; influence on Central Europe and Russia 658, 667, 668; social enterprises 271n8
euvoluntary exchange 116–117, 118, 125
Evan, W. 234
evidence-based theory of management (EBM) 448–449
evolutionary economics 335–336
evolutionary psychology 456
executive pay 16, 48, 52, 418, 419–420, 422, 423, 478
expectations 439–440, 441
expertise 42, 45, 54
explication 6, 39, 51–54, 55
exploitation 11, 362, 412, 490–505; barriers to global business ethics 552; capitalist 32; communist society 659; definition of 491; management theories 447; MBA Oath 203; relations of production 601; rent seeking 368, 370, 371
exploration 5–6, 39, 45–51, 54
external goods 138, 143–144
externalities 34, 229, 333, 351; environmental issues 377, 383, 384; utility maximization 362, 366
extortion 574, 585, 644, 656

Extractive Industries Transparency Initiative (EITI) 583, 587n5
extraterritoriality 549–550

fading 71, 461, 468
Faillo, Marco 109
fair market value (FMV) 498–499
"fair play" 68
fairness 10, 299, 343–344, 565; bargaining problem 108; board diversity 421; Buddhism 160; Christianity 152; compensation 478, 491, 495–496; cultural differences 566; distributive justice 48; economic outcomes 394; efficiency linked to 596; fair distribution 234; finance 346, 347, 351, 355; game theory 297; gift giving 576; Integrative Economic Ethics 209; marketing 507, 509–511; moral foundations theory 456; Rawls 107; role models 467; social contract theory 108; utilitarianism 90
faith *see* religion
Falkenburg, Loren 134
Fayol, Henri 16, 448
FCPA *see* Foreign Corrupt Practices Act
Federal Housing Association (FHA) 395
Federal Reserve Bank 398–399, 400, 407
Federal Trade Commission (FTC) 511, 513
feminine ethic 133
"feminine firms" 136–137
femininity 135, 137, 142, 560
feminist ethics 78, 88, 131–147, 452; business ethics and 134–136, 139–140; ethics of care 133–134, 136–137; virtue 137–139; Wenger 140–143
Fenger, H.J.M. 664–665
Ferguson, Benjamin 412, 490–505
Ferrell, O.C. 282
FHA *see* Federal Housing Association
Fiat 402
fiduciary duty: activist shareholders 420; benefit corporations 261; boards of directors 416; CEOs 423; contractual terms 173; corporate governance 246; duties to employees 412; economics 221; employee compensation 501–503; executive pay 48; fairness 344; management theories 449–450; managers 235; property rights 314; social enterprises 264; stakeholder theory 233, 234; stakeholder thinking 184–187, 189–190, 193, 196, 198, 200n1
Field, Justice 244
filial piety 8, 161
finance 307, 343–358; alternative 353–354; business ethics education 64, 65; derivatives 349; intermediaries 344, 346–347, 352; investment funds 349; Islamic 354; markets 344, 351–353; risk management 350–351; securitization 348, 350; types of banks 348; *see also* accounting

Index

financial crisis 65, 131, 308, 343, 393–409, 573; auto industry bailout 399, 402; ethics of policy response 403; financial industry bailout 399–402, 405, 407; hedge funds 349; housing policy and political interests 404–405; political capitalism 405–406, 407; profit maximization 584
financial fraud 644, 655
financial industry bailout 399–402, 405, 407
firing 476–478
firms 411; culture of business ethics 668; Integrative Economic Ethics 207; labor exploitation 490–491, 493–503; motivation 361–363, 365–367; size of 478; social contract theory 97, 98–99; transaction cost theory 223, 225–228, 235, 298; *see also* corporations; employers
"first fundamental theory of welfare economics" 299–300
Fischel, Daniel 247, 301–302, 417, 418
Fisher, Dann 65
Fleming, A.I.M. 528
Flyvbjerg, Bent 565, 569
FMV *see* fair market value
Fogarty, Tim 525
food 384, 385, 388, 517
Ford: lobbying 359, 360; Pinto scandal 13, 71, 290, 300; rent seeking 370; stealth marketing 510
Foreign Corrupt Practices Act (FCPA) 544, 546, 549–550, 578, 580–581, 586n2
Foucault, Michel 8, 47
four Cs 453–454
"4 Ps" 506–507
Foxconn 548
France: cooperatives 266, 271n10; corporations 244; cultural values 557; liberty 337; particularism 562
Francés-Gómez, Pedro 77–78, 96–112
Francisco de Vitoria 26
fraud: Central Europe and Russia 662, 663, 667; Latin America 643, 644, 649, 653, 655
free markets 50, 328; barriers to global business ethics 552; Lockean liberty narrative 49; social contract theory 97; utilitarianism 450–451; *see also* market economies; markets
free-riding 319
free will 312, 313, 424
Freeden, Michael 48
freedom: Central Europe and Russia 668; employment relationship 475, 477, 486; entrepreneurship 279, 283; financial markets 351; Integrative Economic Ethics 210; stakeholder thinking 191, 192; utilitarianism 89–90; workplace democracy 482; *see also* liberty
freedom of contract 474–475, 486
Freeman, Chris 331–332

Freeman, R. Edward: corporate management 254n9; definition of a stakeholder 185; fair contracts 234; separation thesis 15, 232; social contract theory 97, 100, 106; stakeholder theory 13, 14, 16, 34, 99, 174, 186, 235, 366, 545
French, Peter 170, 180n1, 249, 250, 254n13
Friedman, Marilyn 137
Friedman, Milton 14, 53, 173, 290–291, 300, 330, 359–360; criticism of 30; profit maximization 257, 366, 373n3, 373n4, 502, 584; rent seeking 370; "rules of the game" 321, 578; shareholders 449
Friedman, Thomas 547
FTC *see* Federal Trade Commission
fungibility thesis 493, 494–495, 503

Galbraith, John Kenneth 13, 512
game theory 100–101, 108, 222, 234, 295–298, 299
Gandhi, Mohandas Karamchand 592, 606, 607–608, 610–620
Garff, P. 65, 66
Garriga, Elisabet 172
Gates, Bill 119, 330, 619–620
Gates, Darin 6, 60–76
Gauthier, David 82, 96, 291, 297
GCB *see* Global Corruption Barometer
gender: board diversity 421; critical management studies 449; discrimination 98, 105, 131; gender differences 134, 136, 140; hiring discrimination 476; leadership 440–441; masculine and feminine cultures 560; stereotypes 135, 515
General Dynamics 545
General Mills 385
General Motors (GM) 13, 399, 402, 408n7, 547
"general theory of second best" 300
generosity 25
genetically modified foods 388
Gensler, Harry 70
Gentile, Mary 62–63, 516–517
George, Bill 435
Germany: corporate citizenship 207; corporations 244; cultural values 557; Integrative Economic Ethics 215; leadership 441; social market economy 205, 214; universalism 562
Gewirth, Alan 191, 195
Ghosh, Subratesh 618
Ghoshal, S. 227
Gichure, Christine 629
Gierke, Otto von 245
gifts 17, 465, 569, 575–577
Gilbert, Dirk Ulrich 105–106, 204–205
Gilens, Martin 394–395
Gilligan, Carol 132, 133, 136, 142
Gini, Al 223, 433, 437
Gino, F. 462
Gioia, Dennis 13

683

Giri, V.V. 615
Giving Voice to Values 66
Global Compact 17, 172, 175, 548, 551
Global Corruption Barometer (GCB) 644–646
Global Leadership and Organizational Behavior Effectiveness (GLOBE) study 441, 556, 561, 563
Global Reporting Initiative (GRI) 382, 387, 582, 583
globalization 48, 162, 541, 543–555; Central Europe and Russia 592, 657; China 602; corruption 542, 573; governance gaps 178–179
goals 448
God 28, 29, 337, 576; Christianity 151–152, 155, 157–158; Judaism 148–151; Lockean liberty narrative 49; medieval philosophy 41–42; rules 80; virtue ethics 82
Goel, P. 610
Golden Rule 69–70, 187
Goldman, Eric 508
goodness 193, 198, 450
Goodpaster, Kenneth 165–166, 173, 184–203
goods, production of 230–232
Googins, B. 176
Gordon, Robert J. 338–339
Goss, D. 277, 279, 280
Gould, Carol 233
governance: Africa 626–628, 636, 637; alternative business organizations 222; Community Interest Companies 268; cooperatives 266; Corporate Social Responsibility 177, 178–179; definition of 415; ethics as governance mechanism 301; financial institutions 346; good 583, 625, 631; *see also* corporate governance
government: China 600, 603; corruption 645–646; economic policy 393, 395–399, 406, 407; government failure 361, 363–367, 368, 372, 373n5; human rights responsibility 179; India 609; lobbying and rent seeking 127, 359–360, 367–372; Lockean liberty narrative 49, 52; regulation 44, 45, 360, 373n2; role of the state 615; Rousseauean equality narrative 50–51, 52; *see also* politics
Goyder, George 614, 619
Grameen Bank 258, 354
Gratchev, Mikhail 281
Greece 266, 271n10, 562
greed 153, 298, 329, 343, 351, 420, 585
Greeks, ancient 8–9, 10, 24, 41
Green, Mark 13
Green, R.M. 8, 372n1
Greene, Joshua D. 462
Greenleaf, Robert 433, 434
Greenpeace 388
greenwashing 18
Gresham, L.G. 282
GRI *see* Global Reporting Initiative

Guha, Ramachandra 616
Gustafson, Andrew 77, 79–95
Guzman, R.A. 116–117

Habermas, Jürgen 105, 204, 207–209, 212
Hacker, Jacob S. 394–395
Haggis, Jane 564
Haidt, Jonathan 456, 461–462
Haier 601
Hambrick, Donald 416
Hammurabi, King 8, 573
Hampden-Turner, C. 610
Handy, Charles 424
Hannafey, F.T. 276
Hansmann, Henry 247–248
Hanson, Kirk O. 541, 543–555
happiness: Aristotle 24–25, 26, 82, 452; capabilities approach 27; consequentialism 79; Lockean liberty narrative 50; social contract theory 88; utilitarianism 83, 84–85, 89, 91, 92, 207
Harberger, Arnold 369
hard work 7–8, 10, 560
Hardin, Garrett 296
Hare, Richard 46
harmony 635
Harris, J. 232
Hart, H.L.A. 228
Harter, Susan 435
Hartman, Edwin 27, 64, 85, 89, 115
Harvard Business School 40, 62, 544, 546
Hasnas, John 186, 229, 233, 251
Hayek, F.A. 43, 51, 52, 54
Hayek, Friedrich 14, 254n16, 291, 292, 330, 331, 345, 364, 512, 611
hazards 492
health and safety 379, 380, 492–493, 532–533, 644
Health Impact Fund 321
Heath, Eugene 1–3, 5–6
Heath, Joseph 15, 91, 92, 186; business as "criminogenic" environment 226; economics 222, 290–305; market failures 367, 368; principal-agent relationship 228; rationality 227
Heclo, Hugh 195, 197
hedge funds 349, 420
Heermance, Edgar 12
Hegel, G.W.F. 11, 54, 312, 313–314
Heilman, Madeline 440
Hellman, Deborah 476
Hendershott, R. 422
Heracleous, Loizos 417, 424
Hernandez, Monica 510
Herstein, Ram 609, 610
Hesiod 41
Hesse, Herman 434
Heugens, P.P.M.A.R. 99
heuristic contractarian business ethics 97–98, 106–107

Hewlett-Packard 547
hierarchy of needs 15
high frequency trading 352
high/low context societies 561
Hill, Thomas 46
Hinduism 9, 159–160, 606, 607, 609, 611
hiring 455, 475–476, 669n7
Hisrich, Robert 281
history of business ethics 5, 7–22, 64, 65, 599
Hitler, Adolf 432, 435
Hobbes, Thomas 14, 28–29, 31, 42; consequentialism 91; egoism 83; personal survival 43; social contract 35, 82, 85, 96; state of nature 227, 296
Hofstede, Geert 69, 556–561, 563, 564, 565, 566
Hohfeld, W.N. 310, 323n1
Holcombe, Randall G. 308, 393–409
Holladay, Sherry 137
Homer 8, 41
Honda 121
honesty 114, 157, 343; Central Europe and Russia 665, 668; Confucianism 161; financial institutions 347; leadership 463; moral development 437; performance evaluation 466; utilitarianism 90
Hong Kong 441, 547, 566, 567
Hoopes, James 39
Horwitz, Morton J. 244
hostility to business 24, 39–41
House, Robert 561
housing 393, 395–398, 401, 403, 404–405, 406–407
Hsieh, Nien-hê 85, 88
hubris 438, 439
Hughes, Thomas P. 332
human nature 25, 31, 143, 227
human relations theory 448, 453–454
human resource management 560
human resources (HR) 63–64
human rights 14, 48, 387, 390, 529–534, 551; accounting 413, 524; China 563, 564; Corporate Social Responsibility 172, 178–179; decision algorithms 568; environmental goods 378–379, 381; MBA Oath 199, 203; UN Convention Against Corruption 582; undermined by bribery 578; United States 564; *see also* rights
humanity 437
Hume, David 5, 30, 53; justice 315; laws 230; non-theoretical reflection 51; property rights 229, 314, 323n8, 323n9; sympathy 43; utilitarianism 35
Hungary 657, 666, 667
Hutcheson, Frances 30, 80
Hutchins, Robert Maynard 40
hypernorms 88, 104, 105, 106, 451

IABS *see* International Association for Business and Society
Iamiceli, P. 266
IASB *see* International Accounting Standards Board
IBM 557
ICAEW *see* Institute of Chartered Accountants of England and Wales
ideal communication communities 204, 206, 213, 216
ideal speech situation 209, 213
idealism 11, 15, 43
identity 140–141, 142; corporations 239, 248, 423; ethnic 631–632; feminist ethics 131, 135, 144; moral 437; shared 635; Ubuntu 634
ideology 47
Iliffe, John 628
IMF *see* International Monetary Fund
impartiality 576
incentive pay 423
income inequality 394, 598, 599, 600–601, 620
incorporation 242–243, 244, 246
independence 528–529, 532
India 9, 553, 591–592, 606, 607; Buddhism 160; business ethics as a practice 609–610; business ethics education 608; Corporate Social Responsibility 608; corruption 609, 610; Gandhi's trusteeship framework 610–620
individualism 62, 344; Christianity 628; cultural differences 559, 560, 561, 563, 564; entrepreneurship 276, 277; Europe 638n9
Industrial Revolution 326, 331–332, 339
industrialization 5, 616, 618
industry concentration 34
inequalities: Aquinas 154; capitalism 40; China 600–601; economic crisis 405; feminist ethics 135, 144; gender 560; income 394, 598, 599, 600–601, 620; pay 131, 132, 135; power distance 558, 565; Rawls 33; rise in 339; Rousseauean equality narrative 50, 51; social categorization 440
inflation 345
influence 431–432, 434
informal sector 633
informed consent 494
Inglehart, Ronald 563–564, 666
innovation 119, 307, 326–342; alternative finance 353; board diversity 421; China 594, 598; competing values framework 453; entrepreneurship 277, 278; institutionalization of 333–337; interactive approach 330–333; management theories 447; marketing 507; neoclassical economics 327–330; open systems theory 448
Institute for Business Ethics 546
Institute of Chartered Accountants of England and Wales (ICAEW) 526
institutional approaches 174, 535

685

institutionalism 362
institutions 307, 337, 615; Africa 630–631; Central Europe and Russia 663, 666, 668; financial 346–348, 354, 399–402, 405, 407, 413; institutional design 371–372; social contract theory 97
instrumental approaches 174
Integrative Economic Ethics 166, 204–219
integrative social contracts theory (ISCT) 34, 77–78, 103–106, 108, 165, 173, 205
integrity 68–69, 88–89, 299, 343, 582–585; accounting 524, 527–528, 529, 532, 534, 535; financial institutions 347; Integrative Economic Ethics 208–209, 211; Islam 158; leadership 441, 463; management ethics 454; marketing 507; MBA Oath 203; moral development 437; performance evaluation 466; role models 467; servant leadership 433; utilitarianism 90
intellectual property 63, 307, 318–321
intent: corporate intentionality 170, 249–250, 254n14; Kantian ethics 87; profit seekers 113, 116, 122–125
inter-generational justice 383
interactional perspective 535
interest 9, 26, 27, 156, 159, 354; *see also* usury
interest rates 398–399
internal goods 138, 143
"internal morality" 195–196, 197
internal process theory 448, 453–454
International Accounting Standards Board (IASB) 533
International Association for Business and Society (IABS) 546, 661
International Business Leaders Initiative on Human Rights 530
International Christian Union of Business Executives (UNIAPAC) 546, 649
International Monetary Fund (IMF) 383, 574, 582
International Society of Business, Ethics and Economics (ISBEE) 546
International Standards Association 582
International Telephone and Telegraph Corporation (ITT) 580
internet 334, 513
intersubjectivity 138–139, 142
investment banks 348
investment funds 349
investors 348, 349, 353, 355, 418; Central Europe and Russia 664; private equity 420; social enterprises 264–265, 269, 270; social investor movement 547; *see also* shareholders
"invisible hand" 222, 291–292, 293, 299–301, 328, 366; efficient outcomes 367; free market ideology 552; Mandeville 28, 29; utilitarianism 30
iPhone 514
Ireland 441

ISBEE *see* International Society of Business, Ethics and Economics
ISCT *see* integrative social contracts theory
Islam 9, 17, 158–159, 552; Africa 628; hard work 8; Islamic finance 354; South Asia 607
Ismaeel, Muatasim 158–159
Italy 265–267, 269, 271n9, 271n11, 562, 646
ITT *see* International Telephone and Telegraph Corporation

Jackson, Terence 541–542, 556–572
Jacques, Elliot 16
Jaggar, Alison 88, 132
Jamaica 645
James, William 606
Japan 39, 121, 544, 547; collectivism 559; ethical judgments 566, 567; management practices 299; masculinity 560
Jaworski, Peter 368–369, 373n5
Jensen, Michael 226, 245, 302, 482
Jesus Christ 84, 151–152, 153, 156, 434
Jewish moneylender stereotype 10
job relevant information 483–484
Jobs, Steve 121, 330
Johansson, A.W. 278
John Lewis Partnership 619
Johnson & Johnson 465
Johnson, F. Ernest 12
Johnson, L. 188
joint stock 241, 243, 246
Jones, Thomas 282, 524
Jonker, Jan 171
Jonsen, Albert 40
journals 15, 608, 647–648, 650
Joyner, Brenda 282
JPMorgan 400
Juan de Mariana 26
Judaism 9, 148–151, 158, 159, 337
judges 576
just cause dismissal 476–477, 478
just price 9, 26
justice 92, 343, 534, 565; Aquinas 154; Chinese business ethics 600; Christianity 152, 158; Confucianism 161; cultural differences 566, 567; distributive 48, 101–102, 153–154, 295, 296, 317, 525, 596, 598; divine 576; economic 383, 385; "fair play" 68; feminist ethics 144; financial institutions 346, 347; Hume 315; institutional perspective 535; Integrative Economic Ethics 208, 209; inter-generational 383; Islam 158, 354; Judaism 151; Kantian ethics 86; leadership 437; Luther 155; procedural 433; property rights 316, 317; Rawls 14, 33–34, 109, 207, 403; utilitarianism 84, 85, 89, 90; virtue ethics 138, 452

Kagan, R.A. 362
Kağıtçıbaşı, Çiğdem 563
Kaldis, Byron 1–3, 77–78, 411–413, 541–542, 591–592
Kamal, S. 516
Kaneda, M. 373n3
Kant, Immanuel 5, 17, 30–31, 46, 54, 215, 451; applied philosophy 46; autonomy 481; deontology 606; dignity 35; ethical orientation 206; Formula of Humanity as an End 70; instrumentalism 16; intention 87; Mill on 91; negative influence of 11; non-consequentialism 81–82; rules 80; social contract theory 97; stakeholder theory 34; transcendental reason 43
Kantian ethics 14–15, 46, 251, 451; categorical imperative 204; Integrative Economic Ethics 206, 210; management ethics 453; non-consequentialism 80, 81–82, 85, 86–87; Rawls 34; stakeholder theory 366; Ubuntu 634; *see also* deontology
Karau, Steven 441
karma 9, 160
Kaufmann, Daniel 663
Keeley, Michael C. 107
Kelekar, R. 615
Kellerman, Barbara 437–438
Kemp, L. 563
Kennedy, Paul 628
Kenya 553
Khomba, James 627
Khurana, Rakesh 61, 199, 506
King Reports 627, 633, 638n14
kingdom of ends 81, 86–87
Kirzner, Israel 118–119, 275, 276–278, 280, 331
Kish-Gephart, Jennifer 469
Klein, Naomi 17–18
Kline, Stephen J. 332–333
Kline, William 221, 223–238
Knight, Frank 276, 279, 293, 329
Kohlberg, Lawrence 15, 437, 460, 528
Kolko, Gabriel 405
Koop, Christel 308, 359–375
Korea 567
Korsgaard, Christine 81
Kotchian, Carl 579
KPMG 533
Kraakman, Reinier 247
Kramer, Mark 176, 177
Kramer, Samuel Noah 7
Kretzschmar, L. 637n1
Krueger, Anne 609
Kuhn, Thomas 332
Küng, Hans 551

La Polar 643
labor 32–33, 42; Christian 53; communist society 659; exploitation 412, 490–505; Gandhi 614, 617; property rights 312, 313–314; respect of 98; Smith 327–328; *see also* employees; work
labor theory of value 32, 496–497, 504n8
Laczniak, G.R. 507
Ladd, J. 254n14
laissez faire approach 493–494, 500, 503
Lan, L.L. 417, 424
Lancaster, Kelvin 300
Landes, David S. 337
"landscapes of practice" 132–133
Langlois, L. 63
Langtry, B. 185, 186
language 461, 463, 468
Laos 608
Laozi 160–161
Lapointe, C. 63
Lasch, Christopher 438
Laski, Harold 244
Late Scholastics 26–27
Latin America 592, 641–656
Latin American Association of Ethics, Business and Economics (ALENE) 648, 650
Latvia 667
Lautermann, Christian 222, 275–289
Lavallée, Emmanuelle 633
law: bribery and corruption 574, 579–581, 631; Central Europe and Russia 663–664, 668; common property 240; compliance with 362, 462–463, 549, 550, 552; corporate 246, 301–302; employment 475, 476–477; English 240, 611, 614; ethical climate 469; explication 52–53; financial 344; human rights 179, 530–531; impartiality of judges 576; innovation 326, 336–337; Islam 158; Latin America 649, 650; law-abiding nature of firms 363; legality 193; Locke/Rousseau narratives 52; marketing 507, 508–509; monotheistic religions 162; non-consequentialism 79; property and trade 230; property rights 310, 317, 318; utilitarianism 89; *see also* regulation
Lay, Ken 438
leadership 16, 197, 411–412, 430–446; authentic 435–436; business ethics education 62, 64, 65; Central Europe and Russia 668; character of leaders 437–438; definition of 431–432; ethical culture 455, 463–464; management theories 448; servant 433–434; transformational 434–435, 436, 463; values 188
learning: innovation 332; organizational 139, 448; Wenger's theory 140–143, 144
Lebow, Victor 617
left/right debate 49
legal responsibility 169
legalism 14
legitimacy: Central Europe and Russia 662; discourse ethics 211; entrepreneurs 282; finance 346; Integrative Economic Ethics 206–207,

208, 209, 212; organizational 363; professions 526
Lehman Brothers 400
Lenin, V.I. 658
Lesotho 633
Levi Strauss & Co. 548
Levinson, S. 669n6
Levitt, Steven 294
li 17
Li, Yining 596–597
Libby, Theresa 527
liberal duties 499–500
liberalism 13, 284; Integrative Economic Ethics 205, 207, 210, 215; social market economy 214; Western economic 628, 629
liberty 233, 337, 565; China 594; Lockean liberty narrative 49–50, 51, 52; moral foundations theory 456; property rights 310; utilitarianism 89, 90; *see also* freedom
Libor scandal 573
Licht, Amir 421
Liebowitz, Stan J. 395, 396, 397
life-cycle responsibility 384
lifeworld 207
Lim, Ming 78, 131–147
limited liability 241–243, 244, 246, 247, 252, 259–260, 265; *see also* LC3s
Lipman-Blumen, Jean 437–438
Lippert-Rasmussen, Kasper 476
Lippke, Richard 32–33
Lipsey, Richard 295, 300
Lithuania 667
living wages 23, 492, 495
lobbying 321, 343, 359–360; Central Europe and Russia 663; housing policy 404; political capitalism 406; rent seeking 124, 126, 367–371
Lochner, Joseph 475
Locke, John 5, 9, 14, 31, 35, 53; conquest of nature 32; human labor 42; liberty narrative 49–50, 51, 52; property rights 310–311, 312, 313–314; social contract 29, 35, 96
Lockheed Corporation 544, 579
locus of control 460, 561–562
long wave theory 331–332
Longenecker, J.G. 276
Lorch, Alexander 166, 204–219
love: Central Europe and Russia 665; Christianity 158; feminist ethics 144; Gandhi 616; self-love and love of others 187; servant leadership 434; virtue ethics 138
low-profit limited liability companies (LC3s) 259–260, 264, 265, 270n3
loyalty 299, 459, 485–486, 561, 562, 567
Lu, Dezhi 601
Lu, Xiaohe 597, 599, 602
Luis de Molina 26
Lundvall, Bengt-Åke 336

Lütge, Christoph 99, 100–101, 107
Luther, Martin 154–155, 156, 157
luxury 10
lying 82, 84, 158, 160, 282–283, 438; *see also* deception; dishonesty

Ma, Zhengzhong 224
MacDonald, C. 517
Machan, T.R. 278
Machen, Arthur 244
Machiavelli, Niccolò 5, 9–10, 16, 27–28
Machiavellianism 431, 460, 566–567
MacIntyre, Alasdair 27, 43, 115, 284; neo-Aristotelian ethics 46; non-consequentialism 80; virtue 127, 132, 138, 143
Mackey, John 185
Madison, James 42
Maitland, Frederick 244
Maitland, Ian 227
Malaysia 566, 608
Maldives 606, 607
management: cross-cultural management ethics 541–542, 556–572; global business ethics 552–553; Locke/Rousseau narratives 52; Management as a discipline 40, 41; management ethics 412, 447, 452–457, 459; as a profession 199; theories of 447–450, 453–454, 456
managerial approaches 174, 362
managers 362, 412, 459, 470; appropriateness of management style 559; banks 347; Central Europe and Russia 659, 669n2; character 452; common sense theory 451; corporate ethics programs 548–549; corporate governance 419; cross-cultural management ethics 557, 569; decision algorithms 568; efficiency 525; ethical awareness 460; ethical leadership 464; India 610; management ethics 447, 452, 453–456; management theories 448; moral foundations theory 456; responsibility 449–450; self-interest 416–417
mancgeres (retail merchants) 114, 115, 116
Mandela, Nelson 638n17
Mandeville, Bernard 5, 27, 28, 29, 291–292
Mansell, Samuel 108–109
Mao, Yushi 596–597
March, J.G. 361
Marcoux, Alexei 1–3, 5–6, 165–166, 221–222, 307–308; business 223, 228; fiduciary duty 189–190, 195; stakeholder theory 186, 194, 323n2; veil of ignorance 234
market economies 42, 291, 377; Central Europe and Russia 592, 660; China 593, 595–596, 597, 600, 602–603, 604; Gandhi's trusteeship framework 592, 610–611, 618; Integrative Economic Ethics 207, 208, 213–214; prices 292; self-interest 293; Smith 328; Third Way 618; *see also* free markets; markets

market failures 92, 301, 361, 363–367, 368, 371, 380
market forces 113
market value 193, 198
marketing 63–64, 412, 506–522; behavioral ethics 515–516; consumer sovereignty 516; deception 508–509; definition of 506; false values 514–515; intrusiveness 512–514; manipulation 511–512; stakeholder 516–517; unfairness 509–511; wastefulness 514
markets: Africa 627; China 595–596, 597, 598; environmental responsibilities 376, 377–381, 390; fair market value 499; financial 344, 351–353; "first fundamental theory of welfare economics" 299–300; Gandhi's trusteeship framework 610; imperfect 479, 501; Locke/Rousseau narratives 52; rules 228–229; social contract theory 97; undermined by bribery 578; *see also* free markets; market economies
Marshall, Alfred 335
Marshall, Chief Justice 244
Martin, Charles L. 528
Martin, Kelly D. 469
Martin, Roger 584
Marx, Karl 5, 10–11, 31, 32–33, 35; capital 601; Central Europe and Russia 658, 659; labor theory of value 496–497; needs-based approach to economic justice 383; negative externalities 229
Marxism 32–33, 40–41, 504n8; Central Europe and Russia 659, 661; China 599; critical management studies 449; feminist ethics 135; firms' duties 496; property rights 317
masculinity 135, 137, 142, 528, 560
Mashaw, Jerry L. 531
Maslow, Abraham 15
material ethics 204
materialism 514, 563, 620
Matsui, A. 373n3
Mattel 225
Mattessich, Richard 231
Maugham, Somerset 118
Mauritius 633
May, D.R. 63
Mayhew, B.W. 63
Mazars 532
Mazrui, Ali 629
MBA Oath 199, 203
McBride Principles 548
McCall, John 482
McClelland, David 560
McCloskey, Deirdre 89, 115, 134–135, 138, 143, 337, 452
McCoy, Bowen 197
McDonald, David 636
McDonald, G.M. 566

McDonnell Douglas 545
McDonough, Bill 384
McKabe, D. 469
McLean, Bethany 65
McMahon, Christopher 48
McPhail, Ken 413, 523–540
Meadowcroft, John 308, 359–375
meaningful work 480–481
means and ends: environmental issues 378; Hobbes 28–29; Integrative Economic Ethics 213; Kantian ethics 70, 81, 86, 451; money 345; stakeholder theory 34
Means, Gardiner 227, 298, 418
Meckling, William 226, 245
media 641–642, 644, 652–656
medication 318–319, 320–321
medieval philosophy 41–42
Mees, Bernard 5, 7–22
Melé, Domènec 172
Mengzi (Mencius) 8, 593, 596, 598
merchants 24, 114, 230
Merck & Co Inc. 320
Messick, D.M. 71
Metz, Thaddeus 634, 635, 636
Mexico 641–644, 645, 646–647, 649
Meyer, John 363
microfinance 258, 353–354, 356n13
Microsoft 620
"middle way" 33
middlemen 117–118, 120
Midgley, Mary 200n7
Milgram experiment 438–439
Mill, John Stuart 43, 54, 295; applied philosophy 46; Aristotle's influence on 91–92; consequentialism 80, 91; utilitarianism 14, 33, 35, 83, 84–85, 89–90, 92, 606
Miller, Peter 523
Mingers, John 204–205
Minow, Nell 415
Mirvis, P. 176
misallocations, correction of 118–119, 120, 124
misconduct 462–463, 467, 626, 644, 649
Mises, Ludwig von 275, 276, 278, 330
misrepresentation 644
Mitchell, R.K. 321
Mitchell, William 370
MNCs *see* multinational companies
modeling 65
modernity 31
modernization: China 600–601; India 609; modernization theory 556, 558, 563–564, 568, 569
money 10, 307, 343, 345; Aquinas on 154; Aristotle on 25; Christianity 152, 153; Islamic finance 354; Locke on 29; *see also* wealth
money laundering 343, 644, 662, 667
monism 452–455

689

Index

Monks, Robert 415
monopolies 329, 369, 643, 663
Montesquieu, Charles-Louis de Secondat 53
Moore, Celia 461, 462
Moore, G.E. 194
Moore, Geoff 115
moral agency 169–171, 248–252; *see also* agency theory
moral awareness 62, 63, 65
moral blindness 70–72
moral capital 599, 601
moral commitment 67–70
moral consideration 192, 199
moral development 15, 282, 437, 454, 460, 524, 528
moral dilemmas 30, 67, 366, 459
moral disengagement 461
moral dumbfounding 461–462
moral foundations 456
moral free space 104–105, 551
moral hazard 345, 350, 363, 525
moral identity 437
moral insight 185, 187, 190, 193, 194, 196–197
moral judgments 68, 198, 200n7, 293, 460; Africa 635, 636; China 595–596; cultural differences 565–567; management ethics 454–455
moral myopia 515–516
moral personhood 170, 188, 192–193, 243, 249
moral philosophy 43, 67–68, 77, 191; *see also* moral theories
moral projection principle 188
moral psychology 89, 109
moral responsibility 168–170, 188; China 595, 599–600; corporate governance 411; Gandhi's trusteeship framework 614; management ethics 412; *see also* responsibility
moral theories 5, 77–78, 450–452, 456, 606; business ethics education 64, 67–68; China 599; monism versus pluralism 452–455; overview of 80–81; social contract theory 98; stakeholder theory 232–233; *see also* consequentialism; Kantian ethics; non-consequentialism; utilitarianism; virtue ethics
morality: Central Europe and Russia 668; deontological 293–294, 297; economics 294, 297; feminist ethics 136; Hinduism 159; Hobbes 28–29; integrative social contracts theory 104; "internal" 195–196, 197; Kant 30–31; leadership 432, 434, 435, 437; non-consequentialism 79; positivism 40; social contract theory 97; social nature of 43; utilitarianism 30; *see also* ethics
Moran, P. 227
Morgan, J.P. 126
Moriarty, Jeffrey 233, 412, 474–489
mortgages 393, 395–398, 401–402, 403–404, 406–407

Morton Thiokol 485
motivation: boards of directors 422; Buddhism 160; CEOs 423; firms 361–363, 365–367; Islam 159; leadership 441, 463; Mill 85; social contract theory 102; transformational leadership 434, 435
Mozambique 633
Müller-Armack, A. 214
multi-fiduciary view 189–190
multinational companies (MNCs) 543, 546; bribery and corruption 542, 573, 579, 582; Central Europe and Russia 663; corporate governance 416; cross-cultural management ethics 541–542; decision algorithms 567–568; human rights 530; South Asia 608; *see also* corporations
multistakeholder governance 266, 269, 271n6
Munger, Michael C. 78, 113–130
Munnell, A.H. 396
Murove, Munyaradzi Felix 628, 629
Murphy, Patrick 507, 508, 515, 516
Murphy, P.R. 63
Murthy, Narayana 631
mutuality 142, 158
Myanmar 608
Myrdal, Gunnar 617

Nader, Ralph 13, 14, 406
Nafziger, Wayne 629
Nagel, Thomas 46, 68, 534, 535
narcissism 438
Nash, J. 108
National Security Agency 485
National Semiconductor 250
nationalization 13–14
native advertising 510
natural resources 377, 378, 382, 383, 583, 613
nature 32, 43, 49, 82, 600; *see also* environmental issues
negative externalities 229, 377
negative leaders 437–438
negligence 492
negotiation 234, 235
Nehru, Jawaharlal 612, 617, 618
Neiman, Paul 101
Neimanis, G.J. 567
Nelson, K. 64
Nelson, Richard R. 331, 332
neo-Aristotelian ethics 43, 46
neo-Marxism 449
Neo-Platonism 148
neoclassical economics 307, 327–330, 497, 525
neoliberalism 14, 213–214, 636
Nepal 606, 607, 608
nepotism 559, 562, 564, 568, 574, 585, 662
Néron, Pierre-Yves 363
Netherlands 53, 337, 558

New York Stock Exchange 609
New Zealand 566
Newton, Isaac 42, 44
nexus-of-contracts theory 243, 245–246, 247, 252, 417, 423
NGOs *see* non-governmental organizations
Nider, Johannes 9
Nietzsche, Friedrich 17, 43
Nigeria 559, 627, 631
Nike Corporation 548
Niskanen, William A. 359, 360, 370
Nixon, Richard 544
Nocera, Joe 65
Nohria, Nitin 199, 506
non-consequentialism 77, 79–83, 85–89, 91–92, 451, 565; *see also* deontology; Kantian ethics; virtue ethics
non-governmental organizations (NGOs) 211, 382, 543, 548, 608, 649, 650
nonprofits 258–259, 263, 264, 265
Noonan, John 575, 577
Norman, Richard 196–197
Norman, Wayne 186, 363, 517
normative perspectives 174, 193–194, 198, 459; economics 294–295; Hofstede's theory 558; Integrative Economic Ethics 208, 213; leadership 432
norms 38–39, 42, 44, 298; Africa 592, 626, 628; bribery 574; Central Europe and Russia 663, 668; consensus 139; cultural differences 638n15; decision making 186; discourse ethics 204; ethical culture 463, 468; explication 51, 53, 54, 55; gender 441; hypernorms 88, 104, 105, 106, 451; institutional design 371; Integrative Economic Ethics 212; logic of appropriateness 361; material ethics 204; moral identity 144; ordoliberalism 215; rational choice theory 222; social contract theory 100, 102, 103–106, 108, 109
North, Douglass 228
Northern Ireland 548
Norway 337
Nozick, Robert 46, 49, 313, 408n2, 496–497
Nussbaum, Martha 27, 46, 385

Oakeshott, Michael 42, 43, 51, 52, 54
Obama, Barack 402
objectivity 137
obligations 576–577, 579; Africa 632; common sense theory 451; employees and employers 474; financial institutions 346, 347; Integrative Economic Ethics 208, 210; "internal morality" 195; Islam 159; Judaism 151; Kantian ethics 81, 451; social contract theory 97–98, 99, 102, 103, 107; to stakeholders 187, 190, 198; Trompenaars 562; whistleblowing 484; *see also* duties; fiduciary duty

Occupy Wall Street movement 401, 404, 405
OECD *see* Organization for Economic Cooperation and Development
Olson, J.P. 361
Olson, Mancur 296
O'Neil, Onora 46
online data 513
ontology 162
open innovation 336
"Open Question Argument" 194
open systems theory 448, 453–454
opportunities, seizing 280, 283
oppression 135–136
"order ethics" 107
ordoliberalism 205, 208, 214–215
Organization for Economic Cooperation and Development (OECD) 172, 175, 546, 574, 581, 584, 586n2, 646
organizational culture 16, 459; accounting 528; business ethics education 64, 65; contextual ethics 454–455; entrepreneurship 282; ethical culture 16, 64, 412, 463–470; ethical leadership 439; universities 65–66; utilitarianism 90
orientation 463, 465–466
"original position" 96, 105
Osigweh, Chimezei 134
outsourcing 52
Owen, Robert 11
owner shielding 247–248, 252
ownership 280–281, 309–311

Pacioli, Luca 230, 231
Packard, David 545
pain 30, 83–84
Paine, L.S. 186
Painter-Morland, Mollie 633
Pak, C.K. 566
Pakistan 547, 606, 607, 608
Palazzo, Guido 105, 171, 177, 205, 215
Paraguay 645
Parboteeah, Praveen 624, 631–632
Pareto efficiency 294–295, 296, 367
Pareto optimality 92, 100, 299
Parfit, Derek 46
Parmalat 609
Parmar, B.L. 418
Parrish, Elsie 475
Parsons, Talcott 296
particularism: feminist ethics 132, 139; Trompenaars 561–562, 610
partnerships 240, 241, 243, 244, 246
patents 313, 318, 319–321
paternalism 562, 617
patriarchy 135
Paul (Apostle) 152–153, 154
pay *see* compensation
pay inequality 131, 132, 135

691

Payne, Dinah 282
Peltzman, Sam 364
Pemex 643
performance management 463, 466, 468
personality 27–28, 437–438
personhood 170, 188, 192–193, 243, 245, 249
persuasion 511, 512
Peru 641–644, 645, 649
Petit, Valérie 411–412, 430–446
Petrick, Joseph A. 412, 447–458
Petrobas 642, 646
Pettit, Philip 91, 250, 251, 254n17
Pezoa, Álvaro E. 592, 641–656
pharmaceutical products 105, 178, 318–321, 447, 511, 512, 514, 550
philanthropy 177, 257–258, 269, 632; board diversity 421; Central Europe and Russia 665; China 598, 601–602; definition of 171; Tata Group 619; trusteeship 618, 619–620
Philip Morris 643
Phillips, M.J. 250–251
Phillips, Robert 107
philosophy 5, 23–37, 40, 41–44; analytic 45, 47, 48; applied 46; business ethics education 67–68; explication 51–54; exploration 46; skepticism 291; *see also* moral philosophy; moral theories; political philosophy
phronêsis 9, 16, 284
Piaget, Jean 15
Pierson, Paul 394–395
Piketty, Thomas 44, 394, 399
Pilon, R. 247
Pinchot, Gifford 378, 381, 382
place 506–507, 508
Planck, Max 303
planned economy 594–595, 600, 657, 658–659, 660
planned obsolescence 514
Plato 24, 385, 617; "Forms" 41; motivation 85; needs-based approach to economic justice 383; Ring of Gyges 227; rules 80
pleasure 1, 24–25, 28, 30, 83–84, 90
Plipat, Srirak 607
pluralism 47, 284–285, 452–455
Pogge, Thomas 320–321, 535
Pojman, Louis 69
Poland 266, 657, 663, 665, 666–667, 668
police 660
political capitalism 308, 405–406, 407
political co-responsibility 208–209
political Corporate Social Responsibility 177–178
political philosophy 11, 14, 98–99, 166
politics: Central Europe and Russia 662, 663, 667, 668; corruption 573–574, 642, 645–646, 649; government failure 364; housing policy 404–405; innovation 326; Integrative Economic Ethics 213–214; Locke/Rousseau narratives 52; political virtue 127; rent seeking 124, 126–127; stakeholder theory 233; *see also* government
Pollay, R.W. 515
pollution 34, 301, 362; innovation 327; Latin America 643–644; negative externalities 229; regulation 378, 379–380, 384; *see also* environmental issues
Pope Benedict XVI 157, 194, 200n6
Pope Francis 157, 201n8, 545
Pope John Paul II 12, 157, 194, 545
Pope Leo XIII 11, 157, 545
Pope Paul VI 157
pornography 10, 193, 433
Porter, Michael 176, 177, 335
Portugal 269
positivism 40, 557, 565, 569
Posner, B.Z. 566
Post, C. 421
Post, James E. 545
post-structuralism 525
postcolonial theory 558, 569
power: Corporate Social Responsibility 173; critical management studies 449; employees and employers 474, 475; feminist ethics 135; leadership 431, 432, 438–439; social contract theory 98; stakeholders 212; Wenger's theory 142–143
power distance 558, 559, 560, 561, 564, 565
PPR *see* Principle of Positional Responsibility
practical wisdom 9, 284, 347
pragmatism 283, 606
praise 168
predatory lending 397
preference satisfaction 47
Preston, Ivan 507, 509
Preston, Lee E. 186, 545
Price, Terry L. 70–71, 435
prices: Africa 628; fair market value 499; high frequency trading 352; housing 398–399, 406; liberal duties 499–500; marketing 506–507, 508; profit seekers 119, 120; self-interest 292; speculation 351–352; subjective theory of value 497–498; transaction cost theory 225–226
prima facie duties 451
Primeaux, Patrick 525
principal-agent relationship 227, 228, 298–299, 301, 449–450
Principle of Positional Responsibility (PPR) 485
PRIs *see* program-related investments
prisoner's dilemma 296, 314
privacy 63, 482–484, 487n4, 512–514, 529
private equity 420
private property 31–32, 321–322; Central Europe and Russia 659, 661, 662, 665; forms of ownership 309–311; Gandhi 615; Judaism 151; justification of 311–317; Locke 53;

Rousseauean equality narrative 50–51; social contract theory 97; *see also* property; property rights
privatization 14, 662–663, 664
procedural approach 394
proceduralists 43–44
process-oriented ethics 204
Procter & Gamble (P&G) 643
products 506–507, 508
professions 525–526
profit 26, 35, 40, 52, 247; accounting profits 124; alternative business organizations 263; barriers to global business ethics 552; business as an activity 230–231, 232, 235; capitalist exploitation 32; corruption 584–585; economics 298, 300–302, 328, 525; entrepreneurship 116–120; fiduciary duty 501–502; firms as utility maximizers 361–362, 365–366; Friedman 30, 321, 359, 360, 373n3, 373n4, 584; innovation 329; microfinance 354; private property 309; rational goal theory 448; speculation 352; stakeholder theory 34, 35, 174, 234
profit seekers 78, 113–130, 212, 331
program-related investments (PRIs) 260
Progressive era 405
promises 31, 81, 104, 450, 451, 459
promotion 506–507, 508
property 239–240, 307, 309–325; Central Europe and Russia 660, 661, 663; conventionalist objection 317–318; forms of ownership 309–311; intellectual property 63, 307, 318–321; justification of 311–317; "property deficit" 660, 669n6; *see also* private property
property rights 29, 48, 321–322, 529; Africa 630; Central Europe and Russia 660, 665; corporate governance 418; corporations 243; forms of ownership 309–311; Gandhi 615; innovation 337; Integrative Economic Ethics 207; justification of 311–317; Kant 35; Lockean liberty narrative 49; rules 229–230, 231, 233, 235; Washington Consensus 618; *see also* private property
Protestant work ethic 10, 629
Protestantism 12, 157, 159; *see also* Christianity
prudence 10, 18, 343; Aquinas 154; Aristotle 25; banking 347, 350; Christianity 158; ethical leadership 16; finance 355; Judaism 151; Kant 11; leadership 437; Luther 155; Stoics 123; UN Global Compact 17; virtue ethics 138, 284
Prudential 436
psychological egoism 83
public benefit corporations 262–263, 264, 265
public goods 29–30, 178, 296, 297, 299, 328, 667
public interest 363–364, 367, 526; accounting 413, 524, 527–529, 533, 534–535; corruption 585
public relations 137, 257, 507

puffery 509
punishment 251
purpose-based accounts of CSR 173

"quadruple bottom line" 517
Qur'an 9

race: apartheid in South Africa 547, 627, 638n12; critical management studies 449; feminist ethics 135–136; hiring discrimination 476; leadership 440; mortgage lending 396, 397–398, 406; stereotypes 515; *see also* ethnic diversity
Radford, Richard 116, 117
radical business ethics 32–33
Raheim, Salome 136
Ralston, David A. 566
Ramesh, R.S. 610
Ramirez, Edith 513
Ramo, Joshua Cooper 618
Rana-Plaza disaster 530, 548
Rand, Ayn 80, 83, 294
Rao, Narasimha 609
Rasche, Andreas 204
Rasmussen, Douglas 83
rational choice theory 222, 295–300
rational egoism 83
rational goal theory 448, 453–454, 455
rationality: agency theory 227; Aristotle 25; bargaining 234; contractarianism 97; economics 293, 294; financial ethics 344; instrumental 361; Integrative Economic Ethics 205, 207, 208, 216; Kant 82; moral 47; social contract theory 100–101, 102, 103; *see also* reason
Rawls, John 35, 43, 44, 45; basic rights 233; contractarianism 82, 88; cooperation 316; critique of utilitarianism 80, 85, 91; distributive justice 48, 296; dominance of 49; exploration 46; fairness 107; justice 14, 33–34, 403; political liberalism 207, 210; primary goods 385; procedural approach 394, 407n1; Rousseauean equality narrative 50; rules 80; social contract theory 96, 100, 101, 103, 109; stakeholder theory 366; veil of ignorance 404
Reagan, Ronald 330, 379
realism 41, 106, 424
reason 10, 47, 92; Aristotle 25, 27; Integrative Economic Ethics 206; Kant 11, 43; theory/practice relationship 456; *see also* ethical reasoning; rationality
reciprocity 26, 460, 562; Buddhism 160; Christianity 158; entrepreneurial intent 124; ethic of care 137; financial institutions 346; gift giving 575–576; Wenger's theory 142
recruitment 455, 465, 475–476, 559, 562
redistribution 41–42, 43, 327, 394
Reed, A. 437
Reed, Darryl 204

693

Index

reflexivity 141
Reformation 153, 154–155
"regimes of competence" 140, 141
regulation 44, 45, 301, 308, 359–375; Africa 627, 630, 631; American Recovery and Reinvestment Act 402–403; anti-trust 196; bribery and corruption 544, 549–550, 580–582, 631; Bubble Act 241, 243, 246, 253n3; calls for 60; Community Reinvestment Act 395–396, 403, 406; compliance with 568; Consumer Product Safety Improvement Act 225; corporations 242, 244; emergence of business ethics 544–545; environmental 377–378, 379–380, 384, 389; EU 667, 668; financial 344–345, 347, 349, 355, 401; Foreign Corrupt Practices Act 544, 546, 549–550, 578, 580–581, 586n2; India 608; institutional design 371–372; Integrative Economic Ethics 205, 213, 214; Latin America 649; lobbying 321; marketing 508, 511; rent seeking 367–372; Sarbanes-Oxley Act 60, 90, 609; social enterprises 259–263, 265–269, 270; South Africa 638n10; standards enforcement approach 379; typology of business ethics and 361–367; *see also* law
Reidenbach, R.E. 567
Reiser, Dana Brakman 222, 257–274
Reiter, Sara Ann 528
relationality 131, 132, 136, 137–139, 141, 143
relativism 62, 67, 69; cultural differences 558, 566, 567; decision algorithms 567–568; social contract theory 88, 103, 106
religion 29, 40, 78, 148–164; Asian religions 159–162; Central Europe and Russia 660, 666–667, 670n12; Christian traditions 151–158; cultural differences 563; gift giving 576; global ethics standards 551; Hebrew tradition 148–151; Islam 158–159; Marx's critique 11; medieval philosophy 41–42; South Asia 606, 607; United States 12; Western economic liberalism 628; *see also* Buddhism; Christianity; Hinduism; Islam; Judaism
Renault 664
rent seeking 78, 308, 609; Africa 630; Latin America 642; profit seekers 113, 124–125, 126–127; regulation 345, 360–361, 367–372
rents 360, 368
reporting: accounting 524, 531–532, 533; Global Compact 548; reporting systems 467; Sentencing Guidelines 549; sustainability 382
republican liberalism 205, 207, 210, 215
reputation 175, 207, 211, 228; board diversity 421; bribery 578; entrepreneurs 282; entrepreneurship 277
research: Africa 625–626; China 602–603; Latin America 647–648, 650; South Asia 608
Resick, Christian 441

respect: Central Europe and Russia 665, 668; communities of practice 140; financial institutions 346; Kantian ethics 81, 86, 451, 634; of labor 98; leadership 441; performance evaluation 466; role models 467; universal principles 67; utilitarianism 85
responsibility 92, 343; accounting 413; bribery 577; China 594–595, 599–600; comprehensive moral thinking 197; corporate governance 411; corporations 239, 250–252; definition of 168; discourse ethics 205; employers 486; environmental 376, 383, 385–386, 388, 389–390; feminist ethics 131, 132, 136, 138–139, 143; finance 355; Gandhi's trusteeship framework 614; Integrative Economic Ethics 205, 208, 211, 212; Judaism 151; labor exploitation 501–502, 503; leadership 431; managerial 449–450; moral disengagement 461; Principle of Positional Responsibility 485; shareholders 420; stakeholder thinking 191–192, 195, 196; *see also* Corporate Social Responsibility; social responsibility
responsiveness 447, 448
Rest, James R. 282, 460–461, 528
reward systems 460, 466
Reynolds, Scott J. 461
Ribstein, Larry 247
Ricardo, David 11, 32, 611
righteousness 152, 161
rights 92, 98; animal 192, 380–381, 390; basic 233; contractarianism 82; employees 474–489; environmental goods 378–379; financial markets 351; Integrative Economic Ethics 210; Islam 158; Judaism 151; Kantian ethics 14; legal protection of 318; Lockean liberty narrative 49–50; minority 134; moral 317; non-consequentialism 79, 92; Rousseauean equality narrative 51; shareholders 420; social contract theory 88, 102; stakeholder thinking 192, 195; types of 323n1; utilitarianism 84, 85, 89; *see also* human rights; property rights
Rindova, V. 279
risk: entrepreneurship 279–280, 283; finance 347, 348, 349, 350–351; profit seekers 119; risk assessment 462; risk management 211, 347, 350–351, 386–387, 492, 532; speculation 352
Risse, Thomas 361
rituals 463, 468
Rivero, Andrea 48
Roberts, J. 422
Robin, D.P. 567
Robinson, James A. 337
Robinson, James III 125
Robinson, Joan 490
Rodgers, S. 506
Rokeach's Values Survey 528
role models 463–464, 465–466, 467, 620

Roman Empire 26
Roman law 240
Romania 657, 663–664, 665, 666–667, 668, 670n10, 670n12
Rönnegard, David 186, 199
Roosevelt, Eleanor 551
Roosevelt, Theodore 378
Röpke, Wilhelm 208, 214–215
Rorty, Richard 44
Rosenberg, Nathan 331, 332–333
Rosenthal, S.B. 283
Ross, W.D. 80, 81, 195, 451
Rost, Joseph 431, 432
Rothbard, Murray N. 394
Roubaud, François 633
Rousseau, Denise 48
Rousseau, Jean-Jacques 5, 14, 31–32, 33, 35, 43; equality narrative 49, 50–51, 52; social contract 85, 96
Rousseff, Dilma 642
Roussouw, G.J. 625, 626, 638n8, 638n9
Rowan, Brian 363
Royal African Company 241
Royal Dutch Shell 211
Royce, Josiah 185, 187, 190, 193, 194, 196, 199
Ruggie, John 178–179, 530, 551
rule of law 49–50, 51, 54, 552, 663
rules: business as an activity 223, 228–230, 231, 235; consequentialism 80; corporations 246; cultural differences 562; ethical climate 469; Integrative Economic Ethics 210; Kantian ethics 86; logic of appropriateness 361; non-consequentialism 81, 92, 565; regulation 373n2; social contract theory 101–102, 107; stages of moral development 460; stakeholder theory 233; utilitarianism 84, 85, 90, 91, 450–451; Wenger's theory 141; workplace democracy 487n3
Ruskin, John 611, 613–614
Russell, Daniel C. 78, 113–130
Russia 281, 566–567, 592, 657–673
Russian Company 241
Ryan, L.V. 418, 423

Sableman, M. 513
Sacconi, Lorenzo 99, 100, 102–103, 107–108
Sade, Marquis de 431
safety *see* health and safety
Sagiv, Lilach 421
Saint-Michel, Sarah 411–412, 430–446
Salas, Alejandro 646
Sample, Ruth 495
Samuelson, Paul 296
Santuari, A. 266
Sarasvathy, S.D. 280
Sarbanes-Oxley Act (2002) 60, 90, 609
Say, Jean-Baptiste 276

say on pay (SOP) movement 418, 419–420
scandals 550, 553, 573, 609; accounting 524, 527; bribery 544; calls for reform after 60; CEO incentive pay 423; Chile 647; crisis in corporate governance 415; defense industry 545; demand for ethics training 40; history of business ethics 12; Latin America 642, 643; profit maximization 584; role of ethics in business 362; Watergate 580
Scanlon, Thomas 91, 97
scarcity 29, 150, 314, 319
Schaubroeck, John M. 469
Schech, Susanne 564
Schein, Edgar 16
Schein, Virginia 440
Schelling, Thomas 296
Scherer, Andreas 105, 171, 177, 205, 215
Schmandt-Besserat, Denise 231
Schmidtz, David 315
Schminke, Marshall 469
Scholastics 26–27
Scholz, J.T. 362
Schroeder, J.E. 512
Schumacher, E.F. 620
Schumpeter, Joseph A. 275, 276–277, 279, 326–331, 333–334, 337, 339, 611
Schwartz, Adina 480
Schwartz, Shalom H. 557
Schweiker, William 531
science 332, 333
Science Policy Research Unit (SPRU) 332, 335
Scott Bader 619
SEC *see* Securities and Exchange Commission
secularism 162, 563
securities 393, 395, 397, 400–401, 407
Securities and Exchange Commission (SEC) 48, 90, 419, 580, 609
securitization 348, 350
self 136, 137–138, 140
self-control 25, 28, 48, 437
self-deception 70–72
self-determination 210
self-discipline 48
self-expression 563–564
self-interest 18, 72, 227, 294, 297, 330; Africa 632; agency theory 301, 584; barriers to global business ethics 552; business ethics education 68–69; CEOs 422; contractarianism 97, 99; corporate 177; corruption 585; cultural differences 566; developing countries 666; ethical climate 469; Kant 11, 31; managers 416–417; market economies 293; Mill 33; Rawls 33–34; Russia 567; shareholders 420; Smith 29–30, 292, 299, 328; social contract theory 100, 102; stakeholder theory 34; workers 297–298; *see also* egoism
self-preservation 29

695

Index

self-regulation 251, 365, 513, 627
self-sacrifice 41, 434
selfishness 28, 30, 278, 281, 294, 344, 450
Seligman, Joel 13
Selznick, Philip 188
Sen, Amartya 27, 88, 385, 394, 395
Seneca 123
Senior, Ian 574
Sentencing Guidelines 60, 462–463, 466, 470, 549, 550
separation thesis 15, 232
servant leadership 433–434
service provision 118–119
services, production of 230–232
sex/gender distinction 133; *see also* gender
sexism 132
sexual differences 134
shadow banking 348
Shakespeare, William 10
Shannon, H.A. 242
shared competence 142, 143
shared value 23, 176–177
shareholder theory 34, 165, 309, 359, 362, 366
shareholder value 52–53, 261, 339, 415, 416–417
shareholders 13, 239, 298; Africa 627; agency theory 584; benefit corporations 261, 262, 263; corporate governance 252, 411, 415–420, 423; employees as 619; empowerment/activism 48, 411, 418–420; fiduciary duty to 173, 184, 189–190, 193, 196, 198, 200n1, 221, 246, 449–450, 501–502; financial institutions 347; limited liability 241–243, 244, 246, 247, 260; obligations to 579; primacy debate 416–418; property rights 314, 323n2, 529; rent seeking 125; as residual claimants 482; shareholder primacy 302; social contract theory 108–109; stakeholder theory 35; use of the term 184; *see also* investors
Sharia law 158, 354
Shaw, W.H. 40
Sherk, J. 402
Shiller, R.J. 343
Shutte, Augustine 624–625
Sidgwick, Henry 80
Siegelbaum, Paul 663
Siemens 550, 573, 582
Sikka, Prem 528
Silicon Valley 334, 336, 550
Simha, A. 63
Sims, Peter 435
Singapore 547
Singer, Abraham 109
Singer, Peter 324n11
Singhapakdi, A. 566
Sison, Alejo José 89
skepticism 67, 69, 291–295
Skoda, Emil 665

slavery 10, 150, 529, 532
Slovakia 657, 665, 666–667
Slovenia 657, 667
small businesses 224–225, 478, 633, 663–664, 668, 669n3
Smith, Adam 11, 29–30, 33, 35, 42, 53–54, 296; entrepreneurial intent 123–124; Industrial Revolution 326; "invisible hand" 28, 29, 30, 222, 291–292, 299, 328; justice of government 615; labor and specialization 327–328; labor theory of value 32; market operations 303; meaningful work 480, 481; self-interest 68; small shopkeepers 224; sympathy 43; utility maximization 365–366
Smith, Craig 186, 199, 516–517
Smith, Jeffery 251–252
Smith, Peter 561
Smith, Tara 83
SNC Lavalin 582, 584
Snowden, Edward 485
sociability 25
social action 169
social capital 115
social contract 29, 34, 35, 77–78, 96–112, 545; consequentialism 91; Corporate Social Responsibility 173; elements of CBE 99–103; non-consequentialism 82, 87–88; Rawls 34; Rousseauean equality narrative 50–51; taxonomy of approaches 96–98; *see also* contractarianism; contracts
social enterprises 222, 258; Europe 265–269; United States 258–265
social entrepreneurship 47, 277, 278, 279
social identity 78, 140–141, 142, 144
social intuition 461–462
social investor movement 547
social justice 11–12, 18, 211, 292, 390
social learning 464
social market economy 205, 208, 214–215
social marketing 512
social media 353, 465, 506–507
social mission 258, 261, 278
social responsibility 13, 63, 167–183, 299, 321; Arrow 301; contractarianism 88; definition of 168–169, 171; environmental issues 377; evolution into CSR 224; Friedman 359, 360; human rights 529; management theories 448; market failures 92; stakeholder management 211; *see also* Corporate Social Responsibility
social science 459, 523, 565, 569
socialism 11, 14, 18, 333; China 593, 594, 596; feminist ethics 134–135; Gandhi 615; social market economy 214; soft democratic 48, 49
sociality 81, 139
society 41
Society for Business Ethics 67, 544
Socrates 23, 24

Sogner, Knut 307, 326–342
Soll, Jacob 524
Sollars, Gordon C. 221–222, 239–256
Solomon, Robert 27, 43, 68–69, 85, 88–89, 224, 277
Sony Ericsson 510
South Africa 547, 625, 638n12; corporate governance 627; Corporate Social Responsibility 633; corruption 631; legislation 638n10; Ubuntu 636, 638n14, 638n17
South Asia 17, 591–592, 606–623
South Korea 547
South Sea Company 241
Soviet Union, former 581; *see also* Russia
Space Shuttle disaster 71
Spain 562, 646
specialization 326, 327–328, 334, 335
speculation: financial 351–352, 356n9; real estate 398
spirituality 434
SPRU *see* Science Policy Research Unit
SRI *see* Stanford Research Institute
Sri Lanka 606, 607, 608
Srinivasan, V. 608
stakeholder management 109, 185–186, 211–213, 417–418
stakeholder theory 13, 34–35, 44, 165, 173, 366–367, 545; business 232–235; business strategy 16; Corporate Social Responsibility 174; demands on business 324n12; dialogue 106; discourse ethics 204; feminist ethics 132; hostility to business 40; justice 14; multifiduciary 302; paradox in 189; property 309, 321–322, 323n2; social contract theory 97, 98, 99; UN Global Compact 17; workplace democracy 487n2
stakeholder thinking 165–166, 173, 184–203
stakeholders: Africa 592, 626, 627, 632; Community Interest Companies 267, 268; competing values framework 453; cooperatives 266; corporate governance 252, 411, 415–416, 417; Corporate Social Responsibility 171–172; cross-cultural management ethics 569; definition of 185; ethical climate 469; Europe 638n9; intrinsic worth 195; Kantian ethics 86; management ethics 453, 455; management theories 447, 448, 449–450; marketing 516–517; obligations to 187, 576–577, 579; philosophy 23; public benefit corporations 263; reporting to 532; social contract theory 97, 101; stakeholderism 41–42; trusteeship 619; utilitarianism 90; voice 233
standards enforcement approach 379
Stanford Business School 544
Stanford Research Institute (SRI) 185
state of nature 98, 100, 227, 296
state-owned enterprises 626, 630

status 561, 562
stealth marketing 510–511
Steiber, John 525
Steiner, Hillel 496, 499–500, 503
Steinman, M.A. 512
stereotypes 10, 440, 515
Stern School 67
stewardship 16, 157, 158, 343; CEOs 422; environmental issues 381; Gandhi 615; leadership 434; stakeholder thinking 192
Steyaert, C. 283
Stigler, George 360, 364
Stiglitz, Joseph E. 394, 404, 405
stockholders 184, 186, 187, 188, 449, 618
Stockman, David A. 394, 404, 405
Stoics 24–25, 91–92, 122–123
Stone, C.D. 186
Stout, Lynn 245–246, 302, 417, 420
strategic approaches 174
strategic management 213
strikes 32, 192
"structural restraint view" 170
Stückelberger, C. 625
subjective theory of value 497–498
Subramanian, Guhan 415
substantive duties 494–495, 497–498, 500–501, 502–503
substantivists 43
Suchman, Mark 363
Sullivan, Leon 547
Sullivan Principles 547, 548
Sumeria 7
summum bonum 24–25, 26, 28, 635
Sundaram, Jomo Kwame 631
Sunstein, Cass 44
supply chains 547, 548
Surie, G. 278, 283
sustainability 17–18, 32, 308, 376–377, 381; concept of 386–389; Corporate Social Responsibility 175, 632; decision making 467; Latin America 648; philosophy 23; reporting 382; South Asia 608; undermined by bribery 578; *see also* environmental issues
sustainable development 376–377, 381–386, 387–389, 390, 662
Swanson, Diane 65
sweatshops 171, 495, 498, 500
Swedberg, Richard 277
Sweden 562, 587n3
Swigonski, Mary 136
sympathy 43
Syngenta 388
systems of innovation 335–336, 339

Taiwan 441, 547
Takata 553
Tang, Kailin 600–601

Index

Tanzania 631, 633
Taoism 9, 160–161, 599
Tata Group 619–620
Tawney, R.H. 10, 12
tax avoidance 172
tax evasion 343, 662, 666
tax fraud 643, 644, 649, 653
taxation 17, 44; carbon tax 384; Community Interest Companies 267; progressive 394; small businesses 224; tax benefits for nonprofits 259; Washington Consensus 618
Taylor, Charles 46, 515
Taylor, John B. 399
Taylorism 299
team production 245–246, 252, 302, 417
technology: accounting 534; ethics training 61; financial trading 352–353; food and agriculture 388; innovation 331–332, 333; Lockean liberty narrative 49, 52; marketing 513–514; privacy issues 484; Rousseauean equality narrative 50, 52; Silicon Valley 334
Telefónica 643
teleology 43, 82, 162, 424, 565; *see also* consequentialism; utilitarianism
temperance: Aquinas 154; Christianity 158; Judaism 151; leadership 437; Luther 155; virtue ethics 138, 452
Tenbrunsel, Ann 71
termination of employment 476–478
Tesco 524
Thailand 566, 608
Thatcher, Margaret 330
theft 369
theology 42, 43; *see also* religion
theory of the firm 223, 225–228, 235, 245, 291, 298, 301, 302
theory/practice relationship 455–456, 603
Thomism 9, 11, 15; *see also* Aquinas
Thomsen, Steen 301, 619
Thorne, Linda 527
Thornson, E. 506
TI *see* Transparency International
Tillich, Paul 162
Tokarski, Kim Oliver 222, 275–289
tolerance 69
Tollison, R. 124
Tompkins, J. 422
Tong, Rosemarie 133
Torah 9, 150, 152, 158
trade 29, 240; Africa 629; Aristotle 5; Central Europe and Russia 659–660; Christianity 153; colonial 611, 629; fair 114–115, 116; foreign 328; globalization 547, 548; Judaism 149; voluntary 229–230, 232, 233, 235
trade unions 32, 402, 615–616, 664
trading (financial) 352–353, 356n11

"tragedy of the commons" 296, 314–316, 319, 322
training: Africa 626; cross-cultural management ethics 569; ethical culture 463, 465–466; ethics 40, 60–62, 545, 550
traits 281
transaction costs 248, 334; profit seekers 118, 119, 125; theory of the firm 223, 225–228, 235, 298
transcendence 437
transformational leadership 434–435, 436, 463
transparency 582, 583, 587n5, 648; finance 347; lack of 644, 655, 670n9
Transparency International (TI) 546, 574, 579; Africa 630–631; *Corruption Perceptions Index* 581, 607, 610, 630, 646; *Global Corruption Barometer* 644–646
Treviño, Linda Klebe 64, 282, 412, 439, 459–473
"triple bottom line" 17, 382, 517
Trompenaars, Fons 556, 561–562, 610
Troubled Asset Relief Program (TARP) 400–401, 402
trust: Central Europe and Russia 663, 665–666, 668; Chinese Cultural Connection study 560; entrepreneurs 282; feminist ethics 139; finance 345, 347, 351, 355; Gandhi 616; leadership 440; servant leadership 433, 434; social enterprises 264–265; transformational leadership 434
trusteeship 592, 607–608, 610–620
trustworthiness: accounting 528; managers 452, 464; marketing 507; performance evaluation 466; Prophet Muhammad 158; role models 467
truth 560, 566, 612, 616, 665
Tullock, Gordon 369–370, 609
Turner, Sharon 114
Tushnet, Rebecca 508
Tutu, Desmond 635, 638n17
"two masters" problem 263–264, 265, 271n7
Tylenol poisoning crisis 465

Ubuntu 625, 634–636, 637, 638n14, 638n17
Uganda 631
Ukraine 657
Ulrich, Peter 172, 173, 205–216
uncertainty 276, 279–280, 329, 339, 362
uncertainty avoidance 558–559, 560
unfair business practices 643, 649, 653–654
UNIAPAC *see* International Catholic Union of Businessmen
Unilever 532–533
Union Carbide 224
unions 32, 402, 615–616, 664
United Kingdom (UK): Anti-Bribery Act 549–550; British colonialism in India 611, 612, 616; Community Interest Companies 267–269, 270, 271n12; compliance with legislation 568; cultural values 557; Institute for Business Ethics

546; Modern Slavery Act 532; nepotism 562; universalism 562

United Nations (UN): bribery 574, 582; Convention Against Corruption 582; Global Compact 17, 172, 175, 548, 551; Guiding Principles on Business and Human Rights 172, 179, 530–532; human rights 529, 551; Principles for Responsible Management Education 201n9; sustainability 17, 18, 383, 387

United States (US): American Founders 42; anti-market advocates 39; anti-trust regulation 196; bribery 549–550, 578, 580–581, 586n2; business ethics education 14–15, 60–61, 553; compliance with legislation 568; copyright protection 319; corporate ethics programs 549, 550; corporations 242–243, 244, 334; cultural values 557; economic crisis 393, 395–407; economic growth 338–339; emergence of business ethics 543, 544–545; employment-at-will 476, 477; entrepreneurship 281; environmental regulation 378, 379, 380, 390; ethical judgments 566, 567; ethics training 61; Global Compact 548; history of business ethics 12, 13; human rights 564; interest groups 646; leadership 433, 435, 441; liberty 337; marketing 508, 509; national parks 381; nepotism 562; online privacy 513; regulation 609; rent seeking 124; Sarbanes-Oxley Act 90; securitization 350; Sentencing Guidelines 60, 462–463, 466, 470, 549, 550; shareholder democracy 418, 419; size of firms 478; small firms 224; social enterprises 258–265, 270; social investor movement 547

Universal Declaration of Human Rights 14, 48, 529, 551

universalism 15, 17; ethical judgments 565; feminist ethics 132, 139; Trompenaars 561–562, 610

universality: ethic of care 137; ethical values 551; Golden Rule 69–70; integrative social contracts theory 104; Kant 30–31, 451

universities 40, 42, 65–66

University of California-Berkeley 40

University of Texas 66

Uruguay 645, 647

usury 26, 27, 151, 154, 155, 156–157, 343; *see also* interest

utilitarianism 14–15, 35, 46, 77, 79, 93n2, 450–451; Bentham 30, 83–84, 93n1, 606; in business ethics 89–91; cultural differences 566, 567; economic policy 399; economics 294, 295; environmental regulation 377, 378, 379; ethical judgments 565; Integrative Economic Ethics 207, 208; management ethics 453; Mill 14, 33, 83, 84–85, 89–90, 92, 606; Rawls 34; shareholder value maximization 417; social contract theory 88; stakeholder theory 34;

"stealth utilitarians" 93n3; Trompenaars 561, 562; *see also* teleology

utility: bargaining game 108; consequentialism 79; friendship 1; maximization 227, 293–294, 295–296, 298, 361–362, 365–366, 422, 450–451, 452

Uwimana, Chantal 630

Uyl, Douglas Den 83

Vale 644

value: creation of 125, 173, 208–209, 235, 278, 279, 416; economic and moral 597; fair market value 498–499; labor theory of 32, 496–497, 504n8; social contract theory 106; social entrepreneurship 278, 279; stakeholder thinking 193; subjective theory of 497–498

value chains 178

value pluralism 284–285

values 10, 299, 390; Africa 626, 628, 634–635, 636; Central Europe and Russia 657, 665, 667; changes in 18; China 597, 598, 602, 603–604; competing values framework 453–455; Corporate Social Responsibility 174; cultural 556–565, 569; entrepreneurship 284–285; environmental 381, 388–389; ethical dilemmas 459; false values of marketing 514–515; Giving Voice to Values 66; Integrative Economic Ethics 213; Islam 159; leadership 188, 463; moral development 437; ordoliberalism 215; organizational culture 16; performance management systems 468; religious 162; social contract theory 101; values statements 463, 464–465; World Values Survey 556, 558, 563–564

Van de Ven, Andrew 336

van der Vossen, Bas 307, 309–325

van der Zwan, N. 13

Van Zandt, J. 64

Vandenhole, Wouter 533

Vedas 9, 609

veil of ignorance 34, 107–108, 234, 404

Velamuri, S. Ramakrishna 278, 591–592, 606–623

Velasquez, Manuel 170, 249–250, 252

Velsicol Chemical Corporation 197

Venezuela 645

venture capital 125–126

Vermaak, Frans 627

Vermeulen, F. 584

Vernon, Raymond 546

vice 28, 29, 78, 113, 127, 452

Victor, B. 469

Vietnam 547, 608

virtue: Aristotelian virtue theory 24–25, 43, 46; business and 115–116; Confucianism 161; definition of 114; Eastern cultures 162, 560, 566; feminist ethics 132, 137–139, 143–144; friendship 1; Hinduism 159–160; intellectual

699

and moral 42; Islam 159; Mandeville 28; medieval philosophy 41; political 127; profit seekers 78, 113–114, 115, 116, 122–127; Taoism 161; universal 143; virtuous intent 122–123
virtue ethics 452; Aquinas 153–154; Aristotle 27, 151, 606; Christianity 148; consequentialism 91; entrepreneurship 284; feminist ethics 137–138; leadership 435; non-consequentialism 82–83, 85, 88–89
virtues 27, 138, 452; Aristotle 25; business activities 235; cardinal 10, 154, 155; civic 210–211; feminist ethics 144; financial institutions 347; leadership 437; ordoliberalism 215
virtuousness 436
Visser, Wayne 632
Vogel, David 545, 551
Volkswagen 200n5, 470, 553, 573, 584, 668
voluntary trade 229–230, 232, 233, 235
Votaw, Dow 167, 178
voting, corporate 418–419

wages 297, 475, 478–480, 486; Central Europe and Russia 660, 669n7; firms' duties 494–503; Gandhi 614; unjust 491–492, 503; *see also* compensation
Wal-Mart 479, 510–511
Walker, C.E. 253n2
Walsham, Geoff 204–205
Walt, Steven 500
Walumbwa, F.O. 435–436
Walzer, Michael 103
Wang, Lulu 594
Wang, Jie 594
Wang, Xiaoxi 596, 597, 601, 602
Wang, Zeying 600, 602
Waples, E.P. 63
Warner, C. Terry 71
Washington Consensus 618
Watergate scandal 580
Watkins, Sherron 485
Watson, George W. 108
Watson, T.J. 277
wealth 42, 98; Africa 629, 630; China 600–601; Christianity 152, 153, 156, 157; Hinduism 159–160; Judaism 149, 150; meaning of 424; shareholder value maximization 415, 416–417; Smith 327–328; Taoism 161; trusteeship 611, 614, 618; utilitarianism 207; *see also* money
Weaver, G.R. 61
Weaver, William G. 250
Weber, James 61, 62, 63
Weber, Max 10, 157, 435
Welch, Jack 545
welfare economics 294–295, 299
Wells Fargo Bank 553
Wempe, Ben 99, 101, 105, 108, 284

Wenger, Etienne 132–133, 140–143, 144
Werder, Axel 416
Werhane, Patricia 44–45, 64, 249, 362
Wertheimer, Alan 496, 498–499, 503
West, Andrew 627, 634–635, 636
Western values 10, 558, 559, 560, 598
Westwood, R.J. 566
Wettstein, Florian 165, 167–183, 215
Wharton School 12, 544
Wheatley Institution 67
whistleblowing 63, 131, 467, 484–486, 562
White, Judith 136–137
White, Richard 405
Whitehead, Alfred North 40
WHO *see* World Health Organization
Whole Foods 185
Wicks, Andrew 139
Wigand, Jeffrey 484, 485
Wikipedia 573–574
Williams, Bernard 47
Williams, C.C. 423
Williams, Richard N. 6, 60–76
Williamson, James 618
Williamson, Oliver 226, 227, 298
Williston, Samuel 242
Willmott, Hugh 528
Windsor, Duane 172
Winter, Sidney G. 331, 332
wisdom 452
Wittgenstein, Ludwig 51
Woermann, Minka 592, 624–640
The Wolf of Wall Street (film) 430, 437, 439, 440, 441
women: board diversity 421; feminist ethics 131–147; hiring discrimination 476; leadership 440–441; in management positions 563; *see also* gender
Wood, Allen 81
Woodcock, G. 612
work: Buddhism 160; Christianity 151, 153, 155, 156, 157–158; Hinduism 159–160; Judaism 149; *see also* labor
work ethic 8, 10, 299, 629
working conditions 32, 475; Corporate Social Responsibility 171, 178; firms' duties 494–495; global supply chains 548; labor exploitation 490, 491, 492–493, 503; Latin America 644, 655
working hours 475, 491
workplace democracy 480, 481–482, 487n2, 487n3
World Bank 383, 574, 581–582, 583, 633
World Health Organization (WHO) 388
World Trade Organization 582
World Values Survey 556, 558, 563–564
Worldcom 609
Wozniak, Steve 121

Wright, M. 330
Wurthmann, K. 63

Xiang, Yuqiao 591, 593–605

Yaoming, G. 601
Yates, Sally 549
Yugoslav Republic 657, 665
Yukl, Gary 431, 432
Yunus, Muhammad 354

Zadek, Simon 175, 632
Zaharia, Rodica Milena 592, 657–673
Zahra, S. 330
Zajac, Edward 416
Zambia 633
Zhou, Zhongzhi 602
Zigong 598
Zuckerberg, Mark 620
Zywicki, Todd 402

Taylor & Francis eBooks

Helping you to choose the right eBooks for your Library

Add Routledge titles to your library's digital collection today. Taylor and Francis ebooks contains over 50,000 titles in the Humanities, Social Sciences, Behavioural Sciences, Built Environment and Law.

Choose from a range of subject packages or create your own!

Benefits for you
- Free MARC records
- COUNTER-compliant usage statistics
- Flexible purchase and pricing options
- All titles DRM-free.

Benefits for your user
- Off-site, anytime access via Athens or referring URL
- Print or copy pages or chapters
- Full content search
- Bookmark, highlight and annotate text
- Access to thousands of pages of quality research at the click of a button.

REQUEST YOUR FREE INSTITUTIONAL TRIAL TODAY

Free Trials Available
We offer free trials to qualifying academic, corporate and government customers.

eCollections – Choose from over 30 subject eCollections, including:

Archaeology	Language Learning
Architecture	Law
Asian Studies	Literature
Business & Management	Media & Communication
Classical Studies	Middle East Studies
Construction	Music
Creative & Media Arts	Philosophy
Criminology & Criminal Justice	Planning
Economics	Politics
Education	Psychology & Mental Health
Energy	Religion
Engineering	Security
English Language & Linguistics	Social Work
Environment & Sustainability	Sociology
Geography	Sport
Health Studies	Theatre & Performance
History	Tourism, Hospitality & Events

For more information, pricing enquiries or to order a free trial, please contact your local sales team: www.tandfebooks.com/page/sales

Routledge Taylor & Francis Group | The home of Routledge books

www.tandfebooks.com